D1258098

DICTIONARY OF THE DANCE

Siva Nataraja, King of Dancers. Bronze 11th/12th century, from Madras, now in the Victorian and Albert Museum, London. INDIA

Dictionary of the Dance

Compiled, Written, and Edited

by

W. G. RAFFE

assisted by

M. E. PURDON

NEW YORK : A. S. BARNES AND COMPANY
LONDON : THOMAS YOSELOFF LTD

Library of Congress Catalogue Card Number: 63-18262

A. S. Barnes and Co., Inc.
Cranbury, New Jersey 08512

Thomas Yoseloff Ltd
108 New Bond Street
London W1Y OQX, England

REISSUED 1975

ISBN 0-498-01643-9
Printed in the United States of America

ACKNOWLEDGMENTS

OVER MANY YEARS of research and inquiry into many aspects of Dance, questions have been put to numerous individuals, and some have answered with a phrase or hint, others in longer detailed discussions. Not all can now be remembered, but many persons have given information or opinions, for which we return grateful thanks. No special order is possible; no time or place.

John Foulds (music); Maud MacCarthy (music); Kathleen Schlessinger (music); Dr. Karl Jung (Oriental mandala ritual); Sir John Woodroffe; Sir Francis Younghusband, with Sir Asutosh Mukerji and Sir Jagadish Chandra Bose, Calcutta University, (on oriental topics); Helen Dzhermolinska (former editor of "Dance," New York City); Mme. Consuelo Carmona (Spanish Dance); Dean Inge; Dr. William Temple; W. B. Yeats; The Folk Dance Society (London); Dr. Richter (of "Asia" Magazine, etc.); Shri Aurobindo; Rabindranath Tagore; Uday Shankar Chaudhuri (of Bombay); Anna Varenska (on classical ballet); Lilian Baylis; Ben Greet (the Old Vic); Dr. Rudolf Steiner (of Dornach); K. N. das Gupta; Yussuf Brac (of Putnik, Belgrad); Viktor Semyonof (head of Leningrad School of Ballet); Maud Allan (modern dance); Emil Dalcroze and Percy Ingham (on modern music training); K. S. Stanislavsky; V. I. Nemirovich-Danchenko (on Russian stage); V. Meyerhold and Alex Tairov on modernist theatre); Igor Moiseyev (Russian Folk Dance); Rutland Boughton (choral ballet); G. R. S. Mead (on ritual dance); Angelo Andes (Spanish Dance); Mme. A. Y. Vaganova (on modern Russian ballet education); Natalie Sachs (dance for children); Percy Buck (Woolwich); Bill Court; Christmas Humphreys (Ballet Guild); Bertrand Russell; Rafiq Anwar; Mlle. Simkie; Usha Chatterjhi; Fredk. Joss; Huntly Carter; Jay Hambidge; Aleister Crowley; Mrs. Pratima Tagore (Bolpur); Mohini (Mrs. Sobey Bambay); Nicholas Sergueéff; Baron Arild Rosencranz; Harold Heslop; William Loftus Hare; Sara Jackson (English Folk Dance Society); Dr. Leon Gaster; F. Bligh Bond; Nikita Khrushchev (Moscow Theatres); Sir Stafford Cripps (Theatre finance); Rukmini Devi (Mrs. Arundale); Inayat Khan; Tomas Korda; O. Gangoly (Indian music); H. Coster; G. Sevastianov; Dr. Pierre Tugal (Paris Dance Archives); H. W. L. Dana; British Museum Library Bibliothèque français; Library of the Opera (Paris); Imperial Library (Vienna); Bakhrushin Museum and Library (Moscow); Victoria and Albert Museum Library (London); Leningrad Theatre Museum.

CONTENTS

EDITOR'S FOREWORD

DICTIONARY OF THE DANCE is believed to be the first publication of its kind: objective, far-reaching (if not fully exhaustive) through more than 100 different countries, over periods from ancient Assyria to the fashions of our day. The collection of authentic information covers in candid terms a wide array of facts about the Art of Dance. Of the "three categories"—of Dance, Dancing, and Dancers—only the central and pivotal factor of Dance has been selected; to deal chiefly with the meanings and aims of Dance, in its main modes of the human social form, with a recognition of its cosmic form and its presence in the rhythm of living cells.

The work does not aim to instruct dancers or to teach dancing; what is sought is to rediscover original meanings of rhythmic movement. For the more knowledge the teacher or student can gain on purpose in dance, the better it can be formulated and presented. For tuition the student should find a good school with a competent teacher—and stay long enough to learn. To know what Dance is, almost the only way is to watch a wide variety of performances in many lands.

This book can tell the intelligent student or progressive teacher what to seek and how to analyse a "Work of Dance" above and beyond the technical necessities as usually taught. Consult any desired topic and then persist with all the cross-references. In this single volume much is condensed but many fascinating topics have had to be omitted; yet the would-be producer of dances will find more than enough material to use for new works that are better for knowing the older sources. Those who can create new works more easily are those who know most of the traditional work, in any art; and they, at least, will admit that new ideas are greatly needed in our theatres.

Some attention has been paid to the method of "comparative anatomy of dance form" from which it is found that basic social dance forms are much alike, all the world over, as the human body which dances, is shaped after one ancient pattern. The dance of the living cell and the majestic dance of the cosmos reveal certain elemental laws of rhythm, between which the human form—single or social—must also move; and the revelation of these things was, as Lucian noted, the liturgical basis of religion. Reference to the few items on the topic of notation may show something of these factors. The superficial notion that dance is merely entertainment is obviously an error; but the perception that dance is a many-sided expression of the vital rhythms of the universe, given in terms of human art and social ritual, has mostly been lost from our schools and our profession.

W.G.R.

DICTIONARY OF THE DANCE

A reference in the text marked with an asterisk indicates that an entry on that subject will be found in the Dictionary.

A reference in square brackets, e.g. [See *Duboka*], also refers to an entry in the Dictionary.

To trace dances of a particular place or culture consult the Geographical Index which Starts on page 569.

DANCE AND DANCER

He is now moving
    Yet sees not his own Dance
    Through his Dancing he knows
For He is Dancer revealing Rhythm.

That Silent One sees
    The Dancers body, her Dances and her Dancing
Yet knows them not—he is the Mirror—as
In Song and Gesture they unroll the Dance.

That Silent One watching them
    Quiet in his darkness
Shall Dance with Figures in his Joyous Mind
    When Dancing, Dance, and Dancers all are gone.

DICTIONARY OF THE DANCE

AATTETUR (Norway)

A dance in ¾ time for four couples in a ring, from the region of Asker in South Norway. In a linked circle, dancers move round clock-wise, and then anti-clockwise, with a graceful step in which one heel is raised without the foot leaving the ground, while the other leg swings forward, the toe skimming the ground. There follows a grand chain; partners meet half-way round the circle, form an arch with their arms, then return round the semi-circle to their places. After a curtsey by the girl and a bow by the man, couples dance together, turning clockwise as in an old-fashioned waltz*, but moving anti-clockwise round the circle, to finish with the girl swung to the right of her partner, while he dances on the spot.

ABACUS (Persian origin)

From *abak*, dust or sand. The smoothed rectangle of fine sand, used through the East for casual reckoning, diagrams, or any writing, that is not desired to be retained permanently. The small feather whip or fan, was used to "wipe the slate clean", and a small rod or canon, to pull over the disturbed surface, making it once more smooth. The modern *abacus* (used in Russia and Turkey, as well as Egypt and China), has a strong wooden frame, carrying ten or twelve rows of ten coloured bobbins, on wire. Flicking them from side to side rapidly counts the digits, to the total, without having to follow the reckoning step by step. From the Roman *abacus* we have the geometric terms to *decus* or *decussate*, to divide (and *dekan*, the divider). Many sand patterns were made, from memory, to communicate symbols of good faith; of standing in a society; of rank in dancing relations. Allied with the *abacus* is the chess board, or checkers; the dance-game of *pachisi** and many other disciplined movements over the rectangle or circle. Completely opposite are the modern multiplied drawings known as "blue prints" which are essentially duplicates, and never the original plans, as drawn on tracing cloth. Midway in this history of pattern or symbol transition, comes the *Seal*,* also important in the story of dance.
[See *Sand Patterns; Seal; Pachisi*]

ABEL MEHOLAH (Hebrew)

Dancing Meadow, noted as "the home of Elisha the prophet", and thus possibly his head-quarters for ceremonial. In Coptic, ceremonial, the "meadow for dancing" is a well known and favoured flat grassy field by the bank of a good stream. The space was then used for the important Spring Festival, which included ceremonial bathing, new attire, a feast and a dance. Thus *Abel Meholah* may be in one instance a fixed locality; but it is also by definition a functional name for the favoured site, nearest to any residential district. Probably such a meadow would be a chosen place for the Feast of Tabernacles; a sort of annual picnic celebration, originally associated with sowing and harvesting (much as the Kent hop-pickers operate these days).
[See *Dance of Maskel; Dance of the Priests*]

ABHINAYA (India)

A Sanskrit Theater term, which includes Dance and Gesture. Literally: "All-action" known as "Four Guides", which are: (1) *Angika Abhinaya*, general mode of movements, aiming at real or visual impression; (2) *Vacika Abhinaya*, rhythmic expression, or the "voice" of the whole piece; pronunciation, accent, rhythm (by word or gesture or both); (3) *Aharva Abhinaya*, the decor, character of costume, make-up, implements etc. which combine to suggest the person displayed in action; and (4) *Sattvika Abhinaya*, brings these visual conditions into mental or spiritual expression of the entire character throughout. Literally, *abhinaya* signifies the "explanation of the in-dwelling idea", and affects all theatre action whether in music, dance or voice, coming to its visual apex in *hasta-mudra*,* with its emotional complexus in *raga* (music) with *rasa* (emotional flavour).

ABHINAYA DARPANA (Sanskrit, India)

Means *Mirror (of) Gesture*; using the term mirror in the same manner as it was used in Mediaeval Europe (mirror, *spiegel* etc). *Abhi-naya* means "dance-move", and *darpana* is "reflex". The title implies a text-book on stage action. This work is an abridgement by Nandikeshvara, of an older and far more extensive Indian compilation known as *Natya Shastras, (Verses (on) Dance)*, attributed to "Bharata". An English translation (published 1917 by the India Society, London) by Ananda K. Coomaraswamy and G. Duggirala, is from *Abhinaya Darpana*; and deals principally with the *hastas** and *mudras** (gestures and poses) traditional in Hindu ritual dance, as used in the temple liturgy, the temple mythic drama, and in lesser degree in *hatha yoga* practise. This system of Mime is general through the Orient.
[See *Natya Shastras; Mudra*]

ABKIA FUNERAL DANCE (Southern Sudan)
Ceremonial mourning given for any deceased
member of the Abkia tribe. Music comes from
two long wooden trumpets and gourd rattles; the
women's robes are withered creepers from forest
trees, plastered with mud; yet the melody is gay.
The funeral is at dawn. Thirty women move in
single file round a large mango tree. Though an
expression of loss, these trumpets and rattles give
out a jig, expressed in five descending notes, in a
phrase that has no ending. The feet move in a jerky
double step; and misery is affirmed by monotony
of this shuffling repetition. The funeral dance goes
on for seven days; even when musicians sleep, the
women continue through the night; entirely concentrated on the departing spirit they wish to
assure; while even their wooden rattles do not
break this mood. They not only mourn a departed
soul but, in the concentrated rhythm of the dance,
accompany him on the first difficult stage of his
journey.

ABLI-UMMANI (Assyria)
Picked young men, who in Babylon and other
cities, furnished the *Matzir-bit-Ilu* or Temple
Guard (also for the King). The term means *Sons
(of) Army*. They participated prominently in
festival rituals; they sang in the *Pi-Zalmata* such as
Zalmati-Kurubti (Peace Offerings) or psalms, as part
of the Liturgy (revised and collated in much later
Hebrew versions in the Old Testament). They
served under the *Abra-Khu* or Chancellor; and
were, in part trained in the *Riduti* (House of
Children) or School of Warriors. We note that the
term *abli* continues today, as "able seaman",
while *matzir* has become *matlow*, a naval man
(French—*matelot*); and his biscuit is *motza* or
matzir. Later the number of 25 or 28 (lunar) was
extended; when the younger recruits were named
as *kherubim* (junior choral singer-dancers) or
cherubs.

ABRAXAS, or ABRASAX
A ritual dance of the Greek Gnostics; in Athens,
Corinth and Antiocha (in the "Seven Churches of
Asia"). This serpentine dance has a ring form of
twelve men, and another, the *chantor*, in the
centre. Similar to waltz form, with small circles
round a large circle. Compare with the better
known *Hymn of Jesus;** another closed circle
ritual dance.   [See *Jesus, Dance of*]

ABUANG (Bali, Indonesia)
Second part of an old courtship dance, held yearly
at the village of Tenganan, East Bali. Following
upon the *Redjang,** performed by unmarried girls
at the beginning of the festival, *Abuang* is
accompanied by the *Gamelan selundung* orchestra.
Marriageable girls step modestly forward to show
themselves. With downcast eyes, and arms outstretched, they circle the dancing-space one by
one, each youth making his choice by walking up
to a girl and moving before her in a dignified
dance. If she accepts him, she continues to dance
with him, but if not she returns to her companions leaving her rejected suitor to the laughter
of spectators. Elsewhere in Bali, the *Djoged,** a
dance similar, but less modest and less restrained,
is very popular. In Tenganan, where the real
purpose of the *Abuang* (that of marriage arrangement) is preserved, the *Djoged* is forbidden.

ABUELO (New Mexico)
"The Grandfather" (Old Year). In the village of
San Ildefonso, he acts as does the "fool" or
"man with the whip" (or bladder on a stick) in
the English Morris.* There is a mime to indicate
that after the Old Man kills the Bull, the animal
is cut up and distributed. All through, *El Toro* is
the protagonist of *El Abuelo*. There is only one
girl (like the "Bessie"), but she is always a girl,
not a man dressed up. Much of the dance is
comedy mime; *El Abuelo* makes wisecracks, or he
fights with the Bull; or they dance together; but
then the Bull gets wild. Each character has five or
six aspects, and they are similar to the *matachines**
dancers. All the Matachin tunes are non-Indian in
style, mainly Spanish; short, and much-repeated.

ACADEMY (Greek, French)
The "accepted school" or centre of teaching an
art, hence a classical or conventional mode or
system. From Italian recoveries (stimulated by
Greek learning) the idea of Academie settled into
academies of music, poetry, and finally dance,
when Paris became the setting of Academy
d'Opera; then Academy Royale de Musique. The
Russian School was never named Academy; the
English school gradually obtained the title, long
after we had a Royal Academy of Art or a Royal
Society for Science. As there was no restriction on
the use, we had preposterous dance schools; e.g.
Academy of Choreographic Art. The "academic
style" is settled as Classical ballet style, but in
Theater more than school. Its current name is,
more accurately, *State Choreographic Tekhnikum*.

ACATLAXQUE (Mexico)
"*Reed Throwing Dance*." A dance of the Otomi
Indians of Pahuatlan, Hidalgo, performed by about
a dozen young men and "Malinche" *—a boy in
a long white dress, holding a gourd containing a

painted wood, or articulated silver snake. The other dancers wear white cotton suits, red knee-length over-trousers; red kerchiefs tied crosswise over one shoulder and cone-shaped paper caps with streamers. Each carries his *acatlaxque*—a bundle of ten or twelve reeds lightly fastened together with slip knots and decorated with brilliant feathers. First, to the music of flute and drum, they perform intricate steps in two rows inside the church. Then, in one long row, in the courtyard facing the open door, they advance and retreat with a hopping step, a bow, and a turn. After this prelude the dance, centreing round Malinche, begins. Forming a circle round her, while one man wriggles a snake over her head, they perform various figures, dancing out in ones and twos round her. Finally she is lifted on to a small wooden platform. The dancers stop and, one by one, throw out their *acatlaxque*, so that the reeds extend telescopically to form a canopy over Malinche. This action is repeated several times, the reed dome rotating as the dancers move slowly round. This dance has pre-Conquest origins. *Acatl* ("Reed") was a day and year name in the Aztec calendar, and their fifty-two year cycles were called "sheafs", represented by a glyph showing reeds bound into a bundle.   [See *Aztec Dance*]

ACROBATIC DANCE

Is based solely on physical skill : in rapid, unusual, and even contorted modes of movement. Acrobacy moves midway between real dance and sport or games. The term "acrobat" is said to derive from Greek "to walk tip-toe", which was relevant to *funambules** or rope-dancers. Nearly every mode of dance, when it degenerates into exhibitionism, reveals some kind of acrobacy or personal showing-off; which is neither art nor ritual, as the optimum degree of "command of the body". Basic training (as for the circus) requires limbering (muscle-stretching), with balancing in all positions; next, development of speed in change of movement. At the opposing end are "plastic poses". Most professional dance training borders, at times, on acrobacy —as 'turning out' at the bar, in ballet; the bent-back fingers of Balinese dancers; or *la danse du ventre** of Northern Africa. Some modes of can-can show the acrobatic finale of *grande écarte* or the "splits", and the "cart-wheel". In pantomime, John Rich in London used acrobatic movement for his *Harlequinade*; this pattern persisted until well past 1900, for Harlequin had to dive through apparently solid walls (of stage scenery) to appear or vanish magically. A century earlier, acrobatic dance was linked in Paris with "flying ballet" forms (as in the early *Giselle*).Even in ballet,acrobatic routines have been seen; in *Petrushka*, the Moor is a circus acrobat,

whose worship is his routine; a coconut his deity. In *Scheherazade* was a "big jump" and a head-spin; while we can recall also *Renard* and *Le Train Bleu*, long before the erotic acrobatics of *Carmen*. Acrobatic tumbling and rushing belong more to music-hall and circus than to the art of ballet.

ACTA PILATI (Latin) or
AKTA NIKODEMUS (Greek)

Was a collection of legends compiled as *plauti*, or plays; though a later legend turned the general name into the traditional Pilate—as distinct from the Jewish Saul, who turned into Paul "on the way to Damascus". This *Gospel of Nicodemus* (its final title) serves as a source book for numerous mediaeval Mysteries and Miracle Plays, following those of the famous *paraboloni*, the monk-actors of Alexandria, whose plays became termed *parables*. The collection finally was set aside from inclusion among the chosen "sacred books" and deemed apocryphal, after it had for many centuries been accepted (as indeed it was) as equally authentic. The tradition continued, the plays being located in the *Pilatus Domus* or House of Pilate, with no reference to any supposed individual named Pilate.

ADAGIO (Italian)

Term used in music and in dance; more especially to denote the "slow movement" of two partners in a *pas de deux* in ballet. Derived from Italian *ad agio*—"at ease"—it indicated especially the leisurely entrance of nobles for the *pavane,** as compared with the swifter progress of *andante*. In music, *adagio* is used as a time-indication (though its meaning has changed in precise scale); but in dance the slow body movement is required, regardless of musical speed.

AFRICAN DANCES

No single study or group of studies can cover all the traditional dances of this vast continent; they are still in process of observation and record. Two recent books aim specifically at dance and music. Geoffrey Gorer's *Africa Dances* leads us to expect an exhaustive account of the area covered :[1] in this instance, West Africa in general and Dahomey in particular, but the "travel notes" (apparently from a diary) have been discursive, including comments on politics and economics, yet lacking their underlying connection with vanishing dance ritual traditions. Again, precise facts on time and place, season and function of the ritual noted, are absent or insufficient; while photographs (as reproduced) are lacking in detail of group or person. The reader sadly perceives that an opportunity has been missed for want of methodical training. We turn to the penetrating study by Hugh Tracey of *Chopi*

Musicians (now based in Portuguese East Africa) to delight in the fullness of detail here presented, though the forms and functions of dance receive treatment less adequate than music, possibly because of the recession of older tribal usage, under the pressure of mercenaries and missionaries—the two great destroyers of tradition.[2] The Chopi dance has slowly degraded into a variant of West Indian *calypso*—that is, the lower social traditions of satire and comment continue; while the older and more developed religious rituals have vanished. We have, so to say, a sabbath newspaper but with no serious monthly journals of intelligence. What remains, has been studied with immense care and enthusiasm. Coupled with sound recordings (some already broadcast in Britain) they help to bring to us the reality of this impressive body of musical tradition.

[1] *Africa Dances*: Geoffrey Gorer (Penguin Publication, 1945, first edition 1935).
[2] *Chopi Musicians, Their Music, Poetry and Instruments*, Hugh Tracey. Oxford University Press 1948.)

AFWI, Dance of (French Guinea, West Africa)
Is performed by masked "men-birds" in the "Sacred Forest", or place of children's initiation into the tribe (of Tomo). No drums are permitted. Tattooing, part of the initiation, is the tribal sign; as many as two hundred children, gathered from surrounding villages, may participate. The ceremony takes long to prepare and is held every five years. Music-messages summoning candidates are sent by drum or whistle. Dance music is provided by a small band of semi-professionals who travel where required. All officials of the Sacred Forest enter the final dance before the Feast.

AGAPE (Greek)
From *"agamos"* (Hiero gamos) marriage; the "love feast" of the primitive *Krestiani* of Antioch; and thence among the *Khatakumenoi*, of Rome, who formed an illicit "coll-legia". These weekly gatherings held at night, in underground halls of the *Kathacombs* in ancient Rome, were marked by a feast (the richer people bringing supplies for the *deakons* to distribute among the company); and followed by mirthful singing and dances, ending at dawn.

AGRICULTURAL RITUAL DANCES
Agriculture has developed numerous dance traditions in ritual festival, all rising from the particular social-economic bases of each location. We find rites based on (a) Wheat; (b) Corn or Maize; (c) Rice; or (d) the Yam and similar fruits. Effects known to modern science as "vitamins" or "poisons" are well known to "natives" as spirits, good or bad; they are extracted and prepared accordingly. Important seasons in agriculture are celebrated with rites: especially sowing and harvest—the "death of grain" and its "resurrection", in food for men. Roman rites had twelve sub-rituals, one in each month, administered by the augurs for *Fratres Arval*. Ritual dances arise from the solemn preliminaries: in processional, ring-dance, and square-dance forms. Presently more difficult symbols arise, when mental training is developed, men use tools, processes, and facts, familiar in agriculture, to begin the difficult task of homoculture. The priest-king is known as chief gardener, or as a good shepherd; as a leading musician; as a great soldier; as a grand looter or thief; an agriculturist (Dionysus, god of the vine); cattle-keeper (Zoroaster); warrior (Mithras); administrator (Marsios) etc., in various religious cults. Changes in the year produced a dual-god system— the Egyptian Horus-Elder and Horus-Younger; this in turn incites sadism—a dying, defeated king (or bull, boar, fish, etc.) as the Year End; or a living, triumphant infant-king, as the Year Beginning. These two gods are mutually involved (as, for example, Janus and Johannus). Merged with all was the Great Mother, known under a thousand names; always dual, as Virgin and as Mother, (like Horus and Hera), being attractor or reflector of energy (Hindu *Shakta-Shakti*).

AGUÉ T 'ROYO (Haiti)
The "King of Waters" to whom salutes and prayers are addressed, sometimes in ritual dance with a chant. Usually the *verver** (sign) is made, with corn meal, or in the sand already present; and this Voodoo dance begins circling round it, accompanied by drums. Agué is worshipped at streams or lakes and waterfalls; but his rite is used to follow the preliminary *Rada* chant (*Hélas grand-père*) which begins all *Rada* ceremonies; both in 2/4 time; at the rite of *Tête l'Eau*, or *Maître de l'Eau*. The largest drums are *hountah* (guiding time and giving mood), with bass tone; the tenor drum, *boulatier*; and the medium *sirgonh*. Mambo is the priestess who (second only to the *Houngan* or priest) rules the rituals.   [See *Sect Rouge; Sher-Shay; Guédé*]

AHIDOUS (Morocco)
A Berber dance of Central Morocco. Accompanied by the beat of tambours and clapping of hands, men and women alternate in a circle which closes and widens, as the dancers move in perfect coordination to a vigorous rhythm. Tempo gradually increases, rising to a climax, then slowly decreases to calmness again. It is danced out of doors. The men wear their native dress or woollen *djellabah*

(hooded robes) and yellow slippers. The women (unveiled), in loose robes, are adorned with the many bracelets and gold and silver coin ornaments beloved by Berber women, their dusky skin patterned with blue tattooing, and often wear ear-rings shaped like a tiny hand with a jewel in the centre —"Fatima's Hand", a protection against the evil eye. [See *Morocco, Dances of*]

AHAL OR MAHAL (Arabic, African)
A "marriage market" festival held by the nomadic Tuareg of N. Africa; with a difference. Women arrange the *Ahal* when they need a man. Usually it follows a family wedding; but that is a private affair. By *ahal*, the girl chooses her husband; she may try several; matriarchy still governs tribal descent. They are called Tuareg; by themselves, as Ihaggeren, which denotes their ancient Egyptian origin, as does the ceremonial use of the *litham*, the long head-binding of cotton or linen; once used for the initiates into religion. The girl recites or sings, playing her *amzad* (or *hamzadi*) a primitive violin, for an hour or so. Men ride along, in pairs, riding slow, first in line then in circle. They dismount; drumming and singing recommence. At dusk they stop for a meal; they begin a simple dance form, in pairs, never touching. Women do not wear veils. At dawn men and women pair off. Before all this, the *mahal* player (who first sings) has thrown her small bow towards her chosen man; they disappear toward the desert.
 Touareg—the older name, seems to derive from *Tuat-rehka*—the "Son of the Duat who is Righteous"—an Egyptian term. Amoun is mentioned in some of the love poems, as "the cord"—as *Amoun-Minat*.

AHIR (Uttar Pradesh, India)
To be seen in Lucknow or Cawnpore; an imitation of military drill; swinging or stepping over sword or lance; or combat with *lathi* (a long staff, used by police instead of short baton) like "single sticks" or the now obsolete cutlass-drill. The *Ahir* is performed in smart rhythms (as is *kendo* in Japan) by the small clans who show it, with *dholak* (drum) and *kansi* (gong or cymbal), and usually for their own weddings or birth celebrations. Other male dances in this district include *Kahar*, *Chamar* and *Pasi*. The *Chamar* is a kind of clown dance, like the *Bhanir Nautch*,* there is no technical excellence. The chief dancer in *Chamar* is a boy dressed as a girl, who is the butt of the clown.

AHOUACH, Ahouache, Arhaoush (Morocco)
A "shadow" dance of Shleuh Berbers of the Western Atlas, performed at night in a high-walled courtyard, by fire- or torch-light, which throws huge shadows on the walls. It may be danced in a line by men only (in *djellabah* woollen robes—turban and yellow slippers), with young boys at one end; or in a circle of men and women. Unveiled, the women wear light tunics, scarves and jewelled ornaments. A single piece of material about ten yards long, the tunic or *lizar* is fastened above the breasts with silver brooches. The dancers do not circle the courtyard but remain in one place, dancing consisting of rhythmic movements of knees, arms and hands. Anyone breaking the rhythm by a false gesture is unceremoniously removed by the Master of Ceremonies. Accompanied by the dancers' high-pitched chanting and by the *bendir* (tambour) players, who sit on the ground in the centre of the courtyard, the rhythmic movements change with the music, being sometimes smooth and flowing, sometimes more jerky and violent. Based on a single phrase incessantly repeated, the chant has a theme usually of love or loyalty. The *Ahouach* continues for several hours, perhaps all night, and in spite of its dignified quality is a joyous dance celebrating a good harvest or similar event. [See Morocco, dances of]

ALARIPPU (Hindu)
First of the five basic "movements" of South India classical Temple ritual dance of *Bharata Natyam.** The term signifies the "first borders or boundaries" in this "dance of creation", when Shiva thrusts back the dimensions of chaotic space, forming a localised *mandala* wherein he may dance—"making the banks". (Cp. "*riparian*").

"AL AGUDO" (Spain)
A "couple-dance" of Old Castile. The man and woman face each other with downcast eyes and without touching. In some districts the couples perform the whole dance on the same spot; in others they move in a zigzag procession, each pair at an angle to the others, so that no two neighbouring couples move outwards in the same direction.

ALBORADA (Spain)
From *alba*—dawn, the "white time" or "light", originally a praise song with gesture, after the *vexilla* or "night vigil" in religious ritual. Later, in secular usage, taken over by the jesters and used as a morning dance-song (though somewhat later than dawn), as the counterpart of *serenada* or *serenata*, the evening song. The *alborada* was long popular in Galicia, played on bagpipes and later used at peasant *fiestas*, especially weddings, to awaken the guests; thus becoming the first dance of the day.

ALCHEMICAL RITUAL DANCES
(Europe, Mediæval)
Were evolved by combination of secret Greek rites
with Arabic experiments in physical science (*Al
Khemia*), which thenceforth was communicated in
a dual symbolism. The "Quest for Gold" was followed in laboratories (culminating with Curie, in
discovery of radium, and atomic fission), and in
occult rites for spiritual development. These rites,
using Greek terms (following the Greek books
brought west after 1200 AD) summarised certain
aspects of Eleusinian Mysteries, in which dance
was used ceremonially. These had rites sacred to
Athene (Air), Hephaestus (Fire), Demeter (Earth),
and Poseidon (Water) with Theta. Metals or salts
were named in allegorical terms, while used factu-
ally in experiments. The progeny of this middle
way received names, familiar as sylphs and
sylphides, gnomes or dwarfs or kobolds, salamanders, undines, sprites, or water nixies etc.
These creatures entered into mystical tales, later
termed "romantic" because of allegories; examples
may be found in Scottish ballads, in German
legends, or French romance. Attractions and repul-
sions of chemicals (valencies) were figured as movements of intelligent agents; later these appeared in
allegorical dances and ballets. Alchemy, for two
centuries dismissed as "idle fiction", is re-instated
in atomic science; the mind-creatures symbolised
were ignored as legend, but re-appeared in the
recondite mind-analysis of Freud, Jung, and Adler :
all with newer names but identical relations. Their
single similarity is in their movement seen as
rhythmic dance. One password was *Solve et coagu-
late* (Dissolve and synthesize). For Hymns see
Clothed with the Sun. Anna Kingsford. London,
1912. (3rd ed.).   [See Gabalis, Comte de]

ALCHERA (Australia)
The traditional and secret cycles of legends told in
nine ballet episodes of the "Dream Time" or periods
of world creation. The basic idea is that APMA
the divine snake, dreams the world and man into
existence, each phase with a successive ancestor.
There are nine of these festival dream ballets; in
each one, dance-mime is more important than
words. The Dream Time is a project back in time to
the emergent period of human soul life, as seen by
the Myalls or black-fellows; it is clear that these
are remains of a most ancient religious scheme.

ALEGRIAS (Andalusia, Spain)
A woman's solo dance in 3/4 or 6/8 time. Having
many variants, it may be danced with or without
castanets. In Cadiz or Granada the dancer sometimes wears a dress with a frilled skirt and long
train (also in the *Soleares*), and a characteristic of

the *Alegrias* is the skilful twisting of the train with
the foot, as the dancer turns. Heel taps (*taconeado*)
are also a feature of this dance.

ALEKOKI (Hawaii)
A standing *hula*,* telling in gesture, the love story
of King Kalakaua and the Princess Kamamalu, who
used to meet at the Alekoki waterfall, in Nuuanu
Valley, near Honolulu. With quick, yet dignified
movements, hands and arms describe, in symbolic
dance language, the romantic theme.

ALEUTIAN MASK DANCE (Aleutian Islands)
A mimetic dance, performed with masks of powerful design and rich colour. A hunter has by mistake
killed a beautiful bird. He mimes his sorrow, when
the dying bird suddenly changes into a lovely
woman; the hunter wonders; she explains; and he
now pursues her as a woman, whom eventually he
wins.

ALEWANDER (German and Swiss)
Also named as *Allemande* or *Allemandler* in German dialect. At Appelzell the folk dance form is
called *Schwöbli* (as coming from Swabia). As a
village dance it is in 2/4 or triple time, showing
chiefly the promenade form, but ending in a gallop.
The dance is a measured walk, alternating with a
chain, in which couples turn on the appropriate
note. The Allemandler name runs close to the much
older *Almond*; the current form is late and has no
more than 17th/18th century fashions, known
through Western Europe. There were so many
melodies that some composers found them a "mine
of inspiration".

ALGERIAN NEGRO DANCE (N. Africa)
Dances by Negro men are seen at Algiers, Tunis,
Djelfa, or Ghardaia. The men are usually Sudanese
Negroes; who may suddenly feel inspired to celebrate; regardless of payment for dancing. Six or
eight gather in a close circle; of whom one carries
the *derbouka* (drum), and another, heavy brass
cymbals. These men may stay inside the tight ring.
They begin slowly chanting, marking time with
drum and cymbals; gradually their voices rise in
pitch and increase in speed. The chant may develop
a martial note; or may turn to mourning. They
leave go, and revolve in pirouettes, first on one
foot, then the other; and again join, changing
direction accurately but with no leader and no
orders. They begin to perspire, but continue—perhaps an hour, even two or three, until they are
exhausted. Such a group is composed always of
men who belong to one clan, or work-company;
they will permit no others to join; nor may women
dance with them.

ALLAH (Arabic)
Dance of the Ninety-and-Nine "Sacred Names of
Allah" was performed by the *darawish* ritual
dancers in their *Zhikr*.* Knowing that Allah is not
to be described even by a million names, they select
the most attractive names and recite them, while
dancing in a ring. The dance form is similar to that
of the *valse*, but the men do not move in couples.
They dance alone, perhaps for an hour, perhaps
longer, knowing that possibly at some instant the
incommunicable name, The Hundredth Name, may
be in a flash revealed to them. The Hebrew system
possessed also its Hundred variations on JHVH,
springing from *Tetragrammaton*;* while the Hindu
Sanskrit system actually founded the hieratic
alphabet on the doubling of the "Names of the 49
Fires". These were explicated in sacred ritual
dances. With the ritual we find connected the
famous "*108 Tattvas*" of the universal emanation—
and return. The Chinese used the *Pakua** in similar
fashion; by the fission of the 99 was accomplished
the fusion of the One with the dancer-worshipper.
Modern nuclear physics now has its "98 elements"
—the 10 focal bases are not yet identified.
[See *Dervish Dancers*]

ALLEGORY (Greek *allegoria*)
A description or presentation of one thing, or set
of facts, or relations, under the image of another
balancing thing or set of facts. In dance, an allegory
becomes a prolonged and acted metaphor; it may
partake of mythic character (as dealing with
deities) or of parable (as dealing with human
beings). The principal need is to maintain a con-
sistency of character and relation between the two
sets of facts or entities or situations presented.
John Bunyan's legend of a journey (*Pilgrim's
Progress*) is a fully rounded allegory, having an
essential religious character; but Dean Swift's
legend of the *Adventures of Gulliver in Lilliput*,
has a skilfully hidden political character, so much
so that the main features of the tale can be used
as a story or *Phantasmagoria* play for children.
Rabelais' story of *Gargantua and Pantagruel* today
loses most of its allegorical structure and becomes
a quaint legend; while Anatole France's *Penguin
Island* (on a similar topic) has a more recent freshness. The persistent abuse of alleged Grecian
mythology in ballet form on the modern stage
(presented by those who do not know either the
original allegory or myth or the general meaning),
shows how puerile ancient allegory can become.
[See *Myth*; *Fable*; *Parable*]

ALLEGRO (Italian ballet term)
General term meaning joyful, gladness (esp. as used
in music) or *allegria*. Linked with *adagio* as a con-

trast: slow or quick. Vaganova attached more
meaning: she compared *adagio* with easy work,
pupils' first steps, to "master the body". *Allegro*—
she asserted—is the foundation of science in dance:
its intricacy the mark of future perfection. Where
adagio may mean play, leisurely movement, the
allegro reveals the measure of true style. "When
we reach *allegro* we begin to study dance art; we
reach style or form, as contrasted with play movement". In *adagio* the dancer moves herself; with
allegro she can move her audience.[1]
[[1] *Basic Principles; Classical Ballet*. Agrippina Y.
Vaganova. 1st Russian edition. Leningrad, 1934
(p. 25)]

ALL SOULS FESTIVAL AND DANCE (European)
Ritual or religious celebrations repeated annually,
in memory of tribal ancestors *en bloc*. Thus the
rites go back to pre-history, to those days, "when
no man knew who was his father". The only
memorial was a mass memorial; the modern
analogy is the revived "Unknown Soldier" state
ceremonial (said to be, in Britain, a catholic Irish-
man selected by an Irish padre). The theological
categories have emerged gradually. There are the
"first-class" *persona*, the "saints and martyrs", who
are essentially interred under stone altars; that is a
condition of having any *kirke* or church, the "circle
round the tombe", commemorated by dance and
chant. There are second-class souls: those of
worthy folk who managed somehow to intrude
into vaults, church walls, etc.; and the third-class
souls, permitted in the external "acre". There are
also fourth-class or proletarian souls, or outcastes;
or non-conformists, heretics, and pagana. Many of
the "pagans" (so-called) celebrate their own rites
of greater age and equal potency; and others, such
as the Moslem ritual. In two facts they are alike:
they illuminate burial grounds, they do not emphasise always the mournful aspect. The Romish
church demarcates the Official Dead ("saints" are
admitted, as old ones die out or are found out),
and the Unofficial Dead, or those who may, for
payment, get "masses" at present. Ritual replaces
formal dance, as token bread replaces a genuine
Feast of the Dead, once considered indispensable;
but now apparent only in the Wakes in some English counties. These are not to be confused with
the *Soule*, or the *Soule* Cakes, or the *Soule* Celebrations (in France). The Haitian people preserve a
more realistic approach to the whole basis of the
rite; they understand better what are souls; and
how they live. They use equally dances of exorcism, and dance-chants of invocation.

ALLEMANDE—1 (European Countries: France and
    Italy)
This dance term appears over several centuries, in

different places, with varying usage. There are so many changing streams that it becomes difficult to select any single form as the factual origin; the one certainty is that the name Allemande belongs

One of the modes of *La Danse Allemande* from the mediaeval tapestry *The Court of Love* (see page 131). The dance is accompanied by one female and two male voices, with pipe and mandolina.   FRANCE
(Courtesy of Sotheby and Co.)

only to the latest salon form, having lost all its original meaning. It can refer but idly to any sort of "German Dance."

The last form of the dance tells us little; it seems to have been associated with alms-giving. This clerical rite, used with Maundy Thursday, contained a brief ceremonial. The Chaucerian use of the term *leman* hints at the feminine dominant character of the dance, which may first have been a harvest dance for fertility and "Gifts from the World Mother" latterly a duty charged on ruling families. The Pavan was as essentially masculine — the vahan or appearance of the ruler, moving before or in the circle of this *pavana*.

ALLEMAND OR ALLEMANDE — 2
Also spelled *Almain*; *Allmaine*; *Almond*; *Alman*; or *Almayne*, as well as *Allemagne* (a French form). In its final form (16th century) this was a salon or court dance, but we may examine its Iberian-Arabic sources, in two modes. One was exoteric, from Chapter 107 of the *Quran* (Mecca), being *Al-Ma'Un*; the Alms; and refers to the regular collection of legal alms prescribed. From this association, the term continued in England as *almoner*, almonry, alms and even alimony. The lesser known esoteric parallel was the Sufi one, used in praying for "alms from Allah", and thence derives the term *alma* (soul), still used in Spanish; and *almeh* (dancers of unveiling of the soul). The prophet Mohammed was called *Al-Min* — the "Faithful" or "True One." Cognate terms are Chaucer's *leman* (*Leman*, dance partner); and the University term *alumnus*, or student; also the white-flowered bush, the almond (first to appear after winter), or *amygdal*, from which : Magdalene, another ritual dancer, parallel with Delilah. These chants were also used in the prescribed "seven circuits" of the Ka-aba at Mecca, when ninety-nine of the "Hundred Names of Allah" were recited. One is *Al-Mannanu-el-Qahir* — the All-Subduing Giver. The pilgrims call on *Rabb-ul-'alamin* as Lord, Sustainer, Nourisher of all the Worlds, in the *salat*, or prayer of Islam. In Sufi lore, *Alami-i-Ma'ni* is the world or plane of ideas (compare *Abra-kad-abra**) also *Almensalle* — Table (*Zincali*, or Gypsy); *almendra* (Spanish) *almont*. *Almendra* equals shape of dance-plan.

In her *Legends of the Madonna* Mrs. A. B. Jameson mentions the frequent setting of a picture or "frame" as the "aureole of light". This effect was most obvious in the ritual, being the shape made by the "ring" of lighted candles in the hands of worshippers. When vertical, this effect was less frequently seen (it was done with numerous tiny oil lamps), except in paint or sculpture. These static forms always follow on the dynamic forms that occur in ritual. Mrs. Jameson mentions : ". . .

when in a standing position (it) is of an oblong form, called the *mandorla*, 'the almond' ", (and adds in a note) "or, called the *Vesica Pisces* by Lord Lindley and others."

In this connection, the halo (or *uaello*, the wheel) also ranges from the reality of living light in the lamps of the ritual dance-ring, then to the painted ring round the head in picture or statue, to the final solid form used in sculpture (and also in the mystery plays) as a plate of burnished metal that would reflect light, fitted on as a head-dress. In Andrea Orcagna's relief at Or San Michele, a throne is set within a *mandorla*; attended by "four angels" and two more playing musical instruments. This figures one phase of the ritual dance of the *Almonde*. (One chief festival of Al-Monde was celebrated at "Feast of Assumption — BVM — Aug. 15th). One instrument acquired the name *mandolin* from its usage at this ceremonial. This type of work appeared when the enthusiasm for the Sacrasissima Cintola della Madonna was popular; especially at Prato (Palado) to which pilgrimages were frequent. This *cintola*, or girdle, was merged in the same symbolism. (In England it became known as the *garland* and then *Garter*, especially at Windsor). The latest ritual consisted in granting a material girdle (or sash or riband) as a proof that the wearer had been admitted to the Ritual of the Almond. In this manner, one of the ancient rituals of knighthood was "taken over" into the Latin church in the 13th century.

The last form of *Allemande* is a dignified court dance which spread through Europe during the 14th century. Called *Trotto* (probably from *Tarota*) by Germans; by Italians the name was changed to *Saltarello Tedesco* or *German Saltarello*. In France the *Trotto* was known as the *Allemande* or *Allemagne*; in England variously spelt as *Almain*, *Alman*, *Almand*, *Almond*, *Almayne*. The *Allemande* was the first processional form recorded among social dances. Sung as well as danced, it resembled in this the circular *Branle*,* a form of the *Carole** or linked round dance. Music was in duple time; partners joined hands were held in a raised position, distinct from the *Basse Danse** and *Pavane*.* The procession of couples either circled the hall, or moved forward down the centre of the room, turned, and retreated to the starting point. Sometimes partners separated, women circling to the right, men to the left, meeting at the end of the room and coming up the centre hand-in-hand. The style of dance was smooth and dignified. Although the *Allemande* was introduced into England via France about mid-14th century, the steps were not recorded until the 16th century. A detailed description is given by Arbeau in his *Orchesographie** (1588). The *Allemande* was popular during the reign of Elizabeth I, forming, with the *Courante** or *Coranto*, one of the pairs of dances in duple and triple time often thus arranged. (See *Nachtanz**). By the 18th century, the *Allemande* had again changed into a square dance for eight, like the *Cotillon**, the only apparent link between it and the 16th century dance being the interlacing of arms in a similar manner. When it ceased to be danced the *Allemande* continued in the musical suite, still followed by the quicker *Courante*. Purcell, Couperin, Bach and Handel composed in this form.

ALMACK'S ASSEMBLY ROOMS (London)
Was a centre of dance for London "society" for several decades prior to the accession of Victoria. Founded by a canny Scot, James Macall (he inverted his name for "business reasons") in 1765, it began in a building newly erected in King-street, St. James. This dancing club (as it was in purpose and effect), followed on Almack's success with Brooke's Club (1763) as it became known. Almack's plan seems to have aimed at dethroning Mrs. Cornelys of Soho Square, by providing a certifiably "proper" place, for ladies who wanted to dance, but not in Soho; while Ranelagh was too far distant, and unsuitable during winter. Almack secured the self-appointment of an exclusive committee of *grandes dames*; his hall opened on February 12th, 1765, patronised by dukes and countesses. Subscriptions ran to ten guineas for a ball and supper, once weekly for twelve weeks. Cards and scandal also flourished; but bishops gave the place their blessing; and even Tsar Alexander attended to dance. No sons of commerce entered on those Wednesday evenings. In 1814 Scottish reels were favoured; and English country dances. In 1815 Lady Jersey brought from Paris the recent quadrille; and soon the waltz followed, as a daring innovation, led by Countess Lieven in 1816. Almost by necessity, Almack's was a social marriage centre — a "matrimonial bazaar", one writer terms it. Quasi-fancy-dress balls alternated with plainer affairs. In May, 1826, Tom Moore records seeing a fancy quadrille called *Paysannes Provencales*, though another expected dance, *Twelve Months*, suffered postponement. When Victoria began to reign, obviously a committee of ladies could no longer "run society", and Almacks began to droop perceptibly. By 1840 the exclusive air had been punctured; and though the Rooms continued in use for dancing, the Assembly became more bourgeois. Finally dances ceased; halls were opened elsewhere; and the place was used for lectures or meetings as Willis' Rooms. Almack's had, in its day, "set the tone" not merely for the social dance gathering, but for the style of dance suitable to be performed. This style by usage has also departed; now teachers and competitions try to impose national standards.

ALMTANZ (Austria)
From *Allmande, Alm'Tanz*. Alpine village dance held in September to celebrate the return of the dairy-maids (*Almerinnen*) from the summer mountain pastures. During the day the cattle, decked with flowers, are brought down to their winter quarters, and in the evening the *Almtanz* takes place at the village inn, where *Landlers** and *Schuhplattlers** are danced to the sound of zithers or accordions. The dairymaids are distinguished by their white aprons, in contrast to the black or coloured aprons of the other girls. The *Almerinnen* also celebrate the "Feast of the Assumption" on Aug. 15th, when their friends visit them high on the mountain, to dance either inside the huts or out on the grassy mountainside.

ALPHABET AND DANCE
Early systems of letter-making were, like parallel systems of numerals, first written on the ground in circles; or in square and rectangles. Hebrew names; the *Tetragrammaton* in Greek; and the Latin Augur system, as well as *Runes*, were all set in circles. The clue is the Roman "clock face" in which twelve numerals must rest in a circle for the hours of the day. Roman calendars also were set in a month circle — the median point similarly calculated — the Ides and the Nones. Ritual used the circles to teach, or illustrated by stepping dance forms. Our English form gave us the clock dance (clog, from *eclogue*) as a memory calendrical system. They began with four points (compass) and doubled to eight; then to 16 and ended with 32. Hindu systems have even more set rituals, with letters in geometrical forms.

ALPHABET RITUAL DANCE (England)
Rarely described in the Missal, but said to be remains of a once-magical ceremonial, followed always in the Latinist dedication of any newly-built church. The description[1] reveals a typical forcible jointure of two systems. The dedicating bishop (or archbishop) having given the traditional three magical knocks on the great door of the church, enters and walks, to music, up the central nave. Before the altar he finds a level space of 10 cubits square, over which the grey ashes of burned palm leaves are raked evenly. With his crook (precisely as the Roman *augur*), he then traces two straight lines of letters, in the form of an Andrew cross. One line contains the letters of the Greek alphabet (Alpha to Omega), and the other line has the letters of the later Latin alphabet. This act is said to refer

to the use of letter-symbols as "carrying the message", in words; but as it is claimed that the magical ritual is as old as the church, we have to remember that no scripture older than 9th century[2] is known; that few were written, and none printed. Moreover, the usage of a square of untrodden clean ashes resembles closely the magic circles (of the same kind) used by mediæval alchemists and magicians; but enscribed more often with the "names of gods and angels" (in Hebrew or Greek, rarely if at all in Latin), and merged with Zodiacal symbols. All of these pavement figures provided an essentially magical "dancing ground": the magician moved around, and in, and over them; while the invoked entities entered or surrounded the diagram.

[See *Yantra*]
[1] *Dictionary of Religion*. Ed. Rev. F. Brendan.
[2] Ref. recent discoveries in Ras Shamra (1958/62).

ALPONA (Bengal, India)
A ritual dance-diagram, drawn by girls in coloured sand in the household worship of the ancient gods, usually "Fortune" as Lakshmi, (the diagram sometimes is called "the Lakshmi"). In earlier days, the diagram was drawn full-scale and served to give the form to a solemn ritual dance. The diagram is called also *rangoli** (stage or dance place of the gods), and has many other names. *Alponama*, or the "Little Name" is literally the *Little Altar*, or "space-for-gods". In Tibet it is the *khyilkhor* (place of dance of the mind, see *Khyilkhor**). In Greece it was one of the uses of Geo-Metria or Earth Measure; and was known also in Rome. (See *Augurs' Dance.**) These diagrams are important in choreography.   [Cp. *Rammal* (Arabia)]

ALTRO VOLTA (Italian)
A technical term used both in dance and music, requesting "another turn", or "try again". Later this was heard in the opera theatres, or for a ballet, when the public called for encore (*en chora*). The name *volta* was, during one period (16th century) applied to any turning dance, in which the dancer revolved on his own axis. The *re-volta* required him to turn in the opposite direction.

ALUD BALOK (Borneo)
"No-end-boat" dance, for two men. They sit down, each on the other's feet; and hold arms by wrist or elbow. Then they rock rhythmically until each leaves the floor alternately, in time with chanting and drum beat. Ten pairs thus linked will do a thirty yard race. This energetic dance is one of a cycle "for the dead" for the spirits of the dead are supposed to be carried, one to each couple, in the centre of the "ship". The Punan and Malay groups

in Niah take interest. This "ship-of-dead-man" recalls Egyptian rites; that of the Ngadjhus is most elaborate. All such rites demand rhythmic movement. The form that is drawn (many are pictures) may run parallel with the European traditions of "cat's cradle". There is a similar "ship" used by the Russian *Khrysty* groups.

AMAZONS (Greek term, ritual dancers at Ephesus)
When a Hellenic colony was established at Ephesus in Ionia, they found a sanctuary of Atargatis (Hittite nature-goddess), whose central shrine was at Karkhemish. These Greeks noted one characteristic of this worship, in the many hundreds of ministrant women; and their usual inaccuracy transformed the ceremony into the fantastic legend of "warrior-women". This fact was noted by Sayce, who writes :
"In early art, the Amazons are robed in Hittite costume, armed with the double-headed axe; and the dances they performed in honour of their goddess of love and war (with shield and bow) gave rise to the myths which saw in them a nation of women warriors".[1]
[See also *The Hittites*. O. R. Gurney (1952)]
[1] *Herodotus* by A. H. Sayce (Page 430).

AMBALAVASI (Dekkan, Central India)
Troupes of itinerant dancers, who perform the *Kathakali* and other mythic plays for rich sponsors. Also given as *Amalavasi;* they belong chiefly to Malabar.

AMENER (France)
Dance of 16th-17th century. Usually in triple time, played at moderate pace, written in six-bar phrases. Verses often accompanied the dance; and thus the music was taken into later suite form. As indicated by each verse, the leader changed dance form, so that dancing became a "follow-my-leader" (*a-mener*) variation.

Ā MOLÉSON (Switzerland; Gruyère region, Fribourg Canton)
A round dance in ¾ waltz-time. With couples holding hands in a circle, the dance has six figures punctuated by hand-claps. Walking, Gallop and Schottische steps are used, partners sometimes waltzing together; or the woman, holding the forefinger of the man's right hand in the "Trüll grasp", turns on the spot under their joined right arms. Moléson is a mountain in the district (where the famous "Ranz des Vaches" is heard). The dance has accompanying verses sung in the old Gruyère dialect, with the refrain "Â Moléson, à Moléson". The women wear a bibbed apron over long-sleeved dress, embroidered white shawl and black buckled

shoes, with either a black lace cap or coquettish wide straw hat with flat black bows on the crown and tied under the chin with velvet ribbons. The men's blue linen suit has an Edelweiss embroidered on the jacket and, for special occasions, long white, accordion-pleated sleeves, with a flat cap bound with velvet.

AMORET (French, mediæval)
Generally a love-song (*petite chanson d'amour*) or ballad; sometimes a love affair; also the simple pair dance, or music to accompany the verses, which were supposed to be newly devised by the wooer. Heywood refers in his *Love's Mistress*, to the dancer : —
"He will be in his amorets, and his canzonets,
   his pastorals, and his madrigals".
With them went the *fleurets*—also dance steps, fencing moves, or painted motifs used in costume or inlaid on the dance floor. The *amoret* step had the form of the love-knot, or twined line, or coupled hearts.

AMORINI (Roman)
Literally, the "Little loves" figured in classical mythology of the popular mode, as the junior Cupids, who delighted especially in their duties as accessories and guardians to lovers. They compare with the *puteola* (see *Putti**), who filled a similar function, watching sacred springs and fountains. The *amorini* provided, as essentially dancing creatures, numerous subjects for painters and sculptures for well over a thousand years. The walls of Pompeii were decorated with many of these pagan creatures. Originally they were seen as the "dancers of life" in some opposition to the *mores* (or *morini*) as dancers of death; of youth, as opposed to age; but the metaphorical changes from ritual to popular comedy has obscured this earlier balance. A similar alternation turned *funus* and *funebrus* into *funambulus* and *fun*. Pompeii had many wall paintings of *amorini* and *putti*.

AMOU YOUMAME (Papua)
"Women's Dance". Twice during the *Gabé** festival, the women dance. Just before dusk on the first evening they enter the dancing-ground. About 40 women in ranks of six, in compact *olové** manner, gather at one end of the clearing. Each carries a small "hour-glass" drum to beat the rhythm, and the whole group careers in a hopping, leaping dance, to the other end of the ground, turns, and dances back again, singing and beating drums. (Cp. *Hek-helelean**). This is repeated until sunset, when a more elaborate head-dress is donned, and the dance proper continues until dawn. Spectators chant and beat drums, while young men and girls hold bamboo torches. Dancers wear loin-cloths of white *tapa*, decorated with geometrical patterns; and ceremonial net cloaks which hang from shoulders to calves. Made of fibre-cords knotted together, patterns are made by weaving red, yellow and black-dyed cords with natural gray. Face and body are painted with red ochre, and long necklaces of dog's teeth are wound ten times round the neck. Into armlets and anklets of woven grass are tucked flowers or red and yellow fibre pompoms. Small tresses of hair on the forehead each have a shell or dog's tooth at the end, while on top of the head rests a spreading head-dress of feathers, decorated with toucan beaks. This is changed at sunset for another, more colourful head-dress, more than three feet high, of bird of paradise plumes. For their second appearance, two nights later, the women wear few ornaments. Their dance, performed in silence, is a whirling frenzy of destruction, when they cut down bushes previously assaulted by warriors (see *Warriors' Dance**), trample surrounding plants and flowers, and threaten with javelins or axes the men watching on verandahs. This silent, leaping dance, precedes the entry of Chiefs, for their dignified *Royal Dance*.* Their grave movements contrast with the violent whirling of the women, who continue to dance around each Chief and his two companions.

AMOUR DE LA HAULT PLEASAUNCE (Norman-English)
Title of an allegorical *daunce*, contained in a poem by Stephen Hawes, written in 1505, printed in 1555. This poem has abstruse connections with the "Tower of Doctrine", that was sought in secret mediæval ritual; associated in France with La Belle Pucelle (known also as Jeanne d'Arc). Edmund Spenser contrived his famous *Faery Queene* in the same esoteric doctrine. He and Stephen Hawes, once a celebrated poet who lived in the reign of Henry VII, were nourished on the same secret teaching which gave the knights their rare enthusiasm (culminating in the reorganisation of the Knights of the Garland (Garter) in Winchester and Windsor), and which has left subtle relics in those painted symbols known as *Tarota Cardes*. Hawes described the gaily apparelled puppets used in one of the rituals by the "royalle tower of Morall Document". He tells how in this *daunce* "Fame departed from Graunde Amour and left him with Governaunce and Grace; and how he went to the Tower of Doctrine".
"The little turret with ymages of golde
   About was set, whiche with the wynde aye moved
   With propre vices, that I ded well beholde
   About the tower, in sundry wyse they hoved
   With goodly pypes, in their mouthes ituned,

That with the wynde they pyped a daunce
Iclipped Amour de la hault Pleasaunce".
(From *The Historye of Graunde Amoure & La Belle
Pucel, called the Palace of Pleasure, etc.* 1555)

ANACARA (Greece)
A small military drum, used by the ancient Greeks
in war dances and marches. Women sometimes
played these accompaniments. The single drummer
was named *anacarista*.

ANDAMAN ISLANDS — *Boys Initiation Dance*
During the ceremonies, which last four days, three
men and one young woman, decorated with vari-
coloured clay, dance round the novice, at a ceremonial feast. On the fourth day a great dance
takes place; at the end the initiate's new name is
proclaimed. At one side of the dancing-ground the
women sit, keeping the rhythm of the dance with
vigorous hand-clapping, while an old man beats
time on the sounding board (the only musical
instrument of the Andaman Islands), at the same
time singing a song, usually about hunting turtle.
The women also sing, and vary their clapping by
beating their hands on their thighs. In the centre
of the dancing-ground stands the initiate, with six
men. The six dancers flex their hips so that the
back is nearly horizontal, then with bent knees,
leap upward, both feet off the ground, using much
energy to keep time to the beats on the sounding
board, which are very rapid.

ANDANTE — 1 (Italian)
Term used in dance and music, to indicate progress at an ambling or walking pace. The usual
tempo is that of an easy walk at, say, four miles
an hour. In dance, it is one of the more difficult
of stage accomplishments. *Andantino* meant originally the same pace with smallest steps. That is,
an adult would move *andante* but a child (holding
hands) would perforce move *andantino*, to cover
the same ground in the same time.

ANDANTE — 2 (Italian)
A term of movement (verb *andare*, to go; and,
in imperative, implying "to get a move on"!)
Musicians took the term from dance (and military
orders), and use it as : *andante*, to move at moderate pace; *andamento*, to move firmly and regularly
(as in fugal form); and *andantino*, a feminisation or
"smaller going along". These three terms are opposed by *allegro* (quick), but *adagio* implies still
slower motion. The pragmatic usage of the terms
appeared with the varlets, serving men, when instructed to take in the dishes from the cookhouse;
and the root seems to be in *andres* (Greek), from
which one name for servitors came.
[Cp. *Merry Andrew**]

ANE (Mediæval France)
The title of the dance-song called *La Prose de l'Ane*,
is a corruption of an older and dignified ritual
Paroussia de l'Année — the celebration of the Winter
Solstice, known as the Appearance of the (New)
Year. Like so many ancient customs, it became
denigrated; while solemnity changed to vulgar
humour (partly, doubtless, owing to the customary
clerical attack on all popular customs which
could not be "taken over"). The date affirms the
solstice : the dance ended on Epiphany Day. The
title was neatly Latinised, and so hidden, in
Festum Asinorum; but this has as little to do with
the reality of the celebration as the term "he came
riding on an ass". The "ass" came from Ace — the
"first". [See *Beffany*]

ANGEKOK (Greenland; Esquimaux)
North Polar regions; also called "Tangakoch" —
leader of dance and *Tanga* ceremonial. Greenland
Esquimaux are said to enter their huts for winter
about October; and live there during the cold
months, in such warmth that they need wear little.
They have a favourite chorus-dance, *Amna-aja*, in
which they form a circle, the *Angekok* drumming
in the centre. Sometimes he dances alone; singing
and miming; for the chorus, the circle joins in.
These dances may continue for hours; when the
magician is tired, his assistant takes his place. Other
ceremonies include the typical seance — the "call of
the fathers"; but dancing in this (always by the
Angekok alone) is seldom rhythmic, and he moves
only to his own erratic drumming. Dance and
drum cease when he is "taken in possession", and
falls in trance for his declarations. Similar dances
occur in Ceylon, Southern India, and other tropical
centres. [See *Duboka*]

ANGEL (Theatrical slang, English)
Refers to a Messenger of Midas; the man who
knows the man who will put up the money preliminary to a new theatrical production. Compare
(USA film term) the "sugar daddy" who specialises
in treating feminine dancers with great hospitality.
As a Mediæval theatre term, this name applied to
characters required or allowed to enter on right of
stage (looking outwards), as compared with characters inhabiting the other side, the "hell" corner,
usually the devils. Traditions about this opposition
still linger in English theatre, especially for pantomime.

ANGELS (Greek)
Angellos is the Greek term for one of the nine
groups or emanations, known to Jewish theology
of BC. 100. They were named in three main
classes : (1) Seraphim; Cherubim; Thrones; (2)

Dominions; Virtues; Powers; and (3) Principalities; Archangels; and Angels. In this scheme, only the lowest of these nine classes justifies the name *angellos* as "messenger"; but it was always as a messenger or *nuncio* that the winged form was shown in the miracle plays and dances, and thence copied into the pictures painted by so many artists who saw them. They moved "as light as air", and in later church plays, invariably they danced on wires (that were invisible in the gloom above), as they appeared on their ecclesiastical missions.

ANGLAISE

In France in the 18th century, a general name for dances of English origin or character, such as the *Hornpipe;** and about 1800 for the *Country Dance** and *Écossaise.** Earlier, towards the end of the 17th century, the *Anglaise* was one of numerous dance types used in French ballets. The music was in quick duple time without upbeat, and was later included among those dances introduced into the musical suite.

ANGYLES (Wales)

The clerical actor-mimes, called angels or messengers, and also *gillies* or *giles* (origin of the so-called Saint Giles, and saintgiles churches, which were minstrel centres for plays and parable shows or moralities). The name seems similar to the pre-Roman *anchyles*, the shield-clashing dancing priests at the ceremony of Mars; though the Latinised equivalent to Giles is given as Egidius.

ANIMAL DANCES

Include many diverse styles, shaped according to motive, either immediate or traditional. The oldest are direct mimetic animal or bird dances, known in two main phases: the naturalistic mime of the hunter, camouflaged in hide or feathers, intent on deceiving his prey; and the "festival version" of this hunt, performed after the feast, when the successful hunter is induced by his admiring (and well-fed) brethren, to "show us how darn clever you were!" African animal or bird dances are neat and factual imitations of real movement or gesture; their music also reflects close observations of hoof-beats, as with imitative drum-beats; and modern African tribal music (before it is destroyed by West European or American imports) reveals a keen grasp of these subtle interlocking rhythms. More civilised animal or bird dances (the basis of innumerable mask dance-rituals) appeared in the earliest days of Egypt or Assyria. They show that symbolism has replaced sheer naturalism; that the "animals" now moving in ritual, are not those of Nature but are symbols for human passions. This great development is reflected in scores of religious

rites : from the panther-skin of Bacchic rites, down to modern regimental attire in the futile busby of the Hussars, or the skin used by the drummer as an apron. As a spectacle, animal dances remain with us in ballets: such as the Big Bad Wolf (*Capuchon Rouge*), or the White Cat, and other nursery creatures of ballet fairy-tales. Parallel with these rituals there developed the "heraldic beasts" (from Egyptian originals) on shields and crests; but the greatest (perhaps the oldest) of the animal ritual symbols are found in the mysterious ring of the Zodiac; and the Chinese cycles of years and months.

ANIMAL RITUAL-DANCE (Tibet)

Is derived from their system of chronology, based on the two cycles of Jupiter; of twelve years, and sixty years. The animal masks, used in the public temple dances, most especially for the New Year Feast, are changed with the calendar. The lesser *chakra*, used for measure of short periods, designates the years by animal symbols. As these alter annually, the "leading mask" is changed, like the numbers on European calendars and coins. These twelve "Animals" indicate the cycle of years as: 1. Mouse; 2. Ox; 3. Tiger; 4. Hare; 5. Dragon; 6. Serpent; 7. Horse; 8. Sheep; 9. Monkey; 10. Bird; 11. Dog; 12. Hog. Hence, in the "announcing" of the Birth of the New Year, its characteristic symbol is promulgated by emphasis on the appropriate Mask. To this Dancer-Mask will be added indications of the sixty-year cycle. These are symbols indicating the basic "element" governing the cycle : Wood, Fire, Earth, Iron, Water. Each Element is associated with a pair of animals, the first as "male" with the second as "female" (actually; positive-negative rhythm). The Tibetan Lunar Year is adjusted by adding months, every nineteen years. A year is thus named always with two terms : it may e.g. be "Iron-Mouse", or "Fire-Dragon". These ritual dance symbols were obtained from older systems, the Babylonian zodiac and Chinese-Hindu doctrines of encircling times. These more abstruse doctrines are formulated in typical dance rituals; thus the teaching is conveyed—to those able to perceive it—in essential dynamic mode, as every time-symbol should be apprehended.

ANIMALS IN DANCE

Appear in nearly all religions. Islam is one of the few exceptions. Ancient Egypt, Babylonia and Iran-India have all used animal symbolism, related chiefly to the Zodiac. The Animal form; the head or face mask; and the animal skin—all appear with traditional ritual meanings. They are used chiefly to symbolise the animal passions recurrent in evolved human nature, (*Animus* and *Anima,** is the modernist name for them), and the scheme of the Zodiac is related to a symbol plan of the human body. In the Temple of Egypt, animals appeared as they do now in the *gompa-tsam* of Tibet. From the Hebrew (post-Babylonian plan), they moved into the Christian scheme, as "Four Apostles"—symbolised as eagle, lion, bull, dove etc. From Byzantine and Alexandrian sources they moved into the West European feudal religion, hinged on the Arthurian cultus. Here the heraldry carried on the animal symbolism, painted on significant shields. This form continues into modern British coinage; into traditional knightly language; and seems to expire finally in children's nursery rhymes and games; sometimes exploited in ballet (*Sleeping Beauty*; *Petit Chaperon Rouge* etc.). In India, symbolic animals reverse to demonic angelic forms: *apsara/gandharva* modes, as musicians and dancers, and these entities recur as masks, in *Kathakali** or *Chhau** dancing. The masks become essentially a formal mode of a permanent animalist passion: good or bad. In the Dionysian cult, the panther (spotted and thus imperfect), was slain by the youthful god; who then donned its skin as a signal of his triumph.

ANIMA-ANIMUS (Latin)

Soul is a fund or volume of Ordered *Energy*; its power is the source of Dancing; and all its movements are expressed in dance, so far as they are disciplined by integrated Rhythm. Every mode or phase of Matter has associated energy; a minor or major grade of soul-as-energy. These appear chiefly in four main grades (of evolution) that shade into each other. They are:

Mineral Form. Densest Structure-modes. Stabilized Energy. Corpuscles/Atoms.
Vegetal Form. Structure-mode in Tissue. Lateralized Energy. Plant Tissues.
Animal Form. Structure-mode in Cells. Organized Energy. Balanced organisms.
Human Form. Structure in Body. Organized Instinct/Emotion. Hetero-structure.

Each of these successive modes of Form contains and encloses the lower precedent mode. The Human form thus has four structures—four modes of mind-stuff (one with each), all combined in a fifth structure and a fifth (conscious) mind unit. The Souls, or volumes of energy, associated with each mode, continue in a dual task: to uphold their basic structure; to contribute to the superior structure. The medial movement thus becomes that of *Anima-versus-Animus*, or Animal-versus-Human. The three lower "souls" intensively (by accumulated powers, of millions of years of evolution) against the relatively younger (later) superior form, individuated out of this mass-energy. There are

thus: Four structures; four mind-*forms*; four soul-*energy* volumes, which have to be integrated under the rule of the fifth—Conscious Mind. They all continue their own work; they all contribute; they all sustain; and they all seek to focus energy. This organic contest (inherent in all living bodies) furnishes the basis for the fight: or, when disciplined, becomes the Dance of Nature; and the combination emerges as the living soul, sustaining the Individual conscious Mind. That is the range of single-unit or one-body consciousness. Then we turn to consider Mass Consciousness—the *Group Soul*.

ANJALI (Sanskrit)

Salute; in general; and in all Hindu dance or drama this salute is made to begin proceedings. The gesture is called *Namaska** or *Namaskaram*, as this word is sometimes uttered as well; it means "Salutations". *Anjali* is one of the *mudra** or pose bases included in *Bharata Natyam** and other dances, ritual or dance drama. *Anjali* requires the two hands, palm to palm closely, held before the body. They move to one of three heights, according to the degree of reverence extended. Above the head means a salute to Deity; level with the face is a salute to the *Guru* (Teacher) or parents, or to rulers; level with the breast is the salute to ordinary friends; to an assembly, or in general social life. Sometimes the Salute is made in European fashion with one hand; here the left hand must *never* be used; the right hand alone is the "hand of dignity". The term *anjali* spread Westwards and became *angel,** (Angellos) as it was always used by messengers on approach to rulers or to a gathering.
[See *Kurumba*; *Namaska*]

ANNA LAURIE (Scotland)

Is the legendary heroine of an old Scottish ballad, much altered by the lapse of time, from its stately origin. Anna or Ana, is the "Lady of the New Year", who recurs in numerous West European legends and their ceremonials of song and dance. Her surname of "Laurie" derived from her association with the *lour, loure** or *lourie*—bagpipes that provided the stirring music for the Birth of Ana, the New Year. So it was not for "Bone Ana Loure" that the clansman would "lay him doon an' dee", but the ancient Ana herself—the otherwise named "Auld Dame o' the Mill", the Auld Caillieach, who had to lay doon and dee, on the ending of the fatal twelfth month, the night celebrated in song and story as Hog-Min-Hey. The oldest known form of the "historical ballad" is that by William Douglas (who wrote the popular song version) from older material. Annie Laurie was said to be the eldest daughter of Sir Robert Laurie of Maxwelton; born

December 16th, 1682. In 1709 she married James Ferguson, becoming mother of Alexander Ferguson, hero in Burn's song *The Whistle*. As the name Andrew became a common name for a serving varlet; and Abigail for any lady's maid, so Annie Laurie was the traditional name for a singer/dancer, from the Feast of Innocents on December 16th.

ANTHROPOLOGY AND DANCE
Students or scholars, in the fields of anthropology, should never forget Lucian's pregnant observation : "They dance out their religion". Numerous "travel books" remain content with the superficial comment — "there was some drumming and the dancing began". Even in more exact reports, the omission of essential data is frequently to be noticed, despite its profound importance in relation to all other studies, in these days of increasing de-tribalization; and destruction of ancient records and traditions, with no adequate replacement, save the experience of industrial employment and taxation. Anthropological methods in Dance have resembled the museum system of the precise ornithologist, whose aims required the capture of dead birds, the theft of their eggs to "complete the collection" in some dreary deserted halls. The idea of the "bird-watcher" is recent; but the idea of the "dance-watcher" is barely above the mental horizon. Anthropology has to be more completely rescued from the physiology and comparative anatomy of the *homo cadaver*. The basic commandments of Fleet Street must be taken to heart by all students; they must set forth to answer the fundamental questions which every keen reader will ask :

> *What* is it?   *Where* is it?   *When* was it?
> *Who* was it?   *Which* was it?   *How* was it?
>   *Why* was it?

These are the *Seven Queries* of every efficient reporter. The scientific anthropologist, if he is to deserve that name, is but a more specialised reporter, and in a more intensive mode. His detective work must range from archaeology to psychology; including induction and deduction. These *Seven Queries* have too often been neglected: and until the searcher daily puts them consciously to himself he will not seek and observe the details necessary to provide at least some attempt at clear answers. The components of Dance, covering physical movement, emotional expression and psychic experience, can provide primary material of the greatest sociological value.

AN TOSTAL (Ireland)
Spring Festival; celebrated now from Mid-April to Mid-May, the exact dates varying with locality. Among a welter of sports events, room is found for dance competitions and displays. Other terms are *Cor-Fheile an Tostal* (at Cork City), or *Ceilidh Mor* or modernised dance-hall events, known as *Comortaisi Rinnce* (Dance Competitions) at Dublin.

ANYANGA AND YAO INITIATION DANCE (Africa)
These two tribes of British Central Africa have similar ceremonies for girls' initiation into womanhood. The Yao girls are secluded for a period and instructed by a "Cook of the Mysteries". Anointed with oil, dressed in bark cloth and with shaven heads, they perform a ceremonial dance on emerging from seclusion, at the end of which each girl carries over her head a model of a house or a roof, symbolising her future as a wife and pillar of the home. The ceremony is called "Being Danced into Womanhood". The Anyanga ceremonies last only one day, during which the girls are kept in seclusion. At the end of the day, men (disguised as animals) dance with the girls round figures of animals drawn in the sand. The meaning of this dance is not known.

APACHES, Danse des
Parisian argot (Montmartre slang) from *Peau Rouge* or "redskin" (American). A term that appears to have developed since about 1900 in the working-class cabarets of Paris; applied first to the "toughs" or "wide boys" of the city; then to their dance with their *Femmes des marchands*; thus typically a "tough dance" in which the girl (or sometimes the boy) is thrown about in acrobatic style. Some of these *Danses des Apaches*, when stylised for stage presentation, have shewn considerable rhythmic ability allied with muscular power. The USA *Jive* and *Bop* reveal similar tendencies. The older Irish equivalent is the *Hooligan*.

APARIMA (Tahiti)
A dance of the hands and arms, performed by forty to sixty men and women, sitting in four rows on the ground, the women in the two centre rows. The *Aparima* is a rhythmic, mimed description of some well-known daily activity, such as eating a coconut, or fishing from a *pirogue* (canoe). An orchestra of five or six drums, and chanting, accompanies the dance. With undulating movements, the dancers suggest a coconut falling from the tree, opening it, drinking the milk, eating the kernel and throwing away the shell. Or, arms swayed to one side show the fisherman paddling his *pirogue*; sudden movement of clenched hands and stretched arms suggests throwing the harpoon; followed by the slow, graceful casting of the net. The jerking of fish on the line, and drawing in the catch, follows, ending with the return journey of the canoe. For the annual celebrations at Papeete ("The July

14"), at which dance groups from all the Islands perform, the *Aparima* theme is chosen for each group by a master of ceremonies, and rehearsals, beginning in May, continue every night until July. [Cp. Sitting *Hulas; Himinau; Paoa; Moré; Otea*]

ARABESQUE

Formerly a dance routine (part of a larger ritual dance), but now used to indicate chiefly a position in classical ballet, when the two free limbs are opposed in full extension. In the modern Russian school (USSR), the arabesque is not "held", but appears as the end of a wide movement instantly relinquished. The original term refers to the Ritual of the Great Tree ("Tree of Jesse"), once performed in West European churches. The members of the quire, who danced and chanted, surrounded the Great Tree; and at one point they all dipped towards it from the rim of their circle. They are called the *Arbre Escu* (Tree Company, or people), numbering usually twelve. At the old Easter ceremony, the same attitude was used in *Chanuka* by Jewish worshippers; they leaned forward to gain a light from a central candle, as still done at the Russian Easter Festival. Thus the movement once had a real meaning.

ARABESQUE (French, from Gaelic/Celtic)

A name preserved in Bretagne, relevant to Buffoons. The terms exist in Welsh as *arabwr*, buffoonery; and *araoedd*, arabesque with *escu*, the people who were buffoons, the *arabwr-escu*. The characteristic stretch occurred in their "Tree Dance".

ARABIAN DANCE RHYTHMS

Are not explored so fully as literary comment on musical rhythms and melodies. Sa'adyah of Gaon says (according to Dr. H. G. Farmer) in analysing the "eight modes of music" that they have influence on the emotions:[1]

> "the musician . . at gatherings and banquets and parties (*shurb*) begin with the rhythmic modes (*alhan*) which strengthen the generous moral qualities, and nobleness and liberality, like *Al-thaqil, al-awwal* (rhythmic mode) and so on. Then he should follow them with the agreeable joyful modes, like *Al-Hazaj* and *Al-Ramal* and in the dance and the ring dance (he should use the rhythmic mode) *Al-Makhuri* and so on . . ."

[1] *Sa'adyah Gaon.* "The Blending of the Rhythms." Dr. H. G. Farmer, (p.87)

ARABIAN MAGIC MIRROR

Tropical countries afford an opportunity for display of certain mysterious magical or Zodiac* dances, for which a round pattern is supplied by a subtly contrived mirror. Similar mirrors are known in China and Japan. This mirror (it may be a foot or so in diameter) is made of silver-bronze metal alloy; and bears an engraved pattern; usually of an ancient circular design. The dance takes place in an enclosed courtyard or hall, from which all direct light is excluded. The magician holds the mirror, receiving on the surface a single beam of light, for which the hour is carefully chosen. This may be sunlight or moonlight; both are brilliant in the tropics. This incident beam is then reflected on to a white marble floor, where it appears enlarged as a slightly ovoid form, on which a girl dances, according to the rhythmic pattern of the chant and music then rendered. One of these mirror patterns (Arabian, 13th century) is reproduced on page 104 of *Chinese Thought;*[1] and carries a triple design, the outer circle showing an Arabian Zodiac; next the days of the week; the innermost has the *rukh* bird. The rim has an inscription : "To sovereign Prince Abul Fal'd, Victorious Sultan, Light of the World."
[1] *Chinese Thought.* Dr. Paul Carus (Chicago 1907)

ARABWR (Wales)

A jester or buffoon; from *arab*=joyous or merry. This root is most probably the origin of the familiar dance term *arabesque;** from a Breton version, where the group term *escu* (people) would indicate a group of jesters (in the plural form *arabwr-escu*) whose dances were particularly energetic, especially for the *Gwyl Nadolig*, or solstice feast of winter. Related terms are : *arabawl* : merriness; *arabeddu*, to create mirth (pron, *arabethu*), *arabeddus*, facetious; and *arabeddus*, drollery or joking.

ARBA-KAD-ABRE

The "Magical Dance" from Arabic : *Abrar-Qadir-Abrar*, or the Ritual Dance of Power; known in Spain during the Moslem period from 8th to 12th centuries, and contacted by Hebrew scholars, who used a version in their *Zohar (Qabalah**). Abrar* is Messiah or Saviour, in Sufi mysticism; *Qadir* means "he who is possessed of Qudrat"—Might or Lordliness; hence the sacred ritual is an invocation to the Lord of Might to grant salvation, and was known by the Spanish Jews in their *Sutra Rabba* (Lower Circle) and *Idra Rabba* (Higher Circle), or Ring of the Masters. Their solemn dance is accompanied by secret invocations or chanted prayers; admittance was restricted to genuine worshippers; hence the erroneous reputation for "magic". The famous Abbé Athanasius Kirchner (in 1652-1654) studied and wrote on *Shem-ha-Mephorash** (a ritual letter-dance of transvaluations), which is an elementary introduction to the *Qadir* ritual. Raymond Lull, the mystic of Majorca, (Lullards) made the first connection with Christian doctrine; Pope Leo X and Cardinal de Medici pursued this study with deep interest. The *Dance of Abrar* was connected thus with the famous Arab ritual *Aluma-i-Mina* (or Alemin). This ritual was followed notably by the Qadirite Order of Dervishes (11th century). [Consult: *Kabalah Unveiled* (*Kabbala Denudata*) trans: S. L. McG. Mathers (1892), or *The Kabbalah* by C. D. Ginsberg (1925), and especially see *The Essential Unity of All Religions* by Bhagavan Das (Benares 1939)]

ARBE DE JESSE

Was figured (a) as a Tree, phases of descent; (b) as a sort of genealogy (similar to that contained in the early books of the Old Testament); but symbolic rather than physical; (c) as a mathematical system or method — this favoured by the Islamic Arabs who developed algebra (*Al-Kebra*) while the esoteric cult of the Hebrews was (d) elaborated as a *Skhema* or pattern, in the system known now as *Qabbalah*, as *Gematria* and *Notariqon*. Mathematically it explicated the formation of the world elements, which in abstracted mode was named as a Tree (Chemical Tree, by the Alchemists) and yet was displayed in a ritual dance formation. The remains in Gothic art are (1) in the repeated Rose Window geometrical forms (one of the main choreographic plans) and (2) the liturgical *Way to Jerusalem* along with (3) the *Dance of the Tree*. The tradition goes (says MacGregor Mathers) that none was written down until Schimeon ben Jochai (who lived at the time of The Second Temple); and his son Rabbi Eleazar and his secretary Rabbi Abba, then compiled the *Zohar*. The scripts were kept secret until about the 10th century in Spain, when in the "Magical Schools" of Toledo and Seville, and at Gaon, the circles of students were extended. By the 12th century, combined efforts of Arab scholars with Jews led to a publication of *Qabbalah*,* with some rituals by which the keys were given. One was the famous *Arbre de Jesse*, which like the Rose (taken over by the Rosicrucians) was used in design for coloured windows; the *Arbra* was also carved in wood and stone. The work of Sa'adyah of Gaon was joined with that of Yehuda ben Shemuel ilm Tibbon, of the city of Granada (1130 C.—1190). They translated to and from Arabic, often on musical form, linked to dance ritual that was rarely given in diagram, but more often in algebraic formulae — thus approaching the methods of modern physics though relating to the same material.

ARC (Latin, from Greek *arkhe*)
Has three distinct meanings. Arc is the curve, part of a circle or spheroid; this is the abstract mode. Arch is the material form of construction over and between two pillars or a wall opening (one of the chief elements of Gothic architecture). *Arche* or *arkha* (as in *arkhimandrite*) signifies the leader, the ruler among monks, or governor of ritual (in Greek church) from the earlier Greek; similar meaning in secular mode. In ritual dance, Arc refers both to the "dancing space" (*Vesica*) available in the quire; and thus associated with the Egyptian bark or barque; and joins (in the Christian scheme) as the *navis* or *nave*, theologically listed as the *Shippe of Salvatione*. In it *saltatio* was performed. (Old salt). Early liturgies were never motionless: they were not congregational; they had no seats (except for the privileged officiants, choristers, and canons). The canons "measured out" the Arc; often it was traced permanently on the *navis*; sometimes inset with tiles or bricks; or later (as at York, or Westminster) positions were indicated by brass (latten) insets. This Arc was used for popular as well as church festivals. (Double Arc = Vesica Pisces — at Wells Cathedral.) In Gaul, the ancient worship of Juno, Queen of Heaven, had somehow to be converted theologically into worship of Maria Virginis, also appointed Queen of Heaven, Lady of Earth, Empress of Hell (in *Ars Moriendi*) to cover the three phases of the Lunar deity. She became slowly converted from Juno to Jeanne or Jean (as the male figure Iove or Iovan and Ivan, was turned into Jonah and Johannus). Mostly these rituals had faded, before the triumphant church period of 11th-12th century (before printing appeared), and traces are now few. The church floor retained its last version, the spiraline dance track of the *Way to Jerusalem*,* the *Rouenne* had vanished, as did the Revel soon after.   [See *Arabesque*; *Arbor de Jesse*; *Arch*]

ARC, Danse de l' (France)
Dance of religious ceremony and of tradition, persisting in two main forms, one belonging to the Masque or New Year Festivals (also the Summer *Danse de Feu*, or *Danse de Jean*), and another taken over from the more obscure ritual of the feudal knights, the system of *la Chevallerie*. This ritual had several prominent figures, among whom was one appointed annually as Jeanne d'Arc, or the "Lady of the Arc". In England a similar system for a time prevailed, at last formalised in the Knights of the Garland or Garter, with its headquarters at Windsor. In the older and more public tradition in France and England (and other countries) the ritual settled down around May Day; and also the day of harvest completion, (the Michelmesse or Little

Feast), when the girls of the village performed a dance in which the principal feature was a hoop or arch of (a) green leaves, (b) flowers, (c) ripe fruits, or (d) ripe golden corn. Many traditions have been combined to end in these ceremonials, from the Grecian rite of the *zona* to the mediæval ritual disguised behind *la danse allemande,** in which the floor pattern was clearly marked by two arcs, which combined to show the ancient symbol known as *Vesica piscis*, or (in India) the yantara or *hiranya-garbha*. Formerly, the clerical ritual was performed in the Court of Arches; but it has long vanished from the English scene, though the tradition remains of this place (as at Westminster, merged with Doctors Commons) as the place of matrimonial agreements and disputes. The sole remaining ritual vestige is the "arch of swords" sometimes formed for a newly wedded couple to pass through, after the ceremony; or the schoolboys' (formerly page's) rite of "running the gauntlett"; and the children's game called "London Bridge", or "Oranges and Lemons" (*Oraison pour Leman*). As in the name *Mary atte Bowe* (Church).

[See *Arco, Danza dell*]

Arku Dantza (Dance of the Arches). Basque.

FRANCE

ARCH DANCES

Featuring always some kind of arch, under which a file of dancers must pass. The Arch may be (a) a garland of flowers, a hoop or semi-girdle etc.; (b) an arch made literally "in a moment" by swords, the tools of the trade, or plain staves; all held crossed over the narrow path, seen mostly now at weddings; or (c) joined hands, as in the children's

Feast. In the Orient, the ritual arch in ceremonial varies with the ritual pillar that is its counterpart. Some dances received their "arch" from the devotions to Diana—from the crescent of the New Moon, summarised later in the "lucky horse-shoe". The arch as a flat pattern is assimilated with many rituals of the Cup; so that the drawing is done to recall the Cup. With some enclosed rituals, the principal dancer stands (for one moment or for some time) within the cup form; especially for an initiation.

ARCHE (Latin to French)

Usually mistranslated as Ark, as "David danced before the Ark". The original term means a curve, a symbol of the dance pattern; and was continued into French mediæval period for Solstice dances, done by the elected Jeanne of the Arche. The Court game "Oranges and Lemons". The Arch was seen at the Harvest Festival (on the stage in ballet, as in the last scene of *Coppelia*), and at the New Year of Arches has a parallel tradition (Arch as building, not Ark).

[See *Ark, Dance of*; cp. Bark (Barque)]

ARCHEOLOGY OF DANCE

System and Method; in seeking evidence concerning Dance, a regular scheme is advisable, which necessarily differs from the ordinary "material evidence" methods applicable in most branches of archeological research. Dance is a fleeting art; it has been recorded in tangible or visual form even less than Music; hence evidence has to be obtained by circumstantial factors subjected to induction. Hence we must possess some knowledge of the Comparative History of Dance, so far as it is exact in recent or available evidence. Etymology can be applied only in its functional meanings; and not by syllable or sound. Reference to ascertained regular bases in ancient ritual can be used to place isolated details. Some facts will be gained from (a) implements used in ritual dance, (b) costume or accessories used, (c) and the places used, or specially prepared, for ritual performance. Evidence of time and place, especially as related to actual calendar times and customary (lapsed) times, is always valuable; while the ceremonial relation to agriculture, to the seasons of month or year, according to prevailing lunar or solar festivals, helps to uncover the main character of any located ritual dance. Immense care is required, not to import, unconsciously, any modernist assumptions. Much time has been lost by endless references to "savage dances", or to "fertility dance" as though these terms explained fully the entire purpose, movement, and result of ritual dance. Puerile dismissal of apparently crude movement as "obscene" should be again considered, if only by reference to the Greek meaning of that technical term.

ARCHITECTURE AND DANCE

Express in reciprocal relation, the main functions of the social usage of buildings. So far as the single focus of attraction is within any single construction; these buildings appear in three principal categories: (1) *Temple* (or church etc.) in two or three phases, public and private, based on RITUAL as the central ceremonial function; (2) *Theatre* (or lesser halls etc.) again in several phases; based on MYTH as the central factor of public interest (drama, illusion, etc.); (3) *Circus* (or field games, sports, contests etc.) in display and combat, based on REALITY of Skill etc., exhibited by participants, directly. Thus follow three systems or styles or modes or movements in gesture and dance, guided by three distinct qualities of rhythm. Ancillary arts also include dance, not by actual movement, but in pictures of sculpture (added to the architecture as embellishment or extension of function), while modern invention of mass production has provided (a) books and printed pictures; (b) radio, as the broadcast word and music; and (c) television as the broadcast image. All of these are, in some manner, reproductions of an earlier original creation. Each of these three main modes of architecture-plus-dance has internal qualities; its own terms of reality and of fiction or illusion. In all of them, we perceive more or less the presentation, extension or contraction of this or that mode of elemental dance —the line (processional); the ring (enclosure); and the square (contesting factors), according to the predominance of rhythm in group movement. All three original forms of building (or enclosure) have changed, in many places, from the open-air structure to the roofed and limited structure. This change accords with predominant social and economic conditions; but the basic social contact is recurrent and necessary. In temple ritual dance; in theatre display or expositional dance; and in circus athletic exhibitional dance of skill in technique, we perceive three different and not always contemporary styles, advancing or changing or fading from the social scene. Thus it becomes an error of taste, to attempt to impose one style of dance in the place that is inappropriate to its authentic line of tradition.

ARCHIVES OF THE DANCE

Have been developed principally, as public deposits, only during the twentieth century. The London Archives of the Dance was begun about 1944 by the Ballet Guild of London. After its dissolution as a group, Lionel Bradley was in charge of the Guild's collected material; but since his demise the "Archives" seem to be inaccessible. There is a small Theatre Collection in the Department of Prints in the Victoria and Albert Museum; at South Kensington. London; and in the London Museum; but the proportion of dance material remains small. The ephemeral collection shown in 1954 at the Edinburgh Festival (afterwards at Forbes House, in London), on the subject of the "Diaghilev Ballets", would have been of value if retained; but as most exhibits were on loan from private owners, this consummation was not attainable. In Paris, Pierre Tugal, working with Rolf de Maré, founded *Les Archives International de la Danse* at 6 Rue Vital; but since Occupation and the closure of this centre, the collection also is generally inaccessible. There is a collection at the Paris Opera. In Milan there rest archives, relative principally to the Opera Theatre. In the USA dance archives are collected in the Museum of Modern Art (in part), and in some other centres. The Harvard Collection covers all Theatre. There are some other collections in the USA which have important dance archives. In Russia, splendid collections exist; firstly, at the Moscow Theatre Museum; and also in the Bolshoi Theatre collection; while Leningrad has similar large collections (readily accessible to students and visitors) in the chief theatres (Maryinsky or Kirov Theatre, for dance and ballet) and in some gallery collections.

ARCO, DANZA DELL' (Italy)

Processional dance sometimes performed by peasants in Southern Italy, on their return from a pilgrimage to the shrine of Madonna dell' Arco. They encircle the bullock wagon which has taken them (now emptied of food, wine and offerings) as they return home in joyful mood. This dance doubtless has associations with the almost forgotten French ritual dance of the Sainte Jeanne d'Arc, performed usually in the churches.
[See *Tarantella* (2), *Arc, Danse de l'*]

ARDDANGOS (Wales)

Pron. *Arth-angos*, meaning "illusions" or dramatic appearance, as *phob ardangos*, as distinct from "straight plays". The Illusions always included mysterious dancing figures.
[See *Tango; Tangov*]

ARDJHA (Bali, Indonesia)

The *Gamelan Ardjha* play has developed during the last half century from the *gambuh* common in Java. The basis is provided by romantic legends traditional in the islands; such as *Salya; Galolukuh; Tjandra Lasan; Sidhi-paksa;* as well as Chinese stories, such as *Tuan Wei* or *Sampik*. The *gamelan**
for *ardjha* uses chiefly flutes, with the percussion instruments, gongs and drums. The plays have only

episodes of dancing, for much is explained in recitative and chant.

AREITO (Santo Domingo)
The "ballade of the islands"; forerunner of Calypso and its dance parallel, *La Merengue. Areito* is a "singing dance" of the Indians, popular in the 16th century; then demolished by Spanish music, and next infused with American influence which changes the rhythm of the traditional pentatonic melodies. Here the tribal queen Anacaona, gave what was probably the first "tourist dance" demonstration. Gonzalo Fernadez of Oviedo describes it in his book *Historia Generale y Natural de las Indias.*

ARENA BALLET (Europe)
Was the original form of *Ballet du Salon*, as developed in the ducal palaces of Italy and France. Essentially, the Arena Ballet is a fully three-dimensional ballet (like the *Masque**) having no proscenium or "picture-opening", and being designed for viewing on at least three sides in full. Some space must be reserved for entry and exit. Thus the Arena Ballet has spatial qualities that link it with Circus; these have been extended to "Ballet on Ice", which is a misnomer since the action is not genuine dancing but is skating. The Ballet of the King (or duke) with the Masque of the Queen, becomes Arena Ballet. There is no scenic background for illusion; though in the parallel Masque Ballet, large scenic pieces were wheeled on (with performers hidden inside, coming and going), as set decorations. Often the nobles were acting or receiving characters: without the marked modern distinction of performers and distant audience, separated by a fireproof curtain. Several Russian (19th century) classical ballets have been presented as Arena Ballet; but lacking the picture illusion, are rarely successful. Moreover, the general theme must be well known, in advance, for explicatory action to receive full attention; otherwise there appears a reliance on limited technical exhibition dancing, which at a full distance is never so impressive. Arena Ballet has the commercial advantage of being able to attract a large audience and (if seats are full) becomes economically balanced in cost and income. To devise Arena Ballet for film use is a wrong view of the parallel problem; for the film spectator is psychically placed at a greater distance. A middle mode of Arena Ballet has been formulated, by adding a stage in place where none was built (Albert Hall, and Festival Hall, London), or in large cinema theatres, with the disadvantage of a flat stage of inadequate depth for spectacular dancing. Other types of dancing, notably the Folk Dance Displays (arranged by the English Folk Dance Society), reveal a similar type of Arena Ballet, especially in the *Circassian Circle* for two hundred dancers.

ARGYLL BROADSWORD (Scotland)
Gaelic: *Dannsahd Argyllh Chlaidheimnh*; the oldest form of the sword dance, as the Sun-Dance. Dance performed by four men, who enter, each bearing a heavy polished sword (Claymore). They first carry swords over shoulders, moving in a ring. Then again, beating blades; next with points upright; next lower hilt to mouth (a royal salute of service), and finally lower swords near ground. Then they lay down the swords, all points to centre; and begin the dance proper.

ARIADNE DANCE (Ancient Greece)
Is another version of the ancient ritual dance known as *Labyrinthos,** and *Troy Game** (or *Gamos*). The dance was known in Crete, and danced also at Delos. Sometimes the symbolic name was constituted as Aphrodite-Ariadne (as in Cyprus). Homer gives an account (in the *Iliad*) of the making of a dancing floor, devised for one part of this famous dance. A Latin writer, Virgil, compares it with the winding ways of the Labyrinthos. Some scholars think that the later Greek dance *Geranos** was derived, as the "Crane Dance" from this origin; together with the *Hormos* or Chain Dance.

ARIT (Old Egyptian)
Was the traditional prescribed "ritual space" (the *area*, or *aroura*) in which the worshipper invoked the gods. It may be compared with the Hindu *alponam* or *rangoli** and has a modern analogy in the Muslim use of a portable prayer rug, to represent the same reserved space in his mosque. For public festivals in Egypt, a diamond inside a semicircle was used so often that this figure became the written sign for "Festival"—and the Greeks copied it, as in the Theatre Dionysos at Athens. In later Pythagorean ritual, the pentagon was used as leading figure; this was copied in the Middle Ages as the magician's pentacle, drawn within the "Magic circle".

ARK, Dance of (Hebrew/Egyptian)
The Ark of Noah is the only "square ship" in the legend; in ritual it is the symbolic arch or Great Curve. (As the ancient "Arc of the Covenant", its symbol was a rainbow.) The Coven met within this Arch, drawn on the floor. The Egyptian "Ship of Salvation" was constructed (sometimes in stone) as a "Nile vessel" for popular legends, but in the royal ritual, it was the Arc of the Sun. The "symbolic arch" has persisted for many centuries in its

ritual mode; it was adopted into the Christian system as the mystical *vesica piscis*; and all religious seals followed this arcuate form. The term not only entered architecture as the *arche* or foundation pattern, but continued as the arch or double-curve above the pillars. The Westminster Court of Arches originated within this tradition. At Wells Cathedral in Somerset may be seen this double Great Arche, standing upright as a vast double curve above the nave, built in a reddish stone. The ritual, as derived from Egypt, followed in the Dance of the Zodiak,* which was taken sometimes as a pure circle; in other places, as a smooth egg-shape, in which elliptical form it appears at Easter; and was again symbolised by the use of brightly painted eggs. All the dances began by the affirmation of the main shape: a circle or an elliptical trace on the boundary, to make the basic figure; other figures follow, danced within these closed curves. The term Daoud originally meant "the divider" — he was the "son" of Sol-O-Mon, the sun king; he divided the year, as does the Hindu Krishna with his *gopis*.
[See *Arch*; *Arche*]

ARLEQUIN
Figures prominently in the European "Wild Hunt", in the Scandinavian tradition that stems from the older Cymric doctrine of the "Dying Sun" *versus* the "Boar". This is a myth of the year. The Boar, *Hodur*, of Darkness, seeks to engulf the Sun, and to end *Hoenir*, the "motion for man" — or dance of life. Herthus is Frigga, the "Maid of Life". *Holle* indicates renewed life, by the shining scarlet berries; and thence arises the *Herla* or *Herlathing*, the Wild Hunt — it always follows the Harvest; and is the ancestor of the English custom of the Hunt (following a fox in lieu of a real boar, but always attired in "pink" or red). In France, the tradition became *Mesnee d'Hellequin* (Harlequin) again in the Wild Hunt, as, for example, the *Grande Veneur de Fontainebleu*. The friars tried to confuse the tradition with their Herod's Hunt (of the supposed "Innocents" — in fact, the *Innokente* of Greek tradition, or young candidates, sponsored by Nikolas and Katerina, for baptism). The Swedish tradition continued to name *Wodin's Hunt* (*Asgardreia*), but local English customs continued to show the Wilde Man, or the Green Man, named here as the "Wode House". Thus the merging of several traditions lapsed finally into the magical Harlequin of the London pantomime.

ARLES (French)
Aruels or *Arvals*: The Annual Festival (Agricultural New Year etc.) in this Provençal centre, with a Ritual in a Court, then renamed as Santa Teraphima (or Aruels), which referred to the dancing figures, whether puppets or living dancers (*comedia*), produced and performed by the community of monks and nuns. (Lavra = Arval)

Armenian Folk Dance.   ARMENIA

ARMENIA (Mediæval period)
Was rich in dance-mimes, ballads, and dance
rituals. Every great festival was enlightened by
*Parik** and *hushparik*—professional dancers. The
Festival of Aramazd was earlier celebrated on 1st
day of Narvasard (New Year) in the Mehian
(temple) as at Ani, City of Daramali. Anahit the
Golden Mother was praised as Goddess of Love,
while Tir (or Grogh, Grock) as the great writer,
son of Ahuramazd, recorded deeds past and to be
done, for those who sought Jhennet (paradise) for
Anoush the maid of life. There was also *Tzutzh*,
the dance-mime of all royal weddings.

ARNAOUT (Albania, Balkan States)
A modern version of an older military dance, led
by a couple. The man holds a long whip, cracking
it as he stamps his feet; and then runs from one
end of the group to the other, as though he was
herding sheep or oxen. The melody in 2/4 time,
has a rapid staccato measure. The men usually
wear what arms they possess; knives and daggers.

ARS MORIENDI (Med. Latin)
Literally, the "Craft of Dying", as one of several
similar titles of official Romanist books of scholastic
doctrine, offered as the only available instruction
on the "saving of souls". Many versions existed, in
the form of block books (pictures and words engraved on single wood blocks), of which the earliest
now extant is ascribed to Mathieu of Cracovie,
bishop of Worms, in 1470-1472. Principal titles are :
De Arte Moriendi and *Tractatus de Arte Moriendi;*
or the *Speculum Artis Moriendi*. Invariably they
carried a dozen or so of illustrations, all related to
the death period, of which one was the Demon
Dance around the Dying Man. No definite author
is known; nor artist; though faint indications suggest (via the *Aureum Legendis*) an oriental contact
—as in the conversation of the Image of Death,
with the Dying Man. This was an "official version",
to which the far more popular *Todtentanz** woodblocks replied. William Caxton of London made a
translation from the French version *L'Art de bien
Vivre et bien Mourire*, printed in 1505, from the
Parisian copy of 1493. Unfortunately, these books
told little of value; they are suffused by sickly
sentimentality of the scholastic period; submerged
as it was, in most places, with a leaden realism
that had transformed noble myths into an incredible "history". In the current revolt against this
low standard, the English *Mores Daunce* served
not only to maintain a stout English tradition of
mystical learning, under its apparent village sim-
plicity, but to maintain practical ethics under the
Roman invasion of economic and political authority, imposed on rulers by the cunning of the

Interdict. While the French courts used *Tarot**
symbols, the German centres used the *Todtentanz*
rituals. The final Roman retort was by way of the
Arte revised into *Spiritual Exercises*, in the Spanish
copy by Ignatius; again as a "fear weapon". They
are inferior to the earlier Tibetan recensions of
similar doctrines. From these illustrations, many
"morality plays" took their arrangements; as for
the well-known *Everyman*. (*Elkerlyke*)
[See *Book of the Craft of Dying: and other Early
English Tracts*. Ed. by Francis M. M. Gomper (London 1917)]

A ROSA (Portugal)
Dance performed with poem : "*To Rosa*". A round
dance of the Beira Provinces, in 2/4 time, for
couples facing each other. Using a light, running
step, they move round clockwise (the man moving
backwards); then each partner turns inwards in a
semi-circle to face the dancer behind, completing
the turn to face their own partner. Couples next
revolve together clockwise and anti-clockwise,
finishing with the original circular run. Arms are
held slightly curved, and the fingers clicked on
every beat. The dance is accompanied by drums
and pipe while this simple love song is sung.

ART DIRECTOR (European Ballet)
Is practically an extinct animal. Theoretically, an
individual is thus labelled (by some highly optimis-
tic backer or commercial organiser) in the hope
that he will perform as a sort of Cosmic Cook; and
from a heterogeneous assembly of dancers, producers, and stage managers, combined with scene
painters and costume-designers; and aided by a
conductor with his highly remunerated orchestra
of players, will produce a dish with world-shaking
results. This consummation has not appeared, in
Western Europe or in the USA, since the days of
S. P. Diaghileff. Mostly the primal conditions are
not present : the "art director" is not acquainted
with theatre art, but only with a little dance, a
little painting, or a flair for publicity. Art Directors
who attempt also to work *within* the company
always fail; they cannot hold a balance. Rarely do
they reveal creative power; more often, they show
a good memory of other folks' work—useful, but
inadequate. The Soviet system of equal collaboration appears to produce the best modern result;
there is no dictation; no money pull; no pushing
of inadequate talent by backers; no single boss;
and no failure to seek for new ideas.

ARUNTA "WELCOME" DANCES (Central Australia)
A "play-about" Corroboree* of the Arunta tribe,
performed as a compliment to visitors from another

tribe. Women are present, but men perform the dance. Although many aboriginal dances are basically similar, the welcome dance is a new arrangement for each occasion, being composed in honour of the visitors, who memorise it and add the dance to their own repertory when they return to their village. The hosts, once they have given away the dance, will not again perform it. Usually about twelve men take part on the specially prepared dancing-ground some distance from the camp, the dance often taking the form of two lines alternately approaching and retreating, then passing through each other. Moving with high, prancing steps, the men mark the rhythm with a stick, with which each dancer beats the ground. Single dancers may perform a solo, charging at high speed towards one line or the other, the dancers falling back from him with a peculiar side-step, yelling and prancing. Dancing is accompanied by a chant, with different words for each Corroboree, the sound beginning on a high note and gradually fading to silence, like voices growing fainter as their owners move into the distance. Such festivities may continue each night for two weeks.
[See *Corroboree; Atnumokita; Yoi*]

ARUWALTJA (Arnhem Land, N. Australia)
Name in districts on Gulf of Carpentaria, for the native dance ritual (called *corroboree** by British settlers), as used at Umbukumba. This name applies to the periodical sacred and secret rituals (mainly initiation ceremonial, but sometimes traditional worship), performed in a secluded and reserved site in the woods. The oval clearing is made slightly smaller than a tennis-lawn, fully cleared and level, with three huts alongside for equipment, stores, and preparations. No women are permitted to see the place or the ritual. The legendary dances portray animal, bird and insect characters as symbols. Songs relate adventures of ancient heroes, as the men twist and leap in vivid characterisation. Nearby are other, smaller sites, known as the "dreaming places", where (presumably) the trained leaders undergo their final initiation in the "death sleep" or trance.
[See *Corroboree; Nakumdoit; Honey-Bee Dance*]

ASHAQ (Persia)
The poet-minstrel; singer of praises, usually with a drum or tambour; sometimes accompanied by one or two musicians (*tar*, and reed pipe). The name is spelled *Ashaq* in Urdu (from Persian), but in Uzbek it is *Ashug** or *Ashag*. In North India, the term recognised a high-ranking person; so that Asoka, as an emperor, has the same title. The *ashaq* is the oriental minstrel at the highest, or court, level. The *ashaqi* were dancers with him — minor members of his company.

ASHIKO (Nigeria)
A "square" dance performed by the Yoruba people, although not native to them, having been imported from farther west. Performed by two girls and two men facing each other, the female dancers are chosen to make the set by the Master of Ceremonies, who places a kerchief on the head or lap of the girl required. The music resembles a foxtrot, and is played in unison by five drummers. A carpenter's saw and a nail beaten on a bottle make additional noise. Singing by drummers and chorus boys accompanies the dance, which has evidently been modified by missionary influence, since the songs show religious implications, and the dance is said to be performed only by those who have adopted the Christian religion.

ASHUGS (Armenian USSR)
Is an ancient term for folk singers and dancers, the minstrels of Armenia and adjacent countries. Their calling was highly respected throughout Irania and Turania, two thousand years ago; since, just as the Frankish King Charles was called *Carolos Magnus*, or "Great Singer", so the Hindo-Persian kings were, in one famous dynasty, known as *Ashugs*, or *Asokah*. These traditions have never lapsed; they continue down to the present day; and living *Ashugs* could be seen and heard in the Armenian Theatre Festival in Moscow, when some of their accomplished singers, players, and dancers performed. A few of them later visited London in one of the Folk Dance Festivals. They have been called "Troubadours of Armenia". They are known also in Tbilisi (Georgia); and Baku (Azerbaidjan).

ASSEMBLIES (London)
Soho Square, in West London, was the site of the most notable Assembly, or dance party; setting a fashion for many others. About 1756 or 1757, Mrs. Teresa Cornelys, a pious Bavarian Catholic lady, arrived in London without her Dutch spouse. She had been fired by the success of Handel, and, having a singing voice, secured minor engagements at the Pleasure Gardens of Ranelagh* and Vauxhall.* What she saw convinced her that she could devote her social talents to more profitable purpose; whereon she rented Carlisle House from the Earl in 1760. With some new decoration and furnishing, she opened her House for assemblies, balls, concerts, parties, masquerades; all of which she organised with typical Teutonic thoroughness. Her Catholic husband does not appear in the records. Mrs. Cornelys used publicity then current, in skilful fashion; while her attractions met all tastes. The fascinating Miss Elizabeth Chudleigh (who married later the Duke of Kingston) appeared in a scanty fancy dress. The dances were *cotillon** or

*allemande;** for a Subscription Masquerade "the House of Commons adjourned for the day", when a score of young lords forsook politics for fun and games. Such success inevitably provoked rivalry; there came the Pantheon, and the new Assembly Hall of Mr. Almack;* so that the teams of the righteous and ungodly (who met in Carlisle House) became diverted to different centres of dance amusement. The Bishops disapproved; but their wives went and met Mrs. Cornelys; and this Catholic lady smiled on both parties; while she also aided discreetly the rivalries of the Opera. Eventually the "unco guid" snapped her by means of prosecution for an infringement of a regulation for allowing "dramatic performance without licence". The spiteful ones followed up this assault by others of more flagrant character. Mrs. Cornelys was "sold up", but she started again, now with a "Rural Masquerade", and then a Masked Ball (1776) for which she used the device of a Charity Appeal (this for Infant Orphan Girls of Marylebone). She then retired to Knightsbridge Grove, but in 1785 this was barren; and she ended as a prisoner for debt in the Fleet, where she died in 1797. During forty years she had dominated dance assemblies, from all angles.
[See *Almacks; Paris Gardens; Vauxhall; Ranelagh*]

ASSYRIAN RITUAL DANCE (Ancient Assyria; Babylon)
Had its primal symbol of the threefold ritual displayed in the potent form of "the god in the circle" holding his bow, as a sign of power. Next came the repeated mythos of the royal "lion hunt"; repeated so often that it finally became realistic, losing its original symbolic quality; just as the Cretan bull-fight, or bull hunt, became degraded into the spectacle of the Spanish *corrida*—from a great ceremony to a circus feat. Other reliefs show the Assyrian monarch of the priest—the *miru-dach*—dedicating his trophy to the gods, by an honorific libation. None of these painted alabaster reliefs can show dance; they abstract high moments from the course of ritual; such as the *genies* who stand by the awe-inspiring form of the Sacred Tree. We should have long to seek for ritual movement, without the mythic legend of the hero Gilgamesh, who sets forth on his twelve labours, to pass the twelve stations, gyrating in the twelve modes of dance, on the sacred paths, using now but twelve of the hieratic thirty-two secret ways; coupled with the fact of finding this same Tree pattern engraved or lightly carved in shrine floors; on a scale that shows its usage as a ritual setting. Belus, shown walking, antedated Mars; while the lion, the bull (set at doorways), the eagle-headed priest-mask; and the bearded male head of the

officiating king, give the four standard types for the later "evangelists" symbols of the Greek *parabolos*. They stood also at the four quarters, in a later sacred dance. [See *Qabalah*]

ASTARTE, Dance of (Assyria)
Hidden under traditional vestiges, chiefly in the popular sequences connected with fortune-telling, traces of this dance from ancient Assyrian·ritual of the Goddess Ashtoreth, still endure. The Tarot Dances are one mode. Astarte was (as with the Hindu goddesses Parvati or Kali) associated with both death and fertility. The Hebrew *Ma'gilla* known as *Esther* was derived from the Easter drama-dance worship of Ashtoreth in Babylon; the script (in the biblical form) is a much-edited synopsis of the traditional play. Esther is Istar (who is Isis) and Ashtaroth. In England little girls have a ring-dance game, ending with the refrain: "Ashta! Ashta! all fall down"! which is a relic of ancient Phoenician visitors to Britain; while common words such as tart (pastry), and tart (vulgarism now for "sweet-'eart") recall this distant origin. *Torta* (Spain) is short-cake; *tortilla*, an omelet; *tertulia*, the meeting-place; *tortola*, the dove; euphemism for the dancing girls (as "doves" is for "nuns"). Everyone of these terms came from the dance-rituals of Astarte. The dance-track was *tortuoso*, or "winding." [See *Sacred Dance*]

ASTROLOGICAL RITUAL DANCES
Occur in all religions, with a wide variety of names, forms, and ostensible functions. To understand their primal forms, it is necessary to know the true relation of *Astrologia* to *Astronomia* : to Life and Form of the Makrocosmos. Examination of electrophysics, especially the dual modes of fission and fusion (expansion and contraction), will help considerably. The errors both of astrology (with the wildest of popular superstitions) may be ignored along with similar, but currently more revered, errors in astronomy (e.g. the fantastic assumption of an eternal and never-varying unit called "light year"). Astronomy records the relative shapes, positions, movements, periods, and proportions of the stellar universe in general; with the solar system in particular. That is the Form. Astrology records their balancing aspects of energies, or forces; their directions, phases, and periods, with relations one to another. That is the Life. Every star emits and receives energy from other stars; there is an incessant but variable exchange of forces, in the body of the Makrocosmos, as there is in the Mikrocosmos of the Atom; and, in consequence, there are effects in the world of terrestrial nature, including the body of man. These subjects were the study of the ancient wise men; they

taught much of what they learned by means of ritual, in dance and ceremonial, according to Form and Number (Geometry), in terms of Rhythm (Music and Dance). Thus arose the Sacred Dance; and with it the assumed characters—the mythic figures of the gods and angels—by which symbols their relations were set forth in dynamic ritual. Every religious system has created and sustained an esoteric doctrine, in which some part of these immense schemes are stated and practised. These teachings remain "secret" only because of the difficulty of finding minds able to apprehend them (as with our "atomic fission", there is no final secret that *can* be locked up), but for the unworried masses there are popular projections, consisting of dummy figures and pragmatic ethics, for their consideration. Those who will consent to pursue the apparently frivolous study of "The Dancer, the Dancing, and the Dance", need never stop learning; on the sole condition that they do not expect others to do all the work. Every "dancer" must work out his own dancing and make his own dance; —his own living and his own life cannot be salvationized and done by proxy.

ATINGA (Nigeria)
A war dance, from the name *Nana Tongo*. The wizard doctor assembles the people of the village (or of several villages) and they clear a space thoroughly under a large tree; next day they build an altar of earth only; and perform their dance around this construction to drum music. The local people are initiated into the dance and taught to perform until expert. Breaks are filled by drinking beer made from kola nuts immersed in water, with a few drops of blood mixed in.

ATNUMOKITA (South-central Australia)
"Dance of the Forked Stick". A "play-about" *Corroboree** of the Arunta tribes performed for entertainment, or to honour guests. It may be performed on three consecutive nights from about eight o'clock until dawn, by the light of fires. A forked pole (*Atnuma*), about fifteen feet high, painted red with spots and bars of yellow and white, is set up at the western end of the dancing-ground, about twenty by ten yards area. At the eastern end, round the fires, sit women, children and old men, forming a chorus for the chants. The men beat time by hitting together two boomerangs, while the women clap cupped hands. The performers (ten men, or as many as a hundred) decorate themselves with body patterns in red and yellow ochre, black charcoal and white pipeclay, elaborated with white or coloured down stuck on to the face as a mask. On the head is a cap of twigs, some ending with a plume of Emu feathers. The

pattern of down is continued from the face on to the cap, so that its lower edge is concealed and the whole resembles a long, unbroken mask. Eucalyptus leaves are tied to the legs; in his right hand each man holds a thin wand about five feet long, with red and white spiral bands. Advancing and retreating in transverse rows, the dancers use a rhythmic stamping step, performed in perfect time with one simultaneous impact of feet on the ground. Presently a woman moves to the pole, a man from the chorus group goes towards the north side, and one of the dancers retires into the darkness on the south, suddenly rushing back to the dancing-ground yelling, each yell being answered by a couplet chanted by the chorus. The dancer resumes his place; and the advancing and retreating movements continue. There follow different dance figures, performed as solos, pas de deux, or by several dancers, each figure accompanied by its appropriate chant . . . . and so continued. Each *Corroboree* of this type has its own name, distinctive costumes, chants and dance-figures.
[See *Corroboree*; *Yoi*; *Arunta Welcome Dance*]

AUGURS' DANCE (Roman)
Connected with a system of calendrical forecast for agricultural purposes. The *Augur* was the *Eu-guru*— the "good teacher", who made his compass (step-area) and drew a skilful diagram of the geographical points with his four cardinals (*cardo*, hinges). From this he gave dates, weather indications, and times for sowing, ploughing, harrowing. In this he has been confused with *harospex* (Etruscan mentor) whose functions were divinatory, where those of the *augur* were often political; economic (see *haruspex*). Several terms still continue; as *ochre*, the coloured mud used to make diagrams; *Ogre** the forecaster of trouble (esp. in France). The Augur used his *litra* (or *lituus*) like the *boskop* and *papa*, in moving round his circle. On the rim he probably made symbols. When the Chinese navigating compass appeared in Europe (c. 1200) the familiar diagram, extended to 32 points by division, was used by sailors (see *Lo-Fan, Lo Pan*). The form of dance was a simple *tripudium;** quick or slow. (Boskop = Bi-Scopus = Bishop.)

AUGURS RITUAL DANCE
Associated with "Aruspecus" (inspection), was a slow and stately "walk round" the figured *templum*; an enclosure long retained on the Vatican Hill in Rome; but drawn on the "village green" (on levelled earth, sand, or even dry mud), for some special occasion. The augur was a political prophet —a Roman "Old Moore" who sustained popular superstition by elaborate ceremonial practice; his presence (and his prayers and prophecies) were

considered ritually necessary on the beginning of any new enterprise; hence our modern term "inauguration". His *templum* shrunk to the tiny "mortar-board" which the graduate once had to balance on his skull-cap (not attached then). The modern comedian retains the tiniest hint of the "walk round" by turning right after his verse, and making one circle. This was long called the "Walk-round-Martin". The augur walked round with his sacred wand (*lituus*) and tapped the important spots as he orated. The wand became the bishop's crook; the "walk round" is now only a slow processional. The term augur also now means "to bore" — it was then old; and there is another parallel in the term "hawker", who also "goes round". As *haruspeces*, the augurs went round collecting the "sacrifices", drawing from their condition various conclusions on problems of state (and his own state insurance).
[See *Roman Sacred Dance*]

AURRESKU (Basque)

A ceremonial dance, accompanied by piper and taborer (the *txistulari*), and performed in the plaza before the Alcalde (Mayor) and town officials. First comes the *Aurresku* or *Guison Dantza*. Led by the best dancer (the *aurresku*), a linked chain of young men circles the plaza, salutes the girl chosen by the leader to be his partner, and finishes facing the Alcalde. Flinging his red beret on the ground, the *aurresku* bows to the Alcalde and performs a solo displaying brilliant technique, which is challenged by the *atzesku*, the last man in the line. The two perform a sort of dance contest, each trying to outdo the other in technical brilliance. An arch is then made and the file pass through. Next comes the *Contrapas* or *Andreen deieco sonua*. Four dancers leave the chain and, with ceremony, bring the girl chosen by the *aurresku* to the centre of the plaza, where he meets her with beret in hand and hand on hip. Facing her he performs another brilliant solo, ending with three bows, to left, to right, and to his partner. Then, joined by a kerchief held between them, they take their place in the chain. The *atzesku* then chooses his lady in similar manner, and all the young men should do likewise, but often there is a general rush for partners, the dancers reforming in a long line. There follows the *Zortziko* in 5/8 time. The chain winds in circles, stopping from time to time while the *aurresku* pirouettes. A *Fandango* sometimes follows, the line breaking into couples, to be succeeded by the *Arin-Arin*. Sometimes a *Zortziko* in 2/4 time is danced after the first figure, or *Aurresku*; or, the *Aceri Dantza* (Fox Dance) may come between the choosing of partners and the *Zortziko* in 5/8 time. In *Aceri Dantza*, the first couple dance to the end of

the line each time the tune finishes, the melody being repeated until all couples have completed the figure. The *Aurresku* is performed in the Basque provinces, around San Sebastien and Pamplona. At Villafranca de Oria (Guipuzcoa) on 26th July, a traditional *Aurresku* is danced by young men, married during the preceding year.

AUTO-DA-FÊ (Spanish-Latin)

The corrupted form of *Palauto de Fédèles* or "play of the faithful", developed in this form chiefly in Spain with the spectacular religious murders conducted by the Holy Inquisition. The rapid dance form seldom appeared; the main feature was (after the imprisonment and torture to extract "Confessions") the ceremonial slow march, for which all concerned put on uniform of rank, or, as with the condemned prisoners, attire chosen to mark them for spiteful comment by the admiring crowds. One such dress was the *San Benito*, a dingy yellow garb. The holy fathers often wore hoods completely concealing their features; for, as with the African *ju-ju* doctors whom they copied and surpassed, they skilfully avoided the chance of any identification by relatives or friends. Popular dances sometimes followed the burning of the bodies (books were never burned but "confiscated"), but the street dance (*passacaglia*) of the *Santa Semana* was rarely performed in the same period; though occasionally the great painted wooden idols of the saints would be carried, to the dismal chants of the hooded familiars.
[See *Hist. Inquisition* (W. H. Rule) for plan of theatre erected in Madrid]

AUTOMATIC BALLET DANCER (Paris)

An electrically controlled "dancing" machine (" *Etre Artificielle*") devised by sculptor Nicholas Schoffer and demonstrated in 1957 at a *Nuit de Poésie* at the Sarah Bernhardt Theatre. Tapering to a height of ten feet, with long, thin "arms" and "legs", and revolving coloured plaques, the robot reacted either to music or to colour, spontaneously devising its own "choreography". On a dark, silent stage it showed how a blue spotlight made it advance while making quick turns; under a red light it turned its plaques rapidly; while to *musique concrète* the figure pirouetted and moved round the stage in widening circles. When the music changed, it paused, then continued with appropriate movement : synthetic "dancing" to synthetic "music".

AUTOMATONS, Dances of

Became popular with the virtuosity of the clockmakers of Nürnberg. Besides providing the Embracing Virgin for the local inquisitors they developed chess-playing figures who would play a game with a living opponent. The Dance of the Hours was devised to publicise their excellent clocks, as at Venice, Prague or Nürnberg. They had a Dance of the Apostles, who appeared to strike the hours. This development was noticed by E. T. A. Hoffman, the composer and writer from Königsberg, when he devised his legend of *The Sandman*, or *The Doll with Enamel Eyes*, later (much altered), made into the famous ballet *Coppelia.* In the Second Act we see a Dance of the Automatic Toys, who rise and perform limited doll movements to suitable music. Some dancers find it easy to simulate these figures.

AUTZ-HA-CHAYIM (Hebrew, from Babylonian)
The ritual and symbolic *Tree of Life*—it is composed of the *Sephiroth* and the *Schem-ha-phorasch*—of ten symbols and seventy-two symbols. The seventy-two is the dynamic ritual number: it is relevant to the Secret Paths. These are thirty-two for ritual exposition. We might compare them, distantly, with the Mendelevian "Table of Elements"—but more closely—for the purpose of comprehending the "cosmic dance of Number Word and Form" with the 108 *Tattvas* of the Hindu scheme (as expressed through *Bharata Natyam*). There are two Trees: the Tree of Life (and Death) and the Tree of Knowledge. These cosmic symbols appear in many religions: Babylonian (example of the carved Tree in British Museum); the Norse World Tree *Yggdrasil;* the Egyptian Tree of Hathor (sycamore) or the Aztec Tree and the Druid Oak (or O.K.E.). All have some ritual dance association.

AVAHANA (Sanskrit)
Implies "appearance" in many modes. The idea precedes the "initial dance" of the *pavane* (which has nothing to do with Padua and relates only to *pavo* (peacock) in the notion of display). In Hindu tradition Peacock symbolises the coloured world; the swan is the pure white of the world of peace. *Avahana* has also the idea of mental imagery—the "dance in the mind"—while the *Vahan* is the god-symbol, or his vehicle. In dance—especially in Java—*vahan* is the regular basic image, of the *vayang* or *wayang*, as theatre form or convention. Bunyan has *Vanity Fair*, as also Thackeray, with similar if distant meanings, as illusions.

AVEUGLES, Danse aux (French)
Variation on *Danse Macabre**: Said to be devised as a poem by Pierre Michault (when in service of Charles, Count of Carolois, son of Philip le Bon, Duke of Burgundy.) Under the title *La Danse aux Aveugles* the poet shows that all men are influenced by three blind guides—Love, Fortune, and Death; before whom several persons are made to dance. The form is that of a dream or "vision", described as between the Author and his Understanding. In this form, the theme is a reversal of the *Danse des Bouffants*, in which one or more men (dancers) are temporarily blinded with a kerchief, as an emphasis on the blindness of men in seeking their fortune.

AWISA (Gold Coast, Africa, Ghana)
A dance similar to the social dance *Awassa* of the Surinam Bush Negroes, among whom it is performed as a preliminary to religious ritual. Danced by men and women facing each other, it is said to have originated among the Hausa of Nigeria.

AXE SYMBOL (Crete)
The famous Double-Axe was the sacred symbol of the Minoan Religion (2000 BC–1400 BC). With its simple form went many rituals; in the "Great Hall of the Double Axes" (as recent explorers have named it) at Knossos, and other centres in Crete. At the 1936 Exhibition in London, numerous Minoan relics were shewn : miniature frescoes of "The Ladies in Blue"; and "The Sacred Grove and Dance", with "a Temple and grand stand thronged with spectators; seated ladies in fashionable costume, with an extraordinarily modern touch" (17th century BC). The Minoan Mother Goddess attended by two lions, holds her Double Axe. Boys and girls, clad in long robes, are passing sacramental chalices of gold and silver (may be members of some Sacred College) found in sanctuary in N.W. Palace angle. Women wearing flounced skirts (much earlier than the "romantic tutu") worship at a horned altar; there is a Sacred Tree. Warriors carry "figure-of-eight" shaped shields (as used later in Rome by Saliian dancer-priests). Athletes, in the ceremonial Bull ritual, carry no weapons, use no armour. The Sacral Axe is carried in processions. The Sacred Axe reveals some of its secrets, when inscribed over a lunar circle; but this derives from Babylon; from the labours of the Saviour Gilgamesh. He has two uses for his Axe; with one edge he cuts away the impeding world-forest; with the other edge he slays the enemy world-animals. Holding it upright on bright days (or better still, at night), he learns the period of time by its sharp shadow on the square of the revelation : it is a gnomon; a weapon; a tool; and a profound symbol. Hence the regular appearance of the Shining Double Axe in many rituals and ceremonies. Perhaps it is strange that its modern renaissance should be in Moscow—for the Hammer and Sickle represent two functions of the ancient

Double Axe, now symbolising Industry and Agriculture.

[See Catalogue: *British Discoveries in Greece and Crete: 1886-1936.* (London Exhibition 1936). Notes by *Sir Arthur Evans* and *Prof. J. L. Myres*]

AYRIWA (Peru)

Dance of the Young Maize; also the name of the month of April in the Inca calendar. Performed now by the Quechua Indians on the 3rd May, it is obviously the remnant of an ancient maize festival. Having set up a tree decorated with fruit and presents, the Indians dance round it, afterwards shaking down gifts and distributing them. This ceremony ends with singing of the old harvest song *Aymuray.*

AZTEC DANCE (Ancient Mexico; Abt. 1250-1519)

Was connected principally with religious ritual, although dances were also performed for amusement. Lords, priests, and pupils of the *Calmecac* (school for religious and ritual training) all danced, as did the King himself, both in the temple, and for recreation. (See *Netateliztli.**) Aztec life was dominated by priests, who interpreted an elaborate religion based essentially on rhythm — the rhythm of the universe, of the forces of Nature, with which they sought to keep in harmony and so benefit the nation. The solar calendar of eighteen "twenty-day months" had a ceremony for each month, at most of which dancing took place. Eight were for rain; others were at seed-time; in honour of new corn, of ripe corn, harvest, and "toasting of corn supply". (See *Xilonen;** and cp. *Green Corn Dance** and *Busk.**) Spaniards such as Friar Sahagun[1] and Clavijero[2] left descriptions. Some dances were for men, some for women, some for both sexes. One was in the form of concentric circles, several hundred dancers moving round musicians in the centre. Priests and important people moved with dignity in the inner rings, while less exalted persons on the perimeter circled with greater speed. The dancers kept position behind each other, radiating from the centre like spokes of a wheel. Between the lines of dancers, buffoons cavorted in animal or comic guise. Among Pueblo Indians* of North America, it is still the custom for clowns to accompany solemn religious dances. (See *Koshare:** *Koyemshi**). Costumes were elaborate, with gold and jewelled ornaments, cloaks and head-dresses of brilliant feather-work. Gourd rattles were shaken; bone and clay flutes played; notched bones rasped with a stick. Two types of drum were used — the *huehuetl,* a vertical cylinder with skin head; and the *teponaztli,* a horizontal cylinder with top slotted to form two tongues, and sometimes made like a crouching animal or man. In the rituals, dance-dramas were performed, portraying mythological events, such as that danced by Eagle* and Tiger Knights. At a festival celebrating the passage of the sun through the heavens, they showed symbolically the ritual slaying of the sun and his rebirth the next day. Priests regulated rituals and arrayed dancers. The principal character often represented a god or goddess, and was symbolically dressed in his colours and ornaments. (See *Ilamatecuhtli;** *Xilonen;** *Huitzilopochtli;** *Huixtocihuatl**). An important festival occurred at the end of each fifty-two-year cycle, when the New Fire Ceremony was observed. Altar fires, burning continuously for fifty-two years, were extinguished; also all domestic fires. Houshold effects were destroyed and fasting was observed until a certain hour of the night, when particular stars reached the zenith and the new cycle was inaugurated. On the sacred Hill of the Star fire was rekindled and taken by runners to all temples and homes. Punctuated by special dances, an almost identical ceremony survived among certain North American Indians, such as the Natchez and Creek (see *Busk**). Xochipilli ("Flower Prince", god of pleasure and games), or his synonym Macuilxochitl ("Five Flower") is given as god of music and dance. Ozomatli has been quoted as "Monkey God of the Dance", but in the *Tonalpohualli,* or ritualistic calendar of days, this is merely the name of the eleventh day, whose special god was Xochipilli. Traces of Aztec ritual linger in some dances of Mexican Indians today, while the "Flying Game", or *Juego de los Voladores** has survived almost intact, although its significance is forgotten.

[See *La Conquista; Plumas, Danza de las; Acatlaxque; Quetzales*]

[1] *Historia General de las Cosas de Nueva España.* B. de Sahagun. (Mexico — 3 vols.) 1829.

[2] The *Ancient History of Mexico.* F. S. Clavigero (Trans. C. Cullen — London) 2 vols. 1787.

B

BA'AL — 1 (Hebrew-Syrian)

Is one of the original sources for the continued court institution of Ball and Ballet; which must be examined, if only because of its persistence into Scottish tradition, that continues to modern times, animating the celebration of *Baal-taine. Samhain* etc. *Baal* was a kind of *deus municipium* — asserting and using powers of coercion over ordinary citizens, quite in the manner of the modern "Local Authority" in Britain; or recently in Nazi Germany; invading house and home and possessions. The

Ba'Al "had power over beasts as well as man".[1] These local gods "were conceived of as having their residence and home at certain fixed sanctuaries (*Hotel de Ville*)" while "the power of the gods has physical and local limitations". These *Baalim* were in many respects similar to the modern Town Council, with its Chairman, Mayor, or Lord Mayor (often mentioned in local centres of artisan refreshment as "them little tin gods"). The exposition by W. Robertson Smith[1] is clear. He says:

"In Semitic religion, the relation of the gods to particular places which are special seats of their power, is usually expressed by the title *Baal* (pl. *Baalim*, fem. *Baalath*)—as applied to men, *baal* means the master of a house, the owner of a field, cattle or the like; or in the plural, the *ba'alim* of a city are the freeholders and full citizens".

In ordinary Arabic the word *ba'al* means "husband". "Each of the multitude of local *Ba'alim* is distinguished by adding the name of his own place. Melcarth is the Ba'al of Tyre; Astarte is Ba'alath of Byblus; there was a Baal of Lebanon . . . and so forth". Peculiar is the later *Ba'al-Marcod*. "The Semitic form is supposed to be 'Lord of Dancing', i.e. He to whom dancing is due as an act of homage". Thus the term *Baal* does not merit the angry denunciations shrieked by the Jewish prophets: their resentment of gods other than Jahve was clearly jealousy, evoked by the attention given by citizens to civic affairs, giving second place to financial claims of Levites. The ritual dance of Ba'al-Marcod is but a special example of ceremonial movement, common to most civic occasions of pomp and display. From these rituals we have, in common with the Greek *boule*,* a version probably derived from the earlier Phoenecian ceremonial, and adopted by the "city fathers" of those days.
[1] *Religion of the Semites*. W. Robertson Smith (London 1894).

BA'AL — 2 (Babylonian-Phoenecian etc.)
The ritual dance of Ba-Al is one of the oldest known forms of the circle dance, as antecedent to Ball-et (Little Ba'al). Though most data comes from Syria (later called Balestan or Palestine), because of the highly varied accounts of "Jewish history" the precise origin is not yet ascertained; it seems to be older than the empire of Assyria; and yet there are firm traditions enduring, as far distant as Scotland, in the still active customs associated with *Baal-tinne*. Definitely the religious doctrine was connected with solar symbols of the year; so that four great festivals occurred at equinox and solstice, celebrated with fire and with water; and, despite displacements caused by the shift of the social calendar, in its failure to keep pace both with solar and lunar times, the festival of *Samhain* falls at the Summer Solstice and that of *Baal-tinne* at the Winter Solstice. The copied Feasts of Baal held by the quarrelsome Jews were attached mainly to town feasts, associated with local petty kings and their "circles" (or *gilgal'im*) and were, in effect, little more than municipal gatherings, officially always in the way of the integration into a larger nation, desired by more far-seeing prophets— which is chiefly why these numerous Ba-als were denounced. This Semitic *Ba-Al* had a reflex in Arabia in *Al-Ba* (and the Moslem Allah later), the White God, yet associated with Blood Ritual[1] in tribal fact, and in allegory. The form and function of the *Ba-Al* rituals make it clear that they are precedent forms of much later European court rituals, with Scandinavian "King elections" making a middle period—with another firm circle. The court ballet (varying from rites of procession, of entry, of fealty, and the like) alternated with older traditional celebrations of the *Ba-al* rites, parallel from Egypt in the *Meskhan* rites of the New Year.
[1] *Religion of the Semites*. W. Robertson Smith.
Encyclopaedia Biblica (Ed. Cheyne)

BABBITY BOWSTER (Scotland to 19th century)
Was a ballad dance, usually at "Kirn Baby" Festival at Harvest. This old country dance also followed many a wedding. Girls sat along one side of the barn; the boys facing them on the other side. One boy takes a cushion; the company sings, he replies, on how he learned to dance. After four or five verses the lad has chosen his partner, places the cushion before her; they both kneel and kiss. When they rise, the girl follows the boy; she selects another youth; throws at him the cushion and runs back to her first partner; if she is caught, she pays with a kiss. This second youth then selects his partner in the same round; until all are paired off. Babbity Bowster means "Bab at the Bowster" or Bolster.   [See *Cushion Dance*]

BABORASCHKA (Czechoslovakia)
Bohemian national dance (also given as *Baborák*), joined with a favourite folksong, similar to Styrian style, usually in 2/4 time. These songs (there are variations in verses) show a pattern of three lines. Sometimes we find a succession of single "first lines" with a double-line refrain; but sometimes the other way round.

BABYLON (Assyria)
Was famous for its magnificent spectacles; many rituals with processions, music and dance. Layard[1] recounts something of these in his *Nineveh*:

". . . the Assyrians, as well as those who succeeded them in the empire of Asia, were fond of public entertainments and festivities, and displayed the greatest luxury and magnificence. The Assyrian king, Nabuchodnosor, returning from his victorious expedition against Arphaxead, feasted with his whole army for one hundred and twenty days (also Sardanapalas, after fighting the Medes) . . . the princes and nobles feasted one hundred and eighty days; for one week all the people of Susa assembled in the gardens of his palace, and were served in vessels of gold. Wine was served in abundance; and women, including even wives and concubines of the monarch, were present to add magnificence to the scene. According to Quintius Curtius, not only did hired female performers exhibit on these occasions, but the wives and daughters of the nobles danced before the guests. . . . Music was not wanting".

And again :

"The court of Ahasuerus, the garden of the palace, when he feasted the people of Shusan, was fitted up with white and green and blue hangings, fastened with cords of fine linen, to silver rings and pillars of marble; the couches were gold and silver, upon a pavement of red and blue, and white and black marble".

This inlaid pavement we may regard as the dancing-floor, rather than any grassy sward between trees; on it they danced with bare feet. These celebrations

Pazuzo, the son of Hanput, who was King of the Air Devils in Babylonia. Probably typical pattern for priest mask, and for use as the head of his ritual magic wand. (British Museum) BABYLONIA

were secular in general character; or as near such as any royal festival could be; for every great function had its basic religious form as a thanksgiving or a prayer. Much of the Assyrian life was highly cultured; from them the Greeks obtained a considerable stock of methods and ideas. Among the few certain facts on dance, it seems that any public display was far larger in scale than the almost private ritual duties of the inner temple, whose largest hall measured a maximum of ninety by forty feet.

[1] *Nineveh.* A. Layard.

BABYLONIAN DANCE DEMONS

Performed in temple ritual. Six principal demons were :

1. *Alu* — half human, half animal; hides from view;
2. *Ekimmu* — a restless departed spirit; "to lift", underworld spirit;
3. *Gallu* — a bull form; powerful, sexless; roams at night. *Ilu Limmu* general term.
4. *Rabisu* — a spy demon; in front, as a leader;
5. *Labartu* — daughter of *Anu*; "veracity". (*Labasu*, to throw);
6. *Ahazu* — the seizer.

Sumerian term, *galla* = *Sedu* or *Shed*. Dazzling fiend; some *Shed* were friendly *Shedu* : the gracious genius (Bull-form, at entrance of Temple-palaces). *Asmedaj* (*Asmodeus*, their chief). *Mazzikin*, hurtful spirits (in *Maze*?); *Deber*, demon of pestilence; (Deborah?), *Keteb*, demon of noonday heat; *Alukah*, the leech-like.

BACCHAE (Hellas)

Also known as Maenades or Thyades; feminine dancer-companions of the vine-god Dionysus (Bacchus) in his "wanderings" of ritual form; they are shown as robed in fawn-skins, crowned with vine leaves or ivy leaves; and carrying the sacred thyrsus. The priestesses of the popular cult were called Bacchae; one of the great annual festivals was that of the Vine Harvest. The Bacchic Cult of Dion-Yssus has flourished widely through Europe, in all places where the vine has been cultivated.

[See *Satyrs Dance; Sylvanus*]

BACCHUS (BAKKHUS), Dances of (Hellas)

Were oriental rituals, included in annual celebrations in the winter months, celebrating the Dionyssus (God of the Year), with sacrificial and memorial dance rituals. These are best known today by the numerous remains of sculptures, vase paintings etc., with figures of Bacchantes, the girls who dance in the rituals; and the *thyrsoi* (thyrsus-bearers) which referred to the staff entwined with ribbons, surmounted by a fir cone (a miniature May-pole, in form and symbol). These Greek terms present derivations from earlier Sanskrit (Brahmin-ical) terms, associated with the ancient *Bhakti** Cult of Krishna, whose devotees were famed for their *enthusiasmos* ("god-possession"). Revivals of this cult have again and again revealed precisely similar scenes of devotional worship; and they have affected most other sects of the Hindu religious systems; and others in Europe. The term *Bhagavati* is probably the immediate origin of "Bacchus" (or *Bhikkus*, the Pali equivalent, better known to students of Buddhism), while its last traditional impact is known in France as the dance *gavat* or *gavotte*. The word *Bhagwan* indicates the Lord Krishna; it came into Eastern Europe as *Bhaga* or *Bhoga*—the Bogomiles was the Byzantine (Balkan) version and *Bhog* became the Russian equivalent (satirised by the Latins as "Bogie"). The influence of *Bhakkus* into Hellas probably developed about

Greek bronze figure of Bacchante found at Tetovo, Bosnia. *(Courtesy of Ethnological Museum of Macedonia [Skopje]).*   JUGOSLAVIA

7th century BC (before the Buddhist revolt against the highly developed Brahmin system). Dance ritual was a prominent characteristic of this Hindu system; it is repeatedly mentioned as prohibited to Buddhists (as English Puritans rejected Miracle Plays etc.). For details of this ancient ritual dance we must turn to *Bharata Natya Shastras** and ritualistic details of *Tantra** liturgy.

BACCHUS (Roman)
Same as *Dionysus* (Greek) nominated as "the God of Wine". This is no definition, since it inverts facts : wine was used in the worship of the god, by (a) Bacchae, and (b) Bacchantes—males and females. Bacchus (or I O Acchus) was reputed son of Jupiter (Sun) and Semele (Earth). Celebrations were for sowing and harvest superficially. The servitors became known as *bachelour* (youths unwedded) or university students, just matriculated as Bachelor Artium, thus preserving to some extent the sym-bolic aspect. Bacchus (described by Jane Harrison and Gilbert Murray) was accompanied by his tutor Silenus, his satyrs and nymphs (Bacchantes). Bacchus, the "Ever Youthful" was shown with lions and tigers or lynxes (all cats) and a spear with ivy. The rites should not be accepted as being always "wild" or "licentious"—it is merely a Victorian clerical depreciation.

BACCUBERT (French Pyrenees)
Traditional name given to a vine harvest dance. The Egyptian harvest festival of Pert, was that of "Coming Forth" in the fruits of the earth. Later, it joined with Bacchus, as God of Vine; when the two names merged as Bacchus-Pert. This later change, from Pert to Bert, is marked all through Western Europe in such names as Hu-Bert (masculine form) and Bert-ha (feminine form), as well as the Ru-Pert and the Austrian *Perschten** or Winter Dances. The Bacchus-Bertha showed a couple dance, taking the parts of the god and goddess of harvest, very much as Robyn and Mayd Marion* performed their roles in the Spring Sowing season. Gradually the meaning was obscured and then lapsed into the condensed term *Baccubert*. Sometimes spelt *Bacchu-Ber*, the modern version is a sword dance performed only on the 16th August at the Fête d'Hameau, near Briançon in the Haut Pyrenées. The dance, said to have been performed since 1550, is done by nine or eleven men, who make various geometrical figures, to a chanted accompaniment by five girls. The dancers wear white coats and trousers; and carry brass handled swords, not pointed. Illustra-tions of the principal figures, with some old engravings, are given in Raphael Blanchard's book *Le Ba'Cubert* (Paris 1914).

BACUP "COCO-NUT" DANCE (England)

Performed today by a team of Morris dancers at Bacup in Lancashire. Eight men in black breeches and jerseys, with faces blackened, perform various figures in single file, circles and squares. Wearing white socks and caps, and a short horizontally striped red-and-white skirt, they are accompanied by an accordion player and attended by the traditional Fool, with a whip. But the essential rhythms are provided by the dancers themselves, who beat small domes of wood, like half coconuts fastened to palms of hands, knees and waist. With those on the hands they clap their own and those of the other dancers. A similar dance exists in Provence, performed at Carnival, called *Li Coco* ("The Coconuts"). Men with blackened faces wear half-coconuts on knees, elbows, breast and hands. In the Philippino dance *Maglalatik* the dancers click together polished coconut shells tied to various parts of the body. *El Coco* in Spain means the "bogey-man".

BADINERIE (French)

"Frolic." 18th cent. term used to indicate a quick or jesting movement (*badinage*) in duple time, for salon danse. When in suite, it was one of the *galanterien** as in Bach's B-minor (flute and strings), giving the typical light air.

BAGUETTES, DANSE DES (Brittany)

A stick dance in 4/4 time, having different versions. One is danced by groups of two (man and woman), another by three people (man and two women). In the first version, dancers face each other, at opposite ends of two sticks which they hold parallel. They turn in a circle; then the sticks are raised above the head and, still holding them, the woman turns anti-clockwise, thus crossing the sticks; repeated by the man clockwise. Or they both turn together in opposite directions, without crossing sticks. In the second version, the man stands in the middle, holding one end of each stick, the other end being held by two women on either side of him. First one, then the other woman, passes under one of the raised sticks, the man directing their movements.
[See *Makila Tchuri* (Basque); *Cardadora* (Spain); *'N'drezzata* (Italy); *Paulitos, Danca dos* (Portugal)]

BAHLUWAN (Egyptian/Arabic)

Entertainment form given by gypsies of Cairo. The name is properly applied to a performer of gymnastic feats; a swordsman or champion wrestler etc. But the "modern" *Bahluwan*, says Lane, were almost confined to rope-dancing.[1] The persons who practiced this art belonged to the tribe Ghagar or Ghajar. Their rope might be fixed to a high *madneh* or minaret of a mosque; and extend some hundred feet or more, supported at intervals by poles. The dancer used a long balancing pole; whether men, women or children. The term compares with the Russian *balagan*,* for similar displays at Fairs.
[1] *Modern Egyptians*. E.W.Lane (First Edition 1836).

BAILECITO (Argentina)

A dance in 6/8 time, for four or more dancers, Found in the north-western provinces of Jujuy and Salta, it is well-known also in Bolivia and Peru. Its full title, *Bailecita de tierra* ("Little dance of the earth") may refer to an original rural dance, on to which was grafted, with adaptations, European ballroom styles of the nineteenth century. Most Argentine folk-dances are for one couple only. The chief characteristic is shaking a handkerchief, by each dancer, throughout the dance. There are five figures: 1. *Vuelta*; 2. *Vuelta da pareja*; 3. *Giros a la Izquierda*; 4. *Giros a la derecha*; 5. *Ronda: Vuelta y media*. Using a waltz step, dancers follow each other round in a circle; revolve in couples or individually, and finally form a circle making a turn-and-a-half (*vuelta y media*) anti-clockwise, with a hopping step. The kerchief, held by the corner in the right hand, is waved gently up and down. A song accompanies this dance, together with the *quena* (six-holed pipe of Inca origin), and guitars. The music is in two sections, in different keys.

BAKASURA (Manipur, Assam)

Boys' dance-play, through Manipur province, on the theme of "Krishna kills the Crane". This "crane" is devised (ten or twelve feet high, according to resources) of wicker or light laths, covered with white cotton cloth; with eyes made of black dyed cotton bobs; and long sharp wooden teeth. The strongest dancer carries this Crane; his legs, loaded with jingling brass bells, appear as the bird's legs. The dance is done to a smart rhythm supplied by the *Khol* (drum) and *khanjani* (cymbals), as Krishna draws near for the attack.

BAKONGO "TWELVE MASK" RITUAL DANCE (Congo)

One of numerous different versions of an episodic dance; possibly a local copy of an older *Bapende* dance. Each "mask" enters separately; and characterises not only his part, but a relation among the development. This dance is performed by daylight in the centre of a village, to an audience of headmen and officials; with all other local residents; and culminates in a "sacred wedding" that is factual. (1) Enter "the stranger"—*Tundu* the Uncircumcised. He dances clumsily; has no fine costume; hears jibes and insults. He feigns terror, seeking flight, under blows from spectators; at last he departs when (2) *Kaudumbu*, the Old Woman, replaces him. She is his counterpart, Wickedness and Famine. She is driven back with sticks; for she is *daua* (magical) and contact might be fatal. These two gone, in comes (3) *M'Bungu*, the mighty hunter, armed with bow and arrows, wearing a terrific black/white mask, symbolising death/life. At his waist hang bells made of tiny skulls. He advances in silence, miming a hunt. His dancing steps must be accurate; a mistake incurs the whip. Next comes (4) *Kiwoyo* with *Muyumbo*: these "happy twins" portray "velly good boys", who do their work and pay their taxes. Greeted cordially, nobody has any interest; but attention revives when (6) *Kituga*, the Warrior enters, with full arms, bow and arrow, spear and knife. His mask is a helmet of feathers; he wears lion skin. His dance-mime is a battle; he is killed but revives, eating the heart of his enemy and taking his woman. All is nearly 90% happiness, when (7) *Pumbu*, Spirit of Evil, now appears, throwing his bad *daua* right and left in dance. Yet Kituga and the Two Twins fall on him, bind him and ground him. Now comes the fattest and largest dancer (8) as *Cambanda*, oozing prosperity, and wearing genuine "falsies" (not USA made). He/she distributes antidotes to the bad magic of Pumbu. Hunger will be unknown; gentlemen of the tribe will be both virtuous and strong (at least for a week). Spectators offer two seats to Cambanda; yet he essays to leave, when they threaten his disobedience. Cambanda occupies his large seat. Then (9) *Muluba* the Merchant appears, hidden with wares, offering at velly low price. Everyone imitates his mime of buying and selling. Now we are progressing in this build-up of tribal magic. So (10) *Fumu*, the Chief, arrives, wearing an enormous mask with immense buffalo horns (these denote prosperity and success, as well as potency). Fumu demands tribute; previous Masks and spectators pretend to go to a hut, to bring offerings, which seem to please. At some gifts he is not content, and orders his slaves to give the offender a beating. Thus comes (11) *N'ganda-N'ganda*, the Witch Doctor—who can cure everybody of almost anything. He is usually the real witch doctor; he may not dance, for the audience is afraid. If he is a dancer playing the part, he is cordially received. The feast is now at its height; the tribe has got everything. But it cannot last; so (12) the Great Mumbo arrives, in the midst of mournful cries and deep drum reverberations. The two slaves, serving as a chair for the king, fall over; his wives help him to rise. Mumbo puts *daua* on the huts; and Cadamba is deprived of his bountiful breasts; even the Witch Doctor's body reveals an attack of measles. Spectators seek an offering: "Where are

Tundu and Kaudumba"? But Mumbo refuses this ancient gear; he wants better sport. He demands a virgin; young and beautiful. (Usually Mumbo is danced by a youth, who has already "made an arrangement" with the girl's father). Mumbo becomes pacified; he likes the maiden offered; but a long discussion ensues, between chief and elders. At last they all yield. Candamba returns, newly inflated; the Merchant brings more wares; and everybody feels highly cured. Mumbo takes the girl into his hut as the Twelve Masks all mime a reconciliation; the drums echo jollity; and they form an expectant ring round the Mumbo Hut. Presently the girl returns; her father whispers a question and she says "Yes", so he cuts off her youthful hair crop. So ends the Twelve Mask Dance.

BAKONY HERDSMEN'S DANCE (Hungary)
Is danced now chiefly as a pastime by the swineherds of Bakony district, Mátra and Bükk. They carry axes or long crooks, wearing a festival costume of white, brilliantly stitched with coloured silks. For music they may use a bagpipe, or the long flute. The central part of the dance is a mock combat, using polished small axes, or substituting these with gilded wooden swords. The Herdsmen's Dance also represents the killing of a boar, and is performed by two or more men. Shouting alternates with occasional singing of ancient refrains. The dance, with much stamping, is a display of dexterity in the handling of the axe or stick which each dancer holds. Whirling the weapons in their hands, they throw them to each other, pass the axe under the legs, squat and kick out the legs alternately, or leap in the air, striking the ankles together. In one version, the boar is represented by a hat placed on the ground between two dancers facing each other. A third man, squatting on his heels, tries to remove the "pig" while the dancers whirl their axes horizontally above it, with twisting movements of the hands. Another version has the boar represented by a man, who chases the swineherd. Wielding his axe continually, the herdsman retreats in rhythm with the music, finally killing the "boar" by striking the ground beside him with his axe. In a third version, a youth with an earthenware pot on his head, and enveloped in a sheet, is the boar, which the herdsman "kills" by cleaving the pot on the unfortunate youth's head. A favourite dance of herdsmen and shepherds is *Kanasc Tanc* in which a crude stick cross is made (as a solar cross of the calendar dates) with two axes or crooks. According to season, the steps of the dance (in each alternate quarter of the circle thus indicated) begin and end with the quarter of the year for the celebration. The swineherd traditionally carries his axe (for defence against

attacking wolves), while the cowherds have staves; and shepherds have thinner crooks; but all these may serve to mark the small dance circle.
[Cp. *Goralski* (Poland); *Morismo* (Mexico)]

BAKOROGUI (French Guinea, West Africa)

Are two "masks", male and female; who perform rituals with dances in the villages. Male *Bakorogui* enters from his "dressing room" in the bush, wearing an enormous black mask with great red mouth, carrying a staff decorated with panther claws. He is escorted by three musicians; singing, and hammering with short sticks on a hollow triangle instrument. He darts about the village, in a dance of hops and skips; taking an offering from each hut. This "dance of sacrifice" is done to welcome visitors who bring regulation offerings. Masks are used only to frighten women and boys.

BA-KO-RO-RO (Brazil)

A funeral dance (at Bowro, Central Brazil), held at midnight, for leaders; and lasting sometimes several weeks (forty-nine days). The first dance, at interment, is short; the final dance follows the disinterment (at end of the "time of going" for the departing soul); and represents the final re-assurance to the dead man. Songs are sung to him while realising his invisible presence. The bones or body have been painted with the correct symbols; the skull is given rank with bright feathers. The first dance-song is chanted slowly by the men; the second by both men and women. The bones are re-buried in a pottery urn.

BAL Á DEUX (Brittany)

A dance in two parts; the first in slow 2/2 time; the second, more lively, in 2/4 time. Slow, dignified movements alternate with light and lively dancing. Needing a minimum of four couples, it is danced on the south coast of Finistère, and one version, known as *Bal à Deux à l'ancienne mode*, is known only by the old people of the region of Pont-Aven. There are two figures. In the first, couples promenade round the dancing space. For the second they either face each other, holding both hands; or they dance side by side, the man's left hand and the girl's right hand held in front. The figure consists of steps to the side, half circles and whole circles, both clockwise and anti-clockwise.

BALADINES

Middle French term for those *danses en haute* which were performed by clowns, mimes and *comédiens*, usually for entertainment; and sometimes accompanied by songs, often parodies of graver verses used with the *danse basse*. These *baladines* became energetic; devised to show off this or that special skill in steps or jumps; and thus merged into acrobatic display, lacking in any governing rhythm. On the borders of these *baladines* came the numerous modes of *branle** and *waltz** or *valse*. Usually the dancers were a small group, two or three men who travelled as one company. They were parallel to the English ballads of the style used by John Gay in his famous *Beggars Opera*; and the English revised pantomime, as restaged by Rich, owes some part of its energy to the *baladines*. The German version was known as *die singspiel*. The style endured, more or less, from about the 14th to early 17th centuries.
[See *Balladine*]

BAL DE LA MORT (Spain)

A modern clerical version of a Dance of Death, performed in Easter Week, chiefly in Catalonia. At halts in the village processions (as in districts of Ampurdan), a *compagnia* of fifteen dancers repeats a quadrille dance, with figures for twelve men and three women. They wear black attire, on which bony forms are painted to suggest skeletons; with faces covered by skull masks. The characters indicate Death (with a scythe) and Time (with a pendulum clock) or Fate (with a banner). The single musician carries a drum; he wears armour, with a black mantle. Sometimes additional death figures are supplied by small boys or girls, disguised in identical costumes. The "Death" does not dance, but borders the group, swinging his scythe towards the spectators, in rhythmic walk and movement.
[See *Todtentanz*; *Morts, la danse des*; *Danse Macabre*; *Misère, Danse des*]

BALADOIRES OR PALADOIRES, OR BALATOIRES (Portugal)

Names relevant chiefly to the church ritual dances and processional marches with dances, current from perhaps the second to the eighth centuries (compare the later term *trouba-doires*). Popular travesties of the rituals—here as in the Eastern church at Constantinople during this same period—enraged the clerics so much that they "forbade" dancing and feasting by a Council in 682, without any effective result; while in 744 Pope Zacharius issued a *bulla*, attempting thereby to suppress all *baladoires*—their supposed "religious dances"—on the theory that they had become degenerated. The social fact was that their clerical attempt at control and perversion of far older religious dances had failed; therefore, we learn of these periodical official attempts at suppression. The church ritual dances clashed with popular festivals—those of solstice and equinox—when it was attempted to impose the newer myths and parables. Some success was gained with the Feast of John (summer solstice), which was converted into "Saint" John and Sainte Jean of the Arcus. The Jewish fast of

Pasche at Easter was taken over. *Purim-spiele* was abolished. The *baladoires* remained, as they remain today in Seville, as highly coloured processions with enrobed idols, with singing, but little dancing. Their later forms *passecaille* or *passacaglia*,* had also diminished. Hence the songs developed into *ballades* or *ballata*; instead of being vented in street processions, the singers (*gitana* or minstrel), remained in the inn, the cabaret, the *trattoria*, the ale-house, the *kellar*, as the tavern slowly replaced the tabernacle; and the cloister became neglected as a play-house.

BALAGAN, BALAGANI (Russia)

Were the historical forerunners of Theatre and Ballet in Russia, as Alexander Benois makes clear.[1] They persisted in his youth (round the '70's of last century). He writes:

"The balagani were the covered theatres . . . chief attraction of the Fair . . . the whole Fair went under the name of Balagani . . . the wooden sheds put up anew every year".

These appeared at Easter and Carnival, for the common people. "Berg and Yegarev's Harlequinade were presented", says Benois, ". . . my first experience of theatre. Director Vsevolosky (of Imperial Theatres) saw these Harlequinades in his youth; he desired to revive this impression . . . and created the charming ballet *Les Millions d'Arlequin*". Thus it is obvious that the country-wide appearance of the *Balagani* had an effect similar to that of the Paris *Foires* or the English Fairs, in stimulating a love of Theatre among the people. Certainly in Russia, the "Serf Companies" made little impression; none in the towns (for they existed only in isolated districts) and in any event, the institution of Serfs came late in Russian history. The dukes united the *balagani* tradition with imported ideas, in the dozen or so Serf* Theatres organised for winter pastime. The famous Russian ballet, *Petrushka* (first produced in Paris, 1911), uses a *Balagan*, or fair show, as its setting, from the Petersburg *Mazlinitsa* (Butter Week Fair) of 1840. (*Balaganchik*=a minstrel.) [See *Bahluwan*]
[1] *Reminiscences of the Russian Ballet*. Alexandre Benois (London 1941) Ch. III.

BALANCE MISTRESS (Early English)

A name given to exhibition dancers, who not only balanced themselves, but performed juggling feats with their instruments, especially timbrels. In the *Romance of the Rose*, the name alternates with *tymbsteres* (or *tumblesters*, when male). Chaucer translates from the French poem:

" There was many a tymbestere
Couth her crafte full parfitly;
The tymbres up full subtelly

They cast; and hent full ofte
Upon a finger fayre and softe
That they fayled never mo".

BALATRO (Rome)

Professional buffoons or jesters. They visited markets or the houses of the wealthy. The term *blatea* (suggesting dirt says Festus) is a probable reference to their scurrilous jests with dubious jokes. Possibly the German term *blatt* for newspaper (or page) related distantly to this publication of "society talk" along with our terms blather or blithering: used by the informed electorate in relation to election promises. The Latin *blatero* is "busybody". Their performance was "musichall" in type, with crude dance or vivid gesture; hence the *balatrones* were welcome to the Roman masculine dinner table.

BALATRO (Latin)

A professional jester or buffoon in ancient Rome. One derivation alleges the term is from a proper name, because one Servilius Balatro was a well-known jester; but it seems unlikely. Probably the term is from a Greek root—*boulé*, and *atrium*—the light-hearted comment on *boulé* in *atrium*, court-yard. The Roman *balatrones* were paid for their jests; they entered the dwellings of wealthy people, by permission; they were often companions of the mimes or dancers.

BALE AGUNG BANDJAR (Bali, Indonesia)

The communal, or council, meeting hall. The *bandjhar* is the group, the "bunch" of village people, who build their own hall, used for all kinds of "town meetings". This is a secular rather than a religious centre; but is often the home of the town *gamelan* or orchestra, through which communal emotive feeling is expressed—instead of cricket, although they now play football. This is the "large hall" in the similar sense to the Greek *boulé*.*
[See *Gamelan*]

BALLABILE (Italian)

Is one of the numerous terms associated with *ballad* and *ballare* (to dance). Some musicians apply this term to any piece of dance music, especially for Theatre; but ballet-masters restrict their meaning—for the same word—usually to the final crowd scene in a ballet, implying "general dance". Meyerbeer entitles a set of three dances (*Robert le Diable*) as *ballabille*; but Hans von Bülow later gave the covering term *Ballabilli* to a series of seven different dances (*Carnevale de Milano*). The earlier mode of *Ballabile* seems to have implied a repetition of routine, within any single dance, much as *estrebille* (Spanish) requires a refrain with a repeat of the same melody—and dance.

BALLAD OPERA (England)

An organised stage show; in time preceding *Beggars Opera* (John Gay 1728) which had developed notably in the century before, and following the Commonwealth with its general suppression of Theatre. The new Ballad Opera challenging the imported Italianate form, was a vigorous secular parallel to the salon dances publicised by Playford for worthy citizens, in the Contra-dance. Ballad Opera had spoken dialogue but no recitative; and interpolated familiar songs, often with the simple dance forms that were part of them; and tunes taken from popular songs; or even from Purcell and Handel. In London, Italian opera occupied theatres; but in country districts had less chance owing to high fees. This type of Ballad Opera faded by 1740, but Playford's salon dances — with or without words, continued some time.

BALLADINE (France)

Another general name for *Haute Danse;* or for the form of the *Galliard,** in particular. The principal movement was in the springing step, instead of the gliding step of *La Danse Basse.** During the 15th-16th century period, it was chiefly associated with court and city ceremonial dances. This lively and spirited dance, favoured more by the younger dancers, required steps more varied and difficult in performance than the *Pavane** or *Basse Danse.** The simpler mode (the one that was soonest and most followed in Elizabethan England) moved to a short musical phrase of two bars in 3/2 time. To the six minims, five steps were performed, while the dancer sprang upwards for the fifth, thus missing this note, alighting on the final sixth note. For this reason, this mode of *Balladine* became known as *le cinq-pas* — the "five-step" — and so as *cinque-pace.** Arbeau describes in some detail a dozen basic steps used in *Balladine*, with some enchainements. among which the *Grand Saut* (sometimes extended to a *Capriole*) was the most prominent.(The modern French has *baladeur* — "stroller"; *balade* — "to go for a stroll"; *baladin* — a clown; *baladinage* — coarse buffoonery.)

BALL DE CORRE (France)

Performed on one of the closing days of carnival at Prats-de-mollo and Amélie-des-Bains, in Roussillon. It descends from the old *Ball* which, with the *Contrapas*, are traditional dances of this district. A lively romping dance, its climax resembles a *Square Dance** figure when, in small groups, the men whirl the girls round with their feet off the ground and their bodies horizontal. As the music ends, the girls are lifted above their partner's head. [See *Corranda; Lou Pélédé*]

BALLANT (Scotland)

Used to refer to ballads, or verses and words for popular song or dance mimes. Charles Murray in his poem *The Packman*, has:

"He'd sheafs o' rare auld ballants, an' antrin swatch he sang".

BALLATORIA (Western Europe)

An enclosed or "protected space", before a church or abbey, covering a dancing floor or area; used to present parables or biblical plays (in some, dancing occurred; in the play or as *interludus*). These places were provided by popular custom over a long period: at Cologne the bishop forbade such plays in 1617. Each Feast Day had its appropriate hymn and dance; and as no public theatre (in our modern sense) was known, these sites afforded "holy entertainment" for the villagers. The place was named also as *Choraria* (dancing floors).

BALLET — 1 (from *Balia*, Italian)

Balia was the ruling committee of the Medici family in Florence, developed during 14th century. The *balletto* was the "little ball" or *ballo* — in effect the display of power ceremonially by making a "show of arms" — the *balia* was the fact of rule, the *ballo* was its visual form in the *pallazzo*. A trace still extant may be seen in Siena at the *Palio*, when representatives of the city wards make a show — now mainly a parade like the London Lord Mayor's Show. Many cognate terms descend from this period* — *far baldoria*, to make a feast; *balatio*, power or authority; *ballocare*, to amuse; *ballire*, to govern; *bailo*, a magistrate. From *ballata* — dance or ballad — the dance terms are *ballare*, to dance; *ballatore* and *ballerino*, male dancer; *ballatrice* and *ballerina*, dancing woman. (We may compare ballott, in English, with bailliff, and Old Bailey "on bail").

BALLET — 2 (Italy)

Developed as *ballare* from *balia*, in theatrical aspect as distinct from communal, with names such as *Comedie de la Royne* but also *baldoria*, mainly in Firenze (Florence) by the Medici family, first with Lorenzo il Magnifico and his brother Cosmo (14th cent.). Wealth produced ostentation; permitted elaboration of festivals and celebrations — weddings and funerals etc. Catherine, daughter of Lorenzo, married Henri II of France and did much to develop (1) tournament, (2) masque, and (3) Ballet in France. From political expression of power *de facto* (*balia*) the entertainment became an art of statement of government *de jure* (as ballet) with an absence of arms (though courtiers continued to carry the rapier even in the salon). From masque with words (usually voluble sycophancy, as in England) the songs developed and dance extended. From some time, the rulers themselves took leading parts : this was ceremonial ritual and not yet imitative theatre.

BALLET — 3 (England)
A word used by John of Wycliff in the first English translation of the Latin Bible (Vulgate) approximately about 1382. He applies to the *Canticles*, or *Shir-al-Shirin*, the title *Ballette of Ballettes*. This same term is repeated by Tyndale and again by Miles Coverdale in his complete folio, printed in 1535 — a century and a half later — probably in Zürich. The popular play and mime dance of the *Todtentanz** was then still extant in its ritual or miracle play form; and with it the traditional practice of allotting roles for the New Year Festival mime or Mumming Plays, by means of coloured picture cards (*cartes*). Skeat is thus three centuries late in his attribution of the "first appearance" of the word *Ballett* to Dryden, in *Drama and Poesie*, in 1668.

BALLET — 4
The English word and its origins : William Pickering, printing in 1565 some dance songs, issued "A Ballet, intitled *All in a Garden Greene*". The tune was included in Playford's famous publication *The Dancing Master*, in its first edition in 1651. Poems addressed by Mary Queen of Scots to Bothwell in 1568, were mentioned as "sonnets" or "fond ballads", while Knox refers to "ballatis" made against the four Marys. His contemporary "gude and godly ballatis" were popular songs, parodied for religious edification. The real change from ballad to ballet (as stimulated by Lully) is technical: in its increased speed of movement, leaving words behind. A small book on "Musical Instruction" published in 1597, gives the term *Balete*, as meaning "Songs which being sung to a dittie, may likewise be danced". Ben Johnson mentions "ballett" as a dance song in his *Bartholomew Fair*, but this is construed as a country-dance. Earlier than any of these — more or less professional notes — we find, in Miles Coverdale's Bible (printed in Zurich 1535), following Wyclif, 1382) that *Solomon's Song* is called *Salomon's Balettes;* while Cranmer's Bible follows with *Ballet of Ballets*.

BALLET — 5 (Most ancient religious phases)
Ballet as *Boulé.** the generic Greek term for the town council, in association with the group called *Ekklesia*, and its committee (*Kurios*) (*curia*) and *Prytane*. The *Boulé* was concerned chiefly with secular matters, laws and wars, revenue and activities; and had its own especial ceremonial, notably the solemn entry into session, in procession and costume, prefaced by heralds. This legalistic aspect

founded a long tradition, which endured in parallel with the aspect of display of princely courts in Europe, as the bailey, bailiff, and bail (deposit of prisoner for release). Its religious aspect continues in many ball games, from the method of voting for *boulé* by beans (black and white or red) into bowls, bowling (*ballein*, throwing the ball) and fades into ballistics. All the terms are of motion; verbs or nouns of moving bodies. In Spanish remains *baile*, the dance ceremonial, compared with *dantza*, the dance festive. In slang there is "bully" or the "protector", or the schoolboy "bully for you" (relics of Greek lessons). In Alexandria the term produced from *periboule*, *peribolos*, *paraboloni* (as the players moving on the stage) and again, in slang, "baloney" (nonsense).   [See *Bouleterion*]

BALLET — 6 — BALLET GEOMETRIQUE (France)
Was performed at the Louvre in Paris, in the time of Louis XIV. One noticed by Ronsard, occupied an hour, on the occasion of a reception given to impress the Polish Ambassador, in August of 1573. Sixteen beautiful blondes performed intricate evolutions, without the help of any male dancers. Ronsard comments :
> "Le ballet fut divine, qui se soulois reprendre
> Se rempre, se refaire, et tous dessus retour
> Se mesler, s'escarter, se tourner à l'entour
> Contre-imitant le course do fleuve de Meandre. . . ."

BALLET DU COUR — 1
Principally in Italy and France, but with roots in England, developed from the 15th century in Western Europe from apparently separated sources. They were, in fact, festival celebrations, now dislocated from their original occasions, leaving an array of professional executants seeking for newer modes of social expression. They found these with rich patrons. From the *Entrêmets* (or Feasts), and Tourneys or Tournaments (displays of fighting skill), with *Momeries* (New Year Festivals), and *Moresques* (rituals turned to more varied modes of worship), as well as the *Masques** (which turned slowly into Mascarades) of England, and the May Games or Barn Dances, and *Basse Danse** of France, varied elements contributed to the three phases of *Ballet du Cour*. First it was charged with Ceremonial values; then, with Louis XIV it became a regal exposition, allied with mythic content drawn from Greece or Rome (in opposition to the theological drift of ritual), and finally in the luxury of entertainment or spectacle. Here the *Ballet du Cour* attains almost the same social value as the last days of the Roman Circus with its mimes. Perhaps the first key point can be found in the institution of the *Academie de Musique et de Poesie*, "officially

recognised" by Charles IX in 1570. Original members were Jean Antoine de Baif and Joachim Thibault de Courville; other poets included Ronsard and Jodelle; other musicians were Claude de Jeune, G. de Beaulieu, Du Vaurroy, and Charles Maudit. Their united efforts condensed into the famous *Ballet Comique de la Royne*, performed in Paris. The music was composed by Baltasar de Beaujoyeulx. This production was costly; so a return to the *Mascarade* form occurred. Numerous Ballet-*Mascarades* were produced during the period of Henry IV (1589-1610), but their later form was influenced by the Florentine *dramma per musica*.* Opera had lapsed, like painting, entirely into secular motivation; and only Greek mythic motives appeared. This was the first modern form of melodramatic ballet. In England the older Masque continued at the Inns of Court.

BALLET DU COUR — 2 (France)

The ceremonial manner of ballet used in the French court of Louis XIV, when the system of highly artificial and prescribed movement (developed from the court chamberlain's scheme of etiquette) into a more ornate dance of the company. The second phase appears when the company (the king and the nobles), began to use the rhythm that had been secured from music and movement, to take part in renderings from Greek mythology. This changed the performance from ritual ceremonial to ceremonial *acting* by dance. Thus Louis XIV was noted as *Le Roi Soleil — the Sun King*, because he took part as the ancient "New-born Sun of the Year", once prominent in the Masque celebrated at every New Year. Stage Ballet then separated from the *Danse du Salon*, which became Ballroom Dance.

BALLET, LE OR EL BALLETT (Roussillon, France)

Diminutive of "Ball", meaning "Little Dance". A courtship dance popular in Catalan France, localised in Cerdagne (Haute Vallée de la Segne); in Haut-Conflent (Haute Vallée de la Têt); and in Capçir (Haute Vallée de l'Ande). It is danced in the villages on local fête days. Custom has it, in Capçir at least, that the eldest man and woman of the village dance the first *Ballet* of the fête. Taking the form of many courtship dances throughout Europe, it is performed by either one, or several couples, with a display of virtuosity by the man. Each of the two figures takes the dancers through half a circle, moving anticlockwise, and ending where they began. While the girl strikes a pose, or dances with small steps, skirt held in both hands, head turned towards her partner, the man exhibits his skill in the performance of complicated steps in a wider circle round her. At the end of each figure the man salutes his partner with a kiss, and the dance must

be carefully timed so as to bring the partners face to face at these points. *Le Ballet* demands ardour and brilliance from the man; reserve and grace from the woman; elegance and suppleness from both.

BALLETTI (Italy)

Fifteenth century term, the "little ball" (dances), which defined a routine of nine movements or steps in dance, as the *enchainement*. The *Ballo** (larger form) was the suite of such dance movements; and their display, in sum, the *balli*.

BALLISTOI (Hellenic term)

Used in Sicily to refer especially to pantomimic dancers of *ballistae*.

BALLETTO (Italy)

Term used in North Italy (15th-16th century) to denote a complete arrangement of the formal dances of this period. It still retained the general system of its court origin, but now turned to the purposes of a spectacular dance performed by chosen expert dancers for entertainment. It is thought that the name *Balletto* was first used early in the 15th century, at the Court of Ferrara, by Domenichino di Piacenza, to describe his suite of differently timed dances. His arrangement consisted of an *Intrada*, *Contrapasso*, *Saltarello*, and *Gagliarda*, all repeated and ending with *Finale* and exit.

BALLO (Italy)

A form of *Basse Dance*,* created by Domenico of Ferrara in the 15th century, as a figure dance in which the number of dancers and balance of sexes might be varied. In one example, one lady danced with five men; her partner, and four others who tried to take her away from him. A *Ballo* had its own music specially composed, and could not be danced to any other, in contrast to music for the *Basse Dance*,* which was played from a given Tenor, and one Tenor could serve for any *Basse Dance*. *Prexonero*, a *Ballo* by Domenico, was a dance for two, with music in 6/4 time. Partners stood side by side, lady on the right. They took hands by linking little fingers and bending the forearm back to shoulder level. After the first part, they released hands, when the gentleman went forward alone and danced, followed by the lady who repeated his steps and stood behind him. They turned to face, taking right hands and performing more steps. This was repeated, but the lady went first, the gentleman following, finishing side by side, taking inside hands and going forward together. The dance was repeated from the beginning, the lady going first each time, the man repeating her movements. In *Anello*, a *Ballo* for four in 4/4 time, the second couple stood four paces behind the firsᵗ, ladies on the right of their partners, linking little fingers. After the first part, they released hands, and opened into a square, facing. There followed various figures in which the gentlemen first performed the steps, repeated by the ladies. The whole dance was repeated, ladies doing everything first.

BALLON

"Physical lightness" in dancing; French term adopted into classical ballet academies to signify the dancer's ability to "get off the floor", as the physical or technical precedent to "Elevation" in stylistic practice. *Ballon* was developed along with the "toe-dance", that was stressed in the early Romantic Ballet, when characters of ethereal creatures – the sylphides and undines – had to be revealed in terms of dance that resembled flying through the air. The quality of *ballon* is a particular expression of a high athletic development, not confined to dancers, but evident also in boxing and wrestling (as e.g. in Japanese contests of *Judo*, where a special springy quality is developed through training simultaneously in breath control and double-action muscular motion). Some dancers have been famed for *ballon* and thus elevation, such as Vaslav Nijinsky in his early period; and Riabouchinska at a later date. The Moscow dancer Domashov was reputed to possess enormous *ballon;* he could clear the Bolshoi Theatre stage (thirty metres wide), it was said, in three bounds. The Nijinsky legend of "floating in the air" derived from a technical circus trick (learned from his father), which is illustrated in the Kinneys' book on *The Dance*; it gives the suggestion of flight without the reality of "hovering", True *ballon* gives not only height or elevation, but the essential springiness or lightness of foot, in landing from any jump, resulting in silent contact instead of a thud – the quality of spring in a healthy cat, the precision of a bird settling onto a tree branch without losing balance. The fund of controlled nervous energy is more important than size of body or muscular development.

BALL PLA (Catalonia, Spain)

A couple dance performed at fiestas and pilgrimages, outside the church. In triple time, the music is in two parts, corresponding to the *entrada* or entrance promenade, and the dance itself. Different districts have variations. One, reminiscent of the solemn Catalan *Contrapas* * is the *Ball de Deu* ("Dance of God"), in which men and women, in two lines, move forward and backward in slow rhythm. A more lively variant is the *Ball Cerda*, from the province of Cerdana. After the preliminary promenade, the couples dance in light, quick

tempo, the woman leading, the man following behind her. The dance ends with the couples holding hands in the final promenade.

BALLROOM DANCES – 1

Modern dances comprise two main categories: (1) the "Standard Four" dances of the commercial *Palais de Danse* and the "party evening", including the *Fox-trot; Waltz;* * Tango;* * Rumba* * etc.; and (2) the revived "Old Time Dances", some from 19th century fashions; some pretending to be older, as with the popular *Square Dance* * in favour in USA and wrongly claiming American origins. Ballroom dancing is followed by millions of dancers, mostly with no pretentions to real ability; but in the crowds who attend the popular Palais may often be seen some dancing of real style. Competitions have, during thirty years, raised the dance standards and given British style pre-eminence; but despite this, the teaching element sometimes fails, owing to endeavours to introduce some new quirk, or "fashion" in "new dances". The result is that ordinary people refuse to "go back to school" to learn new pieces; and will cease attending assemblies. The use of "Old Time Dances" has been said to offset this; but changes in them, too, send the older people home. They might otherwise continue to dance, as do the Scots, keeping to approved styles without annual changes.

BALLROOM DANCE – 2

In specialised modes, and connected with some social event: –
(a) *Charity Ball*: A gathering ostensibly devised to attract wealthy people, who will pay high ticket prices (dinner and dance) on the dim understanding that "profits go to the Charity". Actually, the cost of entertainment (band, catering etc.) is so high that little margin is realised; from which the Organisers (professionals) take commission. Possibly the "Charity" may get ten per cent. of the profits, if any. Some of the Charities then subsidise missionaries to destroy native tribal dances elsewhere (e.g. Congo).
(b) *Masonic Ball*: A gathering, originally for male Masons only (very dull), but extended to admit their wives or daughters etc. Admission is gained by fee, ticket, and password. Junior Jesuit apprentices are sent to "spy out the enemy", but learn little.
(c) *Old Tyme Dance*: Gatherings ostensibly devised to permit Victorian or Edwardian dances in modern ballrooms. Sometimes featured on Radio or Television (broken by noxious crooning); and extended to forms of "Square Dance" or pseudo-folk-dance, requiring a "Caller".
(d) *Flannel Dance*: Formerly organised to stimulate

the "Younger Generation" to attend dances (and also dance classes) during summer months. The relaxation from formal "evening dress" was thus suggested, as a means of "not bothering to change". This concession seems to have vanished since 1938.

(e) *Mansion House Ball*: Formerly organised to celebrate the election and inauguration of a new Lord Mayor of London; and attended by Aldermen and Sheriffs and their families and friends. The date was always in November and the rendezvous solely at the Mansion House, City of London. The Mayoral Dinner was celebrated as a more famous event, usually at the Guildhall.

(f) *Hunt Ball*: Normally followed the *County Hunts*, organized in southern shires; (following the fox) attired in "hunting pink", a dance was celebrated for one or more evenings (this by interpoint invitations, one at each centre of the Master of Fox Hounds). For this Hunt Ball it was a convention that men must dance only in Hunting Pink.

(g) *Debutante's Ball*: When a young girl makes her *debut*, her "first appearance" in the social marriage market of her class, by her "coming-out dance". To this a group of "eligible bachelors" would be invited. This dying ceremonial was formerly linked with "Presentation at Court", for which lessons in the formal curtsey were obtained. Lessons in ordinary ballroom dancing are now more prominent. A formal dance for all debutantes, called Queen Charlotte's Ball,* is held annually, usually at Londonderry House. All the girls wear white, and parade in double file down the wide staircase into the ballroom, where they curtsey before a colossal white-iced cake bearing dozens of lighted candles. The name, "Debutante", is sometimes used professionally to indicate a young theatre dancer; but this "first appearance" is also fading from usage. Some of the balls were arranged at one of the royal palaces, merged occasionally with diplomatic occasions.

BAL-NUK-NUK (Arnhem Land, North Australia)
Name of a ritual in a one-day, annual *corroboree*,* at Angaluk Hill, near Oenpelli, and also of the deity to whom the festival of praise is offered; though the rite is basically one of tribal initiation, performed in the secret oval of the *Aruwaltja*.* The rite not only admits the grown youths into full tribal recognition as men, but gives praise that they have so lived and learned as to reach this notable day in their lives. The candidate has to perform new dances; and to learn chants hitherto kept secret. Hopping, twisting, swaying, men depict animal and insects characters in the ancient myths, instructing the young men in tribal legends. *Bal-Nuk-Nuk* is a leading rite with natives of Arnhem

Land. The sacred, large drum, decorated with red and yellow patterns, bears the same name, as the "Voice of Bal-nuk-nuk", and is used also in the initiation of boys (*Nakumdoit**) in the first stages of their education.
[See *Honey-Bee Dance; Oenpelli Snake Dance*]

BALOI (Basutoland, S. Africa)
Witches gatherings and dances. Basuto legends tell of naked witches and their familiars, who gather in a valley to dance and sing. These midnight revels are supposed to be invisible, but travellers have been said to come across them or to hear their singing faintly in the distance. Like their European sisters, Basuto witches fly on wands—or even on the backs of fleas. Their wands are two, one black, one red. With the black wand they cast living people into deep sleep, or raise the dead from their graves as ghosts; with the red wand they reverse these spells. They can turn themselves into monkey, snake, owl, or crow. Their familiars are animals; also a little red monkey-like man, eighteen inches to three feet high, called Thokolosi, "covered with long hair . . . and possessing an enormous penis, which he can wrap round his waist or sling over his shoulder".

BALSERIA (Panama)
Spanish name for the annual festival of Southern Guaymi Indians in the central mountains of the Isthmus. Held about March, after planting, it lasts two days, date and place being changed each year. Indians living on one side of a mountain act as hosts for visitors from the other side. The first day is spent in making camp, visiting friends and dancing. On the second day the balsa-throwing contest is held, starting at dawn and continuing all day. In groups of six or eight, men divide into teams, each team representing hosts versus visitors. Holding by its end a balsawood pole six or seven feet long and about four inches diameter, the leader of one side hurls it at the legs of their opponents, standing ten feet away. The other side retrieve the pole and become the attackers in their turn. Sometimes twenty or more teams compete simultaneously, urged on by festive spectators chanting, shaking rattles and bells, or blowing whistles. While the balsa-game proceeds, the women, forming into lines holding hands, perform a measured, swaying dance, to the accompaniment of conch-shells, flutes, rattles, and ocarinas. Although it has now a Spanish name, the *Balseria* may be the remnant of an ancient rite, perhaps of Maya origin, suggested by the circlet of green *quetzal* feathers worn by the men (some wear Macaw feathers or porcupine quills), and the animal skins worn on their backs over modern dungarees. Mostly skins of jaguar,

ocelot, puma or monkey, the head and paws rest on the shoulders, a small bell being fixed to the tail. It is significant that in Mexico, the Orders of Eagle and Ocelot (or Jaguar) Knights of the Aztecs (heirs of the Mayas) held ritual contests during some of their festivals. The men of Panama wear wide collars of red, white and black beads, made into geometrical patterns, while the women's costume is a dress with long, full skirt falling straight from a tight yoke at the neck. Men, women and children paint their faces with geometrical patterns of red, white and black, as did the Aztecs.
[See *Eagle Knights; Aztec Dances*]

BALZ; *Bals* (Germany)
As the love dance and the love song of the black-cock, is mentioned by Charles Darwin in his *Descent of Man*. The Balzplatz is the chosen place for this vernal exhibition; the male will visit several such places, which are kept year after year by the birds.

BALZTANZ (Austria)
A courting dance, performed by one couple; or several in succession, often in centre of a village ring. The girl accepts the approach of the boy (attired in shirt and buckskin breeches, with a white feather in his hat) and slowly agrees to dance. She wears the festival skirt and white apron, no head dress: white stockings and black shoes. Ring dance and pair dance.

BAMBOO TRAP DANCE (Assam)
Dance form used by Naga tribes of Assam, North-east India, for development of skill, precision, and then show. We might call it a "Noughts and Crosses Dance", since the ground plan is closely similar. Four long *lathis*, or bamboo poles, about two inches thick, are set in a crossed pattern, two each way; the ends held by four crouching men. At the end of these poles, a shorter piece is fixed at an angle, to prevent the poles dropping to the ground. This Bamboo Trap Dance is a sort of "Sword Dance" in which the sword also moves. The drummer stands at one side; the single dancer runs into the centre square, which is never a square for more than two beats of the drum; but becomes a rectangle in two alternate directions. The pole-men raise and close their pair of poles, each two in opposing rhythm, to the simple four-four drum beat. The dancer has to follow this beat, and leap accordingly; he hops twice on each foot, outside the centre cross, or inside it. The central square is the really dangerous part of the Bamboo Trap. Excitement among watchers increases when two dancers join in the same dance; yet, despite the apparent monotony, there can be a considerable

variety of movement. A more deadly form of a similar movement appears in industrial conditions —in timber yards when log-rolling; and in steel-works when pipe-stacking. Both items are liable to roll out of control. At the other extreme are the little English girls' skipping-dance games.
[Cp. *Tini-kling; Singkil* (Phillipines); and see *Naga Dances*]

BAMBUCO (Columbia, S. America)
The national dance of Columbia in 3/4 or 6/8 time. A song accompanies the dance, together with the playing of a *tiple* (three-stringed guitar) and *bandolas* (flutes). Danced by a couple, it is a court-ship dance of pursuit and retreat, until the girl finally allows herself to be "caught", when the pair continue to dance together. The *Bambuco* probably has its roots in the West African town of Bambuk, for it was from this place that the first African slaves were brought to Columbia.

BANDLTANTZ (Austria)
"Ribbon Dance". A dance in which ribbons are plaited round a pole (not connected with May Day), performed at wedding festivities. The pole (like that in the Basque *Cinta Dantza** and the Spanish *Baile del Cordon**), is portable. In the *Bandltantz* the pole is set up, and held by the Master of Ceremonies. The dance round it, in hon-our of the bride, is performed by girls, using a waltz step.
[See *Maypole Dance; Lei Courdello; Danza de los Listones*]

BANJARA (Uttar Pradesh, N. India)
Pastime dance performed by the wandering Ban-jara tribe, principally for their own amusement in evening hours. This nomadic tribe gains a poor living by gathering, and preparing (drying) certain herbs used in Hindu medicine, from roots to leaves or seeds; wild honey; and certain crude perfumes; with illicit deals in opium and *bhang*. They light a fire amid the tent circle, and dance to the *dholak* (drum). Women wear the swinging skirt *lahanga*, with the *choli* or tight bodice (not *sari*, and add a veil—like that of the *nautchee*—if they can obtain material.

BANQUET BALLET (Italian, Mediæval)
Known first from the Festival arranged by Ber-gonzio di Botta in 1489 for the Duke of Milano's wedding. Significantly, the first dance, by related small groups, was called *Entrée**—a name still used on the menu and in music which has forgotten this pragmatic purpose. The general idea was seized upon by courts all over Europe. The "River Gods" brought in the *poisson*; Diana and Nymphs carried

in meat dishes. Pomona with her Maidens brought the fruits of the orchard; and Bacchus naturally was the God of the Wine.

BANSHEE (Ireland)
From *ban-sith*, Gaelic term for feminine fairy. Various legends include mention of their dancing habits; as also their song or cry, known as the "banshee wail", is said to foretell the death of one of the family to whom they have become attached. They have thus some likeness to the Latin *lares* and *penates*, as lesser household godlings, in Irish or Highland Scottish families, provided that they have adequate ancestry. The term in Wales is *Cyhyraeth*, or in English, "wraith". These entities are reputed to be seen most at the period round Hallow e'en, when the ancestral rituals would be performed by way of memorial service.

BANUL MARACINE (Rumania)
A dignified dance in 4/4 time, popular in the east and south—Moldavia, Wallachia, Dobrudja and Oltenia. Having twelve figures, using typical hop and spring steps, including the "spurs" (a form of *cabriole*) it may be danced by any number of dancers in a line or curve, with the shoulder grasp; by two dancers facing each other, the woman with hands on hips, the man with arms folded in front, or as a solo. The music may be played on fiddle and *cobza* (a lute with ten to fifteen strings), a usual accompaniment to Rumanian dances.

BARAMIKER (Egyptian/Arabic)
The name which the dancing-girls of Cairo claim as their original tribe. It goes also as *Barmekees*, and recalls the famous Barmecide Feast of the *Arabian Nights Entertainment*, which they suggest was their ancient line. They are the dancing girls known as *Ghawazee*.* Lane[1] thought they were extremely handsome, "the finest women in Egypt", He recalls the close similarity of Spanish *fandango** to Egyptian dances of the *Ghawazee*. Some gypsies in Egypt claim descent from a branch of the same family.
[1] *Modern Egyptians*. E. W. Lane (First Edition 1836).

BARBE (Orontes, Asia)
A Feast of Barbe (later tacked on to a mythic "saint") is known among the Nosairis, a Semitic tribe inhabiting the Orontes country. Young men and women, after lighting candles, danced round their festive board. Apparently the Barbe is a relic of an initiation ritual, at which the hair was cut or specially trimmed; this cutting is a frequent feature of youth initiations.
[See *Histoire et Religion des Nosairies*. P. Dussaud (1900)]

BARBER'S DANCE (Baghdad)
Many tales from the famous *Arabian Nights' Entertainments* have been utilised for stage productions; but these have been magnificent spectacles. The vocational dances are seen less often. In the "Story told by the Tailor" is a brief account of the *Barber's Dance*, who treated his customers only at dates fixed by astrology. (The same thing is done in Britain, by H.M. Excise, who have a peculiar regard for April 1st). "The barber sung the song, and danced the dance, of the attendant on the baths". He had thus mentioned Zantout (who rubs people), and Salout (who sells beans), as well as Akerscha (who sells greens) and Abou Mecatez (who sprinkles water in the dusty street), and finally Cassam, the Caliph's life-guardsman. "All are ready to sing and dance; each has his own peculiar song and dance".[1] And he performed Zantout's dance; and then all the rest. The "Story of the Barber"; and of his brother, then follows.
[1] *Arabian Nights' Entertainment*, trans. to French by Burton.

BARDO—1 (Tibet)
Thodol Dance of the Soul in the Afterworld, the Bardo, during at least the "forty-nine days of dissolution". This dance, from which the Romish mediæval Devil Dance and Death Dance were derived, is pictured on many of the Tibetan *thangka*, or banners, used in the temples and monasteries. The principal symbol is the Great Wheel of Time (or Buddhist Wheel of the Law) round which humanity dances; and by impulsion the "Desire Dance" continues to dance, in the Underworld of the Bardo, after physical death. Notions of the worst experience are given by symbolic pictures, because the "prepared soul" does not meet them. The philosophy is erudite and requires long study to understand; when it becomes simple, straightforward, and rational in meaning; for natural or slow death is seen as a normal process, balancing with the period of gestation and birth, as a point in human experience. Tibetan scholars figure the process as a world dance, which they know to be rhythmic and gradual. They teach knowledge of the process, and methods of dealing with it; their principal liturgies consist of these practical instructions; their dances show high points in the experience.
[See *Tibetan Book of the Dead*. (Trans. Lama Kawasamdup and J. W. Evans Wentz 1928]

BARDO—2
The Purgatory or "in-between" arena that separates death from the new birth, in Tibetan Lama doctrine. In Tibet this region is said to contain many dancing demons. There is a certain period

(varying according to circumstances of the life now terminated), which must intervene before the reconstructed individuality can gain another birth into the World of Man. This Bardo is often named as a labyrinth. If we here adopt the Western "law of dynamism", which declares that "action and re-action are opposite and equal", we should posit a closely similar period for the "unwinding of mind", as it is required for the living experience that constitutes the "winding". Put in material terms: it would need as long to journey out of the Maze, as to walk in. This exit implies accurate knowledge, but the period depends on tensions. (See *Malekula, Dances of;* *Sand Tracings* etc.) During the Bardo, we unload the "Burden" and secure "Pardon". The Path is traced symbolically, as a Journey by land (Flight into Egypt; or Forty Years in the Desert), as a Journey by Sea (The Iliad) as a passage through Halls of Judgment (Egyptian) or feasting in Heroic Halls (Valhalla). [See *Way to Jerusalem*; and *Tibetan Book of the Dead*. W. Evans Wentz]

BAREBACK BALLERINA (Circus, in Europe)
Circus shows have developed the Lady Bareback Rider into a feminine high-spot of the circus, taking the cue from the great popularity of ballet in the early 19th century cities. The act is technically another extension of the "partner dance", with the male *porteur* as the "guide, expositor, and friend", for he is replaced by a circus horse. Sometimes the act is acrobatic. In Victorian days, the man in evening dress straddled two horses while he supported the girl in the ballet skirt, who did not dance but posed on his shoulders. This *pas de deux* demands a nice sense of equilibrium: the "stage" is always moving and it is more difficult than dancing in an ocean liner; while the act offers the maximum of grace and skill. A young lady rider, dressed in a short tutu, dancer's tights and ballet shoes, is sometimes called a ballerina; she works a "ballerina act", but this term should be applied only to the *Haute École* act, in which a ballerina dances on the ground alongside the horse. Association of dance in ballet shoes with a sawdust ring here seems inconclusive.   [See *Circus*]

BARIS (Bali, Indonesia)
Lit. "In line". A war dance performed at ritual feasts by middle-aged men in two rows facing. Dressed in white, with triangular white hats decorated with a flower at each side, they carry long black and silver spears with which they enact a mock battle. This is *Baris gedé*. Individual performance by the warrior hero in dance-dramas, which includes dialogue, is *Baris pendét*. To be able to dance the *Baris* well in middle-age was a necessity

Baris War Dance, Bali   INDONESIA

for every prince after long, rigid training. Its performance requires full muscular control, since every part of the body is used; ability to express every emotion in his face; and a good speaking voice. Opponents in *Baris pendét* enact a preliminary rhythmic sequence in which tension and ferocity of movement and expression increase to the point where each man draws his gold-handled *kris* and advances upon the other. There follows a stylised duel to accompaniment of *gamelan* gongs, and the defeat of one ends the dance. For this dancers wear tight trousers and jacket, scarf across the chest from which hang narrow strips of gold-leaf-covered cloth; and the triangular head-dress with rows of *tjempaka* flowers in front. *Baris tumbak* is a ritual exorcism; and for *Baris tekok djago* dancers wear costumes magically patterned in black and white chequer.

BARLEY-BREAK (Old English)
Country game, with an associated rustic dance, played by six persons, three men and three women, arranged in couples, placed in three adjoining areas of ground. The central space was named "hell", and the couple here placed tried to catch the others as they sought to pass through. When all four travellers gained their objective, there was a "dance of rejoicing" in which the bystanders joined, to music of fife and drum. Presumably this was a "death-dance" game, with the "three regions" presented as earth, hell, heaven. Many allusions occur, with little description, in Elizabethan literature, as by Sidney, or Massinger; Suckling and Herrick. Recently the game continued, as in Cumberland, where it is called *Burley-Brigs;* while in Aberdeenshire it is known as *Barla-Braks.*
[See Brand's *Antiquities*]

BARN DANCE
A modern pair dance in 4/4 time, which came to this country from America. Although generally supposed to be so-called because of its performance in barns (where, owing to its large size and suitable flat floor, many North American rural festivities took place), this is not so. Many other dances were performed in barns but *Barn Dance* in USA was originally called the *Military Schottische.* Its name gradually became altered, apparently because it was usually danced to a tune called "Dancing in the Barn". It is a simple combination of Schottische hops and waltz steps. The *Barn Dance* is popular in Britain at "Old Time Dances". Teachers of dancing have composed variations, such as the *Esperano Barn Dance,* and the *Progressive Barn Dance,* which is preceded by a Grand March round the room by all couples, forming into a circle, and involves frequent changes of partner.

BARN (Welsh)
A judgment, given in a court, before the *Barnur* or judge. To judge is *Barnu;* and *barug* is to mime or

Barong (Kris Dance)   BALI, INDONESIA

make rhymes. Linked with these old terms are the titles baron or chief, and *baroniaeth* or barony, the district of jurisdiction. Hence it appears that a Civil law association pertains to *Barn* dance, as part of some court ceremonial, such as the measured entrance (with trumpet flourish) of the apparelled judge. Possibly both court and officials joined in festive dance on high occasions (as they did for centuries, at the Inns of Court in London, until the age of the Masque faded out). After the prisoner had duly been relieved of his money (quite legally, of course), by way of fines, this typical legal device then provided adequate funds for dinner and drinks. Possibly the proletarian or peasant Barn Dance — formed on the occasion of harvesting, was suggested by these proceedings of subsidised merriment by their squires and masters. Certainly there was, down to the 19th century, a similar course known in Russia, to the *Barin* and his *Barina*, many of whom retained small companies of trained serfs to provide regular amusement of every kind.

BARONG (Bali, Indonesia)
Symbol of prosperity and health, opposed to the witch Rangda (sometimes called the Black Widow*), symbol of evil and death. The Barong appears at celebrations such as *Galunggan** (New Year), when the mask-figure, belonging to each village, prances and cavorts about the lanes. In a dance-play (which includes the *Kris dance* performed in deep trance), the Barong and Rangda are opposed in the eternal struggle between good and evil. Like the Pantomime horse, he is animated by two men inside a framework, their legs, encased in tight red and white striped cloth, forming the Barong's legs. The frame is covered with long hair, and has an arched tail, with a small mirror and cluster of little bells at the end. Gilt and red leather harness decorates the body; and beneath a high, gilt head-dress is the mask with snapping jaws, from which depends a tuft of human hair, decorated with frangipani flowers. In this beard lies the Barong's magical power. The mask sometimes represents tiger, wild boar, elephant, cow or lion, but the most sacred and important is an unidentified creature called *keket*. In the dance-play, the Barong first entertains spectators with a display of good-natured, humorous antics. With the entrance of Rangda, the two engage in combat. *Kris* dancers, in trance, rush to assist the Barong, their *krisses* drawn. Rangda turns the dancers' weapons against themselves, but the superior power of the Barong prevents injury. Rangda is eventually defeated and the beneficent Barong remains to protect the village and bring prosperity. He resembles the Chinese lion (*Gee-ling*), which

entertains with wild antics during New Year celebrations.
[Cp. *Korean Lion Dance; Prüh* (Burma); *Ryoks* (Java)]

BAR-MITZVAH (Hebrew)
Traditional as the formal "initiation ceremony" among the Jews, marking the time of puberty. The modern ritual is much abbreviated; but formerly it was customary to celebrate the event with a meeting, a feast, and a dance, which was preceded by a parade of youth around the hall. Probably in "early times", this *parados* was offered as a visual proof; but the *mitz-evah* or readiness for *evah* is no longer made evident; though at the festal gathering which is never omitted, red wine is considered essential. *Bar-Mitzvah* was known as a time suitable for maidens to propose marriage.

BARRACK HACK (British Army)
Army slang, relevant to those ladies who were always available for all barrack entertainments, fun and feasting, and as dancing partners. The term has been applied to those "memsahibs" who used to be seen often in the cantonments of the British Army in India; but it was not precisely similar to the *vivandières* of Napoleon's ragged armies. The 1940 term developed as "officers' mattress" when women were mixed officially with men in the armed services.

BARRIERA (Italy)
Was known in Spain as *El Torneo* (circa 14th-16th century), and in France as *Le Tourney*, since it was developed from the mimic form of Tournament, described as the "Ball or Tourney", performed before the Queen of Whims, by Doctor Rabelais. Some of the contemporary illustrations show the required style of chequered floor pattern for *La Barriera* (as in the second volume by Fabritio Caroso, *Nobilita dei Dame*). One of the earliest of recorded versions of this military dance (it is usually scored for trumpet-calls, starting in 2/4 time with ornamental flourishes, suggesting the later divagations of Adolph Sax's 19th century invention), is one to be found in the *Manuscrit de Marie de Bourgogne* (written circa 1440). The last dance there is arranged for three dancers, with the name of *Beaulte de Castillo*. This routine presents but a single section of the whole tourney; since the original complement was thirty-two dancers; and the detailed record by Negri doubtless is offered as a manual of instruction, keeping to but a few dancers for clarity in teaching. Caroso allows six dancers in all — three couples.

BASIC MUSIC (Oriental)
Is ascribed by tradition, in China, to the characteristic "Eight Sounds", as produced by : metal, stone,
wood, and clay; then bamboo, gourd, skin, and
silk. Hence they include all types of drum; wind
instruments or pipes; chimes or bells, gongs; and
finally strings—of silk or metal. Omitted are the
shells known to India; the sacred and primitive
conch; and the whirling "voice", the *Churinga*
(Bullroarer), used by Australian natives; along with
strings other than silk, as animal gut. Original
devisors of ritual paid some attention to the quality
of these sounds, when selecting them to accompany and reinforce particular rituals. The Chinese
priests used a rattle (gourd with hard seeds inside),
to start a ceremony or performance; and a rasping
spine arrangement (something like a huge comb in
form) for stopping it. The "Eight sounds", now
mentioned as timbre or tone-colour, receive less
attention in the modern composer's work, which
prefers (too often) sensation in place of subtlety.
[See *Lithophone; Gong; Gamelan*]

BASQUE DANCES (Pyrenees country, borders of
    Spain and France)
Are called *dantza* (plural *dantzak*). Many traditional
dances belong chiefly to annual festivals; as, for
example, the Masquerade of Soule, including
Gavotta, Satan Dantza, and *Godalet Dantza** (dance
with goblet). Dances of Guiuscaya (*Gipuzkoaka
Dantzak*), include *Ezpata Dantza** (with daggers);
Erreberentzia (Dance of Entry and Salute); and
Uztai Dantza (Dance of the Basket-makers with
wicker hoops). Besides widespread forms of *Fan-
dango** and *Arin-Arin*, there is *Makil Dantza**
(Stick Dance), *Jorrai Dantza* and *Batzan Dantza* (all
dance-songs), with *Arku Dantza* (Flower Arches,
Biscayan version), *Soso Dantza* (Song of Blackbird),
Maigeneko (Dance on Table) or *Kaxarranka** (Dance
with Coffer), or *Sagar Dantza** (Apple Dance),
Others include *Xan Petrike Dantza* ("John-Peter
Dance"—humorous). The various *Inguru* are round
dances, usually with simple rhythm and verse. The
Txakarenkua is "Dance of the Dead Chief", used
at funerals. Another series are called *Banako*
(Dance of one person), *Binako* (Dance of two by
two persons) and so on. The Janus dances are
Otxagabia or "Two Face" dantza, and *Zagi Dantza*
is a comic dance with a leather wine bottle. Musical
instruments used for Basque dances include (as
development from pipe and tabor), the *Txistu*—
predominant flute with three finger holes. The
tambour is *Ttun-Ttun* (tambourine) and *Atabel*
(small tambour). The *Xirula* is a more primitive
form of flute, shriller in sound. The *Dulzaina* is
known most in Navarre; while the *Alboka* exists
only in Biscaya. Accordion players are *Trikitrixak*;

they also sing couplets; and occasionally add the
tambour.

BASSE DANSE (France)
A 15th century court dance, popular in France and
Italy (*Bassa Danza*), usually in duple time. In Italy
it was sometimes in slow triple time, according
to tunes preserved in the lute book of Petrucci
(1507/9). Although generally supposed that the
name refers to the style of dancing, in which the
feet scarcely left the ground, in contrast to *danse
par haut*, which included jumps, some writers
suggest that the name derives from the dance's
lowly origin, being connected in Italy with the
shepherds' dance, *Piva*, and in France with the
"country fashion" of bearing oneself. *Basse Danse*
was for several couples in line behind each other,
and was (according to the *Livre de Basses Danses de
la Bibliothèque de Bourgogne* divided into three
parts, the grand measure, medium measure and
little measure, called by Thoinot Arbeau[1] *basse
danse, retour de la basse danse*, and *tordion*. Some
ascribe the ancestry of *Basse Danse* in France to the
*Branle** and *Estampie,** and in Italy to the *Estampie*
and *Farandole.**
[1] *Orchésographie*. Thoinot Arbeau. (1588).

BASUTO DANCES (S. Africa)
Are group dances, sometimes interrupted by a solo,
after which the group dance is resumed. The most
common are *Mokorotlo,** *Mohobelo,** *Mokhibo**
and *Motjeko.** Invariably accompanied by singing,
in *Mohobelo* and *Mokhibo*, a chorus of women and
girls stands behind the dancers, singing and clapping
to mark the rhythm. The melody is traditional, but
the words are meaningless. The first three were
formerly ceremonial dances, accompanying important rites, but with the decline of native rituals
they are now often performed, solely for amusement. Sometimes *Mohobelo* and *Mokhibo* parties
are held, with contests as to the best dancing.
There are still special dances performed at girls'
initiation ceremonies, when long, thematic poems
are sung as the women rotate slowly round the
fire; and at the *Maqekha* seances, where dancing is
part of the cure of an illness called *motheketheke*.
The patient is said to be visited by a spirit. He is
not only cured, but acquires powers of divination
and second sight, becoming a *Makoma*. The dance,
performed first by an already initiated *Makoma*, is
accompanied by drumming on a dry rolled ox skin.
It has quick, jerky steps, the tempo gradually increasing until one of the dancers suddenly stops
with a cry and chants a song, or rushes away. After
a pause the dance continues, proceeding thus all
night, until sunrise. The next night the patient
himself dances for two or three hours, which per-

formance is repeated for several months until the patient receives dream instructions that the ceremonies may end, when final rites are performed, followed by another all night dance, punctuated by tests of the patient's psychic powers.
[See *Mokorotlo*; *Mohobelo*; *Mokhibo*; *Motjeko*; *Baloi*]

BAT OR BATTE (France)

Harlequin's traditional lath (*lathi*, Hindu), or wooden sword, carried through all the pantomimes in which he appears—and disappears, as his magical wand. Compare the Greek term *rapis*, which became *rapper* in the English sword dance. The *batte* entered the game of cricket; in phrases "to carry his bat", meaning to retire as "not out"; and "off his own bat", meaning the score of runs by one player; while the military bat-man is the servant who formerly carried the weapons (the long lance), but was not a general valet. With this we find *baston*, a card game (Spanish; a stick or wand), which eventually becomes the marshal's *baton*. They are all wands of significance; and in any Ballet should be related to the character in action, not waved about like a baby's rattle.
[See *Rapper*]

BATON DANCE

Name of a traditional *Basque Dance*,* but as a dance with sticks, is widespread. Batons are used professionally by orchestral conductors (not so heavy as the one that Spohr hit his foot with), and are smaller versions of the mace carried by the regimental drum major, who waves it wondrously in display on the march. This display has been copied by troupes of girl dancers. There are numerous types of baton or wand; the bishop's crook; the augur's *lituus*; the king's sceptre; the Egyptian flail of justice; and the *maize* or mace found in English ceremonial, from the gild-hall to the House of Commons. Many of these power-symbols necessarily appear in dance ritual and dance display. The Maypole is probably the largest on record. In India the *Shiva-lingam* is worshipped, as a symbol; here its greatest measure is as the "backbone of the universe". Sometimes the baton or stick appears as a measure of *time*; sometimes as a measure of *space* (the yard-stick was one such), but in other modes it appears as a weapon of defence or an implement of magic. The famous "fairies' wand" is still seen annually in pantomimes; but the Field Marshall carries his baton only at rare ceremonies. The magician's wand is powerful in magic, precisely because it *can* measure, in dance-rhythm and in dance-space. In Morris Dance,* the wands (or rappers), become equivalent to swords, though blunted; while in *chevallerie*,

the knights used the lance and the flag-staff. In the South Indian *Kummi** dance, two girls strike sticks, for time and pattern. In China, sixty-four sticks (sometimes thrice that number) appear in the famous *Pa Kwa* or Trigrams of Fu-Hsi, used for ritual divination, and thence for ritual dance. The modern magic wand is the common pen or pencil; its "choreography" is on paper, as the universal form is in triplicate.
[See *Sword Dance*; *Ezpata Dantza*; *Pordon Dantza*; *Saut Basque*]

BATUQUE; *Butuque*; *Batucada* (Brazil)

A dance of African origin in duple time, performed by Brazilian Negroes. Danced in a circle, the rhythm is marked by hand-clapping, and the dance is accompanied by drumming and percussion sounds made by beating on pieces of iron or wood. This practice of using anything handy that can be knocked together or beaten to produce complex rhythms, is customary in many parts of Africa. In Portuguese West Africa, *Batuque* is a dance resembling the *Charleston*,* performed by a man and woman inside the circle of spectators; and also a term for dances in general. During the 16th century, the *Batuque* reached Portugal, where, according to old records, it was popular in Lisbon as a couple dance resembling the *Lundum*.* These were both apparently of a robust nature, since a law passed in the reign of Manuel I forbade the dancing of *Batuque*, *Lundum* and *Charrada*, in Portugal. The *Batuque* seems to have acquired a more polite European veneer, since in the 18th century it appeared in Spain as a coquettish dance of flirtation, accompanied by finger snapping, with the man dancing round his partner in a winding pattern, the dance ending with an embrace.

BATUQUE (Portuguese Guinea)

A Portuguese term used to indicate all dances in the Cape Verde Islands, and in Portuguese Guinea (West Africa). Also a single dance, which includes the whole crowd, and is performed in the open air, on any flat piece of ground such as the central village space. A big fire is kept going. All villagers stand, chanting and clapping, in a three-quarter circle. At intervals men and girls step out, do a shuffling dance with their feet; waggle their hips energetically, keeping their heads well down. Applause is marked by throwing a hat into the ring; the dancer so honoured retrieves it and makes a graceful curtsey to the owner. The *Batuque* was the ancestor of the *Charleston*.* It was taken by negro slaves to America, where it was learned from them by their white owners and in the 1920's became a popular ballroom dance.

BATUTA (Rumania)

Chain dance for men only. The time is faster and the steps more vigorous than the *Hora** or the *Sârba.** Towards the end of the dance, shouting loudly, the men take flying leaps into the air.

BAYADÈRE (Java)

Portuguese term for any Oriental dancer. The word is not Eastern, but derives from the Javanese term *bedojo* or *bedaja**—a court dancer; which comes from older *Sem-Baja-Deva*, meaning "offering-to-gods", the dancer being one of the ritual bearers of the sacrifices. There was the Sanskrit term *Sang-Beha-Deva*, meaning "group-sacrifice-to-gods". In France the word was used in Auber's opera-ballet *Le Dieu et la Bayadère*. In Russia the term became *bayaderka*. There is no "bayadère dance", as a traditional choreographic form; but to arrange a "dance of bayadères" in classical ballet form is anti-stylistic. *Bedojo* is pronounced as *Be'doy-you*; *deva* and *devi* are Hindu names for "angels". The Dutch in Java continued to use the term *bedojo*, so much so that it gained hold in the courts of Solo and Jokya. The ceremonial of the Nine Bayadères (or *Serimpi**) is itself much changed; once they were more closely equivalent to the Nine Muses of Greece.

BAYLATA OR BALAYDA (Portuguese)

A species of song-dance, which developed in Portugal, as one of the groups of *Cancioneiro* lyrics, or folk ballads. They became most plentiful (as ascertained in extant records) from the eleventh to fourteenth centuries. The dancer was often termed *Bailadeira*, which, when taken by Portuguese sailors to the East Indies, fused into the reference to *bayadère,** as "Indian dancer."

BAYANIHAN (Tagalog)

In Phillipine Islands, implies usually a local celebration for some local event , by a few families, such as opening a new store, a new house, a new school. After speeches comes the feast and the dancing. Over the aboriginal Luzon peoples dances, we find imposed those of successive invaders or traders—Arabs, Muslims, Spanish and finally American. Thus *Jota Moncadena* merges two styles, with long castanets or *Singkil** joins Malayan custom—the bird trapping bamboo poles, with neat footwork. A troupe was seen in USA and later in London, of some 50 dancers and musicians, in watered-down versions of these attractive dances.

BEAMA (Greece)

The raised platform, sometimes called *olithos* (as it was of stone), from which the orators of the *Ekklesia* spoke during the regular meetings of the Athenians at the Prytanie; or the Kuria. At the Festivals it would be used also for singers, and later for mimes—before the construction of Theatres in wood, and then of stone, The *Beama* corresponds to the Latin construction, the tribunal or *tribuna*. In Britain, the term *beama* was used (from the earlier Greek missions, who arrived long before the Latins) to indicate a rood or a similar slightly raised platform, in the early wooden churches of Northern England (North Umbria).   [See *Ruad*]

BEAR DANCE (Sioux Indians)

A propitiatory dance before a bear hunt. The principal performer is the Chief Medicine Man, who wears a bear's skin and imitates its movements. Other performers, and even spectators are also clad in bear skins, and imitate the animal's walk, and his queer way of sitting with drooping paws. The Sioux also have a mimetic dance to attract Buffalo (described by G. Catlin[1]), and some dances are continued by relays of dancers, continuously for three weeks.

[1] *Manners and Customs of North American Indians* G. Catlin. Vol. 1; London, 1841.

BEDAJAS (Java)

Dancing girls, in junior grade, of the princely courts of Solo and Djokjakarta. The senior grade comprised the *Serimpis** in groups of four. The little *Bedaja* girls were recruited by a *guru* (religious teacher) from suitable applicants, from ranks of the nobility. They train in ordinary costume, always in groups of nine; and replaced the Temple dancers who served formerly in Hindu temples in Java. The custom differed, as between the two courts. The ruler (the *soesoehoean*) saw the children, who were accepted into employment; learning dancing, court etiquette, and also household duties. Some advanced to the rank of *Serimpi*; and later they might enter the princely *harim*. Others married nobles. This term Bedaja appears to be semi-Portuguese; and part origin of the term known in Europe as *Bayadère** (Portuguese : *bailadeira*, dancing-girl). The full groups of nine *bedajas* danced on all ceremonial occasions; but never outside the halls of the palace. The general style of dance was based on the South Indian mode of *Bharata Natyam;** and while it included many of the *hasta** and *mudra** forms, was perhaps more delicate if not so symbolically precise, since the girls learned solely by imitation from an older expert dancer; and rarely knew the esoteric meaning of any *mudra*. The *Wayang** dance is, on the contrary, an older mode, especially in its most ancient puppet styles. Some part of the court dances followed the squared movements of the puppet dance, especially in the "strong knee" with the wide-spread feet; which characterises all

Javanese dance (and is seen also in Bali), and is marked in the *Kathakali** styles of Southern India.

BEDE, BEDESMAN (Saxon)
Term used to denote the administrators of the earliest (Grecian missions) church in Northern England, before the disastrous submission at Whitby in 656 by the Abbess Hilda, to the Latin invaders. The duties of the Bede, in organisation of simple festivals, included the New Year Ritual Dance of the *Ruad** or solar circle marking the Winter Solstice, known as the *Hagia-Men*. The Greek term for a similar ruler in church is *Hegumon* or *Hekumen*; and still exists in this form, especially in the Monasteries of Mount Athos. In Scotland the term was changed slightly, into the current Hogmanay. Allied to the *Heguman* was the *Kaedmon*, the chanter or singer. The *bedesmen* are known today as beadles, as lower officials concerned with guarding against intrusion some defined area, or building, as at the Bank of England or the Royal Exchange, London.

BEES, DANCE OF
In their highly organized life, it has been discovered by Karl von Frisch that bees give each other exact information as to a new source of honey by what he called "dances". When a bee returns to the hive from a newly-found flower-patch, she deposits her honey and begins to dance. "On the part of the comb where she is sitting," writes Herr von Frisch,[1] "she starts whirling round in a narrow circle, constantly changing her direction, turning now right, now left, dancing clockwise and anti-clockwise in quick succession, describing between one or two circles in each direction. . . What makes it so particularly striking . . . is the way it infects the surrounding bees; those sitting next to the dancer start tripping after her, always trying to keep their outstretched feelers in close contact with the tip of her abdomen". After her dance she leaves the hive, and her companions set out to find the new source of honey, guided also by the scent brought back by the dancing bee from the flowers.
[1] *The Dancing Bees*. Karl von Frisch. (Trans. Dora Ilse) 1954.

BEFFANY, *Beffanie* (Italy)
Italian corruption of the Greek *Epiphany* or "Appearance", as the conclusion of the "Twelve Nights" Celebration of the Winter Solstice. In Italy, the 6th January is the occasion of much present-exchanging (a variation of the "Gifts of the Magi" theme). The Greek term is probably derived from Beth-Ani (Bethany) or the Beit-Ani, the "House of the Year", celebrated in ancient Egypt as an occasion of hopeful forecasts for the coming year, the "presents" being some of the hoarded surplus from the past year; with the accompaniment of "fortune-telling" as a popular version of the official forecast. Naturally, the occasion ended with merriment and dancing. In Italy the country people journey "to town" for their feasting and begging, some as the *pifferari* or pipers; together with the local *banditti*, who then make a special confession of misdeeds and seek indulgence for the coming year.

BEKSAN (Java)
Ceremonial war dance, performed by men only, known principally at Djokjakarta (now called Jakarta). The nobles of the prince's court numbering forty or so, danced the *Beksan* late in the evening, chiefly as a court ceremonial; and done in the *Kraton*, either in the courtyard or in the throneroom. One occasion for its performance was the prince's birthday.

BELAIRE (Trinidad)
A solo for a girl, who sings or chants; moves her long skirt into curious designs. The steps range from a short shuffle, making a ring, to lighter steps like an Irish jig. The dance is an old tradition of the mountain districts; perhaps its name is from the French *belle air*—a change from work in the hotter climate below.

BELÊ (Trinidad)
A negro dance connected with rituals for the dead and appeasement of the ancestors. Forbidden by law and church, it is now performed secretly in the belief that the ancestors will send ill health or other misfortunes if the appropriate rites and dances are not performed.

BELL (Assyrian—Babylonia. 4000 BC)
One of the oldest dance instruments of percussion. The drum is the Voice—the Bell is the signal of Bel the God; with the Gong in the Far East. The term Bell reached Britain with exactly the same meaning (*angelus* etc.) while in Egypt it gained place as the time-keeper on board ship. This practice endures, with the break known as dog-watch (*Doge* or leaders' short watch). Bell and drum are used much for Modern Dance. Groups of bells, as *carillon*, are familiar in church towers. The kirke and the shippe (once interchangeable) used the bell on a large scale. In Hindu dance, gajja bells possess special importance, tied on the ankles of the dancer on entrance to her profession. Since its first period, the Bell is degraded to factory bell, alarm bell, or telephone bell, along with the Latinist term *belligerant* to offset *belle* or *bella*. For dance, eight bell tones were the limit; but sistrum and castanet, with cymbals, extended this metallic usage.

BELTANE OR *Bal Tanis* (Scotland 300 BC)
Feast of *Bal* or *Tanis*, Goddess of Fire and Life, the
Renewal symbolised as Phoenix by visitors from
Carthage, on May 1st. On the Eve (later to be
termed) Wal Purges* Night, for the cleansing or
purgation) there were dances by the Watchers
(later to be denounced as "witches"). The May Day
celebrations included games, mime-dances, songs
and feasting, with the erection of the May Pole.
This was the Vernal Equinox, balanced by *Samhain* (August 1st). Mainly the dances featured Fire;
but Water was also one of the symbol-facts; and
received veneration. Most of us are still Fire worshippers at December Yule.* Usually there were
twelve fires, sometimes with a large fire at centre;
and at regular sites of worship, they erected twelve
standing stones. At the Bal each man bore an oil
lamp. This Bal of Tanis is one of several sources of
later ballet.

BERGAMASCA (Italian)
Term given to certain Italian dances, wrongly
attributed to a supposed origin in the town of
Bergamo. There are exceedingly few specific dance
names derived from towns or villages : when they
carry this type of name, it is usually by a foreign
reference to a style; or to another error in naming
a place because it was supposed to originate a
style—(*Romanesca*). This name, *Bergamasca*, revised the mediæval *Berger Mascara* (*Berger Mascherata*) (Shepherds' Dance) belonging to the *Noël*
or Nouvelle "New Year Festival". Doubtless there
developed a "country dance" version (which drew
the definite name) in the town of Bergamo. The
dance, done by the miming "shepherds", was
known and performed all through Western Europe,
with the Miracle Plays—in England as *Shepherd's
Hey*; in Germany as *Schäfer-tanz*; in Portugal as
danca-pegreiro, or *dansa-pastora*—and so again to
pastoral. Some 16th century collections of musical
scripts contain examples of *bergamasca* in aural
form (some with words), as *Villotte* by Filippo
Azzaiolo (1569). Instrumental forms appear later,
as in sonatas by Uccellini (1642), repeating the very
simple scheme, with four bass notes kept as
"ground". The later form (freed from the festival
date) is a quick country dance for two couples or
larger groups, usually in 2/4 time. The *mascarade*
had separated before this village usage; and the
Danse Berger had a different mode in the city
salons until, in France, it was celebrated by
Watteau and other painters in pastoral form. In
between, a few poets used the measure with lute
or viol; but its best-known reference is that by
Shakespeare in *Midsummer Night's Dream*—"Will
it please you to see the epilogue, or to hear a
bergomask dance between two of our company"?

Even there, the emphasis is upon "hearing" the
dance measure, rather than dancing it. The *bergamasca* had become equipment for strolling players.
[See *Mascarade*]

BERGERETTA (Brittany, France)
A ceremonial dance which used to be celebrated
inside the churches of the diocese of Besançon on
the afternoon of Easter Day, down to 1738. In
1585 and again in 1601 the dance was forbidden in
the church, when it was reduced to making three
circuits in the cloisters only, and instead of the
dance (*branle*)* airs, the hymn of Lactantius "Hail
Festal Day" was used. Nevertheless, in 1662 the
dance was still performed in the nave of the church
in rainy weather, for an ordinary of about that
time says : —
"After dinner, and when the sermon is over, the
canons and chaplains, holding hands, perform a
dance in the cloisters, or in the middle of the
nave of the church if it is rainy weather. . ."
The *Bergeretta* was last performed in 1737.

BERSILAT (Malaya)
Denotes Malayan sword dances or combats with
staves etc.; in which two youths or men perform a
fight in rhythmic mode. There are two main forms :
Main Bersilat and *Main Ber-Panchak*, which may be
compared with the Japanese *kendo* or the old
English "buckler and staff-play". Malayan fencing
is called *Main-silat*.
[See *Pentchak* (Bali)]

BERUNSAI DANCE (North Borneo)
A welcome or social dance, among the Murut tribe.
The chief performer is a girl celebrated for her
backchat, accompanied by two or three other girls
and twenty or thirty men. They form a circle and
all move round slowly, hands on shoulders, taking
a few steps forward and one step backward, in
unison. In a shrill, nasal voice, the leading girl
chants her questions, to which the men reply. As
the night goes on the fun is faster, questions and
answers becoming more free. Dancing takes an
important place in Murut daily life, every ceremonial "men's house" having its dancing-floor.

BESSIE; *Bes*; *Bez* (English)
From Egyptian BEZ-Beza, God-Goddess of Nature
in primitive Egypt, probably from Sudan. BEZ was
a primitive Festival deity, associated with rejoicing,
food, and sex; and came to Rome when Egypt was
occupied (along with the worship of Isis), and
thence to Britain with the Roman agricultural
festivals of Mamurius (twelve in all), which defined
the successive duties or occupations of the year.

(See *Roman Dance.**) BEZ had a ring or enclosure, later called The House, as *Beth* (Hebrew form), and *Beit* (Arabic form), to which was joined *El Izza* or *Al-Essa*, "the place". The annual Dances of Bez are probably the oldest known dances in the world that have unbroken succession to our own day; though it is hard to recognise in the Man-Woman dancer of the Bessie with the Mummers or Morris-dancers, the jovial Egyptian personification of natural energy. The Egyptians recorded this deity as Seb or ZEB (all god-names can be read both back and forth, denoting dual qualities), (see *Bull Foot, Boustrephedon*) and the same type of Festival became linked with the Sed-Heb Festivals, from which is derived the Hebbe- or Hobby-horse.* (Yorkshire miners refer to their food packet taken to work as "bait" and bait is still 'food for fish"). The term "Nowt" is the Egyptian goddess Nout (Space), implying "Wide emptiness". There are many more derivations from Egypt in Britain; *Huzzas* were dancers (*hussies*; men, *huzzars*). They carry *Bezbeh*, the black top.

BETH-HAGLA (Hebrew)
The basic root *Hag* or *Hayy*, as allied to the place, the *Beth* or house (or reserved site) where, usually, a fountain was associated with a sacred tree. Holy water and holy tree imply each other, since in hot countries, vegetation demands water. Robertson Smith affirms this factor of ritual dance. "The name *Beth-hagla* seems to be based on a local tradition of a ritual procession round the sacred object". (p. 191)[1] The name suggests also *Beth-ha-Gila*, a derivative of far older Assyrian; the *hag* or *hayy* is Arabic and is connected with sacred journey; but the later Greek relates *hagia, sophia* or wisdom — the "journey into wisdom". This journey, on arrival, developed into a dance of triumphant joy.
[1] *Religion of the Semites*. W. Robertson Smith.

BETH-HA-SHAUBA (Hebrew)
The Hall of the Prophetess of *Shauba* (at Jerusalem). She was equivalent to the Greek ritual prophetess, the sibyl. The term derives from *shabal*, "to sprout", having been connected with the spring sowing; a function earlier filled by Ishtara of Babylon, then known as *El Shaballa*, the Speaker. The procession to and from the fountain or pool was always an event to celebrate "with shawms and timbrels on the dance". The word for it was *shibboleth*; or the "out-giving" of the speaker as *profeta*. The dance was performed by a group of "handmaidens" — meaning those who were learning the business; they had accommodation at the *Beth--ha-Shauba*. This term is related also to the Tatar "speaker" or magician, or *shaberon*.

BETHLEHEM (S. Arabic, Coptic)
Also *Beit-Lahem* — the House (of the) Bread. For the church ritual in Coptic liturgy, fresh bread is made (for the *Messe* or Feast) in each service. A small bakery, quite close to each church is called *Beit-Leham*; whence the small loaves are brought in, still warm, to a ritual march and chant by the deacons. Similar — among the Jews of Israel — was the *Dance of Water Bearing.** It is possible that this term gave origin to the earliest British form of Harvest Feast (now Michel *Messe*) but then as *Lehem Messe* — Bread Feast — later T'lammas. Dances of simple style were always associated with the rituals. Part of the tradition is conserved today in the Beit Crosse Bun (from *Buna* or *Abuna*, Coptic, Head Priest) now shifted to "Good Friday" or *Hud*-Friday, preceding the shifting Easter Ritual. They are always marked with solar crosse of the Solstice.

Bez, God of Agriculture. 3000 B.C. Gave name to Byzantium, Bezant (coin), Besant (flag), and finally to Bessie, in the English Morris and Sword Dance.

EGYPT

BEZ (Old Egyptian)

Is the Young Year, whose Festival or Messe was celebrated at the Winter Solstice, with joyful songs and dances. The name and the time came into Britain (known now as Bess or Bessie) as the centre of many rituals and legends. The Bez is wrongly described as a Sudanese dwarf god; he is not a little man but a Shining Boy who sets forth on his Journey of the Year, through which he comes to full age, to maturity, to old age and death, all in the twelve months. He is also the Chylde of English legend, the pattern for Knightly pages in training. From his symbol came the young Iezus, whose father was I O Sephar, mother M A Rhys (Sun and Earth) (Bez ayle=a great grandfather.) From BEZ was named the gold coin of Byzantium, *Bezant*. Bez as the user (destroyer) of his year was Em-Bezzler—or a *bezonian*, a drinker (from later festival excesses).

BEZANT FESTIVAL (England)

Was formerly held (until its abolition in 1830) in Shaftesbury or Shaston, in Dorset, in Rogation Week (the same period for "beating bounds" as occurs at Helston, for the *Furry Dance**). On the Monday, the Lord and Lady then appointed (May King and May Queen) accompanied by mayor and aldermen, with their mace-bearers carrying the Bezant, went in procession to Enmore Green. There the Lord of May with his Lady "performed a traditional kind of dance, to the sound of violins". From the mayor, the manor steward received the Bezant, which was then a calf's head, uncooked; together with a gallon of ale, two penny loaves, with a pair of gold-laced gloves. Permission was then ceremonially given to use all wells, old or new, during another year. Evidently this is a minor part of the ancient custom of Maying, with the Robin Hood Games; concerned intimately with water supplies and green vegetation. The steward took all the gifts, but returned the Calf Head (copy of the Winter Boar's Head, but now a *younger* generation, the "son" or spring character). The Bezant, as lastly constructed, shows the features of the "May Garland"—a frame four feet high, with ribbons, peacock's feathers, and hung with silvery objects (loaned by owners), like that of the Dairymaids.[1] After the people had danced on the Green of Enmore, the procession went back to Shaston; where the wealthier ones attended a corporation dinner. The name *Bezant* was used for a gold coin, once used as rent or tribute payment; and, as its name identifies, was a coin of Byzantine origin, current in Britain during the Greek period of commerce and religious interchange, before some of these scholars settled in Ireland and Northumbria, probably 200 or 100 BC. The British

Museum "Mildenhall Treasure" came from a similar source in Byzantium. *Bezant* may be linked also with the Bessie or Bess of the May Games and Morris Dance.
[1] *Book of Days*. Chambers. p. 585 ii.

BHAGAVANTULA (Dekkan, India)

Players, music and dancing; professional itinerant groups, who perform chiefly at the religious festivals. Their show is open freely, the players being remunerated by some local landowner or other rich person. Many of their plays (in the manner of the Italian *Commedia delle Arte*) are satires, contrived to fix on current local topics. Compare also the Bhagavats, who sing and dance not as spectacle, but as a religious devotion, some of whom came into Europe.   [See *Gavot*]

BHAGAVATA MELA NATAKA (South India)

One of the main forms of classical Indian folk play, as performed principally in Tanjore. Combining music with dance and chanting, they appear at the Spring Festival, month of Vaisakha. Temporary stages are constructed, principally in villages of Uttukadu or Merattur, with an image. Characters are introduced, one by one, by chant of chorus and drummers. Then each performer appears dancing, and with *mudras** of *Bharata Natyam,** beginning with *Konangi* (clown), followed by the elephant-god, *Ganesha;* then Yattakariyan, the king's servant, then the king or hero of the play. The *Bhagavata* follows in style the ancient *Ariyakuttu* of Sanskrit tradition; and is itself being now displaced by modernist modes. These traditions of South India are mutually linked and influenced by their various styles; as we see in the typical *Yaksha-Gana** (through Mysore State), or the *Teruk-kuttu,** in Tamil Nad; and *Vithi Nataka,** that is familiar in Andhra. All these plays use either the small half--screened stage, of bamboo; or the *mandapa*, of circular form.
[See *Bhagavata Mela Nataka*. (J.I.S.O.A. June 1937)]

BHAIJHI; *Baijee; Baiji* (India)

Moslem term for girl dancer, chiefly in Northern India, where Mughal-Arabic influence spread. It is Urdu term for dancer-singers of *Bhajans*, a style of noisy religious recital (somewhat similar to Salvation Army street festivities), following on the revivalist, Chaitanya. As a great devotee for the Cristna cult, he urged the public celebration of adherents, by song and dance as a mode of *bhakti,** or devotional praise. Many of the *bhaijees* became professionals; but wandering women are rarely regarded in India as reputable; normally they travel in groups, from one *mela* to another; they are not admitted to caste celebrations.

BHAIRAVA NATYAM (India)

Are among the Dances of Shiva. Explanation is given in *Lalita Sahasranama*,[1] which affirms severally: "Bhairava is Paramasiva, accomplisher of Creation; Preservation; and Destruction (of the universe). Each letter in the word Bhairava has its meaning: *Bha*, creation (*Bharana*); *Ra*, preservation (*Ramana*); and *Va*, destruction (*Vamana*) to eject. ... Witness to the great dance of Mahesvara in the great cycle ... Mahakalpa; the great dissolution (*Pralaya*) Great Dance, is caused by the fact that Self alone remaining (Kali-as-Shiva) there is no other. She is the witness ... witnessing the dance of the Axe-bearing Para-bhairava (Shiva in his aspect of destruction)". After referring also to description in the *Bhagavata Purana*, the translator continues by mention of Book VI of *Vashishta*, and says: "After describing the wonderful and terrible dance of these two (Shiva and Devi) concludes: 'Having a garland on his breast, having the wings of an eagle as his head ornament, holding in his hand the great Horn of the buffalo of Yama (Death) filled with red liquor, dancing to the sound of his music, such as Dhimba ... may Bhairava with his (spouse) called Kalaratri, who delights in dissolution, protect you'". Then after another mention of Kali ("Time extended and dissolved") as wife of Mahakamesvara, he cites the great "Tripurasundari ... as Tripura, City of the Three (elements) as The Measurer, the Measuring, the Thing Measured". This is directly equivalent to "The Dancer, the Dancing, and the Dance that is seen". Bhairava is known as the Great Yogi (motionless in body, powerful in mind), whose two-fold dance is secret (one is the *Chöd**), and whose *shakta* (Kali) performs the famous "Dance of the Burning Ground" (which destroys all sorrow, all sin, all delusion). These ritual dances of Bhairava are by no means so well known as those attributed to the *Shiva** *Natyam*, where the God is symbolised as performing (in dance) all of the Five Actions; that is, creation as well as dissolution.

[1] *Lalita Sahasranama with Bhaskararaya's Commentary* (translated into English by R. A. Sastry (Benares) 1899).

BHAKTI (Hindu)

In dance is dominance of spirit of devotion of love; thus filled with energy the ritual dancers are known as *Bhagavats* (the Praisers of Bhagwan, the Lord). During the Indian 15th century, there were several great revival movements in this sector of Vaishnavism (or Cristnàs), as that by Chaitanya in Bengal; Tulsi Das and Surak Das in Punjab; and Ezhuthachan of the Tamil country. These leaders recognised the familiar "Five Modes" within the doctrine of *Bhakti*, as modes or forms of love:

Shanti	— Peace of Meditation, or equal love to all men;
Dasya	— Service, or loving help to men and gods;
Sakhya	— Friendship—the power of compassion, sympathy;
Vatsakhya	— Youth; the love of children;
Madhurya	— Family; the love of woman.

Each of these specialised modes was marked by its own measures in ritual song and dance, in fervent *kirtans* and *bhajans*, in the social ethic of *korral* (derived from Jain school). The Tamil *Kurral* descends from the 2nd century AD, written in 1300 *slokas*. Chaitanya (born 1485 at Nadia) recognised no caste; Moslems joined with him. Mira Bai, wife of the Raja of Chitore, wrote her famous Krishna poem in 1420 and often danced its theme (*Krishna's return to Men*). Vallabhai (b. 1470), a cultured Brahmin of Benares, added his lyrical appeal; and stimulated the ritual ring dances (*Tantrika*) to renewed action.

BHANIR NAUTCH (India—United Provinces, now Uttar Pradesh, in Lucknow or Cawnpore etc.)

A mime dance of buffoons. In the nineteenth century, this *Bhanir Nautch* was much patronised by the local Nawabs and Zamindars; they delighted to invite friends whose habits might be gently satirised by caricature in action dance; perhaps with witty quip and repartee. Mostly it is now degenerated, or turned to political advantage as a display before an election meeting.

BHARANG (N. India)

Dance in the Moslem festival of Moharram (marking first month of Islamic year). The *Bharang* is a man dancer renowned as "the foolish talker" (or clown). His head-dress is a shawl attached to a narrow filament, which carries a small flag of green cloth; his body is daubed liberally with red ochre; and his legs carry small brass bells, strapped on. He derives from an old tradition: the "red life arising into green leaf", as a kind of "dance of appeasement", since this feast is associated with the "martyrs" Hassan and Husain.

BHARATA (India)

Fraternity of bards, in Ganges region of India, who became famous for drama and dance. They presented the *Maha-Bharata*, or acted myths of their legendary battles (Kurekshetra, a plain near Indrakocha, or Delhi), eventually being mentioned by other people as "The Bharats". This term is extant in Russia as *bratye* (children) and in Saxon slang, as *"brats"*, while in Western Europe it turned from *bratye* to *fratye* or fraternity. The name *Bharata* denoted the company; later emerged a "Book of Rules", which is attributed to a fabulous writer Bharata, known as *Natya Shastras* (Dance Verses). Similar was the emergence of the theatre term *magadha*; also from the district of the Magadhas or Great Axe People (*Magha-Adze*), who became as famous for dramas, in the various vernacular or Prakrit languages (dialects) of India. These *sanavadas* were composed in Prakriti, not in Sanskrit (the Sacred Tongue), and so abolished the interpreter. The modern Indian actor is called a *bhat*, a term not directly derived from *Bharata*. The principal *sanavada* was *Slaying of Kamsa by Krishna*, but next was *Binding of the Titans*. They were performed in the open air, in daylight, first as simple colloquies, then in wider form.

BHARATA NATYAM (Sanskrit)

Indian term for Devotional Ritual Dance; formulated in worship (chiefly Vaishnava cult) of Aditi or Sakti as the Great Mother; and later with Shiva* as Nataraja.* Aditi is not only the mother of the gods; but "the great mother" of the devotees (*Suvratanam*), the mistress of the rituals, "one strong in mightiness, space-extending protector, and skilful in guidance". This term, *Suvratanam*, contains two important roots: that of *sovran* (still held in the Balkan term *Sobranje*—Parliament; or *sobor* (Slavonic) as "council", especially of the church; and the basis of sovereignty; but also that of *tanam* or ritual, which is also *natam* and *natyam*, or specific "dance". These rules were codified probably about 8th century BC, in the first *Bharata-natya-shastras*, or "Brother's Ritual Verses", and a later reference is in the scripture title *Maha-Bharatya*, or Great Brotherhood. While this *mithya* (being publicly performed as Miracle Plays) was open, the Tantras or liturgies were maintained in private for known devotees. The legends about a sage called Bharata are legends—based only on a small number of exceptionally skilful directors of ritual being mentioned as Bharat-ya or Bharat-ji. The name Bharat is the revived modern name for the Republic—as Bharatyavarsa.

BHAT (Hindu and Bengali; India)

Popular term for an actor or dancer. The family name Bhattacharya derives from it, meaning the "teacher or manager" of the itinerant troupe. Originally they performed the *sanvadas*, a kind of colloquial drama (somewhat akin to the fresher form of the *Commedia dell' Arte*), where the theme was known and the *bhats* spoke or acted or danced,

according to the receptivity of the day's audience; in Prakrit, not Sanskrit.
[Cp. *Bharata*]

BHUT CHAKRAM (Hindu)

Literally "Ghost Circle"; the Dances of the *Pisachas* (or demons); as confused with the slow dance of the spiritualist seance or "ancestral circle". Traditions, legends, and practice of this kind of seance vary enormously through India. The principal sects tend completely to ignore all kinds of "spirit recall", and even condemn the practices; although they do not deny their usual authenticity as "real events". The system is a reminder of far older tribal rituals, mostly of aboriginal peoples, distant from cultural centres. H. P. Blavatsky tells of an instance, witnessed by herself, where a circle of dancing magicians moved in a ring, meanwhile cutting their skins so that blood ran, until presently "each man was joined and then separated by a ghostly figure which danced with him".

BIBASIS (Ancient Sparta)

A popular acrobatic dance performed by both men and women, being little more than a display of virtuosity. Consisting of springing rapidly into the air and striking the feet together behind the body, it was more an athletic contest than a dance, since the number of times the performer successfully beat her feet together were counted, and prizes awarded. The *Bibasis* is mentioned by Aristophanes, when a Spartan woman prides herself on her skill in its performance; while Pollux (iv. 102) gives a verse describing the feat of a Laconian girl who surpassed all previous performers by dancing the *Bibasis* a thousand times!

"BIG APPLE" (USA)

Appeared about 1935 in New York; thence entered England with dance teachers. This "party dance" is said to have come from the "Big Apple" Club (Columbia, S. Carolina) taking its name from the redecorated Mission Hall that sheltered the Club. The form is a large circle for couples; and has a caller (who gives the figure to be done). These figures are lindy hop; shag; trucking, etc.

BIHARI COW DANCE (Bihar, N. India)

Is performed at Sohrai Festival in October, for inauguration of Bir Kuar colours (or of Krishna) celebrated by the Ahir people. The open-air "dance" follows the first ritual; and resembles a bullfight, but a pig is gored by cows, urged by three Ahirs, one singing, one drumming, and one dancing. Sometimes a mock pig is used. Bir Kuar is the "strong man-god", who fights tigers, and induces fertility.

The images are set often in pairs, of rounded tree timbers with primitive heads, much like large skittles (6 or 8 feet high). The dance of cows is *gaidarh*, or *gai nachme ka darh* — a literal equivalent. There is an underlying resemblance to West African initiation rites, devised to teach the meaning of masks in relation to jungle power (as a nature-*mana*-energy).

BILATI NAUTCH (India)
An Urdu term, meaning literally the "Foreign Dance", or the "Dance of Home" (of the former English residents in India). The word *Bilati*, familiar in its British army mode as "Blighty" is known in every cantonment. The native servants of the Civil Service used the term *Bilati Nautch* to indicate any entertainment — at club or Residency etc. — which featured social dancing of the European styles; for "couple dancing" was not (in those days) known generally in India. The classical instance is related of Simla (*circa* 1920), when one of the native potentates had been invited to Government House for a conference. Having ended this talk, the Governor, politely desirous of extending hospitality, took the Rajah "to see the dancing". They stepped out from the Governor's room, on to the dais, whence the Rajah surveyed the solemnly dancing crowd of men in uniform and women in evening dress. Silently he watched for some minutes; then, waving his hand in dismissal, said: "Good, they may now go home".

BINASUAN (Phillipines)
Reminiscent in rhythm and style of the Indonesian *Tari Piring*,* but performed with wine glasses instead of lighted candles. In *Binasuan* girls and men dance with glasses of wine balanced on heads and palms of the hands. Quietly, almost casually, hands, arms and body sinuously twist and turn, without spilling a drop of wine (in *Tari Piring*, without extinguishing the lights). *Pandanggo Sa Ilaw*,* although danced with lighted lamps, is more Spanish in style and rhythm.

BLACK HATS, Dance of (Tibet)
Buddhism was persecuted by King Langa Dharma, about 900 AD. In defence, Pal Dorje (a Lama from Lha-lun) resolved to remove the despot. He devised a scheme of approach, for which he disguised himself as a strolling dancer of the Black Hat sects of the Bonpo faith. Within his great sleeves he concealed his bow and arrows. Dressed in black he travelled on a black pony; and arrived at the Palace of Langa Dharma. His ability in dancing attracted the king's attention; and Pal Dorje was summoned to the royal hall to receive presents.

Darting among the crowd of retainers, Pal Dorje contrived to take out his bow and shoot the tyrant king; and in the immediate confusion made his escape. Though he mounted his pony, he was seen riding off and was soon pursued. He rode into the River Kyi, thus causing the soot he had used to disguise his pony, to be washed off, to reveal its natural white hide. The lama turned his clothes and hat, which he had made white inside; and thus he evaded detection and finally escaped. Lama Pal Dorje has since become a saint in the Tibetan calendar with his festival, celebrated by a pantomime dance which recapitulates the main events. All the chief incidents are included, along with humorous commentaries; while his "unseen attendants" are now made visible as good and evil spirits, solemn demons or buffoons. This annual pantomime is a great favourite with Tibetans of all classes.   [See *Langdharma*]

BLACK MASS (Mediæval catholic legend)
Used as a sort of denunciation by scandale, against scholars who would not accept papal domination. Said to be "unutterably wicked" monstrous details were published : a child had to be "sacrificed" or "a maid had to be mated upon the altar". Then "wild orgies" were celebrated, with witch dances or devil dances. The entire legend is demolished by one fact : the claim by clerics that "Black Marss" could only be celebrated properly (or improperly?) by a defrocked or denigrated "real priest". Thus it was claimed that not only the Barmecide Feast of "White Marss" but the very naughty equally magical ceremony of "Black Marss" was under the sole control of the Latin church. As with their campaign against "Witch-craft" no substantial legal evidence has ever been produced. The custom of "saying mass" equally with the alleged explanation of the basic meaning of the term "mass" (i.e. to dismiss) raises similar queries as to accuracy. The term mass endured for many centuries as *Messe* — the feast (usually following a *Foire*, as present Leipsiger Messe) and derived in fact from the ancient usage of *messe* in Egypt. Later this was used for an actual bread or cake, *maza* (Greek, a barley cake). The term was associated with the Mask, then as a *dromenon* for the dead, at which portrait or ritual masks were worn. The Egyptian ritual was, in Alexandria, joined with the Jewish weekly meeting for a supper or meal; this was by no means an allegorical meal; and it is still followed by the *seder* every Sabbath evening. The suggestion that a devilish inversion was invented by a renegade priest is then seen to be no more than an item of propaganda — or a social masquerade. There was no Black Mass that was blacker than the Holy Inquisition; none more devilish.

BLACK WIDOW (Bali, Indonesia)
The generic term for Rangda, who is the chief personated form of this Nature goddess; she is similar to the Indian Durga, or Kali. The name Rangda means widow; but she is a widow like the famous black spider who devours her mate. This symbol is mythic and not "realism" in the Balinese legends of the *leyaks* (witches or demons). The Black Widow's dance is magical, and she is opposed by the Barong,* as the good influence.

BLAIZE, OR *Balaize* (England; France)
Is a generic term implying the "Dance round the Fire", followed as a bi-annual ritual for many centuries in Britain at the two solstices, thus marking the popular calendar in December and June. These were the ancient Feasts of Johanna (or Anna, the Year Spirit). The sport of "jumping through the flames" was regarded as the big step of the circle dance; but sheep were carried through by way of "sheep-dip" as a protective scorching. The old name was gradually beaten down, until many a "Sant' Blaise" was invented, some becoming "bishops". This Festival of Fire pertains to the most ancient worship, Fire being regarded as the potent symbol of the unseen God of the Universe. Possibly the word itself was derived from Ba'Al-adze—or "Hammer of Thor"; for an allied term is known in Caucasia, in Ba' Al-enchanav-adze (Axe or Adze of the Ring), as the implement necessary for cutting timber for the fires, or making a path through primeval forest.

BLUE BLOUSE GROUPS: SINYAYA BLUZA (USSR)
From 1922 to 1930, roughly, these proletarian "Theatre Groups" developed, chiefly in Moscow and Petrograd, and mostly with "revolutionary plays". Their title originated from their early performances in "workshop kit". While their main emphasis was on the spoken drama, a small number verged towards music hall style of satirical dance. This proletarian culture grew from offices and then factories, using vacated mansions and small halls—one of their chief centres was the Morossov Palace in Moscow—the city is short of large halls. Using vocational movements, these amateur groups gave *Proletcult Teatr* shows, as skits, parodies, and dances. Their principal display was the May First *Krasnya Ploschad* demonstration; in its later modes including some highly skilled technical dance, derived partly from village folk-dance and partly from ballet, with a fusion from the *Modernistiky Tanz*, continued by the Duncan and Vera Maya schools. When *Proletcult* turned to *Matr-Kulturny* Teatr (as war approached and broke out), the Blue Blouse Groups disappeared. Igor Moisseyev turned to Folk-Dance plus Ballet; the Folk Ensembles appeared; and the famous Ten Day Republican Theatre displays occurred annually in Moscow; some of them startling in their advance. [See *Habima Theatre* (Russia); *Serf Ballet* (Russia)]

BLUES (American; semi-Negro origin)
A song-dance form (developing 1925-35), deriving from the Negro *Foxtrot* style, which may justly be termed the Drunk Dance of America (drink) Prohibition. Henry Ford and his political associates, desiring to utilise the full energy resources of his wage-workers on conveyer belts, contrived to get Congress to try to eliminate their access to all alcoholic drinks, by legal Prohibition. The social result was a greater development of "protection" by religious gentlemen, like Al Capone of Chicago (and many others), who considered that Free America should be free to drink at any time (unlike Free Britain). They supplied synthetic liquids; with some stimulation of dreary music and drearier dancing, in the Jazz styles—the Blues; and other decadent varieties of unmusical rhythm. Blues singing could often be heard in London when, late on Saturday evening, the "Drunks" went home; as they sang hymn-tunes of their youth. They danced rarely. In USA the Blues were capitalized; featured in Night Clubs; and finally were permitted by the religious censors to appear in films. Among the very few rhythmic examples may be mentioned *Mood Indigo* (Ellington).

BOAR'S HEAD CAROL AND DANCE (Scandinavian origin)
Has continued traditionally with the Celebration of Yule, later fused with the X-Messe or Feast of Crossing at the Winter Solstice. The Head of the Boar was brought in for the Feast, with an Orange in its open mouth; this symbolises the slaughter of the Boar just before he—as the Beast of Winter—has succeeded in swallowing the Dying Sun. The Pudding was often borne in flames for this reason. The dance march was one of the simple steps of the Scallions or Servitors, from kitchen to table. They encircled the Table singing the Carol—which has been much amended—but it is probably the oldest of the Saxon Carols or Praise Songs for the Chylde or King's Son, the *Kralye*.

The Boar's Head Carol belonged especially to Universities (Oxford) and to the Temple (Law students). They devoured the "chaps" with white bread and mustard, drinking barley-wine. Wynkyn de Worde has a page of Noel in *Carolles*—1521.)

BODNÁRTÂNC (Hungary)
Hoop dance of the coopers in the region of Hegyolja, where Tokay wine is made. Depicting certain operations in the work of cask-making, such

as sawing wood, and fixing the hoops while moving round the cask, the dance has many figures (in Erdöbénye there are fourteen), and is usually accompanied by gypsy music. It is danced at the vintage festivals by five men plus a sixth, who performs the balancing feat of rhythmically swinging a glass full of wine, without spilling any. Danced in circular formation, various patterns are made with hoops, one of which each dancer carries. Holding the hoops low, then high, the men first move round with skipping or running steps, in one direction, then the other, three times repeated, the circle drawing closer each time. There follow various figures—each man jumps over a hoop held low on the ground by his neighbour; an arch is formed with two hoops, through which the other dancers pass; the circle facing inwards, hoops are held as though interwoven, while the ring revolves three times : the interwoven hoops are raised and lowered three times, while the men sing a triple verse; the men dance in and out of spaces made by placing the overlapping hoops on the ground. Change of figure or direction is indicated by a stamp from the leader, and the tune varies with the figures. Finally, a circle is formed and the hoops held high, while the sixth man "swings the glass". Standing in the centre of the circle, he sings "The gentleman drinks from a full glass", at the same time standing a small tumbler brimful of wine on the horizontal base of a stirrup-shaped hoop, which he holds at the top, between middle and forefingers. The glass is not fixed. In rhythm with the music, he swings hoop and glass in a figure of eight several times; then kneeling on the left knee, supported by the left hand, he turns nearly on his back, continuously swinging the glass. This is repeated to the right. Finally, he stands up, hoop and glass still swinging, while the circle of dancers clash their hoops together at the successful conclusion of this feat, which also ends the dance.
[Cp. *Schafflertans*]

BOLERO (Spain)
A dance in 3/4 time for a solo dancer or one couple. The dancers accompany themselves with castanets, the rhythm of which was gradually introduced into the music. The castanet rhythm usually begins at least one bar before the melody. Music of the *Bolero*, like the *Seguidilla*,* is divided into three parts, two main parts each repeated, and a trio or coda. The Spanish *Bolero* has the feeling and grace of an 18th century court dance. According to some, its invention is attributed to a dancing-master of Cadiz (Sebastian Cerezo) about 1780, but as folk dances rarely spring suddenly into being, it probably existed much earlier. Indeed, in support of this, it is also stated to have become stylised

for stage use during the 17th and 18th centuries, which argues its existence long before Signor Cerezo was born.

Spanish dancing figure in the Bolero. Bronze figure in collection of W. G. Raffé; height 8½ins. 18th century, Barcelona.   SPAIN

BOLERO (Cuba)
Reached Cuba at beginning of the 19th century, and was transformed from a medium dance in 3/4 time to a slow one in 2/4 meter, always lyrical, playful and languid. Its form consists of a brief introduction followed by two parts of 16 to 32 bars each. The Cuban *Bolero's* basic rhythm remains unmistakable, and the instrument which most faithfully interprets it in accompaniment is the guitar.

BOLERO DE ALGODRA or ZAMORA (Spain, Leon Province)
Said to derive in music, rhythm, and steps from Arab origins of tenth century form. The dance was much later adopted by the *Cofradia* (Brotherhood) of San Agueda; and thus used as a processional dance when bearing the carved wooden image of the saint. Each line has a group of three, a boy in

the centre, with two men or two girls. Each set of steps ends with a clash of castanets, to resemble a peal of bells. The performance is cut by entry of a major-domo who gives to each dancer a fragment of cake called *miaja* or *miaza* (from Al Khodra).

BOLIM BOMBO (New Guinea)

Performed during *Gol Kerma** ("Great Festival"), in the Wahgi Valley, on the day preceding the great sacrifice of pigs. Its purpose is to drive away evil spirits and bring the ancestors' blessing on the climax of the Festival. *Bolim* is a spirit of evil, whose power to harm must be annulled; *Bombo* is a plant rolled into a large ball and thought to absorb evil. Performed by men round the House of Bolim on the festival ground, the dance begins in the afternoon, when women holding sweet potato green vines, sit in a circle round the House. Men wait, hidden in the bush, then suddenly rush out, in specific order. First come warriors, with spears and drawn bows; then sorcerers—two carrying *bombos*, one dressed as a woman, others making magical gestures. Last come drummers, beating slender hand-drums, and yelling the long-drawn cry called *mangro-mangro*. The dance is a wild charge round the Bolim house (and the women) alternating with sudden pauses, when all men kneel, then charge, then kneel again; and a movement when the warriors run very fast "on the spot". Festival costume includes a narrow apron-skirt in front, with a bunch of leaves at the back like a bustle; collars and ornaments of pearl shell; and bird-of-paradise head-dresses. Beneath the plumes is worn a ceremonial wig (*peng*), reaching to the wearer's shoulders and looking like a judge's full-bottomed wig. Made by special craftsmen called *peng ezim ye*, they consist of a light bamboo frame, covered with human hair (contributed by kinsmen) and dyed deep yellow with a tree gum. The edges are bordered with green beetle shards, or with shells, and the wigs are made specially for the *Gol Kerma* Festival.
[See *New Guinea, Dances of*; *Kip Gamp Gol*; *Gol Kerma*; *Gol Gur Gur*]

BOLSHOI TEATR (Moscow, USSR)

The *Bolshoi* (Grand) Theatre, the largest in Russia, is renowned for productions of ballet and opera. The building was opened in 1825, and was reconstructed (in Ionic *not* Doric style) in 1856 (architects Bové and Kavos). There is a stage thirty metres in proscenium width. Seating accommodation has 2,052 places. The companies include full cast for any opera, doubled by another; a full ballet company, again doubled (corps-de-ballet of 120), with an orchestra of 110, also doubled. These include, with administrative staff, over 3,500 persons. The Theatre has its own workshop, scenic studios, and costume and property factory, employing 400 skilled workers. The Theatre is owned by the Moscow Soviet (Municipal), which receives agreed rentals and undertakes repairs to structure. The staff is controlled by its own administration, from production to sales of seats. Outside contacts are (a) Trade Union units (Theatre Workers Union); (b) city and booking agencies; (c) educational bodies, for block bookings; and (d) transport for tours. In addition, the Theatre (like all regular enterprises) is bound by law to supply housing accommodation for its staff. Many flats are owned or hired, usually within walking distance of the building. Some members of staff have cars allotted (for all usage). Holders of Orders receive free transport; in the city or even over State railways. Performances are held every evening; alternating opera with ballet (usually three times weekly). In the summer holidays, performers go on tour; and have two months rest in the usual thirteen week period, while visiting companies may appear. Little overhead loss is incurred by closure; the only "out" periods are the few occasions when the theatre is hired (as with the Albert Hall in London) for political meetings. The former municipal/state subvention is no longer necessary, income being balanced with expenditure. Differential rates of pay are in force, at levels agreed with the Theatre Workers Union. All stage clothes without exception (including tights and ballet shoes) are supplied to staff by theatre; stage crews have uniforms. All sheet music, with instruments, also supplied. Rehearsals are continued "until ready", with no special pay (but a limit of hours) or conditions; there are no strikes, and contracts must be met. Performers may earn fees outside the Theatre, as in provincial tours; or by giving lessons.

BOMBAY DANCE (India)

The Indian newspaper critics' own term (like "Bombay Duck" on the table), now somewhat derisive in suggestion, applies to those styles of flashy "modern Indian dance", which have developed in the past thirty years. The debasing influences are the modern cinema film, especially the pseudo-Indian dances occasionally shewn by uninformed Hollywood producers, and the "let's be famous quick" style, adopted by too many Bombay or Calcutta "society ladies" who had suddenly discovered that "dance is now quite very respectable", and then took a series of "dancing in twelve lessons" with some Europe-returned master, to be followed (together with a wad of rupees) by "appearance with the Guru guaranteed!" This *Bakshish Natyam** has appeared not only in Bombay, but in

Calcutta, Delhi, Madras, and Colombo, with occasional adventures to Paris (the wealthy groups, with money but no taste), supported by "publicity" supplied by writers having no knowledge of any oriental dance, ancient or modern. Indian newspaper criticism of Indian dancing is far more pointed (and sometimes more accurate) than the usual uncritical adulation that appears in European or American papers. The label "Bombay Dance" is invented by them. They have further comment on exported variations of Hindu music; they remark sharply on some Delhi radio "musical experts" who are copied by the BBC—again, without comprehension of authentic Indian music. Indian writers are even more severe about Indian film production; as, we may recall, their pointed comments on the *Kalpana* film produced by Uday Shankar Chaudhury, the dancer-artist, with its cast of 200, and nearly as many dances, crammed into one oddly modernist imitation American film.

BOMMAL ATTAM (Malayalam Tamil, S. India)
Puppet play and dance in traditional style (now almost obsolete); but probably the source of the extant Javanese *Wayang Wang* puppet plays etc. (*Attam* = Dance-Tamil.) The Bommali are worked by rods and strings from behind, accompanied by music and occasional verses sung to explain the story; usually from the Hindu *Purana* mythos. The style of movement became so familiar that living dancers copied the puppet motion (as in Java they still do). These puppets provided the familiar "Miracle Play" for devotees of Bhagwan throughout Southern India, much as the *teraphim* figures did for the early Christian communities. The name survives in German, to indicate a "gay time", as going "on the bummel".

BÒN RITUAL DANCES (Tibet)
Have two schemes; one general and public, in Bön-Pa system; the other is reserved. The public rites make prominent the Four Queens; while the higher rites include the Four Kings (*Gyalchen De-She*). The director is called Lama Yulgye. These Four Queens belong to the four seasons, beginning with Spring, as:

    Queen of Spring: *Chigi-gyemo* (Red)
    Queen of Summer: *Yagi-gyemo* (Blue)
    Queen of Autumn: *Tongi-gyemo* (Green)
    Queen of Winter: *Gungi-gyemo* (Yellow)

The "fighting dance", or contest, has several forms; one symbolical, based on the known forms, *Perketarioto*. Thence emerges *riota*, or *iota* (the "Small Dance" of Men), and the *Tarota*, or Mediæval Dance of Dead (Purgatorio).

BON ODORI (Japan)
Called also Bon Festival, or Feast of Lanterns; annually July 13th to 15th, as a Buddhist memorial service to the spirits of the dead. A Buddhist revision from the older Bon or Pön faith (as in Tibet). Lanterns are lighted in cemeteries; and in districts a "fire of welcome" is made before the house, to mark the doorway for guests from the spirit world. Miniature family shrines are cleaned; and special food placed before them to entertain the ancestral guests. On the last day the guests are returned to the spirit world in the same pious fashion. All cemeteries in the country have this scene of religious devotion. The *Bon Odori* (or Bon Dance), a traditional primitive folk dance, is performed mostly in country districts by the young people, who gather, not in the cemetery, but at the local temple or shrine and dance through the night, on the last night, the 15th.

BONGO DANCE (Southern Sudan)
With the exception of the musicians, and one solitary man, only women take part. As with the Dinkas (Dinka Virgins Dance), the basis of the Bongo dance action is sexual, but expression is different. The motion appears simple, but is extremely complicated; there are four distinct movements, all of which must occur at the same time. The step is a forward shuffle, feet close together; the women move in a small circle (in the centre is the orchestra) and as they dance round from time to time, they sink slowly down on their heels and rise again, working stomach and thighs in a *danse du ventre*. They wear a long "tail" of grass, at the back. The solitary male has to rush madly round inside the circle, in the direction opposite to the dance. The orchestra has kettle drums, gourd-rattles, and two large bassoon-like wooden wind instruments.

BOOK OF A BALLET
Libretto (Italian, Little Book); or "Program Note" or "Story"; also termed Synopsis; or Plot. Precise meanings vary according to exact usage. The outline of plot, or synopsis, may be printed as "program note" to tell spectators what to expect; it presents the theme of the work to be seen. A complete "Book" will contain more than this: it will have (a) scenario, or description of theme, setting and action in general, as material for the producer. Some alleged "choreographers" never prepare such a book: they "carry the theme in the head"; and "build it upon their dancers", or, "hope for the best". (b) A choreographic outline of movement; (c) some notes on character and costume. Some of the Italian early ballets were recorded in elaborate *libretti*, copies being distributed after performance

to friends through Europe. The rise of "emotional ballet", following the end of court ballet and the partial eclipse of romantic ballet, has led to the offer of a synopsis in about a score of words. Rarely are new ballets sufficiently adequate to make their meaning clear, by such a brief note and carefully designed action. There should be, for a modern three-act ballet (or even for a one-act works) sufficient description for producer and all dancers concerned (as well as scenic designers and lighting experts), to gain a comprehensive idea of what the work "is all about". If they do not know, it is hopeless to expect them to put over the meaning in integral fashion, so that the spectator will understand. The ideal book is thus a "Complete Guide to One Ballet", which it should not be necessary to print.

BORDER TOWN PIPERS (Scotland; Cheviot Hills)

Sir Walter Scott especially mentions these town pipers (who piped for dancing, as for ballads) as the "last remains of the minstrel race".

"The pipers, of whom there was one attached to each Border town of note, and whose office was often hereditary, were the great depositaries of oral and particularly of poetical tradition. About spring time and after harvest, it was the custom of these musicians to make a progress through a particular district of the country. The music and tale repaid their lodging. . . . The town pipers received a livery and a salary from the community to which they belonged; and in some burghs they had a small allotment of land, called Pipers Croft".

These men were expert on the *pibroch* or highland pipes. We find later they were transferred to regimental duties with Scottish regiments; and thus the ancient minstrels were ancestors of the pipers of the Black Watch (the name "waits" in England).

BORI DANCERS (Nigeria)

Hausa negroes, of Muslim faith, use the term *Bori* (or "Children of Bori") to signify "spirit-possession", and thus named are the dancers, when associated with this practice. The adept or dancer is called the "mare", as possession is described alternatively as "spirit mounted her", or as "she mounted spirit". These are mainly "Nature spirits" and they receive praise-songs, which invoke them. Special instruments play the correct tune, and the spirits come to "possess a dancer", being known by distinctive behaviour and gestures. This *Bori* cult is largely held by initiated women of the *karwara* group ("free women"). The initiation ritual lasts fourteen days in all, and is an Islamized version of an older Arabic cult, *iblisi* or *aljannu*, belonging to the ritual of *iskosi*. Formerly there were some male dancers. The "sacrifices" are similar to those suggested by European priests when they require money or food. Mostly these dances occur at night, in the open village arena; anybody can watch. There are certain similarities to the Spiritualist meetings known in England; except that these have music but no dancing; there is sometimes a prescription of herbal medicine. The music for *Bori* is the basic drum, sometimes with a fiddler or piper. The favoured string instrument is the *gage*, a large single-string, played with a bow, to "call the spirits". There may be a group of ten or twelve Bori dancers moving together; also singing; always with their best clothes and ornaments. The dance form is little more than a simple ring.

BORICA (Hungary)

A dance and dance-group of a tribe of Hungarians known as "Csangos of the Seven Villages", near the town of Brassö; danced yearly, on Innokente Day, December 28th only, as part of a traditional Festival, now forgotten. The troupe numbers sixteen selected youths, wearing traditional dress; high hats with bright ribbons, silk scarves over chest and back. They carry polished and beribboned axes, fixed to the outer side of each leg; below the knee are three rattles, while their boots have metal spurs. The leader carries the crown of a pine-tree, decorated with fruits and ribbons, followed by musicians and dance leader. The *Borica* dancers are the compact group; with others as jesters, wearing wooden masks adorned with cock's feathers. Armed with wooden swords and whips, they cut capers as their bells jingle. Another small group, called the "Spit-bearers", control a mime of cooking, subject of many jokes. The word *Borica* means "little pine tree" (like the Russian "little birch tree"—*Beryozka*). The *Borica* dance is grave, precise, and disciplined; not open to the improvisation of the *verbunkos** or *legényes*. This affirms its ritual origin. In the circle dance, each man follows or reflects the movements of the man opposite to him. There are four parts: single *borica*; double *borica*; triple *borica*; and Turkish *borica*. The elements are simple: heel clicking, swinging legs to and fro, right or left; after which they turn right and left. From the single *borica*, the rest are formed by simple repetition; the double simply repeats all the movements twice; the triple, three times; while the sequel "Turkish" increases the *allegro tempo* of the first parts. The Turkish *borica* was formerly a mime dance. The music was, at first, different for all four parts, played on the *koboz* (like a lyre).

[See *Szekler Legënyes; Spiesstanz* (Rumania)]

BOROROMA BOROMSI (Somaliland, N.E. Africa)
Two men surrounded by two lines of warriors,
perform an "attack and defence" so fiercely that
they seem to be joined in a genuine fight. This
Somali war-dance is performed in daylight; the
chorus of spearmen is chanting traditional war-
dance songs to simple drum rhythms; while the
two centre dancers use shield and small cutlass.
There are usually ten or twelve men in the row
on each side; they keep time by beating their feet,
alternately striking their spear or lance on their
cowhide shields.

BORTEN ABTANZ (Rumania)
A wedding-dance among the Saxon inhabitants of
Rumania, to mark a bride's newly married state.
The *borten* is a flower-pot shaped hat worn by unmarried maidens, made of black-velvet-covered
pasteboard, with wide ribbons hanging almost to
the hem of the dress. The colours of the ribbons
vary, according to each village. On her marriage,
the bride lays aside her *borten* which is "danced
off". At midnight on the wedding-day, married
women among the guests join hands, two bridesmaids taking the bride (wearing her *borten*)
between them. In a wide circle, they dance backwards and forwards round the room, sometimes
closing in to a group in the centre, sometimes
opening out, until (either accidentally or on purpose) the ring is broken, when all rush into the
courtyard still holding hands. There follows a mock
struggle in which a young man tries to steal the
bride's hat, defended by her brothers or relations,
but always ending with the loss of the *borten*,
when the bride is led indoors by her bridesmaids
and solemnly invested with her new white cap
and veil, held with silver or jewelled pins.

BOT-MAU (Malekula, New Hebrides)
A torchlight processional dance performed on the
eve of the great sacrifice, the culminating rite of
*Ramben** and *Maki-Ru** on the Island of Vao and
other Small Islands off the mainland of Malekula.
In honour of the tusked boars about to be sacrificed, represented by the symbols held by the
dancers, it is danced as many times as there are
sacrificial boars. The dancers, mainly women, move
in double file from end to end of the dancing-
ground, in a serpentine movement called *tel-telean*.
Each holds in her left hand a branch of the *tawó*
tree, and in her right a torch, the lighted end of
which is dragged along the ground behind her. Two
men head the procession, and two more bring up
the rear, each of whom also carries a lighted torch,
but held high above the shoulder, with the *tawó*
branch. *Bot-mau* interrupts the circular *Taur Na-
mbak,** which continues throughout the night pre-

ceding the climax of the *Maki* ritual-cycles. When
each procession withdraws, the circular dance is
resumed. Wooden slit-gongs accompany *Bot-mau*,
the serpentine running movement of which has its
special gong rhythm called *ril-dralen*.
[See *Malekula*, Dances of]

BOUFFONS (France)
Another name for the 16th century *Mattachins* or
Matassins,* in which men in gilded, mock armour
performed sword dances, or mimic fights. Described
at length by Thoinot Arbeau, the 16th century
writer of *Orchésographie*.* the dance was popular
in France, and in England was known as *Buffens*.

BOULÉ (Hellas)
Athens had various administrative groups of citizens; secular (so far as operations in Greece were
secular at that period, 400-100 BC) as well as
religious. Among these, the principal city group or
gild, was the *Boulé*. This standing committee had
several sub-committees (*prietany* etc.) and a related
group known as *ekklesia*. As the system of the
Khrestiani had settled into usage of Greek language, ceremonies, and doctrines as a core, so their
written documents were couched in Greek. Terms
used in them moved easily from secular to religious
form, and back, during formative years. The *Boulé*
issued its edicts; they were adopted in Rome as
Bullae, later as the "Papal Bull" (as well as charms
for amulet protection, still carried by Italian
children). *Ekklesia* remains (*Ecclesiasticus*, as written), but *Boulé* changed into the Ball (or princely
meeting) and the Little Ball (council) or Ballet. For
all of these organizations there were ceremonial
openings. As Athenian traders and missions had
reached Ireland long before the Latin mercenaries,
so many Greek idioms became established; until
sold out by Abbess Hilda at Whitby in 668 to the
Latins from the south. *Boulé* became overlaid by
Latin forms: *bailey*, *bail*, *bailiff*—again in secular
administration; but in Spain the same Greek remained as *baile*, or dance. Religious groups, using
similar terminology, operated their shows and festival displays: for the *Bouleinoi* they matched with
parabolonoi—the acolytes or monks who acted
parables (see Hook's *Church Dictionary*), and
became notorious in the time of Bishop Cyril of
Alexandria, who murdered Hypatia with their
aid. They had already become the "bullies". The
Christian groups radically abolished the traditional
Greek mysteries; but had nothing much to offer by
way of adequate alternative. Thence developed the
so-called *Mystery Plays* and *Miracle Plays* (Parables),
which are still performed in the most backward
country of Europe, in Spain. The dance *cycles*
became Encyclical—"to send round". The *Boulé*

dropped into the parchment *Bull;* and the Cretan circus from Knossos had its *corrida,* its bull, as the blood sacrifice in the great public ring or *corral.* *Boulé* is thus one of the prime sources of the social function and name of the later Italian court ball and *balletto;** the dance becomes a ceremonial entry extended into decorative dancing, after serious business is completed.

BOULANGÈRE, LA — 1 (French)

A provincial couple dance, now apparently obsolete. *La Boulangère* was a Baker's daughter — who made bread and cakes. With her was the boy from *la boucherie,* who sold meat. Boy and girl, butcher and baker's girl, danced in couples, lighted by the holder of *la candélabre.* Facts are uncertain, but it may be the source of the English version :

> The butcher, the baker
> The candle-stick maker . . . .

This seems to have been a courting dance of familiar pattern in the village; perhaps the girl dispensed rolls or croquettes, to be eaten with snips of meat from the *boucher,* dancing in a circle round the central light from the candelabra.

BOULANGÈRE, LA — 2

La Boulangère was danced in the ballrooms of the late eighteenth and early nineteenth centuries. The music was in 2/4 time, and it was danced by any number of couples in *Cotillion* formation. After the grand round, or chain, each lady progressed from one partner to the next, until she returned to her place. When all the ladies had so danced, the figure was repeated by the men. The *Boulanger* is mentioned in *Pride and Prejudice,* when Mrs. Bennet recounts how Bingley had danced "the two sixth with Lizzy, and the Boulanger".

BOULÉ (Crete)

The Council of Elders who ruled the city of Knossus; much later, in Athens, one such group was named *Gerusia.* The thirty members had been elected from the experienced magistrates. We are not concerned here with the ever-changing balance of political and administrative power that varied the *Cosmi,* the *Gerusia,* and the *Ekklesia;* but to note that, in demands for precedence, this social expression of place and position was always claimed and used — from processional to ritual dance in ceremonial occasions of public character. What happened in the secret meetings, whether of policy or of mystical and religious proceedings, is little known; and must be derived from the known link with Sparta; and the grand affirmation of Lucian : "They dance out their religion"!

BOULEUTERION (Greek)

The House of Assembly (the *Prytane*) of the Athenian Counsel of State, the *Boulé.** The ceremonial entry to this building was the immediate ancestor of the later mediæval Ball, the similar "state entry" of an Italian duke and his company. The Council was broadly equivalent to the modern Cabinet, in relation to the *Ekklesia,* or general assembly of all the people, convened in the Agora (later, in the Theatre of Dionysus, when this was constructed). The Committees of this Ekklesia were the *Kuria,* members of the monthly meetings, called *prytany.* These forms were copied by the groups of the new faith in Antiocha, the Krestianian, when they organised their meetings. A notable fact is that no Latin terms have continued in the local church; but that of the different organisation of the augurs, on the Monte-Vate-Canes. This Grecian period in history is not the earliest origin of Ball, but this is a point from which we can trace related parts of the administrative and political organizations, many of which continue alongside of fluctuating civilian groups or societies.

BOURGEOIS BALLET (France)

Began with Abbé Perrin's theatre in Rue Mazarine, in 1671-2 three years after the last of the royal amateurs, Louis XIV, had given his last public performance in *Flora,* in 1669, at the advanced age of thirty. Within these years, Ballet turned from court to Commercial Theatre, on the financial basis. The Academy had been founded, with its "Table Ronde" of experts; but now the keen commercial sense of the Abbé, united with the financial support of Monsieur Champeron of the City of Paris. With Marquis de Sourdeac as Art Director (scenery and mechanics), and Mons. Cambert (composer) they obtained a *permet* from Louis; and went into theatrical management of the modern style. They produced a pastoral ballet called *Pomone,* for which Beauchamp (of the Academy) was choreographer. The five acts meandered on and off the stage, assisted by the ladies, to the best of their experience; and, we may be sure, of the pupils. The theatre was filled for eight months. This seems to have been the first "Long Run", which is the economic pivot for Bourgeois Theatre. The Abbé secured 30,000 francs, though his colleagues disputed loudly about their "fair shares". There was no touring company; and finally no theatre. Lully contrived to eject the directors. In *Le Bel Air* tennis court (near Luxembourg Garden), with Quinault to supply libretti, Lully produced *Les Fêtes de l'Amour* in 1672, in which the "Guest Artist" was the Duc de Monmouth. Ladies agreed to perform in amateur court ballet, but not on the professional stage; simply because the dancers of "The Theatres of the Fair" contributed their lesser graces. Opera ballet continued, with imported Italian dancers; in

London a similar perversion from National art was affirmed. Display necessities in dance conquered the amateur. In Paris, in *Le Temps de la Paix* at Fontainbleau, the Fair dancers (now mentioned as *femmes pantomimes*), provided the pivotal action, among the titled amateurs who got the "notices". Italian ballet replaced the amateurs for the Court; but the Bourgeois Ballet of Paris was then racing with London. One revolution had come and gone; the French Bourgeois Revolution was to come; in England the Royal Society preceded the *Academy de Danse*.

BOURÉE, LA—1 (Auvergne, France)
Most characteristic dance of the Auvergne, known also in Limousine. *Bourrées* of various districts differ only in the figures, the step being always the same and in 3/4 time. The rhythm, character-ised by numerous cross-beats, is not that of the valse, although in three-time, being harsher and more lively; neither is the step a valse step, although often wrongly confused with it. The beauty of the dance lies in the perfect execution of the *pas de bourrée*, which is used throughout by couples, who revolve *sur place*, move round in a circle, or in a chain. Sometimes they advance or retire, but most often the movement is lateral. Although basically simple, the *Bourrée* is difficult to perform, figures following each other rapidly, and the tempo remaining quick. Dancers' heels are often raised from the ground; the man's knees, slightly flexed, are a little apart; arms bent upwards with hands at shoulder height. He snaps his fingers on each first beat. His partner holds her skirt at either side. There are many *Bourrées*, such as the *Bourrée à Quatre, Bourrée à Deux*. The *Bourrée de Saint-Fleur* belongs to that region and to the Cantal; can be danced by any number of couples and has seven figures plus *entrée* and *sortie*. *La Montagnarde* is a *Bourrée* from the Mauriac region and the Cantal for groups of two couples. It has five figures. In the 19th century the Auvergne *Bourrée* was con-sidered by townsfolk to be heavy and uncouth, being danced in wooden sabots or hob-nailed boots, with a stamp marking every third beat. As danced today it is lively and graceful, with a pleasing rhythmic "to-and-fro" movement of the men's arms. Singing sometimes accompanies the dance.

BOURRÉE—2 (Bourbonnais, France)
An ancient dance, said to have been known by the Gauls. Varying considerably from the Auvergne Bourrée, it is now in 2/4 instead of 3/4 time, and has different figures and different style of dancing, being smoother and more languid. Danced by couples facing each other in a double line, it is preceded by a courtly introduction called *Le Didou*.

When the music begins, each man advances to his partner, hat in hand, kisses her on both cheeks and retires to his place. When the introductory music is finished, the men again approach their partners, take them by the hand and lead them into the dance. The vielle (hurdy-gurdy) or musette (bag-pipes) accompany the dance, which retained its popularity in the countryside until the second half of the 19th century, when it was displaced by the *Quadrille.** This quiet, elegant *Bourrée* became popular at the French court in the 17th century, during the reigns of Louis XIII and Louis XIV, having been introduced to the Court of the Valois by Marguerite, daughter of Catherine de Medici. In the middle of the 17th century, its popularity spread to England as the *Bore*, or *Borry*. Purcell wrote music for the *Borry*, and in France *Bourrées* were written by Rameau and other eminent com-posers.

BOUTADE (France)
A whimsy, an amusement; a term applied to some 18th century dances; or occasionally implying the whole evening performance. Less often, the name *boutade* was used for a light ballet in frolicsome style; or it indicates a musical composition. As a dance, the *affaire* was usually one of the "teen-agers"—it derives from *bout*, the end (of the week); *faire une petit bout de toilette* is to "dress up a bit, for a party", while *boute-en-train* is the "life and soul (of the party)".

BOY BISHOP—1 (Pre-Roman England)
Derives from *Epheboi Episkopas*, the youths of Hellenic rituals, as followed by the Krestiani of Antioch; and thence brought to Britain (first in Eastern Ireland and Southern Scotland) by mis-sions. With this ritual of Initiation came Greek terms, and a basic educational system; from which later developed the public schools (now expensively private) so that principal rites endured in scholastic (as at Winchester) as well as church forms. Thus the Boy Bishop is older, in form and ritual, than any christian *kirke;* though its principal mode dis-appeared from England at the time of the Refor-mation. Lesser details continued.

BOY BISHOP—2 (England)
Refers in its *third* phase to a ritual series of social and church ceremonies that belonged specifically to the 8th to 12th century Latin method of prose-lytising the young; as connected with older cere-monial pertaining to *Nikolas/Katherine** initiation rites. The dance ritual has vanished from England; elsewhere a small part remains, as for example, in Seville, in the *Seises** Dance at Easter. Broadly, the method handed over all the offices of an organised

church to the choristers and novices. For the period, from the day of "Sante Nicodeme" to the concluding day of the *Kantel-Messe* (then February 1st), the youths carried on the offices, covering the transition from the Old Year to the New Year. Finally, these groups were summarised as "Children of the Chapel Royal" or "Children of Santa Powle", and were retained through the whole year, to serve as choristers in liturgical services; and as actors or dancers or pages in the periodical feasts. They became practically professionalized, during the last prosperous period of the Latin church — from the 13th to the 15th centuries; when naturally the character and quality of precise ritual lapsed into abeyance, as the ornamental functions began to increase; so that the legends have lost in clarity while the original social purposes of the rituals are obscured. The inclusion of trained groups of boys or girls in Greek or Latin rites was a similar practice, dating from the foundations of these religions. They are found under many names; their duties are usually as minor assistants; rarely do we find even temporary prominence of the full official performance of duties.   [See *Nikolai; Camilli*]

BRANDO ALTA REGINA (Italian *balleto*)
Is described by Cesare Negri, as arranged for Margherita, Regina de Spagna. The basic dance is a variation of the French *branle** form; and obtained this particular title (*circa* 1598) after the accession of Fillipo III. This *balletto** contained a sequence of dances (in the manner of a modern ballet), which consisted of *Intrada* with *Contrapasso*; then *Salterello**; and *Gagliarda*, all of which were repeated (doubtless with certain variations), and completed by a *Finale*. The *Intrada* or *Entrée** was essential to any *festa*; and, as *Introit*, was used by the church; though this *Brando Alta Regina* was danced by partners as "nymphs and shepherds".

BRANLE (France)
Engl. *Brawl;* Ital. *Brando;* Sp. *Bran.* A French round dance of 12th and 13th centuries, belonging particularly to Poitou. A form of *Carole** (a linked circle dance, with sung accompaniment), the *Branle* was performed out of doors, dancers holding hands or hooking fingers. *Branler* means "to swing", and refers to the characteristic movement of the circle from left to right alternately. Steps to the right were made very small, so that the ring gradually moved round clockwise. Although in a chain or circle, dancers were in pairs, the man having his partner on his right. *Common Branles* in duple time, were the gravest form of the dance, performed in smooth, sedate style, by older people. More sprightly versions were the *Branle Gai* and *Branle de Poitou*, in triple time, the circle moving

always to the left. Younger married people might dance these, while the *Branle de Bourgoyne* for the youngest folk was in still lighter style and quicker tempo. An energetic variety was the *Branle de Hault Barrois*, which required continual hopping, combined with expressive movements of arms and shoulders. Arbeau's *Orchésographie** (1588) gives instructions for dancing the *Branle*, which in France was everywhere popular during the reigns of Louis XIII and XIV. At court it became a ceremonial dance, used to open important balls; and in the Court Masques mimed *Branles (branles morgués)* were danced as ballets. Today the *Branle*, as a folk dance, is still performed in several districts of France. In England, as the *Brawl*, it was much in favour at the court of Elizabeth I, and continued into the reign of Charles II in a slightly altered form. In his *Diary*, Pepys twice mentions the *Branle* — in 1662 and 1666.

BRANLEGAI (Med. French)
The type of French dance called *branle* had many forms; this was resolved from *le gai sabre* — the "secret science" of *chevallerie*; and gradually passed into the modern French crack, *Folle comme le branlegai*, or, in English, "As merry as a cricket".

BRAT (English, from Russian *Bratye*)
Term used earlier to denote junior members of an itinerant company. As they were usually the children of the players — dancers or musicians, the word reverted to its ancient meaning : as in India *Bratye* (from *Bharata*, the socially united company or brotherhood). In Europe, the word turned to *fratye, frater, friar,* or *friere*, denoting itinerant members of a propaganda band, performing plays and dances. In Germany a parallel term *ratye* or *rath* carried a similar meaning, which has endured to this day, to denote the junior members of a dance company (as in France, at the Opéra where they are called, without any disparagement, "rats"). In India the word survives, as in Bengal, where meetings are held with simple ritual dances, to support the *bratya* (religious fraternity).

BREVIARY (Latin catholic system)
Usually compiled in a Book of Hours for individual usage. This scheme follows ancient Egyptian traditions, which prescribed a daily ritual of hourly prayers, chants, or ceremonies. Though considerably modified, the Latin sect lays great stress on the recitation (of extracts at least) from the Breviary by all the *fidelium*. The association of the Breviary with sacred ritual dance is not now so clear as once it was; for it has been led rather in the direction of more complex music, than in the position and gesture of ceremonial. The usage of gesture and dance has remained much closer to the

other half of the ritual process; namely the *mass* (which see), though now dissociated from its original association with a feast or *messe*. The Breviary sets forth an array of "offices" now arranged to begin at sunset (in the Jewish fashion of the day period) with Vespers. Then follows Compline, and the Three Nocturnes (now familiar in musical form), with the sunrise time of Matins; then Lauds (praise), with Prime, Terce, Sext, and ended with Nones. Originally there were twelve periods of the day; and as many by night. Dropped are the Vigils (though followed in consecration of knights), and Orisons or Orantes. Breviaries (*Season Dances*) are printed now in four volumes : one each for Winter, Spring, Summer and Autumn season. Only in mediæval prints of such Breviaries as that for *Sarum Use*, can we find ordinary directions for position and gesture in the offices as ceremonies of movement.

BREZAIA (Rumania)
A festal rite with dance, performed on the day before the Winter Solstice celebrations.

BRITISH FIRE FESTIVALS (Ancient Celtic)
Belonged to the Solar Worship. At first the year was known in two parts : Winter (from November) and Summer (from May) but further instruction astronomically laid down the Four Fire Festivals— at Solstice as well as Equinox, as the grand circle of the year was divided into four. These were
    Samhain celebrated November First
    Oimelk celebrated February First (King of O)
    Beltane celebrated May First
    Lughnasad celebrated August First
All of these feasts had a Fair or Market, a feast and a dance, following the solemn rituals that opened proceedings. This pattern occurs all over Europe. Exact dates have varied owing to precession. Thus the old Winter Yule moved to January 6th, formerly the Messe (Feast of Crossing). Summer Yule belonged on the high-sun-day.

BROWNIE (from Arabic; *al beruni*)
Mediæval West European term, obtained from the Moorish invaders. *Al beruni* were small Arab boys, used as pages or footmen, in most large Moorish houses in Spain. The practice continued in England with the coffee houses; young Arab boys acted as waiters; while, in Russia, aristocratic custom imported a few young Arabs or Negro boys, to act as door-keepers (*dvornik*) or messengers. Then they entered ballet, as in *The Sleeping Beauty*. The name remains as a popular reference in provincial England; whence the notion that "brownie=fairy" Possibly, this is the origin of the family name. Brown.

BROOM DANCE (Scotland, Med.)
Witches' Broom Dance is said to have been a regular practice, (a) on a journey to the coven (monthly meeting) (b) in ring dances in the ceremonial. Accounts make it resemble children's hobby-horse dance games; but the witch used a branch of living broom, with a tuft of leaves at the sprig (as the earlier Maypoles, newly cut, had to be). Later aspirants used a handled besom, birch twigs, and then red ribands were attached. The witch bestrode her magic steed, as the ring of twelve moved rapidly round their leader in the centre. For example, Beltane Eve was celebrated (before Ruad Dag) at Aberdeen on the Hill of Katerina (this, in 1597). They carried fir candles or torches. One dance—done by Isobel Sherrie, was named *Tinkletum-Tankletum*.

BRUICHEATH (Scotland)
Gaelic title of *Battle Dance*; known also as Dirk Dance,* performed by two men or youths, armed with dirk and targe (round buckler, or shield). Danced usually to bagpipe strains, *Bruicheath* requires extreme agility with a marked sense of rhythm; being in this respect similar to some of the Indian dancing combats; and probably much like the old *Pyrrhic** dance.

BRUISH (N. Ireland)
Term equivalent to Scots *infare*, meaning "to haul a wife hame", a rite always requiring the services of the piper for the dancing. There was more or less of a ceremony; but always more of a feasting; beer was home-brewed and even whiskey was but a shilling a quart, for the country had not been "liberated" and *potheen* was held high in estimation in Munster and Connacht. Among the "Dances Home" was the *Jig Polthogue* and the "Dance to Bed" was preceded by *Kiss My Lady*, after which bipartition of proceedings, the guests murmured "Let's dance the *Hora Lheig* in the barn 'idout".

BRUMALIA OR *Bromalaea*—1 (Greek)
From *Brumius*, a functional name of Dionysus, as "The Noisy God", (*Bromos*), alleged to be associated with the typical rejoicings in the Bacchic revelries; probably belonging to the Festival of the Old Year (dying) and the New Year (coming to birth). The name became attached to the bush or yellow broom, said never to be "out of blossom"—that is, eternally returning; and also the brush, or broom, which proverbially when new always "sweeps clean". Hence it is the *bromalia* of Februare or the time of cleaning. The broom (bright yellow) was associated with Diana the Golden Moon (also ever-returning), and belonged to the ritual of the Temple of Diana in London; displaced by a Saxon temple

to Urken-waldus; and this in turn replacing the Apollo dedication by Powles, and the "Paul" (by Mitellius 7th century).

BRUMALIA — 2 (Roman)
Festival of winter-burial, a feast, sweeping out the Old Year. From it comes the ritual of Old Sant Powles and the Abbot's Barumalia or Bromley, Horn Dance.* An old custom, observed for centuries at Saint Paul's Church, London, derives from the Greek sacrifice to Diana, of a buck and a doe. It was ended by W. Baud in 1375. On the commemoration of the later "saint" the processional of schoolboys was held; but the buck was brought now to the West door on this day, and received by Dean and Chapter, giving twelve pence to the hunter. The carcase was "offered" at the high altar, by the Dean, properly apparalled, and all wearing rose garlands on their heads. Head and horns were fixed to a pole or cross-beam; and taken in procession round the church, to trumpet notes. The city guards answered on their horns, for which they had reward. The deer keeper had five shillings and a special loaf of bread.

BUCK-AND-WING (USA)
A vague term that changes according to dances, exhibitors, and teachers; related to tap-dancing crooning or spirituals; cake-walk* dance competitions; and "minstrels" of the American music-hall. This uneasy tradition dates in unbroken but extremely wavering lines, from the first entry of the Irish immigrants; when, in the whiskey saloons of Manhattan — those of Kogan or Moloney or Tom Mooney — the boisterous experts in clog-dancing would mount the wooden trestle tables (as do dancers in Spain) and "show a breakdown". When the Negro element joined in (as it could not in the music-hall shows), then the "buck-and-shuffle" of their work-time imitation gave more syncopated rhythm to clog patter. In 1830, the Jim Crow style emerged in USA, which was what started the music-hall craze for "minstrels". Barney Fagan (about 1865) again developed tap dancing as a show item. Then the Christie Minstrels (in London around 1870-1880) got hold of the styles, to add to their comic songs. Humour gave place to mere technical speed of execution. Many of the troupes then active were white men (blacked out). Finally this amorphous technique climbed into the mime of early films. The Chaplin feet, like those of Little Tich (of Tivoli Music Hall) in London, reflected this extravagant footwork; but long before that, G. M. Cohan billed "Buck and Wing" in 1890. The Negro Cake Walk* had another spell of publicity; no longer in Louisiana but in Harlem; and, later still, this diverged to the ballroom with the Charleston*

(from South Carolina), and that forerunner of Modern Art, the Black Bottom. These are, so to say, temporary solidifications from the general mass of play-game-dance comprised in Buck-and-Wing. In They All Sang, Tom Barratt is summarised as saying:
"Buck and Wing started all the trouble. Buck and Wing is a bastard dance, made of clogs and jigs, and song-and-dance together; and it makes for faking. In a clog or sand jig, you can spot faking in a minute. Well, now they've got no dancing at all; only acrobatics".

BUCKINGHAM PALACE (London)
19th century Balls; Queen Victoria and her Buckingham Palace are almost contemporary. Charity Balls were organised, mainly by Albert, with the stated purpose of aiding depressed trades. The first was the Plantagenet Ball in 1842, to help get funds for the Spitalfields Weavers; dancers had to appear as characters of Plantagenet period. Victoria was costumed as Queen Phillippa, wearing a body girdle bearing some £50,000 value of jewels. Her husband was dressed as Edward III; Duchess of Cambridge was Anne of Brittany, with a hundred companions. In 1845 was the Bal Poudré, costumes temp. George II marked by high heels and high coiffures. Sir Robert Peel was present; and the Duke of Wellington was Butcher Cumberland. In 1851 was Restoration Ball, at which nobody appeared as Nell Gwynne; but the US ambassador was resplendent in blue velvet costume with a scarlet mantle.

BUCKLER AND SWORD PLAY (England)
Continued (after a break) until about 1600, when the change of fashion for "pointing and stabbing" (with rapier and dagger in Italian-Spanish fashion) displaced the older custom. The play of sword and buckler (shield) was a dance in combat form, regulated by music. The buckler was a small round targe, fifteen or twenty inches across, but the sword, probably a wooden weapon for dances, was a broad, flat blade three feet long. This dance was a sport for boys of all ages; probably it resembles the older Dance of the Salii* or the military Corybantic dance of the Mediterranean countries. Many old cuts or drawings in MS, which are preserved in museums (e.g. Cotton collection, British Museum) show youths in combat with sword play; their gestures are extravagant enough to prove that dance, rather than realistic fight, is indicated. Some of these pictures show younger boys; none are otherwise armed. In England the pastime grew so popular (aside from the required exercise of bow and longbow in systematic archery), that schools were founded. In some, the conduct of both masters and scholars became so outrageous

that authority intervened. In 1286 (reign of Edward I), an edict prohibited keeping schools, or public exercise of "eskirmir au bokeler".

BUFFALO DANCE (Dakota, USA)
Annual ritual dance by the Mandan Indians, which celebrated the opening of the yearly buffalo hunt. This animal was highly important in the nomadic economic system of these tribes; but the ritual, as such, was no "prayer for plenty" nor a "fertility dance", because they knew well they could do nothing about it. The dance revived technical methods of hunt for the younger men; they had to learn to "know how to hunt", so the experienced elders gave instructions. Some men danced the part of the buffalo; some as bulls, some as cows (for they had to avoid killing off the females). Buffalo skins were carefully selected and marked; horns were important. The hunters adopted a camouflage costume, also contrived from skins, but now (for the dance) painted in black, red and white. Each hunter held a rattle and a spear. In three days of ritual mimesis, the young men learned. Two grizzly bears (also fully disguised) acted as masters of ceremonies. The central ritual was the chant of success; the approach to the "four points" in search, is qualified by emphasis on the real direction, where they would soon be sought. These Indians wanted food: but they were fully aware that dancing was no way of getting it; the *mimesis* was an introduction of "work after faith". The main dance was a slow circle movement to a simple rhythm; the dance songs were expressed in more subtle rhythm. Catlin[1] thought that "buffalo were attracted by the rhythm".
[1] *North American Indians*. G. Catlin.

BUFFOON (England)
(French *Bouffon*; Italian *Buffone*.) General term for a jester or practical joker, a clown. This is one of a series of terms derived from *Bouphonia* (Greek) related to (a) an Ox-feast, (b) a shepherd or cattle driver, (c) a ploughman; and associated with the merriment of festival games and dancing. Thence are derived *buffet* (place holding food), and the *buffetier*, the servitor, who often "came dancing"; and even Norman "beef-eaters" (this is the original name again). As royal servants in livery, formerly servants for food (Yeomen of the Guard), they were the guard at table. The Grecian priest who slaughtered the sacrifical oxen was *bouphonia*. From his act arose a mock trial (appeasement), which in time turned to comedy. (The axe was "found guilty".) The *bouphon* then turned into the Ritual "fool" whose duty was to buffet the candidate; this, too, turned to comedy when the *Mores* rite came to England, and the whip was replaced

by the air-filled bladder on a string, as the Bessy dances round the Mores ring.

BUFFOON DANCE (Persia)
A comic solo dance performed by a male clown, in which the abdominal muscles were used to create a ludicrous effect. Covering his real head and arms with a black cover, a large face was painted on his bare belly, while false arms were adjusted about his hips, making him appear to be about four feet high. This apparently dwarf figure with enormous countenance, then wrinkled or expanded the muscles of his abdomen, to make the painted face alternately grin or droop.
[See *Danse du Ventre*; *Cifte Tel*; *Muscle Dance*; *Ouled Nail*]

BUGGLE DANCE (Scotland; Celtic lands)
Bugeil, shepherd, *bugeil-gan* a sort of madrigal, pastoral song (as *bugeilig*=bucolic). Buggle Day was celebrated March 17th, Shetland and Orkneys, when young farmers made a special corn row, a test plot. Its crop was taken from the rigg, preserved, and made into a Buggle Cake—a bannock trimmed at edge to be a solar symbol. The dance was a simple affair; music came from pipes or a horn, whence we get bugle, the call to the corn or horn dance. One tune remains in the army cookhouse call—"Come and get it"! and was at one time a march in time to the messe-table.

BUGEILGAN (Wales)
Pastoral song and dance, or the melody used for them; from *bugail*, a shepherd (indicated in *baegeilig* or bucolic), and broadly equivalent to the madrigal of southern countries.

BULBA (Byelo-Russia)
One of the many simple "work-dances" of this region. As *bulba* means potato, the dance mimes the planting, hoeing, or gathering of the vegetable. This folk dance is performed by one man or a group.

BULL-FOOT (step or pace) *Boustrephedon*
Dionyssian Greek ritual dance routine, frequently mentioned in Greek literature, usually dissociated from technical mode, and stated in lyrical terms. This "dance routine" is one of the most important styles of movement in numerous ancient ritual dances, connected with sacrifice of many kinds; and beginning (as its name implies) with the public display and sacrifice of a "prize bull". This ritual was performed in a guarded space, a rectangle, usually roped or walled off, around which spectators gathered. The bull was brought in charge of the *popa* (ritual slaughterer), as in

ancient Rome; and the animal was *displayed*, so that all present could personally be sure that the animal was in fact without blemish. This presentation involved the *boustrephedon* movement (the same as that followed, by necessity, in ploughing), in long rows side by side, and across the full width of the court. The bull walked back and forth, back and forth, until he arrived close before the altar, when the movement became circular, around the altar This movement was copied by the augurs in their inspection of the *templum*. Most important of all : it was followed in many Greek ritual inscriptions, so that we have to read the parallel lines also "back and forth" and not, as we have learned in our modern reading, to begin each line from the left (or from the right if we read Hebrew; or from the top if we read Chinese). The literary value of this *boustrephedon* appears in our "reading" of the god names; they were always functional; they told what the god did; and they told it in several ways, for all god names must be read also "back and forth", to penetrate their secret power. This movement thus became of primary importance in many ritual dance movements. The multiplicity of names (and functions) found, successively or at once, in the same entity, is illustrated in the career of a railway train. Its name at Euston may be "Scots Express", but on arrival at Edinburgh and return, its name, but not its form or main function, changes to "London Express". En route it has minor names : the "One-fifteen" only at a certain place; but it is also named "London train" by those who meet it. The ancient gods, being denominations of energy and function, thus received many names; these were expressed in ritual dance form and title.

BUNDU (Sierra Leone, W. Africa)
Is a name applied to several elements in the Mende women's Secret Society. The groups in the ceremonial are indicated collectively as *Bundu*; the typical ranges of masks worn by the old women (instructors and examiners) are known as *Bundu* masks; and these officiants bear the name while on duty. The tradition shows Ashanti influence; the ritual is occupied chiefly with the training and treatment of the girl novices; they must learn certain dances as part of their tuition, such as the *Buyan* (dance of "passed girls"). There are equivalent dances for boys in the *Poro* Society. The lesser-known dances belong to the older women alone, as mediums, for their spiritualistic seances of invocation and healing. Variations of the *Scarf Dance* ("shunt dem flies"!) are seen on every festive occasion. Four women stand in a facing-in group, each waving a large red scarf to the thump of the *balangi* (the Koranko tribal form of xylophone), along with a great variety of drumming

on different drums, single or double-ended. For the *Bundu* dances, girls act as drummers (they are rarely as good as the men) and the remainder clap hands, for tempo and rhythm. Dances thus form an important part of the women's secret society. Novices are taken into the secret enclosure in the bush, distant from the villages where they have lived, for an initiation period of about four months. They receive lessons, chiefly on the "facts of life", but including domestic chores, tribal legends and other essentials to Mondi life. Some of the instruction is imparted by chanted dances, on the basis that what is learned while singing and moving rhythmically, will be memorised rapidly. The girls, on attaining puberty, and "offered" by their parents, are taken away on a moondark night, coated in white clay, and marched to their destination. They also pass time in plentiful eating and sleeping. The "washing" that removes the clay daubing is equivalent to baptismal rites; by it the girl is "made clean" of all external earlier influences; in the *Bundu* she receives the essence direct of the tribal spirit. Her marriage, later on, repeats the baptism symbolically by white cotton attire; when she is again accompanied by women friends who dance attendance with drumming.

BUREAUCRATIC BALLROOM DANCE
Is the most recent phase of popular or "Social Dance" in Britain. The whole process is heavily draped with Official Organisation, run by Official Boards; and supported by Official Teachers, all duly labelled with their respective accomplishments, cups, certificates, and medals. Thus Dance becomes not only an Indoor Sport, but a National Industry, like horse racing; and almost a national game, like football. Sport Dance is followed in several distinct grades; from No. 1 Society Grade, down to No. 7 Proletarian Grade, each grade being "all very nice an' proper!" in its fitting environment. Apart from medical commendations—"You should dance for exercise, dear sir!"—Dance has not yet been incorporated into National Health, and equipped with Licenses and Identity Cards; but it has got a charter (which King John found to be the First Danger). The "Society Mode" tends to follow a new *basse danse* style; "the feet do not leave the ground!" While the proletarian or G.I. style goes to the other extreme and produces *Jive*, in which all feet are in the air!
[See *Hunt Ball*]

BURMESE DANCE—1 (Burma and Shan states)
Appear in two general modes, meeting in the *Pwe*.* The provincial or agricultural festivals continue : mostly as (a) New Year Feast, or the Water Festival; and (b) the February Harvest Feast when

paddy is reaped after eight months of field work. At the New Year Feast, young men dance along village streets; are caught by elder ladies who bind them and black their faces. They must do the "Monkey Dance" to obtain release by ransom. The obsolete *Nibhatkin** had many mime-dances, with its *Jataka* legends (Buddhist), Another range of village dances portrays the Thirty-Seven *Nats** or Nature spirits, alternated with *hawsa*, or recitations of stories in verse with mime and music (in troubadour style). The animistic *Nat* plays had a parallel in puppet-plays, some with significant animal characters, each of which performed a traditional and typical dance belonging to that animal. Burmese dances, unlike Greek dances, began with women; they have no war dance, no sword dance, as such; but celebrate a popular gathering like the "Feast of Fools".

BURMESE DANCE—2
Modern Burmese dancing then became professional; and helped to develop the *Pwe** or popular fair, with shows, singing, dances and mime, and water sports. Court dance-mimes flourished from 18th century, now revealing resurgent Hindu influence, with tales from *Ramayana*. In the reign of Prince Bodawpaya, a Ministry of Theatre was instituted. Village festivals continued in their folk-dance manner; ceremonial dances and plays developed in court circles; and the town *Pwe** combined all material it could obtain, more in a commercial spirit. Europe has seen very little Burmese dancing. A few individual dancers have visited Paris or London; and the technique has been shewn : it combines Hindu tradition with the Burmese theme in interesting fashion; and a virile influence has become apparent from older dances in the Shan States, showing some parallel with the *Bön** dances of Tibet. The general style is broad, like *Kathakali,** but with many slower gestures and positions. Scenery is unused except in small commercial theatres; while costume is good and colourful. Puppet shows continue their popular welcome.

BUSK (Amerindian)
Harvest and New Year Ceremony of Creek* Indians, held in July or August when the maize was ripe. Meaning "act of fasting", the name refers to abstention from eating maize, until after the ceremony. In large centres the *Busk* lasted for eight days, or four in smaller places, while in the rituals almost everything was done in fours (the sacred number), or multiples of four. Dances by both men and women occurred at points throughout the ceremony, held in the central square. Singing was important; also the drinking of emetics, and the sacred "Black Drink" made from leaves of

the Ilex vine. On the first day were performed "Crazy Dance" and "Drunken Dance", with dancers imitating such movements. These preceded the preparation on the second day of a drink made from roots; and further dancing took place before members of the Four Lodges solemnly drank. In the "Feather Dance", performers carrying wands six feet long, decorated with white heron feathers, danced round the square several times; then, whooping, rushed to the lodges, raised their wands high and thrust them into the ground. Finally came the ceremony of new fire, collected by women from the sacred fire and taken to their own hearths to start the new year. The *Busk* was an annual purification; when all houses were cleansed, old clothes and worn-out equipment were burned, and old crockery broken. The newly ripe corn and relit fires signified a new beginning. After the new fire ceremony, the sacred ball game of *Pelote* was played; then at sunset ceremonial paint was washed off in the river as a purification before the solemn first meal of new corn.
[See *Green Corn Dance; Aztec Dance*]

BYZANTINE DANCE (Constantinople)
Circus, rather than Theatre, either in Greek (Athenian) or modern sense, was the centre of most dance in Byzantium. As in Rome, imaginative drama did not develop; but religious drama continued its schizophrenic existence : turning myth into history and history into myth. Mimes were plentiful and popular. John Lydos says seven main forms of entertainment continued, in his time. The art mime, based on a poem, was danced to music; ranging also from social satire to mere buffoonery. Public scenic plays were performed, for banquet or weddings. Justinian (in the Synod of 591) forbade monks to attend shows or festival maskings. Some mimes, like the later *mezzo* or *interludus*, were used between races in the stadium. Menandros turned from lawyer to poet, and wrote *Death of a Persian Mage*, as a *tragodeia* for singing and dancing. Lindsay says[1] "The *tragodeia* in its dance-form was the ancestor of ballet. Experienced dancers could accompany any poem. Xenophon of Smyrna danced the *Bacchae* of Euripides. Libanios defends the dance-mime as superior to sculpture, as an art; and calls it the "school of beauty and recreation". The church was against dancer and mime alike. By the time of Theodosius the mime had fallen low; under Justin, full degradation had come. In festivals (inherited from Greece and Rome) Olympic games were held (especially in Antioch) with nightly shows. Women competed against men in song and music; probably also in dance. The Kalends (Solstice) gave a five-day holiday (with street maskings and wreathed mimes).

"In the tenth century, at a masked dinner at court, on the eve of Epiphany, the factions danced a war dance of Goths, with shields and staffs. The Goths danced; and the singers executed the 'Musical Alphabet' . . . In the Hippodrome, the Butchers' Gild danced and sang in two groups, an invocation to Spring".[1]

[1] *Byzantium into Europe.* Jack Lindsay (London 1952) p. 304-305.

C

CACHUA (Peru)
Pron. "Kashwa". A round dance performed by Indians in the Andes mountain villages. The music in 2/4 time is usually in smooth rhythm, without syncopation, and the dance is accompanied by singing.

CACHUCHA (Andalusia, Spain)
Literally describes a kind of cap. A dance in rapid 3/4 time, the rhythm being accented by castanets. The music closely resembles that of the *Bolero,** and originally the tune was sung with guitar accompaniment. It can be danced by a couple, or as a woman's solo, in which form it was made famous on the stage by Fanny Elssler. In 1836 in Paris, she danced the *Cachucha* in *Le Diable Boiteux,* a three-act Pantomimic Ballet set in Madrid. The same year, as *The Devil on Two Sticks,* the ballet was given in London, when Pauline Duvernay danced the *Cachucha.* So popular did this dance become that it was frequently introduced into other ballets. The *Cachucha* also forms part of the Catalonian carnival dance, *Ball de gitanes,* while in the Philippines it is known as the *Kuratsa.*

CADETS' SCHOOL (Denmark, Russia, etc.)
17th century. Included training in formal dance as an integral part of the educational system. At Copenhagen, the teacher August Bournonville began a tradition of dance training, during the period when he was engaged at the Imperial Theatre. In Petersburg, a similar system was in vogue for the School of Pages, as well as for the military cadets. Due to these systems, dancing is regarded in those countries as a fitting occupation for the male athlete.   [See *Schools of Dance*]

CAILLEACH AN DUDAIN (Hebrides)
"Old Wife of the Mill Dust". An ancient ritual dance of forgotten purpose. It was performed on St. Michael's Day, 29th September. During the day a special ritual, which always preceded the dance, was performed by the Islanders, who rode on horseback, sun-wise, round St. Michael's burial-place. Then, after cutting with a special knife a cake made with every kind of grain grown in the Islands, they entertained themselves with horse-races. In the evening the *Cailleach au Dudain* (which seems to be an initiation, or "death and resurrection" dance) was performed by a man and a woman. Standing opposite each other they circled and changed places, the man moving a willow wand over their heads. When it touched the woman she fell as though dead. Miming his sorrow, the man began to revive her. Lifting her left hand he breathed on it and touched it with the wand, when it slowly moved up and down. This performance he repeated with the other hand, the feet and finally the mouth, when the woman sprang up, and both danced joyfully together.
[Cp. *Mazurka; Morris; Calusari; Duboka "Dance for the Dead"*]

CAKE AND BREAD DANCES
Numerous dances have been associated with feasting, whether actual or ritual, in which some special item has figured prominently. "Bringing in the Boar's Head", for the New Year's Festival of ancient England, was done in ceremonial that developed into dance from rhythmic marching. The "Feast of the Swan" was similar in Western Europe. In Mediterranean countries, a pastry or cake with fruit was known as *Torte* or *tarte;* and among Jewish people, the *motza* belongs to the Passover and its dance, with the "mass-cake" as a changed relic of the same confectionery. In the South of France, the Carnival or Saturnalia dances were celebrated, with pastry ornaments of phallic derivation, which the dancers carried in the processions. (Italian women wear them today, made of coral.) In Northern England, the proletarian "Parkin Pig"—a slab of gingerbread in porcine form, with a currant as eye, appears as a simulacrum of the festive Boar of Winter; and numerous special local cakes, now famous more by name than by quality, formerly affirmed the celebrations. Eccles Cakes vied with Richmond "Maids of Honour" or Bakewell Tarts. The fearsome confection, enshrined in a sheep stomach and half of oatmeal, is such a festal dish, devoured by Scots at Hogmanay, along with bagpipe strains that keep the dainty a fitting company. This is Haggis. French churches, in their frequent fetes, called for special cakes or new shaped bread : brioche etc. Münich long had the twisted *küchen,* called *Pretzel.* The *marchpane* or *marzipan* is a spicy mixture with traditional associations : it was there as the "First-Bread" or "First man's bread" at the New Year. The Chel's Eye Bun is known as *buna* (Addis Abbaba. The head of the Church (who breaks the

round cake) is called *Abuna*. Nearly all of the associated dances, and their musical forms, as well as cake, have now vanished, before the assault of "homemade" factory-produced dainties, all made to "look like". Yet a few dances remain, such as the Negro-assimilation of the New Orleans *Cake Walk*,* revived by Irish settlers who demanded a bun or dough-nut, to test the required balance of competing coons.

CAKE DANCES (Ireland)
Were known from the early 17th century. They were accompanied by a piper, whose services were paid for by the dancers. The prize was a large cake. Henry Piers, writing on social customs, says of County Westmeath that the local ale-wife provided the cake, which was brought out with ceremony on a board at the top of a ten-foot pike. An advertisement in Dublin *Evening Post* (October 1st, 1734) read :

"On Thursday next, Mary Kelly, at the Queens Head in Glasnevin, near this city will have a

FINE PLUM CAKE

to be danced for by the young men and maidens of the country, who are generously invited by her, not doubting but they will be pleased with her Ale as well as her Cake".

CAKEWALK (USA)
A strutting dance of the Negroes of the Southern States (especially Florida), which probably developed from the dance called *Set de Flo*,* performed by slaves on the big plantations. In Florida classes were formed for teaching dignified walking. Pupils balanced a container of water on their head, and a prize of ice-cream or chocolates was awarded to the one who succeeded in not spilling any. Later, the prize became a huge decorated cake, which the winner shared with the other dancers. The dance which then developed from this special walking became a strut, performed with the arms folded across the chest, the head thrown back, and the whole body arched backwards. Special costume was worn for the dance when Florida became a fastionable winter resort, and the *Cakewalk* was performed for the entertainment of visitors. The men wore long-tailed coats with high collars; the women white fluffy gowns with bouquets. When the *Cakewalk* eventually reached New York (through Georgia, the two Carolinas and Virginia), special clubs were formed and competitions held, the best men performers receiving a champion belt, and the women a diamond ring.
[Cp *Calinda*; *Set de Flo*; *Negro Dancing in USA*]

CALATA (Italy)
A town dance, accompanied usually with lute music; and active during the 16th century through Italy. The form was a grave movement, similar to the *basse dances*,* with music played in duple time. Later a triple rhythm was developed for refrain sequences.

CALECON (French)
White pantalettes, linen or silk, as formerly worn by dancers of the Parisian ballet (compare the masculine version, *culotte*, and the cap, *calotte*), said to have been rendered more visible by Marie de la Camargue. She did not "invent" the garment, any more than the monks invented *la cagoule*; though it seems probable that Mons. Maillol (costumier of the Paris Opéra), helped to devise the *maillot* or longclothes version (later coupled with his name), as a close-fitting garment, more comfortable and more challenging, as suitable attire for dancers. Yet the close-fitting long stocking had long been familiar, even as an item of military attire. The *pantalon* had earlier been used in Italy by the Commedia troupes; the term became synonymous with buffoonery. The Spanish term is *calceta* (stocking, long), and *calcetin* (sock, short). The papal "required" version was *bas bleu*. (This information is added in the interest of H.M. Judges.)
[See *Tights*]

CALENDAR DANCES
From Latin *kalend*, part of the lunar month (ides, nones, kalends) signifying a ceremonial to mark each month. Hebrew forms marked chiefly the New Moon; Hindu, principally the Full Moon; but all the older religions that worshipped Moon deities did so as a recognition of the lunar function in marking earth time. Mexican systems had two calendars, side by side : the religious lunar periods, and the civil calendar of solar periods. Dances occurred at many points in both systems : the solar system is everywhere marked by the equinoxes and solstices; or "the quarters". Between these major points were many lesser punctuations of the year, marked by religious or civil celebrations. In Britain, most of them have been converted into spurious "saints days" — thus the June equinox is labelled "Saint John" as a version of the Santa-annum. Some days were selected to mark legal points, as in the *Foire (Furry) Dance** at Helston, Cornwall, used to re-mark ancient boundary lines. The principal period in ancient history was the Twelve Days Festival, which aligned the solar year to the lunar year, under guise of a feast, to bring the 360-day Year to meet the 365-day Year. In lesser range we find *Clock dance*, and *Tap dance*, used to record in local memories the passing days of the year; they were marked also by a tally-stick.

Further local points—marked by the local saint fabrication—were more ancient specialised market days or Fairs. Most of these have become shifted away from their real calendrical position.

CALENDRIA (Italian)
A famous comedy (including dance interludes) written by Bernado Dovisi (Cardinal) of Bibbiena (1470-1520), first produced at Siena in 1513. Bernardo was secretary to Leo X (in 1513) and helped in the performances of private ballets in the Vatican. The *Calendria* is based on Boccaccio's story *Calandrino*, with some plot from the *Menaechmi* from Plautus. This play is regarded as the earliest regular Italian comedy in literary form. Some hints on the general character of the Vatican ballets have been noted by Joseph McCabe in his *Lives of the Popes*, quoting extracts from Burckhardt's *Diary*.

CALINDA; *Calenda, Caleinda* (USA)
A mock-fight, danced with sticks by the Negroes of Louisiana where, finally, owing to wild behaviour, it was banned by state law in 1843. In the West Indies, where it originated, the *calinda* was danced by men stripped to the waist, who performed with a bottle of water balanced on the head. When any water was spilled the dancer was disqualified. In Trinidad, "Calinda"; and in Martinique "Caleinda", are names for calypso-type songs with traditional refrains, sung by the negroes at their work, with improvised words on topical or satirical subjects.
[See *Cakewalk*; *Set de Flo'*; *Negro Dancing in USA*]

CALOYERS (Greek)
General name of monks in Greek church; in Alexandria and Constantine they played as *parabolonoi* in presenting theological drama as stories of their day (see Dean Stanley, *Eastern Church, Byzantium*) and influenced the Latins who copied them. From this term arose *caloyer-istria*—the "monk-players", and thus their principal place of performance, the *C'lo'ist'ra*, later known as Cloister or Kloster. There were three degrees (corresponding to those in the western sect) called *archan* (novice), *Mikrochemi* (the ordinary or professional monks), and *Meghalokhemi* (the advanced, or teaching monks). With a chief centre on Mt. Sinai, they had large centres at Mount Athos (near Salonica), with buildings such as De La Panagia or Anna Laura (House of the Year). Later in France these terms again became changed: from the canon law came the secular law with L'Oyers; and thence the student bodies at Paris and other universities, with their Pere l'Oyer and Mere L'Oyer, as traditional figures. These monkish bodies were always the leading

itinerant propagandists of the sects, Eastern or Western; and they sought to attract village populations by offering short plays (*ludus*) with dances (some of them comical), and topical songs. During a thousand years, unintended changes were many and various; but sufficient remains to trace the unbroken popularity of religious or secular plays and dances, competing with the remains of earlier religious systems, such as that of Mithra, of Isis, or Apollo or Dionysus, and Manes (of Lydia) whose invisible power developed with the Manichaeans (and also Faustus).

CALUSARI (Rumania)
Calus, "a little horse"; plus *ar* means "Little Horse Dancers". A group of male dancers who preserve an ancient, now obscure ritual, concerned with driving away demons and sickness. Men initiated into the group number seven, nine or eleven. They dance through the countryside at Whitsun, starting on the morning of Whit Sunday and continuing for nine days, dancing from sunrise to sunset. Only pausing for food and sleep, they must never stand still but keep jigging, even when not actually dancing. Dressed in white with ribbons crossed over the chest, they wear spurs, and bells round the ankles, with a tall hat decorated with ribbons and flowers. Besides the Leader, there is a Flag-Bearer, who carries a pole with a cloth and a sprig of garlic attached; and the Dumb Man, or "Fool"—a comic, masked figure, who carries a sword or whip. The Dumb Man takes a vow of silence; and sometimes all the *Calusari* are silent throughout the nine days. Their initiation includes lying face down, close together, while the Leader and musicians (fiddler and zither player) step over and between them. Finally, each man in turn lies on his back, legs upright in the air. Two men hold his ankles between sticks, while the Leader whacks buttocks and legs with another stick, ending with three hard blows on the soles of the feet (shod). During the initiation period they learn the figures of the dance. In each village, they dance in a courtyard, the flagpole set up in the centre. Between each figure they walk round the pole once or twice. Dancing is very quick, with simple steps, but perfect co-ordination and rhythm. While the "Fool" dances alone, the others dance in pairs, side by side, sometimes in a horizontal line, sometimes moving round the yard. Each man holds in his right hand a staff on which he leans, the pairs being joined by a kerchief between their left hands. In Moldavia, in the 18th century, the Calusari wore feminine costume, spoke like women, wore wreaths of flowers on their heads and white veils over their faces, each carrying a naked sword. Now only the Leader and Dumb Man carry swords, except in the district of Muscel,

where all have wooden swords. The *Calusari* at Muscel also include a pantomime scene, in which the Dumb Man is "killed" and brought to life again. In the Banat, where, in late 19th century, the Leader held a carved horse's head, like a hobbyhorse, there is a "Dance of the Rising Sun" and "Dance of the Setting Sun". Other dances are "The Little Horse", (*Câluceanul, Câlusul*); "The Little Flower" (*Floricia*); "The Flower of the Little Horse" (*Floricia Câlusului*). Always connected with the fairies, who are considered harmful (especially during Whitsuntide—*Rusalyi**) the *Calusari* are protected by "the beautiful ones", *Iedele, Dinsele* and *Frumoasele*, and by the *Rusaliile*. Although bringing prosperity and health to the villagers, unless the *Calusari* strictly obey traditional rules, they will themselves be harmed by the very powers that protect them. Thus, at the end of their dances, they destroy and bury all insignia, then run away without looking back, to avoid a visitation of illness. According to tradition the Dumb Man used to wear a stork's head with moveable beak; and in Oltenia he is still called "beak" or "hare", the skin of which animal is carried on the end of a stick by one of the dancers, or by the Dumb Man.
[See *The Romanian Hobby-Horse : The Calusari* by Prof. Romulus Vuia. Journal of E.F.D.S.S. Vol. II 1935—pp. 97-9, 105-7]
[Cp. *Cailleach an Dudain*]

CALYPSO (Trinidad, Tobago; West Indies)
Dance-songs that have now become mainly songdances; that is, movement is slight though rhythmic, yet meaningless; attention being given to words. Topicality is the key note—satirical or humorous is the lilting commentary. South American rhythms are prominent; musical "instruments" are what can be found or easily devised, such as discarded oil drums or petrol canisters, tapped with rubber-headed sticks. The main form is thus the primary need for social back-chat in easy rhythm. Calypso dances include *shango; bongo;* and *limbo,* as danced in Port of Spain night clubs. Calypsonians now run commercial entertainment. Carnival is the high spot when a queen is elected in the New Orleans style.   [See *Mardi Gras**]

CAMENAE (Etruria, ancient Italy)
Also called *Casmenae,* and *Carmanae.* Their name derives from *carmen,* to prophesy. They were a group of dancing and chanting nymphs. Some accounts identify them with the Nine Muses of Greece; they are said to have entered Italy from Arcadia. In Rome their chief was *Carmenta* or *Carmentis;* they had a regular temple at the foot of the Capitoline hill; and festival altars at Porta Carmentalis. This name—and something of the

function—continues in the Carmen of Spain; possibly the *cante hondo** and *cante chico** also stem from the prophetic dancing chants of the Camenae. At the annual Festival, Jan. 11 or Jan. 15, the name was invoked with *Postvorta* and *Antvorta*—to "look back", to "look forward", by the women who attended, to hear chanting and watch dancers. They are especially the "way-finders"—*kamin.*

CAMERLENGO OR *Camarlengo* (Ital. Ren.)
Official in full charge of court ceremonial, feasts, reception and ball; ordered arrangements of visitors, weddings, dances and music; hence prominent in ballet organization. Compare major-domo (firstin-house) with steward, bailiff, *kammer-meister,* canon—all in similar offices.

CAMILLI, CAMILLAE (Ancient Rome)
Boys and girls, trained for help in Roman religious rituals, somewhat equivalent to choristers and acolytes in the later church mode. They were required to be "perfect in form, sound in health, and free-born". They were believed to follow in the traditions of the *kadmiloi,* who served the priests in *Corybantika* and *Curetean* ceremonies; their duties included ritual singing and dancing, in secondary or choral positions; and in Rome they served as pages in the matrimonial ceremonies. Probably they filled duties of bridesmaids and groomsmen, in the two processions to the temple. The name reflects also one of the grades in the Mithraic Mysteries—the *miles;* and this is linked with one of the Roman military ranks; which indicates the origin of the name Miles in Britain.
[See *Korybantes; Curetes*]

CAMPANILLEROS (Seville, Spain)
Companies of carol-singing boys, known as the bell-ringers, parade the city for the New Year *festa.* They sing carols old and new, helping themselves to musical rhythm by beating time on the handbells, metal triangles or spirals (made by smiths for them), and tambourines. Sometimes a talented youth will play a *bandurria* (kind of lute) though they seldom copy the gypsy's castanets; while the encroaching accordion is not thought proper by the older people, whose alms are sought. Before specially favoured houses (when cash donations are likely) some groups attempt a copy of the boys' dance of Easter week (*Los Seises**).

CANA (Spain)
A "couple-dance" of Moorish origin, said to be named from the Arabic *gaunia*—"song". In Andalucia it is accompanied by traditional Moorish songs. Another interpretation of the name comes from the Argentine form of the dance, which the

dancers end by forming a half-circle called *caña*. The *gauchos* who perform the dance call it *media caña*.

CANACUAS (Mexico)

An old marriage dance of Uruapan district of Michoacan, still performed at weddings, but otherwise chiefly danced to honour important visitors. In Tarascan its name means "crowns". *Canacuas* is danced only by young unmarried girls, in charge of an elderly man (a *carguero*), but a young man, *el indito*, dances a *jarabe** with one of the girls at a certain point in the proceedings. Wearing wide, pleated skirt with apron, embroidered blouse, necklaces, and ribbons in the hair, each girl carries a painted gourd bowl of flowers, fruit and lacquered clay toys. Music is provided by string instruments, including a harp. The girls form two lines, at the head of which the guest of honour sits. *Canacuas* consists of ten alternating songs and dances: 1. A song of greeting; 2. An offering song addressed to the guest; 3. A dance with swaying of bowls and skirts to a Tarascan melody *La Flor de Canela* ("The Cinnamon Flower"); 4. A song addressed to the guest, the girls in three lines, one seated, second kneeling, third standing; 5. *El indito* and *El compardito* (good little friend) arrive, the latter carrying a live hen or turkey. He is welcomed with a song, followed by dialogue sung between the *compardito* and one of the girls; 6. A variation of *Jarabe de la Botella,** when a silver coin is laid on the stopper of an empty bottle, and must not be knocked off during the dance; and *Jarabe of the Knot*, tying and untying a knot with the feet; 7. A solo love song, *The Flower of the Changunga*; 8. Another song *La Patera*; 9. Each girl approaches the guest, bows, and empties the contents of her bowl on to the table in front of him. The leading girl dances, holding an *apazaca* flower adorned with corn leaves. Alternately holding out the flower to the visitor and withdrawing it as he is about to take it, she ends the dance by keeping the flower (symbol of her purity); 10. "The petition" when, according to tradition, the guest must grant whatever the girls ask, or lose prestige.

CANARY — 1 (England)

Group dance, from *Carnary*, or funeral dance. Ripon Cathedral had a "carnery" in the crypt, called in 1500 the Crudd, containing an array of more than 9,000 bones and skulls. The *Carnary* was the processional chant sung for the dead, accompanied by a slow dance (like the Irish *caroon* or *croon*). The "canary" was later done in the cemetery dances of the populace, when they came to celebrate the All Souls Day in memory of ancestors, where they sang and danced in the cemetery garth. This slow dance was followed (as was so usual in funeral ceremonies), by a quicker and more lively concluding dance, before the "baked funeral meats" supplied the feast. There is no traditional dance known in the Canary Islands which resembles this "Canary", but Canary Birds come thence. In Ancient Rome, the *Carinae* were women who attended funerals, to march, to dance, and to weep as professional mourners. Later the term attached to *Domus Carinae*, Charnel House.

CANARIE, CANARY — 2 (France and England)

A lively dance in quick 3/8 or 6/8 time, popular in France and England in the 16th and 17th centuries. Shakespeare often mentioned *Canary* as, for example, in *All's Well That Ends Well*—"Make you dance Canary with sprightly fire and motion". Presumably the dance was similar to the Spanish *Canario,** but the name must originally have had a deeper significance than mere reference to the Canary Islands. The dance style seems to have been more or less Spanish and in Spain was thought to be accompanied by castanets. A 16th century description of Africa, translated by Pory in 1600, refers to a dance "which they also use in Spain and in other places . . . and is called Canaries", while an Italian *Dictionary* published at the turn of the 16th century describes castanets as "little shells such as they use that daunce Canaries". In rhythm, measure and character, the music for *Canarie* was very similar to the *Jig,** while almost identical music was used in Elizabethan times for the *Hey** or *Hay*. French and English composers such as Lully, Couperin and Purcell, wrote music for the *Canarie*, and the first musical examples of the dance are found in the harpsichord suites of Champion de Chambonnière (1602-72) and of Louis Couperin (c. 1626-61). With the first note of the bar almost always dotted, the music resembled that of the *Loure,** although differing in tempo, the *Loure* being slower.

CANARIO (Spain)

A couple dance in 3/8 time said to come from the Canary Islands; popular in Spain and Portugal in 16th century. Having much rapid footwork of the stamping, *zapateado** type, it was a courting dance in which the couple first danced together, after which the girl stood still while the man retired, approached, and again retired. The procedure was then reversed, the man remaining still while the woman danced towards him and away. The Spanish Court dance of the 16th and 17th centuries followed this pattern, opening with a formal reverence by partners standing side by side but obliquely towards each other; then advancing hand in hand to the centre of the dancing place. After dancing together with arms linked and then mov-nig apart, there followed the man's first solo dance (*Mutanza*), in which he danced before his partner. The lady danced next, then both together, followed by further variations for each dancer, and ending with both partners again dancing together. The *Canario* as a folk-dance was sometimes performed at funerals in Spain and especially in the Canary Islands, which may be compared with the *Jota Valenciana*,* and the *Jarabe** in Mexico, also occasionally performed as a funeral dance; and with the *Jeunes Vierges** in Mediaeval France.

CAN-CAN

These, and numerous allied words, indicate whole families of old dance forms, most of them distorted in name and in performance. The most famous (or infamous) is the vulgar *Can-Can* of the Parisian halls on Montmartre, done at *cafés-dansants* such as Mabille, Prado or Chaumiére; and the notorious Moulin Rouge favoured by American visitors seeking French culture. The *Can-Can* (also called *Cha-hut**) is chiefly a rhythmic display of multitudinous millinery surrounding a pair of legs partly attired in black silk stockings. For those ignorant of the biological fact that a woman has two legs, it may be an interesting introduction; otherwise as a spectacle it becomes monotonous. The *Can-Can* was performed by a quadrille of four maidens. The original *Kan-Kana* was nothing like this. A court form was known as *Le Beau Cana* (wrongly attributed to one Bocan) and danced in the 18th century at the Austrian court as well as in France. Other forms were those known in Brittany—the dance by the nine Khorrigans (or Khorokhans), or Muses, and those festivals which in Ireland revealed the *Huli-khans*, also becoming debased as *hooligans*. The *Holi* suggests an Eastern influence, as does the term *khan* or prince.

CANDIOTE (Greek)

Dance said to date from 1623 (though this is quite uncertain and improbable), known as a tender and slow, gracious dance for girls. A young girl conducts various figures; they resemble the intricate paths of a labyrinth, with suggestions of the legend as from Homer. Sometimes the girls are clothed solely in white, wearing gilded crowns; while young men appear in light dress of brilliant colours. The dance proper begins with a great circle, danced with full precision; then the circle opens (as does the *hora** or *kolo**), into one or more lines; and moves through numerous variations. The *Candiote* appears at many festivals, both in towns and at rustic fetes. This dance has been compared with the *Farandole*,* but the *Candiote* seems more complex, both in form and meaning.

CANDLE DANCE

A slow dance, when dancers carry lighted candles; a development from candle processions; funeral or celebrational rites. The type of dance is so old that its origins are unknown; probably they date from cave-man days. Some Candle Dances, such as the Sumatran *Tari-piring*,* have been included in London stage shows as "oriental dance", while the processional usage continued in churches of the Romish sect, along with its "other half" of burning incense. Some rituals (as at Easter in the Russian Church), require worshippers to bring a candle in the left hand; these are ignited from the single priest's candle, as brought up from behind the altar. Other forms of the Candle Dance require a candle-lighted hall; or even a town, as in the Indian *Diwali** festivals of The Feast of Lights.

The candle socket is stuck in a saucer; this is turned under the arm by way of gesture; rarely, the candle is swiftly inverted and returned to up-right. It is considered "unlucky" to drop the candle; to allow it to go out; or to spill grease. Other candles, stuck with pins, were used to mark the passing periods of the rite. Traditional customs are explicit on the material permitted for candles; some specify pure beeswax, others are content with pure palm or coconut oil (as in the tropics), but other rites use animal fat as tallow. These recipes are considered important for the numerous Magical Dances in which candles or similar lights, from metallic lamps, are considered to be essential in ceremonial ritual. The early Christian initiation required the *candidatus* to be attired in new, clean, white vestures, carrying one candle which was lighted at the culminating period; when he became *acolyte* as he walked in procession into the central place. On the other hand, the Egyptian *khelu* had candles throughout his ritual; but left the vault to face the rising sun, as his achievement. In some cities, modernist "Fire regulations" forbid the use of naked lights in theatre shows; but the change to electric torches robs the whole scene of its ancient meaning.
[Cp. *Kyndeldans* (Norway); *Domare Dansen* (Sweden); *Ciri, Ball de* (Catalonia)]

CANDLEMASS (English, Mediæval)

A term derived from *Kantel-messe* or "Little Feast", so called (relevant to its date of celebration—2nd February) because only scraps of food are left from the *Cresten-Messe*, or Crossing Feast (December 25th) of the Winter Solstice. The term *kantel* signified small divisions, or sections (also as *cantell*) of the bread; and the *messe* was always the group or company ceremonial *feast* (retained in "Officers' Mess" or "Sergeants' Mess"). The conversion into "candle" might suggest the Widow, searching for her small fragment, her mite. The old ceremonial dance was small in step and movement, as the dancers now carried lighted candles. We may compare the dance form with the *Torch Dance*, or the many modes of *Branle**. *Cantel-Messe* was celebrated in the Inns of Court, at Lincolns Inn, when the judges danced; as forming part of one of the Revels of the Year. This was renamed Purification. *Kantel* is described (*Tekner's Deutsches Worterbuch*) as "*Viertantige walze als lineal; zu kante*". *Kandyl* is an Arabic word for lamp. Kanten is an end crust of bread.

CANDLE RUSH (England)
Also called Leap-Rush, was danced only by young girls (originally for the Sant-Katerina ceremony of Cantel-Messe on February 2nd or February 14th). For this indoor singing-dance, they placed a single, lighted candle, firmly set in its holder, in the centre of the floor. Then they persuaded a fiddler, or other handy musician, to mark the tune for them, drew up their skirts, and performed a round dance, in which all the girls, in turn, must leap over the flame. The words of one song went:
"The tailor in Bicester, he has but one good eye,
  He plies his merry needle, to finish he will try
  To sew us pairs of gallagaskins,
      Green gallagaskins—
To sew up pairs for us, if he were soon to die!"
The words vary, so does the tune, from village to village; it has rarely been heard in this century. Gallagaskins were high leather shoes which were part of the married woman's costume (as snood was changed for coif), at one period.

CANEVAS (Italy)
The painted "chart of plot" used by early Mediæval Italian companies (later known as *Il Commedia delle Arte*), and hung one at each side of their stage, out of sight of the audience. They possessed a repertory of memorised plots; but exploited each theme according to time and place; a short version, or the full (according to the likely income). The *canevas* gave a main *pictorial* outline. For this reason the painters, who delineated these according to instruction (with Interludes, or Dances), referred also to their productions in theological propaganda, as *canevas*, and then "canvas". This profitable use of art for stage purposes was one of the urges that prompted painters to work on the portable canvas (stretched on wooden frames), instead of using solid and heavy wooden panels; or on plastered walls. From the technical term, *canevas* became the thematic term; and thence the verbal term (to "canvass opinion", by argument). We should note contemporary usage of similar devices; but now for each individual actor, con-

taining his main instructions, and given to him in a roll. Hence the parallel term "role". Along with this went the smaller and cheaper *carte*; belonging more to ritual than to public entertainment.

CANNIBAL DANCE RITUALS
Exist in many parts of the world. Human beings are killed, more or less deliberately, for many reasons; but the essential purpose in these rites is a ceremonial feast, concerned with (a) living blood, as the *host* or *sacra*, or (b) the flesh, as part of a sacramental meal. Where these have vanished, references remain in ceremonial chants or hymns (blood of the lamb, blood of the saviour, etc.) and, half-way, animal substitutes are killed ceremonially, instead of human victims. There is often a double form of dance: the processional (to place of slaughter or burning), and the solemn encirclement of the victim on the altar (comp. the offer of Isaac, and others, in Old Testament records). Headhunting is a different phase of the magical process of "eating for strength", and the economic process of eating those who die accidentally (in shortage of food), or the terrible famine pressure on the young, are again events apart from ceremonial cannibalism. These are connected with the immensely widespread ancient knowledge of *mana** (or pranic energy), before the development of semi-scientific agriculture. Modern cannibalism retreats to animal victims; the holocaust of traffic on the roads does not appear.

CANOE DANCE (Sierra Leone, W. Africa)
A dance of the Mandingo people, which combines dancing with rowing. The oarsmen place one leg on the bottom of the boat, while the other is raised to a seat. While paddles are plied vigorously at the same time, with a rapid leg motion, the oarsmen maintain rhythm in rowing, lift themselves on to a seat with both legs, and, still rowing, each throws one foot backward and upward into the air, balancing on one foot and not ceasing to use the oars. A mournful song is chanted, which preserves the rhythmical basis of united movement.
[Cp. *Hula; Uli-Uli Noho*]

CANON, *Kanon* (Greece)
A measure; to measure, or "to set in order"; the implement of measure, in fact, or ethically; in dance, a selection of time-space measure, which seemed to have been used in Hellas as a simple mode of "one step; one note; one syllable", process of the litany. This chanting-dancing was accomplished over the permanent diagram of the *orkestra* (dancing place), in the well of the open-air theatre. Later the Arabic *qanun* seems to have fol-

lowed in a similar kind of system. In modern time, *canon* is a relatively archaic term in music, which refers to musical rhythm and its measure.

CANTAR MAGGIO (Italy)
Literally, "to sing in May" songs called *Magiolati*, also *Maggiore*. *Danza Maggiore* is the dance of May, or the spring season. The names vary from the pure Tuscan (of Dante and Petrarch to the guttural Neapolitan or the sibillant Venetian. These dances appear at Napoli, especially in annual fête of *Piedigrotta*, which falls in summer. New songs are arranged, and some become popular; many are then used for artisan dance tunes; a number have two sets of verses, some are printed, but the others "as remembered" and satirical.

CANTE FLAMENCO (Spain)
Also *Cante Hondo;** these terms refer to "Song of Flamens"* and *Deep Song (Profundo)*. They are both intimately connected with grave ceremonial dance form, traditional in Spain for many centuries. The reading of *Flamenco** as "Flemish", on the supposition that "the song style was brought back by the Spanish soldiers from Flanders", is imaginary. There cannot be found, in Flanders, any similar corresponding song-dance or ritual, in mediæval or later periods. *Canta* is Latin; so is *Flamen* in its ritual association. In Seville, *Giralda* converts with *Hiralda* (the tower and its figure), so that *Honde* or *hondo* also converts with *gondo*. Traditions are these ritual dance-songs are far older than 12th or 10th century; clearly they connect with the Roman-Iberian priests, the *Flamens*. That the forms have been "taken up by the Gypsies" is a natural development — these energetic people appropriate and stylise the traditional music of every country they enter; but Hungarian *tzigane* differs from Spanish *gitana*. In Italy — a more difficult land — *cante* developed *cantata*, as with the Jews they had the *cantor* or *kantor*; and alongside in Italy there came (1) *cantata*, to be sung; (2) *sonata*, to be played; (3) *dansata*, to be danced.

CANTE HONDO OR CANTE JONDO (Spain)
Andalusia is the traditional centre for these songs, now joined closely with *Flamenco** and its style of dance. As Spanish, the term is said to signify the "profound or deep song", but (as with the alleged Flemish origin of *flamenco*) erroneous interpretations seem to have arbitrarily limited the ancient sources of these Iberian modes of dance and song. The attribution of *flamenco* to *cante hondo* is quite modern (round 1870), and is derived from *flamingo*. In fact, the variation *jondo* or *jonde* reveals the older tradition : the association not only with the long-dead rites of Roman priests, the *flamens,** but

with the solstitial festal celebration of Janus (later named as John or Juan). The *hondo* or *honde* belongs with the golden rising god of the New Year (hence *jaundicea, jaune, jonquilla*); but first celebrates the Dying Year in the deep song. After mourning comes rejoicing, with the merry dance. Even the initial invocations of *cante hondo* carry the reminder : "*Aye Aye-ee-Leila*", which vocables recur in the Scandinavian greeting of *Aup-Eeli-Aye*, for the returning sun, after "The Long Dark". The modern developments are numerous : they include the *siguiriyas* (Arabic origin), and *polos* (Greek), with *soleares* (also Greek ritual) and *granadinas, rondenas, malaguenas*; also the *saeta* and *carceleras*, sung during ritual processions in religious fiesta, not accompanied by the guitar, as are the other modes. The *hondo* appears in Italy, in Venezia, as *Barcarolle*, song of the *Hondo-lier* or boatman. The boat or ship is a most ancient religious symbol.

CANTILENA (Italy)
Musical term, modern, derived from ancient chant and slow dance movement — the *Canta-Laena*, or "Song of Mourning". This religious chant was widespread among the ancient people of Egypt and Southern Europe, in two principal modes : the Song of the Dead Horus, and the Lamentation for some recently dead friend. This processional slow dance with chanting was a parallel to the more jovial street dance, which developed into *passacaglia* (*pazza-calle*), and has some relation with other religious and secular chants.

CANTORI A LIUTO AND CANTORI A LIBRO; ET CANTORI A DANZA (Italy)
The mediæval musicians of popular support through Italy — singers and players on the lute and for dancing; some were themselves dancers. There are rare remaining groups, notably the *pifferari,** or New Year waits, who come into the towns, rendering village songs; and dancing in the same traditional style; and, as the players for the *Beffana* (12th night). They can be seen sometimes in the Abruzzi, Umbria, and Marche, going from house to house, playing their *Novena*. These *cantori* correspond to the Provencal minstrels.

CANTRIP (Scottish; Med.)
Dance-song, said to have been used by Scottish witches 14th-15th century. Facts about the genuine witch cult — and dances — are few and rarely reliable, being compiled by their clerical enemies. Village traditions can be searched; but most have been eradicated. The cantrip may be compared with *tripettos** (and St. Martin Dance*) while the

gillatrypes (or gille trypes), seems to suggest an origin in Gillies' Tripetto (*gille* being a name for the Fool, the jester, the servant). Auld Clootie (one of the numerous "divil names") was said to like a dance-tune called *Kilt thy Coat Maggie and Come Thye Ways with Me* (reminiscent of Robbie Burns in style) and another *Wullie the Bed will Fa'*. The song addressed to Maggie is included in Skene MS and the tune in *Ancient Melodies of Scotland* (Dauney. 1838, Edinburgh).

CAOINE (Ireland—Erse)
Pronounced *Keine* or *Kiene*—in Gaelic *Cumhadh*. The traditional ritual of song-dance for the dead; similar to the *Jota** used in Spain with a form of *Cante Hondo*.* The dance is solemn and slow; it may include also the processional movement to and from the grave; but the song rarely ceases. The "keining" is (or was) performed chiefly by professional experts, known as the *mena-caoine* (or colloquially as the "minnies"), usually four or even six in the group. The oldest led off the chant; the others followed in accompaniment; rarely with instrumental music, though a fiddler would be persuaded, if at hand. The *Kieners* followed their own inherited melody and verse; but the burden was always a lament, a continual question—"Why did you leave us?"—with praises intervening. The form is similar to the Roman *funus*; while the ceremony is known as the "wakes" or the "watch", and may (in mourning for a wealthy or esteemed person) last for seven or fourteen days. The custom is dying out; it has affiliations with the *coronach*,* and thus with crooning; with the "musical lament" or *Cumhadh*; and with *ochone*.

CAPRIOLE ALSO CABRIOLE
Immediately from Italian *capriole*, referring to alleged "leaps of a goat", but earlier from *Cap Ruelle*, the "dance of triumph" executed by a university student on receiving his cap (as modern students still rejoice on receiving a "cap" for cricket, rowing, or other sports). *Ruelle* was originally the "dance before the *ruelle*", the "circle of the king". The term cap or head is associated not with a goat, but the position of "first" as with chapter-house, chapter heading (*capitus* etc.), also de-capitation. In ritual and dance-drama, the many kinds of salute or flourish, with cap or hat, are notable in every kind of mime. The Latin *capriolus*, "to move in a spiral" is a more credible source, though limited now to botany (spiral in clinging stems).

CARDADORA, LA (Spain, Segovia)
A traditional dance in which sticks are beaten. Known also as *Paloteo* (analogous to the old par-

able plays, the *Palauto de Fideles*), it belongs still to the church, and as such is performed at festivals during June in the Provinces of Segovia and Huesca. The *Cardadora* is also a processional dance with songs, performed by a confraternity of young married couples; the song is shaped in honour of the last couple to join, who provide a feast.

CARDS, Dances of (West Europe)
Card dances have a certain parallel to figure or puppet dances : the card or figure is used as a symbol or emblem of some entity in a scheme of relations. Many such dances were originally ritual or ceremonial dances by living persons : others, on the contrary (like the flat puppets of some oriental countries, such as Java), have dancers who follow the jerky puppet motion. The *cartes* or cards have a long yet obscure history; they appear to have existed wherever any religious scheme had developed a complex ritual, and there was some material from which small symbols, pictures, *aides-memoires*, could be contrived. Through the immediate and obvious wastage of such ephemeral slips of material, bearing painted and later printed signs, we have few enough to present as direct evidence of their close connection with ritual and secular dance. The once-potent scheme of the Tarot cards has a long tradition, with two main streams : one in the earlier methods of religious divination (the culmination of the *sortes*); and the other in the lesser pack of fifty-two cards, now static in secular games, though used also for "fortune-telling". The card was, in brief, an assignation of character to the individual who "drew it", with his initial position in the course of play. Thus the card indicated his role; his temporary value; his powers in play. Painted cards were rare and expensive; but block-printed cards became plentiful with the advent of press-printing. They were not then newly invented.
  "About the year 970 Bishop Wibold of Cambray recommended to his clergy, instead of dice, a sort of spiritual *bezique*, with fifty-six abstract names represented by as many combinations of cards. *Gesta Episcoper*; Caramracans, in *Mon. Germ. SS.vii.p.433*".
Further :
  "Infessura . . . whose *sortes* point to some instrument, perhaps a pack of cards for fortune-telling".
(From a note in *The Renaissance in Italy* by Jacob Burckhardt. 1929 ed., p. 403, and p. 453.)
[See *Tarot*; *Canevas*]

CAREADO (Spain, Asturias)
From "carear"—to put face to face. A couple dance in two parts, with accompaniment sung by the

dancers. In the first part, the arms hang loosely at the sides, while the body sways from side to side; in the second part simple cross-steps are performed to the rhythm of the dancers' castanets.

CARGON DE LA MOJIGANGA (Southern Mexico)
A symbol carried in the midst of dancing groups at Tlacotalpan (a town about 50 metres south-west of Vera Cruz). The mediæval term means literally : "The Burden of Image of Desiring". The symbol appears (a long pole) carried by four men, who use it as a sort of battering ram as they chase the girls in and out of the bushes. The *huapango** (dances) are interrupted at midnight (just like the discreetly purged tale of Cinderella, who bolts at midnight followed by the Prince), by this ritual of the plaza. When the laughing girls return dancing begins again on the *tarimba* or dance floor.

CARIBBEAN DANCE (W. Indies)
Continues in its three main geographical traditions : in Cuba, Trinidad, and Haiti. All of the music with dance stems from three distinct origins : the native Indian, the invading Spaniards, and the imported Negro slaves. Native religion, with dances, continued in Hayti, as worship of *Le Vieux Dieu* (The Ancient gods) or the *Voodoo*. Over this was plastered a facade of catholicism by the Spanish priests; while equally ancient forms of Indian belief underly most Caribbean dance and music. *Guaracha*, Spanish Cuban in 6/8 alternating with 3/4 is favoured more by bands than popular dances. *Congo* or *Conga* is mainly African, yet centred on "Carnival time" as a processional. The costumed groups, as *Comparsa* or *Conga* dancers, carry great lanterns; and the best may win prizes. *Guajira* is named from the peasants of the interior, "guajiros" but has a Spanish measure in 6/8 imposed over 3/4, with guitar music,

CARILLON DE DUNKERQUE (France)
An old dance of Northern France, for any number of couples, consisting of Entrée, two Figures, and Sortie. The dancers enter "en farandole", and form a circle, men and women facing, hands on hips. The First Figure begins by alternately striking the right and left foot on the ground three times, *sur place*. After a pause, hands are vigorously clapped instead of striking the foot. The figure continues with turns *sur place* in an anti-clockwise direction. Then the previous movements are repeated but in clockwise direction. In the Second Figure the couples form a circle turning clockwise with a galop step. These two figures are repeated as often as desired. The dancers finally retire in line, as they entered, to the same musical motif. For variation, the dancers stand one inside, one outside the

circle, forming two rings instead of one in the Second Figure. The women inside turn anti-clockwise; the men outside turn clockwise.

CARILLON QUADRILLE (Italy)
A popular 16th century dance in Northern Italy (especially in Milano) was known as *quadriglio*, as well as by the French title of *Quadrille;** with the prefix *Carillon* because the music was played on bells, in the form of a *carillon*. This was a *salon* dance in the general form then fashionable as a *quadrille*.

CARMAGNOLE (France)
The modern usage of the word refers to a "Cardigan jacket", but the dance term derives from an older Romance name, linked with *carmen* (France and Spain), and traditionally indicates a chant of phrases and rejoicing. By some the name is said to derive from Carmagnola in Piedmont, across the Alps. The dance of the French Revolution (1792) was said by Grétry to have been brought to Paris from the Marseilles waterfront. In *Farandole** style, long chains of dancers ran through the streets, dancing round the "trees of Liberty" and the Guillotine, catching up passers-by, to the tune of a song by an unknown author, which then became known as "La Carmagnole". After the Revolution there was a change of sympathies, and a dance in *Carmagnole/Farandole* style was used by loyalists of the Monarchy. In 1815, in Toulon, an officer in the Bonapartist Army was caught in its coils and killed to cries of "Vive le Roi".

CARMINA ECCLESIA (Latin)
Clerical term used to denote various ritual-dance songs, in several categories. The accepted chants were relatively few; those cordially denounced by sundry bishops were named *carmina diabolica*; these alleged "devil dances" being those popularly celebrated in the churchyard (where there was one), or before the church building. Clerical denunciations extended to *carmina turpia*, alleged to be "indecent", accompanied by merry dances, similar to those of the modern Victorian music-hall. Some scholars name these *Carmina Saltatio* as incantations, used as conjurations over the bodies of the newly dead; for this purpose, the term *carmina* was most used technically by the clerics. Almost equivalent is the Spanish *jota** or *cante hondo,** or the Irish *crunan*. Regino of Prüm[1] believed that *carmina* were songs of mourning and praise, for the dead, sung while encircling the bier.

[See *Church Dances*]

[1] In *Migne. P.L.* 132 col. 243 (Paris 1853).

CARNAVALITO (Argentine)
Traditional modes developed from the imported Spanish *Tango;* and, like the modern Tango elsewhere, the *Carnavalito* has lost some of its basic twelve figures. The dance is a broad fiesta or "little carnival" dance, no longer with ritual significance. *Carnavalito* is found chiefly in the northern provinces of Argentine, especially Salta or Jujuy, performed as a collective round, danced by couples. In the original form, the company executed any of the dozen basic figures; now some are danced by a couple only, or by couples in succession. Ritual meanings forgotten, all the dances are light and gay. A typical melody of 32 bars is used by *Cholita Traidora* version—this includes eight main figures. They are: *El Circulo* (general circle, men outside); *Las Alas* (The Wings), or two hemispheres; *El Puente* (The Bridge) or "under the arches" of raised arms; *El Molino* (The Mill) with two circles in contra-movement; *Las Volterras* (The Whirling) men swing the women around them, marking the four cardinal points as breaks; *El Caracol* (The Snail) actually the spiraline of the old church dance, "*Jerusalem*"; or as in some forms of *kolo;** and finally *El Circulo* again as the completing round.

CAROLARE (Italian)
"To Dance". This European term appears in all the Romance languages in variant form. Equally it signified the round dance, or the *ronde* as poem, and, as melody. The difference of emphasis is seen in reference to one or other of the three forms. *Carolle* (Old French) moves with *Caral* (Old English), but *Corral* (Spanish) refers to the early theatre form, a closed ring. *Choraules* (Latin) goes back to the music, the flute player for choral dance. The Saxon *ceorl* (the yokel, villager, rustic, or churl) returns us to the country dancer, who also sang his carols. Chaucer writes of *karolling*.

CAROLE (Fr.); *Carol* (Engl.)
A Mediæval round dance performed by men and women in a linked circle, unaccompanied by musical instruments. The dance was regulated by hand-clapping and by accompanying songs, the verses sung by a soloist and the dancers taking up the refrain. The *Carole* was a popular pastime in the 12th, 13th and 14th centuries. In English lordly halls its performance, with other dances, often filled the time between dinner and supper, at 5 o'clock and so general was this simple round dance that the term "caroler" became synonymous with "to dance". During the 15th century, new dances replaced it, and the *Carole* developed into country dances called "Rounds", one of the earliest recorded being *Sellenger's Round** at the beginning of the 16th century. The remote ancestor of the *Carole* was the Greek *Choros,** the ancient round dance from which so many dances throughout Europe have evolved. Percy Dearmer, writing about Carols, says:[1] "The word 'Carol' has a dancing origin, and once meant to dance in a ring: (going back) through the Old French 'caroler' and the Latin 'choraula', to the Greek 'choraules', a flute player for chorus dancing, and ultimately to the 'choros', which was originally a circling dance . . ." Popular in France and Italy, Dante (in the 14th century) referred to the *Carole* in the *Paradiso* (Canto 24) as a dancing choir of saints— "*Cosi quelle carola differentimente danzando*". As a celestial dance it was depicted by Botticelli (in his *Mystic Nativity*). Among spellings given in various dictionaries are: *Carolle, caral, karolle, carowl* (Engl.); *carval* (Manx); *carull, caireall* (Gaelic— "harmony, melody"); *cory* (Irish— *reel* or *round*; Welsh—a choir, a circle); *carola, choraula* (Low Latin) and *Kralye* (Greek church).
[1] *Oxford Book of Carols*. 1928. Preface by Percy Dearmer.

CARRIZO (Venezuela)
A social dance of the Maipure Indians. Arms linked, the couples dance in a circle round three musicians who play six-reed pan-pipes. Spanish influence is suggested by the step used, which is similar to a Waltz step. At the end of the dance, the circle breaks up, couples dancing together, but not in any special formation.

CARROUSEL (France and Italy)
A form of "exhibition riding" to simple march music; done in a great circle or oval field; and marked by contests of two sides, by knights on horses. This tourney succeeded the more bloody contests, when the fights were more authentic, as in the *joust;* and preceded modern football. By the middle of the 11th century, Geoffroi de Preuilly had worked out strict rules for Tourney, which were followed through Western Europe. Dancing followed these tourneys, with the feasting, to which even the defeated men came. Muskets ended the tourney as a practical military method. Ornamental *Carrousel* came in when Henry II of France was killed by a lance while jousting. Intricate manœuvres, parallel to *la danse géométrique** in the *salon*, then replaced joust and tourney; finally the *fola** of the Neapolitan High School of *Manège* culminated in skilled horsemanship, with which circus*ballet was intimately associated, from the displays, as at Vienna. There the Riding School was inevitably used for the stage ballets. In Paris the *Carrousel* became attached to the Foire san Martine (and other *Foires*), with its temporary arch for gay

decoration. The last remnant of this circular dance of the animals is seen in the weary mechanical jig of the "merrie-go-round" of the English Fair-ground; where idlers may ride for a few pence on wooden animals (which rise and fall), to the roar of a steam orchestra.

[See *Horse Ballet*; *Circus*; *Fola*]

CARYATIDES (Hellas, Laconia)

Female figures, for us especially famous from sculptures in the porch of the Erectheum (at Athens), which represent the ritual maidens, bearers of sacrifices, made at the Temple of Artemis Caryatis. The annual Festival of Artemis was celebrated by the Lacedemonian maidens, with ritual dances. Copies of the porch have been made, one for the church of Pancras (Panchorus) in London. Other sculptures exist, showing two of the maidens alongside a small altar, bearing on their heads flat plates with the sacred cakes.

CASCARONE BALLS (California, USA)

Were held, in 19th century, from November to Lent, but were most numerous and gay during pre-Lent Carnival Week. The most brilliant were those at Los Angeles and Monterey; the custom still continues at the latter place. *Cascarone* were coloured eggs, emptied, dried, and with a choice of fillings, from home-made confetti of shredded paper (gold, silver, or many-coloured); to perfume; or, for special occasions, a small amount of gold dust. The sealed eggs were hidden until an appropriate moment during the ball, when a man would approach his chosen lady and break the egg over her bent head. Sometimes a daring girl would slip behind a man, break her egg over him, and disappear quickly among the dancers. In Spanish *cascerón* means "eggshell", while *cascar* is the verb, "to break in pieces".

CASCAVELLADE (Roussillion, France)

A dignified measure performed on one of the closing days of Carnival at places such as Arles-sur-Tech. There are four stages in the dance : —

1. Two lines of dancers face each other, one of girls, one of young men.
2. The lines mingle so that each contains an equal number of girls and men.
3. The two files have completely changed places.
4. They are again as at the beginning, having retraced the figures.

[Cp. *Entrellacada*]

CASTANETS—1

Sp. *Castañeta*; Fr. *castagnette*; Ital. *castagnetta*; Portuguese, *castanheta*—from Sp. castana, Ital. *castagna*, Latin *castanea*, German *kastenien*—"a chestnut" (from resemblance in shape to chestnuts). Instruments used to accompany Spanish dance; a double clicking pair of hollowed wooden shells, loosely linked by cord in facing pairs (one pair for each hand). The cord is looped round the middle joint of each thumb. Made in two "voices", they are carefully tuned by cutting the hollow to approximately a "male" and a "female" note. Best known in association with modern Spanish dancing (*flamenco* style) they are far older in origin and, made in metal (brass or bronze) and ivory, they range into Indian cymbals or North African *neuk'sat*, held on the fingers in similar but not identical fashion. Their probable origin was to enhance the world-wide practice of "finger-clicking" included in rituals used to "banish the dead", and associated with asperging by water. Correct, professional use requires really expert playing. When well played, castanets add a thrill to the best Spanish dance, affirming the time of dance rhythm with ornamental additions, parallel to expert drumming for other dances. The mechanical castanets too often added to a modern theatre orchestra are a deplorable and spiritless imitation. The Arabic/Egyptian name for castanets is *sagat*.

CASTANETS—2

In Spain they were probably of Roman origin. Macrobius, in the fourth century, mentions that formerly noble ladies danced with castanets. That they were used in Greek dancing is shown by vases and figurines, and by mention of them in Greek writings. Athenaeus (*Bk. XIV. Ch. xl*) discusses castanets, and refers to an essay by Dicaearchus (*Manners and Customs of Ancient Greece*), in which they are mentioned. In the worship of Diana they were frequently used by women to accompany dancing and singing. A hymn to Diana says :

"My companion strikes with nimble hand,
The well-gilt, brazen-sounding castanets".

[Cp. *Krembala* (Greece)]

CATHAL (Gaelic)

The minstrel, musician or dancer, as known in ancient Ireland. The term has the feminine *Cathleen* "figure of Ireland". W. B. Yeats had a play on this topic. The abbreviation *cath* is used for a lute string; probably it named also the instrument.

CATHL (Welsh)

A Ballad or *Balad*; a rhythmic song, often with simple dance; but principally a narrative chanted to music and movement. *Cathliad* is singing of narrative; while *Cathlu* is to sing. The traditional Irish name Cathleen, becomes the "national figure" as *Cathleen-ni-houlihan* (Kathleen the Dance-singer), and is linked with this Cymric term. A similar root is found in old Iranian (Zendic) and Hindu, as *Gatha* and *Katha* (thence into *Katha-kali,** also a "dance-story" in India), or in the Parsee system, *gatha* implies a ritual ceremony with chant. *Houli-han* or *Holi-khan* is the dance-leader in *Holi*, the May ceremonial of India.

CATHERINA; *Katherina*; *Katha-rouen*
Italian and French. Was figured as the chief patron of young girls, the *novena* or novices under instruction. She had two "wheels", which originally implied the Wheels of Fortune—the "Wheel of Time Past", and the "Wheel of Time Future". They are shown in many mediæval paintings, as, for example, a picture by Bernardo Daddi (c.1340) where Katarina has an eight-spoked wheel on each side, and holds a feather. Usually she carries a book, ready for the *sortes*, or "choice by lots". Associated with many lights (as is Lakshmi in Bengal, Goddess of Fortune), Katharouene denotes the "play of the wheel", (Rouen was a favourite centre for devotion), and the revolving circle of light thus obtained the name. The alleged "Head of Emperor Maximilian" was the bygone year (now dead), much as the allied figure of Salome is shewn with a "Head of John" (Johannus, or the Year). *Katha rouen*, or *Gatha-rouen*, is the "Song of Time", thus the "dances of the year" are particularly appropriate. There was a ritual dance of the young people, as a circle dance, indicated much earlier in the *parabolos* of the "Twelve Virgins", who came bearing lamps. In some mediæval paintings, Catherine appears with Nicolas (or Niccolo), as in a work by Gentile Fabriano (1360-1427), which approaches the other notion of her "Mystic Marriage", but here shows a youth being introduced, as a novice. These two characters were finally joined with the feast of Valentinus (dated February 14th), as a sign of a betrothal.

CAULDRON DANCES (Many countries)
Belong to pastoral communities, learning to cook food. According to the material being prepared, so the place and time varied; and gradually set verses or chants developed, to note the length of cooking period. Mostly they were women's dances; a slight hint is contained in Act I of *Macbeth* when the witch chant gives recipe and notes the state of bubbling. Two results occur—one for drinks and one for meats. They become "national dishes" such as *Haggis* (Scotland), *Hot-Pot* (Lancashire), *Goulash* (Hungary), *Olla Podrida* (Spain), *Bortsche* (Russia), *Potage* (France). When the mixtures became more complex, each girl brought in her single contribution. This method is featured in the Javanese mode of serving, called *rijjs-tafel*—for this, each boy

carries one dish, all in a train, to the seated diner. Earlier in Europe, this *entrée* was done to simple calls, by flute, drum, or bugle.

CAVE OF HARMONY (London)
Was a 19th century home of midnight mirth, which was developed, partly as a winter-time change from the summer gardens, such as Vauxhall* and Cremorne; and partly as a bourgeoise substitute for such ornate dance salons as the famous Almack's.* Some of the larger Saloons, such as the Eagle or the Grecian, turned into regular theatres, starting as platforms, tented over, in the back gardens. The essential "harmonic meeting", described as a "Cave of Harmony" in *Sketches by Boz*, catered for not-home-going theatre people (or even actors "after the show") with some eighty or a hundred guests, knocking little pewter measures on the table. This was an ancestor of the music-hall; there was a chairman; there was much liquor sold. The dancing was relatively rare; few "ladies" entered; but amateurs with ambition would oblige. Though the *Cave of Harmony* has disappeared (except for one or two brave revivals of highly respectable management), the curious student can find filleted copies in American films; mainly those that present the Wild West, theoretically at its wildest in mid-century. The mining-camp saloon forms the picture; there are songs; there are four ballerinas (or at least chorines) who recall some dance they once saw in Paris or London; and if the platform is well constructed, they will essay a song-and-dance routine—often in full colour.

CEBELL
An old English dance, similar to the *Gavotte,** but quicker. Musical examples of it occur as the basis of Purcell's harpsichord compositions, and among contemporary lute composers. A well-known example for two lutes is contained in Mace's *Musick's Monument* (1676), called "My Mistress". Written for his wife, Mace describes the piece as having all the qualities of that lady, being "lively, ayrey, neat, curious and sweet; uniform, comely, substantial, grave and lovely; spruce, amiable, pleasant, obliging and innocent, . . ." The origin of the name is unknown. For examples of the music for this dance see *Lessons and Aires for Harpsichord and Spinnett*, by J. Eccles, H. Purcell and others).

CECCHETTI SCHOOL
System of classical ballet training; based on Italian (Milano) Academia di Teatro alla Scala. Enrico Cecchetti (b.1850, d.1928) came from a dancing family and spent his entire life in dancing and teaching. In 1890 he was appointed second ballet-master in Petersburg, three years after joining the

Maryinsky company. In 1892 he was assistant instructor under Petipas. Purely technical; and strictly physical, his system was developed from three sources: mostly his own Italian training; the French and Russian systems. He remained twenty years, resigning in 1902 to go to Warsaw. Later he returned to Russia, in a private school; and thence joined Pavlova, becoming ballet master for her touring company, but again left. He joined S. P. Diaghileff for 1909-1914. In London he opened a private school in 1918, returning to Italy in 1923, to join La Scala in 1925. The London Cecchetti Society was formed to carry on his Italian style; a strict routine of five positions and seven movements. His system is entirely abolished from the modern Russian Schools; by the wider methods of Madame Vaganova. Cecchetti's method is most useful for the male students of the under-developed type; it gives them a certain smartness and surety of movement.

CEILIDHE (Gaelic)
Term used in Ireland (pronounced *kay-lee*), for a dance meeting, or social gathering in which singing and dancing usually form a part; and has since found its way into BBC radio programmes in "country *ceilidhe*", relayed from Ireland.

CENSOR IN THEATRE
W. H. Lecky has a note on Mediæval Theatre, as it passed from its earlier propaganda aspect into satire.[1] The priests did everything possible to attract and retain popular interest. Though the old wooden cloisters had been rebuilt in stone, the people would no longer attend. (Cp. Rabelais, eg.) The "histories" were not believed; tithes were regarded by priests as of primary importance; not morals. What was offered as "tragedy" began to turn to "comedy". Says Lecky (p.112):

"For these, though inexpressibly shocking to our eyes, were perfectly in harmony . . . with the time . . . in the gross indecency which the worst days of the Roman theatre had scarcely surpassed with religious terrorism. Soon Satan was made to act the part of a clown . . . he became at once the most prominent and most popular character of the piece . . . emancipated by his character from all restraints of decorum. . . . A spirit of mockery and satire began to play around the whole teaching of authority".

He adds a footnote:

" . . This indecency . . manifest in most of the mysteries (Jacob. *Introduction to Farces*). Where the seventh commandment was to be broken, actors retired, disappeared behind a curtain; this is the origin of the French proverb, on things done 'derrière le rideau". More than once the

government suppressed the sacred plays on account of their evil effects on morals. In England, matters seem to have been if possible worse; Warton has shewn one occasion, in the fifteenth century, when Adam and Eve were brought on the stage strictly in their state of innocence. In the next scene the fig-leaves were introduced".

From the term *interludis*, came our later term *lewd*.
[1] *Rationalism in Europe*. W.E.H.Lecky.1910.p.112.

CEOL MOR (Scotland)
Basic term for music produced by Scottish pipers, for dance and other purposes, also known as *Piobaireachd*, or Pibroch. Pipe music exists in two great divisions; *Ceol Mor* and the lesser *Ceol Antrum*. Donald Main investigated and wrote on the theories of bagpipe music in Celtic idiom.[1] He referred *Ceol Mor* principally to playing Great Highland Bagpipe, as its "art music". This he believed to be harmonic rather than melodic, in form; with groups of chords struck against the fundamental tone of the drones. The dance form would move in unison. The musical ideas circulated round these pedal tones, weaving two dominants and mediants in balance, over the fundamental tone which gives the basic colour. The two alternative dominants carry the steps of man and woman; when the dance is a couple form. *Ceol Mor*, according to Main, could be heard in three modes: the gay *Forghailte* of salutes, gatherings, and war tunes; the solemn *Duin*, of the lament or funeral song; and the lyrical *Breabach*, treating of woman or child. Moreover, Donald Main found, as he declared, strong evidence of variants in time and rhythm, which by other pipers was resented as "Jazzed Pibroch". The old pipers used a system they called *Canntreachd* for the memory and preservation of their best music. This was more easily recalled, when seen together with dance forms. The design of the instrument, it is said, was based on the pentatonic modes of the Celtic harp, with its finger percussion technique, nearer to the dance mode. The lesser bagpipe music is *Ceol Antrum*: used for marches, *reels** and *strathspeys.** The McCrimmon School of Pipers required attendance through a course of seven years' instruction for full qualification.
[1] In *Scottish Music and Drama*. (No. 6, 1951).

CERNA, CERNE (Old French)
Magic circle newly traced with a rod; or counted steps paced over a regular site; pacing passes into dance as speed increases. It can also indicate domain (cp. Cerne Abbas, Dorset) as the "circle" of an abbess.

CHACARERA (Argentina)

Favourite *criolo* dance, usually performed by one couple alone, now in dignified and graceful mode, though formerly often in *burlesca*. Danced principally in Santiago del Estero and provinces more north, it is usually accompanied by a guitar, sometimes an accordion; and often by topical songs rendered by spectators. Though its early history is obscure, the Spanish word *chocarreria* seems to be one root; it hints at mockery or satire, and as such is favoured by lower-class festival gatherings. There are many variations; and, with its simple waltz step, it is much danced by the *gaucho*. *Chacarera* is one of the few dances where men retain spurs as part of their costume; that is, they dance "in their working clothes". Now grave, this occasionally burlesque dance retains a few basic tango* figures—as the *vuelta* or *media vuelta*; but add others, as the *zapateo contorneo*, or foot-turning.

[Cp. Californian *Fandango*]

CHACONNE—1 (French)

(Ital. *Ciaccona*; Sp. *Chacona*; Old English *Chacony*, *Chaccon*, *Chacoon*). An 18th century French ballroom dance, with moderately slow movement, to music in 3/4 time; often the concluding dance of a ball. Dancers were arranged in two lines, men in one, women in the other, and while all danced at the same time, each line performed its own figures. The two leaders occasionally danced alone, or together, and the lines of dancers joined in the final figure. Accompanying songs indicated a particular movement. The *Chaconne* was less popular in England than in France and Italy. Composers such as Lully and Couperin wrote in this form, Lully habitually ending his operas with a *Chaconne*. A dance called the *Chacona* was known in Spain in 1591; and in Mexico, as the *Chacona mulata* or *Indiana amulatada* (so called by Cervantes), in 1599. Cervantes described this dance in *La Ilustre Fregona* (one of his "Exemplary Novels") in 1610. Danced by couples, this was more fiery than the measured dance of French ballrooms, and there is no positive evidence that the *Chaconne* derived from it.

CHACONNE—2 (French)

Chiacona (Italian) and many more spellings and pronunciations, are common modes of *Passacaglia*.* This is essentially the street processional, the dance of the *calle* or way; as farther north we find *ruad*, *rouen*, *rune*, *rad* and a score more allied designations of the circular dance-ritual movement. *Ciacone* stems from Greek *coeana*, "the meal"; and the servitors, the *dia-coena*, or deakons, who brought in bread and wine, tripping rhythmically as they came and retired, more especially for feasts in the larger halls, for the important people. Deacons in the primitive church were in charge of catering: they had the money, bought supplies, and brought them in at the proper time for the *messe*. They "divided the meats"; they also divided the times; as *dia-coena*, or "the courses". They sang as they came across the courtyard (kitchens were always built distant from dining-halls). They had to move quietly, and they sang to let the chamberlain know they were coming. Hence the general usage of street cries in cities. This custom of dancing servants continued in Russia during the 19th century; finally it turned into dining chamber music.

CHAD (Babylonia)

Was a generic term implying "leader in ritual dance". The term (which like most god-names is reversible, as on a clock face), has been thus rendered, in various verbal forms: as *Khad*, *tchad*, or *tchat*, and turned over as *Dach* or *dakhs*. The title is included in such ancient official names as *Nebo-Khad-Nezzar* (Prophet or speaker-leader-(of) Circle or *Raz*), as well as in *Mero-dach* (*Mir-u-Dakh*—displayer of ritual mystery), or *Chad-urim*. Though apparently so distant in the history of ceremonial, as to seem to have little contact with the European lands, the name did continue; and appeared (5th century) as *Khad-Mon*—turned to Caedmon, an alleged "theatre manager" of 5th century Britain; and, later still, it continues as a mythical "Saint Chad". There is a fish termed chad; as well as a family name, Chad-wick. The Cathedral of Lichfield is dedicated to "Saint Chad".

CHAHUT, CHAUT (France)

Appeared prominently in Paris, about 1830, as a "free and easy manner of dancing a quadrille" by four girls, ascribed to one dancer, Rigolboche, a well-known exponent. The later version, in its wilder manifestation, is sometimes called *Can-can*.* The attire required consists of long and flimsy skirts, beneath which an array of white frills becomes apparent when the endless high kicks fling the petticoats into the air. One of the more famous composers of music for *Chahut* was Offenbach, but in his day this quadrille had become a favourite in the public gardens, the opera comique, and the casinos of Paris. Toulouse-Lautrec is the best known recognised artist of the *salon des danses;* while the dance itself has been approved by the Watch Committee of Birmingham, as a part of the art of ballet, in *Le Gaité Parisienne*.

CHAKRA, CHAKRAM (India)

Literally, "Circle" (Sanskrit). It is an erudite symbol used in Hindu worship, as the basis of ritual dance (as *Krishna Radha** dance etc.), and in graphic symbolism; also in architecture and sculpture. The most important dance development is in the divisions of the periphery; the *rim* can present the Zodiac with its "Twelve Mansions" etc.; but the centres of *chakrams* of the body are equally important, in the disciplines known as *Hatha-yoga*; they then refer to nerve centres or glands. Each system of *chakram* throws light on the other systems; the interpretation being necessarily dynamic, the ritual dance has proved the most effective way of communicating the essential knowledge of vital rhythm. All Hindu Dance (above the ordinary folk-dance pastimes) requires a good knowledge of the inter-relations of *chakrams* to present with real power, in true form, and in proper rhythm.

CHAKRA MANDALA (India)
Hindu ritual dance — "Circle centre position"; a peculiar, almost acrobatic "feet and hands down" pose, which starts and finishes certain routines in the Kaula ritual dances of Bengal and Southern India. This *karana* is illustrated in one of the 108 sculptures that were carved on the pillars of the *gopuram* (entrance gates) of the great Temple of Chidambaram in Travancore State. *Chakram* is a generic term for any circle in ritual, whether in dance or in prayer and praise; the ritual dancer moves swiftly through certain positions, ranging from the complete extension to the complete compression (which is this one) and implies any of three modes of symbolism.

CHAKRAMIM (Babylonian-Hebrew — *Exodus* vii, ii)
The "makers of circles" or recorders of the astronomical observations, by way of natural basis; and devisors of the temple ritual (in which these were explained and related as a scheme), by way of ceremonial. Thus they were the designers of the sacred dance ritual, through which the younger priests received secret tuition in astronomy and astrology. Direct facts of the *chakram** system can be obtained from comparative study of Hindu liturgy, which derived ultimately from Iran, whence both Babylon and Egypt exchanged secret wisdom with ancient India.   [See *Chartummim*]

CHAMBER BALLET — 1
As the name implies, is a style of small-scale ballet that is equivalent to chamber music. With a small orchestra, only a small company is required; and they reveal relatively smaller movements, since there is no space for the *grand jeté* or the *entrechat*. In a certain comparative optical sense, television ballet becomes Chamber Ballet, since the physical impact of great extension of high leaps is consider-ably reduced, partly by the small size of the television screen; partly by the psychic distance of the watcher. Chamber ballet offers many opportunities for restoration of the older mode of Troubadour *Ballades;* on the small company, heard at close quarters, whose faces are plainly visible, whose smallest gestures are clear. Character is the dramatic focus; the story is the essential factor of theme; music must support action instead of replacing it; while costume must be apt, even if scenic effects remain sketchy. There is less need for the extravagance of classical ballet; less chance for visual magnificence by sheer light and colour; but far more opportunity for real dancing of a truly expressive emotional character. This requires miniature mime-drama with true rhythm and subtle unfolding by gesture. For the small theatre and audience, Chamber Ballet extended by simple story and graceful action, can supply almost a new style of modern ballet, avoiding both the over-stressed technicality of academic training, or the acrobatic violence of the "modern dance" enthusiasts.

CHAMBER BALLET — 2
The technical difficulty too often outweighs creative ability to select and express a suitable theme. Rarely do we witness a genuine power to construct a ballet for Chamber Theatre; as a composer writes music for a chamber orchestra, instead of a military band or symphony orchestra or church organ. Chamber Ballet requires more attention to theme; abstract technology reveals its poverty when spectators can get close enough to mark its usual pathetic emptiness. Desperate attempts to re-vamp bits of ancient mythology (always misunderstood), or technical fragments (adorned with fanciful French or Italian titles), are accompanied by a terror of modern subjects or meaningful topics. Some producers of Modern Dance have seen these facts: but too many have come down on the other side, with a morbid tendency to pick "sociological" topics, or vast themes impossible to state, much less develop, in an Intimate Theatre. Some Children's Theatres (by not attempting the financially impossible feat) have gained some success by means of simple ballet form. The Children's Theatre (Moscow) showed an excellent *Tsar Saltan; The Golden Fish;* and *The Little Stork;* while Edwin Strawbridge in the USA had equal success with similar colourful themes. Chamber Ballet is not only a most valuable experimental foundation for Theatre Ballet, but has become necessary for commercial shows on Television and for Cinema Film, as being conducive to that compact mode of production (in both time and space) which is a primal essential for modern entertainment. Chamber Ballet can operate economically where Theatre

Ballet is now finding the balance of "income and expenditure" difficult to maintain; but the old-time technical ballet-master-cum-choreographer is here out of place. Chamber Ballet demands a highly expert producer, just as chamber music requires the most expert composers and players.

CHANIOTIKO (Modern Crete)
A men's circular dance from Canea. Said to derive from the Greek *Pyrrhic** dance, it is accompanied by clarinet and small drum. With blue and white-braided waistcoat, and blue cloak slung over the shoulder, the men also wear the black *vraka*, or baggy breeches tucked into white top-boots. Into the breeches is stuffed the end of a long white calico shirt, which fills the "tail" of the *vraka*, and enables it to be swung about in the dance.

CHANQUES Danse (France, Langues dist.)
Done by march hunters on their stilts (the *chanques*). For festivals, they enter villages and, standing on *chanques* before upper windows, solicit contributions. The name got into England as "shanks"—in Yorkshire a journey by foot is called "going by shanks pony".

CHANTY or CHANTRY (Med. English)
May be compared with *Shanty* as the sacred song-dance against the secular song dance or labour rhythmic movement, that imposes regular motion on physical action. The chant is normally slow, solemn, dignified; yet may accompany a procession in due rhythm, or mark some position by gesture and word. Chantry more often has as music; *shanty* has frequently no instrument other than the workers song, along with the noise of the work. From chant and shanty come technical bases which —when imitated in theatre—provide the basis for many a dance, often lacking in real visual conviction because the dancers have never taken the trouble to perform the real basic act. Gregorian chant was introduced to regularise the liturgical usage of song with the Messe or Feast—as may be observed today in the Coptic church—when e.g. bringing in the sacred bread (*leham*) warm from the oven by the baker-priests.

CHARACTER DANCE—1
Belongs primarily to (a) Temple, and (b) Theatre, in the two great modes of sacred and secular dance rhythms. Egyptian temple dance was performed by trained priests, who donned animal or bird masks, to personate "the gods" or "the demons", that belonged to their mythos. In Theatre, Character is (often quite wrongly) contrasted with "classical" dance as a component of Ballet; thus this quality of character is absolutely essential to transfer the academic basis of classical ballet movement into the emotion context of real ballet. With no character in (a) movement, (b) costume, (c) décor, the ballet fails to appear beyond group movement. Character on the stage is obtained by (a) specialised movement superposed on to classical basis, (b) addition of suitable costume, entire or by hints of personality, and (c) background of place character in décor and lighting. Intrusion of dancer's own personality often ruins the clarity of genuine character dance.

CHARACTER DANCE—2
Is usually intended to classify certain dances which the speaker wishes to separate from "Classical Ballet" as a different, even inferior sort of art. "Character" here implies the acting, miming or rendering, of a definite personage within a ballet, which the Classical dancer cannot or will not do, because it interferes with "pure dancing". This contrast, which does exist in some places, reveals how far the abstracted notion of non-meaning dance has gone in "Modern Art". Character in dance is required in many aspects; also in that special group dance known as Ballet. Every factor (to create a true *expression* which in turn provokes a true *impression* upon the audience) must possess and reveal full character. These qualities of character in the contributing factors must be integrated and not contradictory. The form of dance, in position, movement and gesture, must reveal character. The costume, colour and make-up, in all their elements, must concentrate on character. The scenic decor with its lighting, must suggest the character of the selected place. When any one (or more) of these elements is distorted by some demand of some individual artist who wants to "express himself" regardless of the entire presentation, then the character becomes weakened and the total artistic effect is diminished. Character is, in sum, what most impresses the genuinely cultured audience, as distinct from those who view dance or ballet as a sport, with feats to be accomplished, having no other meaning than technical ability. Full integration of character in all the elements permits creation of great style; so that performance within such a production reflects this culmination of profound impression upon all engaged in it.   [See *Mime**]

CHARACTER IN DANCE
Is expressed by Position, Step and Gesture, extended by mime in face and figure; within the setting of costume. Here art separates from traditional usage; a folk-dance belongs particularly to its own natural setting in the normal festal period. Stage dance (whether copying folk dance

or presenting ballet), leaves the external world for the Theatre. Scenic setting of some kind becomes essential, from plain draped curtains to elaborately painted fantasy or realism — together with the now-essential artificial lighting, which either reveals or adds to the show. Character thus ranges from movement and music, to other factors, in which one after another visual quality can accentuate or detract from the total effect. Expression of full character demands much more than what is commonly dismissed as "character dancing", in comparison with the supposed sufficiency of "classical ballet".

CHARAN (India)

The minstrel poet, with a *tamboura;* a one-string gourd instrument, which he twangs as he recites alleged extempore verses (fantastic praise of the persons he seeks to please). A *Charan* was formerly attached to every Indian court (his place is now filled by the P.R.O. who gets more remuneration for doing worse work). He was also a match-maker at times; or a court of appeal for debtors, since he could satirise them in public. Some *Charans* were women; a few were ex-dancers who knew their music.

CHARANAM DANCE (South India religious folk
    dance)

A village processional and circle group dance, often of women only. *Chara Nam* means "Praise the Name (of the Lord)", which phrase is used as a chorus of many traditional chants. — Parallel to *Kirtan* and *Baijan* in Bengal.
[Compare Latin: *caritas*, etc. in Christian ritual dance]

CHARIVARI (Italy)

A version of Mascarade, referring usually to the more popular, extempore, and noisy exhibitions of crowd excitement, for which this term is now best known. The word later became attached to the satirical song-dance, in which some unpopular resident of a village was serenaded, with a "hammer and tongs" band composed of kitchen utensils, accompanied by crude verses; and breaking into dancing. In France, charivari denoted some of the "booth attractions" of the *Foire;* and thence came to England to accompany the itinerant puppet-master, whose mournful music was sometimes called *charivari.* Finally, it gained printed form on comic papers. *Charivari,* irrepressible as a means of interfering with other people and disapproving, was one of the sources of the typical English love of noise. Developments occured also in USA, as at New Orleans where other domestic implements were added, with oil drums and kerosene cans as

drums. The laundry contributed its corrugated board, hence The Washboard Blues were invented. Inevitably in this jazzification (rhythm joins the raucous tones), Europe felt the influence, and the modern composer (such as Hindemith) issued the "Twelve tone scale" with full discords as a contribution to culture. In England, mechanical Town Fair Organs worked on steam or electric motors — the processional Charivari of the circus — and thence to the terrors of "Music While You Work" by radio. The BBC added *"Mobile"* by Piotr Kellerzak, the unknown Polish decomposer.

[See *Mascarade*]

CHARLATAN (Franco-Italian)

Colloquial form of *Carolatanza* — the itinerant vendor of herbal remedies during the Middle Ages; whose partners attracted the crowd by means of patter, song, and dance. They used familiar carol tunes, with parodied words devised to extol their pills and ointments. One familiar centre was the great *Piazza san Marco* at Venice (pictures exist showing these vendors at work). They have been confused with the town characters of the *Commedia dell' Arte;* and also with the bands of monks who travelled from fair to fair, putting on shows based on "miracle plays". Illiterate people gathered around to laugh even when reluctant to pay. The puppet-master was included in these groups of entertainers.

CHARLESTON (USA)

A ballroom dance named after Charleston, South Carolina, where the negroes worked their native African dance steps into a connected dance as entertainment for the passengers on steamers at the docks there. It became popular and in 1925 entered the ballrooms of America, reaching Europe the following year. Danced by couples standing opposite each other, but not with the modern ballroom hold, the movements of the *Charleston* were angular and "turned-in". In quick time, the feet were alternately kicked out, while toes and knees were turned in, and the arms swung in opposition. The origin of the *Charleston* seems to have been the *Batuque** of West Africa, later known also in Brazil.

CHARRADA (Spain)

A dance performed in Salamanca and its surrounding province of Leon, by the Charros, as the men of that region are called. Although a couple dance, most of the dancing is performed by the men. With a table between them, the woman, one arm raised, moves round it with small, shuffling steps; while the man shows off for her with a display of difficult steps as he reaches each corner of the table. Castanets and drums accompany the dance. When performed at a wedding, it is a competition by the men, with a prize for the best dancer. When the *rosca* (a large cake, or "bread with eggs") is placed on the table, a derivation from the Charrada called *La Rosca*, is danced in 2/8 time. A *Charrada* in 4/8 time also exists.

CHARRADE (Spanish)

A dance mime performed as a spectacle at fairs in a clownish style of mimicry; satirical and mocking. *Charro* was sometimes used to refer to the mime, as a churl; *chicolear* is to jest in a bantering mode, without offence.

CHARTOPHYLAX (Greek)

Also spelled *carthophylax;* generally implies "keeper of records", as the function of a certain order or class of officials in the Byzantine church of the earlier period (post 400 AD). This officer had many duties: he entered those "saved" on the *diptych* (two-fold leaf), which was read out in primitive ceremonials; and also prescribed for entry of names on the *triptych*, fixed on the altar. These acts carried on earlier Greek rites. The *charto-phylax* (many typical portraits of whom will be found painted on Greek vases), operated as a chamberlain, or manager of rituals; and as often he acted in mystery plays. The office of manager appears also as Plautus; but centuries later lapsed into the place named Chartres (France) and Charterhouse (London). As chamberlain, when the office divided, part being occupied in the Latin church by *bibliothecarius*, he was governor of manuscripts, in copying and sale, as well as editing old MSS. The management of the miracle plays devolved on other officials, who ruled the cloister and the chapterhouse as Head of the Chapitre, including the ritual dances.   [See *Cloister*; *Miracle Plays*]

CHARTUMMIM (Babylonian-Hebrew. *Gen* xli, 8 and *Exodus* vii. 11)

The makers of sacred diagrams and writing — in Egypt on papyrus, on walls, on sand tables; in Babylon, recorded on clay bricks or stone; and on the temple floor. They were, in sum, the official scribes and chartmakers; so well defined and established that their title and their tasks endure today under precisely similar names. They are most important through the history of all ritual dance. Towns and schools have received their names (Chartres and Chartreuse in France, and Charterhouse in England; and earlier in Byzantium *chartophylax*** was keeper of records, or recorder of the scripts in Greek drama). The term appears to be associated with Hebrew *cheret* — a pen or stylus; and implies a master of enscribed form, a way of movement in ritual. From it comes *khartum*,

and the "great space" of the *khort* (*cour* or court), for which these men laid out the lines of movement and the spots of position for ritual over the broad flat floor. Later terms include chariot or *kariota*; and then many kinds of car or cart. From their ritual then proceeds the enscribed rules or orders; arranged as words, or diagrams and numerals, on all kinds of small fragments — papyrus, linen, thin wooden tablets; then on paper or card — *the carte* or *cartum* — the source of the "cards of the court", and the array of Tarot cards for magical ritual. Ancient tradition can be traced from land to land, from one century to the next, through function and purpose, changing in precise form as adapted to changing rites. The character (an official or mystery play), was denoted by the *carte*, enscribed by the charter. Secular officials followed the same scheme; they indited solemn charters; with them went the seal — another Babylonian practice; and with the "sealing" went the dancing. With the *Chartummim* went their colleagues the *Chakhamim* or *Chakramim*.
[See *Chakramim*]

CHAURI (Nepal)

Male dance of Gurkha tribes, shewn principally by recruits to forces in India. The form derives from a marriage-mart system; and begins with a love song, accompanied by *mridanga* drum. Men sit in a half-moon curve; and, as they feel moved by the song, rise and execute steps, singly or in pairs; while those still seated chant "ho-ho" to the principal rhythm, which the dancers then follow. The dance is vigorous and rapid; with many brilliant turns, leaps, high kicks, and low squatting leg-stretching, like *prisiadki*. Their hands are usually fully extended; movements are short and snappy. In some of these dance-poems, mime enters, but men play the feminine parts today. Formerly, this *Chauri* dance was an alternated man-and-girl dance, in a series of competitive heats; when the final winners were expected to get wed. No weapons are carried; the famous Gurkha *kukri* is laid aside; and only on festival occasions will any special addition to costume be seen.

CHAUVE SOURIS (Russia)

Nikita Balieff's cabaret theatre, *The Bat*, was started as a semi-professional theatre club in 1908, in a large Moscow cellar. Reputedly "underground" and always humorously critical of authority, Balieff used his productions both as political commentary and theatrical experiment. His venture lasted fourteen years; when he pined for fresh fields; and in 1922 the bulbous Balieff "escaped" — complete with company, rail-tickets, and costumes — to Paris, and so to New York. He showed in London; when his extended programs included dancing (ballet and comedy), with some of the ex-Diaghilev girls in his company. He used the French title always outside Russia. Though Russian in its theatrical pungency, his theatre was never Soviet (either pro or against), and he continued to tour until the company closed down, some eight or ten years later. His dance burlesques were original and clever. [See *Crooked Mirror Theatre*]

CHEIRONOMY
Knowledge of Hand Movement, or Hand Gesture, belonging as much to Ritual as to Dance. Probably the two extreme contrasts appear in Classical Ballet compared with Hindu ritual dance. In the academic mode, the use of the hands is severely limited; while in the Hindu dance, immense usage is made of complex hand gestures (known as *hasta** and *mudra*,*) which possess three systems of meaning. The *hasta* is the hand *gesture*, the *mudra* is the hand *pose* or affirmation of the symbol. Various totals are stated by Hindu experts: from 800 to 1,200 different hand poses are stated to be required. In practice, they are mostly slight variations on a smaller basic number: beginning with 24 poses. They are distinguished as one-hand or two-hand *mudras*; Samyuta 2 hand. Asamyuta 1 hand. In Hindu Theatre, the use of hand gesture ranges from (a) naturalistic movement; (b) dramatic or suggestional movements; to (c) symbolic or traditional forms. Many apparently "natural forms" are used as symbols: e.g. the "lotus flower" appears in all three grades; and its reading is thus dependent on its visual context. In Greek dance, cheironomy was an integral part, in much the same fashion; until it degenerated into mere physical display or was diverted into gymnastics for training.

All countries and all religions possess a range of traditional hand pose or gesture movements, which by custom and use belong essentially to each system and can be understood only in due relation to that scheme. Prominent among these gestures are the various "natural salutes" with poses of greeting or departure considered appropriate among the classes or ranks. They belong far more to the hands than to the body; they must be known and used to interpret national dance or religious dance.

Hand poses and gestures may constitute a code: as with the familiar "deaf and dumb" language. In cruder form, similar arm gestures have been used for military or naval signalling. Certain classes of the community possess and use a private manual code, to communicate information; as with the gypsies, and "Tic-Tac men" on racecourses. In film work the hands become highly important, owing to the closeness of view; but this usage has not

been fully developed; and Delsarte's exhortations are unknown to most stage actors of today. [See *Chironomia; Delsarte; Mudra; Anjali*]

CHERKESSKA (Caucasia)
A men's sabre dance, being a solo exhibition to display the performers' skill both in dancing and in manipulating the sword. With many leaps and turns, it is danced in spirited style.

CHERRY BLOSSOM DANCE (Japan)
Modernised form of the *Michiahe*, the ancient popular phallic dance festival of rural Japanese districts. The heavy aesthetic camouflage now used, which is a relatively recent addition (it being impossible entirely to obliterate highly popular traditions from conventional country-dwellers), was started in the towns, with the hope that it would be copied by visiting traders. Suggestion extended to a lady to "Come and see the Cherry Blossoms" still retains its place as an invitation such as "Come into the Garden, Maud?" in Tennysonian verse; or the more cultured 20th century "office conference" or the art gallery sequence "Come up and see my etchings?"

CHESTER BALL PLAY (England)
In the Middle Ages, Chester became the centre of many religious ceremonials; among which is recorded the Ball Play and Dance.
"Ball-playing on Easter Monday was universal in every rank. The clergy could not forego its delights, and made the game part of their services, Bishops and deans took the ball into the church, and at the commencement of the antiphon began to dance, throwing the ball to the choristers, who handed it to each other during the time of the dancing and antiphon. All then retired for refreshment; a gammon of bacon was the standard dish; with a tansy pudding, symbolical of the bitter herbs commanded at the paschal feast".[1]
This ball play (not noticed by Mead in his survey[2]) in England, must have had some traditional and symbolical significance, or the use of tansy would not thus be noted. The ball game of *pilum* was regular in many French churches during this period. Churches were adorned at this season (continues this account) like theatres; and crowds poured in to see the sepulchres which were erected. At three in the morning two monks would enter and extract a large image.
[See *Bergeretta*]
[1] *Book of Days*. Chambers (p. 429).
[2] *Sacred Dance*. G. R. S. Mead.

CHEVALET (France)
The equivalent of the English "Hobby Horse"; he

was acted or danced by a man with the "horse-head", there was also the *Tarascon* or *Tarasque*, which was the opponent dragon, who disappeared from the English dance-drama much earlier. In Belgium he appears as the *Tewrdankch*,* or dragon. The dragon attacked the Foule, who was protected by the Mayd Marrian (or the Jeanne, in France), assisted by *Le Petit Cheval* or *Le Chevalet*. The

casual appropriation of this ritual combat, into festivals which belong to other causes, has produced much confusion concerning its symbolic meaning.

CHÈVRES DANSANTES (France)
The "Merry Goats" are the dancing lights of the arctic north, called in other lands *The Merry Dancers** or *Pretty Dancers.**

The Chhau Dance. Hindu dancers, Seraikella, Eastern India.   INDIA

CHHAU DANCE (Orissa Province, India)
The term *Chhau* indicates "shadow, or cover", though not quite "mask", as is sometimes asserted. The general idea is that the masked dancers who perform annually at Serai-kella Spring Festival are "shadows" or doubles of the figures of the gods; the masks merely point the fact and affirm each character. This dance ritual festival is a three-day *puja* (ritual temple worship) for the Shiva ceremonial. The rite must be performed by thirteen chosen *bhaktas* (devotees), who represent all castes. They move in procession from the town temple to another shrine, where Shiva protects also the river bank (water supply) outside. A sacred pitcher is carried by the chief Brahmin priest. After the procession arrives, another pitcher is brought, now full, by a dancer in female attire; who dances all the way back in delight at the godly gift of pure water. This pitcher has remained a whole year by a spring; it must have filled. The vessel, called the *Jatra Ghat*, is used in sacred rites. The new pitcher,

having been received, emptied and consecrated, is taken back to the river shrine to receive the water, led by *bhaktas* carrying the flag of Serai-kella. This ceremonial is repeated on each of three nights. After they are fulfilled, the Chhau sacred dances begin, in which no women take part; and all dancers wear god-masks. Groups of dancers arrive from surrounding country to take part; each contributing a special episode of the drama of Shiva and Kali or Durga, performed always at night before the Raja. He gives a prize to the group he thinks best.

CHIAPANECAS (Mexico)
A dance belonging to the State of Chiapas, performed usually by girls, but sometimes by girls and men, to a tune in waltz-time. Danced in lines, which form a V-shape, cross and inter-mingle, the climax of the dance comes at a certain point in the music when dancers and spectators clap. Hence it is sometimes called the "Clapping Dance". The name "Chiapanecas" specifically refers to "the girls

of Chiapas". A slightly more elaborate stage version is performed by two dancers in the Mexican theatres of the towns.

CHIARENZANA

A 16th century Italian dance in quick triple time, of which little is now known. Examples of composition in this style for lutes are to be found in Marcantonio de Pifaro's *Intabulatura de lauto* (1546).

CHÎFE DANSE (France, Provence)

Belongs to harvesting of oats, to making and carrying the Sheaf (compare the Scots *Kirn Baby Dance*). The Chîfe Danse Ronde is done (a)round the field, gleaning and (b) round the barn after carting. The name has been given wrongly as *Siva-ai* by some writers.

CHILDREN'S DANCE (England)

May be considered in its three main aspects as dance : (a) technically; (b) as style; and (c) as meaning in ceremonial or spectacle. Educationally, these may all be included; and taught with reference to other subjects of study; for, as any careful reader of this book will observe, the associations of ancient and modern dance are exceedingly numerous; and thus may contact all the arts and many aspects of history, literature, and geography. The technical study of dance may begin with organized games since the playful sport of the isolated infant can seldom be accepted as real dance but remains as natural play, and may develop into rhythmic forms of physical training (with an important bearing on music, both in appreciation and performance), or may in contrast be pursued merely as a pleasant pastime. Dance style brings us closely to every aspect of art; from the style, fashion, or period of any given dance forms, to its associated qualities of costume, music, place; and general form in meaning or spectacle. The third factor, which invariably unites the other two aspects of technique in form and style in design, is the important primary urge now focussed by the meaning or purpose or aim in performing any dance. This factor of theme seems at first simple; but when pursued leads the enquirer to examine the most profound aims of dance in ritual and ceremonial. A few children, once their attention has been caught and their personal interest awakened, find this subject one of enthralling study; and even those who do not wish to perform dances, either as amateurs for pastime or as professionals for ambition, will discover in themes of dance ceremonials a topic that will keep them occupied for many years.

CHILDREN'S DANCE GAMES AND SONGS (England)

Present a full range; excluding some kinds such as hymns, school work. Traditional tunes—and even what seem now to be mere "nonsense words" are inherited. Rarely are their words political; topical terms get in almost "by accident" but personal names enter most of the Counting Out Dances which prevail. Rarely does a melody extend beyond one octave; and even when words are gruesome, violence does not develop. Rarely do children copy adult folk songs but relics of century old rhymes can still be heard. Not yet has the meaning of :

Eeeny meenie minie Mo

been adequately solved. But these dance games escape adult control. School folk dances are "bad medicine" for genuine expression. "Twice one are Two" may make a chant, but African children, as Lucian observed, Dance out Religion—or is it Religion dances out Learning?

Children will copy adult pastimes—nowadays in a crudely commercial fashion—like the Christmas demand for pence for a two line extract from a Carol, badly sung, not understood, and out of tune or time. Similar is the demand "Penny for the Guy Mister!" but the song seems to be lost, like the former Initiation chants that used to accompany the Nicolas rite (for boys) or the Katerin rite (for little girls). We may indeed trace one chant in Oranges and Lemons—*Oraison pour ma Leman*. And we have another distant relief reflex in the little girls ring dance in which they seek to "know who is your lover?" The Hop-Scotch (or Hop Scot) dance is performed over a chalked spiral on a dry pavement (relic of the Way to Jerusalem*) and another half game half dance, is practised with "Bobbers and Kibs"—but there is no song, no tune. These juvenile occupations cannot be "revived" once they have lost vigour; country plants do not grow in industrial towns

CHINELOS (South Mexico)

Dance in the plaza at Tepoztlan, performed by a group of men; evidently a development with a strong Spanish influence. Its characteristic is a high leaping movement of the circle of dancers as they move round. Both dance and dancers are called *Huehuenches* or *Chinelos*. The dancers, middle-class people who take the ritual seriously, perform through afternoon and evening during Carnival, beginning at three o'clock and starting from the courtyard of the church. The *Chinelos*, in leaping groups, wear long gowns of velvet and satin, loose from the shoulder, of red, green and yellow. Each man wears a mask with large white staring eyes, and a long black pointed beard. But the spectacular part of the costume is the head-dress, shaped like an inverted lampshade with the narrow circle on the head; decorated with small pictures, beads, coloured glass and topped with ostrich feather plumes. With half-bent arms in rotary movement, the dancers circulate the plaza, making a little run before each leap. For three hours they may continue before resting.

CHINESE DANCE (China 15th to 19th century)
Followed a presentation method which required a highly active imagination in the audience. Lacking scenery and stage realism, but focussed in magnificent costume, the actor-dancer relied on a subtle and varied system of mime. There was an accompanying tradition of costume, to balance the traditional types of movement and gesture with position, that indicated each character. No horse, but a riding whip, suggests the mount. A flag indicates a regiment; a chair may indicate a hill. The well-marked social classes wear, beyond appropriate costume, further signs of character: the "good official" wears a square hat (university type?), while the bad lad wears a round hat (bowler, bank refusing overdraft?). His face is red, meaning that some noble personage is here; demons are green, but gods are yellow (or gold). A dark face suggests the simple villager; a white face (pallid city office?), a cunning though dignified townsman. Above all, the quality that arises naturally in children's play—"Let's imagine!"—appears in Chinese theatre; the convention rules the scene; the action, music, and dance relate the story. There are a hundred modes of facial make-up; a score of different laughs; fifty gestures of the hands, together with another fifty of a single hand, with as many allied gestures in the adjustment of the robes, swords, fans, and flowers—as they fit the visible act to the invisible suggestion.
[See *Rainbow Skirt and Feather Jacket; Feather Dancing*]

CHINESE DANCE
(China, to Manchuria and Mongolia, as modificatory influences). Has existed in three main systems (with folk-dance as a general substratum), which are (1) Court ceremonial, ritual-dance; (2) Religious ceremonial, dance-ritual; and (3) the semi-secret "Dance of Mind", taught or rather indicated in Taoism. Each has a defined sphere of influence and operation, interpenetrating the others; none are made fully plain; they have to be learned by the dual experience of watching and doing. The first is indicated in *I-Ching (Book of Changes)*, where cosmic, human and terrestrial modes are harmonised in changing vitality, illumined by dance-ritual.

Text is traceable from about 1000 BC. The religious ceremonial was centred in the Imperial Palace of Pe-king (Northern Capital) and has many traces, in document and picture. The "Dance of Mind" is impossible to teach or display; but is indicated by many potent symbols, from the Unity-Duality of the *Yang-Yin*, to the isolated fragments of the *Tao-teh-King*. The world-wide doctrine, called in China as *Feng-Shui* (literally, but not really, "Wind-and-Water"), pervaded all systems, from folk-dance (derived chiefly from work-dance and courting-dance), to the mental system of the inexplicable *Tao. Feng-shui* is called also *ti-li* (geomancy) and *k'an-yu* (chariot). In each system, the dancing entities are different: in the Court system, the state officials (*tchin*) are as the gods (a system now prevalent in Europe); while in the religious system, (re-arranged according to Kung-fu-tse by tabulation) the Emperor was the focal personage. Contrary to both of these, in the "Dance-of-Mind" system, the individual works out his own salvation.
[See *Creative Energy; Introduction to Yih King*.
    I. Mears and L. E. Mears. 1931.
    I-Ching; Book of Changes. From Trans. by R.
        Wilhelm; English by Cary F. Baynes. 1951.
    The Simple Way (Laotze. The Old Boy). Trans.
        of *Tao-teh-King* by W. G. Old. 1905.
    Tao-Teh-King (Lao Tzu). Trans. by I. Mears
        (1922).
    Chinese Thought. Paul Carus (Chicago 1907).
    Chinese Philosophy in Classical Times. E. R.
        Hughes, 1942]

CHINESE DANCE DRAMA
Few facts remain from beginnings in Tang Dynasty period (618-907) enough to prove that fully developed technique then existed. Dance was the central mode. Twelve types were known in *Shen* modes (Masculine) and seven in *Tan* (feminine) relevant to pose, gesture, step, head movement. Women (often played by youths) ranged from *kuei-man-tan* maiden) to *lao-tan* (old lady) with *tao-ma-tan* (fighter) *ch'an-tan* (comedy type) or *chini* (reserved woman and *hua-tan* (servant or "friend") *totsai-tan* (villainess). Each type had characteristic pose or movement, known to every audience. Eight or ten persons would appear in each play; males had wider scope of action. Costume was used to affirm type; also make-up.

CHIROLOGIA
"The Natural Language of the Hand", as developed by John Bulwer (in description) from the basis of current usage in his day (time of Shakespearean acting), with reference to the *Institutes of Oratory*

(Quintilian) Book XI. Bulwer wrote from what he saw on the stage in his day, just before final experiments of Charles I in Whitehall. Oratory was taught as an important part of Elizabethan education, much emphasis being given to the art of rhetorical delivery; and excellence in action was expected of courtiers, as in fence and dance—as "a ready tongue and a ready blade with nimble feet". Universities then put on scholars' plays, with stylised use of voice and gesture: this was reflected on the stage. *Hamlet* refers to gesture more than once. John Bulwer made a thorough study of *Chirologia* (he kept the Latin name throughout) and he distinguished eighty-five definite gestures to be learned. In 1604, one of his teachers, Thomas Wright, wrote in his book *Passions of the Mind*—"In the substance of external action for the most part oratours and stage-players agree". Shakespeare's actors preserved the metre of all his verse; they used prose only when rhythm was silent; and we may take it that their mime affirmed and pointed the action to the word. The Elizabethan stage was a culture in which dance action and a dancing voice were linked by expressive mime.
[See *Chironomia; Delsarte; Mime; Rhythm*]

CHIRONOMIA

"The Art of Manual Rhetoric", which we may compare usefully with the analogy of the Hindu *hasta-mudra* or "gesture-pose", so much used in the Hindu dance, from *Bharata Natyam** to the pantomimic *Katha-kali.** John Bulwer, writing early in the 17th century, adds this "art of rhetorick" as a mode complementary to "Natural Language of the Hand", so that here the studied art advances beyond the incidents of natural expression, which the orator might find sufficient. For his *Chironomia*, Bulwer lists eighty-five basic gestures, most of them in a social relation, or a dramatic contact of expression, made in relation to some other person. Bulwer was a student of Gesture; he had interest in devising a manual language for the deaf and dumb people. *Chironomia*—the presentation of human meaning by correct use of pantomime expressed principally through the hands—gives a valuable addition to the development of dance-mime as a genuine art, instead of the poor parodies so often presented in "classical ballet" on the plea that "the dance is most important".
[See *Delsarte; Mime; Rhythm*]

CHŌD RITUAL DANCE—1 (Tibet)

The general term means "action" or, more definitely "rhythmic action", thus implying a religious dance. The devotee, having received some training, undertakes this solemn ritual, entirely alone and unaided,

in some quiet and solitary place. His purpose is the complete sublimation or sacrifice of his human personality, body and soul, in the finality of escape from the kosmos. For his purpose, he draws and consecrates his *kyilkhor;** chanting the traditional prayers of sacrifice, first from the *Prajnaparamita* (Buddhist doctrine) as a song of praise and submission. The ritual dance begins (as with so many others), by turning in succession to the "four quarters", reciting the names of the "demons" who congregate at each focus. He steps round the circles [with low sounds from his *damaru* (skin drum)], in narrowing phases, stamping his feet in rhythmic beats as he summons the *khadomas* (invisible dancing energies). His drum beats cease as his voice recites the "Praise of Wisdom"—"O Wisdom that is gone, is gone—gone beyond all; beyond that beyond—Svaha!" He pitches a low tent; standing before it he blows challenging blasts on his trumpet of bone (*kangling*), and then begins his chant of destruction, as he offers his bodies to the dissolving powers. This grim *chöd* ritual is said to have been revised by Lama Padma Rigdzin, who lived about 1600, as head of the magical Dzogschen sect of Buddhist-Lamaism.
[See *Kyilkhor; Zodiac Dance*]

CHŌD RITUAL DANCE—2

Chöd means "directed action" or choice. The Yogic consummation in his liturgy of personal sacrifice. This grim ritual follows, in personal form, the mythic mode of the cosmic dance, of Kali, the Dissolvent Goddess of the Universal power; in her traditional *Smashana Natyam*, or "Dance of the Burning Ground". In this mythic dance (which is yet real because it continues as incessantly as creation) the lives and their forms, and mental images that constitute the experimental Universe are dissolved, back to their primal modes as basic energy and basic substance. The Yogi, having realised these facts, affirms his willingness to dissolve his own personality back to the impersonal eternity of the Cosmic Mind. He arranges his own dance: as vigil, as prayer, as submission, in a cemetery during the Dark Fortnight, accompanied only by the corpses of the dead, for whom he feels no fear, no revulsion, but only compassion. While the *Dance of Kali* has been shaped for both temple and public performance, the *Chöd* Dance, from its nature, cannot be shewn. There are literary analogies extant; two known in Europe are the reserved liturgies of the *Naqshabandi* Sufis; and the *Exercises*, copies from these Muslim modes, by one Ignatius of Loyola, written in Spanish and turned to Latin for publication in Rome in 1548. There was a parallel tradition, known earlier (12th century) in England, and derived in part from Raymonda Auliya, which was followed as *De Arte Moriendi*.   [See *Ars Moriendi*]

CHOPI BALLET (Portuguese East Africa)
Is described in detail by Hugh Tracey[1] in a work that is a model of completeness and clarity : *Chopi Musicians*. This Bantu ballet system has been affected by Portuguese music and information; but retains a vital and vivid modernity, expressing topics of its own time and place, as all good dance should. The Chopi do with ballet what the West Indians do with *calypso*,* in a fully matured lyrical form. Dances are *Migodo** (single one is *Mgodo*); the entire ballet is called *Ngodo*. The words are in verse and are sung with dance, mostly to the *timbila** or xylophone. Hugh Tracey describes one *Ngodo* of 1940, in its eleven movements :

1. *Musitso wokata* — First Orchestral Introduction (no words);
2. *Musitso wembidi* — Second Orchestral Introduction (no words);
3. *Mositsu woraru* — Third Orchestral Introduction (no words);
4. *Ngeniso* — ENTRY OF THE DANCERS ("It is time to pay taxes")
5. *Mdano* — Call of the Dancers ("Kapitan, you make trouble")
6. *Joosinya* — THE DANCE ("Oh! listen to the orders . . !")
7. *Joosinya cibudo combidi* — The Second Dance ("Sing Ho! See the Mzeno.")
8. *Mzeno* — The Song ("Katini will not play *Timbila!*")
9. *Mabandla* — The Councillors ("Famboyane would like to be Chief!")
10. *Citoto Ciriri* — The Dancers' Finale ("We hear a Rumour. . . !")
11. *Musito kugwita* — Orchestral Finale (repeats first music)

Other modern Chopi Ballets follow a closely similar pattern. The music retains basic traditional lines, but is enlivened with modern individualist touches; while the poems are prepared anew for each production. The musical form is that of (a) chant, male voice; (b) drums, *ngoma;* and (c) *timbila;* sometimes with rattles. There may be seven *timbila*, with two *gulu* or double bass *timbila* as well, to a company of fifteen dancers. The African musical conventions, like those of the Javanese *gamelan*, or modern European orchestral fugue, have got to be studied and learned. None of the Chopi ballets are religious in theme or form.
[1] *Chopi Musicians*. Hugh Tracey (London 1948)

CHOREGUS (*Korekhus* — Ancient Greek)
The effective "master of the ritual ceremony", who was elected or appointed, to supervise the entire arrangements of a single religious festival in ancient Hellas. Chosen for his wealth, he performed this task as a service to his community; it was the *caritas* of that time and place. He paid for the ceremonial; and devoted his time to the training of the *choroi*, as an amateur, but chiefly as a poet or maker of presentation.

CHOREODRAMA, ALSO COREODRAMA (Italian)
A term used to describe the production of Salvatore Vigano, to the music of Beethoven, for La Scala Theatre, Milan, in 1812. This work, *Les Créatures de Promethée*, was the only one of this style written by Beethoven. This *Ballet héroique et Allégorique* (as it was then styled) was devised to measure with the music already written to the general theme; having its first production in Vienna in 1801, but gained no success until it was repeated in changed form in 1812 at La Scala. Carlo Ritorni, a contemporary critic, used this term in his summary : *Commentarii della vite e delle opere coreodrammatiche de Salvatore Vigano e della coregrafia e de' coropei.* Although this notable work by Beethoven has been taken as an early example of "symphonic ballet", it was, in fact, in the tradition of Noverre in its stressing of theme as drama, as expressed by choreographic means to musical rhythm. The true antithesis to *choreodrama* is the modernist mode named "abstract ballet",* which deliberately rejects all theme or subject-matter or plot; while symphonic music is occasionally admitted, by its composers, to possess some sort of "program".

CHOREOGRAPHY (Modern Term)
Is the Grammar of Dance. Form is given to dance by use of choreography, as discipline of movement, as rational meaning is given to language by use of verbal grammar. Music begins to gain form, when rhythmic beats measure off the quantities of melody and harmony, selecting the notes (equal to words or numbers) in relation to the general meaning to be expressed. The infants' playful dance has no grammar; nor his juvenile attempts to use words. He gets them in the wrong order; or relates them to the wrong meaning; while he takes quite a time to associate a visual image. of letters and words with the aural image of sound, as words. In each effort, he gains help from an unimplied system of grammar; which, however arbitrary it may seem, or be in fact, is a system which a certain social group of people are agreed to use, because the general meaning is known to all. Folk-dance is guided by an inherited form of choreography, which, like most rituals invited no change or devel-

opment. The modern ballet works in schizophrenic
mode : the system asserts its right and its use of
academic dance forms, called "classical ballet", in
its classrooms, while next trying to graft onto these
inherited forms newly invented fragments that are
considered necessary; and which are, indeed, named
as "the choreography" of the piece. Most of these
newly devised actions possess no relation to classical ballet; and often no relation to the theatre
dance, with no meaning concerning the theme. The
sole endeavour is to be "different" — an aim which
is sought while at the same time trying to remain
"classical". The uncomfortable results are then
given second place to the mannerisms of the chief
performers.

CHOREOGRAPHY
From two Greek terms, *choros** and *graphos*
("ritual dance" and "I write"), wrongly given as
"Choregraphy" now implies (a) the plan of a dance
or ballet; (b) the written script of signs denoting
the dance-form or ballet-plan as a record; (c) the
general outline of a proposed ballet, so written
before production; and (d) in a vague modernist
critical aspect, a term denoting the general "scheme
of dance", both as plan and as picture.
[See *Notation; Skhema*]

CHOREOGRAPHY
Design of Dances. Notation of Dance is separately
considered.
Bibliography in Europe :
Le Geste des Nobles Francais. Jean de Angouleme.
   (Paris 1445)
Choreographie. Phillipe Beauchamp. (Paris 1671)
Code of Terpsichore. Carlo Blasis. (London 1830)
Principes de Choreographie. Charles Clement (Paris
   1771)
De Arte de Saltandi et Choreas. Domenico di Pie-
   cenza. (1445)
Choreographie, Raoule Feuillét. (Paris 1700)
Die Tanzkunst ünd Tansfigurin. Karl Gerster.
   (Speier 1780)
Choreographie. Guilleman. (Paris 1784)
Principes de la Choreographie, Charles Magny.
   (Paris 1765)
There are many other books claiming the title of
Choreography, which, in fact, do not deal with
creative design in dance or ballet; but centre upon
record of dance form (new or old). There are a
number of books later than those listed above,
which claim also to comment on Choreography,
but they range chiefly over discussions of general
dance form without explaining principles or
theories.   [See *Notation*]

CHOREOGRAPHY, GRAMMAR OF
Most teaching of Dance is, necessarily, double in
form. The pupil requires to know (1) how to DO it,
and equally important, (2) how to SAY it. This
second requirement is too much neglected. — It is
taught not by principles but by rote. The student
"learns it off by heart". This may pass in chorus;
it will not do for principals, where an important
role is to be both created and projected over to
the audience. They must learn what it means, as
well as "what it looks like". Thus they gain their
real and double pleasure. Dance is for the eye —
yes. But it is also for the mind, for the emotions.
Movement that has no connotation of emotional
relation with the next movement fails to make its
deepest impression. We are back at mechanical
dancing.

CHOREOLOGY
The Science of Comparative Dance (*Choros**),
which is only now in process of definition and formation. The science must rest on the modern
method of Comparative Analysis. As Cuvier, the
celebrated anatomist, was able to offer a tenable
deduction of the character of an extinct animal
from examination of fragments of its bones, so it
should prove possible to arrive at some conclusion
on the character of extinct ritual dances and
ceremonials, by persistent examination of related
fragments, still extant in minor detail. We have
available (a) the human form — the actual dancer
and ritualist — with his stable average of structure,
action, and motive; (b) many of the places (and
the associated place-names) where traditional ritual
occurred; and (c) fragments of pottery, sculptures
in stone or even metal; and relics of building or
architectural form. Together with the great trea-
suries of script, belonging to the great religions of
the world, we are then able to gain some data on
the formation of each mythos, which we know
to have been presented, by means of ritual dance,
to the various grades of the peoples in these cults.
We may even arrive at a few principles in their
secret doctrine, the scientific basis they held (but
could not express fully for want of a symbolic
language easy to state and manipulate — such as we
use in modern mathematics plus the ideologies
possessed by mathematicians). Knowing the elemental modes of human movement, as united with
instrumental sound, we may then be able to analyse
sufficient facts to learn at least the general character and intention of ancient rituals. Even when
one cult sets out to eliminate members of a rival
cult; or to absorb it (as the Mithraic cult was
absorbed into the later Christian system); or to
destroy it (as the Gnostic system was largely
obliterated by their Latin rivals), we learn some-

thing from the denunciation—allowing for the usual exaggeration. Finally, we can trace, behind currently performed rituals, now almost entirely ornamental in their ceremonial (as, for example, a coronation ritual), the original meaning and purpose of this structure, incident to social rhythm; and carrying some associated forms of music, ritual dance or movement, and perhaps religious worship.

CHOROS (Greek): *Xoros, Xorus*)

Classic form: *Choros*, indicates the "Dance in a ring", but stems from an older tradition, surrounding the Festal Dance of Koré. The root radiates into numerous Greek terms, associated with this Festive or Choral Dance, which have spread widely through Europe, from Russia to Ireland especially just as Greek Christianity followed Greek ritual before its forms were superceded by the aggression of the Latin mode. Greek place-names; institutional names; liturgies; and many other terms in Britain, are often disguised behind a coating of Latinist nickel-plate. London was, for some time, a potent centre of Greek ritual, with its gleaming white Temple of Apollo and Diana. There were Grecian choral dances in ancient Lugdinium, two thousand years ago, not entirely displaced by the Roman militia who brought the masculine cult of Mithras; and who built their temple for this Sun worship. The basic term *Xoros* has itself several meanings: (1) ring dance; (2) festive dance; (3) a choir or band, performing these dances; (4) any band or troop, especially of persons or things seeming to move equably together—the stars; (5) a place for dancing, especially the reserved space formed in a Greek theatre. The ancient Greek *choros* originated with the Dorian people; chiefly with their *Xoros kuklikos*, performed during the Athenian *Dionysia*. The fifty or fifty-two persons who moved in this ring dance were inspired by an older Eastern tradition. From it came the Attic Drama, permitting the presentation of a new mythos from Athenian poets, given in rhythmic dance. The Archon of Athens arranged for the *Choros*; the cost being met by a rich citizen, thence called *Choregos*. Three companies were known: the *Choros* Tragikos (of 12 or 15 dancers); the *Komikos* (24 dancers) and *Satirekos*. The poet supervised the specific training, having the title of *Xorodidaskalos*. The public of freemen were expected to attend; foreign visitors were also permitted to enter; there was no admission charge, for this was still a ritual.

CHOUT

Also *Chaud*, India; and *Choud*, England, Mediæval period. A musical joker (as in the Russian ballet *Chout*), who plays tricks on everyone. In India, especially Bengal, there is a clan named Chaud-

hori, or Chaudhuri, which derives from "dance comedians".
[See *Chhau Dancers* (Seraikella, E. India); *Shleu* (Morocco)]

CHRISTIAN DANCE—1 (Developments)

Those rituals and ceremonials, that included regular forms of movement, position and gesture, being accompanied by chanting or music (or both) which we may properly name as dance, were derived from earlier systems. These precedent cults were (1) Israeli or Jewish rituals; (2) Greek and Hellenic rituals; (3) Etruscan or Teutonic ceremonies; and finally 4) remains of Egyptian cults, as imported into Rome and later into Alexandria. Ritual forms; purposes of ceremonial; musical instruments, and hierarchic systems with their traditional titles, were taken into the new cult, according to opportunity and necessity. Our purpose here is not analysis of ritual, or utility of *dochema;* or even the politico-economic aims that become evident to close students of the Primitive Christian church; but rather to trace the forms of ceremonial in their spectacular aspect. These ceremonies, as in all religions, belong to the recurrent facts of life: birth, marriage, and death; the social relations of morals and ethical discipline; with the myths, open or secret, by which the ordinary man was attracted and at times enlightened. We find that three main types of building reveal these principal developments: the temple was merged with the basilica; the kirke or round church adopted the older tomb and memorial structure, long used for ancestral rituals; and thence for the initiations (including the ritual death and resurrection of tribal rites); while the great Egyptian forecourt was adopted (chiefly much later) as the cloister of collegiate church or abbey, as a centre for propaganda. The round church ended with the the Knights Templars (when all initiation rites also disappeared from church usage); but the basilica type was continued and magnified until Bramante planned the Roman centre, the Vatican basilica known as Ste. Petro. The cloister was for centuries built in wood (following, in part, the Roman amphitheatre), but the stone squares were little used. Each building contained definitely stylised modes of ceremonial dance and ritual. The round tomb was skilfully merged with the propaganda of "saints" and "martyrs", because at these annual meetings the recruits (then initiated) gave "witness" or Mar Tyr, to their faith. The scheme of "relic" worship was a later device; transferred to the Latin cross style of building, along with the new style *altara* or stone tomb-table; and the *Messe*, or annual feast, that had belonged to the original memorial round tomb inherited from Asia.

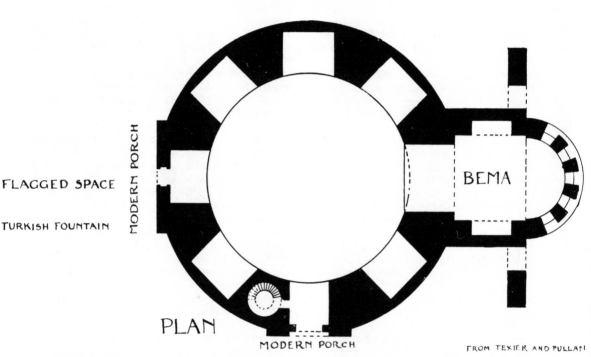

LONGITUDINAL SECTION.

SCALE |||||||||| FEET

FLAGGED SPACE

TURKISH FOUNTAIN

MODERN PORCH

BEMA

PLAN

MODERN PORCH

FROM TEXIER AND PULLAN

Christian Primitive Dance. Characteristic plan of Hellenic Christian Church, Hagios, Georgius, Salonika. The space is always circular. The Beama (High Place) is used by the Master or Speaker, the *Profeta* or "Teacher of Righteousness."   HELLAS

CHRISTIAN DANCE—2 (Eastern form)
Is known in the rituals of the so-called Mandaean of Johana, one of whose centres is at Basra, on the Persian Gulf. They call themselves the Mandaya or Mandaeans, which they take to mean worshippers of Manda d'Haye. Their advanced grade is called *Nazoraya.* Moslems describe them all as *Subba* (Baptists). Their doctrine is said to possess affinities with the ancient cosmogony and theosophy of Babylonia.[1] There are connections of Mandaean system with the Gnostics (2nd century). The term *Manda d'Haye* (as given by Dr. Brandt), reflects the much later *allemande* d'haye*—the dance of the *allemand* or the *Vierge Jeanne.* The cult is connected (by J. M. Robertson[2]) with Ea-Oannes (of Babylon), the sacred Fishman who taught. If we refer to Rome, we note Janus as a collapsed version of a similar god-name; tied to the New Year Festival as *Janus Bifrons,* the Two-faced (Time-past and Time-future). Read as I O-Annus, it is the

"Period of the Moon, or 10". The continued existence of mystery-plays, as acted parables, is attested
by the well-known phrase (Mark iv. 7—Matth.
xiii. 11) "Unto you (disciples) is given (to know)
the mysteries of the kingdom of god; but unto
them that are without, all things are done in parables".
[1] *Die Mandaische Religion.* Dr. A. J. W. Brandt
    (1889) pp. 9, 141.
[2] *Christianity and Mythology.* John M. Robertson.
    (2nd edn. 1936) p. 397.

CHRISTIAN PRIMITIVE DANCE RITUALS(Europe)
Numerous references to the early groups of
religious enthusiasts, who agreed to accept one or
other of the various Christian schemes, mention
rituals in which dance was prominent. These dances
followed earlier customs, now applied to revised
doctrines. (AD 1-400 approx.). The Jews of Antioch,
along with the Greeks of that city, followed the
system of the Tabernacle, or that of the *Ekklesia;*
while the Jews in Rome, along with the slave
women from all quarters, brought in remnants of
the Dance of Isis, and the rites of Carthage (that
city was *delenda,* but their religion was not). Philo
tells of the *Therapeutae* (of Syrian-Buddhist origin),
who used dance; but most accounts come from
enemies or detractors of these groups (wrongly
called "sects", since they had not begun as dividers
of another creed), and we have little description.
1. Euchites: Were the so-called "Praying people"
who originated in Syria as a group; and used to
dance as they prayed or chanted (similar to the
later *karole* 400-500 AD).
2. Choreutes: Other groups of dancing worshippers, in Eastern Asia; their name suggests a continuance of Grecian round-dance ritual.
3. Ascitae: In Galatia, were associated with Mon-
tanists (*circa* 170 AD), as worshippers, following the
Dionysian creed of Bacchus. They used a full-wine-
skin (a lamb-skin) richly decorated, laid before their
altar (on which rested cups of wine and bread),
round which they danced; as a symbol of the
"Wine of the Spirit" ("I am the Vine!").
4. Agonyclites: In Greece and Syria; these groups
objected to prostration (to any image, or officiant)
during ritual worship; and used instead a ritual
religious dance. They were reproved (by the
officials they disliked) in a Synod of Jerusalem in
726.
5. Gnostics: In Greece, and later Rome; also
travelled in missions through Europe, even to
Britain. They used the famous *Dance* or *Hymn of
Jesus** (preserved in *Actae,* or records of ritual
system) as a dance ceremony.
6. Collyridians: Alleged to be (4th century) a
"sect of female worshippers", in "Arabia" (!) who

worshipped with a feast, including little round
cakes, which in some strange way acquired a
Latinist name. The term suggests *colenruada;* but
references from pious denouncers are rarely reliable. The name might refer to a Year-End Festival.

CHUKCHEE ANIMAL DANCES (North-east Siberia)
Mimetic dances of the Chukchee tribe, describing
various animal and bird legends. Accompanying
descriptive songs, the dances are performed by girls
making appropriate animal movements and sounds.
Dancing in a circle, or in opposite rows, they
begin singing gutturally, and then go higher, swaying their bodies in rhythm with the music. Young
boys sometimes take part, lifting their hands,
snapping fingers, clicking tongues. Popular dances
are "Raven Song-Dance", and "Dialogue of the Fox
and Bear". The Fox is a cunning doctor, who pretends to heal the Bear's wounds with hot stones,
but instead kills him. Performers playing the Fox
sing in shrill voices; the Bear dancers reply in gruff
accents, which become feebler as the Bear dies.
Other mimetic dances describe the pairing of the
Fighting Sandpipers; the Long Tailed Duck; Swan;
Seal; Wolves and Reindeer.

CHUKKER (Persia)
A "round" or period at polo-game in Persia. To
Chikker, or *Dhigger,* is "to Jigger", to circle round,
as in the ritual ascent of Ziggurath,* the "circling
path-temple" of Babylon. In seven stages, with a
rising path round each of its four sides; there are 28
inclines in all, to reach the chamber of divination
at the crest.

CHURCH ALE (English)
Was a custom celebrated at Easter, spreading to
Whetsun and then Krestenmesse. A feast was arranged by the wardens, who collected funds
through the parish. Church ale was brewed and
drunk at this feast; which was followed by dancing to hymn tunes or psalm-tunes. Stubbs records
(1585) that a strong ale was brewed (and sold in
the churches) for six weeks, a quarter, or half a
year; to get funds for purchase of necessary service books, or "surplice for Sir John". The origin is
said by Duncan to be traceable back to the Love
Feast or *agape.* The custom obviously spread to the
secular ale-house.

CHURCH DANCES (Western Europe-Latin Church)
Have always been numerous, until comparatively
recent times (17th century), but many still exist,
directly or indirectly associated with Romish or
earlier customs, attached to some point of church
ceremonial. Church Dances may be analysed suit-

ably in their several distinct functional categories:
(a) inside the church, as a basic part of the liturgy;
(b) as part of periodical ceremonial, inside the
church; as a dedication of place or person, a mass,
a baptism, etc.; (c) inside the church, as part of
mystery play or miracle play—as doctrine or propaganda; (d) outside the church, the primary occasion being the initial dedication and opening of the
building for religious usage; usually culminating
with another processional ritual-dance inside the
building; (e) outside the church, the funeral,
burial, or graveyard memorial dances; (f) processional dances, from some gathering place, such as
the fields, a harvest centre etc., then towards and
into the church; or a funeral procession, with
music and solemn dance, (g) popular memorial
dances, arranged and performed without clerical
leave or sanction; these both inside the church and
in the churchyard, usually on traditional dates,
some anterior to intrusive church celebrations on
the site of an older and revered shrine ("St. Martin" from Bacchus, for example). There has never
been a period when there was no dance associated
with the Latin religious system; from its earliest
days, its officiants took over much from the Jewish
and especially Greek rituals, with their dance-forms
of worship; so that the vehement denunciations of
the early "fathers" are invariably against rivals of
their own newly evolved scheme, not against the
ceremonial forms and usage. Successive fulminations are always against popular ceremonials that
were followed without clerical permission (or
remuneration) during the centuries when gradually
the older itinerant bands of players were absorbed
into the newer tradition. The original church ritual
dances maintained several older customs, notably
that of Catechumenoi, "Youth Initiation", for
youths of both sexes (Camilla, Camillae) as innokente (later infantes) received at the fontana or
font. Persistent search into ritual ceremonies reveals a similarity that matches the continuity (and
style changes) of architectural form; of wall paintings (in Catacombs the "Good Shepherd" or
Orpheus becomes Jesus), and of ritual terms and
especially technical language, in this renaissance
of decadent faiths of Greece and Rome. In Spain
and Mexico dances inside the church still continue.
[See Bal del Ciri* Els Cosiers;* Eagle Dance;* Ezpa-
tadanza de Zumarraga; Faixes;* Matachines;* Los
Seises*]
The following dances used to be performed inside
churches: La Bergeretta;* Creux de Vervi;* Marie
Magdaleine, Dance of* (France); Lehenswinken;*
Mailehen;* Moosburg;* Pomwitzel* (Germany);
Danza del Duomo Cintola* (Italy); Jumping
Saints* (Luxembourg); Mourisca* (Portugal); Horo*
(Rumania) at weddings; Dalum Dance* (Sweden);

La Rosca* (Spain); Rush Bearing* (England); Tripettos, Danso De* (France).

CHURCH DANCE CEREMONIAL
Basilican style; derived from the Greek Boulé* and
the Roman basilica or King's hall. The Entry,
Processional, and the Submission (of accused
witness etc.), were the chief events. Some rites
had two entries; one of the "people" or general
assembly; and secondly, of the chief personages,
attired in ceremonial costume. The ceremonial
parade had several forms: public, semi-public, and
private. From the "parade around the great hall",
or "showing of the chiefs", developed the parallel
Trionfo (or street parade), and the interior processional danse basse, preceded only by heralds, and
torch-bearers. The private ceremonials accompanied
the Feast; this required elaborate tables, and
avenues for servants to bring food and remove
dishes. These simple technical necessities dictated
the basic forms of dance and music; finally aspiring
in the 17th century to chamber music; though continued (as in Russia, on country estates), well into
the 19th century. (See Entrée*). The court feast
had its own necessities; the ritual feast (now transferred from the tomb-kirke), now had ritual or non-
real ceremonies; and the church messe* began to
develop as a symbol-feast, the "meal with the gods"
regaining memories of the Egyptian messe or
Meskhen.* Prolonged to more and more "realistic"
devices, the real feast disappeared (though privately continued, as in France by the canons, in
their own manner; until the 16th century period,
as at Auxerre). The concluding settlement of ceremonial produced two processional rites: the
magical dance of dedication, round the new church,
first outside and then inside; and the recurrent
processional, inside the church on any special
occasion. This is extended (where contrived) into
long and elaborate street processions, with symbols,
idols, and music and dancing, as in Spain. Remains
of these basilican ritual dances are frequent; though
the original square form is often lost. The name
survives in contra-dances, parallel with the phon
and antiphon of choral singing; also such dances as
The Seises,* or Els Cosiers* of Majorca; or the play
at Elche (taken from the cloister system).
[See Bergeretta (France); Creux de Vervi (France);
Marcel (France); Marie Magdeleine (France); Pomwitzel (Silesia)]

CHURCH DANCE RITUAL (England)
Internal cathedral pavements when first installed
received well defined marks, cut or inlaid, for use
of the officiants in rituals. At Lincoln, the socket
for processional cross remains near the central
pillar of the chapter house. At York, these circles

were destroyed in 1736; they may be seen marked in old ground plans of the Minster, thus described : "A number of circles which ranged from the west end up the middle aisle, on each side; and in the centre. There were about forty-four on a side, about two feet in diameter and as much in distance from one another." "We take it", says Walcot, "that all these were drawn out for dignitaries to stand in ... or any solemn occasion".[1] He continues (p.119) "It has been suggested that these stones, like the foreign labyrinths, may have served as a compromise for pilgrims 'marking a pace in the length of a nave' which, twelve times repeated, make a mile—twelve little holes against the great door with a little peg (*Antiqepert, ii,* 217) ... in several parts of Westminster, where the old pavement remains, a line of square stones between the ordinary diamond patterns may be traced, which once guided the progress of the procession"
[1] *Cathedrals.* B. O. Walcot.

CHURCH AND TURF-CUT MAZES (England)
Are known only in a few places. They appeared in three kinds of site : (a) within the church, often inlaid in tile or mosaic on the floor of the nave; (b) in the churchyard; and (c) less definitely groomed by clerics, in the village near by. Traditions of Maze patterns are confused with those of *Labyrinth**; and these with others, less familiar in Europe. Some writers believe that forms brought into England were Byzantine. In England, mazes connected with churches were cut in turf. The only example, within a church is one represented in the nave at Hornton in Leicestershire. Church mazes may be seen now at St. Martha's (near Guildford); Hilton (Cambridge); Alkborough (Lincolnshire); Boughton Green (Northants); and on St. Catherine's Hill (near Winchester). The maze cut in turf brings us near to the tradition of the "Nine Men's Morris" (also the Long Man of Wilmington), and its transition into the popular game at St. Andrews, into a longer but less puzzling course at golf. The dance traditions that belong to these mazes remain in the spiraline carol (within the church, as in France), [see *Church Dances*] and in the game of "Barla-brak", now almost lost; for the dances have retreated into barn and ballroom (e.g. *Paul Jones*).

CHYLDE (Old English)
From Greek *Xilias,* a Thousand and *Xiliarchos,* leader of 1,000. The title or rank has been confused with Chylde as a symbol of the Young Year, the Child, for whom was celebrated *Childre Messe* (Dec. 28th) the Feast of Children who danced *The Song of the Lord.* The name exists in English as Chylde Harolde; this was the usage of Chylde

as the pages or sons of knights. This term is ancient; from it we have *Chylde Uren* (the Son of the Wren), again, the Young Year. The 1,000 was a count in the ritual dance of the Shen; from it came the notion of the Thousand Year Reign. [See *Bez; Catherina; Nikolas*]

CHYLDES KIRK (England, Scotland)
Were churches that specialised in the acceptance of children : Nicolas for boys, Catherine for girls. At one period the term *chylde* was feminine; at another (as in France) it was masculine; but the gathering and dance was mixed. Scottish place-names show changes in the spelling : from *Childenchircke* (1160) to *Childenchirch; Chyndlkirk* (1530); and *Chingelkirk* and *Cheinilkirk.* The name was vested in 'Holy Innokentes", but collected also as *Chylde Harolde.* The term *Chield-helles* is "Son of Light"; and there was a *Cheild Lyellies* (Child of Lilies), but it has nothing to do with any "Saint" Cuthbert—this term was *Kath-berta,* the ritual or *kathal.*

CICISBEO (Italy)
Dancing partner, hinting at "a lover" in its earlier usage, a regular Italian male follower of a married woman. We may compare in its dancing sense with the modernist *gigolo** (a partner in the ballroom and elsewhere). From *cicisbeo* we seem to have the term "cissie", as a "too-feminine youth". *Gigolo* indicates a dancer of the jig. In Chaucer's day the analogous term was *leman.**
[See *Allemande; Gigolo; Leman*]

CIFTE TEL (Turkey)
A restrained version of the *danse du ventre,* performed as a solo either by one woman for other women, or by a man for a male audience. While the footwork is of secondary importance, the movement of the abdominal muscles is not as pronounced as in the North African dance. A characteristic of the *Cifte* Tel is a horizontal jerking of the head, and quivering of the shoulders and arms similar to the "shiver" in the dance performed by the *Shleuh** dancers in Morocco. The *Cifte Tel* is also known in the Caucasus, Azerbaijan, Anatolia, Baku and Persia.
[See *Danse du Ventre; Muscle Dance; Ouled Nail; Shleuh Boy Dancers; Buffoon Dance*]

CINEMA FILM DANCE
In Europe, cinema develops in three principal modes, according to the basic technical form of the subject, the dancing figures. These appear in the world which produced dancing figures as dancing puppets, the oldest shadow dances in the world, as (a) figures as shadows on the walls of caves or

huts, or on the flat sands left by receding waters; (b) the extension of flat puppets into flat painted paper figures, as the studio cartoon-caricature, developed largely for children's film shows; and (c) the "straight film" made from human dancers, in the contrasted mode of the photographed ballet or folk-dance, as compared with the three-dimensional film-studio "spectacular" style. Owing to the extreme bias on "motion at any cost" followed by early film producers, the dance (in any style), has received biassed treatment, by regulation production methods from the "chase". This multiple viewpoint has been copied with equally bad results in the television systems. All these producers refuse to allow the spectator to "remain put in one place", to insist upon his viewpoint being forcibly altered, every sixty seconds. Dance cannot be apprehended by violently moving the spectators; hence film-dance has not yet been artistically (or even scientifically) developed as a modern art.

CINQ PAS (French)
The famous "Five Steps" dance, known to Shakespeare also as *sinky-pace*; highly popular in his period. Derived immediately from the tuition of the ubiquitous fencing masters, they were: (1) *Droite*, the straight line, back or forward; (2) *Ouvert*, open sideways, right or left; (3) *ronde*, a circular sweep; (4) *glissé*, a gliding step with foot on the floor; and (5) *tournée*, the turning, also right or left. To these basic five, later teachers have added *Tortille*, winding or twisting; and *Sauté*, the jump or spring upwards; and finally the *battu*, or beat of one foot against the other, which was the finale of the fence exercise, or accompanied *la salute*.   [See *Reverence*]

CINTA DANTZA (Basque)
"Ribbon Dance". Popular in the Basque province of Guipuzkoa, where it forms the last figure of the *Ezpata Dantza** or "Sword Dance". Performed by men, this is no childish game, but a vigorous dance in which the ribbons are plaited into patterns as the men dash round the pole in rapid 6/8 time. The Basque drum and *txistu* (three-holed pipe) accompany the dance.
[See *Cordon, Baile del; Lei Courdello; Maypole Dance; Listones, Danza de los*]

CINTOLA, DANZA DEL DUOMO (Italy)
Processional dance, in Florence, formerly done around and into the cathedral church. The prominent feature was the *Cintola*, made in textile, like the old *fascia* or belt, as a damask *ceinture*, which was unrolled and carried, and hung, on festival occasions, all round the building. Obviously this is a replica of such ceremonies as the Grecian procession with the *peplum*, every five years, to the Temple of Athene Parthenos at Athens. The long scarf, especially woven and decorated with symbolic designs, was carried by the band of devotees. In similar fashion, green branches were carried by an endless chain; or even other items (see *Martial,* Martin**). Smaller cloths were carried as banners (*oriflamme*, etc.), while a famous tapestry specimen is known at Bayeux, made by the Lady Matilda to memorize the Norman invasion in 1066. The symbolism and its dance indicates the investiture of the indwelling deity; as this robe of Minerva (*peploz*, Greek; *peplum*, Latin). It was alternatively a robe and a hanging; a temple veil as well as a statue veil. In Romish ritual it is the *pallium* (stole).   [Cp. *Faixes; Putti*]

CIRCULATION IN DANCE
The first basic Cosmic law of the visible universe. Herakleitus the Stoic phrases the fact as *Panta Rhei*—All Things Flow—but we must balance this assertion with the creative power within "Things" —the Energy inevitable with all Form—for All Energy Flows. The creative Vach (Voice) or Logos or Sokol or Verbum initiates Rhythmic pulsation; and Matter is moved by Energy; as Energy moves Matter into vital form—nuclear, atomic, molecular, cellular, organic and "natural life". With regular pulsation, Rhythm ensues; and so the universal dance emerges. When it becomes irregular (at the point distant from original tension) then discord appears. Our human endeavour in the arts is to perceive, record, and impose a newer order, the apex of which becomes Dance. As Matter opposes Energy (the truth perceived by the Gnostics, Manichaeans—they called it "Evil") so appears the basic condition in which all life becomes possible. A simple fact-symbol is the now obsolete carbon-arc lamp: from its negative current the positive pole emits light; the duality and opposition are essential. The Dancer must have a dancing floor. This knowledge was in the hands of ancient scholars; in India, Babylonia, Iran. Some of it was constructed in Geometrical figures—the plane and solid modes; while the Greeks showed in the Ionic Volute their profound realisation of the "curves of life".[1] which governed their arts. Dances in Egypt were founded on tracing these figures; in Egypt, the Shen was danced by the Phara-Oh—the Neb Sennen, King of the Orbit; and in India, temples reveal their floor patterns, knowledge of the chakram, the circulation (in religion, symbolised as Shiva-Kali-Vishnu) Dances gave dynamic reality to the doctrine of "Circulation-balanced-Rhythm" as the fundamental source of Cosmos—and thus of human life, its reflex in the "Middle Way" between the Makrocosm and the Mikrocosm which is the

Nuclear Energy, hidden in all matter. Along the vast spiraline paths of energy streams are the foci from which the forms we see — and use — and are — come into a more enduring mode of being, development, and change — all symbolised in many modes of Dance.
[1] *The Curves of Life.* Cook. London, 1914

CIRCUS
The Horse Dancer in *La Haute Ecole* (France, Italy, England). One experienced writer on circus bluntly asserts that "Horses cannot dance at all; they have no sense of time". Equally expert artillerymen will state that horses reveal a remarkable sense of timing in many operations. To all circus lovers it is visually evident that they possess a notable degree of the complementary "sense of space". The High School of Equitation is that known as *La Haute École* : in which traditional exercises many names in French are summarised under *dressage*. Like ballet, this discipline derives from military and court necessities, as associated with tourney or tournament; the display of martial exercise on horseback, equally with the display of the *trionfo*. Even the Riding School was the rendez-vous for the ballet — as in Vienna or Moscow (*Ménage*). The Spanish school found a new centre in Vienna; but the German school had military enthusiasts, as had the Milanese school. The *Haute École* had two categories : *Auf die Erde* and *Uber die Erde* — equivalent to *La Danse Basse* and *La Danse Haute.* The score or so of best known "steps of equitation" bear names, which resemble or equal technical terms in ballet; they include :
1. *Pirouette ordinaire;* done as *à droite* or *à gauche*, and *Pirouette renversée* (when hindquarters trace the circle around the forelegs in the centre).
Pirouette en trois jambes (impossible to ordinary ballerinas!) and
Pirouette à pieds croisés (hooves at centre remain stationary, as the legs become crossed when the horse turns about them; this is done both *ordinaire* and *renversée*, which last is easier).
2. *Galops* vary as : *Galop sur place* (gallop without going forward).
Galop en arrière (all movements of cantering, but in fact, moving backwards; very difficult).
Galop sur trois jambes — a three-leg canter, when the fourth leg is extended.
3. *Passage.* A rhythmic trot; forelegs well picked up; hind legs well forward (like a "well-gathered" greyhound stride); *Passage* develops into *Piaffe*, or full-display;
Passage performed in one place; no moving forward, and marking time. In the *Piaffe Ballotée,* the

hind legs are raised and put down in the same place.
4. Instead of *Pas de Basque*, we find *Pas d'Espagne* and *Trot d'Espagne*, along with *Trot Serpentine*; also *Capriole* and *Changement de pieds.* In *Pas d'Espagne*, each step in this walk has foreleg raised extended in front, the whole leg is horizontal; resembling a chorus girl's front kick. For *Trot d'Espagne*, this movement is accomplished as a rhythmic, springy trot (it is seen in any well-trained Tiller-girl troupe) with bent or straight knee. *The Serpentine Trot* is a development of *Travail de deux pistes*, which is an oblique movement where track lines made by fore and hind legs remain distinct and parallel. In "serpentine" the direction is changed at each four-pace beat. In *Changement de pied* there is, obviously, a change in several ways; as for example, a *Changement de pieds galop à temps* alters with each pace. There is a movement known as *pas de polka*, based on changing step, *Capriole* shows the horse with forelegs raised high, quarters raised in jump, and four feet off the ground, kicking with both back legs together.
5. *Croupade* and *Ballotade* are variations, with four legs off the ground.
6. *Lançade* (lancers' move) a leap forward.
7. *Pesade* shows hind legs unmoving, while the forelegs hang vertically, hooves tucked back.
8. *Courbette* keeps rear still, making a set of short jumps, keeping forelegs from ground; while *Mezair* and *Terre à Terre* are other variations from *Courbette. Cabrade* is another : a high rearing position, but now with forelegs outstretched, contrasted with *Ruade*, when both rear legs shoot backwards, forelegs on ground (stable boys beware!).

There are many more terms, based on natural movements, improved by training, that belong to *La Haute École*; but, as with the basic technical steps of the academy of ballet, it cannot be claimed that any such steps express any sort of emotion. [See *Fola; Horse Ballet; Bareback Ballerina*]

CIRCUS RING
Traditional size is always twenty cubits, in modern measurement equal to forty-two feet. At first symbolical, as a "score cubits", the size has been long recognised as a standard dimension, because all horses, and other animals are trained to perform in a ring of just this size, so that one larger or smaller would restrict their accurate movement.

CIRI, BALL DEL (Catalonia)
"Candle Dance". A semi-ritual dance showing traces of an ancient "rain" dance — relic of a pre-Christian ceremony taken over by the Catholic

Church. It now combines ceremony with social dance. At Castelltersol, three retiring church-wardens perform the *Ball del Ciri* inside the church. During the dance, each man carries a glass jar full of perfume (a *morratxa*) in one hand, and a large candle in the other. Arrived at the church porch they throw the *morratxas* on to the roof so that the perfume runs out of the broken jars onto the spectators below. The social dance follows, in which five or six couples emerge from the church into the plaza, to dance, the girls wearing the white lace mantilla without a comb, in the Pyrenean style. Girls moving inwards, men outwards, they revolve in the form of a wheel. Sometimes, with six couples taking part, the first three pairs carry a candle and small jug of perfume with which they sprinkle bystanders as they dance. Half-way through, candles and perfume are passed to the last three couples, and the dance repeated. At Man-lléu there is another variation, when the man offers his partner a succession of *morratxas*, each of which she breaks, finally accepting one.

[See *Cascarone Balls* (California); *Kyndeldans* (Norway)]

CIRIWANU (Bolivia)
Danced by men of the Aymara Indians, wearing white skirts and ostrich-feather head-dresses. Music for the dance is provided by the dancers themselves, each of whom holds a large pan-pipe (*bajones*) in his left hand, and in his right hand a drumstick with which he beats a drum slung on the other side. The Bolivian pan-pipes are sometimes so long that one end rests on the ground.

CLAQUE (French)
A theatre group of paid applauders; the *claqueur* operates in groups, mainly in Paris. *Claque* means "to slap" or handclap by arrangement; it may also, less frequently, be hired to hiss or boo. The French system is logical; it is an extension of *la publicité*, making sure that certain dancers (or other stage artists) get required applause. In England the arrangement is less organized; in USA it is in full swing, with the *shills*; an indispensable group for the TV studio audience. The Parisian *claquement* is carefully arranged—the leader receives 50 or 100 free seats, perhaps also money payment. He receives instructions and informs his little company. With the claque, works also the clique (in USA termed log-rolling). In Paris, critics are "dined and wined" in which S. P. Diaghilev rapidly became expert; though he failed in London, which operates on the "press notice"—as the USA works on "preliminary publicity" free to editors, which allows them to pay no experts.

CLASSICAL BALLET (European)
Takes its rise from the codification comprised by Carlo Blasis, in his academic method and his two books[1] at the Ballet School of the Teatro alla Scala in Milano. This scheme was synthesised during his directorial period, from 1837, but had partially developed before. The academic system was technical dance; there was no school of choreography; no school of décor or painting. The system of *Blasis* derived from the dual French methods, (a) the *ballet de la cour*, or ballet of etiquette and manners; and (b) the bourgeois ballet, developed by Abbé Perrin as a commercial enterprise from the Foires together with the opera ballet which contributed to Perrin's management, along with *les femmes pantomimes*, the dancing girls of the Paris Foire san Laurent and Foire San Martin. In Milan, there was a considerable strain from the Hispano-Italian schools of France, though the duel had almost vanished, except from German *jungers* of university life. This masculine lineage, while valuable for training men in ballet school, affirms the apparently inescapable schizophrenic quality of much theatre ballet: inasmuch as it endeavours to become dramatic or emotional, on a basis of ritual ceremonial movement (that of the courts), and a technical system of fencing school. This male element provided the academic basis of the "Five Positions" which Beauchamp had earlier established in Paris. Blasis took them over once more into Milan; where the fencing masters had, two centuries before, taught these movements of *prise* and *reprise*. Some uneasy realization of this incompatible dualism remains in the emphasis on "classical ballet" as in opposition to "character ballet", or the art of mime, lacking which ballet remains an academic exercise of physical movement, without the emotional factor that energizes character. This: despite the equally "classical" character work of the Commedia dell' Arte; though it was never academic, since it had no school, no *maestro di mimo*, no ballerina but a Columbine. Milanese Classical Ballet reverted to Paris, but in Russia suffered exclusion. The Academy of Leningrad and Moscow uses a unity of French and Italian work, which dismisses the Cecchetti tradition in toto (this by Madame Vaganova), and follows Johanssen.
[1] *Theory and Practice of Art of Dancing*. Carlo Blasis. Trans. Mary Stewart Evans. (Kamin. NYC. 1952).

CLERICI VAGANTES (Latin Church term)
Entered from Greek term *kleros*, meaning "lots" and was clearly applied in the early Grecian communities to those deacons who had to register the "lots" both of the "fortunes" so often told among the faithful and the "lots" of the offerings claimed

by the officiants. The practice of the *clerici sortes* was general. The *vagantes* were probably also *vigilantes;* as later they lapsed into *vagrants.* (*Laws of Elizabeth I.*) Ancients (Latin) another church term. As Anchorite, Hermit, etc. Capitano : vs. *Capellano.* Capella (Chapel). Exorcism.

CLIPPING DANCE (England)

The Clipping or *Clepynge Daunce* accompanied various ritual ring dances in Mediæval England, sometimes round a tree, or round a Maypole. This was associated with the Green Man. The *Clepynge* or "calling" has remained with the old "square dances". The tree itself, and the "spirit of the tree" portrayed by a youth or maiden clothed and masked with foliage, survived in mediæval England as a dance around the Maypole, and as the Jack-in-the-Green or Green Man. The dance was performed (a) within the church, (b) within some local orchard (wassail ritual etc.), or (c) within the churchyard around the building. In another survival the worshippers moved in a circle round the tree, or the ceremony was transferred to the church; the formal dance being then known as the "naming" or *cleping* of the building. This custom continued to the 19th century; it has been revived at Painswick in Gloucestershire. Many stone carved masks exist (a face among green leaves) known as the "boss", itself a significant term; for it was not only a vaulting centre but the centre of every wheel; and every carpenter's gild meeting had the "boss and the fellows". This was the Green Man. To "clip" a youth is to bestow a mild blow (an initiation feature), while calipers are used "to measure" and clippers "to discipline the nippers", or to rule young shoots. Before *Clepynge* of the Church, paths had to be cleared and made level; this was the first essential for the first rite of dedication, in which the building was first officially called by the name of its "Saint".

CLOG DANCE

Or "Clock Dance", an Old English dance, recently surviving in Lancashire, in which the male dancers moved around the circle with heavy foot beats of their wooden clogs. These clogs, worn until about 1920-1930 by the cotton mill operatives, were similar to the Belgian and Dutch *sabot.* The dance step has similarities with the Spanish form of strong footwork, *zapateado.** The clock routine which was worked out in several modes, was in the earliest form a shorter version of the *Dance of the Hours,* in secular mode. The "hours" were marked rapidly in due succession by the required batteries of beats or taps. In a secondary exhibition form the man did the "Minute" steps while his partner did the hours inside his circle. This clog dance was essen-tially a peasant's or artisan's festival pastime; but it was the predecessor of the extensive range of "tap-dances". One of the last modes of the clog-dance was to perform it (like some Spanish dances) on a wooden table-top at an inn. when it became an astonishing exhibition of virtuosity. There are some Irish jig forms which reveal a similar rapidity of footwork; but performed in a soft leather slipper.

CLOISTER (England)

Defines usually the square enclosure where parable plays, miracle plays, and dances were given; alternately by monks, priests, and laymen (according to place and period), which was separated from the precincture of the general building for this purpose. In succession there was (a) the *parvis,* or flat open space before the church; (b) the enclosed space (*corral*) often invaded; (c) the selected space, usually by the south wall of the nave, fenced in, railed in, then constructed, something like an inn yard, with heavy timber; and (d) finally the permanent stone structure. This procedure separated the cloister (*kloster*) from precincture and garth or greensward or cemetery; though local names have been tossed to and fro; before permanent enclosure defined the reserved space. The Close is a favoured name, varied with Precincts (Norwich, Rochester, Peterborough, and Canterbury), at Carlisle, it is "The Abbey" and at Chester, Abbey Square; but at Westminster, the Cloisters. At Wells, "Close" is named Cathedral Green; at Exeter, Cathedral Yard. Then comes the term "cloister-garth". Chester calls its Garth as the Paradise; at Chester, it is Sprice; at Wells, the Palm Court (for Palm Sunday or Green Man Festival), while Peterborough has Laurel Court. Hereford has Our Lady Arbour, like Maid Alley at Durham, and Maiden Alley, the Slype, at Chester. Indifferently, the space was used by monks, citizens, and boys playing at games (as at Westminster, for football). Destruction of many buildings caused changes in name, or even position. Processional rituals commonly passed through, but often into the cloister for a ceremony; and many of these included dances or dancing steps. The name "Cloister" is a collapsed Greek-church version from *kaloyer-istria* (Monk-plays). These miracle plays were devised as popular or propaganda versions, often comical in detail, for attracting possible customers, as compared with the "Mystery Plays" (their final, not first, title), which were enacted in the *quire* of the church. The cloisters were definitely not built as lounging places for the junior monks. The chapter-house always opened into the cloister, being the dressing-room for the various characters taking part. Precisely the same arrangement may be seen at work today in Western Tibet (for example, at Leh in Ladakh), where Lamaist miracle plays are performed. The town criers called "Kal-oyer", drew attention to a play in prospect; gradually, the call became "Oyer! Oyer!" and this in turn gave rise to the term "Mayor Oyer", or Master Player, the tale-teller who managed the productions, finally to lapse into the absurdity of *Mere l'Oie* or "Mother Goose". In Denmark a vestige remained in the term Ole Luk Oieye,* as "dispenser of fairy-tales" — the "Yule Laiker Oyer". "To laik" is used today in Yorkshire, meaning "to play". The Cloister was one of the popular mediæval theatre-houses; by no means a place of silent meditation, until the trade disappeared with the Reformation.

CLOWN

Term referred to Scandinavian *klunni* (a boor) or *klonne*, a clown; and *klune*, a clumsy fellow. The term may relate to Latin Etruscan as *colonu*, a peasant, field worker etc. The content of the term has been widely developed. There are joking clowns and dancing clowns, people chiefly of the Theatre and Circus. Their function here links with the mediæval jester or buffoon or mimic; brought on from Shakespeare's plays into earlier panto-mimes by Weaver* and later producers. Theatre clowns seek to raise mirth by "acting the clown" as inferior persons. Their professional work is often skilful; it passed through the 19th century English music hall and into the film (Chaplin), opera (*Pagliacci*) and pantomime (Joey Grimaldi) with varying styles and periods of dance. Characteris-ation has been more important. Clowns appear now in Circus, music hall act, folk-dance (Morris, with the bladder or bauble), colour-films (Disney animal films, e.g. Donald Duck); and now Tele-vision. Much radio alleged "wit and humour" fails, lacking visual imagination. *Les Forain*, in ballet, had its serious side.

CLOWNS' DANCE (Samoa)

The dance of those who, at a ceremonial *siva* (dance), perform on either side of the *taupo*.* Usually performed by "talking chiefs" (village spokesmen), old men and old women, their dance burlesqes that of the *taupo*, the purpose being, by contrast of age and comic antics, to emphasise her grace and beauty. The higher her rank the higher the rank of those who act as her foils. Leaping about in slapstick antics, the dancers exaggerate the formal style of the *taupo*, pounding on the floor, and making a whooping sound by patting the open mouth with their palm. These clowns are sometimes so skilful and popular, that they "steal the show". Chiefs and older women who wish to dance, may choose between the dignified style of

the *taupo*, and the comedy of the clowns. [See *Samoan Dancing; Taupos' Dance*]

CLUBS, SOCIETIES, GILDS, ETC.

Are organised by enthusiasts for various aspects of Dance — from ballet fans to educational groups. There is often much to be gained by regular meet-ings, poised on the pivot of dance interest. There are Ballet Clubs in most big English cities; some colleges cherish Dance Clubs for amateur ballroom practice. Sometimes activity reaches in too am-bitious directions: where a working professional group is barely able to create and produce a worth-while new ballet, there is little chance of a non-cohesive amateur group attaining such an end. Apart from "lessons" which may acquaint the beginner with names of a few "ballet steps" there is little to be gained that cannot be seen in a good demonstration. More important than this craft of dance is the art of ballet. A library is useful; so are lectures, if real experts can be found (few will give time to provincial groups, and spend a day on British Railways to do it). Films are useful; visits for folk-dance occasions; and to local theatres for ballet or other dance, help to extend knowledge of the great art of dance. Though officers may be honorary, the rent of meeting-rooms; and increas-ing postal charges, combine to make study of dance in club or society more onerous.

COBBLERS' DANCE

Misnomer for *Kobold Dance* or (German) *Dance of Gnomes* (Gnome = Kobold). As *Dance of Three Ivans* it is performed in Russia as a masculine folk dance, and has been used in the *Divertissement* of the last Act of the Ballet *Sleeping Beauty*.

COLEN (Gaelic)

New Year Festival of Solstice (also *Colin*) equiva-lent to *Hogmanay*. Thus King (of) Colen is the elected ruler of the feast (King Cole) and *Kolen* (*Köln*, or Cologne) was one place of meeting for the Festival. *Celyn* is a Gaelic name for holly. *Colen-flower* we know today — *Chou-fleur*.

COLYN (Welsh)

A pivot or point = "cole", the "turning-point of the year" or solstice. Thus Colen-Brenin is King of the Year; or definitely, the elected King of the *Gwyl Colen* or New Year Feast; thus he is the ritual source of "Old King Cole" of British tradition. His "fiddlers three" may have been minstrels — doubt-less master-minstrels — who supplied music for the *Brenin-le ddawns*, for the Winter Solstice: *Byr-ddydd-gauaf*. Probably certain ritual sites, as for example, *Köln*, were so named because there they celebrated the *Colyn Gwyl*.

COMEDIES-BALLETS (France—17th century)
Show the change from court ballet to a kind of opera in secular mode. Extension of the Prologue (a sycophantic affair describing the latest victories) turned at times to neater explanations of themes derived from supposed Greek mythology. Ballet and opera, in the French Court of Louis XIV, were central art forms, devised both as a pastime or spectacular entertainment, and a state institution splendid enough to advertise the stately power. The king and his courtiers took part in the early ballets, but refrained from public song. On the base of Versailles, the composer Lully directed the ballet orchestra and wrote some ballet music, from 1650 to 1660, notable for rhythmic vivacity. Lully matched developing dance steps (*danse haute*) with crisper accents, from his strings, with a syncopation advanced on Handel's simpler 2/2 or 2/4 scheme. The resignation of Louis from active dancing permitted more comedy to appear; hence the success of the collaboration between Lully and Moliére. Their comedy-ballet form was new; it offered an aristocratic variety show blended with the play form. Lully's mature work is heard in *Le Bourgeoise Gentilhomme*, while Moliére's wit lent significance to the parody of an Italian aria, following Lully's *Ballet of the Nations*. Their work was the popular "song-and-dance" brought to a polished perfection, with real comic genius. Lully may be pompous, but in his style he is also passionate; even his church music was operatic in style,

truly baroque. Ballet forms were still somewhat precious; dancers still were advised often to mind their manners; there was no *tutu*. These *comedies ballets* continued to delight the court (and a good many of the people, who contrived "observation posts") until 1671. Then the path of the two theatre forms began to separate—the one into the non-speaking ballet, the other into the virile stem of *Comedie Francaise*. The transition of the royal amateur to the regular professional artists of theatre had been done.

COMMERCIAL BALLET
Implies the use of a dance-group who perform pieces specially devised to gain publicity for some definite commodity. In America, this method has been used by Lentheric Perfume Inc., when two skilled dancers travelled the main cities of the USA, performing in large halls, inside stores where the goods were obtainable. They performed miniature ballets which attempted to stress the character or name of each perfume. Another perfume manufacturer, Houbigant, sponsored a ballet given in 1948 by the Ballets Russe de Monte Carlo, cal'ed after their perfume "Quelques Fleurs". The method has been used for other commodities. For example, in 1950, to boost export trade in British woollen fabrics, a ballet film, called "The Dancing Fleece", was made by Crown Film Unit, to be shown first in America and then in other countries. With the advent of commercial television, we may expect

Moscow, Red Square, 1931. Twelve couples from Minsk performing Fizkultura version of Russian Dance.   RUSSIA

to see really skilful advertisers make more commercial use of this art.

[See *Store Display Dance; Merchandising by Dance*]

COMMUNIST DANCE (Russia, and some other countries)

In the great May-Day Festival (replacing the earlier Spring Festival of the peasants) in Moscow, may be seen huge processions, of armaments and industries. (1) Following soldiers and sailors, many workers appear in gala attire; and at intervals (chiefly in *Krasnaya Ploschad*) many dancing figures will be performed. Some dancers follow the theatre ballet; others display plastic dance; and many develop frankly into acrobatic feats. Dance items are rehearsed in Club or House of Culture centres. Only the best are shown; some reach a high standard in technical skill. These show the Russian versions of the West European *passacaglia* and other processional dances. (2) Competitions of various kinds of dance are held in clubs; or on open-air stages, some in the large arena of the Gorki-park. (3) Special groups, professional or amateur, are invited to give "Ten-Day Festivals" in Moscow, when some remarkable performances of all kinds of dance are contributed by artists of the various Soviet Republics. These may be witnessed, usually, on the Gorki-park wide stage. In most of these Communist Dances, there is no theme distinguishable from similar technical exhibitions that may be seen elsewhere; mainly they dance for rejoicing. At the same time, appropriate flags, slogans and symbols appear on banners; and songs of glorification are endless. Many of the folk-dances formerly practised have been inflltrated with theatre technique (as with the *Beryozka* group, seen in London, 1954), so that stage spectacle replaces group expression.

CONCERT DANCE

A term used to denote specialist performers of some kind of dance, who think they can gain the interest of an audience, apart from a theatre group; or ballet; or folk-dance ensemble. The concert dancer has a task similar to that of the concert singer or instrumentalist. This is chiefly a modernist idea, caused by too highly developed specialization of the arts. Very few artists can do it; for it can succeed, as a rule, only in cities where a changing audience can be drawn; or by constant travel. A dancer, such as Anna Pavlova, worked as near the "concert-artist" idea as was practical, but retained her group and orchestra. The ideal "concert-artist" is one who rarely works in a concert-hall—the experienced music-hall comedian, or the competent circus clown. The intimate dependance of most dance, either as ritual or as ballet and folk-dance, upon a company working together, suggests that

the concert-dance method is rarely worth developing. Among such artists, we can name: Isadora Duncan; La Argentina; Juana; Paul Draper; Himar Kesarcodi; Ragini Devi and others; and as dance-mimes, Angna Enters and Cilli Wang.

CONCHEROS (Mexico)

A highly organized religious society with groups (known as Mesas) in many parts of Mexico. Officials of the Mesa include First and Second Captains, Sergeant (in charge of the group at home), Field Sergeant (in charge of them at *fiestas*), men and women standard-bearers, two Malinches* to supply the censers with incense, and a "devil" to entertain spectators and keep them back while the *Concheros* are dancing. Said to have originated among the Chichimecas during the Conquest, there is evidence of Aztec ritual in the elaborate ceremonial, worship being concerned equally with the Holy Cross and the Four Winds, or cardinal points. (See *Aztec Dances.**) The principal *fiestas*, at which the *Concheros* dance, are those at La Ville de Guadalupe, Chalma, Los Remedios and Amecameca, which lie at the four cardinal points in direct relation to Mexico City. Before dancing, the group honours both the Cross and the Four Winds, by forming into two intersecting lines—a symbol of both conceptions. The same symbol is made by the Captain with each foot as "the sign of the dance", to mark the beginning of the performance. Playing the *concha* (a guitar-like instrument, backed with armadillo shell) from which they get their name, the dancers move in a circle, which none may leave without permission. Steps include springs with legs bent under; marking a cross in the air with one foot while dancing on the other; crossing feet and rocking from side to side; jumping into the air and landing on the toes. Each figure starts slowly, rises to a crescendo in music and dancing, then stops abruptly. Dancing continues for several hours, with an interval at mid-day. All the dancers wear feather head-dresses, decorated with mirrors and beads, and sometimes cover their faces with strings of beads. Costume has varied through the years, but many groups now wear fringed chamois suits in Indian style, although some have Spanish capes of coloured satins. An obligation among *Concheros* is mutual help in sickness and trouble, consideration and respect.

CONDITIONED REFLEX

In Dance would hardly be worth examination but for the pretensions of Marxian experts to lay down rules for art production: notable in the A. A. Zhdanov pamphlet *On Literature, Music and Philosophy*[1] which stretches over decades from Plekhanov's *Art et la Vie Sociale*[2] with Pavlov's experiments on "conditioned reflexes" in between. These did not extend to Theatre until K. S. Stanis-lavsky began work practically with his *Method;* from which Communist art philosophy took — without acknowledgment, their immediate notions of "Socialist Realism". While this basis has some source in many examples of genuine Russian folk-dance, the endeavour to present Theatre realism, as usual in most countries, falls into the dichotomy of theatrical conventions contrasting sharply with the "real life" outside the building.

One Marxian principle : namely that social facts all arise from and return to economic realism and its twin of politics, has not been elaborated into any working philosophy of any art, save propaganda. This is particularly evident in the art of ballet, the theatre art most removed from reality, whether in theme or action. Marx had — as might be expected — little enough to say on art;[3] Lenin expressed his few casual thoughts; while Stalin could not equal his predecessor on the value of imagination; only Tovarish Zhdanov came to help, in 1934 and 1947 on *Literature;* in 1948 on *Music;* in 1947 on *Philosophy;* in which last he lammed "this unforgiveable passion for vulgar naturalism" . . . In deriding Eddington he traces his ideas to "Pythagoras, or the apocalyptic 666". But — asks Zhdanov "does our philosophical front resemble a real front? It resembles rather a stagnant creek .. the field has not yet been conquered . . ." I. P. Pavlov was never Marxist; Anna Pavlova was a liberal; Stanislavsky was temperamentally a realist. But to try to make "realistic ballet" or to put authentic folk dance (in shiny blue satin trousers) on the stage, reveals the absence of any grasp of conditioned social reflex. Accordingly, the Russians who possess what is technically the best Theatre in the world produce some of the worst (home made) plays. They have a magnificent ballet Theatre, but hardly any conception of new ideas, possible to state through Dance. Their excellent Theatres for Children which normally have even less propaganda, are not surpassed. Industrial power is revealed in the main direction of atomic physics; but they do not yet balance atomic materialism with atomic energism; they do not utilise fully their theatre technology for that "engineering of the soul" that was once mentioned.

[1] *On Literature Music and Philosophy.* A. A. Zhdanov 1957.
[2] *Art et La Vie Sociale.* G. Plekhanov. Paris 1949
[3] *Philosophy of Art of Karl Marx.* M. Lefshetz. New York 1938.

CONGA (Cuba)

Originally this Afro-Cuban dance, named after the large Cuban drum, was a street procession danced during Carnival. A 2/4 march rhythm in which every second syncopation was accented, the movement was smoother than in the modern ballroom version, with none of the latter's jerky kicks. When the *Conga* became popular in the USA as a ballroom dance, the "1, 2, 3 kick" rhythm was stressed, the strong beats being violently accented, but Cuban bands soften this exaggeration. The *Congada* of Brazil has no connection with the Cuban *Conga,* being a highly syncopated dance from the Negro ritual *Congo,* which is also the name of a dance in Haiti, when the forms vary with their locality.

CONQUISTA, LA (Mexico)

A dance-play of the Conquest, widespread along the west coast of Mexico, particularly in the states of Jalisco and Oaxaca. Relating the story of Cortes and his men opposed by Montezuma and his court, the historical ending is ignored, in order that Montezuma may live to become a Christian. While Montezuma and his companions wear costumes of gay silks and spreading feather head-dresses in brilliant colours, the Spaniards, represented by young boys, are dressed in drab blue. Malinche* (danced by a small girl), although historically Cortes' mistress, here dances with Montezuma and appears to be on his side. The text used by the dancers of Cuilapan is the most historically accurate. Music is played by a band, rhythms being marked by the dancers' rattles. When the dance is performed without the Spaniards, as in the Valley of Oaxaca, it is known as the *Danza de las Plumas.**

CONTRA-DANCE

English term, from Italian — *contra-danza,* modified into "Countrie Daunce", after the Revolution which displaced the Roman Church as ruler in Britain in the time of Henry VII and Henry VIII. Much argument has continued, concerning the origin of this dance term, which is known thus only in England. No other tribe or nation refers to its own dances as "country-dance". The fashion was set firmly by Playford, who collected current tunes (and sometimes words) into his highly popular succession of volumes, beginning in 1650. From earlier terminology, belonging to clerical usage in Italy, France, and England, it is clear that the choral chanting and church dance rituals commonly had regular reference to the "parts" by the quality of voices : namely, as alto and tenor or bass. The term "alto" is now referred to the "high falsetto voice of men", but boys who sing at this pitch are named contra-alto or contralto; that is, the term implies its opposition, as basso or contrabasso. The terms applied to female voices have a counter-range, from sopra-anno down in tone to the contra-alto, with the mezzo-contra-alto between. Dance terms kept a fair alignment with the music. The *passa-mezzo* is the "step between", both in fence and dance. In England, these musical terms meant first the musical groups who sang certain parts of liturgy; then by usage, they became applied also to the style of step and movement. This begins, apparently, with the ancient Grecian thesis and anti-thesis, when two parts of the chorus sang antiphonally. The Latin church took over this system, with doctrines and ceremonial; finally we get loose copies in secular tradition. In 1600, many church tunes were sung at a quick pace; they could, and did, accompany dance, without alteration. Puritan influence syncopated these to a slower pace; to repress merriment and dance to "a seemlier movement". Then the ancient *contra-danza* became naturalised to "countrie daunce".

CONTRAPAS (Catalonia, Spain)
A solemn religious dance which used to be performed after Mass outside the church. Richard Ford, in *Gatherings in Spain* (1846), notes that the Catalan people are fond of dancing the *Contrapas* and *Sardana*.* Chanting antiphonally a mournful hymn, and led by the priest, the dancers, with joined hands, swung to and fro in a semi-circle controlled by the men at either end. The man at the left (the *Cap*) pulled the line one way; he at the right (the *Cua*) pulled it the other way. According to Gaston Vuillier[1] "it is a sort of round led by two principal performers, who give the time and the step. They perform a few steps to one side, repeat them to the other, and the whole band imitates their movements. This swaying motion . . . . (is) diversified by a rapid *battement* with the heel against the instep. . . ." While the *Contrapas* is not often seen now, it is occasionally performed in small places such as the town of Olot. In some places its form has considerably changed. The *Contrapas de San Genis* has become a dance for six couples in a line; while the *Contrapas de Xinxina* is in semi-circular form (later changing to a closed ring), for six to twenty couples moving with dignified bearing, but of a gay and light character. Where the *Contrapas* is still connected with the Church it may be performed after the singing of a "Divino", directed by the priest and led by the mayor. Beginning solemnly, music and dance become more gay, and some versions contain a figure called "*L'espardenyeta*" after the dancers' canvas shoes. For this each dancer revolves on his heels and then again joins hands in a semi-circle. A variation of the ancient Chain Dance, the old *Contra-*

pas was itself the foundation for the *Sardana*,* the national dance of Catalonia.   [Cp. *Corranda*]
[1] *History of Dancing.* Gaston Vuillier. 1898.

CONTRE-DANSE
Basically "dance against dance", as the term implies; not a "country-dance", except by misunderstanding. The sacred *contre-danse* was from *phon* and *antiphon*—namely the two sides of singers in the church quire (again, from *enquire* and *quire*, "to question" and "to answer"). Later, this basic dance became known as *quadrille*;* also a dance of couples or quartets against a second couple or quarter. Naturally, on this foundation, many dance forms have been elaborated. No solo dance or *danse a deux* can be accepted as a *contre-danse*. Many English traditional dances (some pseudo-Morris forms included) show the *contre* and *rencontre*. The supposed opposition between "town dance" and "country dance" is fallacious; even the term "country" is not found in other languages. The French opposition is *danse basse* versus *danse haute*, as indicating roughly the courtly dance versus the less elegant peasant dance, like the quaint "Gentlemen versus Players" in cricket.   [See *Cotillon*]

CORAL MASTER (Spanish term)
A special reference to a "dancing juggler" said to derive from his tight-fitting garb of scarlet or coral hue, displayed when he threw off his cloak to begin performance. But the term may equally mean "ring-master", since *corral* was the early Spanish circus ring (10th to 14th century period), as the *corrida* was the bull-ring.

CORAULE (Switzerland)
A chain dance from the Gruyère, Alpine district, descendant of the mediæval *Carole*.* Accompanied by songs in the regional dialect, the *Coraule* begins as a circle, but during the instrumental refrain which follows the song, the circle breaks up into couples, who dance a *Schottische** or similar dance.

CORDÃO (Brazil)
Name of a group of dancers at Carnival time, who perform among the festive crowd. In order to make sufficient room for them to dance, some of their companions "cord off" a space round which spectators crowd to watch the dance. Hence the name, *Cordão*. In Rio de Janeiro, Bahia and Recife, the *cordão* groups are renowned for the high standard of their performance and the excellence of their costumes.

CORD, CORDON, CORDING, *the Temple* (Egypt)
Are terms relating to "marking off" the required ritual space; from the elaborate regal ceremony of

Egyptian ritual dance, to the simpler modern lay-out of a sports ground. The Cord was first an implement, then it became a mark of distinction; then it became sacred. The *putser* (surveyor) carried his cord in Egypt, of standard length and material. One form of it became the collar; in India it is the Brahman's triple thread, *vajno-pavita*; the rite of investment marks initiation. The cord was requisite for the *templum* — the "place of measurement". Probably the most famous cord was the knotted rope of Pythagoras: it established the geometrical figures on the ground; it was used by travels "at thirty knots" — the hour is always assumed. The ritual tradition, carried on by the Knights of Malta, is continued by the Grand Tyler of the Freemasons, while practice is in the links of the surveyor's chain.

CORDON, BAILE DEL (Catalonia)
"Ribbon Dance" similar to the Basque *Cinta Dantza*, in that the pole is a "portable" one, and belongs to a special group of dancers. It appears, not in May, but at Carnival, when it is carried about by a man wearing the scarlet Catalan *barretina*, escorted by the group of dancers, some holding the ribbons. As soon as the musicians begin to play, the pole is set down and the dance begins. Men and girls dance round it, plaiting the ribbons into patterns, while the "unattached" dancers perform solos outside the circle, accompanying themselves with castanets. When the ribbons are unplaited again, the dancers group round the pole, while the solo dancers perform opposite them. There is a suggestion of the English *Morris Dance** as the men wear bells on their legs, and a Fool accompanies the dancers; while in one village no women take part, but half the men are dressed as women. (This occurs also in the Mexican *Danza de los Listones.**) The Catalan dance ends with the singing of traditional verses called *dichos*. Performed on June 13 (Feast of Anthony) as at Jaraiz de la Vera (Caceres).
[See *Cinta Dantza; Maypole Dance; Lei Courdello*]

CORDWAINERS' MARCH (Scotland)
A song written by Burns, was adapted to an old tune used for the Cordwainers' March, in their processional rites of Saint Crispin's Day. To some writers it has a Russian memory. With the words of the song it was used later for dancing; it carries the title "O Lay thy loof in mine Lass!" ("Loof" means "palm of hand".) The tune is in *Songs of Scotland*. G. F. Graham. Edinburgh, 1855 (p.135).

COREA (USA)
A local name, given to a kind of "dancing mania" which developed about 1800 among the Funda-mentalists (literally "World-savers") of Kentucky, Tennessee and Virginia. The usual manifestations were seen, in dancing with laughing, singing hymns, and shouting; sometimes ending in convulsions. The term is a change-over from *chorea*, to dance; and some modern versions of a similar kind appear at "revival meetings" — not always with Negroes.

CORELW (Welsh)
A reel or ring dance; from côr, a circle; and related to *Carol.**   [See *Cybol; Rhiol*]

CORN DANCES
Exist in four regular patterns through the world, varied by circumstances of climate as affecting local crops. They give predominance always to the principal grain: wheat, corn or maize; rye or barley; or rice. The rituals that are labelled (by outsiders) as "propitiation" are factual technical needs, or uninformed copies of them. Prominent was the former use of blood as a manure (empirical observation has now returned into modern science; and "dried blood" is again used). The four main patterns, each with its typical dance, chant, and music, are seen at (1) Sowing grain — the recurrent Sacrifice of real food, in the hope of "more to come", followed by (2) Joy for "Green Corn" — the typical "Garden of Adonis" feast, at proven signs of life, the "Resurrection and the Life"; then (3) the Golden Harvest of ripe grain; and finally (4) the Feast of New Bread, the communion in Bread, and often in wine or other liquid — which affirms the security of life for one more year. These four agricultural points of the year, punctuated by changing elements of labour, affirm the ancient calendar of the settled farmer; and provide the technical basis of his religion with its dances.

CORONACH (Irish; Scots)
Gaelic dirge-songs, used at the funerals of chiefs of Irish or Scottish clans; often accompanied during the march to the grave by bagpipes; and then changed into a circular slow dance round the tomb, with the mourning pace known in modern times as the "croon". The crooner then moved also, in mime, with the pipes, recounting at times the splendours of the deceased. Not until recent years has this dirge, the *cronan*, been perverted to announce the woes of a city youth ardently desiring a mate. The *coronach* developed and later merged into the *wakes* (with Saxon associations) celebrated by larger groups of village people.

CORONATION DANCE (England 14th century)
After the Coronation Dinner of Richard II, of England (1377), there was celebrated a magnificent *Daunce* in The Hall of Westminster. The king with

his nobles and prelates, his knights and their ladies, danced in the Hall to the music of the minstrels. In the MS *Poem of Launfal*,[1] there is an account of a similar dance, begun by "Launfal and Gauweyn and her ladies bryghte", for which daunce, through the time after noon, when dinner had been finished, until dusk:

"They had menstrelles of moche honours,
Fydelers, Sytolyrs, and Trompetors,
And all else hyt were unright".

[1] *Poem of Launfal* MS. Cotton Collection (British Museum).

Coronation of Henry IV, Hall of Westminster, A.D. 1399. Heralds' Ritual Dance of Parade and Challenge. They circle the Hall (*Carvell*) and then utter the phrase of defiance to the monarch (Harleian MS 4679).   ENGLAND

CORPS-DE-BALLET (French academic term)
Literally: the "body-of-ballet", meaning a group of trained dancers, serving (during the nineteenth century) chiefly as a background to offset the principal dancers. A well-trained and well-rehearsed *corps-de-ballet* can do much to balance principals who are "not so good", which has led to managers offering performances by "dance groups", who are shewn without principal dancers (as, for example, the famous Tiller Girl Troupes). Normally, theatre employment is first obtained in this general group; from which, in theory, soloists and premiere danseuses are ultimately selected. Selection, like kissing, goes by favour; and we hear of dancers (academy-trained for ten years) going at once to prominent positions, as sons of princes become generals. The formal hierarchy which developed in Paris comprises: *quadrille* (40); *coryphees* (20); *petits sujets* (10 to 16); *grands sujets* (16); *premiere danseuses* (4); *etoiles* (4), with character dancers or mimes (5 or 6). Under M. Petipas, a somewhat similar system prevailed in Petersburg. With the more dramatic modern ballets, the *regisseur* re-

quires more accomplished dancers; hence members of a *corps-de-ballet* take advanced roles in some ballets; the rank is not so rigidly fixed. American "projectionism", which claims full ability after two years training, and demands a solo role at once, reduces the period of essential stage experience, and dilutes the high quality of any production. A good repertory gives numerous chances; a ballet may be killed by unwise allotment of important roles to inexperienced dancers. Hard work in a *corps-de-ballet* is equivalent to the actor's "five years in rep".

CORRANDA (Catalonia)
The name is derived from running steps used in advance and retreat. A couple dance from the slopes of the Pyrenees in North Catalonia, with two variations. In *corrandas bajas* (low *corranda*) the couples, arm in arm, dance through the streets; *corrandas altas* (high *corranda*) is danced by two or four couples in a square formation, the men performing the *camada rodona* or high jump or kick. The climax is reached when the four men lift the four ladies to form a human pyramid; sometimes the lady sits upon the man's hand supported in the air above his head. This is evidently the unnamed dance witnessed in 1835 by James Erskine Murray[1] at Perpignan. He writes that after the *Contrapas** "the women then follow, who, mingling with the men alternately cross and turn each other round; the measure then changes, its sudden stop indicating to the men that they must raise their partners with a bound and place them upon their hand, as upon a seat. ... One of the figures called "Lo Salt" is performed by four men and four women dancing in a circle. At a particular moment the four cavaliers, passing their hands under the arms of the ladies, simultaneously exalt them in the air, thus forming a pyramid of which the crest is the caps of the women". This dance, and the more solemn *Contrapas*, were accompanied by the flageolet, tamborine, two oboes, borassa and bagpipes, which formed the basis of the later *Sardana** "cobla", or orchestra.
[Cp. *Ball de Corre*; *Lou Pélélé*]
[1] *A Summer in the Pyrenees*. John Erskine Murray.. 1837.

CORREDOIO (Italy)
The Romagna has a spirit, a fairy or goddess, of this name—both male and female—who "loves dances and festivals". She is (asserts Leland[1]) a *vera fanatica per la musica*—she is sure to attend wherever there is a frolic or a ball. She had descended from Curitis or Queritis, he ventures; and quotes Muller as saying "Curitis was the name, in Falerii, of Juno". There were magnificent festi-

vals, white carpets were laid in some streets; and white cows were sacrificed. Dancer-maidens, dressed in white, bore as *canne-phore*, the sacred utensils for the Etruscans. Thus *Corredoio* is the modern deity of the Tuscan dance. He comes like *ventata*, a gust of wind, he whirls about the ladies; he flies to the orchestra, the instruments even sound by themselves. So there are invocations to this wild spirit of the dance, who seeks to visit all and make everybody happy.

[1] *Etruscan Roman Remains*. C. G. Leland (London 1892).

Corroboree Ritual. Bankarn Men. Central Australian aboriginal cave drawing. Copied by James Cant. *(Courtesy of Berkeley Gallery, London.)*   AUSTRALIA

CORROBOREE — 1 (Australia)

Said by Morris in *Austral English* to come from Botany Bay dialect, "Corrobbery" being the closest to local pronunciation. Derivation has also been given as *Korobra* ("dance") and *beria* ("to sing"). It seems to be a term used by Europeans, probably as a substitute or mis-pronunciation of a native name. The people in the extreme north have quite a different word, *Yoi*,* with Malay associations. "Corroboree" has curious resemblance to *Khoro-Bori*, an old Keltic name with many shades of meaning: the "dance of the boro" (which we now call borough or town); but also the chorus, or social chanted ritual accompanying an election, a funeral, a wedding. The word is a general white man's name for ceremonies performed by Australian Aboriginals, for entertainment, or for initiation and religious purposes. An essential part of Aboriginal life, they serve three purposes: (1) they teach by dramatic presentation, the creation stories of the tribe; (2) in several stages, they initiate youths into manhood and instruct them in the beliefs and customs of their tribe; (3) they assist the *nungari* ("medicine man") to control forces of nature in an endeavour to ensure food and water supplies. Representations of legends link the tribe with their ancestors from pre-historic "dream-times"; and confirm totemic origins. Among people to whom every natural feature of the landscape is closely connected with remote ancestral adventures, these dance-dramas are a necessary part of every man's education.

They may be in several scenes spread over one or two days. (See *Kipara,* Tjitji Inma,* Nakumdoit,* Resurrection Dance**). "Play-about" *Corroborees* (in which women may participate) are performed to welcome visitors; to celebrate the naming of a child; or simply as entertainment, but each type has its own name, decorations, songs and dances. The festivities may continue each night for two weeks. (See *Atnumokita,* Arunta Welcome Corroboree**). Songs are often topical and may be of the *Calypso** type describing local events. (See *Yoi**). New songs and dances composed by the hosts (among the Arunta) may be given to visitors to take home, after which the donors will not again perform them. Or, as in Arnhemland, the hosts may buy a new dance-song from the visitors, paying with spears or clubs. This buying of dances is also known in the New Hebrides Islands of the Pacific (see *Hek-hekelean**). In the days before European invasion, *Corroborees* were also performed before going to war, to mark conclusions of peace, when seeking revenge, or to seal a blood-brotherhood pact. (See *Wilyaroo ceremony*.) In 1950 a *Corroboree* ballet was performed in Sydney by the National Theatre Ballet Company.
[See *Aruwaltia; Bal-nuk-nuk; Honeybee Dance; Oenpelli; Snake Dance*]

Corroboree Ritual Dance. Warrangan Corroboree, Arnhemland, North Australia.   AUSTRALIA

CORROBOREE—2 (Australia)

"Costumes" of performers consist mainly of body paint in symbolic patterns according to the purpose of the ceremony, dancers often representing totemic birds, reptiles and insects. (See *Tjitji Inma*,* *Nakumdoit*.*) Designs are made with powdered red and yellow ochre, black charcoal and white pipe-clay, mixed with water and painted on a base of grease rubbed into the body. The pigments are applied with the finger, or a piece of bark. The Tiwi of Melville Island (extreme North) prefer variations on the theme of white-on-black; natural or false beards are whitened or reddened, and the effect brightened by topknots of dyed cockatoo feathers, and red or white gooseball neck pendants. The Arunta (South-central Australia) make intricate patterns with tufts of down stuck on to the skin—white or coloured down from the portulaca flower, or from certain birds. Emu plumes are attached to a tall, conical head-dress, while bunches of Euca-lyptus leaves adorn the legs. (See *Atnumokita*.*) Chanting is always part of a *Corroboree*. Some-times, as in the *Yoi** of the Tiwi, striking cupped hands together or against the buttocks, marks the rhythm; or hitting the ground with sticks. Musical instruments vary according to district and tribe. The Pitta-Pitta of Queensland beat an opossum-skin drum stuffed with feathers; and, as do the Arunta, make a percussion instrument by beating together two boomerangs, flat on flat. The Bull-roarer (*churinga*) is whirled in Central and South-eastern parts, but the northern people of Arnhemland have their own instruments, found nowhere else. These are the *Balnooknook*, a hollow-tree drum; and the *Didjeridoo*. With Rhythm Sticks, these play a large part in initiation ceremonies. Decorated with special patterns, the Balnooknook is beaten with the drum-stick, "Labait", and the origin of both goes back to "Dream-times" when all things were created. Rhythm Sticks are short lengths of hardwood, rounded and slightly tapered, beaten together, while a drone is produced by the Didjeridoo—a long wooden tube into which water is poured to give it tone, played through a mouth-piece.
[See *Nakumdoit*; *Aruwaltia*; *Bal-nuk-nuk*]

CORTÈGE (France)

Equivalent to the *Trionfo* in Italy, as the solemn processional movement, usually with music and often with dance *intermedi*; but having a church or ritual character rather than an imperial or military and regal form. Later the term *grand cortège* is applicable, for example, to the movement of a state funeral, but in the ducal celebrations, the *cortège* carried a lighter note, as preliminary or sequel to a masque. The cortège is, to a great extent, the "masque in motion" through the city,

while the masque is the "cortège arrived" at its centre; and now displaying the performers, singers and dancers, with the musicians, within the court-yard or hall.

CORYPHÉE (France)

A leader; one of the definite ranks of the Paris Opera Theatre, carrying a certain status and salary. The term comes originally from the Greek *cory-phaeus*, the poet, as leader in charge of the chorus. [See *Figurante*; *Paris Opera Ballet*]

COSIERS, ELS (Majorca)

Name given to six boy dancers who accompany the procession of the Virgin after Vespers, as it leaves the church on the 15th August (Assumption of the Virgin Mary); and on the Feast of Corpus Christi. Dressed in white, with coloured ribbons and flower-decorated hats, they take their places three on each side of the image. In addition there are two "demons" with horns and cloven feet, who have flexible rods to keep back the crowds; and a "man-woman" called *la dama*, who carries a fan and a kerchief. (Cp. *Malinche*.*) Musicians playing the *cheremias* (bagpipes), *tamborino*, and *flaviol* (pipe), follow the procession. Every few yards the *Cosiers* perform some steps, and in each square, or important place, the procession stops while the boys dance figures similar to the *Morris** dance, with cross-overs and heys, to the accompaniment of pipe and tambor. Returning to the church, the boys dance round the statue of the Virgin. At Alaro and Montiuri, the festival continues next day, when, after Benediction, the *Cosiers*, and their musicians (but without the "demons") dance inside the church in front of the high altar. A general dance follows in the main square.
[See *Church Dances*]

COSMETAE (Ancient Rome)

A class of male slaves who acted (among other duties) as "dressers" for theatrical spectacles of all kinds. The female slaves were named *cosmetriae*; Juvenal[1] shows that there were both male and female experts in make-up, who served the wealthy Roman ladies, or the actor-mimes; and (as now in the USA film business) men or women experts attended both sexes of performers, according to need. The numerous and varied styles of hair-dressing, fully evident in many sculptured extant Roman portrait-busts, indicated the time and skill devoted to public toilette. Only in work such as modern dentistry, optical contact lenses, and plastic surgery, can modern facial improvement be claimed to be superior to Roman practice. Their National Welfare was limited to free *Panem et Circenses*.
[1] *Satires*. Juvenal. vi. 476.

COSMIC BALLET (Plotinus)

The metaphors of this Egyptian philosopher, who taught in Athens and Rome, extended to comparisons of the universal system of stars as a Cosmic Ballet. Passages may be found in his collected *Enneads*,[1] for example:

"We resemble a chorus which always surrounds its leader, but (the members of) which do not always sing in tune because they allow their attention to be distracted to some exterior object. . ."

Then, when we turn to God:

"We disagree no more, and really form a divine choric ballet around Him. . . ." (p.165.)

When he compares the Stars' motion to a prearranged dance, Plotinus says:

"at each of the phases of the circular movement of the world there might be a correspondence between the various beings subject to it, as if, in a varied choric ballet the dancers formed a single figure. . . ." (p.492-3.)

and goes on to compare the movements of the stars to the co-ordinated movements of a dancer's limbs. Dante and other poets adopted similar allegories, some of them used by Renaissance painters, as Botticelli in his *Primavera ("Dance of Spring")*, but older poetical metaphors derive from biblical books, such as quoted by William Blake—the "dance of the morning stars" (from *Job*) and "the little hills clapped their hands with joy and danced."

[See *Mystic Dance*]

[1] *Plotinus Complete Works*. Trans. Kenneth Sylvan Guthrie. 1918 (Vol. 1).

COTILLON (France)

A late 18th century dance, popular in France and England, and forerunner of the *Quadrille*.* A square dance for eight people, the *Cotillon* consisted of several figures preceded by a Grand Round, and linked by "Changes," such as *La Course* or *Promenade*. Each figure was danced by the first and third couples, then by the second and fourth couples. Hence the alternative name of *Contredanse* (in England called Counterpart), which was not simply a French translation of Country Dance. Three usual steps in the *Cotillon* were the *Chassé, Contretemps*, and *Rigadoon*, but dancers chose their own steps according to music and figure. The 19th century *Cotillon* had many steps and figures, but no special music. Waltzes, polkas, mazurkas and galops were used, and the dance became more of a game, with the giving of presents, and many devices whereby the men competed for their dancing partners. A lady would, for instance, present an umbrella to one of two hopeful partners. While she danced with the other, he had to follow them through the figure holding the open umbrella over their heads. The hostess would arrange beforehand with the *Cotillon* leader which figures were to be danced, and the appropriate "props" and presents would be provided. The name literally means "a petticoat", but referred to the dance of the *coterie*, originally a term meaning a gild or sharing company. As each member paid his quote (his quote or gild), so he received dividends or profits, as "gifts", when the disbursement was due, usually as annual, half-yearly or quarterly meetings, when a dinner was held. The proceedings with the company at dance; and the routine of the popular *Cotillon*, mimicked steps of the successive phases of the meeting of the *Coterie*. Later the term became used in reference to an exclusive "social set" of self-appointed ladies.

COUNTING DANCES

With rhymes. appear in many modes of rhythmic ceremonial, from simple children's games, to the serious business, once practised in churches, of the *sortes*. Most familiar is the game *Ten Little Nigger Boys* (selecting deacons etc.) varied by the folk tune of *Ten Green Bottles (hanging on the wall)*. The *Sortes Virgilianae* were magical spell-outs of this kind. Goethe included a basic enumeration spell, for the witch in his *Doktor Faustus*.* Leland[1] quotes a work (Basle 1692) on this subject, in telling us of the use of acorns in the Tuscan peasant magic, in dance-songs; earlier, dry beans, black, white, or red, were used. Johannes Meursis, in *De Ludis Graecorum*, says the Greeks had a game called *Tropa*, played with acorns; the rhythmic term remains in music. English children use a counting dance with "Eeenie-meenie-minie-mo!" in a circle dance-game.

[See *Witches Magical Dance*]

[1] *Etruscan Roman Remains*. G. C. Leland. p.277.

COUNTING IN DANCE

Is for many students an impossible coverage. Yet the system, so helpful to adequate performance and necessary in early rehearsal, can be learned by careful analysis. The "count" can be applied to (a) the physical movement of the single dancer; (b) to the movement of the group of dancers; (c) to the musical beat of a single instrument; or (d) the selected beat of one instrument in an orchestra, which one dancer has been told to follow. Musical counts are always better than body counts, because this implies accepting the domination of leading rhythmic pace in music, to body discipline. Isadora Duncan was a rare example of a dancer who encompassed both modes; even though she switched from movement with one instrument to contrapuntal movement with another instrument, in the same dance; and then

did it differently the next time, to the same music. Musical count, in the mechanical basis permitted by the chromatic scale, can be done by the beat of single notes; by the bar (the commonest, as in marking 2/2 or 4/4 or, as with a song, such as a *carole** with its measured syllables, always the same number to the traditional poetic line. This basis is disturbed by the sharp need to depart from metronome beats to true rhythm, as seen in the phrase, with its subtle changes of pace. Singing lines help to establish the "singing feet" of the true dancer : who emerges with, or even into, the musical phrase. In this consummation all arithmetical counting is lost; having served its purpose. If the dancer uses song, to help musical count, she should avoid all modern crooning dirges and wails; all hymns; all military marches from brass bands; all "multiplication table" school recitals. Syncopation is required, but it must not be mechanical, if the Precision Dance* period is to be surpassed. On stage at rehearsal; or in classroom in advanced class, counting is best done in spatial combination with calculated floor areas. We must recall that certain renaissance dances were named "Measure", for this excellent reason : they measured dancer and ability in movement, against the room and its spaces.
[See *Witch's Magical Dance* for witch count]

COUNTRY BUMPKIIN (Scotland)
Known also as *Ninesome Reel*. A genuine old Scottish dance, for nine persons : three men and six girls, formed in a "square of nine" to begin. The dance was popular in the reign of George II. The centre gentleman wears a "cocket hat" to mark him as the Bumpkin. There are four "reeling figures" to this dance, in which the first Bumpkin "crowns" the man from his rear line, with his cocket hat, as he passes. As the figures change the bonnet is snatched from the head of the previous centre man, so that it is always on the head of whoever is at the centre. The precise significance of this ritual has not been stated.

COURANTE (Fr.), CORANTO (Ital.)
A court dance of 16th and 17th centuries, of a light and sprightly character. Derived from the French verb *courir*, "to run", the name refers to tripping steps, performed with light hops and springs, but not jumping high as in the *Galliard** and *Volta*.* The music was in 3/4 or 3/2 time (although given by Arbeau in duple time), and was in two parts, each repeated. Danced by couples, the early 16th century *Courante** was sometimes preceded by a mimed introduction. In

turn, three young men each led his partner to one end of the room and left her there, returning to the other end. One by one each then approached his lady, inviting her to dance, but she turned her back. The young men then each besought his partner on his knees, when she relented and the three couples began the *Courante*. In England the dance was known as *Coranto, Corranto, Corrantoe, Corant* and *Currant*. Playford's *Court Ayres* (1655) gives 55 examples. Couples advanced and retreated hand in hand; then released hands and faced each other, dancing sideways in opposite directions; finishing again with joined hands. Queen Elizabeth was an expert dancer of the *Coranto*, which endured into Stuart times. (In France it was popular at the Court of Louis XIV.) In 1666 Samuel Pepys attended a court ball, where he found "the Corants grew tiresome", while in Selden's *Table Talk* (1689) the place of the *Coranto* was given as coming between "grave measures"* and Galliards.* Considered by some to have been brought to the French Court from Italy by Catherine de Medici, others consider that the *Courante* may have had a Spanish origin, since a Bodleian Library manuscript includes instructions for dancing the *Coranto d'Espagne*, and it was customary to connect the name of a popular dance with its place of origin. The 16th century dancing-master, Cesare Negri, who had a school in the then Spanish city of Milan, called the dance *Corriente*. This version was danced by three couples and had seven figures. In the customary 16th century musical arrangement of dances in pairs, the *Courante* was the "after-dance" of the *Allemande*.* [See *Nachtanz*].

COURDELLO, LEI (Provence, France)
Called variously "Cord Dance", "Ribbon Dance", or sometimes "Weaving Dance". Each holding a ribbon attached to a mast about seven feet high, the dancers revolve in circles, winding and unwinding the ribbons in a "weaving" pattern. With music in 2/4 time, it is danced by men and women, who stand in pairs facing each other. In the First Figure, they turn round each other, anticlockwise, then clockwise. The Second Fgure is called "Chaine Anglaise", in which the men and women move in opposite directions round the pole, inter-weaving to make a twisted chain, the ribbons plaiting round the pole. Half-way through the 36 measures of the music, they bow to the partner then encountered, and repeat the "Chaine Anglaise", unwinding the ribbons. In the Third Figure, two circles are formed, men inside, women outside, which move in opposite directions. The step is a springy polka. The pole is not planted in the ground, and the dance is not connected with May Day, or confined to the month of May, but is thought to have been a trade dance

of the Cord Makers. *Lei Courdello* is included in *Lis Ouliveto.**

[See *Maypole Dance*; *Cinta Dantza*; *Baile del Cordon*; *Lei Tisseran*; *Danza de los Listones*]

COURT DANCE (Italy : France)
(1) Widely applied term relevant to the three kinds of dancing or rhythmic movement seen in the ducal courts of Mediaeval Italy and France. They are (a) the *entry*, or processional dances of the nobles; (b) the *danse basse* or ceremonial dance of display in the centre of the Great Hall; and (c) the *ball* and *balletto*,* in which some sort of spectacular action was apparent; an approach to dramatic form similar to the clerical miracle plays. There were many variations of *balletto*. One of the earliest known books is that by Guglielmo Ebreo (William the Jew) of Pesaro, who wrote (*circa* 1440) a description of current court dances, including notes on theory. He instructed the famous Sforza family in "social dance".
(2) Modern Court Dance is disappearing : the ceremonial was a long procession (as at Buckingham Palace for "presentations") of young society women (named debutantes), who have learned to make the formal curtsey. The following ball is open only to a few of them; though they may attend the "Garden Party" celebrations. The dances for the selected guests include only the ordinary modernist ballroom dances, notable more for magnificence of dress and costume than for impeccable style in dance. During Christmas festivties it is the custom for the Court household to dance together without guests; master and mistress, with butlers and maids. During the 18th and 19th centuries at the German Court it was the custom to dance the solemn *Fackeltanz** on occasion of a royal wedding; while the *Polonaise** was long fashionable throughout Europe as an opening dance at Court balls.   [See *Cushion Dance, Trenchmore*]

COURT MANNERS (England, Elizabethan period)
Showed a transition in behaviour which reflected Renaissance social conduct. Just as the Latin church had now dropped rack and stake in its political methods, so the Italian courtier was ceasing to rely on rapier and poniard as arguments; and though gentlemen still carried some weapons, they began to develop their verbal celerity with the swiftness of foot and arm. They had their five positions more fully outlined by experts such as Count Baldassare del Castiglione, who published his *Book of the Courtier* in 1528. As with the ideas of Machiavelli, many of its notions were well known. Count Baldassare had much comment on court behaviour at Urbino; he told men not to be too violent in the ballroom; advised women to dance in seemly fashion. Giovannia del Casa followed with *Galateo*; then came an English translation *The Court of Civil Courtesy* (1591). In *Hamlet* we read the advice of Polonius, on similar lines.

The Court of Love. A notable Tournai tapestry in rich colours, from the first quarter of the 16th century when the fashion of the Court of Love was at its height. One of the many versions of *Danse Allemande* is performed to song and the music of pipe and mandolina. The original is 17 ft. 9 ins. long and 8ft. 9 ins. high; the front figures among the court are thus nearly life size. The "modern" style of dance and costume are striking. (*Courtesy of Sotheby and Co., London*).   FRANCE

COURTS OF LOVE (Western Europe)
France: *Cour d'Amour*; Italy; also Belgium. The *Corte d'Amore*—was developed along with the Tourney by Trouvères and Troubadours in the later feudal period. These Courts had much influence on manners and modes; they existed in two phases, the exoteric gatherings associated with the ducal courts; and a lesser known esoteric mode that was cultivated by poets and scholars. Both had dance : in fact or in symbol. The knights, poets, and ladies used the Courts of Love chiefly as amusement, based in music, song and dance, at first in Provence in the 12th century, at Toulouse.

In France the Court of Love was famous under Charles VI; his consort Isabella established her Court in 1380. The last imitation was an "Academy of Love", instituted by cardinal Richelieu (under Louis XIV) as an *assemblée galante*. Though Princess Gonzaga presided, we do not hear of notable awards.

The Court of Love, now in the more settled and far more corrupt period following the Crusades, took in the scholarship released westward into Europe; and so developed *le science gai*. Its display was precursor to the ballet in Italy, the tourney in France and the royal masque (or masking) in England. Music, chants, and dancing were encouraged by the poets. Notable is the *Roman de la Rose*, begun (from earlier material) by Guillaime de Loris (died 1260) on a theme used by the Templars and by the Rosicrucians in ritual; and by the ducal courts in festival dances. The many rooted form of *L'Allemagne* grew into favour from earlier rituals and left church usage. The Rose vied with the Lily; the Gothic church used the Rose Window, as the devotees used the Vesica as floor pattern; and *La Vierge* with Jesus by now fully replaced Isis with Horus. Troubadours found this *Roman* unfinished; later *Jean Chopinel de Meung-sur-Loire* brought the work into popular form, adding 1320 verses (1250 — 1305 AD). In this literature was a firm root of Romantic Love — and of dance in Ballet. The peak of this period was round 1525. Jean de Meung satirised rulers and sought the ordinary people — and the central dance form took one main form in the *aumonier*, celebrating the Assumption (Aug. 15) with a popular form of *Alle Magne*; as in the ducal courts, the poets developed more refined detail. From records in this mode Edmund Spencer got material for his *Faery Queen*, where Rosalind is *La Dame Mysterieuse*, whom Will Shakespeare last recalled as the Dark Lady. Marot added more changes (1527) but the folk romance of *Jeanne d'Arc* could not be continued in the face of bourgeoise expansion. The *Alle Magne* or *Almoyne* collapsed into a polite salon dance, with no song. The Rose has left unexplained traces in England: the Tudor Rose (still on our coins) with the Red Rose of Lancaster and the White Rose of York, as *gules* remains in heraldry, recalling the poet Rumi of Gulistan and the Arab music that spread in Spain.

COVEN (England)
Translation of "teaching circle" as given or implied in *covenant* or agreement. As applied in 17th century legalism to the alleged "witches dance ring", or "witches meeting group" of traditional thirteen members, the word lost savour. But it was a translation of Testament (or: contract, witness, agreement), like the Hebrew *Berith*, or the Greek *Diatheke*. The *Coven* was broadly, therefore, a "Teaching by Ritual", and as such had its practice allied with "keeping watch and ward". Thence came the term witch, as "one who watched" the lunar phases, for illegal time-keeping. (In ancient Rome, the calendar was a state secret, announced in fragments to the howling mob, in case they might derive some unsuspected advantage from "knowing times". In Welsh, *coven* was *cefn*, a haven, a refuge. The *Coven* was also a village refuge, against the ecclesiastical tyranny, operated by infiltration from Rome; and bitterly persecuted; not as a religious rival, but as an economic and political antagonist, in unending cold war that finally burst into flames. The lawyers turned the word to "coven"—meaning "a conspiracy".

COVENT GARDEN THEATRE (London)
Was first opened by John Rich, December 7th, 1732, with Quin as his leading actor. Drama was the program. Garrick played there in June, 1746, and next year joined Rich for his season. Companies and managers alike, at new Covent Garden Theatre and the older Drury Lane Theatre, became bitter rivals. Rich extended his operations; and developed English Pantomime, as well as spectacular presentation of drama, finally leaving Covent Garden in 1761. Most famous English actors appeared there. The first theatre was destroyed by fire in 1808, but it was rebuilt; and opened again within a year. Opera was introduced in 1734 with Handel. Ballet appeared in 1734. After 1826, the management was in difficulty; in 1829 the bailiffs were in occupation. In 1832, Laporte was in control. Drama then varied with opera; but by 1846 the theatre was used for the first "promenade concerts" until in 1848 Ed. Delafield used the house for opera, doing well until fire intervened in 1856. In 1858, the third (present) building was opened; when Gounod and Wagner continued, until in 1888 A. Harris became manager, improving standards to his death in 1906. Covent Garden was famous for its fancy dress balls.

COVENT GARDEN THEATRE (London)

Was built on the site of a Coven, said to have been the garden belonging to a Convent; it is now surrounded by marketing houses for fruit and vegetable produce. Apparently a wooden structure was taken over by John Rich; and his new building opened in 1732. He moved there from the Theatre in Lincoln's Inn Fields. From 1734 Handel was associated; his operas were produced until 1737. The Theatre was licensed for performance of dramatic works; in 1734 Congreve's *Way of the World* was announced as:

"With entertainments of dancing, including Scottish dance by Mrs. Glover and Mrs. Languerre, Mr. le Sac and Miss Boston; Mr. de la Garde and Mrs. Ogden. With a New Dance called *Pigmalion* performed by Mr. Malter and Mdlle Sallé".

It was claimed that in this dance Mdlle Sallé (of Paris) had produced the first complete "ballet d'action" ever presented on the London stage. In 1734 Handel included a ballet, and *Il Pastor Fide*. Between 1826 and 1846 both opera and musical drama were given; in the season 1846-1847 the Theatre was turned over to be an Opera House — it began to use the title Covent Garden Royal Opera House. The building had been destroyed by fire in 1808—September 19th; the new Theatre was opened September 18th, 1809. It again suffered fire in 1856; the interior by Albano was lost. As the Royal Italian Opera House, Michael Costa had been conductor. After the 1856 fire, it was redesigned by Edward Barry and rebuilt by Gye (manager since 1851) Opera was often given with interludes of ballet — but rarely did these fit any part of the chief entertainment. Queen Victoria was a patron until she lost her husband. F. Beale with Michael Costa as conductor continued from 1884, and in 1888 a new opera company was organized under Augustus Harris. Following on the 1939-1945 war, the Sadlers' Wells Ballet, first organized by Lilian Baylis, began to perform — and after variations (as "First Company" and "Second Company") the Royal Ballet emerged as tenants together with various opera companies.

COYOTE DANCE (Mexico)

A ceremonial dance of the Yaquis Indians, performed at fiestas, and also on the death of all soldiers, village chiefs or *Matachines** dancers. Three men representing *coyotes* (prairie wolves, from Mex. *coyotl*), dance to the beat of a drum, which regulates their movements. Dressed in their ordinary clothes, each man has a coyote skin depending down the back from a head-band round the forehead, and a crest of eagle or hawk feathers on hte head. Monotonously dancing in a crouching position, with bent knees and a slow stamping step, each man carries a hunting bow which he beats with a reed. When the drum beats are regular they dance towards the drummer, and when they change to irregular rhythm the three men move backwards away from the drummer, and so the dance continues for hours, sometimes all night. Evidently of pre-Conquest origin and ritual association, the dance has now become attached to Catholic fiesta dates, particularly those belonging to patron saints of soldiers. On these occasions, each soldier performs the Coyote Dance three times, dancing continuing all night. At dawn, the "coyotes" are confronted with three plates of meat placed between them and the drum, when each dancer, without ceasing to dance, must pick up a plate with his teeth and carry it to the drum.

CRAMBO (England)

A mime and dance game; a spontaneous rhyming game, from "cram" — "to tell what is untrue" before it became a preparatory school term; and was mentioned by little Victorian girls as "telling a crammer". *Crambo* means "repetition" and so would apply to lessons by rote; *Crambo* as a play might jog memory. Walter Scott mentions *crambe bis cocta* — twice-boiled cabbage — from a Greek proverb, meaning "a tale worked out"; thus a drama no longer liked, or a "show we have seen before".

CRAMIGNOLE, CRAMIGNON (Holland and Belgium)

A chain dance performed at the Fair held a fortnight after Whitsun at Eijsden in Limburg, Holland, and on festive occasions in other Limburg villages; at the close of the Flemish *Kermesses* (Fairs), and in villages throughout Belgium, where it is sometimes called the *Longues Danse*. It is danced in a long chain through the village, in and out of the houses and inns. In Holland the leader, who is captain of the bachelors' or young men's club, carries a bunch of flowers as insignia of office, while the Belgian leader holds a stick. The dancers, men and women alternating, join hands and proceed with a simple skipping step, the line growing longer as more dancers join in. Everyone is expected to take part. A difference between the Dutch and Belgian versions is that the former is accompanied by the village brass band, while the latter has no instrumental music, the dancers singing traditional songs. [See *Farandole*; *Carmagnole*; *Vloggelen*; *Furry Dance*]

CRANE DANCE (Greece)

An error for the similar terms *Kreion* (ruler, lord, master) and *Karanos* (chieftain). It is clear that

Kreion-choroi signifies not a dance of birds, but a measured Dance of the Lords. The term *karanos* has a Sanskrit parallel in *karana*, basic positions in dance; of which there are 108 codified modes in the system. One who was master of these *karanas* would be termed a *karanos*. Probably from this practical demonstration of ability came *Geranos*, the "elder man", and later the terms give us *coroner* and *crowned*, etc.—one who is recognised, one who can examine.
[See *Geranos*; *Labyrinth*; *Way to Jerusalem*]

CRANE "DANCE"
These birds have a ceremonial "dance", performed by both sexes, singly, in pairs or in groups. Not only connected with the mating season, it is also performed at such times as at big gatherings of the birds on migration. With wings held out the birds move with quick steps in circle, ellipse, or figure of eight; make several deep bows; spring high into the air to right and left; throw small pebbles, leaves etc. into the air, catch them, and stop with a jerk, in an erect attitude. At breeding time the male birds often walk one behind the other, with a stiff goose-step as they follow the female cranes. Spaced out at some distance apart, but gradually getting nearer, each carries his head with bill turned back. If one bird stops, all do so, holding out the wings and touching the back feathers with the tip of the bill. They also have a ceremonial trumpeting, performed by two or more birds with neck stretched and bill raised.

CREEK INDIANS (USA)
With Seminole, Choctaw, Natchez and others, lived along Lower Mississippi in Georgia, and round the coast of Florida. Their culture and language are similar to Sioux; yet town life was more fully developed, and agriculture was their main interest. Natchez (now extinct) and Creek had many elements in common, such as the worship of Fire and Maize. Their towns were laid out in a prescribed plan, with a central square; in the middle burned the sacred fire. At four cardinal points of the square were four lodges—one for the Tribal Chief and Ceremonial Leaders; one for the Warrior Chief; one for warriors; and one for women, children, and visiting strangers. Each town was divided in two sections—the White or Peace Town, governed by the Tribal Chief; and the Red or War Town, governed by the Warrior Chief. The two Leaders of Ceremonies organised festivals; and found leaders for the dances if not dancing themselves. The Creek principal festival was the *Busk*,* when maize was ripe, in July or August (also beginning of a new year). Both Maize and Fire were then honoured in a ceremony lasting four or eight days.

Dances occurred during the rituals, in the central place. The ritualistic ball game, *Pelote*, was played after the peak ceremony, when new fires had been lighted from the sacred fire. Similar ceremonies were held by the Cherokee and Natchez (see *Green Corn Dance**). That the Maya were ancestors of the Creek is shown by their worship of maize and fire, and emphasis on the four directions; while Toltecs and Aztecs also divided their towns into four quarters, and held a "new fire" ceremony.
[See *Aztec Dances*]

CREOLE DANCES (Caribbean)
The term *Creole* (French) or *Criolla* (Spanish), is taken as an American-Negro term, signifying usually a person of mixed descent born in the southern part of America. Creole indicates also a white or near-white descendant of North American states, especially Louisiana and adjacent districts; and finally it names their patois or language, hence denoting their culture, including the range of dances and songs. African rhythmic influence is strong in both musical and dance form, imposed over Aztec and Maya traditions, and modified superficially by clerical diversions. During recent decades, the determined archeological research into early traditions has led to many revivals of older modes of dance and music; some have been seen in Europe, often with examples of more definitely national style.

CRETAN BULL DANCE (Knossos, Crete – 1400 BC)
Masked dance in which two acrobats were disguised as a bull, in a spectacular ritual game. Non-masked dancers, half of them girls, leaped over the back of the "Bull" by grasping the horns when the beast approached. Since the discoveries of Sir Arthur Evans, it has been supposed that the bull was a living animal, as used in the later bull rings of Spain and Italy. Though actual experiment would have dispelled this belief, it can be corrected by examination of recovered Cretan drawings. Here it is clear that the artist can "draw" in the academic sense of that word : that is, he can depict from direct observation. Drawings show the men and girl dancers, well-proportioned and costumed; but the bull is invariably shewn much lengthened. This also is fact : it was the necessary arrangement made for the two athletes hidden beneath the skins, to support the horns and provide a "solid back", on which three points the leaping dancers had to move. Thus the "Sacrifice of Seven Youth and Seven Maidens to the Minotaurus" proves to be (doubled) a Moon Ritual of seven plus seven maids with seven plus seven youths to make up the lunar number; four weeks; two fortnights, one bright, one dark (as in the Hindu system), and

the mouth of 28 days—all finally "sacrificed" to the solar lord, the Bull. Thus the Cretan Bull Dance was a spectacular mode of displaying ruling chronologies and their relations. The Mino-taurus was the Mono-Taurus: the "Bull of the Year." Farther north, he was the Golden Boar, displayed at the Winter Solstice Feast; and he is still recalled by the golden orange placed in the boar's mouth, in England. In Egypt, contemporary with this Cretan Bull, was used a similar model of the Sacred Cow of Hathor, in initiation ceremonies. Other lands show ritual dances of the Great Green Snake—a grand mythic creature similarly made up of a number of disguised dancing men—which may also "swallow up" the candidates.

CREUX DE VERVI (Mediæval France)
An annual dance of the citizens of Verviérs at Liége which flourished from 14th century, and was ended by 1794. This cult dance was performed on Tuesday of Whitsun week, by a deputation from Verviérs, who, accompanied by Mayor, Pastor and Councillors, walked to Liége. Bridge gates were, on arrival, ceremonially opened by the Mayor of Liége; then they passed the Pont des Arches, where the most recently married couple danced in public; followed by other dancers. They then dispersed, fed, and passed the night. Next morning, Wednesday, the people of Verviérs entered the Liége church of S.Lamberte, halting beneath an enormous crown, suspended over the centre. Forming a ring, they danced, all the while upholding their left hands with the thumb pointing up; and singing "Thumbs up! Thumbs up!" Three then entered the sacristy, giving the traditional green silken purse they had brought, and receiving some incense for use in their home-town church of San Remacles. They left the church, going in procession to the palace of the Bishop; and danced before it; next passing to the market place. Here was the final round dance; with a feast of oxen; but the head was carried off, and when they again passed the Pont des Arches, the ox head was severed and cast in pieces into the river, as the returning Verviérs citizens passed dancing over the bridge. The meaning of this dance remains uncertain.
[Cp. *Dalum Dance* (Sweden)]

CROOKED MIRROR THEATRE (Russia)
This *Teatr Krivoe Zerkalo* was opened in Petersburg in 1908, by the actress Z. V. Kholmskaya, as a Theatre Club, mainly to attract professional artists of all kinds. The basis was satire (hence the name) centreing on caricature and burlesque, both of events in real life and current plays or books then being discussed. Some allusions were more than subtle. When later it was directed by Evreinov,

productions tended to mysticism; but the arrival of Kügel again altered the main policy line. Every side of theatre art was utilised; from singing to mime and dancing. The Modernist dancers, then beginning, from Isadora Duncan's visits (the most recent in 1905), attracted the interest of V. Meyerhold. The *Krivoe Zerkalo* shut down in 1928; not before it had stimulated many producers, including Balieff.   [See *Chauve Souris*]

CROWN DANCERS (N. America)
Masked dancers of the Mescalero Apache Indians in Southern New Mexico, representing spirits known as *Gahe*, or "Mountain People". The dancers perform at curing and puberty rites, when they dance for four nights, driving out disease and evil. They must make no mistake in their dance, nor must they be touched. Honouring a fundamental element in Amerindian religion—the four cardinal points—they dance in sets of four, and approach the sacred fire from each direction. Among the Chiricahua Apache, each dancer represents one direction and its associated colour. Wearing a tall, branched head-dress, or "crown'" with a black hood drawn tightly across the face, concealing all features, the Crown Dancers perform high steps, alternating with a squatting step in which the legs are thrust forward. The torso of each dancer is symbolically painted (ritual chants accompany the painting process), and long pendants of eagle feathers hang from the arms. A fringed skirt and soft boots complete the costume. In either hand they hold a pointed stick. They make no sound except a "spirit call". Accompanying the *Gahe* is a clown, *Iibahi*, "the Gray One", who performs humorous antics but remains speechless. He is the most skilled at curing disease, and although possessing more power than the other dancers, he may safely be touched. At Gallup, in New Mexico, where the Intertribal Indian Ceremonial is held, the Crown Dancers perform in the street, one behind the other, arms out-stretched at either side, holding the sticks point upwards.

CSARDAS (Hungary) pro. "Chardash"
A couple dance, now known as Hungary's national dance, which developed from the old, all-male recruiting dance, the *Verbunkos*,* becoming a more regulated and simplified version which could be danced in upper-class ballrooms, as taught by dancing-masters. The word *csárda*, "an inn", is said to denote the type of place on the Puszta (the Great Plain of Hungary), where the dance was performed by the country folk, and the slightly derisive name, *Csárdás*, was given by the aristocracy to the already existing dance. In old records, among names of many Hungarian dances, there is

no mention of *Csárdás*, the first record of the word being in 1835, and the dance became popular in Hungarian Society about 1840. Thus the name is modern, but the basic dance very much older. This basis is thought to have been an "irregular" Hungarian peasant dance. The "irregularity" lay in the improvisation of steps in the quick part of the dance—a fundamental characteristic of Hungarian peasant dances, as in the *Verbunkos*. Some consider the *Csárdás* to have originated from the *Verbunkos* and a Couple dance, called the *Vegyes paros*. Others think it was introduced into Hungary from Bohemia. In Slovakia, which joins the Hungarian border, the *Csárdás* (spelt *Cardas*) is very popular. It is always in two parts—the *lassu*, or slow; and the *friss*, or quick, the two sequences being alternated, as the dancers give a sign to the musicians. The same tune may be used for both parts, provided the difference in tempo is clearly marked. Dancers facing each other, the man puts his hands round the girl's waist, and she puts hers on his shoulders. The basic movement is a sideways chasis on each foot alternately, but skilful dancers add many difficult steps in a display of virtuosity. Music is provided by a gypsy orchestra, led by the *Primás* who, with his violin music, whips the dance into a frenzy. Often the *Primás* immediately follows a *Csárdás* with a slow lament, in order to bring the dancers back to calmness.

CUADRO FLAMENCO (Spain)
Does not mean "Flemish Picture" (as one writer affirms), but the "Square of the Flamens"—the ancient Roman priests whose system went into Iberia, taking their ancient ritual with them. Byzantine forms joined with Roman names, and Moorish music overlaid both. Nor has the title to do with the flamingo bird. These priests belonging to the *Col Legia Flamenina*, in Spain their company adopted the terminal "co" (as "group"), and so the deep-set name has remained. The gypsies contributed their song as *gitanas*—the *gita*, as song, comes from distant India; now *flamen* and *gita* are united by the *cante hondo*—the "deep song."

CUBAN BALL-ROOM DANCE (Havana)
Is encouraged by the Havana Municipal Council, with its annual Rumba Contest. In the city, the *Academia* is equivalent to the *Palais* in Britain; though smaller and not so numerous; while Dance Schools are fewer still. The *Rumba* is called *Son*,* in two phases according to tempo : the *Son-Danzon*, and *Bolero Son* are slow; while the *Guaracha* is quicker. The simple title *Rumba* is reserved solely for exhibition forms of the dance. Cubans have their own main style—neither American nor Spanish; they use the *Sistema Cubano*, in which rhythm is followed by dance on the "off beat". The dance form is energetic, but does not dissolve into *Jive*. The *Foxtrot* style goes in a rhythm style, somewhat like the English *Foxtrot*. The *Paso Doble* is much appreciated, danced in a simple mode; but usual dance programs include only twenty per cent. American or other foreign music, for Cuban music, played by real experts, offers more opportunity for varied subtle effects of rhythm on the basic steps. Cuban dance rhythms are in 2/4 time, with rhythmic accent as : Slow-Quick-Quick. The ballroom dance does not "travel" as much as the ring of the Folk-dance. When the Cuban-Rumba (as it was miscalled) was introduced into England in 1930 and the USA about 1932, it was described as "dancing on a dime". The Cuban phrase is : *bailando en un solo ladrillo*, or "to dance on one tile". These tiles are about ten inches square. The steps are thus all small; opposite to the tango. Yet the accent of the Folk is present, combined with the hauteur of the Spanish aristocrat; for Cuban dance joins Spain with the West Indies.

CUECA (Argentine and Bolivia)
A lively dance in 3/4 time, or in 6/8 time with 3/4 accompaniment, derived from the Chilean *Zamacueca*.* In Bolivia the dance is often in the minor key (as distinct from the Chilean dance, which is invariably in the major key), and is sometimes called *Chilena*. A coquettish dance for partners facing each other, with much flourishing of kerchiefs, the *Cueca* is very popular in Bolivia, while the music of the Argentine dance has occasional syncopation. In northern Argentina a dance in slow 6/8 time, called *Zamba*, is derived from the Chilean *Zamacueca*.   [See *Marinera; Zamacueca*]

CUENCA CARNIVAL (Ecuador)
Belongs to the wrongly-named "Panama Hat" folk industry of Ecuador. These fine straw hats (not made in Panama) cannot be produced by machinery; they are made by skilful hands from *paja*, a fine straw. At Cuenca, the hat-makers buy *paja*, take orders, and return with finished goods. With their pay, they celebrate the Cholo Hat Festival, mainly in the sunny streets. Hats are brought in weekly or monthly; but only at a Hat Fair are definite orders given. They arrange mimes —one dancer will wear a mask as a great ape, leading another disguised as a dancing-bear, who moves to the drum taps, at the end of his short chain. So there are minor dance celebrations every month, but a big one for the chief Fair. The dances are rarely distinguished; they imitate "westerns" to some extent; but they perform a maypole dance with coloured ribbons, by imitation morris men, all wearing new straw hats.

CUENTO (Spanish)

A fable, ballad, story, narrative, esp. *cuento de hadas* a fairy tale. Linked with *cante hondo* (present day form) by *hado*, a prophecy of fate, destiny, doom. The fairy, *Hada*, is the singer, who sometimes dances (earlier form). If current events were related, then it is *cante chico*, the "little tale". Later *cuenta de hadas* dropped into the mime-dance of the *feria*. The village was summoned by a blast on *cuerna*, a hunting horn. *Cuenta*, reckoning, was used in a calendrical chant, for sowing and harvesting. The custom is similar to the Scots *reill*, the reckoning of clan genealogy.

CUIL (Gaelic)

College of religion in Ireland, half-way between *Tampaell* (church) and *schula* (school), and implying a "cell" of advanced student. The Latin *Coll* (association) derives from similar roots—*Col-legia* (or *Col-Licitas*) as a state-recognised institution. The term possibly derives from the ancient Egyptian *Khela*, the place (and *Khelu*, the student); and spread widely through Kymrekh (Cymri) people. Similar terms are known in Tamil (*koyil*) and in Tibetan (*khyilkhor**), with parallel functions in religious terminology. The Arabic version is *khawwal* (singer-chanters), and in Syrian is *cowell* or *kawal*. From it derived the Latin *quill*—the written form of liturgy, by "feather-dance" (writing); *esquillo*, later *tan-quillo*, as dance-song, and *tran-quillo*, "having finished". They are all associated with systems of mind training, or the "dance of the mind" ("association of ideas" is our modern phrase), which involves the perception, holding, and fusing of mental images. The term *Cuil* supplies part of many place names in Ireland; though the same activity no longer occurs; while the *Khela* shares in the base of names such as Kil-kenny or Kill-arne. These schools were, in their great days (500–100 BC) visited by students from all over Western Europe; and from even farther afield. Group ritual-dances marked their festivals.

CUNCA OR CHUNCHO (Bolivia)

Said to be an imitation by the Aymara Indians of the forest Chuncho Indians, but the name of the dance apparently derives from the beans called *cunca* or *cuncu*, strings of which decorate the men's jackets. Feathers ornament their trousers, and all the dancers wear huge feather head-dresses and carry bows and arrows. Accompanied by three flutes and three drums, men and women dance in long lines, their faces hidden behind a mask made of beads, old silver coins and beans, threaded on strings.

CURCHY (England)

The coif or *curchy* was formerly the mark of the wedded woman, as contrasted (more especially in Scotland) with the snood, which was the riband or net used to bind the hair of the nubile maiden. When she was married, she changed snood for coif, or curchy, and thus performed her bridal dance, for the first time in the new attire. Hence the dance-phrase, in a ballad, to "curchy, curchy on the grass", and the parallel ceremonial of "making a curtsey" at the court. All these terms imply some change of condition, a curtain on the past. In several European countries a special dance marked the donning of the matron's head-gear, with simulated reluctance by the bride to part with the sign of her maiden state—the snood or scarf or other girlish head-covering. The ballad is the once famous song—with various titles—celebrating *The Rural Dance About the Maypole*. A current version[1] has eight verses of eight lines each, containing the "names" of twelve couples; which are probably remains of traditional appellations given to characters in a ritual dance; for we have Willie and Jillie, Wat and Kate; Dick and Nick; Batt and Matt; and more significant, Pan and Nan. The second verse runs:

> "Strike up," says Wat; "Agreed," says Kate,
>   "And I prithee, fiddler, play";
> "Content," says Hodge; and so says Madge
>   "For this is holiday."
> Then every man did put
>   His hat off to his lass;
> And every girl did curchy,
>   Curchy, curchy on the grass.

[See *Borten Abtanz*] (Rumania)

[1] *Ancient Poems; Ballads and Songs of the Peasantry of England*. Edited by Robert Bell (1857, London) p. 164–165–66.

CURINKY (Ireland)

16th - 17th century colloquial term for "Dancing master", which remained as a family surname down to 1830 in Ireland. The name is connected with the *rink* or *rinceahhfade*, the *rinkey* or field dance, used at the *kirn* or harvest.

CURRENDE (German)

The band of choir-boys recruited from the ranks of the poor, for singing in the churches, as a lead to the congregation; also organised in the remaining choral dances (*caroles* etc.) prior to Martin Luther's attack on the papal authorities. The *Currende* is directly equivalent to *currente*, *corando* or *coranto*; the tune began in slow and solemn form, but developed into swifter and gayer melodies, as did the movement of the still formal dance. The German term derives from the *kur-*

ruend, the "dance of the font" or "cure" alleged to be gained by this formal acceptance into church; literally, the "dance of the *curate*".

CURSUS (Italian)

A 10th - 12th century term, used to denote the collective arrangement or course of formal proceeding; as in a legal court; a theological dispute; an ambassadorial meeting; or even preliminary discussions for a wedding. We know most frequently the *cursus* as applied to letter-writing; thence it influenced poetic forms, musical forms, and dance forms; and equally was reciprocal in taking their form. In the drama, the *cursus* was the preliminary arrangement of the acts. Leaving the "Unities" of Aristotle it tended to set a new formal scheme, so soon as there was admitted the idea of dramatic development of situation and character. The poem took tenacious root, as in the jolly 12th century dance-song of the Goliards; in reciprocal modes of rhythm and rhyme. The court *camberlengo* was chiefly responsible; but for church, canons (as their generic name implies) had these duties; the "measurement of times and spaces" for necessary ceremonies. With the precipitation of intention into written form, this precept of the "Five Divisions" became established, along with the change of Latin (church language) into Tuscan Italian (language of commerce and war). Court movements and manners emerged, in their answering formal scheme. The *camerlengo* set the scheme; he did not originate it. We see it in the correspondence of the period : a highly specialized activity. Each "proper letter" was designed with five *divisio* :

1. *Salutation:* The Greeting. To or From parties present;
2. *Captatio benivolentae* : The recognition of rank;
3. *Narratio* : The "case" (or *casa*, the house; the tale);
4. *Petitio* : The Request, Suggestion, or statement of solution;
5. *Conclusio* : The final salute, greetings, departure.

These sections followed, in their due and proper course, in quasi-rhythmic patterns, such as would be heard in a well-spoken poem : these are known collectively as the *cursus*. We have remnants in Britain in the procedures of the *Casa de Parlement* —the Houses of Parliament; in the comings and goings of Black Rod and White Rod; the Heralds and the "royal assent" in Norman French, together with the assignation of due territory ("behind the bar"). These court manners exercised a definite influence on dramatic form and balletic form, as well as poetry and music.

CUSHION DANCE (Elizabethan England)

Was usually the concluding dance of a country wake or market, or of a country house dance; it was also performed at court in more solemn fashion; but including master and men, mistress and maid. Playford refers to it (*Dancing Master*, 1698) as a "pretty little provocating dance". This was also called "Joan Sanderson". Begun by one person — man or girl — the dancer took a cushion in a hand; danced a circuit or two, then stopped before his choice. He sang "Then this dance it will no further go"; the girl (or musician) answered, "I pray you sir! why say you so?", to which the stock answer was "Because Joan Sanderson will not come too!" The musician retorted : "She must come whether she will or no!" The man then laid his cushion before the girl; she knelt on it; he kissed her and sang, "Welcome Joan Sanderson". She then rose, both danced, and they sang "Prinkum Prankum is a very fine dance!" Then the woman took the cushion and repeated the circuit and the song. The kissing episode, popular at that time, was perhaps a preliminary to more serious bouts. This dance was probably a tempered English version of an older French *Danse de San Jeanne d'Arc* for which the leading beauty of each town was elected by popular acclaim as "Jeanne d'Arc", who became in England the mysterious Jeanne or Joan Sanderson. In Scotland, this dance was named *Bab at Bowster* and commonly ended a wedding party. As the *Pillow Dance* it is known in other European countries, such as Hungary, and in Austria (*Polstertanz*). The *Siciliana*,* performed at weddings in Sicily is another version.

CYBOL-DDAWNS (Welsh)

Basically a "dance for two" (holding hands) but often read as "pleasure" and wrongly given in English works as *Cebel** or *Sebel*, which does not occur in Welsh, except *sibol* — "onions" (Leek is *ceninen*). *Sillebu* may indicate a children's "spelling dance".

CZECHOSLOVAKIA

Dance of Republic of Czechoslovakia, as listed in three categories of locality : *Tance z Ceskych kraju; Tance z Moravskych kraju; Tance z Slovenskych kraju* — which refer to the Czech western sector of Bohemia; the next sector, Moravia; and then Slovakia. Many of these dances have been "modernised", more in the words of the chants that almost invariably accompany the dance, but most of them are based on the traditional circle of the Kolo. These dances follow three main forms : the circle that breaks into a line and then reforms as a circle; with the alternating "numbers" of the dancing pair; or, finally, the dancing set of four couples. The *kolecka* involves a group larger than eight. There are other circle and square dances for lesser numbers; formerly done before the singing dancers of *kolecka*, who stood still for the period, clapping hands in time with steps and music of pipes and flute. Among these are known the *Rejdovak* and *Rejdovacka* (similar to *Redowa*). Some retain a religious flavour; others are called Tsigane. [See *Lidove Hyr a Tance pro Mladez* (Songs and Dances for Youth). Praha 1952]

D

"D" FOR DELTA (Greek)
Engraved over the Temple of Apollo àt Delphi; as one of the basic symbols of Greek religion, significant of the Trinity. (Compare *triskelion* in Gaelic symbolism). The double *delta* (or Diamond) is set into the dancing floor of the Greek Theatre of Dionysus at Athens; on it the chorus began and ended certain traditional Songs of Dionysus. The figure was used as the basis for obtaining the scales in Greek music; the sides of various triangles (chiefly that in the circle, and that in the square) supplied the lengths of cords for lyra. In writing, it gave the initial letter of many god names—from Diana the Time Measurer, onwards. "D" belongs to the moon-measure, in *three* phases; as the square belongs to the solar-time-measure, with *four* phases.

DABKE OR *DAVKE* (Arabic)
Ritual dance connected with "Water Libation" (with prayers—*salat-al-istisqa*. or Islamic prayers for rain), based on the ancient mode of "leaping dance round the altar." This rite is allocated to the Ba'al prophets. The circle is performed by men, who leap with bended knees; and was done round the great *Ka'Aba*, the sacred stone or *davar*, like that at Mekka.

DACTYL (Greek)
From *daktylos*, a finger. The term was used by Greek poets to signify a certain "metrical foot" or pace, uniting spoken word with instrumental note and ritual movement, in its primitive usage. Greek meters or rhythmic measures were, and still are, important in dance, more especially when the spoken word accompanies stage movement. Most choreographers neglect to examine Greek metre, because of their obsession with "invented movement" to show "something different," thus substituting inferior technology for dramatic meaning or mood. In its training sense, dactyl is superceded by its equivalent "finger", but in Hindu dance, the use of the hand and fingers is extended into the magnificent code of *mudra** and *hasta** (symbol and gesture).

DAGGER DANCE (Georgia, Caucasus)
A man's solo dance, performed to the accompaniment of balalaika, or nowadays probably accordion. Wearing the dark blue tunic and fur cap of the Caucasus, and holding the dagger between his teeth, the man dances round in a circle, arms crossed over chest. The tempo and intensity of the dance gradually increase, until, with arms still crossed, the dancer jerks his head, flinging the dagger through the air until it sticks quivering in the ground. The dance is then continued in reverse, the performer plucking up the dagger and resuming the dance.
[See *Dirk Dance* (Isle of man)]

DAKOTA SCALP DANCE (Amerindian War Dance)
A male dance, performed by successful warriors of the Dakota tribe, when they had achieved ultimate manhood by taking a scalp in warfare. The torchlight dance commemorated their victory while proclaiming their adult status. The men painted themselves with black or other dark colour; chanted a song of mourning to pacify the souls of the slain; yet affirmed their own superior power.

DALCROZE METHOD
System of Musical Training which aims at developing a sense of rhythm, and not dance training, according to its inventor, Emile Jaques-Dalcroze. His aim was "to give musical experience, not musical knowledge", for which he devised a system of "rhythmic gymnastics" based chiefly on musical beat and rhythm. In Switzerland and Germany, it was called Rhythmische Gymnastik; while in England it became known as Eurhythmics. E. J. Dalcroze was born in Vienna, July 6th, 1865; but, as his father was from Geneva, he was a Swiss subject. He studied at Geneva Conservatoire; in Paris (under Delibes) and in Vienna (under Bruckner). His period at Algiers infused him with Arabic rhythms. His method was first recognised, publicly, at a *Musikfest* at Solothurn in 1905. In 1906 the first course was given for teachers of music. In 1910 he went to Dresden; his school was erected at Hellerau, nearby, in 1911. S. P. Diaghileff, contacting Dalcroze, was deeply interested; and asked Dalcroze for an instructor in rhythm for Nijinsky. Before this time, Russian academies in Petersburg and Moscow sought instruction; and soon the Dalcroze system was incorporated in the official syllabus of the State Choreographic Academies (before 1918) along with the Duncan method and the Delsarte system of action-mime. In Dresden,

students like Mary Wigman and others, developed the new German Modern Expressionist Dance, on this basis; Rudolf Laban also studied; and so did Rudolf Steiner, who developed a scheme of Eurhythmik for his Goetheaneum School-Theatre at Dornach near Basle. Dalcroze Schools exist in Geneva, London, Paris, New York and other cities.

DALUM DANCE (Sweden)
In Västergötland, there is a folk dance resembling in some details the church dance of the *Creux de Vervi** at Liége. An old fiddler's melody carries this name "Dalum Thumbs up!" This is sung in a mime-dance, which continued down to 1870. Dancers formed in two groups facing, then in two rings facing each other. The men in the inner ring held up both thumbs before the faces of dancers in the outer ring, as they stepped round. They sometimes sang ancient words; sometimes a gentle parody; when the tune reached the final bar, there was a united cry of "Thumbs up! Thumbs up!", whereupon the outer ring advanced, turned and replaced the inner ring; when the next verse accompanied the next movement.

DAMHSA NAM BOC (Gaelic)
Dance of Goat performed at Harvest Festival in Scotland, as one of the Corn Dances. In Co. Kerry, Ireland, the Crowning of King Goat* is still to be seen, as annual ceremonial with three dances. Gathering, Crowning, Departing. The familiar Goat seems to have become a Mascot of some military regiments, marching with the drums on notable occasions. He appears in ballet in the story of *Esmeralda* (based on Victor Hugo's *Notre dame de Paris*). A goat appears in some Indian dances; and for other reasons in *Voodoo* Dance. In Greece—the goat=satyr.

DANCE—1
Origin of the word is in Zendic-Sanskrit; thence into Teutonic languages; and so into Romance tongues. *Tanha* is the original Sanskrit; it means "Desire of Life". The Zendic *H* becomes *S* in India; India; thus *Hapta* is *Sapta* (Seven) and *Hindu* becomes *Sindhaya*. The *S* continually softens to *H* from Greece to Bengal, from the Caucasus into Egypt. Arabic suspirations illustrate these changes in living fashion. Therefore, when turned into romanized script or print, the roman letters *H–K–S* are interchangeable. *Tanha* becomes then *Tanka* (*Tangka* in Tibetan mode) and then *Tansa*—the European Mode, finally as *Tanza* or *Tanz* and also *Danza* and *Danz*, *Danse* and *Dance* (*Daunce*, Med. Engl.). Every one of these variants retains its root meaning : the desire for action, for movement, for life, for rhythmic dance in the joy and experience of living.

DANCE—2
As a visual plastic fact, is "the Poetry of Motion", as compared with normal (theatre) movement as "the Prose of Movement". Dance is usually referred to human bodies : but the term is used to denote any visually rhythmic motion—the "dance of flames", or the "dance of fireflies",—as physical or biological facts. In Theatre we can see also the Dance of Puppets; and on films, the dance of animated cartoons. In every one of these movements, the elemental nature of all Dance is apparent in *rhythmic motion*. This expressive movement is directly associated with rhythms of emotions—the energic powers that burst forth in periodic rhythms which, when used in art modes, we term dance. Similar factors appear in ritual, though here the designation is not "dance". Primitive neuro-muscular rhythms emerge into primitive dance or ritual, as repeated actions that have been found efficient in producing or evoking a desired emotional result. Mostly they imitate earlier actions such as hammering, throwing, reaping and other acts of primal necessity, which in continuous repetition produce a simple beat of rhythm—as in clapping the hands, stamping the feet, striking a flint to shape it into an axe. Often these acts are accompanied by simple chants; here is the birthplace of music, with its aural rhythm to match the visual rhythm. Dance exists everywhere in the world, from the most primitive to the most sophisticated people, with many forms and many names.

DANCE NAMES
Definitions of dance names depend on being able to find a correct reference, especially for time and place. Etymology alone is not reliable; the term must be linked with function or ritual of the dance, which (before the modern age of Theatre) was joined with aim and purpose. Language variations are inevitable (see changes in the single term *dance*), but change in names of local dances are not so easy to detect (note term *passacalle* etc. and its versions). As important are generic language changes. In Spanish, 'h' may change to 'g' (as in Russian, Hamlet is spelled Gamlet), and 'f' may change to 'h' (*hembra*=*fembra*=woman). In German 't' and 'd' interchange, also 'v' and 'f'. In India, 'h' interchanges with 's' (*sindhu* becomes *hindhu*). From Latin 'v' we have 'w', which derived from earlier 'ae'. Every one of these vocal changes has affected the names of dances, of music, and words in chant or caroles that make up dance-songs. Many of these are noted in this *Dictionary*. Dance forms that remained constant in ritual found their names varied in different countries; and spelling was fixed only with the advent of printing.

DANEGELT DEMON, DANCE OF (England)
Westminster Abbey, London, has (or had) a picture
of an incident alleged to have been witnessed by
Edward the Con-Fossor "in a vision". The substance
of the story is that Edward (or his advisers) became
alarmed at the demands of the invading Danes for
more and more *gelt* (gold). Edward then "saw the
vision" — probably in a little mime-drama suitably
arranged for his entertainment, as a way of
dropping some strong hints on policy — showing
this Demon, dancing on the Danes; and as a result,
he turned down the next "final demand". Probably
this success was celebrated in dance form, with
the inspiration of some artist who made the recording picture.

DANGOS (Welsh)
Also as *Arddangos;* in Mediaeval Welsh implying a
gathering; and thence "to indicate, to show, to
make known, to disclose". This term appears to be
a Welsh equivalent to *tango*, which also implies a
gathering, in which ability in ritual dance is displayed (in twelve orderly movements in proper
succession). A parallel derivative term : *Arddan-
sawdd*, is described now as meaning ontology; but
the individualities mimed in earlier ritual can refer
only to the twelve successive "actions" in the
course of the *dango*. (*Tyngo* means "to give a
pledge"; *Tynged* — Destiny, Fate, or Luck).

DANH-SIO (West Africa)
Are the ritual dancers for *Danh-gbi*, the Great
Serpent God among the Ewe people. As young
girls they are called *kosio* (from *kono*, "without
fruit"), and receive initiation; from ten to twelve
years old. They reside in the "House", learning
during three years, the chants, dances, and herbal
knowledge, useful to villagers. The "House" is a
group of huts in an enclosure; some of these girls
become spiritualist mediums, usually later in life.
They may not be married. The "Great Snake" is
invoked at regular seasons; but especially when
drought threatens, in ceremonials where ritual
dancing appears, usually with chants and simple
drum music. The Python God is a symbol for the
earth rhythms which cause growth. In the "new
millet" season, when green sprouts rise, new brides
are sought for Danh-gbi. A few male priests control
the ceremonial.

DANISH NATIONAL BALLET (Copenhagen)
Den Kongelige Danske Ballet[1] (Royal Danish Ballet)
is an 18th century creation. The first theatre of
prominence was that in Lille Gronnegade (1722),
where we learn of the First French dancing master
in 1726, under Corporation auspices. In 1748, the
King took over; and his Royal Theatre opened in

1784 in Kongens Nytorv (Square), with Mons. des
Larces in charge, giving small entrées and divertissement programs. With frequent changes, other
ballet masters came from France and Italy (Neudin;
Como; Sacco; J. B. Martin; and Gambuzzi). In 1775,
Vincenzo Galeotti was engaged. Born 1733, he had
trained with Angioli and Noverre; he was to work
in Copenhagen until 1816, as dancer, ballet-master,
and choreographer; producing some fifty ballets.
In his last period, the ballet deteriorated. Then
Antoine Bournonville followed; while his son
Auguste had some training at the Court Theatre
ballet school in Copenhagen, before finishing in
Paris under Vestris. Auguste was engaged at Paris
Opéra as soloist from 1826; danced at the King's
Theatre, London, in 1828, and returned to Copenhagen in 1829, when he established the Ballet
School. Until his death in 1879 (with some short
intervals, as in Russia), Bournonville worked with
the Royal Danish Ballet, bringing it to a high level.
Following mainly in a romantic tradition, he was
strongly influenced towards dramatic work by
Noverre, retaining a purely French technical style,
and using full masculine balance. Of his fifty
original works, *Napoli* (seen in London 1953) is
perhaps best known; it carried evidence of the
same underlying clerical bias as does the original
libretto of *Giselle*. He used other nationalist
themes : *La Kermesse* (Flemish); *Le Toreador*
(Spanish); *Le Conservatoire* (French), and *Folk
Legend* (Danish). After his retirement, the Danish
Ballet declined, but Hans Beck, leader from 1894
to 1915, by much hard work pulled the company
together, with his partner Valborg Borchsenius.
Most famous of Danish dancers are Lucile Grahn
(1830?) and Adeline Genée (1880), both well-
known in London. The next impact was Fokine's
visit; and a guest engagement in 1925. Harald Lan-
der became soloist in 1930, and was appointed
ballet master in 1932, experimenting with more
modernist works.
[1] *Den Kongelige Danske Ballet* by Svend Kragh
Jacobsen (Copenhagen 1950).

DANSA (Catalonia, Spain)
A dance for six couples, holding hands, in quick
triple time. Forming various figures, beginning with
a circle and changing to a star-shape, they proceed
with a walking step between the figures. In some
districts in Catalonia, the *Dansa* precedes the dancing of the *Sardana*.*

DANSE MACABRE (Brittany)
Old Breton dance, from *tanz macabh*, "Dance of
lads", in the second half of the Twelve Nights
Festival of the New Year; the name became altered
and shifted to include also the first half, the *Danse*

Ancien and *Danse Noël*, the dance of the Dying Year. The lads presented the Birth Dance of the New Year. The term *macabh* is from the *Geleg* (Gaelic) language of old Brittany and Wales. [See *Dance of Death; Todtentanz; Masque*]

Danse Macabre. The Carthusian and the Merry Sergeant from drawing printed by Guyot Marchant, 1455. Original in Chapel of Innokente, Cloister, Paris.   FRANCE

DANSURINGUR (Faroe Islands)
Dance of the Faroe Islands, performed at Christmas and *Olavsoka* festival (27th to 30th July); after a successful whale hunt, or at weddings. A round dance with arms joined, the step is a sideways "slither" — double left, simple right — easy to do and monotonous, but achieving a certain excitement as the dance gets into its swing, the dancers arms beating vigorously up and down. Sometimes the ring opens into a sinuous chain, winding in and out, around and across the room. *Dansuringur* is accompanied by sung ballads of Danish origin, a special one, *Brudarvisa*, being sung by the men at weddings. On such occasions dancing takes place indoors; each dance may last an hour or more, with newcomers joining in as others drop out, and festivities continue until the small hours, sometimes till dawn. After a whale hunt, people gather on the quayside for the dance. At Christmas, the dance held on Boxing Night (*Annar Joladagur*) opens the dancing season, which continues until *Fostu inn Gangur*, first Monday in Lent. In olden times, on the occasions of the first and last dance of this season only, it was the custom for the men to be hatless. Dancers wear national costume — young men in dark blue knee breeches, light blue hose, black shoes with silver buckles, red embroidered waistcoat with silver buttons, handwoven hat of red with narrow black stripe. The girls dress in dark blue skirt with thin red stripe, black stockings, dark laced bodice, hand-knitted red and blue jumper, small close-fitting bonnet. At weddings they wear the *stakkur*, a long, flowing gown of heavy silk. One of the women's knitting patterns, called *Dansuringurin*, shows a repeated line of dancing men.

DANZA PRIMA (Asturias, Spain)
A circle dance of antique origin; an example, preserved in the Asturian mountains, of the solemn ritual chain of ancient Greece. Men and women alternating, the circle always moves slowly anticlockwise in 3/4 or 4/4 time, with the same step throughout — a step forward towards the centre and a step backwards, moving slightly to the right on the latter, so that the circle gradually moves round. This step is repeated continuously, one step to each beat, irrespective of change of time. Any number of people may join the circle, the dancers holding little fingers. Now danced in the streets, accompanied by a modern song, the *Danza Prima* used to move in a dignified ring round a church or small chapel, singing without instrumental accompaniment. In remote country districts where it is still performed, one of the dancers intones a couplet, the others replying with the refrain.

DANZON (Cuba)
An Afro-Cuban dance in syncopated rhythm, related to the old Spanish *Contradanza*, but with added African elements. Danced by couples holding hands, it was very popular during the late part of the 19th and first half of the 20th centuries, after which it went out of fashion as the more highly syncopated *Son** became popular.

DASI (India)
Dasi or *Das* is, literally, "Servant", thus *Rama-das* equals "Servant of Rama". In the temples the ritual dancers are known as *Dasi*, or *Deva-dasi* (servants of the *Deva* or god), or *Deva-ratial*, ritual-makers of the god. In Bengal, Das has become a general family name among Hindus. In Southern India (among Tamils) there is a class known as *Moylar* or *Muliyar*, sons of temple dancers; often called *Sthanikas*. They represent the male temple element, equivalent to lay brothers who help monks, as the girls are broadly equivalent to the nonnes or nuns. The corrupt or degraded 18th - 19th century quality of the Indian temple-dancer must not be taken as their original purpose or duty — (as with the nuns, those of Chaucer's day had changed considerably from the ascetic devotee of the primitive church; while those of the convents of Tudor days had, in many places, still more changed). The original arcane duty is mentioned in *Isis Unveiled* (H. P. Blavatsky), and a few other works on religion. Among the Mahrattas, such temple servants were

known as *Murli* (a name given also to the flute
used by Krishna, and to the song, also to the bird
—blackbird in Europe, as "Merle"). The dance has
two different forms: one for public ceremonial,
the other for symbolic tuition by means of music
(*raga**) and dance (*yantra* and *mantra*).
[See *Devadasi; Kumbarti*]

DEATH, DANCE OF
Also known as *Danse Macabre,** *Todtentanz;** a
mediaeval allegorical dramatic performance; also
portrayed in paintings, wood-engravings (especially
Hans Holbein), and carvings. This dance-drama was
performed before King René of Provence, as part of
a ballet (*La Lou Gue*) devised by himself, in 1462.
The earliest extant painting was *The Triumph of
Death (Orcagna)* in Campo Santa at Pisa (14th century). Dominican painters depicted it at Basle in
1431 and Berne in 1520. The Tower of London;
Cloister of St. Pauls; Wolsey's Whitehall Palace;
the Bishop's Palace at Croydon; Hungerford Chapel
at Salisbury Cathedral; the chapel at Wortley Hall,
Gloucester; and churches at Stratford-on-Avon and
Hexham, Northumberland—all had pictorial forms
of the Dance of Death. In English drama, it survived as "*Shaking the Sheets, or Dance of Death*"
[see *Dede Dance*] and an old English ballad, *Death
and the Lady*, carries the same theme. This story
is the universal triumph of Death over all manner
and condition of men. The Dutch story *Elkerlikje*
(which has been made into an English ballet,
Everyman) is similar; while the Hindu *kathakali**
dance-drama of Shiva-Kali has a parallel version.
See also *Tarot,** Dance of Cartes (Carthusians).
Bibliography:

> *Dance of Death* (Douce 1832) (1858);
> *Dances of Death* (Deuchar, 1788);
> *Recherches sur les Danses des Morts* (Peig-
> not) (1826, Paris);
> *Explication de la Danse des Morts* (Jubinal
> 1841);
> *Die Todtentanz des Mittelalters* (Seelman,
> 1892).

DEATH, DANCES OF
Are very numerous. Categories range to (a) dances
included in traditional ritual, as those performed
at death of an individual (mourning, funeral, and
festal); (b) dances to celebrate a "martyr" as at
dedication of festival of a single church; (c) dances
included in Mysteries; and (d) in Miracle Plays;
(e) dances belonging to youth initiation rites (i.e. in
Morris* dance, Sword dance*); and (f) dance rituals,
as part of *adult* or advanced initiation rites
(as in Temples of Egypt); (g) popular celebrations,
such as *Todtentanz** (Germany), or the New Year
Masque (England); (h) festal ritual dances, for symbolical or mythic ceremonial (as Dance of Seises at
Seville); or (i) the Hebrew *Megilloth*, or the
Christian Easter celebration.

Death and the Knight. One of the famous series
The Dance of Death; wood engraving by Hans
Holbein.   GERMANY

DEATH DANCES—1
Appear in numerous forms, all over the world;
principally as episodes in religious initiation ceremonies. According to the immediate intention,
they vary in form as ritual or as spectacle; from
"moralities" to rigorous rites of immense tension
(e.g. *Chöd Ritual**). Connected with the Death
Dances are the Wakes which summarise mourning,
praising, and aid to the deceased person, ending
usually with a feast for the living (e.g. Wakes,
Irish) and prayers, sometimes called "saying
masses", or sometimes offered as a series of instructions or guidance to the spirit of the dead man
(e.g. *Bardö Thödol* in Tibet). One of the oldest
known forms is the famous "Discussion of
Nachiketas", found in *Kena Upanishad* (500 BC),
from which various later versions are known,
notably the fourteenth century Dutch morality
play *Jedermann*, taken into English as *Everyman*;
and produced as a ballet (with music by Strauss),
by the Inglesby International Ballet Company. A
German version became famous at *Todtentanz,** a
relic of a much earlier *Tarota* ritual drama that

flourished (in the main, secretly) in mediaeval Italy. A Hungarian wakes dance known as *Matthias is Dead* has been produced by a Polish ballet company; while a modernist form has been done in *The Green Table* (from *Todtentanz*), a ballet by Kurt Jooss; another as *Todtenmal*, by Margaret Wigman, and one in the United States of America called *Dance of Death* by Martha Graham. In Bali there is a Death Dance-drama known as *Rangda*

the Witch; while the Negro people of Hayti have a version, danced to give comfort to the newly dead. Both the Tibetan dance-dramas and the Egyptian dance of the dead are highly elaborate ceremonials. Some Hellenic rituals have the same general purpose, as, for example, in the Descent into Hades in search of Proserpina; and in distant Siberia, in Yakutia, the *shaman* experts perform dance ceremonies for the dead.

"The Burying of Death" in effigy. Spring Festival dance at Helpa, Slovakia.   CZECHOSLOVAKIA

DEATH DANCES—2 (Various)
Include developments of many ritual forms, associated usually with some system of worship. They have three main modes (1) sacrificial rites—death of animal or human being (e.g. Isaac); (2) funeral rituals, dances accompanying interment or cremation; and (3) schematic dance rituals which recognise the inevitability of Death and reveal this fact in formation—as by "Dance of Fate"—*Fatum* or *Moeris.** Mostly they are group dances; a notable exception is the Yogi *Dance of Burning Ground.* The European variations tend to lose the original idea: as in *Todtentanz,** *Dance Macabre,** or Way

to Jerusalem* the *Moeris* (now Morris Dance) and the clerical *Ars Moriendi,** which lost its ritual in its insistence on prayer, culminating in Ignatio's Death Exercises. The most ancient known is that of the *Khelu* or Egyptian confessional dance—portrayed at length in *Book of the Dead.*

DEBKA (Syria)
Pastime dance favoured by Kurds and Yezidi tribes of Syria; men and women join in freely; with music from *zirman* (flute) and *tubbul* (drum). This festival dance occurs in the courtyards of the larger buildings, especially after a wedding.

DEBUTANTE
From French, adopted into English, as the term
given to young girls, daughters of wealthy or "well-
connected" parents, who are making their first
official appearance in society. This system developed
a tight ceremonial during the reign of Queen
Victoria; it involved a "presentation at court"
(arranged in collusion with the Lord Chamberlain,
who issued tickets after approving the parties)
which was a palace reception, when girls, all in
white, moved in long lines, to make an official bow,
called "curtsey". This salute was followed by a
ball. Some girls attended the palace ball; others
had family "coming-out parties" to which short
strings of "eligible bachelors" (vetted as to family,
education, and money) were invited. The main
function was a dance. This remaining fragment of
the matrimonial market customs still exists, in a
lesser degree; but the dances are more widely
attended; while Society is somewhat battered as to
wealth and subdued as to culture. The modern
debutante is the equivalent of the African tribal
initiate, except that the preliminary ceremonies
rarely involve circumcision or taking of solemn
oaths. The male ceremony has vanished, with the
exception of the university rite of conferring
"caps" for excellence in various games; but the
"caps and gowns" ritual for degree receptions continues its chromatic path. This debutante ceremonial is the last remaining rite of the mediaeval
court ball, in which the pavane* or the polonaise*
form of dance processional was used as a frame
for the succession of bows. The term remains in
"reverence" or (in the theatre) the "acknowledgment" bow to applause.

DEDE DANCE (Mediaeval England)
Clerical ritual dance, mostly processional, used in
the dedication of a new church or school etc. The
formal rite was celebrated on the "day of the
saint" whose name had been arranged to coincide
with an older local rite, by Romish invaders.
Usually the old edifice was pulled down, and the
site used for a new structure, to fix the newer invention. The rite itself is from Egyptian sources:
it was then known as the "raising of the Tet in
Tattu", involving the erection of a figure or at
least a column or steeple. This Tet or Ded, brought
to England, gave its name to (a) the original cir-
cumvallation or procession round the site; and (b)
the repetition of this rite inside the completed
building on its opening day (the "saint's day" — or
the day of the company, or sangha). The same
name, as Djed, gives "Saint Chad". Following this
the rite was repeated with less ceremony, on the
annual celebration. Dedication Rite became known
as Dédé Dance. Possibly this originated the term

Tetty or Tutty at Hungerford, with the Tutty men
and their dance. It is also the legal sign of ownership — the "Deeds".

DEDE DANCE (Old English folk-dance)
Known also as Shaking of the Sheets, is mentioned in Misogonous, a comedy dating about 1560,
along with Putney Ferry and the Vicar of Fools,
two popular dances of that day. The Dede Dance
was a solemn "dance for the dead" done in two
portions : first the slow processional of the bier,
taken into the church; and then the circular march
round the bier, as it rested in the centre of the
nave, over the labyrinthine pattern. While this
continued, with intoning of the chanted prayer for
the dead, the deid-bell or dede-bell (passing-bell)
rang its single note at wide intervals. The Dede
Dance was, perhaps, a version of a French Dedale
Church Dance, now turned to secular usage. It is
named in the Complaynt of Scotland (1548) and in
Gosson's Schoole of Abuse (1579). Cecil Sharp says
that the Dede Dance is among the more advanced
forms of Country Dance : [1]
[1] The Dance. Cecil Sharp. (London 1924).

DEER, DANCE OF
A symbolical dance known in many ritual-dances
of various religions. Dances are found today in
America among the Red Indians; in Mexico (see
Venado*); in South Indian (Kathakale : Dance of
the Hunter); and in Tibet in the Lama Dance of
Death where Yama wears a Deer Mask. In the
Hindu Hunter's Dance, the Hunter is simultaneously the Deer, dancing both parts; necessary
to enforce the symbolism (similar to that suggested
in Francis Thompson's poem The Hound of
Heaven).
    "Nada is like a snare for catching a deer, i.e. the
    mind. Like a hunter, it kills the deer, i.e. the
    mind. Like the hunter, Nada first attracts the
    mind and then binds it and then kills it. Thus
    is put to an end the natural unsteadiness of the
    mind (its "dancing" through life) and thus is
    absorbed." [1]
[1] Hatha-Yoga-Pradipika. p.92. Edn. trans, by S. Iyan-
gar, B.A. (1933).

DELSARTE METHOD (France)
A system of rhythmic action, developed in Paris by
François Delsarte (born Solesnes, 1811), where he
taught most of the great French actors and actresses
of France from 1850 to 1870. Théophile Gautier
expressed great admiration for his work; Sir
Charles Bell (seeking facts on "Expression" for his
book) came to his studio. Delsarte instructed in
movement artists like Sonntag; Macready; Père
Lacordaire; Carvalho, and Pasca; while politicians

and royalty came for instruction in elocution and action. Saint-Saëns appreciated his "arts of speaking and gesture". His work was broken by the Franco-Prussian War in 1870; and he returned to Paris in 1871, only to die. His system was highly personal; only a few notes survived destruction; he left no organized school, but a considerable outline has been gathered, from records made by students at the Paris Conservatoire where he taught. Russian students of Delsarte's system took voluminous notes to Petersburg; where later they were incorporated into a part of the training system in the State Choreographic Academy of Ballet.
[See *Science and Art of Speech and Gesture*. R. M. O'Neill 1927]

DEMON DANCE (S. India)
Known through Kanara in the temple, or *Bhutasthanam*, where the priest (*pujari*, who offers the sacrifices), is usually one of the Tullava caste. These structures range from small palm-thatch buildings to larger and solid buildings, sheltering a number of brass symbolic images, which vary according to the *bhuta* who "lives there". The *bhuta* generally are thought of as destroyers, sometimes disease-rulers (e.g. the later European concept of "germs" as efficient causes of bodily disorder). Their principal method is exorcism; the theory is that of powerful animism; there is a concentrated energy which has to be sought, identified and dispersed. From a measure for the ejection of the unwanted demon, the dances may range also into a trance period, by which messages are received.

DEMON DANCE (Paraguay)
Among the Indians of the Gran Chaco, a girl who is to be protected from demons sits in the centre of a ring of women, who dance gracefully a protective ritual. Each performer has a long bamboo stick with a rattle made of a bunch of small hooves from deer or goats. Young boys with feather head ornaments, represent demon birds, whose shrill cries they imitate as they dance up and down the circle of dancing women.

DENDERAH, OR TENTYRA (Ancient Egypt)
Elaborate ritual dance symbolism of period of late Ptolemies was performed in the famous Hathor Temple. A. Mariette (of Paris) who spent much time excavating, removed the valuable Planisphere to the Louvre (post 1823). He records some of the dancers' verses:
"We sound our drums for her Spirit
  We dance by her grace—
  We see her lovely form in the Heavens

She is Our Lady of Sistrums—
Mistress of the sounding necklaces.
                *   *   *
  Hathor is Lady of Delight, Mistress of Dance
Lady of Sistrum and Queen of Song
  Our Lady of Dancing, Mistress of Flowery
    Wreathes
Lady of all Beauty, Mistress of Salutation.
                *   *   *
  When both her Eyes are open: Sun and Moon
Our hearts rejoice, receiving Light—
  Hathor is Lady of the Wreathing Dance
Lady of Ecstasy—we dance for none other
  We praise None other—but her Spirit."
                                (*Denderah*, Mariette III. 1875)

DENGAKU (Japan)
Military ritual dance ceremonial (12th - 13th century) used, like the earlier forms of European ballet, as a basic ceremony of court manners. It was balanced by the spectacular mime-drama, *Kajokubu* dance; this was formulated to show and stress "deeds of loyalty" and filial piety; in settings of famous places (Ashikaga period 1340 - 1570 approximately). Under Prince Shotuku, Kawakatsu was the imperial ballet master; his duty was to "make songs and dances" for the imperial court.

DENGAKU NO NOH (Japan)
Now a mode of *Kabuki* Theatre, formerly part of the peasant Harvest Ceremonial, performed regularly down to 1350, when its practice lapsed. In revived form, this village dance of thanksgiving became a part of *Kabuki* theatre. Costumes still reflect the conventional origin; and include the provincial hats of rough straw decorated with flowers; the farmer's large round straw hat, together with a general form as a "work-dance". Sometimes it is performed together with *sarugaku* ("monkey music"), a comedy form, originally mime interludes in the austere *Kagura** dances. *Dengaku* dances with mime added became known as *Dengaku No Noh*; while *Sarugaku* mimicry with dance added became *Sarugaku No Noh*, *Noh** is the classical lyric-dance-drama of Japan.

DENMARI (Japan)
A voiceless play in pantomime, part of the comprehensive *Kabuki* style of Japanese dance drama. The recent convention is a sort of summary, by all the players of the month, especially all leading actors. Musicians sing a story in verse—of light and inconsequential character—as a general summary of ability. This *denmari* ends with a display of the "star of the month", who is accompanied by drums and flutes, when he performs a version of *roppo** (the "six-directions" symbol of "mastery

over space" suggested by Zen doctrine). The action of *denmari* is marked by long or staccato rhythms; the whole action will stop for a moment (like *tableaux vivants*) to offer the most spectacular "picture-scene".

DEPORTMENT
Is the first technique of the adult, in the carriage of the body; it is studied, first for health and efficiency, then for character and charm—by men as well as women. Dance training will not automatically supply fine deportment; ballet-training is ineffective here, since its work is so highly specialised. Athletic training, and sports or games, will not give good deportment incidentally. Deportment is the basis of personal movement in expression, in social relations; as good acting is a parallel art utilised on the stage. The courts of the Middle Ages, and especially of the Renaissance, knew the necessity of deportment; they arranged ceremonial to teach manners, dancing to teach movement (along with its partner of fencing for the men), but true deportment contains the art of being still and keeping quiet at the right moment; it includes finally, ear and tongue, as well as waistline and hand-shaking. Neither birth nor breeding give the power of deportment by accident; it has to be obtained by conscious work. One sector of good deportment is to be seen at any good mannequin* show; though frequently spoiled by its lack of rhythm, and posing that is too monotonously artificial. Confidence appears at beginning and end of good deportment; though many cats and dogs reveal an immensely · attractive natural grace. Correct and well-fitted clothing is an essential: the usual costume for "time and place" is necessary; this "feeling of fitness" is one of the foundations of confidence. Most of all, health in easy movement, gives the basis; but the final achievement is seen in the true economy of thought, emotion, and movement that reveals (or conceals) an instinctive vigour. Ease in deportment is the sign of the person (of any age) who is fully related to his or her normal social range.

DERVISH (Persian "poor man") DANCE—1 (Arabia)
The name *Derwish* or *Darwesh* is broadly used through Islam for a member of any religious fraternity, and the *dhikr* (pronounced *zikr*), is the religious service lasting about an hour, common to all fraternities, at which spiritual songs and dancing take place, to the playing of drums and pipes. The Dervish Dance is a ritual performed by an Order of Dervishes called the *Mawlawiya*, (or *Mevlevi*) deriving from *mawlānā* ("our master"), a title given to Djal al-Din al-Rumi, their founder. The object of the dance is not to present a rhyth-

mic entertainment, but to induce in the performer a state of ecstasy. Although dancing (*raks*) during the ritual of the *dhikr* is mentioned in Sufi literature much earlier than the time of Djal al-Din al-Rumi, he claimed to have elevated the practice. To the accompaniment of various instruments, each dervish revolves, using the right foot as a pivot, continuing for about half an hour to an hour; although there are legends of saintly dervishes who whirled continuously for many days and nights. Their costume consists of a cap (*sikke*), long sleeveless coat (*tennure*), jacket with sleeves (*destegul*), waistband (*elif-lām-end*), cloak with sleeves (*khirke*) thrown over the shoulders. Instruments played may be reed-flute, zither, rebeck, drum, tambourine, sometimes small cymbals called *halile* or *zil*; sometimes flute, violin, kettle-drum. [See *Zhikr*; *Radenya* (Bulgaria)]

Dervish Dance. Chanting Dervish Dancers, in Tekke at Stamboul. 19th century.   TURKEY

DERVISH DANCE—2 (Samaet, semaet—Arabic)
A round dance performed in the *tekke* (monastery) principally by Moslem devotees of the Mevlevi Dervish Order. They meet each Friday night in the *sinankhane* (a round building with wooden floor), and twelve to twenty men, clad in long, white cotton robes and wearing tall, brown felt bonnets, move in a circle dance to the music of a *ney* (flute). Each whirls on his own centre, for an hour or more unceasing; falling into an ecstasy. Often the "Hundred Names of Allah" are chanted during this religious dance. This Order (suppressed by Kemal Ataturk) survives in Egypt (as Karaouan, for example), Syria and elsewhere. The dance was occasionally performed at the Court (Sergalio) of the Sultan, at Istanbul. Some of the dances resembled *caroles;** they had a chant, rhythmic verses, sung to flute or tambour.

DESGUISER (Norman-French)

From *Das Kaiser*—chief figure in the Mumming Plays of the New Year king and the January 6th secondary play of *Der Drei Köningen*. The New Year Festival continued in West European countries, under various names and with numerous contrived alterations: as *Reye des Havas*, "King of the Beann"; Xmas Lord; the "Guisers" or Geezers (there is a hint of the Gaelic *geasa* or magician here, but he was also a "lord of might"). The habit of dancing and masking existed long before any of these relatively modern names; but the mediaeval meaning was essentially linked with the fading of the individual dancer behind his allotted mask; and so, in modern times, "he was disguised". The New Year Masques, held in the Inns of Court, long retained a wide variety of alternative titles. In the ceremony of Desguising, both men and women entered; their performance was in the *basse danse* category; the Morris Dance followed, but was not part of this Masking. The Scottish term is *guisards* or *guysers*.

DEUTSCHE TANZ (Germany)

At one period, a general term applied, usually by the Germans themselves, to the form of ritual dance known as *Almain* or *Allemunde*. Wrongly, other nations have considered the *Allemande* as originating in Germany because of the apparent similarity of name; but the Italians knew of *mandorla and alle-mandoral* (allemande), without any reference to the *Tedeschi* (Italian name for Germans). *Deutsche* or *Deutsche Tanz* was also another name for the *Ländler;* * and for the similar "turning" or "spinning" dances of South Germany from which the Ländler derived, such as the *Dreher, Weller, Spinner, Schlerfer. Deutsche* was their collective name. [See *Allemande; Landler*]

DEVADASI

Literally, God-servant (Sanskrit ritual dance term) from *Deva* or *Dewa*, a god; and *das*, a servant. The title refers specifically to the servants of the Hindu temple (both youths and girls), who perform the "dance before the gods" among many other duties. European misunderstanding, linked with Indian degeneration, has wrongly permitted this honorific term to indicate "prostitute". In fact, the girl dancer is no more, of necessity, a prostitute, than the *coryphées* of the Parisian *corps-de-ballet;* or the London music-hall performers of the Victorian period. Great temples have a body of *devadasis*, as European churches had convents and monasteries associated; some of these gained unsavoury reputations, but not all. There were three grades or ranks of *devadasi;* the seniors who led the temple ritual dance, and the processionals in which the figures and lights are carried; the larger number, of middle grade, who perform duties closely akin to those of acolytes, or deacons, and choristers or musicians; and the novices, who perform "domestic duties" of sweeping and cleaning. The body may number up to 300 or even 500, dependent on the revenue of a temple from its land possessions. They are named from the celestial nymphs, the *apsaras*, as the musicians are named from the *gandharvas*, who are spirits of melody. The *devadasis* are "consecrated to the service" in much the same fashion as are nuns. We should not confuse them with (a) the *bhaijees* (public singers of *baijans*, or praise-chants), or (b) the *tuwaifs* (Muslim dancers) chiefly for *Nautch;* or (c) the *nattuvans* (Kathakali dancers of the South, who rarely perform in temples). The *bayadère** does not belong at all to India but to Indonesia.

DEVA-RATIAL (Travancore, S. India)

A temple dancer, a "servant of the gods", who in many respects was similar to the *nonnae* of Egypt or the *nuns* of W. Europe. Their duties were as servitors, in and about the temple; and their life began with a formal "marriage to the god" in solemn ceremonial. The girl of ten is baptised or bathed and takes offerings. The priest lights the sacred fire (*homam*) and proceeds with the rites of the *Tiruk-kalyanam* festival. She is then instructed in the basic *mantrams* (musical codes with words of creed) as the *Panchakshara mantra* (five-fold) for Shiva, or the *Ashtak-shara mantra* (eight-fold) for a Vishnu temple. After trial in various duties she becomes relegated chiefly to one or other task: if she reveals signs of proficiency, the girl receives daily instruction in dance from an older retired *Deva-ratial*. Her life is carefully guarded; she leaves the confines of the temple only in ritual processions and other duties; and has to follow temple fasts and watches. A regular rite of a group is *Dipa-radhana*, the "Waving of Lights", that accompanies the *avahana* or invocation of the god; and this is followed by dancing. Though in present times, funds are less and interest diminishes, certain centres still maintain in full power the ancient traditions; but it is rare for a foreigner to see them.

DEVIL DANCE

A term applied to several distinctly different types of ritual dance:

(a) "Medicine dance" used for exorcism of "devils" from some patient; as e.g. by a Shaman (Siberia) or similar expert.

(b) Invocation dance, alleged to be performed by "pagans" for the purpose of "raising the devil". One typical dance of this style is given by Goethe in his *Faust;* the *Tanz im Harzwald* or

Brocken-tanz, said to occur on Walpurgis Nacht.

(c) The mythical Dance ritual of Black Mass, alleged to be performed by "unfrocked priests" in a legendary "worship of the devil"; see Huysman's lurid novel *La Bas* for a specimen description; entirely fictional.

(d) The Monastery Dance of Lamas in Tibet, masked as "demons" as in the Gompa of Leh in Ladakh, designed to indicate the post-mortem world of the *Bardo* (intermediary between death and rebirth once more into this world), as a dramatic mystery play.

[See *The Tibetan Book of the Dead,* Evans-Wentz]

(e) The *Todtentanz,** also known as *Danse Macabre** and *Tarota,** variously performed, described or pictured as a Dance of Death and Devils (see notes under these headings for details).

(f) African ritual dances by masked or disguised figures, performed at puberty initiation ceremonies of admission into tribes as adults.

DEVIL DANCES (general description) — 1

Considerable confusion exists in this term; devil dances are seldom (if ever) accurately to be described as "worship of the devil, or of devils", except by ignorant critics or opponents; and propagandist polemics against alleged "witch-craft". Oriental demon-dances are performed (a) to exorcise a supposed demon which "possesses" some person who is suffering; or (b) to banish "nature-demons", which seek to invade human bodies, animal bodies, or houses. We must here distinguish the banishing from the "appeasement of ancestors" (as in Voodoo and many other forms). Bible accounts contain various examples: e.g. the "Gadarene swine", which took off "devils" from a man (to the loss of the innocent swineherd), or the revenge against Ananias, The primitive church was staffed with official exorcists, whose regular duty was to "banish the spirits", from the gathering, before the "descent of tongues", (in the *profeta,* or *sibyl,* of the meeting). Similar ceremonies are still performed in Hayti and North Africa; while the Siberian *shaman* has identical duties. In Java, one seance, known as *ketjak* (or as "Monkey Dance", to Europeans) deals also with trance, invocation, and exorcism.

DEVIL DANCE (General) — 2

Is a term that implies now as little as its analogue of "God Dance" — it is too vague. We can begin with separation into three large categories of dance ritual. In India, Ceylon, Burma, Java etc. there are many dances which are called by foreigners "devil-dances" and invariably given horrific labels,

such as "grotesque" or "devilish" or "demonic" — meaning that what the trembling observer sees is something he has been taught to regard as "not at all nice". The people who perform or watch have different ideas. There are two main modes of dance here: those which are theurgic or healing in aim (and often in result), and those which present "dark forces" in myths where they contend visually with "light forces". Far less frequent, if anywhere, are those dance rituals alleged to give "worship to the devil", for the simple reason that only the Roman religion has ever made a special personality of this supposed entity, as necessary in its legends of hell and purgatory; and in its political persecutions of satirists as "witches". The mediaeval devil image was superposed on the fabulous figure of Pan, God of Unconscious Nature, in Hellenic mythology. We cannot hope to understand any sort of "devil dance" unless we discard our own narrow prejudice; and see the ritual as it is seen among its own people. Thus the *shaman* or the *godurma* (Australia) does not "dance wildly about" in a "grotesque manner" any more than two opponents in a boxing-ring in England, or wrestling in Japan, mean to fight to kill, like Roman gladiators. The *shaman* has his method of inducing and using certain funds of natural force, which he uses to heal and help his patient. He knows well what he does, though he cannot put it into words, any more than a good violinist can say what he feels: thus he must play it. When the profound ignorance of the half-educated scholar is mounted on slender accounts (for he rarely goes to see for himself at first hand!), it is not surprising that "explanations" are seldom accurate.

DEWINIAD DDAWNS (Welsh)

Diviners' Dance — similar to that of the augurs, as a ritual dance performed by the enchanters or soothsayers — *dewin* or diviners. For these events, they used a ring dance, producing by the *Llinelliad-ddawns* (or *Lliniadu*) the magical diagrams, marked in lines on the stone paving or on the ground.

DHJANGER (Bali, Indonesia)

Is a modern "musical comedy" development from the traditional dance modes of Bali, much influenced by foreign notions and forms. This *gamelan dhjanger* is performed by integrated groups of boys and girls, including periods of modernist dance. The *gamelan** uses drums, songs and flutes, the piece may be of any length, from twenty minutes to four or five hours, though these longer shows are now rare.

DHULI-CHITRAM (India)

Term used in *Silparatna* (an old Indian treatise on

Art) for temporary "powder paintings" done by Indian women, following traditional patterns from memory. These patterns (now called *alpona* in Bengal) are produced for every village festival; and often for special ritual occasions of domestic worship, as those connected with weddings or funerals. They lay down the conventional positions of participants in the rites. Rich people in bygone days, employed skilled artists to inlay these dance patterns, sometimes in semi-precious stones; sometimes in more ordinary substance. Visitors to the Taj Mahal at Agra gain close acquaintance with the magnificence of Indian inlays, where they also appear in many vertical wall surfaces, as they do in the Fort. Formerly, in the Fort, dance patterns were laid by *dhuli-chitram* methods, sometimes for *pachisi.** These patterns are symbolical, not realistic, like the dance.
[See *Vishnu-dharmottoram* (Trans. S. Kramrisch, Calcutta 1924); *Silparatna*]

DIABALADA BOLIVIANA (Bolivia, South America)
Traditional Spanish-American dance and "Morality Play" done in dance-mime before Ash Wednesday, at the mining town of Orura, principally by local citizens. The main form is a processional dance with "devil marches". The way is "cleared" by a condor dancer and bear dancer; Lucifer and Satan lead, elaborately attired. There follows a "devil-dance" (based on the forgotten figures of the *tango*), after which comes the play. The allegorical legend shows Lucifer against Michael; the Seven Vices and the Seven Virtues; together with a local Indian goddess, here turned into the "devil's wife", with the name of Chine Supaye. The dramatic form is a simple contest, obviously devised by some eager padre among the first invaders. Great delight is taken in the evolutions of the Diabalada groups of devils, attired in great masks and costumes bright with glittering glass. The masks closely resemble those to be seen in Tibetan monastery dances; but the dancers wear white tights instead of long red robes; while Lucifer and Satan vaguely recall the Spanish toreador dress, with its heavy red plush cloak, and a trident instead of *banderillas*. Youths of the town, unable to afford carnival gaiety, disguise themselves in hoods as "*pepinos*" (clowns), singing and making quips. They are the last traces of the once-dreaded Familiars of the Holy Inquisition. As well as at Oruro, 12,000 feet up on the Andes range, there are similar dance-plays at La Paz, as a Cemetery Carnival where the Butchers' Guilds play the parts of "devils". This carnival dates only from 1578, when the town was first settled by Spanish invaders.

DIAGHILEV BALLET (Ex Russia)
Existed from 1909 to 1929. This originally all-Russian company went to Paris, in pursuit of the general scheme of showing Russian arts in Western Europe; and, after an Art Exhibition (Pictures and Sculptures) in 1907, there was Russian Drama and Russian Opera (1908), followed by the Russian Ballet (1909). Sergei Diaghileff (born Perm 1871), was employed as a civil servant for this purpose. The outbreak of war in 1914 ended financial support for the dance company, which did not return, then or later. Thus this tsarist Russian Ballet dropped its nationalist character; and gained rapidly a Franco-Russian quality, concentrating on "modern arts" (for theme and decor) and becoming the first Colonial Russian Ballet Company. From its success and influence stemmed numerous "Russian Ballet" Companies, of gradually degenerating quality. Though Diaghileff, who was not an impresario by intention, continued ballet production (financed by various and changing sources), the impact of his work as an efficient "Art Director" roused Theatre in other countries to copying and revival. His first ballets were in newer works that had *not* then been produced inside Russia; yet he revived (in London in 1921) the famous *Sleeping Beauty* (promoted to a Princess), aided by Nicolai Sergueéff. He refused an offer by Anatole Lunacharsky (in 1923) to return to Leningrad to supervise new ballets. Gradually his levels of ambition dropped, under the commercial demands of Parisian art and fashion dealers; his last ballets were inferior, except in technical dance form. The company finally broke up with his death in Venice in 1929. Numerous schools (some of them authentic) sought to carry on Russian *ballet* by teaching Russian academic *dance*: two aims by no means identical. Since 1929 the *Diaghileff* Legend has grown apace; even he, with his skill in publicity, would have been amazed at his fame.

DIAGRAMS FOR DANCE
Used for Ritual Dance; either as familiar symbols of place, or position of dancers; or as guides to doctrines with which the dances are associated. See *Alpona;** *Rangoli;** *Chakram**). Diagrams appear as (a) symbols for festival celebrations, (b) regular patterns made in dance floor, as by marble or stone mosaic work, or parquetry; or (c) temporary diagrams made by a ballet-master in teaching dance form, or by a dance producer in course of rehearsal of dance production. Certain folk-dances (e.g. the *Morris Dance**) produce diagrams or patterns in the course of their evolutions; and affirm these by a final diagram shewn in actual form, as in the star-pattern made with the interlaced "rappers". The single floor diagram is used

in some systems of dance training; as in the circle with four or eight points, used to teach in ballet for orientation of steps or routines. Such diagrams are suitable for one dancer only, in elementary phases of work. In group association, the unit diagram, sited in one place, developed into the stage diagram or choreographic system. The diagram is the letter or word unit, while the true choreographic scheme presents the sentence, paragraph and chapter of the assembled dance. The diagram supplies an essential part in many Magical Dances, and such diagrams may be seen in any complete grimoire and in many books on Alchemy. [See *Sand Tracings*]

DIAMOND SUTRA (India)
Is a sacred Oriental book; known in India as *Prajna Paramitra*; in China as *Chin-Kang-Ching* (trans. by William Gemmell 1910), which has affiliations with the Polynesian ritual called *Tangov;** or, in Europe, the *Vesica Pisces* (and *Al-Munde*). Possibly the term *Sut* is identical with the *Suts* or dance-players, later the *Sotties* of Mediaeval France, in their degenerated form. *Sutra* in Sanskrit implies "verse" (syllables enchained). The main indication is in the term *Vajra Kheddika*, or Diamond Cutter, by which is implied mutual cutting of opposites; or the "interpenetration of opposites". This is performed in dance ritual by the group formation of two triangles, first set apex to apex, which then move into coalescence — one group passing through the other group, until the two have merged and passed; and now show triangles base to base. The central position is that of the *Muhr-i-Suleiman*, or "Rose" made by the Morris Dancers as the Double Triangle. They usually omit to "make" and show the original two separate single triangles; and thus rarely perform the significant interpenetration of the two forms.

DIMENSIONS, IN MODERN DANCE
Occupy some attention in examination of the "Theory of Pure Dance" as the pragmatic base of "abstract dance". As words so readily become confused with facts, several conflicting systems have appeared; diverted according to the principal need before the particular exponents. From the earliest bases (in Europe) pertaining to certain Greek ritual dance and Roman rhetoric (Quintillian) the analysis of dimensional movement and gesture has veered in many modes. Chiefly they appear in three (rarely so named) as (1) physical; (2) emotional, and (3) mental. The Hellenic pre-occupation with physical measure (by unit, scale, and cord), led them to relegate the other two; save a few thinkers like Plato or Plotinus. Concepts of five regular plane

figures, and five regular solid figures, emerged from Euklidian geometry and architectonic practice. The Hindus (through their musical *raga* system) gave much attention to the emotional or vital ranges of dimensions or tensions. Mathematicians have later tried to comprehend physical dimensions as mental dimensions; hence the endeavours of Riemann and others, to fabricate a "curved space" and the curious *eidolon* of "four-dimensional mathematics", ignoring the basic solid concept of di-mension : as "that which can be separately measured" by length, or breadth, or depth, and comprising volume. The modern notion of "mass" tries to supercede this trinity-in-unity, as a disguise for energy, or moving volume, thus bringing in the idea of Time. The "dance" envisaged by Plotinus[1] gained in fact six "dimensions" sustained by a central seventh point; as did the Hindu system of *Raga*, necessarily, being made of music. The twin arts of dance and music depend on a triple perception : (1) as Coming; (2) as Here; (3) as Departed; or, Receiving, Knowing, Remembering. All effects in music (as in dance) depend *relatively* on what has preceded the moment of actual perception, with an echo of what has passed. These are the Time dimensions; essentially triple, as are the Space dimensions; together they sum up to six; united by the inner seventh point, the perceiving point or mind. Thus we gain a total of ten dimensions : three *physical*, three *vital* (tensions), and three *mental*, united in the centre, now the tenth. All of these permit and describe position and movement. Mind reflects or initiates body movement, through the joining vital tensions; contracting or expanding.   [See *Quantum and Dance*]
[1] *Enneads*, Plotinus. See also *The Serial Universe*. J. W. Dunne, London, 1932.

DIMENSIONALISM IN DANCE
Has been approached by various "Modernist" dance teachers and theorists. They have felt the difference that exists : between the predicated "three-dimensional space" as utilised by Euklid in his unfinished summary of Greek geometry, as publicly current in his day. He did not explain the working processes used in architecture and designs of ritual vases.[1] Later mathematicians — feeling similar doubts (Riemann, for example) — have attempted to create a "curved space". One scheme has inverted "right angles", while another has everted "right angles"; thus all surfaces are curves. These schemes evade the eternally repeated fact : the dancer moves always in curves (with a curved body), within the temporary limits of an equi-angular space — beginning with the plane of the floor, the "dancing space", as a prime condition of any continued expressional movement. Here we

have Life Curves[1] moving against the necessity of Formal Shapes, in angles and planes.

[1] *Dynamic Symmetry: The Greek Vase.* Jay Hambidge, 1924. See also *Curves of Life.* E. J. Cook, 1913; and *The Serial Universe.* J. W. Dunne, 1932.

DINKA VIRGINS' DANCE (Southern Sudan)
Is included in a dance series, on festival occasions. Some three hundred Dinka Sudanese girls may be present. Drums are hung on poles and water supplies got ready. Women add paint, mostly red, to their naked bodies. As they begin dancing, they start chanting, becoming louder and quicker. Sometimes a man will grab a girl, and they dance together; these two performers become the centre of an admiring circle, leaping and pirouetting. The movement of their hands strikes observers. It is a childish little dance, like "Here we go gathering nuts in May", but the words they sing are "very naughty". A shout stops this dance; and the warriors come; many of them over six feet tall. Six hundred warriors form in a great circle, while the women stand waiting in a line at the side. A new dance-beat softly emerges; war-cries change to a chant; the waiting girls are chosen and each one with a warrior, joins in the circle. The girls dance, forever retreating and laughing, but always inviting, with outstretched hands. Thus, this scheme is an abstracted love dance; the basic form remains, and is followed, even when there are not enough girls. Different is the *Bongo** dance, done by an adjacent tribe.   [See *Bongo Dance*]

DINKY (Jamaica, West Indies)
Celebration on the ninth night after a funeral. At midnight the mourning period is over, and the festive *Dinky* begins, with much gaiety, singing and dancing.   [Cp. *Nine Night Song*]

DIOMEDE ESKIMO DANCE (Little Diomede Island, Behring Straits)
Before contact with civilisation, a successful hunt was celebrated with dancing, including a "sitting dance" performed by girls. The sitting position was probably made necessary by the low ceiling of the Eskimo hut. Nowadays the same dance is performed at the trading post, to celebrate the arrival of a consignment of American tinned food! Sitting one behind the other, on a shelf above the stacked tins, the girls perform a swaying dance. Squatting with one leg under, they thrust out the other leg in a semblance of the Russian cobbler's step. Arm movements are angular, one forearm is bent upwards at the elbow, the other horizontal across the body. The dance is accompanied by the beating of large, flat tambours, made of walrus membrane stretched over hoops.

[Cp. Sitting and Kneeling Dances—*Kebyar* (Bali); *Puili; Uli-Uli-Noho* (Hawaii); *Kanana* (New Guinea); *Ghedra* (Morocco); *Siberian Kneeling Dance; Otuhaka* (Tonga)]

DIOSCURI (Crete and Ancient Greece)
Twelve deities (of whom Castor and Pollux were two) had an annual festival of worship in Athens, called *Anakeia.* There was a temple named Anakeion. Pausanius is uncertain if the Dioscuri, the Kuretes,* or the Cabirai, were the same deities with different names. They are all various terms for Zodiacal gods or mansions; hence each festival retraced, in dance ritual, the motion of the planets by the Zodiac. This cult was generally adopted through the Doric and Achaean states; but details of ceremonies are few. The tradition was persistent; later its *boule** or council, took on the administrative name of *dios-curia* and then *curia* or subcommittee. There seems to be little doubt that these twelve god-figures appear as the rulers of the "houses of the year", each receiving his due festival and sacrifice in turn.

DIRECTOR OF DANCE OR BALLET
Is the modern equivalent to the ancient Athenian *choregus,* the poet who originated the initial idea to be expressed in terms of dance and drama; and who was thus able to train his chorus gradually to show these ideas in the Theatre. The competent modern Director is rare; far too frequently some limited choreographer or ballerina arrogates the position (by strategy or financial interest), and the consequent dualism of interest produces distressing effects. This is like a bricklayer trying to design as an architect; or a pianist operating as orchestral conductor. Sometimes a paperhanger may for a time direct a war; though his end may be sticky. There have been notable Ballet Directors: men like J. G. Noverre or Carlo Blasis, who had previously gained wide experience and long training; or men like S. P. Diaghileff, who had some experience united with supreme managerial ability; but the person whose practical work has been limited to one sector is rarely able to direct efficiently; while the working dancer, who wants also to appear in the ballet, cannot view any production as a whole, in unbiassed and objective manner. On the other side, the impresario or financial "angel" rarely knows enough to be able to discover or select a real Director; and always "plays safe" by seeking to exploit "names". The successful cinema film director is a man who knows all the technologies involved, but does not himself act leading parts; and even he gains no great reputation with authors. The "choreographer" rarely makes a good director; again being too limited by attempts to

devise quaint technical experiments in movement, offered as "inventive choreography". Though this is in line with "Modern Art" (or "dealerism"), it leaves the general public cold. If we judge solely by artistic results, the Russian methods of integration by a resident directorial combine (Tsarist or Soviet systems are similar in this), which unites, on the basis of theme, the leading experts who contribute to any complete ballet, as though under a working chairman. This flexible method was that followed by Diaghileff; but it requires a permanent company and theatre to attain its achievement. [See *Maitre de Ballet,** *Régisseur**]

DIRK DANCE (Isle of Man)

An old Celtic solo dance, described as "the Dirk Dance of the Kings of Man". It is believed to have formed part of the initiation ceremony of the old Kings of Man when it was danced by the King's sword-bearer. A dance of dedication, it still retains something of its ritual quality. The dancer, holding the dirk with both hands before him, and fixing his eyes on it, circles round with light, springing steps. Then, laying the dirk on the ground, he dances round and over it, finally making movements towards it suggestive of obeisance. [Cp. *Dagger Dance; Ezpata Dantza de Zumarraga*]

DIRK DANCE (Scotland)

The Scottish form of an old Gaelic fighting dance for two men, then called *Bruithheath* or Battle Dance. Dancers carry a short sword (dirk) and a small shield (targe), and perform rhythmic suggestions of a combat. This dance is probably the last remaining form, seen in ancient Saxon/Gaelic sword display pictures, in early manuscripts. The Isle of Man *Dirk Dance** is even later; it has been shewn in London at the Folk Dance Festival, performed by one man alone, and while appearing now merely as a display of virtuosity, it still retains something of a ritual atmosphere. The double Dirk Dance was performed in London about 1850. This dance all Scottish youths were called upon to learn thoroughly. [Cp. Caucasian *Dagger Dance; Pyrrhic Dance; Corybantes*]

DITHYRAMBOS (Greek)

The Dance of the Double Door; or the Festival of the Winter Solstice (parallel with the Roman Janus, and the later "Petrus" who contrived to secure skeleton keys to both doors). Leaping and rejoicing were typical of this Feast, marking the high point of the winter season, after which followed the Solar Epiphane, the "Appearance" that confirmed the Twelve Days of Dancing, with its ritual and its rest. The written symbol was the Double Delta (comparable with the *Tangov** and the later Diamond-plus-Vesica of Gothic myth), which was so revered as to be carved over temple doors. The dancers were groups of youths (*Khrilloi*) and maidens (*Thiades*) as servitors. The Spring Festival, which followed at Eostra, was timed with the Bull of Taurus in the Zodiac.* As the White Bull symbolised the Feast, a real bull was led by the Thiades, garlanded and with gilded harness. This *Delta* was marked in the floor of the *orkestra* of the Theatre of Dionysus at Athens; where it served as the guide to a simple choreographic movement based on the figure eight form. One point must be clarified: these ceremonies were in no sense (save superstition, including modern guesses) performed "to obtain fertility". In fact, they marked the times and occasions for performing agricultural duties, thus enhanced by social approval. Soldiers marching with drums and flags, do not automatically ensure "victories", but they do mark popular expectation that the "enemy" will be defeated. The Greek Spring Festival, in its own ritual, did not "promote magically the food supply", except by the psychological urge to undertake necessary hard work in field and forest. "The gods help those who help themselves" was not merely an open secret of Aesop, with its Buddhist flavour. The dancers of Dithyrambos, called Graces, Carites, Thyiades and other names, personated the Seasons, the Moon-Days, the *Hora;* and they came at the "Time of the White Bull of the Heavens". The Heavenly Bull is considered rhythmically, as dancing. The "Women of Elis" (Hellas) sing the "Bull Spring Song". With this feast is linked the *Bouphonia,* the sequence of sacrifice, not of the Great Bull, *but of his child,* the *young Ox* (the young Year who supplants the Old Year, now dead).

DIVERTISSEMENT (French)

Also *Divertissante* amusement, or something amusing, by way of entertainment or even sport. The term in Theatre is more applicable to Music-hall (or in Paris, *La Cirque*) than to serious ballet or opera. The meaning opposes advertisement, "to draw attention" in its slant of diverting; but it is also intended to divert the "tired business man" from his imperial woes. Many of the examples of dance, presented as "ballet"—especially the classical *pas de deux* as an extract—are never more than *divertissement,* devoid of meaning. The application does not occur in folk-dance. Some readings equate *divertissement* with a one-act ballet, especially of Music-hall type (i.e. *Divertissement Sicilien,* Taglioni). A parallel term in music is *Divertimento,* used to designate a variety of short movements, a cassation, or a serenade; as in some of Mozart's works.

DIWALI (Indian ritual)

"Festival of Lights", marked by the traditional worship of *Diwali Puja*. This last day of the Indian year is celebrated by lighting of millions of tiny clay lamps filled with *ghee* (clarified butter), whose implied purpose is to "light the way" for Lakshmi (Vedatva) as the Goddess of Fortune. There is casual dancing in the streets, while many private *nautch** parties are given.

DIWAN (Persian - Hindi)

Hall of Audience, or of Imperial display etc. in India. Signifies an enclosed area, devoted to justice, exposition, and the display of dance that follows business. The term is parallel with *Devanagari* (script of *devas*=writing) and the Hebrew *schem-ha-phorash*,* the Greek *boustrephedon;* or the Scandinavian *rouen* and *runic*. Symbols, that became letter-numerals, were enscribed round the periphery. Thus the actual movement of the *Nagas* (snakes, possessors of wisdom) across the area and back (plough-like, or "ox-footed") gave rise to ritual which, when made rhythmic by accompaniment of instruments, developed a court dance mode. The officer was *Dewan* (modern France = *douane*, tax-grabber), which in Malay becomes *Tuan* (Master or Manager), and in Java *Dalang*. Chants, recitations (genealogies) or judgments, were announced by the officials, while they moved to and fro across the central space, in "snake-like" progression. The writing, which substituted this oral delivery, followed in this left-right-left transition over the parchment or palm leaf; and so confirms the original physical movement; now performed only by military sentries (centurions) before public buildings, in mechanical ritual form.

DIZARD, DISARD OR DYSARDD (England)

An older term for a court fool; period of Henry VII and Henry VIII of England, mentioned in the Chamberlain's and Churchwardens' books of Croydon and Kingston-on-Thames. The *disard* joined with the "mores daunsers" of the time; some dances were in or near the church, otherwise the churchwardens would not have been concerned in paying the dancers and minstrels, or meeting the cost of their gear.

DJOGED (Bali, Indonesia)

A popular flirtatious dance, performed by a girl to the music of the *Pelegongan* orchestra, with instruments of bamboo. The dancer wears a variation of the *legong** costume and uses traditional *legong* steps, but the character of the dance is quite different. In it she casts inviting glances at a man in the audience, who must dance with her in a love duet of approach and refusal (*nibing*). The Balinese form of a kiss is to approach near enough to the girl's face to catch her perfume and feel the warmth of her skin, and this is the object of the man in the *djoged*. Like a modern "excuse me" waltz, other men may take his partner and dance with her. When it is performed by a boy in girl's clothes the *djoged* is called *gandrung*. It may be a modernised version of the ancient *abuang*,* a mating dance performed yearly at the village of Tenganan, in east Bali.

DOCHE (Germany)

Also *Toche*—a doll-dance; a puppet performing a dance; or a dancer performing in a snappy or puppet-like style of movement, as in the ballet *Petrushka*. Also called *ein springer** "one who jumps or springs".

DODOLE (Serbia)

Rain ceremonies performed in time of drought. A group of girls, headed by the *Dodola*, danced through the village, stopping at each house. The *Dodola* was a girl, naked but completely covered from head to foot in grass, leaves and flowers. Continuously she danced and revolved, while each time the group stopped before a house, the housewife threw a pail of water over her, "in order to tempt the rain to fall". In Macedonia, boys instead of girls went the rounds, the principal one being a poor orphan called the *Dudule*. Dalmatia had a further variant, in that the chief character was a young unmarried man, called *Prapts*, over whom water was similarly thrown while he danced, his companions, also young bachelors, being named *Parporushe*. Similar customs were known in Greece, Rumania, and Bulgaria.
[Cp. *Jack in the Green* (England); *Paparuada* (Rumania)]

DOGE (Italy)

In Venice, the appointed leader of the City Council; and in consequence, leader in ceremonial. Dance form other than the grave ceremonial of the ducal court fell into disuse after the earlier days of the Republic; for more use was made of the gondola in the "processional" around the city. The name Doge is that of the Doge-Star—Sirius the polar star; and is similar to that of *dux*, *duca* or *duke*. The doges became, instead of performers, patrons of the civic shows in the Piazza san Marco; in relation to this, somehow, the term got to Mexico with cowboys, who sing a ballad exhorting "Git along little dogies", to their steers. From their sailing usages came the term *doge-watch* or leading (first) watch of the evening; or *vespers*.

DOINA (Rumania)

A slow march dance tune, used for funeral processions; and the accompanying lament (which the word means). A similar usage is known in Bulgaria; while in Russia the analogous *dumka* fills this function.   [Cp. *Dump* (England)]

DOLL DANCES
Have a very wide range, from dances (as in the ballet *Coppelia*), where a human dancer acts as a doll, to Javanese puppets, where a wooden figure acts as a human dancer. Scales range from the great wicker half-figures—which J. Cæsar wrongly describes as Druid cages "for burning" (Gog and Magog or *Coch* and *Ma-coch* at London Guildhall)— to small dolls carried by children (Dutch wooden dolls) and images used on Mediaeval town clocks (a set in Mercatoria, by *Piazza san Marco*, Venice) which dance the Hours. Religious dolls or *idolas* are now less used in Europe though some, carried in Seville in *Semanta Sacra*, perform a crude dance on a platform. Doll dances are favored for school dance displays, for children to perform. Guy Fawkes or Aunt Sally (Salli) indicate religious parodies, as does Punch and Judy.

DOMARE DANSEN (Sweden)
This ancient Swedish folk-dance means literally "Judgement Dance", but its real meaning is lost. A very simple dance, it consists of a circle of men and women, moving round a central figure holding a lighted candle.
[See *Candle Dance; Ciri, Ball del* (Catalonia); *Kyndeldans* (Norway)]

DOMBA DANCE (North-east Transvaal, Africa)
A dance performed by Zulu girls of the Bavenda tribe, at the beginning of their initiation ceremony. Accompanied by drumming, and the *Tsikhuma* (a slender, undulating horn), the dance includes a ceremonial bow over the drums, in which the girls kneel in a circle bending the body forward over the horizontal drums.

DOMHNULL DUBH REILL (Scotland)
"The Devil's Reel", literally, "Black Donald's Reel". Popularly believed in 16th century Scotland to be the principal "Devil Dance", as performed by Auld Clootie (or Nick, or Hornie), when he attended the Coven. This mythical figure was also mentioned as The Earl o' Hell; or sometimes as The Laird o' Yon Place. His latest title carries only non-commissioned rank: as "The Queer Fella" he was equated by wartime soldiers with the company sergeant-major—if a Scot. Reported to be very industrious (hence his allocation of extra work for idle hands?), he undertakes dancing, in the ring or alone. He pipes or he fiddles, while he drinks long and deep; yet his spare time is filled by courtly

attention to all of the ladies without exception. Against his versatile activities, there was the standard Invocation, whispered by the Unco Guid o' Galloway:
"Frae Witches and Warlocks an' Wurricoes—
    An' evil sperrits an' a' them Things
  That gang Bump! 'i' the nicht—
    Guid laird, deliver us'!".
In 1563, witchcraft became a capital offence, lasting through a century of terrified and kirk-ridden Scots; witches were murdered in the name of high religion. Everybody knew somebody who had heard that the Witches' Coven danced ilka Saturdee nicht—but none had themselves witnessed the *Domhnull Dubh Reill*.

DOMINICANA (Republic of Dominica)
The local version of *Merengue*; a couple dance. It has four basic steps: *Dominicana, La Bota, Santo Domįngo Circulo*, and *Marcando*. Without the 'slouch step' it was turned into an American ballroom dance (circa 1946) described as "gay and folksy". This dance has two periods of sixteen bars, each in 2/4 or 5/8.

DOMINICS (Gaelic, *Domnach* or *Domnagh*)
Organization (*ordo*) of primitive performers of "miracle plays", or chants, derived from contact of Gaels with Greek missionaries, long before the arrival of Latin missions. These bands became merged with incident monachism, and they got the name *Dominic*, and later *Dominicans* (from *Domna-ghans*) when, from wandering bands, they became settled. They took over the older *Teampull* (religious) centres, often on islands with extremely small stone buildings, replacing earlier wooden structures. At Inis-Goil (Lough Corris, Co. Galway) was *Teampull na Naomh* ("Temple of the Spirit"—*neume* means "breath"), while *Teampull Mor* (the "Great Temple") is in Tipperary. The name *Ordo* (Horde), more eastern than Greece, became revised as "Order", and remains in Ireland in its earlier form.

DON JUAN (Spanish Legend)
The modernist legend of "Don John Tenorio", dramatised by Tirso de Molina as *El Burlador de Sevilla* in ponderous verse, was a deposit from earlier monkish legends, devised to ridicule the continuance of the ancient Celtic religion, more especially at the Midsummer Festival of Johannus (or I-O-Annus). Due in part to prominent individuals having been elected to lead these dance rituals, many men had received the honorific name of "Don Juan", and to some of them the name clung, as it did to many other dramatic actors. Success with the perversion of the parallel story

of *Doctor Faustus* led the Spanish monks to consolidate this legend, bringing in (as they always tried to do) a stratum of local facts, "to lend an air of veracity to an otherwise bald and unconvincing narrative". They selected the Sevillean gossip about one Don Juan Tenorio, said to have eloped with the daughter of Commendatore Ulloa, whom Don Juan later killed in argument. His excesses (said the honest monks) continued to be a scandal in the town; so he was enticed by the Franciscan friars to their monastery; and another murder was added to their list. The tale about the "insult to the statue" (used in *The Stone Guest*) and his departure to hell, is alleged to have been added by the friars to excuse their actions. The legend has been framed in verse by Zamora, Moliére, Byron, and Dumas, but latterly its extension into operatic themes has been worked into ballet (as, for example by Fokine, who followed the Russian opera *The Stone Guest* by Dargomizhsky).

DONZELLAS, Danza de (Portugal)
Part of the *Palauto sacramentales* was an exhibition of dancing, especially during the 15th and 16th centuries. In this "Dance of the Damsels" (at Lisbon) eight little girls, attired in white silk, paraded through the streets to the strains of a lute. At certain stations they stopped, to perform a short charade or "play" of a theological character. Frequently the same little dancers formed part of the company for other dances that were included in the *Palauto*, such as *Danzas dos Maryos*; *Danzas dos Espingardeiros*; and *Danzas dos Pretos.** These dances are still performed in the procession on August 15 at Orcozelo da Sierra.

DOOMRINGS (Iceland)
Named so as "Circles of Judgment" by the Icelanders, as they were the appointed places of all trials of justice, held usually four times in each year, at solstice and equinox. In them the kings were elected; the grave legal ceremonial was conducted; and then the merry-making dance and music which followed the final feast. They were marked by circles of upright stones, similar to those at Stonehenge and Avebury.

DORNACH SCHOOL (Switzerland)
School of Mystical Drama and Dance (based on Anthroposophy), founded by Rudolf Steiner in a large double-theatre building of wood, designed by him; and used for the production of (a) modern Miracle Plays, and (b) performance of *Eurhythmy.** This fascinating building was destroyed by fire (probably arson), and was later replaced by another structure (not so well designed), made of concrete.

This Dornach Theatre, situated some three miles from Basle, was built after Dr. Steiner had been ejected from his quarters at Munich during the 1914-1918 war. The elements of dance were linked with vocal sound in verbal form; not music in the emotive sense. In one way, they revived the Jewish *hallel* but more as drama, than as worship or ritual.

DOS-A-DOS (Portuguese-French)
Equals *Deux-a-Deux*, New Orleans term for Two-by-Two, in the "American Square Dance" forms. Simply a dance phrase, as given by the "caller" when he tells the dancers to move two-by-two in procession. The version *dos-a-dos* (USA pronunciation *dozydo*) is sometimes referred to Portuguese; also the name of a horse carriage, either when pulled by two horses, or allowing two passengers to sit side by side. Compare with military drill order "Form Fours!"

DOUBLE FEMMES, LES (France)
A term applied at one period to the "24 Violinists of the King's band", arising from an incident in their occasional double employment in the court ballets. One production (performed in 1625) was named *Ballet des Double Femmes*, when these hard-working non-trade unionists were required to double their double-parts, for no extra pay. The players often acted as "supers", taking small parts in the ballets. On this occasion, their allotted characters were the *Double Femmes*. They entered moving backwards, dressed as old women, with faces on masks over the backs of their heads, yet using their violins, so that they seemed to be playing behind their backs. These masks, apparently, carried indications of characters, not unknown to the audience, though this fact had no relevance when, in 1883, Taglioni *père* revived the ballet for Auber's opera, *Gustave III*.
[See *Vingt-Quatre Violons*]

DOULUKKA (Sudan)
Periodical dance of sacrifice, as an offering to the secret river gods, to preserve the tribe from all evils. After a white sheep has been ceremonially slaughtered, the division is made; and then the tribe forms into a circle for the swift dance in which the ritual culminates. The veiled priestess sits on a special rug, and sips at a bowl of the blood; which contains power that is magically transferred to the dancers.

DOURO-DOURO or DURU-DURU (Sardinia)
Also called *Ballu Tondu*. The name *Douro-Douro* derives from the sound of the tambourine beaten by the palm of the hand. Performed at weddings and at festivals (such as the Day of St. Efisio,

patron saint of Cagliari in the south of the Island), it is a chain dance in circular formation. Now danced by a circle of men and women alternating, with hands or fingers linked, a 19th century description[1] implies that the circle was formed by half men and half girls — "young girls and men advanced to form a circle. . . . . The maidens took hands and stood closely side by side; the young men did the same, the two groups joined by one hand, and the dancers circulated, retired and advanced in a slow cadence, regulated by the melody of the singer. . ." These singers gave another name to the dance, *Boroboboi*, from the repeated sound made by the lowest voices as a kind of drone. Four or five musicians sit or stand in the middle of the circle, playing tambourines, *laudeddas* (triple pipe), or the *sulittu*, an ancient instrument of Sardinian shepherds. Nowadays the accordion replaces some of the older instruments. The dance begins with an introduction in 2/4 time, and proceeds in 6/8 time, the circle moving slowly with two steps to the left and one to the right in an undulating movement. The women keep their eyes cast down, and the dance may continue for hours, becoming more gay as it goes on. While the men wear mostly black and white, the women are magnificent in a double skirt of scarlet, and white silk embroidered with flower patterns; black and white bodice, with a fine white tulle veil.   [Cp. *Sardana; Contrapas*]
[1] *A History of Dancing.* Gaston Vuillier. 1898.

DRAMMA PER MUSICA (Mediaeval Italy)
"Drama with Music". Was one of the fertile roots of modern ballet, associated with the beginnings of opera, oratorio, and the famous *Commedia* in mime forms. In the hands of the composer Benedetto Ferrari of Reggio (b. 1597) this medium moved towards the merging of music with dramatic action by mime and dancing — as opposed to the oratorio which tended to open into action, less and less, as it developed. Benedetto's opera *Andromeda* was performed in Venice in 1637. He remained working in that city until 1645, and then went to Vienna. A ballet devised by Benedetto was performed at the Diet of Ratisbon in 1653, though earlier his *Dafne in Alloro* was produced in 1651 at Vienna.

DREHEN (German/Austrian)
Term used for certain dances, when the partners are "drawn" — originating probably with the mediaeval marriage market dances (in the Lottery), when the chosen girl was drawn forward by the suitor. *Drehen* means: "to turn", "to twist", (Cp. *reihen*, to set in lines; in Scandinavian dance form).

DREIKONIGSFEST (Modern German/Austrian)
"Three Kings' Feast", the general term given to the *Fête des Rois*, or the Epiphany, as the "Day of Appearance" on January 6th, in the Twelve Night New Year Festival. The Kings are Gaspar, Melchior, and Beltazar; bringing gold, incense, and myrrh. They are received with a solemn carol dance.

DRONE DAUNCE (Old English)
The slight dance movement of a singing chorus or burden of a ballad, compared with the mime of verse or reverse; the small group doing one movement compared with the solo dance-singer.

DRMES (N. Serbia, Yugoslavia)
"Shaking Dance". In the Banat, part of the plain of Voivodina in North Serbia, dances are mostly performed in couples or small groups, such as by a young man with a girl on either side. The *Drmes* is danced almost *en place*, with tiny quick steps, the whole body quivering. Dances of the Banat are usually accompanied by the *gadje* (bagpipe) or an orchestra of *tamburicas* (similar to guitar or mandolin).   [Cp. *Troyanats*]

DRYAD (Gaelic)
"Daughter of Oaks" (*Druth*). A woodland creature, who had moved into legend, as being mythical. The Dryades were young priestesses or "virgins" associated as "fortune-dancers" of the "schools of prophecy" formulated by the Druids of Gaul (*circa* 2nd-3rd century BC), and in the College of Druids, as at Arles, or at Tara in Ireland.

DUBOKA "DANCE FOR THE DEAD" (Yugoslavia)
Duboka is a village about fifty miles east of Belgrade on the River Danube. The Vlach inhabitants used to celebrate annually the solemn Dance for the Dead, lasting three days. It was noted for the fact that some of the women fell into a deep trance, in which they were said to communicate with dead relatives. The time of year marked the event; not any long antecedent ritual. Weather at that period (far inland), becomes very electrical in summer heat. The Dance was an Exorcism Ceremony; and began round the prostrate body of an entranced woman, thus resembling closely (as does the whole ceremony), primitive church ritual, for which they ordained an Exorcist for treatment of the *Energumenoi*. A *Hora** was danced, the chain led by a young man; two girls next danced, then a middle-aged woman, then the woman's husband. He and the leader carried a steel knife in their right hand; all the dancers wore bunches of magical flowers, including mandrake, wormwood, garlic and rosemary. After four rounds — men chanting their spell (*Opsa jaresa; Sinko data jaresa; Asa bolesa Daen gure hei; Aide bole hai*) — anointing was done. A sprig of wormwood and a blade of garlic were chewed with a sip of water, and then spat over

the entranced face. The woman's nervous reaction became acute; but subsided with the music. The dancing was mainly a ritual walk; straight or circular; in a "right-left-right", or a "left-right-left" triple step. The rite required placing the entranced one in a series of "stations"; the dance-walk recurred each time and the anointing was repeated. Deep trance might need five or six ministrations to end it, finally carrying the woman across water. The last act was drinking water that dropped from a steel knife, ending the exorcism. Other groups "danced for the dead" to fiddle music; with the same shuffling step. The rite started with the *pneuma*—the "cold wind"—which begins the trance state.
[Cp. *Cailleach an Dudain* (Scotland); and see *Midsummer Fairies; Rusalii; Dybbuk*]

DUCK'S DANCE (England)
Long before Donald Duck incarnated chromatically on cinema screens, a dance-song, sometimes called "Quack-Quack!" was used by children, with the initial line "I Saw a Ship a-Sailing", but this version clearly merges the old *carole** with juvenile dance. Children sing it as they dance in a ring, imitating ducks—not ships.

DUMB DANCE (Old England rite)
On St. Mark's Eve, a group of village girls gather to make a cake, on cutting which they may discover their future husbands. Strict verbal silence is preserved; but an air is used with a simple dance form keeping time with the operations.

DUMP; DUMPE; DOMP; DOMPE
An old English dance of which little is known, but it seems to have belonged to the 16th century. A manuscript of the early part of that century contains a dance for harpsichord entitled "My Lady Carey's Dompe", and the Fitzwilliam Virginal Book contains a "Triste Dumpe". Shakespeare mentions the dance in *Romeo and Juliet* as "doleful dumps and merry dumps"; in *Two Gentlemen of Verona* as a "deploring dump"; in *Much Ado About Nothing* as "dull and heavy dumps"; in *Titus Andronicus* as "dreary dumps". In *Hamlet* the words of the song "And will he not come again?" belong to an old dance tune "The Milkmaids' Dump", included in Playford's *The English Dancing Master** as "The Merry Milkmaids". Queen Elizabeth I had a court official called "Undumpisher"* —apparently a Master of Ceremonies for the court dances. In 1596, in *Have With You to Saffron Waldon*, a 16th century Irish tune called "Peg a Ramsay" (included in William Ballet's *Lute Book*) is called by Thomas Nash a "dump tune", and the dance is again named in *Shepherd's Holiday* in 1598. Musically, the *Dump* was an English or Irish

lament, but the name may be related to the Russian *Dumka*, a folk-ballad alternately sad and gay; known also in Poland, and used by the Czech composer, Dvorak. W. H. Gratton Flood[1] claims that the *Dump* was the music of the *Tiompan*—a small, harp-like instrument very popular in Ireland during the 15th and 16th centuries—"dump" describing the sound produced by plucking the strings.
[1] *History of Irish Music*. Wm. H. Gratton Flood. (Dublin 1905).

DUNCAN DANCE METHOD
Aims to inspire students of Dance with that musical sense which goes with all good dancing. Being so personal Isadora Duncan was never able to organise and devise a general teaching system; she rejected ballet technique (and most other technique) in preference for "Free Movement". With her brother, Raymond Duncan, she tried to run a Dance School in Paris; but apart from some study of Greek dance and ritual, chiefly in museums, the school has not proved able to endure the loss of its founder in 1927. Among the best-known English exponents has been Margaret Morris; who followed the Duncan idea of teaching drawing and music along with elementary dance movement. Isadora Duncan provoked more interest by her performances; especially in France, England and Russia, where all the leading dancers of her period (1905 - 1907) saw her and emulated her free expression. Michel Fokine has admitted his indebtedness to her; while the official Choreographic Academies retain, so far as there is a concrete system, her ideas within their regular curriculum. A Duncan School exists in Moscow. Dalcroze appreciated highly her affirmation of *continued* movement. Isadora Duncan was born in America in 1875 and died by accident in Nice in 1927

DURBARI (India)
From *Durbar*; a royal assembly. The modes or styles of dance, modified for court presentation (either as ceremonial or entertainment) are called *durbari*, or relatively secular, in contrast with basically religious dances. Thus the *durbari* style belong (in Hinduism) to the *Kshattriya* or warrior caste, as opposed to the *bharata natyam*, which belong to the Brahmin or priestly caste. Yet they may be closely similar : though one mode is directed more to ritual form, and the other more to ceremony or mime. Thus the *durbar nautch* is definitely the court entertainment style. Omitted from it are invocations to deities. Lesser in scale are the merchants' dances : until we arrive at the pot-house modes of *bazar nautch*. Curiously enough, style in dance changes with caste far more than language does.

DYBBUK (Jewish: Mediaeval legend)
The Dybbuk, or "Double" is a variant of the *Golem* story, told in a more closely individualised form. This tale has been used by Ludivico Rocca in his opera *Il Dibuk*, as an example of magical possession by a Jewish student, Hannen, of the body of his beloved Leah, by means of knowledge acquired from the *Cabala*. The legend is sited in a "Polish village named Brygnitz"; the opera is cast in three acts, which include several dances. The music covers rituals of marriage and evening prayers, as well as the "Dance of the Beggars" and the final magical dance of exorcism, all in the conventions of mediaeval Jewish superstition, with no genuine comprehension of the *Cabala*. The opera was broadcast by the BBC in October 1953, but has so far received no stage performance in Britain. The Dybbuk legend should be compared with *The Golem* and the tales of Zombies in the West Indies.
[See *Dreigroschen Oper:* Hans Weil and B. Brecht]

E

EAGLE DANCE—HOPI INDIAN (North America)
A modern innovation, performed for the benefit of visitors. The solo dancer imitates the undulating motion of an eagle's wings in flight, to drum rhythm and the jingle of bells attached to his legs. The effect is greatly heightened by the costume, as the dancer's arms are hidden beneath "sleeves" of eagle feathers to resemble wings, and a fan-shaped "tail" of similar feathers is fixed to his waist. Two large feathers are stuck into his head-band, while a large disc, geometrically patterned, adorns his back.   [See *Hopi; Pueblo Indians*]

EAGLE DANCE (Spain)
In Barcelona, the Dance of John the Eagle, performed in the choir of the church; in that city it is the first favourite, appearing in all civic festivals. Two "eagles" dance in the procession, in the church during the service, and sometimes again afterwards. They symbolise the ancient figure of Johannus, taken into the Latin system as John, as an allegory of the flight of the years, but (as with Janus in Roman times), denoting the dual point of the "year-ending and year-beginning", or the "double door". For this reason, tradition requires *two* eagles, formerly men completely disguised as birds and wearing masks. Though "suppressed" in 1753 by the Bishop of Barcelona, the custom continues; and may be seen in Valencia as well; also in the Balearic Islands, Majorca and Minorca. At Pollensa, the custom has thinned out: two girls in festival costume (not in bird character) carry two birds; and they dance with a small figure of the John. The dance is a simple *jota.**

EAGLE KNIGHTS (Aztec - Mexico abt. 1250-1519)
One of the Orders entered by the best warriors, other Orders being those of the Ocelet (known also as Tiger or Jaguar), and the Arrow. In ritualistic dance-dramas performed at certain religious festivals, Eagle and Ocelot Knights engaged in mock combat, symbolising the eternal struggle between light and dark, day and night, north and south, which dual opposition recurred throughout the Aztec religion. Eagle Knights were dedicated to Huitzilopotchtli (War and Sun God), and Ocelots to Tezcatlipoca (Great Sky God). At a festival held to celebrate the journey of the Sun through the heavens, Eagle and Tiger Knights enacted a dance-drama symbolising the nightly slaying of the Sun and his dawn resurrection. The rhythmic mock combats sometimes ended in a gladiatorial fight to the death, with the sacrifice of a captive.
[See *Aztec Dance; Balseria* (Panama)]

EASTER SUN DANCE (England)
In the Mediaeval period, the superstition arose that "on Easter day, the sun danced". Brand[1] mentions this to refute it, saying that the villagers "rise about four o'clock to see the sun dance", and that other people, not ignorant labourers, had asserted that they had "seen the sun dance" on Easter morning. Brand quotes Sir Thomas Browne in further refutation. And again: "In some parts of England, this is called lamb-playing, which they look for as soon as the sun rises, in some clear spring or water, and is nothing but the pretty reflection it makes from the water, which they may find at any time . . . ." In an old ballad, from *Recreation for Ingenious Headpieces* (1667) the popular notion is mentioned:

> "But Dick, she dances such a way
> No sun upon an Easter Day
> Is half so fine a sight,"

which gives us a hint (nearer to its former practice) of the ritual in which the king, or some noble, appeared in the role of the "Sun King". In Spain there was a temporary Easter King; while in France it continued so long that the title was fastened upon the Bourbons, as *Le Roy Soleil*. This was the ceremonial Sun Dance of Easter, which lingered in the folk-memory of England long after the ritual had fallen into disuse.
[1] *Antiquities.* Brand. (p. 162).

ECOSSAISE (France)
A dance of the English Country-dance type, which seems to have little connection with Scotland. Popular in the ballrooms of France and England

in the late 18th and early 19th centuries, it was in 3/2 or 2/4 time, and was at first accompanied by bagpipes, although the music has nothing in common with real Scottish dance music. Schubert and Beethoven both wrote music in Ecossaise form.

ECSTATIC DANCE

Was a regular preliminary in many ancient rituals, to the processes of Exorcism, Invocation, and Evocation. First simple music, chant, and movement were followed, to induce concentrated sympathy within the group. In a large ceremonial fashion, this is the liturgical intention of many a "church service", which is intended to eliminate personal feelings (along with the usual baggage of worries, hopes, and fears) so that the combination of a chosen place and time; soft lights and sweet music, coupled with familiar hypnotic phrases, will induce a feeling of conscious and happy surrender to the mood or emotion of the group. This pragmatic "binding together", is the social purpose of any religion; by it the group is induced to accept the chosen ethical scheme of the moment (usually the schizophrenic morality of civilization : "support your friends, but eliminate the foreign foe"). Participation in the ecstatic dance or ritual will, for a period, lessen the individual tensions inevitably aroused by this constant dual appeal to moral action outside. In the Orient, this is the contrast between group ritual, and yogic discipline of the individual. In ordinary religious practice, the yogi is heretic "self-thinker" — the ordinary group dance is not for him. Rarely, a small group, as in the Moslem *zikhr*, will show ecstatic dance form, in group unison; but the group dance is abolished from the Western church; and any ecstatic experience is confined chiefly to singing or uplift from unusually good exhortations. In Negro dance, this quality remains; it may be seen in Northern Africa; and in Hayti; and occasionally in late-night college dances in USA, marked by excited perversion of ballroom dance forms, often accompanied by distorted and unmelodious refrains. [See *Jazz; Dervish Dance; Hypnotic Dance*]

EDUCATION AND DANCE

(1) Appear associated in several leading systems; some used today, and some forgotten. The most obvious modes — as in P.T. methods — are, in fact, linked with far less easily perceived connections : as in the comprehension of Mathematics or the understanding of true poetry. The central theme is always Rhythm : this factor unites flowing Poetry with Mathematical precision; but their professional separation, since Roman times, has developed too many partial views, until Education is reduced merely to the mode of acquiring sufficient technique "to make a living". This low view may satisfy demands for industrial and military slavery; but does not produce rounded human beings. Methods of mass education may meet mass industry or mass militarism; and even mass religion may help to induce the mass frame of herd mind which can produce ephemeral empires; but they do not evoke men. Education, like dance, is firstly and finally a matter for the free thoughts and decisions of the individual. Real education and real dance have much in common.

Ancient tribal methods invariably utilised dance, as rhythmic motion, or exercise, and training, to develop two skills : the ability to stand and withstand in combat; and the intelligence to join the tribe as a matured adult. We group them as Initiation Rituals : they sometimes appeared singly, but more often in sequence. Dance is a powerful factor in such rituals; at best the dance develops both a swift social agreement (as in warfare), and an equally swift individualisation. Rituals grow around the Tomb, the Court, and the Shrine. Education moves with Dance by the Initiation ceremonies; with careful religious ritual; in the etiquette of social behaviour; in manners, and relations. Many styles, now obsolescent, could be revived with benefit. Professional dance education is seen from "the other end", and is viewed as academic ability and equipment; and, in these days, as "service for sale". At the other extreme we find dance education for health and personal welfare. Whichever mode is examined, other complementary phases must be known for apt comparison.

(2) GENERAL EDUCATION : In schools and colleges, should include some instruction in both theory and practice of Dance. Beginning with elementary play-dances and rhythmic games (not as an art, but as exercise and introduction to group movement and song), the subject will be found valuable in its active association with other topics. Dance is a kind of catalyst. Children begin to enquire into aims and meanings of dances, once they have received a start. Dance touches history and arithmetic (counting steps and beats, in movement and rhythmic sound), and include geography ("where do these dances come from?") as well as languages ("what do these French terms mean, in ballet?"). Production of dance performances suggests design, drawing, colour and making costumes and even scenery. If speech is necessary, then some attention must be given to elocution and gesture or stage movement. For a drama class, dance movement is most helpful. Effects of light and colour extend the visual experience; for no spectacle can be offered without lighting. All this study remains general and does not seek to attain professional

standards; but the ambitious and able students will reveal their aims (despite examinations and scholarships that rarely recognise the arts), and they will try to find opportunities of advanced instruction. Even when a professional career is entered, general education should continue alongside definite dance instruction, including music and rhythm, with design and colour in pattern drawing.

(3) PROFESSIONAL EDUCATION: In dance should begin physically in early years, to obtain and develop bodily power and ability; yet it is not essential to expend the whole time on physical work. Rounded experience should be sought; in particular, early opportunities of appearing before an audience should be gained; at first in school displays and then in Theatre. Nothing can replace this contact. Some few schools are residential; others take day pupils. Sporadic effort in dance is seldom rewarding; constant application is essential; and yet without a basically good physical form, it may be hopeless to expect stage success in dance. But good training is usually of value; many actors and actresses in the "legitimate theatre" owe much to some years of early work in dance, gesture and movement, with the accompanying rhythmic sense. Experience of personal appearance in "real parts" should be sought; but this should be balanced by watching many kinds of show, not merely for amusement but for study : to see "how they work, how they get their results". This is not necessarily expensive; many theatres will permit free attendance to bona-fide students.

(4) SPORT AND DANCE: Find mutual help. Ballroom dance, as a sport, is now well lined with rewards, by way of medals, certificates, and cups; from which, in addition to the fun gained in this pastime, sometimes pecuniary results may flow. Students may train directly with professional instructors, for ballroom competitions. Others, interested in different sports, such as tennis, boxing, or skating, will find that regular exercises in dance technique —both in ballet school or "modern dance" class— will prove most helpful in gaining swift and light co-ordinated movement. In Russia, these dance forms are included in the training of most of their athletes—both men and women—by a basic course in elements of plastic rhythm; while, in the Czech *Sokol,** all women and children were given courses of plastic training, culminating in true dance form. These sports relate chiefly to the physical aspect; though further interest can be found in tracing the various historical and national systems that have been used through the world. More active sport, and less "sport-watching" seems to be indicated in Britain as a national necessity; we spend far too much time sitting, in schools, offices and stores, and then sitting down in transport (sometimes),

and sitting down to watch other people at sport *via* television. Without dashing to the further extreme (Duke of York, his men and his hill) of marching and counter-marching (in *Die Hitler Jugend* style, or the Democratic Catholic *Balilla* of Mussolini and Franco), we can develop some personal interest in rhythmic movement, from exercise to genuine dance.

EGG DANCE (India, at Bhopal)
Performed by one dancing-girl with five male musicians. She has fixed to her head a light wicker frame, some twenty inches in diameter; attached are thirty strings, each with a special slip knot held by a single glass bead. The girl first shows ordinary hen eggs to the spectators. Then she begins to slow music, but quickly gaining speed, revolves rapidly. Taking an egg from the shallow basket she holds, she slips it into a knot, gives a slight jerk to tighten it. The other eggs follow, all slipped in with incredible skill; none are dropped; none are bumped; none are broken. The whirling ring of eggs forms a horizontal aureola round her upright head. Her movement is accurate and smooth; and the dance increases in speed; a remarkable exhibition of virtuosity. Now she has all the eggs in one ring; she has to get them all back in one basket. Swiftly she seizes a single egg and detaches it, again without hindering her dance, without touching the other eggs. At last she has withdrawn them all safely; she stops her dance sharply, advances briskly to the spectators and again submits her basket for examination; some are broken on a plate to prove their genuine character as fresh eggs. There is no trickery but immense skill in this dance.

EGG DANCE (Mediaeval England)
Performed usually about Easter, as a feat of technical pattern memorisation. From one to a dozen eggs were placed on the dancing-board in the approved pattern; each set in a little "dimple" cut in the wood. The truly proficient dancer could "do it blindfold", because he danced it always to his pattern; and thus avoided starting an omelet! The Twelve-Egg pattern was sometimes called the "Twelve Apostles". Beginners restrained their ambitions, and used only one egg. In an Elizabethan comedy "Longer thou liv'st, More fool art Thou!", one character remarks "Upon one foot I can hoppe and daunce it trimly about an Egge!" Having set up the twelve eggs in the form of a Latin cross, the dancer moved between them as though they were posts.

EGYPT (Ancient)
Had dances and dance rituals or ceremonies of many kinds; but broadly in three main categories.

We can classify them according to their place in the temple. Reference to the classical plan of completed temples (developed from the most ancient original rock or cave shrine by degrees of architectural accretion), show a general plan of successional penetration. First come the great propylons; denoting the structure which marked the temple gate from afar. This first gate permitted the "general public" to enter the first forecourt, open to the sky—sometimes surrounded by a narrow collonade. Here short "miracle plays" were performed on the days of great annual festivals. Next we find the Inner Court; in which the "admitted students" saw the Mystery Plays—a grade more refined, more difficult, more instructive. These courts varied: some had wide collonades; some had ranges of steps up to the next Hall of Columns, to which none but priests and dancers were admitted. Smaller and darker, and more withdrawn, are successive shrines or chapels; usually seven in all. To the innermost, none but the priest-king might enter. This principle is common to most religions: the grand secret is hardest to contact. Obviously, the dramatic character of the public Miracle Play, and the instructional theme of the Mystery Drama, are here left, for sacred fact, leading finally to initiation and realization of the esoteric meaning of the whole system. The Egyptian social system was mainly democratic (despite the autocratic rule of priest-kings, and quite frequent revolutions following on corruption and bureaucratic tyranny), and it was recognised that recruitment for the priesthood was always necessary. For the persistent enquirer, the path lay clear through the temple; he had to study incessantly, work hard and develop mind and character, regardless of parentage or money or even "influence". Among his studies were the systems of ritual dance ceremonials, music and chanting. As Lucian later observed, he had to "dance out his religion".
[See *Egyptian Dance; Shen; Masque*]

EGYPTIAN DANCE (Ancient Egypt)
Dates, ascertainably, from seven thousand years ago, known in two main forms for which pictorial or written evidence exists (ritual or ceremonial dance; and pastime or harem dance, in addition to labouring class amusement). Accurate information dates from the early years of the 19th century, when translation began. Leading among experts was Sir E. A. Wallis Budge (British Museum), whose masterly translation of the famous papyrus scripture *REU NU PERT EM HRU* was first published in 1897. He names it the *Book of the Coming Forth by Day* (as more accurate than *The Book of the Dead*, or *Ritual Funeraire*, or *Das Todtenbuch*). In this collection of copied ancient scripts,

Egyptian Dancers. Three female temple dancers with harp, viol, and flute in an interval of dancing. Thebes, 1700 B.C.   EGYPT

there are sundry direct references to ritual dance; and (in distant allusion by name), more hints. Without some understanding of the general forms of the Egyptian religious system, it is not possible to grasp the form and intention of these dances. We quote from the 200-page *Introduction* (p.xxxv. 1938 edition), to which the student is referred for further material:

"Semti (his Horus name Ten) appears with his chancellor Hemaka. To the right is a scene, we see the god Osiris, wearing the white crown, seated in a shrine on the top of a short flight of steps. Before him is King Semti, who is dancing away, out of the presence of the god; he wears the crowns of the South and the North on his head; holds in one hand the object (a mason square), and in the other, a staff or paddle. . . Other examples are known of the kings dancing before their god. . . . Usertsen danced before the god Amsu or Min; and Seti I danced before Sekhet. The reference (text of Pepi I) to the king dancing (before Osiris) proves that the custom was common in Egypt in early dynastic times. . . ."

The king danced "*as* the god" when he did not dance by way of devotion; and again he danced (Sed Heb Festival) *as* the servant and regenerator of "his people". From Egypt comes the dance of masked gods; the ceremony of the *Meskhent* (which evolved into the annual *Masque*) and the Steed of Hapi, which became the Hobby-horse. Greek philosophers early went to Egypt to study (Platon became a commercial traveller in olive oil to defray his expenses), and the imitative Greeks copied much of the Egyptian system, much disguised, under badly pronounced names; while the secret initiation rite (performed within the secret halls of pyramids, using great sarcophagi which never had lids), were copied and recopied into Roman times, with less and less real understanding finally to become a "sepulchre". This is not the place to offer even an outline of the main Egyptian religious scheme: with its firm principle of the surrection of the spirit; of the postponed return to earth; of the routine of accumulating energy by kingly ceremonial, and the usage of dance rhythm for this purpose. Entries under other headings may be consulted.   [See *Shen; Tangov; Masque*]

Egyptian Tambour Players. Four dancers playing different types of tambour, with another dancer and a singer.   EGYPT

EGYPTIAN DANCE (Ancient Egypt)
Belongs principally to religious ritual; but appeared also in regal ritual, as in ceremonies witnessed by the people. Some that appear to be "folk-dance" of the style practised at popular festivals by ordinary workmen, seem to have become mingled with remains of ritual dance; as in the immensely old traditions of Bez. There are temple dance rituals of (a) funeral style; (b) initiation modes; (c) annual "rejuvenation of the king" ceremonies, annual and triennial (Sed Festival). Rhythms in these rituals were highly important; though we have only the great harps (or pictures of them) remaining, to affirm the intricacy of music. Actual pictures of dance rituals exist; though relatively rare; many have been dubiously interpreted. We may take it that no "amusement dances" are likely to have received prominent record in sacred buildings. Lucian tells us of some dances. Apuleius records the *Lamentation of Isis* in his fascinating account. There were mummers, known in various periods as Nemou or Nerue; also Mou-ner and Uren the Bird. Some were buffoons. Others are known to be the

dwarf people from Central Africa, associated with Bez.
[See *Book of Dead*. Trans. Wallis-Budge. *Egyptian Magic*, Wallis-Budge. *Mystères Egyptiens*, Alexandre Moret]

EGYPTIAN TRACES
Can be found in Britain, brought possibly by Phoenicians or Carthaginians; long before Latin looters arrived. The god name Hu remains as Hugh of Lincoln; and Luton Hoo or Plymouth Hoo; while river names like Isis (entirely unchanged) came with Tammuz (for Thames—and Tammuz-Isis) and the Ouse (Ausar—for Osiris). Material evidence—found near Stanhenga—such as blue glass beads, might have been brought by trader or teacher. The stone circle of Stonehenge, the wooden circle of Ave Bury, date from c. 1500, before the Druids arrived (perhaps from Dravidya?) wearing cotton attire; and using terms such as Myzl-el-Tau, "Pearls of Bull" or Wisdom of Thoth—perhaps at Thot-Ness in Devon; or Touten-Ham or Thoth-Ankh-Bekh near the later city of London. Their rituals were Sun dances; they divided the Year in four quarters.

EHARO (Orokolo Bay, Papua)
"Dance-mask", from *e*, "dance", and *haro*, "head". Worn during the long initiation cycle, *Hevehe*.* Whatever their original significance, *eharo* now have a comic quality, and the dominant spirit is one of carnival. They are worn on two occasions —to celebrate a certain stage in the making of more important *hevehe* dance-masks; and much later, near the climax of the cycle, when the young men initiates (*Hii-Kairu-Akore*), appear in tableau. Typical *eharo* masks bear on top totemic effigies of birds, fish, insects, reptiles, trees, mushrooms; or of mythical characters. Made and worn by visiting villagers, *eharo* masks, usually in pairs, accompany their companions in such dances as *Yahe** at the "home" village, dancing round about the concentric circles of the more formal dances. Each pair, sometimes wearing garments of yellow-dyed bark-cloth or sago-leaf, performs its own steps. Each dancer beating time on a drum, they may perform a stationary goose-step, then quickening the rhythm circle round, each on his own spot, in opposite directions; or, in vertically striped garments of red, yellow and cream, dance side by side, first forwards, then backwards, beating their drums alternately; or the two dancers may revolve in frenzied circles. On the second occasion, *eharo* dancers are not so numerous, although the dances they accompany (*Yahe* and others) are on a grander scale. The masks now show no totemic effigies, but all repre-

sent comic mythological characters, such as Evar-apo, Hura and Kapo, all ugly, clothed in dark bark-cloth and with exaggerated genitals, with which they make much play during their slap-stick dancing. Evarapo carries a string bag, lime-pot and stone axe, which he brandishes in mock attacks. Hura and Kapo dance clumsily around, alternately beating their drums over each others heads. Ira and Ope wear head-pieces with huge flopping ears; each carries a spear and string bag. Dancing towards each other, they plunge the spears into the ground, retreat, dance forward, pluck them out and repeat the whole performance. Aikere and Maikere are two men dressed as *idihi vira* (see *Yahe**) dancers with full feather head-dress and cassowary-plume veil. Each carries a shell trumpet, miniature shield, bow and arrows. In company with Evarapo and an "old woman", Haihau'uva, they enact a scene where the old woman is chased, hides, is found and in her turn chases the others. All these comedy "acts" go on independently, like side-shows at a fair.
[See *Poilati*; *Yahe*; *Hevehe*]

EIGHT, FIGURE OF (Lemniscate)

In dance, is a double oval, united at the central point. The term *octra* or *ostrov* signifies "island", or *punctum*; this is that central point about which the dance moves. The dance symbol form then emerges, because the dancer reveals it, moves in and out, between two pillars (of Herakles), which are also symbols of Anna Peranna, the changing Year; or Janus, the swinging door, which rocks back and forth. It is also the door of birth; and as such was later devoted to the gnostic symbol-term Khrestos, as the "bringer-to-birth" of the new man, as "born again". There is a unity in this "Figure of Eight" which compares against the apparent dual-ity in the seemingly single figure of the Ellipse — also known as a *Pisces*. The secret resides in the change from the *single* focus or point to the *double* focus, which creates the opposition of forces that emerges as natural life. Without a knowledge of the functions of the rhythmically dancing figure, it is hard to come by the meaning of the move-ment. In Egypt, the ritual dance was revealed by the two Horus images — the first Horus the Elder (the Dying Year, etc.), and then Horus the Younger (the New Year etc.), who was later known as the Chylde; or The Golden Babe, and some other titles. The essential "crossing" of the continued dance figure is repeated in the lines seen on the Caduceus (*Khad-Dukeus* — the Dance-Leader), but here they separate and then join, as they cross each catalytic point; and then rise to the next of the four ovoid shapes. This world-wide symbol (now seen; and

now fading from the scene) is known in the *Tan-gov*, and again in the *Ankh* of Egypt.

EISTEDDFOD—1 (Wales)

Literally: a session or sitting, from *eiste* to be seated; or, the act of sitting. This term is now widely known as the indicated title of a revived Welsh convention of Music and Dance, organized in 1947 and now held yearly in North Wales. The older mode of *Eisteddfod* is known only by second-ary references, as a convention of Druids and Bards, taken over by later residents. The earliest clearly recorded occasion seems to be that of a convention of Singers and Minstrels (who were also dancers), held at Cardigan in 1176. The prin-cipal ritual is the election or competition among minstrels; the winners are then "given ovations" (*ovate* was one of the bardic titles of rank or attainment), and are then "elected to the chair" or seated.

EISTEDDFOD—2 (Wales)

Pronounced *Es-teth-fod*; at Llangollen (pronounced Thlan-goth-lan) is a modernist revival of 1947, of an ancient exclusively Welsh gathering. This one is International; it features singing and dancing, with competitions on a five-acre level tract (the only place), and has attracted dancers from twenty countries (two thousand persons in all, competed in all divisions), with an attendance of over 130,000 people. International teams of folk-dancers have travelled many miles to enter and compete. The revival was due to Harold Tudor, a Welsh writer; and, like the Henley Regatta for athletics, becomes also a locally sponsored modern event.

EIXIDA (Catalonia, Spain)

A longways progressive couple dance, in which each couple in turn repeats the same routine, until all are in their original places. The first couple lead off, then turn to face the second couple, after which they dance to the end of the line, and the next couple continue.

ELEMENTALS, DANCE OF

Refers to Rhythmic Dance of the Creatures of the Four Elements — Fire and Water, Earth and Air. They include *Air*: Sylphs (male) and Sylphides (female); *Water*: Naiads, Undines, Nymphs; *Fire*: Salamander, Salamandra; *Earth*: Gnomes, Elves or Kobolds. Not to be confused with (a) Ghosts, or (b) Fairies or Sprites. They are not seen as "Evil Spirits".
[See the famous work *Le Comte de Gabalis*† by Abbé N. de Montfaucon (1686). English translation: London 1913]

ELO (Nigeria)

Near Lagos, the Nupe people have mask dance, which appears annually (ninth month) in Mokwa village, its chief centre. Songs, music, and steps are in Nupe style, though the title *elo* is not. All dancers are men; but three masks, highly ornamented and bearing horns, are said to be "female", as is the chief *eloko* (great mask) to which a special salute, *elulo* (Bird of Elo) is given. One elder at Mokwa has charge of masks and tuition. Two males, with simple masks, are *gara* (robbers) and also bogey and clown. Two unmasked youths dance in fringed skirts of leopard skin, bearing white painted spots on their legs. The *elo* has no sacred purpose; it is said now to be "play". The dance movement is *nya-nya*—"dancing". Probably it is, like some English Morris dances, an old ritual; one "on the way out" before the influence of Islam. [See *Bori; Nupe; Nupe Dances*]

ELUSIA (Hellas) (Eleusis)

Religious centre near Athens—Dances of Mysteries were dual in mode : as (a) dance ritual of generation; and (b) ritual dance of re-generation. The third mode, maintained in full secrecy, was possibly not performed at this centre of Eleusis. The initiation dance of puberty, with instruction on generation, human and agricultural, ended with the symbolic Ear of Ripe Corn. Relatively few gained admission to the second ritual, which centred on the culture and birth of mind-soul; it was known to the Gnostics who flourished in the city of Antiocha 2nd century BC.

ENGLISH BALLET—1

Has maintained a general form, some two centuries old, deriving from both indigenous and imported theatre; and comprising the English Masque, the Italian Masque, the *Mores*** and Mumming Dances; and Franco-Italian Pantomime. Certain court dances of Spanish, French and Italian origins also influenced early stage-dance forms, beginning with the Elizabethan plays, where some dances were performed as *Interludes;* doubtless with an elegance in parallel with the poetry and style of acting then in vogue. English Ballet roots then developed in several phases; the first being that of the Pantomime introduced in London (Lincolns' Inn Fields Theatre) in 1756. This activity was soon exploited by David Garrick, who invited Jean Georges Noverre to England; and some French dancers next appeared in London theatres : Covent Garden and the King's Theatre. In these productions, joined with Italian Opera, many English singers and dancers appeared, adorned for the occasion with mellifluous Italian names. This ingenious camouflage continued until John Gay's

Beggars' Opera brought a mighty swipe upon the reign of Italian Opera. Next came English melodrama, presented with Ballet. A small theatre (south of the river, and most unfashionable) opened as the Royal Coburg Theatre, when the 18th century ended in revolution and Napoleon. French and English dancers were all the while coming and going across the Channel, thus continuing the fashion for singing opera simultaneously in four languages (drowned by orchestra). Monsieur le Pic was ballet master at the Coburg in 1821. English Ballet was then in full blast; doubtless with technical equipment just as good as that current at the Paris Opera, if only because the same dancers appeared. Covent Garden and the Kings Theatre could not provide all the ambitious dancers with enough opportunity. French girls came to London; and Cockney maidens (who could show a pretty ankle) took packet to Paris; and some (as Mam'selle Le Beau etc.) got jobs. A writer in *The Theatre* (1885) ed. by Clement Scott, p. 241 - 248, tells of a company of English ballet-dancers who went to Madrid in 1862. The operatic impact of Jenny Lind vanquished the maids of the *Pas de Quatre;* and opera again raised its multilingual head. Ballet turned up again in the Saloons (The Eagle, with Kate Vaughan), and in the Music-halls—the Empire, the Alhambra, or the Gaiety. Though superficial, much of the labour was still in ballet technique; and even in form.

ENGLISH BALLET—2

Began, in its modern aspect, direct from the London pantomimes devised by John Rich and others, during the 18th century. The roots of this form existed through Western Europe; from the old English New Year Masque, which continued after the law students Masques of Inns of Court had lapsed; and from the dancing that had been part of the French Opera Ballet or *Comedie Ballet*, as arranged by Lully and Molière. From Italy came the example and incitement of the travelling companies of *Commedia dell' Arte*, which competed against, and in England joined with, the dancers from the newly formed French *Academie de Musique et de la Danse*. When Garrick and Noverre followed Moliére and Rich, in the invention of the new bourgeois theatre entertainment, they used traditions and notions from all available sources. The ballad opera of John Gay (*The Beggars Opera*) was developed to compete against the invading Italian opera; but there were dance tunes with little dance in John Gay's novel effort; while the singers begrudged any intervention of ballet-dancing in their operatic exertions. Only the pantomime was able to reconcile these contrasting elements of Theatre, and these men began the process that produced what is now called English Ballet. Baroque architecture flourished in Western Europe, contemporary with the ballet; but this style secured no hold in England, excepting for decoration inside theatre buildings, where the tradition of gilded cupids and rosettes, with red plush curtains and upholstery, continued for more than a century, together with the baroque modes of dance that became established as classical ballet. The popular liking for New Year mumming and masque, widespread for centuries through England, united with the newly cultivated bourgeois craze for Italian Opera with its short ballet interval, and the remains of Louis' court entertainment, which crashed finally from 1790. Court masques united Franco-Italian styles with English poetic drama.

ENGLISH DANCE (Post-Mediaeval)
Provided some four principal styles or modes, from which the 16th - 17th century dances were developed in groups. These are comprised in the styles entitled: *Country Dance; Morris Dance; Sword Dance* and the later *Salon* or *Ballroom Dance*. These modes were influenced by imports of European dance styles; including the waltz or valse and galop; which made an almost violent impact on the fashion of "polite country dance" that had (1800 - 1820) arrived at each version in the London *salons*. There was also the *Polka*.* Theatre dance then directed interest away from the dance-hall (Almack's* closed down) and not until the 20th century opened was a new influence discerned, this time from America. The *Carol* and *Noel* had vanished, as dance forms, from popular tradition in England.

ENGLISH DANCING MASTER, THE
A collection of English Country Dances, first published in London by John Playford in 1650. The work contained instructions, with music for 104 popular dances. This publication proved so acceptable that new editions continued to appear, over a period of about eighty years, until the final eighteenth edition had been printed (in three volumes) ,and covering about 900 dances in all gathered over a wide area. Several main styles of dance are described; the elemental ring-dance and square-dance; the square-eights and the couple-dances; and the "longways dances" for files of dancers facing, for varying numbers of dancers. The sources are not stated; but from a few names we can surmise a church or mask origin (*Solomon's Jig*, and *Mask*, are two such names), though the name of dance composers, like music composers, is rarely hinted, except in so far as we may assume that *Dr. Pope's Jig* may possibly have been arranged by the worthy doctor. Dance tunes like *Lilliburlero* or *Pope Joan* we know to possess direct political affiliations; while many extended beyond English borders in origin, as in the *Siege of Limerick* and *Holyrood Day*, or *Irish Boree* and *Bonny Dundee*. Dances such as *St. Alban* or *St. Katherine* imply some church tradition, as also *St. Martins*, and *Parson's Farewell*. A reproduction of the first edition of *The English Dancing Master* has been published in London.

ENGLISH FOLK DANCES
Are said by Cecil Sharp[1] to occupy three categories: *Sword Dance,* Morris Dance* and *Country Dance*. This summation omits the Church Dances, while only the most extensive catalogues of Country Dances (such as that derived from the long series printed by Playford and his successive editors in *The English Dancing Master,*) can venture to include dances which by their names formerly belonged to other lines of tradition, such as *Mask*, or *Solomon's Jig* (possibly a church dance). Again, Sharp admits that Sword Dances and Morris Dances are found widely through Europe, but puts up a good case for the origination of the main category of Country Dances, in England. This argument is recounted under *Contra-Danse*.* Country Dances almost died out (the last was dropped from fashionable London when *waltz** and *quadrille** entered from Parish about 1812 - 20), but in villages of some English country districts, both the Morris Dance and Sword Dance continued to be performed on traditional festival dates. Country Dances were consciously revived, due chiefly to the work of Cecil Sharp and his colleagues, from about 1920 onwards.

[1] *The Dance*. Cecil Sharp. (London 1924).

ENGLISH SWORD DANCE
Was once part of a dramatic ritual performed at New Year and on Plough Monday. The play, embodying a ritual death and resurrection, has survived only at Ampleforth and Revesby; and in Scotland only in the Shetland Island of Papa Stour (described in Scott's *The Pirate*). A mock death is simulated by the "lock" made by dancers' interlaced swords, placed over the candidate's shoulders, and the swords suddenly withdrawn give a vivid impression of decapitation. The "hilt-and-point" Sword Dance has survived among the miners of Yorkshire, Northumberland and Durham, the area of Danish settlements, from whom this dance may have come into England. In Yorkshire, it is danced with long, rigid steel swords; in the other two counties a short, flexible "rapper" is used. Because of its shortness, the dancers (usually 5) are in a compact group, their intricate dance patterns being closer than the more open dances of Yorkshire.

Traces of accompanying drama have mostly disappeared, but the dance of Grenoside shows a remnant of ritual. Performed by six men wearing clogs, it is accompanied by dialogue, and has a "calling-on" song by the leader, who sweeps a clear path with a curved sword. On his head is a cap of rabbit or hare skin, with the head in front. He is "decapitated" by the "lock" of swords at the beginning of the dance, and withdraws without being "resurrected", while the dance continues. At Handsworth, the "lock", made at the end of the dance, is placed over the leader's neck but he is not "killed". Each of these eight dancers wears a cap dyed half red, half white. The "lock" (or "rose") is itself of ritual significance, with its shape of Solomon's Seal, two interlaced triangles (6 points), or a seven- or eight-pointed star, according to the number of swords. At Flamborough Head, eight fishermen dance, linked by wooden "swords", held in the left hand. The figures (called "threedlings") suggest operations in net- or mat-making. Men in Northumberland and Durham are "step-dancers", and clogs were formerly worn for Sword-dancing, but are now mostly replaced by light shoes, and a portable "tap" floor for exhibition dances. Teams of Sword-dancers exist at North Skelton (6 men), and Lingdale; at Loftus (6 men); at Earsdon, High Spen, and Newbiggin (each 5 men), and many other places. Not all the teams have an unbroken tradition, many having been formed, or revived, during recent years.
[See *Sword Dance; Pace Egg; Ezpata Dantza* (Basque); *Ouliveto* (Provence)]

ENRAMADA (Spain — Neila district of Burgos)
La Enramada is said to have originated in an incident of the 16th century, in a combat between Neila and other villages, in which the women helped by brandishing branches from the pine woods. Women, each bearing a pine branch, mark the rhythm of the *dulzina* and tabors, in the present day dance.

ENSALADAS (Spain)
A mode of burlesque madrigals with a curious history. Those that were written down (and thus traceable to a single composer) were often "not performed", as in some works by the musician Mateo Flecha. Those that were performed, without notice or permission, in the *romeria* canvas theatres, were not written; and, like the Italian Commedia, were framed on slight points, danced and mimed with plentiful topical allusion. They were constructed on the technical style of the madrigals; but, with a vastly different content. Hence, the continuance of the term "salad", meaning fresh — very fresh — greenstuffs, for immediate consumption!

L'ENTRALLAÇADA (Roussillon, France)
"Interlacing", a "French Catalan" dance, performed most often by six couples (minimum), or not more than twelve. Danced by men and women with light, springing steps, each dancer holds a tambourine in the right hand. Without music the couples enter the dancing place in line, then partners face each other. The music begins only when the dancers are in place; they stand still for fifteen measures, then all together the tambourines are shaken in the air, and from that moment they remain upraised till the end of the dance. It is performed in a vertical line, with short and long sideways movements, partners changing place, men and women working towards the end of the line. The music is repeated until each dancer is back with his original partner.
[See *Cascavallade*]

ENTRÉE — 1
For "Dance of Entrance" in which the "entrance" was not that of the dancers but of the men-servants who brought in the dishes from the kitchen. As such, the term remains on every French menu; and thus connects with the dance term *menuet* — the small tripping step necessary in carrying a heavy dish without disaster. The musicians "played them in", either from their seats in the minstrel gallery; or by dancing ahead and behind the dishes. This custom was maintained in Russia until 1912 or so, principally on the country estates of the dukes and boyars; we have a reminder in England with the famous "Boar's Head Carol". This melody, with its original words, was used to "give the entrée" to this principal dish of the New Year Festival; it signified the slaughter of the menacing boar who sought to dissolve the Year by gripping the sun. Now symbolised by a golden orange, or latterly a lemon, the head was carried in triumphantly and taken round the room in circuit, three times for all the diners to see. The dessert, was the last dance tune of the dinner, for similar reasons; the dancers deserted the company.

ENTRÉE — 2 (Fr.), Ital. *Intrada;* Sp. *Entada;* Eng. *Entry*)
Before the Court Masque developed as a separate entertainment, it was part of the banquet, with guests at table, seated in the midst of an appropriately arranged scene. Dishes were brought in ceremonially by servants moving in rhythm to music. This was the *entrée*, exemplified by a 16th century entertainment given at the Court of Mantua. "Orpheus", accompanied by shepherds and

shepherdesses, summoned the guests to the banquetting hall, arranged to represent a moonlit pastoral scene. When all were seated at table, courses were brought in to the accompaniment of music, by servants dressed as hunters and country-folk, who presented the dishes with appropriate verses and music. The name, *entrée*, has moved from the occasion or function, to the food itself, applied to the dish served between fish and meat. When the Court Masque became a separate production, performed on a stage, it was usually divided into several "Entrées". Dances were performed by ladies and gentlemen of the Court, who afterwards descended from the stage to rejoin the audience. Later, in Ballet, the *entrée* came to mean a solo dance performed in a divertissement as a separate, complete item. In music, the *entrée* signifies the first piece after the overture, which begins an opera or ballet. The term also applies to an opera-ballet where each Act is separate and complete in itself; or to one whole Act of an opera. This name was also formerly given to music played for the entry of a procession in ballet or other theatrical production, usually in slow 4/4 time, in march rhythm.
[See *Stuart Masques—The Dancing Place**]

EPIDEMIC DANCES (Med. Europe)
Is a name given to some sporadic outbursts of popular energy—perhaps by way of discontent—which took forms of dance, either on journeys, or near churches in towns. Accounts differ very considerably, together with reasons alleged for these epidemics. There is some likeness to the parallel outbreak of alleged "witchcraft" that occurred over the same period; we can note that, during the religious burnings, there were less "epidemics". On the supposed witchcraft, the only certain historical facts concern the endless trials; and the devilish retribution meted chiefly to poor and friendless people. Rich people, who used "magic" or witchcraft, like Catherine de Medici, were never brought to trial. Though many trials did take place, it is utterly uncertain what was the alleged crime. So also, with these dances; crude enough in form and aimless in performance. Possibly they were parodies of the "pilgrim traffic" which was the current term for "tourist trade"; and satires of the mystery and miracle plays, which also included dances. Clerical accounts of these dances; or fanatical legends of "sins" are incredible inventions; they were the "yellow press" of their day. Restriction of these epidemic dances to certain localities (mostly in South Germany and Northern France or Flanders), is itself suspicious; like the sudden appearance of "witchcraft" and the equally sudden lapse, when popular support failed, which

recalls the convenience of this clerical method of revenge for political and economic opposition. Modern missionary accounts of "native dances" contain equally queer descriptions.

EPILENIOS (Greece)
"Dance of the Winepress". Described by Longus (4th - 5th century AD), in his *Pastoral of Daphnis and Chloe*. It was a solo mime of the process of wine-making, depicting the gathering of the grapes, carrying them in baskets, treading them down, pouring the juice into tubs, and finally drinking the new wine. Originally danced by members of a household at private entertainments, it was later taken over by professional dancers, when it became more acrobatic.

ERZULIE (Haiti)
A ritual dance used in the "Voodoo" system (*Vieu Dieu*) derived from Europe, where the name was Ursula or Ursulie. There was in Venezia the famous brotherhood (also nuns), *Scuola di santa Orsola*, which is linked with several mediaeval legends. The original name is Latin—the *Ora-salii*, and refers principally to the ritual dances in pagan Rome, of the attendants upon the famous Vestal Virgins, who had charge of the City Sacred Fire (*Vesta*), and the fountains. One of the Latin titles of the "Blessed Virgin Mary" is *Vesta Matutina* or "Morning Fires". Much of this catholic ritual was taken to the islands of Haiti by French and Italian settlers; thus Ursula was changed slightly into the goddess Erzulie. In the catholic form, these became the dance ritual "Dance of the Hours" and Vesta (or Hespera) became Vespers, the "evening light-up" period when a nun circulated, with torch or taper, to light lamps.

ERZULIE FREIDA (Haiti)
The Voodoo "Goddess of Love" (from Ursula, notorious in the Mediaeval pantheon of Rome, famous at Cologne, with "many virgins"). Erzulie is worshipped by men only; by those who "have a vocation", for after acceptance they remain (theoretically at least) celibate; and no woman can claim them in marriage. She opposes all women; she is one of the Petro group of gods. Drums play after her ceremonial, never during the liturgy; and dancing goes likewise, chiefly among upper-class Haitians. More care and talent has been expended, it is asserted, on songs for this initiation, than for any other Voodoo ceremonial. "Erzulie ninnin, oh! hey!" is the most popular of all Haiti folk songs.

ESCONDIDO, EL (Argentina)
Sp. *Esconder*, "to hide". A lively but dignified dance in 6/8 time, for one couple. Originally a gaucho

dance of the pampas, known all over the Argentine, today it is chiefly found in the north-western provinces. Danced also in the cities by folk dance groups, its name "the hidden one", refers to the 6th and 8th figures (*Escondimiento-Búsqueda*). The woman kneels with bent head, shading her eyes with her hands. Her partner dances round with a waltz step, snapping his fingers and appearing to look for her. On discovering her he makes no sign except a pleased expression, dancing *zapateo** in place, arms hanging at his sides. The woman remains "hidden". This is repeated in reverse in the 8th figure, the man hiding and the woman seeking him. During the first four figures (*Giro-Esquinas*), dancers gradually progress in a circle, anti-clockwise. Standing facing, they dance towards each other slightly diagonally; when nearly touching each revolves and moves out and round a quarter circle. This is repeated three times, until they return to their starting points. In the 5th and 7th figures (*Vuelta*), they dance anti-clockwise in a circle, always keeping on opposite sides, but in the 9th figure (*Media–vuelta*), they make only a half-circle. The whole dance is then repeated, which finally brings them to their original starting places. There seems no explanation of the "hiding" episode, which may once have formed part of a mime-dance or game, now forgotten.

ESPRINGALE

Mediaeval round dance for couples, popular in Europe about the 14th century. The step used was a little spring or hop, and the dance was introduced into England by the Saxons from the German *Springentanz*. The dance-song accompanying it was called *For-Gengail* and dated from about the 12th century, when the simple round dance, or *Carole** was popular. Verses addressed to Nature were sung by the leader of the dance, who was answered in the refrain by the chorus making sounds similar to yodelling, or imitating musical instruments.

ESQUIMAUX DANCE (Behring Straits, Arctic Ocean)

In December, Esquimaux in this area hold a festival to ensure reincarnation of sea-creatures killed by their hunters. Believing that the souls of seal, walrus and whale linger in the bladder, these are retained during the year by each hunter, who, on the appointed day, brings the inflated bladders tied to a hunting-spear, to the dancing-house, where the ceremony is held. This *Kashim, Kassigim* or *Kassigir* is a spacious semi-underground chamber entered by a tunnel. The spears, with their bunches of bladders are hung round the walls, and after the "souls" have been offered food

and water, the men dance. Accompanied by drumming, to the rhythm of which they keep perfect time, they first move slowly with a jerky action, from side to side; then change to an oblique gallop with arms tossed up and down, ending the dance with hops and jumps. Supposed to imitate the movements of seals and walrus, the dance is performed for the pleasure of the souls in the bladders. A *shaman* leads the dancing and directs the ceremony, which ends at night, or at sunrise, with a procession across the snow, out on to the ice, led by the *shaman* carrying a large torch. At an already prepared hole, each man rips open the bladders and thrusts them into the water under the ice, so that the souls may be reborn.

ESQUIMAUX DRUM DANCE (Greenland)

Held at the height of summer season. Principally they "let off steam" by bandying satirical songs, while dancing rhythmically, on grievances or disputes or criticisms. The men dance, singly, from the groups they represent; then in parties; so that the group which continues the longest, or provokes the most and loudest laughter, is regarded as "the winners". Naturally the missionaries tried to interfere with this relatively peaceful manner of settling disputes; trying to introduce their theological system of verbal dispute.

ESTAMPIE (France — *Estampida* Provençal)

Evolved by Provençal Troubadours in 12th and 13th centuries, and performed by one man and one lady or, more rarely, by one man and two ladies. The accompanying music, in 3/4 time, was instrumental, not vocal. Made up of several little strains, each followed by the same refrain, the music resembled a *rondeau*. The *Estampie* was danced round the dancing-place, partners side by side and holding inside hands, without raising the arms. In *Estampie Gai*, after sixteen bars, partners faced each other and took right hands, later making a half turn to take left hands, and finally returning to the original position, side by side. After the Albigensian massacre (begun in 1208), fleeing Provençal Troubadours brought their songs and dances to other European Courts, in Italy, Germany, France and England, where the *Estampie* (among other dances) developed according to different influences in each country. In England the same 13th century dance survived into the 16th century; while in Italy the *Estampie* was danced in the 14th century, and in Spain traces of its form appear in later dances.

ESTRADA (USSR)

Estrada means "platform", but is the general name

now used for "parks entertainment", developed in Russia for summer shows in the green spaces, also on the wide Moscow boulevards (here mostly for children). The companies of five or six persons (including one or two able to play musical instruments), construct their own approved show, and contract for a "city tour" (meaning any park in Greater Moscow, perhaps fifty places), or take on a provincial tour. They play a week (or, in town perhaps only a half-week) at each place. The type of program is, briefly, "music-hall style", ranging from song and dance—solo, duo or company—to juggling and acrobatics. They may perform thrice daily; or only twice (if lighting is not adequate). Broadly, they correspond to the pre-1939 English seaside "concert parties" and the general standard is, if anything, somewhat higher than the BBC"*Light Programme*" offerings.

ETHIOPIAN RITUAL DANCE

Is said to have been organised or reformed by a priest known as Yareed. This account is mainly legendary; but the tradition of three main systems or modes exists. Their musical forms, called *Araraj*, *Esel*, and *Geez*, appear to be equivalents to certain Hindu *raga** modes. They serve to indicate a placing of music, relative to a phase of ritual dance. In this Coptic tradition, the formal dance is important. The company of priests and deacons form one or two circles (the outer ring of deacons only, if there are enough of them). Inside this ring dance, two higher priests perform, with a third man beating a drum for rhythm. The dancers in the circles clap their hands, as they intone chants. Chief is the *Beit-Lahm*—Entry of the New Bread from the *House of Bread* (final celebration of the New Corn). The written notation is relatively modern, and naturally does not carry the neumes that were so essential. Ethiopian religious ceremonial was formulated mainly in 7th century, energized and opposed to the newly risen Moslem system. Festal dance chants, used during all the year, are known as *Miraf*; while the principal ritual chants, used for peak periods, are called *Deghuah*. Additional are the "Praises of Maryam" (made over from Isis) called *Malkutha Maryamma*, (or *Malkousa*—a type of *raga*)—"Legends or Plays of Maria". These sextuple-verses remain from playlets, performed in dance-mime; but obsolete since the 15th century. A few paintings have been reproduced, from such episodic shows, by E. W. Budge, and others.
[See *Maskel; Dance of Priests*]

ETHNIC DANCE (USA)

One of a set of allied terms, developed in the USA, attempting to provide definitions of "dance material" obtained from other countries. These categories have their own distinct interest. An American writer comments: "Critic and public . . . as yet know little of the shadings of ethnologic dance. Traditional forms are seldom recognised, being confused with the authentic. Ethnological departures are misunderstood. . . . the creative artist is many years ahead of public and critics alike". That is the complaint of a dance expert, who seeks to offer these various modes to the American public. In these definitions, new meanings are given to technical terms. In the USA, there are no poor: they are the "under-privileged". Dance advertising is "promotion". Again it is claimed (same writer) that "It is being recognised more and more that ethnologic form is a *science* of movement; and need not necessarily be a racial heritage", meaning: that any national traditional dance can as well be performed by foreigners. Instead of explaining, says the dancer, that many styles of national dance had been studied, and imitations were offered, an attempt was made to summarise this eclectic system in single terms. They "emerged with 'ethnologic' ", and next it is stated "we use ethnic for the exotic primitive or communal forms; ethnologic for the traditional and authentic forms; ethnological for the departures from traditional or authentic techniques".[1] (This claim for "authentic" for admitted variations seems hardly "ethical".) From these three contradictory terms it would appear that an ethnic exotic form is not always authentic; and that an "authentic" form is never exotic; while a technique can be diverted to sustain a new kind of theme, still claiming to be ethnological.
[1] *Twenty-five Years of American Dance*. (Ch.: *Theatrical Ethnic Dance*. p. 182) 1951.

EUCHORICS (England)

Dance-mime system for "the representation of Poetry and Prosody by means of Expressive Movement", developed as a method for use in stage training, chiefly by Eve Acton Bond. Her book, bearing this title, was published in 1927.
[Cp. *Eurhythmics; Dalcroze*]

EURHYTHMICS (organised 1900-1905)

Professor Emil Jaques-Dalcroze devised his system of training in apprehension expression, and appreciation of musical rhythm, working chiefly in Switzerland (after he had come in contact with Arabian music in a period at Algiers). The Dalcroze system was exhibited in many cities; it has directly influenced the Diaghilev system of Russian Ballet (and was taught to their dancers as part of their work), while the method has been added to ballet schools in Russia and in England.
[See *Eurhythmics*. E. J. Dalcroze]

EURHYTHMY (Rudolf Steiner's system)
Devised as a system of theatrical expression, about
1912, by Dr. Rudolf Steiner of Münich, and later
of Dornach, near Basle. In that village was built
the interesting wooden "double theatre" called
Goetheanaeum (later burned down and replaced by
a new building in concrete, of different design). In
this theatre Dr. Steiner, as a mystical philosopher
(a some-time follower of Theosophy — he called his
system Anthroposophy) gave his *Mystery Plays* and
readings in verse, in his system of *Eurhythmy*. He
explained to this writer (visiting Dornach) that the
sonorous verbal form was accompanied by the
visual gesture — each sound had its own appropriate form or movement. Some exposition was given
in German, from Goethe, Schiller and others; but
it was never explained how the same work, translated into French or English could equalise different
sounds (with the same basic meaning), in similar
gestures. Displays have been given in London and
other cities; and two books were issued, further to
explain the method : *Eurhythmy as Visible Song*;
and *Eurhythmy as Visible Speech* (both from lectures given at Dornach in 1924). Dr. Steiner dis-
claims any direct approach to ballet, or even dance
form; as does Dalcroze.   [Cp. *Eurhythmics*]

EUROPEAN BALLET — 1
Has developed into various related "national"
phases after the preliminary separation from the
Masque and religious festival ceremonials, in particular those of the New Year and the Paschal
period of Easter. Thus the religious element was
dropped, for the court ceremony of secular intent;
and this in turn was superceded by the "diplomatic entertainment" or feast, on the occasion of
receptions for foreign ambassadors, weddings of
great families, and similar gatherings — including
even the Council of Trent, when it met to decide
(in 1545) its politico-economic policies, under
guise of religion. There was a performance of the
Capture of Troy included in the lavish entertainment. Ball or social dance was complemented by
ballet or spectacular dance, beginning where there
was most money to spend. This financial aspect
originates and then haunts all developments of ballet. The national phases developed first communally
in the minor Italian states — Milan, Padua, Mantua — and then were seized upon by the Medici
family in Florence; and exported thence to France
by Catherine de Medici, principally for propaganda
amusement. Musical forms had developed in
parallel, from liturgical forms into court ceremonials; but, like ball and ballet, were long fused
and interchanged through the years. At the French
court developed another communal Italian notion
— the Accademia, here turned to nationalist form

in the succession of Academies formulated under
Louis Quatorze, among which the last was the
Academy of Music and Dance, organized in 1661.
The nationalist impulse had come from Elizabethan
England, with the Royal Society; the teaching and
guiding form — in opposition — came from catholic
France. The first notion of every French Academy
was to impose standard forms — from architecture
to language and the dance. On this firm stem
developed the theatrical forms of ballet from court
ceremonial; the professional actor-dancer (who
pretended to be a prince) in place of the reality
of the nobles as dancers around the ample form of
Le Roi Soleil. This title affirms the last trace of the
traditional connection of dance and ballet with
the Masque of the Winter King. When Louis retired
from active service, the stage ballet "went professional". It entered the closed theatre and thus
started on its European commercial course. The
different "Schools" that developed we must examine in their nationalist centres.

EUROPEAN BALLET — 2
Began in Paris; followed in Vienna and Milan (then
Austrian), and then in Denmark and Petersburg,
followed by London and Moscow. In these cities
academies were founded; though London did not
have a national academy, but remained in the
hands of private enterprise, visited by the experts
of Paris and Milan or Vienna. This rise and fall of
ballet can be traced in its various sectors : sometimes the scale develops and then fades; sometimes
the technical standards improve and then begin
to lapse, as direction fails to sustain the high attainment. Popular approbation also becomes variously
directed to ballet or opera, to drama or social
salon dancing, according to the peculiar excellencies or tastes of reigning monarchs. From Bordeaux
to Moscow, from Copenhagen to Milano and
Venice, various theatre companies flourished for
their season, and gave way to other entertainments.
German States were late in admitting the interest
of ballet, but at Stuttgart, performances were
inspired by Noverre; as later, notable dramatic
work was encouraged by the Dukes of Meiningen.
Russian ballet, again as a direct court pastime,
flourished from the time of Empress Anne, until,
in the 19th century, five Russian royal theatres
received official guidances and support, with annual
cash subsidies to offset any losses. The clash of
events from 1900 (from war with Japan), the first
revolution (1905) and the expectation of attack
upon, or from Germany) directed exhibitions of
Russian culture, in plays, in opera, and lastly ballet,
as well as pictures and sculptures, with participation in the international exhibitions, centred chiefly
in Paris. When the first European war broke down

empires, the Russian export ballet company remained, now centred in Paris; and its influence impinged on most other ballet centres, from the music-hall traditions of London to the effete opera styles of Paris. Danish ballet had continued in Copenhagen; while two companies remained active in Russia; with another in Milan, and one in Vienna. Minor companies aggregated and disappeared in most countries; then small groups of dancers began touring. Denmark and Russia competed in London against Paris and Vienna, with their dancers; not as full companies. Style of dance was exhibited; not style in ballet, which is even more important. The USA had been invaded by dancers since about 1830, in various small companies, led by ambitious dancers; in a few eastern towns — New York to Boston or Philadelphia.

"EXCISEMAN AND DEATH" (English 17th century)

A typical *interludus* — a satire of its day, in which two characters, Death and the Exciseman, chant a dialogue with a slow pas-de-deux, to one of several current tunes (and sometimes with more virile additions). The version in *Ballads of English Peasantry* (1857) carries about 100 lines. *Death* bids the *Exciseman* end his duties, with a writ.

Exciseman replies:
> "A writ to take *me* up, excuse me sir!
> You do mistake, I am an officer
> In public service, for my private wealth; . . ."

Death answers:
> "I know thy office, and thy trade is such
> Thy service little, and thy gains are much . . ."

Finally, *Exciseman* (seeing no escape) surrenders:
> "My office sins, which I had clean forgotten,
> Will gnaw my soul when all my bones are
> rotten . . .
> Let all Excisemen hereby warning take,
> *To shun their practice* for their conscience
> sake".

The dance executed by both characters is the simple circle walk, still practised by a few comedians, in which they cease singing (or patter) and turn upstage always to the right. This is called the "Walk Round Martin". Here they move both ways. [See *Dance of Death*]

EXECUTION DANCE (Persia)

At Schah-al-Bunder, records C. J. Willis[1], a deep well was cut in living rock; no water was found, so the shaft was used for executions; it was more than 600 yards deep. About 1850, a friend of his witnessed the Persian Execution Dance:
> "The woman was paraded through the town (Shiraz) bare-headed, with her hair cut off, on an ass, her face being to the tail. She was preceded

by *lutis** or buffoons of the town, singing and dancing, while the Jewish musicians were forced to play upon their instruments and join in the procession. All the rabble of the town thronged round the wretched woman. The ass was led by the executioner; it was nearly dusk when the place of punishment was reached. The victim had been mercifully drugged with opium, and was probably unaware of her fate; she was ordered to recite the Mussalman profession of faith; this she was, of course, unable to do. Her hands were bound behind her; a priest recited the profession of faith in her name; and the executioner, saying *Be ro!* ("Get thee gone") by a touch of his foot, launched her".

[1] *Land of the Lion and the Sun.* (Persia, 1866 - 1881). C. J. Willis, M.D. London 1891. p.275.

EXPOSITIONS (International)

Have for more than a century been centres in which enterprising people have organized some strange form of dance and music; partly as a "side show" but also as an entertainment that might help to convey suggestions of a different cultural system. From the "Great Exhibition" of 1851 at Hyde Park, London, in the Crystal Palace devised by Paxton for the show, to various French, Belgian, Dutch, and Italian Expositions Internationales, we have records of commercial displays of materials and methods of industrial use, rounded with exhibitions of the arts — painting and sculpture, dance and music. In particular, Europe has been enriched by glimpses of various styles of Oriental dance. Even where the shows have not been entirely authentic (as with the amazing "hootchy-kootchy" shows that stemmed from the USA Philadelphia Centenary Exhibition) the public interest has been caught and even roused to take interest in the foreign cultures thus concentrated in sound and movement. Following the Great Parisian Exposition of 1900, both Indian and Russian arts came again and again to Paris. These static centres proved to be the culmination of the enterprise of the 16th century "Companies" such as the Hudsons Bay; the Merchant Venturers; the Honorable India Company; and those who sailed to the White Sea and eventually got to Moscow.

EXORCISM — 1

Ritual dance (in various periods) when performed as a healing rite, is sometimes called "Devil Dance",* on the supposition that the sufferer is "possessed by a devil, or evil spirit". Formerly the Primitive Church groups used this ritual exorcism, as a matter of weekly practice. The third grade of deacon was an amateur; and then, later, became a professional theological exorcist; and his status was

held to be affirmed by his proven ability. Obviously it was associated with *charismata*, or natural "healing grace" based on strong personal physical magnetism. The dance was used, along with much impressive gesture, as a preliminary to the actual mesmeric contact. We have many descriptions of healing methods used in oriental countries, some closely similar in form and method, though differently decorated by way of costume and accessories. As European clerics have dropped mesmeric modes of vital healing for hypnotic modes of suggestion by word and music; so their power to obtain results in physical healing have vanished. The last period in England was in the days of Charles II, who gave the "royal touch" alleged to have cured a few diseases, notably scrofula. There was no dancing. In Ceylon, in contrast, there is a regular village system of "cure by dance", which ignorant missionaries term "devil dancing" because they are told that (as in their own older writings) "devils are driven forth". This priestly cure is a powerful system of suggestion by means of music and dance, with continued chanting (or prayer), which frequently, when the ailment is nervous or mental in basis, cures the victim by literally "changing his mind". But he himself rarely joins in the dancing; that is done by the doctor as a part of his bedside manner.
[See *Devil Dancers; Mummers; Witch Dance; Hexentanz; Energumens; Magical Dance*]

EXORCISM — 2

(Of power — *Ex-orchema*) and its polar opposite INORCISM (Invocation and Excovation) — which are known as invocation and revocation, present the two most important phases in all religious ritual. They are formulated in India as *avarahana* or *devahana* — or, as *avahana*, which is described as "calling in the deity". Those phases known as expulsion (of power) are named as "exorcism" (when done by *our* cult) or as "devil-dance ritual" (when done by "pagans"). The ritual process of Invocation (prayer for help etc.) is accepted as holy, as done by our cult; but as black-magic when done by un-official rituals. Exorcism was an office of the primitive Christian *kirke* (a ritual dance-prayer of chanting (*litorgia*), because it was a regular ritual in all religious ceremonials; as part of the preliminary process of purification of the place, done by circum-procession. The participants had been purified by previous attention to diet, behaviour, washing, and clean garments; but the place of ritual had to be cleared of all lurking invisible "devils" by a similar process of cleaning. We call them "germs", and we sprinkle "disinfectants" — they called them "devils" and sprinkled "holy water"

or cleaned the air with "holy fire" by incense. These magical practices are still followed.

EXTRAVAGANZA (English)

Theatrical term, chiefly 19th century, denoting the "musical comedy" productions of the first half of this period; especially those devised by Planché. The name derives from *vagans* (Latin) to wander; and *vagari* (Latin) the wanderers. In one aspect, this became a musical reference — the "wandering" or uncertain *motif* — given as a name to the *quinta pars* in a mass; and thus stating that the melody line could be taken by any singer, at any part of the scale. The voice could wander. Precisely this wandering occurred in the "musicals" called *Extravaganzas*: the songs were "passed" from one singer to another; and so were the dances. The minstrels had also collected this term, in their final period of decadence; being classed as *vagabonds*; or wanderers. After a long period of obsolescence, the system, but not the precise name, now returns to the stage, called "musical comedy". or just plain "Musical".

EZEKIEL'S RITUAL WHEEL (Babylonia, into Hebrew)

Derives its *Merkabah* (Chariot) from the Zodiac designed by the Chaldaean *magi*. If given dates are accurate, Ezekiel, last of the "Four great prophets of Judah", was born *circa* 620 BC, as son of Buzzi, a priest of the Zadokite clan. Trained in the Babylonian temple, he became a friend of King Nebu-Chadrezzar; and, as a sacerdotal official, sought to centralize Jewish worship, in the scheme to abolish the numerous local Levite shrines, to concentrate later at Jerusalem. His ritual was thus formulated on the secret Babylonian scheme of monotheism, though it was publicised in a pattern of apparent polytheism. (The Hebrew Bible scheme of *Genesis* has both accounts, from Babylonian originals). His Yahwe was symbolised as in the Chariot (*Merkabah*) which was, astronomically, the Zodiak of Twelve phases, seen in Twelve Patriarchs (and later, "Apostles"). The four annual feasts (public versions) were allocated to *Marqod*, the Lion (of Judah); *Matthai*, the Worshipper; the Bull, or Ox, as *Lukious* the Light Bringer (symbol of Spring); and *Iohannus* or Midsummer, the Eagle. These are parallel to the Four Spirits of the Tomb (in Egypt). They marked four points of the Great Wheel of Ezekiel; four points in the seasons; four points in the ritual life of man. Later the Chariot, after a phase in Greece as Apollo and Quadriga, became the *Navis* or Ship of Salvation; also with Four Points. The ritual retained the hidden pattern, through all phases; and revealed them by the movement with music, that we call dance. Dr. Cheyne[1]

refers to "symbolical actions, dramatically representing a siege . . . a dithyrambic ode . . ." and is clear that "no psychological basis can be admitted for the "visions" which are elaborate and composed" — they are incidents of ritual — mythic statement. The king is allocated to the Tree. The precise patterns of the ritual dances can be gained only from lengthy examination of Babylonian texts, chiefly by indirect reference; and by analysis of the Babylonian Sacred Tree (and *Qubalah** diagrams or paths).
[1] *Encycl. Biblica* (Art : *Ezekiell* p.1460 - 3. Ed. Cheyne.

EZPATA DANTZA (Basque)

"Sword Dance". A ceremonial dance of dedication, once performed by Basque soldiers before going into battle. To the music of pipe (*txistu*) and drum, young men in the white and scarlet Basque costume, perform various figures with swords and with staves, but the first figure, the *Danse du Drapeau*, is sometimes performed separately on both sides of the Pyrenees. The *Ezpata Dantza* belongs especially to the region round Pamplona, in Spain. First the entry (*Mutchurdinak*), with dancers in double file, flag-bearer (with furled flag on one shoulder) coming down mid-way between them, where he remains while the men perform various jumps *sur place*. They jump first with feet together; then again as high as possible; next making a complete turn; then two jumps raising alternate legs in front as high as possible. The first pair then dance to the end of the line and the same sequence of jumps is repeated — continued until all dancers are back in their original places. On the last jump, the men fall on to one knee, body bent forward, head low. To the roll of the drum only, the flag-bearer slowly advances between the lines waving the flag horizontally over each pair of dancers in turn. Arrived at the top pair, he kneels between them and sweeps the flag over his own head. The sword dance follows, with various figures, including *Zortikoa* and *Ezpata Jokul*, when swords are clashed together; and *Makil Aundiak* when the swords are changed for staves. It is in this dance that the famous Basque high kicks occur, when, with body poised on one foot, the other leg is thrust upward in front of the body so that foot and ankle rise above the head. In the last figure, the solemn dedicatory mood returns, as the leader is lifted, and held horizontal on the upraised arms of his companions.

EZPATA DANTZA DE ZUMARRAGA (Basque)

A dance for four men performed inside the church at Zumarraga (Guipuzcoa), in the chapel of "Nuestra Senora la Antigua". Dressed in white,

each dancer holds upright in either hand, a dagger with the hilt wrapped in a white kerchief. Dancing always on the spot, with the neat footwork of the Basque, the most noticeable thing is the constant flourish of both hands, in which the kerchief-wrapped daggers are swept in graceful curves and lines, across and round the body. There is a dignity and air of dedication about this dance, which recalls the solo *Dirk Dance** of the Isle of Man, although in form the two dances are not alike. The dance at Zumarraga is performed at the *Romeria* (festival) of Nuestra Senora of Antigua, on 1st July.

F

FABLE in Dance

Is a form essentially suitable for presentation in dance and mime, provided that the producer has a lively imagination, able to convert some ancient set-up to convey a modern and topical implication. Fable (Latin *fabula* or *fari*) has already devised, for example, the *farina* or *farruca** — the *Dusty Miller's* dances. The term means generally, just "talk" or "gossip over the beans" (*faba*), for we must recall that ancient voting was often done by means of beans (black, white, red), as it is still, in voting in some clubs (black-balling=non-acceptance). Hence we may assume much pot-house talk, coupled with "election promises" ("war to end war" etc.). One of the main Pythagorean instructions to young students was "Refrain from Beans". This was not on account of the comment (recorded by Culpeper, the herbalist) that "Beans be windy meat", but concerned with futile strife of elections. The "Morale Tayle" comes over well in fable; and if joined with wit is received with a merriment, conspicuously absent from modern ballets. The Atellane Fables, and succeeding Italian Comedians, relied much on the topical fable, especially in its satirical form. The "fabulous" is now essentially perverted to imply the "astonishing"; this quality should not be monopolised by film advertising, political yarns about the "Freeworld", or claims for cosmetics and breakfast foods, all of which make the tall tales of Baron Munch-hausen seem very modest. Some recent fables in dance include *Chout* (Diaghilev ballet); *Peter and the Wolf* (Stravinsky ballet); *The Seven Heroes* (Jooss ballet); while a 17th century masque — *Cupid and Death* (1653) — derived its story from Aesop's *Fables*.

FACKELTANZ (Germany)

"Torch Dance". A ceremonial court dance of 18th and 19th centuries, performed at a royal wedding. A relic of mediaeval tournaments, the dance was

particularly favoured by the Prussians, and took the form of a stately procession to a Polonaise* played by a military band. In 1742 at the marriage in Berlin of the Prince of Prussia and the Princess of Brunswick Wolfenbuttle, the *Fackeltanz* was danced after supper, in the candle-lit White Hall of the Palace. In a letter by Baron Bielfeld, who attended the wedding, the dance, "of extreme gravity", was described as "a ceremony used in the German courts on these occasions". The band was placed on a stage made of silver, and the "clangour of trumpets . . . rent the ear . . .". Strict court etiquette governed the order of the dance, which was opened by the newly married prince and princess. Before them went six ministers of state and six lieutenant-generals, two by two, each holding a lighted white wax torch. After making a tour of the room, "the princess then gave her hand to the king, and the prince to the queen; the king gave his hand to the queen mother, and the reigning queen to prince Henry; and in this manner all the princes and princesses . . . according to their rank, led up the dance, making the tour of the hall, almost in the step of the Polognese". Strict order of precedence was similarly observed in France at the court of Louis XIV for performance of the *Minuet.** In 1791 the *Fackeltanz* again appears at the wedding of the Duke of York and Princess Frederique Charlotte Ulrique Catherine of Prussia. As before, it was danced after supper, in the White Hall of the Palace in Berlin, and its performance marked the end of the wedding festivities.
[See also *Gavot*]

FACTIONES (Early Latin)

The four organized Parties of the Circus Maximus, who competed when clothed in recognisable colours. These companies provided horses, drivers; and for interludes, pipers and dancers who wore their "company colours". In Rome the Factiones wore *russata* (red), *veneta* (blue), *prasina* (green), or *albata* (white). In Byzantium similar schemes prevailed for contests in the *Hippodrome*—games and shows. Contests were frequently riotous. From horse or chariot racing came our modern usage of jockeys' colours; also the prominent use of "Blue" for caps at university games; and then to elections, with the "favours" worn as badges, or attire in dances. In competition, churchmen favoured Black Freres, White Freres, Grey Freres, leaving brilliant colours to bishops and cardinals; these have gained ritual observance in processional ritual-dance usage.

FAIRS, Dancing at

Before the period of enclosed commercial theatres, the numerous mercantile Fairs, established at town centres all through Europe from London or Paris,

to Leipzig or Nijni-Novgorod, attracted providers of amusement as well as merchants and caterers. At Paris, the *Foire de San Germain*, of *San Laurent*, and of *San Ovidius*, were the principal centres, each on its customary date. In London, at Southwark Fair, Bartholomew Fair, and later the May Fair attracted thousands, while Nottingham had its Goose Fair in October. Theatrical booths varied with puppet players; games of skill and chance; while outside spectacles included invariably the "rope dancers". Dancing entered into many of the shows : from the humble acrobats to the skilful step-dancers of various styles. The records of rope-dancers reflect the high degree of technical skill, which was equally apparent in those who did not perform on stretched ropes. Fashions of dance movement, of costume, and of tunes, were carried from Fair to Fair more rapidly, to the people, than from Court to Court; indeed, the more expert performers received "commands" for court shows, both for the princes and for the wealthy bishops. At the Fairs (*La Foire, Die Messe*) the popular amusements found a centre and reputation, which had deserted the Market Square before the church; or the Miracle plays inside the church or the cloister. Possibly the term *Leipsiger Messe* was derived from the "leapers" and their bi-annual feast.
[See *Rope Dancing; Church Dances; Miracle Plays; Puppets*]

FAIXES (Spain)

"Sashes." The name refers to sashes held by performers of a religious dance at Malda, Province of Lerida, on 2nd January, in honour of St. Macario. At least twenty-four dancers, all married men, perform various figures in a line outside the church, each man holding a sash in his right hand. Entering the church, they are joined by the sashes in a long procession, and as they go out each man, in turn, dips under a scarf. Outside the church once more they continue their longways dance.
[See *Cintola, Danza del Duomo; Church Dances*]

FAN DANCE (Japan)

Fans are important ancillaries in most Japanese dance forms. The *ogi no sabaki** (fan techniques) are significant emphases of character and action. Symbolism governs many fan movements; but long experience tends to provoke a virtuoso mannerism, bringing the fan movement suspiciously near to conjuring. Some dancers use two fans, with a to-and-fro movement, from one to the other fan; or both fans will move identically. The fan may suggest many things—a turning wheel, a letter, a sword, a musical instrument, a falling leaf. Colour and patterns on the fans may have some subtle

relation to the dramatic theme; or may have none, being of a single unpatterned hue. The fan may be tossed freely in the air, and caught; or be taken thus by an attendant, near the end of a routine. In the Filipino dance Singkil* the dancer manipulates a fan with each hand.
[Cp. Feather Dancing (China)]

FAN DANCER (USA, chiefly)
Solo dancer, invariably and definitely feminine, touring the Carnival Circuits, Fairs and Burlesques, through USA. The principal equipment requires two large ostrich feather fans, with which the dancer endeavours to remain in what (astronomically described) may be called a state of permanent, but variable, occultation. That is : the dancer performs as partially invisible, though not in the same manner as that indicated in H. G. Wells' story of The Invisible Man, for there is never 100 per cent. visibility or 100 per cent. invisibility. This dance has no relation to the famous game of Fan-Tan, as followed in the mission settlement of Macao; though it is probably one of the oldest dances of the Christian world. During the classical period the dancer Theodosia, later official wife of the Emperor, was renowned in Byzantium for her terpsichorean display. The alleged original performance—that in the Eden Campus, BC 4004, was achieved (it is related in the myth) by using leaves of ficus religiosa, which became ficus proletarii, when the current Zionist Agricultural Board ejected these amateur farmers for incompetence. This primitive ritual dance was revived, in similar form, during the English Mediaeval Plays, being received with applause (and much box-office benefits); then to travel to the USA as a more open method of dollar acquisition.

FANDANGO—1 (Spain)
A dance for two people in quick 3/4 or 6/8 time. Said to be of Arab origin, the first mention of it in Spain occurs in the early 18th century. Lane[1] mentions the similarity between the Fandango and the dance of the Arab/Egyptian Ghawazee,* or dancing girls. Belonging to Andalucia, local variations take the name of their district, as Malaguenas (from Malaga), Granadina (from Granada), Murciana (from Murcia), Rondeñas (from Ronda). Farther north, it is danced in Castile and Leon, while variants are found in Valencia. In Basque provinces the Fandango is extremely popular, being very similar to the Jota,* which is said to derive from it. Danced by a pair (usually a man and woman, but sometimes two men), the Fandango is accompanied by guitar and castanets, alternating with sung couplets. With very quick, intricate footwork, the dance becomes a contest of skill. The man (or

the first dancer, if two men) sets the rhythm and steps, which his partner takes up and elaborates, the two dancers taking turns to display virtuosity. On the stage, Gluck used the Fandango in his ballet Don Juan (1761), while in the finale of the third act of Figaro (1768) Mozart used a popular Fandango melody. Rimsky Korsakov and Granados have also composed in this rhythm.
[1] Modern Egyptians. E. W. Lane (1836).

FANDANGO—2 (French-Basque)
A couple dance in lively 3/4 time, with four figures. The first three figures may be repeated to make seven. It is followed immediately, without a break, by the Arin-Arin, in lively 2/4 time, which has two figures repeated twice, the last two increasing in speed. Known all over Spain, the Fandango is also danced along the Basque coast on the French side of the Pyrenees in the region of Saint-Jean-de-Luz, where it is performed by groups of two couples with castanets, often accompanied by an accordion. Throughout the dance, arms remain in the air, open and rounded; the dancers marking the rhythm with castanets or clicks of the fingers. The most characteristic dance of the Basque country, it is performed with the enthusiasm that the name itself implies (Fandango—"fait danser"— "compel to dance"). It demands from the dancers vivacity, suppleness, sense of rhythm and grace. The French-Basque Fandango uses four steps—le pas latéral, le pas pointé, le pivot, le pas recule. In the Arin-Arin two steps are used—le pas latéral and le pas sur place. The Fandango is almost identical with the Jota, which is said to have derived from the Fandango of Andalusia.

FANDANGO—3 (California, USA)
On the ranches of early settlers (18th and early 19th centuries), a fandango was a dance party, or any event where dancing formed an important part. With the development of towns and "Society", fandango meant dances of the lower classes, while those more formal functions for which an invitation was necessary were known as Bailes. Dancing, on the ranchos (when not out of doors) was in the sala, a long room with benches on either side, and a place for musicians. For a big fandango, a special arbour (ramada) was built outside the house, open on three sides, with a slightly raised platform for musicians. Women sat round the sides, while the men either stood in the open fourth side, or sat on horseback outside. Dancing was directed by the Master of Ceremonies El Tecolero, who, in formal rhythmic mode, introduced each lady. In time to the music, he approached the first lady, clapping his hands several times in front of her. She would then be

escorted to the middle of the floor, dance several turns in place, and be returned to her seat. Always moving in time to the music, *El Tecolero* progressed round the room, introducing each lady in this manner. When the dance needed male partners, men would dismount, remove their spurs, and take the floor. When the dance ended, ladies returned to their chaperones, and men remounted. Until about 1817, a *fandango* was over by 10 or 11 o'clock, but later the time became extended, dancing sometimes continuing till 9 or 10 in the morning, while a big ball might last for three or four nights. Among dances performed at the earliest *fandangos* was the Spanish dance of that name, and others such as *El Cuando*, *El Jarabe*, *El Son*, *Jota Aragonese*, *La Malaquena*, *La Cachucha*, *La Paloma* and the *Minuet*. Later dances included *Vals Jota*, *Sombrero Blanca*, *La Contradanza*, *Spanish Waltz** and *La Varsouvianna*, while finally there arrived the *Mazurka,** *Polka,** *Schottische,** *Lancers** and *Waltz.**

FANDANGUILLO (Andalusia, Spain)
Literally, "Little Fandango", but while the *Fandango** is a lively dance in triple time for two people, the *Fandanguillo* is a woman's solo dance, slow and dignified. With erect carriage, mask-like face devoid of all expression, and staring eyes, she moves with long steps but covering only a small area. She kneels, arms sweeping wide as fingers clack the castanets; or her body quivers as heels tap out *taccheos*. Sometimes she simply walks with dignified grace, and this can be the most difficult thing to do. Not spectacular, it is fascinating in its slow rhythm. The *Fandanguillo* is a test of a dancer's skill and artistry, since it is far more difficult to achieve the slow rhythmical walk, maintaining the proud carriage and expressionless face, than to move in the quicker rhythms of the dance.

FARANDOLE, FARANDOULO (Provence)
A chain dance for men and women, who, holding hands, wind through the streets on fête days, in the manner of the *Furry Dance** at Helston in Cornwall. A descendant of the ancient Greek *Choros** and the Cretan *Geranos,** the *Farandole* chain is drawn by a leader through arabesque and serpentine patterns to lively music in 6/8 time, played on pipe and drum. Three figures, The Snail (*L'Escargot*), The Bridges, and The Maze, indicate the winding evolutions of the dance, different steps being introduced by the leader. Among steps used are *le pas Niçois* (one leg crossed over the other at knee height, first in front, then behind), and *le pas Arlésien* (one foot crossed over the other, the toe touching the ground). Special *Sociétés des Farando-*

leurs keep the dance alive in Provence, as at Arles, Tarascon, and Aix. In French Catalonia the *Farandole* begins with dancers in pairs, walking round the town Square. Then, still in pairs, they run under an arch made by the first couple holding up the man's scarlet sash. There follows *L'Escargot* when, in linked single file, all follow the first lady, who turns under the sash. The first man then leads the winding dance through streets and houses, returning to the Square, where each man shows off a variety of steps to his partner, and a final galop ends the dance. The French Basque *Farandole* to lively music in 4/4 time, also winds through the streets on fête days, taking young people from the pelota ground to the dancing place. Men and women alternate in a line, linked by scarf or kerchief, the man at the head being the leader. Steps include *entrechats* and *pas en quatre temps*, and the dancers follow similar figures, including the passing of the line through an arch made by the first couple, and back again. A fourth figure consists of jumps and turns *sur place*, the last jump being as high as possible. The Basque *Karrika Dantza* (Street Dance) and *Soka Dantza* (String Dance), are both of the *Farandole* type. In the theatre, the *Farandole* has been introduced into the operas *L'Arlèsienne* by Bizet, and *Mireille* by Gounod.
[Cp. *Furry Dance; Carmagnole; Cramignole; Fröhntanz*]

FARRASH (Arabic-Persian)
Literally : a carpet or *kelim*. The carpet or rug has been for centuries important in the East, as a portable "marked place". In ritual, the *farash* (*frash* or *farshi*) thus possesses an intrinsic value as the *gadi* or seat (or throne), much as the "chair" has been in Europe. In Arabic Egypt, this place of honour became *seggadeh* (or *saqadeh*), thus being the focus of ceremonial ritual and dance, as was the throne in a cathedral, displacing the *altara* (high place, or mount). The *farrash* was copied on the marble pavement of every mosque : every man had his allotted place, or rather space, indicated in the traditional pattern, whereon to bow and chant his prayers. The *farrash*, whether in religious or secular usage, thus carries its own pattern. Many ancient Persian carpet patterns repeat a *paradis* (or pleasure park), while more modern (post 15th century) *kelims* carry the copied mosque pattern; hence called prayer-rugs, by Europeans. In the ritual dance, the large carpets (as, for example, the *Ardebil*) shows a larger *paradis*; on it, dancing girls might move, singing and dancing, precisely as they did over the alabaster pavements of the ancient Assyrian temples.

Lane[1] gives a version of *Dus-ya Leila* (Dance, my Joy!), in which one verse goes :

"*Ya benat Iskenderreyeh; Meshyukum 'ala-l-farshi gheyeh;*
Telbisu-l-Kashmir bi-telee Wa-sh-shefaif suk-kareyeh!"

("Oh ye damsels of Alexandria! Your dance on the carpets is alluring; You wear embroidered Kashmir shawls; your lips are sweet as sugar!") Persian carpets carry half-forgotten ritual designs, merged with tribal signs and special symbols of their deities, inherited from the ancient doctrines of Zoroaster and Bel of Babylon. As with the Arabic *ramal** (the small kerchief), with its mnemonic patterns, so the *farrash* carries the temple designs through the East, to every corner of the desert; reminding men of music and dance.
[See *Schem-Ha-Phorasch; Rammal*]
[1] *Modern Egyptians*. E. W. Lane (First Edn. 1836).

FASCHING (Germany)
Throughout the Black Forest, *Fasching* is the three-week pre-Lent Carnival. At week-ends during this period, towns and villages hold their celebrations, with masked dancers collectively called *Narros* ("Fools"—an old name for Minstrels, giving "narrate") but each mask having an individual name. Each village has its own characters, the dancers wearing carved and painted wooden masks, with elaborate costumes. In one week-end, groups gather from all over the Schwarzwald (at a different town each year), for the high-light of Carnival —*Narrentreffen,** or "Meeting of the Fools". *Fasching* is a time of general relaxation of in-hibitions, of hilarious behaviour and general gaiety.
[Cp. *Mardi Gras; Tlustni Dni* (Poland)]

FASTNACHTSBAR (Germany)
"Eve of Lent Bear", or literally "Festival Bear". At Shrovetide in country districts of Bavaria and also Bohemia, it was usual for a party of young men to tour the village, leading the *Fastnachtsbär*. Usually a man or boy, covered from head to foot in pease-straw and wrapped in straw ropes, he was led from house to house, to the accompaniment of music and singing. At some places, as at Leit-meritz, he wore a bear's mask. In every house he danced with the wife and daughters, and drank to the health of all the household. He and his com-panions were given food and money. When they had made the round of the village, they went to the inn, where all the villagers gathered to dance, for it was the custom at Shrovetide, and especially on Shrove Tuesday, that everyone must dance.
[Cp. *Tlustni Dni* (Poland); *Fasching* (Germany); *Mardi Gras* (USA)]

FATES, *Moriae* (Greek mythic symbols)
Three maidens, accompanying Ilithyia, who pre-sided over child birth. As sybils, oracles (later *orantes* or *adorantes*) they chanted destinies of the new infant. Their ritual extended to the Birth of the New Year in the annual Festival; and early spread into Britain (probably 3rd cent. BC) giving the source of the *Moeris;* but now seen with three opponents. The Latin name was *Parcae*, the Scandinavian name, the *Norns*. The contest was mimed in ritual dance form; but this earlier feminine form gave place to the masculine *Moeris.**

FAUST (Opera)
(Composer, Gounod). Has dance music written into the story as rendered by Wolfgang von Goethe. In Act II, the *Kermesse* scene, there is a Waltz; but the principal dances appear in Act V, in the devel-opment of the *Walpurgis Nacht* celebrations, as seen by Doktor Faust under the guidance of Mephistopheles. There are seven distinct dances, which are (1) Les Nubiennes; (2) Adagio; (3) Danse Antique; (4) Variation de Cleopatra; (5) Les Troyennes; (6) Variations de Miroir; (7) Danse de Phryne. These are arranged for performance in the style of French classical ballet.

FEATHER DANCING (China)
In the Chinese classic drama, the manipulation of two pheasant plumes worn on the head. Seven or eight feet long, the feathers were formerly worn only on the helmets of robber chiefs or rebel generals, but were later displayed by any com-mander. Feather dancing manipulates the plumes in such co-ordinated movement that they make curving patterns in perfect rhythm and symmetry. These patterns resemble a formal mime language, each set of movements having its name and sym-bolic meaning. Thus, "Winding the feathers" indi-cates anger or determination, shown by dropping the head forward and moving it round so that the feathers describe a perfect circle. Immovable deter-mination is indicated by taking the tips of the feathers between the teeth. "Nodding the feathers" shows surprise, contemplation or recollection. The dancer's head is lowered until the feather-tips touch the floor, being then thrown back as the head is raised. The two feathers must move in perfect unison. "Dancing with the feathers" describes the circular waving of the feather-ends. Holding the plumes about a foot from the tip, the hands are moved in circles, left hand inward, right hand out-ward—never both inward, or both outward. Spec-tators thus take a two-fold pleasure in feather dancing—understanding the emotional meaning, and enjoying the rhythmic and synchronised move-ment of the two plumes.
[Cp. *Fan Dance* (Japan); *Ogi No Sabaki* (Japan)]

FEATHERED TIGHTS (England)
Mediaeval church plays and dance-mimes included performers, in the character of angels, wearing garments described as "feathered tights". Over the west door of Sall (Norfolk) church, dating from c. 1419, are carvings of angels in the feathered tights which are considered as originating in the plays. Angels in feathered tights can be seen on bench-ends at Warkworth (Northants), Haverfordwest (Pembroke) and Withsfield (Suffolk); on an alabaster font at Clifton Campville (Stafford) and in windows at Long Melford (Suffolk), Methley (Yorkshire) and in York Minster. Similar styles of costume, though they resemble scales more than feathers, have been recorded on painted rood screens, at Hexham-on-Tyne, and at Barton Turf in Norfolk. This costume is known much earlier, as in Constantinople (Stambul) under the auspices of the Eastern Church. Dean Stanley comments on these angelic actors[1].

[1] Lectures on the History of the Eastern Church. Stanley. 1861.

FEIS, plural FEISANNA (Irish)
A festival held on annual holidays, including Music and Dancing with drama. The style is said to derive from the first great "Feis of Tara" held there in 130 BC, when Ollamh Fodhla was King of Ireland, after which it was celebrated every third year until about 500 A.D. The Feis Bheal Feirste (at Belfast) begins on May First and continues for a week.

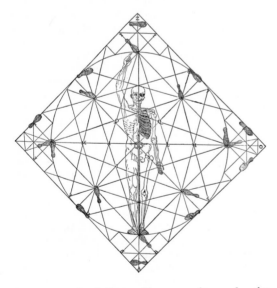

Fencing and Ballet. Choreography of the Fencing Masters; from a plan by Gerhardt Thibaut of Anvers, printed in his instruction book of 1650.
FRANCE

FENCING AND BALLET
Court Ballet first arose chiefly as a system of etiquette and manners, from a combination of their earlier techniques, and fencing, with the ceremonial ways of court gatherings. All of the famous "Five Positions"* were known; and were used in the technique of fence, long before any academy of dance existed. Many of the same technical names remain, alike in ballet and fence, revealing the rudiments of the same positions and movements. The culminating period of Fence developed in Spain, France, and Italy; and later in England, in the 15th/16th centuries. This height of formal fencing is well illustrated in the great folio volume issued by the famous fencing-master, Gerhardt Thibaut of Antwerp.

FERREL'S FIGHT (Paris)
Jean Francois Ferrel, a Parisian musician, published a pamphlet in 1659, which opened a conflict in the city, between musicians and dancing-masters. Le Roi Ménétriers, chief of the dancing men, had earlier claimed jurisdiction over all musicians as well as dancers. Ferrel rebutted this professional claim by affirmation of demarcation (quite in the modern trade union manner) in his saucy, if verbose, retort:

"A savoir que les maistres de danse qui sont de vrays maistres larrons à l'endroit des violons de France, n'ont pas royale commission d'incorporer ès leur compagnie les organistes et autres musiciens, comme aussy de leur faire païer redevance, démonstré pas J. F. Ferrel
Practicien de musique à Paris, natif de l'anjou".
The contest (no strike or lock-out being practicable) lasted about a century, and included several law suits. Paris Parlement decreed in 1750 that Messieurs les Musiciens could not be ruled by Le Roi Ménétriers.

FÊTE CHAMPETRE (French custom)
Literally a "Feast of the Field"; (now turned to "pic-nic"), arranged as a Spring Festival, usually by groups of persons (artists, writers, etc.) in honour of one of their number. The 17th century court Fête Champètre involved more time; more trouble for servants; and more expenditure; often without the central meaning. The 18th century painters (Fragonard, Watteau, Lancret, and others) sometimes recorded a scene that struck them. The custom took hold in Germany, always with its serious side evident: Munich artists, for instance, planned the event for months ahead, taking barrels of spätanbrau and boxes of würst. Speech-making preceded the Feast, music started during the eating and drinking; and "field dances" ended the public proceedings. These secular Fêtes had no

calendar day; they awaited the weather. From this cause, sprang the provision of a "hall in the country" to prevent postponement; and thence came the secular dancing customs associated with the Folks Hall (Vauxhall, Volks Halle, etc.), from which developed the popular London centres of Ranelagh and Cremorne; though tapered off with the spring customs of Visiting the Wells — Bagnigge Wells, Sadlers Wells, Bath, or Tunbridge Wells — itself a culmination of the ancient carnival of Well-Dressing that preceded the spring rites of the bright Fountain of Water. The term *champetre* seems superficially to be *Champs-etre*, but equally well may derive from *Cham-Petre* (as Cham-Border, Cham-bertin, Cham-berlain etc.), and thus connects with the autumnal "Feast of Peter", or the Ancestors, later turned into "All Souls Day". This feast was celebrated by a memorial of prayer, followed by dance rejoicings.

FÊTES DES FEVES (Algiers)

This "Feast of Beans", a traditional Negro festival, is to be seen on the first Wednesday in April; the rites are performed on the seashore, near the Marabout of Sidi Bellul, near Jardin d'Essai and the village of Hussain Bey (he was the last ruler of Algiers). The ritual, which invites comparison with the English "Beanfeast" — originally a harvest festival, ranges from dancing to drinks

FÊTES DES FOUS (France)

General term for the mediaeval version of the Roman *Saturnalia*, a festival of the "turn of the year", when all values were inverted. This word may come from *foule* (the crowd), but D'Israeli[1] ventures the opinion that *fou* equals "bull"; though the Greek is *bouph* and *bouphon*, which marked a similar celebration called Bouphonia. From this feast were derived the *buffoons*. But *fouiller* is "to excavate", and, at this time of year, agricultural digging was arranged — ("Fool Plough" in England). A *fouleur* is a wine-presser. Bacchic festivities entered France, and were converted to mythical "Saint Martin" celebrations at harvest time. Possibly the *fouleurs* danced as satyrs.

[1] *Curiosities of Literature.*

FÊTE VINOCOLE (France)

Is a modern revival of the ancient Feast of Bacchus, formerly converted into the Feast of "Saint Martine" for November 11th, and now turned into a two-day festival at Beaune in Burgundy, noted by modern reporters as "almost a sacred occasion". Banners of Sainte Vincent (newly appointed patron saint of vine-growers) are carried through the streets by local damsels, attired in traditional blue and white. The display is frankly commercial; admission to the formal opening of *séance particulière de degustation* costs a thousand francs — but continues seven hours. There is a wine "wick auction", copied from the ancient "lots by candle" formerly held in the parish church of Notre Dame. Dancing formerly took place in Rollin's Chateau. The *salon*, now *grande salle des malades* (it is *L'Hôpit*al) had a mediaeval judgment *danse des morts* picture (though a modernist dauber covered the nude forms of the *damnée*), since Beaune was an ancient centre of Gaulisme. The dances are now smaller and less fantastic, for the rite now is "rolling the pearl" — the former libation to Bacchus — in expert wine-tasting.

FEU DE LA SANT JEAN (France)

Ritual fires at the solar solstices are traditionally celebrated by dances for Johanne and Johannis (from the Roman Janus, the dual-faced god). Brand describes a print owned by Douce : "In the centre is the fire made of wood, piled up regularly; having a tree stuck in the midst. Young men and women dance round it, hand in hand. (This is on Midsummer Eve, the June solstice). Herbs are stuck in their hats and caps, garlands surround their waists, or are slung across their shoulders. A boy, carrying a large bough of a tree, is watched by several spectators. Beneath the picture we find :

"Que de feux bruians dans les airs!
Qu'il font une douce harmonie
Redoublons cette melodie
Par nos danses, par nos concerts!"

FEUILLET'S NOTATION

This curious system of noting dance steps was invented in Paris, by Raoul Auger Feuillet; and published by him in 1701, with the title : *Choregraphie; ou l'art de décrire la danse par caractères, figures et signes demonstratifs.* More complicated than Beauchamps' earlier scheme, Feuillet's technicologies comprised something like a secret military code (Top Secret), which some modern critics have compared to the meanderings of a bar fly. They show, mainly, the tracks of one dancer. The book was translated by John Weaver of London in 1706. By then Feuillet had published (in this script) his versions of some English *contra-dances*, called thus to establish an English origin for *contre-danse* as country-dance.

FEULATARE (Switzerland)

Meaning "La Folatre", this frolicsome or "crazy" dance, belongs to the district of Champéry in the Valais Canton, and is danced by couples in a circle. Movement alternates between fast spinning and more gentle movement. While the circle moves round, two or four couples in the centre spin on their own axis, with short rapid steps. When they tire, they move to the outside and revolve more gently in the outer ring, the original circle breaking up into couples who, in their turn, spin round in the centre at high speed.   [Cp. *Folia; Coraule*]

FIDDLE (Old English term)
Belongs to dance, to the instrument; and to black-marketing, which last tradition confirms the basic European meaning, as allied to jig or jiggle. Several instruments reveal close connections with the group for whom they are played: e.g. *crewth*, the *cruth* or crowd; the viol and violin as the vial or vessel (of the group "filled with grace"). The ecclesiastical origin of fiddel or fiddle is from *fedele* (*fideles*), the "faithful". Arabs use *el-fida* to indicate "ransom" (i.e. "saved"). (There was a Chapel de Fedeles ranged with Olde Saynte Powles, London). Modern financiers know the term in relation to monetary and commodity operations; while lesser folk emulate the Victorian grocer. An allied term fake or faking, is distantly related to the form fugue; but the German *Geige* and *jig* (and modern *guage*) indicate other reflexes for the measure of music, of goods, of finance. Hence the term of curt dismissal "Fiddlesticks", when a fake argument has been rumbled.

FIGURANTE (French)
A dancer, a supernumary (in drama, a "small part player"), and in ballet, styled "small soliste", or one who figures in a small character for a few minutes, as compared with *Coryphée*,* a leading ballet dancer, first in chorus or more prominent as *soliste*. The word may come from *figure*—once a "court card", or *figurine*, a little figure and *figurer*, to imagine or create a form. This group of terms ranges from realism to metaphor; but in English drops to slang: "A fine figure of a woman", with the word turned to "figger". In Spanish, *figurar* has a more emphatic sense: to make a shape or form. With less bombast, it implied what is now called "creating a part", in being an interpreter of a role.

FIGURE DANCES
Usually for more than one person, where the dance is divided into sections instead of being danced through without a break. With each section, or figure, the dance pattern is changed, different steps and sometimes different rhythm or tempo, are used. In figure dances it is the figure, or pattern made by the dancers as a group or team, which is the essential part, as distinct from solo step or tap dance, where the emphasis lies on the technical skill of the dancer in executing different steps.

FIJI HEAD-HUNTERS DANCE
A vivid drama of attack, pursuit, capture, slaughter, beheading and devouring; seen by Sir Basil Thompson at Nandrunga, and described in *The Fijians—A Study of Decay in Custom*.† Visiting dancers from the mountains perform at a great Council of Chiefs. Warriors and dancers marched into the village square in twenty ranks of ten, then squatted with spears poised. A quickening chant was sung, and, after a brief silence, singing started again as one man fluttered a fan. Singing shrilly, to rhythmic beats on war drums, suddenly a mighty deep-toned shout was the signal for a third of the party to leap up, spears poised, march the length of the square, then retire to allow another section to follow. All warriors then knelt, bodies bent, spears poised, ready for stabbing or hurling; legs like steel springs, suddenly tensed, caused the men to leap in open order. There followed a realistic mimicry of pursuit, dodging blows by sideways jerk of the head, stabbing at foes, running with heavy rhythmic tramp, so that the audience of plainsfolk (hosts to the dancers) retreated in headlong flight.
† (London 1908. P.584 - 6).

FILI, plural FILID (Ancient Irish)
Professional poet-singers of the courts of Ireland, organised in close corporations, First to Fifth Centuries (perhaps over a longer period); equivalent to the Gaulish *retorics*; or the bards among the Druids. The *filid* were, official historiographers and genealogists, before the days of written history. Their training was long and arduous; the meters they learned were difficult and complex. At great festivals, the *fili* would recite, with mime and gesture, to instruments, from his store of learning. The lower grades filled intervals with more vigorous modes of dancing. In Eastern Europe, the Slavic tongue turned *fili* to *vili*; this term denoted the groups of traditional poets who held festival meetings in their own land, or midnight meetings in countries over-run with enemy invaders. The same term *vili* descended in Georgia, to be a family name, by way of suffix; such as Djugashvili. [See *Vili*]

FILM DANCE—1
Like camera photographs, provides more a record of dance performance than any creative art. So far, dance on cinema film is a compromise, the film camera makes a record, often incomplete, of dance material, such as a ballet, a folk dance, or a "documentary". In this ethnological phase, filming of dance is most valuable, if done direct from native dancers in the country described; and far less useful when made from touring groups of

Siamese Hunters Dance from the film ballet
Sinatleh (Light), Georgia, U.S.S.R.   THAILAND

students. Too often cinema conventions intrude;
the ever shifting view point; the distant or close-
up. This studio trick—convenient to suggest speed
in "Westerns" is futile for dance that has its own
order and style of movement. We have seen a few
designed dance films, such as *Red Shoes*, *Invitation to the Dance*, which did attempt consideration
of the new medium; it pleased few more than a
few discerning critics who say it helped professionally and educationally. Every film, like the
television, gives us the frame proscenium.

FILM DANCE—2
Is most likely to succeed in this modern medium
if technicians will agree to "work their way up"
starting with puppets (wayang wang, e.g.) or silhouette stencil material. Both puppets and the
moved silhouette possess the rudiments of essential
esthetic appeal; and if the artificial demand for
"modern chorreg-raphy" can be diverted, optical
requirements will probably blend with newer and
genuinely expressive design. As vehicles for fantasy
—which is one of the traditional styles of effective
ballet—puppet or silhouette can take full advantage
of their miniature theatres, which the projector

can reasonably enlarge. Ballet is best designed for
the moving dancer watched by the seated spectator;
but the inevitable reduction in scale (or variation
to larger-than-life episodes) challenges instead of
convinces.

FINGERS in Ballet training
As between training for ballet dance and training
for piano or violin, there is the most complete
contrast. For the instruments, the fingers have got
to work, sensitive and accurate; while in ballet
they have been relegated to the position of futile
ornaments. There is some argument whether the
fingers shall remain in the ornamental *port-de-bras*,
open and separated, or slightly closed and touching. The technical means is "holding a penny" or a
button, during practice. The vast neglect of manual
gesture in ballet helps to empty it more of human
feeling and meaning; which along with the banal
code of facial indication, lowers the entire display
from a possible art to that of technology. Fingers
are used chiefly to hold a ribbon, a wand, or a
skirt. Not until we move into genuine dramatic
ballet do we find that fingers belong to hands,
expressive in action or restraint. Rarely do we
observe any usage or fingers for symbols; for that
we must examine the Hindu *mudra;** or a system
like that of Delsarte.* Some dancers—and the
ballet-masters who fail to instruct them—are occupied with technique so exclusively that they eject
meaning from passages which originally had some.
Thus, in the Prologue of *The Sleeping Beauty*, one
of the "variations" takes the dancer to "four directions". She is supposed to use the "magical act" for
expelling spirits; the snapping of fingers with the
outward movement. Everywhere this action is reduced to caricature; the dancer clearly thinks it
enough to show an imitation of an imitation. Then
it is proudly named as "*My* finger Variation".
[See *Castanets* (1) and (2)]

FIRE FESTIVALS (Britain)
Date from periods older than the arrival of Greek
and Roman missions or armies, back to at least
2,000BC. With the Festivals, solemn ceremonials
were performed, with ritual dancing; relics of
which carry down to modern times; as, for example, in the Brittany "Pardon" rites, formerly the
Pyr-Dune or Hill of Fire, known as Montreff in
Brittany, with the Prayer of Fire. Owing to calendar shifts, the precise earlier annual dates have
become uncertain. Those fixed by solstice and
equinox (Samhain and Beltane) became attached
more closely to the social gatherings. These are
given as :—

Oilmelc : February 1st. *Cantel-Messe* ("Candle-
mass", Little Messe).

Beltane: May 1st. May Day/*Walpurgis* on May Eve.

Lugnasad: August 1st. *Lammas*/Michael Messe.

Samhain: November 1st. Ancestors; Fawkes/All Saints.

By the calendar shift, two more dates seemed to be essential; and were reinserted with differing name. Hence, the Scottish festival of Hagmanhay (made into Kresten-Messe farther south), covered the very ancient Festival of the New Year, which became coalesced with the Winter Solstice, instead of (as formerly) noting the Spring Equinox, for which Easter or Pasch was celebrated. Over Midsummer was laid the vague figure of Johannus (both as Johan and Jean), from the earlier Janus or Ionis (Roman and Celtic). Thus, there seemed at one time, to be six annual festivals instead of the European seasonal four. Fire was for a long period called *Tan* or *Tein*. This fact is recorded in the name Teampull-na-Teinead, at Inismuray; Tan Hill (Ross-shire); Tan Hill (Wilts.), and hundreds more such names, including Tanei (Etruria) and Ti-Tania (Bretagne), as well as the deviations: San Tann turned to "Saint Anne" or Mar-Tinea (St. Martin) Bel-Tain is the "Fire of Bel", of Babylonia.

FITT (Old English)

From the Welsh or Cymric *Ffith*, meaning a "gliding motion". The term *fitt* occurs frequently in old copies of dramas or ballads (as of *Robin Hood*), heading the sections as *Fitte ye Firste*, indicating the outburst of action, and was sometimes applied to dance form. The word appears in terms like "fitte as a fiddle".

FIVE POSITIONS (18th Century)

In academic ballet of the Franco-Italian schools, are taught as the essential elementary positions of dance for classical ballet. These Five Positions derived from the earlier Schools of Fence, developed by the expert swordsmen of Spain and France; later of Flanders and England; as the most expedient stances for successful combat with the rapier. These positions were not arbitrary in the sense of fashionable dictates; but as found most effective by masters of fence. In later academic dance, which was at one period taught along with fencing as a fashionable and necessary court accomplishment, the Five Positions rapidly lost their pragmatic meaning. When the dancer ceased also to fence, he forgot the meaning of movement in combat; and as the purpose of the "positions" was then obscured, so also was the movement of his body. In this loss of meaning, the ballet suffers as a convincing spectacle, just as failure in precise and well devised mime ruins its aspects in terms of character.

FLAGELLANTS, Dance of (Spain)

Pictured by F. Goya (1793) as part of the peculiarly Spanish institution of the dramatically arranged burning of "heretics" as a public entertainment, *Auto da Fe (Palauto de Fideles*, "Play for the Faithful"). This painting (now in San Fernando Academy, Madrid), portrays the ring of white-clad "penitentes" wearing the peak-caps or *benito*, imposed by the torturers or "familiars" who dance round the half-clad victims, and before the idol carried by other Familiars of the Holy Inquisition. This picture, *Dance of Flagellantes*, contains one of the last phases of the realistic dance of death to be seen in Europe, for at the conclusion of the dance, the victims were burned on the famous Quemadero in Madrid.

FLAMEN (Ancient Rome)

General name for all male priests, devoted to service of one particular god. The most distinguished were *Flamen Dialis* (Diiovis or Jove), *Flamen Martialis* (Mars) and *Flamen Quirinis*. Some date from Romulus. Three selected from patricians were styled as *Majores*; the rest, *Minores*, were plebs. These names have persisted into West European mediaeval religions (for example, minor canon, majors in rituals, etc.). When elected, by Comitia Tributa, they were "capped" and then inaugurated by Pontifex Maximus; they served under his authority. Their highest rank was *Dialis*, the lowest *Pomonalis;* their office was for life, save for dereliction of duty, or offences. They had a uniform costume, including the *apex*, with a woollen cap, or wearing the *filamen* (a thin headband of white wool) in hot weather; whence, it is said their name is derived (probably wrongly, as this inverts values). They were, in political fact, members of such *parlementa* as the Romans permitted; the priest belonged to the Senate, but under many restrictions, relevant to duties of priesthood. His wife, called *flaminica*, had to help in his duties. Her hair was bound in conical form, with purple conical band (*tutulus*). Municipal towns had smaller bodies of the *Flamen*; and as they were appointed in Roman provinces, we may assume that in Iberia the title, if not the office, continued for centuries. Somewhat transformed as to duties, the dancersingers still held sway as *flamenco*. The girls brought in to learn duties and help, were named *flamina* (this name persisted as *mignon* and *minion*).

FLAMENCO

Modern Spanish Dance song; ancient Roman-Egyptian term for ritual dancers of the Temple. In 2500 BC the term was *ko-hen* or *hen-kau*, the body of priests. Another group was *Shu-heni*. All these professional groups came to Rome as *kau-heni*; legalised as *kau-legia* (basis of our college). The professional group became individualised as *Cohen*, to this present day, in a score of variants as: Kahn, Cowen, Koon, Kohan, etc. The Roman gild associated with guarding supplies of (a) Fire, and (b) Water (highly important in those days) for the city was the Flamyamen-kau; in Iberia they settled into *Flamen-kau*, as in Gades (Cadiz) famous as a centre of Spanish dance, which sent dancers to Imperial Rome. The chief ritual of the Flamenco was the re-kindling of the Sacred Flame at the beginning of each New Year; and the re-dedication (after ritual and factual cleansing) of the fountains or springs of the water supply. Hence the connection of Vesta with Hygeia. Ring dances were alternated with processional dances. With the ancestors of the Basque people was the god Jinco (British form, "By Jingo!") or Zhenkau (Ruler of the Ring or Zhen). The graceful cranes of the Camargue are called "Flamengo", and in Spain the terms of Min, Minco and Minho remain.

FLEA DANCE (North Queensland, Australia)
Travellers report that certain tribes in North Queensland gyrate in a slow circle to drum-rhythm, while they enjoy life by removing lice or fleas from their partners. The famous Russian bass, Feodor Chaliapin, used to sing a merry verse anent *The Flea* (it exists on records), but these particular insects were *pulex irritans rex*, which were alleged to operate by excising their victims, in the courts of the monarchs, to obtain revenue.

FLEUR DE LIS (French)
From Gaelic/Welsh—*Ffilores de Llys*, meaning "dancers of the palace" (5th - 6th century), derived from Flora and Roman games of Spring etc. The term *Ffilores* applies to the female dancers, part of the retinue. From their badges of connaissance came the heraldry symbol of the *Lys* (known in Wales, as the emblem of the "Black Prince" (Winter Prince, in Solstice Festival, or May Games). The term endures in modern Welsh as meaning a "female fiddler", but earlier implied a dancer-singer-instrumentalist, a player on the organ and an expert in ball games. The badge continued as "Prince of Wales Feathers", but in France remained as the conventional Lily. The *Ffiler* was then the minstrel; and the *ffillis* was a winding or twisting dance. Probably our term *flirt* derives from this root; the modern French term *faire flores* means "to cut a dash!" In Italy the cult had a centre in Firenze (Florence) as companion to Lorence or Lorenzo; and familiar as "Florrie". The *fleurs-des-llys* were chiefly dancers in the Spring celebrations or May Games. After the Gallic period, the term

continued in ceremonial; whence we have *fleuret*, both in court fencing and court dancing, as a "little flourish of the foot", or of the foil (epée). Names such as De Lys (Alicia, Delicia) seem here to originate.

FLOOR
The surface of any "place for dancing" as distinct from the site or period. Technically, the dance floor and the foot with its covering must always be adjusted to each other. Floors have been made of (a) natural materials, and (b) artificial substances. Earliest dancing-floors were, and still are in some places, the natural hard earth or firm wet sand left by the tide; the firmly trodden floor of a primitive-style hut (cow-dung pressed hard, dried in tropical heat, is the actual floor of native dance schools in India). Homer tells of the dancing-floor as the circle where grain is threshed out. In Northern Europe, frequent rain prevents such a floor remaining; so it is covered and then fitted with wooden planks; thus arise the barn and barn dances. This offered the best level surface, of sufficient area in the village. In temples, and then churches, paving was introduced, partly to receive the chalk or sand markings, required in different rituals; partly to offset the wear of many feet. Burned bricks, sun-dried bricks, stone or marble (sometimes inset with metal, like the silver lines in Egyptian temples) gradually developed the "permanent pattern" floor, in paving blocks or in mosaic work. In Northern Europe, plentiful timber provided for cut slabs, to make a pattern floor in measured marquetry. This method still offers a characteristic stage pattern in many city theatres; in the same hardwood. Highly polished materials are unsuitable for dancing. Professional ballet dancers habitually use the "resin-box" placed at the side of every well-equipped stage, to coarsen the soles of dance-shoes and lessen the chance of skidding on a too-much polished wooden floor. Resin gives a slight grip, as it does to the bow of the violinist. Many American theatres have bad floors, suitable for a circus or baseball, but dangerous for dancing of any kind.

FLORAL DANCE (Cantabria, Spain)
A garland dance of the *Mayos* and *Mayas* (young men and maidens) performed at weddings. Representing triumphal arches in honour of the happy pair, the garlands are covered with large paper flowers. Led by the bride and groom bearing white garlands, the dance follows country dance figures. The arches of the other dancers are coloured. At the end, each person holds one stick of his partner's garland, so that the flowered arcs are brought together, and all promenade under double arches.

FLORALIA, OR FLORALES LUDI (Ancient Rome)
A festival celebrated in honour of Flora or Chloris, during five days, 28th April to 2nd May, and said to have originated at Rome 238 BC at command of the Sibylline oracle. Similar Spring festivals were celebrated throughout Greece and Italy. The *Floralia* included games and dancing. Valerius Maximums indicates that theatrical and mimic representations were a principal attraction, when nude female dancers entertained the audience.
[See *Church Ale*]

FLYING BALLET
Methods of stage mechanics whereby dancers may be shewn appearing to "fly through the air". This usage in ballet has often been attributed to Didelot; but though he made much use of this mechanical device, he was not, by centuries, the real inventor. Dean Stanley refers (*Eastern Church*) to the use of dancers on concealed wires (as angels) when the early Russians visited Constantinople in the 8th century. These actor-dancer-priests were lifted and moved by wires. Generations of European "rope-dancers" had also much ecclesiastical employment (see *Rope Dancing**). The device was widely used in Victorian pantomime; perhaps the last production dependent on this "flying" has been the Barrie play *Peter Pan*. Some ballets which could use "flying" with advantage (*Giselle, Swan Lake*, etc.), fail to add this suggestive device to their stage effects. Cinema films have used it; but as any sort of fake can be introduced, audiences are correspondingly less impressed. The "flying trapeze" artists of the circus are nearest to the actuality of moving unsupported through the air.
The so-called "flying movement" attributed to V. Nijinsky is chiefly a publicity legend. Though he had good elevation, a trick taught him by his father—formerly a circus expert—of raising the knee at the top of a jump, gave a slight suggestion of pause. In Moscow there was a dancer named Damashov, who had a phenomenal leap, said to cover the Bolshoi stage (30 metres wide) in three bounds.

FÔFA (Portugal)
An old dance-song performed by two people, with guitar accompaniment. So popular was this dance towards the end of the 18th century, that it was described by travellers who saw it as the national dance. Possibly it resembled the *Lundum*,* which was popular in Lisbon at that time, but with a more gay character, since a contemporary account referred to people who "ran about here and there, singing and dancing the *Fôfa* . . ."

FOLA (Italy)
Mentioned by Lewisohn[1] as "art of riding to musical accompaniment", in 16th century. He says :—
"A feature of court and popular festivals . . . horses had to bring their feet down in exact time with the music; or musicians had to adjust their timing so skilfully that the horses seemed to show a good musical sense. To this day, equine ballet is still part of any good circus . . ."
The *fola* (from Portuguese *folla*—"to dance, to rise and fall like the sea", as in the *follia;* which motion is seen when a body of horsemen ride in rhythmic time, also in movement of horses on a roundabout) was developed in the Neapolitan "High School" of horsemanship, begun by Federico Grisone. Gentlemen came from all Europe to Naples. His successor, Pignatelli, sent equestrian experts to perform in all capitals, giving stimulus to horse ballet in circus. This branch of *manége* was very popular. All this was most probably done earlier in Babylon; and possibly in Minoan Crete. Riding horses were known in the days of Ammu-Rabbi, *circa* 2000 BC.   [See *Horse Ballet; Circus; Carrousel*]
[1] *Eine Geschicte der Tiere*. Richard Lewisohn (Hamburg. 1943).

FOLIA OR FOLLIA (Spain)
An old Iberian dance accompanied by mime and dancing songs (*cancionero*) which arose during the New Year Festival. At this annual celebration of the Solstice, the tradition of Saturnia or social inversion had been general for many centuries. The masters waited on the slaves; and the servants sat in their chairs at table. Naturally the release from constraint permitted the temporary outburst of satirical comment by song and dance; which became labelled as *Folia* (and later, folly or non-sense). Mediaeval melodies are later records; so that 15th or 16th century specimens of written music tell us little; and when they become serious organ music, they are far from their original function. They were then known as *Folies d'Espagne*. In Italy, the term *fola** was applied to a style of horse-riding at a famous Neapolitan riding school, where horses were trained to move to music.

FOLIA (Portugal)
"Madness", sometimes known as "Folies d'Espagne". An old carnival dance, of which the earliest musical examples exist in *De Musica Libri Septem* of Salinas (1577). The term *folia* was used for several lively dance measures in triple time, the most famous being Corelli's Variations. In the 17th and 18th centuries one particular *Folia* tune was popular with composers, who based many

variations on it. Originally the *Folia* was a wild and noisy dance accompanied by tambourines. Performed at a furious pace by men dressed as women, the dance was so named because of the extravagant behaviour of the dancers, who appeared to be out of their senses. Some carried masked boys on their shoulders; others whirled to the clatter of castanets. Its performance seems to have been connected with ancient fertility rites. In France and Italy the *Folia* became a couple dance, and in Spain it was performed either solo or by a couple with castanets and accompanied by flutes. The character of this dance was much changed, having become more subdued, more graceful and alternately grave and gay.

FOLK DANCE — 1 (England)

Has several recognised branches or divisions, noted by modern practitioners. These are mentioned as (1) Country Dances; (2) Playford's; (3) Community Dances; (4) Traditional Dances; (5) Sword Dances; (6) Morris Dances; (7) Mummers' Dances; and (8) Children's (Nursery Rhyme) Dances. These groups interlock and intervene; names and locations change slowly in the course of time and dialect; with quicker exchange in the travel from country to town, and back again. The principal change from, say the 16th century or 17th century fashions in popular dance, is in the more highly conscious usage of dance as a pastime to follow, by way of learning and practice, most of the year round. This does not imply that the old-time dancers of the 15th century never did any practice "between times", but there was not the same amount of movement by travel; and the village troup who presented each dance normally scorned to copy or to let others easily imitate them.

lk Dance Festival in Ooster-Park, Amsterdam. *De Gorsselsche Boeren-Dansers* (The Farmers' Dance).
NETHERLANDS

FOLK DANCE — 2

Is a modern term for "vocational dance rhythms" known all the world over, based on the daily or seasonal toil of peasants, in agricultural and handicraft occupations. Festivals afford opportunities for rest or change from labour; but most of the rhythmic movement was little more than technical motions of familiar work, with the addition of a simple musical discipline or beat. With agriculture, as a religious basis, merged with a traditional worship of the lesser divinities of field and forest, the essential processes of sowing and harvesting gained a social emphasis marked by festivals. Cunning rulers, such as the ancient Romans, devised a series of notable events, to affirm the social importance of field labour. These became settled and gained traditional form; the "Twelve Months" are recorded in churches, or Books of Hours, along with the Signs of the Zodiac, or the mythical Patriarchs and disciples; and appeared again with the New Year Festival of the *Masque*,* thus developing more specialised bands of Mummers, Guisers, and Sword Dancers — with occasional accessions from earlier religious rituals, half-forgotten but with external modes tenaciously remembered. This origin of genuine folk-dance is affirmed now that the English peasantry is obsolete; and handicrafts are replaced by machine production, to which people neither sing nor dance. Older folk-dances are recalled or revived as pastime pursuits or museum exhibits; while former court dances take on proletarian uniformity in the *palais de danse* as a spare-time hobby; or a system of sports competition. In these dances, movement is meaningless; the former carols are dissipated in monotonous drivel called crooning, with melodies hewn into jig-saw dissonance to replace the simple direct round dance or song. Some European countries, not yet infested with industrial mechanism, retain parts of their traditional dance systems; but many examples are trimmed when they are "produced" for Cultural Exhibitions by touring propaganda parties. Folk dance loses its countryside freshness and vivacity when translated into city surroundings; and, like the "old masters" of painting, exchange values of meaning for cash values when torn from their original setting.

FOLK DANCE—3
Is essentially the "Dance of the People" as opposed to ritual dance (of the church or temple), and aristocratic dance (of the court), or professional dance (of theatre and music-hall). Folk-dance belongs to tradition and to festival; to custom and to popular ceremonial of the village. Like wild flowers, it tends to perish in towns; and is obviously out of place when brought in slabs for view in some city concert hall. Folk-dance is almost invariably an open-air and country style of dance; essentially it is a dialect form, that possesses its own local authenticity, and it has only its own integral standards, since it is not academic and obeys no national school. Hence folk dances tend to exhibit innumerable variations, all of which can claim an equal correctness, though we may by long search discover some slow changes that have crept unseen into traditional forms of dance and costume. Like authentic sacred ritual, folk-dance is conservative, and admits change unwillingly. Folk-dance is simple in its passion, even if its form waxes into intricate modes that may require very considerable physical skill to perform accurately and well. Music is almost always simple in form, and orchestration is absent. Costume is followed on regional lines; though in England where handicrafts and gilds (that tended to support the dancing life of villages) perished before the onslaught of factory productions, local costumes perished by the way. The term folk-dance is itself a modernism; tradition knows no such name; while "folk-lore" is even more bookish and more removed from life.

FOLK MOOT (Folcmote; Saxon)
A local tribunal, lower than the Witenagemot, for administration of justice. Attended by all freemen of a shire, it was held at quarter-day intervals on the moot hill. A sort of processional ritual dance was formulated, as the entry and closure; the officials concerned were the judge, as the burlie-

man (from Greek boule*), the radman or raadman (the travelling supervisors) as councillors; and the slattere, or steward. The modern legal term "circuit" remains; now the judge and his retinue travel; the ritual movement is much diminished, but the pomp or gesture and position remain inside his court, along with the fancy costume so much admired by American visitors.

FOOTMASTER (USA)
American term (1954) applied to (a) successful competitor in ballroom dancing; (b) teacher who can make $2,000 weekly by teaching others how to dance; (c) hobo gentlemen who make annual trips on foot across USA for fun; (d) college chiropodists; (e) travelling salesman for footgear; (f) Army sergeant in charge of drill.

FORLANA, FURLANA (Italy)
An old couple dance of the north-eastern districts, particularly associated with Friuli, where it is called Furlana Ziguzaine and danced in 3/4 time. A courting dance with lively mime, for one or several couples, it is danced with skipping and waltz steps, with much coquetry on the part of the woman, pretending to evade her partner, who begins the dance by presenting her with a posy of flowers. The dance known outside the Friuli district, is in 6/8 time, and probably of Venetian origin, being a favourite with gondoliers. The music, which follows the Jig* rhythm in triple meter, appears in 16th century dance collections with the more even character of the Passamezzo.* The Forlana was used by Bach in his Orchestral Suite in C Major, and the dance appeared in Campra's ballets of the late 17th and early 18th centuries, such as L'Europe galante (1697) and Les Fêtes Venitiens (1710). Occasionally the name appears as "Furlong", probably an English mispronunciation.

FORMATION DANCE (England 1958-59)
Became the apex of stylistic exhibition dance, ballroom modes; as teams after solo or duo displays had attained their limit. From accomplishment it was developed to a spectacular attraction, under a semi-military type of discipline. Personal expression is abolished. Some thirty teams of eight men and eight girls exist, a few securing low paid jobs on television. They appear also in hotel cabaret. The dances are chiefly the "Standard Four". Beyond pastime or amusement, the social dance here passes into professional display, balanced by teachers of equivalent skill.

FORTUNA (Greece and Italy)
As Tyche, the Goddess of Fortune, was widely

worshipped in these countries, especially by women; being associated with many ritual dances. Many ball-game dances were followed by the devotees of Tyche. She came to her optimum in Rome; and even reached Yorkshire with the Roman Legions, where the familiar name remains as Tyke. She was called Daughter of Zeus the Liberator (by Pindar) while elsewhere Fortuna dances with the *Moerai* or Fates. Fortunata Virginensis was worshipped by newly married women, who dedicated their maiden garb in the temple. Great temples of Fortuna were built at Praeneste and Antium, where *sortes* or oracles were consulted, during ritual dances. This custom endured for many centuries in Roman Gaul, and lingered as the Wheel of Fortune in many churches; its more modern name is roulette. The history of playing cards – especially Tarot, is associated

FOSSOYEUSE, LA (Mediaeval France)
One of the many terms used to signify "Death the Reaper", in Moralities and Sotties. The name derives from *fossor*, the digger, who was necessarily so active in the Roman catacomb revival meetings. Later he became a purveyor of bones ("relics") as Chaucer (*Canterbury Tales*) relates (of Pardoner), but in the rituals, was elevated to the duty of *con fossor* or listener (reporter), as well as digger. With this name, he acted in the miracle plays, for the burial scenes. Around this burial came the Dance of Death.

FOULA REEL (Scotland, Shetland Islands)
A reel, also said to be a Norwegian dance brought to Foula. This dance was familiar in London about 1900 as a ballroom "Scottish Dance".

FOUR KINGS : *Gyal-chen De-shi* (Tibet)
Performers in mystic ritual drama; as at *Dung-kar Gompa* (White Conch Monastery) in Tibet (*Gelug-pa* sect). They balance the Four Queens, of the Bön cult, that existed widely through Europe, before the emergence of Buddhism. These "Four Kings of the Directions of Space" have echoes in many religious rituals: they are creatures assumed as guardians or protectors of the Four Quarters. The East is seen always as auspicious; the West, as the way of darkness (taken from the solar rising and setting). The Japanese call them *Shi-Tenno*. Disguised under Hindu terms: they are known in Tibet as (1) *Kuvera* (N) always in yellow, who carries banner in his right hand and a mongoose in his left hand; (2) *Virudhaka* (S), usually in green or blue, carrying a sword, and wearing an elephant-shaped helmet; (3) *Dhritarashtra* (E), shown in white, playing on his lute; and (4) *Viripaksha* (W) painted red and bearing a small *chorten*, here as a

death or memorial symbol. The Four Kings appear often as dancing masks in (a) mass ceremonial, (b) personal ritual, in study and practice; (c) in seasonal celebrations, popular rituals; and (d) in mythic dramas, with episodic dancing in character or each change, each season, each esoteric meaning. The colours seem to have been changed.

FOXTROT OR FOLKS' TROT
From Norman-French *Faux-Droite;* the dance of annual meeting of the Folk (*Volk*) People. (Cp. Polish : *Polk* = regiment, group). Modern snob term *faux-pas*, indicating a "fault" means a folk-step, declined as "clumsy", vulgar, etc. Down to the 16th century a Faux Hall existed south of the River Thames; from which the district took its name of Vauxhall, but the Russian term *Voksal* (rail station) retains connection with a large building. Connected terms are *faux-bourdon*, a folk-melody, standard, or chorus; *fauteuil*, a seat in a theatre; *falluting* or *falutin'* (to "put on airs") – retort to "*faux-pas*". Foxtrot has no association with fox; mediaeval satirical term here was Reynard (the Red Sly One). Current versions of term exist in family names : Vokes (famous 19th century London theatre family), Foulkes, and ffoulkes (also place names such as Folke-stan/stone). The dance, now used as one of the Standard Four of the modern ballroom, is merely a congregational shuffle to commercial low-grade music. The new terms Folk-lore and Folk-dance are modern inventions.

FRANK-ALMOIGNE (Norman-French)
A term literally meaning "Free Alms", but significant in law, as the name of land tenure granted to religious corporations; and stating the area over which they could have mastery. Related as such to the ritual term *allemande* or *allemoigne*, as a basic figure of sacred dance ritual.

FRÖHN-TANZ, "Early Dance" (Germany)
A traditional dance performed on Whit Tuesday at Langenberg in Germany, said to be a civic imposition on the town as a feudal obligation. *Fröhn-tanz* is a pair dance, round the linden tree and through the main streets.
[Cp. *Farandole; Furry Dance*]

FROTTOLA (Italian)
Literally, a "swinging" or "rubbing against". The name is best known today, as related to the late books of the music pieces which became popular in 15th century Venice (and other Italian cities). This *Frottola* "rubbed up" the citizens, much as does the Yellow Press of Bouverie-street and Shoe Lane in London. The gestured-song was essentially a street show, similar to those of the *carala-tanza*

who sold remedies and liqueurs in the Piazza san Marco; and alongside the broader comments voiced by the experts of the *Commedia*. The melodies are are mid-way between *villanelle* or *passacaglia*, and the more cultured *madrigal*. Obviously the verses were usually comic; though many were sentimental and thus ranked with Tin-Pan Alley crooning-fox-trots. They included sometimes animal or bird imitations. Usually a group of three or four youths would perform: sometimes hired, sometimes for fun, and sometimes simply seeking cash returns. The dances were taken from traditional forms and caricatured or fitted to the newly contrived verses. Some of the *Frottola* books of music were printed by Petrucci at Venice in 1505 - 1515. A form of verse called *Strambotto* was used for the *frottoli* in the 15th century. This was eight lines (*ottava rima*), the first six rhyming alternately and the next two consecutively.

FUFLUNS (Etruria, Ancient Italy)
Is described sometimes, as "one of the Folletto", being known by many similar names. Leland[1], quoting from Müller, says that these were: *Fuflun-us*, or *Fuflunu*, *Fufluns* or even (on goblets) *Funfunl*. Another was *Fuflunsel* (suggesting *Rapunzel?*), but it was agreed that *Fufluns* was the Etruscan *Bacchus*; and thus fond of revelry with music and dancing. He was then the leading spirit of the vineyards; called *Fardel* or *Flavo*; but the *stregone* named him *Faflon*. This generic term seems linked with the psychomantic condition attained by some revellers, in a state of inebriation; with results known today in colloquial terms as "faffling or fuffling". (This comment is frequently heard in modern London, in connection with the peculiar divagations of bureaucratic dic-tatorship, as seen in "foffling of forms" or formula, in which the Lunar worship changes from He-kate to Triple-kate). Leland relates a story of *Fufluns*. A *contadino* had several vineyards—and a daughter. She was courted, she told her father, by a strange and beautiful youth. The peasant was angry; denied the youth, and scolded his daughter. The youth answered (said the girl), that if he could not have the daughter, neither should the peasant have any vintage. Angrily the father sent her to bed, and descended to his cellar. There he saw "On all the barrels devils were frolicking; fire flashed from their eyes, and their mouths, as they danced and sang:

> Give Faflon that girl of thine
> Henceforth thou shalt have wine—
> If the maiden you deny,
> As a beggar you shall die!

The *Contadino* relented, gave his daughter to *Faflon*; when all his barrels were filled with the best wine; and all his vintages were abundant". So the peasants recite invocations to *Faflun*! The Scandinavian godling called Fafnir was slain by Sigurd; he also was a treasure-hunter or hoarder; but a closer local connection is evident in the Por-tuguese dance *fofa*; while in England, we have records of a children's dance-game with a chorus "Fee-fi-fo-fum! I smell the blood of an English-man!" Shakespeare uses the name *fardel* (*Hamlet*) to indicate similar burdens: Hamlet has just been filling in his tablets, relevant to the local, smiling *Fufluns*. The term turns to "Fluff"—another symbol of lightness. *Faflun* "lives in the grapes", but he seeks the *contadino's* daughter. He was (says Leland) known also as Vertumnus in the Romagna, allied with the goddess Voltumna (also a patron of dancing), whence *Volta* or *Volto*, at whose shrine the princes of Etruria held their solemn councils. In any council, or conference, *Faflun* is the revered Spirit of Circumlocution.
[1] *Etruscan Roman Remains*. C. G. Leland. London. 1892.

Funambulus. Pompeian dancer on the tight rope. (*Above*) the Pan pipes for Dance of Bacchus; (*below*) the dancer shows his skill by pouring wine. Mural painting, Pompeii.   ITALY

FUNAMBULUS (Rome)
A rope-dancer; a technically advanced mode of rhythmic exhibition, much appreciated by Romans. Paintings discovered in Herculaneum and Pompeii provide excellent notions on this type of entertain-ment. Characters, mostly single males, but some-

times two or three acting together, were attired and made-up or masked to represent satyrs, bacchanals, fauns, and other creatures of legend. Every sort of variation in gesture was included in the elementary process of crossing along the rope; while jests of all kinds pleased the uncritical Roman taste. Instruments were played, with or without songs and parodies; the thyrsus was misused, for a balancing rod; but experts showed how to pour wine unspilled from one vessel to another, while still moving. They had no nets; they were rarely high up; but Emperor Antoninus ordered that feather mattresses must be used. This tradition of rope-dancing exercised notable effects on later presentations of church miracle or mystery plays, where entries of angels, on invisible ropes high up, caused a great sensation.[1] The Greeks knew the rope dancer as *kalobates*.

[1] *Lectures on the History of the Eastern Church.* Stanley. London, 1861.

FURIANT (Czechoslovakia)

A rapid, fiery dance of Bohemia, in quick waltz time. Accompanied by singing in a three-beat rhythm, the dance steps steadily follow the 3/4 time of the music. Dvorák and Smetana often used *Furiant* rhythm in their compositions, while an eighteenth century example exists in a piece called "Furie", in Türk's *Klavierschule* (1789).

FURRIERS' SWORD DANCE (Hungary)

In the days when craftsmen's guilds were responsible for the defence of the city walls and ramparts, the Furriers (both Saxon and Hungarian) of Brassó, in south-eastern Transylvania, performed a dance with drawn swords. Practice in the skilful handling of weapons, necessary for the defence of the town, was thus provided. The dance took the form of a mock-fight with swords, between two men, each man carrying a shield. Preceding the fight was a dance containing running steps, leaps in the air, and passing under each others legs. They wore tight-fitting trousers, old-fashioned military tunics, and tasselled shoes. This does not seem to have been a true work dance (which usually mimes the processes involved in any particular labour), but rather resembles the old fighting dances, part of Hungary's restless past (see *Bakony Herdsmen's Dance**). It is reminiscent of the mock-duel popular elsewhere in Europe—the *Matassins** or *Bouffons.** The Furriers' trade did provide them with a weapon in the tool they used to soften raw-hides. In 1744 the dance was forbidden, perhaps because it had become dangerous, since fighting on the city walls no longer occurred, and the old skill in sword-play was less evident.

FURRY DANCE or FLORAL DANCE—1 (England)

Descriptions vary in detail, but all agree that it is danced at Helston in Cornwall, on the 8th May; that it is of the *Farandole** type; and that it has ancient origins. Its original purpose was probably connected with the Rogation or Ambulation of the Parish, to "beat the bounds" (see *Youling**); while some connect it with May rites and the ancient Feast of Beltane (May 1 - 8). The name, once known as *Faddy* may derive from the old Cornish *Fada*, which recalls the Irish *Rinnce Fada,** "Long Dance". But in some quarters it is considered that "Furry" may derive from the ancient word *fer*, a fair or festivity; or from the Latin *feria*, which originally meant a holy day.

FURRY DANCE or FLORAL DANCE—2

The dance also has connections with the old custom of "Bringing in the May", or the "living green". According to descriptions, first comes the ceremony called *Hal-an-Tow*, referred to in the accompanying song:—

> ". . . . And we to the merry greenwood . . . .
> To chase the buck and doe,
> With hal and tow, jolly rumble O".

At 7 a.m. the townspeople return laden with green foliage (oak and sycamore), and the houses are then decorated. There used to be a children's procession at 9 a.m.; and another procession containing a suggestion of the *Furry Dance* as a comic country entertainment. This included a Mock Mayor and a "man/woman" such as accompanies many an old English Morris Dance as the "Bessie", but here known as "Aunt Mary Moses". This procession danced along to the beat of a drum. There was also a tradition that anyone found working on Floral Day was ducked in the river.

FURRY DANCE or FLORAL DANCE—3

The dance begins at noon on May 8th. Headed by the Mayor and his lady, and accompanied by the town band, the chain of dancers moves through the town by a traditional route. Spectators join in the dance, which lasts about an hour. Ladies wear summer dresses with flowery, wide-brimmed hats; men, black coats, top hats and spats, all having buttonholes of lilies of the valley. According to tradition, the first two couples should be of Helston birth and the first lady the most recent Helston bride. The dancers frequently stop to clatter knockers or ring bells, while an open door is a sign for the whole chain to dance through house and garden and back into the street, singing a simple verse. In two lines, men on the left, women on the right, the chain swings forward, backward, then circles round. The dance is, or was, in two parts. In the first, couples walk forward, hand in hand.

For the second part, dancers form into groups of four. Men change places; turn the women by the hand; change places again, and turn their own partners. The procession then continues. But this may have been a Victorian addition to the simple processional dance.

FUSTANELLA (Greek, from Albanian)
The unpatterned white linen kilt of the Albanian hillmen, latterly adopted into the Greek army because recruits from this part of the Adriatic wore it; and is now familiar in many styles of modern Greek folk-dance, as well as on the stage. The term is close to the English "fustian", a cotton/linen cloth imported from Fostat, a suburb of Cairo, where it was formerly made. The "fostan" was the long garment of the *hadji* (Muslim traveller) and the *fustan-ella* was its diminutive form, more suited for ranging in scrub covered hill country. The white garb was liked for its camouflage qualities in snow-covered hills. Forty yards of material make the many layers of the Greek *fustanella*.

FUTORK (Scandinavian term)
A made-up word, using the first six signs of the Runic system (like *alphabet*, the first two Greek letters, give for us). The phonetic signs show the same order in Northern runes, Old German, or Gothic. Names derive from trees or other natural objects used as symbols. The word *Futork* comes from the Maeshow inscriptions, found in 1861. The dance form is similar to that of the Roman *augur* or *harospex*. The circle is marked, like a compass, with 8 or 16 or 32 signs, similar to the Trigrams of Fsu-hsi. The mystical dance served to convey some basic principles in relation. The *rune* becomes *rouen* or *round*, the circle. The Norse *Futork* has sixteen basic rune signs. The Greek mode was *boustrephedon*; the Jewish was similar; the Egyptian hieroglyphs were set round the *Shen*; or at places in a square. The Roman capitals were later "born of the square" (cp. Trajan's column letters).
[See *Ogham*]

G

GABALIS, Comte de, ou Entretien sur les Sciences Secretes (Paris 17th C.)
French romance dated 1670, which was written by Abbé de Villars (1640 - 1675). This work is important as a survey of the "creatures of the elements" first made public by some of the Alchemists. They became favoured characters in many of the Romantic Ballets, a century and a half later. Though it is asserted, by some theological critics, that the book "ridicules the Qabbalah", there is little internal evidence to be found. The author presents a fictional Comte de Gabalis, who reveals to him, in five long conversations, certain features of mystical philosophy, mainly concerning these entities of the terrestrial elements: those of the air (Sylphs and Sylphides); of the waters (Undines); of the earth (Gnomes); and of the fire (Salamanders). The book was multiplied so rapidly that copies became favoured reading in French salons; while some reached London, where Pope (who refers to it in *The Rape of the Lock*), used it for his verse; when numerous romantic writers followed his example. The work, wrongly alleged to be based on *Chiave del Gabinetto* by Borri, was fraudently displaced by the back-dating of this later volume—which knows nothing of any Qabbalah. Apart from a very few references to these elementals (such as Benvenuto Cellini's tale in his *Memoirs*, of how his father showed him a salamander sporting in the fire), there is little public information. Those who seek to understand the source material of the Romantic Ballets of Paris should consult this volume; there was an English translation published in London in 1913.
[See *Zanoni*. Bulwer Lytton. 1842]

GABBERLUNZIE (Scots)
Refugees (15th; 16th century) from Romanist persecution. J. M. Robertson refers (*History of Freethought*) to a careful writer, Domenico Berti who recounts details in *Il Processo di Gelileo*. He mentions in particular the destruction of Il Accademia dei Lencei (unique in its time) and Il Accademia del Comento. As strangers they came into England, playing instruments in return for food and shelter. The "Gaberdine" was for them a kind of blue uniform; this style is carried on by the "Blue-coat School". Blue cloth (linsey) being a general garb of the poorer classes, carried on to (a) navy, and (b) police. The chants and dances of the Gabberlunzie men were often simple marching songs. Walter Scott shows some confusion with the King's Bedesmen, also attired in blue gaberdines.

GABÉ (Papua)
Dance festival of the Fuyughé people, held in honour of the dead. "Fathers of the Gabé" decide which villages to invite, and runners take ceremonial invitations. After months of preparation— growing special vegetables and fruits; gathering feathers for head-dresses; training dancers—guests assemble at the home village. Each village sends its Chief and about ten warriors (the "night dancers"), plus a retinue of relatives. Dances occupying two nights, with two days rest between, are held

on slightly sloping ground, about fifty yards long by twenty yards wide. Graves, and hurdles laden with fruit and vegetables, surround the clearing; while the whole village is enclosed by a ceremonial fence of scented wood. The first dance, *Amou Youmamé*,* or Women's Dance, begins at dusk and continues till dawn by the light of bamboo torches. Two nights later, the important male dances take place, culminating in an impressive *Royal Dance** of the Chiefs. First the "night dancers" perform their *Warriors' Dance*,* at dusk. In complete silence they give a violent representation of an attack on an enemy village, ending in a song of triumph. Silent again, they line the square, as women, armed with javelin, axe or sharp stick, whirl through a dance of destruction, smashing grave fences, trampling flowers and plants — all without a sound. This frenzied silence, prelude to the stately *Royal Dance*, may be broken only by the Chiefs, whose solo dances are accompanied by muffled drum beats. Each Chief, in towering head-dress and cloak of parakeet and bird-of-paradise feathers, swings at his elbows two skulls — those of former Chiefs not yet given ceremonial burial, and taking part in their last Gabé. The climactic *Royal Dance* is followed until dawn by *Olové** dances, performed by the "night dancers". Each dance, lasting eight or ten minutes, mimes the movements of animals or birds. Danced in a compact group, with co-ordinated movement, these are accompanied by drums and chanting. (Cp. *Naleng** dances of Malekula). At sunrise the solemn *Aï' olo*, or Dawn Dance, is performed, with a grave ritual chant and subdued drumming. This ends the *Gabé*.
[Cp. *Hevehe* (Papua); *Gol Kerma* (New Guinea); *Maki-Ru* and *Ramben* (Malekula)]

GADABAS, Dance of the (Mountains of Orissa, in Eastern India)
The Gadaba tribe, fond of music and dancing, have wedding ceremonies lasting several days. A thin, one-sided tambour is used to announce feasts and ceremonies. A dance by about ten girls is performed in the village square, round a brazier. Standing close together in a line, with arms linked behind, they move at the direction of their leader. Beginning slowly, and hesitantly, the tempo quickens, until the dancers hesitate, retreat and begin again. Gradually moving round the brazier, this is repeated several times. Wearing tunics woven in horizontal stripes of white, red and blue, the girls have many necklaces of red and yellow, while a single string of red beads binds their black hair. They wear huge ear-rings of copper wire, three strands threaded through the upper part of each ear and reaching to the shoulders;

and on their arms heavy silver bracelets, eleven or twelve between wrist and elbow. A silver rupee mounted on a ring, adorns each of the four fingers.

GAELIC FOLK DANCE (Scotland)
The *Dannsahd Gael*. Many traditional dances are now obsolete; though persistent research might enable qualified students to recover some of the forms; as probably certain melodies, still played for songs or chants, were used for dances. Some have continued or changed to modern names; but many of the old Gaelic names are descriptive:

Dannsahd An Dubh Luidnach (Youth's dance, clay daubed);
Dannsaha Na'am Boc (The Goat, or Buck's dance);
Dannsahd Cailleach (Old Woman's Dance);
Dannsahd Chlaidheimnh (Dance of Claymore-sword);
Dannsahd Na Cleoka (Roman Cloak Dance);
Dannsahd Na'n Coileach (School-Cock Fighting Dance);
Dannsahd Na'an Gurraigh (Lamenting Woman's Dance);
Dannsahd Bhiodaigh (Youth's Dirk Dance, finale of initiation);
Dannsahd a Chroigh Leith (Grey Bucks Dance — Winter);
*Dannsahd Cailleach an Dudain** (Old Woman's Dance with Doll);
Dannsahd Na Tunnaig (White Duck's Dance);
Dannsahd Croit an Drovigheann (Dance of Thorny Fort);
Dannsahd Fidhe na Goon (Weaving Dance for the Gown);
Dannsahd Chriosgaidh (The Golden Warrior Dance).

In addition there are larger group dances:

Dannsahd Bualidh mi thu's d'cheann (Ballet of Attack and Defence (Skye));
Kath-na'n-kuraidh (Contest of the Warriors);
Ruidheadh-na'n-coileach-dubha (Circle of the Black Cock's Dance — Reel).

GAGAKU (Japan)
Refers to the musicians and dancers of the Imperial Palace, Tokyo, usually as the group, but also as their traditional style. This group is said to be founded about 700 AD, but this date is doubtful, since it belonged to the shrine of Ise and of Nara. *Gagaku* is not a specific dance but means the entire spectacle, or ritual, or entertainment done for the Palace. The movement resembles *Noh Dance*:* it is slow and stately; and does not always carry a discernible theme. It has an analogy in the *Bedajas** or court dancers of Djokjokarta in Indonesia.

GAGOSA (Amerindian)

"False Face" Society of the Iroquois Indians.* Members wear wooden masks, black, red and white, usually with twisted features. The masks represent semi-human "faces" seen in dreams; spirits with the power both of curing disease and of causing it. The dreamers must make a mask in the likeness of the "face", which when worn by him, will give him power to heal, if also accompanied by the right songs and dances. In Spring and Autumn the *Gagósä* wearing their masks, visit each house in the community, shaking turtle rattles and uttering cries, to ward off sickness. (Nowadays Iroquois dwellings are scattered, and the "False Faces", instead of walking to them, make their rounds in open cars!). They participate in the Mid-Winter Festival in the village "long-house". Assisted by the *Gadjisa* ("Husk Faces"), they perform their healing ceremony in five stages. First a song to sooth hostile spirits, as they go to the house, or to the "long-house". Next come three dances—"Dance of the Common Faces", "Picking Out Partners", and General Round Dance. The first, performed inside the house after knocking for entry, is a heavy hopping dance, with turtle rattles and staves, during which hot ashes are rubbed on the patient's hair. The second dance is performed, opposite the patient, first by two "doorkeepers", then by two men and two women of the Society. The round dance is for all, the doorkeepers seeing that everyone joins in. At some part of the proceedings the leader makes a short speech. The fifth and last sequence consists of a noisy dance for all, which is heralded by the *Gadjisa*, who straddle a bench and beat it with turtle rattles or wooden paddles, at the same time singing loudly. All make animal noises, no doubt to invoke the animal spirts, and dislodge the sickness from the patient's body. The *Gadjisa* wear masks of braided corn husks (hence "husk faces") and have the names of plants, thus associating themselves with the vegetation spirits. They dance stiff-legged; and sometimes circle round their staves in a fast dance. In some festivities they join in the social dances.
[See *Iroquois Indians*]

GAJO (Arabic, Spanish)

A magical wand or twig, or a fresh green branch, used to draw traditional magical patterns in sand for divination; used to outline a place for dancing, as the *roza*.*

GALANTERIES (France)

Also as *Galanterien* (German). Dance tunes, added with the formal classical suite. The term probably derives from *kalendas* (similar "free dances"), and is now far distant from the English "gallant" (French *galant*), meaning ceremonially polite; or the nautical term "t'gallen'sails" or even the rodeo wide-brimmed hat, nominally the "ten-gallon". This calendar association follows upon developments of suite-form in music, in a roll of "Dances of Four Seasons" (from Roman times, as affirmed by their mosaic pavements), with a special dance for each three-month season. The conclusion of calendar thus gives this popular name to an "extra dance". Musical forms used might repeat any preceding air, with different tempo : *courant*,* *gigue** or *sarabande;** a *minuet** or *bourrée*.*

GALANTERIEN (German-French; 18th century)

Term used for a suite of dances, when the regular four were extended (from *allemande*,* *branle*,* *courant** and *gigue*.*) These extra dances ranged from *minuet** to *sarabande;** but there was always a Prelude and often a *bourrée*.*

GALANTY SHOW (W. Europe)

Old English dancing puppet show; so-called after the wandering *kalavants* from Syria and East (another term is "gallivanting", meaning for youths to wander "round the town" flirting and joking, in 19th century England). The Galanty Show was done with crude puppets, shown against a stretched cotton cloth, with oil lamps or candle-light; usually at Fair grounds like May Fair or Bartholomew Fair. The *Kalavants* perform today, wandering in Southern India, giving plays and dances, half folk-dance, half legendary topics, with local and topical jokes.

GALLEGADA (Galicia, Spain)

A couple dance, popular in Galicia. Dancing back to back, men and women move at first in slow rhythm, the music gradually quickening until, reaching its climax, the performers dance away to the furious clacking of their castanets. The dance may be accompanied by bagpipes (*gaitas*), the characteristic musical instrument of North-west Spain; or by guitars. Costumes are bright, with red or yellow full skirts, wide shawls and coloured head kerchief for the girls; mostly black and red for the men.

GALLIARD—1 (Fr. *Gaillarde;* It. *Gagliarda*)

A gay 16th century dance in 3/2 time. The music was often derived from that of the *Pavane** usually danced before it, the *Galliard* being lighter and quicker. An example is the *Earl of Salisbury's Galliard*, which was danced after a *Pavane* of the same name. (See *Nachtanz**.) Usually performed by a couple, it began with a salutation, partners facing. After circling the room hand-in-hand, the couple separated, to dance facing each other. The dance consisted of many variations of the *cinq-pas*, performed first by the dancers together, then separately as a florid solo. The lady charmed by light and airy grace in a number of variations or *mutanze*, while the man dazzled by his strength, virtuosity and agility. The *Galliard* was sometimes danced as a solo by a man, who exhibited his skill in executing numerous types of the *cinq-pas*. A characteristic of the *Galliard* was a jump called the *cadence*, which Arbeau describes as "a high jump followed by a posture", which when sufficiently high to allow the dancer to "agitate his feet in the air" was called a *capriole*. Many *Galliard* tunes exist, and instructions for performing the dance are given by Fabritio Caroso (*Il Ballerino* 1581); Thoinot Arbeau (*Orchésographie** 1588); and Cesare Negri (*Nuovi Inventioni di Balli* 1604). A version which came from Rome was called the *Romanesca*. The Italian *Gagliarda La Tamburina* contained six figures, while in the *Gaillarde à la Lyonnaise* the man left his partner, who danced alone for a short time, then chose another partner. When they had danced together she retired, leaving him to choose another lady, and so on. A lively version was the *Frog Galliard*, danced at a quick pace, with hops replaced by springing steps from foot to foot. The *Galliard* was popular at the Elizabethan Court, and developed into the *Volta*,* with its much criticised high jump.

GALLIARD—2 (Italy, France, Spain)
Was, for a century or so, a highly popular "students' dance", which varied in form and name. Known as "the Merry Galliard", it was performed usually in two phases of twelve bars each, using 3/2, 3/8, or 3/4 time; or sometimes 2/4 common time, in fact, according to the memory of the musicians available, The phrase went "For every Pavana, we do a Galliard", meaning that the slow and grave processional-dance of the seniors was to some extent parodied (as certainly were the verses) by the students. The dance was called *Romanesca*; or, by the duffers, the *Cinque-pas* (Shakespeare has *sinky-pace*), because that was all they could recall. In Scotland, the name of the dance, taken there by Spaniards and French, was corrupted into *kailyard* (as a cemetery or funeral dance).

GALLICENAE (French—Bretagne, 5th-century)
Was the dancing group of the Nine Priestesses of the Gallic oracle; they seem to be partly Grecian in tradition (like the Nine Muses) and partly from an older, less traceable derivation. In Brittany, or on the coast islands, were the *Nine Khorrigans* or *Khulikans*, who also were religious ritual dancers; they were also sibyls in the ritual, or in secular mode, "tellers of fortunes" for the curious.

GALLIMAUFREY (English, Mediaeval, from French)
Meant, finally, a medley or confusion of—foods, or dancers, or of word meanings, in talk of players. Seems to have arisen from the final "dance of the fair", after the "packing-up" was completed; when the odds and ends of viands of all kinds were sold off cheap, to be eaten by the artisans who had set stalls etc. for merchants (who probably paid, as a general tip). The French term *galimafree* alludes to "scraps of the larder", and the dancing was doubtless as rough and ready. Political ballads that carried dance tunes (like *Greensleeves*, and *Jo Anderson*, or *Pudding-Pies*) were favourites at this period of the Reformation.

GALUNGGAN (Bali, Indonesia)
New Year Festival of the Balinese year of 210 days. Lasting ten days from Galunggan Day to Kunninggan Day, it is the time when ancestral spirits revisit their homes, where elaborately arranged offerings of fruit, flowers and rice cakes are made to them, and to the gods at the temples. On roads and at house gates stand tall, bamboo poles (*penyor*), decorated with flowers and woven coconut leaves, with dangling traditional figures, cut out by women from young palm leaves. With feasting and dancing this gayest time of the year is celebrated. Throughout the period, *Barongs** cavort about the roads and paths, their accompanying musicians preceding or following them. A shaggy beast, with long hair and harness of red and gold leather-work ornamented with small mirrors and frangipani flowers, the *Barong* as a symbol of beneficence, is animated by two dancers inside the framework. Celebrations vary in different parts of the Island. Plays may be staged; the *Kris* trance dance is given by young men; or the stately *Baris;** a mock battle with long spears, the dancers (older men) dressed in black and white cloth chequered in magical patterns.

GAMBOR (Malaya)
A dance belonging formerly to female puberty initiation ritual, by way of invocation of *Hantu Gambor* (Spirit of Gambor Play), is danced solely by young girls. They are attired in yellow sarong, coat and drapery, with a yellow (royal) sash, elaborate head-dress, crescent-shaped pendants (*dokoh*), over the breast; and a fan. The essential "property" is the "Pleasure Garden" (*taman bunga*), in which the Spirit is to be caught; it is a large water-jar (or similar vessel) with many long sprays of real (or more often artificial) flowers, fruits and birds. The inevitable brass tray has sacrificial rice and incense. The girl to be initiated lies down, covered with a plain sheet; music starts very softly, incense is burned; and invocation is chanted by a woman

who taps a tambour. Presently, the ceremonial evokes its effect; the girl rises, the "spirit of Gambor" descends and moves her into her dance. After a period that varies considerably, from three or four minutes to a whole hour, the Spirit is exorcised, back to his "seventh heaven", and the ritual is over. The chants used, before and after, are from poems belonging to the *Panji* cycle, with many old Javanese terms.

GAMELAN

Javanese orchestra, used for dancing. The most developed and complete form of Javanese music, is of very high character, especially when its basic principles are understood. Percussion instruments dominate, mostly as gongs; some hang vertically; some, more like kettles, rest on cords across a wooden frame (*bonangs*). Other percussion instruments are *aron* and *gambang*, having metal or wooden sound staffs; and the *gender*, with metal keys resting on cords, under which horizontal sections are placed vertical pieces of large bamboo as tube resonators. Instruments are played with hammers of various types (*taboeh*). Flutes are of bamboo and metal; a kind of zither; and the latest (Arabic) item, a *rebab*, a two-stringed violin played often by the conductor, who thus leads the melody. The orchestra may number ten to fifty players; to hear it on a warm evening at Soerabaya, played on the *aloon-aloon* (public square before the palace), is an artistic treat. Music follows the five-note or seven-note systems; none is written down; and all is learned, rehearsed and composed solely by ear, and long experience. The seven-tone scale is *pelog;* and the five-tone scale is *salendro;* the tone intervals are not European, not arithmetical. Indonesian music is not an individual art; this music grows, it is not designed, even from the primitive form of pipe and drum. *Gong* is a Malayan (Polynesian) word and form.

GANDY DANCER (USA)

Proletarian term for combined rhythmic movements of a gang of workmen, necessary to perform some heavy job without mechanical appliances William Edge[1] describes the method as applied to laying or straightening rail tracks. Ten or twelve Negroes would stand with crowbars; the foreman was fifty feet away; and at his signal, they would pull together. Often they sang snatches of hobo* songs "faintly similar to those of a college cheer leader". He compares them with sailors' chanties. This job was "shinin' de rails an' gettin' out der kinks"—and as each slight fault in the rails is different, it remains a manual task; even with use of cramps. Later this term, or a similar one—"sky-

dancin'" was used for steel construction men; for which they had a familiar hobo song:

> "Eat your hay, work all day,
> You'll get pie—in the sky—
> When you die-ee-e!"

Modern "steel men" disdain "dancing on girders". They like to be called (and paid) as "spider-men". [1] *The Main Stem*. William Edge. New York. 1927.

GANESHA DANCES (India)

During the Ganesha festival, in Bombay district especially, there are endless processional dances through city and village. Ganesh or Ganesha is the "Elephant God" (similar to Atlas in Greek mythos), whose strength gives aid in trouble, and brings fortune. He was known to British soldiers—*pace* Kipling—as Gunputty (Ganpati). Every Mahratta family contrives an image, shown during the three days celebration. Singing, and beating small drums, the devotees march and dance, eventually (on the third day) to the seashore, where they cast in the sacred image, to end the festival. The meaning is: they know the image is but an image; they destroy physical form to retain the memory, in the greater reality of the mind. "The god has come", they say, "now the god is gone!"

GANGAR (Norway)

A sedate, aristocratic couple dance from the districts of Telemark and Setesdal. It belongs to those dances (such as the *Springar,** *Halling,** *Pols*, and *Vosserull*) influenced by Polish styles and rhythms brought into Norway by mercenary soldiers. These dances supplanted the old type of dance-ballad formerly popular in the Scandinavian countries until the 16th or 17th centuries, and still to be found in the Faroe Islands. (See *Dansuringar**). The women's costumes in Setesdal region feature a short skirt, under which is worn a longer white petticoat with black ribbon round the hem. In Telemark wool embroidery brightens the costumes, one of the most striking being black embroidery on white cloth. A scarlet bodice or very short jacket sometimes contrasts vividly with a black skirt.

GARA YAKUMA (Ceylon)

Ritual of exorcism of the Gara demons requiring performance of twelve rituals (*dolaha pelapaliya*) in honour of the twelve entities. The gods invite these demons to clean the *magul maduva* (great hall). There is a great deal of dramatic dancing; by exorcists wearing costumes and masks. Six or twelve dancers begin at *Yagapala;* a square enclosure open on one side. They are attired in white, with halves of coconuts to suggest femininity, under their jackets; they are the *Giri* goddesses;

whose wedding festivities are celebrated in mime. Many episodes follow, ending with a distribution of paddy—with sowing and reaping done in mime. The *Gara Yakuma* is sometimes performed as part of a much longer series in the *Kolam** religious rituals, in which the *Yaka* or *Yaksha* demons, and the *Gara* demons, appear frequently. The whole system belongs to a system of Natural Health Service—confusing at first to the stranger; but logical enough (when the real nature of the *mana** energy is studied and fully understood) from the practical experience of the priest-magicians.

GARCON (French) or GWASAN (Welsh) : A youth Both from Cymric basis; a page, a waiting man (as, for example *Ysgar* and *Ysgario*, to separate or to cut food shares; to spread the table). Attendance was formally developed, at notable feasts, to a marked walk or dance movement (often with chants), to *Ysgariad* (waiting etc.) with *son* (beat of the tambour) then used to mark time; *ysgar-son*, the ceremonial service of the dining hall. Analogies are numerous; as in the "Entrance of the Boar's Head" (with carol), while a faint reminder continues in commercial dining-rooms, when the waiter "calls" to the servers, in brief professional patois, the precise dishes ordered, which call is repeated to avoid error; with the refrain "Comin' up, Comin' up!"

GARS DE LOCMINÊ (Brittany)
A round dance, in lively 2/4 time, still performed in the Vannetais and Haute-Bretagne. Having clearly marked rhythm, it is danced with firm steps but without stiffness, and was doubtless connected with a process in the treatment of flax and hemp, after which there would be dancing. Although the accompanying song refers to "The Lads of Locminé, who have *de la maillette dessous luers souliers*" (large, square-headed nails under their shoes), which suggests a heavy tread, some steps are on tip-toe, and the jumps, although sharply stressed, are not "weighty". There are several versions; for men only or for couples, in a circle, facing inwards and revolving clockwise. Dancers hold hands, or little fingers, and the arms swing in rhythm with the body movements. Steps include *le pas latéral*, found in other Breton dances; *le pas sur place* in which, the weight of the body being on the right leg, the body is raised four times without leaving the ground, the pointed left foot grazing the ground each time; and *l'appel du pied*, performed by men only, in which one foot sharply strikes the ground, the other being briskly thrust back, almost touching the buttocks. These *appels du pied*, performed in absolute unison, mark the strong beat of the dance, and give the characteristic rhythm of many Breton dances.

GATHA (Zend-Iranian)
Ancient ritual dance with chants, used in the religion of Zoroaster, the earliest known in Persia; having influence on and with the early Brahmin rituals (their form is *Katha*). Most of the remaining forms suggest sacrificial modes; thence came into Europe and into Buddhism, the idea of *Kata-tharsis;* and the *sangha-katha* (or wheel of *kata*, the *ruena* or round). Essentially the ritual form follows primitive movement : the gatherings of the sacrifice, the processional approach to altar, the sacrifice, the thanksgiving and the return. The Zoroastrian priest, as regent of fire, was the *hotar;* this rite has endured to our own day, much changed in detail, as *iota* or *jota;* as its mythos has lived on, in India as the Katha. A perverted form developed, more openly than before, into a rite indicated by the reversed name—from *ga-tha* to *tha-ga* or *thugee*—a system of plunder excused by the "sacrifice to Bhowanee". In Biblical legend, we recall the phrase "Tell it not in Gathas, nor (show it) in the streets, by Askalon", thus prohibiting certain shows by name, not by some obscure places (Aschelon is probably a processional display). The mediaeval "Sainta Katherina Wheel" is traditionally linked with fires; and as the Zend used fire as a symbol in worship, they carried torches and moved in the sacrificial circle. There is an Irish version : *Callaieach, (The Old Woman, Queen of Winter)* with similar meaning.

GATO, EL (Argentine)
"The Cat". A pair dance in rapid 3/4 time, known also in Chile, Peru, and Paraguay. This flirtatious dance is performed by two couples, either in the *kururu* style (accompanied by a song, and in smooth rhythm), or in the *siriri* style, which is more lively, with vigorous *zapateado.** During a pause in the dance, partners recite verses to each other. The *Gato con Relaciones* is "with stories", which may tell of love, politics, or life in general. In rhythm and choreography, *El Escondido** is similar to the *Gato*, but in 6/8 time.

GAVILAN, LA DANZA DEL (Mexico)
The name given by the Huasteca Indians of San Luis Potosi, in the Sierra Madre, to the *Juego de los Voladores** ("The Flying Game"). *Gavilan* means "sparrowhawk", and refers to the birds whom the four dancers represent. They wear a feather jacket and a crest of feathers on their head, while their Captain has red shirt and trousers, with a white diagonal band. All are barefoot. A special ceremony attends the felling of a suitably tall tree each year, prayers being offered to the god of trees,

together with explanations of the ceremonial purpose for which the tree is to be used. A libation of brandy is spilled before the first blow is struck. When the tree is felled, it is carried (it must not touch the ground), to the village, and set up in the plaza after a sacrifice of a live hen placed in the hole into which the tree is thrust, "to give the tree added strength". The four "Flyers" and their musicians must fast before the performance. The pole, with a liana wound round for foothold, may be 70 or 80 feet high. At the top is a small, revolving platform, two feet across, to which four ropes are attached. Having climbed to the top, the four "flyers" sit on the frame below the platform, while their Captain, the musician, dances on the tiny stage above, playing his flute and drum. When he has finished, the four men tie the ropes round their waists, and launch themselves into the air, flying upside down, spirally round the pole, with the rope between their closed legs. There should be thirteen revolutions. When nearing the ground they right themselves, and land on their feet. Meanwhile, the musician waits on the platform until the flyers approach the ground, then swiftly slides down one of the ropes, continuing to play his instruments, and arrives at the same time as his companions.
[See *Voladores, Juego de los; Tocotines, Los; Otomi Voladores*]

GAVOT OR GAVOTTE—1
Said to be a "French peasant dance", known about 14th - 15th century in Provence. Derives from South Indian religious dance used by Bhagavat sect, with boisterous singing; and still continues in India in this style. In time, in a foreign land, the first half of the term became detached; and *Gavat* remained, as a circle dance of rejoicing, used by the *Albe-Genses* (The White People). They adopted also the cotton robes, together with a knowledge of papermaking from the same (used) material, and many oriental symbols, which were used as paper marks.

GAVOT, GAVOTTE—2
A brisk dance in 2/4 time, popular in 17th and 18th century France until the Revolution in 1789. In England, it was in vogue at the end of the 17th century, and beginning of the 18th. Said to belong to the people of the Pays de Gap, in Dauphiné, who were called Gavots, the dance choreographically developed from the old duple *Branles.** Arbeau's *Orchésographie** (1588) gives a set of Branles to which "they gave this name of Gavotte". From a country round dance, the Gavotte became popular at fancy dress balls, and gradually became more stately and dignified as it entered the repertoire of Court dances. Eventually it closely resembled the

*Minuet** in style, but the feet were lifted off the floor instead of walked or shuffled and it was in duple instead of triple time. In its gay country version the *Gavot* was a kissing-dance, which no doubt helped its later popularity in the ballroom, but the bestowal of a kiss was presently changed to giving the lady a bouquet, or crowning her with a chaplet. Popular in the reign of Louis XIV (1643 - 1715), when Lully composed many examples, the ballroom custom grew of following every *Minuet* with a *Gavot*, but in its early stage as a form of *Branle*, it seems to have preceded the *Minuet*. At the time of Louis XIV *Gavottes* were a collection of round dances known as *Branles*, not one single dance. In the Court Balls rigid etiquette was observed. King and Queen led the Court in the opening processional *Branle*; then followed the *Gavottes* in the same order of couples, who afterwards bowed to the King and Queen and to each other and retired to their places, when the *Minuets* began. (Cp. *Fackeltanz**). In France after the Revolution an attempt was made to revive some of the former fashionable dances, but they no longer suited the changed times and, with others, the *Gavotte* died out. In England, the 17th century *Cebell** was a type of *Gavotte* but in quicker time.

GEISHA (Japan)
The trained professional singing-dancing girl of the country. Her junior apprentice is called *Miko* or *Maiko.** They learn traditional (and modern) poems which they recite; or they will sing to the *samisen;* or they will offer discreet and charming dances, performing on call at restaurants or hotel; or sometimes at special gatherings in private houses (usually for a male audience only). More recently, commercial companies have offered *geisha* performances for the *Odori** style of dance (as at Tokyo, Mintogawa Theatre; or Shochiku Gekijo Theatre). In Osaka, at Takarazuka (near Amusement Park), there is a large theatre with three stages, where "Girls Opera" is performed. Included with famous Geisha Dances is the Cherry Dance at Kaburenjo (Gion), April 1st to 30th, and the *Kamogawa Odori*, similar to the Cherry Dance, at Pontocho (May 1st to 20th, annual season). Geisha girls do not appear in the *Noh* Dance-mime plays; nor in sacred ritual dances. These girls were formerly recruited by Tokyo entrepreneurs, trained in dance, in etiquette and dress. Many of them joined the famous Yoshiwara—formerly the great municipally owned "House of Red Lights" in Tokyo (now de-nationalised, but many smaller establishments replace it in other civic centres). Many small towns can supply a company of Geisha girls, who are skilful in entertaining their hotel guests with song and dance. Many of these

girls proved to be accomplished students of literature; to know many plays and much music; and even themselves to write good verse for their own songs. They have probably helped as much to refine the somewhat boorish "all-male" *samurai* culture of mediaeval Japan, as did the *hetairae* in ancient Athens.

GEISSLER LIEDER (German; 13th - 14th cent.)
Rhythmic dance-singing by "Flagellants" in processional movement. For some, the refrain moved at double tempo, in which the groups paused for whip-swinging or a fragment of mime-drama, before moving on. This practice was in parallel to the town "miracle plays", which at *festa* occupied Spanish towns with costumed players and their painted wooden images. In Italy the *laudi spirituali* were similar; though even at Napoli the misery aspect was not so predominant. The tone and stress is exactly opposite to the *trionfo;* but the Italian *laudisti* were semi-professional in their later period. From their practice sprang an impulse to dramatic form in Oratorio (as at centre of Fillipo Neri in Florence, from 1560) and so gave direction towards opera with dance or *balleti.*

GELOSIA, LA (Italy)
Literally "the jealous woman". A dance for four couples. Standing in a line, the first man dances in turn with the lady of the other couples. Between these progressions all eight dance in quick triple time, the men performing turns and jumps, while the ladies parade. *La Gelosia* has distant relations with the fifteenth century Italian court dance, the *Ballo,** in one version of which one lady might dance with her own partner and four other men, and, in fact, one of the *Balli* devised by Domenichino Piacenza was called *La Gelosia.* It was a court dance for three men and three ladies, in 6/4 time, with three figures.

GEOMETRY IN DANCE
Appears from several distinct sources, usually governing its basic pattern. Most common is the Round Dance : in modes (a) Natural, (b) Social, and (c) Ritual. Architectural design may impose dance form (as in numerous round wooden churches of Northern Europe). Many Hindu temples were constructed on a mutual basis of symbol-ritual and its liturgical reflex completed in dance movement. Thus Jewish temple dance was based on double-hexagon (six point star, Magen David) from the Elohim (six foci of power with seventh in centre). Theatre dance forms are formed or restricted by stage dimensions—by size of company; by type of performance; by style of dance selected. Geometry is closely linked with dance notation. Geometry as a pattern basis is less seen in folk dance; and in much Modern Dance, is rarely found, though used in some training schemes.

GEORGIAN FOLK DANCE (Georgia, USSR)
Is chiefly masculine, developed on simple forms in virile movement. *Partsa* is a round dance (20/30 men) changing from one circle to two rings. *Kartuli* is a pair dance, on the basis of courtship, elegant and seemly. *Dhzeirani* (antelope) has been shown with eight men and one girl; she flirts with all but chooses none. Among wedding dances the *Ossetian Semed* is attractive. *Khessur* is a pair dance for two men in a sword duel. *Khorumi* (circle of men), is a battle dance, while *Mekhed-ruli* imitate horse riders slicing down enemies with cossack sabres. A dance from Tbilisi affirms Persian intrusion, in its name (which can be heard in Urdu) as *Khabadar*—"Take Care !" or "Look out" as a street warning. A Russian flavour is in *Karascho-kheli* (which could be given as "Good! Kelly !") —it was actually in football "good pupil."

GERANOS (Ancient Greece)
So-called "Crane Dance". Supposed to have been performed in the Island of Delos until the time of Plutarch (first century AD), and to have been danced by Theseus when he returned to that Island from Crete. Consisting of gentle movements of the body and many turnings and windings, it was said to describe the twisting of the Cretan Labyrinth, where Theseus sought the Minotaur. The leader of the dance was called *geranoulkos,* and the form was presumably the simple chain which characterised Greek religious dances round the altar. More properly, *Geranos* was 'eranos, dance of the 'eranoi or "social" or group dance; symbolic of the "world-dance", and thus attributed to the dance of the Labyrinthos, or a "winding dance". This name is wrongly translated as "crane dance", or even the "dance of the old men". It belongs, in ancient Athens, to the numerous clubs, called *Eranoi,* which had a fluctuating membership, "in and out". We can discover several parallel terms, especially in the Sanskrit term *sangsara,* "the world dance", from which Buddhists wished to escape. This same term endured into Mediaeval Chivalry, in the term "Knights errante", or "wandering knechts", who were at the same time, members of the group, the club, the society of the true knights; but also went wandering through the world "seeking the perfect maiden", who in Greece was Athene Parthenos. One of the principal dance forms used was the lyrical *hyporchema.** A description of a dance engraved on Achille's shield, in Homer's *Iliad* (Book XVIII) may have been the

Geranos. A. T. Murray's poetic prose translation[1] describes how Hephaestus (Vulcan) "cunningly wrought a dancing-floor, like unto that which in wide Cnossus Daedalus fashioned of old for fair-tressed Ariadne. There were youths dancing and maidens . . . holding their hands upon the wrists one of the other . . . Now would they run round with cunning feet exceeding lightly . . . and now again would they run in rows towards each other. And a great company stood around the lovely dance, taking joy therein : and two tumblers whirled up and down through the midst of them, as leaders in the dance".   [See *Troy Game*]
[1] *The Iliad*. Bk. XVIII. Trans. A. T. Murray, Ph.D. 1925 (p.333. 590 et seq).

GHARBA DANCE (Gujerat, West India)
Is the famous traditional Pot Dance done by village women, dancing in a circle to their own chorus singing. Mostly the songs pertain to *Krishna Lila* celebrations; they have been called *Rasa Lila* or *Rasoda Lila*; and they carry verses which describe the months of the year (something like the famous Kalidasa poem *Rituhara*, or *Song of Seasons*). The great brass pot, carried full of water or milk, is said to typify the cosmic *Hiranyagarbha* or the Golden Womb of Creation. Mostly these songs are slow and the dance even stately, with regular pulsating rhythms, with subtle variations fascinating to watch. They begin with the month *Kartika*; they solemnize periods of love and times of separation.

GHATU (Assam, India)
Generic term for the popular boy dancer, as in the Sylhet Valley (a well-known tea district), who is hired professionally as a home entertainer. He visits any home on request (like the Japanese *geisha*) to sing and play and dance for the company.

GHAWAZEE or GHAZEEYEH (Egypt, Modern Arabian)
The professional public dancing girls. Lane describes them as a distinct tribe; then to be abolished (as were the *devadasis* of India) in 1834; but the prohibition extended only to the darker side and dancing in public; dancing in house or café etc. continues. When Lane wrote, the *Ghawazee* performed in the street, unveiled, usually in pairs, with two male musicians. The male is a *Ghazee*. In Iran the song developed into the famous *Ghazul* or love lyric. The musical instruments are : the *kemengeh* (or *kemanchi*) or *rebab*; and the *tar* (tambour) or again, the *darabukkeh* (drum) with *Zummarah* or *zemr*. The *tar* is usually played by a woman. The dance itself lacks real grace; it is merely undulation, with the characteristic hip motion, beloved of American theatre managers as being the "real Oriental dance". These dancers call their name as *Baramikeh*. Lane says that the Spanish *fandango** was, in his time, very similar in style. The *Ghawazeeyeh* attended all great camps, festivals and fairs; but in towns they live in a distinct quarter. The more accomplished girls equal the *'Alawim*; they use profuse make-up. As Muslims, many go to Mekka with pilgrims. There are a few male performers of similar dances, known as *Khawals;** they dress like women and parody their dances, using castanets. Another class of male dancers in Cairo are known by the title of *Gink* (Turkish term), who are not Muslims, but Turks or Armenians etc. The term *Almeh* is by no means identical with *Ghawazee*.

GHEDRA or GUEDRA (Morocco)
A solo dance of ancient origin, performed only at Goulimine on the edge of the Sahara, and (outside Morocco), in Mauretania. A dance of seduction, its chief characteristic is that it is danced entirely on the knees, with closed eyes, the dancer performing subtle movements of head, shoulders, arms, hands and fingers. In former days of nomad tents, with no room to dance upright, this ritualistic Moorish strip-tease was developed by the most expressive possible use of the upper part of the body. Then probably performed by one woman before her lord, dancers now are courtesans, trained from childhood as a dance-troupe by a former dancer, who accompanies them to the dancing-place when the *Ghedra* is performed. Danced indoors, at night, it is accompanied by one instrument, the *ghedra* (from which the dance takes its name)—a bowl drum covered with sheepskin and beaten with the fingers. Besides the *ghedra* player, about twelve other Arabs (in blue robes and turbans) sit in a circle, chanting and matching the rhythm with hand-clapping. For about ten minutes each, the girls dance, one by one, in the circle, the next taking up the rhythm as each one retires. At first completely enveloped in a long blue hooded robe, soon the hood falls back, when the mistress takes the cloak, leaving the dancer in blue skirt and full-sleeved white blouse. Wearing necklaces and bracelets, her hair is dressed in many tiny plaits threaded with small silver ornaments, one plait wound round the head like a coronet. Hairdressing takes six hours preparation by an expert (*mallama*), and the ornaments are sewn on to the hair with a large needle and wool. Keeping her kneeling posture, with closed eyes, the dancer throws off her blouse as the dance becomes wilder, leaving the torso naked except for necklaces and tossing plaits. Having no special

climax, a dancer withdraws as she becomes exhausted, but during several hours the tempo becomes faster and the dancers fall into a trance or ecstasy. Though intense, movements are jerky, each one being built up of short, rapid jerks; tiny staccato movements of fingers, head, torso, arms. Although the basis of each dance is the same, there is a subtle variation in rhythm and movement as each girl performs.
[See *Morocco, Dances of*. Cp. *Mokhibo* (Basutoland —Kneeling Dance); and *Rishi* (Arabia)]

GHILLIE CALLUM (Scotland)
Sword dance, done solo over two swords laid on the ground. The music moves to a slow Strathspey, or "Scottish Measure", usually in 4/4 time, and the foundation step most used is the *pas de Basque*. The garbled traditions concerning *Ghillie Callum* (even the name is variously spelled) take us back to AD 1054, where a Celtic prince is named as Calum-a-Chinn Mohr, who fought Macbeth at Dunsinane in that year. The words of the song, sometimes hummed with the dance-tune, reveal merely a silly parody of a real ballad that is lost.

GHOSTIE'S DANCE (Scots)
Has many styles if not forms : *Sciomachia* Festival in Rome derived from the annual "Ghost's Return" (September) in the Burial Ground Mourning Dance. 17th century verses :

"From Ghosties and dark ghoulies
and glaring eyed rowlies
From long leggetty beasties
an' a' rum things that goes bump
I' the nicht
May the Guid Lord
Deliver us all!"
(Litany from Inverness)

GIANTS AND DWARFS IN DANCE
Belonged respectively to Summer season, and Winter season (as Shadows). The tradition of the *kobold* or *gnome* (so-called "cobbler's dance") shows the male dancer squatting to make himself as short as possible; while the opposing tradition (at six months distance in the year for its true period), shows tall dancers, often leaping but usually helped by stilts. Neither form has any direct reference to "making the crops grow" by jumping, just as nobody wishes to "stop the crops" by non-jumping and by crouching. The real mythic reference is to the length of the day. These dances formerly had association with the *eclogue* or clog dance of calendrical counting.

GIENYS (Isle of Man, England)
A Manx dance performed on Twelfth Day (January 6th), when the *Mainstyr*, or Master of Ceremonies

appointed to every young man his *tegad* (valentine or sweetheart), for the following month or year, according to whether they "hit it off" well together. The rite seems to be the remainder of an ancient practice in which the local priest took on himself to pair off the couples of his district, according to his own notions. On this day, was the ceremony of Lackets or Plackets. Youths of both sexes were invited; after supper they joined in dancing, in the process of which the couples were "tried out a wee bit". If they did not get on well as dance partners, it was assumed they would probably not do so well as sweethearts. In an interval between dances was introduced the *Lavare Vane*, a hobby-horse carried by a mimer concealed under a white sheet; the jaws were hinged so that they could snap. The dances were jigs and reels; with music from fiddles.

GIGAKU (Japan)
"Skill-music". Buddhist temple dance coming to Japan in 7th century, via India, South China and Korea. First performed in Japan in 612 AD by Mimashi, a Korean, *Gigaku* was danced to the accompaniment of flute, hand-drum and cymbals, the dancer wearing a mask covering the whole head. From these masks derived the later elaborate make-up of *Kabuki** and puppet theatre. The Buddhist Prince Regent, Shotoku, founded a school for *Gigaku* with Mimashi as principal, and proficient dancers were sent to temples throughout Japan. There seem to have been ten varieties of the dance. Although not now a living dance-form, *Gigaku* influenced later styles, and one type remains in the *shishi-mai*, or lion dance, now known as *shakkyo-mono*. This Buddhist guardian animal, now secularised, appears in many *Noh** plays and *Kabuki* dances, always associated with peony flowers which sooth him (symbolising repose), and butterflies which irritate him (symbolising anger). *Gigaku* was followed during the T'ang dynasty (618 - 907 AD) by the ceremonial *Bugaku.**

GIGOLO (French *argot*)
Dancing partner; from *gigoter*, to dance; also *giglot*, frivolous girl (who giggles) or *giglet*, a wanton. Associated with *gille*, a clown (music-hall or circus), and *gillie*, a servant (origin of Sante Giles). *Mère Gigogne* (figurative term) a woman in charge of a troupe of youngsters; broadly equivalent to Dame Trot, as village schoolmistress. Thus a partner in the Jig; but not always a dancing jig.

GIGUE (West European)
Or *Jig,** *Giga*, *Gigua*, *Geige* and many other variants. These dances, in triple time, are often referred solely to the Irish, but they had a wider

usage, traceable in 13th century customs. The name *gig, giga, gigue,* or *geige* became appropriated to the stringed instrument used for accompaniment — a fiddle, the player of which (in 15th century) was called the *gigator.* The dance-style was similar to the *Galliard** (known in England as *Cinque-pace,* the Five Step, or "Sinky-pace". In his play, *Much Ado About Nothing,* Shakespeare refers to "Wooing, wedding, and repenting, as a Scotch jig and full as fantastical; the wedding mannerly — modes as a measure, full of state and ancientry; and then comes repentance, and with his bad legs falls into the *cinque-pace,* faster and faster till he sinks into his grave". (*Act II, Scene1.*) That the *Jig* was known in Ireland in mid-16th century is evidenced by a letter from Sir Henry Sydney to Queen Elizabeth I, in which he refers to the dancing of Irish *Jigs* by the Anglo-Irish ladies of Galway.

GILGAMISH (Assyrian - Babylonian; 4000 BC)
Is the oldest extant creation myth, 1500 years older than the Iliad of Homer. Gilgamish (or Khilkamisch, formerly named as Izdu-Bara) is the hero of this Epic, known from fragments (now in B.M.) from legends originated at E-Rekh. Significantly the tale is enscribed on twelve regulation tablets; whence we see Ghilgamish as the "World Traveller". With his friend Ea Bani he kills Khum-baba of Elam; and then the "Bull Alu". Horns of this Bull were dedicated by Ghilgamish to Shamash the Sun God (an origin of the Boars Head Legend). But Gilgamish now seeks immortality visiting the palace of Sabitu in the Mountains of Sunset. With his great axe he cuts his path through dark forest after passing the first Gates. There is a great banquet with the ritual dances. Further legends follow (including that of the Flood) and the magical initiation into the secret of the 'food of the immortals' (also an Egyptian quest). Ghilgamish finds the secret food; but on his homeward journey is robbed by a serpent-demon. The god Nergal then brings up the spirit of Ea Bani, who tells his old friend of the horrors of dissolution. These ancient myths — which are projected statements of far greater facts than are contained — are related in triple terms of (a) god-names of symbol images, (b) Forms, diagrams, places, known as seats of the gods, and (c) the weapons, tools, implements proper to each of the god images as concentrating upon his usual function. "The god is the name within the form but what he does is his divine power, his being and his life". Ghilgamish is therefore one of the earliest culture heroes; he dances in ritual at each banquet; he makes the Great Journey, renders the great sacrifice and attains the Great Consummation. Some knowledge of these things came to Britain; possibly with the traders of

Carthage — who gave the name Tammuz to our river Thames?

GILGOLEM, GILGAL, GIL-GALILU (Hebrew, from Babylonian)
The Cosmic "Dance of Souls", symbol of the process of Birth, Death and Re-incarnation, repeated until wisdom is obtained. This idea, familiar in all the great Eastern religions, is conveyed within the hidden teachings of *Qabbalah,* in Europe. The Jewish story of *Die Golem* (placed in Prague) in the best known version is a lesser tale, of the tribal "blood avenger". The term *Gal-Ilu* (much later) became Galilee, the "Chapel of Waiting", constructed before the entrance of many mediaeval churches; there the applicants for baptism awaited their turn. In some places they passed the period with itinerant entertainers; thus probably came the term *glee* and *gleeman,* and *gala;* also the much later reference in theatre to the "gods" in the gallery. Another adjacent term is that of Golgotha;* rendered often as "Place of Skulls", but also meaning the Gal Gatha, or "play" (Indian : *Kal-katha).* At Gilgal in Palestine are the remains of a "Circle of Twelve Stones".

GILLATRYPES (Scotland)
Colloquial term for an alleged "Witches Dance", traditionally performed among the "lower classes" in Moray-shire. The accompanying ballad, which gave tempo and rhythm, was said to be "varry low".

GILLES (France)
A band of youths, players, dancers, singers, in mediaeval period; vaguely associated with system of Chevallerie. The name reached Scotland, so the boy who carries the implements essential to golf, is called a gillie; formerly he helped the gamekeeper. Possibly the term is the masculine complement to giselle; a parallel term for the feminine company. Probably from Julio (Yulio) the New Year Dancers (fem. Julia, Juno etc.). They carried a flower as symbol (gilly-flower) and had only small drinks (gill). Earlier still, the twin terms were Jacques and Jilly. The *San Gilles de Retz* were the Players of Retz. In England the term Giles marks many places (church etc.), where a Band of Players performed or resided. The Latin term Egidius is substituted to disguise it.

GINK (Egypt — Turkish/Arabic)
Described by Lane[1] as a class of male dancers, performing in Cairo, as "almost exactly similar to the *Khawals,** though distinguished by this different appellation". The term is Turkish — "and has a vulgar signification". These youths were, in his day

(round 1830) Jews, Armenians, Greeks and Turks. They danced chiefly as "female impersonators", or the reverse of the English "principal boy" in pantomime; but similar to such roles as Widow Twankey (*Aladdin*), played usually by a male comedian. Again Lane mentions Greek dancing boys, or "*gink*", elegant but effeminate, performing to the accompaniment of mandolines played by two of their countrymen; a crowd of admiring Turks surrounding them, dancing before a coffee-shop.
[1] *Modern Egyptians*. E. W. Lane. (1836).

GIOCOLINI (Italian)
12th - 14th century term; equivalent to the French and Norman *trouvère* and *troubadour*. Troupes were formed for acting dance-mimes or plays. Some of the later Commedia delle Arte troupes of players bore names from this term : as the *Giocosi*. The famous picture by Leonardo da Vinci, *La Gioconda*, was probably suggested from one of these players; perhaps as "Theyre Lady".

GIUSTINIANA (Italian. 16th cent.)
Generic term for song-dances used in Bergamasca festivities. They had words, arranged in three-part versions, with an easy street dance. Thomas Morley who had direct acquaintance, characterized them as "wanton and rude kinde of musicke" in his collection (1597) *Plaine and Easie Introduction to Practicall Musicke*. These Bergers are village actors of the "Shepherds" of the Lamb Play at XMesse.   [See *Bergamasca*]

GLAGOLITHIC RITUAL (Slavonic)
This corrupted term is met in references to early Slavonic music; or in later compositions, said to relate to the same rite; this is essentially an open-air or field celebration of mass, on a customary stone table. The original term is thus *kulak-o-lithik* or the "Peasants' stone", which was the centre of a rite accompanied by the usual solemn circle dances with processional chanting. The West European analogy is seen in the Field Preachers, centred at many a Gospel Oak (originally *OKE*), as by Wycliffe's "Poor Men"; or the later Wesleyan itinerant preachers; and the Protestant Field Preachers of the Netherlands.

GLAMOUR (Old English)
A magical term, in vogue among Irish and Welsh minstrels, signifying skill in a kind of group hypnosis. By Glamour, the magician could "cast his spell" (this spell or *spieling* being his impressive chant), and gradually persuade his attentive listeners that they actually saw what he described or "suggested". Modern medical hypnotism provides a parallel example; though doctors are not able to delude more than one person at a time, thus having no advantage on the priest, who can. Welsh stories (Mabinogion etc.) occasionally mention Glamour; and through it the Magician (Merlin or another) could suggest beautiful scences, fairy dance etc. An example is given in Goethe's *Faust;* while the famous "Indian Rope Trick" is effected thus.

GLOCSEN (Wales)
Dawns y Glocsen is "Clog Dance", now known as an old Welsh tune, formerly used for dancing. The *Dawnsio Haf* are Welsh May Day Dances.

GNOSIS (Hellenic)
Religious ritual symbolism, sometimes expressed in ritual dance and chant. A corruption of an earlier, fuller term, perhaps from Knossos in Crete, this term is related to Diagnosis, Prognosis, Agnosis, and so forth; and finally implies a real "knowledge-by-experience" in religion. Belonging to, or parallel with this doctrine, are such fragments of ritual as *The Hymn of Jesus*, the *Shir-al-Shirin*, and the legend of *Yusuf and Zuleikha*, which endured into the Christian, Hebrew, and Islamic systems respectively. The *dochema* appears in several modes; as a ritual (dance-mythos)· for the initiated; as a parable (more obscure in meaning, but realistic in presentation) for the people; but as a rare initiation for the advanced scholar, following upon his study of "twelve years in the desert", requiring him allegorically to "cross over the red flood of the Jordan". The term probably takes origin from the Sanskrit *agni* (fire, who is god of fire, a symbol meaning "intellectual mind") which produced also *agon* (as the name of a ritual) and other terms. Deriving from the great city of Alexandria, possibly there the scholars united Egyptian Isis (Great Mother) with this Fire of Mind, Agni.
For data see works by G. R. S. Mead (with bibliographies containing further references).
Hastings *Encyclopaedia of Religion and Ethics*. (Art. *Gnosis*, etc.).
Cheyne's *Encyclopaedia Biblica*. Art. *Gnosis*, etc.

GNOSTIC SACRED DANCE (Hellas)
Receives mention in several documents; while dancing postures are sometimes depicted on sacred gems (cornelian, intaglio) used as passports or secret signs. Notable is the *Shepherd of Hermas* (dated conservatively 130 - 150AD, but probably a century earlier), in which the symbolic dance is declared. Hennecke translates (in ninth simile) how Hermas visits the divine mount.[1] There he beholds twelve virgins, clad in white raiment, who receive him with affection. Some of them perform a simple carole* or round dance, others a straight-formed dance; and all of them sing. They symbolise twelve

powers that emanate from the hidden secret source. In Antioch, one Theodoretos, a Syrian churchman who lived about 393 - 457 AD, tells us of rejoicings of his colleagues in that city, when they celebrated the death of the Emperor Julian with festivals and banquets, in church and theatre. Further he relates about the Egyptian Gnostics, in his fulminations *On Hereticks*. He described the followers of Bishop Meletius and the Messalians (who accepted the Messe). "In Alexandria appeared Bishop Meletius; from his teaching rose the sect in Egypt. In accordance with their doctrine, they were so foolish as to wash their bodies every other day; to sing hymns to accompaniment of hand-clapping and dancing; and they rang suspended bells". All this was, at that time, ordinary Christian practice, except the bath. Theodoretus says of the Messalians : "But they did many other things in their madness. They began suddenly to dance; and urged themselves against demons while dancing (that is, on the sick men who were "possessed") and held their fingers as if they were arrows ("powers") to shoot at demons. This act indicates the usage of mesmeric energy for healing purposes, as was the custom of the Therapeutae (instructed in Syria). These healing methods were tried in many places among Christian communities; they ended (in England) with the "royal touch" for scrofula, as by Charles I.

[1] *Neutestementliche Apokryphen*. Ernst Hennecke (Tübingen. 1924).

Mithrai Ritual Dancer, a member of the cult of Rome. The Dance of Miles the Soldier. A gem ring in low relief, probably used as a passport of admission.   ROME

GOA (India, former Portuguese settlement)
Missionary Dance, devised to placate and to replace (if possible) older genuine dances. "Pretty dances", says Lily Grove (in *Dancing*) "were performed in Goa, about 1650, by pervert boys, who held garlands and danced round a pillar crowned by a huge flower in the shape of a tulip, from which became visible the figure of a maid with a child". This local church dance is clearly a revised version of the far older ritual of the *Vishnu lingham*, a venerated symbol rarely understood by invading missions. Yet we are told "the Jesuits were of opinion that such dances were useful in existing conditions", which was considerate of them; but we are not told to whom the dances were most useful.

GODALET DANTZA (Pyrenees)
A Basque dance of the Soule, performed by five men : — 1. *Flag-bearer*, carrying a small souletine flag; 2, the *Tcherrero*, carrying a stick with a horse's tail at the end; 3. "*Gattia*" ("the Cat"), holding a sort of hook on a spring, with which he catches at the head-gear of the spectators; 4. *La Cantinière*, dressed as a woman, carrying a small keg slung over the shoulder; and 5. the *Zalmatzaim*, or hobby-horse. A glass, half-filled with wine is placed in the centre of the dancing-space by the "koblari", a local character who accompanies all Basque festivals, reciting appropriate stanzas. The music is in lively 2/4 time. The dancers form a circle round the glass, then one by one, in the above order, while the others stand and watch, they approach close to the glass and perform a solo. The *Flag-bearer*, *Gattia and La Cantinière*, each dance round the tumbler, and over it, but not touching it. *Tcherrero* and the *Zalmatzaim*, while dancing round the glass, twist the right foot in a circular movement which just grazes the glass. Each dancer must approach the glass as near as possible, and with great skill, execute steps over and round it, without upsetting it. When each has performed his solo, they continue to dance in a circle, facing the glass.

GOG AND MAGOG (England—First Century BC)
Festival derived from those Greek missions who preceded Roman invasions into Britain in the south, and who installed the worship of Apollo in London and other cities. The basic festivals for Grecian Aphrodite were named severally as *Anagogia* (its name, known in Sicily, is from Paphos), and the *Ma-gogia* and *Gogia*. These terms equal *Boule* (council) in *metaboule*, *anaboule*, and *kataboule* now better known in relation to biology or metabolism. Pigeons were used as "white messengers", and, being released at a distance, they returned

Godalet Dantza. The Basque "Goblet Dance" with Hobby Horse Dancer.   PYRENEES, FRANCE

(*katagogia*) after the ritual nine days (months). Most probably the tradition of pigeons at "Sent Powels" church, which was built over a destroyed shrine of Apollo and Diana/Aphrodite, dates from this period, one or two centuries BC. In the ceremony, these were the wicker figures carried in procession; and wrongly described by Julius Caesar (whose Brittanic News Agency was inadequate), as containers of men, burned alive. To construct wicker baskets, strong enough, is technically not possible. The legend is a version of the Persephoneia, and her visit to Aides each year.

GOLGOTHA (Hebrew - Iranian)
Erroneously translated as "place of skulls". No such place has been located geographically; because any such "place" was in fact itinerant; a moving *theatrum* or a place of ritual display. The term derives from Assyrian *Gal* and *Gatha*—the Ritual of *Gil* (*Gamisha*) and, if anything, indicates the "Place of Skills", in acting-dancing, in yet another "Mystery". Another phrase : "Tell it not in Gath, nor publish it in the streets of Eskelon", refers to a similar prohibition of the older rituals. The *eskelon* become *echelon*, not *e'skullon*. In India, the Zoroastrian *Gatha* changes but slightly to become *Katha*—a story or legend, but then returns once more to Europe as the *Sainta-Katha-Rouene;* the "ring of the story-teller" (with lights). The principal Indian legend is performed in *Katha-Kali* style—or *Kali-Katha*, directly equivalent to *Gali-Gatha;* but in many suitable places. A similar origin of ritual drama accounts for the allied term (not a place, but a mythical ritual) or *Kali-varius*, and this term moved into Europe to give a central name for *la chevallerie;* nothing to do with horses; but more with the *miroire de cheval*. Its Hindu source is the notable term *kaivalya*, "eternal peace" or "equilibrium of soul" (*valiante knecht*).
[See *Katherine*]

GOL GUR GUR (New Guinea)
Danced by men during the Festival of *Gol Kerma.** At a certain time, some months after the start of the Festival, the House of Bolim (evil spirit opposed to Geru, god of prosperity) is built on the festival ground. Supposed to be made by spirits, it is erected secretly at night, and later the *Gol Gur Gur* is danced by the "spirit" builders. In addition to their festival costume, each man has slung at his waist a slender, "hour-glass" shaped drum, which he beats during the dance. The monotonous form is two steps forward and one back. Accompanying the dance is a high-pitched, long-drawn cry called *mangro-mangro*, heard in many cere-

monies of the people of the Wahgi Valley. (Cp. *Yoi*.)

[See *New Guinea, Dancing in; Gol Kerma; Kip Gamp Gol; Bolim Bombo*]

GOLIARDOIS (French) OR GOLIARDENSIS (Latin)
Mentioned by Chaucer (in *Canterbury Tales*) as a pastime of the Miller, who "was a stout carle", and "was a jangler and a goliardeis . . . a baggepipe wel could he blew". Tyrwhitt adds a note, "This jovial sect seems to have been so called from Golias, the real or assumed name of a man of wit towards the end of the 12th century, who wrote the *Apocalypse Goliae*, and other pieces in burlesque Latin rimes, some of which have falsely been attributed to Walter Map". Golias is a name found on early Tarot cards. Students in University of Paris (circa 1250), were sometimes known as Goliards; and the travelling singer-dancers were *jongleurs* (sometimes rendered *jogeyleurs*, or jugglers). They had a known pattern of dance and jingle-music.

GOL KERMA (New Guinea)
"Great Festival". Ritual cycle (now dying out) for initiation of youths. In Nondugl (pron. NONd'g'l) area of the Wahgi Valley (5,000 feet up, and known to explorers only since 1933), it used to occur about every twenty years, over a period of some eighteen months. The headman announces the start of *Gol Kerma*. On the festival-ground a Geru-house is built, 40 feet long, 20 feet wide, of specially selected wood. Geru is the spirit of fertility and prosperity, and in his house initiation will begin. A week later, when building is finished, the men dance before it, in a silent line, without drumming or the usual high-pitched cry called *mangro-mangro*. On a tree called the *mongoi-ont*, "decoration tree", set up outside the house, are hung bird-of-paradise head-dresses to be worn at the big ceremony. Various ritual preparations, and small sacrifices of pigs follow, and more than a year after the first announcement, the date is decided for the great sacrifice and climax of *Gol Kerma*. Word is sent to villages, and a House of Bolim is built, when several dances take place. Bolim (called *Kip Bang* —"Red Spirit") is evil and the opponent of Geru. His house, in the centre of the festival ground, faces the Geru-house, and round it the main ceremonies take place. Before building begins, men perform the *Mont-tree Dance* in honour of Bolim. Next night, secretly (Bolim-house is supposed to be built by spirits), the circular house is erected. Made of Mont-tree wood, it is five feet in diameter with conical roof on five poles. The central pole is a phallic symbol and protrudes above the roof. Ceremonies are two-fold—to placate Bolim and honour

Geru, for whom the *Kip Gamp Gol** is now danced. That night the "spirit builders" place diamond-holed boards on the central pole of Bolim-house, and then dance the *Gol Gur Gur.** Next afternoon (eve of the great sacrifice), the *Dance of Bolim Bombo** is performed by warriors and sorcerers in plumes and shell ornaments, to drive away evil spirits and bring the blessing of the ancestors on the Festival. No further dancing occurs. Next day many pigs are killed and eaten, and initiation called "Seeing the Flutes" follows. Formerly never seen by women or boys, these "spirit flutes" are the "voice of *Ka*", Bird of Life. Made of bamboo, 12" to 30" long, 1" to 3" diameter, they are played in pairs, one player producing a counter-melody to the other. Candidates, entering the Geru-house in pairs, are each given a flute, which they play during part of the ceremonies and endurance tests that follow.

[See *Bolim Bombo Dance; Gol Gur Gur; Kip Gamp Gol; New Guinea Dances*; and cp. *Ramben* and *Maki-Ru* (Malekula); *Hevehe* and *Gabé* (Papua)]

GOMBEYS (Bermuda)
Festal dance of Negro workers in the Islands. They have three musicians; the dancers are tall Negroes wearing masks, sometimes of white painted wire mesh. They use a turban with peacock feathers, up to four feet high, covering head and necks with brightly coloured scarfs. The syncopation is African. Capes of black velvet, sequin dotted, whirl as they move vigorously. Symbols in gold stitch are added, also small round mirrors. Knots of ribbon are added to fringed aprons, leggings, wrists and ankles. The dancers carry bows and arrows and wooden tomahawks (these due to admixture of Red Indian blood, and acquisition of this weapon). The main form of dance is a mock battle, stylised to fife and drum.

GONDHAL (India)
Dance of the Gondhalis (or Ghonds), performed by men in the district of Ahmednagar (south-west Nagpur) during the Hindu festival of *Dasehra*. During the Nine Days (as *navrati*) the men, wearing special long coats, with shell necklaces and ornaments and ankle-bells, move in this ritual circle dance, applauded by watching women. Through the day-time they sing chants in honour of Devi; followed at dusk by the dance.

GONG (Malay)
Generic term applied to metallic plates; or shallow dish-forms, used for percussion in (a) ritual summons, as a bell; and (b) in dance orchestra, in numbers, as in the *gamelan** of Java and Bali. The usual form is round; the most frequent metal is

"gong metal", which is a hard bronze (78 per cent. copper and 22 per cent. tin), emitting a steady sonorous note. The gong-stick is bamboo (or other springy wood) with head covered in leather. An expert player can get three notes from one gong, by striking on different parts of the disc, sometimes with different sticks. Chinese gongs have been made of silver, or even gold; this change of metal varies the note slightly. Burmese gongs are seldom round but usually triangular, or the shape of a flower petal. In India, many gongs are made of brass; and thence they slide into the smaller varieties, as the cymbal, or finger-gong, with a high note. Some Japanese gongs have been produced, made of iron. The Javanese orchestral gong is tuned by filing or scraping after casting; usually by matching "by ear" to an older standard. They have no traditional scale relation.

GOOSE DANCE (Scilly Isles)
Was celebrated as part of the New Year Festival by young people. They followed the Saturnalia custom of exchanging clothes: so that boys were dressed in girls' attire; and for the day the girls "wore the trousers". In companies they paid visits; related humorous yarns that were interspersed with dancing. When music and dance were finished at one house of call, they went on to the next.

GOOSE-STEP
A stage dance, apparently of comedy character, in which the famous Vestris is depicted in extravagant gesture; possibly he did it by way of satire on his rivals. There is also the military goose-step, formerly favoured by German army drill-sergeants; and responsible for the somewhat ridiculous high-step required. It could be seen practised by *Die Jungerbunden* (Youth Clubs) of the Nazi period. In England, a version of the same "military step" can be seen in the "slow pace" required for ceremonial "slow march" of the Guards; and again in the fancy stepping produced as a spectacle, for sentries on guard, who must perform a goose-step, turn round "smartly", and smack their rifle as they shift it up and down. Kaiser Wilhelm II was extremely fond of ceremonial march-dances and drill; but never did any himself. In America, dance is taught in a number of colleges; it is customary with some writers on education in that country to refer to this dance by way of metaphor. No survey of modern education in the USA can be complete without careful perusal of the leading work on this subject, *The Goose Step: A Study of American Education*, by Upton Sinclair (edition 1923).

GOPAK, ALSO HOPAK (Ukraine, USSR)
Traditional folk dance for a man; marked by vigorous high leaps, with feet and arms outspread horizontally. This dance, being very spectacular, is often performed for festivals; and has been included in some ballets. On holiday occasions, it may be seen in a street procession. In Czechoslovakia the *Odzenmek* is a leaping dance similar to the *Gopak*.

GORALE (Poland)
People of the Tatra Mountains. They have vigorous male dances, accompanied by singing, such as the *Goralski** and the *Harnas*, which require great agility and skill. Proficiency in dancing is a social necessity, and boys begin dance training as children. Women take part in some dances, but in a secondary capacity, the man being the chief performer. Unlike other parts of Poland, where most dances are for men and women in pairs, the Gorale prefer the male solo dance. At festivities held in the villages on all holidays, a young man may pay the orchestra for a special tune, to which he must compose and sing topical or humorous words, before dancing. There is a traditional formality about the choosing of partners. When a girl is chosen by the first dancer, two other girls dance with her before she joins her partner. Another man wishing to dance with her must first seek permis-

Members of *Mazowsze*, the Polish State Dance Company, performing a dance of the Tatra mountains in traditional Gorale costume. Men carry the mountaineer's axe vigorously wielded in the Goralski Dance.   POLAND

sion to "dance for her". Men wear the Goral costume (see *Goralski**), while the women's dress is white blouse, with many-stranded bead necklace. a full, patterned skirt, laced velvet bodice over Over white stockings they wear either soft mocassins (*kierpce*), or high boots. Their head-covering is a coloured kerchief, not the elaborate head-dress favoured elsewhere in Poland.

GORALSKI (Poland)

Brigands' dance performed by the Gorale (dwellers in the Tatra Mountains), particularly in the Podhale region round Zakopane. The dance is accompanied by violins, in brisk 2/4 time, with perhaps flute or *gensla* (zither), bagpipes or accordion; and by the singing of spectators. A very vigorous dance, it may be performed by a group of men, or solo. The group dance is performed in a circle (formerly round a fire), facing inwards, and contains much leaping and crouching; springing with bent knees, kicking the heels in the air; and other expressions of fierce virility. An essential part of both dress and dance is the *toporek* (mountaineer's axe), which dancers strike on the ground, cut through the air, fling up and catch, or clash together. In the solo dance, the man leaps high, crossing his legs and (in brigand days) firing a pistol before landing. Although a man may choose a girl as partner, he concentrates on his own performance. She performs less spectacular steps in the background. The men's white wool trousers are embroidered in front with red and blue patterns, called *parzenica*, characteristic of the Gorale and varying with each group. Mocassins or white felt boots cover the feet. Over a white shirt, the fur-lined jacket, or *serdak*, is worn cloakwise, while round the waist is a broad, brass-studded belt, ten or twelve inches wide. Eagle feathers and mussel shells adorn the round black, felt hat.   [See *Zbójnicki*]

GOSHIKI (Japan)

Court ritual ceremonial dance, formed chiefly in the Ashigawa period (1340 - 1570). The mediaeval costume, with wide sleeves and full skirts, had to be handled gracefully; as the opposite of the much tighter fitting scale armour, then used in combat. This was essentially a ceremonial dress. Hence movement of the nobles in the court hall was governed by unwritten rules, as to "advance to the Shogun" (there was then no Mikado on the scene) and the great sleeves, especially, required much slow manipulation. This mannerism was later transferred to the *Noh** stage, to depict a character of nobles or heroes. The robes are heavy silks and brocades, elaborate, and adorned with family symbols. They are most voluminous; the dancer while wearing them is correspondingly slow, and graceful as possible. Many such costumes can be seen in Japanese prints.

GRACE DANCE (England)

15th - 17th century : was an informal dance after supper, performed by youths and maidens who had just eaten at their master's table. This gild custom was continued in all towns and cities where craft or merchant gilds operated; when the dancers were the apprentices, and the relations of the merchants. Sterne[1] refers to this dance, while Stow's *Survey*[2] says "The youths of this city (London) have used on holidays, after evening prayer, to exercise their waisters and bucklers; and the maidens, one of them playing a timbrel, in sight of their masters and dames, to dance for garlands hanged athwart the streets".

[1] *Sentimental Journey*. Lawrence Sterne.
[2] *Stow's Survey*. Strypes edn. p. 251.

GREAT HARMONY OR TA-TAO (Pekin, China)

Ritual dance or sacred ceremony, said to date from 2450 BC. According to Charles d'Albert, it has the essential character of the *Tango*.* There are eight principal movements :

    1. The *Ta-tao* (rhythm or cadence);
    2. The *Ho-ang* (the Phoenix of Fire);
    3. The *Ho-ang* (another version);
    4. The *Ho-ang* (a version *a cote*);
    5. The *Ta-kuen* (*a grand tournant*);
    6. The *Ta-ou-ken-tche* (*la vague*, "the wave");
    7. The *Ta-hyen* (*le tout ensemble*);
    8. The *T'chen Ou* (*solo pour l'homme*).

GREEK DANCE (Modern Forms)

There is in Greece no "Revived Greek Dance", of the style popularised by Isadora Duncan and her brother Raymond; probably there never has been this artificial mode, at any time, in Hellas. The ancient Hellenes would be somewhat surprised if they could, after two thousand years, see the performance called Greek Dance, in other countries. More still, the exponents of these divagations, seen in modern capitals, would be astounded if they knew what the old Hellenic dances implied and sometimes revealed. Vigorous folk-dances do exist today in Greece, performed exclusively by men, with one exception. There is not the mingling seen in the *kolo** or *hora** of other Balkan countries. The social dance now called *Balos*, performed by a couple in the ring, is the only dance where man and girl join in the same movement. There are many dances, in softer style, for women only. There is not much theatre ballet performed in Greece; the population is too small to support large theatre companies through the year. In recent years, a small company of fifteen women has developed out of the Nichols school; now named Kosta Nichols Athens Ballet Company. This group perform in Athens in the winter; in open-air theatres in summer, and they have already a "tourist connection". Their style is chiefly Modernist Central European; they add some folk-dance forms to their program; classical Greek themes (as now understood), and Byzantine themes.

GREEK MUMMING PLAYS (Northern Greece)
Can be seen today in Thessaly; Macedonia; Thrace and Epirus; and in some of the Northern Islands. Chiefly they are performed at the Spring Festival; when work is done to secure healthy crop growth, especially the "cleansing of ground" (in Roman terms, the *Fevruare*). Few peasants are so dull as to believe that crops will appear, merely by praying and singing, whether in terms of supposed "magic" or by sacerdotal "blessings", unless they put in days of preliminary hard work. Their Mumming celebrates the occasion. Originally the great time was the New Year Festival; now the periods occur at Epiphany and May Day; or "Cheese-Monday" at beginning of Lent (Cp. "Butter-week" in Russia) as well as the solstice. The play has many local variants; but there is always a Bride and a Groom, always a ritual death and ritual resurrection of one character by the Doctor; with the pantomime of "distributing the forces" (a realisation of the reality of *mana**). Many such plays are now fading out; but some were seen by Wace and Dawkins[1] at Hagios Georgios (Viza, Thrace) in Skyros; and on Mount Pelion, on May Day. In the Pelion Mumming were seen the First Man, the Old Woman, and the Doctor who performs the ritual. The fact that they carry on a tradition closely similar to that of the Mumming Play in Northern Britain appears to indicate a direct influence from Grecian visitors; certainly before the Latin invasions in the south in the 6th century.
[1] *Journal of Hellenic Studies*. R. M. Dawkins and A. J. B. Wace. XVI. XIX *Annual*.

GREEN CORN DANCE (Amerindian)
Performed by Natchez Indians (now extinct) as a culmination to their feast celebrating the newly ripe corn. After ceremonies lasting all day, in which their Chief, the "Great Sun" participated, there was a general dance by torchlight on the dancing-ground. In his *History of Louisiana* (reprinted London 1774), Du Pratz describes the dancing-ground, lit by some two hundred torches standing all round it, "each the thickness of a child". The dance continued all night, to rhythms

beaten on a drum made from a pot covered with deer skin. With the drummer in the centre, women formed a circle round him, not joining hands, but at some distance from each other. Round them again the men formed another circle, each holding a calabash with a stick thrust through it for handle. The women moved anti-clockwise, the men clockwise, the circles sometimes narrowing, sometimes widening. Next day, the ritual game of *Pelote* was played. Similar festivals at the ripening of corn were held by Cherokee and Creek Indians.
[See *Creek Indians; Busk; Aztec Dance*]

GREEN GARTERS (English traditional dance)
Also "Green Garlands"; known as a three-form dance (a) round the living tree before cutting; (b) processional, to village green or other place for erection; and (c) the finale, round-dance of triumph. The name derives from the widespread custom of the dancers, taking small twigs from the newly-felled tree, and placing them in the bands of their knee-breeches; their armlets, their hats, as symbols of their devotion to the "Green Life". This *Green Garters* belongs to the same traditions which urge the use of mistletoe and holly in churches etc. at the Winter Solstice Festival of the New Year; the carrying of vine garlands at the Harvest Festival; the decoration of wells or fountains with profusion of new green leaves; and the ancient Festival of Horus the Younger in Egypt. These dances originated Jack-in-the-Green, and similar characters, such as "Green George", in Carinthia.

GREENWICH FAIR (London)
Early 19th century writers (including "Boz") describe the current innumerable attractions of the famous old Greenwich Fair—that same festival that brought King Henry VIII to see the Morris Men and Robin Hood with his archers. Copies of *Sketches by Boz* (written early in the career of Charles Dickens) are plentiful; last "corrected" in 1869. Greenwich was ever the home of folk-dance; its early-Victorian Fair was no exception, except that it had become commercial and was organized. Let us quote:
"The grandest and most numerously frequented booth in the whole fair is The Crown and Anchor—a temporary ballroom, we forget how many hundred feet long. The price of admission is one shilling . . . a refreshment place, at which cold beef, roast and boiled, French rolls, stout, wine, tongue, ham, even fowls, are displayed in tempting array. There is a raised orchestra; and the place is boarded all the way dawn, in patches, just wide enough for a country dance. There is no master of ceremonies; all is primitive, unreserved, and unstudied. The dust is

blinding, the heat insupportable, the company somewhat noisy; and in the highest spirits; the ladies in the height of innocent animation, wearing the gentlemen's hats and the gentlemen promenading the 'gay and festive scene' in the ladies' bonnets; or with the more expensive ornament of false noses and low-crowned hats; playing children's drums, and accompanied by ladies on the penny trumpet. The noise of these various instruments, the orchestra, the shouting, the 'scratchers' and the dancing, is perfectly bewildering. The dancing, itself, beggars description—every figure lasts about an hour; and the ladies bounce up and down in the middle, with a degree of spirit quite indescribable. As to the gentlemen, they stamp their feet against the ground, every time 'hands four round' begins, go down the middle and up again, with cigars in their mouths and silk handkerchieves in their hands; and whirl their partners round, nothing loth, scrambling and falling, and embracing, and knocking up against the other couples, until they are fairly tired out and can move no longer. The same scene is repeated again and again (slightly varied by an occasional 'row') until a late hour at night. . . .".

[*Sketches by Boz.* (p. 67)]

GREYSTEIL (Scotland)

A Minstrel poem, used as a dance-song, traditional as a mime in Scotland from 1497. In the *Buik* of Lord Treasurer of Scotland, when James IV was at Stirling, appears an entry of payment to "two fithalaris that sang Greysteil to the King, ix.s.". These fiddlers had recited this Metrical Tale; and a few years later (1508) it is said that one of the royal lute players bore the nickname of Greysteil —either in consequence of his skill in performing this mime-dance; or in reflection of the character, in his own appearance and manner. Thus the tradition was far older, for it was then a high compliment to offer this name. The tune in the old tablature, was re-scripted in modern form by William Dauney, in whose *Ancient Scottish Melodies* (1838) it is given. The melody is not truly Scottish, but resembles Spanish airs. Satirical versions were later written, intended to be sung to this old tune; which suggests not a complete rendering, but a prelude, probably for a ring-dance or reel of early type. *Grey-Steel* was, literally, the famous "Sword of Kol" as related in the Icelandic *Edda*. This weapon always proved finally fatal to its owner and user, for it could be carried and used with impunity only by a "Galahad".

GRIM (Russia)

Means the craft of make-up for the stage. Under this name, the practice is taught as a regular subject in all Russian Theatre Schools or Academies. The term is allied to the French *grimace* : to distort or alter the facial expression; but when done by inexpert hands, the result is "grimy" or merely dirty.   [See *Make-up; Mascara*]

GROSSVATER TANZ or "Grandfather's Dance" (Germany)

Used frequently at weddings—16th and 17th centuries—as the final dance of the celebrations. The traditional tune is in three parts: the first being *andante* with a couplet; followed by two quick phrases in 2/4 time. The verse carries a triple meaning :

"*Und als der Grossvater die Grossmutter nahm*
Da war der Grossvater ein Bräutigam".

(Bridegroom)

Because of its humorous drift, this dance was named also as *Kehraus*, or "Clear-out dance" (*kehren*, brush or sweep), so that when the familiar melody was heard, everybody emptied the last *stein* and went home.

GUABINA (Columbia)

Song-dance in 2/4 time and quick tempo, popular in provincial towns. Couples, holding hands, or separated by a kerchief held between them, dance round a hat on the ground, approaching and withdrawing. Guitars accompany the dance, playing in 3/4 time.

GUAHARIBO DANCES (Venezuela and N. Brazil)

Among the most primitive people now existing, Guaharibo Indians live deep in the forests, eating only forest foods, and going naked except for painted patterns and feather ornaments. At the beginning of the evolutionary scale, knowing nothing of knives or hatchets, or how to build a solid hut, these people yet have their own songs and dances. In simple mimetic form they imitate the forest animals, and their own customs. Thus, their most important ceremony, the *Monkey Dance*, performed by men decorated with black and white feathers, imitates the walk and movements of those animals. It lasts all day. The women, dressed in special skirts of banana leaves, take part by singing and dancing round the men, waving fringes of palm leaves. In their *War Dance* six men, flourishing bamboo-tipped arrows, defy each other; while a curious item is a "trading" or "bargaining dance", in which two men squat opposite each other, holding arrows, a bow and a cudgel. Swaying their bodies rhythmically to right and left, they wag their heads violently, beat themselves on the chest and thump the earth with the palms of the hands, talking and shouting. Decked with red and black feathers on arms, in hair and ears, with tufts of white down stuck on to their bodies, the climax of the "dance" arrives when, flinging away his weapons, and tearing off the feathers, one of the bargaining adversaries rolls over exhausted. Having no musical instruments, *Guaharibo* dances are accompanied only by singing and shouting.

GUAJIRA, QUAJIRA (Cuba)

A peasant dance of Spanish origin, in which the tempo changes from 6/8 to 3/4 or 2/4. The style sometimes resembles that of the *Conga.** The *Guaracha*, by some considered to be the same as the *Guajira*, is a song-dance, also of Spanish origin.

GUARACHA (Cuba)

A song-dance of Spanish origin, in 6/8 time, with lively rhythm sometimes resembling that of the *Rumba*. A dance musically similar, is the *Guajira,** also of Spanish origin, but with rhythm reminiscent of the *Conga.**

GUARDS' MARCH (England)

Dance is often used in drill for war fitness; ritual dance is often used for military display, from the Roman *trionfo*. The four regiments of Guards have special drill modes for ceremonial usage. They are relatively modern; (a) Grenadier Guards (raised 1660 by Col. Russell, for bodyguard of Charles II), (b) Coldstream Guards (Gen. Monck 1650), Scots Guards, 1660, and (d) Irish Guards, 1900. All regiments drill in slow march, quick march, sentry change, chiefly with drum and fife tunes. The stride is standard at 30″ measured by the sergeant major's "walking stick". The exaggerated swing of arms is recent. A notable ceremonial is "Trooping the Colour"—they take sentry duty at royal palaces; and at Whitehall.

GUARDS' CEREMONIAL MARCH (London)

Is a military semi-ritual march performed in public by guardsmen of the four principal regiments detailed for ceremonial duties, such as Palace Guards (Buckingham Palace; St. James' Palace), where the rite called "Changing of the Guard" has become a tourist attraction. The training includes intricate routine resembling that of a corps-de-ballet, in a marionette mode of perfection of organised movement. Learning to walk—the first lesson—occupies the recruit five hours daily, five days a week, for at least a month. He is forbidden to swing his arms (precisely the opposite to A.T.S. drill for girls), and holds them, like the Irish clog-dancer, by his sides. This develops carriage. Then he learns the "set pace" guided by metronome

beats, and a pace-stick for length. He must step precisely thirty inches. The Sergeant-Major's "walking-stick" is, in fact, a measuring or pace stick; it opens on a hinge to give exact measure. The time has two standards: "Quick pace" at seventy paces per minute; and "Slow pace" at forty paces per minute. The speed of pacing is tempered by metronome beat; then by a drummer; which beat, being learned by rote, remains constant. Carriage of the head remains regular. Sentry duties are learned in barracks; and repeated "by the gates"—two men when the palace is in use, one man when not. Duty period is two hours on guard. The timing of the sentry walk is given by the senior man (called Old Soldier). He crashes his rifle butt on the pavement; and moves in counts of three for each single gesture. The men move seventeen paces away, in opposing direction (by the count), halt, crash arms, reverse position, and return. The number of such marches is indicated by the Old Soldier, who spreads one finger, two fingers, or even three fingers, over his rifle butt. To encourage ciné-cameras. the sentries may do a triple march.

GUDOK (Russia)

Minstrel of the Mediaeval period, usually strolling and mendicant, in groups of two or four men. They played, recited legends, and mimed at village taverns. The term seems to derive from a version of *Kathak* (Indian) and appears as *Hudok* or *Ghudoka*. Two *gudoks* appear in *Prince Igor*, the opera by Borodin. In Serbia, these minstrels are named *Guslaks* or *Guslari.**

GUÊDE (Haiti)

Pron. *gee-dee*. An annual carnival, celebrated "for the ancestors" in early November; yet recurrent at intervals through the year. The feast, similar to that of Hallow-Eve, has a rite, a dance, and a feast. none of them very definite in form, except that there is a saturnalian exchange of partners—the men dressed as women, and women dressed as men. This is a localised cult, connected with those of Baron Samedi and Baron Cimitière, but limited to the "common people", originating at Miragoane among the Bossal natives. The slogan is *Parlezcheval*, or "Tell my Horse", and includes a certain rite of mediumistic activity. In its social form, Guéde finds opportunity for much satirical comment. He has no definite centre; but his rite requires twenty white candles burning round the cross dedicated to him. As with similar Moslem cults, the rite involves a visit to the burial ground, which for the night is blazing with light. Processional dances may occur on the way to and from the country. "Brave Guéde" as opponents of the *Sect Rouge,** have a similar but secret ritual.

GUELSA (Morocco)
Arabic term for the "sacred square" used in Western Morocco (as at Marrakesh). This square of white cotton cloth, elaborately embroidered in deep blue patterns, is spread on the stone or marble floor of Arab houses, to indicate the special seat reserved for the honoured guest. Thus it is the *Seguidilla** of Arabs from Cairo who went to Spain. Broad bands of blue border frame the *nekhla* device, which is a *motif* characteristic of Fez. The cushion-covers on the divan carry similar traditional patterns, always purely geometrical in basic design.
[See *Arts and Crafts of Morocco*. Prosper Ricard (French official, Casablanca) Paris 1918.]

GUERRE DES BOUFFONS (France)
War of the Buffoons (1752 - 4); a name given to the contest provoked in Paris by the invasion of the Italian theatre people (opera, dancers, comedians, etc.), in which the cardinals sponsored Lully and his friends. Parisians knew of the underlying papal propaganda; and resented this cold war on their religious opinions. The Jesuits had operated a similar scheme in Austrian schools and colleges; while in England, the flow of Italian papal propaganda (carried by numerous artists in all fields) was finally perceived; hence the immense welcome extended to John Gay's *Beggars' Opera;* or the rebuff to Noverre's *Fête de Chinois* (ironically, non-political). Naturally. many dancers were involved (mostly without the slightest idea of their exploitation). This particular 18th century contest culminated in the French Revolution.

GUGU DRUMS (Southern Sudan)
As made by the Azande, are produced in three sizes, each with a greatly different main note. They are made from hollowed logs of trees, and each drum is shaped like a pig or a horse, standing on short wooden legs, with a flat wooden head, and a slit in the rounded back. The largest is the size of a bullock; the smallest the size of a sheep. Using different tones and rhythms, messages can be sent over considerable distances—a good drummer can produce something like the actual words. This feat is done also with Yoruba "Talking Drums".

GUIA DA DANSA (Portugal)
Leader of the dance, especially ballroom dance; as *Guia regulamentar*, or master of ceremonies; whence (from New Orleans) a "Reglar guy" at the *fiesta;* one who does the ruling or regulation.

GUIMBARDO, LO (Limousine, France)
"The Goad". An old dance of cowherds, performed by two men (or several groups of two), holding a

"goad", or broomstick about two metres long, with a bunch of ribbons tied to the middle. With music in 2/4 time, a polka step is used throughout. Dancers enter in couples, each holding opposite ends of the stick. Arrived in place, they raise the stick above their heads, and face each other. Four figures follow : 1. Each dancer pivots clockwise *sur place*, under the raised stick. 2. The stick is lowered, and on the first beat of the measure each dancer throws his right leg over it, changing the stick to the left hand. This is repeated with the left leg. These two movements are repeated four times, on the first beat of each measure. 3. The stick is again raised, the dancers moving round clockwise in a half-circle. 4. The same as the Second Figure. These figures are repeated as often as required.

GUISING (England)
Guiser is from *Kaiser* (King Dances). A term varied with Disguising (or Masking) to denote periodical performances of traditional legends, through most of England and Scotland. What material we have (now most fully detailed), is but the end of a long tradition, which has to be examined centuries prior to these precise records, to discover what was the real meaning and purpose of the *Guisers*, who appeared at the great country festivals. The legends and their intent remain embedded within the rough exterior of the old popular versions; while the name of the performance itself suffers occasional change.

GUIZARDS (Scotland)
The country rendering of De-guisers or Guisers, who belong (north of the Border) to the Yule Season, recalled by troupes of children who perform mumming plays, with more or less talking or chaunting, and feeble musical rhythm. These masks, or "false faces", came in also at Hallow E'en, for the vigil of the Feast of the Dead, or "All Souls".

GUSLAR (Yugoslav)
A minstrel who sings and dances, with his *gusla* (or *guzla*), which is a primitive type of stringed instrument somewhat like a Russian *balalaika*. The *guslari* are hired for village weddings; they appear at festivals, but rarely enter churches to play. They furnish music for *kolo** or *hora,** along with a pipe and drum or tabor, but their chief tradition lives with their folk-songs and ballads, which they can sing, in a kind of recitative, by the hour, if fortified by suitable libations of *rakhya* (plum brandy). The *guslar* is often made of a gourd or coco-shell fitted with skin or parchment, and played with a bow, or plucked. Its string is usually horse-hair; and its tone rarely pure.

GUSLARI (Serbia)

Musician, usually fiddler, player of *guslar* music for song and dance. *Guslar* was for centuries chief minstrel or bard of Serbian people; singer of folk epics, dance songs, funeral chants; marriage ballads; equivalent to Scots piper or Indian drummer in his leading position. The original *guslar* was tuned in pentatonic scale; but many forms were reduced to one string; scale was maintained by the songs; instrument has affinities with the Arabic *rebab* or *rebec*; so also have a few songs (possibly imported by Moslem invaders).

GYMNASKA (France)

A Breton dance of the Basse-Cornouaille district. To lively music in 3/4 time, dancers (any number) move round clockwise in a linked circle. There is only one figure, and the step used includes *sauté croisé*, the "crossed jump" so often occurring in Breton dances. The dancer jumps first on left foot, crossing the right leg with foot pointed, in front of the left leg; repeated with left leg crossed over right. While executing these crossed jumps, the girls pivot lightly on themselves, first to left, then right. The tune is also sung.

GYMNOPAEDIA (Ancient Greece)

An annual festival of "naked youths", held at Sparta in honour of Apollo, Pythaeus, Artemis and Leto; said to date from about 665 BC. Round statues of the deities, which stood in the *choros* or open forecourt of the Agora (collection of temples, legislative buildings etc.), the young men danced and sang. The dances were rhythmical, mimetic representations of the *palaestra* (wrestling matches) and the *pancration* (athletic games), and also included movements reminiscent of dances that occurred in the worship of Dionysus. The festival lasted several days; on the last day choruses and dances were performed in the theatre. The leader of the chorus wore a wreath to commemorate the victory of the Spartans at Thyrea.

GYPSY DANCE (Spain)

In Spain is mixed up with Spanish styles (*Flamenco*,* *Baile*, *Danzo* etc.), and has Eastern affinities; seen in the terms *Gitano*, male dancer; and *Gitana*, female dancer; also *Zincali* (*Dzyan-Kali*=Circle of Kali), probably of Oriental origin, relevant to a famous Hindu dance-ritual. Gypsy names for dance (from George Borrow's glossary in *The Zincali*), give these equivalents: *Quelar*, to dance; *quele*, a dance; *quelabo*, *quelaba*, dancers; *panelar*, to leap; *guillabar*, to sing; *chaseos*, exercises; *burlo*, play or sport; *Boltani*, a turn; *Baricuntus*, "Count", or Captain of Gitano troupe; *duquendo*, a master among *gitanas*; *tarquino*, a parable or play, shewn; *tinbalo*, music. The term *quelar* is obviously akin to *wheel*; and this belongs to Provence (*langue d'oeil*). The traditional Spanish gypsy centres are Cadiz, Granada, and Seville; their dances include *Buleria* (a fast solo dance, from Cadiz, with finger clicks); *Farruca* (Andalusian dance, adapted by gypsies from Galician music); *Polo** and *Romalis;** *Manguindoy*; *Zorongo* (a solo dance, with accompaniment of cymbals or tambourine). In Hungary the gypsy is called *Zigeuner* or *Tsigane*, the gypsy king or queen being *voyvode* or *voyvoda*. Most Hungarian dances are accompanied by a gypsy orchestra, the leader (*Primas*) often whipping the dance into a frenzy with his fiddle-playing, as in the *Csardas*.* In England the gypsy calls himself *Rom* or *Romani* (*Rom* or *Rum* is a Byzantine term). In France they are *Sintes* or *Sinti* (considered by a gypsy writer to derive from the *Sindhu Ghonds*, or Ghonds of the River Sind, in India). Provençal gypsies are *les caraques* (singular, *caraco*). In Persia, Indian origin is also given to the gypsies (*Luri* or *Luli*), said to descend from the 10,000 minstrels called *Luris* brought to Persia by the Shah, Bahram Gur. In Greece the gypsy is the *gyphtoi*; in Scotland, the *caird*.

GYPSIES (Russia)

Moscow and Petersburg, in 19th century, were centres for resident groups of professional entertainers (much as Seville is now). Their singing and dancing attracted wealthy patrons. They lived in the Novaya Derevnia (on The Islands) in Petersburg; in Grouzini in Moscow, during the winter, living patriarchal lives. In summer they left the big cities. The men wore Russian-style attire; bright blouse, long sleeved black kaftan, high top-boots, wide black hats. Bright colour adorned the women, with full long skirts and shawls; head-scarves tied at the back of the neck; with many heavy (and genuine) ornaments. Gypsy songs were traditional; rarely varied by newer topical verses. Their expressive dance was accentuated with mime. This Russian gypsy tradition as in Britain, has almost vanished through assaults of civilization, education, registrations, and other evils. Many gypsy artists continued for a time in the Gypsy Theatres (provided by Soviet care for theatres of all kinds), but the war dispersed them.

"GYPSIES IN THE WOOD" (England)

This traditional folksong-dance seems to have belonged originally to the rituals of Santa-Katerina;* being "suitable advice to young ladies". Despite the mention of "gypsies" these wanderers have nothing to do with the rhyme; they are dragged in, as was "Old Boney" before Waterloo. In printed form, these verses have a brief life. One grandfather, born 1818, had learned to play the tune (usually standard) described as . . . "still a favourite at village weddings or merrymakings, whenever a lively jig or polka is needed". The tune is identical with part of *King Pippen's Polka* (c. 1870), and is heard as a gypsy dance in Smetana's *The Bartered Bride*. Possibly it was once part of some dramatic *joie de vivre*, as part of the Katherine initiation ceremonial, once given to girls :

"My mother said : I never should
   Play with the gypsies in the wood;
They steal my lunch, they break my chain —
   I'm never going there again !"

"Lunch" or "*lanch*" is a gypsy Romany term.

GYROMANCY (Greek)
Said to have been a method of divining, or prophesy (enchanting) by the practice of *gyromanteia*, or performing a magical ring dance. Much depended on the time selected for the enquiry, which had to be balanced with period of day or night, term of the month, and the particular rhythm of the musical beats, given by song or instrument. This magical dance appears to be a Greek version of the regular practice of the Roman *augur* or *aurospices*.

GYROVAGI (Latin)
Also *Gyrovagantes;* said literally to mean "circuit-wanderers", but probably derived from *Korybantes*, the protagonists of an earlier doctrine which supported much ritual dancing. They were known to the monk Benedict (*circa.* 500 AD), who was naturally in competition with them as showmen. He apostrophises their wandering habits (necessary since they lacked a permanent town centre, having been driven out by aggressive christians), and refers also to the Sarabaitae, as a similar "class of monks". All these monks, the "Bene-Dictines" included, got a spare living by touring round, with plays and ritual dances, to the various traditional festivals; not by any means then always christianized. There were numerous bands of wandering devotees, who were displaced by the breakdown of the Roman empire; some of them visited Britain and certainly they moved all through Europe from Byzantium to Iberia.

H

HABANERA (Cuba) (Fr. *Havanaise*)
Song and dance of Havana. With music in slow to moderate 2/4 time, and rhythm similar to the *Tango,** the *Habanera* is danced by couples facing each other. They accompany the singing of *coplas* (verses) with expressive gestures. Dance style is slow and stately, with langorous movements of arms, hips, head and eyes which hint at Moorish or Oriental origin. Some consider that the *Habanera* was introduced into Cuba by African slaves and later imported into Spain; others that it came from Spain to Cuba and was re-introduced into the Peninsula about 1850. The earliest known *Habanera* is *El Areglito*, by the Spanish composer Yradier, which appeared in the 1840's, sub-titled *Chanson Habanaise*, and was used by Bizet in *Carmen*. About 1900, the *Habanera del Café*, prototype of the *Tango*, became popular. Sometimes called *Contradanza Criollo*, the Spanish *Contradanza* of the 18th century may have become the *Habanera* on arrival in Cuba.

HABANEIRA (Spanish, from Arabic *Ha'Abuna-eira*)
The ritual dance of the Abuna (Chief Priest), when making his sermon or prophesying, similar to the term *Min-eira* or *Mun-eira*, applied to the women; and still celebrated as a dance in North Spain. The meaning of "dove" was concurrent, as applied to the trained women mediums (or sibyls) as those who went from Africa (Oasis of Amoun) to Dodona in Greece. Others went to Iberia. The term "*Abuna*" refers to the head in the Coptic church; from this term came our word *bun*, as a small round loaf, impressed with a cross inside a circle. The traditional time is at Easter. The same term *bun* is used to denote a tight wad in hair-dressing, much used by dancers. In Latin it became *Tu Buna*.

HABBÊ DANCES (West African)
Dances of the Habbé mountain people who live in cliff dwellings some miles south of Timbuctoo. Many dances show in pantomime legendary and possibly historical events. Costumes include highly stylised, tall head-dresses in brilliant colour, some hiding the face. Several of the dancers have wooden "crocodile" helmets, with crosses several feet high, modernist art in motif. Symbolical masks indicate ancestors, or enemies; with many animals, including antelope or hyena, bustards or rabbits. Enemy Peuhls are marked by close brown netting hoods, over face and head, with eye holes, outlined in white shells. Dancing takes place in full daylight with firing of muskets, before great crowds in the public square, as for example, at the town of Sangha. The "dance season" is about January; the chief piece mimes the ancient history of the Habbé people and their wanderings in West Africa. The Habbé religion is monotheist, with a symbolical trinity.

HABIMA THEATRE (Russia) (Ha 'Bima, Gr.)
Was established first in Moscow as a "Studio" of the Moscow Arts Theatre (that is, a branch of the

Stanislavsky groups), and attracted many Jewish players. All available plays, mimes, and dance-plays were produced; but the spoken word was Hebrew. The professional development (post 1917) brought into being the Moscow State Jewish Theatre (G.O.S.E.T.), which opened on January 1st, 1921, which then acted not in Hebrew but Yiddish. Most spoken dramas then used were written originally in Yiddish (as, for example, plays by Abraham Gold-faden), but this fact obviously had little bearing on dance episodes; such as the Gipsy musical play *Life on Wheels*. When Granovski departed, his

place as director was filled by the accomplished Jewish actor Mikhoels. Vahtangov, the first direc-tor, died in 1922. They produced *The Dybbuk*; and *Sulamith*. Most plays had musical settings and many had some dance; but all spoken rhythm, and stage movement, was dominated by notable rhyth-mic phrasing, in an intense style of acting, often exaggerated. Mikhoels shewed a moving production of *Macbeth*, dominated with his rhythmic mode. Some of the *Habima* group returned to Palestine. [See *Blue Blouse Groups*]

Ritual Ring of the famous old ceremony of the *Hag Ha' Mayim* (Feast of the Water Festival) celebrating the time of the New Year when fresh water becomes available for the Spring crops.   ISRAEL

HAGG (Hebrew, Arabic) (*Haji & Hajji*)
Implies the sacred ritual dance, coupled with the name of the feast. This term is regarded by Oesterly[1] as the chief original word for a religious

dance, though it is used also to indicate festival. The dance form implies a circle, usually around some sacred place; or person; or object. With Moslem Arabs, the term was used to name the

ritual of circumambulating the sacred Kaaba Shrine at Mecca. This was the factual *Hagg*, accompanied by chanting suitable passages from the Koran. In time, the term was extended, to include the journey made by the pilgrim to Mecca, who is today named as a *hajji*, or "one who has journeyed, or danced", at Mecca. In the *Targum* on Isaiah lxvi. 20, the noun *kirkeran* (feminine plural form) means "dances", and *kirker* is used (describing the famous "Dance of David" (*2 Sam. v. 14 - 16*) where it clearly implies the circle (as in Greek : *kirke*), and not merely a "dance before" an altar. David is dancing round the *kirkeran*, which contains him and the sacred centre. This same term, *Hagg*, is connected with *Hagia*. the holy wisdom (*Sophia Hagia* Church in Stambul) and notably names the New Year Festival, celebrated by Scots, as *Hag-Min-Hay* or *Hagmanay*.
[1] *Sacred Dance*. W. O. E. Oesterley. 1923.

HAGGIS (Scotland)

Part of the Ritual "Dance of the *Hag-Men-Hey*", or New Year Festival of the Scottish clans. The haggis a concoction of prepared offal, was cooked during the performance of reels* and strathspeys,* and devoured with acclamation when ready, with the accompaniment of *usque-baugh* (whiskey). This Feast was, particularly in the period preceding 1914, celebrated by the London Scots on December 31st always around St. Paul's Cathedral. Proceeding there on foot, or by any sort of vehicle — riding clustered on the tops of cabs. Each man carried a bottle of whiskey, waited for the midnight chimes, drained the liquid with many a loud cheer; and dashed the bottle on the ground. Then they broke into song, and removed themselves somewhat for a ring and chain dance, afterwards repairing to the adjacent restaurants (booked in advance) for steaming portions of the national Haggis. Thus the *Hag-Min-Hey* is, in this relation, similar to the Boar's Head Carol-dance of England, or the *paulenta messe* of Italy. In Greenock, "Burns' Night" is celebrated annually on 21st January, birthday of the poet in 1759. The meeting includes reading of poems; the "Address to a Haggis", with a piping-in of the haggis dish, for which the piper gets his "dram o' whusky". The feast is traditional; it has Cock-a-Leekie Soup (chicken broth). Salt Herring. boiled Haggis wi' Neeps (turnips mashed), and Champit Tatties (boiled potatoes), while the drink is whisky. The traditional toast is *Deoch-slainte*, meaning "Drink at Door". There follows group singing, pipe music, dancing of reels and strathspeys; and Burns' "Auld Lang Syne", in this meeting for adult Scots only. Haggis is also a local product, exported all over the world to brave Scots, both for Burns' Night and

for "Sant Andra's Nicht", on 30th November. The standard national recipe requires :

> A sheep's bag (stomach);
> the pluck complete (lights, liver, and heart);
> beef suet, onions, and oatmeal; seasoning of salt and black pepper.

"Wash bag twelve hours; boil for two hours; remove 'gristle and pipes'; mince half liver, grate it; mince heart and lights; mix half pound minced suet, two finely chopped large onions; large cup of toasted oatmeal. Moisten with stock from pot; shovel into bag, sew up and boil in large pot. Prick to prevent any burst. Boil three hours, while dance proceeds. Serve hot".

"HAI-YA"

A "welcome" dance of the Wapisians, an Indian tribe of South America. The chant accompanying the dance consists only of the two syllables "Hai-ya", repeated in the rhythm of the dance, with little variation. The dance is performed on arrival of a friendly tribe, to celebrate conclusion of a hunt, or building of a house. To mark the rhythm rattles are attached to legs and hands of the dancers, while an improvised solo is sung by one man, old men and women swelling the chorus. The dance is accompanied by one musician, playing a flute engraved with intricate designs, and made from bamboo or the leg bone of a jaguar. An improvised "trumpet" is made like a megaphone, by coiling up long strips of palm leaf, giving a low tone to mark changes of rhythm.

HAJDUTÂNC (Hungary)

An old military dance of the *Heyducks*. Hajto, hajduc mean "cattle-driver" and the *heyducks* (pronounced *hoidoos*) were originally herdsmen, who became mercenary soldiers. Their dance, related to that of the herdsmen (see *Bakony Herdsmen's Dance**), became more military when they took to soldiering. Descendants of the early *Heyducks* still live near the town of Debrecen, but the dance is forgotten by them. First mentioned in the 15th century, it was danced with drawn swords, as a mock combat. The English traveller, Edward Brown, in 1669 compared the *Hajdutánc* to the Greek *Pyrrhic** dance, and described in his book (*A Brief Account of Some Travels in Hungary — 1673*) how the men danced "with naked swords in their hands, advancing, brandishing and clashing the same . . . singing withal measures in the manner of the Greeks". A very swift dance, performed with heavy swords or battle axes, it was danced to the music of the pipe, and later the *tarogato* (a wooden instrument like a large clarinet). The *Hajdutánc* apparently developed into a regulated dance with figures in a set order, since part of an old song contains instructions to dancers suggestive of the "calling" in American Square Dancing. By the beginning of the 19th century, the dance had become more military and was directed by a leader. [See *Verbunkos; Furriers' Sword Dance; Bakony Hehrdsmen's Dance*]

HAJNALTUZ TÂNC (Hungary)

"Dawnfire Dance". One of the many ceremonial dances proper to a traditional Hungarian wedding, known as the "singeing of the bride". On the second day of the wedding, the bride and her companions would dance around a fire in the courtyard, the bride herself jumping through or over the fire, for ritual purification. Similar jumps were made by maidens through the Midsummer Fire at the June Solstice.

HAKA (New Zealand)

Maori dance, described by some as a "posture dance" because its variant positions are sharply emphasised; performed as a war drill or as a sport, chiefly by the younger men. The *haka* is not restricted to any age; women sometimes perform, but only in their own groups. The fiercer development of *haka* is in the *peruperu* or *tutu-ngarahu* (war dance). *Haka* is now frequently performed in Maori villages as a "Dance of Welcome". The women and girls meet the visitors on the village boundary with a *powhiri*—with much waving of shawls and green branches; while the *haka*, as the men's greeting, follows immediately. The dance form of the *haka* is mainly in rhythmic loud stamping of the feet, gesticulation and slapping of sides or thighs, accompanied by a loudly ordered chant. These words are usually from ancient war songs; but special *haka* songs are composed for any great occasion. The dance appears in daylight as a rule; the men range in two to four or even six level lines, facing the visitors; clad in shorts and wearing *tapa* kilts, with no head-dress.

HALAU (Hawaii)

In old times, the hall or temple of the *hula*.* Originally part of a religious ritual, *hulas* were performed in the sacred *halau*, which contained an altar (*kuahu*) decorated with foliage and flowers. They told, in symbolical gesture-language, mythical stories of the gods, especially of the volcano goddess Pele, and her companions. Laka, symbolised in the *halau* by an uncarved block of wood from the sacred lama tree, was goddess of the *hula*. In prayers, dancers besought her spirit to enter their body and so give inspiration to their performance. *Hula* dancers, trained in the *halau* school by the *kumu*, or *hula*-master, belonged to the group of

temple dancers, with right of free entry into the *halau* during a performance, on giving the correct pass-word. Part of a chant was sung outside the door; when recognised by the doorkeeper and answered, the door was opened and the dancer admitted. Modern *hulas* are danced out of doors; and the earliest legend of the dance tells how the youngest sister of Pele danced and chanted for her on the sandy beach.   [See *Hula*]

HALCYON (from Greek *Alkhyone*, White Mother Goddess)

Traditional "Twelve Days of Xmesse" of Feasting at Winter Solstice, marked by a series of twelve different dances. The name was later given to kingfisher as "the Blue Bird of Happiness" and the period is associated with "good fortune". This long festival was an extension of the Egyptian Five Day Feast of the Gods, filled by worship and ritual dance, in which the tiny wren (*Uren*) was freed for flight. In its final version, came the carol-dance called *Twelve Days of Xmesse*, with the symbolic presents named in mounting succession, by the circling dancers.

HALL OF THE DOUBLE AXES (Crete)

Name given by Sir Arthur Evans to one of the principal halls excavated at Knossus in Crete. The Double Axe was the chief sacred symbol of the Cretan religion. As such it figures prominently in most of the important rituals. It was accompanied by the shields of the Minoan eight-shaped form, suspended on the walls; or held over the arm by the celebrants during the ritual dance. The key to this Minoan symbolism is : The sacred axe is used by Humanity to cut through the "world forest"— and it is illustrated as axe-plus-plant, emphasising the use of "wood as handle" to cut "wood as branch". The innumerable *Phoria* (later becoming Feria or Fairs) that affirm this duality by the "Carrying of the Branches", persisted in Greece, and came thence into Latin ritual. The Axe was usually held by the Minoan Goddess; but not by the great Snake Goddess (The Earth Serpent). She held golden snakes. There was (says Sir Arthur Evans) a shrine of the old Cretan Goddess at Delphi; where later the Temple of Apollo was erected, with a shrine for the Sibyl. One intaglio shows Edipus, in his encounter with his father Laios in the "Hollow Way" of the underworld. Later the "Forest" became summarised in a "Tree of the World" (*Iggdrazil*), in its ritual form, within temples.

HALLING (Norway)

A dance of the "showing-off" type, performed by a man before a girl. Usually in 2/4 time, it is danced generally by one dancer, or by two or three dancing in rivalry, and is accompanied by the "Hardanger-felen", or Hardanger fiddle. This is a violin dating from the 18th century, with eight strings, four of which give a drone effect. The dance is very energetic and acrobatic in form. Sometimes the girl, standing on a chair, holds a stick with the man's hat on the end of it, which the man, keeping the rhythm of the dance, must kick off with a leap coupled with a turning movement, or with a cartwheel. If he succeeds the couple dance together; if not, she walks away in disgust. The dance begins and ends quietly, rising in the meantime to violent acrobatic movement by the man in his efforts to impress. Sometimes the dance is performed by the man alone, without assistance from the girl. It is said that the *Halling* derives both origin and name from Hallingdal, between Christiana and Bergen. It is one of the dances, such as the *Springar** and *Gangar,** which developed from a merging of Polish dance rhythms with the old Scandinavian ballad dances. In music, Grieg has used the dance in many of his *Lyric Pieces*.

HALLISAKA (India)

Or *Gallisekka* — an operetta or musical play, performed by a travelling troupe of professional artists in Mediaeval India. The company had seven, eight, or ten female player-dancers, with a masculine manager. Two companies are recorded in wall paintings in the Caves of Bagh (Gwalior State, between Gujarat and Malwa), a former Buddhist monastery, flourishing about 8th to 10th century. One company shows six players; the other seven; all elaborately dressed; singing and performing with enjoyment on drums, cymbals and other instruments. Their shows seem to denote secular topics despite their religious situation; probably they resembled, in this, the entertainments furnished to abbeys in Europe, where monks gave hospitality to any troupe who could fill an evening jovially. These paintings give the forms but not the true colours of dresses: in black and white with touches of Indian red; and blue with yellow and another red. Similar paintings exist at Sigiraya in Ceylon. See *Théâtre Indien* (Sylvain Levi).
[Cp. *Yatra*]

HALOA (Ancient Greece)

A rustic dance belonging to harvest of corn and vine; uniting a song or chant of praise and thanksgiving with renewed worship to Pan and the gods of field and forest. This dance was performed normally on the threshing floor, as the only place sufficiently large and hammered flat; and able to accommodate a circle of dancers.

HAMMOCK DANCE (Sierra Leone, W. Africa)

A male solo dance of the acrobatic, circus type. Accompanied by a noisy orchestra, vocal and instrumental, the man dances first on the ground. A grass hammock is stretched between two poles, twenty or thirty feet above the ground, and as his dance becomes more wild, he scales one of the poles and begins a gymnastic dance in the hammock. Frequently he pretends to fall, recovers his balance, hangs by one leg, swings round it, rolls up in the hammock and makes it revolve, and all other variations of the flying trapeze known to European circus. The dancer continues till exhausted, to the great excitement of the crowd.

HAMMOSELIM (Hebrew) (Selah)

Or *Ammo-Tzelim* (in *Num. xxi. 27*). Indicates individuals who filled the function of minstrels. We may compare with *Tzaliim* in Rome; but the Hebrews were probably organised at this period (7th century BC), as the *Sons of Korah* or Choral Gild; who operated along with the Gild of Prophets.

HANSWURST (German, Mediaeval)

Literally, is "John Sausage", but sometimes translated as "Jack Pudding", and possibly related to the earlier Jack Horner (Jack Herne, the Hunter) who "ate the pudding". *Hanswürst* was the traditional dancing buffoon in the old German comedies and *puppenspielen*, long popular among the townspeople; but his supremacy was challenged in mid-18th century by the Neuber company plays; and later by Gottsched. His boisterous character was that of a clumsy and greedy clown; active in many folk-dances as the fool, or the butt of the circle of dancers. In France the name was Jean Potage; in Russia he became Ivanushka Durutchek, also Petrushka or Little Peter. The Zanny of Italy has a more inclusive tradition.
[See *Harlequin*; *Zany*]

HANUKKA (Hebrew; Dedication)

Also *Chanuka, Hanukah* etc. ritual feast of dedication of temple, centred on 25th Kislev, approx. December, enduring eight days. The feast arose with older Solstice rites before days of the Maccabees; it figures with Halkyone, the White One, the Goddess of Light (Alynyone-Alkh-Yoni); and pre-dates the "Twelve Days of Kresten-Messe". Every day had its ritual dance.

HANTU MENARI (Malaya)

Malayan "Spirit of Dancing" — who is invoked and welcomed as inspiration of the dance, which enters and "possesses" the girl dancers during their performance. (Compare *Voodoo* forms, Hayti); also the primitive Greek modes, e.g. of Bacchus and Dionysus, when Maenads or Minats — from

Egyptian *Menats*—women ritual dancers; and the *mignons* of Spain.

HARANGUE (French from Old High German *hring*)

A ring, a circus or arena, circus ring for display; a place for a circular processional dance, or entertainers; also a place where a talk is given. Also called harangue.
[Cp. H'arrange, arrangement; "hangment!" an interjection in Yorkshire]

HARBINGER (English, Med.)

Also *herberger, herbergeour;* an official (royal or ducal etc.) who journeyed one day ahead of the monarch, to arrange lodgings, food and entertainment. In this sense, an *impresario* who "impressed" persons as well as fire and food. Any important official sent his own messenger. (In Africa, this duty was performed by "talking drums" so that dancers and retinue went out to meet the visitors). He arranged a spontaneous welcome by drum and dance. When payment was not certain, performers were sometimes evasive; they had "gone away" and thus "led the man a fine dance".

HAREM (also *Harim, Hareem*)

Arabic—"reserved, secret". (Compare older Sanskrit *H'rim*, "keep out",* also the mystical "Urim and Thummim".*) In relatively modern times, the harem dance is exclusively a pastime show for the sultan. Many Muslim paintings (17th - 18th century, India) record such a dance; a female array of trained dancers, musicians and reciters of poems, with attendants in charge of swords and sweetmeats, or peacock feather fans, putting on a "one-spectator" show. In more liberal communities, the ruler would proudly display his harem dancers to visiting potentates; but they, if arriving in martial mood, would confiscate the company and take it home! Harem dance is almost obsolete, though still existent in partial form in Thailand, Java and a few other lands. Some African queens collected an all-male harem; they also danced "on demand". Relics of this tradition remain in North Africa, with boy dancers attired as girls, who pretend to offer "genuine harem dances".

HARLEQUIN (England)

As a stage character in London, Harlequin (apparently nationalised from the Italian Arlecchino), appeared with Rich, and with Garrick about 1750, when Garrick had to drop Shakespeare in favour of Pantomime. Garrick first employed Henry Woodward: an actor able to write as well as to pose and dance; he wrote the pantomime *Queen Mab;* then left for Dublin, to return to Covent Garden. Garrick recruited a famous Italian clown from the Fairs, named Giuseppe Grimaldi, for Drury Lane. With him the "clown tradition" became firmly founded. He first appeared in an interlude, a dance called *The Millers,* performed between two acts of *Richard III.* Thenceforward, he continued to serve Garrick at Drury Lane Theatre with great versatility: besides dancing, he was *maitre de ballet,* acting also as Harlequin, Pantaloon, or Clown. This phase of pantomime continued some tradition of the *Commedia dell' Arte,* merged with those of the English mummers. Grimaldi senior became *maitre de ballet* at Astley's Circus; and then at Sadlers Wells, where he performed in a number of pantomimes. His even better-known son, Joseph (born in 1779) maintained there the same tradition in its Anglo-Italian form. Harlequin became naturalised: the clown had long been in England, left by the Romans. Columbina settled first in Paris, where she was transformed into the romantic ballerina; they had both come a long way.

HARLEQUIN (English), ARLECCHINO (Italian) and ARLECHU (Welsh, from Cymric)

All signify an elusive dancing figure, belonging essentially to the Masque of the New Year, or the Feast of the Winter Solstice. Meanings now seem to remain most clear in Welsh. *Arlecchu* is "a hiding one", seclusive; but *arlachar* implies one very glittering; while the related word *Arlais* is Temple (possibly Arles). The traditional figure changes in detail; but essentials are (a) the parti-coloured costume; (b) glittering fragments of mirror or sequins or polished metal; and (c) the dark mask over the face. The dance, even in fairly recent English pantomime, down to *circa* 1900, had the same characteristic: the bounding and restless figure, alternately appearing and disappearing —as the Sun may well do, not only in the winter, but at any period of English climatic conditions. There may have been an earlier contact with Herakles, a Grecian sun-god who went through Twelve Labours in his twelve months; again, coming and going from his homeland on devious journeys. The Victorian pantomime Harlequin was seen in the "Magical Transformation Scene", dancing in and out of the scene, up and down, through walls as well as doors; though more as a virile male fairy than as a solar god; but he was forever dancing, swishing his lath or magical wand, sometimes seeking Columbine (Psyche) in competition with the pale Clown (Dead One), who could only fail.

HARVEST MOON BALL (USA)
Is a ballroom "dance contest", held annually in Madison Square Gardens, New York City; usually before a capacity audience of 18,000. Finals only are danced here; the preliminaries are completed in local halls. This program, including amateur teams as well as professionals, is sponsored by the *Daily News*. There are some display dances by "Guest Artists", who receive fees. Originated nominally as a genuine dancing competition, it is said by professionals of the city to have become entirely devoted to stage or cabaret experts, and "not-ballroom" exhibition dancing, with most amateur couples following only a set routine. Six routines are set for competitors; but too wide a margin is permitted for "fancy steps" (sometimes shoes are raised to waist level) to remain entirely within the range of normal social ballroom or pastime dance. The routines are named as : Fox Trot; Tango; Rumba; Waltz; Polka; and Jitterbug Jive. No other country admits this last performance as a ballroom dance; but relegates it to musichall.

HASIDIN, Dances of (Poland)
The Hasidin, or Chassidim, were a Jewish mystical sect founded by Rabbi Israel Baal-Shem, or Baal-Shem Tov ("Master of the Good Name"), just before mid-eighteenth century. Baal-Shem (born 1700) believed that laughter, song and dance were the highest forms of prayer, and dancing to sung melody formed part of the worship of the Hasidin. His fundamental teaching was that of love—of God and of men. Although condemned by Talmudic traditionalists as heretical, Hasidism grew in popularity, until towards the end of the nineteenth century half the Jews in Europe belonged to it, but corruption within itself brought about its downfall. During services, many Hasidic melodies (*niggunim*), especially the more meditative tunes, were sung without words, it being considered that words stood between man and his communication with God. The more joyful melodies were sung as an accompaniment to the dances of the mystic circle, among which were the *Dance of Teb Mayer* and *M'la-Veh Mal-Koh* ("Dance of the Departing Sabbath"), both in 2/4 time and both "la-la'd"; Hasidic Round also in 2/4 time, and *A Radel Fun'm Libavitcher Rebbe*.

HASJELTI DAILJIS (New Mexico, Arizona)
Amerindian Apache tribe, Dance of Hesjelti, or *Hezyelte Dailyes*. A Dance of Renovation, held always in Autumn or early Winter, annually, "when the Thundergod sleeps", to pray for health of all the *Dinne* (Indians' own name for "People") known as Apaches (*Apaches del Navaiu* is the Spanish term). This rite is a "medicine song", done as the opening of *Yei Bit Chai** ceremonial gathering, lasting eight or nine days. The twin deities Hasjelti and Hosthoghon (medicine priests, masked in deer skin) rule the ritual. Weird hooting is peculiar to Hasjelti, who leads in the cure of sick men. Part of the rite requires the making of Sand Pictures.

HASSAPIKOS "Butchers' Dance" (Crete)
A chain dance for men only, or for men and women alternately. Each dancer with hands on the shoulders of his neighbours, the line or curve, facing inwards, moves slowly round counter-clockwise, in 2/4 time. With small steps and regular foot-beats, the chain moves in perfect rhythm, frequent knee-bends (from a slight flexing to a deep squatting position) causing it to dip and rise as it progresses. The leader sometimes crouches and revolves in solo exhibition. Originally from Constantinople, the *Hassapikos* was danced by butchers on their feast-day, and is found also in Armenia. It was known in Byzantine times as the *Makelláricos*.

HASTA-MUDRA (Hindu)
A dual term, uniting a Sanskrit word, *mudra,** (seal) with a Prakrit word, *hasta* (gesture), has usually been confused in the study of Hindu ritual dance. Both of these two terms comprise more than is indicated in their translation into English. The closest approximation to *hasta* in "gesture"; and this, as part of *abhinaya** or general acting, applies first to *movements* of hand and arm, but also of head and limbs. The older term, *mudra*, should not be used to indicate movement, but the temporary motionless result of movement. Originally it meant a *seal*; a fixed and permanent form, able to repeat only its own design. The *mudra* is the word; the *hasta* is the articulation that creates the word in action. The *mudra* is the symbol; the gesture or *hasta* moves and draws or directs attention to it, in place and position. The *hasta* is the dance; while the *mudra* affirms the ritual. These elements are so closely united in Hindu dance, that their relative and relating importance has rarely been analysed. The *samyuta* and *asamyuta* define *hasta* as "made with one hand", or "made with two hands"; while the immediate meaning of a single *mudra*, selected from its score or more divergent meanings, is located by its position in the dance, in the routine, in the hands, in the contrasting relation to any other dance character.

HARUSPEX (Roman ritual)

The rustic "dance of divination" said to be done from "inspection of entrails of birds, animals, etc." but just as likely to be examination of their crops, as determination of pests to food production. They used a *litra* (like the Augur*) but as a dowsing rod, as the modern dowser seeks hidden water. The term is probably connected with *arval*, and harvest and *rustica* (country-side matters). The ritual dance in a closed corde drawn in dust or mud was doubtless an ornamented *tripudium*, to increase their impressive statements.

HAUSA DANCES (N. Nigeria)

Dancing occurs at the two *Salla* Festivals: the *Babba Salla* (Greater, is *Id-el-Kabir*; and Lesser is *Id-ul-Fitr*); but also in the ordinary week—"Thursday night is Music night". On Tenth day of *Zul-Hajji* is the *Babba Salla*; it begins in prayer and ends in music with dance; the Koranic rule against dancing is not so rigidly maintained. The New Year Festival, called "Feast of the Full Stomach", literally means just that. There is dancing at the Initiations (only for girls, in these days), when the phrase goes: *Aka-girka-ta*, meaning "She was cooked!" This is sometimes an initiation into the Bori women's cult. For weddings, they have special dances: each vocation has its special dance, and relatives in these revel in their imitative skill. Some of the brides' "mothers" or sponsors will dance with her, as in the dance of the blacksmiths; when a tomato is held in the mouth to represent the red hot iron. At the butchers' feast they dance with mouths filled with porridge and mime the selling of meat. The *algaita*, an instrument like an oboe, though sounding like bagpipe music, is reserved chiefly for dances connected with officials; and is heard at the *Salla* Festivals, with the *kirari* or praise song.   [See *Bori Dancers*]

HAY (England)

Has had many meanings, direct and derivative, including that of dance forms and places. As a place, the hay (or *hagh, haugh, haigh*) was a fine royal pasture; later "rich pasture land", but then "hayward" turned to mean "keeper of cattle", or of a common herd. Then the word *hay* came to mean "hedge"—the fence of the pasture; and then of its crop of mown grass, dried in the sun. Anglo-Saxon *hay* was *heq* or *hege*, meaning "hedge". All these terms, by festal usage, became indicative of dance and dancing-places. The prime, the middle day, was called hey-day (Saxon *heh-daeg*) in a parallel term; the German was *hoch*, from which comes the *Hoch-fest* or high feast, again with rural dancing and sports. Thence we come to *Hagmanay*, and the *Hegmonath* of July.

HAYATO (Japan)

Court mime-dance, described at length in mythic tales, *Nihongi* (720 AD), and in *Kojiki* (but not now performed), as a "dance before Mikado". The tale has some resemblance to the Russian story of *Sadko*; modern Japanese critics admit recent foreign influence. There is a submarine palace of the dragon-king. The theme develops as a result of the adventures of the hero Hohodemi, who consults the Old Man of the Sea; visits King Toyo-tama-hiko (Jewel Prince), and marries his daughter. Family troubles ensue, with his elder brother, who was defeated, and whose family and guards then became court servants. They are the dancer-mimes; they perform the "drowning and struggles" of the ancestors. [See *Shinto*. W. G. Aston, (London 1907)]

HEAD HUNTERS' RITUAL DANCE (Polynesia, Brazil, etc.)

Was arranged and performed chiefly for propaganda. The whole aim was proving success in aggression; looting and plundering, by exhibits of the enemy's heads. Heads on show were irrefutable proof of the death of the "other side"; proof of great valour (or more cunning treachery), and thus the heads (it being unnecessary to display the entire body) were the first item of evidence—"Exhibit A in the case". All subsequent displays of similar type, shew progressively more and more symbolical substitutes: the standard, the flag, the "colours", or even trophies taken into battles (regimental mascots etc.). In the dance aspect of the ritual display, the head was shewn in various ways. It was carried in the first *trionfo*, the triumphal "entry of troops" back from war, together with plunder and captives in chains, to be used as slaves or as craftsmen etc. The head of a slaughtered general was (a) empaled above a gate; (b) retained in a shrine (relic of overcome power), or placed "on a shelf" in village ritual. Eventually the game aspect displaced the solemn ritual aspect; and the head was thrown about (comp. Green gourd, and "king's strength") among the troops. They played then in two groups, each trying to place the head in their own shrine (goal) (comp. Rugby football), and so began the long series of ball games. Football was sometimes "played through the town" instead of on a reserved green field, with an inflated ball to replace the head, but always approximately the size of a human head.

HEALING BY DANCE

Is accomplished in several widely different methods; from the basic positive mode, in which the sufferer makes his own endeavour to regain health, to the basic negative mode, in which treatment is given to the patient who is more or less helpless. In the positive mode, the person makes his own efforts to regain energy, by using what power he has, in a discipline by which more power is received, as it flows through the organism. This is an extension of the normal system that occurs in sleep and waking, by systole and diastole of natural tensions and relaxations. The ancient negative method of treatment is for the expert "medicine man" to direct energy (through his own channels) into the weak organism, without its own conscious effort. This flow of energy, directed by will power and accumulated by ritual dancing in a ring surrounding the patient, is a skilled usage of natural magnetism, sometimes known as "devil-dancing". The primitive Christian method, connected with those known as "energumens" was carried through by appointed exorcists, who followed a routine similar to that of the "pagan" devil-banishers. Less drastic are physical training methods, which include use of musical rhythm with dance movement. Direct

healing is rare; it is practised by Harry Edwards of Shere in Surrey.
[See *Devil Dance; Rhythm; Relax*]

HEAVENLY DANCES, The Seat of ("—in the Six Heights of Osiris". Ancient Egyptian)
An expression contained in and relevant to the Rituals of the Temple; meaning the rhythmic movements of certain star systems, in the "six modes of the tropical heavens". These are named in the great "Planisphere of Denderah" (now in the Louvre), where the *Akh* (points) are marked for the *Annua* (Year); for Horus, the Entrance of the Golden Heaven; for the Seat of Sacred Dances of Horus, Son of Osiris; followed by the whole series. The higher priests, wearing appropriate god-masks, performed the solemn ritual for the dual need of devotion and instruction for the junior priests. Later this became *Tabla Ronda*.
[See *The Book of the Master*. W. Marsham Adams. 1898. Ch. VI]

Ritual Temple Dance. The Judgement of Osiris. Luxor.   EGYPT

HEBREW DANCE (Ancient modes—BC 300 - AD 400) Is a fusion of Semitic - Arabic forms with those of Babylonia. There are eleven distinct Hebrew roots, which describe variant characteristics of dance, cited by Oesterley.[1] Most of them occur in the intensive modes of speech. Among them, *dalag* and *tzala* both refer to ritual steps. The oldest root is *ragad* (used as *riqqed*), meaning "to skip about joyfully". The Assyrian is *rakadu*; this survives in our common term "racket" (kicking up a noise), but is deeper hidden in "rigged" (to fake or "arrange" some delusion). The most frequently used root in the Old Testament is *hul*; it expresses the whirl of dance, and implies always highly active movement. This same root lies in Arabic as *hul*,

making *hul-ab-alou* (the noisy dance), or the market crowd; and comes up again in *Holi* (India) and *huli*, into (Irish) *huli-khan* or *hooligan*. This same whirling idea is more firmly contained in *karar* as *kirker* (*pilpel* form), meaning "to rotate", and as such is used to describe the "Dance of David". "Going round " is implied by *sabab*, and crops up as *sabathat*—the round of the week. In *Canticles*, *dalag* is used to denote some joyous form of dancing, as a processional movement. The term *pazaz*, mostly as *pizzez*, implies leaping (possibly an ancestor of *pas* or *paces*). The term *hagag* occurs but once; it means "to make a circle". The term *tzela* may be a re-spelling of the terminal (often found at the end of Psalms) *Selah?*, which most

scholars evade. Possibly it means or implies: "Having sung, Now Dance!" (The ruler of Abyssinia has, as title, *Haile Selah-ssie!*). *Saheq* means "to make merry, to laugh, rejoice, or playing". It comes as *siheq*. The Egyptian *heq*, leading into Arabic *heqh*, connotes magical dance (*Heqh*=Magic in Cairo). *Qaphatz* occurs rarely; it may mean the dance step of servants?
[See *Hastings Encyclopaedia of Religion*; *Encyclopaedia Biblica*; Cheyne; *Religion of the Semites* (Robertson)]
[1] *The Sacred Dance*. W. Oesterley.

HEBREW RITUAL DANCE
Operated through three distinct phases. The doctrines, taught by the Chaldaeans in the great city of Babylon, were not conveyed to the immigrant Jews too readily; as the two different accounts of creation, contained in *Genesis*, clearly reveal. The secret doctrine of Emanation (not an "instant creation") though covered in the ciphers of the "patriarchal genealogy" (which gives cosmic rather than clan history), was never published freely; nor is it easy to understand. The teaching was thus given (as in Hindu system) in three phases; according to the comprehension of the disciple. The external form was that for Jawhe of Israel; the next inner mode was El Shaddai of Abraham (known to Babylonian educated men), and the inner intellectual mode was that of Elohim (male/female, as the term conveys) allocated to the mythical Noah by the Magi. *El Shaddai* somehow got to Britain; where this God is memorised as Chad or Shad (in Babylon as Chad or Dach). Rituals carried the meaning of relations (highly important in all god systems), and the Elohim (Seven, or "Six in One") is symbolic in the Hexagon badge, used by Morris Dancers with six *rapirs*.

HEK-HEKELEAN ("Settling Down". Malekula, New Hebrides)
A circular dance which occurs during the fourth year of the ritual cycle called *Ramben.** Performed when the day of the culminating rite is approaching, its name signifies that henceforth the "Maki-men" (initiates) will "settle down" seriously to the performance of the ritual. Its name, therefore, refers to its place in the ritual sequence rather than to the form of the dance. Contrary to usual custom, the first performance of *Hek-hekelean* takes place in daylight, from noon till about 4 o'clock, after which it is danced in rotation by each village, at intervals of from five to ten days. It is then replaced by *Taur Na-mbak** which it closely resembles. (See also *Turei Na-mbe**). Although ritually not as important as *Taur Na-mbad*, *Hek-hekelean* has a status of its own, in that it

holds the position of sanctioning more important dances that follow it. Before it can be performed, the right to dance it has to be bought by the Maki-men from their own sponsors and from members of all other villages on the Island, which act is symbolised by the handing over of the bamboo stick called *Ne-mbal*, with which the leader of each village beats time during the dance. This stick, representing the whole dance, is paid for with money-mats. As the buying of dance copyrights is not again repeated during the rest of the two-part cycle, the right to perform *Hek-hekelean* also confers the same right on *Taur Na-mbak* which follows it, and even on the most important dance of all, *Taure,** which occurs years later, at the peak of the second part of the ritual cycle, *Maki-ru.**
[See *Malekula, Dances of*]

HENXMEN (England)
Court of Edward IV, were pages, sons of noble families entering system of knighthood. The regular number was twenty-four, under charge of a Master of Henxmen who sat with them at the royal table, to observe their manners. They had to study languages (English, Latin, French) and the use of weapons. On this basis they had lessons in music (piping and drum) dance and singing to instruments. They were required to read books on courtesy and manners, rules of procedure and address. They danced as required with the Maids of Honour, and foreign visitors. Besides these "henchmen" the Master ruled the Choir of the Kings Chapel; they also learned comportment.

HERMITAGE THEATRE (Leningrad)
Is a former imperial-private Theatre, designed by Guarenghi, and built-in as part of the Winter Palace (now the Hermitage Museum of Art), for the delectation of ruling class families. The stage is an exact replica of that in the Maryinski Theatre, enabling a complete production to be transferred without change of scale; the auditorium, not much larger than the stage area, seats only some four hundred persons. Obviously, such an arrangement has no economic basis; this Theatre is now used, at intervals, for giving special concerts of classical music, to selected audiences.

HERMITAGE THEATRE (Moscow)
Is a large wooden structure, used only as a "Summer Theatre" (it has 1,600 places), situated in one of the smaller parks, off the Sadovaya Boulevard. During hot summer months, many performances of ballet are given, interspersed with other entertainments. Dancers of the "big theatres" may appear with these companies; the same high standard of production is normally visible. This theatre is a

simple rectangle in shape, having only one balcony, as compared with the other ballet theatres, which follow the West European opera house "Renaissance style".

HEVEHE (Papua, New Guinea)
An initiation ritual-cycle of the Western Elema people of Orokolo Bay. The shortest time for its completion is seven years, the average being fifteen or more. Strongly connected with Elema mythology, it is concerned with initiation of young men, particularly into knowledge of the *Ma-hevehe* sea creature. Very large, upright oval masks are made, representing daughters of *Ma-hevehe* who, at intervals (in a noisy ceremony called *Hevehe Karawa*) comes up from the sea to bring the necessary materials to the *eravo* (men's lodge) for making the masks. After years of preparation, the climax comes when the masks are ready to emerge for their ritual dance. Made of bark-cloth over an oval cane framework, they average ten feet high, with a projecting rib rising another six feet. Having projecting jaws, they are painted with symbolic patterns, and each is named according to the totem it represents. Awkward to dance in, they are balanced by a sago mid-rib between the thighs, and a conical framework at the back which fits the head. Long mantles of frayed sago-leaf and white bast hide the wearer's body. Each dancer beats a drum slung horizontally in front of him, with the particular rhythm of his totem. These rhythms have special names, such as "Sky Thunder", "Sea Waves", "Tide Rushing Up-Stream", "Whirlpool" (when the *hevehe*-dancer revolves first in one direction, then the other); and each dancer performs the steps belonging to the totem of the mask he wears, as do the groups of girls who attach themselves to each mask as it descends from the *eravo*, dancing lightly round him. Some masks have a special song, sung by men, while the mask-wearer performs a stationary dance. After the first dramatic appearance at dawn on the appropriate day, dancing continues each day for a month, the *hevehe* dancing singly, or in pairs; sometimes in groups; on the beach or in the village. At the end of that time, dancing ends with a ceremonial procession, *Laraa*, when drums are surrendered, and later the masks discarded. With modern influences, and missionary disapproval, the *Hevehe* cycle is now disappearing. Dancing also occurs earlier in the cycle, when masks in-the-making have the sago-leaf overmantle fixed — see *Eharo;** *Poilati;** *Yahe.** [Cp. *Malekula, Dances of; Golkerma; Maki-Ru; Ramben*]

HEY, HAY, HAYE — 1
A round dance and also a figure in Country Dances.

An early mention occurs in 1564 in a Morality Play by Wm. Bulleyn, in which a minstrel is described as "dancing *Trenchmore** and *Heie de Gie*", or (according to Flood[1]) "Hey of the arms". This may refer to the *Bouffons** or *Matassins** (16th and 17th centuries), which was a mock combat, one part being called in Arbeau's *Orchésographie** (1588) "Passage de la Haye". Flood mentions that "in a book printed in 1588, the Irish Hey is illustrated as danced by four men, with bare arms, in imitation of a combat, and the music played is printed in Playford's *Musick's Handmaid* in 1678".[2] He also asserts that the "Irish Hayes were Irish Round Dances, the round being the old Irish *corr.* or reel".* Chappel's *Popular Music of Olden Times* says that "Dancing a reel is one of the ways of dancing a hay . . ." Shakespeare mentions the dance in *Love's Labour Lost* with "I will play on the tabor to the worthies and let them dance the Hay". In 1957, notes to Spenser's *Shepherds Calendar* refer to the *Hey* as "a country dance or round" which recalls Percy Grainger's composition *Shepherd's Hey*. As a figure in Country Dances, the *hey* is a "winding in and out", frequently mentioned in Playford's *Dancing Master,** as when "the women stand still, the men giving the hey between them". The "whole-hey" is a figure of eight. Derivation of the name is uncertain. Dr. Johnson's Dictionary of 1755 suggests that it refers to "dancing round a haycock", while other have given the French word *haie*, "a hedge", as a possible origin. For older meanings of the word see *Hey* — 2
[1] *History of Irish Music.* Wm. H. Gratton Flood (Dublin 1905).

HEY — 2 (or *Heye*)
Is not merely a rustic dance, of mirth and jollity; but originates in an ancient and stately ritual, namely "The Journey", (*Yerne Hayy*), which has an analogy with the Dance of the Labyrinth. *Hey* is the same as the Arabic Moslem *Hajj* — the popular name for the Journey to Mecca, but allied also with Greek mystery doctrines which continued with a similar name (the *Hagia*), associated with *Sophia Hagia* (i.e. the great Byzantine church, now a mosque, in Stambul). *Sophia* is Wisdom and *Hagia* is the way or journey to it. Thus in the primitive Christian ritual, the *heyya* of the shepherd was the ritual dance of the leader of the group of worshippers. The Moslem pilgrim rightly uses this name for his long journey to his sacred centre. In West Europe, this was the *pelli-grin* (*pella-guerin*) later *pelegrin;* though in French churches, the symbol was laid down in a spiraline path as the Path of Peace. At centres like La Haye (now La Hague), this was a devotion, long before the form was left to country villages or gathered into the pages of

Shakespeare's folios. From Alexandria, this ritual spread—north into Western Europe, and south into Abyssinia, where it merged with older Egyptian traditions. In the Coptic round churches we find the chancel (chant-cell) is called the *hey-kell;* and there it is that the priests repeat the ancient mythic chants each festival. Here the shepherd is the *Abuna* (or *Abouna*) known as Abbatachen—the Father of the Circle, allied with Matta-chin, the Mother of the Circle. From this Alexandrian term (the chief bishop, the Abouna, is appointed thence to Addis Ababa, no native may hold this post), we cherish our familiar term *bun*—the circular festival cake (as once it was). In Ababa, the ritual is still followed; the dance is still performed.

HEY—3 (or Heye, Haye and La Haye—Hague)
Various spellings of *Al Hayy* (Arabic-Islamic chant) meaning "Praise to the Living One", recited in the devotions of Moslems of Southern Spain. The intertwining form arises by the dance circulation in a round church or temple. Needing a longer movement yet in a small space, the worshippers danced "in and out" of the ring of pillars, instead of remaining in the central space. With a second chain moving in the opposite circular direction, the "*intrecchia*" is produced. Compare this form with the spiraline "Way to Jerusalem" ritual dance (see Hughes *Dictionary of Islam,* also *Islamic Encyclopaedia*). Coming to Britain with Arab traders, the dance form was repeated in the open—Village Green—and became *Shepherd's Hey,* and other variations given by Playford in his *Dancing Master.* These are the final forms. The Balkan *kolo* has a similar out-door form, affirmed by the exchange of hands as the two rings circulate in opposing directions.

HEY! DIDDLE DIDDLE (From Welsh *Daedol,* "to right")
Tudor period. The term Hey is admonition to dance, Western Europe. The lines belong to a ballad, probably satirical, *Ye Hey diddle diddle,* the Cat and the Fiddle etc. in which Cat=*catachumenoi* and *fideles*=faithful who were told to separate (usually at church porch, for the students were not admitted with the Faithful baptised). The violin itself got named from the *Fideles* who danced to its melodies.

HIGHLAND FLING (Scotland)
A group dance, usually by four or eight men, known from 16th century in the Scottish Highlands. Some dancers refer the name to the special step called *fling* (or *flank*), when the performer stands on one foot while moving the other leg back and forwards. In French dance there is a similar step, *la vache,* thus blamed on the cow. The phrase "to fling like a cow" was used by Scots grooms, concerning awkward horses. The music is usually a *strathspey,** and the dance carried in its traditions a number of melodies regularly used. Small children may be seen doing this step during their dance-game of Hop-scotch; and it used to be done during footballers' training.

HILDE (German)
Also *Gilde;* as for example, Brünnhilde, *die brünnen-hilde,* the group, entrusted as "guardians of the spring". In countries further west, as *Kilde* or *Kilda;* and *Gilda;* as one of several gilds of companies, each with their typical ritual, with a processional dance movement. Before communities obtained (a) regular access to rivers or (b) an ever-flowing spring; or (c) constructed reservoirs, the problem of water supply was as urgent as the conservation of Fire. Hence every such community deputed several trusted members to "keep watch and ward" over these supplies. Hence, the fountain, the spring, the stream, was highly important, both for supply and for purity. In Greece the village maidens arranged a regular supply; the well or spring became a centre of gossip; the walk to and from the village a routine that developed simple song and a dancing step, enhanced on ceremonial occasions. Mythology kept pace with the "unseen guardians" of the Water and the Fire; these were then pictured in the festivities; and we find undines and sylphs, gnomes and naiads, appearing in the dance.

HIMINAU (Tahiti)
Performed by some forty dancers, in two concentric circles, directed by a master of ceremonies. Rhythm is given by the inner circle, who kneel, facing inwards, and beat the ground in unison with half coconut-shells. The outer circle of men and women revolves, stopping at intervals, when partners face each other and perform the hip-rolling, gyratory movement called *upa-upa.*
[See *Otéa; Hula; Paoa; Aparina; Moré*]

HINA MATSURI (Japan)
Festival for girls, March 3rd. Annual celebration, to be compared with the boys' festival—*Tango-No-Seku.** Traditional religious festival. now mainly a children's game, to encourage filial piety and loyalty. Daughters of the houses exchange visits at homes of friends; and partake of delicacies placed on the shelves for the puppets (cp. *Alpona** and *Lakshmi* in India). The puppets do not represent deities, but imitate, in splendid old-fashioned costume, Emperor and Empress, high-court officials and heads of noble families, with their court minstrels and dancers. The end of the gala day is occupied with simple dancing.

HISTRIONE (Ancient Rome)

Term used in Etruria for actor-mimes, who performed usually in ceremonial; from *histor*, meaning a dancer. This root is important, since from it stem many derivatives: from "history" to "minister" (Min-Istria),, and "minstrel". Rome knew the "Istrione" first, it is said, in 364 BC, when ceremonials then performed in Rome, for some religious purpose, required instruction. Ordinary performers were not accepted as citizens; they were considered as servants; yet, later some men of talent were distinguished, such as Roscius and Aesopus.

HISTRIONES (Latin, from Etruscan)

Assistants in the Roman *funus* or burial; they were hired, along with the *scurrae* or buffoons, to recall and represent the character of the deceased person, by giving vivid imitations of word and action. The religious theory originally formulating this custom is allied with the recondite system held by the Egyptians concerning the post-mortem world, as presented to us, chiefly, by their paintings and temple-carving. The funeral was arranged by Dominus Funeris (Funeral Lord or Master) who also hired musicians (*cornicenes, siticines*) who played mournful strains; while the *praeficae* (women) sang the funeral song (*naenia* or *lessus*), and sometimes moved in dancing steps. Some of the *histriones* walked, bearing masks (imago) of the face of the deceased person's ancestors, and attired to suggest them. The bier was *vilis arca,* carried by *vespillones;* the coffin space was also called *arca*, or *loculus.* A wealthy person had perfume or incense thrown on the fire (Pyra) when burned, which the *vespillone* walked or danced slowly round. Later called *columbarines*, they assisted at private tombs for burials.

HOB-BIDI-DANCE (Old English)

A term applied to silent gesture or mime — one who "acts dumb" — denounced by the clerics (rivals of the secular mimes) as a person "possessed of a devil". Thus the term came into legend as the "fiend who possessed Poor Tom", as given by Shakespeare (*King Lear*, iv. 1). The parallel name appears in fairy-tales as Hoppety Thumb or Hop o' my Thumb.

HOBBY HORSE

A man carrying a framework, roughly cut to suggest a "Horse". This was not a single dance; it has a basic ring pattern but much "ad lib" Basque dancers use it; but in England it was associated with the May Games and the Moeris, sometimes in combat against the Bear (who devoured the Old Year). The dance may stem from *Hapi* (Egypt). In Austria, the Perchten* dancers ride the Hobby Horse.   [See *Godalet Dantza*]

HOBBY HORSE DANCE (England)

Traces of ancient traditions remain in the children's *Hobby Horse Dance*, performed usually with a broomstick captured from the kitchen. Great pretence is made, at intervals in the ring dance, about the difficulty of riding; and this may be a nursery pastime recalling the adult hobby horse of *Morris** or *Sword Dance** groups. There are sundry four-line verses: some invocations, some parodies; such as:

> "Matthew, Mark, Luke, and John —
>   Held my horse till I got on!
> When I got on, I could not ride
>   'Cos I fell off, and broke my side!"

In the West Indies is a more serious invocation, when Negro worshippers repeat similar verses, until one of them is "mounted", or possessed as a medium.

Hobby Horse Dancer in Basque Godalet Dantza. The *Zalmatzaim*, or hobby-horse, leaps above the half-filled glass of wine.   **BASQUE**

HOBO (USA)

Modern North American term for the "industrial gypsy" or tramp, in the mechanised slave system, which he aims to avoid. Bordered in the South by the remainder of the Negro slave system, the roaming hobo refuses to take any permanent job. He may be a cow-hand or harvest-helper; or he may join some great industrial unit; but his method is to wander during the summer, taking jobs only in the hard winter months, when hitch-hiking or train "rod-riding" drives him to towns. His songs are well known : they touch the Negro spiritual on one side, or the bawdy saloon melody on the other; or often sentimental, he will echo some chapel hymn-tune, but not the words. His dances are a medley : a mixture of the country or square dance (seen in the farmlands at harvest) or parodies of some town music-hall. The rhythmic music may be supplied by a jews-harp, an empty tin for a drum; or rise to an accordion melody from some amateur expert. There are no women; they rema'n in the towns. The hobo comes from all classes; the anarchist artisan, or the broken professional man; they refuse all allegiance to governments or their agents. Their dance occasions appear only during summer; usually round a camp fire; mainly spontaneous. They never dance for money, only for fun.

HO-BO (Thailand)

This fête is celebrated in April - May in Thailand (Siam) at many local centres. The French writer, Bonifacy records *Fête de Ho-Bo* at Binh-lieu;[1] at Dong-trung-po; and at Na-thuoc. They are agricultural festivals of fertility type; the term *Ho-Bo* means or implies mixture. Young girls and matrons take part; they walk about in parties, varied by simple dance circles; the young men move in other similar circles, but they do not mingle the sexes. The festival is popular as a means of "meeting people"—a permanent marriage may follow.
[1] *Bulletin Ethnologique, French Extreme Orient.* M. Bonifacy. (1915- p. 17).

HOLIKA-DAHA (Northern India)

Belongs to *Vasant-Otsava,** the Hindu Spring Festival. Known best by the familiar abbreviation *Holi,* the people celebrate the joys of Spring as Vaishnavites, for Krishna. The original *Holika-daha* were the bonfires, lit to burn rubbish accumulated in the winter season; thus began the preparation for general cleansing of home and temple. There is associated the rites of the *Chatuh-Shashti Devi*—goddess of the "Sixty-four Arts" which serve *Kama* or enjoyment in life. Generally, the modern *Holi* shows that religious inspiration and meaning have dropped to a low level; the *mela* or fair becomes

an occasion merely for coarse merriment and horse-play, marked by squirting coloured water from large syringes. Dances belong to the Krishna cycle, while too much of the music is a blare of horns, a jangle of brass, with a wheezy gurgle from a German harmonium.   [See *Krishna Dances*]

HOMUNCULUS (Mediaeval Europe)

The tiny "Mannikin" or "dancing creature" first endowed with this particular name by Paracelsus, the Swiss doctor (15th century) becomes the Guide in Part II of Goethe's drama of *Faust,* conducting the *Walpurgis Nacht** ceremonial of the Eve of May (second of the four annual festivals). He replaces Mephistophelius, who was Master of Ceremony for the Winter feast, the Classical Masquerade. This "tiny" dancing creature, made by alchemy within a glass viol, symbolises the "higher mind", which dances, not in glass but in the bony "vessel of the skull", drawn alternately between the shadows of Mephisto and the light that is 'Elena (or Wisdom). He is at once companion (as with the Prodigal Son), and tempter (the women), and the mystical "swan-prince". In Part II of *Faust,* the guide Homunculus says (just after he has commented on the "swan-prince with plumage white")·

> "Command the warrior to the fight,
> Conduct the maiden to the dances;
> And all is finished; all is right.
> Just now, there breaks on me a light—
> 'Tis Classical Walpurgis Night".

Then follows Scene III of the *Walpurgis.*

HONEY-BEE DANCE (North Australia)

Harvest "Dance of Thanksgiving" performed by the Australian natives at Yirrkala in Arnhem Land. They prepare special patterns, enlarged symbol-pictures on the basis of the honey-comb shapes, in yellow and black, painted on their bodies; and dance to music, which they believe resembles the humming of bees, from the droning *didgeridoo,* and small drums. Their story is one of thanks, of explanation and expiation, for having taken the preserve of the honey-bees; and thus caused some of them to die. They hope the bees will recognise their need; will accept the brotherhood of the tribe; and will "rise again". Thus the body pat-terns painted on, invite the Bee spirits to partake in friendship. The man is but a greater bee, eating the same food. No technique of bee-keeping exists; no offerings are made save flowers; but the song is considered important. Women are excluded.
[See *Corroboree; Oenpelli Snake Dance; Nakum-doit*]

HOP (England, Lancashire)
Local term for a dance, as "Sixpenny Hop", in bygone days when sixpence was the admission charge. The step also is called "hop"; while the village "wakes" in parts of the North of England are retained under the title of "hopping". The Swiss educationist Jaques Dalcroze, favoured the term "hopp" when giving instruction in his Eurhythmic system. A country couple, on a courting ramble, will invite any curious small boy, to "hop it, quick", to expedite his departure out of sight and sound. The term possibly derives from Saxon *hoppan*, to leap; but there is still extant a pavement game (pursued by small girls) known as "hop-scotch". An allied term, *hobble*, means to hinder movement.

HOPI (North America)
Pueblo Indians,* living in seven villages in north-eastern Arizona. An agricultural people, living on arid land, their religious ceremonies emphasise the constant need of rain. Ceremonial races to produce showers (by sympathetic magic) are still run; but the most famous "rain-making ceremony" is their *Snake Dance,** performed in alternate years, on the last day of the nine-day ritual. On preceding days, secret ceremonies take place in the *kiva,** or underground ceremonial chamber. The *Powamu* ceremony for abundant crops, held annually in February, is also a puberty rite. Among all Pueblo Indians, ancestral spirits, or *Kachinas,** who visit the earth for the winter, are impersonated by masked dancers at rites to ensure growth of crops, or rain ceremonies. Their arrival and departure, at winter and summer solstices, are occasions for dramatic ceremonies. The Hopi *Kachinas*, who arrive in January at the *Soyal* ceremony, stay until July, when they return to the spirit world at the *Nima'n* ceremony. During the summer months they are replaced by the Snake-Antelope or Flute Societies. *Powamu*, *Nima'n* and *Soyal* all last nine days, and include dramatic presentations, and *kachina* dances, as well as religious ritual. Accompanying the *Kachinas*, and providing burlesque interludes between their dances, are dancing clowns known as *Koshare** or "Delight Makers"; and *Koyemshi** or "Mudheads", called by the Hopi *Tachuki*. The most important event of the Hopi calendar is the "New Fire Rite". This elaborate ceremonial includes songs and dances, culminating in the ritual rekindling of fire with drill and stone. The rite suggests the remote ancestry of the Hopi in the Maya, who, followed by Toltecs and Aztecs, had a similar fire ritual. The Hopi evolution story tells how humanity emerged through three successive underground worlds (or cycles), on to the earth in the fourth, and present, cycle. In the third world of darkness, a madness seized the women, who left husbands and children in order to dance. In the *kivas* they danced almost ceaselessly, stopping only to sleep and to feed their babies, brought to them by their more domesticated husbands.   [See *Aztec Dance; Eagle Dance*]

HOPKE (Yiddish)
Term used in East London (19th century) to refer to a cheap "song-and-dance" show, patronised chiefly by Jewish visitors. Many were given at the old Pavilion Theatre in Mile End. They ranged from solo dancers to comedians who did a dance — Schilling or Schatz; and Joseph Sherman, a notable dancer and jester, who appeared at the Grand Palais in Commercial Road. Two other veterans, Axelrad and Markovitch, also appeared there, or later at the "Alex". (Stoke Newington).

HOPPESTERES (Anglo-Saxon-Norman)
Term used to denote female dancers, at Fairs or other gatherings for festivals; derived from *hoppan*, "to leap or dance", mostly remaining on one leg, swinging the other to various positions. Chaucer names his dancers as *tomblesteres* or *saylors*. The term *hopetan* or *hoppian* implies movement on one leg; but there is also the West European legend about "Hop-o-my-Thumb", a kind of elf, known as *nix* or *nixie* (French *le petit pouce*, and German *daumling*), which some dancers may have presented in mime. In Lancashire, the weekly dance meeting, or the dance at the wakes, was known as the "sixpenny hop", while small girls continue a hop-dance-game which they call "hop-scotch".

HORA (Rumania)
Popular dance, known all over Rumania. Deriving from the old Greek *Choros*, it is a linked circle similar to the *Kolo** of Yugoslavia and the *Horo** of Bulgaria. Performed on special occasions, such as weddings (*Hora Miresei* danced outside the bride's house before the ceremony, and afterwards by bride, groom and parents round the altar in the church), it is also the popular form of relaxation. On Sundays and holidays, young and old alike join in the swinging *Hora*. For young people it has a social significance, since a youth joins the *Hora* circle when approaching manhood, and a girl when she has reached marriageable age. It also censures bad behaviour, since if anyone joins the circle who has sinned against local moral standards, all the dancers stop until he or she has withdrawn. The dance, in 6/8 time, is begun by the young men, who are soon joined by the girls, then by married couples, and later on by the old people. The *Hora* continues for hours, accompanied by gypsy musicians (*lautari*) in the centre. The linked

circle, dancers facing inwards, moves one step forward, one back, three to the left, five to the right so that the ring gradually turns anti-clockwise. At times the circle rushes in towards the centre, shoulders almost touching, then opens out again. This large circle, which may contain several hundred people, is the *Hora Mare*, or *Great Hora*. At the opposite extreme is a version for two couples only, in a small circle with hands crossed behind the back, called *Tărăneasca*, which is danced with increasing speed. The form of the *Hora* varies slightly according to district but remains a closed circle, unlike the *Kolo* and *Horo*, which open into a linked chain. About 1600 *Hora* names or variations have been identified. In some parts of Transylvania it is called *Joc Românesc*, Rumanian Dance. A Rumanian chain dance for men is the *Sârba*,* with a leader at either end. [Cp. *Sardana* (Catalonia); *Kolo* (Yugoslavia); *Horo* (Bulgaria)]

Hora. Greek Easter Festival. (Athens, 1868)   GREECE

HORAE (Hellas)
"Orai" — a goddess of nature and the seasons; later abstracted, to symbolize rule, order, and justice; and thence probably seen as the source of the "Hours" celebrated in Christian doctrine, as in the *Book of Hours*. Homer gives them as divinities of weather, as ministers of Zeus, for whom they guard the doors of Olympus. In Grecian popular doctrine, they are guides in the course of seasons; their action is described as *Dance of the Horae*. At Athens were two: Thallo (Hora of Spring); and Carpo (Hora of Autumn). Thallo accompanied Persephone each year, in her ascent from the lower regions. They adorned Aphrodite, as she rose from the waves; and garlanded Pandora with flowers. Ethical notions were soon associated; they are confused with the Charities. Hesiod names three, in this sense, whom he calls Eunomia, Diké, and Irene.

HORN DANCE (England)
Performed at Abbots Bromley, Staffordshire, on the Monday following the first Sunday after September 4th. The dancers consist of six men with deer horns, three sets painted black and three white; a Fool; a Man-Woman or Maid Marion; a boy with

a bow; another boy with a triangle; accompanied by an accordion player. Kept in the church all the year, the horns vary in size, the heaviest weighing 25¼lbs. Together with the deer head which they surmount, they are fixed to a short wooden handle, held before the dancer's face. Dancing through the countryside in single file, the group stops before each farm. Beginning with an open round, at a word from the leader they form into two lines facing each other and, to a simple rhythmic tune, the six horned men advance towards each other, slightly tilt their horns forward, and retire again, in a gentle suggestion of combat. There is some controversy as to the origin and purpose of this ancient dance, but whether it was "sympathetic magic" to ensure good hunting, or a "beating of the bounds" to confirm villagers' forest rights, there is still an atmosphere of mystery about the *Horn Dance* which suggests a ritual origin. Although the old tune is no longer used, and the costumes are of recent date, as the six horned men silently dip and sway towards and away from each other, there is a subtle feeling of something no longer understood; an almost dreamlike quality, apparent even in the uncompromising setting of the Albert Hall arena. The costumes, many times changed, were last renewed in 1950, when they were based on those of the Morris dancers in the famous Betley Window in Staffordshire. An account in 1686 by Dr. Plott, in his *Natural History of Staffordshire*, says that the dance was performed at New Year and Twelfth Day, and it is not known when the date was moved to September. Hobby Horse, Maid Marion and the Fool dance round about the horned men, and sometimes in line with them, the boys twanging the bow and striking the triangle, and the Horse snapping his jaws. What may have been ceremonial antler masks of prehistoric times were recently found by archeologists in the Vale of Pickering in Yorkshire. [See *Prehistoric Dance*]

HORNPIPE—1
Is not originally a sailor's dance, but derived from the ritual festival dance *Herne-Pipe* of pre-Saxon days in England. Herne was the great god of harvest (*Gerne* or *Grain* is another name), who is sculptured on English hillsides, as at Cerne Abbas and Wilmington, in giant form. This ritual was a Harvest Dance done to pipe and tabor; the long-remembered "tummy patting" motions signify delight after a good meal. Herne was also the "Great Hunter", as of Cerne Abbas, revered in Britain and also in Gaul. In German, the word *gern* means pleasure, while in late Latin *hernia* indicates one result of too much food. *Horn* equates with *corn;* relates also to *cornucopia,* or

Horn of Plenty. Some of the *Cotton MS* (British Museum) carry pen pictures of dancers performing the *Herne Piping.*

HORNPIPE—2
A solo step dance claimed by England, Ireland and Wales, now associated with sailors although in origin it belonged to the countryside. If the dance was named after an old musical instrument made from animal horn, its origin must have been Celtic, the "horn pipe" being known in Wales, England (Cornwall) and Brittany as Pip-corn, Piob-corn or Corn-bib; and in Ireland as Cornphioba. Chaucer translates "Estives de Cornwailles" in *The Romance of the Rose* (13th century) as "Hornpipe of Cornwailes". Although popular in the 16th century the form of this early dance is uncertain, only the music in triple time having survived. About the middle of the 18th century the time signature changed to duple time and the character of the dance became altered, but it seems to be unknown when or why the *Hornpipe* forsook the land for the sea. A theatrical version became popular and up to the 1840's it was the custom to dance it between the acts and scenes of a play. As a step dance it remained popular in the North of England (Derbyshire and Lancashire—home of clog dancing) after it had faded away elsewhere. Step dancing proper is a matter for the feet and legs alone, arms hanging straight at the sides; but the *Sailor's Hornpipe* uses the arms in a series of movements descriptive of ship-board tasks.

HORO (Bulgaria)
The most popular Bulgarian dance, corresponding to the Yugoslavia *Kolo** and Rumanian *Hora.** As a development from the old Greek *choros,* the form is a linked chain or circle in 2/4 or 3/8 time and quick tempo, in which everyone may join. Every district has its *Horo,* danced in the village square on Sundays and all holidays. Besides being a means of "letting off steam", it forms a sort of marriage market, where young people can meet, although the sexes seldom dance in couples; and, in the linked chain, hold one another by their belts. *Horos* are sung as well as danced; words, and the form of the dance, vary in different regions. In Thrace they are slow and solemn, in western districts quick and with small steps. In some, the women dance together with simple, earthbound steps, while the men perform virile stamps and complicated movements. Chain *Horos* are called *vodeno horo* ("led *Horo*"), having a leader at one or both ends, who draws the chain in and out of curves and spirals, often at high speed, as in the "Crooked *Horo*" in 11/16 time. Sometimes the circular *Horo* will rush in towards the centre, and then slowly open out.

A men's *Horo*, danced in a straight line is called *na prat*, "on a stave", while other forms show mime, from the work of various trades. In the rose-growing districts some women's *Horos*, performed at the time of gathering the flowers, depict the processes involved in making *Attar* of Roses. Whatever the variations in the dance, there is always a basic and instinctive co-ordination of movement, with a perfect sense of rhythm.

HORSE BALLET — 1 (France)
In the famous entertainment *Le Carrousel de Louis XIV*, in 1662, were combined the two basic notions of a court ballet and a triumphant procession. Many of the designs still exist (they can be found in museum collections), such as the engraving of Duc de Guise as "King of the Americans", with costumes for horse and rider, designed by Henri Gissey. The drawing is totally devoid of mythic accuracy; but full of the desired theatrical quality. Jean Berain, another famous designer of this period, produced extravagant costume designs for these spectacular processional ballets; while even the architects joined, for one of their works was the *Arc de Triomphe de Carrousel*. The source of the quadrille dance form, on its pragmatic military basis, could be seen, as in a *Quadrille of Turks*, when four foot-soldiers led a curvetting horse. The imperial Horse Ballet has vanished from Paris; but in England we can see the military circus known as the *Tattoo* — with no sort of ballet, except horses parading neatly in step to military band strains; and instead of dance, the development once more of the dramatic *interludus*.

HORSE BALLET — 2 (Savoy)
Military evolutions in drill, and dance evolutions in quadrille have sometimes been close. The addition of music brought them together, as in the famous mounted ballet, performed on the occasion of the arrival of Prince d'Urbin at the Court of Savoy in 1615. The spectacle was devised in the form of an attack with a combat done to music. Three hundred men on foot opposed mounted men; who formed companies in different shapes : round, oval, square or triangular. It was said that the horses had been drilled so well (like modern circus steeds) that their paces kept perfect step. Processional cars drawn by "animals" show the *Four Quarters of the World*, or *The Triumphe of Love*. Another similar "ballet and tourney" was produced in 1618 by the Duke of Savoy and his son, the Prince of Piedmont. There were many of these *Ballets des Chevaux* [See *Fola* (Italy); *Carrousel*]

HORSE BALLET — 3 (Modern Form) OR QUADRILLE
In London (Harringay), in October 1954, the "Horse of the Year Show" included a *Riders' Quadrille*, in which four instructors from the Swiss Cavalary School mounted on chestnuts, led by a Major on his grey, offered a *Horse Quadrille* to music. This was said to be similar in movements and figures to the quadrilles danced at the Royal Courts of Versailles and performed in the famous Riding School at Vienna, in the early 18th century. All uniforms, saddlery, and accoutrements were "in period style", while the musical tunes used for accompaniment were traditional airs always associated with these displays. The horsemen are called "dressage riders". Musical times are found parallel to movement times. Experts say that a canter is distinguished from a gallop by the style of movement. The legs move in three-four time at a canter, but at four-four time in a gallop. Weight is extended forward in a gallop; but at a canter, the weight is held backwards. The polo pony is not put to a gallop; the circus pony never moves at more than a canter; in the ring this becomes slower and goes into trot. The gallop gave its name to the *galop* in dance; as a swift "all out" movement at speed; rare in the modern ballroom.

HOURI (Arabic)
Creatures of Moslem legend; said to be seventy-two lovely damsels, whose companionship in paradise is one of the rewards of every true believer. Endowed with every charm, and perpetual youth, they sing and dance, recite poetry and play enchanting music. Cultivated Sufi poets assert that the *houris* are symbols or allegories of spiritual life. They have been featured in Western songs and dances; even in ballets of oriental themes; usually with considerable inaccuracy.

HRINGBRÖT (Iceland)
A dance (usually with song), similar in form to the *polonaise*.* Ten or twelve men make a chain, when the first couple dive under the arched arms of the last couple; the remainder follow, still holding hands.

HUAINO (Bolivia)
The Bolivian version of the *Sanjuanito** of Ecuador. Rhythms of the Huaiño are fundamentally Indian, the dance being originally a funeral procession of the Quechua Indians. With added Spanish influence, it has become a social dance of mild flirtation, with music in 2/4 time and lively tempo, although less gay than the *Zamacueca** of Chile, which it resembles. The *Cacharpaya* ("Goodbye" in the Quechua language) and the *Pasacalle*,* are Bolivian dances of similar type. In Peru, the *Huaiño* or *Huaiñito* is identical with the Bolivian dance. This basic dance form of partners facing each other but not touching, advancing and retreating or

moving round each other, with kerchiefs flourished, thus appears all along the western side of South America, from Ecuador to Chile and the Argentine. A similar dance in Panama is the *Tamborito*,* and in Mexico the *Jarabe*.*

HUAPANGO (Mexico)

A couple dance, much favoured in modern Mexico, especially in the South. It is performed out of doors on the *tarimba* — a special wooden floor laid down solely for dancing, and easily portable. On this *tarimba* are danced also the *jarabe** or *bamba*. Sometimes, in the *fiesta*, dancers see the notable Spanish symbol (brought centuries ago with the *Sandunga**) known as the *Cargon de la Moliganga*.* The *huapango* is a "small dance" for, say, six couples, and rarely seen solo or duo. In two rows facing, the dancers weave in and out but without any arm movements or facial expression. Body is held rigid and arms hang stiffly at the side, for the *huapango* is in the category of the Spanish *Zapateado*,* a dance for the feet and legs. Each dance lasts about twenty minutes, with frequent change of partners. There is also a reminder of the *Fandanguillo** in that no expression of feeling is permitted. The fire of the music is suppressed in the dancers, who perform with a strongly controlled intensity and mask-like face.

HUB (Mediaeval English)

Means the centre of proceedings, equivalent to *Boss*. This Saxon term was used for the hub or nave of a church; but especially of a ring dance. Hub is the hilt of a sword : the farthest attainable point with a thrust. Hub was sometimes the *tar* or target centre. A woman refers to her husband as "hubby"; but it is uncertain if the far older word *Hobby-horse* or *hubbi-horse*, has a direct connection, since he traversed the outside of the dance ring. All wheelright terms appear to have been copied in dance positions and movements; as well as in gilds — as *felloes* or *boss*, etc. [See *Wheel*]

HUETA-MADL (Austria)

Dance of the Shepherdess, or the Goat-Herd *Mädchen*, known through Upper Austria, but in Lower Austria called *Strön-schneider-tanz* (Straw-Cutters' Dance). The form is a couple dance for a group, usually in 2/4 time; using polka steps in lively fashion. The whole body is in movement; the men often add improvised steps or jumps, with shouts of "Yu-hu !"

HUITZILOPOCHTLI'S FESTIVAL (Aztec-Mexico)

Used to be held in May at Tenochtitlan (Mexico City), in honour of the War and Sun God. At the end of ceremonial dances a young man, who for a year had personated the god, was sacrificed. On the preceding day he led the dances, dressed in paper robes painted with black circles, with golden bells on his ankles, wearing on his head a paper mitre decorated with eagle feathers, among which was fixed an obsidian knife. Holding hands, in lines, the dancers, young and old, moved in winding figures. Specially chosen young women (considered to support and sustain the god) accompanied the young man. Their faces were painted in the god's symbolic colours; red feathers ornamented their legs, while garlands of maize hung from their shoulders and crossed on their breasts. Dancing ceased at nightfall, to be continued next morning; when the young man was put to death. [See *Aztec Dance*]

HUIXTOCIHUATL'S FESTIVAL (Aztec-Mexico)

A festival in honour of the Goddess of Salt, held at Tenochtitlan (Mexico City) in the seventh month of the Aztec year (June 12th to July 21st). For ten days before the festival day, a woman personating the goddess led dances performed by women and girls of the salt-makers. Wearing yellow robes embroidered with "sea waves", with flower-shaped gold ear-rings and ankle bells; and a head-dress of iridescent plumes, she danced in the centre of the circle. Holding a round shield, painted with leaves and fringed with parrot feathers, she marked the rhythm of the dance with a stick decorated with artificial flowers and feathers. Moving in a circle round her, the dancers, wearing garlands of Artemisia, held a cord and sang as they danced. On the tenth day Huixtocihuatl's representative danced all night, without rest, aided by old women who danced with her and supported her as she grew weary. At dawn she was sacrificed at the temple of Tlaloc (God of Rain), whose sister the Salt Goddess was considered to be.   [See *Aztec Dance*]

HULA (Hawaii)

General term for a performance that includes dancing, gesture, and chanting. There are many *hulas*, standing or sitting, performed by both men and women. Descriptive dances, they portray by imitative and symbolic gesture, natural phenomena (fluttering leaves, or the flight of birds); sports (surfing, canoeing); historical or mythological stories; or the detailed beauty of a queen. The story is sung by one or more chanters, or by the dancer herself. Of religious origin, old *hulas* were part of a ritual performed in the sacred hall, or *halau*.* Laka (equivalent to Terpsichore and Euterpe, Greek Muses of dance and song) was goddess of the *hula*. Her priestesses wore skirts of yellow tapa cloth adorned with green *ti* leaves. Singers and story-tellers gathered at the King's

Hawaiian Dance at Waialee, near Honolulu. Full company of Hawaiian dancers with orchestra. HAWAII

palace, and from young men and women at Court were chosen those to dance the *hula*. They received thorough training (including the art of gesture) in the school of the *halau*, from the *hula*-master, or *kumu*. When competent, they graduated at a ceremony called *Uniki*. Dancers were divided into two classes: the *olapa* ("agile ones")—young people who performed the dances; and *ho'o-paa* ("steadfast ones")—older people who chanted and played the heavier instruments. Traditional costume was the same for both sexes—a knee-length skirt (*pa-u**) anklets and wristlets (*kupe'e*), a flower wreath on the head (*lei poo*), and one round neck and shoulders. Ceremonial chanting accompanied the donning of costumes. The skirt was of *tapa* cloth, or *ti* leaves (mid-rib of 40 - 80 leaves woven on to a vine waistband). Only in modern times have raffia skirts been worn because they last longer. A *ti*-leaf skirt lasts three days, and must then be remade. Anklets were of whale teeth, bone, shells or fibre. Modern dancers wear a sleeveless bodice (*mu'u-mu'u*) of red, yellow or purple (royal colours). Six steps form the basis of all Hawaiian *hulas*, with countless variations and combinations making up the dances. 1. *Kiiwawae*—a movement forward and backward of both feet and arms; and swaying of the body; 2. *Hooleielei*—swaying of hips; arms outstretched in front; 3. *Wawae Holo*—a side step with hip-movement; 4. *Uwehe*—a hop step with knees bent, hands hovering over them; 5. *Ami*—a turning, undulating step; 6. *Ami Poipoi*—a repetition of *Ami*, with pivot in complete circle. Instruments accompanying, occasion, or

words of the chant, determine the name of a *hula*, such as:—

Pahu: Chanter uses a *pahu* drum; also plays the *puniu* or small coconut drum; both with sharkskin drumheads.

Pa-ipu: Calabash (*ipu*) is held in dancer's left hand and struck on the ground, while right hand drums upon it.

*Puili**: A sitting *hula*. Name refers to one or two split bamboo sticks struck by the dancer on the ground and on her body.

*Uli-uli**: A sitting *hula*. Dancer uses one or two gourds, decorated with coloured feathers.

Ili-ili: Dancer holds small, flat, polished stones (*ili-ili*) using them like castanets.

Ka Laau: Dancer or chanter uses *ka-laau* sticks; sometimes accompanied, in old chants, by the Hawaiian footboard.

Paiumauma: A sitting hula; the dancer rhythmically slaps her chest.

The traditional pose for ending a dance is—both arms extended in front, one hand over the other with fingers outstretched; the gesture which says —"And thus my dance is finished—I hope it has pleased you".

[See *Alekoki*; *Halau*; *Kawika*; *Liliu E*; *Puili*; *Ula No Weo*; *Uliuli Noho*; and cp. *Laka-Lakas* (Tonga)]

HULLACHAN (Scots-Irish)
Is the earlier form of the Scots dance called *Reel of Tulloch.** In Ireland, there is a series of names, referring to the dancing group; such as *Hoolichan*

or *Hoolikhan*—more recently given as *Hoolighan*, owing to the disreputable behaviour into which the fairs and *Feis** sank. The name has affiliations with an old Breton dance and its ring, known as the *Korrigan* or *Khorikhan*—probably earlier as *Khor-Regan* (as in the tale of Lear or Llir). W. B. Yeats had a play entitled *Kathleen ni Houlihan* (yet another variant), where the Kathleen was presented as "the spirit of Ireland" by the poet. In the *Reel* form there is not so much emphasis on the round as on the intervening figures.

HUNT BALL (19th century England)
Described in terms Dickensian by R. S. Surtees (1854) in fictional mode.[1] At Handley Cross, the Hunt Club required members to wear morning, undress uniform consisting of scarlet coat with blue collar; and evening or dress uniform of sky blue coat, lined with pink silk, canary coloured breeches, and white stockings. The ballroom order of dance varied; but usually opened with Country Dance; followed by Quadrille,* a Waltz, a Galop; a second Quadrille, a second Waltz; and then a Reel.* The supper dance (at about 1.0 a.m.) broke the routine; and dancing was resumed until dawn. Mr. Jorrocks is the hero—the M.F.H.
[1] *Handley Cross*. R. S. Surtees (illustrated John Leech) London 1854.

"HUNTING THE WREN" (Isle of Man, Britain)
A ceremony, ending with dancing, performed up to the 18th century on Christmas Eve. After a midnight service, people went out to find a wren, which they killed and fastened it, wings extended, on top of a long pole. This was carried in procession from house to house, the people singing and collecting money from householders. When the round had been made, the wren was laid on a bier, carried to the churchyard, and solemnly buried with dirges (called "her knell") sung in the Manx language. Christmas was then considered to have begun; people formed a circle outside the churchyard, and finished the night dancing to music. It is obvious that this ceremony has nothing to do with Christmas, belonging to a much earlier period and religion, and perhaps connected with the ancient Egyptian *Uren* (also a small bird released at New Year). By mid-nineteenth century, the ceremony was performed by boys on St. Stephens Day (December 26th), and the wren was no longer buried in the churchyard, but on the sea-shore or some waste land. A similar custom was known in Ireland, Essex, Pembrokeshire, and France.

HUNGARIAN FOLK DANCE (Budapest)
Has seen energetic renewal. Revival of folk music stems from Bartok and Kodaly. From the central

Folk Art Institute (in Fö Utca) is organised the Hungarian Folk Dance Eensemble, which has toured in many countries. Many provincial groups are encouraged to work in dance ensembles and orchestras, many based on factory groups or farm collectives. Specimens can be purchased at the large folk art studio in Vaci Utca. The city has about twenty theatres and concert halls, at any of which some form of dance may appear during the year. The State Opera (and Ballet) House, with the Erkel Theatre, has its own academic school.
[See *Pearly Bouquet*]

HUNZA SWORD DANCE (Pakistan)
An annual winter-solstice festival in Hunza Valley (a small kingdom in the Karakorum Range of the Himalayas), is held throughout the month of December, when Sword Dances are performed each evening. In days when the mountain kingdoms were often at war, the dances were performed by warriors, to show their strength and prowess. Now that there is no army, the Hunzukut men perform their Sword Dance for pleasure, to the music of pipes and drums. Dancing first in line, the men divide into pairs, and perform a vigorous mock-fight. Their circular leather shields, and long curved swords, are heirlooms handed down for generations. With trousers and cap of white handwoven wool, and soft boots, they wear long coats of rich Chinese silk—red, blue or gold—relics of the days when such robes formed part of the tribute paid by China to the Mir of Hunza, to safeguard her Turkistan settlements from raids. The Hunzukuts are Moslems of the Ismaili sect, and their women go unveiled. Religious ceremonies include Consulting the Oracle—a man who chants his prophecies after having inhaled Juniper smoke and performed a vigorous dance. The whole proceeding is accompanied by music.

HUPPLEKEN (Sweden)
Said to mean "Hopping Dance" or *Hop Laiking*: but reveals many characteristics of the older "Bride Fair" or "Girls Market", once known all over Europe; (see *Marriage Market**) and was probably known earlier as *Cupple-ken-dans* or Couple Dance. This dance is best known at Floda in Dalecarlia; danced by couples. The girl wears fairly long full skirts of gay embroidered or woven floral patterns; a red over-stitched stiff poke bonnet; and an apron. Apart from silver brooch or neck ornaments, she has little jewellery. The man is attired in a long open coat; plain, with a low stiff small collar, but decorated cuffs; with a vest of similar material. He wears leather or cotton breeches (according to season) and simply-cut leather boots (like the girl's), with a sort of bowler

hat with curly brim. His breeches show each calf in bright blue socks. This is called Wedding dress; they are named "Bridal Pair" and are accompanied by bridesmaids and grooms-men. Dancing is thus stately. The Hopping step is done by men only, while girls pace out the notes. Many couples now face to centre; men inside of ring. Then they clap hands; the bridal pair begin dancing and every other couple follows. The dance concludes with a running step; and the Dalacarlia *polska*.*

HYPNOTIC DANCE

Some kinds of dance have been produced under "suggestion" or hypnotism; both in religious ritual and in commercial music-hall mode. In London an untrained girl, advertised as "Madeleine", was exhibited as a subject under control of a hypnotist. Music was played (sometimes selected at the wish of members of audience, and thus impossible to rehearse), and the girl moved in sympathy with the melody. In conscious mode, this was much what Isadora Duncan displayed; for she rarely danced the same music twice in exactly similar form. The production (when genuine), proves simply what all good teachers and producers know: that a dancer moves better when "relaxed" from all external inhibitions and when concentrated on movement alone. In religious ritual, imposed hypnosis (by a master) or auto-hypnosis (under personal suggestion) produce a kind of ecstatic concentration (see *Dervish Dance**) when bodily energies are devoted to one purpose. Hypnotism should not be confused with Mesmerism. Hypnotism operates through mind and its ideation (sometimes upon the emotions), while Mesmerism begins with the body and its nervous energies, but may contact emotion via instinct. The technique of psycho analysis hovers between, while the doctrines publicised as "Christian science" have something in common. Attendance at a *Palais de Danse* may, at rare intervals, induce a similar mood of hypnosis, under which young men are induced to commit rash acts such as proposing marriage. The use of "martial music" is an accompaniment of military training or action, though movement rarely goes, in unison, beyond the simple march. Zulu warriors beat the tom-tom to induce similar hypnotic unison when whipping up the fighting spirit.

HYPORCHEMA (Crete, later in Greece)

A lively mimetic dance that accompanied the worship of the sun god Apollo, in Crete and among the Dorians, performed by men and women. A chorus of singers danced around the altar, while actor-mimes carried on the action with mimetic performance (*hyporchesthai*). Thus it was a lyrical dance. The *geranos** was similar; but the *hyporchema* has been compared with the *kordax*.* Fragments of *hyporchemata* by Pindar reveal light rhythms in graphic style. The later forms of *hyporchemata* may have followed an earlier *geranos*, based on the allegory of the Cretan labyrinth, for it was performed in winding mode (much as the *hora** or *kolo**), about a large circle. The *Hyporchema* was performed until some time in the second century AD.

I

IACCHOS or IAKKHUS (Hellas)

Was the principal "call" of the Maenads and other dancers, in the vine cult of Bacchus, which came to Hellas from Syria and India, before the period of Buddha, fifth century BC. The term transfers the Indian call of celebration "Yakkhus" from the worship of the Nature spirit of *Yakku's*, which festivals still recur to this day, with the dancing troupes known as *Yaksha-gana*, or *Yakusha-Khana*, the *Feast of Yakku*, prevalent in Mysore and Southern India. The parallel term Maenad would indicate an Egyptian source, from *Min* or *Maen*. The Dionysian vine cult had two great annual celebrations, the spring planting and the grape harvest, both marked by libations and drinking of wine. *Dion-Isseus* (also *Dhyzan-Isseois*) was the "God born of the Purple Grape" (or *Agrape, agape*, the felicitous time), he was in a sense the anti-god to Apollo the Sun god, but also to Diana, Queen of the Moon. Each of these Hellenic deities had his own cult and ritual dancing, in solemn worship and celebration.

IBERIAN DANCE (Ancient Spain)

According to Richard Ford,[1] the form that is now named *comparsa*, or national quadrille was "undoubtedly a remnant of the original Iberian exhibitions, in which, as among Spartans and wild Indians, even in relaxations a warlike principle was maintained. The dancers beat time with their swords on their shields; and when one of them wished to show his contempt for the Romans, he executed before them a derisive pirouette". Ford describes the modern dance he saw in his journeys through Spain, in a chapter on dances:

". . . performed by eight men, with castanets in their hands; and to a tune of fife and drum; while a Bastonero or leader of the band, directed the rustic ballet. Around were grouped *payesas a aldeanse*, dressed in tight bodice, their hair hanging down and their necks covered in blue and coral beads. The men bound up their long locks with red handkerchieves, and danced in their shirts, sleeves puckered up with bows of different-coloured ribands, crossed over back and breast, and mixed with scapularies. Their drawers were white, and as full as the bragas of the Valencians, like whom they wore alpargatas, hemp sandals laced with blue strings. The figure of the dance was very intricate, and accompanied by loud cries of *viva!* at each change of evolution".

[1] *Gatherings from Spain*. Richard Ford. 1846.

ICE DANCING (England)
Has developed chiefly as an entertainment, since 1947 - 48, when *entrepreneurs* sought to combine the ice-rink (as used for ice-hockey or skating, indoors), with semi-choreographic evolutions. Lacking full knowledge of the spectacular principles involved in what is necessarily a large-scale show, they tried to adapt what they thought were "ballet steps" to skating. The scenic element was kept also in theatre terms for some time, though the "optical background" was always the artificial ice, for the spectator who kept his eye on the principal moving figures. In this, good colour was absent. The variety of movement in figure skating is limited. The skater-dancer can move at a speed much greater than the stage dancer can traverse, but after making a number of curves, forwards or backwards, the interest drops with repetition. The principal "dance figure" utilised is the arabesque — now completely devoid of any thematic meaning. Movements have become standardised as much as the costume; so that the display offered is one of moving legs. Facial expression cannot be seen at the sixty-yard distances; and any vocal attempt is similarly limited. Portable microphones will alter this defect; we shall have the muffled boom of the railway station announcer. This mode of entertainment, from the scale of the rink, must be essentially one of mass movement — as in football. Humour is rare; it can derive only from a circus-clown basis, which the skates do not help. What is wanted is a carefully devised dumb show, with really good music; based on a technology of masks and mime. The supposed need of high speed all the time must be varied. Thus treated, the ice-spectacle may offer a change from stage pantomime (though it can never be a successful rival), but above all the ice show needs a new tradition of characters, situations and episodes; new ideas on this different basis, starting not from a pseudo-ballerina, but from a skilled corps-de-ballet with good comedians. Refrigerated fairy-tales may supply some plots, but modern schemes are essential Otherwise we are back at the Russian Ice Mountain; a children's game in which we can't take part.

ICHIMBWASA (Rhodesia)
A general dance of the Bantu people, used in many tribes, such as the Lamba, in Northern Rhodesia. Usually it is danced to honour a girl initiate, by two older women, in the centre of a ring of chanting friends. This dance is ordinary movement, without mime; men do not join it and rarely watch. Traditional chants are sung.

ICHIN SENGWE (Rhodesia)
The professional Hunters' Dance among the Bantu people. No women may join. The Hunters (*awapalu*) dance singly, in close succession; sometimes ordinary men may join in. *Ichin-sengwe*, a rite in honour of *Ka-aluwe*, Guardian Spirit of the herd of game (whose creatures are despoiled by hunting), is performed usually while head and heart of the slain animal are being cooked. Typal mime in this dance ritual follows (a) the hunter, in his actions of stalking, finding and killing the game; and (b) the gait of the animal, in character, and as it is wounded and dies. We may compare this living Hunters' Dance (besides the mythic mode of certain Indian "Hunters' Dances") with the similar scenes found in ancient cave paintings; where they denote magical ritual. Music is provided by *timbila*,* calabash and gourd piano, and hide-headed drums, with a large voice drum, standing four or five feet high. This dance is performed also for the *Imipashi* (departed spirits), along with a beer-drinking festival.

ICONOGRAPHY OF DANCE
Includes all forms of permanent record — usually works of art or prescribed ritual indications — which carry information or instructions about dance. Art works range from sculptures or mural paintings and floor patterns, to manuscripts drawn in older books or mass-produced pictures in modern books. They include paintings and sculptures, sacred or secular; some that summarise dance (as the *Shiva Nata Raja* of India) and others that portray some individual dancer. The most modern of all Iconography is cinema film; even this does not tell the whole story. One phase of dance iconography, as yet little investigated, is the category of temple floor pattern (as in India) with geometric kernel (see *Yantra*)* on which the dance moves. At the other extreme we find the movement of the hands, as *Cheironomy*,* and the whole language of gesture, realistic or symbolic. From these the artist selects what seems to him to be most characteristic — as in early printed books on dance.

IJO ODE (Nigeria, W. Africa)
A "hunter's fire-dance", said to take place a week after an unusually triumphant "kill", when the

tribe celebrates its admiration of the successful hunter. The traditional mark of success was the slaying of some human tribal enemy, whose skull was stripped and polished, to form the focus of the ritual. The first part mimes the hunting, by stalking, and the encounter; the second part, the triumphant return march, singing and dancing; while the last part shows the "quieting" of the defeated enemy, whose soul is now placated. The dance has been produced in a toned-down stage version (in Paris), in which too many different features were crammed into one display.

ILAMATECUHTLI'S FESTIVAL (Aztec-Mexico)

Ceremony held at Tenochtitlan (now Mexico City) in the seventeenth month of the Aztec year (December 29th to January 7th), in honour of "The Old Princess", a goddess of ancient times, related to corn and the earth. A woman who personated the goddess was sacrificed, and on the morning of this day she danced alone until noon, weeping. (During this period other women and children wept, in order to "bring rain by sympathetic magic"). The temple image of the goddess wore a two-faced mask (in the manner of Janus) but her representative had her face painted in symbolic colours, the upper half yellow, the lower half black. Dressed all in white, with white sandals, her leather tunic was edged with a fringe containing small shells, which clashed together as she danced. She carried a round white shield decorated with eagle feathers and white heron plumes. Music played by old men accompanied her dance. At sunset priests dressed to represent all the gods, led her in procession up the steps of the temple of Huitzilopochtli (God of war and the sun), where she was sacrificed by a priest wearing the costume and mask of Ilamatecuhtli, the goddess she represented — victim and slayer being thus identical.
[See *Aztec Dance*]

"ILKLA' MOOR" (England)

This famous folk-dance, associated with Ilkley Moor, near Bradford, in the West Riding of Yorkshire, lost its ring-dance during 19th century, and retains only some of the essential verses, though the words remind us of the movement :

> "Wheer war ta bahn when Ah saw thee?
> on Ilkla' moor baht hat?"

(meaning :

> Where were you going when I saw you
> On Ilkley Moor without any hat?)

for in the ring-dance, one of the dancers had to enact this mime of the departed one; and, returning, sang the reiterated query. The song contains, in fact, subtly worded hints of the doctrine of

reincarnation, similar to the longer version embedded in the *Alf Leila wa Leila*, or *Arabian Nights*; and that to be found in the *Mabinogion*, in the transformation of Taliesin the Radiant-Browed. Here it is more direct — it centres on the "gobblin'-oop" of the "dook", but the final meaning affirms the rhythms of the "ring of return".

ILLUMINATI (Roman Latin)

The *ambulando illuminati* was the rhythmic procession of the newly baptised *catechumens*, attired in fresh white robes, as they were each issued with a lighted candle, given them as a symbol that their minds had been newly enlightened. They must be distinguished from the acolytes, who bore both lamp and censer, in the ordinary liturgy. The earliest processional dance form was the triumphant march, from the investry, to the space around the altar; where it turned as a ring to the simple circle dance, later known as the *karolle*. The occasion and the act was so important that four religious societies founded their ritual with this ceremony as one of the high points. These were (1) the *Hesychasts*; 14th century; (2) the *Alumbrados*, Spain, 16th century; (3) the *Guerinets* of France, 17th century; and (4) certain Mystics of Belgium, following one branch of Beguines, 18th century. The *Alumbrados* had a mode of torch dance; this ritual was also used by *Rosicrucians*. Similar lamps were important ritual items in the crypt ceremonies of the Mithraic and Gnostic devotees.

IMANENJANA (Madagascar)

Malagasy term for a spontaneous "dance of revolt"; which came to notice in 1863, in strong popular rejection of unwanted innovations, brought in (under missionary pressure) by the late King Radama II. Another account calls the dancers "patients". Parties of Malagasy came to the capital town, Antananarivo, bearing pieces of sugar-cane (as weapons of defence) and danced for hours at a stretch. Others of the party sang; some played the simple music, which regulated the speed, always very quick. They assembled at a Sacred Stone (some professed to hold seances), and they disliked black attire (as worn by parsons). Dancers were called *ramanenjana*.

INBAL "Tongue of the Bell" (Israel)

National Dance Theatre Group of Jews of the Yemen, in the south-west corner of the Arabian Peninsula. Isolated for many centuries, these people (now mostly repatriated to Israel) yet preserved their own culture, although naturally tinged with Arab overtones. In 1949 the Company of eighteen Yemenite dancers was founded by Mrs. Sara Levi-Tanai (Artistic Director), in order to present their

living tradition of folklore, song and dances in theatrical form. Both Hebrew and Arabic were used, while speech and song, acting and dancing, were combined in Old Testament stories, wedding festivities, and scenes depicting modern Israel. Some music was recorded, but more often provided by the dancers themselves, using small hand-drums, tambourines, flute, two tall standing drums and the pounding of silver pestle and mortar.
[See *Pearly Bouquet* (Hungary); *Masowsze* (Poland); *Bayanihan* (Phillipines)]

INCWALA (Swaziland, S. Africa)
"First Fruits Ceremony". An annual festival held in January about the time of new moon, at a village near Mbabane (capital of Swaziland). Ceremonies last six days and celebrate the new year; authority of the Chief; and renewed energy symbolised in the sampling of new crops, and in the rain-making ceremony. Thousands of Swazi people gather to take part in the singing and dancing. The Hereditary Master of Tribal Ceremonies conducts the necessary ritual in a specially built ceremonial hut, and on the third day the sacrifice of a black bull is the occasion for dances by the Chief's warriors. These men pay particular attention to their hair, which is worn long, bleached with soda, and "set" into ringlets; sometimes tinted with ochre. The climax comes on the sixth day when the Chief, dancing before the people, shows his strength and skill, in the rain-making ceremony. Afterwards he samples the "first fruits" and gives assent for all to partake.
[Cp. *Amerindian Green Corn Dance; Busk*]

INDIAN DANCE (Hindustan)
Comprises many more than an alleged "Four Schools of Indian Dance", named in a phrase, too often repeated, by uninformed writers. There are fifty languages in the peninsula of the Indian sub-continent; almost as many different races; and many more than that number of different cults, with their rituals. India includes (1) the Hindu systems; the famous *Shat Darshanas* (Six Doctrinal Systems, literally "Views"), and their derivatives; (2) the Moslem systems, from Sunni Shariat to Sufi cults; (3) the surviving Dravidian cults in Tamil Nad; the numerous secluded tribal cults, as e.g. in Orissa, at Seraikalla (the Chhau* Festivals etc.), and (4) many borderland cults, as in Manipuri, only half Hindu. In addition, India has as many bordering religions and cults, beginning with the modified Buddhism (mainly obsolete within India's mainland proper), such as Tibetan Buddhism; Nepali Buddhism-Hinduism; and Manipuri Hinduism, as well as Bengali Islamist-Hinduism; and then Buddhism in Ceylon and the cults of

Burma, the Shan States, must be considered as well as the small communities of Jains (in Punjab), and Parsees (in Bombay district). Indian ritual and dramatic dance extends further into Indonesia, as a former colonial dispensation, into the Islands of Sumatra, Java and especially Bali; though in the western sectors Hinduism, already infiltrated with Malayan cults, has been dispossessed by Islam. Every one of these living cults maintains some form of ritual and rhythmic dance, sometimes several forms, in its own different social classes. The aims and rites of the millions of people within India (well over 350,000,000 in all), are more diversified than those either in all Europe or all America; and range from relatively simple "animist" practices (though with profound ancient traditions behind them), to the most refined subtleties, as apparent in the rituals and doctrines of the great Hindu system of monotheism-pantheism. Many of these rites are not open to members of external sects; still less to Europeans; it is hard to learn enough of them to ascertain more than their main form and ceremony; still harder (though not impossible) to comprehend their intimate functions.   [See *Kamakala*]

INDIAN DANCE IN USA (Hindu style)
Was known in New York in 1881, when Augustine Daly, the impresario on the look-out for anything new, brought a troupe of *bhaijis** from Bombay, calling them "East Indian Nautch Girls". Some writers think that the American version of Skirt Dance may have been influenced by the visit of this group. They were not "temple dancers", and offered no religious dances. Most probably their work displayed the magnificence of Marwari Nautch, which is also a skirt dance. The pseudo-Indian show, *Lalla Rookh*, was staged in New York City in 1872, evidently "inspired" by an earlier presentation in London, of a play with the same name. This American show had absolutely nothing Indian about it; even the scenery was a mess.

INGOMA SHAYAMA-OMBE (Rhodesia)
Celebrates a Bantu girls' initiation. One or two expert old women dance alone in the ring of chanting women; there is no mime. They wear regulation dancing-skirts of grass (*awu-yumbo*). Drummers provide the rhythm; one male drummer, standing, with double-ended drum; and two men with ordinary drums (*imikunte*). There are rattles (*insangwa*) in addition to the clapping hands. Dancers and drummers are paid by the girl's father. Their songs are in the *Ichimbwasa** style.

INGUANA, OR INKWANA (Bantu Africa)
A Swaziland Festival, performed for purpose of "making the king strong". The warriors dance, passing round a large green gourd, which is

revered and thrown high. The king then joins in the dancing and hurls the gourd even higher. It must be caught and never allowed to touch the ground; or the *nyama* (energy that is drawn into the living fruit) will be dissipated, instead of lodging within the king.

INITIATION DANCES (Christian scheme)

Were taken over and re-formed from earlier ceremonials; have disappeared behind a facade of superficial ritual; so that we possess only slender clues in names, annual dates, and associated customs that remain, some detached, but most considered as meaningless. The basic names are : for the Boys, the famed Santa Nikolaus; and, for the Girls, the balancing figure of Santa Katerina. Neither of these supposed "saints" was, in fact, any historical individual; the term *sant* is derived from the basic Latin *centa;* and the name Katarina is foreshadowed in the *centa-ruena* (centurion); or the figurative "hundred of the ring". The *santa* term is equivalent to the Buddhist group term, the *sangha,* the assembly of novices. Our terms indicate connection with Greek forms of religions. The revived traditiona of the Santa Nikolaus belong with those of the Sacred Tree; the illuminated Tree of the Winter Solstice, now devoted to children's parties; while the *Katha-rouene* (wheel) is the play of the ring; again, represented as a symbol of light, as its dissociated name Catherine Wheel (a symbol of the Guy Vokes now) begins to disclose. We have, then, the upright Tree and the horizontal Ring, both enlivened with fire; and both marked by circular dances. Formerly, the children bore the small torches; as now they carry candles, in a more sedate and less meaningful ceremony of "confirmation". The legend of "children in a tub" replaces the rite of ceremonial "washing" now a baptism by symbols. Spain preserves the terms, *novio* and *novena,* as the youthful equivalents.
[See *Boy Bishop; Nikolai; Catherine*]

INITIATION RITUAL DANCES

Are common through history, in all kinds of social organisation, usually connected closely with religious ceremonial. Boys and girls are put through various tests—of physical endurance or skill; of obedience and intelligent behaviour; and of elementary mental powers. For these, some form of dance ability is often required, as one of the important tests, since rapid learning and performance of new motions can indicate to the experienced master, the general ability of the candidate. In many religious societies, this overall summation is neglected, as it is now in many secular schools of today. There is undue emphasis on one subject, to the neglect of others. Initiation as an event is

known by many names : a familiar one is "matriculation", which is technically an admittance to the care of *alma mater*—usually a university organization. Here we find an example that studiously omits all physical tests, from vision or hearing to sports and games. For military admissions, the tests incline to the other extreme—the results of modern over-specialization. Older communities had their own initiation systems, usually well rounded. Many modern social systems, especially those in countries not yet industrially infested, retain their older bases of operation. By study of these forms (as, for example, in South African native tribes) we can perceive more readily the general lines of operation. In Europe the early religious ceremonials are almost obsolete; and where they exist, are moss-grown with superstition and ignorance. A curious perfunctory rite called "confirmation" replaces the former initiation, in Christian Europe—which was tied to the ceremonials of Santa Catarina and Santa Nikolaus,* for girls and boys respectively. The "Wheel of Catherine" is a wheel of dance ritual; and "three boys in a tub" attended by the mythical Bishop of Myra, shows a formal baptism by immersion. From these propaganda rituals are derived the effusive legends; with them were the processional ceremonies; the solemn dances; the examinations; even to the imitation of adult rites, as in the long-continued traditions of the Boy Bishop.   [See *Boy Bishop; Catherina; Nikolai*]

INITIATION RITUAL DANCE (Australian; Aboriginal)

The ritual site—clearing or platform—is carefully arranged from traditional patterns. A large circle is made of separated stones, each circular in shape, the size of a large plate—that is, accommodating two feet of one man. They are twenty-five inches apart, rim to rim; and are quite flat white stones. Twenty-one men can stand in the larger circle; ten boys in the smaller circle. The two circles are connected by a long corridor, about a hundred yards, permitting one boy and his sponsor to walk side by side. In the large circle, three stones omitted permit entry or exit, without stepping on or over the choreographic forms of the double circle. The initiation rite begins with the boy in the small circle; he is gradually introduced to the larger circle (the tribe) and out of it (to the great gods). A near-by rock pile often contains certain ritual implements, pointing bones, *churinga* stones; or weapon heads.

INSECT DANCES

Reveal instinctive modes of motion that we compare immediately with human dancing, chiefly because of their rhythmic expression of vitality.

The great naturalist, J. H. Fabré, observed this fact: he writes ". . . I went to Carpentras, to see the entrance of Sitaris into the Bee's cells. The works were in full swing. In front of a high expanse of earth, a swarm of Bees, stimulated by the sun, was dancing a crazy ballet". He notes "the Cricket still waiting for the few lines needed to bring his merits before the public". He recalls the Sacred Beetle of the Egyptians (which later inspired Karel Capek in Prague to write his *Insect Play*) who does not dance but walks, rolling his great ball of treasure, wrestling with robbers. Men dig gold from one hole (called a mine) and bury gold in another hole (called a bank vault), but the Beetle digs his funeral dinner; and so doing told the Egyptian of reincarnation. Fabré, in his Provençal home, turns from the lighting expert, the Glow-worm, to that traditional clerical worker, the Praying Mantis: "In the days of ancient Greece, this insect was named *Mantis*, or the prophet. The peasant saw her, standing half erect in a very imposing and majestic manner, her broad green gossamer wings trailing like long veils; and her forelegs, like arms, raised to the sky as though in prayer. To the peasant's ignorance, the insect seemed like a priestess or nun; and so she came to be called the Praying Mantis. There never was a greater mistake!" Then "The Mantis has her good points; she makes a most marvellous nest (but) has no heart. She eats her husband, and deserts her children". Like the Inland Revenue, she has teeth in triplicate, and devours every living creature. "She is the only insect that can divert her gaze wherever she will". The Beetle is the Eternal Gymnast Pilgrim; the Mantis, the goddess of destruction; the Bee is the sunlit dancer.
[*Book of Insects*. J. H. Fabré. *Dance of the Bee* Carl von Frisch. 1954] [See *Bees,** *Dance of*]

I OLACK MICHEIL (Triumph Song of Michael, Scotland)
The ancient Feast of Mikahiel *biadha Michiel* carries many indications of Indian origin. Its principal name as *Michiel nam Buahd* remains as Mikael in the name of Buddha (Golden Victor) and he carries a three-prong trident (like Avalokiteshvara of Tibet) and lives on a Mount. The festal cakes are *Struans*, made in quadrant form of all cereals; races were held—he rides a White Horse. The feast is followed by a ball with many dances, from *Cailleach an Dudain** to *Cath nan Curaidh* (fight of warriors). The male dancer carries a white wand—*slachan druidheachd* or *slachdan geasagach* (magic wand) and there is this dance of death and resurrection. *IO lekh* is the straight spell or, the wand that "spells out" on the ground the ritual diagram.   [See *Augurs Dance*]

I-O (Europe [I-O-Bal=Jubal=Moon Measure]
I-O is the primal symbol of all Moon Dances; and appears in numerous god-names which originated with the Lunar Calendar. The two vowels are sounded usually as "eee-yoo"—they resound in the Grecian cults of Pan or Dionysus, as the Bacchantes cry (or pass word for entrance into the dance), as "IO Pan! IO Pan! !" Then these vowels energize the stable names IONO and IOVO or (as Romanised) in *Juno* (Iuno) and *Jove* (Iove); while in the earliest Semitic form the symbols are *Yevah* and *Yevoi* (later becoming scripted as *Yod-He Vau-He*), still as part of the Lunar liturgies. In India, the moon rituals, again with expressional dances that affirm the numeral and formal values, form their basic geometry. This is easily seen, by super-imposing the letter forms; the single line decussates the full circle (the full moon orb) in two halves, or (as repeated at right-angles), in four quarters, or four watches, or wakes, or weeks. Thus it is seen that counting joined with dance and the primal circle to elucidate the lunar calendar of *IO-tara*, thus forming the pragmatic foundation of dance in the *Yota-ra* or *Hota-ra*. The counts are thus: seven for the watch, fourteen to the "full through waxing and then another fourteen by waning, by two "sevens" to the "dark o' the moon". From Dione, D-IO-ne or D-IAN-A came Luna (Bright) and Hekate (Dark), and thus IO was the Triple Moon Goddess, whose completion was called *Moonde*, *Munde* or *Montha*. The ritual dance taught and impressed these facts. Finally, the difficult "conjunction of times" was attempted—the lunar convention was joined with the solar calendar of the year: thirteen to twelve. The summary was given in *IO-Dasa*—the Servants of IO—whose bright thirty pieces of varied silver (the "moon surplus") to the great Solar Count of Twelve gods, had to be "taken away" to the "dark field". This mutual conversion: the count of the month and that of the world year, was hard to learn; but in the sacred ritual dance, the changes could be estimated visually.
[See *Calendar; Moon Dances*]

IONIKA (Primitive Hellenic term)
The "Image of IO",* the Moon Goddess; figured ritually in dance, and physically in the column symbol that was carried into Grecian architecture; the double volute or spiral. One mainland centre was Salonika; but in the Islands were the chief sanctuaries. Compare this feminine cult with the masculine (northern invaders) of the *Teutona*, which settled at Dodona, and founded the Taurich or Doric cult, with its "order" of the single capped or male column. The tribes of the Iones became the "Jones" of Kymry, from Wales to Rumania.

INTONATION
In Musical Form (from Greco-Egyptian) is the derivation of a series of related scales (from a monochord unequally divided — by geometry instead of arithmetic or anti-rhythm) — and so producing the *tropoi* or "turns" (cp. Atropos, the weaver goddess). Natural Intonation compares favourably with later modes : "Just" or "Mean" or "Tempered" — as in the flattening or sharpening of notes to meet a harmonic need. *Tropos* depends on harmonics not harmonies. The unequal intervals must therefore be given also in dance, by unequal steps. Natural Intonation lingers only in folk tunes, in some Oriental music such as the older Hindu *raga** forms (it is lost in modern modes). The *tropoi* did explicate the motif (*Raga*) by turns. Scientifically it has been demonstrated by Chladni (with sand on metal plates and violin bow vibration) while psychologically C. G. Jung shows results in *mandala** forms — in line and colour, balancing the sound effect.   [Cp. *Ancient Music,* Canon Galpin]

IRISH DANCES
Follow in much-obscured traditional lines. Country Dances were introduced last. Many forms of dance, as *Rinnce** (anciently known also as *Chor* or *Cor*) have been known. These were usually with a regular beat and regular number of bars : the Jig or Gigue, Double or Single; the Hop Jig; and the *Monoen* or Green-Sod Jig. The *Reel** is similar to the Scottish form; there is also a *Hornpipe** which is like the English versions. There were older forms known as *Irish Hey* and *Irish Trot* — the emphasis on the national mode indicating that they competed with English Hey and English Trot; these are included in Playford's book *The English Dancing Master.** The Fair competitions or *Feis* gave rise to renewed Feast dances, such as the *Cake Dance,** known from 1680. An Irish *Dumpe** was known : one called *Ho Hoane* (*Ochone*), and *Colleen* (Wm. Byrd), printed in the Fitzwilliam Virginal Book. [See *Dance Music of Ireland.* Ed. B. M. Levey. London, 1870]

IROQUOIS INDIANS (USA)
Occupied what is now New York State, Pennsylvania, and Ohio. In 18th century, the Iroquois (among whose leaders was Hiawatha), joined with Mohawk, Onondaga, Seneca, Oneida and Cayuga tribes to form "The Six Nations". An agricultural people, their religion and festivals centre round the solstices, life cycle of plants and animals, and five seasons — Spring growth ("Green Corn"); maturing of Maize; "high-sun-time"; "leaf-fall-time"; Winter. They believe in a life-force called *orenda* (see *Mana**) which permeates all Nature. Chief agricultural spirits are a triad of sisters, Corn, Bean and Squash, representing the chief crops, while alternation of seasons is symbolised by struggles between the God of Life and the Destroyer ("Great Good" and "Great Bad" Spirits). Iroquois possess many dances — social, curative, ceremonial — nearly all in circular, anti-clockwise form. Richard Wallaschek[1] mentions twenty-one out of thirty-two known dances being in use in 1893, all accompanied by music, with song and dance alternating. Most dances are of the stamp-and-shuffle type, with a twisting of the feet in and out; accompanied by water drums, rattles and chanting. In the social dances, men and women perform together, either in pairs, or alternating, or men leading and women in the rear. The Pigeon, Coon, Robin, and Fish Dances imitate movements of these creatures. Curative dances are performed by members of Buffalo and Bear Societies, but especially by the *Gagosa** or "False Faces", who hold exorcising ceremonies in Spring, Autumn and Mid-Winter with special dances. There is an Eagle curing dance, and a "Dark Dance" performed in the home of the patient, in the dark. Ceremonial dances are included in seasonal festivals, such as the three-day Green Corn Festival in Spring, and the Mid-Winter Festival. At the latter a Buffalo dance is performed, both mimetic and curative; while the women's dance, *Eskänye*, in honour of the spirits of Corn, Bean and Squash, takes place at both festivals. These are generally held in the village "long house", and all include the Drum Dance as a dance of thanksgiving. Iroquois and Seneca live now in Reservations in New York State, while the Mohawk's Reservation is across the border in Ontario, Canada.
[1] *Primitive Music.* R. Wallaschek. 1893.

ISHTAR (Assyria BC 4000)
Is the origin of the Salome myth; described in tablets from Nineveh (in B.M.) and was associated with the Gilgamesh* mythos. The Queen Goddess Ishtar sought her young husband (possibly seeking him in Hades. Tammuz (as the Year God) had been "lost"; but the tablets recording his death, burial and resurrection are not available. The porter of Hades (Kingdom of Underworld), Allatu, permitted Ishtar to enter, if she performed the correct ceremonial. This involved removing her "seven garments" (six in fact — she was the seventh). As the Welcome Dance (Shalomé = Welcome) Allatu mocks Ishtar. In the absence of Ishtar from Earth, love is dormant. Shamash the Sun god orders Uddushu-namir to provide Allatu with the Waters of Life. Namtura sprinkles Ishtar; who returns through the Seven Gates, restoring her "raiment".* So "Spring is born again" and is celebrated now as

Easter. The mythos of Ishtara penetrated into all of the lands of Europe: for the later Jews as Esther (M'-Gilloth), for Eire as 'Tara; for the Latins as Eastrea; and for us as Easter—and the strange cell-substance "Yeast which Rises". The lover Tammuz, who is like Horus, who is leader of the Khoroi interchanges as often. The mythos of the Rising and Falling Year is used as a factual basis for the symbols of the Rising-Falling Soul, who dances on the Journey through the Seven Gates; and the Heraklean Twelve Months (of Zodiacal time). Ishtara-Salome is herself the soul, seeking the bliss of the Garden of the Gods. At every great banquet is a feast, a song, a ritual, a dance; as we see with Khil-kamish—who is "one third mortal and two parts divine" (that is, material body with vital soul and indestructible spirit). In this fascinating 6000-year-old Sumerian legend we can find many origins of recent tales: they belong to the same humanity, the same problems, the same Way. [See *Quanta*]

ISOLANO (Greece)
Peasant dance performed in the Islands of the Aegean Archipelago, as in Casos. Some twenty girls, clad in white, enter the room; leading a youth playing on a lyre. They make a circle and invite the principal guest to dance. Dancers in this circle hold hands, not of the next dancer but those beyond these dancers on both sides, so that the arms pass across their backs. In the centre stand the musicians, playing and dancing at the same time. The step is the simple two or three steps clockwise, and then one step back; with a swaying motion that varies according to the development of merriment.

J

JABADAO (Brittany)
A dance in lively 2/4 time for men and women (minimum of four couples), still danced in the Cornouaille. "Jabadao" is said to come from "Jabad" which, in the Breton language, means *Sarabande*,* but there seems little connection between the two dance forms. With slight variations, it is in two figures, the women making a progressive clockwise round, until each returns to her partner. The *Jabadao* contains a suggestion of miming, which may point to an old, now forgotten, purpose in the dance's original form. In one version, while the girls dance *sur place* in the first figure, the men advance to the centre with hands on hips in defiant attitude, strike the ground sharply with the right foot and raise the right arm

in threatening gesture. Returning to his partner, each man passes her in front of him from right to left and back again, after which she moves on to take the place of the girl on his left. These two figures are repeated until the girl returns to her first partner. In another version, the first figure, using the Breton *pas de gavotte*, is a closed round, the dancers linked by little fingers and facing centre. In the second figure the men advance towards the centre, turn the body and head back, and each beckons his partner, who advances, giving him her right hand, the left remaining on her hip. They then perform steps together, before she passes to the left as before. These movements are repeated until each girl has returned to her partner, when the round is then danced again, as often as required.

JACARA (Spain)
A pair dance, considered in the 18th century to be a variation of the Sarabande.* Partners dance facing each other, but without touching. *Jacara* means a merry ballad, country song or dance tune, while *jacarear* is to sing in the streets at night, which suggests a serenade.

JACK IN THE GREEN (London, 17th century)
The principal "mask" of the chimney sweepers' companies, when they celebrated the First of May. They paraded the streets, disguised more or less completely, decorated with gilt paper, fancy buttons, sprigs of flowers. Taking shovels and brushes, they knocked out a crude rhythm, to which they danced. Some larger companies paid a fiddler; and had a Lord and Lady of May with them, to follow the dancing Jack in the Green.* "This mask was contrived", says Strutt,[1] "as a piece of pageantry, consisting of a hollow frame of wood, made in the form of a sugar loaf, but open at the bottom, sufficiently large to receive a man. This frame is covered with green leaves and bunches of flowers interwoven, so that the man within is concealed, who dances with his companions. And the populace are mightily pleased with the oddity of the moving pyramid". This is one of the ends of a most ancient tradition; found over many parts of the world—the "Green Man" of living nature.
[Cp. *Dodole* (Serbia)]
[1] *Sports and Pastimes*. Jos. Strutt. 1801.

JAGAT (Sanskrit) (India)
The World as a "Living Thing"—the "Dancing Life"; also termed *Samsara*, the net or whirl in which mankind is caught. Compare *Jahan* (Arabic-Persian) with the same meaning; further extended to *Jahannum* (purgatory or Lower World), and *Jinnie* (genie), some of the inhabitants (as in

Arabian Nights Entertainment). These ideas served to originate the pervasive terms of John, Jan, Yan, Ian, Jean or Jeanne, and Janus, all mythic personifications of the world process; and all of them apparent in ritual and traditional dance ceremonials. The term *Jagat*, which gives us *jig* or *gig*, appears at the ancient Indian centre Puri, as the great Car of Jaganath (Lord of the Mountain), symbolising the Chariot of Time—beneath whose wheels all forms are destroyed. The missionary tales about Hindus "throwing themselves under the car" are—just legends; the great wooden car moves at about one mile an hour; and weighs much less than a London motor-bus.

JANOSCHEK (Czechoslovakia and Poland)
Legendary mime-play, merging the Solstice Carnival with one of the traditional Czech and Polish heroes of the Tatra Mountains, who acted as a "Robin Hood". (Some men received this ancient name, through acting this leading character in the two Carnivals—Summer and Winter). There are many poems and pictorial works (from peasant sketches to painted windows), which record Janoschek; while he has naturally appeared on stage and film. He was renowned as a dancer through Bohemia and Poland. When he was captured, he was permitted to perform "one last dance", at the end of which he jumped higher, and dived through the window, to disappear from sight. His costume has the close-fitting white felt trousers, with gaily embroidered vest and coat, and a high hat with designs and feathers or leaves; with leather mountain shoes. This semi-legendary hero is said to have been finally caught and executed in 1713.
[See *Zbójnicki* (Poland)]

Scene from Noh dance-drama. (Tokyo 19th Century).

JAPAN

JAPANESE DANCES
Exist now in three main forms: (1) the ceremonial of the courts; (2) the popular festivals, religious and social; and (3) the commercial theatre, which has extended into imitation of European ballet. The Miko or Maiko* girls perform the *Sacred Mirror Dance* at many a village shrine. The social *Dance of Thanksgiving*, or "Harvest Festival", is celebrated under the full moon of that month; while on the *Feast for the Dead* in the Autumn, scores

of white-clad girls issue from the silent cemetery, to perform the *Dance of Welcome for the Ancestors*, or the *Ghost Dance*, in this old Shinto ritual. In Kyoto at the Temple of the Green Lotus, there is the *Butterfly Dance*, which is the last dance of the Spring Festivals, to welcome the summer season, after the pilgrims have danced their last *ondo* as they journey to the Shrine of Ise. Numerous are the series of *Odori** or ritual dances; from the *Geuoka Odori* (or *Kuroka Odori*), which celebrated the royal umbrella as a symbol; to the ancient *Dance of the Mothers* on the femininely attributed symbol of the two-breasted summit of Mount Tsukuba. At the courts, the stately war dance *Hayato-Mai* was formerly celebrated in mediaeval uniforms. The popular theatre is presented in the *Kabuki* form of dance-drama; while the reformed *Noh Dance-dramas*, entirely different, are better known to foreign readers. The *Ota-gaki* was the dance of adolescence, clad in blue silk with scarlet *obi* or girdles. A gild dance of Kyoto, first celebrated in 795, was devised to mark its promotion to be the capital, in the *Honen-odori*. Associated with the impulse of imported Chinese music, the *Saibara* were pantomime dances, skilfully joining Japanese words to the older rhythms—on those same topics which appear in Chinese paintings. *Genon odori* is a dance performed in Wakayama by a hundred gild merchants, in ceremonial costumes. *Tanabata odori* is the children's festival dance (seventh day of seventh month), marked by the heavenly approach of two stars : Prince Shepherd and Princess Weaver.

JAPANESE "MODERN DANCE"
Japanese modern dance schools follow both traditional and modernist modes, even ballet and ballroom and cabaret. The gilds of Geisha—at Kyoto and Tokyo—maintain the old classical system : with *maiko* (juniors), *geisha* (trained) and the rare *Tayu* (ballerina standard). Of the 5,000 in all Japan, most *Geisha* were trained by Matsuogi-san, in *Chayu Yugetsu* (Tea House of Friend of Moon). The ten year course includes Dance, *cha-no-yu* (tea ceremony), *ikebana* (flowersetting), musical instruments (Koto) calligraphy and singing. The school is in Pontochu (Gion) for girls 10 to 18 years.
[See * *Of Geisha and Gangsters* (Illystrated fully) by Frederick Joss London, 1962 (Odhams)].

JARABE (Mexico)
In its basic form, a simple pair dance performed by partners facing each other but not touching. As in many such folk dances, the man's steps are more spectacular than the girl's and performed at greater speed. Holding himself stiffly above the waist, he executes *zapateado** steps, while his partner dances modestly with down-cast eyes, her skirt slightly lifted at each side. In its simplest form, the *Jarabe*, together with the *Son*,* forms the basis of many Mexican folk dances. In more elaborate versions the man may emphasise the steady immobility of the upper part of his body by dancing with a glass of water on his head, or by tying and untying with his feet a knot in a scarf or kerchief. A stylised version, *Jarabe Tapatio** has become known as the national dance of Mexico, while at weddings and at the funeral of a child, a more ceremonial *Jarabe* is danced. (Cp. *Jota Valenciana;** *Canario**). A descendant of the Spanish *Zapateado*, the dance is in combined 3/4 and 6/8 time.
[See *Jarabe de la Botella; Jarabe Tapatio; Canacuas; Son—2½; Huaiño*]

JARABE DE LA BOTELLA (Mexico)
One of the slightly stylised *Jarabes* of gay and humorous character. Popular in Jalisco, it is danced by one couple. After performing an ordinary *Jarabe*,* the two drink from a bottle of tequila, which is then stood on the ground and they take turns dancing over and round it. The accompanying musicians exhort them not to upset the bottle or spill any of its contents, the penalty for which is provision of a full bottle. This dance occurs in one of the sequences of the girls' marriage dance, *Canacuas*.*

JARABE TAPATIO (Mexico)
A dance of the *charros* (horsemen) of the State of Jalisco. "Tapatio" refers to anything from that State. In Guadalajara about 1920 it developed as a stylised form of the simple *Jarabe** upon which many Mexican folk dances are based. *Jarabe Tapatio* became popular in theatre, cabaret, secular *fiesta*, and rodeo. Theatre audiences in other countries were shown it as a "Mexican dance", and it has become known as the national dance of Mexico. Pavlova and Argentina both performed it. A coquettish pair dance, it lasts about ten minutes and consists of nine figures and melodies. Partners dance facing each other, but not touching, the man with his hands held behind his back, the girl holding the front of her skirt. Dancers advance and retire, then circle round each other, always some distance apart. In one figure, the man winds his *sarape* round the spinning figure of his partner; repeated with the *sarape* wound round the man. In another, "The Dove", the girl dances round the brim of the man's sombrero, thrown on the ground, while he follows her round; as she stoops to pick it up he swings his right leg over her. She puts on the hat and, partners facing the same way, they perform a final figure, ending with the man falling

on one knee upon which the girl rests her foot, while he kisses her hand. The *charro's* costume consists of long, skin-tight trousers and short jacket, both heavily embroidered with gold and silver; broad-brimmed sombrero with silver cords and tassels. In the cities, girls wear the "China Poblana" costume. (*China*=Chinese woman; *Poblana* refers to Puebla de los Angeles, a city eighty miles from Mexico City). The name derives from a 17th century lady, Sor. Catarina de San Juan who, although traditionally regarded as a Chinese princess, was an Indian girl of high degree. After many adventures she devoted herself to good works and bequeathed her costume to her adopted city (Puebla de los Angeles). Now a popular form of *fiesta* dress, but not a true peasant costume, it consists of spangled green and red skirt; low-cut white blouse, silk- or bead-embroidered; lace-edged drawers. In country districts, the *Jarabe Tapatio* is more fiery, and is danced on a wooden platform placed over a pit to give resonance. After a rodeo, *charros* and *charras* (girl riders) perform *Jarabes*, the man sometimes spinning a rope throughout the dance. Country *charras* do not wear the China Poblana dress, but their regional costume.

JARANA (Mexico)
Literally, "a merry noise". A couple dance of Yucatan in combined 6/8 and 3/4 time. Songs accompanying the dance often have words in the Mayan language. Dancers facing each other in pairs, form two lines, which cross and recross, the dancers curving their arms up and snapping fingers as the lines cross. While the *Jarana* thus shows Spanish style and is a popular secular dance in the towns, the expressionless face and downcast eyes are characteristically Mexican. In the villages there is evidence of its ritualistic associations; when danced on ceremonial occasions such as religious *fiestas* or weddings, it is performed always outside the church, being danced four times during the *fiesta*.

JARDINEROS, LOS (Mexico)
"The Gardeners". A burlesque dance, performed by men in villages of the Oaxaca Valley. The sole connection with its name seems to be the garland of flowers which each dancer holds in an arc above his head. In a burlesque of court dance style and behaviour, the men perform polkas, waltzes and mazurkas, to the music of string instruments. Mimicking the elegant manners of lords and ladies, the two groups of dancers, wearing masks, are headed by a "king" and a "queen". The "king" and his followers have short trousers and brightly coloured shirts; while the "ladies", with wigs of long hair, wear short red silk dresses.

JARDINIERO, LI (Provence, France)
"The Gardeners". A dance in 4/4 time, from districts of Apt, Draguignan and Marseilles, and other country districts. Having seven figures plus entrée and sortie, this dance is similar to *Les Treilles,** of Languedoc. Men and women enter and form two lines in couples, women holding garlands over their heads. 1. Dancers move into two single lines, each girl in front of her partner. 2. Dancers cast down the line, and then out, to finish in a double circle, facing centre, men outside. 3. "Arches". The women's inner circle being joined by upheld garlands, men dance in and out of these arches. 4. "Bower". A bower is formed by one man moving to the centre and holding one end of each garland as the girls dance round him, the other men remaining in the outer circle. 5. "Round the Bower". Centre man and girls remaining still, the other men dance round the bower, sometimes facing it, sometimes with backs to it. 6. Women take back their hoops and the double circle is reformed, men on outside. 7. Each man taking the left side of his partner's garland, all move into a straight, horizontal line. For the sortie, a Tunnel is formed with the garlands, through which each couple passes in turn. A song accompanies the dance, sung during the entrée, and the seventh figure.

JAVA (Indonesia)
Is rich in traditional plays and dances; many still performed though some have been injected with modernist political themes. Many people dislike this change; preferring the legends: morality plays, mythical tales told in dance, and the famous shadow plays. Broadly they operate in three main systems: the court systems centred in Suryakarta and Jogyakarta (now much disturbed); the temple and festival ritual system; and the general public or pastimes and entertainments. The religious forms are oldest, in two modes: the ceremonial form of ritual-dance (inherited from Southern India, chiefly Shivaite, in Java and Bali), and the *Wayang** or shadow plays, which are possibly older still, also recounting traditional stories. Governed in movement mostly by the *gamelan** music, they become rhythmic in general character, a factor accentuated in chanting of verse forms by the *dalang* (manager) or, in the temple festivals, by the priests. The historic bases are Hindu with Malay-Polynesian influences, later infused with Chinese and Moslem-Arabic streams of tradition and music; finally with Dutch, Japanese and lastly modernist Euro-American contacts, as with films, in the large towns.

JAVANESE DANCE — 1
Has three main styles, or design modes governed

by technical qualities. These are 1. *Aloes*; 2, *Gagah*; and 3. *Kasar*. The *Aloes* style of movement is that of women and the refined hero type; it is slow and not emphatic or energetically stressed. The *Gagah* movements reverse the *Aloes*; they are the expression of great and proud heroes; thy move more quickly, in broader lines, and more emphatic gesture, though fully controlled and graceful. Finally the *Kasar* style has the highly energetic, broad, and aggressive movements, suited for the *Kauravas* — evil characters, giants etc., with arms lifted speedily and high. Some similarity with this system is visible in the characters played in the South India mask dance of *Kathakali*.* All of these three styles are found especially in *Wayang Wong* — the "human-shadow" mode of developed Javanese dancing — though earlier derived from the symbolic dramas expressed in puppet forms. The Javanese dancer indicates emotions only by conventional gesture; the face remains expressionless and mask-like.

Serimpi Dance. *(Courtesy Eastern World.)*   JAVA

JAVANESE DANCE — 2
Is comprised in its three main modes of Theatre, known as *Wayang*, or Shadow-Dance (but similar to its origin in Hindu *vahan* or *avahana*, meaning "an appearance" or forth-showing). These Shadow Plays began with the simple wall or screen, and puppet; possibly in the depth of the primitive cave, starting with holding up hands and face (or extempore mask-forms, an animal skull or wing etc.), between the flickering light of a cave fire and a smooth patch of wall. Thus originated the *Wayang Poerwa* — the Shadow of Action; and next the *Wayang Kulit*,* Leather-men Puppets, contrived of cut leather, and manipulated by short rods, so that shadows fell on a cotton screen. From these origins came the ritual drama of *Wayang Wong* — danced in mime by human actors, who still obeyed the older rules of symbol-movement in

the stiff style imposed by puppets. This puppet-action governed the human dance for some centuries; and is only now being extended into naturalism or realism, losing the symbol character. During the development of the *Wayang Kulit*, each character had its own costume, style of dress and of movement, easy for the people to recognise. For the *Wayang Kulit*, men sat on the puppet player's side of the screen (with the light source and the *dalang*, or story-teller), while the women sat on the other side; and saw only flat shadows. This same cult did not require facial expression; none of it was personal, and the later dance form of *Wayang Wong* kept the dancers' faces as unemotional masks.   [See *Wayang; Srimpi; Bedaja*]

JAZZ (Arabic, N. Africa)

From *Jazba* ("Delight"), *Dzhajasbah* in Islamic ritual prayer; used of ecstasy produced by circle dance and chant in mosque. Taken to New Orleans (and Southern States) by Negro slaves; gradually displaced by Christian hymns which produced "Negro Spirituals". Jazz then turned more commercial, in dance halls, to refer to the freely syncopated rhythm linked to steps of popular dance, by Negro dance-bands.

JESUS, DANCE OF, Hymn of Jesus (Hellenic BC)

Sacred ritual dance, partly described in the *Apocryphal New Testament* (Ed. Dr. M. R. James), also included by G. R. S. Mead in his work *Thrice Greatest Hermes*, transcribed from the *Actio Johannis* (*Actio* or "Play of IOhannis"), which was rejected from the orthodox bible, because of its Gnostic associations in superior teaching. In this ritual dance, Jesus, standing in the centre of a ring of the twelve apostles, is chanting a litany of initiation, as a slow round dance proceeds. The sole reference in the orthodox script is "I have piped unto you and ye did not dance". Only the few key lines remain in this text. A more recent commentator (Jean Delaire), says that "The magic circle drawn on earth represents the shape and orbit of the celestial bodies, the cyclic processes of the universe : the measures of the sacred dance repeat the movements of the satellites around their central sun". (p. 170, *Mystery Teaching in the West*). The whole dance, even as a real ritual, was entirely symbolical. The round ritual dance of the Durweshes (Mevlehvi Order) of Islam shows a similar sort of sacred dance; and there were many other similar rites".
[See *Pagan Christs*. J. M. Robertson]

JESUIT BALLET — 1 (France and Austria)

When the Society of Jesuits (formerly *Gesuati*) was formally organized in 1564, the change of policy moved from the terrors of "Holy Inquisition" to methods of persuasion and propaganda, through schools and theatres. For this purpose, leading Jesuits were detailed to seek, learn, and schematize various cultural systems; from current education to methods of propaganda, of ideology by infiltration. Several men were instructed to learn about dance systems, dance training, and dance use, for schools and theatres. Best known are the writers Kircher and Arbeau (pen-name of the Bishop of Langres). Claude Francois Menéstrier was another Jesuit writer, whose book *Des Ballets Ancien et Moderns Selon les Regles du Theatre* is the first printed history of ballet known to us, published at Paris in 1682. The work by Thoinot Arbeau is earlier : his *Orchesographie** was published at Langres in 1588 (date of "privilege") and 1589 (issue for sale). His "church name" was Jehan Tabouret. He describes twenty-six dances, music of drum and fife. Cardinal Richelieu and subsequently Mazarin gave close attention to stage propaganda, whether by drama or ballet; and in company with the Italian Medici family did much to develop and change this former court amusement to wider aims. This was often influenced by Jesuits, when not under their direct control. The rapid infiltration of Jesuit members, into schools, led to the use of ballets as "moralities", in this newer "educational" form; chiefly in Austria, some in France and others in Switzerland. Kircher's influence was in the direction of scenic stage display; his perspective effects attracted attention; and this careful design of stage illusion led the way to the "realistic theatre" later at its optimum at Saxe-Meiningen.
[See *Power and Secrets of the Jesuits*. Rene Fülöp-Miller. Vienna. 1929. USA. 1930]

JESUIT BALLET — 2

Culminated in Paris, about 1840, after their triumphant return to France, and successful invasion of the realm of Romantic Ballet, which was mainly instigated by J. G. Noverre. We have it brought sharply to attention by the "critical" writing of Theophile Gautier, whose skilful theories supported the notions of "Art for Art's Sake" (to offset the reality of its use in propaganda), and were rivalled only by the young curate who (at this time) used the pen name of Eliphas Levi to publish scholarly volumes, ostensibly "all about Magic" (Magic for Magic's Sake). We note Gautier coming to the surface for occasional air, in his sharp contrast of the catholic dancer Marie Taglioni, against the protestant dancer, Fanny Elssler. The first was praised as a "Christian dancer", but the other was denigrated as a "pagan dancer". The Jesuit policy (since transferred with more success to control of film censorship board — the Hayes

Committee in California), then secured the use of an alleged German legend, to formulate the famous ballet of *Giselle*. The theme revolves round the capture (and recovery) of the Christian village maiden (despoiled by the naughty German princeling), and her suicide, yet restored by the virtue of christian symbols. The original finale of this ballet was altered; either in rehearsal, by those who saw the point; or soon afterwards; and Giselle was allowed to return to her monumental tomb. Another similar ballet, *Napoli*, was produced at this time (1892) in Denmark. A few years later, the use of Hoffman's story in *Coppelia* (with its original and greater subtlety) put an end to this submerged influence in Paris. The Hollywood film factories have given the policy of the "priest as the good man" prominence in hundreds of bad films; much as G. K. Chesterton contrived his little Father Brown in propaganda romances of detection.

JEU DU BERGER ET DE LA BERGÈRE (France)
This pastoral play of *The Shepherd and the Shepherdess*, known in written form in 12th century Paris, comprised the residues of some far older traditions; and continued down to the period of the Bourbon courts at Versailles, where pretty ladies and ardent gentlemen pursued the sheep "into the fold" of the *Parc au Cerf*. Adam de la Halle is believed to have written music for some special performance, at a spring festival. The principal characters in the play were Robin and Marion. Warton thought our English legend might be derived from this stem, but Ritson did not assent. In England, Mayd Marian appeared in the countryside May Games; but by Shakespeare's time, the legend had much faded. She appeared also in the Morris Dance. Earlier in France, we learn of the May Game of Martinisme; but this festival was in September, being taken over from the wine harvest Feast of Bacchus. Dancing was associated with all of these plays and games as a matter of course; as well as in the dramatic unfolding of the central theme.

JEUNES VIERGES, La Danse des (France)
Early Mediaeval religious dance, performed usually at the funeral of a young girl; but traditionally in the old church choral dance of *La Rosalie*, when a village girl was crowned; also for the solo chant, the *Way to Jerusalem*.* A group of twelve unmarried girls sang their chant to a slow dance. This version came from Flanders:

"La Demoiselle has gone away, Alleluia!
And in heaven will dance today, Alleluia.
All young maidens dance and play,
Singing as they dancing go,

Alleluia! Alleluia!
Dancing *Rosalie* they sing, Alleluia!
She has done with sorrowing. Alleluia!
With the dancing maidens play.
Alleluia! Alleluia!"

Another ceremonial with this name was recorded as being performed in 1840 by the lacemakers of Bailleul. Of this is said:

"La cérémonie religieuse terminée, et le cercueil descendu en terre, toutes les jeune filles tenant d'une main le drap mortuaire, retournèrent a l'église, chantant la *Danse des Jeunes Vierges*, avec une verve, un élan et un accent rhythmique, dont on peut se faire difficilement une idée, quand ne l'pas entendu".

Closely similar are some forms of *Jota* (*Jota Valenciana;** also *canario**) in Spain; the *Danse* of *Matthieu* in Hungary, and the earlier mode of the *Wakes*, in Ireland and in Lancashire.

JEWISH DANCES (Poland, *Yiddsche* dance in)
Exist in Europe and USA (and elsewhere—naturally in Israel) on two main systems: in (a) the ancient ritual dance form; and (b) the traditional dance forms, still widely performed. Many of the current popular Jewish dances are related to folk songs or poems by Warshafsky, known under the Yiddische names of *Dee Muzinke Oisgegeben; Yoshke! Yoshke!; Dreydl Tanz; Machetom Geyen; Der Becher; Finf un Tzvantziken Beim Rebns Tish; Dee Yomtovdike Teg; Achtzik er unzibetske Zee;* and *Gey Ich Mir Shpatzirn.* Most of the music is traditional; but from the pipe and flute melodies, modern tunes have been arranged for simple pianoforte rendering. *Die Dreydl Tanz* is a circle dance that accompanies the famous ceremony of "Lighting the Candles" or *Chanuka*. The ancient words are lost and newer versions prevail. *Beim Reben's Tanz*, for males only, is a "Hassidic dance of the *schule*", led by the Rabbi on Friday evening, as he chants the traditional melody *Shalam Alechem* (Salute, or Greeting of Peace). *Der Becher* (The Beaker, or Cup) is filled with red wine to celebrate Seder Night of the Passover Ceremony. *Achtzik* is a Golden Wedding Dance.
[See *Jewish Dances*, Ruth Zahava]

JEWISH RITUAL DANCE (Assyria)
Was developed (400 - 50 BC) mainly in Syria, partly from Egyptian sources and partly from Babylonian doctrine. On an agricultural basis (formalised in the local Ba'Al cults for many centuries) grew three principal festivals: (1) *Massoth* (the *Passover /Pasch*); (2) *Pentecost* (the Feast of Seven Weeks); and (3) *Tabernacles* or "Feast of Booths" (Harvest). To these were added the "Purification of the Temple" (Spring-clean rites) and the Ceremonies of

First Fruits (Osirian tradition); Feast of Trumpets; and the At-one-ment or Feast of Ancestors. These annual Festivals were superimposed on far older Semitic traditions, the Feast of New Moon (lunar calendar), and that of Wool-Shearing. Later than the Babylonian celebrations were arranged *Purim* (new form) by the Maccabeans, as the *Legend of Esther*. From these and other writings, mythic and legendary, were drawn the material for the famous *Five M'Gilloth** (Rolls of Script). At no period were these annual festivals rigidly fixed; though changes occurred more speedily after revolts and journeys. We can estimate them only by reference to (a) their technical origin in agriculture, (b) the doctrinal origin in cults derived from Egypt and Assyria; and (c) the internal origins devised by Levites and other priestly castes of ambitious temperament, assisted by propagandists down to Josephus; yet illumined by such scholars as Rabbi ibn Judah ibn Hillel, who is said to have co-ordinated the public legends (of *Genesis* and *Exodus*) with their real meaning, as partly set forth in the *Qabalah**. Certain ritual dances were devoted to exposition of these secret doctrines. [See *Zohar*]

JHUMMIR DANCE (Punjab, Pakistan)
Originally a Beluchi dance, brought in by traders and camel drivers, from the nomads of Beluchistan, where it goes by names of *Dzhumara* or *Chumamir* and other local variations. Punjabis use this dance for their weddings. There are three main forms of this circle dance, each influenced by varying mood; with some intricate developments of pattern in rhythm and tempo. Girls and men join; though often in different circles; men are esteemed highly if they can show complete ability in the *Jhummir*; the girls sing a couplet of satire, directed at the inexpert: *"Na Jhummir na tari—Na ajai mukh te darhi,"* meaning "You can't dance *Jhummir* and clap; you cannot grow a beard!" The Rebabi musicians supply the usual *tabla* (drum), but lead with their stringed lute, the *rebab*. There are local chants for accompaniment; while watchers add to rhythm with their hand-claps.

JIBIRI, LE (France)
A simple round dance of High Brittany — Cornouaille, and the Vannetais district. To lively music in 2/4 time, the linked circle revolves clockwise, dancers making a little jump on each step. This circling alternates with dancing *sur place*, when the left and right foot are alternately brought forward with the heel on the ground. At the same time, arms are raised when the left foot is advanced, lowered with the right foot. The tune is also sung.

JIG (Irish)
Is danced with arms at angles, hands on waist (called "akimbo", from *on kenbowe*), with legs crossing every other step, moving in a quick and lively rhythm. Two partners also dance; the man brandishing a *shillelagh* (thorn stick), shouting and slapping his legs or snapping his fingers. The girl keeps both arms akimbo.   [See *Gigue*]

JIG, GIG OR GIGUE (Europe)
European peasant festival dance, known all through Western Europe and Ireland. A dance for couples or a number in a group; in rapid 6/8 time, usually from bag-pipes, sometimes fiddle. The ancient name derives from *Jagat* (Indian) the "moving thing", i.e. the "whole living world", seen in vital rhythm; from the widely celebrated Festival of Jaga-nath (Lord of the World) at Puri in Eastern India. Many festival dances occurred; with gay processions and feasting, to very simple music form with an equally simple dance mode. The name *gig*, as meaning a two-wheeled vehicle, may also derive from the famous Car of Jaga-nath, in which the figure of the god is carried through enthusiastic processions, sometimes entailing accidents through vast crowds pressing closely. This festival reached into Europe, probably before, but certainly with, returning Crusaders from Syria; giving such names as *juggler* or *jongleur* (experts with moving things), and the popular dance itself. Lapsing into slang, the generic term gives many derivations, implying something that moves regularly, from the "jig" used in workshops as a pattern-piece; to "jigging", or "I'll be jiggered!"; or "jiggle" to move rapidly, and "jig-saw" cut (as a puzzle) with ever-curving steps or movements.

JITTERBUG (USA)
Modern American variety of Australian native Corroboree; done usually to Negro jazz syncopated rhythms. This combination of topical song, acrobatic gyrations, and swift whirling of the mingled sexes, supplies the youth population of American cities with a more intimate method of "getting acquainted" than is afforded by the co-educational system used in some towns. While the night-club patrons prefer to watch the dancing "done for them", the Jitterbuggian devotees demand to do this exercise for themselves, claiming it is "healthy sport". In some of the New York City halls "jitterbugerese" is spoken, in combination with *marihuana* (clubs for smoking Jimson Weed cigarettes) or even for more efficient narcotics, to provide the maximum contrast to the craze for "excidement". A typical example of Jitterbug "dancing" was shewn in the colour-film *Living It Up* (shewn in London, September 1954).

JITTERBUG (USA)

Derivation of this name is uncertain; in the USA there is frequent reference in Spring to the May-bug. That genial Victorian scholar Thomas Wright, refers in his *History of Caricature*, to similar names, as nicknames, or name of qualities. He writes :

"An Anglo-Saxon abbess of rank, whose real name was Hrodwaru, but who was known universally by the name of Bugga, the Bug, wrote this latter name in signing charters. We can hardly doubt that such a name was intended to ascribe to her qualities of a not agreeable character, and very different from those implied by the original name, which meant, perhaps, a dweller in heaven".

Perhaps he refers here to the Slavonic *Bhog* or *Bhoga*, their term for God; hardly to the name Herod-varu (or Grodvara). Or the USA term may stem back (by way of immigrants) to Rumanians, who had the Bogomili and their traditional dances. The one certain fact is that current USA versions are (a) not religious in origin, and (b) partake of the fanatical character so often ascribed to "native dances" by missionaries.

JOCULATOR (English, from Latin)

Joculator Regis, the King's Jester, is mentioned in Domesday Book (the first great tax registration imposed on England). This court office developed from the Harper, one of the ancient titles. *Gleemen* and *Joculators* were Saxon and Norwegian entertainers —tumblers and dancers who performed with the *Minstrels*.

JOGET, OR JOGED (Malaya)

In several modes, this is the most typical of Malayan dances. *Joget*, the most accomplished, is done for rajas or for rich people. Probably this form comes from Java; since many of the melodies used are frequent in Java and Sumatra. *Joget* is performed by a group of four girls (the *Budak Joget*), two about eighteen, two about twelve, wearing very pretty costume, and head-dresses of flowers in gold. Costume, alike for all except that elder girls wear white silk bodices with red-gold kerchief, with its knots in centre of back. Younger girls wear dress of one material; usually gold cloth; heavy waistbelts have buckles (*pinding*) right across middle; diamond studs in ears; bare feet. The dance begins with them sitting, before audience enters, their faces partly hidden by fans of crimson and gilt paper. Their orchestra has two principal musicians (*klempong*, struck with sticks, and *gambang*, inverted bowls), boys for gong, drummer with sticks; and several boys for *chanang*

(triangles). Music is vigorous. The dance begins with *sembah* (ritual salutation), then slow swaying movements; much play with the scarf after they rise erect; moving through many positions in slow and graceful style, with hands, head and body being moved, the feet seem hardly to change. A performance will have five (or six) different dances, each twenty or thirty minutes. Themes are symbolical, but are expressed in "work-dance motion", that is, miming of sowing seed, tending rice, reaping grain, carting, winnowing and storing. Attendants hand them "properties" from time to time— a fan, a mirror, a flower, or a small cup; but usually the empty hands show *mudra* poses. Last is a war dance; a wand represents a sword; it is faster. The dance develops into real meaning as elder dancers affect to be possessed by the "Spirit of Dancing" (*hantu menari*), and they are restrained by attendants who lead them out. This *Joget* is performed usually in a small hall, *asthana*, partly as a ritual, in some festival period.

"JOHN ANDERSON" — "My-Jo !" (English)

Reformation period, popular dance melody or ballad that became (with parody) a political ballad. This song, with others such as *Maggy Lauder* and *Greensleeves*, was sung in derision of the Romish sect, hated for its corruption and pretensions. The name possibly referred to the disastrous list of popes named John : twenty-three of them.

"JOHN CANOE" (Jamaica)

A festival dance of the Negroes, held annually at Christmas. The name is uncertain, theories advanced being that it is a corruption of the words "carrion crow", explained by the West Indian pronunciation of these words; or a corruption of the French name for the Midsummer Festival of John — "Jean Cano" — taken to Jamaica by French immigrants. This seems the more likely, although the dance has a derisive and frivolous character. The dancers wear bright costumes consisting of printed cotton jacket with large bustle; brilliant cotton drawers, edged with lace; white cotton gloves, white shoes and stockings; and their faces are hidden behind painted masks.

JON-NUKÊ (Japan)

A popular tea-house "forfeit dance", performed by girls. They pay a forfeit for every failure to imitate each other's gestures when challenged by a loud "Hoy !", by throwing off one article of clothing each time until nothing remains, when they disappear behind a curtain at the back. Part of this Japanese "strip-tease" performance is a song beginning with the words "Jon-Kino ! Jon-Kino !"

JOROPO (Venezuela)

The national dance of Venezuela. A quick waltz for one couple, with steady rhythm in 3/4 or 6/8 time. The dance has four main figures: 1. A waltz turn as in the ballroom, but stamping on the first beat of each measure. 2. Partners, face to face, combine a scissors step with zapateado.* 3. Turning under each other's upraised arms. 4. Holding hands, partners perform stamping zapateado steps with alternate feet, the right and left shoulder being thrust forward with the corresponding foot.

JOTA (Spain)

A couple dance claimed by the Aragonese to belong specifically to Aragon, but acknowledging its arrival there from Andalusia. Said to have been brought north by the Moorish poet, Aben Jot, it is known nearly all over Spain and in the Basque country on both sides of the Pyrenees. There is some contradiction as to its actual origin. Generally believed to have derived from the Andalusian Fandango,* some claim that it originated in Aragon, but the Aragonese themselves sing a copla, or verse, which says:

"From the banks of the Turia to the banks of the Jalon,
Singing the Jota came the exiled Aben-Jot".

In the twelfth century this "Moorish poet" was exiled from Valencia, and took refuge in a village of Aragon. Some authorities state that the Jota was at that time called Canario.* Very popular in Aragon and Valencia, the Jota is danced by couples facing each other, the woman following the steps chosen by the man from a selection of about forty. In quick 3/4 or 3/8 time, it is danced in flat rope-soled shoes, partners facing and moving in opposite directions. The same step is always used for the opening, after which any may be chosen, the dance being broken by the estrivillo—an interval during which a copla is sung while the dancers rest. The dancers sometimes accompany themselves with castanets, or tambourines, while the music is played by guitars or pipe and drum. The chief characteristic of the dance is a light, springy agility, with jumps and kicks to the side, in front and behind. In the Philippines variations of the Spanish Jota, having alternative grave and gay moods, are Jota Purpura, and Jota Moncadena which is danced with elongated bamboo castanets.

JOTA ARAGONESE (Spain)

Aragon possesses several different styles of Jota, classified into: rabaleras, golondrinas, zaragonzanas, femateras, etc. The man (maños) approaches his maña (girl) and, taking her by the hand leads her to the dancing-place, where they wait facing each other, until the musicians (playing guitars, lutes, mandolins), strike four vigorous chords, when the dance begins. Havelock Ellis describes Jota Aragonese as "a kind of combat between (the partners) . . . advancing and retreating in an apparently aggressive manner, the arms alternately slightly raised and lowered, and the legs, with a seeming attempt to trip the partner, kicking out alternately somewhat sideways, as the body is rapidly supported first on one foot and then on the other . . ."[1]

[1] The Soul of Spain. Havelock Ellis. 1908.

JOTA VALENCIANA (Spain)

Differs from the Aragonese dance, the most popular version being the Jota del Carrer ("of the street"). Leading his partner to a suitable clear space, the man spreads his striped blanket on the ground and the couple dance up to and away from it. Accompanied by the dulzaina (pipe) and tabalet (drum), guitars and the singing of coplas also form part of the dance. The style is softer than the Aragonese Jota. In Valencia the Jota is also a funeral dance following the death of a child. With guitars and castanets, a man and girl dance in gala costume, to the singing and clapping of the funeral guests. It is an expression, not of grief, but of joy at the escape of the innocent child from tribulations on earth.   [1]Cp. Canario; Jarabe; Jeunes Vierges]

JOUET (French)

The "second clown" who mimes misery (as a plaything) in a circus, the victim of japes. From joute, a tilt or fight; and jouteur, antagonist; now popularised as "Pal Joey" and formerly used by Joey Grimaldi the clown of Sadlers Wells; the "victim" in the Harlequinade dancing.

JOY OF HOUSE OF WATER DRAWING (Jerusalem) (Hag-ha-Mayim)

The most elaborate ritual performed in the second Temple of Jerusalem, connected with earlier Feast of Tabernacles, over seven days, at the beginning of the Hebrew Year in Autumn, onset of the rainy season. At this "Ritual of Water Libation", Messav was the additional festal sacrifice. The shofar horn was sounded: teqi-ah (long blast), a teru-ah (tremulous blast), and again teqi'ah, to initiate the walking dance round the altar; done every day with brief chants. This altar was hidden in fresh green willow branches of ten cubits, placed standing, so that the younger leaves hung over. On the seventh day the ambit was done seven times, with another rite, that of the lulabs and ethrogs. This means that each devotee carried a small swish (lulab) of palm or willow twigs, used to beat the altar (i.e. to make it clean), while the ethrog was a citron, suggesting the desired fruitful results. The Mishna has it:

"Whomsoever has not seen the Joy of the House of Water Drawing has seen no real joy in his life". The principal dance was the Torch Dance; but there was also the Levitic *Songs of Ascents,** or steps. The daily routine required twelve acts: 1. Covering of altar with green boughs; 2. ambulation of altar; 3. brushing of altar with *lulabs*; 4. lighting of lamps; 5. torch dance; 6. songs (with lesser dancing) accompanied by instruments and trumpet blasts; 7. processional dance to Siloam at daybreak; 8. ritual water drawing and libation on altar; 9. libation of wine; 10. the tumult or fight with *lulabs* (Sabbath day); 11. the culmination (*qaluth rosh*) with the women (or the *saturnalia*); and 12. destruction of *lulabs* (by children) and eating of *ethrogs* as symbol fruit. Venerable Rabbi Simeon ben Gamaliel danced with eight burning torches. He threw them high in alternation and caught them; further he threw himself down in acrobatic dance. While this Torch Dance continued the Levites took positions on the fifteen steps leading from Women's Court to Inner Court; holding harps, lyres, cymbals and trumpets. There they sang the *Songs of Ascents*. This dance preceded the procession to Siloam. The whole ritual marked the desired invigoration of Nature for harvest; in this, ritual and myth grew together like two walking feet, on the factual earth.

JUDAS (Hebrew-Etruscan-Latin)
This name is taught as a term of reprobation; yet its origin proclaims a realistic basis in ritual and dance. Strong hints from the earlier story of the Indian Cristna tell us of his lunar dances with the *gopis* (Shepherdesses), of whom half wore dark attire, and the other half, white or silver. There were thirty. The distorted remains of the legend, added the tale to the mythic parable. *Das* or *dasi* in India means "servant" (as *deva-dasi*, servant of the gods) and, for the Hebrews, *I O* was the lunar goddess, whom they as Semites followed for many centuries, as they adopted the Golden Cow (of Egypt) of Hathor. This ritual dance then set forth the Round of I O, as the Moon, and her "thirty pieces of silver" are thirty nights of lunar light, of tropical brilliance. *Io-dasa* is thus the Thirteenth Lunar month, which does not equally fit the twelve-month Solar Year; and has to be "cast out" or not reckoned, as a named month. The emphasis on the date for Easter reveals the still powerful influence of Moon worship, in current ceremonial. There may be an Iberian connection of *Io-dasa* with *Iota*, as a funeral dance: for "one who had now gone forth". In the Greek · system, *iota* is the smallest letter, while in Hebrew it is important, as *Yod*.

JUGGLERS (English term); JONGLEURS (French version)
From *Joculatores*, Latin; signifying originally the all-round entertainer who could dance and sing, mime and fight in rhythmic combat. The jugglers (notes Strutt) were sometimes called gladiators by the early historians, as: "*Mimi, salii; balatrones; emiliani; gladiatores; palestritae — et tota joculatorum copia . . .*"

JULSDANS (Sweden)
General term for Winter dances, now semi-ritual in mode, known in about twelve main patterns. They were performed during the New Year Feast celebrations. The term is connected with Yule, for December - January; but has another reference to Midsummer or July. These dances were almost all round in form, as singing dances, with a fire in the centre.

JUMPING SAINTS (Luxemburg)
Traditional ceremonial "dance to church" known humorously as *Die Springende Heiligen*, celebrated on Whitsun Tuesday at Echternach in Luxemburg. The lower orders of clergy hustle crowds of people into some sort of line of march, near the River Sure Bridge; whence they proceed dancing with simple, but noisy, musical strains, to the church, up to the altar (and formerly round it three times), and thence out again to the cemetery cross, to the supposed grave of the mythical saint Willibrordus. As many as 10,000 persons, mostly from the surrounding country, may participate in this traditional Benedictine mirth-making.   [See *Church Dances*]

JURUPARI (Amazon District, Brazil, S. America)
Annual fertility festival performed by the Uape people (on the Uape River, tributary of the Amazon River), which is a tribal dance of all adults. They hold a feast for Jurupari, chief member of their Trinity, when the young men go through initiatory rites. The women are then invited to a "great sacrifice" like the Hebrew *Hag*.

K

KABIRI (Crete)
The "Dancing gods of Crete", brought by Phoenicians from Egypt (Memphis Temple) into Crete and Thrace. There are said to have been originally three males, then three females were recognised; then a seventh. Names given for them are: Axierus; Axiekersus; and Axiokersa. These approximate (functionally) to the Three Fates (Clotho, Lachesis and Atropos), especially if we read Axio-Eros,

Axie-Cursus, and Axio-Cussate—The Binder, The Marker, and The Divider. The Flamens of Roma celebrated them in their songs Axio-menta; especially Axio-kersa. The fourth (or seventh) was Kada-Milus, the uniting principle or Dancer. *Kibbirim* (as a Hebrew term) was translated by Gesenius as "The Mighty", while Fürst says that the *Kabbirim* were the "Seven Sons of Tzadik", in the Phoenician system. If then Tzala was the partner of Tzadik (as Mother of the *Kabbirim*), we have the origin of the *Sala* from *Tzalaiim* (and *Salomai?*). Finally, the *Kabbirim* became twelve (like the *Korybantes,* *Curetes** and *Flamens**). The original three were said to be sons (grandsons?) of Phthas (Pthah?). He was Ha-phaestus, Ruler of Fire and Light, whence spring the long tradition of the *Faustus* legend.   [See *Walpurgis Night; Homonculus*]

KACHINAS (N. America)
Ancestral spirits of Pueblo* Indians (especially Hopi* and Zuni*), thought to dwell in the "good" or western direction, and to visit the earth for six months of the year, when they are impersonated by male masked dancers. Primarily concerned with bringing rain and increasing crops they are beneficent spirits, anxious for the well-being of man. Different varieties of Kachinas include *Long Horn Kachinas; Manas,* or *Maiden Kachinas; Shalako** etc., and in some pueblos they are divided into summer and winter groups. All men and boys belong to Kachina Societies, the initiated, *si'cti,* being "those who know" that the Kachinas are men disguised. Even so, dancers as well as spectators believe in the identification of the ancestral spirit with the mask while it is worn, although dancers do not go into trance. For four preliminary days initiates are secretly prepared, masks painted and dances practised. On the fifth day the medicine man leads them into the plaza. They divide into two groups—dancers in line behind each other, all wearing identical masks; and attendant dancers at the sides in varied masks. *Maiden Kachinas* take their places behind the men. Following the movements of their leader, the Kachinas shake their rattles and dance in a sunwise circuit of the plaza, facing in turn each direction. Singing as they dance, they monotonously repeat the basic steps of stamp and raised knee. At a signal from the leader they turn and dance towards the next wall of the Square, for the dance must be repeated towards all four directions. This fourfold dance ritual is performed four times in the morning and four times in the afternoon. Accompanying the Kachinas are dancing clowns, *Koshare,** *Kurena,* and *Koyemshi,** who provide burlesque interludes in the otherwise serious ceremonies. Kachina masks are carefully stored away between rituals, and

consecrated before use. Elaborate ceremonies mark the arrival and departure of the Kachinas at Winter and Summer solstices. Small dolls, also called Kachinas, are made in their likeness, and given to children. Visitors are not permitted to see the masked dances, but unmasked dances having the same form may be witnessed at various times of the year.
[Cp. ceremonial masks in the *Hevehe** cycle (Papua)]

KADESH, KADDISCH (Hebrew)
Term relative to ancient ritual dance; has now a general meaning of "holy" yet from it derives the slang term (in Oxford dialect) "You cad!" among schoolboys; as well as the Scoto-Gaelic term "caddie", or "attendant on course". The original term is Babylonian; an honorific title of kings; as in Nabo*chadrezzar*—or *Nebo* (father, prophet), *Chad*, ritual leader of *Raz* (or circle), and *tsar* or *zar* (ruler of circle). These symbolic names may spell, reversed, as in dance, both back and forth—*Chad* is also *Dach* (as in *Miro-Dach*, again "Ritual-Leader"). Later there was in Syria a high goddess named as Kadesh, of whom some statues have been found in Egypt, probably taken by Assyrian invaders. From these sources, the Hebrews inherited many of their great rituals and their dances (see *M'gilloth,** Hebrew Dance, etc.), including the mystical *Urim-Thummim,** or *Mimuth-Miro*, the Play of Mythos, the diagram of which ritual was preserved in the breast-plate design, with twelve gems. The basis is a circle-plus-square—a centre with twelve lights on the *rim* or circumference; these indicated twelve Patriach or twelve prophets etc.; later as twelve Apostles in the *Dance of Jesus.** The term relates also to *Katha* and *Kathak;* masters of religion interchanged many of their symbols, for their basic facts were identical.

KEDUSHA
Hallowing or sanctification; *Kaddish*, Assyrian, Holy; *Kuddsha*, Assyrian, hallowing. Group of closely associated Assyrio - Hebrew rituals in which dance movement belongs to "messengers" (who come and go). Two loaves are "blessed" with wine. The goddess Kadesch (Crete) had her ritual and dance forms like those of Aphrodite.

KADRILJ (Sweden)
Includes the national and local forms of dance summarised as *Quadrille.** There is a dignified form, followed at Ovraby (in Halland Province), danced usually by eight couples. In the Ovraby *Kadrilj*, the dance begins with a Big Ring, when all turn out, women inside and the men outside, pulling outwards. In this, the movement goes at

walking pace. Next follows Chorus, in which formal bows or curtseys (compliments) are exchanged. Six figured steps ensue, couples separated, with men's arm folded; and the girls holding skirts. The Ladies' Chain requires the girls to cross, clapping hands with their men as they pass. Then the men swing the girls by the waist as they meet; repeat and return; and swing their own partners. In some *kadriljes*, the Arches movement (*bägdans*) follows at a walking pace; and then comes the Women's ring; a repeat of the first chorus; and finally the *kadrilj* turns into a gay galop, including circle and cross-circle movement.

KAGURA (Japan)

Sacred dance of the Shinto ritual; the legend tells that Ama-Terasu (Light of Heaven), evading her brother (The Impetuous One, Susa-no-no) retired to a cave, leaving the world in darkness. The concert of high gods assembled before the cave mouth, dancing and playing instruments. At length, slowly emerging, she saw her image as in a mirror; and the *Kagura* dance is attributed to the rejoicing that followed. This appears to be a celebration of the Winter Solstice, as in Europe. Groups of girls, trained for the purpose, are retained at certain principal temples to perform the *kagura* at intervals through the year. A permanent dancing stage is part of most Shinto Temples; it is the *kagura-do*, or sometimes *bugaku-dai* (for *bagaku* dance). There is a usual programme of five sequential *Noh* plays, of which the old *Kagura* was formerly first. Modernist forms are influenced by Buddhist tenets; while they have been heavily biassed for imperialist propaganda on behalf of the ruling house. As a pilgrimage display, the *Kagura* has great attraction and succeeds in extracting numerous "offerings". It is performed on festival dates at Yamada (near the Temple of Ise) for payment, by groups of girls. There are three grades (of completeness and company) known as *Sho Kagura* (the simplest form); *Dai Kagura* (medium form); and *Dai-Dai Kagura* (most complete possible). Formerly prices were five yen, ten yen, and twenty yen. Post-war prices have risen accordingly. At this pilgrim centre, there is literally "all the fun of the fair", calculated to part visitors from their money. Another popular dance in Tea Houses, called *Ise Ondo*, antique in tradition, is graceful in form, dubious in character. In some dance booths (fair-ground style) is performed *O Sugi O Tama*, in which it is the custom to donate money to the orchestra by throwing it.

KALACHAKRA (Sanskrit)

Broadly the "Wheel of Time", but includes also notions of time-rhythms, made manifest in ritual mode by construction of the *Mandala*—either painted as a *thang-ka* (or *tang-kar*), or constructed in temporary modelled form as a sculpture in cold butter or an arrangement in coloured sand (in Tibet). Controlled by the *sadhana mantrams* (*shastras* or verses of discipline, stating the typal designs) these *mandala* forms of *Kalachakram* set forth in visual mode the symbolical order and relations of the intercalated modes of time, which the human consciousness has to study and master. Hence ritual dances are controlled by the same disciplinary modes; both music and dance movement must conform to each successive phase of sacred expression. The system is related to the Chinese sixty-four *trigrams*. The *Sidhe khorlo*, "Wheel of Transformation", is related closely to the "Wheel of Time"; and both to the popular Buddhist symbol of the "Wheel of Law"; as three aspects of one unity of form and motion. Other religions use similar symbolism as the Zodiac or the Wheel of Fortuna etc.; and in mythic presentation, they invariably take the form of rhythmic dance with music or chant.   [See *Tangov*]

KALAMAJKA (Czechoslovakia)

A pair dance in 2/4 time with the same tempo throughout. Couples face each other, with hands on hips (not touching), but the form of the dance varies in the West (Bohemia and West Moravia), and in the East (East Moravia and Slovakia). The western *Kalamajka* is in two parts, the first using a stamped polka step, and the second the *holubicka* step ("the dove"), in which partners, facing each other, link arms and revolve with a running step clockwise, then counter-clockwise. In the eastern version which is quick and vigorous, polka steps are followed by the *pritukávany* step in which hops are combined with the clicking together of heels. The couple then circles the room clockwise, inside hands joined, with stamping steps. Elaborate costumes are worn in both East and West, the men with embroidered breeches and and waistcoats; the girls with pleated skirt, white blouse with large puffed sleeves, lace apron and embroidered headscarf (in the West); or (in the East) full skirts, embroidered sash, top boots, and white blouse with sleeves pleated like a Chinese lantern. Large red tassels adorn the bodice, and the man's waistcoat. On the other side of the Carpathians, in Poland, a similarly named dance is found—the *Kolomejka*,* which is a coquettish courting dance; while in the Ukraine is the *Kolomaika*, a pair dance in circular formation.

KALAMATIANOS (Greece)

National dance of modern Greece, popular with the Evzones (the famous Greek regiment with the kilted uniform) in their leisure moments. A vari-

ation of the ancient *Syrtos*,* it is performed in a circle, the leader singing and flourishing a kerchief; the girls following, holding hands. To music in 7/8 time, the chain moves slowly round, the men elaborating on the basic step. From time to time the leader moves into the centre of the circle, to perform complicated steps and movements called *scherza*, passing the kerchief to another man when he grows tired. The new leader then performs the *scherza* in his turn, making leaps and turns, and lunging as if holding a sword. The change of leadership in chain dances, and the purpose of the spectacular steps, may be an attempt to ensure that the life-force at the starting-point, passes from one man to another. Such dances derive from the ancient magic-circle dance. When performed in cafés the *Kalamatianos* is accompanied by fiddle, mandoline and zither.
[See *Mana*]

KALELA (African; Rhodesia)
A native dance done in the "Copper-belt"—a tribal form but re-organised to satirise or comment on Europeans. In the *Kalela* European clothes are worn; European roles are the King, the Doctor, the Sister. Rhythmic form is given, sometimes by xylophone but recently by European instruments— saxophone and drum being prominent in the larger gatherings, as in Lusaka.

KALI-KANZAROI (Greece)
Greek - Turkish term for dancers or "sprites", who appear at the great Kalikanzaros, or Great Feast of All Saints (Ancestors). A double ring was used in traversing the dual path (this world-next-world idea). Thus the "figure-of-eight" was traced; shouts of "Hai" or "Hui" accompany the processional (Alay) to and from the selected place.

KALLAI KETTOS (Hungary)
A couple dance (*kettos* = "double") performed today at Nagy-Kálló in the Szabolcs country. Formerly a vigorous, acrobatic dance (a poem in 1790 compares it to the Slovak "squatting dance"), its chief characteristics now are lightness, suppleness, and dignity of bearing. Requiring great skill, only specially chosen young men of sufficient ability may dance the *Kállai Kettös; also the Borica.* The clicking of their spurs forms part of the rhythmical accompaniment—(among musical instruments used for Hungarian dances, spurs are included). Like most Hungarian dances, it is in two parts; slow, and quick. The music begins slowly, while the couple stand facing, swaying rhythmically for the first line of the song. As the song belonging to this dance is sung by the dancers themselves, the tempo is less wild than in some dances. The words are generally about the fickleness of women. After the

first line, the dancers move apart, then come together, embrace and whirl round. There is little difference in the dance form of the quick part, except that it is more gay, the tempo faster, and the accompanying words more pointed, but the essential dignity of this dance is maintained.

KALU ISHTARA (Babylon : Sumeria—*Circa.* 2500 BC)
"Priest of the Call" or the leading priest in the ceremonial chanting and movement. He was specifically the "First worshipper" of Ishtara as Mother Goddess, protector of the people; so that his recurrent duty was "to call". This rite seems to be the origin of the term, as it changed into Kalliope, who was the recorder or caller among the much later Grecian Muses; and then the same functional term continues into Etruria, as the "*istrionoi*", the actors of the sacred mythic drama; and in Greece, later still, as the itinerant monks, the *kaloyers* (who became *klephta* or wanderers); and who in Europe originated the monastery play-house, the *cloister* or *kloster*. In Assyria were several ritual duties: that of the drummer (an important official), the flautist, and the dancers. Having "praised Ishtar Goddess of Stars", the *Kalu* then cast the lots, or indicated the "fortune" of the claimants. Possibly, this function was carried out in the great public forecourt, where stood the Great Drum (six feet wide), with its bull-hide surface painted with the twelve figures of the Zodiac (which was devised in Babylonia). The "Priest of the Call" appears frequently mentioned in the Hindu *Songs of Gritsamada*; song of *Bharadwaja*, as ancient poems of *Rik Veda*.
[See *Hymns of the Mystic Fire. Rik Veda.* (Trans. from Sanskrit by Shri Aurobindo. Pondicherry, India, 1947)]

KAMA KALA (Hindu) (Book of Love)
"Love Times". Includes the four subtle relations of the art of dance to the arts of love. *Kama* means, among other things, the Hindu God of Love; thus it indicates "desire". The four great ideals of Hindu life are *Dharma* (religion and morality); *Artha* (wealth and prosperity); *Kama* (desire of increase); and *Moksha* (manifestation of full power, ending in release). Thus four different phases of desire appear in varying proportion in all modes, in all directions of mental attention. The books called *Kama-shastras* are verses describing aims, means and methods of gaining success in love. Among them are the *Kama-kala*—the sixty-four arts of personal and social life. They begin with *Gitam* (singing), *Vadyam* (playing instruments), and *Nrityam* (Dancing), and continue with *Chitra-kala* (Painting); going on to the inlay or design of wall

and floor patterns; perfume-making; puppets; recitation of verse; and other minor arts and crafts, to the total of sixty-four. Hindu dance, most especially any performance of ritual and religious dance, cannot properly be presented unless the *sutradhara* (manager) has full knowledge of the *Kama-kala shastras*. The art of dance is then used (a) for religion, in symbolism; (b) for feasting and social entertainment; (c) for aspects of love-making; and (d) for a subtler mode in gaining release from worldly affairs, that attainment of "happiness in bliss", which is called *Moksha* or is known as *Nirvana*, where the human "Dance of Mind" is brought to the subtle mode of *Kaivalya*; or broadly "equal values", or balance, or equilibrium and peace.   [See *Karmakala*. D. Thomas]

KAMLANIE (Siberia)
Includes invocation of "Spirits" and then prophesy-ing by the *shaman*. Drum or tambour is "tuned up" by warming before a fire; hand or stick is used for beating. The Chuckhi shaman uses a slip of whale-bone. The *kam* uses the tambour in several ways; an extraordinary range of sounds can be produced; in it he collects power; it becomes heavy. He dances for part of the ceremony. The tambour could be found in a belt around the northern world—from Siberia through Asiatic Russia, Finn-land (Suomi), Lappland, among Mongols and Tartars; each place having its traditional tunes varied by the individual expert. The Yakut may have small vibrating stones; the Lapp shaman's drum has brass rings loosely attached to the head of the drum. Many drums bear pictures or occult diagrams (Red Indian, Tartar and Mongolian pat-terns) while some have facial masks of the local gods. The term *shaman* is indifferently (and wrongly) used. The Haida (Indians of U.S.A.) call him *ska-ga*.   [See *Lapp Drum; Shaman*]

KANANA (New Guinea)
In the Wahgi Valley, 5,000 feet up in the Kubor Mountains, villagers hold a weekly social gather-ing in the firelit, thatched dancing-hut. A sitting dance—the *Kanana*—performed by young men and girls, is the chief event. Accompanied by drum rhythms and chanting, it takes place on a low, horse-shoe shaped platform in the centre of the hut. Older people sit round the sides, laughing and chatting, while children run about. Girls, aged from 13 to 17, take their places about eight o'clock, wearing skirts of casuarina fibre, bracelets and arm-bands, and collars of pearl-shell. In flat discs, one over the other, the amount of shell worn by a girl indicates her father's wealth and her own marriage price. On the head is a cap of cowrie or tambu shell, sometimes decorated with golden mapul fur. Faces are elaborately "made-up" with pig-grease

and ochre cosmetics. When the men enter, orna-mented with Bird of Paradise plumes, they circle the U-shaped platform until each stands behind his partner, according to precedence. At a signal, the men sit between the girls, so that men and girls alternate, but facing in opposite directions. As the chanting begins (by men, women remaining silent), all begin to sway. Moving in rhythm, each girl turns her head and lightly rubs noses with the man on one side of her, then on the other. At the begin-ning there is only momentary contact. Then the girl, with eyes closed, sways ever more rapidly from the man on her left to the one on her right, although noses touch for longer periods, ultimately for as long as five minutes. But the dance retains an informal and pleasant character. When each session ends, girls break into peals of laughter. Only noses and faces may touch. Any other contact is taboo, except that the girl may grasp the man's shoulder with one hand. The *Kanana* continues for several hours, a matron "Mistress of Ceremonies" seeing that partners are frequently changed. The dance serves as a kind of marriage-market.
[See *New Guinea, Dancing in; Paradise Birds*; Sitting Dances : *Kebyar* (Bali); *Otuhaka* (Tonga); *Puili; Uli-Uli-Noho* (Hawaii)]

KANTEL (German)
Four dancers in a waltz form, dancing in a line; thus a "small dance" in relation to the usual larger company which dances in a waltz. *Kantel* (or *Candel*) *Messe*—"Little Feast" is held February 14.

KARAGIOZ (Turkey)
Puppet Play, Mime and Dance, known as *Khayyal-el-zill* (Arabic title), or "Shadow Play", as men-tioned by Umar-el-Khayyam, the poet of Naishapur. Puppets are played through the year, but especially at Ramazan (the month of the fasting ritual). The puppets are played before a white linen or cotton screen, lighted from behind to show the figures. Similar forms exist in Java, taken there by Hindu and Moslem experts. The figures are usually flat, cut from stained camel-hide leather, played at the ends of strings by a ventriloquist, who recites all the parts. Traditional plays exist (as those by Hasen-zade), for example, *The Beautiful Ass; The Dumb Man; The Negro; The Arnaut* (Albanian); *The Prodigal Son*, etc. These all have one principal character with a half-dozen supporters; his adven-tures are recited. There is a permanent comedian : Karagioz himself, and Hajji-Aivat, the wisecrack man. They correspond to Arlecchino and Panta-leone in Italian Commedia. The original Karagioz is said to have been a Gypsy (or Greek), Sofioglu Karagos Bali Chelebi (of Thrace), who met at Konia the Sultan's courier, the Hajji-Aivat, with

whom he exchanged jokes. Stories without mime are told by *meddahs*.

KÂROK (Amerindian)

Annual Ceremony of the Yuma tribes of California. Each year a solemn feast follows the cremations of the preceding twelve months. All families go into mourning, until the *Károk*. Images are contrived to resemble the dead persons. Then a series of formal dances of praise and prayer are performed, ended by a sacrificial fire in which the images finally are burned. This act ends the period of mourning, after which the names of the dead are never again spoken publicly in the tribe. Among the dancers, four carry bows, shooting at a "life symbol", followed by a dozen men who carry the costumed images. They pack closely together, dancing with a restricted step and holding the images upright above their heads.

KAROLE (Western Europe)

Romance term for the ceremonial "song of praise" formally adopted at the Frankish court of Charlemagne (*Karolus Magnus*, the "Great Singer") founded on much earlier systems, from *Ka-Ruelle* or *Khor-Ruelle*—the chorus of the "kingly circle". The *karole* was essentially a solemn ritual dance that followed the unanimous election of a new king; but as this election was then avoided, the ceremony took on the form of acclamation and praise without the reality that should have preceded it: the selection and voting. The "king's song" was, in earlier periods, an important feature of the "King of the Year", who was elected at each New Year Festival. This ancient tradition was skilfully merged with the clerical scheme in which Charlemagne went to Rome for a coronation; and since that date (AD 800) the traditions have remained confused. Later the *karole* was adopted in the system of Chevallerie, as a "knights song of praise", and it is chiefly from this that more modern traditions arise, marking the basic ring dance form as a dance-song or praise. In the Balkans, the term as *Kralje* was given to the prince's eldest son; in the older ceremonial, he was the "Young King" who was popularly "elected" to follow his father, the "Old King". In Spain the term drifted to the enclosure, which was called *korrale*, corral.

KARPAIA (Ancient Greece)

A mimetic dance which belonged particularly to the Aenianians and Magnetes. Performed by two armed men, accompanied by a flute, it mimed a story of industry and brigandage. The first man, laying down his weapon, indicated the ploughing of his land with yoke of oxen, and the sowing. As he danced and mimed, he continually looked nervously around, as though afraid of attack. When the second man appeared, as a robber, the first man seized his weapon and fought the robber, who sought to take away his oxen. All these incidents were performed with rhythmical dancing movements, and the dance was frequently performed at banquets for the entertainment of guests. Sometimes the robber won, tying up his opponent and driving away the oxen; sometimes the farmer won.

KATE KENNEDY CELEBRATIONS (Scotland)

At St. Andrews, every April, are held the town proceedings summarised as the "Kate Kennedy". The basis, as half legend and half mediaeval history, is referred to one James Kennedy, then bishop and chancellor of the University, about 1450. He had a daughter named Katherine, "beloved (says tradition) by all the students". The ceremony dates, in its revised pattern, from 1926; blending town traditions with those of the University, laid over an ancient Gaelic Spring Festival and the "Initiation rites" associated with Catherine* and Nicolas.* Katherine, now becomes The Lady Katherine, goes in procession with her court, led by a figure of St. Andrew, followed by eminent townsmen and visitors, as well as the Bishop. The ceremony is organised by the Kate Kennedy Club. A young student (a Bejant) takes the part of Katherine, while her uncle Bishop Kennedy (here replacing Nicolas) is played by the President of the Club for the year. The earlier celebration, which became too wild after 1840, was banned in 1880. The revised form follows the general line of a Masque; the local Salvator rules, forbidding masks, being set aside. Critics assert that Lady Katherine never existed—which may be correct as history—but the figure of Katherine has moved alternately with Nicolas through many an ancient college ceremonial. "Kate Kennedy" apparently comes from Katha-cuno-Edda (play or drama from the *Cuno Edda* or saga). (The game of *gowf* or golf appears to be an extension, from the ancient Andrews game of Nine-Men-Morris—beginning with the square "Course of Nine Holes").

KATHA-KALAKSHEPAM (Malayalam-Tamil, S. India)

From Maharashtra district; and described as a kind of musical story telling. Some incident taken from sacred lore, is narrated by one musician accompanied by one or two others. The narration is prose, interspersed by music. The songs may be *kirtanams* composed by some famous person, or pieces made for the occasion. A large number of *shlokas* (vernacular verses) also are used. This "cantata" or "oratorio" style is thus parallel with the pantomime or miracle play form that centres upon dance, the *kathakali*.*

The Dance of Mohini. Kathakali style. The God Vishnu appears before Bhasmasura, the Demon King, in the form of Mohini, a temptress.

INDIA

KATHAKALI (Hindu)

Indian "Miracle Play", performed in Southern India. The term is said to mean merely "story play", but in Bengal the *kathak* is a poet-inter-preter of legend (*Purana*), often an accomplished scholar. In the very old religious system of Iran, the scheme of Zoroaster set its scriptures as *Gatha*; probably this ritual element continued. There is even a reflection in early English, in the term "Quotha!" meaning "he said", or "he spake", and we still use "quote". The word Kathakali may then mean the Ritual of Kali (the dark goddess, wife of Shiva). It is pronounced Kat-ha-ka-lee, not Katherkali. These plays are vigorous presentations of various Hindu myths in masterly dancing with immense emphasis on movement and gesture. They are essentially plays for the people; in this they contrast strongly with the solemn *Bharata Natyam** or symbolic temple dance.

KAWIKA (Hawaii)
One of the fastest *hulas,** with lively hip movements. Performed to instrumental music, with a tune of the same name, the dance describes the adventures of King David Kalakaua. (*Kawika* is Hawaiian for David). Vigorous dance-action symbolically portrays his mountain climbs; travels to various places; his favourite haunts; and visit to the volcano. A more subdued *hula* called *Kalakaua* is also connected with this king. With dignified movements the dancer describes his prowess and strength, and the magnificence of his feather cloak.

KAXARRANKA "Coffer Dance" (Basque)
A man's solo dance, performed annually at Lekeitio (Biscay) on the Feast of Peter (29th June). This festival is organised by the Brotherhood of Fishermen, when the new head of the community takes office. Said to have been performed yearly for five hundred years, the *Kaxarranka* requires excellent balance, as it is danced on the flat top of an oblong wooden coffer, borne on the shoulders of four or six sailors. Accompanied by the Txistu (a three-holed flute) and drum, the dance shows very neat and nimble footwork on the confined and unsteady dancing space.

KEBIYAR (Bali, Indonesia)
A modern dance, a solo performed sitting, by a boy or man, who demonstrates the character of the music, as interpretation of musical mood. These dances are individual rather than group productions; so that the *kebiyar* of one season is rarely repeated during the next year. It is a pastime or entertainment dance needing great facial mobility and general suppleness. The dancer may have the support of a full *Gamelan** orchestra. *Kebiyar* was evolved by the Balinese dancer, Mario, who combined the nobility of the *baris** with the delicacy of *legong** and was a most expressive exponent of the dance.

KEISEI (Japan) (Korea)
Girls who follow the profession of courtesan; hence the generic name of such parts, as played in Theatre. The *Keisei* have gilds; and formerly were given municipal trade union status and protection, living in a quarter denoted *yoshiwara*. They are not to be confused with the *maiko**, apprentice *geisha;* or with the *geisha** themselves. All of these categories include, if they can, some training in singing and dancing, to extend their professional equipment. The *Keisei* girls wear *Genroko* costume, highly ornate and magnificent, and so they appear in the Kabuki theatre. Many plays are written with a *Keisei* as the leading character. A typical convention in their dance is *obi-hiki*, the flirtatious unrolling of the long *obi* or sash, as a preliminary to a love-scene in a *Kabuki* dance-play.

KELPIE (Gaelic, Scots)
A fairy creature, a spirit of the waters, who appears as (a) pony, or (b) girl riding a pony; somewhat similar to the Irish *phooka*. Said to live in every lake or stream in lonely glens; on the kelpie-steed, the foreign fairies come riding to the meet for the nocturnal dance.

KEMP DANCES (Northern Ireland)
Down to the 18th century, there was a general custom for unmarried girls to gather at the largest house of the local farmers, to hold a "spinning meeting". This was called a Kemp or Kemb (probably from the place, a Coombe or shelter; or from the combing of wool and flax). The saying went, "Every kemp must end with a dance", though we are not told if the girls danced alone, or if their farmer boy friends came to collect and take them home at dusk. Among dances mentioned was always a *Jig,** such as *Jig Polthogue;* or perhap₋ the *Saltehorum Jig*, proverbially "danced on the bottom of a barrel, so neat were the moving feet of the dancer, so little space did he need".[1] There might be the *Cannie Soogah* or the *Screw-Pin-Dance;* and possibly *Shaun Gow's Hornpipe*, or *Pease upon a Trencher*.
[1] *Irish Peasantry; Traditions and Character* by William Carleton (Dublin 1854).

KEMP'S DANCE or KEMP'S JIGGE (England)
Refers to the "long-distance dance" performed by actor William Kemp in 1599. Accompanied by a piper (tabor with pipe was usual), he danced from London to Norwich; afterwards publishing details of his adventure (complete with woodcut picture) "to refute the lying ballads put forth concerning this exploit", and to mark (by sending copies of his pamphlet) his gratitude for all favors received on the way. This same actor gained renown by dancing with his "Men of Gotham" in the popular Morris, when his "newe jigge" rivalled the fame of his earlier performance as the dancing Peter in *Romeo and Juliet*.

KENGEKI (Japan)
The "Sword Theatre", equivalent (by sword-play) to the USA "Western" films as "shooting wars" in Wild West camps; similar in theme to the recurrent combat theme in European theatre; as exemplified in *Hamlet* or *Romeo and Juliet*; in Henry Irving's play *The Corsican Brothers*; Dumas' theme of *The Three Musketeers*, but more especially the Robin Hood *gestes* of mediaeval England. These plays were not stylised into dance; but the *kengeki* is made rhythmic by music and dance form, though they centre on gang leaders and touch on a distant symbolism only with "The 49 Ronins", The Japanese gang boss (*Oyabun*), in these *kengeki* plays follows a theme "out of this world", and this is the quality of the sword dance, which is not precisely *chambara* (realistic sword battle). The weapon has had much influence on subsequent dance-drama, much as the rapier fights of Italian communes had standard training poses (now bereft of meaning), which came into the classical ballet basis.

KERALA, Dances of (South India)
Include Kathakali, the mythic drama-dance or Miracle-play form, one of many varieties formerly practised through India. In Kerala, control is vested in (a) the Nayar aristocracy, in the politico-economic rule, through administration; and (b) the Nambudiri Brahmins, who control the Maths (Temples) and the religious system generally. Thus the Nayars pay (or transmit revenues) while the Nambudiris arrange rituals and festivals, including forms of dance, in private ceremonial or in public display. Certain village celebrations escape their immediate domination, such as the seance-dances (spiritualism) and others included under the term folk-dance. The religious balance is sustained as between Shaiva and Vaishnava (the latter with *Krishnattam*) and the *Bhagavatis* rituals; as well as the older veneration of the Great Mother, now presented as *Mohini-attam*. There are also ritual dances known as *Pattu* and *Pana*; *Kaniyar Kali* and *Tiapy-yattu*; *Patha-kama* and *Eta-mutti-pura-patti* or *Muti-yetti*; with the popular *Tullal Koratti-attam* as quasi-religious forms of celebration. These are based on themes drawn from the *Puranas*, the ancient religious legends of the Brahmin code, a mythic form of literature devised for mass acceptance. Commensurate forms exist in Ceylon, Burma, and especially Indonesia.

KERDAUER, KERDORYON (Wales)
Minstrel; minstrels; in ancient and mediaeval Wales; players and singers, accompanying the dances, particularly at the Festivals, such as *Diw Calan Ionawr* (New Year's Day). The minstrels were mainly secular, as compared with the bards, who were religious teachers and singers.

KERMESSE, KIRMESSE, KIRMES (German, Netherlands etc.)
A Mediaeval term meaning an annual Feast or Fair (French *Foire*, German *Messe*), as a Trade Fair (*Die Leipsiger Messe*). Possibly this ancient city-name (1200 AD or so) was derived from "Leaping Feast", but the ancient term *Messe* was encroached upon by persistent clerics, who tied the Winter Messe, or X-Messe (The Feast of Solar Crossing, rightly named X), to their much later-devised celebrations. Hence the Greek title *circe* or *kirke* has been linked with the *Messe*, and produced as *Kirkmess*. This was essentially a traders festival; of buying and selling, accompanied always by singing, feasting and dancing. There were four *Grosse Messe* in each year in Teutonic lands; the two solstices (Iolo and Iohannus, winter and summer) and the two equinoxes, Pascha-Messe and the Michel (Goose) Messe. The dances are but slightly named as associated with *Kermesse*; they retain mainly their own names.   [See *Walpurgis; Reigen*]

KEY NAMES IN DANCE
If followed carefully through their change and development, will reveal many of the fundamental realities of the art and science of dance. A few of these words are : —

Ba'Al: Ball:	Babylonian-Assyrian-Jewish
Boulé: Ballet:	Greece to Italy
Tanz/Dance	German-English
Meskhen to Mask :	Egypt to Britain
Natyam/Nautch :	India
Gig/Jig :	Assyria/India/Ireland
Xoros/Chorus :	Greece
Mimos/Mime :	Greece/Rome
Allemandus :	Europe
Ruad/Ruelle :	Europe
Tangov: Tungku	Polynesia-Malaya

KHADDI (Bengal)
Annual festival of the Oraon Hill tribes in Bengal, which celebrates the sacred marriage of Sun and Earth (*Bhagwan* and *Dharti-Mai*). This ritual occurs in the month of May. when the *sal* tree is covered with its *khaddi*-bloom. Chief priest and priestesses impersonate the sacred characters. Drum beating announces gathering of sacrifices from the village during the morning. In the afternoon, a white cock and a black hen are sacrificed in a symbolic marriage-and-death. *Khaddi* flowers surround the ritual. Then priest and priestess perform a ritual marriage (as deputies). Women of the village carry winnowing fans; one for holy water, one for rice beer. The marriage dances follow. Missionary

descriptions of these rituals are rarely reliable; in general they are similar to an English Bank holiday, with some local variations according to the current factor of prosperity or famine.

KHA-RI-MA-TI (Assyria)

Ritual dancer of Ishtara in Babylon. She appears as mythic goddess; and as "servitor or devotee" in the Temple. Samkhat and Karimat are handmaids of Ishtar, goddess of Erech; who, as the "Heavenly Twins" attempt to lure the solar hero Gizdhubar and to entice Hea-Bani (his "Moon-maid" companion) into Erech. These twins in turn had maidens: these appear as temple dancers in the mythic drama. The chief event is the contest (*Lakham*) or fight or contention, of Gizdhubar (Master of Fire), against Khumbaba (Lord of Darkness), in the world *labyrinthos*. He is mythic equivalent to the Greek Herakles or the Hebrew Samson (or Sol-om-on) in his path round the Sun, which is his symbol. The turning points are Ni-Piru, the "four directions" on the road, *Khar-Ruan-Shamsi* (Car-Round (of) Sun). The *Khari-mata* bands—dancers and musicians—are women consecrated to the temple service; they aid to fight the *atal limnuti*—spirits of evil, in the *hekal* or *heykall* (temple palace). They are also called *Khadistuv* in some inscriptions.

KHATMEH (Arabic)

Another term for the ritual ecstatic dance, usually known as *Zikhr*.*   [See *Dervish Dance*]

KHAWAL (Muslim Egyptian)

Are Muslim young men, who entertain (as in Cairo) by singing and dancing. In England the same name became Cowell. They impersonate women dancers, accompanied by a reed pipe, perhaps a tambour, and brass castanets* (*sagat*). Lane[1] remarks that, in his day (c. 1830) the class was small and perhaps not increasing. Their dances are exactly the same as those of the *Ghawazee*,* their dress is partly male, partly female; a tight vest, a girdle and a kind of petticoat. They suffer their hair to grow long and braid it. The hair on the face, when it begins to grow, they pluck out; and they imitate women by applying *köhl* and henna to eyes and hands. They even veil their faces. They are employed to dance before a house or in its court, on the occasion of a marriage fête or birth of a child; and frequently perform at public festivals. They dance in groups of three or four.
[See *Shleuh Boy Dances; Ghawazee*]
[1] *Modern Egyptians*. E. W. Lane. (First edition, 1836).

KHAYAL ED-DILL (Egypt, Cairo)

Is the local Arabic term for the imported puppet show, the Turkish *Kara Gyooz;* "who perform by mime and dance, with dialogue in *Turkish*". They were conducted in the style of the "Chinese shadows", and thus seen only at night. As the term *khayal* refers specifically to dance, the part of the name *ed-dill* is said by Lane[1] to be more correct, for puppets. Was this name given to a street in London, as *Pike-edh-dill*? The name for *lute* (*el-ood*, Arabic), endures as *liuto, luth, lute*.
[1] *Modern Egyptians*. E. W. Lane (First Edn. 1836).

KHIDR, EL (Muslim Egyptian)

El Khidr, the mysterious "Green Man" of Moslem tradition; who is seen at rare intervals, mostly about festivals. He is always attired in green; but reports make it uncertain if the green is textile, in the sacred colour of Islam; or green boughs, in the manner of popular folk traditions.

KHLYSTY (Khristy) (Russia)

Russian religious sect, who use sacred ritual dance within their own communities. Operating in secret worship, they gather in quiet houses, garbed in long white robes, beginning their meeting by chants sung with immense fervour. Presently they start up with a swift tripping song about the "little ships" that sail the world's oceans; then the rhythm moves some worshippers to dance, first one and then another, in a movement governed only by the rhythm. They dance in pairs, in groups, in rings; or all together "as a ship" in an oval form; or as two walls (contra-dance form) or again jumping up, in position. They claim that some men attain the spiritual standard of a Christ (this is, like Buddha, a title and not a personal name), and say the term *Khlysty* was a malicious police change of term from "Chrest". Shrewd women leaders gain the name of *Bogoroditsy* (madonna, or godmother). These dances follow their ritual mythos: as "Ship of Salvation" (used in Western Europe up to 10th century), or "The Garden"; and "The Vineyard". Thus the presiding elder becomes a Steersman; or a Gardener; or a Maker of Pure Wine. They sing of "apples (and butter) on a lordly dish", (whence *Maslanitsa*—Butter Week). Mime enters these dances; but many elements are real enough. Many adherents of this *Khristy* sect are intelligent people in prominent positions;[1] they are still active in Soviet Russia, and various sub-sects have developed.
[1] Nicolai Sergueéff, former *régisseur* of Maryinsky Theatre, told the present writer that he was a Johannite—a follower of the famous Father John of Kronstadt, renowned for his gifts of healing. Many mystics appeared among poets (Alexander

Blok, e.g.), and musicians (Scriabin) and others, who, according to Sergueéff, had contacts with the Khristy. Stanislavsky was himself a member of the *Raskolniki* (Old Believers) in Moscow; he studied Eastern Yoga.

KHUMBABA (Babylonian)

Ritual Dance of the "Demon" named Humbaba or Khumbaba, in the mythic contest of Gilgamish. This ritual is one of the "world-wandering" myths; consequently it takes on the characteristic form of interlacing or labyrinthine path. Some Babylonian artist-priest took the floor diagram and merged the pattern with a mask-head of the Demon. He worked with a thin line of clay, much as some ancient pots were built up without a wheel, and in this manner contrived a solid head. One in the British Museum (116624) is attributed to Abu Habbah, and thought to be Babylonian *circa* 700-500 BC. The linear character here allied to the solid, describes the face in terms of an endless path of macaronic quality. This clay head was probably used as a passport to enter the ritual — it is but three inches high, devised as a miniature half-mask. The blank eyes were probably painted with the rest of the form.

KIBBY DANCE (England)

Saxon period (10th century), is mentioned by Strutt[1] as a popular folk dance in villages. The chief step is similar to that of the *kobold* or "cobblers' dance". The name appears also as "kibbers" or "cobbers" (which name is known in Australia — from London, as "comrade"). Cecil Sharp records having seen the *Kibby Dance* in Somerset and Devon, where it was called *Monkey Dance*. English children have a skill game called "Bobbers and Kibs", with the use of "dancing stones" — also known as "Five Stones".

[1] *Sports and Pastimes of the English People*. J. Strutt (1801).

KIMFUDSE (Ecuador)

August annual festival of the "scarlet men" of the highlands of Ecuador, following the wet season. This fiesta is the celebration of "coming of age" and *kimfudse* is the "nose-puncturing" ceremony of the Colorados people, in this province of Esmeralda, about seventy miles from Quito. Men and women dance together (unusual in such rites) in a *cholo* (imitation fox-trot), while more attention is paid to drinking *nepe*. Music is obtained from two *marimbas* (instruments borrowed from the Negro), with drum and pipes; and chanting. The *puna* (witch-doctor) makes the puncture with a sharp black thorn. All men's bodies are dyed scarlet, and many carry intricate painted patterns.

KING GAME — 1 (England, Mediaeval)

A court game of dancing skill, resembling both chess and checkers; and played in a large hall. The floor was covered with a single painted or woven cloth, stretched tight, over which the thirty-two characters moved. This great area of sixty-four squares gave rise to a traditional pattern of stained cloth, the popular name of which continues in our stores' reference to *gingham* cotton, which is made always in contrasted squares. There were many games of movement during these centuries; some related to the tourney or tournament, and others distantly reflecting the oriental royal game of *Pachisi*.* In other aspects, the *King Game* had traditions that connected it with the *Troy Game*,* (the *Ludus Regis*) the *Arithmomatica;* and finally the arcane *Tarot*,* which became popularised as the *Todtentanz** as the "Peoples Game". Doctor Rabelais (1483 - 1553) has an excellent description of the *King Game*, in his collected works,[1] covering five pages; too long to reprint here. The jovial cleric begins :

"Now there was a Ball in the Manner of a Tournament, at which Queen Whims was present. After supper there was a ball in the form of a tilt or tournament, not only worth seeing but never to be forgotten. First, the floor of the hall was covered with a large piece of velveted white and yellow tapestry chequered, each chequer exactly square, and full three spans in breadth. Then thirty-two young persons came into the hall, sixteen of them arrayed in cloth of gold; and of these, eight were young nymphs, such as the ancients described as Diana's attendants; the other eight were a king, a queen, two wardens of the castle, two knights, and two archers. Those of the other band were clothed in cloth of silver".

The human "pieces" were not "played" by an outside character, as in *Pachisi*, but moved according to the music. At Marostica, Province of Vicenza, Italy, an annual commemoration is still held in the Castle Square, of a human chess-game played in the 15th century. Each move of the contestants is duplicated by human players on a chequered "board" covering most of the Square. The original game was played by the Counts Rinaldo d'Angarano and Vieri di Vallonara for the hand of the lady Lionora.

[1] *The Works of Doctor Rabelais*. Bibliophilist Society Edition (London, New York). Chapters XXIV/XXV — pages 588 - 593 inclusive.

KING GAME — 2 (Western Europe)

Has three scales of playing or dancing. The greatest scale is, or was, the open-air contrivance of tour-

ney or tournament, which existed in Western Europe; and may be compared with the large-scale open-air game in the Orient, called *pachisi*. The medium scale, is the form operated in a large hall, which is the style known in Mediaeval Europe chiefly as the "King Game". The *Troy Game** was related to the *King Game*; but had also a Maze or Labyrinth as part of the ritual equipment. In the *King Game*, the ritual semblance of this Labyrinth was produced by a code of stepping, or dancing, from square to square. This system had a close association with the sets of symbols we now call "Playing Cards". At one time, these cards were mentioned as "Books of the Four Kings", while Chess was referred to as "The Game of the Four Kings;" and the earlier cards (attributed to India) had been known as "The Four Rajahs". These cards indicate one of the smallest scales. The middle scale was *The King Game* itself. The unsettled point in all these names, is the fact that chess, checkers, and the usual *King Game*, were devised as the opposition of two parties (or kings), and not four, as exist in the traditional Pack of Cards. Brewer[1] says that the Indian pieces (Four Rajahs) were named as *fierche* (king or general) − vizier?; *phil* (knave, turned by the French, also, to *fol* or *fou*); and *ruch* (*rukh*), as rook, the camel or horsemen. The French turned *fierche* to *Vierge*; then to *Dame*. Wardrobe Rolls (*temp.* Edward 1, 1278) record that Walter Sturton was paid 8s. 5d. for *ad opus ad ludendum adquator reges*. This *ludendum* appears to refer to the King Game, not to chess; for *opus* would mean work on the floor, in this connection. We may discover connection between *verger* or *vergier*, and *Vierge*; as the rite was performed in the church nave. The third, or smallest "scale of play" is the use of small symbols − the cards, or chess pieces; or checkers, etc. Sets of cards were called "pairs".
[1] *Dictionary of Phrases.* Brewer.
Playing Cards. W. Gurney Benham (Ward Lock)

KING'S SON'S RITUAL DANCES (Europe)
Appear in almost every country, with the Son as the leading dancer under a great variety of names. Sometimes the name informs us about the dance; sometimes the dance name tells us of the relation of the Heir. The title we know best is Prince. In its French pronunciation it is Prance; and that is what he does. Spain had the Infante (and the *Meninas* of the court); France had the Dauphin and the Charol − belonging to the Carol. Hungary had the *Kralya* in common with Slavonic lands. Germany had Kron-Prinz and Greece has *Kuros* or *Kurios*. These are relatively secular terms, related to legal claims of rulership; but many such rituals had their religious aspect. In Egypt the Pha-Ra-Oh danced as "Light of the Oh" (Shen*). In Italy, Dux and Duce become Duke; or, older still Caesar and Kaiser (and in England villages, Guizar). Dux became the still familiar mode of Cockaigne, as "Ducks" while Gaelic *Coch* is Old Cock. Dance rituals appear in all these, usually circular.

KIP GAMP GOL (New Guinea)
"Dance of the Great Spirit". Performed by men during the Festival of *Gol Kerma*.* Months after the first ceremonies, *Kip Gamp Gol* is danced in honour of Geru, god of fertility and prosperity. Performed to drive away evil spirits from the newly-built Geru-house, and to ensure virility in the warriors, it is danced in splendid head-dresses of bird-of-paradise plumes. Into each head-dress is fixed a small decorated board called *gerua* (associated with Geru), worn as a fertility talisman. Painted with geometrical patterns, the pre-dominant shape is the diamond (or *tangov**), the female symbol. Immature girls wear the *gerua*, as well as all men. With an apron skirt in front and bunched leaves at the back, together with collars of pearl-shell, the men dance round the Geru-house, then rush to its entrance, where an arrow is shot in the "bad" direction, and a *bombo* bundle is thrown on to the roof. The *bombo*, a plant rolled into a large ball, is thought to absorb evil magic. *Kip Gamp Gol* is followed by the *Gol Gur Gur** dance, and next day *Bolim Bombo** is performed.
[See *New Guinea, Dance in; Gol Kerma; Bolim Bombo; Gol Gur Gur*]

KIPARA, "WILD TURKEY MAN" (Central Australia)
A story of the Pitjendadjara tribe, told out of doors with dance, mime and chanting. Divided into eight scenes, it tells how Kipara, of the Wild Turkey totem, stole fire from the only men to possess it. Meaning to extinguish it in the sea, he was foiled by two Hawk men, who snatched the fire-sticks from him. Each scene has its own chant which describes the action, the chants being sung by men sitting in a circle, and beating the ground with sticks to mark the rhythm. Not until the fourth scene does Kipara steal the fire-sticks. *Scene 1*: Describes how he tried to attract some women by his antics. He calls them, then hops towards the chanting men, hips held stiffly and feet close together, finally falling over backwards, feet in the air, copying the behaviour of the Wild Turkey when courting his mate. *Scene 2*: Watched by Kipara, a man representing a Blind Wood Pigeon, mimes his search for water, and his joy when his groping hands find a water-hole. *Scene 3*: Continuing his journey, Kipara releases two *kuran* (spirit doubles; *kuranita*="life essence") from his

body, but instead of hunting for him, they quarrel, when Kipara re-absorbs them. *Scene 4:* Having stolen the fire-sticks, Kipara becomes the essence of vigilant stealth, as he dances in perfect time with the chanted rhythm, on his way to the sea. *Scene 5:* Another wayside incident, in which a dancer skilfully mimes the cautious actions of Wara, a young wallaby, invited by Kipara to come down and dance with him. *Scene 6:* Hiding the fire-sticks in his hair, Kipara seeks food for his supper, but falls writhing to the ground as the wind fans the fire, which burns him. *Scene 7:* Several dancers, and his own *kuran*, try to persuade Kipara to return the fire-sticks, but he pushes them aside and rushes into the bush. *Scene 8:* Climax is reached as the Hawk men stealthily creep up on Kipara, rush in with yells, and tear the fire-sticks from the Turkey-Man's hair, whereupon he dies, and fire is restored to mankind.
[See *Corroboree; Tjitji Inma; Nakumpoit*]

KIRIBOTO (Nigeria)

A men's solo dance of the Egba tribe of Yoruba people. Mimetic and near-acrobatic in form, *Kiriboto*, needing great skill, is performed at the dictate of the "talking" drum. Three drums accompany the dance, the leader beating drum instructions to the dancer, who may imitate the movements of various animals, or spin on one foot for several minutes, then reverse the direction in order to "unwind". Singing also accompanies the dance, the Master of Ceremonies first singing a song to the spectators, who then join in. The dancer wears iron rings on both hands, and leather belts called "Ighadi", which carry charms. The excellence of a performance is best gauged by those spectators who know the drum language, and can thus appreciate how skilfully the dancer is interpreting the drummer's instructions.

KIRKE OR KIRK (Jewish/Greek/Saxon)

Saxon term (from older Sanskrit) meaning Circle (of stones) and later (especially in Scotland) the church. Hence the ritual circle form was more important than their Latin cross or Greek cross form; thus came the earliest church forms (especially in Northern Europe), which were built round, of timber. *Kirke* is also *Kirkle* and *Chircel* (an offshoot is *kirtle*, the round garment) and (German) *kirche*. Chaucer gives us *chirche*. The *kirke* affirms the ritual nature of innumerable round dance forms.

KIRN BABY DANCE (Scotland)

To 19th century, for end of Harvesting. The country ritual of "Crying the Kirn" celebrated conclusion of reaping. The last sheaf — as the "Corn Spirit" was shaped — in Galloway as the Hare, in three strands, tied in a knot. Sickels were thrown, to cut it below the knot. Round dancing was done on a nearby hill, in views of many farms, to the Lowland bagpipe. Three shouts began, with three tossings of sickles in the air; and three rounds at least were made, deosil. The Kirn Baby was the centre; she was the new born Maide; the *Cailleach** was the Maide grown. After Harvest Home — the Clyack, was Winter Supper — the Kirn Maid was planted above the kitchen door. Sometimes Home was preceded by a minor affair called Bere Barrel. The end was often the dance *Babbity Bowster.**

KISAN (Korea)

Dancer, equivalent to Japanese *geisha*. At the age of thirteen or fourteen years, girls began training in a special school. During a course lasting several years, they learned dancing, Korean music, and other *kisan* accomplishments, for their career of formal entertainment. In Korea, as in Japan, it was customary for a *kisan* entertainment of singing, music and dancing, to form part of any important men's dinner at a restaurant. Often the *kisan* were known by name to the guests; and, on being summoned to perform, would travel from school to restaurant in *rikshas*. Prices of entertainment varied, according to the size of town or village, averaging about 1s. od. to 2s. od. an hour. *Kisan* also took part in festivals, such as that held annually at Shariin, a village five hours train journey north-west of *Keijo* (Seoul), on August 30-31st. Festivities on the first day were held in the courtyard of the *kisan* training school, one of the dances consisting of four girls in wide white dresses, with hoods and very long sleeves in kimono fashion, moving in a gentle rhythm, to the accompaniment of two drums, three bamboo flutes and a fiddle, their long sleeves swinging. In another dance at this festival, twenty *kisan* performed in more elaborate costume. With a coloured tunic over their white dresses, they wore a wide sash tied high under the breasts, and on their heads flat hats adorned with peacock feathers, with strings of beads passing from side to side under the chin. Their feet were clad in Korean white cotton boots.

KISMET AL REML (Baghdad)

Also given as *Kismut el Reml* (Turkish) is the name of the process of sand divination; as related in the *Arabian Nights Entertainment*, in the lengthy story of "Aladdin or the Wonderful Lamp". The young brother (we are told) carried a geomantic square; he prepared the sand (by levelling it off, quite flat), cast the points, and drew the figures. Then he examined the planetary crystal. When the divination was done for great rulers, the magicians used a private room in the palace, having a floor already inscribed or inlaid, with elemental lines and circles. On this, the servants moved, holding fine threads of silk, as directed by the *Rammal.** The *Kismet* (or Fate) from the *Reml*, allows a middle sort of divination, in which a client can be consulted in his own home, needing but the usual sand *abacus** of Eastern countries. The third (and smallest) method for the *Rammal* is to draw his figures on paper.

Dancing Cherubs; Nymphenbad, Dresden (1930).

KISSING AND CUDDLING DANCES

Have appeared in various lands at various periods, usually charged with highly divergent views on social morality. England reveals a peculiar history in this phase of dance. Elizabethan England knew no *Cuddling Dances;* but the *Kissing Dance* was in high favour. Says one writer: "It were unmannerly, Kate, to take you out to dance and not to kiss you!" In *Joan Sanderson* (another name for the *Cushion Dance**), and numerous other English Country Dances, this public salute was considered a normal courtesy; and even at Court, the ceremonial of "kissing hands on appointment" is still a phrase familiar in our ears. In Europe, the ballerina is saluted with a kiss by admirers—on the hand; but rarely in England, while she resents any reality of kiss during performance: it disturbs make-up and interrupts rhythm. Yet when the English *Country Dance* was going out of fashion, around 1800, and the *Waltz* was "coming in", the embrace of the couple was denounced, as obviously immoral, even by such a spark as Lord Byron. Kissing was then abolished from the ballroom, as the Kiss of Peace had been abolished from church gatherings. Children still play at "Kiss in the Ring"; and (we are told) some staid and stodgy lecturers (on ballet) receive fervent kisses (as in Stuttgart), while the current practice is not to cuddle during the dance (especially in American dance halls), but to reserve kissing ("necking" it is inelegantly termed), for intervals of "sitting out". Oriental races rarely permit any contact in dance, even where male and female dance at the same time. Japanese people are horrified at "kissing" and all such scenes are cut from their films. There are British critics who would like to see "close-up" salutes omitted from all films and dances, in favour of more subtlety in treatment. In England, most kissing is reserved for the hypocritical affection of election candidates for voters; and the mistletoe of the Commercial Christmas season. Many Folk Dances throughout Europe contain a "chaste salute" either during the dance or at the end, such as *Le Ballet.**

KIT (English), POCHETTE (Fr.), TASCHENGEIGE (German)

Small violin, used by dancing teachers during private lessons. The kit gave the advantage of slight change of tempo or stress without waiting for a pianist to respond. Making no pretence to excellent tone, the instrument was about 15"-16" long— able, as the name indicates, to slip into the tail pocket.

KIVA (North America)

An underground ceremonial chamber of Pueblo* Indians, in which religious rituals are held. Entered by an opening in the roof, the *kiva* was originally circular but today is usually rectangular. The chamber symbolises the universe—the ceiling and walls are the heavens, the floor is the earth; while a hole in the centre of the floor represents the exit (*sipapu*) through which men first emerged from caves on to the earth, according to Pueblo Indian creation legends. Members of the society performing the rite sit on benches round the walls, while it is believed that the gods themselves honour the *kiva*, sitting on invisible benches called "cloud seats". Near the *sipapu*, a "sounding-board" on which the dancers stamp, consists of a larger hole covered with a plank. The resonant pounding of feet informs the spirits of the underworld that a ceremony is in progress. These ceremonies usually depict stories of the creation and migrations of the tribe. Often they last several days, sometimes ending with outdoor public performances, as in the *Hopi Snake Dance*,* performed to bring rain. In some pueblos, the *kiva* is also used as a men's social club, or as a place of retirement during ritual purification.

KLATSCHWALZER (Switzerland—Valais Canton)
A simple couple dance in 3/4 waltz time. Dancers proceed round the room, first with walking steps, punctuated with hand claps; then waltzing with the girl's hands on the man's shoulders, the man's hands on the girl's waist. The girls wear a striped apron over their dress, long-sleeved white blouse with kerchief crossed over bodice, the main feature of the costume being a wide black straw hat with ribbon bows.

KLONDIKE CAN-CAN (Canada)
In 1898, with the Gold Rush at its height, the boom town of Dawson City was flourishing. To the Nugget Dance Hall and the Floradora came prospectors who had "struck it rich", to drink champagne and to watch the nightly performance of the *Can-Can*,* by Klondike Katie and Diamond-tooth Gertie. Yukon counterparts of Parisian dancers such as La Gouloue. Population dwindled from 40,000 to about 500 but both dance-halls still existed in 1953, when the Floradora was sold by its original owner, a veteran of the Yukon trail.

"KNEES UP MOTHER BROWN!" (England)
Modern English folk-dance (originating probably in London) performed on occasions of national holiday or festival, by purveyors of whelks and other comestibles; especially in the broad Whitechapel Road in East London. There is a popular chant which carries the words; some versions (as with mediaeval dances) are rarely, if ever printed. The dance form generally consists of two long lines of dancers, hand in hand; who alternately advance and retire. The lines are usually male and female; maybe twelve or twenty couples. Music is provided by accordion. There is an older similar dance form, known as "Nuts in Maiye!" popular in the same quarters. Research students have not been able to discover who was the original "Mother Brown" though some say it is an endearing reference to Queen Victoria and her Scots servant John Brown

KOBEUA MASK DANCES (Brazil)
Performed in honour of the dead by Kobeua and Kaua Indians of north-west Brazil. Masks represent birds, animals and insects, with the spirits of which the wearer identifies himself, through the energy possessed by the mask. As in Australian *Corroborees*,* dancers imitate the actions and habits of forest creatures. Flight of the large, shimmering blue butterfly of Brazil is portrayed by two men; others, dancing side by side, imitate the darting of swallows; a group of dancers represent the swarming of sandflies in the air; and the static role of the sloth is played by a man hanging by a hooked stick from the cross-beam of a house. The owl, vulture, jaguar and other forest inhabitants are represented in rhythmic action. These Indians see themselves not as superior to, but as part of Nature. Their mask dances are performed to restore the rhythm or life-force (see *Mana**) lost by the death of one of them. When the dances are over, masks are burned and the spirits are thought to return to their own place, exactly as with the *kachina** spirits of North American *Pueblo** Indians.

KOHOMBA KAMKARIYA (Ceylon)
A dance-mime ceremonial, done to please the nature-deity known as *Yakka Kohomba* (or as *Kohomba Deviyo*). Here *Kohomba* signifies much the same as does Combe in Western England : it is a "pleasant place" for dwelling, essentially sheltered. The King of the Flower is invoked at the effective beginning of the rites, which continue for several days (like a Wake), and they contain a number of different episodes (see *Yakkama**). Twelve sylvan gods seem here to indicate the changing duties of the twelve months; and may be compared with the similar early Roman cycles of agricultural rites.

KOKOSHNIK (Russia)
National head-dress worn by Russian ladies to 1917, and often copied for Russian dances abroad. The *kokoshnik* signified "ladies of the household", as a kind of uniform tiara, except that it was usually fan-shaped, and stood up vertically. Jewels were stitched on to a solid background of cambric.

The *kokoshnik* was a ritual necessity for the Russian court dance, which varied between *polonaise** and *mazurka** in style, but was equivalent in purpose to the *pavane** in Western Europe, as a processional dance of display. The *kokoshnik* was, in effect, the court tiara. [See *Polonais*]

KOLAM (Ceylon)
Generic title for a whole series of (a) religious plays, and (b) derived folk-plays, that stem from ancient traditions. The Sinhalese term *kolam* means "acting" by means of an "appearance" or personation; a masquerade or masque (since *kolam* implies a group, *kolama* is the single character), which in its current form leans heavily to burlesque, and is offered chiefly as entertainment. We have arrived here at a level with Aristophanes : the deities and demons are now popular subjects for laughter. Despite this humorous aspect, there remains the serious side of exorcism; under this are pregnant mystical doctrines, with meanings hard to gather. They are in fact dependent on a keen grasp of the meaning of *mana** (to give the Polynesian term as one better known), for (to state the basis in one phrase), these ancient people contrived to do with "natural or plant electro-magnetism" more or less what we have contrived (in our industrial civilisation) with metallic-mineral electro-magnetism; and what we have only recently touched on with the polar oppositions of "Poison x Vitamin". The rites were devised to attract, induce and direct natural energies : an accomplishment possible only away from large cities and their accumulations of metal. Thus *kolam*, originally was to deal with "tone" or vital energy; we know this now only in spiritualist seance, the phenomena of hysteria or schizophrenia; or the pranks of *poltergeist* entities. The *kolam* characters, their meaning, their dances and their mime, all revolved on this foundation of "personified energy". Parallel are (a) the trance dances of Bali, *sanghyang* (see *Sanghyang dedari**); (b) the *shaman* healing of Siberian tribes; (c) the primitive christian rituals, as the *agape;* and (d) the later rites of Russian *khlysti sobors;* (e) the hysterical mediaeval "plague dances"; (f) the Jewish dances of the Polish synagogue (Cracow, etc.); (g) the induced murmuration of the sibyls of Delphi; (h) and even the less systematically controlled divagations of Lancashire spiritualist mediums in the cotton towns. All of these require the shifting of the energic focus; or the skilful usage of *mana.* [See *Nadagam*]

KOL ATTAM (Tamil Nad, India)
Several dances (traditional, ritual and folk dance) bear this name; latterly serving to indicate only "Stick Dance". The stick, or *kol,* was (in some places still is) a standard of length measurement, defined as a "rod of sacred bamboo", with a length of a span between every two joints; and having twenty-four thumb breadths in each span. This *kol* was used as a unit of length, by which the space required for a new theatre was laid out on the selected "suitable site" (there are standards also for this). After the theatre was arranged, the juniors entrusted with the "hold sticks", celebrated the fact by a simple dance in which they tapped the sticks. Thus it was a sort of ceremony parallel to the "laying of a foundation stone". The *Kol-attam* is a "circle dance" for sixteen (sometimes more, even numbers), done to *Adi-tal* (time-beat) danced by young girls who hold sticks in each hand, at festivals, local or national. They begin with a single circle, partners facing; there are five figures each of eight bars. Some of the popular titles include : *Subrah-manya; Lord Gurunatha; Koladittivaduvom* (Stick-Dance). *Kolattam* implies "Stick-Dance"; these pairs of sticks are eight or ten inches long; three-quarters inch thick; *Pinal-kolattam* is a circle dance with ribbons (like English Maypole circle dance). *Pinnal* equals "plait". This dance has two chant forms : one with *pallavi,* followed by *anu-pallavi* (like Greek *phon* and *antiphon,* or Latin *bass* and *contra-bass*) followed by a chorus or *charanam. Pallivi* and *anupallivi* are one verse line each; *charanam* is four times this length. The *Pinnal-kolattam* has two parts—the weaving and then the unwinding. Sometimes *pallivi* is the chorus.

KOLENDAS (Poland)
General term for carols; many are preserved in old Polish song books called *Kancyonaly;* they served for dance tunes. They are song-dances regulated by the calendar.

KOLO (Yugoslavia)
A national dance form, similar to the Rumanian *Hora** and Bulgarian *Horo.** *Kolos,* with many variations, are danced in all six Republics—Macedonia, Serbia, Croatia, Slovenia, Bosnia/Hertsegovina, and Montenegro. An open or closed linked chain, the *Kolo* has a leader, who directs movements and steps. The leader may begin the dance as a solo, others joining him until the chain or circle is complete. Dancers may leave or join the circle, which moves a few steps to the left, then to the right, forward or backward. Steps are generally simple, and the dance style forceful. Interest lies in rhythm, and co-ordination of the linked dancers, who move as one unit. This precision is emphasised in the *Kolos* of Montenegro and Bosnia, which are danced without musical accompaniment

other than singing. The thudding feet in absolute unison, keep perfect rhythm. (See *Silent Reel*.*) In the Slavonian part of Croatia, the *Kolo* is in two parts—first, slow movement accompanied by singing of humorous words; then at greatly quickened tempo, the dancers shouting mocking verses. Some *Kolos* move in spiral or "snail-trail" patterns. In some men and women stand alternately; in others women form half the circle, men the other half; or circles may be all men or all women. In one version of the *Zetsko Kolo* (Hertsegovina), two circles of men are formed, one standing on the shoulders of the other. Dancers in the lower circle cross hands behind the back, then grasp the hands of the men on each side; while those in the top circle place hands on the shoulders of the men on either side. The double circle slowly revolves, only the lower ring of men performing steps. Women's movements are always more restrained than the men's. In Serbia the leader is called *Kolovogya*, and during a quick *Kolo* the young men burst into *poskochitse* ("springing recitals"), being a few recited lines expressing high spirits. Formerly danced with no accompaniment other than singing, in Serbia musical instruments are now added. At weddings *Kolos* are danced at various stages of the proceedings, while ritual *Kolos* are performed at Whitsun, Easter and Midsummer.

KOLOMEJKA (Poland)

The "marriage-market" or courting dance of the village, (*Kolo-maika*), known on both sides of the Carpathian mountains. After bartering was ended, on the commercial side, men and girls (often as new acquaintances, though shepherded by fond parents), linked up. Partners did not hold hands or touch; they held a kerchief or a green branch; or a fair ribbon. The dance is silent except for one instrument (a simple drum rhythm) to begin. When the pipe enters, after the drum, girls let go and run off with graceful gestures. The boys follow, with entreaties to return (supposing they do want the girl). When the girls are finally persuaded, they dance slowly back, faces hidden in kerchief or apron. Partners again dance together, in ring and square. Finally ribbons and twigs are cast away, to the centre; girls and men come closer and the dance rhythm moves more and more speedily. Then they go for a drink. Latterly, this dance has seen changes, as the old marriage-market is modernised; and "patriotic motives" replace the courting mime; flags are waved instead of plain kerchieves; and songs that mark the middle of the dance break into nationalist refrains. In the Ukraine, the *Kolomaika* is a couple dance in circular formation with contrasting high leaps and crouching movements.   [See *Kalamajke*]

KONGO-PI (Brazil, Amazon River)

Is the chanted dance used by the Jivaro Head Shrinkers as they finish off a ritual trophy. The head of a witch-doctor is requisitioned (owing to his own misdeeds). When he has been induced to part with it, the process of reducing the head begins, with the idea of so diminishing his *tunchi* (*mana** power) that he will cause no further trouble. This process was watched in Huambiza Indian territory, near Rio Santiago, in the upper reaches of Rio Maranon (Amazon). They remove the skin and scalp; then thrust this into boiling "Water of the Boa" taken from the river. By reducing the size of the head—the seat of the spirit—by mummifying it, by sealing its lips, they can imprison its supernatural powers. Next the killers are "purified" by tobacco juice. Then follows painting of magical designs on their bodies, with a skeleton shape in black paint. The flayed scalp (with all bones removed) is then turned into a kind of bag or pocket; and filled with hot sand; driving off all fat, as it is held on a spearpoint. Massage follows, to restore original form; but two-thirds smaller, in two days work. The reduced head is called the *tsantsa*. On the evening of the third day, the head is hung on a new spear. Two warriors with the headman perform the *Kongo-pi*, chanting slowly "*Kongo-pi; Tawao—Tawao*!", being stylised imitations of forest animal cries, as an invocation to those who might have given refuge to the dead man's spirit, to give it up. *Kongo-pi* is danced again in the communal hut, the men donning red and black feather head-dresses, ear ornaments, and face paint. The headman with two warriors dance round the *tsantsa* on the end of an upright spear. Everyone joins in, tempo increases, and dancing lasts till middle of the night. After an interval for eating, there follows the *liste* dance—the "display dance" for the head. Women dancing hand in hand in a single line, rush from end to end of the hut shouting *liste! liste!*—"See! See!" Urged on, they continue for hours, the chorus shouting *liste!* as the dancers rush one way, imitating the barking of a dog as they return. At dawn comes the *wambo*—purification—when the *tsantsa* is held under water, in a large jar. This is a rite of fear and dread. Next the *tsantsa* is "held to the sun", fixed to a spear and lifted towards the east (rising sun), and the west, the women chanting *Etsa iista*—"see the sun". Then comes the final dance, to shouts of *Tuyung! Tuyung!*—"Let the head dance"; and *Tutor! Tutor!*—"In my father's house we dance!" The *tsantsa* is suspended on a red-painted cross of wood, nine feet high, hung on its left arm. With magical red paint (*piako*) on the cheeks; the lips are sewn with red threads. Bathing in the river ends the ritual.

KORAI (Hellenic)
Trained groups of Athenian virgins, dancing or
chanting in ceremonial procession (but not in the
Mysterion). They gave origin to the figures of
Karyatid sculptures (as seen in Erechtheum). On
their heads they bore sacred baskets or vases, with
sacrificial elements. The marble figures were
finished in pigment and gold. Their dance was slow
and regular, with flutes and lyre.

KORDAX (Ancient Greece)
A Satyr* dance said to have been taught by
Dionysus; performed by youths at Dionysian festivals. In ancient Greek comedies, it was the dance
of the Chorus (which numbered twenty-four).
Wearing masks, they reeled about in imitation of
drunken men, and performed other supposedly
humorous and "broad" antics. W. Smith[1] says that
"for a citizen to dance the *Kordax* sober and without a mask was looked upon as the height of
shamelessness". Dancers were naked or very scan-
tily attired, with tails and horns of satyrs. Aristophanes did not always include the *Kordax* in his
Comedies.   [See *Satyr's Dance*]
[1] *Dictionary of Greek and Roman Antiquities*. W.
Smith, LL.D. 1861.

KOREAN LION DANCE
"Lion" dances, centring round an elaborate creature, similar to the Balinese *Barong*,* were performed in Korea for more than a thousand years,
gradually dying out; until, before the recent
Korean war, they were to be found in only three
places. One of these was Shariin, a village five hours
train journey north-west of Keíjo (Seoul). Here, on
August 30 - 31 a yearly festival was held. One item
was the "Lion Dance", when a "lion" four yards
long, led by his master carrying a cane, went
through a comical pantomime dance. His body was
made of strips of paper, he had a long mane, rolling
eyes and lolling tongue, with a long, moveable tail
which he switched about. The dance consisted of
antics by lion and master. The lion would refuse
to dance, rush his master, agree to dance and perform some steps, bringing shouts of laughter from
spectators as he swung round to bite his tail, or
turned his head to survey the audience as he withdrew in a dignified walk. The lion was animated by
two dancers inside the framework.

KOREAN SORCERESS DANCE
An invocation dance of Old Korea, performed by
a sorceress when consulted by a client. Travellers'
accounts confirm that it was still being performed
in 1930. The dance took place in the consultant's
house, with accompaniment of drums, cymbals
and flute. One account describes the sorceress
as a woman over fifty, dressed in a blue silk

skirt, short coat of golden-brown lined with
bright blue, and white cotton heel-less boots,
holding paper streamers in both hands. The
dance began slowly, worked up to a crescendo
of both sound and movement and again subsided. Throughout, the sorceress sustained a nasal
chanting addressed to her client, who replied
in a similar way. To the sound of cymbals
and one drum, the dance began with a ceremonial
bow and salutation of joined hands, the paper
streamers mingling together. The dancer swayed
and rose up and down; then, as the drum rhythm
increased in speed she began to revolve, twirling
faster and faster, and waving the streamers alternately over her right and left shoulders. From time
to time she brought one foot down hard upon the
floor, and as other drums joined in her chanting
grew louder. During the dance an assistant handed
her a little brass rattle with six small bells attached,
and a large fan, and threw over her left arm a long
piece of yellow silk. Presently the intoning and
cymbal-clashing stopped. One drum continued, and
the dancer gradually slowed to a light floating
movement, and then ceased. The ritual garments
were removed, the sorceress continud to question
her client, and began fortune-telling with counters.
[Cp. *Oracle Dance* (Tibet)]

KORMAGYAR, KORTANCZ (Hungary)
"Hungarian Circle". A dance for men and women,
fashionable about 1840, at the same time that the
*Csardas** invaded the ballrooms of Hungary. A
product of the dancing-master Lajos Szabo Szöl-
lösi, the *Kormagyar* retained a hint of the spirited
*Verbunkos** which influenced its creation and by
then it had become a regulated, circular dance led
by the Corporal in the centre. Arranged for four
couples in two facing lines, the *Kormagyar* was in
six parts—*audalgó, lelkes, toborzó, ömledezö,
három a tánc* and *kézfogó*. It ended with the
dancers forming two concentric circles, which revolved in opposite directions, the women inside
going round clockwise, the men outside moving
anti-clockwise.

KORSI-KORONI FIRE DANCE (French Guinea,
    W. Africa)
Danced in a state of exaltation by the *Korsi-Koroni*
—athletic male dancers who perform, naked, for
three hours without pause. About ten men, accompanied by an orchestra of tambours, cymbals,
flutes, big drums, coras and balafons, dance round
a large brazier kept at white heat. With leaping and
jigging steps, they dance without sign of fatigue,
becoming more frenzied as limbs and head are flung
in jerky movements. At the climax they seize fire-
brands and rub them over their naked bodies and

on their tongues; then, one by one, each dancer leaps into the fire and rolls slowly over until dragged out by spectators. No sign of burns is afterwards apparent.

KORYAK WHALE DANCE (Siberia)

In north-eastern Siberia, the Koryaks used to celebrate the capture of a whale. Conveyed over the frozen sea on a sledge, it was greeted from the shore by women, wearing ceremonial dancing-coats and masks of sedge-grass. In one hand they carried sacrificial alder branches; in the other, lighted fire-brands, as a gesture of welcome. Singing, "Oh! a guest has come", they performed a vigorous dance, with arms out-stretched, sometimes squatting, then rising and swinging the whole body, head shaking, shoulders swaying. On reaching the shore, the whale was cut up, but not before one of the women had made a ceremonial speech over its head, and the alder branches and sacrificial grass had been thrust into its mouth. For three days ceremonies were performed in an underground chamber, containing a wooden image of a white whale, the head of the real whale being placed upon an altar. Treated as an honoured guest, the whale was welcomed with presents of food, and invited to visit them often. Two women kept vigil; on the fourth day the spirit of the whale was considered to have returned to the sea. The essence of the ceremony was appeasement of the whale's spirit, so that it would not be angry with them for having killed it; the idea being that it had merely come on a visit, and had returned to its own land, where it would tell its kindred of the good welcome received from the Koryaks, and induce them also to pay a visit, thus ensuring food for all without incurring the anger of the gods. The Koryaks performed a similar dance of appeasement when a bear or wolf was killed, one of them being dressed in the skin of the animal.

KORYBANTES (Crete)

Ritual dancers in the solemn ceremony *Korybantika*, celebrated in the Mysteries at Knossus in ancient Crete. They are said to be associated with the *Couretes* (*Kuretes*) brought by Zeus. Another legend states that the "Nine Korybantes saved Zeus". A third legend says that Corybas (whom they commemorated) was father of the Cretan Apollo, who disputed the kingdom of the Island with Zeus. These allegories are uncertain; facts are rare. At Cretan initiations, it is known that the candidate was seated on a throne inside a diagram circle or *kirke* (after long preliminary trials) when Nine Korybantes, led by their priest, danced round him, chanting their initiation song. This part of the rite was called *dronousis* or *dronismos*, according to Plato (*Euthydem*), and Dion Chrysostom. The Korybantes were deities, acted by priests in ritual mode, as ministers of Rhea or Cybele (Koré) Great Mother of the Gods. Many of the ritual dances were done in armour, with music of drums, flutes and cymbals (Strabo). From Crete the cult spread into Hellas; the term *Ban* spread widely through Europe; turned to *Pan*, as the collective earth-god who partnered Cybele. *Korybantes*, *Koré-Bante*, *Koré Bantu* etc. (Greek, Phrygian, Cretan) were variant names for youths in the devotional service of the Earth goddess, *Koré*, the "World Mother", who guided agricultural rituals.

KOSCHEI (Russia)

Is the principal remaining entity of the old Siberian shamanistic Death Dance, belonging mostly to their *Bön-Pa* cult. *Koschei* is the term used now in Tibet to mean "Master", translated into English as *Kushog*. While *Koschei* is relegated to realms of legend or fairytale, the *bilyni* is still relished by Russian children. He has appeared to adults only in one version : in the ballet form *Firebird;* and the curious *Legends of the Bogatyri*, staged and then hastily taken off, at Moscow. Tibetan painters repeat his antics in tempera painting (miscalled *fresco*) on temple or monastery walls. One of the strangest forms is the *maithuna* (embrace) of Kastchei and his wife, who danced in a delirium of ecstasy, clad only in their bones. In Tibet, the myth retains far more of its esoteric meaning : it is a version of the *chöd;* or, again, the culmination of an older *Dance of the Burning Ground*, since it presents the last energies of Shiva revolving in the final whirls of creative dissolution. Here *Koschei* is indeed the Master of Kosmos; in dissolving, he is dialectically producing the seed of the new world from the body of the old world; a work of art that should be appreciated by all who read Hegel or Marx.

KOSHARE (N. America)

Literally "Delight People", these clowns dance in many ceremonies of the Pueblo* Indians in New Mexico, Arizona and Colorado. By burlesque antics and joking with spectators, they provide comic relief in the otherwise serious religious rites of thanksgiving, or supplication for abundant crops or rain. At the winter and summer solstices they perform their antics in the ceremonies to welcome and bid farewell to the *Kachinas.** In some pueblos they dance separately (as at Santo Domingo, in February). Their performance is individual buffoonery rather than a formal dance. Having distinguishing body paint of black and white horizontal stripes, they wear a kilt and a band of rabbit fur from shoulder to waist, with many neck-laces, and green leaves in their hands or tied to their legs or arms. Sometimes they hold a rattle of deer hooves. Unlike the *Kachina*, they wear no masks, but paint circles round eyes and mouth. In their spirit existence, they are thought to live in the east, the "bad" direction, and although pro-viding humorous interludes, they are feared as bad spirits, in contrast to the good *Kachinas*. In the Taos and Isleta pueblos, the *Koshare* are called *K'apio*, and are divided into two societies—*K'apio chifunin* (Black Eyes), and *K'apio shureno* (Red Eyes), according to the circles painted round the eyes. The *K'apio chifunin* accompany the Deer Dance and Spruce Dance of the Taos Indians, and at certain ceremonies the two "sides" perform alternately. With the Apache and Navajo Indians, the *Koshare*, as the "Summer People", dance against their antagonists the "Winter People". Ten *Koshare* dance outside the main line of dancers; as clown figures, with bodies painted white. The dancers may number two hundred, led by tribal elders, who stand aside as the lines of dancers move. A man and a woman alternating makes one forma-tion; the other group, has a line of men opposite a line of women. Male dancers' costume includes a head-knot of brilliant plumage, with long curly hair hanging loose. [Cp. *Koyemshi*]

KOSHIN KAGURA (Monkey Dance (Japan)
An ancient ritual-dance form formerly performed on the "Day of the Monkeys", and presented as Three Monkeys (*sam-biki-zaru*), thence known, by a play or punning on the three calandar words, as Blind Monkey (*mi-zaru*), Deaf Monkey (*kiki-zaru*) and Dumb Monkey (*iwa-zaru*). These three popular animals are seen as roadside objects of devotion in Japan, carved in stone on slabs. Their fame has spread to Europe as "Three Good Monkeys": "They Hear no evil, Speak no evil, See no evil!" which has been turned into another dance form.

KOUROI (Greek) *Kouro-Bantes* (Cretan)
Bodies of youths who acted as priestly attendants, guards, stewards (at the Boulé). Known as "Sons of Koré" (the Virgin Mother) they ranked with young women who had parallel duties. They derived from the Egyptian bands, The Sons of Horus, the *Horoi* or *Khoroi*, who "hurried" the watching people, along with the Usher. Part of their duty became ceremonial, moving into dance form. They shouted at the beginning and end of meetings *Kuroi Elysen* (The "Court is Risen"—or Assembled . .) as did the later *Oyers*; they had to watch the time. Their great dance was the *Horo*, as the time circle; and in particular had a Spring

Dance to welcome the Green vegetation—again with the cry *Kurie Elysen!*—Horus is Rising!

KOYEMSHI (N. America)
Dancing clowns of the *Pueblo** Indians of the South-West, who perform between the serious *Kachina** dances. Generally known as "mudheads", they are masked with cloth stained pink with sacred clay, and each has a special name. Molan-hako, Father-Koyemshi, is their leader. They are feared because it is believed they have power over people, given to them by virtue of a small quantity of earth (soil from the village on which people have walked) which they carry in a pouch. Par-ticularly associated with the *Zuni*,* these clowns accompany the *Shalako*,* and dance at night with the *Kachinas* at the summer solstice. Their per-formance consists of leaping about and over each other, juggling and general buffoonery, and they have phallic associations. [Cp. *Koshare*]

KOYIL (Tamil, India)
Also as *koyyil*: is the Temple, centre of Shiva's Cosmic Dance. Compare *kyilkhor** (Tibet) as the symbolic centre of ritual dance; also *Feis-ceoil*— an Irish assembly for musical culture. The Temple of Chit-ambaram is the principal Shivaite *koyil* in Southern India.

KRAKOVIAK (Poland)
Couple dance, mentioned in records in 1510, be-longing originally to the region of Krakov, where it was danced by everyone. Later it was adopted by the nobility, in a refined form; and is now danced all over Poland. To gay music in 2/4 time, the couples dance in circular formation, the man with his right arm round his partner's waist, the girl with her left hand on his right shoulder. The couples move into a large circle, then into lines behind one another, moving again into a linked circle. Satirical or flattering songs accompany the dance, the man of the first couple starting the song; or a ballad or madrigal may be sung, the dance varying according to the song. The *Krak-oviak* may also be danced by one couple, when it has more dramatic action. The clink of metal heels, and jingle of brass and silver rings on the men's belts, mark the rhythm of the dance. Costumes are colourful. For the women a patterned skirt with yellow waistcoat over white blouse; high red boots and a head-dress of flowers with long rib-bons. The men wear striped trousers tucked into high boots, long tasselled coat, and red cap with peacock feathers at one side. The *krakoviak* (called in France, *Cracovienne*) became famous on the stage in 1839, when Fanny Elssler scored a great success in the ballet *La Gypsy* at Her Majesty's

Theatre, London, with this dance. Contemporary prints show her in vivandière costume of blue skirt, braided tunic, and boots with metal heels,

dancing before a background of Edinburgh Castle, since the ballet was set in Scotland.

A vigorous Krakoviak performed by members of *Mazowsze*, the Polish State Dance Company. Men wear striped trousers and wide-skirted coats, with peacock feathers in their hats. In the background girls in full skirts, high red boots and flower head-dresses await the moment to join the dance.   POLAND

KRALJICE (Yugoslavia) "Little Princess"
Near Pojarevach, North-east Yugoslavia, the ritual healing of the *Dubovka** ceremonial is performed. This Dance of the Little Princesses is done as a preliminary "exorcism of the way", or a leading of the pilgrims. There are two small girls, twelve or fourteen years old, attired in an all-white gala costume, and carrying swords. They wear a small crown, and have a mirror pinned behind their shoulder blades. Three small girls supply a chant, while an old woman directs "The Little Queens". Variously, they are said to present Sun and Moon (in friendship or combat) or, traditionally, two local queens who fought over the spring of the River Dubovka, one being slain; the other declared that all her posterity would dream of the contest on the anniversary of their fight. The dance goes with a peculiar step, which suggests that they are both riding horses. This may be a mode of the *Calusari*,* in Rumania, who use a similar step, or an actual hobby horse. The rest of the dance consists in waving the swords in circles and "figures of eight", with a mutual clash at the end of each verse of the chant.   [See *Dubovka*]

KREMBALA (Greece)
Ta'kremballa are the castanets, much used in many of the ancient Grecian dances and rituals. They were adopted, instead of the drum, for keeping time in the dance; with the term *krembaliastus*, which indicates the "rattling of the castanets". [See *Castanets*]

KRIDA BEKSA WIRAMA (Java)
Dance Society and School founded in 1920 by Prince Tedyokusomo of Jogya in Java, for preservation and teaching of the old arts of Theatre in the Island. The K.B.W. thus continues the ancient court ballet forms, rather than folk-dance; and also maintains the attractive *gamelan* music. The best show is for *Lebaran* (Java is mainly a Muslim country, though the players give Hindu legends) which is the end of the Feast. From Solo come professional dancers; from Jogya mainly the traditional aristocratic "amateurs". The various Wayang* styles have some affinities; but modern influences have provoked different modes, such as *Langendriya*, a fusion of dance and song, devised by Prince Mangkunegoro of Solo, as a kind of

modern opera. The *Sandiwara* came in from other lands.

KRISHNA DANCES (India)
There are several principal modes of Krishna dance, bearing many titles, in the various languages of India. In the North, a generic term is *Krishna Lila*, while in the South (Tamil Nad) there are the *Krishnattayam*. The first mode is usually Krishna with his Flute—(as the *avatar* or deputy of Vishnu the creator)—he dances in his musical creation, playing his flute as he moves, alone or with the *Gopis*. The next mode is the *Krishna-Radha Lila*, of the "Blue god", with his feminine counterpart, Radha (*ruadha*, or the round), as the principal *gopi*. There are latest folk-lore dances of legendary style, as the "boyhood of Krishna", in which his youthful sports are detailed in song and dance. The Krishna cult is many centuries old, from at least fourth century BC in its early form; it is especially promoted by the *Bhagavats* or devotees; it has a

Bala-Rama, the Dancing Krishna. Copper figure in the Madras Museum. The base is designed for two ropes to be inserted so that the figure can be carried through the sanctuary.   INDIA

ritual "dance of ecstacy". Literature is extensive and detailed; but the esoteric meaning of symbolism is harder to attain. The temple dances in these modes are less extensive than the Shiva* ritual dances, or even those of Kali; having gained such a deep popular hold that separate rituals are unnecessary. These rituals are religious dances in every meaning of the term; they are not everywhere submerged in flat realism. *Bhagavad Gita* (Song Celestial) is the principal scripture of the cult. (Trans. in English available.)

KRISHNA-RADHA NATYA (India)
The principal ritual drama dance of the devotees of Krishna in India (properly spelled Cristna) and performed at *Dasehra* (Hindu Festival). Krishna stands erect in the centre of a ring of "Milkmaids of Brindaban", who dance mystically with him, and around him, simultaneously. There are thirty or three-hundred-and-sixty of these *gopis* (nights of moon, days of sun). The dance belongs chiefly to the Bhagavata cult, which spread widely from India, first into Asia Minor (as at Antiocha, where the *Cristanees* were known as *khrestiani*—a term still existing for some obscure Russian sects)—and into Spain. Their song, the *Bhagavad Gita* (Celestial Song of the Lord), gave rise to the *'gavad* dance (as the *gavot**) in Provence and to the group name of *gitanos* (singers and dancers) in Southern Spain. Krishna is portrayed in Hindu sculpture as four-armed : two hands carry his *murli* (flute), on which he plays the dance melody; two more carry the *chakram* (ring or *ruad-ha*) and the conch (sacred sound). Krishna is an *avatar* (a reincarnation of the God of Salvation, Vishnu the Preserver). (See Hindu *Puranas*). Krishna and Radha are favourite subjects in the later Hindu *rag-mala* paintings of Northern India (16th - 19th cent.), where the seasons of the year and the phases of love are symbolised in delicate colour.   [See *Kama Shastras*]

KROUNO TEKHNOPHAGIA (Greece)
One of the ritual dances of Kuretes, priests of Kybele. As recorded, this dance was a mythic display, in Crete, of the solar Dance of Zeus as infant; the title means literally "Time-Eater", and was part of the Ritual of the Year (end of year, "time is gone"; opening of year, "time is to come"). In India, the Dance of the Golden Garuda is similar, while the Dance of Krishna and the 360 Gopis has similar elements.

KUDUKUTTA (Dekkan, India)
A version of the *Gharbha*,* or Pot Dance (Tamil name). Originally a pastoral dance of the Krishna legends, this is a dance of his victory after the defeat of the demon Banasura.

KUJAWIAK (Poland)

A peasant couple dance belonging to Kujawy, in north-eastern Mazovia. A slower variant of the *Mazurka*,* it is less vigorous, being danced smoothly, without emphasis or stamping. Dancers move round in a circle, partners facing each other, each with their hands on the upper forearms of the other. The dance has no particular ending, but continues indefinitely. The true *Kujawiak* begins with the *spiacy*, or "sleepy Kujawiak", in which the couples circle slowly to the left, beginning lazily but quickening the tempo and then turning first to the left, then to the right. The people of Kujawy favour dark blue in their costumes. The men wear long coats of this colour, with stiff, high-crowned hats, and at weddings they perform a dance with a full glass balanced on the straight brim.

KUKRI DANCE (Assam; Nepal)

A solo dance of technical skill. The hill man desires to prove his strength and agility: he practices with two bottles tied firmly to his waist by a short length of rope. The object is to revolve quickly, to keep them moving in a circle through the air, without clashing and breaking, without holding or touching them. Incompetence is marked by a heavy blow. When proficient, he ties instead of smooth bottles, the heavy curved sword, the *kukri* (familiar as the chosen weapon of the Gurkha troops of Nepal and Sikkim), and now he has to whirl (occasionally bending forward to touch the ground and then springing sharply back) to the instant challenge of the sharp blade. As the blades swing past, he raises alternate arms and legs, in one version.   [Cp. Mexican *Morismo*]

KUMBARTI (Hindu)

Temple dancer, the "junior handmaiden"—of twelve years or so—whose chief duty was to prepare and carry the temple lights; and to hold them during ceremonial. Thus the duties were equivalent to those of the acolyte in the christian organization. The *kumbarti* carried lamps during night processions, at certain points; preceded and followed by men holding the less manageable torches. The name is given to the sacred lamp, filled with *ghee*, or coco-oil.

KUMMI (Malabar, S. India)

Folk dance; popular village or household dances; in which simple ordinary duties are mimed to soft chanting; almost all circle dances, varied by processional forms when some celebration requires girls to gather at a centre. These duties such as: drawing water, cleaning pots and pans, preparing rice and grinding rice, grinding spices, winnowing grain, milking a cow. Other *kummi* dance forms show picking flowers for altar adornment; most include saluting when they indicate religious festival. *Kumm* or *khumb* equals "home" or "home-like" (Old English: Combe). Other *kummi* include Snake Dances, and Lamp Dance, *Mavil-akku*.*

KUNCHUNEE (Hindustani or Urdu)

An ordinary dancing girl (not in temple service). [Cp. *Bhugtiva*, dancing boy.] They are seen chiefly in the *Nautch* (*nach*) or entertainment dance of the town; but in recent years have invaded the cinema film industry. For village celebrations, they used to perform on a newly built (wooden) *chabutra* (platform), made about three feet high. In the centre of Baranesi (Benares) there was a black granite structure used for this purpose; also in other places. Patterns were made over it, for some dances, in white rice powder (*Alpona**).

KURETES (Hellenic)

Legendary people (acted by boys of priestly caste) said to come from Aetolia (that country was sometimes called Curetis on this account). More definitely, the Kuretes appear in Crete (Krete or Kurete) as the Island priests of Zeus; and are mentioned with the Korybantes, and the Idaena Dactyli. In the allegory, the infant Zeus (now as sun god), was entrusted to the priests by Rhea ("Who Flows", Time, the Year). They are famous for their Dance of Shields, in which the clashing of spears on shields was said to be done to "drown the cries" of the infant; and so prevented his father Kronus (Time Eternal) from learning where the infant was, so that he could not be disturbed until the year ended. This is a myth of the round of the year; and the dance ritual doubtless followed in this circular form, with the usual twelve stations or changes of rhythm.

KURUMBA (India)

The regular "salute" before and in Manipuri dance. The term has parallel forms: in Tamil, *karamba*— "now dance!"—and it seems to have reached Spain as *caramba*, now used as a mild swear; while Lascar seamen brought it to London, where it is repeated by Cockneys as "Crumbs!" or "Kerumbs!", as a note of exclamation or astonishment. The hand salute, single or double hand, is a simple circle, fore and aft, of out-stretched arm. The comparable Indian (Sanskrit) salute is *anjali*.*

KURUVANJHI (India)

Allocated by some to the Korava people, who are the gypsies (wanderers), fortune-tellers, acrobat-showmen, and snake-charmers in South India.

Their dance-mime plays use a theme mostly from their own lives. Despite this apparent proletarian concern, the *Kuruvanjhi* plays are repeated at certain festivals in the courts of the Temple of Travancore and other centres, here under control of the *devadasi* dancers. Women only perform, and they use more or less the *Bharata Natyam** technique. Their chief festival is usually that of the *Mahasiva-ratri* in March; here the hero is the elephant god Ganesha.

KUTTU-AMBALAM (Tamil, S. India)
The temple dance-hall. Not many dance halls are accessible to strangers. Those in the ruins (Halebid) and at Belur, or in the *Padmana-bhapuram* Palace (between Cape Comorin and Trivandrum) show the final style, constructed in stone. The hall, some fifty by thirty feet, has in front a portico and roof also of stone. Its floor is hard Indian cement, stained black and smoothly shining; with a bluish tinge from the indigo dye used to get the dark surface as a foil to the brilliant hues of the dancers. Most of the *mandapa* slabs, usually circles of twenty feet in diameter, were finished with this indigo-tinted cement. The surrounding sculptured stones were originally painted and gilded, mostly with dancers as the artists' subject. None of these dance-halls were in theatre form; they occupied a centre (some were oval in plan), and dancing could be watched from all sides, and from above.

KUVERA RITUAL (Sikkim)
Is held at Gangtok, the capital, in the space before the principal temple. An orchestra first appears: six lamas, two with the *tung-chen* (sixteen-foot long copper trumpets, used chiefly as signals), others with *gyaling* (small silver trumpets) supported by drums (*damaru* and others) and cymbals, which dominate the rhythm. The ritual dance, in honour of Kuvera, is done because he resides in the immense Mount Kanchenjunga, near by; and though his companion is *Maha-Kala* (The "Great Darkness"), it is performed in day time. Thirty monks, attired like Kubla Khan's soldiers, wheel rhythmically in measured and solemn step (named *dorje-dro*—the "thunderbolt pace"). They cleave the air with bright swords, slicing evil spirits apart. The sacred music is in spondaic rhythm. The chief heralds sing the Invocation to Kuvera:

"Destroyer of enemies, guilty of ten sins
Prince of guardians, this country of rice!
Lord of all Spirits
    Known as High Summit of Yunjga
Martial Divinity of warrior youth!"

Soon Kuvera himself appears—a majestic and big lama, splendidly attired in brocade of silk and gold,

wearing a polished red mask. An excellent dancer, he performs a long series of evolutions, with many pauses, in slow balancing movements, the results of long training. *Maha-Kala* stands by the temple door, awaiting the final invocation—"Glory to *Maha Kala, Kiki huhu*! Great One, of Triumphant Time!

KYILKHOR (Written *kyilkhor*; Tibet)
General ritual term for diagram constructed for various modes of ritual and liturgy, including certain magical dances, for which they supply "paths" or matrices. They exist in two great categories: the objective material and tangible forms; or the subjective and imaginative forms, usually derived from the visible experience of the ritualist or his master. Again they exist physically in two modes: the full-size diagram, drawn or cut or painted on a temple floor, or on a large wooden board; and the small-scale diagrams drawn or painted on paper or cotton (as the ritual banners), or cut into metal or sculptured in stone or wood. Large *kyilkhor* diagrams may be constructed or suggested by hinted lines or points, using vases filled with water or grain etc.; or small flags set in order; or lighted lamps, or even an array of incense sticks. The word means "circle" but this implies a container or holder of power; as we say "magic circle" when the form delineated is, in fact, a pentacle. The principal *kyilkhor* of Tibet is the *Maha-Mandala* of Avalokiteshvara (the chief patron deity of Tibet), often seen on the temple banners, with its great square, four-gated city; and enclosing lotus. When drawn for the *chöd** ritual, the *kyilkhor* is made in a size large enough to perform the requisite dance movement. The initial purpose is to "fix attention", and then to supply a root of meditation; a process of mind training (summarised in AUM), implying (a) Analysis; (b) Meditation; and (c) Understanding. The principal symbols of each great religion are summarised in a diagram that may be taken in precisely the same way as the Tibetan *kyilkhor*; all of them have been used in their liturgies.

KYNDELDANS (Norway)
A Candle or Torch dance, dating from the thirteenth century, performed at weddings. Brought to life again since the revival in Norwegian dancing began about fifty years ago, it is danced to the traditional historical ballad "Falkvor Lomansson". After performing country dance figures, the men kneel in pairs holding above their heads flaming torches, while the girls, carrying small flower garlands, dance a winding way between them.
[Cp. *Domare Dansen* (Sweden); *Ciri. Ball del* (Catalonia); *Candle Dance*]

L

LABAN NOTATION SYSTEM

Was devised by Rudolf Laban Varaljas (Bratislava, 1879 - 1958) on a basis from Dalcroze Eurhythmics, Delsarte stage mime, and the work of Duncan, Fuller, and Maude Allan (as "Free or Modern Dance"). This synthesis was used in the development of Kurt Jooss and his 1932 modern ballet productions (*Green Table* etc.) and reduced to a tangible teaching system. Next the mode of Notation, taking in systems from Feuillet to Stepanov, were combined and re-stated in a text-book format for ballet students. The perennial difficulty in all such written systems is the use of the "third dimension" of space, which has to be interpreted, much as the player has to interpret the musician's ideas of time progression. But steps, musical notes, and words for the actor can all be provided—as a basis of production.

LABRYS (Greco-Cretan)

Term used to signify the Assyrian "Double-Axe" by later writers. This sign resembles two equal isosceles triangles, having a common apex, through which runs the line representing the haft of the weapon. Remains of the ruined Palace of Minos (Knossos), were called the palace, the labyrinth, or *House of Labrys*. The word came to mean a maze. With the Double Axe we find the Queen Mother; and the Bull-Man-God,—the Mino-taurus. As several doctrinal ideas are fused in these symbols, their meaning has been too much simplified. The Double Axe goes back (older than Crete), to Babylon and Gilgamish. With these symbols we have the ritual dances: especially the "Dance of Winding" (The World-Dance) mythologised in Theseus and Ariadne. *LabRhys* became *Lavra/Arval* (in Rome), *Rhys* in Wales; *Labyrinthos* in Greece; *Rouen-Theoi* (the gods "going round"). This symbol (it gives also double *Delta*) is similar to *Tangov** and the *Muhr-i-Suleiman* of sword-dancers. The haft is the *rapir*, once more.

LABYRINTH (Crete, early Hellas etc.)

Is a symbolic pattern that carries one of the most important keys to ancient dance ritual. We know it from the days of Babylon, where it appears with the legend of "The Man with the Adze", called Gilgamish, who cuts his way through the Underworld or Labyrinth with this primal weapon-tool. Then follows Theseus, later known as Jesse/Joseph (tree-cutter, carpenter), and Jesus. This pattern appears repeatedly in various modes: as the dancing-place (Tibet, *mandala**); or dance-pattern (*Na-Leng,** Malekula), or dancing-shield (Maori), and the Grecian shield-symbol (Achilles and Perseus, who gets it from Minerva), and again in Rome (where it is reversed: *Lavra* X *arvaL*), and indicates the Sacred Ploughed Field (as it does in early China). The term *Labyrinth* is not Greek, but derives from much earlier form: *Labya*, the Axe; and *Ruentha*, the round, or "going-round". The Egyptian form *Maze* does not touch it for centuries; though the basic idea is identical; but they come closer in the Latin church, as in the *Way to Jerusalem** (a later post-crusade term), laid down in mosaic, in many churches. The oldest known labyrinth (4th century) is in the Basilica in Orleansville, Algeria, made over from Roman usage. Western European churches contained many such formal patterns; many large enough to dance or step over, while chanting. One at Amiens (13th century) is twelve metres diameter; that at Chartres is forty feet. One at St. Michaels dates from 11th century. In Cologne, the parallel symbolism of Zodiac and of Seasons appear (11th century) in the crypt of S. Gereon, surrounding the labyrinth. This symbol governs the central ceremony of the "ritual death" so often a part of initiation. The famous Cretan Labyrinth emphasises this factor: the "seven youths and seven maidens" were the candidate's "powers and possessions", which he had to "sacrifice" to reach and slay the Minotaurus, the bull-god.

[See *Architecture Religieuse (Rudiment d'Archaeologie)* by M. A. de Caumont (Caen. 1870) p. 510 - 513; *Way to Jerusalem; Shields; Mandala; Tangov; Maze; Sand Tracings; Geranos*]

LADAKHI MARRIAGE DANCE (at Leh, in Ladakh or "Little Tibet")

Follows the simple ceremony. This is performed on the symbolical *lakshmi* or *rangoli** (long used even in Buddhist weddings), where the man enters, bows to priest and bride's family, and sits on a swastika pattern drawn on the floor with coloured chalks or sand. Chanting begins; then the bride is brought in by her friends. She salutes priest and man, and places herself over a similarly drawn pattern, now the symbolical lotus (there are millions in the lakes of Kashmir). The married couple then dance with relatives and friends; in a circle dance, moving slowly, with music from drums and pipes, and an occasional cymbal, with verses. The dance follows a circle, with small three-step pirouettes. The inevitable *khatak* (white silken scarf, gift of greeting), is raised and lowered by the men, in time with body movement. The women raise their arms, using the *lotus-mudra* (as a symbol of marriage), opening and shutting their slim fingers. They all wear red leathern slippers for this indoor dance. Feet are kept supple (and clean!) by massage with butter; there is much dust, which gets inside their heavy outdoor *pabbues* (leather soles, with woollen tops, felted).

LADDER DANCE (England)

Strutt[1] describes this "because the performer stands on a ladder, which he shifts from place to place; and ascends or descends without losing equilibrium. . . . This dance was practised at Sadler's Wells, at the commencement of last century (17th century) . . . James Miles (temp. Queen Anne) declared himself to be a performer from Sadler's Wells, and kept a music booth in Bartholomews Fair where he exhibited nineteen different kinds of dances; among them a wrestler's dance; vaulting on the slack rope; and dancing upon the ladder". An *Inventory of Playhouse Furniture* (quoted in the *Tatler*) specifies masks, castanets, and a ladder of ten rounds. "I apprehend", (says Strutt), "that the ladder dance originated from the ancient pastime of walking or dancing upon very high stilts."

[1] *Sports and Pastimes.* J. Strutt (ed. 1898).

L'AG-YA (Martinique,, West Indies)

Ritual dance of Negroes, invocation of the "King of the Zombies". These rituals were held throughout the West Indies, where Negro slaves were brought in by the Spanish and French Christians, so that two cults have mingled, along with many cult names and terms. "L'Ag-ya" may derive from *agir* (French—"to work", "operation") or from Spanish *aguardar* ("to expect", "to await"), with inevitably slackening accent, due to Negro usage. In the stage version (Katherine Dunham's Company) *L'Ag-ya* was presented as a "tale of magic" from the Island of Martinique, so small that it is completely permeated by French catholic culture. African religions have largely died out, but a strong belief in magic remains. There are two rivals for a girl, who uses the *cambois* (a love charm), but the Dance of the *Mazouk* culminates with a love dance, *Majumba*. The second scene shows Dance in the Jungle, where the Roi des Zombies uses ritual to arouse the "half-dead" called Zombies, as his new slaves. In this result is the "expectation" fulfilled —as in *Shango**.

LAI HARROBA (Manipur province, Assam)

Traditional Manipur dance, belonging to the local shrines in all villages; a ritual of devotion at the Laipham or god's-place (particularly at sowing or harvesting), where the Imung-Lai is given offerings. He is similar to the Roman Lares and Penates. The term is said to mean "Gods making merry". The chief dance, performed after all family groups have made their devotions at home, begins with offering of fruit and flowers, led by the Maibi (Priestess). Gaily dressed girls perform first; they select local youths; another dance follows. Then comes the traditional story dance of "Khamba and Thaibi" (a Princess loved by a poor but noble youth).

LAKA-LAKAS (Tonga Island)

Danced and sung descriptions of legends and historical events, performed by groups of men and women. Arranged in rows, men to the right, women to the left, performers sing traditional stories as they dance, symbolical gestures bringing vivid illustration of the song. Costumes are made of *tapa* cloth decorated with leaves and fruits, and whale oil is rubbed into the body. A chorus accompanies the dancing, one chant sometimes lasting twenty minutes, with several voices carrying one note while other voices continue the melody. Singers stand round three large drums which mark the rhythm. All vocal and instrumental music is subordinated to the dance, which includes very rapid movements of arms and head, always in perfect rhythm. Dancing in Tonga, considered an essential part of education, was learned by chiefs and other important people.   [Cp. *Hula*]

LAKHON (India)

From Sanskrit, *Lekha*, to engrave, or "cut out". A sacred play, performed as in a concentrated act of ritual symbolism, intended to "cut into" the living mind; in later centuries, applied widely to many modes of drama, dance and ritual; is related to the Egyptian *rakhon* (to calculate, to prepare for, to plan, to devise by synopses). The word penetrated to Britain, and is used in Northern England, as *laike*, meaning directly "to play"—or, by negation, not to do physical toil. "Laiking" or playing in this sense is not to be working. The term implies the first beginnings of sculpture (seals etc.) in contrast to a parallel term *lipi* (to daub superficially, to write on a surface) which is the beginning of painting; as in *lipimara* ("word-sound-create") and held "in between" carving and painting by the immense impact of dance-drama and ritual dance, by the later term *lipimudra* (the "drawn seal", instead of *lekha-mudra*, the carven seal) in Lalata-vistara. *Lekha* and *lekhon* (or *lekharna*) has two phases: the static mode in the carved object, seal or figure; and the dynamic mode in the ritual dance of the living body. Thus *lakhon* and *lekha* are the oldest known dance terms; and equally, they display, in India, the origins of writing.

[Cp. German *lehr*, *lehrer*, "to learn", "learner with learning"; *rakhon* and *trakhon* (raconteur), *narra-khon*]

LAMA DANCE (Tibet)

Meaning of the word Lama is important: in popular Tibetan, *lama* means "path" or "road"; but (as in other doctrines) The Path (as in Buddhism) means The Way to Wisdom, to Salvation. Yet *lama* means also "cross" for, like the Roman X as Ten or 10, the figure (as form and as quantity) is an emblem of perfection. Egyptians, Chinese and Phœnecians of Carthage also used X, yet it appears in Mexican secular calendars. Tatars call it *lama*, from the Scytho-Turanian word *lamh* or hand (from ten fingers on the hands); it is the same as the *jod* of the Chaldees. Thus *lama* becomes the name of a cross; of chief priest of the Tatars; the Lamaic messenger of God says one writer. In Ireland, *luam* denotes "head of church", a spiritual chief. *Ollomh* was the Druid chief. The name of the chief among the Druses of Lebanon is El Hamma.

Tibetan Lama Dance. *Tsam*, the ritual dance of the Bhorkans (The Hidden Ones) drawn at Lama-Sarai, south of Lake Baikal about 1880.   MONGOLIA

LAMA DANCE RITUAL (Tibetan, *blama* or *lama*)
Lama is the qualified priest in the Tibetan Buddhist Church system; but as the Lama himself is usually a dignitary of high qualification, he governs the ritual dances (though he may have helped in his undergraduate period), which are performed chiefly by junior members, the *trapa* or student body. The rituals of the *gompa* (monastery) are entirely religious in action or theme, or both; they include the actual rites and festival performances of popular legends (we should call them "miracle plays") shewn at the annual celebrations at Lhassa, Ladakh and other centres, to be seen over an area much wider than Tibet. Most of these rites and plays include masked dancers, gorgeously attired, who dance to the music of gongs and trumpets in the courtyard of the monastery; or, as for the *Tsam*,* in the centre of a semi-permanent group of tents, at sites in Mongolia. The purpose of performance is apparently single, but in fact has meaning within meaning, according to the competence of spectators to perceive and to grasp what is presented. While the external display is offered to attract and retain the attention of the simple householder or shepherd, the symbolic content will not immediately become apparent to the most astute Western psychologist; for it is focussed in the profoundly powerful system of mind training and evolution, controlled by the Lama body.
[See SHAKTI and SHAKTA (trans. from *Shakta Tantra Shastra*) by Sir John Woodroffe (Arthur Avalon) 4th ed. Ganesh, Madras]

LAMMAS (England)
One of the four principal Messes or Feasts of the Year (now August 1st). This term seems to derive from *Leham-Messe* (Bread Feast) and is appropriately a celebration of a Corn Harvest, to mark a "Quarter" of the Year. It is probable that the Horn Pipe Dance (*Gern* or *Gerne*, Grain) was originally one of the Lammas dances. The Coptic Church has a ritual processional, from the Mread House (*Beit Lehem*) into the church at Easter.

LAMENTO
A fourteenth century European dance was called *Lamento di Tristan*, and in music the word signifies a mournful character. An old Celtic dance called *Planxty** was also sub-titled "or Lament", and both terms seem to be connected with the Provençal word *planc* or *planh*, meaning Troubadour songs of a mournful character.
[See *Planxty*; *Planctus Karoly*]

LANCERS, LANCERS QUADRILLE
A 19th century square dance, for eight or sixteen couples. The five figures, performed at a brisk walk, in strict musical time, were called *La Rose*; *La Ladoiska*; *La Dorset*; *L'Étoile*; *Les Lanciers*. The dance appeared in Ireland and in Wales (at Tenby "as danced by the nobility and gentry") in 1817 and 1819 respectively, but it was not seen in London until 1850. John Duval, a Dublin dancing-master and Joseph Hart (of Tenby) both claimed

its invention. Their versions had similar music and figure-names, but the figures themselves differed. From a newspaper account in which the dance is called "Hart's set", it seems that this was the version introduced into London ballrooms in 1850, by four young Society ladies, who learned it at the Hanover Square Rooms, where the then fashionable dancing-mistress, Madame Sacré, gave instruction. The same account gives the figures as *La Chaine; Zodorska; D'Orset; L'Étoile; Finales les Lancers. Etoiles* is sometimes called *Les Visites.* By 1860 the *Lancers* was included in Queen Victoria's State balls.

LANDLER (Austria)
An Alpine dance from *das Ländl* in Upper Austria (variously spelled *Länderer, Länderli,* or *Ländlerische Tanz*) which developed from the 14th century "turning dances" or *Deutsche** of South Germany. These were performed by couples revolving in a circle, mostly in triple time. Singing often accompanied the dance, the tune being played on a fiddle or Alpine wood instrument, with music in two parts of eight bars, each part repeated twice or more. These dances were known also in Bavaria, Tyrol, Styria, and Carinthia, with local names. In Upper Austria, in the early 19th century, the *Ländler* rhythm became slower, turning to a heavier dance in 4/4 time; the 3/4 version developing into the lighter Viennese *Waltz.** In the *Ländler,* partners face each other, the girl's hands on the man's shoulders, his hands on her waist; or she is held by one hand, and twisted and turned by her partner in various ways. As they revolve in a circle, the man breaks away to display technical virtuosity, while the girl spins by herself, and the pair end the dance together with a slow waltz step. Local variations occur as in the *Steyrischer** from *Styria,* and the *Schühplattler** from Tyrol. The Swiss *Ländler,* a vigorous dance similar to the Austrian, is popular in the German speaking Cantons. In Central Switzerland it is called the *Gauerler;* in Appenzell the *Hierig.* Mozart and Beethoven wrote in this rhythm, while Schubert composed the *Wiener Damen-Ländler.*

LANGDHARMA (Bhutan)
Dance of King Langdharma—known also as *Black Hat Dance,* this semi-historical 9th century legend relates how King Langdharma, who ruled Tibet at that period, brought the country to ruin; and was liquidated by a "great lama" who was leader of the Black Hat Monastery. Disguised as a minstrel, he attended the Court of King Langdharma, offering to perform a valuable magical dance. Receiving permission, he was given the time demanded. The lama, wearing his black robes,

began the dance. Suddenly he drew from under the voluminous cloak a short bow, fitted an arrow, and shot the monarch at close quarters, as he knelt at the final point of his dance. Then he fled. In a corridor, he turned his robe, leaving the black exterior now as lining, and showing the white silk. He leaped on his pony; which had been coated in soot; and headed into a stream, where the water washed away the black leaving the animal its natural white. Thus the lama made his escape. This legend is danced as a festival Miracle Play, in Pharo Dzong, played solely by men (novices and lamas), from the monastery of Tashi Chho Dzong. The Bhutanese dancers follow mainly the older Hindu-Buddhist *mudra** system. The dance of the Lama is slow and dignified, accompanied by powerful rather than melodious music from long trumpets (up to fifteen feet), bells, conch shells, cymbals, and drums of several sizes. Other dancers are clad in scarlet and black, with wide fur-trimmed hats, mounted with a miniature skull; and even the short version (sometimes repeated for a wedding festival) will last three hours. Girl dancers accompany a bridal procession, with monks beating small drums; but this is not part of the ritual play; nor are the "animal dances" (by bare-footed hunter tribesmen), as done to entertain visitors, in the fields. [See *Black Hats, Dance of*]

LAOUTARI (Rumania)
Literally, "Lutists", a name given to bands of gypsy musicians, singers and dancers, who, receiving news in advance, travelled to weddings of wealthier folk to provide an entertainment. They improvised music, on folk songs; and did a similar development of traditional dances, but having once got a group style tended to repeat it, so that they became known by special names. They visited other Balkan countries on the same mission.

LAPP DRUM—1 (Lapland)
Magical or *Runic* drum, used by the *angekok* or master of ritual to ascertain distant events. One form of runic drum was known as the "Dancing Stones". On the wolfskin used for the drum-head, magical diagrams of geometric form were drawn or painted, with the sixteen runic characters in their proper original positions round the circle. By drumming the correct rhythm, to meet current astro-magnetic conditions, the *angekok* caused vibrations on the skin, which in turn induced the "talking bones" to take up new positions. (This was probably the origin of the more sophisticated dice cubes). From the position of these bones (usually the small knuckle-bones of deer), could be deduced certain information from the Dance of the Bones. Chanting went on; also, at intervals,

the prayer dance round the drum. Gourdon in 1614 described Samoyedes (N. Russian Lapland) as using a large hare's foot for drumming the rhythm, on a "great tabor made with wolf skin". Missions destroyed the practice; but specimens of Lapp drums can be seen in some museums (British Museum, e.g.).

Shaman Dance of Invocation (He "talks" to the Deer). From a silver vessel found in Gundestrup, Jutland.
LAPPLAND

LAPP MAGICAL DRUM—2 (Lapland)

Some of these drums may be inspected in museums; but not sounded or used. If they are not seen in action, their purpose cannot be fully appreciated. The writer, Meinhold (who seems to have had this privilege) describes such a drum in his accounts, said to be founded on facts, of witchcraft in Pomerania[1]:

"This drum . . . a piece of hollow wood, either fir, pine or birch, and which grows in such a particular place that it follows the course of the sun : that is, its pectine, fibrae, and linae in the annual rings must wind from right to left. Having hollowed out such a tree, they spread a skin over it fastened down with little pegs; on the centre of the skin is painted the sun, surrounded by figures of men, beasts, birds and fishes. All this is done with (paint of) the rind of the elder tree, chewed first by teeth. Upon the top of the drum, there is an index in the shape of a triangle, from which hang little rings and chains. When the wizard wishes . . . he strikes the drum with a hammer of reindeer horn (not to procure a sound) to set the index in motion, that it may move, and point to what may give the required answer. The magician murmurs conjurations, springs up from the ground, screams or laughs, dances and reels; and falls at last in ecstacy, dragging the drum down on his face . . . Anyone may then put questions . . . all came out true".

These drums seem to mark the end of an ancient Babylonian ritual.

[1] *Sidonia the Sorceress.* Dr. William Meinhold. Trans. by Lady Wilde. (2 Vols. London, 1894). (Vol. 1, p. 51).

LAPP DANCE DRUM—3

The form of incantation used with the drum, for spiritualist seance or for healing, or for prophecy of events, is called *jojk* (pron. *yoick*). It is chanted usually by a single male voice using only seven notes, in a monotonous rise and fall, though occasionally inflected with tensions of emotion; and consisting almost entirely of vowel sounds. When the drum is used, rhythm is more marked in the *jojk*. Presumably, this rhythm is an accentuation of steps and arm movements, in the dance circle.

LA SCALA (Milano)

French name for *Teatro alla Scala*, the famous opera theatre. After the burning of the *Teatro Duca Regio* in 1776, this building was erected on the site of a former Church of Santa Maria alla Scala ("of the Stairs", metaphorically—there are no hills in Milan). The Theatre was rebuilt inside in 1867 and newly equipped in 1921; and remains open during the winter season, though damaged during the war.

LASYA (Sanskrit)

Hindu Temple ritual dance. The feminine, or negative part of the Brahmin ritual of *Samaya*. See *Saundarya-Lahari* (*Ocean of Beauty*). Shankara; trans. Sastri and Ayyangar. p. 160. [See *Tandava*]

"LATIN AMERICAN" TOWN DANCE

Ballroom versions extant in Europe (1955), included arrangements of *Mambo; Samba; Son-Rumba; Guaracha; Baion;* and a *Bolero-Rumba*. As is usual, the commercialised versions are all crushed. within the limitations of a ten-piece band with its piano and saxophone, so that the special local qualities of these South American dances are lost in a smoothed orchestration of the style alleged to be "demanded" by ballroom dancers of the European capitals. Hence the dance rhythms are reduced to common standards, similar to those found in factory-made automobiles; most of the instrumental playing rarely ranges above mechanical treatment.

LAUTERBACH (Switzerland)

Traditional wedding dance in the Canton of Berne. Accompanied by the zither, it is a couple-dance with simple miming, the rhythm marked with hand-clapping. Using a waltz step, partners dance round the room, the man turning the girl under his arm with a spin. A promenade and the mimed sequence follow. Arms round each other's neck, dancers circle the room, the man pretending to smoke his pipe, the girl giving coy side-glances. After coldly refusing an imploring invitation to accept the advances of her partner, the girl relents, when they whirl away together in a waltz. Then the man kneels while the girl dances round him, and the dance ends with a final waltz. The man wears short-sleeved black velvet jacket over white shirt, with bands across chest and round waist embroidered with patterns of edelweiss and gentians. Over full skirts, the girl wears brocaded apron, black bodice and the traditional black lace headdress.

LAVANI SAVAL (India)

Dance-song performed at Kama Festivals in Deccan.

(Kama is the God of Love, the Indian "Cupid"). This Spring festival is in honour of Krishna and Radha. The performance is called *Lavani*, with a special type known as *Saval;* and is sung by two separate parties. One party, called *Turai*, recites the questions (or replies) of Krishna, while the other party called *Kalki*, recites the answers (or questions) put by Radha to her Lord. Where the tradition is strong, and "everyone knows the words", the song is more or less extempore; but for a performance of any pretensions, some rehearsal is done the day before. The performance is simple and popular; there are also more finished versions offered by professional travelling groups of dancer-players. The ordinary folk-songs are *lavanis*. A similar celebration is known as *Kabi* or *Kavi* (the poet) in Hindostan.

LAWUNG (Java)

Military training dance, instituted by the Sultan of Joghya, for developed ability in use of weapons, and "unarmed combat". The *Lawung* company has four soldiers and two clowns, who attack another group (or divide their own in two) to commands of a *dalang*. This system developed into *Pentchak*[*] a scheme of wrestling and dance movement (we may compare with *la savate* in France). With dance prevailing the exercise is *Lawung;* with fight dominant, it becomes *Pentchak*. The *Taman Siswa* school of sport, started in 1922 by K. H. Dewantoro, made a point of including dance. We may compare with the Czech *Sokol*[*] Movement

LAY (Saxon)

Old French songs were called *Lais;* the term may perhaps derive from *lessus* (Latin) lamentations, complaints. In German there is *leich* (compare lych-gate, the place of pausing) connected with *reigen*, ring dances; and the song name *leid* (also a dance tune) was used by the *Minneleider*. Böhme gives a list of dance tunes, as *ringel* and *reigentanze*. In Hindu (Sanskrit/Prakrit), there is the widespread term *lasya*,[*] for the feminine dance.

LAZZI (Italy)

The lesser members of *Il Commedia dell' Arte;* also of similar itinerant companies (the Monte Banco, etc.); also the *Ge-Lazzi*, or *Le Gelosi*, one of the later companies; then, by derogation, the *lazzaroni*. The team probably originated with itinerant dancers from India—companies of low caste women, who offered the generic women's dance or *Lasya*,[*] (later "lasses"). Later, the term *lazzi* indicated the "actor's business", or stage movements or mime.

LECHWALLEN (Sweden)

"Death Dance". This funeral dance was celebrated

regularly in Bjuraker. For example: at the lake-side town of Norra Dellen, there is a grey stone wall, stretching from the shore to the church; this is for the "way of the dead", which is called *Lechwallen*—literally, the dance of the dead, the *lekha*. This funeral dance was performed until about a century ago. The dead person was conveyed to the outer end of this wall, either by sledge over the winter ice; or in summer, by rowing. The dance was started immediately, always on the Saturday evening, for burials were done always on Sundays. The mourners held each other by the hands, in pairs facing each other. These pairs took positions, side by side, in a great circle round the coffin which stood on a low bier or trestle. Then a slow ring dance followed, moving to the left, to music provided by a fiddler acquainted with the custom. This custom ran parallel with an old English rite, which began at the *leich-gate* (Lych-gate), the term *leich* or *lekh* shifted from the "display" to the dead man (as with mumming). For this reason, the body resting at the "gate of the last field", the wide cover was erected. The church porch (*perke*) had the same meaning. In Denmark a similar custom (bordering on *Wakes*, is called *ligvejt*.

LECTISTERNIUM (Latin, from Etruria)

Literally a feast of the gods at rest. The date BC 365 is noted as the introduction into Rome of a company of actors who performed in a *lectisternium*. In dumb show, with no verses in accompaniment, they danced to flute music. This was one of the earliest theatricalised Roman amusements from an older religious basis. The form suggests an imitation of a Hindu *scena*, in which the dancers performed on Kailasha, a peak of the Himalayan mountains, in a sort of *Götterdammerung*. In the Roman form, images of the gods were placed, reclining, and receiving sacrifices. For the *Epulum Jovis*, the god was shewn on a couch with Juno and Minerva seated on the sides. The later modes had three or four gods, all seated, around whom the dancers moved, inviting them to feast.

LEGAT BALLET SCHOOL SYSTEM

Carried on at school, Tunbridge Wells, Kent, by Madame Nicolaeva Legat, wife of Nicholas Legat, former dancer and first ballet-master in the Petersburg Academy. Nicholas Legat (1869 - 1937) was a son of dancer Gustave Legat (Swedish) and graduated in 1888. His method was the finest development of the Russian school—from Johanssen, Petipas and others—as opposed to the elementary Italian method used for the younger boys by E. Cecchetti. Nicholas Legat was appointed (on the

advice of C. P. Johanssen) as teacher of the Class of Perfection, in the Academy. His method combines the best of the Swedish School (of Bournonville and Johanssen) with the best of the French school from its prime period. Legat is the "teacher of dancers" rather than of students.

LEGONG (Bali)

A dance-pantomime by three girls between eight and twelve years old, performed at feasts, generally in the late afternoons. Lasting well over an hour, the performance is accompanied by full *pelangongan* orchestra, and relates *Lasem* and *Semaradhama* stories. The two principal dancers (*legongs*) are dressed from armpits to feet in tightly wound silk, overlaid with flowers in gold-leaf, and wear golden head-dresses with rows of fresh frangipani flowers. Their attendant, the *tjondong*, is similarly but less gorgeously attired. The dance is in four parts: (1) *tjondong's* dance with two fans, which she later gives to the *legongs*; (2) introductory dance of *legongs*; (3) the story; (4) final dance by all three. In the *Lasem* story (which is best known), after the *tjondong's* dance, two *legongs* perform with open, fluttering fans. When the orchestra plays the *Lasem* theme, the actual story begins, telling how Princess Rangkesari is

Legong Dancer.   BALI, INDONESIA

stolen by King Lasem, but will not yield to him; how he wages war on her father, but is foiled by a blackbird which flies in front of him (a bad omen), and Lasem is killed. The *legongs* portray Princess and King, a closed fan representing a *kris*; the blackbird is danced by the *tjondong*, who puts on a pair of gilded leather wings, and dances while sitting on the ground, fluttering her wings and advancing on her knees with birdlike leaps. While the three performers dance with economy of gesture, refined and stylised movement, the *djoeroe* tandak (a member of the gamelan orchestra) recites the story. A relaxed dance of farewell, by all three dancers, ends the performance. There are three *Legong* dances without a dramatic story, the dancers representing butterflies (*Koepoetaroem*), herons (*Koentoel*), and monkeys (*Djobog*). The origin of *Legong* is uncertain, but virtually the same dance is performed in trance by young *sanghyang dedari** at religious ceremonies, and it may have developed from a temple dance. According to legend it was, like the Javanese *Serimpi** and *Bedaja,** first danced in heaven by goddesses, who taught it to the dancers of a favoured earthly king. The dance is *Legong*, dancers *legongs*.

LEGONG DANCERS (Bali)

Begin training between five and eight years of age, and retire from *legong* performance at about thirteen, although they continue in other dances, and teach younger girls the graceful *legong* movements. Besides natural grace and physical perfection, those choosing young girls for training look for facial resemblance, since it is considered that if dancers can be found who look alike, their *Legong* will be good. Although but children, they perform the long dances without fatigue, falling into a semi-trance induced by hypnotic rhythm of music and movement. Formerly every raja had his own *Legong* group. Being beautiful and highly regarded, the girls often marry into a high caste on ceasing to dance. *Legong* dancers are treated as privileged people, being exempt from heavy work in the village.

LEG SHOW (American term)

Equivalent to English (Victorian period) of Art Dance; also among USA press photographers, known as "cheesecake" (Brooklyn term), in photographic prints for local culture. During the English Victorian period literature never referred to Legs (especially the feminine variety), as they were always "limbs"; and in theatres, the revelation of ankles was considered "daring". Even bedroom furniture had its "supports" carefully veiled in lace. Some historians believe that this fashion originated in the fact that Queen Victoria had bow legs; and never appeared publicly except in long skirts; and never rode a horse or a bicycle. Consequently masculine education had to be completed in Paris, as French ladies (before Sartre) admitted the material existence of legs; and proved the fact in music-hall dancing. Nottingham lace manufacturers particularly approved this fashion, alike for theatrical shows and for suburban front windows. Unfortunately the monopoly, once enjoyed and exploited solely by theatre managers, has been ruined, partly by Hollywood films and partly by modern seaside summer fashions. Some American managers; and European ballet producers appear so far to be unaware of these advances in human knowledge. Though it was known in proletarian quarters, the casual reference to a "leg of mutton" or a "leg of pork", was in polite circles qualified in literary terms as a "shoulder" or a "ham". G. B. Shaw portrayed this "fear of limbs" in his character Liza Doolittle, the chaste flower-girl of his play, *Pygmalion*. She covered the bathroom mirror with a towel, thinking it vulgar to look at herself. The last faint reflex of this social tact appears at Royal Academy Dinners : there is never a "nude painting" in the gallery where the guests are seated at the annual banquet.

LEHENSCHWINKEN (Germany)

Popular 16th - 17th century church dance, connected with traditional weddings. This dance, along with a parallel dance called *Kronentanz*, was forbidden by the Archbishop of Cologne in 1617. The name repays analysis since *lehen* connotes : "feudal rights" and a *lehensmann* is a feudal vassal (liegeman), this hints at the older Norman/French custom of the *droite du seigneur*. The term *schwingen* or *schwinken* is broadly the English "swinging" (known to military men as "swinging-the-lead"), and it indicates "to swing oneself" or to move in dance rhythm; but *lehen* is said in this connection to mean "to lend", or "to grant". *Lehenschwinken* may be compared with *Mailehen,** and both seem to suggest the familiar "trial marriage" or betrothal for a year. Nevertheless, the ceremony and its purpose were accepted by the church, as its performance within the building confirms, through the 16th century. The dance was in three routines : the march to the church, with martial music; the procession within the church to the ritual positions; and the ring dance in the centre, around the bridal pair, concluding the main ceremony. The arch of swords (or pikes, or flagstaffs etc.) was sometimes included, as part of the entry.

LEICH (Germany)

Tanz-spiele—a dance-song with uneven lines and

varying melody. In earlier Gothic: *laiks*=*tanz*; in Anglo-Saxon mode, *lac*=*spiel* or play (modern Yorkshire, "to *laik*" is "to play"). In modern German, *leichengesang* is a funeral or mourning song. Compare *Lakhon*—general oriental term for "play".

LEKOURI (Georgia, USSR)
A dance for men and women, usually performed after the *Lezghinka*,* in which the man has shown his prowess. During the *Lekouri*, partners never come face to face, as the dance pattern is continually changed with swift turns by the girl, followed at once by an equally quick turn by her partner. The girl dances, with downcast eyes. The quality of the dance is smooth and lyrical, in contrast to the vigour of the solo *Lezghinka* which precedes it. *Lekouri* is said to represent the cautious following of a treacherous, zig-zag mountain path.

LEKSTUGA (Sweden)
Winter Dance Meetings, formerly traditional; now organized by various national or local societies, as *Samkvams* or *Gilledanser* (social or festive dances) principally round about the New Year holidays, but through the long winter. The visitor may see such dances as *Renningen** (Weaving Dance), the various *Kadrilj** forms, and many steps of *Polska** (as well as the *Waltz**) which originated (it is believed) from the *Hambo* (*Hamburger Polska*), in variants like *Tyska Polska*; or others associated with certain towns; or even the *Halling*,* which is a Norwegian dance. For men are several acrobatic styles of dance, which include vocational miming, such as *Kopparslagaren* (Coppersmiths) or the *Skobodans* (Hunters' Dance). Even more agile are *Orfiladans* (Boxers' Dance) and *Dans pa Stra* (over narrow lines, made of straw or chalked on the wooden floor to represent these limits), ending perhaps with the *Josseharads-polska* (cartwheels, in between polka steps). The *Svenska Folkdanzens Vanner*, now over fifty years old, was the first group to sponsor national interest in Swedish dance traditions, led by Artur Hazelius.
[See *Skansen; Svenska Tans*]

LEMAN (Mediaeval English)
Term frequent in Chaucer's writing, indicating sweetheart or partner; but derived as short for *alleman*, the dance partner in the Easter ritual, when the *almes* were distributed (Maundy Thursday or Allemaunde Thursday), and the recipients promptly celebrated their wealth with drinks on leaving the Almonry.   [See *Allemande*]

LEÓTARD
The close-fitting garment, of wool or cotton, widely preferred as a basic dress for ballet or other dance school practice. This item is made in a size and shape closely resembling the torso which it is intended to cover; and without buttons or tapes for fastening; the natural elasticity of the material being relied on for its remaining in position. The name derives from the acrobatic dancer Léotard, who is credited with having introduced "the flying trapeze" with the exchange jumps from one trapeze to another.

LESGAFT ACADEMY (Leningrad, Moscow, USSR)
An important Russian training school, concerned chiefly with (a) the training of athletes, and (b) the training of teachers for physical culture. Lesgaft, pioneer in Russia of such systems (apart from theatre and ballet-school training), was a student of the Czech *Sokol** Movement; and contemporary with Dalcroze and others, who influenced developments in the German schools of Modern Dance. In Russia, he came in contact with Isadora Duncan, but he was then young; and she was interested in poetry, not work. Soviet development of the Lesgaft system has been thorough and extensive, from primary schools to students of theatre. There are few schools which omit periods of well devised physical training; it is a regular occurrence in the great May Day Parades of Moscow (and other cities), to see groups of students appear. They will cease to march onwards, halting at suitable places (especially in the wide Red Square), and taking form, will display exercises and evolutions, many of them based upon or showing folk-dance and ballet movements. Working between the Lesgaft academicians and their schools, we find the few Modern Dance Studios, partaking of the qualities both of athletic work and the broader portions of ballet training; while the Circus Schools, who regard rhythmic physical training as an essential basis for their work, also make use of numerous dance exercises. Even footballers find that dance training helps their speed and accuracy.

LETTER AND NUMBER
All letter-systems had alternative usage in calculation. They were all associated with temple plans or ritual charts; they were large enough to dance over, across their basic circle or square, or along the perimeter. The plane figure supplied geometry; the count around the rime or across, the step of the arithmetic. These gave Space and Time; the *litra* further symbolised the Sound. Sanskrit had 49 letters—Sound, Position, Value. These are often included in the Dancing figure the *Nata Raja*. Hebrew has 22 main letters; points were added to Sound or Numeral values. The Latin system, or our "Roman Alphabeta" or "First-and-Second forms" replaced the Greek Omega circle or *Alpha-*

Beta-Omega count. The Roman *litra* system carried a brief set of Numerical values; these we still find on our clock face in circular layout; also on tombstones and some publishers' dates. The Roman letter-numbers are not consecutive beyond the first decade; nor derivative in geometrical form. They were used in the Augur's Dance; they belonged to his calendar, for hours, and days, and years.

I   II   III   IV   V

X ten   C hundred   M thousand

D five hundred   L fifty (half of ☐)

LEVÊE (French)

Term used, and originated in France, for a court morning reception; and so copied in Britain for the same ceremonial; thus giving rise to the phrase, "to dance attendance". Formerly the levée was a semi-military occasion; and "dress parade" was held, with a display of drill and manœuvres, approaching a choreographic system. This parade ground was much loved by Louis XIV and his son; and was equally enthusiastically adopted by Wilhelm II of Germany. The Levée was often the occasion for a luncheon (more especially for ambassadors thus "received") and in Russia (also France, for a time), was followed by a visit to theatre for a ballet. Paris also had, for a short period, formal afternoon dances. The distant original term appears to be connected with regal interviews with revenue officers; concerning the levying of loot by way of taxation, either regal or legal. This court ceremony has seen constant change; and in Britain is almost obsolete in its earlier form.

LEVENTIKOS (Modern Greece)

Also *Levantikos*. A couple-dance performed by two men or two women, moving side by side. They perform the same steps, but neither look at nor touch each other. The traditional steps are quick and smartly done, varied in character and precise. The influence of ancient ritual continues in the etiquette; the dancers always gaze straight before them. The music is supplied, usually, by the ordinary "dance band" led by a fiddle, with a zither and clarinet, or reed pipe. The dance music carries always a strong rhythm, often with a light gaiety.

LEZGHINKA (Caucasia and Georgia, USSR)

A male solo dance originating among the Lezghis of Daghestan in the Caucasus, and adopted by the Georgians. A wild, vigorous dance, it is said to imitate the attack of an eagle on its victim. Circling on tip-toe, with small, swift steps, round a dagger on the ground, the dancer suddenly kneels, seizes the dagger in his teeth and rises again.

He wears the Cossak dress of long, belted coat, with soft heel-less boots and fur hat. Because of their mountain homes and the necessity of balancing on narrow paths and ledges, the Cossak can rise easily on to his toes, and the dance shows rapid footwork with little movement of the body. It is sometimes given, without the dagger, as a courting dance. With swaggering gait, the man dances with swift, neat steps, this tip-toe progression contrasting dramatically with the vigorous, wilder steps. The *Lezghinka* is often followed by the *Lekouri** (a more lyrical pair dance), in which case the first dance takes the form of "showing-off" by the man, before he and the girl dance together.

LIBRETTO (Italian)

"Little Book", in effect, the creative synopsis of the theme of a ballet or other mode of dance-drama. Ballets must reveal some sort of "development by action", which is dance; but not all of these are accepted as "plots". The so-called "abstract ballet" is the modernist type which eliminates meaning, in preference for movement; it has no "book" or libretto; it cannot be explained; and it cannot receive adequate description (which militates heavily against ultimate publicity). As with music, such ballets have to be spoken about mainly in technical terms: minor criticism of technique replaces the major criticism of art. There is an effort to replace or reinforce *libretto* with notation; which is as acceptable as, say, the creation of a work of architecture, which also can rarely be explained in words: it must be experienced. Yet most stage works are better produced, if everyone concerned knows what is attempted; this can be told, sometimes, in a few words with some action, such as the synopsis of mythic drama or plays, known as parables (*parabolos*). However much the creator or producer rejects words, he cannot reject usage of some formal devices (outline drawings, stage plans) in association with the music, to fix main points of time, place and change of position. Thus a full "notation chart or book" will contain these elements, as did the system used by Stepanov in Petersburg. The French analogy was called *prétexte* ("excuse for action") or *intrigue* ("the winding"). The fact remains that, according to its genuine historical development, a good ballet should make itself clear in and by and through its complete action, in dance and music, mime and setting.

LIFE, Dance of (Egyptian)

Was summarised in the apparently abstruse hieroglyph (priest-notation) of a dance diagram—the ritual dance of ten loops known later as the sign for *sa-en-ankh*. This we should pronounce as essans (life). This ritual was one of the movements performed by the Phara-Oh as king-priest. By it he received the "strength of Osiris" which he was able to conserve and render to his subjects—it was in fact an action of mana, representing a real life daily occurrence. It gives the formula for ingestion of food (alternate rhythm, alkaline saliva, acid stomach and so forth). When the ten-loop is laid over the form of a body; or on the Tree of Babilu, its rhythmic swing affirms the flow of food into blood, illustrated by an example of circulation. This was one of the patterns drawn on the temple floor, probably thirty feet long; and rendered to a chant.

LIFT
In Dance is featured as a feat in ballet (usually too often)—an action that requires as much technique as mere strength. Male students are set to practise, in some schools, with sand-bags, or canvas gunny-bags. These should weigh less than the ninety pounds of a dancer, being a dead-weight; harder to shift and lift. The "dance lift" demands close co-operation. The moment of "breath intake" is important, since the slack or "dead weight" body remains heavier. In addition, the girl has to make a slight spring (which should not be so vigorous as to be noticeable), which takes her a few inches upwards. The dance lift is not similar to those used in wrestling or *judo*, where the basis is contest rather than agreement. The male part of the effort is closely connected with the rhythm of breathing (and consequent state of energy), so that the upward movement must be correctly timed, in relation to the full lungs. It is also advisable for the male partner to know where he is taking the girl, and why.

LIGHT ON THE DANCE
Is a primary modern problem, since most theatres display performances only under artificial light. Open-air daytime theatres, like the *stadium* or *corrida*, or the imitation "Greek Theatre" are relatively few. From the erratic illumination of the *café chantant* or the *cabaret*, we move from the naptha flares of the Victorian Fairground, to the contrived electrical glare of the up-to-date circus, or other itinerant display. Their aim is solely and simply to illuminate; to let the audience see what is going on. This remains as the highest aim with nearly all displays of dance. Film directors must arrange their lighting, to reveal action and to affirm colour; yet they seldom proceed to incorporate light and shadow consciously into their drama. Almost all entertainment remains at this store-window level, with the notion "Show the goods;

flatter them; conceal their innate faults"—but no more. The dramatic theatre puts on its frank imitations of daylight or moonlight; or may give hints, along with painted colour, to imitate winter or summer; yet rarely proceeds beyond this feat. Some mask dances have been shewn, with skilful beams of light, devised to enhance expressional character. One show arranged to change the hue of electric light in order to change the apparent hue of costumes; yet this was technical effect rather than dramatic expression. Scientific theories of light remain still uncertain. Impossible standards of alleged speed of "light" (through the universe) are stated, as though they never changed. Two "theories of colour" contend (as if one *or* other must be correct, not both, in their own action; as in fact, they are). These are seen in the "additive light" or the "subtracted colour" experiments. While gas-lighting continued, subtle effects were few (Irving delighted in them) but the extreme flexibility of electric light has not been utilised by the stage director so much as in films; and not much in them. The conventional notion of "showing line" in ballet rules to the exclusion of emotional impulse and effect by means of light and colour. Technical means now exist, but they remain unexplored in terms of psychology, though examined in terms of vision. The folk-dance, as done in full daylight, retains the traditional advantage of light, while the enclosed theatre lags behind; it is behind even the artfully devised effects of ritual in religious ceremonial—as in the *Lux in tenebrae* ceremonial.

LIMERICK SONG DANCE (England)
Despite the Irish name, there seems little connection between this verse form and the town of Limerick. Though Edward Lear wrote some, they existed long before his time. Many are contained in collections published through the 19th century. (*Adventures of Fifteen Gentlemen*; Marshall, 1822, and *History of Sixteen Wonderful Old Women*; Harris, 1821, give the oldest known array in print.) This verse form has few tunes; one is almost the standard; and this was used, about 1910 - 1920, by sundry groups of seaside entertainers called Pierrots. They used a white clown costume. Using the basic tune, they gathered in groups of five, each singing one line, followed by the chorus, in refrain:

"That *was* a nice little song;
So! sing us another one! *Do*!"

Following this came the dance, based on the perennial music-hall circle known as the "Walk-round Martin"; always clockwise, done by one dancer, here the chief singer, the bass. The Limerick was highly popular with troops, in 1914 - 1918 war, usually with libellous verses that never gained publication; many written by camp poets, especially for some unusual occasion and sung at camp concerts.

LIPSI (Poland, East Germany, etc.)
Term derived from Calypso,* for a new socialist dance" described by Kurt Henkels, dance band leader (1959) as a kind of calypso "with a strong propaganda content, set to music in six-four time". An "instruction" had been given that over sixty per cent. of his tunes must be written by communist East German composers (*D. Tel* report. 22nd July, 1959). The "Youth Festival" then organized for Vienna, declared the "Festival Dance" to be the *Blue Danube*. There are no words. The *Lipsi* was to supplant rock-an-roll or *cha-cha-cha*.

LILIU-E (Hawaii)
A popular women's standing *hula*.* Steps and arm movements describe the beauty of the Hawaiian Queen Liliuokalani. The *olapa* version (danced without musical accompaniment other than gourd beat and chanting) is in lively tempo, but is slower when danced to instrumental music. The solo dancer uses symbolical gesture language in which hands, feet, face and eyes convey the desired meaning, so that the dance may be "read" by the informed spectator. The Queen is described sitting on her throne. Flowing, graceful movements refer to her kind heart; her large, beautiful eyes always seeking the truth; her plump cheeks and well-shaped face; the graceful swaying of her shoulders; her dimpled knees; the music of her voice; and the crown of flowers on her head.

LIMBO (Trinidad)
Solo male dance—relic of a ritual; performed in a ring or before the group. Clad in white trousers, with bare torso, rubber shoes, the male dancer shuffles in narrow "eights" before a bamboo "bar" painted white. This indicates his spiritual troubles, in approaching salvation. To end he bends far back and passes under the bar, held about three feet high by two watchers.

LISHKA (Hebrew)
The Banqueting Hall, in which many feasts were held, with appropriate music and dancing, (*Sam.* ix, 22), similar to the Grecian *lische*. Ceremonial circuit of the large hall was the basic movement, first with some trumpet (or announcement for readiness), and then of the dishes of cooked food. This form is the origin of the *entree** in later festal dancing; it derives from this semi-religious observance, that stems from the idea of sacrifice. This was practised in the libation (pouring out the first drops "to the gods"), and continues now in "drinking toasts".

LISTONES, DANZA DE LOS (Mexico)
("*Ribbon Dance*".) Similar to the modern *Maypole Dance*,* though more vigorous, it consists of winding and unwinding ribbons round a pole. Usually performed by men, the dance sometimes forms a figure in a longer dance, such as in the *Negritos** and the Yaquis *Matachines*.* When performed as a separate dance, half the men dress as women, in the local female costume—full skirt, and *quexquemetl* (cape-like, sleeveless blouse); wig of long hair, many bead necklaces, and an embroidered kerchief on the head. The other men wear bright coloured suits, with wide-brimmed, feather-decked has. *Danza de los Listones* is performed at *fiestas* in Yucatan, Campeche and other districts.
[See *Cinta Dantza; Courdello, Lei; Cordon, Baile del*]

LITHOPHONE (Greek roots)
Literally: "Stone-sounder", a name applied to a set of five stones, excavated in China; and believed to present a set of ancient musical notes, since their sounds give an octave. This percussion mode of sound-making is an oriental form, followed into modern times by the so-called "wind-bells", made by the Japanese; usually from a set of rectangles of thin glass. Hung in a breezy position, they move with a tinkling sound. Pieces of jade will also emit notes, usually too high for musical use, since the sections are too small. These five stones are in the *Musée de l'Homme*, in Paris. We may compare the usage with (a) xylophone bars; and (b) metal bars, or round plates, then called gongs;* and (c) metallic tubes, as originators of percussion sound. More developed is the Hindu use of a set of porcelain bowls of different size, *jalta ranga*, filled with water until each one gives the required note. All these percussion instruments are used to accompany dancing. Chinese chimes were angular or circular discs of marble or jade, tuned to various notes, suggestive of toy dulcimers with metal slats; they were hung on a frame and tapped.

LLAES LODRAU (Welsh)
Typical professional attire of the mediaeval minstrels, strolling players, and others (distinguishing them from itinerant monks), and known in English as *galligaskins*. Their last relic is in gaiters, as foot covers (part of Bishop's uniform). The *galligaskins* demanded no great skill in fashioning from the mercer; they indicate "loose breeches". Later they were adopted by women; and so began another aspect of fashion in attire that has appeared in various modes connected with dance; until, in modern stage usage, they have disappeared from public view, after having become—from *Llaes lodrau*—a filmy garment known as lace-drawers.

In parallel, are the more tightly fitting integuments favoured by Italian male comedians, and named pantaloons, from their use by one leading character, Panteleone (of Venezia). These became known to store-drapers as pantaloons; again to be seized by women under the appellation of "panties".

LLAMDDAWNSIO (Wales)
A Quick Dance, or Jig : and, more closely, a "striding dance", used to describe the Welsh mode of Galliard;* alternatively noted as Hoyw-ddyn (Hoyden)—a "gay, sprightly dance".

LLONG (Welsh)
An ark or box, or a ship; sometimes a strong chest made in the form of a ship. This compared with the silver nef or "Great Salt" made for mediaeval tables, also in the form of a ship, a galleon in full sail. As ark or arkha, the Greek applied the term to a sacred chest (also kista or cista). In Druid and later Welsh ritual, the "arc" was made as a form of the dancers, surrounding the wooden arka or arche. Earlier in Britain (from Greek influence) the ark was the symbol of doctrine, containing sacred implements. The Latin arceo signifies "to enclose": the "ship-shape" enclosed the ark-as-altar. The term is widespread; in Gothic as arke; in Gaelic as airc; in Irish as airg; while it gives place names like Llanark. In secular Welsh, ark means a coffer with a lid, a container for meal or flour. The older Egyptian form was bark or barque: both as ship and container. The essential symbolism was that the ark was a holder of souls, the soul-power. In the Latin system, the secret doctrine was by later men named arcana, and Bible translators used the term to indicate the sacred Jewish coffer, the box for the sacred scrolls; thus a moveable altar equipment, a centre for sacred dance; also carried in processions.

LLONG-GRAWYS (Welsh)
A Ship Festival: or Company Feast. This is probably the origin of the unexplained term found in association with the 17th century books of Country Dances, compiled in the Restoration Period for town usage; and usually given as "Longways, for as many as will".

LLORONA (Mexico)
A pair dance in the State of Oaxaca. Although meaning "The Weeper", Llorona is a courting dance of pursuit by the man and mock elusiveness by the woman, and the accompanying song tells of Latin passion rather than sorrow. It seems to have no connection with the melancholy figure of Mexican folk-lore, La Llorona, a weeping, shrouded woman who wanders at night in lonely places, seeking her lost child. To music in three-time, the man moves in a circle pursuing the woman, who glances provocatively back over her shoulder. The step resembles that of the Waltz. Sometimes partners separate and meet again, their movements in duple time forming a counterpoint to the triple beat of the music. The dance is similar to the Sandunga.* In Tehuantapec, the splendid costume of the Tehuanas (native women, famous for their beauty and grace), adds to the effect of the dance. Moving with haughty carriage, they wear a long, full skirt with starched and pleated flounce twelve to fifteen inches wide at the bottom. Over the huipil (a loose, sleeveless blouse), is worn the curious bidaniro or head huipil—a white, stiffly starched garment shaped like a small jacket but never worn as one. For fiestas it falls back from the head, the starched frills flowing down like an American Indian feather head-dress; but for church the stiff frill of the neck opening frames the face, the garment falling over upper arms and torso like a cape.

LOBSTER QUADRILLE (England, Victorian period)
Is first reported in the classical school book[1] by one Lewis Carroll (pseudonym of a famous Oxford don, skilled in mathematics). Though the quadrille dance formation appears to have been suggested by the current interest in Fourth Dimension (Dr. James Hinton or Babbage etc.), the historical fact is recorded in this famous work: Alice in Wonderland, that the actual dance form was a round, and that no lobsters were dancing. The Lobster Quadrille forms Chapter X of the twelve, where the dance routine is fully described, though difficult except for Abstract Ballet. Said the Mock Turtle to the Gryphon: "We can do without lobsters, you know!" and then "they began solemnly dancing round and round Alice . . . waving their forepaws to mark the time—while the Mock Turtle sang this, very slowly and sadly:

"Will you walk (i.e. dance) a little faster, said a whiting to a snail,
There's a porpoise close behind us, and he's treading on my tail.
See how eagerly the lobsters and the turtles all advance!
They are waiting on the shingle—will you come and join the dance?"

Then follows the stately lines of the chorus—which at a Festival Hall (London) production of the ballet, was skilfully recited in Chinese by the Director of Art. He said, distinctly and mournfully:
"Wei-ul-yu, won-chou, wei-ul-yu, won-chou, wei-ul-yu joihn the darns?"

and so forth. Later in this descriptive chapter, the Dance of the Lobster Ballet is mentioned, again in verse, concluding:

"so he with his nose—trims his belt and his buttons, and turns out his toes".

All ballet students will recognise this exercise. The Mock Turtle enquires:

"But about his toes? How *could* he turn them out with his nose, you know?"

"It's the first position in dancing, Alice said . . ." She has previously referred to a dance critic, renascent in the ballad (given in full Ch. V., *Advice from a Caterpillar*) which begins "You are old Father William . . ." This Grandfather William, who sported a resplendent scarlet vest, appears to have been a ballet-master, but fell into advertising and journalism. For further information, the student is referred to the several books by this Victorian master, necessary in all dance academies and garages.

[1] *Alice in Wonderland.* Lewis Carroll. See also *Alice Through the Looking Glass* (C. L. Dodgson).

LOCHABER SWORD DANCE (Scotland)

Said to be the same as the Eightsome Reel, reported to have been danced when Prince Charles Stuart landed, in 1745, at Moidart. There were then "Eight Men of Moidart", selected as a bodyguard, who danced this Reel in the celebrations.

LOKUTA (Sudan)

Tribe living in the Torit District (one hundred miles approximately, east of the Nile and north of Uganda); Hamitic-Negro people, who wear little, and favour a pair of rubber shoes and necklace. Christian converts have clothes imposed on them (by missionaries) which they discard on return to their village. Lokuta girls walk in the village attired in rows of watch-chains fixed to a narrow belt of beads; and, behind, a bandanna square. At a hunting-dance, observers noted blue-tinted skins (alleged to derive from laundry blue). They are polite; kissing is immoral. The rain-chief, *kobu*, controls some dance-rituals; they will operate only just before the regular rainy season. There is a New Year Dance, following a ceremonial foray, *netabiji* ("Shed blood now!"). For the Hunting Dance they have long oval shields of white buffalo hide, marked with a huge black half-ball of ostrich feathers (probably symbolising enemy heads), and carry long, thin spears. They wear tin helmets with great black and white plumes of feathers. The great New Year's Dance is a ritual of worship to Hollum (creator of the people). The women use everyday costume (goatskin skirts), but add make-up of red ochre or white flour paste. Music is led by a high drum (some have identity names), whistle, and low-toned trumpets. Men ranged in age groups step high in a circle; before them the women stand, swaying, urging on masculine vigour; while on the side lines, small village maidens copy intricate steps and body rhythms. They will dance for hours in silence; but the men shout martial songs. The drummers are at the centre, lavishly decked, beside the sacred vertical drum poles; each man with his special melody. All men carry ivory or tusk arm bands; many have a brass tomahawk. One dance costume is a cattle-horn trumpet, held by a chain on the neck; strings of jingling bells; a leopard skin casually tied on; or a colubus monkey skin (black and white) tied to the waist. Hair tufts taken from dangerous animals are trophies of a real chase. Wealthier men favour large plates of shining brass: neckband or pendant on the chest. Missionary medals are hammered into necklace discs. There is a regular funeral dance, done around the compound of the dead man's hut. The rain dance fills in intervals marked by the conclusion of all jobs possible in dry weather: they "sit and wait" or "run and dance". Married women join the dances. One drummer stands exhorting, on top of a pile of drum poles, bearing two white feathers on his head; ivory collar and armlets; white socks.

LOLLARDS (or Lullards) (West Europe)

English version of name of followers in doctrines of Raymon Auliya; known in France as Goliards (see *Galliard**) or Holyards. The Lollards were effective forerunners of the English Reformation, with centres in London and at Oxford, where John Wyclif, as Master of Baliol, was one of the best-known leaders. Raymon el Auliya was born in Majorca, son of a Moslem mother and Christian father; he learned both doctrines, and sought at times to unite the best from them. After studying and teaching in Paris, he visited Oxford, and first instituted there the study of oriental languages. With him came friends, bearing Arabic songs and music, and ritual dance forms. Few musical historians know of the immense debt they owe to the Lollards, for the metrical versions of the Psalms introduced by them; and later accepted and spread by other reformers. The decline of ancient minstrelsy that had accompanied the 14th century decline of the Roman church, left room for newer church music. Popular songs and dances at that period retained true rhythmic melody; though the court musicians disdained to cultivate melody (as they do now) in their work. During the reigns of Henry VII and Henry VIII, to those of Mary and Elizabeth, English music knew a complete change. The Persian-Arabic culture that had ruled in Spain for eight centuries was destroyed; but its vast influence remained in France, and moved into England.

In churches, the Psalms were sung to dance melodies; while in secular feasts the dancers used
church rhythms; though the days of dancing in
church (which had formulated the early mass ceremonial) were ended. We know only fragments,
such as the Easter mass dance at Seville, where the
Musarabic system had ruled.

In France, the *galliard*; in England, the *Lull-abye*
(*zhikr* melody).

[See Trans. by John Wyclif of *Song of Songs* (*Shir
al Shirin*) entitled *Ballete of Ballettes*]

LONGWAYS (Folk-dance term, England)

Means "ship-wise" or shipways, with the dancers
placed in the outline form of the "Ship of Salvation" formerly used in church ritual dance. The
name derives from the old Welsh *llongsaer*, and
the Gaelic *longsaor*, both meaning ship-builder, or
a resident longshoreman, as opposed to a ship-
sailor who travels. The 19th century Russian
peasants had a dance in the form of a ship. In
modern folk-dancing, the dancers are in two long
"sides" facing.

LO PAN (Ancient China)

Is the most ancient schematic plan of ritual in
existence. This net-tablet (also called *lo-king*, net-
standard), appears to have been co-existent with
the *Ming-T'Ang*,* and has continued its tradition;
while that of the Temple has been almost lost. The
Lo-Pan contains the scheme of the *Pa-Kua*, the
trigrams; and the total popular modes of *Feng-shui*
—the dance of "wind-and-water" (to use the superficial version), while it carries also, at its centre,
that strange yet familiar instrument, the Mariner's
Compass, known symbolically as *t'ai-chih* or the
"Great Origin". Pragmatically, the *Lo-Pan* (copies
of which can be purchased in any populous Chinese centre, by a persistent enquirer) carries their
basic scheme of divination. Behind this, the religious
scheme of the *Yang-Yin*, whose eternal "Dance of
Energy" is established, and set forth, in a general
mode that offers the expert diviner a possibility of
"reading" for his local time and place set forth in
dance. The work is neither simple nor easy. A
picture of a modern *Lo-Pan* will be found in a
work by Dr. Paul Carus,[1] who says further (concerning the south-pointing needle) that :

> "It is a Chinese invention, which seems for some
> time to have been forgotten. Prof. F. Hirth
> (Columbia University) says it was employed in
> ancient times by travellers through the desert
> . . . it . . . became known in Europe after the
> time of Marco Polo . . ."

The name *compass* seems similar to that of the
Tibetan *gompa* (monastery), but the *Lo-Pan* offers
direction through the mental world, being connected with the ancient *Zodiac** for adjustment of
Time. The *Pa-Kua* presented a mathematical cor-
relation, similar to half of the *Muqabalah*, or
the artificial Hebrew script system, which was
earlier sustained by its "Urim and Thummim"*
divination method; with a peripheral division in
twelve (the "jewels"). The *Lo-Pan* seems to have
provided a "ready-reckoner" mode of calendrical
adjustment to the *Ming-T'ang*, which gave general
principles; so that the rituals of the *Yueh-Ling*
could be worked out by minor officials. In this
manner, the *Lo-Pan* would give "place and position" for the conventional ceremonial of any year
or month—certainly it contains symbols somewhat more complicated than a logarithmic table,
combined with chemical signs, related by atomic
formulae; as well as twenty-four constellations
and the magic square.

[1] *Chinese Thought*. Dr. Paul Carus. Chicago, 1907.
Science and Civilization in China. Joseph Needham,
1962.

LORD OF MISRULE (Mediaeval England)

Name wrongly applied to the elected King of the
Revels, customary for the "Twelve Days of
Cresten-Messe" during the Middle Ages of England. This name is a perversion of the original
title; which referred to the Lord of the *Messe
Revel* (or *reulle*, for the mediaeval spelling often
exchanged *v* for *u*, as the letter *u* was not known
in Italic manuscript production). The whole festival naturally surrounded the great Feast traditional
to the Winter Solstice, for which Twelve Days
Feast a King was elected. He was variously called
the Prince; the King of the Messe; or the Lord of
the *Messe Ruelle*, the circle (or square hall). The
term *Messe* (which survives in Germany as the
Trade Fair or *Messe*, as at Leipzig twice yearly),
implies the real original reason for gathering for
the Supper, alike on religious or secular occasions;
and has nothing to do with missions or dismissal,
or like alleged derivations. The Scottish equivalent
was the more obvious fraud of the title, "Abbott
of Unreason". During *Twelve Days Festival*, dancing was seen on each day. The Lord of the Messe
Ruelle faded from the English scene with the
Reformation, along with the Masques; its last home
in London was in the Temple of Gray's Inn.

LORENZO, DANZA DEL (Italy)

Children's Festival dance, performed always on the
"appointed day" of the "San Lorenzo", who was
guardian of the children's maze (popularly known
as the "grid-iron" which "puzzled", that is "tor-
tured", the children). The day is August 10th "when
innumerable children visit his church, and turn
(or dance) three times before the altar; or go round
it (walking or dancing) thrice for good luck, recit-

ing *orazioni*, incantations, and prayers. "*E ciascuna volta far mostra d'uscise de chiesa*" — this turning round for *luck* is a remnant of the old worship of Fortuna, with the turning of her wheel".[1] This children's dance is a forerunner, in the course of the year, of the regular occasions devoted to *Katerina** (for girls) and Nicodemus or *Nicolas** (for boys).

[1] *Etruscan Roman Remains.* C. G. Leland. London, 1892.

LOURE (France)

An old country dance with music similar to that of the *Gigue** but slower, usually in 6/4 time. The name of the dance was probably taken from the instrument which accompanied it, the *loure* being a bagpipe in many parts of France, especially in old Normandy, *loureur* being the player. Little is known of the dance form, but it is thought to have resembled a jig or waltz. The air *L'Aimable Vainquer*, said to have been a favourite of Louis XIV, was one of the tunes for this dance. *Lur (Luur)* was a great horn of prehistoric times in Scandinavia (Denmark and Sweden), shaped something like an S made of bronze.   [See *Musette*]

LUCIA, LUKHIA, LUGHAD, Etc. (Scandinavia, Ireland)

Belongs to the festivals of the Winter Solstice, particularly in northern latitudes. In Sweden, the celebration is accepted chiefly as the "Festival of the Long Night", though it is now dated chiefly for December 13th. As one of the principal symbols is the "Bride of Light", it is probable (before it was distorted by the irruption of Latin doctrines) that December 13th marked the beginning of this period — the Dark Month. The Bride Lucia wears a crown bearing six lights; she is herself the seventh, attired in white robes. The candles are fixed in a coronet of living leaves — sometimes whortleberry, dug from under the snow. Their dance, when these crowns are donned and lighted, is a slow movement, now rarely performed; and usually replaced by an entrée to a family feast, itself mingled with the garden visit to the *Vard-trad*, a tree especially denoted to represent that family; and by a ritual song or circle dance similar to the *Was Heil* of Teutonic lands. Cakes are eaten at the feast, with biscuits made to follow the svastika pattern, in four whorls. Some of the emblems are heart-shaped; and among others we may note the familiar *pretzel* — bread seen in Munich and other German towns. This Feast of Light should be compared with Asiatic rituals of similar character; also the Italian rites of "Lukhia, the Lamp-bearer" (and Luke, the painter etc.), who led in the Goddess of Fortuna; and the Celtic Feast of Lugh (Hu or

Hugh). Neapolitan singers repeat, as a popular ballad, the traditional song-prayer to "Santa Lucia". When these dancing ritual figures are detached from the pseudo-realism of supposed "saints", and replaced as the symbolical presentations of magnificent myths, we see them in their true proportions, and on a grander scale.   [See *Diwali*]

LUNDU (Brazil)

A song-dance in 2/4 time with guitar accompaniment. In varying styles, it shows a blending of African and Portuguese characteristics. Performed by a couple, the dance may be a charming display of graceful movement with a melancholy song, or a more vigorous dance with occasionally syncopated music. Predominantly European, the movement shows traces of African influence. The *Corta-Jaca*, in rapid time, is a variation of the *Lundú*. Both dances, are the prototypes of most Afro-Brazilian dances.   [Cp. Portuguese *Lundum*]

LUNDUM (Portugal)

An old song-dance for two people, popular in Lisbon from middle of the 18th to middle of the 19th century. The langourous dance accompanied by guitars, and a melancholy song, is referred to by the poet, Nicolau Tolentino as the *dolce lundum chorado* — "sweetly weeping lundum". The dance came to Portugal from Brazil, which country in turn had it from the West Coast of Africa. Portuguese writers refer to the melancholy character of the music, which was closely connected with the *Modinha* (a sentimental song in minor key). While the *Lundum* dance faded, the song grew in popularity, and some writers consider it to have been the forerunner of the famous *Fado*, the nostalgic singing of the poorer quarters of Lisbon. The *Fado* was, at one time, a dance closely resembling the Lundum; the two may have been identical.

LUNG (China)

Is "The Dragon" celebrated in three great festivals; and recognised in numerous aspects. The abstract analogue is *Pa-Kwa* : the "Diagrams". The natural aspects are observed in world phenomena : of *Feng-Shui* (Wind-Water) and many more, all amoral in action, affecting man as giving him locally joy or sorrow. Thus *Chu-Lung* is "to come forth in floods", which may become disastrous; but water in moderation is essential. The *Lung* is cognized (not "worshipped") at the Chinese New Year, and the following Lantern Festival, 15th day of First Moon. Thus "much light" is joined; natural light, and man-made. The processional dance of New Dragon is performed by twenty to forty men, dancing under a gigantic cloth or paper dragon, mounted on bamboo ribs, with lights in mouth and eyes. To drum and flute, this momentous figure dances merrily through the streets, swaying from side to side (*Sua-ung-t'eng*). Passing through many houses on the way (as with the "Furry Dance"* at Helston), it is welcomed, as its power banishes misfortune. Small boys imitate as best they can; wearing paper dragon masks, and doing their share with fireworks. Next comes "Fifth Moon Festival", now celebrated on water, as Dragon Boat Festival (*T'ang-wu*) said to have originated in Hunan, at Tung Ling Lake. The large boat is decorated in green; its steersman, dressed as a clown, gesticulates with humorous intent. Several boats may race; and many small boats carry spectators. In the Autumn comes the Festival of Eighth Moon, on 15th day (*chung ch'iu*), when it is traditional to ascend a hill or pagoda; and young people build an "auspicious fire". Dancing at these Dragon Festivals follows folk tradition, not aristocratic and solemn ritual. In Britain, the Dragon appears (as in Wales) as the Wyvern, the Red Dragon of the "Shield of Wales". The *Lung* of China signifies their conception of the electro-magnetic cycles of the natural year : to name them as "cyclones or anti-cyclones" does not further elucidate their cause and action.

LUTA, DANÇA DA (Portugal); (Fr.: *"lutter"* = "to struggle", or "to contend")
A mock battle in the form of a sword dance, given by two groups of men. One side, called *lutadores* ("wrestlers"), are dressed in tights and spangled black velvet, and carry clubs; while their opponents wear cloaks and helmets, and carry swords. Various figures are performed, with swords clashed against clubs, the climax being reached when the *lutadores* climb on to each other's shoulders in the form of a pyramid. This dance is a diluted version of the wide-spread *Mourisca* — a contest between "Moors and Christians". [Cp. *Perkhuli* (Georgia)]

LUTI (Persia)
A buffoon, a festival or market dancer, who carries a lute or rebab. He performs professionally at the *Chai-Khana* (or Tea-room).

M

MABCHA (Tibet)
"Peacock Dance". One of the dances performed during the Festival of New Year (*Losar*) by groups of dancers and musicians going from house to house. To a flute accompaniment, the dancer, inside a peacock figure made of *papier maché* and bamboo, imitates the bird's movements of strutting, pecking the ground, flapping wings.

MACABRE DANCE
From Arab symbolism, of *Magh Arba*, the "*Great Square*", as the formal symbol of the World of Man. Some religious systems present the *Circle* as the typical form of "heaven", with the Square as fourfold mode of Earth. Developed from *Rammal** sand divination, by dance tracks of four seasons, revised by impact of Roman augurs and their twelve seasons or tasks. The figures in the older (and most complete) form of the sacred ritual dance were four series of twelve in each, with another pivotal or moving figure, who appeared as a Jacque (Iacchus). Each of these series presented (in the "Mode of World") one of the four annual seasons, two in black and two in red, arrayed in a single line along one side of the court or ritual square. The last man, the thirteenth, stood at the end.
1. The square Table or place, the site of the New Year ritual, was the full scale mode of the world symbol with its fifty-two performers, plus the Joker.
2. The smaller Table symbols were made on cards, first drawn and painted, used by the actors; then later utilised in a schematic "play of fortune" by four players over a table.
3. The greater Table was the *Lauh mahfuz*, as the Cosmic "Tablet of Memory", but also, here, the Tablet of Divination — (the Past recalled to reflect the Future).

MACCABEE (Hebrew)
A much disputed term. First the word indicates a famous Jewish family (Asmonean) but the five *Apocryphal MSS* consist of allegory merged with pseudo-history. (Two are accepted by RC as canonical). The period of compilation is taken as 175 - 135 BC onwards, written by an Alexandrian Jew. Its ethic is chiefly Stoic (the "Straight Men") which runs with the brief note in *Kabbalah*. The word *MKBI* (*Maccabee*) has a numeration value of seventy-two which is the same as Schem-ha-phorasch, the *Divided Name* ("We represent the three columns of the Sephiroth"). This scheme of the *farrash* (Carpet) invariably indicated dynamic action, in pursuit of *Daäth* (which is Knowledge). The Rabbis then were members not so much of a "family" as a College, some possibly at Qumran (Koomb-Iran). Even today, the rabbi in the synagogue tends to break into some rhythmic movement as the cantor recites. But "*Maccabee*" is not a "Dance of Death".

MACE AND MAZE (Europe)
Parallel with the ancient tradition of *Mask*,* run allied ceremonials and rituals of the Maze and the Mace; with still further proliferation, into the terminology of May, mayestie, mayor, major, and

others. Associated with all of them we find ceremonial which frequently is dominated by rhythm in music and movement, bringing their form within the range of dance. The maze is a two-dimensional route, intended to delay and puzzle the candidate who enters its narrow ways; and we may say: "Straight is the Mace and narrow is the way that leads thereto; and few there be who find it!" For the dual symbol of Mace and Maze has continued to our own days. Many a full-scale Maze form changes from material obstacle into mental form, symbolised not by thick green walls of close-cut shrubs, but of printed papers (dancing in triplicate) in a "rule-and-regulation maze" of interminable hindrance; where the great Mace of the "council chamber" now changes into a smaller instrument, the pen-and-ink, which moves with erratic certainty here and there, leaving traces of letter and numerical in static form, sufficient to allay the demands of the lesser demons of the Bureau. This exemplifies the Maze of Civilization; here its institutions each wear a Mask; and each moves through endless corridors, similar to the Egyptian After-world of the Tuat, which swallows up suns and souls with eternal facility. This symbolism endures within the secret doctrine of many religions: Gilgamish wanders through the living world; or Persephone returns each half year; or Theseus ranges through the Labyrinth; or Loki wanders in the ways of Nifelheim; or Arthur's knights seek from the Round Table after the glittering Graal, as Herakles toils in similar fashion to accomplish Twelve Labours; or Jesus sweats through a series of stations of a Passion; or Krishna dances round his annual ring of smiling *gopis*, who ask no better heaven. Mace and Maze appear (masculine and feminine) in a hundred guises, for ever seeking and forever evading solution, in the eternal Dance of Hunger and Love.

MACEDONIA (Republic of Yugoslavia)
Has numerous traditional dances, many no longer connected with the ceremony that originated them. One is the "twelve-day" ceremonial (of the New Year) named *Rusal* or *Rusaliye*,* in mediaeval times associated with magical dances of exorcism, as well as dances of invocation. The centre with the tradition most clear is the district of Djeved-jeliya (Southern Macedonia), where the *Rusal* ritual still remains, though without the full equipment of costume and implements. These dances belong to the modes known as *Lesnoto* and *Teskoto*.* Older forms now danced only for festivals of any kind, include the *Petrovsko; U mensko; Kavadarsko; Tikvesko; Zlata; Todore Biro Kapidan; Saridjol Avasi;* and *Karajusif Avasi*. The *Kolo** (danced throughout Yugoslavia) appears in many

forms. Often traditional dances are accompanied by the singing of national poems, and the greater dances now exploit the heroic epic, the *sestna-esterac* (verse of sixteen syllables in line, sixteen steps in dance), and the *desetrac* (verse with ten syllables and ten steps). There is now a popular society for folk-song and dance, named *Bratstvo Jedinstvo*. Wedding dance-songs are accompanied with guitar and tambourine, as well as reed pipes or bagpipes. Sometimes the modern violin will lead instead of a singer, or fill intervals with the melody. The large primitive drum, *toupan*, is not heard so often.

MACHOL (West Africa: Portuguese Guinea)
In Nalú tribe is "god of dance", who appears at the youth initiations. These "mystics of Guinea" have been discredited with ceremonial cannibalism (by Landerset Simoes) through Southern Guinea, prepared by the witch doctor, or Babesse. They deny the accusation. They make elaborate dance masks, conventionalised pelicans and twining snakes, beautifully coloured in pale reds and greens, and purples, contrasting sharply with uncompromising black and white.

MACUMBA; or Ma-Khumba (Brazil)
Dance of the "Mother of Khumb" (or Cave Secret). A Brazilian dance liturgy called *Macumba de Exu* or Devil's Macumba, is cynically asserted to be devoted to "devil worship" on the theory that "the devil is kept in a good temper by propitiation", but it is not "devil worship". The dance ritual derives from the more ancient modes of worship of the Great Mother, a ritual systematically denigrated by opposing devotees of the Great Father, which generally displaced and evicted the older rites, hence denounced as "evil". *Macumba* is mainly a spiritualist séance, having as its pragmatic object the evocation of the ancestral spirits; thus giving them an outlet for their sorrows; and so causing them, when all is over, to retire in peace. It is a lustration exorcism, in one way, but a social form. Red and black are used as symbolic colours of blood and darkness. Songs used in the ritual often refer to Afro-Brazilian gods, such as *Xango** (in Nigeria, god of lightning). *Macumba* is known also as *Candomblé, Babacué, Catimbo,* and *Pagelanca,* and many Brazilian dances showing marked connection with African style, derive from it. Among them are the *Catereté, Chiba, Cururú, Coco de Zambé, Embolada,* and *Maracatú*. The *Cucumbi*, an Afro-Brazilian pantomime, similar to the *Congada*, is also closely connected with *Macumba*. (Ma-Khumba is the name of a Brazilian secret society with quarters in Rio de Janiero.)

MADAI (Central Provinces, India)
A Diwali Festival dance, performed by the Ahir (who are *dudh-wallahs* or milkmen). These men borrow or make the most highly coloured garments, adding peacock-feather crests (it is a Krishna Festival), with quantities of noisy ornaments, shell necklaces, and brass anklets or bracelets. Thus arrayed, they call on their ordinary customers (preferring the richer houses), and also others; where they dance and chant topical songs. They will visit also the local markets, with the same object of securing rewards. Their show has a form similar to the London *Dance of the Milkmaids,** which ended in the nineteenth century.

MAENAD (Greek)
Accompanied the worshippers of Bacchus, companions of Satyr or Faun. The term is from Egyptian *M'nit* or *Menat*—broadly a "girl with a necklace". As servants they had many subsidiary functions, similar to the Nurse or Hindu *devadasi*. Their tradition was in line with the doctrine of *Min*. We seem to have from it the term menial and the Scottish *meine* or Servitor, also the *mignon* (France) and *las meninas* (Spain).

MAGEN DAVID (Israel)
"Shield of David". The symbol formed by a pair of equilateral triangles, sometimes drawn with double lines; and (usually in the Brahmin form) interlaced so that the lines run over and under. These are said to indicate the Spiritual World (white triangle, apex upwards), merged closely with the Material World (black triangle, apex down-pointing). This pattern is famous in India as analogous to the "Great Mother Pattern", *Shri Yantra;* where it is used to supply original points in many ceremonial ritual dances. Another name used by Jews, for this pattern, is "Seal of Solomon", and the Arabs, who also use it, called it *Muhr-i-Suleiman*. Along with the pentagram, this hexagonal form was treasured by the students of Pythagoras of Samos; thence both have been adopted by modern Freemasons. The hexagram appears once more in the *hexantanze*, and it is "made" in *Morris Dance** as "The Rose".
[See *Yantra; Tangov*]

MAGGID (Jewish)
Generic term for a "preacher"; much used in the 17th century (post-1657) of the few Jewish preachers who founded the first synagogue of London after the resettlement. It was their custom to speak in eloquent terms, breaking into rhythmic motions (as did the rabbis of Warsaw and Lodz), as they chanted rather than talked. They used familiar exhortations so frequently that their congregations would recall and sing them, even in the street markets. By this means, there rose an array of rhythmic melodies, used later for dancing, as "Mr. Levy's Maggot", or similar terms. During this same period, church preachers frequently interchanged popular ditties for psalm or hymn tunes—they were sung much quicker than now. Precisely the same exchange of sacred tunes and secular words occurs now in Kenya, at the missions. [See *Maggot*]

MAGGIOLATE (Italy)
The May-day dance-songs, used by the *pagani* of the *campagna* (countryside), and often adopted and adapted by the *trovatori*, or itinerant companies.

Bushman Magical Dance. Four Bushmen of the Kalahari Desert seek to lure a boar. The chief waves the bright light, his second has the smaller light, the first female continues, while the line ends with the solitary spearman, cloaked. From a cave drawing in red ochre, Kalahari Desert.   SOUTH AFRICA

MAGICAL DANCE

An important part of all ceremonial magic; ancient or modern. Movements of the body, subjected to meaningful rhythm, are described as (a) position, (b) gesture, and (c) dance. All these may be artificial, or natural. Gestures are defined (by A. Crowley) as attitudes, circumambulations (and similar movements); changes of position; with knocks or knells. Magical signs are artificial or required gestures, belonging to ritual or liturgy. Circumambulation is performed *deosil* (sunwise, as clock hands move) or *widdershins* (reverse direction). There is also the spiral : centripetal or centrifugal. This movement approaches the dance. "There is also the dance proper; it has many different forms, each god having his special dance. One of the earliest and most effective is the ordinary waltz-step combined with the three signs of L. V. X."[1] Again this writer avers "All art is magick. Isadora Duncan had this gift of gesture in a very high degree; let the reader study her dancing; if possible rather in private than in public; and learn the superb 'unconsciousness', which is magical consciousness, with which she suits the action to the melody".
[1] *Magick*. A. Crowley (Lecram. Imp. Paris, 1926). Ch. X, p. 79.

MAGICAL RITUAL DANCE

Rhythmic movement in or over squares or circles, exemplify the schematic bases of (a) the religious mythos or concrete doctrine; and (b) the religious cosmic scheme, in its abstract doctrine. The principle linking them, and their parts, is the essential relativity of their "life and form", and affirms the necessity of explaining function by relation, as well as use, by form. Thus ritual dances, and mythic or dramatic dances provide the sole means of group exposition. Individual knowledge is gained, after this initial experience of mythos, by extraction of *dynamic* meaning out of apparently *static* forms, i.e. the god figures, their special arms and implements, their houses and their adventures. The key to this task is mentioned by K. O. Muller,[1] when he affirms the contrast of chthonic elements with terrestrial or heavenly elements. For us, an array of symbols can be gained, from comparative religion. We find a number of apparently diverse schemes; always backed by hidden abstract systems; just as "finance" is clarified by essential existence of commodities or services (*relations* of things, sellers, buyers, users, consumers). Here we find an array of Magic Circles, Magical Squares, Magical Octagons, or Magical Cross and Star forms. When dynamised by grasp of *function*, and their *relations* proved, they reveal the mystery behind god forms and god names. The preliminary task is that of dramatic ritual; as exhibited in terms of dance, with and without masks and disguise. The Circle may appear as a Shield (Apollo, Achilles, Hercules, the Salii* of Rome, *ankhiles*); or as a *Mandala** (Hindu, Tibetan); while the Square is seen in the *Templum*, the *Ming T'ang** (China), or the *Troy Game** (Crete). There is an apparent union of concrete/abstract symbol, when these Magical Circles or Squares are constructed in full-scale mode, so that devotees may enter them. Hence we have the Labyrinth,* the Maze,* the Pyramid, the Hindu temple, and the Egyptian temple, with successive sections and ritual performances pertaining solely to each phase. In some of these full-scale symbolic structures, the ritual dance appears as a journey (*Book of the Dead*, Egypt), or a double journey (*Prodigal Son* parable), or a ring-dance (*Krishna** and *gopis*), or a forest search (*Gilgamish* and his world maze), or a passion (Christian mythos), or a sea voyage (Ulysses), and in numerous half-obscured relics, known to us as fairy tales, or *märchen*, or *contés*. The magical "count" occurs in nine-celled squares (same addition any way), or round circles (chanting letter-words-numbers), and these enumerations rule the dance forms. The Hebrew-Arab *muqabalah* was an attempt to gain this knowledge by reckoning, on parchment or pavement.
[1] *Greek Literature*. K. O. Müller. 1840.

MAGGOT (English)

Country-dance of 16th - 17th century. Many dances are listed as, for example, *Isaac's Maggot*, or *Lang's Maggot*, or *Betty's Maggot*, *Captain's Maggot* — and many more. Though *Maggot* is the substantive noun, the term in general means a "caprice", defined as a fantastic notion. The equivalent French term *magot*, declares it to indicate a grotesque figure; though the word also means baboon; and, in connection with money, a hoard. Probably this series of dances lapsed occasionally into the jive or bebop of the period, when the Mohawks (the contemporary "tough guys") 1710 - 1715 were dancing. [See *Maggid*]

MAGI REX (Latin term)

Meaning the "Legend of Three Kings"; in celebration by a mime play with dancing at Epiphany on January 6th. The remains of the original legend are much distorted, chiefly by insistent realism. The first form celebrated the fact of three doctrines being united within the newer christian scheme : the teachers who brought them respectively from India (Buddhism to Syria); from Iran (to Asia Minor, Ephesus); and from Egypt (to Alexandria), were symbolised, partly by colour (Jasper is the dark man of Egypt), and partly by characteristic gifts. These three symbolic figures became known as the Kings of Colen (Köln, Cole, etc.). Jesus was himself named as the bringer of the revised Jewish "Law of the Prophets". In Hungary, these players are known as *Rëgos*, or Kings. The three kings in the popular legend were Jasper, Melchior and Balthazar.

MAGILLUH DANCE (Celebes Island)

A women's trance dance, performed during the annual *Ma-Maroh* festival for curing the sick. (See *Maroh Dance**). Accompanied by drumming, the dancers form a circle round the drum, moving elegantly, with small tapping steps, arms outstretched, and hands performing delicate rhythmic movements. As the drum rhythms increase in tempo more girls join in, the dance becoming faster and wilder, until some of the dancers fall into a trance. Considering this state to be an essential part of the *Ma-Maroh* ceremonies for expelling evil, the girls are treated by the medicine man, according to whether they are under the spell of good or evil spirits.
[Cp. *Sanghyang Dedari* (Bali)]

MAHAMANDAP (Hindu)

Or, *Maha-mandar*; *Mahar*=Great, *Mandar*=Circle. Traditional style of dance platform, provided for Hindu ritual ceremonial, inside a temple (as at Belur in Mysore state) or outside, as in Benares city on the Ganges. (There are many at temples through the Dekkan). At its best, this circle was contrived of black marble, perfectly level and smooth, elevated only a few feet above the open space. On it, in the fullest ritual, were drawn symbolic patterns, mainly in geometrical forms (*yantra*) with fine meal, white and coloured. The single dancer moved in and over these without disturbing the lines; from her movement, direction, position and gesture, erudite religious codes conveyed the arcane doctrine to the *adhikari* (enlightened ones). These dances were seen in Benares; in Mysore (especially during the dynastic reign of the Hoysala Ballalas, who ruled from about 1000 AD to 1300 AD. King Vishnuvardhan, last of the line (before the Moslem invasion) was building his greatest temple—on its ruins we find numerous sculptures expressing the profound symbolism of the Hindu dance-ritual. The use of some of the floor patterns was revived by Sri Aurobindo (in 1945) in his *ashrama* at Pondicherry; and his students danced over them.
[See *Yantra*]

MAIBA (masc.) and MAIBI (fem.) (Manipura, India)

Are the Hindu priests associated with all rituals; from exorcism and trance (including certain modes of hypnotic dance), and the oversight of the festival dance, *Lai Harroba*. Women predominate, after passing through a long probation, including ritual dances, of some nine months duration. Not all are chosen. Part of their tradition is concerned with telling fortunes; but, apart from running the ceremonials, she joins in spiritualist seances, with their complementary aims in exorcism.

MAIKOS (Japan)

Apprentice *geisha** in Kyoto, the old Japanese capital. Contracted by her parents to the manageress of a Geisha House at the age of about five, the *maiko* is educated, and trained in the arts and ceremonies that will make her a *geisha*. Lessons in dancing, singing and playing the *samisen* are of first importance. Traditionally her kimonos are brilliantly coloured, with long sleeves touching the ground, and wide brocade belt. Small bells adorn her lacquered pattens; and her hair, ornamented with trinkets and silk tassels, is worn in a bun or "half-peach". She is engaged at restaurants, to dance, accompanied by "elder sister" *geishas* as musicians; to hand dishes and serve *sake*. The money she earns goes to her manageress. At the age of sixteen or seventeen she becomes an "*ippon*" *geisha*, changes her style of hair and dress, and develops the wit and accomplishments of a successful *geisha*. In Toyko these children are called *hangyokos* ("little jewels").

MAILEHEN (Germany)

A popular wedding dance, which entered the church via the *Lehenschwinken** ceremony, as a survival of feudal "rights" parallel to those exercised by *die fürsten*; but here as the *Mailehen* for the villagers. The dance is one of matrimonial adventure; originally celebrated on the eve of May Day, sometimes called *Walpurgis-Nacht* (then transformed into the mythical "Saint Walburga"). and danced on Easter Monday. The centre of the occasion was the "auction" of the girls to youthful bidders; when the girls accepted the obligation to come to the village for a year, to dance with the youth to whom she had been "loaned". This was called "Betrothal-for-a-Year". The first dance preceded the May Day rejoicings; but the Easter dance, in church, became merged with *Kronentanz*. The *Mailehen* custom lasted until 1870. The auctioning of maidens was customary throughout Europe, as, for example in Poland during *Tlustni Dni** at Easter, and at the Rumanian *Tergul de Fete*,* or "Maidens' Market" on June 29th.
[See *Marriage Market Dance*]

MAIN B'ROK (Malaya)

Monkey Dance, *Main*=game. A dance which preserves older rituals. The rite is to cause the "Monkey Spirit" to enter a young girl of about ten years. First she is rocked in a Malayan infant's swinging cot (*Buayan*), while fed with areca nut with salt (*pining garam*). Gradually she becomes dizzy or dazed (*mabok*), when an invocation to the Monkey Spirit is chanted by a woman with a small tambour. Then the child climbs out (the swing having halted) and performs a dance, sometimes with unusual climbing feats, none of which she could do if not "possessed". When she droops, it is time to banish the Spirit, and the child is recalled by chanting her name. If this fails, she is bathed completely in coconut milk (*ayer niyor hijau*).

MAÎTRE DE BALLET
French technical term, which defines changing duties in the teaching, rehearsing, and production of a ballet. This "Master of the Ballet" is not expected to be "the poet" or creator of the whole enterprise (as was the *choregus* in Athens, who originated the basic idea, trained his chorus, and finally paid their expenses). The *maître* was essentially the stylist teacher; the corrector of technical style in the accepted conventional and "classical" form of movement. In this, he was the *maestro* in Milano; the ballet-master or ballet mistress in London. With the production of a ballet, his duties change; his name becomes *regisseur*,* the controller of the ballet form, as distinct from the ballet dance. In recent years, the choreographer has intruded into this domain, with results that can rarely be commended; while the final achievement has been for the dancer (or ex-dancer) to become the "Art Director", with even worse results, far from the efficiency of the experienced film director, who seldom endeavours to act as well as direct. In Russia, these distinctions are observed with more clarity; the ballet master directs "the class", but the producer directs "the ballet", while the choreographer contributes his formal expression in routine or group dance of the theme given to him. The *regisseur* in Russia commonly directs rehearsals, in part, in chorus, and in complete stage, and controls rehearsal music, but not the full orchestra. This system of integration works extremely well : the inevitable overlapping moves into consultation, and avoids dictation that elsewhere ruins ballet production.

MAKAVITZA (Ukraine)
A cake-dance of Russian Ukraine and adjacent countries, at village feasts; harvest festival, or at a rich wedding. This "dance of cakes" is performed by a ring of twelve unmarried girls; each one carries a piece of cake (made of flour and honey, and flavoured with poppy-seed) which she is required to bite, with the rhythm of the dance.

MAKE-UP
Began with ritual practice. In ancient Egypt, the Spring Festival required dancers with green attire and faces : they had to suggest new vegetation. Tribal rituals all over the world demand plentiful red; and in dark races, application of white clay for leading ceremonials. (See *Corroboree.**) In Aztec ritual (Mexico) the face of the dancer representing god or goddess was painted in the colours symbolical of the deity. From religious practice, the usage of facial make-up spread to secular dancers—in Egypt, India, Persia, Assyria, and other lands; and thus to palace dancing and eventually to occasions of home life. Inevitably this method of enhancement entered Theatre, first in court ballet and then in the modern bourgeois performances; thus it became necessary to analyse the various systems, to meet the different needs. The personal stage performance is the principal guide; but here, the precise quality of make-up must vary according to (a) audience distance, and (b) basic lighting conditions. The broadest mode is the Music-hall or circus style, where burlesque and caricature demand full accentuation. Rarely can the experienced circus clown be recognised without his professional make-up. Musical comedy (in theatre terms), comes next in scales of exaggeration; while the cinema film requires the paradoxical application of a definite scheme of make-up that shall, in most instances, "look natural". Here it is true that what does "look natural" varies with the spectator, producer, or actor; hence the need for one expert to oversee all the members of one company, so that their grades of naturalism shall be in agreement. Basically : the stronger the direct light, the more in contrast must be the hues and tone applied. For studio work, strong make-up must balance the heavy lighting used to light the scene for adequate photography; and here comes a difficulty : that of using an out-door (sunshine) make-up on a single character who appears in the next scene in some interior, under artificial light; a problem that does not arise for ordinary Theatre. Make-up must agree with (a) the character dramatically portrayed, as balanced with the person underneath; (b) with the particular costume, which may accentuate the person or the character, but can rarely do both; (c) the historical or modern "period" of the play setting; and (d) the particular setting—artificial or natural, stage decoration or studio set, selected as the container of the production. From this analysis it becomes clear that make-up is a wider term than at first appears; and that inaccurate make-up (not necessarily faulty, if considered for one person) may be inappropriate in relation to the rest of the production. Finally : the needs of personal make-up, when not

playing any dramatic character, must be met in
(a) the street or home life, as now thought essential
for the feminine population; or for (b) Television
appearance of public persons who are shown in
their individual character. In either environment,
qualities of facial form — or even anatomical form
— can be modified; and for Television must be
equated with the strong direct lighting used. The
fundamental principle in every aspect of make-up
is : "We see form by colour and tone, not by light;
we see reflection, not the original source".
[See *Grim*; *Mascara*]

MAKILA TCHURI (Basque)

"Stick Dance". Performed in France around St.
Jean-de-Luz, in the Labourd region; and in Spain,
near Saint-Sebastian, in Guipuzcoa. Danced by
men, in multiples of four (and sometimes by girls),
each man holds two short sticks, painted, and
decorated with short ribbons. *Makila Tchuri* has
more than one version; and can have five or seven
figures. Dancers enter two by two, arms at the
sides, sticks held vertically against the body.
Having formed two lines facing, the sticks are
struck together in various ways — against each
other before and behind the body; under the knee;
against their partner's singly, or while held together horizontally; swung in a small circle round
the head; and finally held crossed to form an arch,
through which the dancers pass in twos, and so
end the dance. The various changes of partners;
quick succession of figures; and variety of steps
performed in conjunction with striking the sticks,
call for concentration and make a spectacular
dance. The usual accompaniment is the Basque pipe
(*txistu*) and drum.
[See *Baguettes, Danse des* (Brittany); *Cardadora*
(Spain); *'Ndrezzata* (Italy); *Paulitos* (Portugal)]

MAKI-RU (Malekula, New Hebrides)

The second part of a two-part ritual cycle of death
and rebirth native to Malekula and the Small
Islands. On Vao it takes place a year or two after
Ramben,* the first part of the ritual. On similar
lines to *Ramben*, *Maki-ru* is more magnificent and
ritually more important, since it symbolises the
entry of the reborn man into a life even fuller than
that he attains at the end of *Ramben*, both cycles
being connected with the native belief in the
journey of the soul after death. (See *Malekula*,*
Dances of.) The main difference between the two
lies in the place of sacrifice; in *Ramben* the dolmen,
in *Maki-ru* the stone platform and monolith. *Maki-
ru* takes from seven to twelve years to complete, the first four (or more) years preparing
for the great sacrifice, followed by a period of
retreat for the chief sacrificers. Dances, occurring

at stated intervals, have special places in the
sequence of events. As in *Ramben*, the circular
Velal* introduces important rites, being danced
by all villages in rotation, when coral blocks have
been collected and a date is to be announced for
building the platform; again when a day is to be
appointed for setting up the monolith; and finally
in the last year, to close the cycle. When the monolith stone is hauled to the dancing-ground, a
few important Maki-men (initiates), dance *Taure*
before and round the stone as, at a similar point
in *Ramben*, the same men danced *Taur Na-mbak*.*
The fifth, most important year, opens with the
planting of an Erythrina tree in the centre of the
dancing-ground, which ceremony takes the place
of the dance *Hek-hekelean** in *Ramben*, indicating
that the Maki-men will now "settle down" seriously
to the rites, with no further delay until the final
great sacrifices of pigs. The feast, *Vin-vi-ghih*, follows, on the night of which *Taure* is danced round
the Erythrina tree, and subsequently at intervals
of five to ten days by all villages in rotation. About
five days later *Vin-buel* ("Dance of No Consequence") is performed by the home village and a
day appointed for the announcement of the date
of sacrifice. After the date is made known, *Taur*
is danced all night, and thence until the day of
sacrifice it is performed nightly from dusk to dawn.
On the eve of the great day, all villages join in this
dance, which is interrupted at intervals by the
women's processional dance, *Bot-mau*.* At dawn
on the day of sacrifice, a women's *Na-leng** figure
dance called *Rokaik** is performed in full, thus
differing from *Ramben*, when a fragment only is
danced. Parties from other villages arrive for the
great ceremony in procession, dancing the heavy-
footed *Na-rel** and, as in *Ramben*, there are no
further dances until thirty days after the sacrifice,
when *Na-leng* mumming plays and figure dances,
and the *Le-tean* song-and-dance cycle, are performed. *Velal* introduces the final rites that bring
the cycle to a close.
[Cp. Ritual cycles *Hevehe* (Papua); *Gol Kerma* (New
Guinea]

MALABAR DANCES (South India)

Folk Dances, *Kummi*,* *Kolattam*,* *Pinnal Kolattam*,
Mavilakku.* See also *Bhagavat*, *Bharata Natyam*,*
Kathakali,* *Kuruvanche*.* Most of the Folk Dances
are performed at Festivals, National or local, in
simple form and ordinary costume; usually with
accompaniment of song or chant; the music is
rarely more than a tapping of sticks, a drum-beat,
or a few cymbals.

MALAGASY DANCE (Madagascar)

A popular simple dance, in which men and women

join; formerly held each Thursday in the Queen's courtyard, as part of the general entertainment. Only at national festivals can the old traditional music now be heard; most of it has been destroyed by invading missions, infiltrating into schools.

MALAGUENA (Spain)

A local version of the *Fandango*,* belonging particularly to Malaga; also the name of an emotional type of Southern Spanish song. Théophile Gautier, visiting Spain in the mid-nineteenth century, found the *Malagueña* "poetical and charming". "The cavalier", he writes,[1] "appears first with his *sombrero* slouched over his eyes and his scarlet cloak drawn round him. . . The lady then enters draped in her mantilla and with her fan in her hand. . . The cavalier endeavours to catch a glance of the mysterious siren, but she manoeuvres her fan so coquettishly . . . that the gallant is baffled and retires a few steps . . . He rattles the castagnettes under his cloak . . . the lady pricks up her ears, smiles . . . throws aside her fan and her mantilla, and appears in a gay dancing costume glittering with spangles and tinsel, with a rose in her hair, and a large tortoise-shell comb at the back of her head. The cavalier then casts aside his mask and cloak, and the two execute a deliciously original dance".

[1] *Wanderings in Spain*. Théophile Gautier. 1840 (1853 edition).

MALAYAN DANCES

Were, until this century, performed almost entirely for ritual purposes, as a functional part of some festival ceremony, rather than for any commercial exhibition or even as a pastime. The "social dance" was unknown. These dances include some still practised at appropriate times; such as *Joget** (or *Joged*), similar to one of the same name known in Java and Bali; the *Main Gambor** or initiation ritual for girls; the *Monkey Dance* (*Main B'rok**) (another trance ritual); the *Henna Dance* (*Menari Hinei**) performed chiefly at weddings; and others such as *Palm Blossom Dance* (*Main Mayang*) and the *Dancing Fish-Trap* (*Main Lukah*), which belongs to a "spiritualist performance". *Main Dabus* is similar to a fakir dance.

MALEKULA, Dances of (New Hebrides)

On Malekula and the Small Islands off its northeast coast, there are three main types of dance—processional; circular; and the mumming plays and maze-dances called *Na-leng*.* All are connected with the long ritual cycles called variously *Maki*, *Mangki*, *Mangke*, *Menggi*; with the Gong-Raising ritual, *Turei Na-mbe** and with lesser rituals per-

formed at times of death, initiation into manhood, launching a new canoe etc. They are performed on the Dancing Ground (either rectangular with gongs along the upper side, or circular with gongs in the centre), but the processional dances also take place along paths leading to the dancing-ground or on the beach. Of these processional dances, *Na-rel** *Ro-mbulat*,* and *Bot-mau** are the most important; while the five circular dances *Velal*,* *Hek-hekelean*,* *Turei Na-mbe*,* *Taur Na-mbak** and *Taure*, though similar in form, each hold an important position in the prescribed arrangement of rites and dances; opening and closing the cycle, or preceding important rites. The dances are usually performed by men, accompanied by singing and nearly always by the slit-gongs made from tree-trunks and either erected upright or laid horizontal. Women sometimes take part, as in *Bot-mau* and *Rokaik*,* a women's *Na-leng*. On the Small Islands the *Maki* ritual, which may last from fifteen to thirty years, is divided into two parts—*Ramben** and *Maki-ru*,* with an interval of a year or two between. Each part takes a similar form, culminating with the same series of ceremonies and grand sacrifice of tusked boars, but *Maki-ru* is more elaborate and its ritual benefits greater. The whole double-rite is performed by each village on its own Dancing-Ground; and most of the sub-rites leading up to the final sacrifices have their appropriate dances. A year or two after the close of the double-cycle, it begins again, the men who "sponsored" the Maki-men now becoming the initiates, and vice versa. The principal figures are the *Mara maki* or Maki-men who, through a series of sacrifices, ensure themselves a place with the ancestors after death, and against annihilation. A mystical conception of the ritual considers that, at the moment of sacrifice, the ghost of the boar (itself identified with the Guardian Ghost who bars the way to the Land of the Dead) enters into the sacrificer, who thus becomes one with the Guardian Ghost, and filled with a power which will give him new life. After the great sacrifice the Maki-men go into seclusion, are "reborn" and take a new title and name. A physical and symbolical distinction between *Ramben* and *Maki-ru* is shown by the place of sacrifice—in the former a flat dolmen; in the latter a stone platform and monolith. Both are connected with the journey of the soul after death, the former symbolising the cave which the dead reach after passing the Guardian Ghost; the latter the greater paradise in the volcano on Ambrim, which higher initiates attain, where they dance all night and lead a life of bliss, with the ancestors. The *Na-leng* maze dances, performed after the great sacrifice in both *Ramben* and *Maki-ru*, sym-

bolise the passage of the soul through the bewildering maze set by the Guardian Ghost.[1]
[See *Sand Tracings; Labyrinth*]
[1] For full descriptions see *Stone Men of Malekula*, by John Layard. 1942.

MALEKULA—Dancing-Grounds (New Hebrides)
In Malekula and the Small Islands off its north-east coast (Vao, Atchin, Wala, etc.), there are two types of dancing-ground—rectangular and circular. Each village possesses one dancing-ground, which is the centre of the Maki* ritual cycles. Here the stone-platforms, dolmens and monoliths for the sacrifices are erected, gongs are set up and the chief rites and dances of the rituals are performed. On Vao, Atchin and Wala the long, narrow type is found, with wooden slit-gongs set up along the upper or men's side; while the circular kind, with the gongs in the centre, are found all over the south and centre of Malekula, and in the Small Islands as well. While on Vao and adjacent coastal villages on Malekula the dancing-ground is called *ne-sar*, the usual term is a variation of the word *(h)amal*, used alternatively for the dancing-ground and for the structure connected with it, i.e. the men's lodge called *ghamal*. Its general meaning seems to imply "the sacred place of the community". On Atchin the dancing-ground is called *amal*, on Wala *n'amil*, on Lambumbu *na amel*; on Lagalag *hamil*. [Cp. *New Guinea Dancing "Parks"*]

MALINCHE (Mexico)
Said to be the Indian pronunciation of Doña "Marina", the name given to the Indian princess who became Cortes' mistress, aiding him against her countrymen by acting as interpreter and intermediary, during the Conquest of Mexico. Malinche appears in several present-day Mexican dances, as a boy, or man in woman's clothes, wearing a girlish mask. In some she represents the Indian princess, as in the *Negrito*** dances, where accompanying songs refer to the treachery of woman as personified by Malinche. Huasteca Indians have a solo dance called *La Malinche*. Performed by a youth in woman's clothes, the dance conveys the remorse of Malinche (Doña Marina) for betrayal of her country. But in some dances she seems to be honoured. In *Acatlaxque*** the dance revolves round her, until the telescopic reeds held by the dancers are extended to form a canopy over her. Sometimes she is called Maringuilla ("Little Mary"), but this is obviously a Catholic addition. In *La Conquista*** Malinche appears as the companion, not of Cortes, but of Montezuma. Connection with pre-Conquest Mexico is suggested because she is often accompanied by some form of serpent —made of painted wood or articulated silver, or

even a small live snake. In Aztec religion, the serpent was the emblem of Quetzalcoatl ("Feathered Serpent", God of Wisdom). They were twined into a garment for Coatlicue ("Lady of the Serpent Skirt", Mother of the Gods), and recurred often in temple architecture. A high male official who supervised temple rituals was called "Snake-Woman", and at the Festival of Tlaloc (Rain God), among accessories of the dance were wooden snakes. In the dances where Malinche appears, she sometimes carries a snake in a small bowl. At a given moment, the snake escapes and must be killed either by one of the dancers or by Malinche herself. In describing the *Juego de los Voladores*,* contemporary historians such as Clavijero and Torquemada made no mention of such a character, although in some villages today she accompanies the "flyers". She may have been added after the Conquest, or the name Malinche may have been given to an already existing "man-woman" figure similar to the European "Bessie". Some sources give "Malinche" as the Spanish corruption of the Indian name Malintzin, belonging to Cortes' mistress, but confusion of Indian and Spanish cultures makes her origin obscure. Malinche appears in : *Los Negritos;*** *Acatlaxque;*** *Las Palmas;*** *Los Voladores;*** *La Conquista;*** *Danza de la Culebra; Conchero*** dancers have two Malinches among their officials.

MALKA NAGIRI (India)
Circle dance, seen in Malka and at Nandapuram. This women's dance is light and dainty, hands on shoulders only (no men) in short sari of white cotton. They have bells on their fingers and toes or ankles; their tattooed limbs move gracefully from ankle to knee; from wrist to elbow; with the left arm bearing many brass bracelets; and more on the ankles. The drum orchestra (three or four players), beats a rhythm for assembly; then another for the first circle of dancers; then they make a long straight line, headed by a leader who carries a wand with peacock feathers; this is used to indicate movement right or left, quicker or slower. As they dance, the girls sing a traditional song, all the while making the ring, with intervening curves, spirals and figures of eight. The drums quicken up each successive routine; until they are moving at full speed; and with larger and higher steps.

MAMA QUILLA (Peru)
Inca name for the Moon. In villages high on the Andes, the *Dance of Mama Quilla* is still performed on moonlight nights. Accompanied by flutes, pan-pipes, clay *occarinas* or *quenas*, drums and rattles (all known in Inca times), the adult population of the village begin a stately, rhythmic measure, which

gradually increases in tempo and fervour. With ever-increasing speed, men and women whirl round the square, until a climax of excitement is reached, when the dancers drop exhausted as the music dies away. Men wear striped ponchos; women long, full skirts, braided jacket, and vicuna-wool shawl close round head and shoulders against the cold Andean night. All wear the flat pancake hat of the Peruvian Indian, decorated with brilliant red, yellow and blue. In the Columbian Andes, on the borders of Ecuador, live a tribe called *Quillacingas*, meaning "Moon in the Nose", from a former custom of wearing a golden crescent as nose ornament, perhaps as worshippers of *Mama Quilla*, the Moon. The Chief's family wear a halo-like crown from which depend at the back, looped, coloured ribbons of various lengths. Each streamer tells an ancient tribal legend, reminiscent of Inca *quipus*—coloured knotted cords used as records. Their musical instruments include a three-foot long flute, giving bassoon-like notes.

MAMBILA MOON DANCE (British Cameroons, Africa)

There is a "Moon Society" or cult of moon worship, in which the Moon God is personated by a leading priest, who wears a string costume and animal mask. He appears at the rising of the New Moon; and is ceremonially given beer. The sacrificing priest then asks that by his grace they may have prosperity during the "month that he gives". Then follows a feast with circle dancing, fourteen dancers for each of the two phases. When the period is ending, the Moon Masker again appears; but now he acts the part of a "Dying God", bidding farewell to his people; desires them not to grieve, for "In three days and three nights I shall arise and bring you new life!"

MAMBO (Haiti)

Ritual dance of Voodoo; an initiation ceremonial which follows the ancient *Danse Shalame* (Salome) in its symbolic-realism. "Mambo" is the official name for the chief priestess. In the slow rhythm of the dance, she discards six veils; until the final phases when the priestess falls, herself entranced, to the ground. There sometimes follows a second phase in which she sits enthroned—similar to the ritual of the Christian *Agape* (of the first century), or the Hindu *kaula chakram*. This phase includes the worship of Damballah, chief of the pantheon, whose principal symbol is the "Serpent of Time-Eternity". "There is but one Damballah and Moses is his prophet"; around him he gathers the simple worship of all that is most beautiful in Nature; his secret symbol is much like the Staff of Hermes, the rod of Mercury, with its two intertwining snakes

which unite at the crest. His feminine counterpart is Aida; his time is at the Sunrise. Hence the priestess Mambo is his deputy, the servant of his church; revealer of one part of his hidden mysteries.

MAMBO DZHAMBO (Western Sudan)

Usually called *Mumbo-jumbo;* a masked dancer of the local secret societies of men, who used this means of compelling refractory women to obey tribal rules. Being fully disguised, the authorized wielder of the wand of justice could inflict the punishment decided upon by his council, without possibility of reprisal. Meetings were held usually once monthly (full-moon night), when the council assembled outside the village; and sent their masked dancers to huts designated.

MAMURIUS VETURIUS (Rome)

Broadly he was the "Smith of the Year" who "hammered out" the twelve months (symbolised as *ancile*—*Ankhele*—"time fragments"), whereby their bearers, the Saliian dancer-priests then "danced out" in succession, their prognosis of the coming Months of the Roman Year, beginning with the portentous Ides of March. Mars, progenitor or ruler of Mamurius, the Old Smith, was "born on March 1st" from Anna, goddess of the Eternal Year Recurrent. This date was the official beginning of the Roman Year. The dance, doubtless in some sort of consultation with the Collegia Augurum, was devised to indicate the probable course of the coming period, by slight changes in the ordinary course of the ritual. Closer to myth, the dance symbolised the "death" or departure of the Old (Veturius, the Veteran), and the coming of the new and better period. This change was indicated by a ritual death, burial, and resurrection; which tradition continues in the modernist version in England, known as the Morris Dance. (Danza Ma-Murius Romanus—brought during four centuries by the Roman invaders of Britain.)

MANA (Polynesian)

A term first made popular by Codrington in his travel books about the Pacific Islands. *Mana* is the "native name" for the electro-magnetic forces of nature, for the use of which much of their magical ritual is devised. Since the natural fact exists everywhere, there are numerous names (*Orenda*, or *Uskanda*, Amerindian; *Feng-shui*, Chinese; *Grace*, Latin countries; and many more). This discovery formed one of the centres of Tyler's famous work, *Primitive Culture;*[1] from which emerged the "Theory of Animism", thenceforward consistently denigrated by the philosophers, until Freud broke one of the medical unsound barriers, followed by Jung. The facts within "animism" appear usually to be misapprehended; not least by Frazer, who tries to show that "magic is an illusion, is 'false science'". Andrew Lang cannot understand how "the natives" took so long to "discover that magic does not work", and went on using rituals for *mana*. By it they ("the natives") mean (a) the collection of energy; (b) the conservation of energy; and (c) the use of energy. This is biotic energy; a phase of natural-electro-magnetism. *Tapu* or *taboo,** and *totem** are intimately associated. *Taboo* = insulation (danger), and *totem* implies use (or readiness for use). As there are several grades of natural electro-magnetism; and as we use the mineral grade (crudest mode) extensively in all electrical engineering, we may eventually give the "primitive man" due credit for knowing what he is about to do, when he uses plant energies or human biological magnetism. This he does, in one range, by means of ritual dances. The dance-ring operates like a Wimshurst machine: the moving circle induces local collection of energy as precisely as does a metal turbo-generator. This tension is the energy called *mana;* it is dissipated by contact (as is crude mineral electricity; or as the mimosa plant, when touched). *Mana* can heal, or it can injure (the ecclesiastical "curse" or the "blessing" are intended to work in this manner). The conscious control of *mana* by the *tohunga*, gave him the operative centre of his dance ritual. Rhythmic movement is essential; belief in the reality of the energy each man can feel, speeds the process of magical operation by means of group dance. In lesser fashion, the same instinctive act appears in group work (hauling etc.) when a shanty and its rhythm guide the human wave action of pull and rest.

[1] *Primitive Culture.* E. B. Tyler (2 vols.), 1887.

MANDALA — 1 (India)
Basic Sanskrit term with diverse meanings. The place of ritual or liturgy; or portions of the ritual in verbal form. Varied as *mandapa*, it implies also a hall or place; but with secular meanings in addition. As Mandalay (Burma) it denotes an ancient ritual centre; while as an adjective, it appeared as *Mandalai Lama* — head official of celebrations, shortened to Dalai Lama. Another semi-secular mode referred *Dalai* to *talai* as a count (for taxes), while in much later European usage, *mandala* indicates the use in painting or sculpture of a sort of radiation or halo, round a figure, usually in ovoid form (*almandala*), though this line has possible associations with Egyptian *Min* (with numerous derivations into *min-istria* etc). All of these are linked with sacred ritual dance.
[See *Allemande* — 2]

Mandapa, a traditional dancing platform for *Bharata Natyam;* invariably of polished stone, usually black granite, sometimes white limestone. This Mandapa was made for Kashi (Benares), the Holy City of Hinduism, and is near the Golden Temple on the bank of Ganges River.   INDIA

European form of the Mandala, with four dancing angels. A sculpture of Allemande Ritual Dance, by the "Gislebertus Guild" over the West Porch of Autun Cathedral. 12th century. Originally gilded and painted.   FRANCE

MANDALA — 2 (Sanskrit)
In Hindu ceremonial worship Mandala is a place (usually square, round, or star-shaped) for the dancing mind to receive its discipline (*sadhana*). The *guru* (master) constructs an altar in an approved "beautiful room" having a fine ceiling cloth, scented with incense . . . then he should with rice, powdered and coloured yellow, red, black, white and dark blue, draw the *Mandala* called *sarvato-bhadra*, beautiful and auspicious in every way. This preparation for ritual precedes the "mental worship" during which further marks are made in vermilion Sandal paste, on the diagram, in devotion to Lord of the Chakra (Supreme Lord) by which the rite proceeds to a mode of "mass" or symbolic intaking of food — after which "the *Rudra-dakinis* and *Rudra-bhairavis* dance in joy. These are angelic figures or ideas. *Mandala* is a technical ritual dance term of "position"; also a ritual term that indicates a "place of dance ritual", or circle of ritual. The dance term is broadly equivalent (in the *Shas-tras*) to the "Five Positions of Ballet", for a *Mandala* means one of the "Ten Attitudes" which define an attitude or position of body, linked with the proper position of the feet and hands. Thus the *mandala* is a more comprehensive term than 'Ballet Position", since this indicates only the legs; while the Hindu term includes upper body and arms. The classical Ten *Mandalas* are: *Sthanaka; Ayata; Alidha; Pratyalidha; Prenkhana; Prerita; Svastika; Motita; Samasuci;* and *Parsvasuci.* There are in addition six "simple attitudes", or *sthanakas* (stances) which refer chiefly to the legs, and thus are nearer to our familiar Five Positions.
[See *Tantra of the Great Liberation (Mahanirvana)* Trans. by Sir John Woodroffe, p. 329). *Integration of the Personality.* Dr. Carl G. Jung .London, 1940. (Ch. on Mandala Symbolism, p. 127 - 130)]

MANDUCE (Mediaeval French)
Described by Dr. Rabelais[1] as "the ridiculous statue Manduce", was a French parallel to the wicker figures, known in London as Gog and Magog, and carried in Carnival street dancing processions then, as many centuries before similar wicker figures were carried by Druids. The term probably derives from *Min-Duca* — the Duke or Duce of the *Min* or meeting place or hall — thus prominent in civic processions. Rabelais tells of the *Manduce* at the Court of the Master of Ingenuity :

"In this order, they moved towards Master Gester, after a plump young lusty gorbellied fellow; who, on a long staff, fairly gilt, carried a wooden statue grossly carved and as scurvily daubed over with paint; such a one as Plautus, Juvenal, and Pomp-Festus described it. At Lyons,

during the Carnival 'tis called Maschecrouste, or Gnaw-crust; they call this Manduce.
"It was a monstrous, ridiculous, hideous figure, fit to frighten little children; its eyes were bigger than its belly; and its head larger than the rest of its body; well-mouth-cloven, however, having a goodly pair of wide broad jaws, lined with two rows of teeth, upper tier and under tier, which, by the magic of a small twine hid in the hollow part of the golden staff, were made to clash, clatter, and rattle dreadfully one against another; as they do at Metz with St. Clement's dragon".
[1] *Gargantua and Pantagruel.* Dr. F. Rabelais, Lyon, 1542. Paris ed. 1927 (p. 643).

MANIPURI RAS MANDALA (Assam, India)
The principal Krishna-Radha dance of the great annual festival. Every village in this province has a small temple devoted to Krishna-Radhaka; or Krishna-Balaram (as a youth); or Krishna-Chaitanya (devotion); and usually there is a small hall reserved for performance of episodic dances from the life of the young god. Always there are musicians, usually with *khol* and *cymbals*, sometimes a *been* or pipe; and often there is chanting as well. Costumes are rich and beautiful. Many dances are done by girls alone; their attire is in traditional style; a close-fitting velvet *choli* (bodice) with short sleeves, carrying a two-inch band of gold embroidery. A wide and full skirt swings in flowing curves (the limbs are rarely seen) of many yards length. This skirt of red or dark green silk carries hundreds of glittering sequins like tiny mirrors; while largest bits of glass mirror are fixed here and there, adding much to the weight and flamboyant effect. A wide piece of white silk or cotton muslin is tied close to the waist; its light folds contrast neatly with the heavy skirt. Thrust into this waist-band, and drawn over the carefully dressed hair, is a veil of finest muslin, marked with narrow bands of silver stripes, or attached ribbons. This is a moonlight symbol. The short skirt, falling over the full-length brocaded silk, provides a magnificent effect, extended sometimes by a light form of cane, fitted beneath the full skirt (like a Victorian crinoline), which forms the skirt into a square at the feet. The small conical cap of velvet has a narrow edge of pearls, usually with a spray of pearls dropping from its peak. These colours and folds move continuously with the slow rhythms of this fascinating dance. Radha wears the most magnificent costume; on the same style. Krishna is covered in his usual yellow silk (he is the sun god) as a *dhotie*, tied at his waist with a silken scarf. His chest is free of costume, save for necklaces and armlets; but his high head-dress carries his symbolic peacock feathers for, like the Greek goddess Hera and

Argus, he "has a hundred eyes" (days of the year). This Ras Lila continues without cessation during the Twelve Days; and being centred in Vishnu worship, is accompanied by music, songs and chants by celebrated Vaishnavite poets, especially from the great Bengali reformer, Chaitanya.

MANNIKIN (Europe)
Is the artificial creature, rarely life-size, used for a variety of purposes, including entertainment and commerce. The mannikin ranges from the automaton, capable of movement, to the still-life figures beloved by drapery stores, on which to display feminine garments for sale, more or less the size and shape of "real life". In theatre, the mannikin may appear acting as a character, as a part to be danced, as in *Coppelia*; or again, in some other ballets where the "sculptor's figure comes to life" —a notion for a story derived from very ancient legends (Pygmalion and Galatea). The mannikin has a long history as a puppet in religious propoganda display; and in modern Spain, these wooden figures (often arrayed in costly draperies and jewellery) are shown to the cheering populace as the idols or symbols of the popular gods, carried through the streets on the annual festivals. Thus the mannikin appears as a useful accessory, devoted to the creation and support of social imagery, from religion to commerce, and in Theatre. The immense range of puppets* —figures usually less than life-size —accompanies the mannikin or mannequin as a minor competitor for interest, dating from days of pre-history, with the shadow forms seen in the secret shrines in deep caves. On the debit side may be cited the use of the mannikin in magical rituals —from prophecy or fortune-telling (Urim and Thummim*) to the half-fictional usage of the Italian *strega*, which has drooped into the modern phenomenon of the newspaper strip-cartoon and caricature, with mannikins drawn flat in the briefest outline, or filled with lurid colours.

MANORA OR MINORA (Siam)
A highly popular dance-pantomime, performed in Thailand. Originally a group dance, or Min-Hora. The frequently chosen "finest dancer", who was featured in the annual New Year festival performance, gradually took on the name as a character; and "she" is now recognised as a "national heroine". This festival began as a circle dance around the symbol of the Min —the dancers formed the Hora, the group of praise and prayer (later still recalled in the Latin phrase *Ora pro Nobis*), while the ritual dancer was known as the *orante*, the circle becoming the Hora. Sometimes it is called *Lakhon Minora* (the play or Ballet of Minora).

There is also the *Lakhon chatri*. In Indonesia, the term extends from *ora* to *orang* (ora-ankha, or "live play", as compared with the puppet play).

MANX FOLK DANCES (Isle of Man)
Include traditional dances, such as Peter O'Taby — *Eunysagh Vona*—; and *Hunt the Wren*.* They are performed now at the annual festival in July. The New Year dance, "Hunting the Wren",* performed also in Wales and Brittany, continues a most ancient Egyptian tradition, when this "Bird of Happiness" was called *Ueren*, and flocks were released to celebrate the New Year; only later were these tiny birds killed.

MAORI DANCE (New Zealand)
Native festival and ceremonial dances with song. Principal remaining modes are *poi* (for women), and *haka* (for men). *Poi* is an action-song-dance; some modes use a light ball of dried *raupo* reed or ornamental flax, on a string. New *rangi-poi* are devised, but the *waiata-heehee-wake*, or canoe-paddling chant, is ancient. They are all group dances. Sacred dances were controlled by *Tohunga** (the tribal priest). The men's *haka* (pron.: short, "ha-ka") includes fierce martial dances, the *peruperu* or *tutu-ngarahu*, with strenuous action. *Haka** contains rhythmic foot stamping, slapping of sides and thighs, with a loud impressive chant. Words are sometimes ancient war songs, sometimes modernistic versions (calypso style) or special songs are made for great events. The "village welcome" dance, *powhiri*, is performed by women and girls, with shawls and green branches; the men's greeting follows. The *hongi*, or nose-salute, is not rubbing; it is contact (like two friendly cats!). *Hongi* means "to smell". The *ruwahine** (wise woman) trains girls, gives advice; and controls certain modes of *tapu* (house-warming acts). The *rangatira* is the tribal chief; he sits with *Kaumatua* (the elders) who, besides ability in *haka*, show skill in poetry, history, oratory; and they know all tattoo patterns used for identification. Dance garments of coloured woven flax (formerly finished with *kiwi* feathers), and vegetable-dyed, and beaded head-bands, are worn. Maori dance has certain origins that affiliate with those of Honolulu.

MAQUARRI (Guiana)
A dance for the dead, among the Indians of Arawak.[1] This ritual dance aims to provide fresh blood, with the usual purpose of stimulating the returning life of the departed man, and is danced at a funeral. The name derives from *maquarra*, the whip of oiled hide, about three or four feet long, which serves to mark time by cracks in the air; and

to lash the legs of dancers, making the blood flow. [Cp. *Sudanese Whipping Dance*]
[1] *Indian Tribes of Guiana*. W. H. Brett. 1868.

MAQUIRITARE "SCHOOL" DANCE (Venezuela)

Maquiritare Indians use dance to educate their young men in tribal knowledge. Traditions of hunting, warfare and other matters are taught by chants and movements of the body, at the chief festivals, when "lessons" are given daily. Moving in a circle round the village dancing-space, wearing long "skirts" of split palm-leaves, and each with one hand on the shoulder of the man in front, the young men are led by one who marks the time with a staff on which rattle small hooves of deer. The dance is accompanied by *uanas* (bamboo flutes) and a drum of stretched monkey-skin. Each time the circle approaches the village Chief, he gives a verse of the chant, which is repeated by the leader and then taken up by all the dancers. In this way they gain their tribal knowledge, except history, which is so bound up with religion and sacred things, that instruction in it is reserved for the last night of the festival, when the *Sun Dance** is performed.

MAQUIRITARE SUN DANCE (Venezuela)

Performed on the last night of an important festival, it celebrates the mystery of the Sun God. Round a large fire in the village square, circle young men in split palm-leaf skirts and wicker crowns, their leader chanting and the men repeating each verse after him. No instrument accompanies the dance. For the instruction of the young men, the leader, who is also the Chief, chants the story of the world's creation by the Sun God. Then he crouches down near the fire, facing east. Forming two parallel rows, one behind and one before him, the men now alternately move towards and away from the fire, rhythm being marked by the thudding on the ground of a staff wielded by the first dancer, and the clicking of small deer hooves attached to it. Presently these rhythmic sounds cease as the staff is thrown into the fire, to be followed by the men's skirts and crowns. The naked men, still in two files, dance round the square, then, to quickened rhythm, converge face to face on the fire, crushing out its glowing remnants until only darkness remains.

MARAICHINE (France)

Dance of the Market Gardeners (*maraicher*) and sometimes associated with the Chife Danse Ronde. In its earlier phases, this Danse Maraichine simply copied the elementary moves: round the gardens, picking produce; tying or sacking it; carrying to waiting carts and dance after being paid.

MARCEL OR MARCELLA (French)

In the Church of S. Leonardi in mediaeval Limoges, the townspeople celebrated the festival of an obscure "Saint Martial", variously known in the circle dance as Marcel or Marcella (probably from Mar-Salii, the Roman dancer-priests). This was a popular round dance, performed in the choir or nave of the church. Gallini records that the Hebrew psalms were chanted; but instead of singing at the end, the prescribed *Gloria Patri*, they followed the exhortation of the ancient term *Selah* (Now Dance!) and intoned their own traditional song:

"Bon Sainte Marcel, pray for us, Sainte Marcel
O Sainte Marcel!

And we will dance in honour of your name!"
There are a dozen or so of assorted saints and martyrs bearing this name and similar appellations, with dance rituals, probably all deriving from the ancient Roman Festival of Mars in the month of March. All the known dances are circular and had a wavy motion in movement. Later the wardens were known as *marquiller* or *marguillier*.
[See *Church Dances; Tripettos*]

MARCH

A regular imposed rhythm, de-marking local time and local space, with local movement in and over it. March or *marche* is the essential polar opposition to *jig*, or irrythmic movement; both in their "natural state". March implies a procession: a movement towards some destination. In the Roman mythos of the year, March was essentially the Month of Opening, to begin to move towards gaining crops, food, or plunder. In ritual dance, March affirms this repeated movement; this organised and determined progress in one direction; which *marks* the start of war, the return in *trionfo*, or the sacerdotal triumph, through the streets with the idols. All of these are affirmed in some regular music; accompanied with weapons. March and mark are limitations (Hermes, God of Boundaries Markurios armes); hence Ares (or Mara in India), is god of death; and as such, *tempo di marca* is in the underlying beat of every genuine *Mores* dance. Mars is thus god of emergent agriculture and finishing war; of the rising warrior, who contrives to oppose and subdue that which is unorganised; the Jigs or Jags who move, yet not in social order. March is fundamentally a group movement; while the Jig is personalised (as in Ireland, France, centres of individualism). The *gig* is a "carriage for one", which can go almost anywhere; the *march* suggests the Roman road, the Roman field. Compare plough with sickle: straight lines and unrepeated curves.

MARCIA (Moslem villages in Eastern Bengal, Pakistan)
Though dance is not widely approved in Islam, yet the festival of Moharram exhibited mourning dances called *Marcia* and *Pari*. These are to be seen chiefly at Mymensingha. Women dancers move in a ring, holding the hem of their ample *dhoties* with one hand, and waving scarlet fragments of cloth; they stamp the rhythm noisily to sound their ankle bells; following the chant sung by the leader, who stands outside the circle. Their subject is the "Death of Hassan and Husain" at Kerbela, one of the few Moslem legends with some historical basis.

MARDI GRAS (New Orleans, USA)
From French, literally "Fat Tuesday", the *Grace Mardi* or last Day of Grace (Indulgence). Festival during the period from Twelfth Night to Ash Wednesday. The modern carnival is in the hands of numerous catholic bodies, called *Krewes*, who compete in arranging (a) private balls; and (b) decorated trucks in public procession. The Carnival is in fact descended from the *ballet ambulatoire*, but presents a more baroque aspect. Each *krewe* has its own king, queen, retinues and tableaux, and there is much rivalry among girls for the position of queen. In older organizations the daughter of a former queen will "inherit" the right from her mother, but many families save up for years, for the time when their daughter may be chosen queen. Girls thus chosen are sometimes taught deportment and how to walk "regally". Of about sixty Carnival *krewes*, the oldest, founded in 1857, is known as the "Mystick Krewe of Comus", and the most coveted social honour in New Orleans is presiding over such a *krewe*. The Negro community have their own Carnival with a Zulu "king". As Lent approaches, processions begin through the streets, with elaborately decorated floats (prepared in great secrecy) and on "Mardi Gras" itself the whole town is *en fête*, with everyone masked and in fancy costume. With darkness masks are removed, but dancing continues till midnight. Shortly before midnight "The Lord of Misrule" and his court formally visit the "Krewe of Comus", which marks the end of *Mardi Gras* and the beginning of Lent. New Orleans is the home of modern jazz, or baroque in music. Dance has not changed so much; but the South American tribal dances have merged with the North African forms, to challenge the voodoo dances of Hayti. Unfortunately the domination of saxophone destroys the best part of the South American rhythms of string and drum; though the whole endeavour of synthetic jazz is to break through the mechanical beat of modern civilisation. As one of the principal catholic centres in USA, the priests have had much to do—pulling their strings in approved democratic fashion—so that the local Ku Klux Klan was defeated, while the gangsters of St. Louis type have been ejected from salon or ballroom control. Existence of several distinct communities also influences local dance fashion in Basin Street and other local centres of joy. New Orleans has thus had considerable influence on the swing of modern USA ballroom dances; and, to a lesser extent, in England.
[See *Tlustni Dni* (Poland); *Fasching* (Germany); *Fastnachtsbär* (Germany)]

MARGUILLIERS (France)
Equivalent to English wardens of the church; formerly had the duty of "marking out" the respective positions and routes of various rituals; and thus developed into conservators of repairs, having to observe and note defects in the fabric. Many of them, being ignorant of symbolism, failed to maintain the proper floor patterns that earlier were deemed of such importance in ritual. (See *Breviary of Salisbury*, where place and position are indicated in diagram—*Sarum Use*.)

MARI LLWYD (Wales)
New Year's Festival Mummers, once performing at various places in the Principality; now to be seen at Llangynwyd in Glamorgan. The play and dance formerly showed both a Mores and Sword Dance, with the chief symbol of the White Horse of Death, now carried as a horse skull by the principal Mummer, who wears a smock similar to a shroud. The earliest form was the ritual combat of Winter versus Summer, marked by barring of doors against the dancing mummers in the street. They are admitted or greeted after their song. *Mari Llwyd* does not mean "Holy Mary", but the Play of Maria (*Ludi*). The Sword Dance has vanished; and even the street dancing steps are rare.

MARIE MAGDALEINE, Dance of (France)
This ceremonial dance was performed on Easter Day, apparently at St. Stephen's in Vienne and at Bale, in the 15th century; also at Besançon. Church dances were then fading into disuse. Pierre Bonnet mentions several services with dance, including the *Bergeretta** and the *San Martial** celebration at Limousin. At Besançon (records Bonnet) the custom was continued outside the church, after due celebration inside had ceased. The dance was reduced to making several circuits (*tours*) in the cloisters; and instead of the dance (*branle*), the hymn of Lactantius—"Hail, Festal Day" was sung. A French book of ritual (early 16th century) used at St. Stephen's, Vienne, says "After nones, the clergy assemble in the cloister with the singers to

chant the music. The choir begins *Salva Festa Dies* and MM respond *Qua Deus*, going (in procession) round the cloister. Then the choir sings again (*Qua Deus*) and MM sing back the other verses (of) *Salva Feste Dies*. Thus these two verses are sung alternately by MM, who make the circuit of the cloister three times". This account, leaves us in doubt if "MM" presents Marie Magdaleine with her attendant choristers. A note on the ritual at Besançon states that "in spite of vigorous synodal diocesan decrees (of 1585 and 1601) which threatened severe penalties against enthusiasts for ancient customs, the dance was still in full force at Ste. Marie Magdaleine's, danced in the nave in rainy weather, down to 1662". If this dance (part of a much longer structure, evidently) was, in fact, the *Dance of Marie Magdaleine,*, we can suppose only that it recounts the post-passion incident of the Meeting of Mary with Jesus; and that this is why it was placed on the Monday. This dance has links with the *Bergeretta*, and with the Easter Day "Sun Dance" as with the *Pelota* and the *Labyrinthine Dance.** [See *Church Dances*]

MARIMBA (Portuguese)
Name given by West Indians to the African xylophone brought by the Negroes—an instrument made with several keys of flat wood, suspended over gourds as resonators. The tone is broad and mellow; the tuning can be chromatic or pentatonic in scale, according to the maker's wish and skill. The *marimba* is widely used through Africa for dance accompaniment; it has been dubbed "Kaffir piano" by Europeans. In the West Indies, where it is very popular, it is said:

> "*Marimba, que cantan vos de mujer,*
> *Marimba, que bailer con pasos de angeles!*"

MARINERA (Peru)
A lively song-dance in 3/4 and 6/8 time, performed by couples waving kerchiefs. Of Spanish extraction, the *Marinera* came to Peru from Chile and was originally called *Cueca Chilena*, or *Chilena*, the name being changed to *Marinera* during the 19th century when Peru and Chile were at war (1879 - 1883). The new name honoured the Peruvian Navy, but the dance remained a version of the Chilean *Zamacueca.** Danced and sung in lively tempo, the dance is one of pursuit and retreat. Dancers face each other, but without touching, each flourishing a kerchief. The form of the dance varies in different districts. A similar dance exists in Bolivia and the Argentine.
[See *Cueca; Zamacueca*]

MAROH DANCE (Celebes Island)
Part of the annual *Ma-Maroh* ceremonies (among the West Toradjas of Central Celebes) for curing the sick and expelling the evil spirit ("Maroh"). In a ceremony to invoke the aid of the *Dewatas*, or good spirits, a dance is performed during which one of the performers falls into a trance to communicate with the *Dewatas*. A few weeks later the villagers gather for the two-day feast and healing ceremonies, which are opened with the *Maroh Dance*. Performed only by men, they form into two lines facing each other, later changing into a circle. Singing a monotonous song to invoke the *Dewatas*' aid in driving out Maroh, they take short, bobbing steps forward and back. The dance continues for some time, being interrupted three times by loud yells. After the second yell, the sick are placed inside the circle of dancers; the medicine man, chanting, covers them with blankets, while hand-in-hand the dancers, still singing, move round this group. After further treatment by the medicine man and an interval for rest and refreshment, the festivities continue with the women's *Magilluh,** a trance dance. On the second day more trance dances are performed by men and women, the trance being an essential part of the proceedings, under control of the medicine man.
[Cp. *Sanghyang Dedari* (Bali)]

MARRIAGE MARKET DANCE—1 (Europe)
Is the culmination of the ancient process of *homo-culture feminis*: the peak of the "grooming" of marriageable daughters, by the numerous peasant families of Europe—and most of the other parts of the world. This is the show or display, set forth in some public mode, usually at one of the Fairs held for cattle or merchandise, at recognised centres. Closely connected with Initiation ceremonies, this public display of charms and wealth has accompanied the parallel social traditions of Theatre. Where once it was an attendance expected of all male citizens (as in ancient Hellas) now the show is surrounded by walls and protected by a box office. Theatre and Market have been related for many centuries, after escaping from sacerdotal control; and having thrown off temple schemes for gaining revenue from social necessity, in this direction. European Marriage Markets, with their show of fine costume, ending in dances with selected partners, are still active in country districts in Europe. From the sabbath "Monkey Parade" of northern English industrial towns, to the *Romerias* of Spain, we may turn to the native jaunts of South American tribes, or the ceremonial walking dance, active in Polynesian Islands. Their sociological meaning is centred in selecting and mating. The French have lapsed into monetary discussions, on *dot* or dowry; even that is fading out. With the industrial *civis* in operation, the

churches fail by undue interference; and matrimonial offices appear in business. The alternative is often the local *Palais de Danse*, varied by a summer trip to a Butlin Monastery; eliminating the *pelerinage* or the crusade, which never helped towards settled family life. In the dance displays are groups of maidens or bands of youths : they never join until the end. Each show their paces, much as the dealer brings cattle or horses into the ring. Good appearance, with grooming, is accepted as a sign of vitality; costume as indicator of wealth; and accessories as examples of craft skill. Farm life demanded a many-sided ability; but the handicraft marriage market is dying, before the deadly pressure of mechanization; so that the arrangement for life is displaced by a film-system of annual wives, like annual new models of cars—and new fashions in dance try to keep up with this meaningless rush. In the Hungarian language a marriageable girl is " a girl for sale", while *völegény*—bridegroom—literally means "buying man".
[Cp. *Mailehen*(Germany); *Tergul de Fête*(Rumania); *Tlustni Dni* (Poland)]

MARRIAGE MARKET—2 (Nigeria)
Authoritarian interventions have contrived to change the traditional methods of wife-finding and wife-purchase, as known through Africa; and, until recently, in countries like Hungary or Rumania. In Nigeria, the municipal and government officials have surpassed parsonic novelties such as white cotton nightshirts. There has been a Conference, to consider modern methods of wife-buying. Instead of the Hollywood method of "Trial, Error and Alimony", the sale of wives on the hire purchase system may return to Nigeria. Says a London newspaper,[1] (omitting the necessary reference to festal dancing, which still occurs) : —

"A Government committee, inquiring into the current prices paid to parents for brides, has recommended a price freeze of £30 and a return to instalment payments". (Economic repercussions of war had altered market values). "After the war there was pronounced inflation in the marriage market. This was a result of soldiers returning from the war with enough money to buy wives outright, and to pay above the usual rate". (We recur to GI brides in England; same basis!) "The Committee, in its report (22nd July, 1955) said that every man should now be content with one price-controlled wife".

The local festal dance had also gained in size and extravagance; but the Government committee has so far refrained from imposing more regulations; or devising more licences. The dancers and drummers still obtain excellent fees.
[1] *Daily Telegraph*. London. July 23rd, 1955.

MARTIAL (France)
Many stone churches in France have replaced earlier wooden structures; and with their expansion, the legend of Charles Martel was slowly transformed into a clerically qualified saint. Charles the Hammer (as *Martel* then meant) was instrumental in halting the last northern thrust of the Moslem invasions into France; and thus became a national hero; yet it was considered (by the modest propagandists of the church) that his glory could suitably be converted; and bring grist to their mills, replacing also the notorious Vine Harvest rites of Bacchus, already allotted to Martina. So the celebrations were duly arranged; and a new dedication day fixed; and his annual festival celebrated by merry songs to the "Little Guts of Saint Martial"—the *cervelas* or potted small meats of the peasantry, preserved in long skins from cattle (known in England as the festive though humble *saveloy*). So Martel and Marshal or Martial displaced Mars, by Roma and Amor. In 1955 a similar invention was devised in Italy, for May Day, with a new "Saint Joseph the Workman".
[See *Church Dances*]

MARTIAL MARCH AND DANCEC (Europe)
Has developed with the egoism of Princes and potentates, from the relatively simple "Salute" formerly accorded on the election of kings, to the pompous displays devised for Louis XIV, or Kaiser Wilhelm II. The Roman *trionfo* retained a slight functional aspect, in that it was primarily a display of the looted goods and enslaved captives, brought home and thus shewn as a proof of the Glories of War. The parade-ground display gave no such proof; but conversely was shewn as a potential threat to the foreign ambassadors invariably invited. This juvenile system still exists in "Military Exercises", as a sort of rehearsal for "battles-to-come", and a highly magnified and civilised War Dance, to which civilians (who merely pay) are not invited. To understand thoroughly the varied functions of dance and ritual in social extension, we have to examine military march and dance as well as ecclesiastical forms; often the two are united, as modes of power display or power-threat (see T. Veblen's works). The large pictorial publicity, devised by Hans Burgmair for Emperor Maximilian in 1512, in woodcuts of large size, indicates what "the public" was required to see and applaud. We are scientifically advanced : we have films for power-publicity; and the "march-past" is done by aeroplanes at high velocity and cost; we have advanced in military music to the atom-bombardon, the trom-cross-bones, or to jet-wind-instruments that scream and roar like the Australian corroboree call. The scale of lethal science

has expanded; the early forms of military ritual now appear solely as ornamental affairs of "Guard Changing", or "Colour Trooping" or "Gong-Giving" (as named in the services). These functions are associated with more or less music, quaint ceremonial gestures and howls, with various modes of salute and step. The nearest successor of the savage war dance—i.e. the simulated slaughter of any potential enemy—is performed privately, as in "bayonet drill", when stuffed dummies are penetrated with steel. The dance element has disappeared from this ritual murder rehearsal.

MARWARI (Bikanir, Rajputana; Gujerat, in India)

A style of traditional dance, followed chiefly by women of the Province of Marwar and Kathiawar in Western India, whence it has spread to other parts. Fairly simple in form, its gorgeous costume and accessories make it irresistible, as a dance to copy, whether by native film producers or foreign visitors. The chief attraction is the *gargari*—a skirt of light silk with an enormous width (anything from forty to a hundred feet around the edge), while the dancers wear numerous jewels, some of them real. *Marwari Nautch* is chiefly a *pas seul* of the *Kathaka* type—a whirling and dipping; but it is done also by groups of ten or twelve, during the festival periods. Rarely is any great technical achievement visible; nor is much use made of the classical *mudra;** it may be taken mainly as a folk dance for women.

MARWYSGAFN (Welsh)

The traditional "Death Bed Song", or Lament, familiar in several aspects: (a) the religious ritual accompaniment for a funeral (the *Wakan* or *wakes*), as well as (b) the liturgical form used to emphasise church doctrines and legends; and (c) the more intense usage, in the initiation ritual of the secret discipline, when the *candidatus* was reduced by a mock death. This remaining mode constitutes the central action of the older English (and Welsh) Morris Daunce; while its earlier Tudor form is stressed by the "Making of the Rose" with five *rapirs* or interlaced "swords". With the *Marwysgafn* is the ritual of the Death Parting, known as *Marwysgar*. These rites spring from most ancient traditions, stemming from Greco-Egyptian doctrines of the *Moirae* (Fates, Destiny, etc.) associated with Isis-Hathor (cow-goddess), or dissolution; and the *Mari* or Maria, associated with the fount of life, as Isis and as Meri. Moving into England, the term is found frequently in mediaeval documents as *Mores;* and in France as *Maur* (later a Benedictine centre) and *Mauric* from *Maur-Rhys*. From this ceremonial is derived the term *Moreske* or *Moresque*. *Mawlad* is "praising".

MARYINSKY THEATRE (Leningrad)

The principal theatre for ballet and opera in the city (formerly Petersburg) and now named Kirov Theatre; it was named first for Grand Duchess Marie. The former Bolshoi Theatre, after burning, was rebuilt as the Conservatoire of Music; and no theatre of that name now exists in Leningrad. The Kirov Theatre is smaller than the Bolshoi Theatre of Moscow; it holds 1982 seats; and is definitely a more workable size, for ballet theatre, than the Moscow building. Here the original Russian classical ballets were first produced, mostly by M. Petipas, some by Lev Ivanov, with a company ranging from ninety to one hundred and forty dancers. There is a fine Ballet School associated. The site is open and spacious; the building designed by Rossi, was opened in 1860. Regular ballet began in 1880. The building is now owned by the Leningrad Soviet (Municipal) which receives an agreed rental, and undertakes structural repairs; otherwise the whole administration is run jointly by delegates of the staffs. Everyone has a voice, and there is no arbitrary dictatorial harshness, since everyone may be, and is, criticised. Official intervention occurs over choice of subjects or treatment of a few themes. In the main, Soviet ballets and operas are produced for home consumption; not as "propaganda" and productions have got to satisfy their public; who are free to attend or stay away; or to voice disapproval in the local press. Despite this day-to-day freedom, creative ability is as rare as ever; partly because of the failure to encourage it; and (in the dramatic theatre) the disparity of reward to producer v. translator. Hence the trend towards Pushkin etc. as a source (*Fontan Bakchiserai; Prisoner of the Caucasus*). The five "imperial theatres" received (19th century basis) a subvention guarantee of two-million roubles annually between them (equal then to £200,000). The *tchinovniks* saw that it was "just necessary" (like English "Excess Profits Tax" worked—there were no "excesses"), but today, this guarantee is unnecessary; and working expenses are met by takings. Other theatres in the USSR (mainly those newly developed) do receive state and municipal subsidies. There is no heavy ground rent; no impresario; no leaseholder; no extravagant "film-star" salaries or trade-union demands; and n o strikes.   [See *Hermitage Theatre*]

MASCARA (Spain)

A mask; a cover or disguise, as used in a masquerade. Now applied also to stage make-up (or even street make-up, used by women), in the specialised item of eye-paint.   [See *Make-up; Grim*]

MASCARADES (Italy)

Social spectacle, that verged into deliberately designed entertainment, separated from any religious or family occasion; and in 15th-16th centuries freely produced for enjoyment, in professional experiment of the new race of artists, who served rich patrons in secular works of art, instead of providing religious propaganda or embellishment. The swing of thematic content veered sharply away from "religious" subjects to the mythos of Greece or ancient Rome. In Florence, the Mascarade system permitted the *Dramma per Musica*,* forerunner of Bourgeois Opera; precisely as in England, the Masques (in the Inns of Court and other centres such as Oxford) stimulated the dramatic theatre in verse. Italy had no verbal drama: that had expired in laughter with the satirical commentary of the Italian Commedia upon the wearisome rag-tag left by mendicant friars in miracles and mysteries. These faded from Italy before they disappeared from Elizabethan England. The *Mascarade* was a social product; the *Dramma per Musica* was an experimental product by scholars; but the *Ballet du Cour* which emerged was a joint affair, attracting a wider range of interests. The *Ballet de la Reine* was, in France, the first peak; the Florentine *Mascarades* returned —costs were high and performances were limited, but the visit of Mascaraders to Paris stimulated the nobility to turn to *Ballet du Cour*, further urged by Richelieu (and then Mazarin), on the same theory in which cricket and football are artificially stimulated by the modern Press, to keep "the minds of the masses" occupied with juvenile interests. These developments occurred in the period just before and just after 1600, contemporary with the Elizabethan period of modern England. Italy produced Opera; France produced Ballet; and England produced Drama. The century saw Oliver Cromwell in England; Richelieu and Louis ruling France; and Italy, slowly being reduced by the Vatican, along with Spain, to lesser dimensions. Rulers used a *Mascarade* in politics, as the people did in their pleasure parks.

MASCOT OR MASCOTTE (France)

A folk-dancer leading the crowd, for "good fortune", as opposed to one tailing it, as *Jettacotte* or *Jettatore* (bringer of the "evil eye"). A large wooden image, known as *Masche-Croutte* or *Casche-cotte* was carried "dancing" round the city of Lyons during Carnival; it would seem to have some relevance to the Guildhall figures (of London), known as Gog and Magog. The Welsh *Coch* means "leader"; the term may derive from *Maes-Coch*. The Mascot now remains chiefly in two forms (the ancient god-figure head of ships

now being obsolete), as the "regimental goat", or the small figure mounted on the bonnet of an automobile. The array of papiér-machè dancing or strolling figures, with huge heads, is annually a feature of the *Riviera Carnival des Fleurs*.

MASK—1 (African styles)

Are used by elders of tribal communities as a means of assuming traditional legal power, over the people who infringe accepted custom. The Mask thus disguises effectively a person—otherwise well known—and, like the legal wig and gown disguise adopted in British courts, invests many quite ordinary brains with a temporary power of punishment. The African type was called *fetiche* by Portuguese travellers; oblivious of their own usage at home, with idols or images or *fetiches* of their own faith. The Ibo or Yoruba Mask is a head cover with eye-slits, either half-mask covering the face, or helmeted covering the entire head. There is always a conventional costume; and often a weapon that goes with each figuration. Many of the African Masks possess extraordinary plastic or glyptic vigour in their formal expression, some of them far superior to the rubbish that masquerades as "Modern Art".

MASK—2 (from old Egyptian *Meskhen*)

Is a group term which has for us many related meanings. The Mask in its intimate form is the facial cover, the disguise of the man but the exponent of the assumed character. It is a trivial social cover—the *bal masque*; it is the sculptor's name for a face, or a hunters reference to the forefront of animal. As masquerade it becomes the group term for a pleasure dance gathering (ridotto*) but in detective novel fairy lands, it refers to the disguise of the "villain". As a Masque *tem*. Charles I, England, it is an entertainment by poets and painters, luxuriant in form and sycophantic in content, for intimate court circles. For the small boy, the mask is a cheap paper face, behind which he can bargain for pennies. For the feminine beauty expert, the mask is to be hidden in a mud-pack part of "The Treatment". For the Japanese, the mask is an essential item in Noh Play; while the tribal medicine man—whether in Sinhala or Ghana—uses the mask to disguise his own face, to frighten the victim (patient or village sinner). According to the central aim so is the mask designed or selected and used.

MASK DANCES (Japanese)

In *Noh* Dance-Drama. Wooden face-masks (covering the face, not encasing the head) are used frequently in playing the *Noh* dance-drama. These are used, where necessary for the character, by the

Masks in Temple Ritual Dance. Osiris and Hathor,   1250 B.C. Dynasty XIX. Wood, painted and gilded.
(Courtesy Cairo Museum.)

shete (chief actor), and his two colleagues (tsure and tomo), not by waki or other characters. Masks are used for "old men", or women parts. They are made usually of paulownia wood; many are two centuries old. They are egg-shell polished, rarely paint is added, but some are all-white (for ghost parts) or red (for demons etc.). The classes of traditional masks (developed from Gigaku and Bugaku, early dance forms), include *rojin* (for aged men, nobles, etc.), the *No'otoko* (male dancers), and *N'onna* (females), the *shen-butsu* (deities of Buddhas); and *s'henge* (demons). Hair is sometimes added; slits allow for eyes; some masks belong only to one play. Plays are seen mostly by lamp-light; which helps mask expression considerably. Among the female of *N'onna* masks, many single types show various women : young and beautiful; happy or sorrowful; mothers, or very aged persons. One main emotion is the motif; there is rarely a full gamut; so the mask may thus concentrate upon this single feeling. The male or *No'otoko* masks are much helped by helmets or other head-dress, rarely permissible for female parts.

MASKEL, Dance of (Abyssinia)
Sacred Dance of Priests in Ethiopia (Abyssinia) when celebrating the New Year Festival at Addis Ababa. The term means : *Mass*, the birth, or renewal; and *kell* or *khel*, the place or cell of celebration. The form of the dance (done in the open in daytime) is a great hollow square, attended by the Emperor who sits at one side, on a throne. This dance is formed by chanting to simple accompaniment of large drums, cymbals, and beating of sticks (prayer-sticks of silver, or ivory, or horn etc.). The ceremony ends with loud reading from portions of the Coptic Bible. A lesser ritual dance is performed at other points of the year, within the round or octagonal churches; in a chancel called *heykell* : place of *hey* or "dance". The rite and the name derive from ancient Egypt; from the New Year Festival of the "Birth of the Year" or *Mas Skhen*. In this tradition the mediaeval mask or masque was developed.   [See *Masque*]

MASQUE (English - French from Arabic)
Is a term used in three main modes : (a) the popular masque of the festivals of the people, culminating (in England) with the Masque of X-Messe or the Winter Solstice, the Crossing. This developed (about the Reformation, rather rapidly) into the Court Masque, while the village Masque dropped into the Revel (also Lincoln's Inn) or the Mummery. Long previously, Arabs in Spain used their own terms : *maskharat*, a buffoon or jester, a sportive fool or zany, from *sakhira*, to ridicule. English Court Masques (inspired in part by the visits to Italy of Inigo Jones) were mainly acted pageants, each designed for some special court occasion and often devoid of plot. Ben Jonson and Fletcher supplied poetical bases for Masques, acted out by the children of His Majesty's Chapel Royal (or the Savoy) and the Quire School of St. Pauls. One named *Comus* was done at Ludlow in 1634 by John

Milton; another at Kenilworth was seen by Shakespeare.
[See *Entrée; Stuart Masques—Dancing Place*]

MASSAGE— 1
So valuable to all professional dancers, is best given by technically trained anatomical experts. The French system comprises scientific manipulation : (a) surface friction (*effleurage*); (b) muscle kneading with relaxation of tension (*petrissage*); (c) finger-tip striking—*a la piano* and (d) percussion, striking or slapping with the hands (*tapotement*). Massage is used in Polynesia as a mode of relaxation of muscular tension (*mana*) with the name *lomi-lomi*; in Tonga Islands it is used as *toogi-toogi*, or *mili*, or *fota*. These were used to alleviate cramp got in swimming; similar massage can be used in Europe beneficially, especially with High Frequency treatment. Dr. Mesmer used in his medical practice a parallel operation on the nervous system; it is not hypnotism, but a direction (or an alternative re-direction) of emotional imagery, which causes involuntary neuro-muscular tension.

MASSAGE— 2
For professional dancers is an indispensable treatment, as between the hard work of dancing and the period of complete relaxation that should precede every performance. There are numerous systems, from the heavy pummelling given to the football industry, to the delicate touch of an accomplished Japanese *masseur;* or the commercial method of the Turkish baths attendant. All have their uses. The female dancer should be massaged by a *masseur*, the male dancer by a *masseuse* (there are very few competent). If breathing exercises can be added, so much the better. As athletes, dancers are a suffering crowd of performers. Chiefly, the feet, ankles and limbs need most attention. The small "High-frequency" apparatus is extremely valuable for foot relief (as footballers find). Oriental *masseurs* use some oil (usually coconut) as an aid. Facial massage is another branch of feminine treatment.

MATACHINA (New Mexico)
(Spelled also *Matachen, Matachena* etc.). A medi-aeval Spanish dance form, *Los Matachines*, found active in New Mexico, but obsolete in Europe. Originally this dance belonged to the New Year Feast celebrations; though even the Spanish form had changed much before it was taken to Mexico. The leaders, in pseudo-traditional costume, include. a sort of bishop, a male named Mananca; and his partner, a small girl named Malinche.* The man is sometimes named El Monarca. The dance is a New Year feature, now tied to December 25th, and per-

formed in the open, during the morning, and again in the afternoon. The mitred men begin the dance with Mananca; the others are in two lines facing; at the other end sit the musicians, with violin and sometimes a guitar as well. Finally comes in the bull, who fights the Old Man; when he is killed the Matachines all kneel. The girl child in bridal white moves up and down the two lines. The original Spanish term has been defined as meaning : a joker, or buffoon; a grotesque dance; a masked dancer or group of them; and has also been applied colloquially to the butcher. (This may indicate the slaughter or End of the Old Year, paralled with Herne the Hunter, farther north in Europe). A more probable origin is from Arabic : the words *motawajjihn*, or *muta-wajjihin*, means "maskers" or "He with mask".

MATACHINES (Mexico)

An old dance now entirely overlaid by Catholic influence. It is also a Society of dancers among the Yaqui and Mayo Indians, called "Soldiers of the Virgin" and part of the church organization, with life membership. The group is directed by a chief with two assistants. The chief dancer, called *monarca*, also has two assistants. Dancers wear white shirts with red ribbons crossed over chest, a small crown of flowers over a red bandanna, carry a wooden rattle in the right hand and in the left a three-pronged wand, adorned with feathers. The *monarcas* of some villages wear black velvet over-trousers open on the outer side from thigh down. The *Matachine* organizations of the Tarahumara Indians (neighbours of the Mayos) are differently arranged. Their costumes differ in various villages. In Samachique dancers wear a red cloth cape with blue or white lining, reaching to the knees, over a white cotton shirt; red trousers over white ones, which show through openings at the knees; red bandannas hung from belt, long coloured stockings, with shoes. In this village each dancer is in charge of a *Chapeon*, who stands to one side of him, marking the rhythm of the dance and "calling" the changes in figures in falsetto. The leader of the *Chapeones* wears a wooden mask on the back of his head, painted with white lines, with false white hair and beard. In New Mexico *chapeones* under different names mime bull-fighting in the *Matachine* dance. The Yaqui *Matachines* is danced in two lines, an assistant *monarca* at the head, the chief one in the middle, performing simple steps and figures. Two violins and the dancers' rattles accompany the dance, which is performed at fiestas, funerals of all members, and at the church every Sunday, taking part in the procession to the cross. At Bacun and Corcorit the *Matachines* perform a Maypole dance. At sunrise, in the former village,

six dancers, in two opposite lines, wind ribbons round the pole; in Corcorit three on each side wind the ribbons, while six more braid the ribbons without winding them round the pole. The Mayo Indians at St. Ignacio and Navajoa, instead of the Ribbon Dance perform *Mo-els** (Bird Dance) and the "Sleepy" Dance.* [See *Listones, Danza de los*]

MATASSINS OR MATTACHINS (France)

A dance in imitation armour, representing a mock combat, popular during 16th and 17th centuries. There were four dancers usually all men, but sometimes two men and two women. The dance contained several figures (in which, no doubt, the ladies danced), between which mock combats took place. Thoinot Arbeau in his *Orchésographie** (1588), gives an illustrated account of the dance. He describes the performers as wearing a short tunic (*corcelet*) bordered with taffetas below the waist, and a gilt-paper helmet. Arms were bare and bells were tied to the legs, while they carried a sword in the right hand and shield in the left. Movements of the fighting part of the dance resembled fencing, and the phrase "To dance a mattachin" meant "To fight a duel". Up to 1735 the dance was popular in Bordeaux, Marseilles and Strassbourg, and was sometimes known as *Les Bouffons.** Two 16th century examples of music for the *Matassins* exist in the *Mattasin oder Toden Tantz* in Nörmiger's tablature (1593); and *Matachina*, contained in a French guitern tablature of 1570.

MATELOTTE (Holland)

A sailors' dance performed in wooden shoes, with arms folded behind the back. The music, in 2/4 time, is in two parts with definitely marked rhythm. *Die Tanzmusik* by Schubert gives a good example of this rhythm.

MATELOTTE, LA, OR MACLOTE, LA (Belgium)

A dance of the Ardenne, to be seen at Stavelot on the Fête de la Journée Ardennaise, held on the Sunday after August 15th. Very gay and quick, in 4/4 time, it is performed by four couples standing opposite each other, each man on the left of his partner. Once known in the whole of the Walloon country, *La Maclote* may have reached Belgium during the 18th century, from Provence. There were then two versions—a slow, graceful style; and a quicker, springing version, as performed at Namur, Liège and Stavelot. The latter style developed variations called *Aredjes* (rages), each variation being called after a different village. The dance as performed at Stavelot has six figures, and is immediately followed by a Second *Maclote* having eight figures. In Provence a popular dance is *Les Matelotes* once performed by sailors on board warships in Toulon.

MATHEMATICS AND DANCE

Becomes first apparent in "counting" to musical beats; and then in "stepping" to space. This may remain half apprehended; merely as a pragmatic usage of arithmetic, but not known as a principle. Yet dance is the finest method, both primitive and final, of obtaining the ultimate principles of all mathematical thinking. Mathematics rules in two modes—apparently opposed, but in fact essentially integrated. Commercial reckonings, long ago, were compared with architectural or building reckonings, without wide realization that both of these systems depended upon movement. While the temple was deliberately erected, as a shell in which basic ritual could then properly be performed or acted through, the trader accepted unconsciously the movement of wares in barter, and credits in separated transactions (which are the basis of world trade, on credit-confidence). Commercial arithmetic, for long gripped by local standards, was slow to expand to national standards. (Precisely the same variation is seen in local or national moral standards, which receive expression at festivals in folk dances, as well as in other actions). Mathematics is the logical process of the mind in precise reasoning: at first it was occupied with sensory data; with things, with quantities ,or services; easy to see, and to measure. Clever traders caught their profits, by personal adjustment of natural rhythm to fixed quantities ("buy up corn when plentiful and available; sell corn when scarce; and demands increase"). This "dance of trade" (fluctuation is its economic name) serves material gain or loss. Historic change, to reckoning of abstract quantities, then led to extended credit, to a wider choreography of commerce. Much later, came the general concept of abstract or real energies, which gave birth, mathematically, to the "quantum theory". So modern mathematics works in four main modes: two of *quantity* or solidity of form; and two of *quality* or energy. There is a dance, typical of each, in terms of orderly movement of the entities engaged. These comprise the Dance of Mathematics. In Europe, it clings to geometrical concepts; in India the philosophical grip still utilises the traditional figures of personalized gods and lesser entities, the population of Hindu mythology. In their functions and relations, they dance or fight.

MATRAN AND KRODISH (Tibetan Dance)

Are two demon figures slain as a cosmic sacrifice by two Boddhisatvas. Krodish and his wife were noted as particularly horrible monsters, not at all nice, whereupon their destruction was determined. The two beneficent masters, the Boddhisatvas, first approached in their "mild aspect", but being un-

able to become victors, they transformed their shapes into a Head of a Horse and the Head of a Sow, respectively. This tale is forcibly expressed in mythic terms. Soon the contest was over, the demons were destroyed; and the two victors celebrated their success by a solemn religious dance. From this legend derives the fame of Dorje-Phagma (Sow-Thunderbolt, literally), who, as Lady Dorjei is now asserted to be re-incarnated in the person of the abbess of a famous Tibetan convent. As a festival, this dance is said to have been performed firstly by the great Lama Padma Sambhava (Lotus of Equilibrium), to overcome the devices of numerous malignant entities who sought to prevent the building of a new home for the Samyé Gompa. Padma Sambhava is shewn in some temples as the wizard priest in place of Gautama Buddha. He is presented, sitting before a lotus-screen, wearing a mitred hat, holding his *dorje* (thunderbolt mystic weapon) in his right hand; and a skull libation vessel in his left hand. His two wives attend him; one bearing an offering of blood, the other with an offering of wine. The two wives were Khando Yeshe Tsho-gyal (Tibetan) and Lha-chen Mandarawa (Indian). Padma Sambhava was said to be a graduate of the great University of Nalanda; to be a native of Ghazni (born about 720 AD), and to have gone to Tibet in 747 AD.

MATSURI (Japan)

Annual festivals held at various dates, in honour of the local god (equivalent to the Jewish Ba'Al, known as the Ujigami. They were state Shinto ceremonies, run by *Matsurigoto* (the Government). The god, or his emblem, was taken in solemn procession (like a French carnival scene) from temple to temple. *Kagura** performances (mime and dance etc.) went on all day and late at night, supervised by *Nakatomi* officials. There were booths for the sale of toys, mascots or pilgrim tokens; wrestling; fireworks; races; conjurors; tumblers, and itinerant musicians with dancers. Some of the liturgy (for the serious part) mentions the *Michiahe** (always prominent in Spring) and others, in the Book *Yengishiki* (tenth century). Some of the official liturgies are called *norito*.

MAUNDY (English)

As applied to Maunday or Maundy Thursday, it signifies today the time for an ornamental "bestowal of Maunday money". This is the last feeble trace of a Latin doctrine: namely, that this was the day (or evening) of the *Coeni Domini* or (Last) Supper of the Lord. The action still followed is the "washing of feet", now a highly bureaucratic process, more scientific than any surgery, entirely without any technical meaning. In ritual, the Supper was supposed (by some writers) to be the time when the *Hymn of Jesus** was last sung; or, according to officials, both occasion and action were "instituted", though not the slightest historical reference is adduced. The modern difficulty of accepting this *Coeni Domini* is that the day now follows instead of precedes Easter or the Paschal period; though this kind of separation is not unusual in theological doctrine. The dance was later connected with the *Allemonde** (and still retains an association with an Almoner or dispenser of alms).

MAVILAKKU (Malabar, S. India)
Processional Dance of Carrying Lighted Lamps, usually at Festival of *Diwali** (Festival of Lights). Performed usually by groups of young girls, a version of *Kummi.** Flowers may be carried and scattered on the way.

MAWL-GERDD (Welsh)
Carol, especially a love-song, with its rhythmic dance melody; also called *carawl*. The basic term *molianna* is "to give praise". *Mawlrhodfa* is "praising in a ring" of dancers.

MAXIXE (Brazil)
A pair dance, first mentioned in Brazilian records in 1884. Said to have derived in some part from the *Batuque,** the music, according to musical authorities, was a mixture of Spanish and American styles, with rhythms borrowed from the *Catarete* and *Embolada.** In 1905 the *Maxixe* was performed in Paris as an exhibition dance; and, in modified form, later became popular in ballrooms of Europe and America. In England in the years before the 1914-18 war, as a ballroom dance, the *Maxixe Brésilienne* was well known; and in Paris about 1921, the music of the earlier exhibition dance reappeared in more rhythmical form as the Samba.* The *Maxixe* is in moderate duple measure, with simple syncopated rhythms.

MA'YONG (Malaya)
General theatrical performance, of Siamese origin, often including dancing, posturing, and singing. Numerous tunes have special apposite action.

MAYPOLE DANCE (England)
Mediaeval rural dance, practised by villagers (and some townsmen) for May First as a Spring festival celebration. The centre was the tall May Pole, which by rights should be a newly cut, living tree, bearing a green bough at its summit. This essential symbol was gradually forgotten; the Pole was a fir scaffold, preserved from year to year, especially in towns where a great height was thought most desirable. At the period of the anti-Rome revolt through Europe, in England the May Pole was included in rejections; to Puritans the Feast was especially offensive. The pastime was forbidden by Parliament in 1644; but on the return of Charles Stuart, with lady friends who liked dancing, the rural festivals also revived in every respect (and disrespect). In the Strand in London, a tall pole 134 feet high was erected, supervised by the Duke of York (later James II), and duly celebrated. Many other English towns celebrated May First in this way; the date has now turned into a semi-political artisans' rite, though deferred to the nearest Sunday. The Maypole dance is now performed principally by school children; its proud and ancient history is tactfully set aside; its connection with the Assyrian *Asherah* is never mentioned in schools. The old Maypole was decorated with two or three flower wreaths of graded size, and with streamers, but ribbons for plaiting were unknown until late in the 19th century. Plaiting is first heard of at Whitelands College, in 1888 (where John Ruskin introduced May Queen celebrations), and later became popular in schools as a students' pastime, with no special significance. Plaiting occurs in several European countries (and in Mexico), the ribbons being attached to a short, portable pole, and having no connection with May Day celebrations. They are "Ribbon Dances", rather than "Maypole Dances", and sometimes illustrate the processes of weaving.
[See *Cinta Dantza; Courdello, Lei; Cordon, Baile del; Listones, Los*]

MAZE—1 (from Iranian Zoroastrian mythos)
From A'Hora Mah-azhada—the Ritual Dance of the Axe; the religion of Northern Europe/Asia in the time of the great forests. The symbolism branched off, on the south to Crete, where it developed the Sacred Double Axe; and the *Labyrinthos* (or ritual maze). The term survives in "adze". The full-scale Maze form was then planted in artificial labyrinth design, to repeat the world-forest or labyrinth, through which Early Man had to fight his way with a stone axe. When personalised in the myth, Ahura Mazda had to fight his antagonist, A'Rimmon—the "god of circumference", who forever enclosed and prisoned Ahura, as god of light. Through Scandinavia, the artificial maze was contrived; one term is *Volland-haus* (in Iceland), but when this became a Vallhalla, it turned to a place of shelter; not a maze or place of ritual testing. The existent Maze at Hampton Court (near London) shows one quarter of a decussated square and circle pattern. The maze patterns, still made (as the *Tangov** pattern etc.) by the Polynesian people of Malekula (New Hebrides), show the same primitive ideas as a mode

of control : the soul has to find a path through a linear pattern which must previously be practised and learned. The Myth of Theseus and Ariadne at Minos is a narrative of the same form. Spiraline "magical patterns" or "spells" follow in the same tradition; in European ritual, the last remnant was "The Way to Jerusalem"* inlaid on the nave of some French churches. See *Maze and Labyrinth.* W. H. Mathews.
[See *Labyrinth; Malekula, Dances of; Na-Leng; Geranos*]

MAZE—2 (Ancient Iran)
Is the schematic or ritual form of the "World Puzzle" of *labyrinth,* which was used in connection with the disciplinary trials of the religion of Ahura-Mazda, known in North Western Europe, later as the doctrine of Mithras* (the Mediator). The disciple was required to find his way, within a set period, to the centre of the tangled Maze. Numerous "trees with shields" occur in mediaeval design; this particular arrangement is a record of the symbol; when the "worthy knight" had arrived at the centre, and had there hung his shield. Previous instructions had given him some clues, doubtless with "orientation guides" from sun and shadow, as he twisted and turned. The whole scheme is a localised symbol of the world-forest; through which primitive man had, in fact, to cut his way with an axe. From this grimly necessitous basis, the axe became ritualized; symbolised and shewn with leaves engraved on it, memories of real leaves on a real cutting axe. The patterns of ritual dance-form then left the walled maze and became a checker game; then the spiraline dance of the church; and finally, a dance with no visible lines at all. Britain and northern countries long retained the formal Maze; and when the forest lost its terror, the formal well-clipped Maze and its setting provided the basis of the "Pleasure Garden"; yet still with "shepherds and sheep" wandering the formal paths in formal joy. The oriental religions used the same symbol and the similar discipline; as in the Hindu *sangsara;* the Buddhist *Wheel of the Law;* the Egyptian *House of Labyrinth* seen by Herodotus; but the Tibetan development is into a dancing nether world, as a realm of the unliving soul, enveloped in its own images. Traditionally, the centre of any such Maze was called "Home". In Crete, the legend of the Minotaurus carries the basis of the Maze.
[See *Tibetan Sacred Dance; Labyrinth; "Way to Jerusalem"; Bardo*]

MAZE DANCE
One of the oldest religious dances performed ritually in three different main modes; and publicly

in one of these modes at the four quarters (seasons) of the solar year; the two equinoxes and the two solstices. Their chief ritual value was to symbolise the labyrinthine process of involution, of revolution, and of evolution, in dance processionals and ceremonials that go back to the age of the great Stone Circles, such as that at Avebury in England; at Carnac in Brittany; possibly earlier at Karnak in Egypt; and on other sites now destroyed. The doctrine that surrounded these Maze Rituals requires study. (See also *Labyrinth;* Troy Game;* and *Way to Jerusalem.*) Remains of vegetation Mazes remain in England; some were newly constructed merely for pastime, at dates much later than the accompanying rituals would justify (as at Hampton Court). Some were built in stone lined paths (specially in Scandinavia).

"MAZOWSZE"
Name of the Polish State Dance Company, referring to Mazovia in the great plain of Poland, home of the *Mazur,* Kujawiak* and *Oberek.** In 1948, at Karolin Castle in Mazovia, about twenty miles from Warsaw, composer Tadeusz Sygietynski and his wife, stage designer Mira Ziminska, established the nucleus of the Company (singers, dancers, musicians), selected from many hundreds of young people in the villages of Mazovia. Today (1957) the Company numbers nearly 100, with ages ranging from sixteen to twenty-five. Living at Karolin, they receive a general education as well as tuition in music and ballet, with a month's annual vacation. Aiming to present the folk songs and dances of Poland in a theatrically acceptable form, the founders have collected a repertoire of highly effective items firmly based on tradition. Mira Ziminska has produced brilliant versions of authentic regional costumes, and the choral and dance numbers make a highly coloured and vivacious performance. Besides appearing in Poland, "Mazowsze" has performed in Europe and in Pekin.
[Cp. "*Pearly Bouquet*" (Hungary); *Inbal* (Israel); *Bayanihan* (Phillipines)]

MAZURKA, MAZUR (Poland)
Found throughout Poland, but originating in Mazovia, where it is known to have been danced in the 16th century. A peasant dance for eight or sixteen couples, it then had a circular formation, and was accompanied by the singing of national songs. The melody of the Polish national anthem is based on the *Mazurka* rhythm, and its vital connection with the people is expressed in the verse :
   "Matthew is dead
   And laid out on the board,
   But if they would strike up a tune for him
   He would dance;

For such is the soul of Mazur
That though dead
He will not be still".

Danced at all social gatherings, the *Mazurka* is started by the leader and his partner, followed by the next couple in order, until all are dancing. For the man it has spectacular steps, but the girl is not ignored during these displays, being continually brought into the dance as a partner and not merely a background for his brilliance. To music in 3/4 or 6/8 time, the dance is now in line formation with a variety of figures and steps, and a strong accent on the second beat. Steps include *holupiec*, in which dancers take a small sideways jump, clicking heels together in the air; and a leap by the man, dropping on to one knee while his partner, whose hand he holds, dances round him. Tempo is much slower than the ordinary *waltz*. In the 18th century the *Mazurka* was introduced into Germany by Augustus III, Elector of Saxony and King of Poland, later becoming a popular dance in the ballrooms of Paris and London, where it arrived about 1845. Whereas the stately *Polonaise** was used to open Court balls, the *Mazurka* often concluded a ball. When Poland was annexed by Russia in 1832, the *Mazurka* became also a Russian dance, but was performed by an indefinite number of couples, whereas the Polish dance was limited to four or eight couples. The Polish *Mazurka* has three variants—*Mazurek, Kujawiak** and *Oberek.**

MAZYA (Bantu, S. Africa)

Dance of Initiation for girls; belongs to the *kusolola* or "coming out ceremony". The term *mazya* indicated (for the Bantu tribes who hold the *Ndola** initiation ritual—as among the *Nsenga* (Patuaka) in N. Rhodesia) the collective dances which the young girl is required to learn and perform. This rite is controlled by a *nyapunga* (midwife), who first takes her small fee; and begins with the pubescent girl by giving her a herbal bath. Prisoned in her grandmother's hut, the girl remains there up to three months, during which time she is taught *sisikanya*—"to behave", with the traditional dances (notably *mitunga* with its drum music). Equivalent to the "court curtsey", the girl begins practice while kneeling; she swishes her grass skirt to and fro with increasing skill (*nyung'ula*) and finishes by doing it, standing (*Kutendekela*). The "coming out", in fact, does mean coming out of the temporary prison; then the great Mazya drums boom and the dance begins. [See *Ndola*]

MEASURE—1 (England)

A court dance of the 16th century, which grew out of the French *Basse Danse.** Of dignified character, it seems to have resembled the *Pavane,** since little special music was written for it, *Measures* being generally danced to *Pavane* airs. The phrase "to tread a measure", indicates that this was no lively tripping dance, but a stately progression, as indicated by Shakespeare in *Much Ado About Nothing*, when Beatrice compares "wooing, wedding and repenting" to "a Scotch jig, a measure and a cinque a pace; . . . . . the wedding, mannerly-modest as a measure, full of state and ancientry . . . .". Measures were danced at the Courts of Elizabeth I and James I. In the later reign elaborate figure dances in the royal Masques were called *Measures*, but as the term was sometimes used to signify a dance generally, these may have taken any form. *Measures* were danced against, instead of with, the tempo of the music, and this dancing in cross-rhythms gave the *Measure* its character. At the "Revels" occasionally given at the Inns of Court by the Societies of Law and Equity, *Measures* were popular, the dignified progress of the dance no doubt being considered appropriate for performance by legal dignitaries. The term "Measure" is significant in relation to *La Danse Geometrique** and, in the sense of division into sections, the term was used in the older *Basse Danse*, which was divided into three "Measures"—Grand Measure, Medium Measure, and Little Measure. One example of music specifically called "A Measure" exists in the Giles Lodge Lute Book (1570) and has been set for keyboard by Arnold Dolmetsch.

MEASURE—2

In Dance has three main features: (a) Technical; (b) Stylistic; and (c) Thematic. The measure or canon may refer to the actual distance used; the length of pace, and its direction. Technically this movement derives from the human body and its norm of measure; thus we can expect to find slight difference in the dance-paces of a grown man, a woman or a child. Combined with the Measure of space and direction, we have the measures of music, in beats or speed and rhythm. These may be simple or complex; one or two instruments or an orchestra; measure in melody, or multiple measures in harmony. Stylistic measures belong partly to exposition; they arise in gesture and position, as in ritual dances; always they tend to follow in a known tradition. Or in some modern works a localised style may be imposed. This form belongs to dramatic elements of dance; it governs the unfolding theme, in the contrasts of emotion, swift or slow; and obliges both technical method and stylistic form to submit to its drive for adequate exposition. In ritual, this canon is ruled by the ceremonial and its import.

MEDIAEVAL DANCE STYLES (England)

A circumstantial and mirthful tract, printed in 1609, was entitled: *"Old Meg of Hereforeshire" for a Maid Maryan and Herefore Towne doe a Morris Dance; or Twelve Morris Dauncers in Hereforeshire.*

After a long dedication come the ascriptions of current styles:

"The courts of kings for stately measures; the city for light heels and nimble footing; the country for shuffling dances; western men for gambols; Middlesex men for tricks aboue ground; Essex men for the hays; Lancashire for hornpipes; Worcestershire for bagpipes; but Herefordshire for a Morris dance, puts down not only all Kent but very near (if one had time to measure it) three quarters of christendom. Neuer had sainte Sepulchers a treuer ring of bells; neuer did any silk-weauer keep brauer time with the knocke of the heel; neuer had the dancing horse a better tread of the toe; neuer could Beuerley fair giue money to a more sound taborer; nor neuer had Robin Hood a more deft Mayd-Marian".

This Morris had "two musicians, four whifflers (marshals with long staves, white and red) and twelve dancers".

MEDIAEVAL DANCING (England)

Was of three kinds: that of the *jongleurs* or minstrels; country dancing; and social dances of the nobility. After the Crusades, repertoires of the jongleurs, besides tumbling and acrobatics, included dances with an Oriental tinge. Many lords had their own troupe, such as John of Gaunt, who had a Court of Minstrels at Tutbury in 1380. Country dances were the simple round, or *Carole*,* as were also the social dances of the 12th century and earlier. Knights and ladies standing alternately, took hands in a circle, and moved round to the accompaniment of songs or of rhythmic hand-clapping. Verses were sung by a soloist, the whole company joining in the refrain. In the great halls, the time between dinner and supper at five o'clock was often occupied with dancing *Caroles*, which became a general name for dancing, so that "caroler" meant "to dance". In the 12th and 13th centuries, the *Branle*,* a linked circle variation of the *Carole*, became popular. The *Espringale*,* introduced into England by the Saxons, was danced with a little spring or hop; while the *Estampie** of the Provençal troubadours was also danced in England in the 13th century. Later dances became more sprightly, and in the 15th century moralists, alarmed at their lively character, warned young ladies "not to be too eager in dancing", and "to dance with moderation . . .". In the Interlude *The Four Elements*, there is a reference to people—

"That shall both daunce and sprynge,
And torne clene above the grounde,
With fryscas and with gambawdes round,
That all the hall shall ryng'".

Cp. the later Elizabethan dance, *La Volta*,* against which protests were also made.

MEDIAEVAL MIRACLE PLAYS

Along with Mystery Plays and the Moralities, were urged by intermittent means by many clerics, in two principal modes: those on behalf of their own propaganda; and those which seized on older legends and re-arranged them. With the revived Grecian myths of the Renaissance they had little success; these were not understood by the people. One source was the *Golden Legend* collection; this was extended by Lope de Vega and Tirso Molinos in Spain; and even Cervantes had an unofficial attempt in his satire *Don Quixote*. Many of these plays included dance episodes (*interludus*) or stressed heavy mime; some performed inside the churches, others in the specially reserved spaces of the cloisters. Among the revised older legends we find (a) Robin and Marian; (b) Jean d'Arc, another Marian cycle), the Doctor Faust story (from Ha-Phaestus, cherished by Stoics) and the Don Juan story (from John, or Johann, the June solar festival). The Winter *Agon* was turned into "Moors *versus* Xtians; and the old *X-messe* into Christmas.

MEGISTER KOUROS (Ancient Hellas)

The "Greatest Youth" who led the sacred Spring dance of the *Kuroi* (company) of the Initiate Youths. The concept is close to the splendid dualism of the Egyptian "Son of God", who was Horus Twofold (though not as Kronos or Janua, the god of time-past-future of the Roman year or *Annua*). Horus was the Dying God of the Old Time (some rites affirmed the Solar Year), and the New-Born God, Horus the Younger, of the New Year— the shining "Heavenly Babe". These Hellenic *Kouroi*, were the human counterparts, the strong among men, now become lesser gods by initiation: yet were also the Aphiktor, the Suppliants. (It later became noted as "Saint Viktor"). Gilbert Murray, in a notable passage, remarks on the ritual projection of mass emotion[1]:

"A similar projection (to the Aphiktor) arose from the dance of the *Kouroi*, or initiate youths, in the dithyramb—the magic dance which was to celebrate . . . the coming of Spring. The dance projected the Megistos Kouros, the greatest of youths, who is the incarnation of spring or the return of life; and it lies at the back of so many of the most gracious shapes of the classical pantheon. The *Kouros* appears as Dionysus; as

Apollo; as Hermes; as Ares : in our clearest and most detailed piece of evidence (in *Themis*[2]) he actually appears with the characteristic history and attributes of Zeus".

Megistos remains with us in *magister* as it does in *magician*—inheritance from the older Sons of Khaldu in Assyria; from their magical secret of how to induce and gather and focus the tension (sometimes called *mana*,* sometimes *mania*), that vitalises a group of human beings when possessed by one idea, and moved by one passion. This is the meaning of *orgia*; as revealed in the dynamism of ritual dance.

[1] *Five Stages of Greek Religion*. Gilbert Murray. London, 1935.
[2] *Themis*. Jane Ellen Harrison. London, 1927.

MEJORANA (Panama)
A traditional dance, probably of Spanish origin. In square dance form, with partners facing each other, *zapateado** steps are used, and the *paseo* or promenade. Five-stringed guitars (Mejoranera) take their name from the dance which they accompany. There are many traditional *Mejorana* airs, sung during the dance, the melody being in 2/4 time with an accompaniment in 6/8 time. Usually in the major key, when it is played in the minor key its name is changed to *Gallino*. The *Mejorana-Poncho* is a slower version.

MEMORY TRAINING and Use in Dance
Should begin, yet never end the actor's development. Without mastery, he can never be a master. The human memory is not single, but multiple; yet despite this fundamental factor (which always helps to divide, disperse, and destroy memories) the various complications of memory must be analysed, studied, and thoroughly learned. Ordinary dance-training rarely includes any attention to memory, except by merely empirical devices. Rarely does it help a girl to remember her steps or routine, by throwing a stick at her. Such incivility is merely an abject admission from the ballet-master that he does not understand his subject; and, not understanding, cannot expect to teach it. Many people can do a piece of work, but far fewer can teach others how and why and when to perform it.

Memory operates in the complete human being, on four main levels :

1. The basic *Cell Memory* : it keeps our tissues alive;
2. The *Organic Memory* : it keeps our body organised and in health;
3. The *Emotional Memory* : it dominates our social relations and formulates our desires;

4. The *Intellectual Memory* : it makes conscious our ideas, aims and methods.

Every one of these phases of memory must operate in dancing. Kinaesthetic rhythm moves in cell, tissue and organ. Emotional rhythm energises the entire body with its external relations. Intellectual rhythm controls the sanity of the mind and soul by its regular rise and fall. Every aspect of these memories must be trained. Though the sub-conscious rhythms—operative in cell and tissue—may be trusted to maintain balance and progress, interference with them from within or outside may provoke disturbance, loss of memory, absence of imaginative power. Kinaesthetic memory governs the technology of all dancing. Without its control the body is paralysed. Yet this kinesis is subject to emotional impacts—again, from inside and outside the single body; it has to be trained; or powers of Mimesis fail. We cannot focus the image that we have to seize, to make, and to present, if memory source is lacking. Dance has to present an image; an emotion or mood, an idea; or (in ballet) a character in relation to other characters. Memory must dominate and control all of these relations.
[See *An Actor Prepares*. K. Stanislavsky. New York, 1936]

MENARI HINEI, Henna Dance (Malaya)
Performed chiefly at weddings. A small cake of henna, held in a brass cup (*gompong hinei*) is surrounded by candles on a small tray. This cup is carried by the girl dancer, who must turn it over and around without allowing the candles to become extinguished. (Cp. *Tari Piring**). There is a special step, *Langkah tar' hinei* or *tari hinei*; while the traditional melody is *Laghu berhinei*. This ceremony is called *Menyelang* or *Berlebat* : the dance over, the rice—also henna stained (cp. Cornish saffron stains in eatables, or Hindu usage of turmeric in ritual), is eaten by guests; the rest being given to those engaged in *Main Zikir* (the chant or prayer circle).

MENDET (Bali, Indonesia)
A temple dance of offering to the gods, performed by women, in slow tempo. At Asak, during a festival, it follows *Redjang*,* danced by the village girls, and these two dances recur at intervals during the day and night of the feast. After dancing *Redjang*, the girls join the older women, and all advance slowly towards the altar, in twos. The offering of flowers and food in a silver dish, is held in the right hand, while the left hand moves gracefully with raised fingers, as the body sways slowly twice to right and twice to left. With slow, rhythmic movement, the double line of women advances. During a festival any girl who wishes may become

a temporary priestess, first undergoing a ritual purification. These girls, who perform the temple dances, are called *Njoetri* or *Soetri* (*Soetji* meaning "cleansing").

MERCHANDIZING BY DANCE

Has been developed anew, in terms mainly of small ballet or dance-groups. The basic idea is to attract the dance-conscious public; to formulate a display in dance, which shall combine some aesthetic appeal with a more or less subtly integrated presentation of the sponsor's merchandise or services. This basic idea is not new; for the scheme was used all over Western Europe by the various itinerant vendors of numerous commodities. Italian bands of monks toured from town to town, selling medicines. The famous liqueur (with its claim to eighty ingredients) was developed by bands of Benedictines, who carried a line of patter and dance; while the Gesuati (known as Acquaviva Brothers) were famous for alcoholic merchandise in Mediaeval Italy. The Montebanqui succeeded them; and then the *Marchandes des Foires*. The modern form has shown us perfumes, receiving publicity through a repertoire of a dozen simple dance-sketches, performed in large halls in USA department stores (Lentheric), while the Ford Company arranged its own ballet company for a World Fair. Bakery and confectionery has been featured; and from England, an organization devoted to wool publicity, has used dance in a film show. Diaghileff more skilfully combined the merchandising of Paris fashions in two of his ballets with subsidies from Madame Chanel (*Beach* and *Train Bleu*). The Shell Oil Company also used dance film for publicity; but the theme had no sort of relation to any kind of oil. [See *Commercial Ballet; Store Display Dance*]

MERENGUE (Dominican Republic)

A song-dance in 2/4 time, usually in the major key. After an introductory promenade, or *Paseo*, come interludes called *Jaleo*. In Haiti the dance tune, otherwise identical in syncopated rhythm and musical structure, is called *Meringue*, and is in the minor key. The song in Haiti is sung in French, the Dominican in Spanish. A gay and vigorous dance, showing marked African influence, it seems to be a mixture of African and Spanish styles. In Haiti, a more dignified version is performed in dance-halls and ballrooms, than the freer dance of the streets. Origin of the *Merengue* is uncertain. Dominicans believe it to have come with Negro slaves from Cuba, or from Puerto Rica or Haiti. Some consider it to derive from an African dance in duple time called *Meringha*, while it has also been asserted that the name comes from a verb "*merenguearse*", meaning "to dance with great abandon". It seems

possible that the verb may have come from the dance style. The *Merengue* folk dance is very popular in the Dominican Republic as a favourite example of Caribbean rhythm. The ballroom version is sometimes called "Dominican One-Step". It is danced "on the spot", as contrasted with the *Paso Doble* or *One-Step*, which travels round the room. Tempo is an even beat in 2/4 measure. Many of the variations in this dance rhythm carry popular songs, such as "Te Lo Dije"; "El Conquistador"; "Recuerdos de Infancia"; and "Merengue Nacional", which all possess the basic lyrical quality of this folk-dance-song.

MERRY ANDREW (Mediaeval English, from Greek)

Leader of the group or band of servants who brought in the dishes at a ceremonial meal. The term derives from *meristes* (dividers), or *meris* (share, or portion), and *to Andreia*, the public meal, followed by the Greeks from earlier Cretan tradition. Hence : *meris-andreia*, the "meal-sharers", equivalent to the *dekans*, who served up the church meal or feast for the poor. Ancient custom provided for musical entries (followed down to late mediaeval times, and still later in Russia), where the Tweenies, who brought meals from cookhouse to table, sang and danced to announce their coming. The *Boar's Head Carol* is a late example of this custom; another is used by the Scots to "pipe in the Haggis". The final term was given to the jester or buffoon who accompanied the string of servitors (*sirventes*), at a court or baronial dinner; but originally it came into Scotland with the Greek missions. In 16th century England it signified a court buffoon, a dancing mimic who acts as a clown. Though this referred to one Andrew Borde (physician to Henry VIII, who admired his wit), the term Andrew is very much older; in Greek it seems to denote a group : "the others"; (in German, *die andere*); and in mediaeval England served as a generic term for a varlet or manservant (as did Abigail for the maids). Most probably it denoted the four ritual dancers who stood at the ends of the Andrew Cross in primitive liturgy (Roman style, following the augurs), indicated as "one dancer in the centre, and the andrews at the points". Andrew Borde wrote *The Merry Tales of Gotham*.

"MERRY DANCERS" (*Aurora Borealis*; also *Aurora Australis*)

The "Merry Dancers" is the name given by the Shetlanders at Uist, and by peasants in far northern latitudes, to the electro-magnetic phenomenon seen soon after dark on many winter evenings. First appears a dark circle segment followed by a brilliant arch of fiery light; often several concentric

circles separate rings of this arch. From the arch rise columns of visual light, variegated and beautiful in colour, shooting towards the zenith. Sheaves of light scatter in masses in all directions, when there is a general undulating of the light. This is the feature that has been called "Dancing Lights" or "Fairies Lights" and a score more poetical names. A fiery coronet finally forms about the upper ends of the columns; they all meet in vibrating flame, but periodic renewals occur, until all of the light collects over the north and it fades into rising daylight. Frequently the brilliant light is attended with crackling noises, hissing and explosive sounds. The Aurora has four annual points of maximum appearance, the greatest being in October. Sometimes one or two can be seen in a year in London; three or four in Edinburgh. The precise reason for the Polar Lights is not yet established. Kastner assigned them to terrestrial electricity; and Franklin, with Bailly, to magnetism. Probably both modes of electrical action are included, as part of the cosmic circulation of energy to and from the sun. The attribution of dancing is of great interest in relation to seasonal earth rhythms and their traditional association of dance and music.
[See "Chèvres Dansantes"; "Pretty Dancers"]

MERRY-GO-ROUND (England)
Colloquial term for a masque-dance in which ten or twelve dancing animals (horse, dragon, unicorn, and the like) moved in a rapidly dancing ring. When the dance form became obsolete, it was taken up by the Fair entertainers, who contrived a large mechanical wheel, made as a ring with horses, on which juvenile riders could sit, and whirl on the "Merry-go-Round". The first form was simple; with perhaps six or eight seats, propelled by a hand-turned winch in the centre; but the highly efficient modern form became steam, then electrical, with a loud organ to increase the merriment; and the horses not only move round the circle, but bob up and down. This is known in France as the Carrousel.

MERRY MESSE (Scotland)
At Irvine in Ayrshire, is celebrated on March 25th the ancient Merry Messe (Spring Feast), now revised into Mary Mass by clerical enterprise. Nine-Anne (Fire Festival), as the traditional name of Nunian is given as Saint Ninian or Ninianne. The pageant is now transferred to August (usually better for weather), and a Marie Messe Queen is elected from schoolchildren, supported by four attendants or Maries. They, with Wallace and Bruce, are prominent in the town procession; while Brothered Carters of the local union, ride the marches or boundaries. The Captain is "lifted"

and after the crowning of the Queen at the Town House, there is a civic processional, costumed in historical attire, from the Fiscal and his Axe Bearers to the Burgh Halberdiers; the Provost and his fellow magistrates. Following the Races, there is a festal tea and dancing at the Town House. It is clear that several ceremonies have been coalesced into one occasion; though it is admitted (or boasted) that the origin of the Merrie Queen of Messe derives probably from Druidical rituals.
[See Marie Llwyd; Kate Kennedy]

MESHICHOYO, MESHIGOYO (Syriac) (Goyim)
Also as Mashijoyo; ritual term indicating the dancing participants in the primitive Syrian form of Mass or Messe, the fraternal supper, held weekly as part of the Chaldaean Rite; and continuing thus into the primitive Syrian mode of the christian system. So important was it esteemed, that the current Arabian reference to early chrestianoi was as Ya Meshichoyo. The form of dance was usually extremely simple; it occurred with the entry of the plates of bread and salt, and of wine or water; this was for long continued in rituals of the Russian church, as the same rhythmic movement remained part of the Rabbinic ceremonial; and is still apparent in the ritual suppers of the Coptic Church, when they bring in the "sacred bread" from the Beit Leham (the "House of Bread"), with dancing steps; and, on festival days, with appropriate chanting.

MESS OR MESSE
The Communal Feast; followed by a dance; sometimes including the ritual ceremony or dances of the servitors. This term belongs to a most ancient lineage of functions, all connected with the festival rituals of civilised peoples, beginning (so far as we can say now) with Meshken, the great temple feasts of Egypt, from some 5,000 years BC. With Meskhen, the "Feast of the House of Birth" alternates the "Feast of the Mastaba", the Sacred Stone Table of the Dead. From these came the shorter term Messe, and Mass or supper, finding a regular practice in Alexandria. The Greek inner court Messaulon was used for dining and then dancing; while in Abyssinia the Coptic church calls its chancel (used for the ritual meal) the Maskhell. The Hebrew term Ma'shhiakh or M'Sheik meant primarily "lord of the feast" (from Arabic, sheik), but was rendered in Greek as Messias, master of the feast (of masche or barley-cake), which in Latin became Messiah, "ruler of the feast" (and by symbolism, "master of the feast of life" with heavenly dance). In Northern Europe, the ritual labyrinthos* was renamed as maze;* and from this lateral line developed mace, maize, mazer (the bowl of wine),

and other terms associated with ritual dance and ceremonial. In the Greek *kirke* or Latin *chiesa*, the weekly supper became the *mess* and then *mass*, as it atrophied from a real feast into a mere token celebration. Thence the term, having spread into England, was satirised as "Lord of Misrule", from the functional term Lord of *Mess Ruelle* (or Supper-circle), in mediaeval times. The military followed the university students and law sergeants in maintaining their communal or regimental *mess;* and, down to these times, it is insisted that a student must "dine with his fellows" as a sign of his communal life. In secular terms, the Winter Feast of Solstice (the clerics having imposed on it the term *X-messe* or *Kresten-messe*), turned to *Masque** (in France) and *Masking* (in England), and *Mascherata* (in Italy) from *Masca-ruad*. In Germany, the term *Messe* remains now as the title of Trade Fairs (*Leipsiger Messe*, twice yearly), still associated with a mayoral dinner. Theatrical modes cover the *Mascarade** and the "masked ball", now as empty amusements, with no ritual meaning. Islam retains the term *Massjd* or *Masjid* (or *Massyid*), as the sacred place for its worship; there is no feasting, but it signifies the "place of the people", as *Jumma Masjid* (Messyid) in Delhi, the largest mosque in India. The finality of the line is heard in *mask*, the secondary reference to the disguise or covering; though it is applied by Europeans to the ritual cover-symbols used in their religious ceremony by Africans and others. The scientific world uses the word *mass* to denote the "attractive power" of a certain element of energy or quantity of material, instead of "weight".

MICHIAHE (Japan)

Phallic Festival (with worship of Sake-no-Kami, phallic symbol deities), formerly held in great esteem through Japan. The Kannushi priests advertised it as a ceremonial prayer "for prevention of pestilence", when all the local "ladies of joy" turned out in full regalia in ornate processional marches, through every town of note, from their official quarters, the Yoshiwara. In recent years, the realistic figures and the forms of dance have been "toned down", and now the ostensible Cherry Blossom Festival is the chief replacement. The festival was one of the many *Matsuri*. [See *Mitaka*]

MICHI-YUKI (Japan)

"Journey of Love". Descriptive dance-interludes in Kabuki* theatre, between acts of historical plays, as a relief from intense drama. They usually depict two lovers who pause in their journey to describe past events, make love, or comment on the scenery, and then proceed towards their destination. Sometimes, instead of lovers, the characters

may be a mother and daughter on their way to a wedding, or a concubine with her servant proceeding to their master's secret hiding-place. Now often performed as a separate item, the "travel dance" was originally part of the play itself, as in *Yoshitsune and the Thousand Cherry Trees* (1747). The fourth scene shows the concubine Shizuka and retainer Tadanobu, who rest in the forest while journeying to rejoin their lord, Yoshitsune. They dance together, describing their journey and the virtues of Yoshitsune.

MIDSUMMER FAIRIES (E. Yugoslavia)

General name given at Duboka (near the Danube) to "occult powers" known as Ielele, believed to visit the village in a period (following the Trinity Feast), called *Rusalii** or "Rose Time". They are shown in the processions or dances, by men bearing three typical styles of mask, said to be servants of three mysterious women called "The Emperor's Daughters", the dancing *Rusalii*. The fairy groups are known as *Vintoasele* (The Windy Ones) who wait for the trance (probably the same as the *pneuma* of Corinth, centuries ago); the *Frumoasele* (The Beautiful Ones); and the *Bunasele* (The Well-wishers) — probably the last two, as "bearers of wine and bread". The opera *Rusalka* by Dvorak uses these legends.   [See *Duboka*]

MIGNON (French), MENINAS (Spanish)

A girl, servant, courtier etc. parallel with Greek chorus; a dancer for the Minne ballad singers of 12th century Germany; but earlier with *Minnistria* (Etruscan players) *Mignone* (Ital.) *Minne* or *Minna* or *Minne* — to remember, to recall — as did the ballad singers (Genealogies). The mignon was traditionally "small and delicate". They endured into the Spanish court of 17th century with this name. The flower mignonette (N. Africa) was named after them; while the basic minuet and menuet doubtless derived from the later court dances. In England, the term degraded into kitchen help — the minion, but in Scotland minnie was used for a nursing mother. The dance has small steps, in parallel with the host of related terms for minishment or "small-making" as in musical Italian, as *diminuendo*. Along side the minion dance was the dance of the hour, and the seconde (necessary in every duel).

MIGODO (Portuguese East Africa)

Are the "orchestral dances", or opera-ballets of the Mu-Chopi people (Bantu race), who live in Zavala district (about 200 miles north-east of Durban). The Chopi people of Portuguese East Africa are famous for their orchestras of xylophones (*Timbila**), and their orchestral dances, *Migodo* (singular *Ngodo*). Both these are advanced examples of African artistic effort. As in Bali (with the *Gamelan** orchestra), a *Timbila* orchestra is found in every large village. The term *Ngodo* implies the "whole show", including dancers, *Ba-sinyi*, and players, *Waveti*. None of the music (or the dances) is written down; and the themes are mainly modernist, rarely legendary or ritual. New productions are regularly heard; new music is devised, with new words, in chanted poems; often political and frequently social commentary. They are not pre-occupied with sex; and there is a wholesome absence of dreary crooning or similar animal wailing, with a balancing presence of good humour. There is no press, no stage, no church; yet there is a general thematic form of expression in all *Migodo*, accompanied with superb dancing. The dance tradition itself seems to derive chiefly from war dances (there are comic dances also), since shield and spear, with decorative plumes, are almost standard equipment.

MILITARY DANCES
Or Rhythmic Exercises, have been included in the training of youths, at all times and in most lands. These we may view as distinct from War Dances; the Military Dance belonging to the general scheme of education, but the War Dance usually pertaining to immediate preparations for some definite contest. Egypt is one of the few ancient countries in which no specific military training was imposed on all citizens; but in Hellas this system was developed to a high degree. The Spartans devised the *Gymnopedeia** and the *Enoplian* military exercise is said to have been invented by Pyrrhus of Epirus, as a drill in four parts. In Gaul, several muscular dances were used, including the pragmatic Sword Dances, from which many movements were borrowed for the ritual initiation ceremonies connected with the symbolic Sword Dance or Dance of the Rose. The Japanese united quarter-staff or long-staff training (these are English titles for similar movements) with rhythmic movement, named *kendo*. Fencing is closely similar. The ancient Germans had many military variations, including ring dance and sword dance; these were known in Britain, though practical defence soon developed the "Bokler and Targe" exercise. When the bow or longbow came level with the short sword (used for in-fighting) there was not so much opportunity for close personal combat. This play of thrust and parry returned when the Italian rapier came into fashion. The basic positions of court and modern ballet were, in fact, derived from Hispano-Italian fence with rapier and dagger. In Spain appeared the *escu-da-ruelle*—a small "mass movement" which developed on one side into army drill, and on the other into the square dances of the early quadrille. There are many highly technical feats with swords or daggers (especially in the Caucasus, the ring dagger-dance etc.) but they display precision rather than attack; and lead to knife-throwing, or other circus feats, rather than dance.
[See *Fencing and Ballet*; *Buckler and Sword Play*; *Pyrrhic*; *Sword Dance*; *Pentchak*; *Ezpata Dantza*]

MILITARY RITUAL MARCH
Develops from the Gesture, the Step, and the group walk, into the quadrille square, moving in march tempo. This is one of the simplest human rhythms, consonant with the normal stride of adult men; but taken over from the far older town bands or Waits (*Wights* in Saxon, *witer* or waiter in Cockaigne)—as deacon, deakon, turned to dicken or dickens (the food bringer), at the communal messe. The military march settled into three main forms: the Slow March (German parade march), the Quick March (*Pas redouble* of the French), and the double quick march, or *pas de charge*. The comparable Spanish dance form was *paso doble*; this also had a reverse movement. The Slow March was taken at eighty paces to the minute in Britain; a pompous progression with plentiful jingle, at leisure. The Quick March (as used by the *Entrée* of the Tiller Girls *circa* 1880) was in metronome = 100, played in 2/2 or 2/4 time, though the old British march in 6/8 time was in vogue, fascinating the German *hauptleutenants*. Not much musical advance was made on the wind-band favoured by Lully, until Mozart gave the matter his attention. In Britain, the puppet-masters' tradition early captured the drill sergeant: his insistent demand for immediate, blind, and faithful obedience was obtained (as he thought) by his demand to "make it snappy", especially in endless salutes; joined with the heavy stamping of sentry feet (not merely to keep up circulation, as thought by A.T.S. girls), and summarised in the "big bangs" of cannon salutes, now outmoded by Big Bangs of Hydrogen, heard in several countries. The troops "big salute" was done by "Trooping the Colours" once a necessary process, in showing to the illiterate mercenary scoundrels who fought through Europe, the particular "flag" they were hired to defend. Gestures and noise comprise elementary training; but commando gymnastics now replace dance, except for canteen or *palais* off-duty periods. The march tunes and steps re-appear frequently with dance troops; the uniform attire follows precisely the same tradition of "one design for all persons".

MILKMAIDS' DANCE (England)
Festival dance celebration by groups of milkmaids (farmhands in country villages; milk-sellers in

towns). They borrowed many silvery objects, polished them for symbolic adornment, and performed a processional street dance, stopping to dance before houses where they expected reward. Origins are obscure; but it seems to be a lunar Dance of Diana (restricted to women and marked by carrying of silver),

MILONGA (Argentine)
An old countryside dance in 2/4 time. About the beginning of the 19th century a dance called Milonga, long popular in Buenos Aires and said to have originated in the low quarters of that city as a popular song, became merged with the *Tango*.* Today, a version of the *Tango*, called *Tango-Milonga*, combines the older dance of the countryside with modern *Tango* rhythms.

Pulcinello, one of the principal dance-mime figures of the Italian *Commedia dell'Arte*. 17th century. ITALY

MIME (from *Mimoi* — Greek; or *Mimus* — Latin)
From earlier Egyptian *Mumia*, the "Actors of the Dead". *Mime* differs from *Pantomime*;* mime includes dialogue; but panto-mime is the "all-mime" or all-action; it is prose stage presentation today; with dance, it becomes rhythmic presentation. Mime is not necessarily imitation; not a blind copy of natural action; in theatre it is an "extract" from

Nature; it has to be, because all drama etc. is a condensation from "real life". We learn from Roman custom that the funeral mimes were called to the procession, to enact (it may seem to us now, as extraordinary) by a sharpened presentation, some of the chief characteristics of the deceased person. This is not the place to explain why this was done; or what they believed it meant. This act was the original and serious ritual aspect of the social custom, which in the Roman theatre went to the opposite extreme, and caricatured the living man. We see, sometimes, the politician, and always the leaders with whom we are currently at war, neatly "taken off" by slick comedians. In fact, the more talented of the modern music-hall comedians is the nearest to the Roman mime; he gets many effects with a nod or a wink, without speaking; by innuendo, without verbal statement; by movement, by costume, by setting, without explanation. These facts remain still as the essence of genuine Mime.

MIME (Grecian)
Is compared by J. E. Harrison[1] with *methektic* ceremonial, as a contrast with "utterance of a common nature" (of the self, or group-mind) with the *mimetic*, or imitation of alien characteristics. In this fact resides the profound difference between sacred ritual and theatre presentation. The priest does not mime; he does not "imitate", but his movement is (or should be) *methektic*, or expressional. The feeble following of this expressional act is a factor in rare examples of "modernist art", but lacking power because it has, in fact, little to express. The priest has the whole liturgy of ceremonial form, in which he is a potent part, not as actor but as officiant, not as *mimos* but as *methektikos*. He is direct, and not reflex. The muddle of modernist "self-expression" aims to combine both, but fails; and dance relapses into merely technical movement.
[1] *Themis (Social Origins of Greek Religion)*. Jane E. Harrison. London, 1927.

MINARI, also *Mirani* (North India) (Minara, male)
Singer-dancers of mourning bands, paid as professionals to provide the requisite ritual chants. They dance in a circle, singing cheerfully. In Siam the *Minari* is a prominent ritual dancer at all festivals. We may compare the *Maneros* or "song of mourning" for Osiris, heard in North Africa by ancient writers, Greek and Roman; as well as their arrival in England centuries later, as nuns, e.g. in the Minories, London. The name and the office keep close together in many lands. In Spain and France they appear as the *mignone*, and then as "minions of the court," as Velasquez has *Las Meninas*.

MING T'ANG (China)
Is the Hall of Light,[1] developed first as an institution for religious and regal usage; then furnished with reserved building or temple. At first a crude hut, the *Ming T'Ang* slowly changed into a splendid set of palace halls, planned on the basis of the Magic Square; in which the Hall of Light (one of five equal halls) was southernmost. The word *Ming* is written in two graphs : *Sun* and *Moon* (indicating full brightness), with *T'Ang*, which means *Hall*. In and from this hall, calendar calculations were made and issued. With it was associated a Hall of Audience; near by was the Sacred Field; and schools, developed for religious education. The chief rite of the primitive Hall of Light was ancestral worship; as *Shih-shih* it was "House-of-Generations" or *Ta Miao* (House of Fathers), with eight names but only one entity. The performance of ritual comprised music, ritual dance and gesture, at solstice and equinox, done originally to invoke the "spirits", but differently for (a) *ch'i* or terrestrial nature spirits; (b) *kuei*, or the ancestors; and (c) *shen*, celestial spirits, or the gods. By music and dance, the young princes were taught how to perform rituals; and mime-dances or opera-forms, of semi-mythic or symbolic legends : called the *Yun-men*; the *Ta-hsien*; the *Ta-hsia*; the *Ta-hu*; and the *Ta Wu*. The first *Yun-men* (Cloud-Gate), followed musical form by *Huang Ti* (Yellow Emperor) as a magical rite, or as a mystic symbol ("Cloud of Unknowing." Penguin Classics).
[1] *Hall of Light.* W. E. Soothill. London, 1952.

MINNESINGER
Special titles of German lyric poets, about 11th to 13th centuries; but much older in derivation and wider in form. These *minnesingers* belonged to the traditions of Chevallerie, as men of noble descent, moving from one baronial court to another; and receiving hospitality and often money rewards for their tuition and entertainment. Their own name for their verse was *höfliches gesäng*, or "courtly songs". This was the final mode; they had by then discarded the older dance measures; and we have only songs in Middle High German, as from Walther von der Vögelweide or Wolfram von Eschenbach. Wagner celebrates them in his opera, *Die Meistersinger*, with its "Prize Song".

MINOAN DANCE (Crete)
Flourished about 1400 to 1200 BC. Accounts have been published which relate to two main styles of ritual dance known in the Island of Crete, by Sir Arthur Evans,[1] of which traces have been found at Knossos. The principal religious ritual dance was that of the Serpent Priestess. She wore a long chequered skirt (illustrating symbols of moon

phases, in strong contrasts), with an overlapping open bodice displaying the breasts; and holding in each hand a small serpent. She was crowned with a head circlet bearing the sacred dove. The apron of the ritual costume bore symbols of the worldwide *tangov* elements—the "triangle-plus-diamond" figures; while the long skirt carried triple-cut squares. The other principal ritual was a gymnastic bull-vaulting display, in which youths and girls leaped over the backs of charging bulls; from some

Minoan Priestess, wearing the ritual costume of Koré, as the Great Earth Mother, in a mode of lunar worship. The beasts typify abundance; the alternated patterns of the six-pleated skirt record the lunar phases and changes. The two serpents are the "Earth Powers" or magnetic cycles. 1400 B.C. Temple of Minos.   CRETE

rite such as this the modern *corrida* (bullfight) must have descended. There was also the *Labyrinth** Ritual or World-Illusion Dance.
[1] *Knossos: The Palace of Minos.* By Sir Arthur Evans.
[See *Labyrinth; Cretan Bull Dance*]

MINOS, Sun Dance of (Crete—1400 BC)
Accompanied the Spring "ritual marriage". The word *Minos* is, like the word Christ, a *title* and not a name, denoting the Hellenic dynasty who ruled Crete (second millenium). Each king wedded the Moon Priestess of Cnossus; ritually he "spent his life in the maze", in the heart of which he concealed Pasiphae (as a Moon Goddess) and the Mino-Taurus. This mythos is connected with that of *Ha'Phaestos* (the Lover of Light and seeker after Elen, the Light). In the rite which included sacred dances, the Minos king met the Priestess; he wore a bull mask and she had a cow mask. Says Robert Graves[1] on the suggestion of Sir Arthur Evans that the Palace of Minos at Cnossus was itself the labyrinth (called so from the sacred Double Axe*), this maze had a separate existence; it was a true maze; and "seems to have been marked out in mosaic on the pavement as a ritual dancing pattern . . . a pattern which occurs in places as far apart as Wales and North Eastern Russia; for use in the Easter maze dance. This dance was performed in Italy; and in Troy, and seems to have been introduced into Britain towards the end of the third millenium by neolithic immigrants, from North Africa". Homer describes the Cnossus maze: "Daedalus in Cnossus once contrived a dancing floor for fair-haired Ariadne" (*Iliad xviii.* 592); and Lucian refers to popular dances in Crete connected with Ariadne and the dance (*On the Dance.* 49).
[See *Maze; Labyrinth; Hall of Double Axes*]
[1] *Greek Myths.* Robert Graves. London, 1955.

MINSTREL—1
From *Min-istria*, Etruscan-Latin term for actor-singer-dancer. Generic European term, including many more localised persons; implying travelling groups of singers and dancers who moved through Europe between 5th century BC and 15th century AD. The word itself derives from an early Egyptian festival god of ritual, the famous Min; and passes finally into the Latin-English term Minister, belonging to a Minster. There were, during these centuries, many variations, many grades of minstrel; and many duties expected of them. Principally they were distributors of news and fiction, and were replaced by modern books and newspapers in these same functions. They included: the *skald* (Scandinavian); *skomorakhy* (Russian);

caloyer and *kalephta* (Greece); *guslari* (Balkans); *scopas* (Asia Minor); *gitano* (Spain); *jongleur* (France); *minnesinger* (Germany); *bard* (English); *Ollamh* (Ireland); *gleeman* (Saxon lands); *Mimus* (Rome); *Choroi, parabolos* (Alexandria); *trouvére* (Normandy); *troubadour* (Provence); *Comedien* (Italy); *shaman* (Siberia); *dalang* (Sumatra and Java); *buffoon* (from *bouphon*—France); and many more. All of them had some connection with popular dance and music of their time. They are all related, in agreement or in opposition, to the religious groups of their time. The Minster was the church belonging to a monastery, which specialised in performances, as of miracle plays and festival "saints" celebrations at the local trade fair—they were the minstrels of English legend.

MINSTREL—2
Mediaeval inclusive term, including many European closses of itinerant entertainers; related also to the somewhat earlier terms of Trouvere; Troubadour; Gleeman; Skald; Rymour and Harper. Bishop Percy (whose original work *Reliques of Ancient Poetry* (1765)[1] should be consulted), investigates these titles in dating his collection of ballads, as originating soon after the period of the Norman Conquest. In fact, the radical term *Min* in Minstrel proves a far older source; but we have to examine !the various professional names as each term becomes prominent. Bishop Percy stipulates:
"It is well known that on the Continent, whence our Norman nobles came, the Bard who composed, the Harper who played and sang, and even the Dancer and the Mimic, were all considered as of one community; and were all included under the common name of Minstrels. I must, therefore, be allowed the same application of the term here, without being expected to prove that every singer composed, or every composer chanted his own song; much less that every one excelled in all the arts which were occasionally exercised by some or other of this fraternity."
[1] *Reliques of Ancient Poetry.* Bishop Percy (p. 27, edition of 1880; ed. E. Walford).

MINUET (Fr. *Menuet*)
An 18th century Court dance, introduced into England from France late in the reign of Charles II, by the Marquis de Flamarens. Its popularity increased at the courts of the Georges (1714 - 1820), where a special *Minuet* was composed for each royal birthday. At Bath, Beau Nash's balls usually began with two hours of *Minuet* dancing. To dance it well was a sign of gentility, here as in France. Most *Minuets* were in 3/4 time. Music was usually arranged in two sections of four or eight

measures, each repeated. Danced by two people, the *Minuet* was stately and elegant, with none of the affectation often associated with modern versions. Rameau's work *Le Maître à Danser* (1725) gave a full description of the *Minuet*. He laid special emphasis on the need to avoid all affectation, and he required the dancers to preserve a calm bearing with an air of natural dignity. The earliest written example occurs in Feuillet's* *Chorégraphie* (1701). There developed two forms— the Ballet or Opera version, and that of the ballroom. The stage *Minuet* contained many different steps and figures arranged by the choreographer as he wished. The ballroom dance was simpler; the figures were fixed, and only one basic step was needed, although skilled dancers might add other steps. The main figure was in the form of an "S" or "Z". Although thought by some to have derived from the *Branle*,* it seems more likely to have developed from the *Galliard*,* which is nearer to it in form. The *Minuet* was popular at balls, from the Court down to the "Assemblies", where a "king" and "queen" were chosen, and the same precedence and order of dances was followed as at Court. (Cp. *Fackeltanz*.*) By 1820, in England, it was still used to open a Court Ball, although no longer danced elsewhere; while in France it ceased with the Revolution in 1789.

Miracle Play Ritual from scene in Canterbury Church. The mother of Becket is submerged in Holy Water; a symbolic scene. 15th century (Royal MS, Bodleian Library). ENGLAND

MIRACLE PLAY (Including dance, and "interludis")
One of three main forms of religious propaganda. The miracle is the most public form; usually given in the courtyard of a temple (Egypt), or formerly in the Cloister* attached to a church or monastery. This system still continues in Tibet with the *Tsam*.

Miracle Play Mime. Adam and Eve in the Garden of Eden with three dancing devils. A typical scene in Monastery Play. ENGLAND

The term is from *miraculum*, from mirror (cp. *spiegel*, *speculum*). The Spanish say "O! Mira que la"! "Oh! Look at that"! The "Miracle" was offered as the "image" of the legend; it had not at first the connotation of the "supernatural", though doubtless the general notion of something unworldly was inculcated. The centres in England possessed their own collections; later termed "cycles" as at Winchester, Coventry, Chester, of which we have only the final forms, as written down *after* numerous performances. The subjects were the myths of scripture; or imposed "lives of saints", and were intended to displace the older legends of older doctrines. Then it was seen by bright-eyed traders that the production of a notable Miracle Play would attract visitors to a town'. (The Tale of Thomas Becket and his decease served thus; the date was changed from winter to summer to accommodate productions). Some towns grew up, with Fairs, around a monastery famous for its spectacular performances (Oviedo in North Spain did this). There was always included some popular appeal : all kinds of dancing or tumbling; and even "cabaret", for Adam and Eve appeared *in puris naturalibus*, at Coventry at the show in the Cathedral Cloisters; but that was no miracle. The Miracle Play is extant through the Orient, as the *Tsam* or open air theatre. The "Lives of Buddha" supply the main topic, from the *Jataka* stories; but Tibet adds some local legends. Burma celebrates the events of the Natural Year, often with dance of the *Nats*. In Italy the Miracle Play was early changed; the legends derided; and from the debris sprang up the Compagnia of the Arte, the Commedia players, who celebrated local events and nationalist doctrines. [See *Religious Dance*, *Ritual Dance*]

MIRIAM (Hebrew)
Also given as *Maryam*, *Meriam*, and other variants.

The "Dance of Miriam" is an allegorical triumph, said to have been performed "after the crossing of the Red Sea". Bishop Colenso had the fact demonstrated conclusively to him by one of his Zulu students, that to attribute any "historical realism" to the account of a large processional march of Israelites, actually crossing an arm of the geographical Red Sea, as told, is a factual impossibility, in relation to the numbers, the time, and the place. Taken allegorically, the Dance presents a portion of an initiation ritual (like the story of *Job*), and though a real dance might be performed, it celebrated a victory not over a blue sea of ocean waters, but over a sea of red blood. As with the title *Virgo Marina*, turned to indicate a Virgina Mariam (as in the Coptic church), the whole meaning is not realist but symbolical; and this symbolism was at some points expressed in terms of priestly dance; as was done with similar dances of Moses, Aaron, and Joshua (his circuit of Jericho, with blasts on trumpets etc.).

MISÊRE, DANSE DE (France)
Also called *Danse Triste*; a popular performance of a Dance of the Dead, known at Besançon. E. Male[1] relates, that church archives (later lost) described a dramatic dance often performed in the town church of St. John at Besançon. The actor-dancers represented various ranks and professions; and after each turn of dance, and verse of chant, one of these dancers withdrew and vanished. This was known in 1393. Later, at Besançon (1453) the Franciscan friars had a similar *Danse Misère* in their Church of Sant-John, for which suitable verses were sung. This was the form that originated the famous series of wood-cut pictures by Hans Holbein (and other artists) and paintings in various churches. The "Odd-man-out" emphasis was derived from the belief that the newly dead returned, to drag the living to join their company : hence the skeletons who begin and end this dance-drama. This tradition runs close to the Negro dance propitiations in Hayti, where ritual prayers are sung with dancing, to "make quiet the dead man". This *Danse Misère* is rendered, at least in paintings, as a line dance, not a ring; sometimes the figures in pairs (leader and the led), and occasionally in processional form, as a group is taken away by the dead men. These pictured dead men hop and dance in lively style; the living move slowly, with reluctance. Possibly the Moslem custom, widespread during four centuries in Spain, of feasting, singing and even dancing on memorial days for the dead, helped to evoke this churchyard tradition. Certainly the underlying theology is one with the gloomy scholastic doctrines of that period; though dance is rarely mentioned save in the

famous phrase concerning "how many angels might dance on the point of a needle".
[See *Todtentanz; Morts, la danse des; Danse Macabre; Misère, Danse de; Bal de la Mort*]
[1] *L'Art Religieux de la fin du Moyen Age en France.* E.Male. Paris, 1908.

MISTLETOE (Britain)
"Miz-el-Tau". Ritual dance, used by Druids who held the plant as a sacred symbol (the glistening berry was a vital symbol of life, as gold (torque) was a symbol of former life). *Mistle*, German *mista* — the rain deposit of Mother Nature — and by a transfer, rain of wisdom *Myzl-Tau* (Wisdom of Gods) giver of life. The plant grows 'without roots' on the (World) Tree, here the oak; it has three berries in a cluster. In Scandinavian myth, Loke hurts Baldur, beloved of the gods, with the plant, by Hadur of Darkness. Freya restored Baldur to life, saying that all passing under it (i.e. acquiring wisdom) should live. Druid dance had three phases; processional approach; circle, to cut with gold blade; and triumph with the crop. Pearls were held sacred in similar fashion in Britain; to *mizzle* then, is to depart (Heb. *sche-mozzle* — Go !).

MISTLETOE RITUAL DANCE (Britain)
This Druidic ritual (belonging to the sacred Oak) was probably the precursor of the better-known *Wassail* ring dance, done round the biggest apple tree of the orchard. The name is a collocation of *Myzl-Tau* — the "Hidden Wisdom of the Gods", and its only connection with "mist" is the dispersal of ignorance. The Russian word for wisdom is *Myzl*; centres like *Pre-mysl* (Poland) were probably Cymric places of regular ritual. The symbol is in the glistening white berries : bards were crowned with slim wreaths of leaf and berry. In Ancient Britain, the symbol of Hidden Wisdom (to be gained by long and arduous study, ten or twelve years at the least) was the Pearl. British pearls were sought by Egyptians and other inhabitants of the "Great Green Sea" (Mediterranean Sea), as the first of three connected symbols. The second was the pearl-like berry of the apparently rootless, suspended plant; not hard, but soft and living; while the third was rarely mentioned, though familiar to some Druids. This triple symbolism was affirmed by three rites, of which we know only a reflex in the *Vasa Heil* (King ! Hail !) for the second; and the "Shore Journey" of the first. Amber and jet were used, for their colour and for quality. The third rite, not described, can be learned only from far-distant analogies. Biblical language of 16th century England refers to the "Pearl of Great Price" and, with many reference to the "Pearl of Life" in Wilhelm and Jung's *Secret of the Golden Flower*, we

may add the quatrain of the Persian Sufi poet Omar Khayyám, who sang (it is told) many wise verses. One version from Fitzgerald's freely rendered English may be noted :

"With Them the Seed of Wisdom did I Sow —
And with my own hands laboured, that it grow;
Yet this was all the Harvest that I gathered —
I came in Water but in Fire I go!"

One aspect of its symbolism is that (a) it breaks light into colour; and (b) that it reflects pure white light. Of the dance form, we assume that it was a simple ring dance (perhaps in concentric circles) round a great Oak, or an altar piled with cut Mistle Tau, accompanied by chants and harp music. Layers of dancers represented layers of *nacre*, which gradually lay down the shell and the seed pearl found within. *Mazul-Tov* as used in Yiddisher "Good Luck" greeting; *Mazul-Toy* = "Master of Wisdom" — may also have some earlier connection with *Myzl*; also *Mazer, Mazul* — "He who arrives at the Centre" (of the Maze).   [See *Uchellawr*]

MITAKA (Japan)
The annual celebration of the Phallic Festival; now largely abolished, but the calendar period itself is now celebrated by the popular custom of "Visiting the Cherry Blossoms". The Pink Blossom is that of the goddess Amatecsu; and the White Blossom is the symbol of the "Impatient God". These characters led the Shinto rituals. In a few places, this spring period is celebrated by a solemn Procession of the Town Courtesans. In Tokyo, there was a special Feast in the Yoshiwara (and in the smaller establishments municipally governed in other towns) to celebrate the resumption of business. [See *Michiaha*]

MITHRAIC RITUAL DANCE (from Iran. Roman period)
Spread with the masculine religion of Mithras. Remains of centres have been found in Britain : at York and recently in London; at Margate and Albana (later 'St. Albans'). San Clementa church was built in Rome over a notable Mithraic temple. One found at Ostia reveals 'seven phases of initiation' as marked for dance in stone pavement. Over these, the candidates moved. In *History of Roman Society*, Dill gives the seven phases : 1, Corax (Raven); 2, Chruphius (Veil); 3, Miles (accepted soldier); 4, Leo (the Lion); 5. Perses (the Phrygian); 6. Heliodrumos (The Solar Runner or Dancer); and 7. Pater, or Ha-Phaestus (Father of Fire). In Britain, the name Miles has lingered, while Esmothras (member of Mithra) is now "Smith". The Leon *candidatus* assumed his "white robe" while the Phrygian obtained his cap.

MITHRA, MITHRAS — 1 (Roman, earlier from Persia)
A religious system, apparently derived from Iranian scheme of Zarathustra. In ancient Rome, the cult of Mithra as Sun God was highly favoured by the Roman armies; so that wherever they moved on military missions, they took with them their disciplines and rituals. Remains of Mithraic temples have been found in London (1954) and York, and several other centres in England. Some details are known, which make it clear that only adult men were admitted (never any women), and that ceremonials covered seven grades in all. Ritual dance was not large in movement, or great in numbers; it is doubtful if any public processional movement was made in display (as with the Salii,* Kuretes* and other masculine cults).

MITHRA, MITHRAS — 2 (Greco - Roman, from Iran
The Cult of Mithra - Mithras (masc. fem.) as *Helios Invicta*, the "Unconquerable Sun", was widespread in the Roman armies, as an ascetic militant faith followed only by men, chiefly by soldiers (*solidarii*), who had the grade of *miles* (in Greek, *emiloi*; Latin, *emilianus*). Mithra was the sun as creator-producer (gave the later Scots *mither* or mother; also "to míther", to worry, to investigate). We know the cult worked in small Mithraeum (one was discovered in London in 1954, causing great interest), for its small and secret rituals, in seven grades; but some of the ceremonies were undoubtedly held in the open, of a semi-military character. In this, we can trace origins of the masculine *col-legia* cry "Mithras! Mithras! Mithras!" (see W.R.S.) (coalescent into "Smith-ras"). The terminals indicated the circle or ring of the ceremony; *Mith-Ra* was the centre — the "raying sun", or Helios (Apollo) who reversed into *Souleh* and eventually *Soule*, seen as the symbolic gilded ball of later church ceremonial in France. The primitive Christians of Rome copied much of the aggressive quality of Mithraism (hence "Christian soldiers", the 'faith militant', etc.). The solemn dance-ritual sometimes was also military; from it descends the "drum-head court martial". The arcane aspect of Mithraism was bound up with the secret tenets of Gnosticism; they are as inner and outer forms of the same doctrine. The *labarum* of the Christians was taken from the Roman soldier's standard (as SPQR in one form, was copied in INRI). The ritual which is most preserved in its symbol form is the Conquest of the Bull (still living in Spain as the *corrida* vastly changed), which which was, as with all the "animal skins" seen in sacred ritual, used as a symbol of the subdued "animal nature". The Spanish *corral* (theatre) preserves the form of ring; the still-military ritual

reflects faintly the Roman ceremonial, formed as a march round the enclosed ring of contest. We know that the Gnostics had chanting dances. Some dance ritual figures are to be found in some intaglio gem rings (that gave admittance to members on showing), and a trace remains in the traditional *Hymn of Jesus*. [See *Gnostic Sacred Dance*]

MIYAKO ODORI (Japan)

An *Odori* or Ballet, given in Kyoto (5 p.m. to 10 p.m.) at Hanami-koji, near Gion-za Theatre in this city. The season is in April, for twenty nights. Girls are trained (for this and other *Odori* dances), in the *Nyokoba* (School) adjacent; they learn also about *Cha-no-yu* (Tea Ceremony) and Flower Arrangement. Commercialism of theatres, and especially of films, have developed this system considerably during the last half century.

MODERN DANCE (London and USA)

Has moved from the period of Kate Vaughan (plentiful skirts) along to Loie Fuller (maximum of skirts), to recent film dancers (no skirt at all) in terms of costume. But its full contrast, according to its advocates, arises in a need for broader technical expression to fulfil the primal necessity of sociological thematic expression. Modern dance has tended to drop the threadbare revival of "classical mythology" (which modern ballet still regards as a classical basis for classical style), and to turn to current social themes. The difficulty comes in the fact that neither ballet nor dance can "explain" a plot or theme, as words can sometimes do; and that the symbols used must already be familiar (a) by traditional inheritance by education, or (b) by acquaintance with current events, by propaganda or advertising etc. Some teachers of Modern Dance technology, in the classroom, make great play with claims for extended movement; for a theoretical multi-dimensionalism, more obvious in words than in movement. Some claim "six-dimensional projection" as the very newest parallel with scientific psychology; but examination of the ballets as produced fails to sustain this ambitious exploitation of "space and time". Moreover, it is not even new. The Japanese have long since developed their own theory of the classical movement of the Superman: it is known as *roppo*,* not as a "space module", and presents the character as *arropo* (arrogant) with clear motions in all "six directions". The Japanese invented the revolving stage; aiming also at full directional movement; this device included scenery as well as the dancer-actor. Modern dance, as presented by Isadora Duncan, was more effective since a single dancer moving to a single composition could concentrate attention on emotional repercussion from aural

impression to visual suggestion. This result has rarely been gained in the Modernist Dance Ballet. A welter of meaningless movement disperses, rather than integrates, attention (as does the *Noh* drama dance), while elemental motion is rarely used to state basic emotion; as happens in Hindu dance drama and especially the *raga* music. An abstract "space module" will not remedy this lack.

MO-ELS (Mexico)

A dance forming part of the Mayo Indian *Matachines*.* *Mo-els* are small birds which eat the farmers' corn and vegetable crops, and the dance may be performed to scare them away (Cp. *Montoneros**), or it may have had a ritual significance now forgotten. Performed early in the morning, it is a round dance in which the dancers jump vigorously as they circle. The chief dancer (*monarca*) carries a small boy sitting on his shoulders, said to represent the bird.

MOERIS, DANCE OF FATE (Greek)

The Three Fates (*Parcae*, in Latin) who as daughters of Zeus, controlled the destiny of Man. Brought to Britain by Greeks, it eventually became the Morris Dance, with its three dancers moving in mythic opposition to three Ereinyo—the creatures who sought to disturb rhythm and destroy dance. The typical Moeris Dance is the unending linked chain—the six initiated youths about to bring in a seventh, or five admitting the sixth. The *Moira* was one with Homer, triple with Hesiod; they carried the *raper*—the short sword of the *epheboi*. The Fates were: Clotho who spun the Thread of Life; Lachesis, picture maker or pattern-setter who gave the plan; and Atropos, who severed thread or pattern as destiny had decided. The Moeris Dance portrayed the Pattern of Lachesis—weaving over and under, in three styles; Harvest and Winter.

MOERIS (in Egypt)

A lake which had the great Labyrinth on its shore —as described by Herodotus (*Book II*). Lake Moeris illustrated with emphasis the 'Law of Circulation'— for six months Nile water flowed into the Lake, for six months it flowed out again. In the Twelve Great Courts of the Labyrinth, many instructional ritual dances were celebrated; and we can see that the lake title could be taken for some of them—especially that of the Double Spiral (so often included in temple decoration—the "watch spring" line). Greek religion came mainly from Egypt; names, with it, went over the long periods; but in England, Egyptian names remain to this day. The Salute to Ra is *Hu Re* or *Hu Ra*. (Hu was also the Sphinx or Teacher). Our river Thames is

Tammuz-Isis; Ausar becomes the Ouse (Osiris) and Hu is Hugh of Lincoln. Many terms in Welsh from Celtic reveal Egyptian influence — Taffy for Tefi. Suten (Royal) is in Sutton Hoo, and twelve more Sutton places. And Maat Goddess of Truth becomes Maid (Mari-Anu-Bez).

MOHABBAZEEN (Egypt)

Modern Egyptian players of low comedy farces, which often include episodes of dancing, both straight and burlesque in style. The travelling groups give performances at weddings, in courtyards; or in public squares in Cairo. These actors are men and boys. They have a sort of hautboy, a drummer and two or three who may dance, one attired as a female.

MOHARRAM (Persian - Arabic)

Mourning; Month of Seal; year end; *Mohr* is Seal of Solomon. This is the period of the Tazzia, now transferred to the legendary "Death of Hussein and Hassan", which is performed in dramatic mode. Instead of "Death of Winter and Birth of Spring" we see, in the revised miracle play, that both individuals must die. This celebration was, therefore, varied tremendously during its long tradition. In Arabia, and then with the Arabs to Northern Africa, the *Tazzia** was extended as a term to Tazzia, a Cup; and thence (with Greek prefix) to *Phanes* or *Pan-Tazzia*, the "appearance of the Cup", from which we have the old term fantasy and fantasia (see *Tazzia*). This, at Moharram, is the Cup of Jamshed — the Cup of the Year, which Omar celebrates; it is also another cup, served by the Sufi mystics of Islam; for which the beauteous lady, the Saki, is the mysterious ever-feminine whom they regard so highly.

MOHINI (India)

Hindu ritual dance term = The "Temptress", as in dramatic myth, or in course of ritual; comparable with Delilah (Assyrian) or Salome (Arabic-Hebrew mode), or Eve (O. T. Legend). The central idea is one of allure and temptation. In the Indian legend, Mohini is sent to tempt Indra from his meditations. Mohini is South Indian, allied with Egyptian ideas; she was The Great Cow Mother (Mow-ni) consort of the Great Bull (Mautt), and there are traces in Western Europe of similar traditions; as in the names Moyne (Ireland), Mona (Angel's Eye) or Mignon and Minne, related to the ancient Egyptian *Min*. The dance is performed by a pair, man and woman, as a dramatic mythos; she tempts the man, as in the legend of *Samson*, who was here the sun-god who "lost his hair" — rays or light and power. There are scores of versions of this primordial theme; they have two endings, according to

the success of Mohini, or her failure and repulse. The Christian scheme has two tempters — a male (Mara) and a female (Mag-Dalini), who both proved (it is said) unsuccessful, precisely as in the comparable Buddhist legends of Gautama.

MOHINI-ATTAM (Tamil, South India, in Malabar)

Literally, "love-dance", but on a mythic basis. Mohini is a favoured women's name; meaning "enchanter" or "fascinator", for she is known as the Hindu Delilah, the "heavenly temptress". The term signifies a whole repertory of dances on the *sringara* or love theme, given according to audience and festival period. The itinerant group is managed by a *Nattuvan* (dance-leader) and dancing has gone up and down in public favour; it is now returning to "respectability".

MOHOBELO (Basutoland, South Africa)

A men's vigorous dance requiring much energy and endurance, nowadays performed by young men solely for recreation and amusement. Girls clap and sing an accompaniment. Formerly it was a ceremonial dance, part of a rain-producing rite. [See *Mokorotlo; Mokhibo; Motjeko*]

MOKHIBO (Basutoland, South Africa)

Formerly danced after a women's rain-producing rite, this is a girls' dance, performed entirely on the knees. Discouraged by missionaries because of the prominence of breasts and thighs, *Mokhibo* is seldom now seen, but when well done it is a graceful and attractive dance. The girls dance in a long line facing outwards; behind them stand a chorus of women, singing and clapping to mark the rhythm. Beginning slowly, knees beat the ground, as the body rises and falls, accompanied by a graceful lateral and upward sweep of the hands. As the tempo quickens, movements become faster until, with a whoop, the climax is reached, body erect (still kneeling), and arms flung upward fully extended. In the accompanying singing, the melody is traditional, but the words are meaningless. [See *Mokorotlo; Mohobelo; Motjeko*; and cp. *Ghedra** (Morocco — Kneeling Dance)]

MOKOROTLO (Basutoland, South Africa)

A men's dance, performed on important ceremonial occasions, such as the Chief's attendance at boys' initiation; after the ceremonial first planting of the year in August; or, latterly, at big political meetings. A slow, impressive dance, the performers move back and forth, with regular slow foot stamps, the leader singing in a high-pitched voice, the men answering with deep-voiced refrain. Now and then they stop dancing, to urge on one of their number, who breaks rank to leap and prance before the Chief, with mimic thrust and parry of battle, reciting the praises either of the Chief, himself, or a character of the past. His companions shout encouragement, using his special dance name. These names sometimes refer to the character being danced, e.g. *Sea ja, sea rora, sebata* ("It roars, it devours, the wild beast"); *Chomporo* (Headman); or *Offisiri* (police officer). His solo finished, the dancer prances back to his place, when the slow movement and chant of the main *Mokorotlo* is resumed.   [See *Mokhibo; Mohobelo; Motjeko*]

MOLECH (Babylonian-Hebrew)
Is *Melekh*, "the king" or the ruler where "passing the fire" is first a ritual dance, but this rite is a symbol of the spiritual "fire baptism", or regeneration of the mind, by the dissolution of false ideas, or the "burning of ancient (mind) images". The term, as slandered by the Jews, is related (by them) to "sorcery". The root is the same as in *Malchi*, or *Malekhi*, the prophet; — "he of burning tongue".

MOLUCCAS (Indonesia)
The Ternate group and Ambon group of islands between Celebes and New Guinea; have several traditional dances. Best known are a series of *Tjakaleles* or War Dances, performed as sham fights in Ambon, Banda and Ternate. They are religious in basic character, performed only on high festive occasions. In this *Tjakalele** dance, ancient clothes are worn; it is marked by vigorous jumps and loud shouting in concert. Heads are covered in polished helmets of light brassware; armour of similar kind is carried, frequently with long shields. Some patterns (it is said) are reminiscent of military wear used by past invaders: Dutch, Portuguese or Spanish. Preparations for these dances are costly and occupy much time. Only men perform them. The *Menari Dance* is the complementary performance by girls and women, as a national dance, with music of violin and native instruments; and singing. The unmarried girls of the Islands are called Djodaros, supervised by an older woman, the Captain Djodaro. Chants are sung in chorus; as simple in form as the dances.

MONFERRINA (Italy)
Country dance of 17th century Piedmont. Known also as *Monfarina*; introduced into England late in the 18th century; and in London performed as *Montfrina or Montfreda*.

MONOGATARI (Japan)
"Narration". A mime-dance sequence in a *Kabuki* play, describing a past event relating to the story of the play. Sometimes the *Monogatari* comes as climax to the *Michiyuki** or "Travel Dance", as in

the play *Yoshitsune and the Thousand Cherry Trees* (1747), where a character describes in dance the death of his brother in battle. In *Battle Chronicles of the Two Leaves at the Valley of Ichi-no-Tani* (1751) the warrior Kumagai, using only a sword and fan, "narrates" his contest with Prince Atsumori. The twisting and flourishing of the open fan represents the meeting of the two warriors on spirited horses; the closed fan brandished or held against the side symbolises their swords; Atsumori pinned to the ground is shown by the open fan pressed to the floor; when Atsumori flees Kumagai brushes the dust from his erect sword with the open fan. The *Monogatari* is accompanied by music, and sometimes interjected dialogue and singing.   •
[See *Ogi No Sabak; Fan Dance; Feather Dancing*]

MONTEFERINA (Italy)
Il Danza Montferine (or *Montfarine*) appears to be a town version of a harvest dance, known in Milan during the 19th century. The form, which includes a promenade, is somewhat similar to the *Bourrée,** being danced by two or four couples, in which the ladies are "exchanged". The name seems simply to imply the "little hill" or mount of grain, produced after the harvesting.

MONTONEROS, DANZA DE LOS (Mexico)
A mimetic harvest dance performed in the church-yard. Dancers (young men and boys) are in two groups, representing harvesters and guardians of the corn. The first group perform a dance with hoes, among stalks of maize brought from the fields and stuck into the earth to represent the cornfield. The other dancers, dressed in rags, carrying stuffed badgers and weasels, and with long whips, dance to the music of fiddles. From time to time they crack their whips in unison, to frighten away vermin (or demons). These dancers are ceremonially identified with the animals against which they protect the crops, since they wear masks of animal skins, and at one point in the dance each in turn is seized by the harvesters, thrown on the ground with a stuffed animal laid upon him, and beaten. The dance, evidently a relic of pre-Christian ritual, ends with the "harvesting" of the maize and carrying it in procession into the church.
[Cp. *Mo-els*]

MOON DANCES
Belonged, all over the world, with the I.-O. manifold cults of The Great Mother. "I.O." The Moon is an obvious and persistent Recorder of Time, with three definite phases, marking the hours, the fortnight, the month. So the Moon as Diana was "worth-shipped" or valued; and known as Luna and Hekate (Light Moon and Dark Moon). All

Semitic tribes followed the Moon; and, until later in their history, they revered most the Great Mother, giver of increase. Hence their monthly festivals rested on (1) the New Moon, the Lunar crescent of Diana and Maria; the Full Moon of Ishtara, Kybele, Kwannon, or Magh-dalini; and the Dark Moon of the Destroyer—from Kali to Klementa. Even now, in Moslem lands, the appearance of the Crescent Moon marks festivals, whether of Feasting or Fasting, such as the Moharram; and the Silver Crescent is carried on the sacred green flag. Ritually, this same crescent formerly appeared in dances; but the stricter usage of Islam has thrust them in the background, along with all the minor gods: "La ilaha, illa Allah; Mohammed rasul Allah!" is the cry from the Minar or ancient moon tower, erected in four corners of the plangent square of the Mosque; on which the mullah calls in monthly succession. Lunar dances were performed more successfully by the women of the tribes; men were the musicians, the Sons of Korah; gatherers of tribute (as Levites). Even in the great annual festivals; which came to be called Meghilla (Magh-El-La) the great days of El-La) four times in the year; tradition became so strong that the goddess IO or EO, developed in the rite for IO-estra, became personalised as Eostra, and dated into Easter—its date always settled by the "first full moon" after the Spring Equinox. The Moon Dances were ritualised for praise and worship, for counting off the sacred calendar; thus, without excessive mental agony, the more intelligent sector of the population came gradually to learn; and even to adjust the human rhythms—of body and emotion—to the imposing rhythms of natural life as displayed in the time keepers of moon and sun.
[See Calendar; I-O; Sun Dances]

MOONSHINE DARLINS' (Jamaica, West Indies)
Open-air dances held at full moon. Dancers bring their own refreshments, and "gate-crashing" is in order, since anyone may join in, whether invited or not.

MOOSBURG (Germany)
In the small town of Moosburg or Moisberg (between Regensburg and München) there was a church dance (14th century) chiefly of priests, recorded in a dance-song, written by the deacon in 1360, urging the plebs Mos burgae—doctrinata, Gaude sub perita. The custom was a town processional dance, first to and then inside the church, while singing this: Geistliche Tanzlied aus dem Mosburger (graduale des Dekan Johann von Perchausen, geschrieben 1360). The dance had the three forms of procession, line, and ring, boys and girls holding hands, and led by the bishop.

MORÉ (Tahiti)
Dancing-skirt worn by men or women. A kind of white raffia is made from bark of the burao tree, which is soaked in sea water for fifteen days, then cut into fine strips. For an ordinary, tourist-trade moré, these strips are plaited into a plain waistband, but for ceremonial dancing morés this is covered with a band of white cloth on to which is sewn a pattern of red, white and amber-coloured shells. The moré is nearly ankle-length; and sometimes dyed red, yellow or green. To complete the costume, a "sash" of shell-work is worn diagonally across the chest (from right to left), and into the shell-patterned head-band is tucked a tuft of dyed coco-nut fibre. [Cp. Hawaiian Pa-u]

MORISMO (Mexico)
"Knife Dance". A gay but dangerous dance performed at Jalisco and other parts of Mexico. It can be danced by a man and woman, or by two men, the men wielding knives or machetes. As they dance, each man whirls two machetes, knocking them together under each leg in rhythm to the music. The dance is said to have been introduced into Mexico by the Spaniards.
[Cp. Bakony Herdsmen's Dance (Hungary)]

MORNA (Cape Verde Islands)
From Portuguese; described as "universal song and dance of these islands, doubtless a development of the fado". They alternate as a sad song, as a traditional melody, as a dance, or all three together. Equivalent to the Afro-American "blues" favoured by the Creoles, one is well known, in Forca de Cretchen. (Cretchen is Creole for "sweetheart"). Music is provided by a guitar or two, perhaps a fiddle. Along with the Morna, on the Midsummer Day of Johan, there is the coladeira, dance with obscene verses. Ethnologically Cape Verde is not Europe, but West Indian. On the mainland Morna and coladeria give place to batuque* in Guinea; and these dances celebrate the tabanca (village feast)— a local jollification like an Irish wake.

MOROCCO, Dances of
Among the inhabitants of Morocco, the Berbers, especially the Shleuh tribes of the Atlas Mountains, have many dances. Though best known for their boy-dancers on the famous square Djema el Fna, in Marrakesh (see Shleuh, Boy-dancers*), the Shleuh also possess other dances, such as the Ahouach* and the Gliding dances. With all Berbers, dancing is still a living thing, part of their daily life, familiar from earliest childhood. In mountain and desert villages children very soon learn traditional songs and dances, every festival or anniversary being so celebrated. There are no special teachers,

the knowledge being handed down from generation to generation. Among the women there are groups of "strolling" dancers and musicians, who go from village to village performing at weddings and other festivities, the members being divorced women, who often choose this means of livelihood. The dance form is often a line, curve, or close circle (all men, all women, or men and women alternating), with musicians in the centre. Sometimes the circle remains almost stationary, the dancing being rhythmical movements of hands, arms and knees (the *Ahouach**); sometimes it shrinks and widens, or breaks (the *Ahidous**); or a circle of men or women will move in a gliding unity of movement, varied by the curious "shivering" of head, shoulder or hips seen also in Turkish and Albanian dancing and called in Morocco *Shtah del Khzem* or, if done while moving backwards or forwards, *Shtah atemshi-uji*. A characteristic of Berber dancing is the sudden stamp which marks the rhythm; their dances show that fundamental unity of movement that comes from a living tradition and much practice together. Accompaniment is provided by the *bendir* (a single-sided tambour two feet across, struck with the fingers), and the high-pitched chanting of musicians or dancers; other instru-

ments include flutes, three-stringed *lutar*, *rebab* and the *neuk'sat*, which are three small cymbals worn on the dancer's fingers. Troops of dancers are hired to perform at private houses, when dances seldom seen in public may be given, such as the Berber *Dance of the Year*. Accompanied by flutes and drums, but no singing, twelve male dancers representing the months, and carrying orange blossom, remove their white outer garments to reveal red, yellow and green robes beneath, symbolising the colours of earth, sky, and grass. Other Moorish dances include the frankly seductive *Muscle Dance** found in the cafes of Marrakesh and other towns, but the equally provocative *Ghedra** (a women's solo dance with African characteristics) is performed only at Goulimine, in the South. Also from the South come the black-skinned dancers seen on the Djema el Fna and at Mogador, and as far north as Tangier. Some villages of the extreme South, such as Tinerhir in the Sahara, have their own troupes of dancing-girls.
[See *Shleuh Gliding Dance*]

MORRIS DANCE (English)
From Greek *Moira*, *Moiridios*, the Goddess of Fate or Destiny. (Also: *Moiridios* 'fated from birth' and

Whitsun Morris Dance at Bampton, Oxfordshire, England. 17th century version for two-couple dance, with one musician (pipe and tabor) and, at right, The Hobby Horse and The Fool. The traditional bells are stitched to leather puttees, not ribbons. *(Courtesy Travel Association.)*   ENGLAND

Moiro-kratos, 'ordained, or destined'). This dance has two thousand years of tradition; it has no sort of association with 'Moors'—it was a dance of Initiation (the New Born One) having two main forms: that of the Individual, and the Birth of the New Year. Six main dancers performed (or five with one Candidate). The original three *Moirae* were *Clotho*—or *Kalotho*, the Spinner or Weaver; 2. *Lachesis*, Maker of Life Pattern, writer of Destiny; and (3) *Atropos*, the One who Turned (*trope*) or cut short the life or ended the Year. In early form, they had three opponents, who sought to avert, to delay or counter these Measures of Fate; hence the use of six *rapers*, short swords. This profound ritual came into Britain with early Greek traders. The rite has no parallel with later Latin "Fortune Dances". The hexagonal Rose was used widely through the Orient; but is unknown to Rome. The hexagonal "Rose" appears on a fine silver bowl (probably from Byzantium) excavated at Mildenhall, Suffolk, 1942, now in British Museum. In the ritual dance, this Rose is again made by the interlaced six *rapers* (this name in Greek)—not the *rhabdos* or *lituus*. The Initiation Ritual was a "mock death" in which the Candidate is "killed" and then restored; he was "fated to anticipate" his real death; on the weapons that attacked him he was next elevated by the "six powers". They reflect the ancient Hindu rites, also a double trinity. The style of dance still remaining is affirmed in interweaving by hand and by sword—the interlacing ways of Fortune. Along with the Mithraic system (which belonged chiefly to the invading Roman armies) this Hellenic ritual of *Moires* probably came to Britain about 3rd century BC, when the Temple to Apollo and Diana was erected on the site where the Saint Poweles church later displaced it, on Ludgate Hill in the City of Londinium. Normally many of the Greek religious dances were performed there.

MORRIS DANCE (England)
A spring dance performed usually by a band of six countrymen, furnished with short blunt swords (rapers) and dancing in an endless slow stepping entwined movement. This is broken by a few mime episodes, which present the death of one (candidate) and his resurrection by Doctor; he is then hoisted on a shield made of entwined six rapers to head level. Music is supplied by pipe and tabor. Around the dancing chain we sometimes see a Fool and a Bessie (Old Woman). The "Morris" will sometimes be danced for the X-Messe Masque, but except for modern displays, it does not appear at other seasons. The dance has also been known in Europe (as at Munich, e.g.), but it is not known in Scotland nor in Ireland. Traditionally—and with

no good reason—the dance has been assigned to the fight of Moors versus Christians; it does not stem from any of the Winter-versus-Spring contests. It was introduced into England by Greek teachers and traders—and the name was *Moirae*. [Cp. *'Ndrezzata; English Sword Dance; Ouliveto*]

MORTS, LA DANSE DES
A dramatic oratorio composed by Paul Honegger with a libretto by the poet Paul Claudel, based on the bible myth of Ezekiel. Meant to be sung in the concert hall, it usually contains no visual dancing, but the music has many rhythmic passages confirming the "Dance of the Dead". The work, written in Paris in 1938, may have been stimulated by the performance in 1933 of the Kurt Jooss ballet *The Green Table* (a modern version of the *Todtentanz**), but as a Catholic form rather than anti-Fascist. This necromantic drama begins with a vision of Ezekiel: "The voice of the lord was within me; then was I carried out, and set down in the midst of a valley full of dry bones". Ezekiel is then adjured to exorcise these bleached skeletons; and he witnesses the revival to a great army of the once-more living men. The prophet is now told to take two tablets of wood; to write on them the names of Judah and Ephraim; then to unite them to a dyptich, to signify that these two tribes of Israel are now to be one; now ruled, not divided, by David. This musical work is arranged in seven sections; after the opening dialogue comes the impressive *Resurrection* and *La Danse des Morts* as they are reclothed with living flesh. Skilful use is made of traditional French tunes, such as *Sur le*

Greek Dance. A mosaic picture by Dioscorides of Samos. The male singer keeps time with the tambour; the next with cymbals, while the female plays her twin flute and the infant follows on a horn. GREECE

Pont d'Avignon and *Il Était une Bergère* —both
with earlier dance significance. In 1954 *La Danse
des Morts* was performed at the Salzburg Festival
in the open-air Riding School. This version contained dancing, with choreography by Margarete
Wallmann, and dancers from the Vienna State
Opera-Ballet took part.
[See *Todtentanz; Misère, Danse de; Bal de la Mort*]

MOSAIC (from Early Hellenic *Musaeikon*)
A geometrically patterned style of dancing-floor,
frequently laid down in halls where the elements
of Grecian culture were taught. The associations
were at first three, and ultimately nine topics, each
being figured by a "Muse" or symbolic leader in
each subject. These patterns were used in teaching; and the festival rituals were performed over
them. Roman imitation turned the meaningful
design into technical ornament; and, when the
inlaid patterns departed from geometrical bases on
the floor, to realistic pictures on the walls, the
entire purpose was destroyed. The last reference
was in the so-called "Mosa-arba" rites; sustained
by small groups of Arab-Christians in Spain; while
the highly glazed and minutely fragmented mosaic
pictures in St. Peter's at Rome present the modernist decadent mode—a mere pictorial imitation of
realistic painting in oils. A few designs of Roman
mosaics, laid down in Britain, retained the later
Musaeian traditions, with their symbols of the
Seasons.

MOTHER GOOSE
Named by Charles Perrault in his first collection of
Contes, as Mere l'oie, as the source of the legends
among the French children. Perrault published his
short collection of eight tales in 1696[1] by way of
pastime; though his success was rapidly imitated
by other authors, some who collected and some,
such as the Countess d'Aulnoy, who (in part) invented or severely edited their stories. "Mother
Goose" as Mere l'oie is a corruption of an older
term, *Mayor de l'Oyer*, or the Mayor of the Law-
men. This Norman French term *oyer* lingers in
British courts as "Oyer et Terminer", to "Call and
Determine"; and we may take it that the stories
belonged to their idle hours when legends replaced
scandal as a topic; or when the form of legend was
carefully devised to caricature some current scan-
dals, by way of "problem plays". Thus, *La Petite
Chaperon Rouge*, worn by the unnamed maiden
who visits the Big Bad Wolf; she told other tales
to the laughing audience of Parisian students. The
tale of *La Belle au Bois Dormant* carried two, or
even three, different satires, according to the conscious possession of the current key. These
reformed legends (their topical features lost with

the passing of time) lapsed into *Legends de la Foire*
(for they were copied merrily by the *Comediens*),
and dropped finally into French nurseries. Thence
the literary researches of Charles Perrault recovered
them, as from the treasury of Mother Goose, the
dame whose festival fell at Lammass, the Feast of
Michel Messe, and the high period for the goose
(or swan) on the table.
[Cp. Grimm's *Fairy Tales* (Marchen) 1812]
[1] Perrault's *Tales* appeared in Moetien's *Recueil*
—1696 (in Vol. 5 of this magazine) was published
La Belle au Bois Dormant; 1697 (Vol. 5) *La Petite
Chaperon Rouge* and other stories. The *Tales* were
republished at the Hague in 1742, illustrated by
Fokke. An English translation was published in
1745. First English version translated by Samber,
printed by J. Pote, was advertised in London in
1729.

MOTIONS (English; from Latin *movere*, to move)
Has had two general theatrical meanings. The
"Motions" was a colloquial name for any sort of
puppet show. From that, the term has been applied
to ornate ritual or futile pomp (foundation-stone-
laying; speech-making at lengthy dinners, etc.), as
"he was going through the motions". For a time it
had relevance to the film industry—"Movies" or
"motion pictures" are American terms for Cinema.
The more precise language of Elizabethan scholars
referred the term to the dancers of the Masque.
D'Israeli quotes *Memoirs of Ben Johnson*:

> "In curious knots and mazes so
> The Spring at first was taught to go;
> And Zephyr, when he came to woo
> His Flora, had his motions too".

Here the meaning of "motions" implies both the
figures and the actions of dancers in masques.
[1] *Curiosities of Literature*. Isaac D'Israeli (Masques).

MOTJEKO (Basutoland, S. Africa)
A term covering all dances in which men and
women take part; also a dance with a jerky step
performed as a solo, or by couples holding hands,
but bodies not touching. There are various *Motjeko*
dances—one performed at the concluding feast of
girls' initiation; another at modern weddings,
where it is performed first by the groom's men
and bridesmaids, and later by the guests at the
wedding feast. It is sometimes accompanied by
modern European instruments, such as concertinas,
mouth-organs and police whistles, which latter may
accompany all dances other than *Mokorotlo*.*
[See *Mokorotlo; Mohobelo; Mokhibo*]

MOUNTEBANK (West European term)
The English term copies generally the Franco-

Italian, as the wooden bank or *banque* or *banco* (trestle-table) on which travelling vendors displayed their wares for sale. To attract the crowd, it became a custom for one of the assistants to mount the *banco;* to dance, and sing, and finally to end in loud verses, puffing the particular merchant. This was "advertising art" in an early state. The Italian term *montanbanco* indicates a quack doctor; the *banco* also accommodated the *banquette.* An Italian term *cantambanco* named the singer-dancer; while the French *saltimbanque* signified mostly the dance. *Patter* named both the tapping feet on the thick planks, and the stream of verses, wisecracks and bawdy jokes, that held the rustic crowd, and urged the sales. When the itinerant bands of monks were merchants, they used exactly the same method. Thus the Gesuati, or "Aqua-Viva Fathers" (who sold liqueurs, as do their successors of La Benedictine) in Venice, they sang and danced on the *banco* in the Piazza san Marco.

MOURISCA (Portugal)
An obsolete church dance, which used to be performed inside the church at Pedrogão Pequeno, on "John's Day". Six men carrying decorated staves and musical instruments, led by a seventh man called *Rei da Mourisca,* entered the church and proceeded to the altar, where they bowed low to the statue of "John the Baptist" and then performed a slow, dignified dance. Two of the dancers played guitars, and two tambourines, while the remaining two carried staves decorated with a bunch of carnations. All six were dressed in be-ribboned suits, with diagonal shoulder straps and a pointed hat decorated with flowers. The seventh man, the "king", wore cloak and crown, and carried sword and shield. At the end of the dance all bowed before the altar, and the "king" shouted *"Viva meu compadre São João Baptista!",* while pirouetting on the left foot. [See *Church Dances*]

MUDGE, MUTCH or MUCH (England)
The Miller's Son in the Robin Hood ballads, whose dance is accompanied with his bladder (blown up, or with rattling peas added, for noise), which he uses to shower blows on other dancers or spectators.

MUDRA
Sanskrit theatre/temple term, meaning "seal". In Hindu dance this word is used (often carelessly) to denote a position of the hands; each such *mudra* has many meanings, according to its "context". *Mudra* means the pose but not the movement, for which *hasta* (gesture) is more accurate. The temple *mudra* is always symbolical; and belongs to the intricate iconography of the sacred ritual dance—

Natya Tandava and *Natya Lasya.* Copies of the symbol then become used in the *Kathakali* (miracle plays), and thence enter ordinary popular shows, with diluted meaning; or are shewn merely as "cleverness".
[See *Mudras: The Ritual Hand-Poses of the Buddha Priests and the Shiva Priests of Bali.* By Tyra de Kleen. 1924]

Mummers, A party of New Year Mummers, three wearing animal masks, helped by two singers and one musician. 14th century (Bodleian MS).

MUMMING PLAYS (England)
May be seen in some villages, celebrated on dates that often belong no more to their original usage. The term "Mummer" or "Mumming" is of uncertain derivation: it may stem from Egyptian *Mumia,* as "Image of the Dead", and be related to "mummies" as "remade images". The Romans had a festival that had images of deceased relatives carried in procession; and sometimes kept in houses. This tradition continued in London, when images of dead sovereigns were made, clothed in their own attire, and kept in the Islip Chapel at Westminster, down to the period of Elizabeth. The plays were connected originally with the New Year Festival; then with Easter and Whetsun; sometimes with the ancestral celebrations of November First. Most of them carry a play, which contains (a) an elected king, sometimes also a queen; (b) a Fool; (c) doctor or magician; and (d) sword dancers, numbering a team of six. Thus the Mumming Play is related on one side to the *Sword Dance,** on the other side to the *Morris** or *Mures Dancers;* though the Play may be mythic while the other two are rituals. The Mummy is thus related to the Dummy —the tradition of ancestral images, carried on by waxy facsimiles of the famous, continues to this day in popular places of exhibition; while the rite of the Burned Image has lapsed with the exception of the supposed Guy Fawkes Night of November 5th. The image was formerly carried round while the youths solicited contributions for this *Auto de Fedélé.* Mediaeval Catholics frequently fabricated

the burned images of rebels they failed to catch, and burn in reality at their Palauto de Fedeles, as in Madrid; but these events were rituals, not mumming. We arrive thus at the distinction between the rite and the mumming—the rite is real and present; the play is an imitation, or a presentation of a myth.   [See *Revesby Play*]

MUNEIRA (Galicia, Spain)

"Miller's Wife". A dance in 6/8 time, with smooth flowing movement. The oldest dance in Galicia, it is a brisk dance of the mountains, performed with castanets,* either by one couple or by three couples as a figure dance, partners facing. After an introduction, in which partners skip towards each other and back, the "chorus" is performed, which afterwards is repeated between the five figures, and also closes the dance. The body is held bent slightly back from the waist, arms above the head. Steps are high, the foot being raised to the knee in each skip.

MUSCLE DANCE (Morocco)

Called variously "*Danse du Ventre*",* "Abdominal Dance", "Stomach Dance", it is performed also in other countries. The North African version is a dance of seduction, performed by women in small cafés of the towns along the coast. Their costume, resembling that considered by wearers of fancy dress to be "Arabian", consists of baggy trousers fitting low on the hips, with transparent apron overskirt; brassiére and gauze veil floating from top of the head over arms and shoulders. Sitting on one side of a small stage, an orchestra of stringed instruments and drums accompanies the dance, the main feature of which is a rhythmic "rolling" of the abdominal muscles. Beginning slowly, in a stationary position, the dancer first rolls her belly in a circular movement; but as the tempo increases, arms and feet come into action and hips and buttocks join in the rhythmic revolving, together with shaking of the breasts. The primitive form uses not only the abdominal muscles, but the entire pelvic region (known in America as the "Pelvic Roll"). In the USA an exaggerated version of this dance is performed at burlesque shows and circuses, where it is known as the *houtchi-koutchi*. In Persia, the stomach muscles are used in a comic dance, performed by a male clown with a face painted on his bare belly (See *Buffoon Dance**). The Algerian *Danse du Ventre** includes a tour de force when the dancer fills one wine-glass from another by manipulation of the stomach or abdomen muscles. [See *Ouled Nail; Cifte Tel; Danse du Ventre; Buffoon Dance*]

MUSES (Hellas)

The *Musae*, or the "Nine Muses" said to be inspiring goddesses of song, dance and poetry, as daughters of Zeus and Mnesomyne. Hellenic legends on the Muses vary considerably; it seems to be an inheritance from a far older Egyptian doctrine. Homer mentions, but does not name, Nine Muses, whose titles Hesiod first gives in detail. His names are Clio; Euterpe; Thalia; Melpomene; Terpsichore; Erato; Polymnia; Urania; and Calliope. As such, they would appear to have been patrons of Egyptian sacred colleges; while those gods or heroes, said to be "sons" of this or that Muse, were probably famous students from these colleges. They were connected with the Sun god, Apollo; he has the name Musageta from this association. Each Muse appears with symbols or implements; thus Terpsichore, Muse of the Choral Dance and Song, appears with lyre and plectrum; but all three original Muses carried musical instruments: flute, lyre, or barbiton. Much of the doctrine and ritual connected with the Muses has been lost. Thespians celebrated a solemn festival called *Musea*, on Mount Helicon. It seems probable that the *Musaeikon* or "muse-images", the traditional patterns (many of "The Seasons" still remain) originated the term *musaic* or *mosaic*, to denote these celebrated inlaid designs. The Cult of Orpheus is especially connected with the Muses, as that of Dionysus (or Bacchus) was with the dancing Maenads (whose name also arises in Egypt, as Menat).

MUSETTE (France)

French bagpipes. In music, the name of a dance with drone-bass. A *gavotte* with a drone-bass, in an old suite, was called *musette;* and was arranged between other gavottes as: *Gavotte - Musette - Gavotte.* In old Normandy, the bagpipe was called *loure.**

MUTCHICO (Basque)

Traditional dance of the Basque people. May belong to the better known *Danse Mattachins* (still performed in Mexico), but has a seasonal form related to solar celebrations. The Symbol is made of two sticks, a metre long, placed crosswise on the ground. The old man, as leader, sings; clasps his hands, and as the *biniou* gives the time, a young man dances, making ceremonial circles or pirouettes in each of the four quarters.

MWGDD-DAWNS (Wales)

General term for a masquerade; the term *Mwgdd* means a mask or disguise. Allied terms include *Ffug-lyrfa* and *misyrn-dorf*, where mask equals *Ffug* or *miswrn*. A horse-mask (that is, a horse-head as used in Hobby-horse danse, usually in Morris dance), is called *canwyl* or *wynel-ffugio*.

MYALL (Australia)
Generic term for the "blacks" or aboriginal people of this continent. They possess a remarkable tradition, acted out by rituals, framed in chanting with dance. These mime dances belong to the "three great occasions" of birth, wedding, and death; with battle, and the two initiations intervening in secret rites. *Atna-arita-kuma* is sex initiation for girls; and for men, it is part of Ingwara Festival. These traditions are manifest in the Nine Alchera, or phases of evolution in which the Great Snake (E. M. Energy) takes form as APMA. The bull roarer *namatwinna* or *tchuringa*, is used. There is a dual soul : united, it is *Kurunga*. They are *Arumburingo*—the group soul (resident in *tjurunga* cave) and *Ulthana*, spirit which lives in man, but returns to the Cave of Heart, then it takes a new body. These episodes are danced forth.

MYL NOS (Welsh)
Funeral watch or Wake, held in Wales and Scotland, for the period of a funeral. *Myl Nos* is the term still used in North Wales; it includes a vigil, filled by singing hymns or psalms, followed by a picnic feast or supper. The burial feast was called *Arvel*. A *Myl Nos* was recorded in 1882, by Mac Mhic Allister (chief of Macdonald Clan, Glengarry) when 150 clansmen sat to feast, and 1,500 attendants and servitors were filled with bread and cheese and whiskey. Many of the *Myl-Nos* were marked with a ritual dance or procession, to and from the burial ground (like an army march). In Ireland the wake has deteriorated.

MYSORE STILT DANCE (India)
Reveals an extreme emphasis on the ritual quality of "cleanness" as related to the temple figures. One of the local sects requires the dancer-priests to walk and dance, from temple to sea-shore, solely on stilts. The main idea is to lessen the contact of the sacred images they carry — via the body — with the unclean way. They carry wooden panels, draped with cottons and silks, with the metal images balanced on top. The occasion is the annual baptism of the god figures (a technical necessity, to wash off the year's accumulated dust or "sins"), and the dancing procession thus makes its way to the sea. [See *Stilt Dances*]

MYSTERY (Greek mode : *mysterion*; Latin mode *mysterium*)
Was in general a religious ritual or religious drama, to which only the accepted students were admitted, as the *mystae* or *epoptae* ("those who have seen"). The term is associated with *mazla* (Hebrew, "good fortune", as from wisdom), and *myzl* (Celtic) im-plying wisdom. The Chaldaic root *mazla* appears again in Russian as *mazla-nitsa* rites (popularly called "Butter Week" (Easter with its great rituals), but carrying the meaning of anointing (with oil, butter, chrism) which is removed with the initial cleansing. At Eleusis near Athens, the Greater and the Lesser Mysteries were celebrated; always, as Lucian affirms, with dancing. In later Latin usage, the term was fused with the Egyptian *Min* into *ministrium*; at first as a ritual and later as a service to the group. Thus the term became an official title. Still later, in France and Mediaeval England, the term mystery was appropriated by gilds, who called their craft secrets the "mysteries", and the accepted expert as the master (mister, mistress). The final deposit is in the term mystic, now often used by way of depreciation (if modernly applied), or by way of authority (if quoted in reference to alleged church authorities, who were always reprobated in their own life-time—as Suso, Taylor, and Eckhart etc.—as naughty heretics). In this sense, mysticism and mystic are set in opposition to occultism and occultist, as if comparing theory with practice; or, as "one who ponders secrets", as against "one who knows and uses them". Dance or ballet can be used with tremendous effect in formulating again a religious mystery—either in some revived ancient form, or in some re-designed modern mode—if only the producer is fully informed on what it means and is clear how to express that meaning.

MYSTERY PLAYS (French, 19th Century)
Continued, or were revived, after Napoleon's defeat, in Paris; with every theatrical advantage, including dancing. Thomas Moore (*The Fudge Family in Paris*) writes of his own observation, which William Hone quotes in his famous work *Ancient Mysteries Described* :

"It might be supposed that mysteries had made their last appearance on any stage; yet the author of *Lalla Rookh* records the performance of scriptural and apocryphal subjects at Paris, in the year 1817. One of his later pieces introduces an English girl, in that metropolis, relating epistleways for her female friends in England, that :
'They call it the playhouse—I think—of St. Martin,
Quite charming—and *very religious*—what folly
To say that the French are not pious, dear Dolly,
When here one beholds, so correctly and rightly,
The *Testament* turned into *mélo-drame* nightly;
And, doubtless, so fond they're of scriptural facts,
They will soon get the *Pentateuch* up in five acts.
Here Daniel, in pantomime, bids bold defiance

To Nebuchadnezzar and all his stuff'd lions;
While pretty young Israelites dance round the
    prophet,
In very thin clothing, and but little of it; —
Here Bégrand, who shines in this scriptural path,
As the lovely Susanna, without even a relic
Of drapery round her, comes out of the bath
In a manner that, Bob says, is quite Eva-
    angelic !' "

William Hone observes that Madame Bégrand, a
finely formed woman, acted in *Susanna and the
Elders*. "Madame Bégrand lately left the pious
audiences of the Théâtre de la Porte St. Martin, for
an engagement at the King's Theatre, London,
where the apocryphal story of *Susanna* is not
acted."

MYSTIC DANCE (European)

Is especially examined by R. P. Knight[1] as an
accompaniment of all religious cults. He refers to
the Greek systems, quoting Lucian (*De Saltatione*)
agreeing that "Dancing was a part of the ceremonial in all mystic rites". Dance was held in high
esteem; so that the philosopher Socrates and the
poet Sophocles cultivated dance as "a useful and
respectable accomplishment". The author of the
Homeric Hymn to Apollo describes that God as
accompanying his lyre with the dance, joined by
other deities. A Corinthian poet, cited by Athenaeus, introduces the Father of the Gods and men,
as employed in the same exercise. The Knossian
dances of the Greeks, sacred to Jupiter; and the
Nyssian dances, devoted to Bacchus, were directed
by Pan (principle of universal order). Lucian affirms
that "No ancient initiation can be found where
there is not dancing" (*De Saltatione*), and further,
the same writer says :

> "The choral dance of the stars, the orderly concert
> of planets, their common union and harmony of
> motion, constitute the exhibition of the Dance
> of the First-Born".

[Cp. *Cosmic Ballet*]
[1] *Symbolical Language of Ancient Art and Mythology*. R. P. Knight. New York. 1876.

MYSTICAL DANCE

Traditional forms. An expert 19th century writer
on occultism devoted an article to "Mystical
Dance", bearing as title the quotation, "Praise Him
with the Timbrel and Dance"[1] from *Psalm cxlix*.
In her current reference to some new Hindu cults
then emerging (*Brahmo Samaj*) H. P. Blavatsky
refers to "Mystical dancing as a practice hoary
with age and pregnant with occult philosophy
. . . ." and mentions the allegorical King David
saying : "Jesus dances, Moses dances . . . . . Old
King David dances . . . And with him Janak and

Yudhistir". "And why not ?" "The mystics and
devotees of nearly every religion and sect", she
writes, "have at some time adopted the salutary
exercise. There was the Dance of the Daughters of
Shiloh during the Jewish Mysteries (*Judges xxi*)
and the Leaping of the Prophets of Baal (*I Kings
xviii*). From the Sabaean dances—denoting the
motion of the planets round the sun—down to the
American Shakers of Old Mother Lee, the truly
religious bodies found themselves occasionally
possessed with Bacchic frenzy. During their
religious meetings, the Shakers first sing a hymn,
then form a wide circle around a band of male
and female singers, to the music of whom they
dance in a solemn rhythm, until "moved by the
spirit they begin prophesying and speaking with
tongues". Dancing was established as a rite, together with the *kiss of charity* by the Agapæists,
the venerable members of that primitive Christian
institution called the Agapæ, which counted
Augustine among its influential members".
[1] From an article in "The Theosophist" by H. P.
Blavatsky (Vol. II No. 9. June 1881, p. 201).

MYTH AND DANCE

Ballets have been, for three centuries, concerned
with performing legends of Greek and Roman
"mythology", just as the Miracle Plays were concerned with presenting later forms of myth,
revised from earlier projects. The myth is seen
essentially as a dramatic legend : it tells of events
and personages—the gods and their activities, in
terms of action. (Pictures and sculptures appear
later). Only in this manner can the essential dual
quality of "function and relation" be stated (it
cannot be fully explained in any other manner,
than by experience). The term myth (Sanskrit
mythia—the "not-true") is said to be "invented to
explain ritual" but this notion is inadequate. Myth
and ritual are counterparts : the dramatic myth
provides basic sense-data, for the formation of
mental images; while ritual (in its genuine modes)
provides sensation and image, by way of direct
inner experience. These two series of images are
fused, to provide that basic knowledge, from which
illumination can sometimes be gained. The most
potent world method we know is in the duality
of dance : in *watching* events unrolled, as mythic
drama, and in *performing* events, as mythic ritual.
In both modes, the universal quality of dynamic
rhythm rules figure and function; eventually the
mystery is penetrated, yet only when the seeker
becomes able to "ride the storm" by relaxing his
own personality in exchange for the reality that is
concealed behind myth and hidden within ritual.
For this purpose the Hellenes devised their *theatrum*—the display of the gods; for this, the Hindu

priests projected their magnificent sacred dances — to unroll the mythos-curtain of the "not-true" and reveal the ever-present yet invisible reality. In the *dromenon* (the "thing done") was projected this drama of the gods, as in the *natya* of India was shown the veiling form that hid *nitya* (eternity). In drama or dance, the insistence on dynamism is potent: events must move, images must reveal character in function; and the whole series of images and functions (which cannot be shewn except in a very long series), when rejuvenated in the living and moving mind of the observer, bring him to the hidden wisdom, which neither *mythos* nor *mathematikos* can state in any completeness of images — whether seen, remembered, or imagined.

MYTH IN DANCE (Greek, *methos*, a tale; Sanskrit, *mithya*, the "not-real")
Essentially: a substitute, usually in a sensible reality of form, for a thing, entity, relation, or power that is not physically apprehensible. Hence, any myth is fundamentally a mental concept, though presented in some physical mode, of a fact (not a non-truth) that cannot be directly perceived by the senses. Because the myth is not the fact it contains, reveals, and conceals, it has the quality of a symbol; in that some lead has to be given, by which to follow, in a concatenation of formal ideas, until the individual mind does seize the inward reality. For this reason, dance is used in religious association; both as a ritual and as drama (*dromenon*). Usually, the broad terms are rendered extravagant: so that the rational mind shall feel unwilling to accept the ostensible presentation, for the fact. Thus the apparent relations among the "families" of Greek gods and goddesses were stated or hinted in such startling manner as to cause the beholder to seek for some other connection. This quality appears in all religious myth: the apparent form and motion is never the real form and motion. The dancer presents a character; or the ritual group present situations, which *must* be examined and pondered to yield the invisible realities. In this sense all religious dramas, literature, symbols, and legends are given to students; in myth, allegory, fable, miracle play or mystery dance; parables; pictures or sculptures. The inner facts, relations, and powers of any myth *are real*, as compared with the external forms. The only reality of religious history is in the history of its changing mythic forms.

MYTHIC DANCE
Or Dramatic Religious Dance of the Gods and Goddesses, moves along with its counterpart of RITUAL DANCE or the dance of religious action in worship. Every religion develops its own typical scheme, balancing its technical-material basis against its emotional-mental desires. The doctrinal scheme thus contains an ethical system (group behaviour) often mingled with a salvational system (for personal behaviour) and, less often, an intellectual system, or world-explanation. These mythic ritual dances appear in: —

> *Egypt:* Isis/Osiris/Horus scheme;
> *India:* Brahma/Vishnu/Shiva;
> *Moslem:* Hassan/Husain/Allah;
> *Mexican:* Toque Nahuaque/Tonacatecuhtli/
>   Tonacacihuatl;
> *Greek:* Zeus/Athene/Diana;
> *Assyria:* Ishtar/Bel/Belus;
> *Hebrew:* Elohim/Shaddai/Yahve;
> *Christian:* Jesus/Chrestus/Maria;
> *Icelandic-Scandinavian:*
> *Roman:* Jupiter/Juno/Mars
> *Gaelic:*

The most complete scheme of myth reveals a double "trinity in unity", such as the complex Hindu system. Some attain only to an all-male scheme, like the Jewish Jahvé system. *Lunar cult* (Dianic) has an all-female scheme — Hekate-Diana-Luna.

MYTHIC STRUCTURE
As apparent by analysis of dance and ritual or mythic drama, is known in two immensely different series; which we may, in comparative study, align with the physiological world of vital structure, also as 1. *Exo-skeleton*, and 2. *Endo-skeleton* in archetypal form. This factor arises in the circumstances from which each mythic system develops. The technical myth, as developed from harsh necessities of life, in hunting or agriculture, is based on the *material* weapon, tool or implement, the *material* food and shelter. The typical hero of such mythic extensions of knowledge (as systems of understanding and use of daily life and action), is always the Strong Man, the Great Hunter, the Military Victor. The psychic-mythic structure, with its *endo-skeleton*, carries its structure hidden within; and derives from mental power. There is a third type of structure which unites both phases, in the form of the Social Myth, requiring the Saviour or Messiah or Mediator. The core and the frame are here united in supernal Toughness. Sometimes three phases are held in one mythic structure; apparent in gods as a Creator, a Sustainer, and Dissolver; and each of these again, in two balancing modes: positive-negative, formulated in myth as male-female, the god and his spouse (*Shakti-Shakta*). By their relation in structure, and dynamic *movement in rhythm*, is conceived the World Dance.

N

NA'AT KHAN (Turkey)
Singer-dancers in ritual; professional reciters of stories (in India, *Inayat Khan*), probably associated with *Natyam* and *Natya*; and thence to *Narr*, narration, etc. (in Germany).

NACHTANZ (Germany)
"After-dance". European court dances during the 15th and 17th centuries, were often arranged in pairs, a slow dignified dance in duple time being followed by a more lively dance in triple time. In the music for these dances, the second, gay dance was called the *Nachtanz*, the melody often being a rhythmic variation of the music for the first dance. *Nachtanz* was sometimes called *Proportz*, in which case the melody for both dances was the same but in varying meter. The usual dances performed together were : —

> Pavane* and Galliard*
> Passamezzo* and Saltarello*
> Allemande* and Courante*
> Sarabande* and Gigue*

NĀDAGAM (Ceylon)
Mode of "folk-opera" or "country-song-dance", which was reformulated in 19th century, on an older and vanished basis. This "reform" (properly, deformation) was initiated by a half-caste, Pillipu Siñño (Philip) born 1770, apparently with a Croatian catholic parent, of which many traces are evident. The form is a developed sort of "Calypso"* or Negro spiritual; with more dancing and action strongly propagandist in thematic content. Several still continue, not thus spoliated (*Kapiri Nadagamâ*, and *Dinatara*) with fairy-tale elements; and older in their own mythic meaning. Many "new words" were coined by Sinno; as *Salila liya*, for dancing girl. The music was similarly defaced by use of German harmonium (locally, *seraphina*), to accompany drums (*maddala*), called *demala bere* (Tamil drum) by players. The *caroli* style was imposed on the ancient tradition (*kirtanam* or sacred chants) of the Tamil folk play. The "dancing place" is called *karaliva*, as a platform, circular in shape, under a shed roof, raised with sand above the level of the seated audience. Curtains, or even painted scenes are used. Performances begin about nine and continue to dawn. The chief, or "presenter", is called *Pote Gura* (? Peter Guru), who contrives to assimilate the *kantaru* (cantor-tones) with the two drummers. There are two Fortune-tellers intermixed (as in some New Year *noels*), and the inevitable jester; who between them, relate or carry the story, as *Desa-navadis*. Stock characters enter, each with typical tune and dance; some wear masks. The main form is lyrical; changing from verse to declamation; from mime to dance (similar to the Tamil form *Teruk-kuttoo*). In a full performance there may be eight or ten musicians and five dancer-characters; but all actors enter dancing, even the *Pote Gura*; but the jester (*komali* or *konangi*) does most. The *Nadagam* may be compared also with *Yaksha-gana*.* This missionary intervention even developed a "Nativity Play", but, "after all", says Prof. Sarathchandra,[1] "gradually the *Nadagam* went into non-catholic hands . . . and and it was not held in high repute; it died out after about one-and-a-half centuries of existence".
[1] *Sinhalese Folk Play and Modern Stage*. Prof. E. R. Sarathchandra. Colombo, Ceylon. 1953.

NAGA (Burma)
Is familiar to all Burmese. Like all snake or serpent spirits, he is hard for the foreigner to identify, since snake is by no means identical with serpent; while *Nagas* exist on many scales of proportion. Often he is a dragon, somewhat like the ancient Chinese dragon; yet he dances with the *Nats** in their mythic drama. In some folk-tales, the hero always had to kill a *Naga* before he could be a king. The worship of the *Naga* elementals differed from the worship of the *Nat* spirits; both belong to pre-Buddhist lore, though temples devoted to both were permitted to remain when the big change occurred (dated at *circa* 1044). The battles of Hero versus Naga prince were often produced in a mock battle-dance form   [See *Toe-Naya; Nats*]

NAGA DANCES (Assam, India)
There are many closely related Naga tribes in the hills, who continue their simple traditional dances. They have a war dance in ceremonial attire; dancing as successful head-hunters at a full moon night in the Spring Festival. Each man carries a plaited basket decorated with bison horns (a substitute for the grisly "new head" trophy formerly necessary). Brass medals show by number the record of victims claimed. Decorations of silver or brass set off these ritual elements; they are skilful craftsmen. The Konyak Naga people hurl their spears, to show how they transfix their victims — if they don't miss. Small boys copy all these dances; and prepare for them with immense delight. The Naga maidens do their dance before the Chief's house. To simple rhythms, they sway in graceful rhythm by the hour, sometimes singing, grouped on a new platform of heavy bamboo especially erected for the dance. Simpler dances are more social in character, where young men and girls dance to simple melodies on moonlight nights just for fun; though much earlier ritual was by

way of placation of the nature spirits. There is a Spear Dance where, in one routine, the soloist plunges his spear at his feet, kicking back and forth; while next he leans back so far that he seems to be suspended in air. The numerous rapid hopping movements contribute to this effect. Or his legs swing alternately, de-tensed so that they appear dead; he is miming the "toe touch" for bamboo traps which enemies use to defend their villages. Another *Spear Dance* shows the attack-defence moves, familiar in numerous weapon dances. Long spears are swung with incredible skill and accuracy; the dancer will combine a move of evasion with his legs, with an attack by his spear. The Kabui Naga women perform an abstracted magical dance, making geometric aerial patterns while seated, but rising to affirm, by a smack on the thigh, the use of the magical force thus induced.   [See *Bamboo Trap Dance*]

NAGARI (Hindu)

Refers directly, today, to the alphabet derived from Sanskrit and used to write or print Hindi. The ancient terms had many more meanings: at one time, *Nagai* implied the town gentleman, *nagari*, who used writing in *nagari*. But *naga* is serpent; the original track of letters was made in the *anda* (egg or sphere) and implied the whole culture; hence the *nagar* was a "serpent-master" or scholar. Yet the *naga* was not the familiar snake; but an erudite symbol of natural forces; hence the scholar in *nagara* was master of some of them. Theatre as a basic of culture was inclusive. In Persian and then Arabic, the drum ("talking-drum" of dance and code) became called *naqqara*. The opposition of these terms is equivalent to the derogatory term *pagani* (villagers) used by the Roman city people, even by slum dwellers.

NAIN ROUGE (France)

Literally "Red Dwarf". A *Lutin*, or dancing goblin, traditional in Normandy, and helpful to fishermen. Another goblin is *Le petite homme rouge*.

NAKT REVUE (Berlin)

Typical German entertainment in a number of small theatres (mostly along Friedrichstrasse) between the wars. In the *Revue*, a number of girls (usually heavyweights) danced lustily to easy tunes, which the simple audience (*aus provinz*) was invited to sing; and, having sung, *etwas bier trinken*. The largest of such establishments was *Haüs Vaterland* (Potsdamer Platz), where food and music, song and dance were provided *fur die Provinz*. Berliners rarely patronised these shows. They are parallel with the typical American *burletta*, or the Montmartre cabaret *pour les Améri-*

cainos. In England, almost the only remaining one operates just off Piccadilly, though with a higher artistic standard. In practically all of these kinds of show, the dance is simply "movement to music", more or less with rhythm, seldom for any expression of any idea, even by way of satire. In this manner the Revue follows in the ancient tradition, as known in Rome or Byzantium. There it must have been good, for the Christian Emperor Theodoric married the chief star of the Constantine theatre. In the Middle Ages, similar entertainment was provided in the Kloster by mercenary monks, especially in literal representations, as in the Morality Play of *Adam and Eve;* or the highly popular *Salome and Herod.* Many Dutch or German "altar-pieces" were obviously inspired by similar moral plays.

NAKUMDOIT, Ceremony of (Arnhemland, N. Australia)

Initiation ceremony of youths of the Gunwinggu tribe, depicting appropriate totemic myths. The boys (*Nakumdoit—"to-be-initiated"*) hear for the first time the *Balnooknook* drum and songs connected with it. This hollow-tree drum (whose sacred name is *banagaga*), is painted black, red and yellow, with white dots, and is beaten with "Labait", the drum-stick—a piece of pandanus palm frayed at one end. In addition there are two rhythm-sticks beaten by the Songman; the *Didjeridoo* (a long, narrow wooden tube, played through a mouthpiece and giving a droning sound); clapping and chanting. The *Balnooknook* and *Didjeridoo* are found only in Arnhemland. The ceremony (forbidden to women) takes place on a cleared dancing-ground, beginning in the morning. When the men are gathered, the *Nakumdoit* are led into the clearing, and the "spirit of the Balnooknook" is "sung" into them. There follow short, swift solo dances. Then men of the *Kalahara*, red Kangaroo totem, perform. Painted with red ochre splashed with white, they imitate movements of the Kangaroo, hopping round in line behind each other. Then squatting, each man grasps the waist of the man in front and they move round on their knees. In the afternoon two *Gau-bi*, or "Bee-men" (painted with yellow and white circles made of small dots to represent the honeycomb); and two *Barangbang*, "Snake-men" (painted with a yellow "snaky" line, and having grey feathers on their heads), perform their "dances". Each pair sits back to back, feet tucked underneath, arms at sides so that each man's hands grasp his partner's. The Snake-men sway forwards and round in imitation of the python in their legend; while the Bee-men represent the flight of bees by a continuous quivering of the muscles of chest, arms and shoulders. Part

three depicts a myth of *Kalahara*, watched by the *Nakumdoit*, who later are "walked along" by the Kangaroo men, as they imitate that animal in a crouching line. Each holding the man in front, they proceed in perfect rhythm, jumping with both feet off the ground, like the Kangaroo, their heads rolling rhythmically from side to side. The ceremony ends with a ritual "singing" of all the men. Forming two lines facing, in pairs, the squatting men quiver their shoulder and chest muscles, while the Songman walks between the lines and "sings" each pair of men.
[See *Corroboree; Wilyaroo; Tjitji-Inma; Aruwaltja*]

NA-LENG (Malekula, New Hebrides)
Mumming plays and "maze" dances performed on the Dancing-Ground at dawn on the day of an important rite during the Maki ritual cycles, following the all-night dance. (See *Turei Na-mbe,* Rambden,* Maki-ru**). The plays, either mythological, or comic skits on everyday life, are mimed by dancers wearing ankle-rattles; and performed in rotation by visiting villagers. Each actor/dancer wears a mask, or veils his face with strips of white bark, fixed to a frame, on top of which is a model of the character he represents. He must never stand still, but continually dances, moving from place to place with swift, shuffling steps. After the mimed plays a "maze" dance is performed by the Maki-men (initiates), who form the "chorus" with four solo dancers. On the island of Atchin this dance is followed at intervals of several years, by four others, the whole sequence illustrating the gradual initiation of the Maki-men; but, in the south-west bay of Malekula, the whole series is given as one dramatic performance. The first dance of the sequence shows the Maki-men defenceless, because uninitiated, and symbolises their passage through the Maze into the Land of the Dead, from which they will eventually be "reborn". *Na-leng* dances thus slightly resemble *ballet d'action* in that, although having a ritual purpose, they portray a theme. The dancers should ideally number a hundred men, in a square with ten lines of ten men; but may be seven lines of seven; or five lines of five. The leader beats time on a portable bamboo slit-gong, and the dance is divided into sections, growing to a climax. Representing unfledged birds (symbolising their uninitiated state), the men break their square formation, as line follows line in a spiral movement, down the Dancing-Ground, forming into a square again at the other end. Then, in single file, they move from side to side of the ground in serpentine course, and with a swimming movement, again forming into a square. Now two men enter with bows and arrows. They dance round the group of men in a mock battle, and

retire, to be followed by a single dancer representing a hawk (a symbolical motif that runs through the Maki ritual), arms outstretched as wings. He threads between the ranks of men and also retires, but is followed by another "hawk" dancer called "the hawk pouncing on his prey". He also dances in and out of the lines of men until, at a given moment, he becomes threatening, sways from side to side, beats his "wings", dances a short way away, then turns and swoops down upon the "unfledged birds", who cower in a mass at his feet as the "hawk" stands triumphant in their midst with outstretched arms. So ends the dance. Its form and movements connect it with the Malekulan "Journey of the Dead". The "swimming" movements of the Maki-men represent the channel to be crossed before the dead man reaches the rock where the female demon, Temes Savsap, guards the entrance to the Land of the Dead. The dead man must know how to complete a design which she half draws in the sand, before he can pass through the maze into the other land. In the dance, the Maki-men, in their square formation, represent the framework of straight lines, on which the design is based; while the solo dancer who threads between the rows, symbolises the design, made by one continuous line interweaving through the framework. In 1776, on Tonga, Capt. Cook saw a *Na-leng* dance of this kind, with 105 men—100 for the square, with five solo dancers.
[See *Malekula, Dances of; Sand Tracings; Olové*]

NAMASKA (India)
Also *namaskar*: general term used as "salute" or greeting, in active sense. The *anjali** is the pose or position arrived at (the *mudra**), as compared with *namaska*, the gesture or act. In dance the verbal greeting (in the North) is *Sala'am*! (from Moslem Persian) or, if sent by servant: *Sala'am do*! ("Gives greeting"). Another Punjabi mode is the *salam-rei*; while in the South, a term used is *charanam* (abbreviated from *chara-namaska*). In dance or drama, words are used or indicated in *abhinaya*; for the audience is always first saluted at the opening of proceedings.   [See *Hasta*]

NANIGO (Cuba)
Cult dance performed secretly by Cuban Negroes. They belong to the traditional *Shango* (or *Xango**) category of West African tribal rites, mainly from the Yoruba country. *Naningo* is principally an invocation dance, performed only by men. A watered-down stage version (derived from the *Santos*—Spanish spiritualism) was presented (London 1948) by Katherine Dunham's company.
[See *L'Ag-ya; Xango*]

NANNAR (Babylon; Chaldea)

The Moon God was the earliest "Measurer of Time". Sayce says:[1]

"According to the official religion of Chaldea, the Sun god was the offspring of the Moon God . . . such a belief could have arisen only where the Moon God was the supreme 'symbol' of worship. To these Semites the Moon god was lord and father of the gods".

Egyptian astronomy held that Thoth was Moon God (also male) was "measurer and regulator of the seasons". The Eye of Thoth was the Full Moon; as the Eye of Re was the midday Sun. From these factors was constructed the first (Lunar) Zodiack as the measurer of world-time. Hence these secrets were set forth in precisely measured ritual, to give the known facts of astronomy. The moon moves over the space of its own width in one hour; that gives the twenty-four hours. The Rite of Nannar gave the apparent Paths of Moon and Sun, in the girdle of the Zodiacal belt and Ecliptic at its centre. Periods were marked by total lunar eclipses: from which the Moon gave the Times and Rhythms; this continues now in the fixation of Easter by the first full moon of the Equinox; and this point gave the date for the Great Feast of Ishtara, "Mother of Stars". The lunar eclipses define the Ecliptic; successive full moons; and these (when known) give the imaginary anti-sun which marks the boundaries of Zodiac. From Nannar came the Lunar Annum; and also the Triple Hecate or Lunar phases, so important in "fortunes", and thus materialised in dance modes. In these dance rituals, imaginary animals etc. were shewn by masked priests, led by the Bull Taurus. In this setting (the secluded temple circle) came the Ritual of Urim.*

[1] Hibbert Lectures.

NA-REL (Malekula)

A simple processional dance of Malekula and the Small Islands of the New Hebrides, danced at the culminating rites of Ramben* and Maki-Ru,* a two part ritual initiation cycle. Guests from neighbouring villages arrive dancing Na-rel, and it is also performed at the final rite of Maki-Ru, when tusked boars are brought up for sacrifice. During Turei Na-mbe* (Gong-Raising ceremony), songs and dancing of the Gong-Raising and Na-rel cycles are performed by the "Maki-men" (initiates) as the logs for the new gongs are ferried across from the mainland. The name, derived from a root meaning "to walk", indicates the characteristic movement of the dance—a heavy, thudding step, each foot being brought down with the whole weight of the body on heel and sole. [See Malekula Dances of]

NARREN-TREFFEN (Germany)

"Fools' Meeting". Throughout the Black Forest at pre-Lent Carnival (Fasching*), masked dancers prance through the towns in a leaping dance. On one week-end during the three-week period, people from all over the Schwarzwald gather, in a different town each year, for a mass Narren-Treffen. On Sunday morning, rehearsal, or Probe-Sprung ("practice springing") is held, and at 2 p.m. the procession begins. Each village has its own characters (all men), collectively known as Narros ("Fools"), but also with individual names. Principal characters are Schuddig, Federhannes (Feather John), Hänsel (Tease), Schandle (Scandal) and G'schell (Bell-Fool). The last two each carry a book with records of moral lapses in their village over the past year, which are read out after the procession. G'schell, with slightly legal appearance, wears a mass of bells on his chest, while Schandle, dressed as a woman, holds up a parti-coloured, open umbrella. Schuddig, the most ferocious, has a grinning cadaverous mask, and a hat thickly decorated with snail-shells. He belabours Narros and spectators with a bladder tied to a stick. Federhannes, with feathers sewn to his suit, wears a tusked mask; and springs at bystanders with a long, feather-tufted pole. There are witches with broomsticks, who raise bystanders in the air. Nearly all Narros wear bells which ring rhythmically, as they dance with the traditional springing step. Some carry pretzels strung on a stick, which they fling to the crowd. Masks, carved in wood may weigh up to two pounds. Some are heirlooms two hundred years old. Costumes are hand-made of white linen, brightly painted with symbolical figures, the pantaloons sometimes padded out. One or two are made all of playing-cards; or of strips of paper sewn on to the linen. At Rottweil there is a hobby-horse called Brieler Rossle, after the village of Briel, now vanished. His arrival in Rottweil used to announce the beginning of Carnival. Another village has a hobby-horse shaped like a cock. The festival is the old yearly cleansing—ridding of Winter evils—reminiscent of the ancient Roman February festival of purification, februare meaning "to purify". [See Fasching; Perchten; Schemenlaufen; Rollelibutzen]

NATARAJA (Hindu)

King of Dancers, is also Narayana (the "good power") who urges on the world dance, with Kala (understood as "Time") but drawn from: Kala yati iti Kalah, or "that which moves all things". The effect of Time-Space-Motion is originated by the appearance of innumerable "ego" or "eka" selves from the Cosmos; thus giving (to any single one) the idea of duality and objectivity. Hence we see

"Dancer-Dancing-Dance" as a triple entity that is yet but One in dynamic being. This is the essence of *Nataraja*. Writing on this profound topic, Bhagavan Das says:

"the great Jaina writers, whose versions of the *Mahabharata* and the *Ramayana* are more "rationalistic" have a very illuminative theory that *avataras* always come in opposed pairs; as Narayana and Prati-Narayana, the former representing the Good Forces and the latter as Evil, as Rama and Ravana; and history is fullest and vividest when the two forces are battling most strongly. Time as the Oversoul makes the man; time as an era is made by the man".[1]

The theory of *avatara* (the "coming of a messiah" or a prophet, or a conqueror) permeates many religious ideologies. In modern times it has been seized by Friedrich Nietzsche and implied rather than expounded by Oswald Spengler,[2] as it was re-stated alike by Jews (Messiah), Greeks (Soter) and Christian (Saviour) or Hindus (Krishna), as an *avatar* of the god Vishnu. The profound symbolism of Hindu sacred dance expresses in its liturgy the same general scheme: "He comes dancing, that he may save this world!"

[1] *Krishna Avatar*. Bhagavan Das. Madras, 1924 (p. 6).
[2] *Die Untergang des Abendlandes*. Oswald Spengler. Munich, 1925.

NATIONAL BALLET (Europe)
Has developed chiefly by reason of State, Ducal or Municipal, subsidies; some direct; but this fact cannot be a complete definition. The National French Ballet* dwells at the Paris Opéra, municipally subsidised. Italian (National?) Ballet developed at Milano; but lapsed considerably, though subsidised (as also companies at Venice, Naples, and even Genoa), by occasional or continued municipal subventions, granted mainly to opéra. The English National Ballet is a compromise: one or two favoured companies, which cannot now operate commercially, are state-subsidised for home losses; but not for profits made abroad. Commercial companies (visiting in USA) now fail to do more than provide operating costs and profits to American managers; for the principal self-contained company, International Ballet, found mounting costs too much to cover expenses. American "National Ballet" is subsidised solely by private parties, individuals or groups; and has no "home theatre" for permanent occupation. Russian National Ballet continues, with much less state guarantee than in Tsarist times, as a state-controlled set of companies. The Danish National Ballet receives certain state guarantees; but the Swedish National Ballet, formerly supported by private persons, has relapsed. There is no German state ballet, though attempts

are being made to revive companies; while the Austrian National Ballet (supported by Vienna) has shewn signs of revival. Certain other countries have made attempts to form National Ballet companies; sometimes with financial support; as in Australia; while in Canada the effort is solely private. The Indian Government has made no attempt to form and support a State Dance Company (the impediments are tremendous, as organisation difficulties seem insuperable); Hungary has a State Ensemble, also Yugoslavia, and Rumania, each featuring Folk Dances but not ballet, although Zagreb in the Croatian part of Yugoslavia, has a State Ballet Company. Spain has no National Ballet. The company at Prague in Czechoslovakia is moribund; though there is dance activity. The Polish National Ballet remains inactive as such; while that in Finland at Helsinki does not yet show much

Bilu or Nat. Burmese dancing figure of extraordinary vigour in carved teak, gilded. The Nata is one of the powerful dancing Nature Spirits. From Rangoon, Burma; 18th century, height 19½ ins. Collection of W. G. Raffé.   BURMA

development. Centres in South America receive occasional aid: Argentine, Peru, and Cuba; but remain far too much on technical lines.

NATS DANCE (Burma)

Before Buddhist missions arrived (200 BC) in Burma, with the *Hinayana* system (Little Vehicle), there was a mode of Nature worship prevalent, which had two aspects. In this the *Naga** "serpents" or earth powers were reverenced as entities of power; while the *Nats* were esteemed as nature spirits, both good and evil, who were able to "communicate" or to enter female mediums to give advice. The *Naga* godlings had a leader named Milind or Milinda (known in the time of Buddha); they lived in Patala, the nether regions. Their rituals comprised sacrifices and dances. Their ministers were a *shaman* type of priest or wizard; he also contacted King Thakia Min, ruler of the *Nats*. They also held festival dances. When Buddhism advanced, this nature worship receded, as it did elsewhere; but the official religions have never abolished entirely this elemental spiritualism and ancestor worship; and the simple dances, which induce and end the trances, still continue in remote villages. It is a moot point in etymology, if the Saxon *gnat* was not derived from this ancient shamanist source. [See *Burma, Dances of*]

NATTU-KUTTU (South India)

Type of religious folk-play, related to the *Terukkuttu* of the Tamil Nad; or the *Vithi Nataka* plays seen in Andhra. The small group of male players consist of the *guru*, with musicians and actor-dancers. They perform in a *mandapa*, or circular stage, with a conical thatched roof. This floor is raised by banking up sand or earth, trodden flat and hard. Four or five musicians sit on the back half of the *mandapa*, each side of the actors' only entrance, at back centre. Two boys hold a curtain; the dancer enters, the curtain is dropped; and he begins. Each actor dances in a small ring movement, with music from drums and *kaitalans*. The *guru* or Announcer is here called the *Annavi*; he is general conductor and manager. The *Nattu Kuttu* may be seen in Jaffna and Batticoloa. The chief dance in it is *Cellep-pillai Vacantam* (meaning "Dance of Playful Boy", possibly originally Krishna as the boy god). The play themes are mostly from *Mahabharata* and *Ramayana*; while the dance reveals forgotten traces of *Bharata Natyam** classical dance form. Some of these dances are simply "work dances", like cutting grass, rowing a boat, or riding a pony. *Tenmodi Nattu Kuttu* (South) is the older form; while *Vadamodi* (*N-Kuth*) (Northern) is more influenced by modernist ideas.

NATURE DANCERS (General)

Comprise the vast range of living and moving entities (*other than* human beings and animals), who are referred to in ritual and drama, in popular traditions of legends and dance. While most of these creatures possess local names and places, many are known over wide areas (as in Asia), and though some are mentioned as being apparent at certain periods of the year (or month), others are taken as "characters" by human dancers, who act in these parts after the supposed manner of the non-human creation. These nature dancers thus occupy a borderland between human beings and the more fully formalised "afterworld" postulated in the various religious schemes. Some of these non-human entities are again accepted as denizens of the lower world, having the power to move in and out; to become visible at will to human eyes; or to specially gifted groups, or to single persons. To dwellers in commercialized modern cities, it becomes quite difficult to know that particular condition of mind which can accept these "nature dancers" as real entities; so it is usual to refer them to the "poetic imagination", or simply to show them as "delusions or illusions". Despite this modern tendency, the names and places, with the appearance and the characteristic acts of these creatures of the half visible world, have occupied a considerable space in most popular traditions. As in consequence, it has been considered possible to portray some of these fairies or demons, as stage characters, it seems necessary at least to attempt a classification. They reveal, to the observant eye, totally different characters, by their regular forms and modes of movement; and so long as romantic theatre endures, so long it seems advisable to examine these nature-dance traditions. We have then to glance at the kingdom of faerie used by Shakespeare; at the realm of demons beloved by witch hunters; at the glossy circles of angels portrayed by theologians; or the elemental spirits, used symbolically by the alchemists. Many of these entities have descendents—parallel figures— in some department of our modern mythology, disguised by more familiar names. Today there may be no Dame Trot in villages; but there is Dame Fashion in cities; she has two seasons annually, dancing or moving in quaint costumes and styles.

NATYA VEDA (SHASTRAS) (Hindu)

"Dance Scripture". Said to be derived, in legendary accounts, from a synthesis or extract of the original Four *Vedas*, as *Veda* of Theatre. Dance came from *Rig Veda*; song from *Sama Veda*; Mimicry from *Yajur Veda*, and passion or duty from *Atharva Veda*. The term *natya* is Prakrit, not Sanskrit. In the great *Natya Shastras*, the account referred to the

legendary sage or manager Bharata, and abounds in technical Prakrit terms. The languages are mixed. The *Prakrit* (almost equals "dialect") existed in Magadhi, in Shauraseni (Agra district, home of Krishnaism), and *Yatras* are known in Bengali, which is used for the part of the jester (*vidushaka*) who is one of the basic characters.

NAUBUT KHANA (North India)
Town "Musicians' Gallery"—arranged as an open balcony, always over the town gate of Indian cities, where important visitors entered. Here a company of the local gild musicians would gather, to perform melodies suitable for each occasion. The *naubat khana* is exactly similar to the Minstrels' Gallery in England (or France) of mediaeval times; or to the earlier "Waits Lift" of Norman-Saxon days. One of these was pictured in the famous *Dance of Death* painting (known as the *Doom Panel*) which portrayed scenes from miracle plays, in Gloucester Cathedral. The "blesséd" were ushered past the heavenly gates, over which a group of angels played on trumpet and viol, while others sang appropriate verses. Over the opposite entrance, to hell, the devil-musicians were producing a *charivari* chorus on kitchen implements. In the Indian ceremonial, a *nautch** party met the distinguished visitor; instead of "taking the salute" the dancing girls took charge of him, dancing before and through the archway of the town gate, as they led him to his ceremonial bath.

NAUTANKI (Mathura, Uttar Pradesh, India)
Is a traditional ritual drama-dance, celebrating episodes about Krishna and Radha. The dancer is a boy attired in girl's garments, with a veil. The dance begins with would-be elaborate footwork similar to Kathak, but seldom so good, accompanied by *tabla* (drum) and that horrible instrument the harmonium, now disappearing from India.

NAUTCH (Northern India)
A corruption by Moslem invaders of the older Sanskrit term *Natyam*; refers now solely to entertainment or pastime dances, performed by professional dancers in cities like Lahore, Agra, Lucknow or Delhi. Traditional performances are usually dull for Europeans; it is like watching a chess game, demanding considerable experience to appreciate the "fine points" of each move. Nautch has not for a century been considered "respectable" by Hindu matrons; but it has recovered, to a cabaret style, and entered into Indian film production. The 19th century style (itself a development) required one girl, supported by three to six musicians and sometimes a singer. She dances in the centre of a room,

on a small platform some four feet square, covered with hard red cotton cord carpet. With bare feet, and jingling anklets, she dances usually in modest costume but loaded with jewellery (often genuine and valuable) to familiar melodies and topical chants. The speciality is to begin at a slow *tal* or beat; then to double it and again to double it in speed, without committing an error of footwork. For a very special Festival Dance, the *nautchee* will spill a pattern in fine coloured sand;* and dance over it without breaking it; or make one while dancing; or gradually kick one pattern into another by gentle taps of her toes. The dance had affiliations with *pachisi** (16th century Mughal-Kshattriya style) but, apart from certain esoteric uses of varied beats, this has been lost. Formerly there was a tap-code similar to the modern Morse code; a dancer could convey information to instructed members of her audience—useful in times of trouble.
[Cp. *Alpona; Rangoli; Sand Tracings; Pattern (Sweden)*]

NAVAJO (North America)
A semi-nomadic people of the Pueblo lands, who lived in one-family huts, or *hogans*. Now more numerous than when the Spaniards came, in 1940 they were the largest tribe in North America, numbering 50,000 and occupying territory in northeastern Arizona and north-western New Mexico. After the Conquest, they became more pastoral, weaving blankets and making jewelry of turquoise and silver. Their ceremonies are connected with the curing of disease, of which the painting of sand patterns forms an important part. Painted by the medicine man on the dry sand floor of the ceremonial lodge, the elongated designs symbolise scenes and figures in Navajo mythology. While tribesmen chant and shake gourd rattles, the masked shaman moves over the pattern (on which the patient sits), touching both the patient and various parts of the design, so that the disorder will enter the painted symbol and be carried away when the pattern is erased, as it is after each day's ceremony. Next day a different pattern is painted. The most impressive Navajo ceremony is that of the *Night Chants*, a religious rite performed at night in the open air. Including many dances, prayers and songs, the climax is the *Fire Dance,** in which white-painted men dance round a fire with lighted torches. As with the Pueblo* Indians, *Koshare** (dancing clowns) accompany the solemn dances, burlesquing the actions of the priests and joking with spectators. They provide a light-hearted complement to the more serious aspect of the ceremonies. The Navajo origin story affirms the importance of the Four Cardinal Points, prevalent

The Nautch. "Dancing Girls at Night Entertainment." Miniature painting by Maharaja Abhan Sing 1724–1750) 43.5 cm. by 34.5 cm. Sardar Museum, Jodhpur.   INDIA

throughout Amerindian cosmology. As with the Cherokee and Pawnee Indians, they associate a colour with each direction—white in the east (first light, or dawn); blue in the south (day-time); yellow in the west (evening); black in the north (night). The Navajo also give appropriately coloured ornaments to the cardinal points—rock crystal; turquoise; haliotis shells; and black stone. Besides being shrewd traders, the Navajo are also poets, and their legends and ceremonies are in poetic and symbolic language.   [Cp. *Navajo*]

NAVAJO FIRE DANCE (Amerindian)
Formed in a circle, some twelve to twenty men, naked save for a thick coat of white clay, dance in a long striding step, with increasing tempo, nearer and nearer to the central fire. They carry in each hand small bunches of coloured feathers; then hold torches ignited in the fire. As each man dances, he strikes the back of the man in front with the lighted torch. This *Fire Dance*, performed in the open air, at night, is the climax of the tribal *Night Chants* ceremony, which may fill ten or twelve days, between new and full moon. [See *Navajo*]

NAZUN (Srinagar in Kashmir, India)
A hybrid Hindu-Moslem festival dance, performed solely by men, who sing love poems as if uttered by a girl. Young boys dress as girls; the words are in Urdu; or in Persian, derived from the great poets; and are sung as *ghazals*. That is, they resemble the carol; the dance (as now) is subordinate to the chanting. The *Nazun* dance has *nautch*** affiliations; being performed mostly at parties, and belongs to no special festival or religious occasion.

NDOLA (S. Africa)
Is the general Initiation Ceremony among Bantu tribes of Rhodesia and neighbouring territory; and signifies the "state of adolescence"—the period of the girl's life betwen puberty and marriage; and is thus broadly equivalent to the European notion of the debutante and her "coming-out" (*kusola*) as an accepted member of her society. More than in Europe, the Bantu girl must become proficient in feminine traditions, exemplified in "good behaviour" (*sisikanya*), and consummated in ability to perform the accepted dances—the *kutendekela*, and the *kunyun'ula* in particular—which she must display before the critical eyes of older women. This public ceremonial follows upon three days almost unbroken dancing and singing of the *kusola* proper, which occupy the period required for guests, relatives, and friends to assemble, with the customary presents. This preliminary period to the grand final day, has its private dance, inside the

grandmother's hut; here perform the *nyapunga* (midwife in control of teaching) with the *achembles* (one or more "passed" girls, who act as instructors in "home management") in which dance the novice joins. The dances to the *Mazya*** drum fill these three days; and the girl changes from her earlier *mitungu* dance (drummed to calabash instrument melodies of simple character) to the *kusola* dance. This dance is performed, not in a ring or a row, but in a half-circle, with the *mazya* drummers at its central focus. Both sexes now take part; the novice does not appear; her teachers are occupied in receiving gifts, as a side issue to their own hut dance. The final dance of display is performed in a more elaborate setting—the *vilenga*—meaning broadly the "stage propertues". They are small mounds of differently coloured soil, forming the dance centre. These mounds have names : one is *nsato* (Python); another is *nzovu* (Elephant); and the next *ngwena* (Crocodile). A stick with branches, bearing lumps of earth (*ntowe*) is also in the *vilenga*. There is a *chiselo* (small basket) for gifts to the girl.

'NDREZZATA (Italy)
A sword and stick dance belonging to Ischia. Although all the dancers (numbering sixteen to twenty) are men, half of them are called "women", and the leader is the "Corporal". In two concentric circles, revolving in opposite directions, the dancers move round with a running step, each holding in the left hand a wooden sword, in the right a short, heavy stick. With a leap, dancers change from one circle to the other, hitting swords and sticks together with rhythmic precision, turning and striking again. Flute and drum, and humming by the performers, accompany the dance. Wearing white knee-breeches and stockings, rope-soled sandals, doublet and sash, the "women" have a blue doublet with red sash; while the men wear scarlet doublet and blue sash. Once performed on Easter Monday or "John's Day", the *'Ndrezzata* now has no fixed date. It retains a ritual element in the making of a "lock" of swords upon which the Corporal is hoisted, from which position he harangues spectators at the start of the dance. Afterwards he encourages the dancers from outside the circles.
[See *Makila Tchuri* (Basque); *Cardadora* (Spain); *Baguettes* (Brittany); *English Sword Dance*]

NEB-SENNEN (Ancient Egyptian)
"Lord of Orbit" (*Ora-beit*, the House of Ra, also known as the *Shen*). Described as "one of the proudest titles of the Pharoah, proclaiming at once their universality and their dominion, from it, the Initiate in Egyptian Ritual obtained his illumin-

ation in celestial things".[1] This Orbit is the origin of the cartouche or the "sacred ring", which supplies the symbolic line surrounding all the royal names in Egypt; it continues in coinage. The Orbit is highly important, since its ovoid form dictated the principal "line of ritual" that was daily enacted within the temples; and, on great festival dates, in the open courtyards. On this spherical path was performed the solemn ritual dance : the passage of Ra, the Sun God; the moving of Thoth, the Moon God; and the still more secret rhythm of the stars. From Thoth, the "Lord of Measures" as the "God in the Hour — secret astronomical rites, danced out — (later followed by the Christian *Book of Hours*) the Egyptians went to the *Book of Cosmic Time* in rhythmic measure. The midsummer Solstice was for them the "Opening of the Year". From the Red Crown and the White Crown of Egypt came the Red Rose (Al-Ankh-Istria) and the White Rose of England, and their ceremonies — Hathor became Ar Thor. Zodiac=Tabla Ronda.

[1] *The Book of the Master*. W. Marsham Adams. 1898

[See also *The Gods of the Egyptians*. E. A. W. Budge]

NEGRITOS, LOS (Mexico)
"The Negroes". Groups of dancers found along the coasts to which Spaniards brought Negro slaves. They perform a dance-mime which retains pre-Conquest elements in the invocation of the Four Winds and inclusion of the serpent. It also contains a "Man-Woman" and a mock death and revival, as in the English *Morris Dance.** Dances and costumes vary according to locality. In Papantla, Vera Cruz, *Negritos* wear black velvet trousers; short jackets over white, embroidered shirts, and wide-brimmed beribboned hats. Ten men represent field workers and a foreman; two clowns in ragged clothes have their faces painted with black lines, dots and little snakes; a man in woman's clothes and wearing a rose-coloured mask is the Maringuilla (See *Malinche;** Los Viejitos**). He carries a whip in one hand and in the other a gourd vessel containing a small, live snake tied with kerchiefs. Maringuilla is part of all *Negrito* dances of this region. In some groups the snake symbolises the treachery of woman (personified by Malinche, the Indian girl who helped Cortes conquer Mexico), which it is the purpose of the dance to kill; but in Papantla it merely represents actual danger to workers in the forests. The vigorous dances are accompanied by violins, a big guitar, sometimes a harp. Dancers move in single file one behind the other, or form a circle round the "woman". During a pause, the foreman chants; dancers repeat the verses, and the dance is then renewed. Maringuilla lets out the snake's head, one of the workers pretends to be bitten, falls to the ground, is taken into the centre of the circle where, after making his will, he is cured by a "doctor-priest", who invokes the Four Winds to aid him. The clowns dance about, as they please, among spectators. Finally the snake escapes and is killed by all the dancers, to a general acceleration of dance-rhythm. Some *Negrito* groups conclude with a dance weaving ribbons round a pole. (Cp. *Listones, Danza de los**). At Papantla a single *Negrito* dancer accompanies the four *voladores** in their Flying Pole Dance.

[See *Tocotines; English Sword Dance; Aztec Dance*]

NEGRO DANCING IN USA
When the first slaves entered America in the seventeenth century, they brought their own songs and dances. In New Amsterdam (later New York), Christmas and Pentecost became holidays (known as "Negroes' Days"), with dancing in the streets, to music of three-stringed fiddles, and drums made from eel-pots covered with sheepskins. Dutch farmers and their families travelled to the City to join in the festivities, dancing with the Africans. Later, City Negroes began to gather at Catherine Market (now Chatham Square) to dance and sing; and here first developed this type of Negro entertainment in New York. The Market eventually became famous as a meeting-place for dancers, jockeys and boxers. When New Amsterdam became New York, the English discouraged "fraternisation", so that mingled dancing between whites and blacks no longer occurred, and the Africans developed their characteristic dance style. In their "off" time, country slaves from Brooklyn, Long Island and New Jersey, competed with their city companions. To the accompaniment of chants and drums, they danced on an improvised floor of wooden planks called "shingles", held down at the corners by four men. The City Negroes were more expert than the country slaves, but rivalry produced high standards and accomplished dancers. Reputations were made and clubs formed, until legislation by nervous Europeans prevented Negroes from congregating at night. This may have forestalled any attempted rising, but it did not prevent the Negroes from dancing; and after the abolition of slavery they began to "break into" the American Theatre. From the *Blackbirds* musical show in the 1920's, Negro entertainments have appeared regularly on Broadway, establishing the loose-limbed tap dancing now inseparable from films and variety performances. In recent years, a more ethnic approach to West Indian and African dancing in the theatre, has been developed in New York by Katherine Dunham and Pearl Primus, both of whose Com-

panies have toured Europe as well as America. [See *Cakewalk; Calinda; Set de Flo*]

NEMBUTSI ODORI (Japan)
This term is a Nipponese version of the Buddhist phrase: "Name (of) Buddha", added to *Odori* (dance); and indicates a shrine ritual (prayer to the Buddha) performed at first by one dancing girl, who did it daily. The traditional departure from this form derives from O-Kuni, a dancing girl who, in 1586, said she came from the Shrine of Izumo. Her performance at Kyoto was marked by her choice of "river bed" to display her dance; possibly because the river centre was free of police supervision. O-Kuni added to the elementary ritual of the Shrine; giving *shite* (leading character of *Noh*) excerpts. Her ability attracted other actors; and writers; so that gradually her "theatre" developed from the "Calling Prayer" to the broader character of *Kabuki.** The end of her "river bed show" (*Kawara moni*) resembled the West European Masque; in that actors and chief spectators joined in a general dance: *so-odori*.

NESTINARI FIRE DANCE (At Vulgari, South-eastern Bulgaria, near the frontiers of Turkey)
These people called themselves *Iconobori*: meaning, not image-bearing, but image-revering people. *Ikonophoroi* is Image-bearing. Villages within a twelve-mile circle of Vulgari, on a date they say is the Feast of Constantine and Helena, build great fires and two girl dancers move through them, carrying ikons dedicated to these two persons. This cult dates certainly from the days of Leo Isaurian; holding its faith against the *ikonoklastes* (image-breakers), who sought to impose ceremonial changes. The name Nestinari suggests both the early Nestorians (who went into China) and the far older Nusareni (who came from India into Syria, and founded the Nazareni). Fire-walking occurs to this day in India. A service begins in a small chapel; the melody follows *ratchenitza** rhythms. Then there follows a blessing of dancers and water at the well-head; this is for asperging; and the dance through the street now is a *horo** snake form. The fire is lighted at six, at dusk. The pile of wood is five feet high, twenty feet along each side. Another *horo* follows, round the rising flames; and two men ikon-carriers appear with the *papa* (priest). The ikon-bearers walk round to the huge pile of glowing cinders; *ratchenitza* melodies start again. The two women are again blessed, now dancing, now still. They go into a trance, then dance three times across and three times round the fire, leaving no blister on their feet; not a touch of fire on their black dresses. It is recorded that on one occasion some Roman priests brought a boy to show how they could also command fire. The boy was horribly burned. The women's feet were examined within a minute of leaving the fire. The Nestinari ritual dance of fire had left them unharmed. The rest of the villagers formed six circles; and now danced round the glowing fire, three times counter-clockwise and one clockwise circuit, then returned to their favourite *ratchenitza*. It seems tolerably certain that garbled versions of this Nestinari Fire Dance (or others similar) provided the propagandists with some material for fiction about Witch Dances in Western Europe.

NETATELIZTLI (Aztec, Mexico)
Festival dance, performed before the Palace of Montezuma by Aztec nobles. Opening with a long chant of praise and genealogy of the Monte Zuma two long lines of dancers entered, headed by two skilled professionals. They began slowly; dancers in the lines copying the movements of their leaders; then the pace quickened. Drums, with soft-toned flutes, provided music. Occupying all day, there were breaks for rest. Finally, there were swifter songs, with chants and buffoonery; with clowning done by other characters who joined at the tail end. This dance existed down to the time of Cortez' invasion and destruction.

NEW GUINEA, Dancing in
In Wahgi Valley, 5,000 feet up in the Kubor Mountains, annual celebrations may last for weeks, while villages hold three-day festivals from time to time. In these men dance each day from dawn to dusk, followed in the evening by the sitting dance *Kanana,** for young men and girls. For the large festival, families may travel five or six days to the meeting-place, and villages compete against each other with dances. The main object is to display gorgeous Bird of Paradise head-dresses, since a man's importance is judged by his plumes. After lengthy preparations in the forest, the men emerge in lines of four, stamping and yelling to announce their arrival. While chiefs intone a long, restless chant, dancers pound the earth with heavy steps varied by movements imitating the "display dance" of the male Bird of Paradise.* Drum rhythms mark the beat, from a small, horizontal drum, one end closed with python-skin, slung in front of each dancer. To frighten away evil spirits, a clown provides comic relief, capering among the dancers. Covered with yellow mud and dead grass, he wields a stone axe, with which he charges spectators, pretending to attack them. Dancing continues monotonously for hours, unless it rains, when the men run for shelter to preserve their plumes, which are carefully kept in pandanus-leaf cases. Each man wears an ankle-length apron of casuarina-fibre in

front, and at the back a "bustle" of twigs and leaves. Faces, coated with pig-grease, are painted yellow and red, while slivers of pearl-shell through the nose septum curve up and down, like tusks. Collars of pearl-shell adorn the neck, while some wear long chains of palm-nuts, which click as they dance. The head-dress towers from a cap of cowrie-shells or fur. Feathers of eagles, parrots, owls, cockatoos and cassowaries are used, but the Para-dise Bird provides the most spectacular. Flame-coloured plumes from four birds of the "Greater" species may spread in a wide fan, while the black "cape"-feathers and turquoise breast-shield of the "Superb" lie flat below. Or skin and plumes of a complete bird may be worn upright, beak-down on the dancer's head, plumes soaring up and back. But only chiefs may wear the pale blue curving quills of the "Saxony", forming a circular sweep from septum to forehead, and framing the face. Some chiefs also wear two quills horizontally through the nose.
[See *Gol Kerma* and cp. *Malekula*, Dances of, *Maki-ru* and *Hevehe*; *Gabé*]

NEW GUINEA—DANCING "PARKS"
In some parts of the Wahgi Valley, the natives, who are good gardeners, make well-kept dancing-grounds for their "sing-sings", or big dance gather-ings. Usually rectangular, the "park" is a smooth lawn, with wooden stakes spaced down the centre for the tethering of pigs to be sacrificed; or a row of ornamental shrubs. Tall casuarina trees are planted in straight rows on the sides, and paths leading to the dancing-ground are bordered with bamboos, flowers, and ornamental shrubs. Mick Leahy (who discovered the Wahgi Valley in 1933), has described the best ceremonial ground he saw. About 150 yards long and 30 yards wide, beneath the casuarina trees on one side was a shady path. A bed of shrubs and flowers separated it from the lawn, while at the other side groups of shrubs and foliage plants were evenly spaced between sym-metrical clumps of bright green bamboo. At one end stood the round, thatched ceremonial house, with two clumps of bamboo at the entrance.
[Cp. *Malekula—Dancing Grounds*]

NEW YEAR FESTIVAL (Ancient Iran)
The Greek writer Athenaeus (*bk. x. 45*) cites Duris and Ctesias on the New Year ritual of Iran. On the First Day only the king was active; he was the only performer of the ritual dance, the sole applicant at the sacrificial bowl; no other of the priestly retinue was included until the second day of this Festival of Mithras. Besides this New Year Festival (when initiates were recorded) they kept also the Easter Feast (when initiates were tested and accepted).

They performed in *Garoue-manem* (House of Songs), the dwelling of Ahura Mazda.

NEYMARTIN (Upper Amazon River, Western Bra-zil)
Is a tribal war dance of the Jivaro Indians, per-formed when two or more groups wish to unite for some foray. The rite begins with a chant by the visiting group: *"Neymartasin Winaie!"*—"We come to dance *Neymartin*", or "You are called to the fight!", as the visitors raise their spears, hopping from one foot to the other. Each group speaks alternately, still dancing. *"Amue okamue?*—"Do you seek us?" *"Nanki sorusta!"*—"Give me your spear!" *"Nanki susaie"*—"I give you my spear". This assent is given, spears are waved; suddenly chanting stops, everyone has a drink of *yamanche* and the war-pact is sealed.

NIBHATKIN (Burma)
A play: literally, "moment of joy", in forms similar to European miracle plays; and popular during the same period. They ended about 1750, having developed from Buddhist processionals used for *Wezak** (Full Moon Festival), and other cele-brations. The *lu-byet* (clown) as attendant on the princely hero, was the favourite figure. Jesting with the princess's maid, these two dancers satirised audience and other players. From 1717, Siamese influence became stronger (after conquest), so that impacts on *Nibhatkin* resulted in a change like that in Japan, when the *Noh* plays merged with other forms. Burmese dance-drama became, in later 18th century, as important as cricket or football; but later lapsed into *Pwe.** Ancient festivals continue, mostly away from the few big towns.
[See *Burmese Dance*]

NIGERIAN SOCIAL DANCES (Africa)
When a dance is given, drummers, singers and Master of Ceremonies are engaged by the man organizing it, who pays them a few shillings and provides them with refreshments and cigarettes. During a dance lasting several hours they earn more money from the dancers. To make up sets for dancing, as in the *Ashiko,** the Master of Cere-monies chooses a girl from among the guests, by placing a handkerchief on her head or lap. If she does not wish to dance, she returns the kerchief with some money; if she has no money she must dance, the penalty being inclusion of her name in an uncomplimentary manner in the accompanying songs. Other people enter the ring, dance a little, and give money to the musicians. Dances are mainly accompanied by singing and drumming, but the Ilorin people in the north use an instrument like a very small violin, of which the strings are

plucked. Most important are the "talking drums", which, beaten in the special drum language, often instruct the comprehending dancer in the form of his dance, as in the *Kiriboto** and *Sakara.**
[See *Saki Acrobatic Dancers*]

NIKOLAI (Greece)
The "leader" of ritual in the Youth Initiations, of the primitive Greek church groups. The term derives from *Innokanoi* — the prefix dropped from *Innokoloi* (the group) to *Nikolai* (the youth). The main ritual was formed as a simplified copy of the adult ritual: as this was the social *kirke* form into which they were then being inducted. The term continued as *innokenta* — as in Iberia it was *inphanta* — "he who appeared", or *infanta*, the "new born". Allied terms are in *dokent* or *docent* (decent, is the modern term). From the rite grew the legend of "Bishop Nikolai of Mira" — this "real history" was, in fact, the office, not the person; the youthful leader as *Episkopus*, the financial overseer. Allied is the term for the girls: *Katha*, and their *rind* (round), the *Rouena*, which together make Katherina (or Catriona) and similar names. The Irish masculine term is *cathal* — level with Eastern *Kathala* (*Kat-hala*) — story-teller, reciter of the sacred *parabolos*. These two rituals (initiation for boys, and another for girls), constituted the earliest "ritual of reception" into the *kirke* or circle, at a time when adults only were normally admitted.

NINE DANCERS
Occur as a specified ritual or magical number by traditional terms. There were Nine Muses in Hellas (though three, like the Fates or *Moirae*, were the original set). Nine virgins danced as the *Gallicae-nae*, or temple priestesses of the Gaulish oracles; while in adjacent Armorica, there were nine *khorrigans* as dancers. Nine *devas* appear often in Hindu myth. In *Macbeth*, the poet says, the Weird Three Sisters sang as they danced around their cauldron of magical herbs: "Thrice to thine and thrice to mine, and thrice again to make up nine", and then declared "the charm wound up". As Roman numerals were devised, at their basis, to run to nine before the *decem* or X, so the augurs danced in and over their floor diagram. Lawyers retain to this day a similar superstition of "nines", when they impose the peculiar figure of "ninety-and-nine years" as the period of a lease; while they stress "nine points of the law" as the legal obstacles between an appellant and justice — sometimes called also Dance of Inns of Court (or Law Court Dance). From this legal cauldron the police seem to have got their 999 symbol, while doctors demand that we "Breathe deep and say ninety-nine".

NINE MEN MORRIS (England)
The game Nine Men's Morris (or Nine Mena Merils) was played on a turf cut square, containing more squares. Nine stones or men were used by two players, inwards from the angles, moving in alternation. The aim was to get three stones in one straight line (removing opposing pieces) and finally one player lost all his men. There is a simpler form called *Noughts and Crosses*, that is played by schoolchildren; there was a larger scaled form, using live boys who moved at command. This was (French) *mortaise*; (Spanish) *mortaja;* and (Arabic) *murtazz*, meaning "fixed by mark," i.e. a dance of destiny. Probably it was associated with the large turf-cut Maze. *Meril* (or *me'relle* or *marella*) is "hop-scotch" also known as "Fivepenny" (children's game). [Cp. *Merry Andrew; Merry Dancers*]

NINE NIGHT SONG (Haiti)
The Ritual of the Death Wake including chants and dancing. Groups of Negro dancers encircle the tombs. Often the "shuckers" do a "muscle dance" of African type. Often the rite passes (like the trance dancing of Bali) into a ceremony of possession, or what in Europe is called a spiritualist seance. The chief woman dancer-singer is named "La Gouvernesse". Poltergeist phenomena become evident, proving the presence of condensed invisible powers able to move objects. [See *Dinky*]

NINYA (Central Australia)
Mythical Ice Man who, according to the Aborigines, lived in ancient "dream-times". Legend tells that two of them made their camp where Mount Connor now stands. When they struck camp and moved on, the Mount rose from the ground. Flat-topped and 800 feet high, it rises straight out of the surrounding sandy plain. It is believed that the Ninya still dwell in icy caverns beneath a salt lake inside the Mount. In hot, dry weather, aboriginal women dance and sing to persuade the Ice Men to emerge and cool the air, while in winter men chant to drive the Ninya (who remain invisible) back to their caves.

NIPPON Festivals (Japan)
Other than local celebrations; or those connected with guilds, families etc., there were traditional rites, all showing some form of dance. The mythical ruler Jimmu Tenno had (a) his birth date, (b) an accession or initiation date, and (c) a death date. These came: Winter solstice, Birth (December 24th); February 12th, Initiation; and April 3rd, Death. As the rites are attributed to 600 BC the actual year dates are uncertain; they appear to relate to a traditional deity. Harvest has two Festivals, October 17th, to the deities of Ise (*Shinjo-*

sai, also called *Kan-name Matsuri*) and the second, on November 23rd (*Shinjo-sai*, or *Nil-name Matsuri*). Owing to the shifts of precession, these dates are only approximate. The New Year holiday is called Shogwatsu, for January 1st.

NIRAJANA (Sanskrit)
Hindu ritual term, indicating a rhythmic dance in which there is "waving of lights", which for this ceremony form "dazzling bright crowns" of light, that illuminate the dancers.

NIZZARDA (Italy, France)
"Dance of Nice". Popular from 14th century, alternating in its precise form by sequences of Italian or French influence; known also as *La Niceois*. This cheerful dance resembled *La Volta** — a similar version is treated by Arbeau in his book; while Caesar Negri's version shows the main Italian form of *La Nizzarda*, which existed within the brief category of "court dances" as a dance for couples.

NOEL (France)
Was broadly equivalent to the English *Carol;** though usually it was limited more closely to the New Year Feast, from which the ancient French term derives: as *nouelle*, the new or novel period. Taken over by the clergy, the dance songs were attached, instead, to their newly invented Christmas celebrations (round 4th - 5th centuries), though many vestiges of the older forms long remained in Spain and Provence. Lope de Vegas, marking the end of the thousand-year tradition that was at its apex in Rome with Pilates (Pylades) and Beth Ilius (Bathyllus), affirms the transference from the Roman year of Mars to the Latin year beginning with Janus; so that the new year was now made to mark a person instead of a solar period. This fact remains vaguely in Lope de Vegas' *Nacimento de Cristo*, where the last act concludes with the appearance of three kings (or *magi*), but preceded by merry dances of Gypsies and Negroes (the white men of New Year versus the black men of the departing year). These three Kings of Colen (or Colyen, or Köln etc.) symbolise three qualities of man; while the gypsies occur frequently in both Provençal and Spanish *chansons de noelles*. Some are sung especially for Epiphany (Twelfth Night), where the gypsy girls sing their *cante hondo* at the "Gate of Beth Lehem" (The House of Bread), as they welcome the Three Kings, with dances and refreshments. Here the *Noël* comes even closer to the earlier *carolle*, which was especially marked as the Song of the King's Son — the *kralje*.

NOH Dance-Drama (Japan)
The typical opera ballet of Japan, which includes dance, mime, singing or chant; and music, rendered in rhythmic mode. Formulated about middle of 15th century AD, from the *Saragaku*; which had earlier united parts of *Dengaku, Kowaka, Kusemai, Ko-uta, Bugaku;* and the Buddhist ritual form of *Ennen-Mai*. The *Saragaku* was prominent during the Zen-influenced Ashikaga period; performed at Shinto shrines. At the ancient Ise shrine, three different schools prevailed; at Nara, four groups arose which became bases for present-day schools called Komparu, Kwanze, Hosho, and Kongo. The material of *Noh* dance derived from Shinto forms and Buddhist teachings, particularly in the Zen sect. Chinese influences underlie these earlier forms; and behind them are powerful Indian traditions in both Brahmin and Buddhist modes. *Noh* became a court study and accomplishment (much as *ballet du cour* did in France during much the same period). Scripts of *Noh* plays are written in alternating prose and verse, both rhythmic; they are untranslateable, because meaning depends on tone, scale, and tempo. Rhythmic movement has similar variation; a pose is held for some moments, while others are swift gestures. They range from solemn and serious themes (*shinji*, a divine play), to *ki* plays (demon topics), or from romantic themes (*katsuramono*) to farce (*kyogen*). Allowing for oriental differences, they may be compared to the Mystery Plays and Miracle Plays of mediaeval Europe, though less proselytising and more artistic forms. They are performed (as were the Miracle Plays in earlier modes), solely by men and boys. The traditional *Noh* stage (a village form) is an eighteen-feet square (of cypress wood), with audience on three sides; connected with actors' room by a gallery nine feet wide and eight long (here ends much action). There is one main character (*shete*), who bears the full action: his two supporters (*tsure*) and secondary parts (*waki* or *hysaheta*) and occasional comics (*kyogen*). The orchestra is *hayashi* (four instruments), and these players also sing. Drum is basis of the rhythm. A chorus may sit on the right. There is no scenery, but costumes are magnificent and elaborate in court Mediaeval style. Dance comes at most important periods of the *Noh*.

NOH DANCE (Japan)
Modern program, as given in Tokyo etc. Performance usually offers six or seven different plays, of as many traditional styles. They begin either at 10.0 a.m. or at 1.0 p.m.; less often at four in the afternoon. The full program covers seven to eleven hours (as in the earlier history of the *Noh* drama). They are not given in ordinary theatres, but in an enclosure (usually in temple grounds, not always), with a small *dai* or stage 18 feet square, surrounded

by the audience on three sides. The program contains (1) *Shinji*; a Shinto or "divine play", showing Shinto gods; (2) *Dan* or *Dengaku* or *Shuara-mono*; a "warrior play" including evocation of some dead warrior who appears in the second half; (3) *Katsura-mono*, or *Jo-Noh*; a romantic mime drama, the principal character is a woman and the topic is love. This play is the longest in most programs. (4) *Kyo-Noh*; a tale in which the chief character is unbalanced, often a woman grieving for a lost daughter; a prodigal son type of play. (5) *Ki-Noh*; in which style some demon (not a devil, they have no Satan in Japan) is prominent. (6) *Shugen-Noh* depicts a victory celebration; a military achievement, etc. Sometimes this appears as No. 1 in a program; usually it ends the day. Occasionally, in place of the *Kyo-Noh*, there is presented a *Genzai-mono*, a style nearer to what is accepted in the West as realistic, though *Noh* plays are never realism, but are always deeply symbolical. The Demon play provides a comic element of relief. Festival dates (*matsuri*) at famous shrines provide for the *Noh* plays as the latest mode of *Kagura* or religious dance; they are here like the Masque. At other times of celebration, a program will be given unattached to a known festival. There are nine kinds of dancing in a *Noh* drama; and dance is important, for it appears at the climax; every play (but one) has a dance or rhythmic mime passage. The song-forms, which go with dance, are : *shidai*; *nissei*; *suta*; *sashi*; *kuri-kuse*; *rongi*; *waka*; and *kiri*. There is no scenery; costumes are gorgeous, colourful and spectacular. Players are of four ranks: *sheta* (chief); *waki* (second); *hayasheta* (supports); and *kyogen* (comics).

NONGKREM (India, Assam, in the Khasi Hills)
A tribal folk dance, performed at the great festivals, belonging essentially to the ancient goat sacrifices formerly offered by the Siem of Nongkrem (Priestess, attendant on the deity). Ashes from the burned goat are solemnly placed on the chief sepulchre of the tribe, with a slow dancing circle following the first procession. The Siem leads the twenty-two male dancers, armed with swords and circular shields; and, having performed the ceremonial of fire and water, the Siem returns with the men to her house. In her large courtyard, more ceremonial dances are performed by a party of boys and girls. Finally, the men dance alone, concluding with a mock combat or sword-dance.

NORNS (Scandinavian mythology)
Known in the epic *Voluspa*; which tells of the sacred World Tree Iggdrasil. They are like the (Greek *Moirae*) guardians of human life; with Urd (the Past), Verdaudi or Verdanoi (the Present), and Skuld (the Future). Poets foretelling the Future are the Skalds; hence also, the toast "Skoll!" The Norns live by the Urdar Fountain; in this lake live two white swans. Some scholars say the two Swans are symbols of Sun and Moon; others believe they signify the human dual-soul. These Norns have dances—sometimes single but more often the Three; for each man has a personal Norn. Their dance form creates the Runic circle, with its characters of destiny. In Greece Apollo as Sun God (or Diana as Moon Goddess) danced with the Muses —three or nine.

NORTHERN LIGHTS (Aurore Borealis)
The Dance of Electrical Lights in the atmosphere over the polar regions, said to range to some 600 miles in height; and occasionally visible in the most northern isles of Scotland, Norway or Finland. The Greenlanders call them "The Dancers". Legends with "dancing princesses" have been developed on this natural basis.
[See *Merry Dancers; Chèvres Dansantes; Pretty Dancers*]

NOTARIQON (Hebrew, from Latin *notarius*)
Letters - words - numbers regarded as mnemonic condensations of sentences, recipes, formulae etc. Dance ritual is mentioned. Speaking on the *Arcanum of Tetragrammaton*, one of numerous four letter (and four-number) symbols Rabbi Schimeon said further "He who walketh, going up and down (from one house to another) revealeth the secret; but the faithful in spirit conceal the Word. (16)
"He who walketh up and down : this saying merits question, because it is said going up and down . . wherefore then 'walking'? (17)". ". . certainly we are (the symbols of) the pillars of the Universe". (*Kabbalah Unveiled*. Mathers). The dancer must return along the alternate row—the reading eye jumps. *Notariqon* is the system of making these notes of the condensations.

NOTATION—1
From Latin *notarius*, a writer. The term is specially applied to (a) the written record of dance form on paper; and (b) the process or scheme of "dance-writing". Traditional dance required no written scheme (popular songs or chants were also remembered, in parallel). thus no recognised mode of notation appeared, until the requirements of the *Academie de la Danse* trained dancer-teachers who needed records (a) to comply with the "correct form", and (b) for ceremonial and stage production usage. Various schemes have been proposed for recording dances, beginning with Arbean's *Orchesographie* (1588) and continued by Feuillet and

others, down to Stepanov, who compiled (in 1892) the system used for record in Petersburg, and by Nicholas Sergueéff for his revivals of classical Russian Ballets in Western Europe from 1921. [See *Feuillet*; *Stepanov*]

NOTATION—2
English method. In 1954-55 another system was published in London, devised by Rudolf and Joan Benesh, which has been adopted by some dance groups. They claim an "innovation" in the use of musical staves; and the abolition of a ground plan. The method is technical; related only to body movements; and not (as with the *hasta-mudra* systems) to any emotional or symbolical usage. Like earlier systems, this one moves on the single dancer, in academic ballet style. Records of a collection of separated dance-routines does not necessarily supply a record of a ballet, in which relations of dancer to dancer (in a real ballet, not merely technical exercise) gives the foundation of this theatre-group mode of dance art. Any complete Notation for Ballet must supply (a) space and space movement, in three dimensions; (b) music and musical rhythms, in time dimensions; (3) movements of any single dancer; with movements of these dancers in temporal and spatial relation to all other dancers on the stage. An orchestra, in contrast, uses time; while space is but lightly indicated, as in positions of instruments for tone in relation to merging, particularly for microphone transference.

NOTATION in Pattern for Choreography
Pattern is part only of choreography; even so, pattern is required both in plan and in picture—a dual composition, setting forth a third aspect disciplined by musical rhythm, which thus develops into full choreography. Notation has had many modes. There is the single track of a single dancer —the famous "fly-track" of Rameau and his colleagues. This developed once more to the stage plans of Stepanov, the nearest factual approach for the scriptual notation of academic ballet. Ancient notation was evolved otherwise: it grew on sand drawings and in marks or badges, and prospered. Two systems flourished, one semi-pictorial, and the other as numerals. These were the oldest notations of identification, direction and movement. Ritual choreography failed to become transferred to parchment or papyrus; but remained on the ground, on the pavement, for its pattern was useful only in its full original scale. In smaller size, these patterns could be used only for tuition, for memory, for record. Dance thus lost its immediate modes of notation, when the rituals changed and floors became worn out; while letters and numerals

flourished in the banker's commercial accounts. He had survived the change in trade, from identification of *things* to identification of *money* ownership, by symbol in letter, word, and numeral.

NUDE DANCING
With varying time and place, public movement, ritual, and dancing in a nude state, is done in accord with current fashion; and not considered to be in any way disreputable, much less a crime. In Britain, it would be considered unwise, even flighty, to appear in Piccadilly Circus (in the centre of London) in a slight "bathing costume", but at almost any seaside resort, or on the Thames in summer, the garb passes with little notice. This fashion compares with that in vogue a century back; when to reveal an ankle was indiscreet, and a visible knee was inviting ex-communication— except on the stage. A French writer, M. de Sade, recalls some historical facts: —
"Lycurgus and Solon, firmly convinced that results of immodesty maintains citizens in that immoral state essential to the laws of a republican constitution, obliged young girls to appear naked at the theatre. Rome copied this, and there was dancing in the nude at the Games of Flora. (See *Floralia*.*) Part of the pagan Mysteries were celebrated in this manner; nudity even possessed virtue among several peoples".[1]
[1] *Writings of de Sade*. (Trans. L. de S. Yves.) London, 1953.

NUMBA (Kenya, E. Africa)
A jumping dance performed by Masai warriors. Very tall and with long legs, the men jump in turn, vertically from the ground. The dance is an athletic contest to see who jumps highest, spectators chanting cadences to keep the rhythm. No musical instrument is used. A length of calico wrapped round the body leaves arms bare; while feet are shod with a sole of cowhide with thong and ankle-strap. Long hair, braided into a stiff, pointed pigtail, extends from the back of the head. Living on a reserve of 38,000 square miles, the Masai are a proud race, more Semitic than African in appearance, with rigorous tribal discipline. Lions are hunted when they worry cattle. The lion's mane, awarded for special bravery, is made into a tall, busby-like hat called *olowaru*, to be worn as a mark of honour at the great Masai initiation festival, *Unoto*.* They never dance to drums, and have only one musical instrument, the *kudu* horn.

NUMBER (English usage)
In a certain Theatre usage, is connected with music, and thus music-halls, by a simple technical practice. Composers and copyists of long compositions

divided their work by an assessment of portions (rather than parts) much as a printer divides his work, technically, in relation to the "sheets" a book may require, in multiples of eight or sixteen or thirty-two pages. These portions received a regular sequence of numbers, as identifying symbols (as do "sheets"), and so the position of any "Number" could be immediately recognised. In music-hall practice, a number of different persons as "turns" were assembled; and, placed in working order by the manager, again were numbered, and so repeated on the program, if any. Each singer's accompaniment of music thus received one or more "numbers", and then "Mister Joe Johnson's Numbers" were given in a single batch to the hard-working conductor, for trial at rehearsal on Monday morning. This simple theatre arithmetic then gave a working guide to sequence and position. Thence the practice has travelled back into the superior concert world of symphony and sonata; still attired in numbers; and in relation to sheets of "band parts". The experienced dancer relates her own work to the managerial number sequence; or to parts of a long composition.

NUPE (Nigeria)
A masque of Dancing Giants. These disguised figures are made about fifteen feet high, of bamboo or heavy twigs etc. topped by a mask. Members of the Poro Secret Society dance in these, during daylight, in parades through the villages; at nightfall this procession ceases, and one or two of the giants will wander here and there, peering over fences "smelling out" the unknown local "witches" — meaning women they don't like, as busybodies etc.

NUPE DANCES (Nigeria, West Africa)
In and near Lagos, the Nupé people use numerous dances and dance rituals, from those of the *Gunnu* initiation; and its adult link *Ndako gboya* (a secret society), to the simplest dances such as *Sorogi* (tortoise) done for entertainment; and one called *Kutukpa* (denoting the noise made by a galloping horse), and the unique mask dance *Elo.** Trance or spiritualist dances of the *Bori** cult are also known; from the Hausa people, farther inland. Some dances, such as *Elo*, are influenced by the Yoruba people, adjacent on the southern district, who have one called *Gugu*. These tribal dances range from agricultural ceremonies of traditional type, changing very slowly; to initiation dances connected with ancestral cults, preserved in some essentials but with some meanings forgotten; and the "policing" dance-rituals which are the external or public activities of the *Ndako gboya*, through which tribal rules are enforced by elders.

NURSERY RHYME, Dance-songs
Numerous traditional dances are maintained by brief songs used as Nursery rhymes, distinct from children's games or mere experimental play. They are found in the three basic technical forms of all dance; the processional or linear form; the circle dance; and the square form, this last being the rarest. These nursery rhymes possess a certain seasonal character, as do some games, and in some strange manner they appear and fade out from the months of the year, without any adult prompting. They vary in the countries of Europe; but in general they tend to contain and to carry on rituals that have been dropped from adult usage. In them we find many strange phrases that are known as "nonsense words", which remain as evidence of age and purpose, when we penetrate to their factual origins. Thus "hey nonny nonny!" used by Shakespeare, is first an exhortation to Nunnes to dance—"hey" is to dance. In the "ring-a-ring-a-roses" (similar to the French-Basque refrain "Arin! Arin!") we have hints of a much older tradition, reflected in the phrase "Asha! Asha! we all fall down", for which we have to seek origins in ancient Iran. Although nursery rhymes are most useful as sources of "material" for overworked school teachers, it seems that it would be fatal to tradition to bring these social child memories into scholastic schemes. The school type of "nursery rhyme" should be devised within the school system; this can be used for its good effects on other "subjects" of our mercantile culture.

NUSSLER (Switzerland)
Masked dancers who perform at Schwyz during pre-Lent Carnival. Dressed as representatives of Spring in leaf-covered clothes known as *Blätzlichleid*, they carry a birch broom, with which they make sweeping movements, and wear over their shoulders a leather band to which is attached large bell. Moving about the country-side from house to house, they dance in groups called *Rotts* from dawn to dusk, the dance consisting of much leaping about. Although there is no cohesion of movement among the dancers, each man performing individually, each *Rott* remains united and progresses as a whole. Dancing is accompanied by drummers. With different costumes are the *Sylvester-Kläuse*, who dance in Canton Appenzell on New Year's Eve—Sylvester's Day. Using similar leaping movements and wearing large bells, their costume more nearly resembles that of the Austrian *Schemenlaufen** or *Perchten,** with elaborate head-dress.
[Cp. *Röllelibutzen* (Switzerland); *Narren-Treffen* (Germany); *Schemenlaufen*; *Perchten* (Austria); *Suruvakary* (Bulgaria)]

O

O (Gaelic, from Egyptian)
Appears in numerous clan names in Ireland, to signify which "circle" or "Caleann" the people are affiliated with, e.g. The O'Brien. The "O" comes into the appropriate place-names, as the centres of these particular *clans;* where they meet for the annual festivals. Some belong to the plain (riverside) etc., which more definitely equate with "O", while others belong to the mountain tops — the *Baal Tene* (equinoctial fires). (*Rinnche*=rink, and ex *Renn* (Egypt) as the *O-Mor* circle, the "Great O" of *O-Magh*.)

OBEREK, Obertas (Poland)
From *Obracác*, "to turn round". A wilder variant of the *Mazur,** it hails from the same area — Mazovia, in the central plain of Poland. A gay and spirited dance, in 3/8 time, it contains intricate steps and many figures. Couples dance side by side, the man's right arm round his partner's waist, her left hand on his shoulder. Turning from right to left, they dance in a circle, following a leader, as in all Polish group dances. Sometimes a song accompanies the dance. The girl may dance round the man or vice versa, the man performing leaping and crouching steps. From a nearly horizontal position, one hand and one foot on the ground, the other leg stretched horizontally back, he will spring into the air making a half turn; or he will jump, knocking heels together sideways in the air (*holupiec*). His partner may be whirled round, while he kneels, first on the right, then the left knee. More showy than the *Mazur,* the *Oberek* is one of the most popular dances in Poland.

OBERON (French)
Appears in *Huon de Bordeaux,* a mediaeval romance,, with his consort Titania. They are known to England through Shakespeare's play *A Midsummer Night's Dream,* for which Felix Mendelssohn composed music, including the dances; though traditional English songs have also been used. In the play, the fairies dance, as Oberon holds his court. The name varies through Western Europe: as Auberon, or the still older Alberon, indicating "the white ones", of the German Alberich, as King of the Elves. Oberon as the fay is a dwarf, less than three feet high; he was the friend of Huon in the legend.

OBI (North Africa)
A generic term for many tribal dances that are connected with séances in specific operations; and with the annual ancestor-worship rituals in general. The *Obi* are the dead; the *Obeah* is the expert who gains connection. In European studies of this nature worship, the term *Obi-ism* has been coined, to indicate "serpent-worship", where ritual also includes circle dances. There is no serpent actually "worshipped" though one may be used (as with the Druses of Lebanon) as a symbol; and as it was seen in metal on the erect staff alleged to be prohibited by the mythical Moses, as worship for the Israelites. The subject is still obscure for Europeans. A distantly parallel tradition is that of the faeries, whose chief in France was Oberon.

OCCHIU DRACULI (Rumania)
"Eye of the Devil" (*Dracu*— "dragon"; *Draculuj*— "spirit of evil"). A dance of exorcism by the power of music, said to purge the evil from a person bitten by a vampire. A special tune in 4/8 time must be played on a violin, until the rhythm compels the afflicted person to dance. Gazing deep into her eyes, the fiddler plays faster and faster, never letting her rest until she falls, exhausted, to the ground. This rapid, fiery rhythm must then be followed by a slow, sad tune to induce tears in the patient, as a sign that the evil has left her.

OCTOECHOS (Greek, from Egyptian *Ogduad*, the World Pattern)
Egyptian temple doctrine taught that Ogduad (or Oke-Duat) was the world-form, created by vital world rhythms of a pattern to be expressed in temple ritual dance. The aim was to show worshippers how their individual rhythm could be accommodated to cosmic rhythm, by music and dance. This discipline was manifested in "Eight Modes" of their liturgy, subsequently giving basis to Byzantine and then Christian worship. Mythic god-forms summarised all the dual powers (four pairs, male-female) making, dissolving. Later *Octoechos* entitled "Right Tones" has poems (hymns) of Severus of Antioch, used on eight sabbaths, each with one dominant mode of music/dance. They appeared in the dual Tetrachords of Greek music, formed in two squares. Compare Hindu diagrams (*Yantra*) and *raga* music system. Octoechos provided the basis of the Gnostic dance-hymn as in Sacred Dance of Jesus.* (Octo-oikhos= eight houses). *Oichos* Byzantine ritual became The *House* (in Latin, the *Stanza*); the place of dual dance, (in Coptic, the *Hey-kell,* sanctuary or chapel, and *Beitha,* the House (Beth-El).

ODORI (Japan)
Secular dances by Geisha girl dancers; usually accompany religious festival periods; Seasons are held in commercial theatres; and small groups can be hired at most times, in principal centres. Charges

vary according to place, number of girls, their reputation, time required. Some *Odori* dance displays are especially produced for delectation of foreign visitors, as "Geisha Dances". In TOKYO: the *Azuma-Odori*, April 1st - 20th; KYOTO: the *Inuyama-Odori* and *Miyako-Odori*, April 1st - 30th; and *Kamogawa-Odori*, May 1st - 20th; OSAKA: the *Konohana-Odori*, March 10th - 30th; *Naniwa-Odori*, April 1st - 24th, and *Ashibe-Odori* (rival company) also April 1st - 24th. These are the largest troupes of dancing girls displayed in Japan. They are trained in the various Dance Schools, and appear in companies from ten to twenty-four, or rarely thirty girls (according to size of stage), dancing in "unison style", mainly, in what is known in Europe as "Tiller Girl style". Until recent tours by European ballet, there were no "leg shows", but these now appear; just as American ballroom dance style infests the popular social dance halls. The *Odori* lacks dramatic interest; the songs are popular ditties; the costumes are charming. Scenery is often a single painted sheet, nailed over the back stage. Music is played on *koto* and *samisen;* or, is relayed from radiogram records, amplified.

OENPELLI SNAKE DANCE (North Australia)
Occurs at Oenpelli, in Arnhem Land, as part of an all-day festival, usually in Spring season, celebrating the awakening of the earth-snake or dragon. The dance is a single file or string-line dance, winding incessantly. The men bend their heads, each clasping the one in front lightly on the waist; and so dance with uniform step, making a huge snake figure. From ten to twenty men will unite in one snake: they twine in many floor patterns over the dancing-ground, to the music of *didgeridoo* (drone trumpet), and the log drum, with time beats by stick tapping. The drums are made from hollowed logs, some nine inches across, and five or six feet long, covered with skin at one end. They are painted in symbolic patterns, in brilliant colours — red and yellow, with white and black.
[See *Corroboree; Nakumdoit; Honey-Bee Dance; Tjitji-Inma*]

OGHAM OR OKEHAM (Old Saxon, Gaelic, etc.)
The traditional letter system of Britain before Greek or Latin appeared. Signs are used as symbols, set in a circular arrangement. Ogham inscriptions exist on many ancient monuments in Britain; as a language it is obsolete save for a few terms in Zincali; or single words like "Oke" or okey-dokey (meaning "all right Dux!"), but gave many place names such as Oakham, the Druidic Oak, and villages (centres) of Oke turned by the prefix into St. Oke or Stoke or St. Oke-Umber. Ogham is comparable with Norse *Futork.** There were several

schemes of Ogham—the Wheel Ogham (said to be learned by Columba of Iona) the Tree, and others. Ritual dance movements ensured that boys learned to recognise the signs. Some became capable scholars—we recall William of Okhham who wielded 'Occam's Razor. Tradition persisted and much later John Oghilboy, a dancing master interested in notation, sold maps and road books.

OGI NO SABAKI (Japan)
Name given to the many variations of fan manipulation in Japanese dancing. Used to supplement dance-mime, the fan may represent innumerable objects—a sword or mirror, the moon or a horse, a door sliding, or rikshaw wheels turning. Open, closed or half-closed, the fan is whirled and twisted, sometimes tossed into the air; sometimes a second fan in the other hand repeats the movements. In *Kabuki* plays fans may be used in the *monogatari** or mimed "description of a past event". The use of fans is not merely a decorative addition, but part of the gesture-language of the dance. Teachers of this difficult art assert that in movement the fan and hand should be one, the fan being an extension of the arm. The long sleeves of the kimono are also used symbolically.
[See *Fan Dance* (Japan); *Feather Dancing* (China)]

OGRE (France)
The Dancing Ogre, creature of later fairy tales, and villain of many *contes des enfants*, is a perversion of the Roman *augur*. His social function was to act as calendrical prophet or adviser for the villagers. This he did in a ritual dance, a compass he set up at the appropriate season (using ochre or yellow wet earth as marking). When *ides* and *kalends* were kept more or less secret, dates for planting remained uncertain. In England the watches (witches who were also denigrated) performed this agricultural function. The promise of bad weather—frequent enough—gave the augur a bad name, countered by the *haruspex* or soothsayer. The compass dance is a type of all circle dances; it was parallel with many a magical circle with its ritual of "divining" done with a rod or *litra*. So deeply did this term remain in France that it was used in state weights and measures as *litre*. Jacques the Giant Killer is the fable hero who "climbs the beann stalk" and discovers the hidden grain.

OHORODNIK (Ukraine, Russia)
Popular at weddings, performed by twelve dancers in square formation of four groups of three. Usually each group has a man between two women, but sometimes the reverse. The dance has two figures. In the first, using a running step, two opposite trios advance towards the centre; as they

retire the other two groups move inwards, so that two sides of the squares are advancing while the other two retreat. In the second figure, the girl on the right of each man hooks elbows with him and vigorously turns him round; repeated by the girl on his left. Although the name "Ohorodnik" means "gardener", there is no suggestion of miming in the dance.

OKINA (Japan)

A ritual dance symbolising long life, performed as a propitious opening ceremony, as on the completion of a new theatre-house. A full series of *Noh** plays, lasting all day, must be preceded by *Okina* dances. They represent three stages of man's life, from age to youth. First enters the principal actor, without make-up, carrying a black and gold lacquer box tied with thick purple cord, from which he removes the *Okina*—a bearded wooden mask of a very old man. Tying on the mask he dances with slow, dignified movements, carrying in one hand a fan, and chanting ancient words. Two drums and a flute accompany the dance. The second dancer, Senzai ("a thousand years") always wears an elaborate costume of blue patterned with white storks, symbol of eternity and good fortune. His dance is more lively, while the third character, Samba, performs a humorous, swift dance of youth. Wearing brocaded clothes, and a conical hat of black and silver bearing a large red dot, he carries the Buddhist *juzu*, or handbells. There are many variants of *Okina*, but the general arrangement is the same.

OLD TIME DANCING

Is a phrase used in Britain in a sentimental and commercial sense rather than with any historical reference. The "Old Time Dances" thus indicated mean the style familiar to the older generation; which they first knew in their youth; when the same dances were not "Old Time" but the "fashionable style". There are some sixty ballroom dances included under this title, of which the oldest is the *Lancers*, said to have been invented about 1730 by Joseph Hart; or alternatively by Duval of Dublin. A later mode, with the same name, was current from 1895 to 1914, with variations in different parts of Britain. The *Waltz* (or *Valse* in France) has endured since 1895 in current style; but is older in name and form. (See *Almacks**). At Almacks Rooms there also was danced a *Quadrille*,* erroneously said to be originally an English country dance, while the very name affirms its more Southern origin. Versions of *quadrille* appeared in the French salons about 1700, when it was brought to London; sometimes danced as "Hart's First Set". Another form settled down about 1895, which endured until 1910, about the same period as the

Old Time Waltz.* The *Polka** is older; it was seen on the London stage in 1830 as the *Styrien*, danced by ballerinas. The *Schottische** is a Teutonic version of an earlier Highland dance; again revised, while the *Waltz-Minuet* is a hybrid. Most of the current three-score "Old Time Dances" are no more than half-a-century old; indeed, it is claimed in one manual that ninety per cent. of the dances in this book were invented, arranged, and orchestrated by members of the British Association; there seems no reason to dispute this claim. We find the *Boston Two-Step* or *Gay Gordons*; *Maxina* (1917); *Empress One-Step* (1912); *Florentine Waltz* or *Progressive Waltz* (1922), with modes of *Barn Dance** or of *Tango** and a *Mazurka** (1906), and even a *Toledo Valse* (1920). About half of these ballroom dances are "variations on a theme", contrived with the laudable objective (from the professional teacher's point of view) of offering some new fashion or twist which the eager dance enthusiasts will pay to be taught. Subtler is the appeal to older people to "keep dancing", by the suggestion that they may like less vigorous dances instead of the versions of *fox-trot*; *tango*; *jazz* and *bepop* which are favoured by adolescents, although many a *Galop* and *Polka* need far more energy than some sedate modern ballroom dances.

OLD VIC THEATRE (London)

Popular name for the Royal Victoria Opera Theatre, Waterloo Road and New Cut, S.E. 1. In this proletarian centre, three eminent Old Victorians laboured conscientiously to produce Drama (chiefly Shakespeare) and Opera (chiefly Italian or French) at low admission prices. They were Lilian Baylis (1874 - 1938) as general manager; Ben Greet, as producer and actor in Drama; and Eugene Corri, as conductor for Opera. Ballet was included in minor opera presentations, arranged post-1918 by Lilian Anderton. There was a fairly regular drama company, liable to frequent change of principals; and a similar operatic company. Dancers were recruited from schools; there was no school of any kind at the Old Vic, either drama, opera, or ballet. Desiring to expand her operations to north of the Thames, Miss Baylis had the idea of buying up the then derelict Sadler's Wells Theatre; to rebuild as a Theatre for Drama and Opera. She collected £10,000 in funds. By 1928, the opera-ballets had been expanded; for the Christmas season, panto-ballets were devised, for Miss Baylis had now developed the idea that she could add ballet performances; and three were offered in the December 1929 - 30 season. There was no plan for British Ballet; or for a regular company or school; these slowly appeared. The new Sadler's Wells Theatre opened January 6th, 1931, appropriately enough with *Twelfth Night*; followed two weeks later by *Carmen*. The scheme envisaged by Miss Baylis required a transfer of the two companies, plus scenery and costumes, from north to south and back, since no scene-dock had been included in the new Sadler's Wells plan. A short ballet, *Job*, mounted on Ralph Vaughan Williams' *Masque for Dancing*, was arranged by the Camargo Society (which had no contact with the Old Vic), which Miss Bayliss saw at the Cambridge Theatre. The failure of the drama-plus-opera scheme induced her to try her newer scheme, for opera-plus-ballet. There was no government subsidy, except remission of Entertainment Tax; but she lived long enough to see her scheme for Opera and Ballet replace Opera-Ballet.   [See *Sadler's Wells Theatre*]

OLE (Spain)

A woman's solo dance with castanets, similar to the ancient *Romalis** gypsy dance. Of oriental origin, with movements of the body rather than of the feet, the dance is accompanied by rapid vocal acrobatics or colaturas to the syllables "ay" or "olé" (from which the dance may take its name); or by verses sung in unison by a chorus, who mark the time with hand-claps. Although identified by some with the *Polo*,* there is some doubt as to whether these two dances are the same.   [See *Romalis; Polo*]

OLE LUK-OIE (Denmark)

Hans Andersen wrote his collection of children's stories chiefly in Copenhagen. One of his "tale-tellers" was the famous *Ole Luk-Oie*. He is important because he seems to be the Danish counterpart of *La Mere Oyer* in France, on whom Perrault relies as a source. Probably the most famous of the Andersen stories of dance is *The Red Shoes*, made into a colour film; but there are other tales in which dancing appears, such as *Little Ida's Flowers*, in which all the flowers have dancing parts, with roses as king and queen; the tale shows also a wax doll, and then a chimney sweep who wants to dance. There is dancing in *The Little Sea Maid*; in *The Elf Hill* (torch dance and the *kalling* dance); in *The Fir Tree*, where is Klumpey-Dumpey; and in *The Puppet Showman*. In recent years we have seen flower dances rarely—those in *Alice in Wonderland* (done as a ballet) may be recalled; but any producer with imagination could follow the versatile Hans Andersen into modern themes, equally fanciful and suitable. *Ole Luk-Oie* does mention that he has a brother, who had another name, but who never comes more than once.

OLOVE (Papua)

General name for group dances of the Fuyughé people. Performed by a compact group of men, they mime the behaviour of birds or animals; or express a mood. (*Dance of the Areca Nut* symbolises happy tranquility). Each dance lasts from eight to ten minutes and each, with its accompanying chant, has an individual name (*Oundoulou falamame*—Cassowary Dance; *Ourouve*,* Toucan Dance). The group containing from thirty to fifty dancers in lines of six or eight abreast, follows the example of a leader, who indicates with drum-rhythm the chant about to be sung and consequently the dance belonging to it. In short, rapid zigzags, each beating his drum with the flat of the hand, the dancers proceed from end to end of the dancing-ground, with brief pauses to chant. Rhythm governs movement, chanting, drum-beat. Steps include a light hop, sideways glide, forward or backward run, while rolling and nodding movements of the head cause plumed head-dresses to describe graceful curves. The whole group moves in perfect co-ordination. *Olové* dances are performed during the *Gabé** festival, and last from nightfall until dawn. Women torch-bearers move up and down the dancing-ground beside the group of men. One of the best dances imitates movements of the Birds of Paradise,* whose brilliant plumage supplies glowing colours for head-dresses and cloaks (worn in the *Royal Dance**). Another shows the withdrawing of a snail into its shell, when dancers crouch and curl up in front of each other; or the sinuous movements of a snake, with the dancers in a long file. Sometimes the group breaks into two opposing sides, advancing and retreating. [Cp. *Naleng* compact dance of Malekula; animal dances of Australian *Corroboree*, e.g. *Oenpelli Snake Dance*]

OMAL (Greece)

A women's dance of the Pontos region, along the southern shore of the Black Sea. Although outside the boundaries of Greece, this area has been the home of Greeks for centuries, and many ancient Greek dances survive there. The *Omal* is a linked chain, each dancer holding with her right hand the left hand of the girl in front. With downcast eyes the dancers move slowly along with a "dragging" step Accompanied by singing and music of the *lyra*, the *Omal* has a liturgical quality. The costume consists of a straight, wide-striped skirt, sometimes with a check "apron" draped round the hips; a short black jacket over a blouse; and a patterned kerchief binds the hair in a snood. Ear-rings, necklaces and forehead ornaments add to the effect.

OPERA BALLET

A term continued in use to refer to a combination of dramatic singing, as opera, with interludes of dancing, as ballet. The term *opera* (a work) has changed its meaning with each century. Once it meant a ceremonial piece of work, a chanted ritual, such as an admission to a company or academy, with a meaning similar to that used by Freemasons when they speak of "working a ritual". As with musical form, once subjected to similar limitations, the opera, losing its solemn religious connotations, became entirely secular. The dance was once an integral part of the "work", but rarely of the theatrical opera; where technical voice exhibition became more prominent. Ballet then became an intrusion into the operative theme or story; not part of it; and was as such resented by the "music lovers", who attended to hear music by song and orchestra. Ignorant producers of opera, who know nothing of the constructive meaning of dance; ignorant dancers who know nothing of musical themes; and ignorant ballet producers who do not know how to integrate rhythmical movement with operatic singing, are severally and together responsible for the gradual loss of reputation associated with "opera-ballet". Comedy ballet has been far more fortunate as an acceptable development of song accompanied by dance.

OPERATIC BALLET DANCE (England)
Derives from the several theatre schools of classes maintained during the 19th century, chiefly in London, for rehearsing dancers to perform the ballet interludes sometimes offered with operatic productions. The schools concerned begin with Mrs. Conquest at her Eagle Saloon Theatre in City Road; and continue with the productions at the Empire and Alhambra Theatres, with many incursions into Covent Garden Theatre Royal. Katti Lanner came from Vienna to the Empire; after her were Malvina Cavallazi from Milan, with Lucia Cormani and Francesca Zanfretti (Naples, Venice), and Alexander Genée. Predominating influences thus were French and Italian, as subdued by the opera managers and producers. English girls commonly took foreign *noms-de-theatre*, though the famous Kate Vaughan took an English name to replace her Danish one of Candelon. No special demands were made of operatic dancers, except that they move rhythmically; many of them took jobs in the then flourishing pantomime seasons; sometimes with more new names. The Association of Operatic Dancing was formed in 1920, after which some efforts were made to upgrade and standardise teaching and performance, since no accepted standards existed. The appearance of Russian dancers, first in 1908 and then the (1910) Diaghilev company, did much to convince those interested that something remained to be done and could be done. Eventually the network of examinations

developed, with demands on teachers for accredited ability (more in performance than in teaching, for long), and very slowly, productions improved. Finally the Operatic Association itself swelled into the Royal Academy of Dancing, though demands for dancing in connection with opera are much less in proportion. The English system is still limited by adherence to the Cecchetti School (ex Milan), and has gained almost no contact with the fully developed Soviet style.

ORACLE DANCE (Tibet)
Performed when consulted by the State Oracle, in trance. At the Nechung Monastery, near Lhassa, the lama, dressed in gay silks and seated on a throne, falls into a trance. As the spirit takes possession attendants place a huge head-dress on his head and, hissing and trembling, he rises from the throne and begins to dance to the accompaniment of oboes and drums. Apparently unaware of the great weight of the head-dress, he rotates on one foot, beating on his breastplate with a large thumb-ring. As he turns attendants fill his hands with barleycorns, which he throws among the suppliants bowed before him. As he becomes calmer questions are put to him, often by Cabinet Ministers on important Government matters. While holding them in high esteem, Tibetans have the capacity of laughing at their own institutions. During a "drama week" held yearly at the Dalai Lama's summer palace outside Lhassa, religious plays are given, with dances accompanied by flutes and drums. As comic relief, a group of mimes (the Gyumalunma) give highly popular parodies of church and government dignitaries, including the Dance of the Oracle, complete with trance.
[Cp. *Korean Sorceress Dance*]

ORANTE—1 (Greek)
Term, later Latinized, for the "caller" of the primitive Christian sacred dance; later the first ritual movement of the gathering, as formalized in the period of Charlemagne. Remi of Auxerre (AD 880) first gives the much later verbalized form. Gradually the control of ritual dance was taken from the lay officers. Missals of Sarum, Bangor, and York, carry only the phrase as revised: "*Orate, fratres et sorores*", but this could not mean (as it seems superficially) "Speak, brothers and sisters!", since clearly they could not all speak at once. The real tradition is indicated by the development of the song form called oratorio. Where the priests once said *Orante!* or *Orante pro me!* after the *lavabo* (or cleansing preliminary of the feet), the word was neatly turned to *Orate*, when the one person who did, in fact, orate, was the priest himself. The developed form was the early Mystery

play—oratorio as distinct from oration; and implies a more or less dramatic poem on some biblical subject, set to music with recitative, airs and chorus; but essentially without full action (or gesture), and with no scenery or even costume. This we might name as the non-conformist shape. The other traditional line can be observed in the Miracle Play. Many pictures (mostly in mosaic) of the *Orante* (almost always a woman) were made in catacomb shelters; and have wrongly been labelled as "The Virgin". Her office was, in fact, closely allied to that of another ancient female officiant, the Sibyl. For long periods, the hall called oratory was a place devoted to the dual purpose of the Feast or Messe, and the liturgy of prayer and ritual dance that followed. Thus the *Orante* was parallel to the secular *Naranta* or narrator.

ORANTE—2 (*Adorante*)
Developed into the chanter-dancer in primitive Christian ritual; especially one who pronounced the *oraison* or *orison*; as one of the *'ora* or hours. The term moved into early French as *Igun-orante* (from Greek sources), as a "friar who taught the poor"; the French term exists as *Ignorantin*, in this sense. The office was marked by excessive gesture and much movement; and later developed, with music, into *oratorio*. In England the term remains in "rant"—to talk at excessive length with excitement. Many figures of the *Orante* are seen in the Roman catacomb paintings, often wrongly labelled as "Virgin", or passed off as "saints" by attachment of the name of the prayer: as *Perpetua Felicity* —the Prayer for Happiness—to the unknown ritual dancer.

ORATORIO (Italy)
Was a 16th century reply of the Romish sect to the development of *Chorale*, inspired by Martin Luther, which was instituted about 1524. Dance music or airs had been used considerably, in and out of churches; and increased since the breakdown of brief Latin rule in Constantinople. Incipient origins of oratorio, opera and ballet had almost eliminated plain-song, until this liturgical music was renovated by Palestrina in newer mode. The "Greek Peace"—from 1265 to 1396—concurred with the defeat of papal power after the Crusade aggressions; many Greek scholars with their books, music, and painting, came into Italy from Constantinople. Jewish *Psalms* and Romish plain-song gave place to chorale and hymns; while ritual dance moved with them in parallel form. When in 1453 the Turks attacked Constantinople for the third time, the end of the Byzantine rule brought newer life to Italy, with refugees. All the arts began to flourish in Italy, mainly on extortions

from the rest of Europe, including England; cut short by the rejection of papal rule by Henry VII and Henry VIII. Then the urgent need for propaganda developed oratorio and opera, centred in theatres, replacing miracle plays in the forsaken cloisters. The oratorio (or *orante*) gave its name to the Oratory (place for teaching rhetoric etc.), prompted in the scheme by Philip the Black (Neri) at Rome, from about 1560. He provided dramatic pieces in this Oratory. In 1600, Emilio Cavaliere produced *L'Anima e Corpo* (*Soul and Body*) at a Roman church, with a small orchestra; but his rival Giacomo Carissimi won attention with a scenic play on *Jonah*. They used interludes of dance. Oratorio is a sung mode of drama, based mostly on old religious myths, as an improved form of miracle play. The *passion-spiele* continued in a few places in Germany; but the religious church dances (especially celebrations) provided the Lutheran chorale (not so named) by devotional song and dance. The Ommergau Fest is a revival.

ORCHESOGRAPHIE (France)
One of the earliest printed textbooks on dance, was written by one of the canons of the church at Langres, as a commission from the recently formed Compagnie de Gesuita, following their policy of using dance as an element in their educational schemes. First printed in 1588, the original work is naturally scarce; but it was reprinted in Paris in 1888. The *nom-de-plume* of the compiler (born Dijon 1519) still hides his identity. Given as *Thoinot Arbeau*, we are told that this is an anagram of the name *Jehan de Tabouret*; yet this is not an individual name, but the title of a ritual office, similar to Jeanne d'Arc. "Tabouret" then meant not only the small drum or tambour, but indicated a court position "next the king"—either for man or woman. The canon studied dances (16th century) known to him directly; but he paid even more attention to older dances; and refrains from giving us the ritual and ceremonial usage of the current church dances, in his immediate technical interest in steps and appropriate musical form, despite the claim to tell about *danses du XVIieme siecle*. He has retained the visual association of step and musical note, placing the airs in vertical columns to accentuate these facts. John Weaver, the noted London ballet master of the early 18th century, also wrote a work named *Orchesography; or the Art of Dancing*, publ,ished in London in 1706, and again in 1710, following Feuillet's book of 1701, entitled *Choreographie*. Weaver translated it into English.

ORCHESTRA (Latin, from Greek *opxestpa*)
Hemi-circle in the public Greek theatre, paved as

the special place for dancers of chorus. This space was at the lowest level, before the proscenium. In Roman theatres, the corresponding place was used to seat dignitaries in the audience. In modern theatres, it is the space (often a well) occupied by the musicians. Sometimes, by popular reference, used to refer to "orchestra stalls", as the seats adjacent to this space; and finally the word means now the company of musicians who perform on instruments; not singers. The derivative term, "to orchestrate", means to arrange music for perform-ance in another form; as to add "accompaniment" to piano works, to provide more volume in a more important manner. Such an example is the well known treatment of Chopin's piano music to provide orchestral form for the ballet *Les Sylphides*.

OREAD (Greek)

The dance-singer of the rituals of Dionysus (the Grecian Festivals of the agricultural year), as the nymph of the grassy hills, especially in the great Spring Festival. These ring dancers were associated with the Oracles, who practised by every fountain or spring. They are broadly equivalent to the Gopi or milk-maids of the Krishna mythos in Northern India.

OREIBATES (Greece)

A mountain dancer, known in the *Oreibasia* or Mountain Walk or Dance, connected by Gilbert Murray[1] with "hallucinatory gods" in Crete. This god is "spirit of the Mountain Dance, Oreibates", and was known "in a social custom we have almost forgotten, the Religious Dance". Concerned at that point with emergence of a god-form and a god-power, from traditional custom, he says:

"When the initiated young men of Crete or else-where danced at night over mountains in the *Oreibasia* or Mountain Walk, they not only did things that seemed beyond their ordinary strength; they felt also led on and on by some power which guided and sustained them. This daemon has no necessary name : a man may be named after him *Oreibasius* (or) "Belonging to the Mountain Dancer", as others may be named Apollonius or Dionysus. The god is only the spirit of the mountain Dance, Oreibates . . . . . This spirit of the dance, who leads it off, personifies its emotion, stands more clearly than any other daemon half way between earth and heaven. A number of difficult passages in Euripides' *Bacchae* and other Dionysiac liter-ature, find their explanations when we realize how the god is in part merely identified with the inspired chief dancer; in part he is the intangible projected incarnation of the emotion of the dance".
[1] *Five Stages of Greek Religion*. Gilbert Murray. London, 1935 (p. 27 - 28).

ORGANIZATIONS

Organizations for Ballet range from the religious ballet (not so-named, but like it in form and action), to the court ballet (Italy and France), then as Masque in England, and the court ballet as enter-tainment in Russia. Followed by Bourgeois Ballet, Theatre-managing enclosed the production, impos-ing admission charges, thus making the organiza-tion commercial. The search for profit in Ballet has been multifarious; but has rarely been successful in doing much more than pay its way as a com-pany of salaried artists, with perhaps a modicum of profit in addition to satisfactory managerial commissions. In the USA, the ballet has to find heavy charges of theatre staff, large fees for agents, and publicity; and transport charges, before any surplus can be seen. Further, all persons are mulcted by income-tax impositions. The Russian court ballet did not produce profits; but, along with all five imperial Theatres, received subsidy to offset loss. The USSR have turned this into at least a balance, by eliminating all middle-men, agents, *entrepreneurs* and high staff charges. Despite this, the high-fee artist has returned in some places. In Britain, no ballet company now makes a com-mercial profit; and the two London companies connected with Sadler's Wells Theatre receive excessive state subsidies, for remarkably little en-couragement to British art and British artists.

ORGIASTIC DANCE

Does not mean what the modern word implies, such as "an orgy of crime etc." but derived from the ritual process of *orchestrion;* namely the delib-erate invocation of (a) the *manes* or departed spirits; (b) the ancestors; (c) the elemental spirits of nature, or (d) (rarest and most difficult of all) the invocation of a higher divine spirit. Thus the rite is the opposite of exorcism or compelling un-wanted entities to "depart in peace". Frequent references to "wild dance" are due mainly to mis-understanding or mistranslations of the brief descriptions of ancient authors; who perhaps never saw what they describe.

ORIGINS OF DANCE

Can usually be found in their social function, if this can be traced. Thus : many forms are ritual dances. If we know the intention and shape of the ritual, we can discern the dance form that ex-presses it. There are many Work Dances; Military, Agricultural. There are social dances, half ritual, half local ceremonial, that belong to birth, initiation (tribal, secret society, trade or gild), marriage (market and wedding), death, coronation, funeral; and memorial or ancestral dance rituals. Some ornate dance rituals belong to temple and church; entrances, dedication or consecration; enthronement; liturgic; festival; excommunication (as e.g. *Auto-de-Fideles*); street processional (*Puri, Jaganath*, or Seville, Santa Semana etc.). Some semi-dance rituals are developed military forms; e.g. the Tattoo, the "Salute to the Colours", the Parade, slow march with band. All these must be considered with Dance Origins because human movement is subjected to regular rhythm. (For details see under topics mentioned). Dance rituals become obsolete when the social form or the work task itself is dropped or changed; thus the "Industrial revolution" (from craft to machine production) eliminated many familiar work movements (it is rare to see a woman spinning in European cities and towns), and many agricultural operations (ploughing by hand and horse), became scarcer. New habits are often too new to be accepted into ceremonial form. "Laying the foundation stone" is now a futile ceremony of advertising and blah; the stone is not a genuine central stone; but a feeble slab covered with gilded names; it is more a trade mark than a solemn memorial. So the ritual is changed; the tools are useless for real work, as is the "layer"; and real workmen rarely appear. Similar changes have occurred in the religious ritual dance of the Freemasons.

ORLANDIADES

Festivals held at Munich and other German centres (14th - 15th century), said to be "named after the tone-master Orlando Lassus", but in fact he got his name from his prominence in organizing these festivals, at which the plays (e.g. on *Orlando*, or *Rolando and Oliverus*) were a regular feature. Boys from the *Currende* or school choirs were enlisted for singing and dancing in the Festivals in which Martin Luther participated as a poor boy, as in Magdeburg or Eisenach.

ORLIANCE (Scotland)

Dance step, mentioned in a Scots ballad, repeated by Sir Walter Scott in *Ane Interlude; Of the Laying of a Gaist*, as a satirical account of current superstition. This ballad is short (it conjures the "dancing ghost"), and the penultimate stanza runs:

> "This littel gaist did na mair ill   (p. 269)
> But clok lyk a corn mill;
> And it wald play and hop
> About the heid ane strop;
> And it wald sing, and it wald dance
> Oure fute, and Orliance".

Possibly the "overfoot" and the "Orliance" came with the French to Scotland from Orleans.
[See *Essay on Minstrelsy*. Sir Walter Scott. 1834]

OSCHOPHORIA (Ancient Greece)

An Attic festival, celebrated in honour of Athena and Dionysus, or of Dionysus and Ariadne. Although ancient writers do not mention the date of the celebration, it was a vintage festival, said to have been instituted by Theseus. On the day of celebration two youths, called *oschophoroi*, headed a procession from the temple of Dionysus in Athens to the ancient temple of Athena Sciras in Phalerus. Disguised as women, they carried branches of vines with fresh grapes, and were followed by persons also carrying vine-branches, by a chorus singing hymns, and by dancers who moved in rhythmic accompaniment to the singing. Women representing the youths' mothers carried provisions for them, and related stories about them. Races were run from the city to the temple of Athena Sciras, the victor receiving a cup filled with five ingredients — wine, honey, cheese, flour and a little oil.

OTEA (Tahiti)

Danced by men and women, in four rows, the women forming two inside rows. To drum rhythms, the men perform one dance, the women another. With bent torso suddenly drawn erect, half-bent knees opening and shutting, the men spin round rhythmically; while the women perform their dance of the hips. The upper body is held stiff, head high; arms, with closed fists, slope towards the ground in front, while the hips move in the undulating, gyratory movement known as *Upa-Upa*. (Cp. *Hula**). While the lines of dancers move in co-ordinated rhythm, only one, the best dancer, may leave her place and dance alone, approaching spectators, advancing, retreating, then returning to her place. Both men and women wear the *moré,** or dancing-skirt.
[See *Himinau; Aparima; Paoa; Pa-u*]

OTOMI VOLADORES (Mexico)

Otomi Indians, in the mountain village of Pahuatlan, Hidalgo, vary the traditional *Juego de los Voladores** ("Flying Game") by having six flyers, instead of four plus the musician. The additional man is dressed in skirt and blouse, as *Malinche,** who accompanies many Mexican dances. The other five wear red suits with two bandannas crossed at the back. All have bare feet. The musician carries a flute and small drum, the other five have gourd rattles. Careful ceremonies attend the felling of the tree and carrying it to the village, but the Otomis use the same pole for three years, if it is sufficiently strong. At Pahuatlan the same men

"fly" every year; some until well past middle age. The framework is hexagonal, instead of square, to accommodate the six flyers. It is fixed to the top of the pole just below a small, revolving platform, the *tecomate*, to which six ropes are attached. Having climbed to the top of the pole, the musician plays for the other five men, each of whom dances in turn on the twenty-four inch platform, high above the ground. The others, meanwhile, sit on the framework just below. For about ten minutes, each man performs a stamping, jumping dance, shaking his rattle in rhythm, and turning to each of the cardinal points. The musician changes the tune slightly for each turn. Malinche's dance, which lasts twice as long, is more intricate, and four different tunes are played as "she" dances towards the four directions. At the end, she leans forward on top of the eighty-foot pole, in order to pass a large kerchief over the head of each man. Finally, all six tie the ropes round their waist, fling themselves into the air, and "fly" in wide circles, making thirteen revolutions round the pole, towards the ground. All except Malinche fly up-side down, the musician continuing to play his pipe and drum with increasing tempo. When near the ground, the men right themselves, and land on their feet.
[See *Voladores, Juego de los; Gavilan, La Danza del; Tocotines, Los*]

OTTHUN-THULLAL (India, Malabar)

Is a version of *Kathakali** dance-drama, but is much simpler, being performed by one mime-dancer who elaborates the whole play, assisted by one musician, perhaps two. Thus it becomes equivalent to the English Punch-and-Judy street show, as compared with the work of the larger company in the tent of the bygone "penny-gaff"; and, as with the puppet-play through Europe, it has been used widely for satirical commentary. A revision of *Otthun-thullal* (Tamil term) is attributed to Kuncham of Kerala, a century back; but the form existed long before, much as it is operated in Indonesia today. This itinerant dance form has been called "the poor man's *Kathakali*", as it is obviously less costly to provide a performance. In Malabar, it is customary for a rich landlord or farmer to defray the costs of a *Kathakali* troupe; but he will seldom reward the village *Chakyar* (story-teller), who elaborates this Tamil social criticism in action. It can be seen at Quilon in Travancore.

OTUHAKA (Tonga)

A sitting dance in which the performers, glistening with scented oil and decorated with garlands, sit in a long single line. Consisting of rhythmic ges-tures, in which all parts of the body, even the toes, have their rhythm, the dance has extraordinary precision. Before the dance begins, a long drum solo is performed, the same bar of music being insistently repeated about thirty times. The gesture dance begins in silence, to the same monotonous accompaniment, then the leader bursts into song, punctuated by drum rhythm, which varies only towards the end with a slight increase in speed. Following the leader's singing of the melody, all the other performers sing the second part in chorus, repeating the same theme until the leader gives the signal for a change. Striking a higher note, the gestures change, time quickens, chorus breaks into a coda, ending with a long-drawn note and a final gesture as the voice goes down the scale.
[*Sitting Dances; Kanana* (New Guinea); *Kebyar* (Bali); *Puili; Uli-Uli-Noho* (Hawaii)]

OULED NAIL (Algeria)

A name often given to any performer of the *Muscle Dance,** but properly belonging only to girls of the Ouled Naïl people, an Arab tribe living in the hills of the Sahara. With headquarters at Djelfa (about 250 miles south of Algiers), girls come to the towns (such as Ghardaia, Bou Saada, Bog-hari), often accompanied by their mothers, to live in the "reserved quarter" as dancers and prosti-tutes. Encouraged by their parents in this traditional mode of living, no dishonour is attached. When they have earned enough money, the girls return to the mountains to marry, and bring up their own daughters in the same way. After marriage they are kept strictly secluded. Their dance, a version of the *Danse du Ventre,** is accompanied by an instru-ment like a clarinet; a tambour; and a skin-covered bowl drum similar to that used in the Moroccan *Ghedra.** Wearing a flowing muslin dress, with many necklaces and bracelets, in one hand they flourish a kerchief, while a coloured scarf is twisted into a rope and wound round the head. Their feet are bare. About the hips rests a silver belt which plays its part in the dance, since owing to wriggling muscles, it gradually rises. The dancer then stops to adjust it, which is the oppor-tunity for spectators to applaud or to slip money into her head-scarf. Formerly girls were paid in gold pieces, which they wore as bracelets, anklets, and necklaces, both as ornament and evidence of solvency. Nowadays, paper money is changed into gold to make the necessary jewellery. In the walled "reserved quarter" (introduced into desert towns by the French), are cafés, small streets and squares, where the Ouled Naïl girls dance, while patrons relax over mint tea. The girls have small apart-ments, where they entertain friends and visitors.
[See *Muscle Dance; Cifte Tel; Danse du Ventre*]

OULIVETO, LIS (Provence, France)
A ritual dance once performed at the time of olive harvest, but now on any special occasion. In two parts, the dance includes (1) *Les Epées;* (2) *Lei Courdello.** After an introduction by men and women in couples led by the Fool or Arlequin, there follows *Les Epées,* a hilt-and-point sword dance for eight to sixteen young men, accompanied by the Arlequin. While various figures are performed the Fool skips about in a dance of his own. Then , dancing round him, each man lays his sword on the Fool's shoulders until the "lock" is made, which is slipped down over the Fool's body to the ground, then raised shoulder high with the Fool standing on the locked swords. *Lei Courdello,* performed by men and women weaving ribbons, or cords, about a pole, sometimes comes in the middle of the sword dance. A third dance, called *Arlequin,* may be included, performed by about ten girls and the Arlequin.

OUROUVE (Papua)
"Toucan Dance". One of the story-dances or *Olové,** of the Fuyughé people, depicting a legend of the Toucan bird. When fledglings are ready to leave the nest, high in a tall tree, says the story, the male bird, or *isio,* flies away to tell other *isios.* Male toucans then gather in the next tree; two fly to the nest side by side, making a platform of overlapped wings. On to this a young toucan steps and is flown round about by the adult birds, to show him the world he must live in. Pairs of *isios* follow, each with a young bird, and all return, not to the nest, but to the next tree, for the fledglings are henceforth "on their own". To illustrate this, dancers move in close single file, in a serpentine course over the dancing-ground; then two move forward on either side of the dancer in front, the three dance a few steps together, then return to their places. This is repeated several times. *Ourové* is danced by men to accompaniment of drums and chanting, and with graceful waving of plumed head-dresses.
[See *Olové; Gabé* and cp. *Kipara* (Australia); *Naleng* (Malekula)]

OWCZARZ; "OVCHAZH" (Poland)
"Shepherd". A dance for seventeen people—eight couples and the *owczarz,* who leads, carrying a heavy stick. A very old dance, which survives only in a few places, it is part dance, part game, reminiscent of our children's games with an odd man out. The couples, led by the *owczarz,* sing as they dance. At the end of each verse the *owczarz* bangs his stick on the floor, dancers form into two lines facing each other, and the young men bargain with the "shepherd" for the "sheep"—i.e. the girls. The

merry business over, the *owczarz* throws his cudgel on the floor and seizes one of the girls. There follows a rush by the young men for partners, the odd one out taking up the cudgel to be in his turn, the *owczarz.* And so the dance continues. This, and the Shrovetide custom of bargaining for partners, are probably relics of the old "marriage market".* formerly common in many parts of Europe, such as the *Tergul de Fête** held in Rumania each year on the 29th June, at the top of the Gaina Mountain. In Bulgaria there is a dance called *Ovchata,* "The Sheep's Dance" but the form is quite different, being danced in a linked line.

OXDANSEN (Sweden)
"Ox Dance". A humorous dance performed as a sham fight by two men. Said to have originated among students of Karlstadt, it is performed to lively music, the dancers miming during the "verse" and dancing together during intervening "refrain". Pulling hair and ears, sticking out tongues, boxing ears, bumping into each other, opponents dance out their burlesque contest. One will sometimes clap his hands to simulate a blow, at the same time bending sideways to avoid it, and during the "refrain", which is a sort of lull in the proceedings, the two glare defiance at each other, while performing their dance.

P

PACE, OR PAS, OR STEP
Provide the elemental basis for nomenclature in associated dance and music, with the limitations of the human form, which makes both. Much mystery has been created by professionals who seek to obscure the simple facts. Return to the Greek basis recalls once more the intimate association of (1) Voice, as the single Syllable; (2) the Pace, the single Step; (3) the Musical Note, the Measure or Beat. These have not, and cannot, disappear; since they exist in the fundamental character of these three factors. All dance is built up from that basis. Hence titles of apparent dances are named for accompanying music; and both these categories belong to the Step or Pace. The *passepied*—the pace-foot; the *passa-mezzo*—half-pace, half-foot, half-beat; and so on to the cinq-pas or step (by) five, the "sinky-passe". The *passa-caglia, passe-caille,* and the rest, evolve on the same basis : the *"calle* is the "street" or way or progression inside a hall. The musicians play a simple melody to give them their pace, their cue, their measure. Pace in dance is thus commensurable with music, first in the *beat,* then in *phrase.* African drum

music reveals complex pace records; often like the hoof-beats of cattle, sometimes one or two, sometimes a herd; yet both are rhythmic, in contrapuntal beats.   [See *Horse Ballet; Carrousel*]

PACE EGG (England)

A Mumming Play—formerly with a Sword Dance—performed now at Midgley, near Sowerby Bridge in West Riding of Yorkshire, at Easter. The modern theme is a merging of the Paschal ritual with the older Egg or Arc ritual of the Spring Festival, here symbolised (as in Preston, Avenham Park) by the appearance and use of many eggs. Balkan countries retain more powerful traditions, in precisely the same character. The text of this play is a much revised version, dating from 17th - 18th century period. The hero is now Saint-George; who fights nobly against Bold Slasher, Black Prince of Paradise, and Bold Hector (or Arkter). From the Sword Dance remains the Fool and the Doctor, along with the King of Egypt, Bugler, and the quaint Toss-Pot, who can "drink all". When the play is given, on Good Friday, the players use brightly coloured coats, with many rosettes; and have large helmets with more decorations. They wear bells. The Doctor sports a top hat; but Toss-Pot is by way of being a ragged devil of straw-tailed satire. He carries the wide basket to receive egg offerings; and also collects money. The martial characters bear their wooden swords, led by Saint-George and his merry men, slaying the Prince of Morocco.   [See *Morris*]

PACHESI (India, Uttar Pradesh Province)

Dance-game played with human "pieces". This courtly pastime was played at Agra and Fateh-pur-sikri in the time of the Muslim Emperor, Akbar (1600). In the great court of the Fort of Agra, lines incised on the sandstone paving can still be discerned, about a metre square. On these sixty four squares, the two opposed players seem to have had sixteen girls, as pieces, on each side. The king or nobles called out the moves; the girls went to the square as a chess-player moves his pieces; usually chanting to some musical rhythm, supplied by drum and vina. At Agra, the rival players sat outside the great square; at Fatehpur-sikri (Akbar's new city) they sat on a low pedestal in the centre. This game is still played in similar fashion in Indo-China, where a match may be followed on a rice terrace, with temporary squares laid in strips of bamboo—as between the Man-Coch and the Man-Tien people. The players sit under a shelter close by. Girl dancers attired in silver gauze or gold, with tassels and pompoms, move as ordered; and when "captured" leave the board. These games appear among the Thai and Annamese people. In the USA,

a domestic board game, faintly similar in system, is known as *parchesee.*

PAIKHA (Oraon, India)

Relic of a fight and "marriage market" contest similar to those formerly danced in Europe. This *Paikha* is arranged as between the two villages, where bride and groom come from. The men in the girl's village array themselves in "armour", as warriors, but with wooden swords and bamboo shields. They practise among themselves by way of rehearsal; then sally forth to meet the approaching groom's party; and a good time is had by all in the "fight" with subsequent refreshments. By an imitation raid, the bride is borne away to the house of the groom.
[Cp. *Borten Abtanz* (Rumania); *Marriage Market Dance*]

PAIXTLE DANCE (Mexico)

"Paixtle" is the Aztec word for "moss" and the dance, performed in Tuxpan and villages of Jalisco, is evidently of pre-Spanish origin. Danced now at Catholic fiestas, its purpose is forgotten, but it obviously once had a magical or ritual significance Each dancer, concealed beneath a cloak made of moss, wears on his face a mask of wood or paper, and in addition covers his head and face with a large kerchief. Encumbered thus, he can only perform simple steps, but forming into a line, the dancers move through a dignified dance, accompanied by a violin. The rhythm is marked with a shepherd's crook hung with bells and carved with an animal's head, with which each dancer strikes the ground. From time to time they utter cries, which the muffling mask and kerchief make strangely animal-like. The Spanish name for the dance is *El Heno*, "the hay", referring to the cloak of moss or hay.   [See *Aztec Dance*]

PAJARO BOBO (Spanish, Estramadura)

La Pajaro Bobo Dantza, means "Stupid Bird", and is a juvenile Sunday afternoon "courting dance". Village girls (with some incitement from the clerics, doubtless), take drum and tambour, pass into the village and sing, inviting the boys to join them in the street dance. The youths, already lingering round the corners, do not move, but add their own refrain :

> *Ya esta el pajaro bobo*
> *Puesto en la esquina!*

admitting that

> "Here is the stupid bird,
> Already in his corner!"

and for a few minutes the flirtation continues (before the whole village), when the couples dance together, until the church bell rings for vespers, thus drawing the apathetic males into the service.

PAK-DON (Santal Tribes, Bengal)
A sword and shield dance, formerly performed on the eve of battle, or in triumphant celebration of returning warriors, by the Santals, living in the hills bordering on Chota Nagpur. Performed at night, by torchlight, the dancers moved in an uneven circle, waving shields, but using sticks instead of swords. In the middle were the drummers. Each dancer wore loin-cloth, anklets, and necklets. As they danced, onlookers passed round the circle with jars of rice beer, pouring libations from a rolled leaf down the thirsty throats of the performers.

PAKHTA (Uzbekistan, USSR)
Utilises movements, in a traditional folk-dance, of the rapid motion of the hands, as in cotton picking. *Pakhta* means "cotton". Five or six girls move slowly down, as along a row of cotton plants, turning from side to side, sometimes carrying a basket; and following the vocational gestures of picking cotton.

PALAIS
The Commercial *Palais de Danse* is a 20th century institution. The first one was opened at Hammersmith (London) in 1919; then another in Birmingham. Mass Ballroom Dances, held in Covent Garden Theatre (1925) were followed by the Mecca Cafés scheme starting at Brighton (1927). Then the Ritz (Manchester) and Locarno (London) were added, with Lido (Croydon) and in 1936 Locarno at Glasgow was opened. Several other Palais Halls were organised: at Edinburgh, Leeds, and Manchester. The Paramount Hall (newly built) was opened in 1938 for dance; but closed by the police in 1952 owing to invasions by the "Roebuck Boys" (chiefly Jamaicans). The Mecca Dancings, mostly in the modern *Palais de Danse* provide millions of dancers annually with space for pleasant dancing. With them must be associated the Blackpool Tower Festivals and competitions; and those held in London; usually at the Albert Hall; some sponsored by the London *Star* newspaper.

PALAIS DE DANSE (West Europe)
General term, from French, given to the modern large-scale commercial ballroom where amateur dancers may enter, on payment, for the evening. There are many in Britain. Usually a good ten-piece band is provided (sometimes two, who play alternately), and often the style of dancing is considered good; that is, up to a high standard in currently accepted conventional style. The present custom is

for a young man to escort his own girl friend; but often parties are made up; and it is rare that one couple will dance together during the whole evening. The *Palais* is an accepted town centre, replacing the mediaeval marriage-market, or the Victorian Assembly Rooms, as a place where eligible young people can meet matrimonial partners. Normally the four types of ballroom dance are followed; or the "Old Time Dances", or versions of Country Dances and Square Dances. Lately Scottish styles have spread more (*reel*,* *jig** and *strathspey**) as well as extending in Scotland. In Ireland it is the *Feis*.

PALIO (Siena, Italy)
A city celebration dubbed Palio occurs every July, in the chief square before the Town Hall, which has a long and often obscure history. The present form, which features a horse race, was pushed forward by clerical interests in the seventeenth century. This race takes the form of a competition between the parishes (*contrades*) which formerly competed by way of procession and mimic dance. A wagon drawn by four white oxen, with the *palio* flag, is the most ancient feature now preserved. The imposition of the name Palio, from the supposed banner that bore the name, to the race, is recent. The parishes (now seventeen) once numbered twelve, carrying the mediaeval "Signs of the Zodiac", as their emblems—a dragon, a goat, a unicorn, a goose or a wolf (also having been altered). The selected horse is taken into the parish church, and is there subjected to ritual magic, ending with "blessing". Formerly this was the ordeal of the principal mime-dancers. All the costumes used today are copies, more or less accurate, of Renaissance designs. There were formerly two such celebrations annually; they belonged once to Etruscan festivals for the solstices of June and December; but they are now held on the 2nd July and 16th August. The procession through winding mediaeval streets still continues, but nearly all the public dance has disappeared; it is seen only in restaurants or cafés.

PALMAS, LAS (Mexico)
"The Palms". A rain dance of the Cora Indians. Although now performed at the Catholic fiesta in San Miguel on September 29th, the dance (especially the costume) suggests pre-Conquest origin. Ten young men, led by the *viejo* (old man), who wears a wooden mask with horse-hair moustache and carries a whip, perform elaborate figures to music of violin and flute. They are accompanied by Malinche,* a small girl wearing adult female clothes, who dances at intervals with one of the men. In addition to cotton suits, they wear a

crown of flowers and tall blue feathers tipped with down. Over their face falls a fringe of blue beads reaching from head-dress to middle of the chest, and symbolising rain. Each dancer carries in one hand a painted rattle, in the other a fan-shaped palm, decorated with artificial blue and yellow flowers. In Aztec times, several festivals during the eighteen-month year were connected with Tlaloc the rain god, who is pictured in some codices with blue garments, his face painted black and yellow. Blue symbolised the colour of water, and his face the thunder-cloud. Many dances occurred at the festivals, and poles were erected with paper streamers coated with liquid rubber or *ulli* gum, to represent rain-drops.

[See *Aztec Dance; Huixtocihuatl; Ilamatecuhtli*]

PAMPERRUQUE (France)

A chain dance of the *Farandole** type, belonging to Bayonne in the Basse Pyrenees. Dancers, linked by kerchiefs (or, as in 1781, when it was danced before the Dauphin, with garlands), move in a winding pattern, the leader and the last dancer sometimes carrying beribboned wands. It used to be danced in honour of any distinguished person visiting Bayonne; a description is given by Mdme. d'Aulnoy in her *Memoirs*.

PAN, DANCES OF (Hellas)

Pan, or Sylvanus, has been associated chiefly with Greece (and Etruria, as Sylvanus) while in fact this Nature worship existed widely through the whole of Europe, before the name of Hellas became known. The system is still living today in Tibet as the cult of *Bön-Pa*, preserved as the oldest and indigenous religion of Bod-gyul. In Western Europe, the cult, probably gave part of the foundation of the Druidic cult remaining virile in Brittany, Wales and Cornwall until relatively recent times. In Wales it had the triple terms of *Tre, Pol*, and *Pen*, all prominent in religious ritual dances; and they remain in numerous place-names, as well as family names. The nature dances of Pan (or in Italy, of Bona Dea), celebrated in Syria (by Lucian), have been confused with different distinct orders: as those of Orpheus and of Bacchus (Dionysios), to that considerable investigation is necessary to distinguish the basic elements of each system. For all of them, it is an error to begin with assumptions of "wild" or "frenzied" dances. Doubtless, some rituals culminated in fanatical behaviour; but we can see similar incidents today. These cults celebrated two modes, known later in Greece as the Lesser and the Higher Mysteries; of Generation and Re-generation; and found also in biblical terms, the Lesser as the "Old" and the Higher as the "Novum". Myths differ, but the theme remains. Examination of the Tibetan

Bön-Pa reveals some traditional parallels with Hellenic rites; some names remain similar, as with the seminal title of *Pan* or *Pön*. This moved into later cults as *Pan-aghios* and *panakea* ("All-souls" and "All-healing") as well as *pantheon*, a survey of "all gods united in one unknowable supreme". All modes were expressed in dance and chant with simple music.

PANDANGGO, SA ILAW (Phillipines)

"Dance of Lights". A Spanish-style dance in *Fandango** rhythm. Girls and men dance in pairs, the female dancers balancing lighted oil lamps on their head and backs of hands. *Binasuan*,* in quite different style and rhythm, is danced with glasses of wine balanced on the head and palms of the hands. The Hungarians also have a dance for women, with wine bottles on the head, said to originate from the practice of carrying bundles and baskets on the head.

[Cp. *Tari Piring* (Sumatra); *Cakewalk; Calinda* (U.S.A.)]

PANTO-MIME — 1 (Early Greek form)

Indicated "The World Spectacle" — the "playing out" of life in forms, a dictum held by the *Stoicheion* (The Straight Men). Their phrase ran: *Ex auton — kai de auton — kai eis ta panta* which we may render: "Out of Self, through Self, in Self all things are". If we add the "dark saying" of Hera Kleitus: *Panta Rhei* — "All things Flow", we come close to modern physics; we can perceive the swiftly moving hands of the devoted expert in Mime (as also in *Bharata Natyam**). They postulated three modes of Mime or reflection or "material imitation"; done as (a) Mimes of Things, actions, remembered, from the *Past;* (b) Mimes of Things *Now* perceived, reporting, comment etc.; and (c) Mimes of Things, projects, Events, to be seen in *Future*. In this *panta ex mimos* he could reveal more than in words. With this subtle *Stoicheion* view we may add the more familiar Gnostic Christian phrase: "In him we Live; and Move; and have our Being." Turned to popular amusement, Mime no longer presents these values.

PANTOMIME — 2 (Italian)

Stage show by full action, without words or song, but with simple music; this term is equivalent to *Saltatio* (Latin) or *Orchesis* (Greek) and the modern stage *Ballet*, in contra-distinction to *Mime*, which in Greece and Rome included speech. The pragmatic distinction appears in the contrast between prose movement (quasi-naturalist) and rhythmic movement (stylised modes), together with the stress on (a) speech, as against (b) suggestional action. That is: the poetry of speech is compared with the poetry of motion. With the use of music to provide rhythmic stress, or emotional mode, we move to the form of oratorio and then opera, contrasted with the use solely of words as in modern drama. Then the prose action of drama receives the term "business", which the experienced actor may devise for himself, or be required to accept actions as dictated or suggested by a "producer". In modernist stage performances, there has been a strong tendency to reduce movement (at least in British theatres) to a pseudo-naturalist range; and this style has been widely adopted in cinema film production, owing to the tendentious use of the "close-up", which reveals every flicker of an eyelid, no longer as pantomime, but as mimic action of unadorned naturalism, requiring little skill in personal acting, but much in "production" and episodic assembly.

PAOA (Tahiti)
A woman's solo dance, performed in the centre of a large circle of kneeling men and women. In contrast to the *Himinau*,* where the inner circle beats the rhythm with half coconut-shells while the outer circle dance, in the *Paoa* it is the outer circle who provide the rhythm by beating the ground with the palms of their hands. They kneel facing outwards, while the woman in the centre performs an undulating dance of the hips, arms raised, top part of the body stiff.
[See *Otéa; Aparima; Moré*]

PAPARUADA (Rumania)
An invocational rite, danced by Gypsy girls in time of drought. They dance through village streets, pausing from door to door, singing the chants invoking rain. This usually occurs in Autumn, after a hot summer.   [Cp. *Dodole* (Serbia)]

PARABLE (English - Latin, from Greek *peribolos*, an enclosed space)
Literally, an early "miracle play" or "morality play" acted in mime, probably with tambour to give rhythm emphasis; as "an item thrown out" by way of propaganda. The form was known in (a) proverbs or couplets; (b) short narratives, recounted in the *tavern* or *taberna* or *capella* (various sorts of Roman shops) and, for festival occasions, elaborated on a small platform, in a hall or in the squares. The terms are numerous, surrounding the Grecian *boulé** or council group. *Peribolos* was thus the space roped off; or the *pergula*, the small booth (tent for the Fair). These playlets were popular in Alexandria. Bishop Kyril (who ruled the city) had a large gang of *paraboloni*, who alternately performed *parabolon* stories, or acted in buffoon comedies for rich private persons. Their tales

became so wild that the term "boloney" is now a comment for the incredible. These monks sometimes added women as dancers to their secular groups. After the transfer of these plays to itinerant monks, the term given in scriptures as parable was sustained in written form; though never as "history".

PARADISE BIRDS (New Guinea)
Living in the Kubor Mountains, Central New Guinea, the male Birds of Paradise make elaborate display in the mating season, before an audience of one or more females. Ornithologists call these rhythmic movements a "dance", and the displaying place is the "dancing-ground". Choosing a thin, high branch, the bird struts and hops, spreading its plumes. Bringing his wings together across the back, he thumps the "wrists" rhythmically together, and when greatly excited, tumbles over, hanging head down, his plumes sweeping out below. The "Saxony", robin-size, yellow and black, carries on his head two curved quills hung with pale blue translucent "flags", which sweep forward and back, as he displays. The "Greater" species, with long flame-coloured plumes, hops up a pencil-sized sloping branch, twitching partly opened wings. At the top he turns sideways, and jumping with both feet together, descends the slope with little leaps. Then with raised wings and curved neck, he flings his plumes upward and back in a cascade of orange and flame hues. The dance of the velvet-black "Stephanie", on a bare branch eighty feet above ground, makes much play with the tail-feathers, nearly two feet long. Curving the tail inwards, he spreads the central plumes, and waves tail and wings in rhythm. In full sunlight he shines greenish-blue. Most theatrical is the "Magnificent", who seems to stage-manage his performance, given in early morning, and again later in the day. Thrush-size, with golden-yellow plumage and green chest-shield, he carefully prepares his stage. He selects a tree of broom-handle size, deep in the forest, usually on a steep slope. He clears the ground beneath the trunk and snips the leaves overhead to spot-light its arena with shafts of sunlight. With a screeching call, he promenades proudly up and down his sloping stage, flexing his wings and pausing to spread his plumes. Then, circling the trunk, he repeats the performance. Plumes of the Paradise birds are much prized by New Guinea natives, forming splendid head-dresses, and this bird's courtship dance is imitated in movements of native dances. A dance performed in Ambok, Molucca Islands, is *Tari Tjenderawasih*, Dance of the Paradise Bird.
[See *New Guinea, Dancing in; Kanana; Olové; "Royal Dance"*]

Paradise Birds, from a drawing by M. E. Purdon.   NEW GUINEA

PARAGUAY (S. America)

Missionary dance propaganda was utilised by the Jesuits on both banks of the River Uruguay. They used music and dance to attract the natives (Guarnis and Chiquitos), Church choirs were developed, with the use of imported instruments. "The Indians fell into the trap", writes Chateaubriand,[1] "and they descended from their hills to hear. F. Charlevoix relates how the Jesuits introduced the custom of celebrating with dances the church festivals. "Sometimes", he says, "they performed complicated dances . . . walked the tight rope, or tilted with lances". During the Easter procession were carried life-size figures, made by the Indians, portraying various Passion episodes. The Fathers made use of statues of saints with moveable limbs and eyes. Thus arose the Jesuit republic of Paraguay, a communist state; which was later attacked by Spanish and Portuguese forces. When, in 1759, the order was banished from Portugal (in 1767 from Spain — where it now rules, with Franco), the Spanish premier, Aranda, began to demolish Jesuit rule in Paraguay. The religious dances continued to be performed for decades afterwards, much as they are now in Mexico.

[1]*Spirit of Christianity*. F. R. de Chateaubriand. Paris, 1802.

PARCAE (England)

Latin name of the three Greek *Moirae* or *Fates Moirae*. Greek rituals account for the Dance of the Perke (known in Teutonic countries) made over from an ancient Dance of the Fates (Lachesis, Atropos and Clotho), which became traditional in rites of Perchta, Perkun and Parke. These are also the *Morae* (see *Morris**). In England, the rite lingers in the North-country fabrication, each November, of "Parkin Pigs". This little brown animal, made in flat cakes with a single currant placed for the eye, celebrates the once-dreaded boar. This Cosmic Boar sought to diminish the Sun each Autumn; and there was a feast of prayer with dance and chanting. For this, the little "parkin pigs" were made, at first of honey and oatmeal, later of treacle. The Greek Fates were Clotho, with her Spindle (Of Necessity) Atropos, who draws the thread of human life; and Lachesis, who cuts the line (or pattern). Homer knows one Moira; Hesoid names three, Moirae "daughters of Night" as Clotho who spins thread; Lachesis who mixed with "weal and woe" in pattern; and Atropos who cuts at the hour appointed. *Moeris* therefore came into Britain from some Greek sources; not Latin.

PARIK (Armenia)

The general name of Mediaeval girl dancers, who performed for various festivities; also *Hushka Parik* the "mournful dancers" under control (as a rule) of the *Vahuni* (priests). The groups of minstrels (*ashoughs* or *ashuk*) composed and recited dance-mimes. For some important feasts, the *Katholikos* (head priest) was deputed to arrange the ceremony.

PARIS GARDEN (London)

This London pleasure resort began as a bear-garden; animal show; and general noisy rendez-vous for the teenagers of that period. The place was started by Robert de Paris, in the time of Richard II, on the Thames Bankside. The owner of the bears (usually two German brown forest bears) had them chained with a light link; and he carried a stout staff. He was known as bear-ward. Ben Jonson describes the entrance of the two bears: "Very sufficient bears, and can dance at first sight —and play their own tunes if need be. John Urson the bear-ward, offers to play them with any other city dancers for a ground measure". So says Slug; when Notch returns: "Marry, for lofty tricks, or dancing on the ropes, he will not undertake, for 'tis out of their element". Then John Urson sings a ballad, to the same shrill piping, while the patient bears perform their slow clumsy dance, reared on two legs. Later the bears and their dancing disappeared, and the place took on the character of a fair, with itinerant showmen coming and going (chiefly during the summer months) when the gawping youths could see the tumblesteres and posture-makers and rope-dancers do their tricks. Many other "gardens" started from copying this crude enterprise; until we arrive at Cremorne, Ranelagh,* Marylebone Gardens, and Vauxhall.*

PARIS OPERA BALLET (Professional)

The ranks of dancers in the Opera Company were in 1954 as follows:
Female dancers: five danseuses étoiles; four premières danseuses; eleven grands sujets; ten petits sujets; eight coryphées; ten premier quadrille; twelve deuxième quadrille.
Male dancers: five danseurs étoiles; five premiers danseurs; four grands sujets; six petits sujets; seven coryphées; three premier quadrille; six deuxième quadrille.
Officially there is one ballet master, two choreographers, nine teachers, three stage managers and four pianists. The salary of the étoiles is equivalent to between £120 and £150 a month, the minimum is £45 a month. (In 1789, Vestris, danseur étoile at the Paris Opèra, received the equivalent of £300 a year.)

PARVIS (France)

The clear, level, paved space, kept in front of the West Front of a French cathedral; and some other churches. This central space was used for (a) the annual festival markets and fairs; (b) the religious plays and ritual dances commonly celebrated, at least in part, in the open air; (c) for town meetings. Said to derive from *parevis* or paradise, from Latin (Persian) *paradisus*. The traditional scene of the parade or *parados;* the display of troops, or of clergy; or latterly of municipal pomp, The *parvis* is the primal scene for the town versions of Basque dance, especially the *Erreberentzia* etc.

PASCOLAS (Mexico)

Ceremonial dances of Yaqui Indians; also Spanish name given to the dancers who perform them. Originally a pre-Conquest ritual concerned with the hunting of game, the *Pascolas* (which include the *Deer Dance*, or *Venado**) are now performed at Catholic religious fiestas, especially on Easter Saturday—hence the name, *Pascola*. In a few places they retain something of their original character. *Pascola* dancers begin their training as children and continue dancing until past middle-age. At fiestas they perform in an *enramada* (an open-sided thatched bower, sometimes containing an altar). Preliminary ceremonies mingle Catholic and Yaqui ritual. All kneel before the image of the saint. The eldest *pascola*, his face masked, is led three times round the *enramada* anti-clockwise; then he puts a stick into each hole of the harp which will accompany their dancing, at the same time naming all the animals of the woods. After shooting off three fire-crackers the dances begin, accompanied by harp and violin. Having bare torso and feet, the men wear trousers fastened with a belt from which hang brass or copper bells. Round their neck is a bead necklace, and strings of *tenabari* (cocoons filled with gravel) are twisted round their legs. They shake wooden rattles, and on their head is tied a small wooden mask with shaggy eyebrows and hair, no longer worn over the face as in the introductory ceremony. The Pascolas dance one after another, each with the mask on his head and each adding variations to the basic steps, which are of the stamping variety. While one is dancing the others amuse the spectators with clowning antics. When all have danced, there follows the dramatic *Deer Dance*, in which the *Pascolas* join, representing *coyotes* or other animals who hunt the deer. They are expert at imitating the movements of many animals.
[See *Venado, danza del; Coyote Dance* (Yaqui Indians); *Matachins*]

PAS DE QUATRE (French)

Technical term, denoting a connected dance usually referred to four *premiére danseuses;* but equally applicable to any four dancers in any academic style of Ballet (e.g. the "Cygnets' Dance" in *Swan Lake*). In 1843 Fanny Elssler and Fanny Cerito were presented in London in a *pas de deux*, and in 1845 a display called *Pas-de-Quatre* was performed at Her Majesty's Theatre by four famous ballerinas—

Marie Taglioni, Fanny Cerito, Lucille Grahn and Carlotta Grisi. These performances have been acclaimed as the "Height of Romantic Ballet", which is an over-statement. Such an academic display, however technically excellent, can no more be given such peaks of art, any more than a display (equally neat technically) of the "Changing of the Guard" can be admitted as "military strategy". Both are ornamental shows; not artistically fine achievements.

PASILLO (Spanish)
"Short step". Latin-American dance found in Venezuela, Columbia, Ecuador, Panama and Costa Rica, with slight local variations. Of Spanish derivation, its music is in combined 3/8 and 3/4 time. Known also in Columbia as the *Vals del pais*, the *Pasillo* there and in Venezuela is in the major key, but the Ecuadorean *Pasillo* is in the minor. In Costa Rica, there is a variation in the music, the melody being in duple time, while the accompaniment remains in triple time, and the dance is called *Pasillo Guanacasteco*. When performed to a Mazurka rhythm it is known as *Pasillo-Mazurka*.

PASSACAGLIA, PASSACAILLE
An Italian dance form, in slow triple rhythm, dating from about 1600. In musical construction it closely resembled the *Chaconne*,* but was different in mood and spirit.

PASSACALLE
(Sp. *Calle* = street; *paseo* = walk, promenade; *paso* = step.) A Latin-American dance of the *Huaiño** type found in Bolivia, Ecuador and Peru. Also a serenade. The dance, in 3/4, 6/8 or 2/4 time, is a Carnival processional dance through the streets. In Bolivia, although in slow time, it is gay and carefree; while in Peru it is a Carnival march-dance. Couples perform this dance of flirtation at intervals during the procession.
[See *Huaiño; Sanjuanito; Tamborito*]

PASSEPIED (France) (England : *Paspy*)
A gay and spirited dance popular at the courts of Louis XIV and XV, but belonging originally to the people of Haute-Bretagne. At first in duple time, the 17th century dance was in triple time, and was not sung, as were most of the old dances. In character it was light and gay, and in form resembled the *Minuet*,* although thought to have descended from one form of *Branle*.* It reached England (as the *Paspy*) some time before the end of the 17th century. The *Passepied* is described by Niedt in *Handleitung zue Variation* (1706) as being very quick, the feet showing great agility—hence its name. As a folk dance, performed today in

Brittany, the *Passepied* is danced to lively music in 4/4 time, the tune being sung, and the name referring to one of the two steps used. Found throughout the mountain region of Haute Bretagne, and in the Trégorrois district, the *Passepied* has two figures in contrasting styles. (1) *Promenade* using *pas marché*—a rhythmic walk, slow and dignified, either in a circle, or couples in line behind each other. (2) *Passepied*—of light and lively character, partners facing each other but moving on a slant towards the right. They make four *passepieds* (using *sauté-croisé*, "crossed-jump"; an open jump; and steps backward), which is fully danced only by men, the women merely "sketching" it. Thus, as the two figures contrast in style, so does the dancing of partners in the second—men showing virtuosity and vigour, women remaining gentle and reserved.

PASSOMEZZO, PASSAMEZZO
"Half-step". A 16th century Italian dance very similar to the *Pavaniglia** or *Spanish Pavane*, which was quicker than the *Pavane*.* The name, "half-step", indicated the quickened movement and tempo, and the consequent greater number of steps per beat, in contrast with the more solemn *Pavane*. Partners stood face to face, without holding hands, for the *Grand Reverence*. There followed a number of figures, in which the dancers wheeled round together, clockwise or anti-clockwise; alternating with ornate variations for the man while the lady moved more sedately, facing him; and similar variations for the lady while the man danced from left to right opposite her. The dance ended with another *Grand Reverence*. Music for the *Passomezzo* was in 2/4 time. In 1550 a collection of melodies, published by the Gardano press, contained three *Pass'e mezi* described as "new", suggesting that the dance already existed. Examples were also included in the *Intabolatura del Lauto* by Anton Rotta (1546). The *Passomezzo* was popular in Elizabethan England. In Italy it gradually superceded the *Pavane*, which continued to be danced in France and England. In the custom of that time, when dances were often arranged in pairs (see *Nachtanz**), the *Passomezzo* was the slow dance in duple time followed by the *Saltarello** in triple time.

PASSOVER (Pesach; Seder) (Hebrew)
Dance ritual included in Jewish celebrations. Passover had two modes or forms : one lunar and one solar; the first lasted only one day (or night) and the other, the vernal or sowing (Easter) was annual. Latin terms include pask; pasch and pasque (cp. with Basque) while Wycliff uses (*Matthew xxvi*) the phrase "The Maister saith my time is nigh

with thee I make *paske* with my disciples". Whether they used the Egg symbol is uncertain (used by Russian Church) but it seems probable that a ring or oval dance was used by twelve men. The first barley was ripe; the "lamb" of the legend belongs to the Zodiac; no real animal is eaten in modern Judaism; but wine is used (with unleavened bread) which begins to approximate the Latin *Mess* or Supper. The monthly supper gave place to the *Seder* of each Sabbath.

PASTORAL (French)

Has had many dance phases and forms. Rousseau in his day saw the pastoral as music, accompanied by words, suggesting the vocation of the shepherd. But the court thought that "playing shepherds" was also a pastoral delight. Alleged to derive from simple rustical songs and dances, the pastoral in music developed to the cantata, sonata, and ended in the triumphant splendour of Beethoven's *Pastoral Symphony*. In Napoli, in 1285, Charles of Anjou saw at his court Adam de la Halle's arrangement of the traditional play *Le Jeu de Robin et de Marion*. According to Tiersot, this was a simple pastoral comedy, using a string of folksong-dance tunes that had long been popular; much as John Gay did for his famous *Beggar's Opera* centuries later. For more precise origins we have to connect this dance-song with the church pastor; or with the celebration of harvest with *Pasta* made into new bread. The carol *Angelus ad Pastores* refers to a religious play version (AD 1624).

PATCH TANZ or PASCH TANZ (Jewish)

"Clap Dance". A progressive round dance performed at weddings, and other festivities. In three or four figures, it begins with couples facing in a circle, moving slowly round in a clockwise direction. In the second figure, the circle closes to the centre, where all clap their hands; then opens out again, and dancers stamp three times. The circle then breaks into couples, facing each other with arms joined at shoulder height, who revolve as in the *waltz** or *ländler*.* At the end of this figure, the woman moves under her partner's arm to the next man on the left, and so the dance continues with new partners.

PATTERAN (Europe)

Has many meanings. George Borrow (*The Gypsies in Spain*) explains how Gypsies use the "patteran" or trail. These companies use a system of special marks or trails as signs, at cross-roads or turnings, to indicate what road they had followed, and the "fate" that their colleagues would find. These *patterans* follow the oldest "scout trails" known to Europe; markings not only by simple indications —wheel tracks or hoof marks such as the Red Indians could "read like a book"—but signs deliberately made, according to the Gypsies' scheme. Cleft sticks, stuck in a bush, or on gate-posts, with one tiny arm pointing to the commended road, offered a tribal signpost, not easily observed by the *gorgio*. Modern theatre knows *patteran* in different codes. Rehearsal is helped by chalk marks on the stage, which indicate the position of some characters, places for entrance or exit in non-existent scenery; the place for some important stage property. Ballet masters use temporary chalk lines for the precise place of direction of their *corps de ballet*; though the lines vanish "before the night", yet repeated use in rehearsal has helped the dancers to maintain formation.

PATTERN (Floor)

In dance has one well-known meaning, and several meanings not so obvious. The usual reference is to floor pattern : the track, or footsteps, traced by the dancer on the stage. The active sense of this movement is called "choreography", while its static record (seen "in plan") is called Pattern, or (on paper) Notation. The easel-artist or picture-painter sees a different pattern; his vertical view, framed by the proscenium, reveals a picture pattern which he can record in his three-dimensional suggestion, as a basis for his painting. Pattern in an older and frequently forgotten sense, implies the actual pattern set out by means of diagrams or designs on the floor, or other dancing surface, such as squares of marble in alternating black and white, as used in Italian halls during the Renaissance period; or wooden parquet from suitably arranged sections of pine as used in Russian halls or on theatre stages and rehearsal rooms. These horizontal permanent patterns were found useful in arranging for position and movement over them. Other patterns are more complicated, both in form and meaning.   [See *Maze; Labyrinth; Alpona*]

PATTERN (Sweden)

Skarva (join) or *Dans pa Skarven*; also *Dans pa Stra* (Dance on Straws). Swedish dances when men are required to dance with great attention to the fragile "floor pattern". These patterns were made with (a) cracks in wooden floors, (b) lines drawn with chalk, (c) straws laid in geometric patterns, (d) crossed clay pipes. They may be compared with dancing over crossed swords (see *Sword Dance**) and the delicate sand patterns used by Nautch girls in North India.
[See *Alpona; Nautch; Rangoli; Sand Tracings*]

PA-U (Hawaii)

The knee-length skirt of the *hula** dancer. Tra-

ditionally made from *ti* leaves, it is only in modern times that raffia has been used, mainly for costumes sold to tourists or for stage performances. For an authentic skirt, mid-ribs of from forty to eighty *ti* leaves (according to hip measurement) are woven on to a waistband of vine, taking about three hours to make. These long, green blades last only three days, so that the tougher raffia is more practical for a costume that has to endure. In old times, *hau* bark, banana fibre, or a fine rush were also used. On ceremonial occasions the *hula* dancer's *pa-u* was of fine *tapa* cloth (made from bark)—a strip several yards long wrapped round the waist, and reaching nearly to the knees. Special chanting accompanied the donning of the *hula* costume.
[See *Hula*, and cp. *Moré*]

PAULITOS, DANÇA DOS (Portugal)
A stick dance performed in Miranda do Douro and neighbouring districts, on the last Sunday in August. Danced by eight or sixteen men (*Pauliteiros*) in front of the church, this is a ritual dance accompanied by drums and bagpipes. The men wear white starched petticoats and skirts, scarves over a shirt, zig-zag stockings and garlanded hats. Each man carries a short stave, and the dance consists of many figures or *llaços*, sticks being struck together in the course of winding in and out of complex patterns. A movement common to all the figures occurs when staves are tucked under arms and, to the clicking of castanets, the dancers move into line while a tune in 6/8 time is played on the pipes. The *Pauliteiros* who dance at Cercio, south of Miranda, have over twenty *llaços* all named after the verses the dancers sing when no instrumentalist is available, e.g., *Carrascal, Senhor Mio, Carmelita, A Verde, O Touro, Enramada, A Lebre, A China, O Caballero, O Mirandum, Vinte Cinco, Volticas, A Puentes, As Aguias, As Bichas*. Miranda de Douro, where the Mirandez dialect, scarcely intelligible to other Portuguese, is spoken, is near the Spanish frontier—hence the use of castanets.

PAVANE—1 (From Greek *Epiphany*)
"Dance of Appearance". 1. The ceremonial "entrance dance" of Italian courts (14th century). 2. The "Appearance" of the New Year King, on Twelfth Night (the Masque of the Year), known in modern Italy as Beffany, the day of giving presents, on January 6th. In Mexico there is *Baile Pifana* on the same date. The attribution to "peacock" from *pavo*, is less accurate than that from *pavi-mento*, the path, way etc., or pavement, *pavimentum*. The duple *Pavane* was often followed by the triple *Galliard*.*   [Cp. *Polonaise*]

PAVAN, PAVANE—2 (French)
(Ital. *Pavana, Paduana*; English, *Pavin, Pavine*.) Court dance of the 16th and 17th centuries. A slow, solemn procession in duple time, used to open a ball; and, in a masque, as an entry for deities, emperors, and kings. In the ballroom, couples moved clockwise usually; two or three times round the room, men on the outside. They sometimes sang as they danced. As a variation they might come up the centre of the room, cast off separately to the other end, and come together again up the middle. The *Pavane* was sometimes danced advancing and retreating, while in the simple *Pavane*, as a set dance, couples danced opposite each other, both couples and partners changing places. In England, the *Pavane* was popular at the courts of Henry VIII and Elizabeth I, and continued to be danced into the reign of James I. Arbeau, in his *Orchésographie** (1588) describes the processional *Pavane* as being suitable for ceremonial occasions. ". . . it serves", he writes, "for the kings, princes

The Dance in the Garden of Pleasure, an incident from *The Romaunt of the Rose*. Toulouse, 15th century (Harleian MS 4425).   FRANCE

and grave noblemen to show themselves on days of solemn festival, with their grand mantles and robes of Parade. And then the queen, princesses and noble ladies accompany them with long trains . . . sometimes borne by damsels. The said pavans are played by hautboys and sackbuts . . .". Popular at early 16th century Italian courts, the first known music for the *Pavane* is in the *Intabolatura de*

Lauto of Petrucci (Venice 1508), where the dance is named *Padoana*, so that some consider the dance to have originated at Padua. The Italian *Passamezzo** was a more lively version of the *Pavane*, while the *Pavaniglia** ("Spanish *Pavane*"), arranged by Cesare Negri at Milan in the 16th century, was an elaborate variation, popular throughout Europe, and particularly in England. Although sometimes described as a simplified *Basse Danse*,* the *Pavane's* immediate ancestor may have been the *Quadernaria*, an Italian court dance slightly quicker than the *Basse Danse* but heavier in its rhythmic accentuation.

PAVANIGLIA (Italy)
Spanish *Pavan* ("Little Pavan"), as arranged at Milan (16th century) by Cesare Negri. The *danza* so named is given by Fabritio Caroso, with this simple title; but Negri, at a later period of development, offers two variations, which he names as *Pavaniglia a la Romana* (apparently as the fashion in Rome), and the other as *Pavaniglia al modo di Milano* (as the slightly different fashion approved in Milano). These dances moved at a livelier pace than the earlier mode of the Processional *Pavane*,* the *Danza del Intrada*, or "appearance", whence the *Pavane* dances derive their name (epiphany), when used for the masque. Here the dance is devised for a couple; in the *Intrada*, the couples follow in through the great door, two by two.
[See *Passomezzo*]

PEACH GARDEN (China)
Is an allusive classical term for any Chinese school of acting and dance. The original Peach Garden was said to be an actual fruit garden, devoted by a famous mandarin to training promising students for the Theatre which he loved. Associated with this term is the name "peach gardeners", in reference to the students. Probably the initial symbolism goes further back than this charming legend; for it is not unknown in Europe when a maid is sometimes described as " a peach". There appear to be other similar names for Chinese schools of acting and dancing.
[See *Rainbow Skirt and Feather Jacket*"]

PEACOCK DANCE (India, Greece, etc.)
Has deep roots in symbolism through the East; but it has nothing to do with *pavane*.* The secret basis can be traced in the usage of the all-pure-white swan, as against the chromatic bird called peacock, with its fantastic tail feathers. The usage in Greek shows the peacock as the symbol of Hera, known as "Argus, of the Hundred Eyes", who could see anywhere and everywhere. This bird depicts the "Soul out-turned", or the concentration of the ego

on sense data, on the outer world. Thus the peacock feather is used as a crest by Krishna in his dance; it is used in royal fans (even in European churches), while it is superstitiously "deemed unlucky" to the ordinary man—because the terrible eyes always see him! On the contrary, the pure Kalahansa (Swan of Time) is divested of all colour, is indifferent to all worldly attractions; and thus becomes the "clear unspotted soul" (among other arcane meanings). The peacock is thus given to display (especially about the mating season), while the white swan is evasive. This bird appears in heraldry (as at Cleves), not the peacock; and these stories wax into legends, such as the pervasive story of The Twelve White Swans (or The Dancing Princesses), held in the power of a highly chromatic magician—sometimes the Rot-Bart (Red-Light or Red-Beard—the colour-displaying Sun-rays) and pursued by a prince of this ordinary world.

"PEARLY BOUQUET"—Gyöngyösbokréta (Hungary)
A folk-dance festival held annually in Budapest around the 20th August. Founded in 1931 by Béla Paulini, who travelled all over Hungary encouraging villagers to preserve their songs and dances, the first festival lasted two days and represented ten villages. By 1937 sixty villages took part, and the festival lasted nearly a fortnight, performances being given twice daily in Budapest's largest theatre. With the object of preserving all branches of Hungarian peasant art, the General Hungarian Bouquet Association was formed in 1934, with Government approval. To maintain a high standard of dancing, small village "Bouquets" invited each other to dance at local festivities, while the larger country towns organised exhibitions of peasant art and displays of dancing, as preliminary rehearsals for the great August "Pearly Bouquet" in Budapest. These gatherings were generally held on the national feast dates—Easter Carnival, Whitsun, First Fruits, feast of Peter and Paul (June 29th), Vintage and Christmas. The August festival, held on the Feast of St. Stephen, is now replaced by the "Day of the New Bread", held on the same date (20th August) to celebrate harvest.

PEEVER (Scots)
Children's dance game, performed usually over hastily chalked lines drawn on stone paving (notorious for ruin of their shoes!). Said to exist in ten or twelve variants in Scotland; two forms in England; and two in France (*Marelle ordinaire* and *Marelle en ronde*), it is the equivalent to the game called "Hop-Scotch". The two English patterns are those (a) on a square or rectangle, with nine inscribed square spaces; and (b) on a spiraline series

of nine steps. Another source indicates twelve modes in France.

PELATO (Portugal)

Pron. *pelotam*. A group, squad, or small company formerly of girls who played with balls (pelota) as as itinerant jugglers (*pelotica*). Their short dress was called *pelote*. Between juggling and dancing, they achieved fame for filching (*pelotiquira*). This occupation had only a distant relation to the Basque court game of *pelota;* but a clerical game, similar to the *pelatao*, was followed ceremonially in churches. Possibly this continued a Greek tradition.

PELELE, LOU (France)

"The Jumping Doll, or Puppet". The most widespread and celebrated dance of Limousine. Of Spanish origin, it is still danced at weddings, and with variations at Berry and Rousillon. Danced in waltz-time, by numerous couples to the hurdy-gurdy and "chabrette", it consists of an *entrée*, eight figures, and *sortie*. Couples enter the dancing space one behind the other, the man holding his partner's right hand at face level. After executing a gliding step, waltz and boston steps, they form into two lines, facing each other. The First and Third Figures are the same. Partners' left and right hands joined, are swung in rhythm; the man pivots his partner clockwise under his right arm; and the movements are repeated to the left. The Second, Sixth and Eighth Figures are an ordinary *Waltz*, while it is from the seventh figure that the dance takes its name. Two couples face each other in a square formation. The two men hold the girls under the arms, their hands on the men's shoulders. They sway rhythmically, then the men lift the girls as high as possible, and after this jump the swaying is repeated. The *Sortie* repeats the *Entrée*. The lifting of the girls by their partners may be a relic of the old custom of elevating a newly appointed king (or other official), done partly (a) "to be seen", and (b) as a trial of good temper. While this elevating was originally on a shield, or on the "lock" of swords, it later turned into tossing the person, or his effigy, into the air. Goya has a picture of the *pélélé* puppet or doll, being tossed from a blanket held by four men.   [Cp. *Corranda; Bal de Corre*]

PELORIA (Hellas)

The splendid Sacrificial Meal offered to Zeus Pelorios in Thessaly, in which dancing slaves were attendants, while their masters (including the king) served the feast. This was the year-end Saturnalian custom, of inversion of duties (like the Roman festival of Kronos. In Crete it was known as *Hermaia* (a terminal). Athenaeus quotes also the *Trophoniads*, as equated with *Idaean Daktyls* and the youthful *Korybantes*, as dancers. At times they were vegetarian feasts; the slaves carried in these foods on splendid dishes, stepping to music.

PENDOZALI (PENTOZALI) (Crete)

Modern dance form of the warrior dance of old Crete; very energetic and working up to a great speed. Performed by men, it begins with a chain moving mainly to the right, the dancers following a leader with hands on each others shoulders and stamping hard on the ground. They may circle in a small space that is itself defensive; or the chain may break into small chains. The leader leaps high, slaps his leather boots as his feet rise behind, turns in a circle in the air, and comes down in rhythm with the often blaring music of saxophone or accordion and drum. He repeats this leap until tired, when the next man follows. Between dances onlookers sing *mandinatha*, rhymed couplets of ten, twelve or fourteen feet; topical, often pungent in comment. The small chains usually re-unite into one when the music is at its fastest, and finish dancing on the spot.

PENNY HOP (England)

Victorian term, usually applied to a rustic or village pastime dancing occasion, for which each person dancing pays one penny to the fiddler. The method was used in small towns, where private dancing parties were arranged at short notice; and admission charged at the door was one penny. Similar was the "Penny Wedding" in Scotland.

PENNY WEDDING (Scotland)

Dances appeared at the nuptials of the lower classes in Scotland. Each guest contributed a coin (in earlier times it was "one silver penny"—hence the traditional name—but later up to five shillings), as a wedding present and recognition. After clearing expenses, the surplus went to purchase household necessities. The dances were popular jigs and reels. Many such events have been painted, as by David Wilkie. The first reel was danced by the bride with her male relatives as guard; after the first couple-dance, by bride and bridegroom. Later was a torch dance, preceding the six-some reel, following which the chief dancers put a silver piece into the musician's "kitty". He was usually a piper, playing with a garter ribbon ornamenting his instrument. The first reel was called *shemit*; and the last dance was *Bab at Bowster* (same as the English *Cushion Dance**). These ceremonies are now rare. The original reel was *reill* or *reyul*—the "regal" or "Lord and Lady's Dance", as the couple were, for the wedding, then "king and queen" and thus royal.

PENTATONIC MUSIC (Five Tone) (Asia)
Has been very widely practised for Dance; it was popular long before the modern arithmetical "chromatic scale" came into use. Much of value to delicate music has been lost with the abandonment of the true Pentatonic Scale; which is not derived from a single chord, by any equal divisions. The supposition that the Pythagorean Monochord is the only basis for string musical scale is inaccurate. Also wrong is the teaching that a scale must be made of equal intervals of a single taut string; or even such a scale "tempered" to lessen dissonance. The Pythagorean school used for their music, the Pentagon. This five-pointed star offers a series of scientifically based modulations of tone. We may compare decimal line measurements with those made on the yard and foot, arithmetically.

PENTATONIC SCALE (Five-unit) (Asia)
In Oriental music, is not originally derived from any arithmetical division of the basic linear unit, though European musicians always endeavour to read the pentatonic intervals in terms of chromatic or arithmetical intervals, as used in the European octave. Because this pentatonic music has its direct reflex in what might be termed pantomime dance, the "irrational" nature of the proportions of intervals demands close analysis and understanding. The "furthest west" approach of this three-dimensional geometry appeared in Greek architecture and sculpture; later it vanished, to be replaced by the Gothic style of design, and the chromatic scale in music. Two modes of music in Java utilise the pentatonic scales; but their original source from strings is obscure; and must probably be traced to Southern India and possibly to Egypt or Babylonia. The gong (orchestras of gongs appear in Bali —the gamelan*) cannot convey a scale from one instrument; a set of gongs must be tuned from some external basis. The pentatonic scales range from South India through Indonesia to China and Japan.

PENTCHAK (Bali, Indonesia)
Rhythmic combat of two men with staves; a stylised mode of semi-military drill or exercise. The word has several slightly different pronunciations (like all words through Indonesia), and is heard as pent-chak; pong-jack; pent-chek; and even ponj-jaq, according to the origin of the speaker and his dialect. The form is important. European ballet had originally some close associations with etiquette du cour, which included fencing and dancing. Pentchak is somewhat like Japanese kendo; mediaeval English single-sticks; or even naval cutlass-drill. The Zen sect of Buddhists at one time utilised some rhythmic exercises, attributing

this source to the mysterious Tao. As with Italian-French fencing and its fleuret, pentchak has its "ornaments", called kembang'an; these are both deceptive and diverting. Men at pentchak use drums, sometimes a flute, usually cymbals; these keep time and rhythm. Like judo, the more subtle modes are kept secret. The advanced mode uses pedangs, imitation or real swords of bamboo or steel; or weapons are discarded, for a turn at wrestling. Speed is not the first essential, but accuracy. Pentchak is one of the rare heights of fine animal rhythm, such as we see in the movements of cats in contest, especially during their spring season. In recent years, a "girls' style" of pentchak has appeared; but this movement is closer to the trance modes than to real rhythmic contest. Pentchak is performed all over Indonesia, being developed along local lines in different places but all following accepted national principles.

Winter Perchten-Spiel (New Year Carnival) at Badgastein, Austria.   AUSTRIA

PERCHTEN (Austria)
A band of male, masked dancers who, in Salzburg and Tyrol regions perform a ritual driving out Winter and welcoming Spring. Taking their name from the mythical old woman, Perchta, Berchta or Percht, who is associated with the twelve days between Christmas and Twelfth Night, they usually

appear on Perchta's day, 6th January, but sometimes on Shrove Tuesday. In two groups, Beautiful and Ugly Perchten, they career through village streets and over fields, stopping to dance before a farm, sometimes entering houses, making a great noise with bells attached to their costumes, their attendants blowing horns, cracking whips, shaking rattles. Usually performing in daylight, in Salzburg Province the Perchten appear, in procession, at night, headed by drummer and torch-bearers, their antics ending at midnight. They are accompanied by Fools, with sausage-shaped rolls, or a swaddled "baby" on a string, with which to strike at women spectators; or by clowns in white with tall pointed hats who sometimes blow ashes and soot at people through a blow-pipe. At St. Johann the Perchten used to carry drawn swords, and were attended by a "man-woman" and followed by masked men in black sheepskins, holding chains. The Ugly Perchten wear hideous masks, long sticks with demon heads, tall pointed caps. In Salzburg Province they are twelve young men in black sheepskins, with hoods of badger-skins and wooden masks with hideous human features, or animals with moveable jaws. All carry bells fixed to broad leather belts. The Beautiful Perchten are sometimes masked. At Linz they wear tall, pointed caps with bells; ribbons and braid adorn both costumes and the long sticks they carry. In Pongau district they wear a large head-dress—a framework nine or ten feet high, weighing forty or fifty pounds, covered with red cloth and silver ornaments. Resting on the shoulders with iron supports, it is too heavy to allow the wearers to dance, merely turning slowly round and round. The Beautiful Perchten of Pinzgau district dress in scarlet, with red shoes and white stockings, and wear straw hats with fan-shaped white feathers.
[See *Schemenlaufen; Nüssler; Röllelibutzen; Narrentreffen; Suruvakary*]

PERCUSSION DANCE

Refers chiefly to the instruments used to give tempo and rhythm. These begin with the drum and gong, extend to cymbals or castanets, even to plain wooden sticks—all of which noise-makers have a long history in association with dance. The human elements of percussive rhythm include (a) the stamping foot, (b) clapping hands, also claps on thighs or on feet; and (c) the staccato call of the voice. Some of these regular rhythms are contributed by the bystanders, along with periodical calls or continued chanting. Percussion is the earliest and simplest mode of all dance rhythm; it continues in the marching soldiers at drill; and in our modern industrial civilisation has extended from the ancient hammer-and-anvil beat of the primitive smith, to the recurrent clank of many machines and wheels.

PERCUSSION IMPLEMENTS (Dancers)

Appear in two distinct categories : (a) those which are carried by the moving dancer; and (b) those which remain with the orchestra or accompaniment. A third similar element is (c) the ancient practice of the spectators, who supply hand-claps; foot-thumps; stick-rapping; finger-snapping; and even syllabic shouts or hissings, enforcing only the main line of rhythm. Dancers may carry : castanets of wood or metal (Spain); finger-cymbals of metal, brass or silver etc. (Egypt, India, and the *Nak-sut* of Morocco), spurs attached to boots (Hungary, Argentina etc.) or small bells, tied to the legs (India, anklets; England, Morris bells); short wooden sticks (Malabar); rattles (S. American *maracca*, or gourd); circular tambour covered with skin, parchment, sometimes with timbrels (Jewish, Egyptian, North African, Gypsy, etc.). Percussion instruments used in a dance orchestra cover a wide range; from metal or wood gongs, xylophone or dulcimer notes; bells or glockenspiel tubes; or the accompanist may use a simple metal triangle, merely to mark time.

PEREHARA (Ceylon)

Annual series of ceremonials, processional and temple, now performed at Kandy. The present form is the result of an amalgamation of older local rituals with later modes of Buddhist (*Mahayana*) rites, evolved for *Pattini* (local Nature goddess); Kataragama and Natha (hill deity), were connected for long with Vishnu, in the South Indian Brahmin faith. In 1775, the King Kirti Sri Rajasinha joined the Hindu cult with that of Buddhism; and included Pattini. He ordered the famous relic, called Sacred Tooth, to be carried along with the god-figures in the popular ceremonial. The *Perehara* is accomplished with much gaiety, singing, and dancing; and a procession of the finest elephants, as well as the rite of *Giribandha* (Circumambulation of the temple, or *Cetiya Pabbata*). The institution of the Buddhist *Sangha* had then ceased; monks became priests. The focal points of dance appear to show a character of sun symbolism.

PERICON (Argentine and Uruguay)

A lively round dance in 3/8 time and steady rhythm. In the Argentine it is a dance of the gauchos of the pampas, performed with a flourish of kerchiefs, to the jingle of spurs and the songs of wandering musicians (*payadores*). The *Pericon nacional*, the national dance of Argentina, is a lively quadrille, for which the figures are called. In Uruguay the *Pericon* was an old round dance,

Kandyan Dance, Ceylon. The "Dance of the Queen" in *Birth of Sinhala*. Danced on a sand foundation.
(Courtesy British Lion.)   CEYLON

forgotten until it was revived in 1889 by a theatrical company in Montevideo, since when it has remained popular. The name, *Pericon*, means literally "a large fan".

PERICOTE (Asturias, N. Spain)
"Little Peter". A courting dance of the Llanes district, taking the usual form of showing off by the man ("Little Peter"), in this case before two girls instead of one. The Music, in 2/4 time, is played on bagpipes (*gaitas*) and drum, the dancers clicking their fingers in rhythm. The ground pattern is interesting. The two women stand opposite each other, the man dancing between and at right angles to them in a figure-of-eight form. As the girls advance towards each other and retire, the loops of their progress interlace with the man's figure-of-eight, forming a love-knot. The steps for the girls are modest and unspectacular, but the man may

use any steps he likes to show his agility, drawing the attention of the women to his skill as he passes between them.

PERIGOURDINE (France)
Village festival dance, showing dialect forms of current *rondelette;* popular in districts of Perigord from 17th century. A few composers began to write suitable tunes, usually in 6/8 time, taken at a quick pace.

PERKHULI (Georgia, USSR)
A traditional male folk-dance, in which one set of dancers is borne on the shoulders of as many more men. Probably it was once an imitation team-fight (such as is done by boys in Europe), when one combatter, borne "piggy-back" endeavours to unseat his rival, mounted in similar fashion. Here it is made into a dance pattern.
[Cp. *Luta* (Portugal)]

PERRAULT (Paris)

Is remembered as the source of many plots for ballets (or other stage shows), the stories issued first in magazine and then in book form, as *Contés de Ma Mére Oyer*. Charles Perrault was born in Paris, January 12th, 1628, and died in 1703. He got his *licenses*, in law (cash down) in 1651. Then he got a government job (1654 to 1664) which, as do many similar jobs in Britain, left ample time for study. He then became an architect (1657), from which effort Colbert made him superintendent of royal buildings. (Clearly, he knew people who knew people, who . . .). Finally, he was elected to the Academy; and thus to Versailles. He helped Lully to a monopoly at the Opera, *adversus* Moliére. Thus after twenty years of service, he withdrew; wrote little comedies; ended his censored *Memoirs*. His leisure gave him time to read *Abbé de Villars* (see *Gabalis, Comte de**), and romance was in the air along with amateur shepherdesses at Versailles. He mocked people who think it a fine thing "to publish old books with a great many notes" — (he should see some academic books on anthropology!) and then, resorting to the *Foire san Martin*, saw dancers and heard many strange tales. Madame de Sevigné knew of them in 1676 — the *Contés* were fashionable before Perrault took hold. In 1694, Moetjens (of La Hague) published a magazine; and Perrault contributed to it. Some stories were printed in verse, in 1695; but in 1696 came *Le Belle au Bois Dormant*; in 1697 *Le Petit Chaperon Rouge* and *Le Barbe Bleu*; then *Le Maistre Chat ou le Chat Botte*, and *Les Fées* with *Cendrillon* and *Riquet la Houppe*, ending with *Le Petit Poucet*, Abbé de Villars wrote appreciations (1699) and the *Histoires et Contes du Temps Passé* began to be copied, everywhere; though a century was to pass before Planché gave them full scope on the London stage. Imitators flourished. Perrault's *Contés* were republished at the Hague in 1742, translated into English with Fokke's illustrations, in 1745. Andrew Lang published (1888) a copy of the French text (with translation) with admirable discursive notes, as *Popular Tales*.

PESSAH (Phoenician - Hebrew)

Danced in Canaan, by the Twelve tribes, as part of the *Pascha* or Passover spring festival. Similar Greek dances are drawn on Greek clay vases; many dancers had costume with *ruber porrectus*, as Horace tells us. *Pesselim* with *Masakah* were the chief symbols (*Ency. Biblica.* 2148) similar to the Roman Lares and Penates, used as figures in the domicile. The whole festival was in one aspect phallic, and in the other agricultural. The cloak or ephod (as worn by David in his "Dance by the Arche"), made in scarlet and gold, was the main garment. *Hosea. iii*, 4, affirms that *Ephod, Teraphim** and *Massebah* were essential to these religious rites.

PETENERAS (Spain)

A couple dance of Andalusia, developed from the *Seguidillas Sevillanas*, and called *Peteneras* after a flamenco singer. A typical step includes the *flores*, familiar in Andalusian dancing, in which the free leg is lifted and twisted before setting down again. The dance became known in Cuba, where it received some African characteristics, and the *Peteneras* rhythm became incorporated in the Cuban *Guaracha*.* In Mexico, *Peteneras Zapoteca* is danced in 6/8 time, to Spanish guitar music.

PETRONELLA (Scottish Country Dance)

Described as a favourite in the nineteenth century; and notable for featuring the "Diamond Figure".

PETRUSHKA (Russia)

Is the traditional leading puppet of the Northern Slavs, who acts and dances, chiefly in satirical comedies, reflecting on the incompetence of *tchinovniki*, officials of the state. The name denotes "Little Peter"; but we must not assume that he is Holy Peter, that same mythic entity who took over the functions of Janus in Rome, with his two doors and two keys. His name is *Petrushka* (not *Petr* "ouch" *ka*, as it is so poorly rendered in English from second-hand French forms) and he was unfairly treated by Benois in the famous ballet, except in the fact that he can't be killed. Petrushka lives in many peasant legends; some could be told only by Gogol; but he turned up in every Fair, from Kiev or Moscow to Nizhni-Novgorod. There he danced and mimed in the booths; much as his fellow travellers did in London in May Fair or Southwark; or in the Pincio in Rome, or the Piazza san Marco in Venezia. Petrushka is the eternal clown, whose misfortunes (except in this one-act *Scenes Burlesque* of the Russian Ballet), turned out right in the end, long before the birth of that depressing eunuch, The Average Man.

PHALLIC DANCE — 1

Common to all early religious tribal gatherings through the world, phallic dances can be discerned under numerous modern names, customs and implements; and yet are not necessarily to be confused with the "wild orgies" automatically denounced by the "unco guid" who would still retail legends of Ye Fertile Gooseberry Bush (19th Century). These dances were intimately connected with orderly ritual, and the annual "marriage market" or "bride fair", which developed in the peaceful relations between early small communities. The frequent and unthinking reference of all such clan ceremonies to "fertility dance" alleged to be done "to make the corn grow", is chiefly repetition of misunderstood traditions of what is summarily termed "Animism", but which are in fact, remainders of the pre-historic comprehension of the dynamic powers of Nature. The dance forms were attempts to realise, in action, the reflexes of these vast natural rhythms. We have now, in the main, only the ends of such traditions; often deformed and frequently misunderstood; none of them should be examined superficially or judged hastily. In the Hellenic Mysteries of Eleusis, these facts were better understood. In the Greater Mysteries (reserved for the competent), the facts of material nature were used as potent symbols for teaching the principles of immaterial nature. In the solemn words of Plotinus, it was realised that the whole Kosmos was not only a dance of perfection, but that in the relevance of the sacred Dance of Shiva, it was also a universal phallic dance of creation; or, in the christian legend a "heavenly marriage". Only by clear cognisance of these allied mythic factors, can we analyse and classify the many traditional ceremonies; discern their masterly design and follow their gradual fading into modern customs of popular ignorance. These dances have existed in all religious communities in the early period of nations. Numerous traditional modes still exist; many of them semi-obsolete as ritual; and revised as to dance. Frazer mentions many in his *Golden Bough*, usually under the title of "Fertility Dance", but these rituals that connect agriculture with homoculture are numerous. Blood offerings and substitute offerings (of milk, honey, special cakes or bread etc.) often accompany these rites for increase of crops and children. Fertility dance and phallic dance appear in the three primal technical modes: the ring, square, and processional. Some of them developed into peasant "Marriage Market Dances", and others endured as secret rituals with symbolic associations. In Assyria, one of the god-priest's duties was the fertilisation of date trees (a basic need in its culture), which is portrayed on sculptures (some in British Museum), while another duty was the Puberty Initiation (instrument shown in British Museum *Guide to Babylonian and Assyrian Antiquities* (1908, p. 146). Egypt had regular phallic dance rites, with the most primitive gods: Bez or Bess, and Min with A-Mena (some statuettes may be found in British Museum galleries). The traditional duty of the king-priest to fertilise women endured through many centuries, until relatively recent times; when the feudatory ritual of *jus prima noctae* was ended, though the privileged men of some families claim "morganatic" wives. India has had widespread systems of sex-worship;

they existed through Asia (especially in Japan), but also in Europe, for which the reader may consult J. B. Hannay's lucid work: *Rise, Decline and Fall of Roman Religion* (Religious Evolution Research Society. London 1925)—also G. Roheim's book *Animism, Magic and the Divine King* (Kegan Paul, London 1930)—psychoanalysis, somewhat over-emphasised views. In Greece, the Lesser Mysteries (Youth initiations) preceded the Greater Mysteries (of Regeneration), which matched broadly the Older Testamentum and the Newer Testamentum; as phallic ritual and far harder symbolic ritual that referred to the Mind (or Soul).

PHALLIC DANCE—2 (Japan)
Memorial dances, with dual phallic significance, were performed in Japan to the end of the 19th century. At Nikko is the Futara-san Shrine (Shinto) where a ritual dance by one girl is performed daily; but for the Futara San-Jinsha Festival (April 17th) a full company dances. There is a shrine Tosho-gu (Iyeashu) rebuilt 1624-36. Passing through the famous Yomei-mon (the feminine symbol) Gateway, the visitor, doffing hat *and* shoes *and* overcoat, can find the Dance Hall. There is also a well-known carved panel of the familiar "Three Monkeys". Near the Toshu-gu stands the Sacred Sorinto—a huge phallic column of copper, forty-four feet high and twelve feet round. The dancers at Shimonoseki hold a great memorial festival (April 23-24-25 annually) at the Akamagu Shrine, called Senta-sai. Says the tourist bureau, "The gorgeous procession of the local courtesans is the chief attraction of the occasion". The mediaeval processions of similar ladies, from the Great Yoshiwara in Tokio, are no longer seen going through the city; but they celebrate in their own quarter.

PHALLIC RITUAL DANCES
Depend on the interaction of homoculture and agriculture, dominated by the contest of human sex life. The masculine is influenced by solar rhythms; the feminine by lunar modes; and, as with the calendar, complete balance is rare. These facts indicate one of the sources of bygone "astrological" ritual dance—lost after the Mediaeval period of "magic circles" and the hora-scopes inherited from Greece and Rome. In ancient periods, when "Mother-Right" ruled the tribes, one symbol predominated, now known in the *Alle Monde* with a basic oval form; and when "Father Right" came to control, the male symbol replaced the ovoid (as the Roman remains, now in Napoli, prove fully). Less physiological usage began to devise "Mysteries" (as at Eleusis) of Generation and Regeneration; while later the church symbols of Western

Europe alternated or combined doctrines and rituals.

PHANSIGARS (Bengal)

Were the semi-religious sect, worshippers of Bhowanee (Kali, goddess of destruction) in 16th to 18th century. Originating in the Mughal capitals of Delhi and Agra, being provoked by excessive tax demands, they began as a joint Moslem-Hindu secret society, having the political aim of liquidating heavy-handed revenue officials. In this natural retort, they achieved considerable success. They gained their basic information on (a) location and direction of tax accumulations, and (b) description of officials and their guards, from *tuwaifs** or *nautch girls*, who being in contact with such officials at parties, were able to obtain facts. Though it is possible that in their early days, the *phansigars* (stranglers) permitted the dancing girls to attend some rites, the actual initiation (with the Sacred Pick Axe) was limited to men, though by no means hereditary. Like the sacerdotal officials of the Holy Inquisition at Goa, the Thugs did not shed blood, which in view of the usual "sacrifice of blood" to Kali is in itself surprising. The chosen official was strangled in silence with a sacred *ramal* (silk kerchief) as swiftly as an official hanging at Pentonville. Later the sect extended its operations from officials to the merchants : and waylaid caravans of commodities; and so degenerated (as did the ancient monks) from members of a sect into gangsters. They occupied a village twelve miles north of Calcutta, named Titigarh, as headquarters in Bengal. The family names of Thakkur or Takore and Tagore appear to derive from the group name of Thuggee.[1] Finally, they were eliminated as an organised body by Col. Sleeman (early 19th century) with special police.

[1] *The Confessions of a Thug.* Col. Meadows Taylor. Calcutta, 1837; London, 1839.

PHOENIX (Arabian)

The Newly Born or newly arising One—the prime symbol of the fire worshippers known as Phoenicians—given publicly sometimes (as in coins) as a flourishing Date Palm, erect with a crest of virile foliage and fruit. The mythic or ritual symbol was the "Bird of Heaven," known in China, also, as the *Fo* or *Foh* Bird or Dragon, which was forever consumed in the Fire, yet arose again from its own ashes. The third symbol was revealed in the Mystery Schools as the Secret Phoenix. Later the *Fo-Nix* or *Fo-Niche* was mentioned, as *Niche* or *Nika*, the "Image", and thus entered into Initiation Rituals, as a potent factor. With these rituals were performed Dances of Fire, and Dances of Light or Illumination—the lesser and the greater mysteries;

again symbolised in action by torches, and then small lamps with clear flames.

PHONEY DANCES

Have developed apace with commercialization of Theatre, especially in conjunction with the modern Tourist Industry. New "Festivals" are contrived to attract and to sell to the Traveller. Some become respectable; the Henley Regatta was originally a trade effort. During the Middle Ages, the Tourism was called Pilgrimage; at Canterbury, the date of the demise of Thomas a Becket was changed from the authentic day of despatch to the summer, as Pilgrims would not attend in mid-winter. The manufacture of "Holy Relics" is indicated by Chaucer, who was a reporter of the delights of travel. Connected with Mediaeval Fairs and Festivals, we find all sorts of "attractions" from two-headed mermaids to rope dancers, whose agility was real enough; but in modern time the Phoney Dance has seen peculiar styles. In the USA, the Trade Fairs, and then the Burlesques offered "Oriental Dances" of a strange character. One dancer, who worked out the "Dance of Isis" and "Dance of Krishna-Radha" from imagination, was surprised on later visiting India, to see real oriental dances— some quite good. This followed the mediaeval tradition; even Dürer drew a rhinoceros he never saw, from vivid description. We must distinguish between the Phoney Dance which pretends to offer (a) a genuine foreign dancer, (b) a genuine foreign style of dancing, and (c) a genuine portrayal of a foreign theme. We have seen a "Hindu Dance Company" in which one dancer out of nine was, in fact, an Indian; but he was a Moslem, not Hindu. We have seen "Greek Dances" done entirely from imitated poses seen on vases, with no idea of the original meaning (they would be highly shocked sometimes, if they knew it). One such was *Le Dieu Bleu*, an "Indian classical ballet" done by Fokine, whose entire knowledge of Indian dance was obtained from museums. Even genuine Indian dancers have offered dubiously contrived dance (e.g. *Garuda*, or the "Eagle Dance").

PHYLAKES (Greece)

A watchman, a guard; an inspector in Athens. From these guards come several traditions associated with ritual and dance. Hebrew temple rituals were "watched" by guards (of Levites appointed for the task) as "men entrusted". As signals, they wore the beaded armlets and brow circlets (familiar still in Arab-Semitic dress over the *haik* on the brow), which gave them the Greek title *phylactery*. The badge has no original religious significance. The *phylakes* were satirised (they may be seen in caricature on many a Greek vase), for as inspectors they were not regarded with sympathy), but their name is conserved as the Watchmen of the New Year Festival. Penetrating into Western Europe, the name of the guards, *phylakes*, was diminished to "fullakies", and then fools; their watch became the "Feast of Fools". (Also *phalankies*). The *phylarchos* was their chief. They filled much the same town function as the Saxon *waits* or *wyghtes* (turned to witches). Their drill included the Spartan military dances.

PICKELHERRINGE (Holland)
The typical "boy of the town" — the dancing, singing buffoon in the Netherlands, alike in the market place or in the puppet show. *Pickelherringe* is the direct equivalent of the German *Hans-Würst*, the Russian *Petrushka*,* or the French *Marian* or English *Punch*. In England also, a character called *Pickleherring* is one of the six sons who behead their father with the "lock" of swords in the Revesby Mummers Play.

PICOULET (Switzerland)
A singing-dance which may have had ritual origins, now little more than a children's game. Popular among young and old at local dances, the dancers skip round in a ring, holding hands. It is a sort of mimed "Follow My Leader", with cumulative effect, in the manner of the farmyard song where a new animal sound is added with each verse. The dancers must follow exactly the gestures of the leader in the centre of the circle. His gestures follow a set order, being made first with fingers, then hands, fists, elbow, feet and head. Between each mimed example, the circle skips round, the leader adding a new gesture each time.

PIFFERERI, Danza del (Italy)
In the traditional *campagna* Italian New Year Masque, there were simple peasant dances, accompanied by tabors and bagpipes (hence their name — "pipers"), who sang *caroles* and sometimes acted in little plays or sketches. They reside during the year in the *Campagna* round Rome, and in Calabria, retaining their primitive costume when they make their annual visits to the towns. They end their Twelve Days Festival with *Beffani* (Epiphany), when presents are exchanged. Many of them were used as models by eminent painters (especially in the *bottegas* of Bologna), such as Annibale Carraci. One of their dances is the *Tarantella;** another was the *Romanesca*.*

"PIGUE, PIGUE" (Upper Amazon River, Brazil)
A women's dance of the Jivaro Indians, performed to celebrate the killing of an enemy witch-doctor.

Women emerge from the communal hut, wearing only a white loin-cloth. Hand in hand, in a line, they face the ring of supporting posts outside the hut, against which the men lean. At a signal from the oldest woman, they leap into the air together. Their feet strike the earth in rapid rhythm, dancing and chanting *"Pigue! Pigue!"* (meaning "struck down") — and so they dance all night, urged on by the men if they shew weakness. The purpose of the dance is to deter any demons (*iguanchi*) from invading the hut, while in another, distant hut the shrinking of the witch doctor's head proceeds. This ritual has its own ceremonial dance of invocation, *Kongo-pi.**   [See *Kongo-pi; Neymartin*]

PILATUS, Domus (Latin)
"House of Players". The root term *Pila* equals "Ball" and develops into many variants, as does ball-ballad-ballet, etc. The plautus (or Palatus) was a kind of chamberlain, who controlled the plays of the King of the Year (familiar in the Reveles of Dionysus). When the "ball" is seen as the symbol of earth, we can grasp the association of *pila* with the ritual; it remains in the coronation "orb", but is now static; the moving ball is used in the games (cp. *Hiero-gamos;* sacred wedding; the spectacle or sport that followed a solemn ritual). The term grows to : applaud, laud, ludus, interludus, lude, or lute (or lyra), and Plautus (the official manager of the *Plaue* or Play). In and out of the "church", ritual and game and proto-drama continued. The tenacity of tradition appears in the *Domo Pilatus*, numerous in Latinised countries; in Seville, in Barcelona, in Granada (now *Corte di Naracion* or *Niranges*), called House of Pilate, thus referring to a non-existent personage, in this connection. The ball game continues with the Basque people as *pelota;* it had court contact with Charlemagne (*Carolus Magnus*) and his twelve Paladins (in England, Palatine) of the current ritual mode. It had come a long way from the *paludumentium* and *pileus* garb. Ritual dances, usually of serious but rhythmic character (being accompanied by measured chanting) marked these ceremonies. The building became known as palace (as do music halls now), or *palazzo*, or *palais* (dance). This tradition of function related to place was so strong that no "Saint Pilatus" has emerged; but we may ask if the Paulus (who resigned his position as Saulus (*Salii*), was one such person; known variously as Paolo, Pablo, Pavel etc.? He became domo-major; chambre-layen; kellner; and "master of revels".

PILER-LAN (Brittany, France)
Fr. *Pileur d'ajoncs* — "gorse crusher". An old Breton dance, still performed in the Léon district, for any

number of couples, in lively 4/4 time. Danced either in straight lines or in a wide circle turning clockwise, partners face each other. Steps for the men, although not heavy, are lightly stamped, reminiscent of treading the furze before giving it to the animals to eat. The dance is accompanied by a song about the rest and good meal which await the dancers when they have done their work of crushing the year's supply of gorse; modestly claiming to be the best dancers in their province, and to sing so well that they need no bagpipes. A similar term *pileur-lin* applies to flax-crushing, done over a paved floor to prepare linen.

PILLI YAKUN NATIMA (Ceylon)
A magical ritual of resuscitation, by which a magician (*kapurala*) secures for his service a sub-human slave. The process is broadly parallel with that of the Zombie ritual used in Hayti in the *Voodoo* magic, where a mesmerised human is subjected to drug treatment that deadens the will. The "possession" here implied is not that of some erratic natural entity, but a projection of the magician himself, combined with a specialised demon—a method called *avesaya* or *bandanaya*. Carefully selected time and place are the first essentials.

"In preparing *Pili*, the most dreaded Sinhalese magic, a dead body is wanted . . . is submitted during preparatory ceremony (the first circle dance) to a special operation called *jivama*, i.e., restoring of its life . . . a demon is introduced . . . becomes bodily receptacle of the demon, the body is restored to life and obeys the sorcerer; and according to his orders, inflicts disease, kills his enemies, destroys crops etc."[1]

This operation of *kora pilli roga* (magic) uses also diagrams and waxen figures; along with *Sitimaya* (magical geometrical designs or patterns) of Tantrika origin. These are used as the sand patterns,* for the ground course of the ring or square dances. For full understanding of this process, it is necessary to study all aspects of *Mana*,* as the manipulation, transfer, and concentration of *quanta*,* or the natural energies of animal and plant life; while some comprehension of modern electro-mechanical engineering is useful in grasping the forms and functions of mineral magnetism. "It gives", reports Dr. Pertold (a close student of Sinhalese magical dance), "much trouble to the plain man of a Sinhalese village to explain his ideas to an inquisitive European". The native imagery of his mind has grown on a basis different from that of the sceptical city-dweller, where "demons" are now germs and microbes; and instead of holy water he uses equally holy disinfectant, but gives pills and ointments still, constructed from obscure Latin spells

that are called prescriptions, and kept very secret. [See *Spell of Seven Steps*]
[1] *Archiv Orientalni* (Praha) No. 2 (p. 319) June 1929.

PIN MEN
As Dance symbols, are small "basic drawings" of slight reference to human shape; but made significant of human place, position, gesture, and motion in relation to the dance. Efforts have been made to incorporate these semi-pictographs into dance notation systems. The most effective known traditional use has been the Amerindian "letters" or notices, or records; some done for records of dance-songs (as among the Dakota Indians).[1] Wide knowledge of tribal customs, dress and domains, is considered necessary for due interpretation; but this is true of any dance system. Every Indian draws these pictographs in the same manner. They may be compared usefully with heraldic animals or birds; and "Supporters" in Europe.
[1] "Pictographs of North American Indians". Carrick Mallery *Fourth Annual Report;* Bureau of Ethnology. 1886 (Reference in A. C. Haddon's *Evolution in Art.* 1895).

PIPE AND TABOR (Mediaeval England)
Two simple instruments, used to accompany many of the dance movements of village minstrels or gleemen. The tabor, used for percussion, marks the basic beat, while the pipe or flute allows an expert player to suggest rhythm, by means of the musical phrase. The unaccompanied bagpipe omits the beat, since the drone is continuous; but the beat is filled by the marching feet of men, while phrases are carried not in their movement but their song. Hence two bagpipes are required to fill the same needs. This pairing of percussion and phrase occurs all over the world. Yet in modernist Irish dance, the movement phrase disappears, leaving a heightened sense of percussion in foot movement.

PIPER (England)
Tom Piper is the traditional name for the player of the pipe and tabour accompaniment to the Morris Dance. He also received the money collected for performances, acting as treasurer—hence the phrase "Who's to pay the piper?" and the answer "He who pays the piper, called the tune!" There is an older Tom Piper, mentioned by Drayton the poet (16th century) who seems to have been a *raconteur;* possibly as the reciter of the "Tale of Sant George" :

"Tom Piper is gone out, and mirth bewailes
He never will come in to tell us tales".

The player plays the pipe with the fingers of the left hand and beats the tabour, slung under his left arm, with a stick held in the right hand. In Provence, players of the three-holed pipe and drum are called the *Tambourinaires*.

PIROUETTE

From Mediaeval French *pirouelle*, or *pieretta*, the "Pier that wheels" in a company of twelve (as, for example, Piers or peers of Charlemagne). Ritual in dance requiring revolutions (a) *sur place*, or (b) in making progress through a circle. Both modes of this dance are used in ballet as a routine, rarely as a displayed dance form. The form is a complete spinning turn of the body; most often done *sur place*. To gain speed, the leg is extended — the dance comes close to *fouetté* (whip thrust), and often the female dancer is supported during a pirouette by a partner. Mostly they are meaningless, except as feats of technical brilliance, The "Whirling Dervishes" of the Mevlevi Moslem sect (at Karouan and other places) far exceed any ballet dancer; since they circle, spinning like silent tops, for an hour or more without ceasing, in a state of unnaturally composed calm, as a religious exercise.   [See *Dervish Dance*]

PLANCTUS KAROLI (Latinised term)

Equivalent to Lamentation, or Song of Mourning, variously used in ritual; chanted sometimes as a slow dance round a bier. This *Incipit Plancty Karoli* became in Ireland a secular dance mode, known as *Planxty*,* in addition to the clerical modes; and in France was included in the *Chansons de Quête* (songs of the choral deacons).
[See *Planxty; Lamento*]

PLANE FIGURES

Governed each great series of Sacred Ritual Dances. The Pythagorean Pentagon/Pentacle ruled both dance and music — the pentatonic scale, as used by many Greeks. The Ellipse supplied Egypt with the *Sennen* or oval (cartouche) inside of which were laid the two axes, making the "cross" which was taken over by the *Khrestianoi* at Alexandria and Antioch. The Square was used by the Stoics (or Stoichion) as "the square Men" — they founded the Trajan alphabet on it and the circle. The Heptagon was used by the Spanish Jews, got from Islamic sources, to contain the "Holy Name". Both Square and Pentagon have been used later by Freemasons; while the Oval was shewn as the symbol *Vesica Pisces* by Gothic builders when they used the Diamond (from Dionysus Temple, Athens) as the rule of building style. All of these forms were used in dance ritual. The cross form was picked up, from the *Sennen*, in the robe adopted by the presbyter; and today appears on episcopal uniform attire —

its two halves are "cope" and "drag". The Chinese symbol form of Yang-Yin is more dynamic, in its duality. Plane figure symbols gave basic dance forms; the circle gives kolo or khoro, as "round dance" which, at rare intervals, reveals a spiraline change. Egyptian designs repeat the straight or circle pattern, now called meander, because that river moves in wavy pattern. The Egyptian standard was a watch-spring double spiral — the dancer moving in and then out. The great Gothic spiral — as laid into some French church floors — was used for the ritual dance of "Way to Jerusalem".* The square with two sides emphasized was the elementary "contest" pattern — used for ritual combats — Black versus White, Winter versus Summer, Men versus Girls in village wedding dance form; and, more static, as the "running of gauntlet" for the bridal pair on leaving the church; the schoolboy entrance rite.

PLANIPEDES (Greek and Latin popular term)

Literally, "the flat-feet" (as modern police are called "flatties") so-called because these *mimoi* did not use the *cothurnus* (high heels) or *buskins*, to make their height more, or to seem important and pompous. Doubtless they found, in practice, that bare feet or soft leather sandals gave them more facility in their dance, than the hard iron-shod leather, similar to the sandals of the soldiers; and made less noise.

PLANXTY, or Lament (Gaelic — *Planxtae*; Provencal — *Planh*)

An ancient Celtic dance of the Irish and Welsh harpers. In 6/8 time, the music possessed phrases with an unequal number of bars, but the character of the dance was apparently not as mournful as it sounds, since in Bunting's *Ancient Music of Ireland*[1] several examples are described as "brisk" or "lively". These harp airs, arranged for piano include *Planxty Charles Coote* "very quick and sprightly"; *Planxty Burk* — "very quick" in 12/8 time; while *Miss Burk's Planxty* was to be played "gracefully and distinctly". Two others are given — *Planxty Hugh O'Donnell* and *Planxty Toby Peyton*, both in 6/8 time and described as "quick", "brisk and lively". All the *Planxty* tunes in this book are by Carolan.
[See *Lamento; Planctus Karoly*]
[1] *The Ancient Music of Ireland*. Edward Bunting. Dublin, 1840.

PLASTIQUE POSES (England, France)

A theatre display of "near-dance", for which Regulations of the London County Council (Fire Brigade Department) strictly forbid movement. This injunction follows those traditional in sentry or Whitehall duty for regiments of Guards (who contrive immobility, even on horseback, much to the admiration of feminine visitors), and the more easily secured endurance of the ladies of Madame Tussaud's famous Exhibition, who are present not in *puris naturalibus* (nor are the Guards), but in comely resemblance of modelled and tinted wax. *Les Poses Plastiques* developed from charades. Scientists of the 19th century made the great discovery (despite the crinoline used by Victoria to conceal her bandy legs or the kilt worn by John Brown to expose his tanned limbs) that "Woman Had Legs". From then on, as with the discovery of Aniline Dye, the discovery was commercialized, chiefly in Music-hall shows; then once more in ballet at the opera. Seaside costumes were still voluminous (good for the cotton trade), and no American coastguards went on inspection with tape measures. The female form was to be revealed —beyond the feeble limits of antique statuary or French Salon paintings. As with the dyes, Teutonic enterprise leaped in, and they had *Die Akt Plastik*. This developed into sun-bathing and *La Nude*— dancing in the fields, in summer camps and in winter halls; and thus breaking the city market for artistic views of slender ladies. Paris was taken at great disadvantage; the principal industries being dress-making, and un-dress-taking, traditional at *La Folies Bergéres* since the court vacations (at Sceaux and the rest), but Paris was not hindered by any L.C.C., and Gallic plastique never stiffened into poses. Despite all this, the system goes on within English art schools, under the innocent title of "Life Class".

PLAYFORD DANCES (England)
Term used by modern folk-dance enthusiasts, to denote the groups of "dancing-master" sophistications, exploited first by John Playford from 1650. After the Commonwealth gave way to the "Restoration", town life settled down again to enjoyment. This fact was perceived by John Playford, printer and publisher, of the Inner Temple, London. He collected his first batch of popular dances (omitting the parodies and more scurrilous versions) into his original book, *The English Dancing Master.** This title sufficiently emphasises the fact guiding his selection: he wanted to sell his book; and he printed only the townee versions, established in favour, and then fashionable. Many visitors took dances and books away with them, when his first collection appeared (with simple music) in 1651. Some had been brought from country towns; but many were "new dances" devised by ambitious dancing masters—much as versions of foxtrot and rumba are made now—such as *Mr. Draper's Saraband*. These Playford "Town dances" contrasted with court dances and Morris dances; but from church came the term *contra-dance** (choral form implied). Playford published six further editions (constantly amplified), and his son, Henry, added five more; his successor John Young completed the long run with a final five editions, with some 500 dances in all. John Playford incidentally records, in his publication, a parallel to the work of Molière in France: the advance of bourgeois sentiment against that of the court. The culmination of revolution in France was later than Cromwell's revolt in England, by a century; but England was in advance in the economic change—from agriculture and its trade (as in wool) there was the great change over to handicraft and industrial production. The social centre shifted, from the court and its taxes to the trader and his profits—and so the fashion for dance began, almost as a reaction against the Puritans, in the midst of the 17th century. The "country dances" came to town with the country merchants and their dames; and religious church dances and plays had ended; the court dances waned, after Charles I lost his "divine right". Thus the Playford dances began the essentially modernist shift of dance fashion for town use (under the sway of the dancing master) for the bourgeois citizens; while Morris and Sword dances continued in the distant villages, still attached to festival dates. The Inns of Court lost their Masques; these rituals returned in the Masquerade and Masked Ball—also bourgeois modes.
[See *The English Dancing Master*. Reprinted 1945. Kellom Tomlinson]

PLAYING CARDS
Carry a wealth of information on Mediaeval French Dance-Mime legends, of the Trouvere or Troubadour schools (especially of Provence), and the Italian esoteric legends (especially those prompted by Picus of Mirandola). Their other presentation remains in the much-edited words of the *Chansons de Gestes*. The same heroes and kings are named in the *Legendes*, and on the Cards. The reason is that the Cards were first devised to give out roles, in mime plays, acted and danced. There were three main series of the *Chansons*: Those of Charlemagne, of Alexander, and Arthur, all fostered by the system of Chevallerie. The stories of "Huon of Bordeaux" (John or Juan de Bordeaux) carry on the same series, though many have been lost. These "card characters" are still continued in some Basque Dance-Mimes, given as traditional plays. On the other side, the clerics had devised their propaganda Miracle Plays, also in three cycles: the Noël series; ending with the Epiphani (Sages and Shepherds— Magi and Mutton); the Esther series or Paschal plays, with *Trois Maries* and a *Ressurectio*, ending

with the Whetsun Gala; and those which tried to displace the Midsummer Games of Juan. With these went the *Book of Hours*. Both antagonists used the *Arc** (Joan of Arc=Juno, or *La Vierge*, the Dark Lady), and the sacred *Arbre* (Tree of Jesse), as well as the various Bright Swords, starting from the *Escu-L'Arbre* (done by the Duc d'Aubre). They also used *Jean de Vigne* (John with the Vine, replacing Bacchus), in various modes, from Bacchus to Santa-Martine (Martini). While the Tree of Jesse was carved and painted in many a church, the Arc never was, despite the sacerdotal French title of *Arc-Eveque* as the chief bishop or minister. These legends of *La Chevallerie* were painted on the rolls or roles; then printed by woodcuts on thousands of cards for popular usage, for the Noëlle Play. Many remaining cards (few indeed of those first printed) show the figures of the various heroes; and their ladies or queens. The Double-Arc—or *Vesica Pisces* has another meaning —it was carved over many church porches.

PLEROMA (Babylon, Greek)

Is a term variously adopted by later writers of scripts; into which one strange error has entered. The word is translated as "Book of Stone", and thus has confused scholars. The original meaning is *Script on Stone*, which makes some difference. The Mosaic reference is to Tables of Stone, but the original is Tables ON Stone. Egypt reveals hundreds of these carven inscriptions and pictures. They belong to ritual ceremonial and dance : they indicate movement *over* the stone paving; which elucidated the meanings of symbol forms, especially that of the Zodiac discovered and devised by these Chaldaean masters of astronomy. Merged with the frequent reference to *Pleroma* or *Palé-Roma*, we find the misconstrued Foundation Stone read as "corner-stone". This *Pinnah* stone, in fact, received the builder's pin or peg; the upright metal rod, whence he stretched his Measuring Cord, to lay out the foundations of the Temple; or any great building; to plan its site in the full-scale model. The term is thus *kernel-stone*, not corner-stone : and it is the primary stone in the "writing of the book on stone", repeated with the diagrams incised into the Assyrian alabaster slabs, inlaid with blue and gold. Readers should themselves make experiments, using *solely* a knotted cord. Take a cord of twelve divisions with thirteen knots (one at each end, having a small pencil or scriber-loop, for marking), in length about the stretch of the extended arms (some five feet or so). Make true circles; then all five plane figures : triangle to hexagon. This teaches something of ancient prac-

tical geometry : the ritual dancers moved along such lines, though drawn on a larger scale. [Cp. *Sulvasutras*; *Schem-ha-Phorasch*]

PLOUGHMAN'S FESTIVALS (England)

Tusser in his work *Five Hundred Points of Husbandry*, tells of the six regular Feasts of the Ploughman. Most are now vanished; all have changed. The six days of this agricultural ritual were : (1) Plough Monday; (2) Shrove Tuesday; (3) Sheep Shearing Wednesday; (4) Wake Day; (5) Harvest Home; and (6) Seedcake—end of Sowing. For each of these rites (inherited chiefly from the work of the Roman year) there was a rite, a chant, and a simple dance, all featuring the principal implement used in each successive agricultural operation. Of all six Feasts, that of the Fool Plough, on Plow Monday, is still observed with rural song and dance, in which Bessy is seen, even with a sort of *Sword* or *Baton Dance*; while the Harvest Home was one of the parents of the *Barn Dance*,* preceded by a processional as the "Kern Baby" (the last sheaf) was borne home from the fields. This, with Shrove Tuesday, remains connected with church ritual, as a Harvest Festival. Shrove has nothing to do with "shriving", or "confessing", but is far older; and wider in scope. As the term Shrove-*tide* implies, it is seasonal, not clerical. Separate are (a) the village rituals, and (b) the town rituals, from (c) the church rituals, all with processional movements and dances.

PLUGGE DANSE (Netherlands)

Traditional peasant dance, performed at the *Kermesse*, or series of annual festivals, held as markets in various towns. The form follows that of the *Fandango*,* possibly it was influenced by the Spanish invasion.

PLUMAS, DANZA DE LAS (Mexico)

"Plume Dance" of the Zapotec and Mixtec Indians surviving in the villages of the Oaxaca Valley. One date for its performance is the 8th December, when dancers from Zaachila usually dance in its honour of Our Lady of Juquila. Although often performed alone, the *Danza de las Plumas* is part of a dance-play, *La Conquista*,* which takes place at saints day fiestas in the states of Jalisco and Oaxaca, when the dancers, in tall feather crowns, take the parts of Montezuma and his court. Holding gourd rattles they dance rapidly in a crouched position, with bent knees, yet as they dip and turn the plumes on their heads never touch. These huge head-dresses are made of tall feathers in brilliant colours, mounted on a band decorated with mirrors. In Aztec Mexico feathers were much used for ceremonial head-dresses and shields, and whole

cloaks were skilfully woven of them in "feather-mosaic" patterns. The metallic green of the Quetzal or Trogon bird (Quetzalcoatl – "Feathered Serpent" – was God of Learning), and the multi-coloured plumage of Parrots gave the featherwork craftsmen rich colours with which to work. The tradition survived into this century.
[See *Aztec Dance*; *La Conquista*; *Quetzales*]

POCHETTE (France)
Literally, a "little pocket", in reference to the *viol de pochette*, a small instrument (similar to the English *kit*), used by French dancing masters during 17th - 18th century, mostly for "private lessons to the gentry" since its tone was light and small.

POILATI (Orokolo Bay, Papua)
Are clowns who come in pairs from each village to the village celebrating the long initiation cycle, *Hevehe*.* Arriving in advance of the *eharo** and *idihi vira* dancers (see *Yahe**), who later take part in the festivities, they are traditional characters belonging to this particular stage of the *Hevehe* cycle – (fixing sago-leaf over-mantles to the ceremonial *hevehe* dance masks, and fitting a door to the new *eravo*, or men's lodge). Before sunrise the first pair of *poilati* arrive along the beach. Dressed from head to foot in sago-leaf dyed red and yellow, their faces hidden behind a small mask with staring eyes and crooked mouth, decorated with coloured spots. they wear at wrist, knee and ankle *harau* rattles filled with seeds, and carry full-size bow and arrows. They first perform before the *eravo*. Revolving face to face, they quickly turn and revolve back to back, all the time leaning to one side as though about to fall over. After repeating this dance once or twice, they sharply twang their bows and, having been given food, set off to repeat the performance before one house after another. Pairs of *poilati* from other villages quickly follow, perform their dance, and receive food, with which they retire to the forest, where the other dancers are encamped before making their entry into the village. The clowns may receive their name from their function, *poi* meaning "sago," and the whole word, *poilati*, possibly meaning "sago-fetchers". [See *Hevehe*; *Yahe*; *Eharo*]

POISSON D'AVRIL (France)
Formerly a traditional initiation preliminary, in which a youthful candidate as a monk was tormented by his older fellows, as an "April Fish". At one time this was a dance of buffetting, which became varied into the "fool's errand" (*Foule errante?*), and so passed into the recently known English practice of more or less cruel joking on the first day of April, thus labelled All Fool's Day

(*Jour des Folies*). Here the dance disappeared; it survives only in the children's game of *Bouffant*, or "Blind Man's Buff", which in France continued as a parallel version of the same ritual – the teasing of the candidate, when blindfolded, or "hoodwinked" by drawing the monk's hood over his head, on first donning the garment. In some English public schools, a similar "new boys" ritual was called "running the gauntlet", as the youth was sent down an alley of older boys armed with knotted cords or kerchieves, with which they aimed blows at him. This mediaeval ceremony has passed in and out of the realms of youthful custom, of dance form, and of school form; then of games detached from meaning. Probably the earlier name was *Poisson d'Avril*, or the "Monks' Fish," meaning the new candidate; attracted, caught, and drawn into their net, for the monastery. (*Les Poissons*=*Pisces* =*Vesica Pisces*. The "fool" is in French, *sot* or *sotte* – another term derived from a company of players of *sotties*.

POKLADA (Hungary)
Festival of Winter, celebrated mainly in Mohacs district (on Danube) by descendants of Southern Slavs. At "Carnival Time" they dance in processions, ending around a large bonfire, first Sunday of the period. Masks are important; these present the two sides. Another familiar name is *buse*. The Saturnalian transformation is affirmed by inversion of clothes; especially in the children's version, when boys and girls exchange attire. The term *poklada* means a rebirth or renewal. Adults stuff old coats with straw and carry a large carnival horn. Children rattle sticks on tins. Presents are exchanged like Italian *beffana*. Formerly they took a plough, to cut up yards where they were not well received. They seek rewards of cakes, doughnuts, wine and sausage slices.

POLITICAL BALLET
Seeks to present a theme with a definite bias (for or against) some subject accepted as "politics". Strangely enough, the twin topic of "Economics" is rarely cited. The Kurt Jooss arrangement of the old political work *Todtentanz*,* as *The Green Table*, was followed by an anti-Fascist work, *Chronica*. In Russia, we have seen such productions as *Flames of Paris* or *Red Poppy*, with definitely political themes, intended only for home edification. They are no worse, as works of art, for setting forth a current theme; for the sedulously cultivated theory that "art has nothing to do with politics" is cited by the complete ignoramus; or by the wily propagandist who seeks to disguise his views with art forms. Any topic of human interest is adequate for Theatre, providing it can be presented in action.

The mediaeval Masque was entirely sycophantic (that is, political) and the early Court ballets revolved around sun kings and their mistresses. The Jesuits were so well aware of this that they produced dance text-books, and offered political ballets later.

POLITICO-ECONOMIC BASIS OF BALLET

Reveals an extension, more fully marked in modern social environment, of the sociological factors that impinge upon, select, and govern all the arts that are based in dance. We call the social or mass-mode of art impetus by many minor names: such as propaganda, education, advertising, and the like; hence it becomes important to examine these bases. The emotional elements which we name as desire or repulsion in the individual, become hidden in class or national guise, in which the "rulers" try to divert the masses, in the quest of power and position and prestige for themselves. This stimulates the formation of those predatory social systems known as "empires". The individual emotion becomes an expression of mass desire called "policy", formulated in politics, which is eternally linked with aids and hindrances, weapons and instruments, summed up as "economics". In Athens, *Ekonomia* was the guidance of the household, done by women; but the administration of the *Polis* was done by men. These facts are expressed in every mode of art: in large and costly forms, consciously; but reflected in all minor forms, as a matter of course. Dance and ritual express *economia* and *polis* by way of place, prestige, movement, rank and power—in Athens, via the *Boule*,* the *Ekklesia*, the *Agora*. Individual and social emotions sway the choice of policy, expressed in methods called politics; as desires accumulate and turn to expend this or to save that, in an economic system adjusted to the major desires of the people. Hence it is not only desirable, but inevitable, that "art forms" shall express social desires and methods; the emotion and its fulfilment; peace and war; in sex and sustenance. The technical facilities of each time and place now extend or limit these desires; which in turn sustain or destroy moral standards. The Spartan respected successful robbery (so did the *klephta;* so also did the sailors of Britain bearing "letters of Marque" to license national piracy; and as the modern motorist may kill or maim on the highway, against the slightest of deterrants. These moral standards receive expression; in ceremonial, in ritual, in what we now call "art forms").

POLKA

A 19th century dance in 2/4 time. Origin is claimed by Poland and Czechoslovakia, but the Polish *Polska** was more likely the foundation of

17th century Scandinavian dances of that name. A country dance popular in Czech villages in 1830, was in *Polka* rhythm and used steps fundamental to the later dance. In some villages it was called "Polka", presumably after the particular step employed, since other village dances in the same rhythm, such as *Trasak*, *Britva* and *Kvapik*, were so called. This seems to have been the source of the dance which first caught popular attention in Prague in 1835. Developed by professional dancing masters, it was taken to Paris and shown at the Odéon Theatre in 1840 and the Theâtre de L'Ambigu in 1841 by M. J. Raab, ballet master from Prague. Paris dance teachers (Cellarius, Eugene Coralli (Paris Opera), Lucien Petipa etc.) turned the simple Czech *Polka* into a dance with five figures, which so took popular fancy in 1843/4 that a "Polka mania" swept the ballrooms of Europe and America. Commercial commodities were called after the dance, and *The Times* complained that interest in politics was temporarily eclipsed by the all-absorbing new pursuit. M. Cellarius came to London in 1844 and the *Polka* was danced at Almacks,* then at Cremorne, Vauxhall,* the Argyll Rooms, and at balls from Windsor Castle to small-town Assembly rooms. At the Paris Jardin Mabille dancers such as Céleste Mogador and Rose Pompon performed a showy solo variety. Theatrical versions appeared the same year (1844) in Paris and London by famous ballet dancers—Mlle. Maria and Eugene Coralli; Carlotta Grisi and Jules Perrot; while Fanny Cerito and Arthur St. Leon gave a version in 3/4 time called the *Redowa*. The *Polka** was a sprightly dance for couples proceeding round the room. Dancers faced each other, the man's right arm round his partner's waist, his left hand taking her right. The main feature was a hopping step ("polka step") and a "heel and toe" step. In one figure the man. leading his partner, danced backwards round the room; repeated with the lady dancing backwards. Duration and change of figures was decided by the man. As the fever died down the figures disappeared and the later *Polka* resembled a vivacious waltz having two versions —one retained the "polka step", the other the "heel and toe". Smetana and Weinberger included *Polkas* in "The Bartered Bride" and "Schwanda the Bagpiper".

POLO (Spain)

An Andalusian gypsy dance in moderate 3/8 time, accompanied by singing; said by some writers to be similar to, or identical with, the *Romalis** or *Olé.** Other sources give separate accounts, describing the *Polo* as an 18th century dance for one couple, and the *Olé* as a solo with castanets, which seems to show no connection between them. Possibly the name (Polo) is from Persian, due to the rapid passing of the *motif* (like the ball in the Persian game) from one dancer to another. In this sense, the term seems to have passed into German music, as *polo* in the structure of the fugue. Here the subject receives orderly transition, in *polo* and *senga*. In the Prelude to the fourth Act of Bizet's opera *Carmen*, the composer used a *Polo* composed by Manuel Garcia, called *Cuerpo Bueno*.

Russian Court Dress. Typical court dress worn by ladies of the Imperial Court at Petersburg about 1890. The *kokoshnik* head-dress was always ornamented with pearls. The stately dance at court was polonaise or mazurka in form.   RUSSIA

POLONAISE (Poland) *Taniec Polski*

An old Court dance, not of peasant origin (See *Polska**). Said to have derived from Court processions in the late 16th century, its true home was in "Great Poland", between the Rivers Oder and Warts, where the country's earliest capital, Poznan, is situated. With music in moderate triple time, the dance is a rhythmic processional march, with emphasis on the second beat and step. The *Polonaise* was used to open a ball at Court, or at houses of nobility. Partners side by side, danced in a line behind each pair, in order of precedence, and in olden times it was the custom for the cortège to pass through all the palace rooms. In the ballroom, couples danced down the length of the room, led by the most important person present. With flourishes, bows and dignified movements, he led the dance through its stately evolutions, and because the others followed his lead, he was called *rej wodzic*, or "lord commanding the dance". The *Polonaise* was at first performed, only by men, as a dance of knighthood. Wearing long, close-fitting coats, wide coloured sash and top boots, at appropriate moments in the dance, they swept off their plumed hat or, with a flourish, drew sword from scabbard. The popularity of this dignified dance of rigid etiquette, spread in the 18th century. Bach and Handel composed music in *Polonaise* form, but better known are the piano compositions of Chopin and Tchaikovsky's *Polonaises* in ballet and opera. [Cp. *Minuet; Fackeltanz* (Court dances of strict etiquette)]

POLSKA — 1

A country dance in Denmark, Finland and Sweden, coming from Poland (about 1600). *Polski* or *Polska* was an old Polish peasant dance. The Polish name for *Polonaise** is *Taniec Polski* (Polish Dance) and tradition has it that the 16th century Court processional, ancestor of the *Polonaise*, was based on the old country dance. Early Scandinavian dances called *Polska* probably derived from this country dance; while the 19th century ballroom *Polka** from Czechoslovakia has returned to the countryside in relatively "modern" folk dances in Denmark, Finland, the Netherlands, Sweden and Switzerland. In Denmark *Polska* (or *Polsk*-dance) seems to have been a pair dance in 3/4 time, containing a walk forward and turning on the spot. At Odense, in 1674, wedding celebrations included this dance. In Sweden *Polska* steps included springs and hops, a slow introductory part and many figures, and the dance has been popular in the countryside since about 1600. Modern Sweden has many variations of the old *Polska* (see *Polska* — 2). Its use in Finland suggests a certain dignity of style, since until early in the 19th century *Polska* was danced as a preliminary to a banquet. The original Polish *Polski* must have had something of this quality to enable it to be adapted to the stately processional dance which led to the *Polonaise*. When, in Finland, the *Waltz** superseded the *Polska* as an introduction, it became the last dance, known as the *Parting Polska*. Today in Finland there are pair dances, and round or square dances with many figures (generally in 3/4 time) derived from the old *Polska*. *Hollolan Polska* ("Nine Persons") is for three groups of three, two lines behind each other facing the third.

Female Dancer from the House of Dancers at Pompeii. About A.D. 60.   ITALY

POLSKA—2 (Sweden)

Has developed in this country, from an admitted Polish origin, into many interesting national and local modes of group dance, from about 1600. Dalecarlia (famous as a district that retains folk customs) has *Dalpolska*, also called *Slangpolska* (Swing Polska), as well as *Hupplek* (another dance, ending in *Polska* form) at Floda. The Leksand district has *Leksandlaten* or *Lekslanddans*, in which the "Excuse me" exchange of partners is a feature;

though in Leksand, two or three couples may dance together before the change-over (or two or three men and one girl). Similar is the *Trikarlspolska* (Three Lads' Polska), or the *Fyramanna-dans*, which shows similar groups; but even this is surpassed by the "unknown man" who springs suddenly into the midst, for *Rysska-polska* (Russian Polska) to grab the girl. Quite different is *Värmland-polska*, noted for its etiquette. The main form of *polka* underlies these variations: the alteration of slow walking paces and quicker turns. Usually the music runs in 2/4 time, but changes to 3/4 if the *Crooked Dance* is used; and may continue for the pair dancing in *Dalecarlia Polska*, especially if the pace is altered to three-step.

POMPEIIAN DANCE (Italy)

The small town of Pompeii (near Napoli) was destroyed by eruption from Mount Vesuvius in AD 79. Much of it has since been excavated; among many items recovered are some records of their dances. These consist of wall paintings; and works in bronze (occasionally fragments of pottery), which depict dancers, their rituals, their implements; and hint at their doctrine. The adjacent town of Herculaneum has also been partly excavated, and many of the works are now in the *Museo Reale* in Naples. Some of the more interesting can be found in the large salon *Camera Segreti*. Numerous examples of dance, in bronze and painting were reproduced by careful engravings in two volumes: *Antiquities d'Herculaneum*, drawn by P. T. Piroli, published in 1805 by Piranese Frères of Paris. Figures of eight muses are included, with Greek lettering; and two paintings of the dance-rituals of Eros. Pompeiian dances ranged from several religious styles, to spectacles done solely for amusement. Some shown in paintings and bronzes were records of "Dances of Isis"; others were rope-dancing or tumbling; and some clearly offered all the resources of the most modern cabarets of the USA. Acrobatic performances were welcomed. Pompeii was a kind of Brighton or Southend "suburb" from the "big city" of Rome, where many of the moneyed men would ride down for the week-end, to be near the sea, instead of visiting Ostia; and its standard of entertainment was "provincial"—not so magnificent as Rome could provide, but just as salty, possibly even more vulgar. These traditions remained in Rome itself, right down to the 16th century. In the Foro Triangolare, was an open-air theatre built during the 2nd century BC, and showing Greek influence in its original plan. Altered, and added to at later times, it seated about 5,000 people. A small, covered theatre next to it, for musical entertainments, held about 1500, but it was at the Forum

in the centre of the town that religious festivals, pantomimes and musical festivals were held. In the 1st century BC an amphitheatre was built in a corner of the town walls for gladiatorial shows, which housed an athletic-cum-military organization for educating sons of the well-to-do.

POMWITZEL (Silesia)

An ancient New Year Festival Dance, taken over by clerical interests and shifted slightly in date to December 24th. Originally the dance celebrated the *Chylde*, the New-born Year, who was rocked gently—as the days themselves tend to swing slightly in climatic tension (though much more so in Spring and Autumn). This dance was known (15th-16th century period) at Hofstadt, near Leipzig and Regensburg. The liturgy (dating from 4th century) consisted then of songs of praise for the young Jesus, in the midst of which the organist turned to a traditional local dance tune (for which newer words had been provided). Boys and girls, awaiting their cue in the church, then walked slowly to the altar, dancing round it, performing the act of swinging a child to sleep. Later a few adults participated; but in the end the custom lapsed. [See *Church Dances*]

POPPYCOCK (England)

Equals *Poupée-coch*, the "puppet-master", who in mediaeval England recited a good deal of topical nonsense and quips, to attract customers. The colloquial term "old cock" simply means, as much as to say "Oh, Sergeant!" for it comes from the Welsh *coch*, the leader. In architecture this puppet term lingers as "poppyhead", meaning the images once carved and painted, built on the end of church pews, alleged to be "saints" or doll-heads (*poupée-head*). These *poupées* were once the familiar "dancing dollies" of the market place or the annual festival, as the Aunt Sally (Ante-Salii).

PORDON DANTZA (Basque)

Dance of the Lancers in Basque ceremonial; it varies from slow march time to rapid and vivacious rhythms. The regular date is on the Midsummer Feast of John, when hill fires celebrate the solstice.

PORTUGUESE DANCE

Includes a wide variety of traditional and ritual dances. A festival of thanksgiving, after the plague in Lisbon in 1570, was marked by ceremonies and dancing. They were performed as *Pal-auto sacramentales*, and included: *Danza de Donzellas** (of the Damsels); *Danzas dos Maryios*; *Danzas dos Espingardeiros*; and *Danza dos Pratos*. The *Donzellas* were a group of eight or a dozen small girls about ten years, dressed in white, who marched and danced through the streets to the rhythm of lutes; stopping at certain squares to mount a platform, to give a playlet on some moral topic. The *Baixa*—a dance series— included *Chacota*, *Villao* and *Mourisca*, performed at weddings, as religious ceremonials. Cervantes refers to *Danzas Habladas*. The *Fado* was an old inheritance (it is known in Sicily), while the *Batuque** (danced today in Portuguese and French Guinea) has been subjected to African influence. The *baylata* or *baylada* is closely equivalent to the French *carolle*. *Folias** and *Bailes* were danced by the nobles. In the Azores, the traditions of *charambas* and *zapateados** continue, especially at church feasts. Through Portugal and the Azores, the fiestas of *Fogueiras de san Joao* have accompanied a fire tradition, in which (as the parallel French *Danse de san Jean*) the dancers jump through the *Bonne Feu*. There were also the *Fôfa** and the *Xacaras*. The church promulgates widely the *Ballets Ambulatoires*, when the wooden idols, richly carved and painted, are carried through the streets on festival days. Conversely, at the *Romerias*, the great secular markets and popular feasts, the chief dance is the *Fôfa.**

POSTURE MAKING (England)
Was combined with various elementary modes of dance during the Middle Ages (and probably before, as a crude entertainment). In *Old England* we are told :

> "Posturing was a favourite exhibition; the art had its great man in Joseph Clark. No motion, however unnatural or preposterous, was impossible to him. He could be a cripple, a hunchback, a big man, a little man, and in short, set at nought all the laws of anatomy in so complete a manner, that he deceived one of the most celebrated surgeons of the day, who dismissed him an incurable cripple. Scientific men were interested ... In the *Philosophical Transactions* it is stated that 'Clark had such an absolute command of all his muscles and joints, that he could disjoint almost his whole body'".

This unusual anatomical ability has been rivalled— and in some aspects surpassed, by the *yogi-chelas* of India, as reference to the methods of *Hatha-yoga* will show. The ability, when facial, begins to connect with drama; while in Japan, some acrobatic troupes learned to move as a group, in unison. This rhythmic display, done to music, brings it within the scope of dance; and it was in this less complete style that some of the *Commedia* troupes in Italy used the body to express exaggerated emotion. Artistic records of facial distortions appear in many plastic or graphic works of the Italian Renaissance. Court reaction was such—to

accentuate the princely dignity—that all facial movement was obliterated; (this gave the style of the blank mask to the Court Ballet)—while bodily motion was slowed down to *basse danse*. In England, the mobs and the yobs delighted in watching the posture-makers at May Fair or Bartholomew Fair, at Nottingham Goose Fair or Hull Fair. Then the artists Hogarth and Cruikshank, seized upon these shows, as a realistic basis for their political caricatures; while William Blake was the only one who turned them to the expression of dance in pictorial mode. The politicians have closely studied conjuring.

PRAYER STICKS (Amerindian - Zuni)
Are the principal implements used through the dance and rituals of Zuni Indians; as important as the sceptre of the Phara-Oh, or the *Lituus* of the Roman augur. Great ceremony is devoted to their preparation, with prayer and statement. Fresh willow wands are cut—both "male and female willow" goes the song. They are chosen long, white, and straight; and adorned with feathers; first of turkey and eagle; then with added colour from jay, hawk, oriole, and humming birds, on a background of "Old Mother Cotton". The craftsmen refer to making the wand "in human form", but it is a totemic mythic form—the essence of the turkey or of the eagle. These wands vary according to (a) the social standing of the owner and user; and (b) of the gods to whom each wand is dedicated. With these Prayer Sticks are sung the chants asking for three chief blessings : for corn, for game, for children; as they are used to "direct" the sacred breath of the ancestors, and the nature spirits. For some consecrations, two wands (male willow and female willow) are ceremoniously bound together; while the concluding dance affirms the same necessity of "holding hands" in a series of ring dances of unification.

PRECISION DANCE (USA)
Is the general basis of what is termed "Musical Comedy Choreography", founded on the unison movements of a group of girls, selected for their close similarity in height, weight, and figure. Precision dance in the New York music-hall compares with classical ballet in the opera theatre, and "Modern dance" in the concert hall—before these forms became less distinctly followed. This dance mode, insistent on strict discipline in movement and gesture, represses the eager American individualist on the stage, in meeting the demand of the "Tired Business Man", who wants to see a show he doesn't find thought-provoking. Much the same need was met in Germany with military drill at Potsdam; and appears in England with the public

performances given by the Guards regiments. All of these have long been preceded by Zulu or Maori male dances, which are just as precise and just as spectacular. For the musical comedy theatre, the English tradition was formulated in London productions (some on the naive *schühplattler** style imported by Viennese ballet mistresses, who developed in USA also, with the "hoofers"), by a Lancashire business man, John Tiller, who was responsible for the sharpening of the training system to a close precision. His son, Lawrence, continued the system; and Lancashire girls won fame in Parisian shows; and were hastily copied in the USA, where the term "Precision Dance" was widely adopted. The system is the old "Geometric Ballet", speeded up and shewn, not as manners, but as "spectacles" with authentic legs on view. Precision dance has usually "nothing to say" in relation to any theme requiring dramatic expression, for it is an exhibition of technical movement in unison. In street carnival processions are seen the girl "Drum Majorettes".

PRE-HISTORIC DANCE
Must be a matter for research and deduction from remains of other arts and comparison with vestiges of primitive rituals still extant. Certain facts can be gained from (a) principles of Animism; (b) places used for meeting, rituals etc.; and (c) symbols, pictures, carvings, etc. found in these caves or constructions. In the Island of Jersey is the tumulus of La Hougue Bie, examined in 1924, as one of the most notable megalithic monuments of Europe. The date assigned is Neolithic Bronze Age. The gallery measures thirty-two feet, main chamber thirty feet long by about twelve feet wide, with three side chambers; constructed of massive supporting stones roofed with huge capstones (some estimated to weigh fifty tons). The cave of Altamira (N. Spain, near Bilbao) has an array of painted animals (now widely known from copies by A. Breuil). It was discovered first in 1879. Near Bayon is the cave of Isturitz, known to have been inhabited from Mousterian epoch to Gallo-Roman times—here is the "real home of the Basques". In the celebrated Dordogne, near Perigeux, is the site known as the "Capital of the Pre-Historic World", now called Les Eyzies. Breuil asserts (see his book, 1952) that the "cave masters" travelled from one of these cavern centres to another; that they probably possessed and taught a distinct doctrine, even a magical system; and we may feel sure, from evidence in living "primitive ritual" that dance appeared prominently in this system. Pictures of dancing magicians and dancing women support this thesis with abundant visual evidence. The course of direct evidence in caves is further supported by the available pictures (with traditions) known in the Buddhist caves of India, in some of which magnificent pictures of dancing girls are known. These are not pre-historic, yet they continued an ancient tradition of cave usage. In North Africa and Syria and Arabia, sacred chambers were cut into living rock in an external form copied from constructed architecture. The cave tradition was older and stronger. At Ellora, in India, the same method was followed; it is certain that ritual dance ceremonial was followed in these impressive vaults; for some of them reveal sculpture on the walls (as at Elephanta, Bombay Island). In Rhodesia Prehistoric Dance is exemplified in cave and rock paintings found near Salisbury, which are copied, in examples now in Salisbury Museum and Bulawayo Museum. Experts who have examined these paintings note their varied character. They are executed mostly in dark red monochrome (silhouette or outline) usually with striking individual attitudes; but compositional grouping is rare or absent; the relation of groups is apparently more narrative than dramatic in intention. Colours include yellow ochre; dark-red; brick-red; usually one colour to one drawing. The scale is important; most pictures are "one-man paintings" and "one-man views"—that is, the small size (often no more than 20" x 30") is not devised for group viewing; but for inspection by one, or two at most, privileged persons. The subjects present varied scenes: men, animals, masked or costumed dancers, mostly in vigorous action. One man from Glen Noran Farm has a group of twelve figures, of three sizes; one is a masker wearing some animal skin and skull. Two of them dance, apparently in a high jump, with separated feet; another whirls a club or hurls some missile. Some are hunters; but, says E. Goodall,[1] "we can only conjecture . . . it is impossible to 'explain' them". There are "persons wearing masks performing dances and acting as the animals themselves . . . they must have played a prominent part in a possible social structure and, perhaps, pantheon, of prehistoric man". These drawings may be compared with the still existing dances and cave paintings among the aborigines of Australia. In England, recent excavations of Megalithic culture (7500 BC) in the Vale of Pickering, in Yorkshire, discovered among other things, stag antlers attached to the frontal part of the skull, which had been thinned and made lighter. This, with the fact that protuberances inside the skull had been removed and smoothed, and the horns lightened, suggests that these may have been ceremonial masks.

[1] *Pictorial Documents of Prehistoric People.* E. Goodall. *NADA* (Salisbury) No. 24: 1947.

PREMIER DANSEUR AND PREMIÈRE DANSEUSE
(French)
Correct academic terms that refer to the leading
members of a ballet company, in the "language of
ballet", which has stemmed chiefly from French
institutions. To use the name *ballerina* (singular)
or *ballerine* (plural) and *ballerino*, is to accept
Milanese terms. At their top we find *prima ballerina*, and *prima ballerina assoluta*; also *primo ballerino*, a term not much used. There are no precise
English equivalents, unless we turn to the dramatic
theatre, and mention "leading lady", or use the
American music-hall term "star" (derived from the
addition of printed stars on program leaflets or
posters). But to adopt a journalese lack of accuracy
and professional discrimination, and to write of
"baby ballerinas", is nonsense.

PRESS REPRESENTATIVE
A person whose general job it is to secure mention
(preferably highly favourable) in the morning newspapers immediately after the opening night of a
new show. Some press-representatives are highly
capable journalists, knowing every sector of their
task; others (usually ambitious females) contrive to
compress the job into a dull routine. They view it
as solely commercial—as "selling seats for that
show"—and nothing else; they take no "long view"
of the sheer need to obtain every possible reference to their clients. Technically, the job involves
(a) getting facts about the show, the performers,
the ballets or other items; and (b) distributing these
facts in easily assimilable form to newspapers and
magazines (as well as to a small number of expert
and knowledgeable private writers) so that they
can select and reprint. Next it requires a parallel
system for photographs, which is complicated by
the need to pay fees to expert photographers. The
regular press routine differs in each country. In
Britain, there is relatively little corruption, though
the absence of the companionable welcome with
a drink before the show, or in the intervals, has
lapsed into a cold commercial store-front attitude.
In Paris, the manager or his deputy may lunch or
dine the critics. In the USA, he has to bribe the
union boys and invite critics to "receptions" beforehand. In some places, the company's travelling
press-representative will have to take a hand, helping to unpack and pack the show for the "one-
night stands", as well as supply drinks to the local
editor and his spouse. In the USA, often the impresario's press-representative will undertake the
major part of a nationwide publicity racket; he is
expected to do this by newspapers, on the basis of
"No advert—no notice". In Britain, papers in the
provinces expect a small advertisement and a
couple of seats; they play fair as a rule.

PRETOS, DANCA DOS (Portugal)
Performed by men during the procession of the
"Assumption of the Virgin" (August 15th) at
Arcozelo da Sierra, near Gouveia. The procession
includes different groups of dancers, called *charolas*,
who perform at intervals, and of whom the *Pretos*
form one group. With blackened faces, and wearing red costumes ornamented with bells, they dance
the *Fandango** to music of guitars, in between
performing clownish antics. Other *charolas* in the
procession perform the dance of *donzelas* (six or
eight small girls pretending to be Moorish maidens);
dance of the *marujos* by boys representing sailors;
and *danca dos espingardeiros*—a mock battle between eight or sixteen young men, representing
Portuguese and Spaniards.
[See *Donzellas, Danca dos*]

"PRETTY DANCERS" (N. Scandinavia)
A term used, like "Merry Dancers",* to indicate
the brilliant "dancing" of the Northern Lights—an
electro-magnetic phenomenon that appears at the
poles, as the negative discharge of solar energy,
producing extreme coldness with a surplus of
electrical energy. Along the north Norwegian coast,
the glow which appears about midnight is called
Tussmorke; the dancing lights, making small crackling sounds, leap and waver in shafts and curtains
of violet and yellow, orange and green. In Arctic
Norway, the return of sunlight, marking the
warmer season after the "Long Darkness" (*Mor-
ketiden*), is a time of general holiday. Schools are
closed and everyone waits in the streets for the
sun. Called "Sun Coffee Day" (a modern tag), it is
a festive occasion, when people visit each other
for coffee and cakes, and a general feeling of hope
succeeds the depression of the "Long Darkness".
In Greenland, the return of the sun is celebrated
in a festival called *Qartsiluni*—"The Long Silence"
—which provided the theme for a ballet in the
repertoire of the Royal Danish Ballet.
[See *Merry Dancers; Up-helly-ah; Chèvres Dansantes*]

PRIESTS, DANCE OF THE OR DANCE OF DAVID
(Abyssinia)
A religious dance of Ethiopia, performed by priests
and scribes on the principal feast days—at New
Year, and Feast of the Cross or *Maskal* (both in
September); at *Temkat*, or Epiphany (January); and
at Easter. It takes place in the precincts of the
church, or, during *Temkat*, in the open air, after a
ritual procession to the river for purification and
re-baptism. The priests stand in two lines facing,
each holding a small sistrum or rattle, and carrying
a long, ivory-handled praying-stick over one shoulder. Low chanting at first accompanies the dance,

then joined by the rattle of the sistrums and the boom of drums, which give a high or low note according to which end of the drum is struck. The two ranks of chanting priests approach and withdraw, cross, turn and approach once more, their bodies swaying to the slow rhythm. As the lines move to right or left, the dancers pause with one foot raised; then, slightly bending the knee, the praying-sticks, held in the middle, are lunged forward towards the ground. The slow rhythm quickens, chanting grows louder, and the dancers move faster and faster to a climax, when quite suddenly, with a final boom of the drums, all movement and sound ceases. The dance is performed in the Church of St. Giorgis at Addis Ababa, and at Addis Alem, where the crown of Menelik is kept.

PRIMITIVE DANCE
Is usually referred to "Ancient Dance" but some primitive forms are extant today. They may be (a) traditional in technical form, in pattern or style; or (b) in meaning. Primitive dances occur also in children's play, often with some reflex of current adult dance, or inherited school play, or feeble copies of film or TV displays. Primitive forms appear also in course of movement done for other aims—as in "physical exercises" or moments in football matches (often interesting in line but with no art meaning, only emotional and physical tension). The chanty develops some modes of primal dance, as does liturgical pose and gesture. Vocational village dance forms frequently show a primitive imitation of tool usage, often with simple chant, as in weaving (some Scottish songs; S. Indian rhymed verses) or sailors' chants to operational movement. Hunting and fighting evoke primitive dance form, sometime developed by virtuosity to symbolic expression (Indian Hunters' Dance, when one dancer mimes both animal and hunter).

PRINCE (Celtic, from Ap-Rinnce)
Means the first dancer, "the prancer", leading in dance ritual, in Rinnce fahda or Rinnce Teampall. As the East European title kral came from kuriol, "leading in the circle song-dance", so also this West European title prince (eldest son) developed. One is Grecian; the other Gaelic. Another such title is Dauphin, D'Auphin, the "first" (also known as D'Auban, and De la Vigne).

PROLETARIAN BALLET
Is an appendage of Bourgeois Ballet.* Their basic need for numerous "repeat performances" arises in the commercial need to spread the initial production costs, as an overhead charge, by showing the single theatrical production to the largest audience it is geographically possible to contact. The Bourgeois Ballet thus becomes Proletarian and Pedestrian, in the technical sense; it has to travel far and stop often. There are two sources for inflow of Maximum Audience. First: use a city theatre of good capacity, set in the midst of a large population. Any great capital, from London to New York, Moscow to Buenos Aires, fills these conditions.

PROLETARIAN DANCE THEATRE (London etc.)
In the period "between the wars", small groups in big cities sought to develop what they hoped was "Revolutionary Theatre". As a rule, the shows were satirical; but otherwise more divergent in technique than in theme (much as a great deal of the so-called "Modernist Art", that reveals incompetence in technology with aridity in ideas, in futile lumps of stone or messes of tangled wire, as, for example, "Political Prisoner"—nevertheless hailed as masterworks by national guides in art, intent on destroying standards). The chief centre in London was the Unity Theatre (holding some 320 seats) near King's Cross. Their programs included witty music-hall turns. Owing to the small stage (some twenty by twelve feet) large-scale dance shows were impracticable; while there has been no development of a suitable scale in mime-dance of theatre form. Performers tend to mistake violence in movement (modernist dance) for real power in thematic expression; just as in the London ballet theatres, a similar error (as in Job, or Everyman) substitutes physical eccentricity for a suggestion of profound strength. We have seen no use, in London (as there has been in Moscow or Kiev) for adequate processional dance or mime elements, on national festivals. In Russia between about 1922 and 1930 the Proletarian Theatre (including dance) was represented by the Blue Blouse Groups.*
[See Blue Blouse Groups; Habima Jewish Theatre]

PROPAGANDA BALLET
Satirical Mode. While most propaganda is positive and active on behalf of its chosen theme, the turn of events allows occasional opportunity for the "other half" of favourable publicity, by way of satire or caricature. In Britain this usage of theatre appears chiefly in Music-hall entertainment, especially (a) satirised during one or other colonial war, when the current "enemy" is invariably satirised by comic songs; and (b) less notably, at election periods, when both parties are liable to receive some public censure. The ballet, being more expensive to produce, less often appears with satirical theme. One of the renaissance performances was The Alchemists, in 1640, a satire by Ben Jonson on the current fashion for alchemy.

PROSE DE L'ANE (Mediaeval French)
A corruption of an older term, used in the New Year Festival, as *Paroisse de l'Année* — the "Prayer for the Year". This distortion is similar to the English displacement of *Lord of Messe Ruelle** by the meaningless term "Lord of Misrule". Accompanying this once-solemn royal festival, the words of the chant have suffered change : and "Heye! Seignior, Heye!" was perverted into "Hez, sire Asnes, Hez!" — the exhortation to dance, thus altered to animal cries, in the dog-Latin verses as preserved. The former celebration, as at Beauvais or Sens (near Paris) included a village maid, riding on an ass, with a dancing procession, chanting this patois of Franco-Latin doggerel. Though alleged to present "the flight into Egypt", it was a replacement of the far older hobby-horse that belonged to the ancient New Year Festival; just as circumsession has been replaced by circumcision; the dance around the sacred place replaced by the *Fata de l'Année*, or *Fête of Fürst* (the prince, in Norman-French), turned into *Fête des Fous* (not "fools" for this is *sot* or *sotte* in French; but *fou* has been made to imply "mad". The Prayer for the Year was a ceremonial contained with the French Masque or New Year Festival, *Fete du Fürsten*.

PRUH (Burma — Shan States)
A children's ceremony among the Palaungs. Spread over many weeks, it is their first introduction to discipline, and the behaviour of the sexes towards each other. They learn courtesy; and ceremonial modes of address in rhyme and symbolic language, culminating in the October festival held at full moon. After an exchange of presents between boys and girls (chosen for their size rather than age), and many other ceremonies, parents, children and their special teachers go in the early evening to the open monastery courtyard — a railed enclosure, its floor spread with bamboo mats. Boys gather at one end, girls at the other, with *Pak-ke's* (elders in charge) between. Besides full moonlight, the court is lit with pine torches. Performances alternate between dances by young men and boys (the girls do not dance, but sit and admire), and a comic procession of animals made of strong paper over a bamboo frame. Larger than life and able to stand alone, each animal is "animated" by one or more men walking inside it. First come several pagoda-shaped erections, twelve to twenty feet high. There follow a half-human bird (*king-ga-ra*); a Chinaman; a white and gold deer; and a real man dressed as a hunter with bow and arrows. He provides the comedy, for after him comes a snarling tiger with snapping jaws, which the hunter, while trying to shoot the deer, seeks to avoid, with many antics. The procession ends with a white-paper elephant,

and two monkeys walking side by side. These creatures circle the monastery three times, then rest while the men and boys dance. To the rhythm of drums and gongs, the dancers move round one behind the other in large circles, outside the enclosure, arms waving and bodies twisting. They dance either round the musicians seated in the centre, or round the bamboo structures that led the procession. After about an hour the boys rest, while the animal procession begins again, and so on until midnight, when the children sleep in their separate groups. At dawn the boys dance again for an hour before eating, then all go into the monastery for reading of Buddhist scriptures; the festivals end about noon.

PSALM DANCE TUNES (England)
At the time of Henry VIII these were used for village dancing; as the clerics had taken folk dance tune to use for psalms and hymns in their church liturgies. This interchange between secular and liturgical music seems to have been frequent. The English literary form of translated Old Testament books hides their rhythmic form. Originally Hebrew works were devised to be chanted in rhythmic phrases, as poetry; often to simple instrumental music. Thus we find a direct parallel in Persian poetry. There is the *Qasida* (Epical Ode of Praises) similar to some of the psalms, the *Ghazal* (lyrical love song), like the *Song of Solomon*; the *Ruba-i-yat* (quatrains, as popular verses) like *Ecclesiasticus*; and finally the *Mathnawi* (or *Mesnevi*) as familiar couplets (like *Proverbs*), which still continue, in the flamenco rhythms of Spain as the *copla*. Hence many of the mediaeval folk-dance tunes, that remain in use, have been played in two modes. The slow and simple beat was the hymnal pace; while the same melody played twice as fast, is the dance tune. Skilful syncopation is the basis of this apparent change from sacred to secular music.

PUEBLO INDIANS (N. America)
A collective name given by the Spaniards to tribes living in *pueblos*, or communal houses of two or more stories. Built of plaster and poles, the upper rooms were reached by a ladder through the flat roof, as was the ceremonial chamber, or *kiva.** Principal tribes are the *Zuni** (whose buildings sometimes reach five storeys), and the *Hopi,** who, with other Pueblo tribes (Taos, Isleta, Acoma etc.), live along the upper Rio Grande and Little Colorado River in New Mexico, Arizona and Colorado. In 1940, the total population of 15,000 lived in twenty-six pueblo towns. In this region, also, but living in one-family houses, are the *Navajo** and *Apaches*, both influenced by Pueblo Indian culture. From

1100 - 1400 AD the great communal dwellings were built, such as the 800-room Pueblo Bonito in New Mexico and the "Cliff Palace" of Mesa Verde, Colorado, ruins of which still remain. In 1540, the Spaniards found in the Zuni pueblo of Hawikuh, two hundred families living in the three-storeyed building. Evidence suggests that the Pueblo Indians are descended from the Toltecs, in the long, gradual spread of Maya and Toltec culture from Yucatan northwards through Mexico into Arizona and New Mexico. Developing a theocracy, all pueblo tribes have preserved elaborate ceremonies, with priestly and curing societies. Maize is the sacred emblem and a pre-occupation with the bringing of rain and fertility of crops characterises dances and rituals. At the head of the fifteen groups of priests, four groups of rain priests are associated with the four cardinal points, while one priest called "the Speaker of the Sun" sees that all festivals are observed on their proper dates. Adult men belong to *Kachina** Societies. *Kachinas* (ancestral spirits) attend most ceremonies as masked dancers. Dancing clowns known as *Koshare,* Kurena* or *Koyemshi** often accompany them. Altars are made of ground-patterns of coloured earths, with screens of painted symbols; and sand paintings (see *Navajo**) are used by the curing societies. Tribes possess sacred "bundles" called *mile* (*ettonne* among the Zuni) containing essentials for life such as meal, pollen, seeds, etc. Pueblo tribes venerate ancestors and have a deep faith in the Nature gods (of corn, rain, hunting), and in the life-force (*mana**) known to most primitive religions.

PUERTO RICO (Caribbean, America)
Uses the generic term *plenas* to indicate folk-dances, most of which follow the mingling of native Indian mixed with Portuguese styles; and most modern dances (at San Juan) chiefly of South American style. Folk-tunes or song-melodies, used for dancing, are *plenas*. Similar to the Trinidad *calypso*, as a song-dance with topical relevance, is the *decima*, here limited to the "ten-verse" as suggested. A guitar is named a *cuatro* (four-string), though its current form has six strings. The pervasive rattle, once the dominant time-maker in Aztec dances, is the *maracas*. Made from a *gourd* and dry peas or glass beads, one is held in each hand. Carols are named *aguinaldos*; the ring dance re-appears with them at New Year Festival. Miracle plays are still produced by the local clerics at Easter. At Bayamon is the largest procession, featuring many school children fixed up with chicken-feathered "angel-wings", to play in *El Santa Entierro* (interment). Feasting and dancing follow the processional display.

PUILI (Hawaii)
A women's sitting *hula** taking its name from the split bamboo sticks used by the dancers. Seated in pairs facing each other, the girls sway gracefully as they mark the rhythm with the sticks. In an intricate sequence of taps they strike the *puili* on the ground, on their own shoulders, heads and arms, or cross them with their partner's. There is no other musical accompaniment than chanting, and the rhythmic beat of sticks. Chant and dance describe the Hawaiian Islands, and in particular the flowers and *leis* (garlands) symbolic of the different islands.
[Cp. Sitting Dances : *Kanana* (New Guinea); *Kebyar* (Bali); *Otuhaka* (Tonga); *Uli-Uli-Noho* (Hawaii); *Diomede Eskimo Dance*]

PUNG CHOLAM (Manipura, India)
The *pung* is a medium-sized double-barrel drum, usually suspended from the neck of the single male performer of this dance, by a leathern thong. (*Cholam* means "smart action"). The drum is perhaps a foot wide at its centre, tapering towards each end. Both ends bear deerskin covers, tightly stretched. The *pung cholam* is essentially a virtuoso performance, intent on display of all the varied technical means of obtaining rhythmic tones from a single drum. The skins are struck with one or several fingers; with palm or side of the hand; with two hands on one end; or tapping the wooden sides of the *pung*. The dancer selects his own rhythms, usually increasing speed towards the end; he jumps and turns or dips, as he beats intricate cross rhythms; in which the drumming is usually better than the dancing. *Pung cholam* belongs to no particular festival or time; and has been seen in London.

PUNJABI FOLK DANCES (Punjab, Northern India)
Many hundreds of villages throughout the Punjab province, perform pastime circle dances, in elementary form, all much alike. The usual three modes are present : (a) men alone, (b) women alone; and (c) mixed social dances. Many of these *Nautch tamasha's* are accompanied by traditional legends rendered in easy melodies with perhaps a drum (tabla) and flute. These village dances are known variously as *Dhris; Bhangra; Dhamal;* or *Semmi;* and many more local names; and begin spontaneously, at weddings, local fairs, and other celebrations; or just for fun.

PUNTO (Panama)
A rapid song-dance in 6/8 time, performed by engaged couples in the villages of Panama. Spectators throw coins at their feet, as in some European countries it was the custom for guests at a wedding to give the bride a present of money when dancing

with her in the Bride's Dance. The music of the *Punto* is usually in the major key, but when played in the minor key it is called the *Coco*. Cuba and the Dominican Republic also have the *Punto*, which is similar to that of Panama. The Dominican dance is called *Punto Cibeano*, in 2/4 time.

PUPPETS—1

Dancing, Miming: have been known in almost every country of the world, in every period of history and even pre-history. In Java, in particular, the dancing puppet preceded much of the living dancers' style. They have existed in two main modes; and in several scales, some miniature, some human scale. While most puppets portray the human form, often distorted in form and action, there have been many puppets made to suggest animal, bird, or insect forms. There is a ritual relation to the mask; which may be accepted in some modes as a partial puppet. The two principal modes of puppets are (a) the solid or three dimensional puppet; and (b) the flat or two dimensional shadow figure. In Java, the flat puppet has been developed to a state of artistic perfection, simple though its basic style is, in form and manipulation. The dance styles of puppets vary; but all can be said to be happily nonrealist, with action devoted solely to the expression of the main theme, sharpened by the special character of each different puppet in the small company, instead of perverting the basic quality of Theatre by trying to project the "personality" of the actor. Normally, the puppet theatre or display can satisfy only a relatively small group of spectators; though this limitation has been ended in the cinema theatre; yet it should never be assumed that the puppet show is only for juvenile entertainment. The puppet has been, and is, used widely in popular shows of the town and market-place, for satire and commentary on current events; while at the other extreme, puppets (now called "idols" if part of some other person's ceremonial) have been utilised frequently for religious ritual and mythic presentation of popular legends; finally they have been conscripted into the Export-and-Import Dance of modern merchandising, by way of publicity and advertising, in store and exhibition display. Puppets still remain as symbols, with a neat little story to tell; but not all of them venture into the sophisticated rhythms of dance. Known by many names, they have been used for displaying mythic legends and modern satirical comedies in all lands. Dance is a familiar feature. In Java the puppet influence was so strong that its slow movement imposed a similar convention on the human dancers, who later developed a religious dance form. The puppet dance-play has several different technical bases that determine the

mode of presentation. They begin with the shadow play of simple hand-gestures on a whitewashed wall. They develop in stronger light, and the stretched cotton sheet, with flat cut-out puppets made from dried skins. Presently the notion of more enduring and solid puppets emerges; they become a regular stock of the familiar repertory of the professional player—the "Teller of Tales" who requires illustrations beyond his ability in gesture and grimace. From the small-scale puppet then develops the mask disguise of the grown adult; and the simple form of the earliest "god figures"—the *eidolon* in symbolic form—as with the Greeks who clothed a selected tree with drapery. They knew it, and we must accept their idea of this object, *not* as "idol for worship", but as symbol for concentration. Missionary ignorance which denounces all other creeds as "idol worship" knows not the first thing about real religion; not even when puppets are adopted, and then called Marionettes, or used in churches as "poppy-heads" (poppets). The puppet is essentially a materialised visual focusser of ideas (or imagination, which most small girls display in dealing with their family of dolls). In dance, especially in choreographic planning, puppets can be useful. In display, as on shadow screen, puppets can bring back the producer from his concern with unimportant details to the central meaning of each episode.
[See *Wayang Kulit; Noh Dance Drama; Teraphim*]

PUPPETS—2

England knows her more recent puppets as Punch and Judy; the older images were Gog and Magog; or the Green Man; and several more, now faded from the scene. Old England had the *mommet* or *mammet*. France knew her puppets as *Marionne* or *Marianna; Poupée, Marotte* and *Marionette*; also as *Polichinelle*, and *Dame Gogone*. She also has the *mannequin* to the English *mannekin*. Germany has a string—some relatively recent by name, such as *Hanswürst* and *Pickelhering;* there is also *Dattermann* or *Tatermann* and *püppen-spielerin*, while *Kasperle* belongs in Germany and Switzerland. Italy has a lengthy roll of puppets. Many are known only in local places, such as the *Girolamo* of Milan, whence *Fantoccini* are much more famous. Rome has the *Buratini* and *Cassandrino*. More general are the *Pupazzi*, the *Bamboshie*, and *Fantoches*; also the *Magatelli* and *Pulcinella*—in Turin, the *Gianduja* or *Gianduca*. Hungary has some called *Manush Mulengra*, a special one, the "dead man". Latin stages knew the *Neuropastes* (string-puller), as India had the *Sutra-dhara* (string mover). Germany also has *Kobold* (gnome or dwarf *puppchen*) and *wichtel*. In Spanish houses are the Images *de vestire, Ikono* in Greece. Sierra Leone (Africa) has *nomore.*

PURGHIS (Perke, Perchte, Perga-Mum, etc.)
All personifications of the Dark Trinity of the *Parcae* or *Moirae*, the Grecian purgators or purifiers (from life and its evils) as the Three Fates, or *Norns.* The ritual origin of the *Mores* Dances consists of an endless circle and its incessant windings, in which the "candidate" is caught; and there endures a ritual death, in preparation for the discipline which later shall bring him peacefully to his physical death, but with soul survival. The *Wald-purgis* Meet and ritual dance followed in this ritual on the Blocksberg (Hartzwald, Brocken) on the Eve of May First—the purgation of Winter now ended by the outburst of Spring. Hence the jovial dance and feast, to which the maidens came in dark (winter) clothing, which they discarded in the course of the Ritual. The men's secret *Mores* ritual dance was performed chiefly on the following day, beginning with the dawn of the First Day of the May Blossom, or the "Green May". Perga-Mum was an ancient Greco-Asian centre where rituals of Purgation were held in high honour. The name parch-mentum (Latinised form) denoted the script given to visitors of the Temple of the *Moiraie* (also Diana of the Ephesians).

PURPURI (Finland)
A popular dance which is a "pot pourri" of many figures and steps from dances of other countries, although the figures seldom resemble the Polska, Russian Quadrille, Mazurka, Cossack, after which they are named. Simple walking, running, hopping, galloping, stamping, springing and valse steps are used. The number of figures varies from nine in Nyland to only one in villages of the East, and each figure has its own tune and tempo. The dance sometimes begins with a square formation of eight couples.

PUT-SER (Ancient Egyptian)
Literally: to "Stretch Cord" in surveying the temple site and its subsequent construction. The cording method, as used by the *harpeno-doptae* (Greek term for surveyors in Egypt) in ritual of orientation of the site and its courts; hence the original geometrical method of choreographic layout of a courtyard. Main facts are quoted by Sir Norman Lockyer (*The Dawn of Astronomy*), from inscriptions found in Temples of Edfu, Karnak and Denderah. The King, or *Para-Oh* ("Great House", or "Ruler of O", the circle of the "stretching"), was the principal officiant, assisted by the chief priestess in the character of a goddess, Sesh-Eta, as "Mistress

of Foundation", while the *Kher-Heb* (Chief Priest), recited the appropriate text from the scriptures. This technical use of the rope was found also in the re-survey of the Nile banks after every flooding erased the owners' marks. Later the rope became an instrument in many public announcements; it circumscribed the *corral* in Spain, and finished as the standard twelve-cubit measure of the traditional circus-ring. Numerous dances reflect the use of a rope, or a kerchief, as a measure; the dancers grasp and pull the rope into a ring; or hold it in serpentine linear advance. Numerous temples were founded on the circle and its ritual, from Avebury or Stonehenge to the wooden churches of Scandinavia or the Round Churches of the Templars.

PUTTI (Rome, Italy)
Mythical protectors of a sacred enclosure; often a well or fountain, but sometimes a sarcophagus. They danced round the centre to keep out "influences". An example in the British Museum (from the Villa of Tiberius, Capreae) shows five groups of fauns and bacchanalian nymphs. Their children were named *puteoli* or *putti;* always dancing, and bearing garlands of living branches or flowers and fruits. This rite was dramatised, as in Florence. In this form, they re-appear incessantly in Renaissance art; while their analogues continue in church ritual as "Children of the Chapel", (see *Cintola, Danza del Duomo**). They have been named *amorini** from their guard over the nuptial couch. A writer on art says:[1]

> "Donatello uses garlands and *putti* much as they were used on Roman sarcophaghi. The boys supporting festoons, as on tabernacles in Sta. Croce and Or San Michele, should be compared with garland-bearers on the Roman sarcophagus in the Metropolitan Museum . . . the *putti* are singing, dancing, and making wondrous merry (Cathedral at Prato)". Della Robbia followed with pottery.

[1] *Essentials in Art.* Osvald Siren. London, 1921.

PWE (Burma)
A Fair; a popular holiday gathering, including all kinds of amusement; song and dance, puppet shows and various sports. The *Pwe* is largely a commercial fair, arranged not by priests (there is no appointed priesthood in Burma), but by various patrons or providers of these entertainments. The main idea is having a good time, with suitable profits for the promoters. Town celebrations, as in Rangoon, have deteriorated and are sometimes caught for propaganda usages; yet popular visits to *Shwe Dagon* (the great monastery centre) continue.
[See *Nibhatkin*]

PYRE (Egypt)

Ritual dance with sacrifice made at time of Spring Festival, at Heliopolis; it is similar in some respects to the Fire of Baaltinne. The description given by Lucian shows it to have been more magnificent in his day :

> "Greatest of the festivals is that held at opening of Spring; some call this the Pyre; others, as The Lamp. The sacrifice is performed in this manner : They cut down small trees; setting them up in the (temple) court. They bring goats and sheep and cattle; and bind them living to the trees, adding gold and silver decorations. After all is finished, they carry the gods (images) around the (pyre of) trees; and setting a light under, all is ablaze in a moment. To see this solemn ritual, a multitude gathers from Syria and regions around. Each party brings its own god, as the statue which they possess".[1]

The dance movement was clearly in three parts : that long and slow period, while the day's preparations were being made; the serious circumambulation of the finished Pyre, ending with the priest bringing the sacred fire; and the more joyous proceeding, which ended the ceremony while the huge fire was blazing, lasting long into the night.

[1] *De Dea Syria.* Lucian (XLIX). *The Syrian Goddess.* Wm. Strong, 1913.

PYRRHIC DANCE (Hellas)

A military dance of ancient Greece, part of the training of young soldiers. From it the youths learned by rapid body movements, how to avoid blows, weapon thrusts and missiles, and how to attack the enemy. In very quick, light tempo, it was danced with shield and spear, to flute accompaniment, and is described by Plato in *The Laws* as the representative of all war dances. Of Doric origin, some accounts give Crete or Sparta as its native place, but some assign the dance to Pyrrhicos, and its invention to Pyrrhos or Neoptolemus, son of Achilles. In Athens, from the 6th century BC onwards, it was performed by the Ephebi (called Pyrrhicists) at the Greater and Lesser Panathenaea. At Sparta, in 7th century BC, the *Pyrrhic Dance* was an important item in the military curriculum, taught to boys from the age of five. Athenaeus records that it was still danced at Sparta in the 3rd century AD by boys of fifteen upwards, but elsewhere it had become one of the Dionysiac dances, with torches carried instead of weapons. Its military character disappeared (and also its purpose) when women performed it as a dance of entertainment, as mentioned by Athenaeus. Apparently also known as the *Sousta,* it became a pair dance. In its late form it is found now principally in Crete, where it is performed by one or two couples at a time. In Rome the *Pyrrhic Dance* was introduced into the public games by Julius Caesar (100 - 44 BC), when it was danced by the sons of leading men. It continued to be shown by Caligula, Nero and Hadrian, and spread through the Roman Empire. Traces of it survive in Europe in various mock-combat sword and stick dances.

Q

QABALAH (Arabic - Jewish)

From *Muqabalah*—"permutations". This term is persistent in Arab mathematical books, from the 11th to the 15th centuries. While this process of calculus, by combination and permutation, was applied chiefly to arithmetical quantities, by way of Al-gebra (or *Al-Kebra*) the esoteric Qabalah system, as re-founded by Moses of Leon (12th century) turned once more to geometrical values, relations, and symbolisms. Some parts of it were expressed in abstract dance ritual (later merged into "magical dance") and derived ritually from the older *minyan* of the *schul*; the provision that every religious meeting of Jews must have a quorum of ten adult men. Thus we have the *Idra Rabba* and the *Suta Rabba;* as the Great Circle (or The Masters) and the Small Circle (Students), formulated for study of *Qabalah.* These combinations and permutations lie at the formal foundation of the Hebrew letter-system; and were combined with fragments that had been preserved from the erudite symbolism of the Assyrian "Holy Tree" (with *Asherah*) with its "32 Paths". These were danced over, in Assyrian ritual; and, in some degree, Jewish students followed this movement in their endeavour to visualise the inner reality of the 32 Paths; and, most important factor of all, to grasp their values and relate their meanings. The *Qabalah* —written in Hebrew and translated into Latin by Rosenroth—was made over to English by S. L. Mathers; but as the whole available material is not complete, considerable aid must be derived from the earlier sources in Egypt and Assyria. In one view, the *Qabalah* may be accepted as an attempt to view the Kosmos as a "geometrical construct", in much the same manner as modern physicists view the Universe as a "construction" of vast and intricately related mathematical series; or the chemist, from his view, sees it as a coherent range of material structures, consisting of elements, moving by dynamic forces of repulsion and attraction, cohesion or explosion. In all of these modes, the prime difficulty is to see and grasp the principles that control the process as a *dynamic* structure. Plotinus saw this movement as a Cosmic* dance; Heraklitus affirmed, in allied terms, *Panta*

Rhei "All Things Flow". Some scholars assert that the *Qabalah* is the essential key to the mythology of the Jewish Old Testament. The term *Muqabalah* belongs to the mystical interpretation of the Hebrew scripts made in Galilee, in terms of the *quadrivium*. This numerical term *Muqabalah* implied an algebraical permutation of (a) syllables or letters, and (b) their corresponding numerical values, in religious symbolism, for interpreting Bible myths. As expressed in motion, over the "Magic Circle" (supplied by drawing geometrical figures—the square, the pentagon or heptagon, and especially the hexagon or "Shield of Solomon" or *Muhr-i-Suleiman*), and then "dancing" along the lines or spaces thus obtained, the permutation revealed certain key words or symbols of interpretation. This is the principle of mathematical notation. This ritual was one of the secret modes of Magical Dance, also denoted by the collateral term *schem-ha-phorash.** For this scheme, the "carpet" (or *farrash*) was prepared by writing down the twenty-two letters of the Hebrew alphabet; round (a) a circle; or (b) a square; or (c) a hexagon. Similar usage was connected with Chinese rituals *Ming T'ang* based on the trigrams *pakwa* of *Fu-hsi*. The reckoning associated with *muqabalah* was taken into the secular process of algebra and its later quadratic equations. The pentagonal equations have not yet been operated; they belong, for example, to music (as in the pentatonic Hindu *raga** system of music), but the mediaeval dance rituals made use of the pentagon; note Albert Dürer's famous drawing of the male figure, imposed over a pentagon; or Honecourt's architectural *Notebook*, where he used a pentagon as a design control.
[See *Yantra*, Raga,** Indian Dance,** Ming-T'ang**]

QATNI (Cotton) DANCE (Arabia)
Performed in groups, to a quick tune, the groups visiting each other as in the *Lancers*. The local poet stands and sings a verse, such as "I left my loved one in the Wadi al'Ain", which is repeated or given refrain by the audience.

QOSEM (Babylonian - Hebrew)
Khosem (*Chozen Bakko Khabbim*) a diviner, by observation and record; a poet or "maker of praise", and thus a creator of songs, for chanting and dancing. Later, the *Qosé* (*José*) was himself an actor or a "revealer" by mime and suggestion; and a ritual dancer (again, as an actor), which is possibly the source of the *ghazi* and *ghazal*, or the lyric and the reciter of poetry and a link with Horoscope makers, with *chakramim.**

QUAALTAGH (Isle of Man)
New Year Festival, formerly observed in this Island. A party of young men assembled at mid-night; proceeding from house to house, they executed a simple dance known as The First Footing. The steps were across the thresh-hold, for which rite it was essential that a dark-haired lad should be first, with his right foot. A similar ritual was long followed in the West Riding of Yorkshire. The Quaaltagh Boys were invited to partake of cake and beer, or bread and cheese. The Quaaltagh actors long ceased to dress their parts, like the Mummers of England, or the Guisards of Scotland. With the Manx Quaaltagh, an older rite followed by the canny housewife, was to "track the Fairy Dancers". For this, she spread fine white ashes from the dying fire, over the floor. She hoped to find next morning the tracks of tiny feet; if the toes pointed toward the door, then it was taken as a sign that the fairies would dance away with one of the residents, during that coming year; but if the footprint pointed inwards, then the family might that year be increased.

QEDISH'IM (Hebrew)
Lit: the "Holy Ones"—a term applied (as in *Zach.* 14. 5) to some of the temple servitors; in its original sense, broadly equivalent to the Hindu *deva-dasi*, "Servants of the gods". Usually feminine, they worked with the Levites in daily practice; but are, like the *mal-keth*, as much mythic angels as human beings, in the manifold allegories presented in script. The term *Qadesh* or *Kadesh* was one of many epithets given to Syrian Astarte and Cretan Aphrodite; it survives in the word *Kaddish*, now meaning a song, a prayer, or a thanksgiving; no longer associated with actual dancing. A parallel term, *cadi* or *kadi*, in Arabic signifies a magistrate, as "one deserving respect", and belongs in the group marked *Ket-ub* (a ritual centre).

QUADRILLE
A French dance for an even number of couples in square formation. The name, parallel with Italian *squadra*, refers to French and Italian *Carousel** or *Horse Ballet,** popular in the 17th century, when a group of from four to sixteen horsemen, elaborately caparisoned, performed rhythmic figures to music. In 18th-century French opera-ballets, the *quadrille* was the group of dancers (numbering four, six, eight or twelve) for the *Entrées** preceding each of the five Acts. The dance, popular in 19th-century English ballrooms, is said to have come from a *Contredanse,** seen in 1745 in one of Rameau's opera-ballets; and thence taken into Parisian ballrooms as the *Quadrille de Contredanse*. *Contredanse*, indicating the dancing of couples *contra*, or against each other, was an alternative name for Cotillon.* The French *Quadrille* continued in popularity through the Consulate and

First Empire, and was introduced into England at Almacks* by Lady Jersey in 1815. This dance had intricate figures and many difficult steps, but the style of dancing became more and more casual, as deplored by the Hon. Mrs. Armytage eighty years later, who complained of the "lazy nonchalant fashion of walking through the figures". The French *Quadrille* could be danced by any number of couples, each couple dancing with its opposite pair. After eight introductory bars of music, dancers began the five figures, which were : 1. *Le Pantalon;* 2. *L'Eté;* 3. *La Poule;* 4. *La Pastourelle* or *La Trènise;* 5. *La Finale* (called, by modern "Old Time" dancers, *Flirtation*). The last figure had many variations, and the dance often ended with a galop. Customary music was a medley of popular airs, mostly operatic. An American version, considered too lively for Victorian ballrooms, named the figures : 1. *La Promenade;* 2. *Les Moulinets;* 3. *Les Chevaux de Bois;* 4. *La Passe;* 5. *La Corbeille.*

QUANTA, the Dance of Energy;
QUANTUM, the Dancing Atom of Mass-Energy; and
QUANTOI, the Dancing Entities
Concepts following on discovery of Radiation (Curie and Rontgen) by Max Planck of Berlin (round 1900). Though barely recognised as such, the Quantum system reveals the balancing concept of the Cosmos (Nebula etc.) or the "Infinitely Small" against the "Infinitely Great". In both, the triple concepts of "The Dance, the Dancer, The Dancing" are excellent guides; and examples may be seen in the Cyclotron, the appearance of Isotopes; and some other operations in nuclear physics. Discoveries are hindered by several assumptions (a) the notion that the supposed "speed of light" is unchanged throughout all space and time, (b) suggesting it is the sole unchanging factor in a changing universe. Scientists have much to say about "solar energy" (or supposed "light") arriving at the Earth but do not say what energy (which must be equal or nearly so) is returning, in obedience to the law of circulation on which the Quantum Theory is constructed if rarely acknowledged. After Planck's Theory came Böhr (studying radiation but not absorption) and then these apparently disparate theories on Quantum Mechanics (in 1926) :

(a) *Matrix Theory* (Max Böhr & W. Heisenberg)
(b) *Wave Theory* (de Vreghl & S. Schrodinger)
(c) *Transformation* (D. Dirac & P. Jordan).

None tells us what occurs in the Nucleus. The source of form out of energy may be noted (by analogy) to the whirling string with a glowing end : it makes a circle visible by the eye but not actual — an "optical illusion". Planck then touched on "Harmonic Oscillation" which is nearer to the Cosmic Dance posited by Plotinus.* "The reality of Quantizised Position is the Essence of the theory"; but according to more advanced thought (Principle of Uncertainty), the Energy-Mass moves into Form (gaining position) and then *out* of Form (releasing energy, losing its place). Here again the defect is in reckoning on units of identical mass-energy : the charge, the change, the channel. According to the fairly well-known Hindu theory of world or cosmic creation, *Shakti-Shakta* or Form-Energy, the entire cosmos is dynamic, in a state of continuous oscillations : in (a) Creation, (b) Maintenance, and (c) Dissolution. This movement is figured as the Cosmic Dance — with Nata Raja as King of Dancers. In this movement sound (*Vach*) is important as a mode of Energy; so the Universal Dance exists because of its own music. Put otherwise : Name is Form.

In 1925 Uhlenbeck & Soudsmit demonstrated what they termed Electron Spin (the miniature pirouette of atomic energy around its nucleus — the spin upon an atomic axis which in the next second was itself spinning, in its positive-negative interchange. "Nature says one writer, has a penchant for an anti-symmetric wave function". This we find when a *straight* light-wave is repelled in *curved* colour waves or corpuscular expansion. Balanced between Cosmos and Atom lives the body of Man; in it all these phenomena also occur : this is the price of life, and its exhibition. Thus the Quantum active in the brain, is the seat or focus of Soul-Mind — of soul as Energy, of Mind as Form. Its appearance and continuity depend on oscillation (hence two halves of one brain). No Adaptation is complete without Reception or Inception. Here the Isotope which in chemical form carries Energy, in mind-form carries Energy-Images as Mass (positive or negative, never still, always dynamic, always dancing). Isotope is the rocking balance — like the cyclist who balances on two wheels at the price of motion. More complex modes exist, for the mental isotope — we have an allegory in the gyroscope, apparently still, yet moving. It is not possible to reach a finalised picture (there is none) by using static mathematical symbols to illustrate an essentially dynamic system.

QUATTRO CORONATI (Med. Italy)
The "Four Crowned Ones" dubbed (12th century) as "saints" but derived from older Egyptian legend, as the "Four Guardians of the Tomb". This ritual had three versions : two for initiation (one by water, and again by fire), and the funeral version at death. These four entities, known in symbolic form as "four evangelistica" or four apostles (visitors), stood in the four points of the symbolic compass circle, as protectors of the soul within.

Their dance was solemn and stately. Remains of some mediaeval records can be seen on the sarcophagus of Augustine at Pavia. The *Quattro Coronati*, as the "Four of the Crown" appeared post-1777 in Masonic symbolism; standing by the prone form of the candidate when he was "admitted" and hearing his responses. Hence the relic in nursery rhyme, requesting the Four to "guard the bed that I lie on". This esoteric ritual dance has long been forgotten in Italy; though there remains in Rome a small church bearing their name. They were linked at one time with Olimpici of Mirandello (known as "Pico"), and with the restoration of Greek studies at Pavia and Vicenza.

QUEEN CHARLOTTE'S BALL (London)

Later version of "Coming-Out Ball" or "Court Presentation" (discontinued) for young girls first making a "social appearance" in the upper class "marriage market". Annually held at Grosvenor House, some 1,600 persons may attend; of whom 350 to 400 young girls of about twenty-one will be sponsored. Queen Charlotte had her Birthday Celebration at St. James' Palace; then the Palace "Presentations" were organized; now it is a Private Ball every spring. In the Great Hall or Ballroom, some 160 Maids of Honour descend the double stair, to march music from Handel's *Judas Maccabeus*. Lights are dimmed, cymbals clash, the Maids wheel forward the Birthday Cake; and the presiding duchess makes an incision. Maids receive portions; then all the debutantes. A dress of long white tulle is almost uniform, mostly white, wide skirted, with very little jewellery. A few men are permitted at the dinner following. Foreign girls can now attend.

QUEEN OF THE MAY

Dances are traditional over Western Europe; while May Day celebrations, practically co-extensive with white races, follow many lines of design. Dances occur the previous evening; early morning; during some processional displays; and finally after the May Day Feast. Best known today are alleged May-Pole dances, with children twining ribbons; but there is no early trace of this pattern series; for in the older dances it appears to have been accepted that "This is no place for children!" The principal ceremony was to go to the woods to bring in the Merry Pole, as a newly cut tree, from which branches were lopped, leaving a green bough at the crest. This was then "erected" by setting in its annual pit on the village green; and circle dances were then performed by relays of excited people. It remains uncertain if the month gave the name, or if it is *Queen of the Mayers*, meaning the leaders of all the local gilds.

QUEEN OF MEASURES (Italy)

Generic term aplied to *Bassa-danza* by Domenichino of Piacenza (15th century Italy) to the fashionable group of court dances, which he set forth in diagram form. This term is in itself probably a late version of a far older original, as *Regina di Mezze* or *Regina da Messe*) — the factual "Queene of the Feast", here converted by the professional dancing master to technical description. The court dances were essentially part and progress of the high social feast; the basic term *basileus* (the house of the king was *basilica* since Roman times) affirmed the grave and solemn dances as *danse base*, as in parallel the vocal part of *basso profundo* was "king's voice". Domenichino states a series of six measures — here in tempo relation, descending from the gravest measure, from *capo* (the *bassadanza*), by *secto* (the measure called *quadernaria*); then *terzo* (which is *salterello* called *passo brabante*); to *mezzo*, "called *piva* by name" (holding half only of the *bassadanza*), and so down to *salta-terzo-rello* and *quader-sexto-naria*. Like the Greek measures of feet, the pace of the music marked the strict tempo of dance; naturally, the high personages of the court desired to move in slow and solemn rhythm. This 15th century Franco-Italian period, though a culmination of court dance, was itself changed in its long progress of gradual development; not less in name than in style; but if we retain in mind the social necessities of feasting and movement, we shall be able to ascertain the authentic relations of dance movement; and to note how they ranged from the etiquette of social precedence, to the flourish of social display. Here the turning routine was the *reverinza* — the punctuation of position and salute — to prince, to ladies, to men, to spectators; and thence it turned to the *bassa et alte* — the dance with leaps.

QUEEN'S OFFICERS' "COW DANCE" (France)

Notoriously one of the effective causes of the French Revolution (*circa* 1790) was the inexorable looting of the "taxpayer" by officials. This predatory system resulted in a national French habit of tax-resistance, which endures to this day (in 1955 it provoked organized strikes), though its origin was earlier than the plunder-system of the Louis Bourbons. Hence Dr. François Rabelais, in his satirical masterpiece, *The History of Gargantua & Pantagruel*, included a commentary on the "Queen's Officers", marked by reference to the popular dancing then prevalent at Court (Turin). He described the *Cow Dance* in a passage that could well be dedicated to the "Crichel Down Department" of the Ministry of Agriculture and Fisheries. He writes :

"I then saw a great number of the Queen's Officers

... others taught cows to dance, and did not lose their fiddling. Others sheared asses, and thus got long fleece wool .... Others, out of nothing, made great things; and made great things return to nothing ... Others on a large grass plat, exactly measured how far the fleas could go at a hop, a step, and a jump; and told us, that this was exceedingly useful for the ruling of king-doms ...."[1]
When Lewis Carroll described the *Lobster Quad-rille*,* he had no such vivid satirical notions. Neither has any ballet-master, from Moscow to Manhattan except Lt. Kije.
[1]*History of Gargantua and Pantagruel*. Dr. François Rabelais. Lyons, 1542 (English edition 1927, p. 584).

QUEEN WHIMS' COURT DANCES (French, Medi-aeval)
As listed by Dr. Rabelais,[1] include familiar and strange names. Says he, telling us how Queen Whims passed her time after dinner:
"When we had dined, a chachanin led us into the queen's hall, and there we saw how, after din-ner, with the ladies and princes of her court, she used to sit .... we perceived how they revived ancient sports, diverting themselves together at it :

1. Cordax	6. Phrygia	11. Monogas
2. Emmelia	7. Thracia	12. Terminalia
3. Sicinnia	8. Calabrisme	13. Floralia
4. Jambics	9. Molossia	14. Pyrrhice
5. Persica	10. Cernophorum	15. Nicatism

and a thousand other dances".

This was followed by the sports of the Queen's Officers* (which see) and a ball ("in the manner of a tournament").
[1]*Gargantua and Pantagruel*. Dr. F. Rabelais. London ed. 1927.

QEMAT OR QUIMATI OR QUIMAIT (Old Egyptian)
The chief "Singing Priestess", a temple servitor who sang to a harp, or danced with sistrum. As a priestess of Amen the God of Secrecy, she was usually of royal birth; her services were used in the lower grades of temple initiation as instructor of young priests. Quimait was leader of the "ven-erable women" in the *Hymn to Osiris*, aided by Tehuti the Measurer, God of the Moon. They measured out the dance floor of the "Secret House" prepared for Osiris. At Abydos (one of the three great religious centres) ceremonial began in silence. No singer nor player on the pipe, nor on cithara, was permitted to perform at the commencement ... as usual in rites in honour of the other gods. This was the Silence of Mourning; it was only a solemn dance movement.

QUETZALES (Mexico)
Performers of the *Quetzal Dance* in villages of Vera Cruz, Puebla and Hidalgo. Of pre-Conquest origin, it probably had connections with the cult of Quetzalcoatl, Toltec god of learning, and with the Mexican Quetzal bird, which has brilliant plumage of red, green, yellow and blue. This bird was sym-bolically associated with the "Lord of the House of Dawn", a variant of Quetzalcoatl, and one of the gods governing the thirteen periods of each day in the complicated Aztec calendar. Its feathers were used by the Aztecs to make ceremonial cloaks and head-dresses. The present-day *Quetzal Dance* is notable for the spectacular head-dress (the "Splendor") worn by the dancers. While this may once have been made entirely of feathers, only the outer rim is now feathered, the rest of the "Splendor" consisting of a circular frame, five feet across, of thin reeds, through which are threaded bands of coloured ribbon or paper, the whole supported on a conical cap fitting the dan-cer's head. The rest of the costume consists of fringed trousers and cape; white or coloured shirt, embroidered or trimmed with ribbons; long coloured stockings and sandals. Accompanied by drum and flute, and marking the rhythm with their rattles, the dancers (about ten or twelve men in a group) form two facing lines, and move with dignified steps through several figures, each figure beginning with a "reverence" and having a different tune. Using simple steps, the dancers change places and form patterns, such as a cross or a chain. In some villages, the last figure is a turning wheel, made by four dancers; and another figure, the "serpent chain" to a tune called "Little Snake" again points to Quetzalcoatl, whose name means "Feathered Serpent".
[See *Aztec Dances; Malinche; Plumas, Danza de las*]

QUINQUATRIA (Roman)
Days of the Feast of Pallas, celebrated during the ancient "Twelve Days of the Winter Ritual". They were filled with singing and mumming, dancing and feasting, attended by players hidden in vizors and painted masks. This custom was continued in Rome by the *catechumens* who were roped into the new religion; they held the Hebrew "Day of Circumcision" (really, circum-cession of the sol-stice), on the New Year's Day; while the Epiphany —the Twelfth Day, when the sun had definitely "turned the corner" from the solstice—marked the end of this ancient ritual. In England there was a famous *Golden Carol*, in which danced Melchior, Balthazar and Kaspar, singing the words as they moved.

QUIPU OR QUIPO, OR KIPU (Peru)
A knot. The Chinese name is *chieh-sheng*. Cords with regular knots have been used widely as a method of mnemonic record and repetition. Herodotus mentions that King Darius, fighting the Persians, gave orders to Ionians by thongs carrying sixty knots: the expected period of his return. Dance forms used close circles with a knot for each dancer: the rope, or the dancers, moved on. The Peruvian system was developed to a kind of tree, or main cord with offshoots (the human nerve system is similar). The *quipo* operate much as the Red Indian *wampum*, the Tibetan or Latin:st *rosary* or Hindu *vajnopavita* or Egyptian *putser* cord. In folk dance kerchiefs have been used. Knotted memory cords are known also in Mexico, Asia and Africa. In ritual, the "folded cords" were used to mark out a *templum* (*rincke*) or the Templar's house or *meissen*.

QUIRE (Latin, from Arabic *Quhar*)
The place in the *Navis*; the place for ritual dance; the place essential "For the Question"; the examination of the ritual or ceremonial; the place of attendance for roll-call (the *tychus* or list of members)—to "enquire". The older Roman ritual had the same unit: the *quirinus* (a place named as *quiranalius*). The term is related to the Greek *choir* and *chorus*; to the Eastern *khor* and the later Spanish *corral* (which preceded in use the term theatre); also to the Basque *escu-uar* (square). The Saxon *squire* is the "master of the place"; to re-quire is to demand attention. Paper-makers refer to a numbered pile of flat sheets as a *quire* (usually twenty-five similar pieces). *Quietus* is "the end", and *equerry* (*equerria* in Basque) is the attendant at the enquiry; nothing to do with "horse", but as a *querent*. The "esquire" was one competent to attend; or who had attended.

QUITO Y PON DANTZA (Spain, Estramudra)
Means "Put and Take" dance; or is termed *Son brincao y son no brincao*, ("Jump or No-Jump Sound"), or else *La punta y el pie* ("Foot and Point"). These dances move with a bright foot rhythm, but, like so many Irish jigs, keep the arms quite still with the body upright. The emphasis is thus technical brilliance; the music is from drum and tambors. They are contests held in public places on holidays, but especially for the Festa de San Bartollomeo at Montehermoso.

R

RABBA (Israel)
The *Idra Rabba* and *Suta Rabba* signify the Greater and Lesser Schools of the Hebrew rituals, connected with *Qabalah** on one side and synagogue on the other hand. Each *Rabba* had a ritual dance system.

RADENYA (Bulgaria)
An excitable religious circle group dance, in swift rhythm, used by the Khlysti sect of the Eastern Orthodox Church (though they are not there accepted as strictly orthodox), and followed, under this name, in Valcov. The dance is performed by an "admitted group", with the direct purpose of inducing a trance condition, in which they can forget all worldly affairs. The Khlysti were persecuted by Russian tsarist government officials. Many of their ancestors were deported from Russia into Bessarabia (mostly 1860 - 1880). They retain their dogmas and ritual most tenaciously.
[Cp. *Dervish Dance*]

RADESHORI KIRTANS (Manipura, India)
This localised term for a special Radha's *Hori* — the round dance of Radha-Krishna; performed invariably with a chant known as *kirtan*, belongs to the *Nyupi Pala*, or Women's Songs of Lament. There was a renaissance of the devotional singing of *kirtana*, about 1740, by Jey Singha, stimulated by the earlier poems of Jaya Deva in Bengal, the famous *Gita Govinda*. Descendants of Jey Singha perform this *Kirtan* at funeral festivals. About fifty women and girls sit in the *mandala** with their drummers; two more men blow conches as signals. They perform, after a long chanted introduction, the dance *Chali Shabha*. The name indicates "The Fourfold Praise" (*Shabash*), and the *chali* is a four-four rhythm, difficult to perform. *Chali Shabha* is performed as they stand, mainly with softly curving arms and hands, as the singers move in a semicircle; the dance is one of noble grief, great dignity, and intense emotional expression. This *kirtan* belongs solely to this family group; being performed on the twelfth evening (or day following) after the death of a descendant of Jey Singha. This particular chanting dance as a *kirtan* is not aligned with the joyous dances of Krishna and Radha.

RAEGO DANCE (Celebes)
A dance of the West Toradja tribe of central Celebes, performed at a two-day festival to seek the favour of the gods in a good harvest. On the evening of the first day, young men and girls assemble in the ceremonial house (*lobo*) to sing love songs, and dance round a fire till morning. In the early afternoon of the next day everyone assembles outside the *lobo* for the ceremonies, during which the *Raego* is danced. Wearing short black jackets, embroidered with gold, striped knee-

breeches and bright head-cloths, the young men form a semi-circle, each with his left hand on his neighbour's right shoulder. The girls (in long dresses of bark-cloth, round bamboo head-dresses, bracelets, a collar of beads with a fringe of coins and bells, and a bunch of scented leaves tied at the back), walk in a close row, their arms crossed behind. Forming a circle round the line of girls, the men (one behind the other, each with one hand on the shoulder of the man in front) take four steps forward, stamping the left foot on the ground and whooping in time. The girls take four steps sideways and a short step backward with the left foot. Thus the dance continues, with no change of figure, the dancers singing all the time, occasionally one taking a rest, to be replaced by another.

RAG FAIR (Old English) OR RAGFYR (Welsh)
The last Faire of the Year, held in December; probably both from *ragna*, twilight (Scandinavian) or "end of reign" as being the fall of the year. *Rhaca* or *Rhaga* (Welsh) is a "spectacle", once connected with miracle plays, hence the term "rake-hell" or *rhaga*-hell (their furious presentation of "hell fire for the sinner", in the Christian manner). The gradually worsening of these itinerant shows gave rise to other terms, often used to indicate dancer-mimes; such as *rhaca-muffin*. The college boys' term : *Rag* or *rhaca*, is the same : a spontaneous "bit of fun"; *rhag* is also "an entrance". Thus the Rag Fair was the last chance of buying and selling at the end of the year; play or dancing booths were always in evidence. The dozens of derivatives show that the term and the occasion were traditional.

RAGA (India, Sanskrit)
Is emanation in emotional terms of Sound (*Bhava*). In this music, delicately balanced and originally fully organized, we have the direct parallel to the Brahmanic-Hindu doctrine of the dual emanation of energy-substance; of force-matter; of life-form. *Raga-ragini* retains this same balance; has this same eternally rhythmic quality. In Europe this doctrine was taught at Krotona, in the school of Pythagoras; as the "One evolving into the Many", while eternally pervading the All. This profound fact is expressed again in geometry; and in certain associated numeral forms we know in the Roman system of Trajan. In this simple, yet erudite series, we proceed from cipher to ten; "circle to square to circle" — not by finished line added to line, but by the dynamic inscription of lines from the *laya* point; in lines made by points always moving as "traces of force". Thus every genuine *raga* scale has a unity-in-multiplicity. Heard within the octave; it may be first noted as unity-to-unity : the simple side of the square (as a line) is sounded against the opposite side of the same square. The sound is identical; it is equilibrium; and nothing happens. There is no departure from the basic note; no origin of form; no step to that disequilibrium that is essential to all life and living. All music is emanation : all sound begins with a vibrating surface, whether of gut or metal, or a column of air in an organ pipe. In *Timaeus*, Plato says :
"Zeus formed things as they first arose,
   According to forms and to numbers".
Aristotle, misunderstanding, mispresents this statement, saying that Plato stated "forms *are* numbers", or that "ideas have substantial existence, are real things". *Raga* is the schematic basis of Hindustani musical song and dance, in terms of traditional or ritual motifs. The *raga* is a "group of notes" (never any single note) that belong essentially to one scale (grama). Originally the intervals were not equal in tone, but modern practice tends to adopt the chromatic European scale, as far as the arithmetical intervals of the string are concerned. This defect ruins the quality of *raga*, which is associated with *rasa* or emotion, as displayed in music or the dance. There are six "principal *ragas*", from which "motifs" are derived the *ragini* series, each in groups of six. There are then thirty-six, if the original *raga* is included, but forty-two if new groups of seven are heard. The six *ragas* are allocated traditionally to the *bhava* or nature-mood of the three seasons of the Indian year; while they possess also more recondite and esoteric qualities, hinted or described in Hindu scriptures. Indian dance systems have tended to forget the dominance of the *raga*; but it remains in the *mantra*, or chant system, associated with the religious liturgies, in some sects.
[See *Raga and Ragini*. O. C. Gangoly (Calcutta); *Raga and Ragini* (Am. Jrnl. Aesthetics) December 1952. W. G. Raffé]

RAG-MALA (Northern India)
Generic term for "dance-pictures", which developed first in the hill-country, on the southern side of the Himalayan range. This branch of painting became possible by (a) provision of paper, from China originally; and (b) traditions of religious paintings, stimulated by Tibetan temple banner paintings (*tsangka*); combined with (c) ancient traditions of the Hindu musical system of *raga-ragini* modes, in figures known mythically as *gandharva* and *apsara*. These creatures were painted in Hindu cave or built temples; but paper, and painting on paper was then new to India. Manuscript writing and drawing had been limited to palm and other leaves; parchment had already developed in Persia. The

invasions of the Mughals (Mongols) brought Persian painting, and manuscript production, into the great courts of Delhi, but then chiefly in secular (*durbari*) mode. The meeting of these technical and social factors allowed the emergence of the *ragmala* — painted presentations of the imagined "creatures of music" believed to be summoned by correct playing of the Hindu *raga*.* Thus in the Hindu valleys — Kangra, the Kulu Valley, and in Kashmir, there grew this North Indian school of "musical dance painting". From these paintings much can be gathered on Hindu dance (*Krishna-natyam*) and the Purana play mode, as cultivated by the *Kathaka* mime-dance form; which was then receiving the Moslem impact in the cities of Delhi, Lahore, and Agra. The cycles of *ragmala* paintings provide a visual mode of Hindu ritual, especially as repeated on festival days.

RAIGOE (Japan)
Ritual dance, said to have been performed annually for more than a thousand years (since the Fujiwara period), in the province of Nagano, Central Japan. This Buddhist rite includes only young unmarried men; for them it is a kind of initiation. After a three-day fast (with other preparations) there is a procession from temple to dancing ground; in which youths wear masks (as *bhikkus*, or disciples entering the *Sangha*, society), and they appear as birds, or angels (*kinnara*). Some masks show them as aspirants to the Boddhisattva attainment. Some dances show *kinnaras* — with fans instead of wings — moving as if floating through the air. Many youths in the procession wear a fixed golden halo (like those used in mediaeval Florentine plays and shewn in paintings), while male Buddhists of all ages are indicated by masks, finished in smooth white, or in lacquered gold.

"RAINBOW SKIRT AND FEATHER JACKET"
  (Mediaeval China)
Dancers of the T'ang period (AD 620 - 900), when Chinese civilization reached its height. The patron of actors was Emperor King Huang, according to the legend of his "visit to the Palace of the Moon". When he returned to his own Palace at Chang An, the Emperor recalled the twenty maidens he had seen, performing the Phoenix Dance, clad in their ceremonial "rainbow skirts and feather jackets", dancing under a beautiful cinnamon tree. He founded an Academy, called the Bountiful Pear Garden, for training of theatre people. Actors and dancers were called "Disciples of the Pear Garden", or similar charming names according to their particular theatre school. They began to develop a system of opera-ballet-drama, apart from religious ritual dance.   [See *Peach Garden*]

"RAISINS AND ALMONDS" (Jewish)
A folk dance, popular during the 19th century in East London, entitled *Rozhinkes un Mändlen*, with a plaintive traditional melody, formerly (chiefly in Poland), led by the Baal Shem Tov. Probably this once-ritual dance was derived from *die reisen von Alle-mande* — the journey around the sacred circle of the *Allemande*,* during which slow and sorrowful rite the mourners' prayer, *kaddish*, would be heard; or give a final benediction to *Chasaneh* (wedding ceremony), as for the required march round the hall; or to follow *Maoz Tsur Y'chuati*, the leading hymn of *Chanucah*, or Feast of Lights, alternating with a familiar *Leibgesang* (song of praise).

RAJASIKA PUJA (Hindu)
Ritual devotion which includes dance, as the "Dance before the Devi". Says Sir John Woodroffe : "In full worship there is always dancing and singing before the Devi . . . this is *rajasika puja*. The *puja* of the text here, is *Sattvika*, the dance being the ideal one of the mind and the senses. All the things offered are in the human body, which is called *kshudra Brahmananda*, or "small egg" or spheroid of Brahma".[1] The ritual dance is thus a royal (*raja*) worship (*puja*), in which the whole being of the worshipper is devoted and offered to the Devi.
[1] *Tantra of the Great Liberation* by Sir John Woodroffe (p.123)(Trans. of *Mahanirvana*). Madras, 1913.

RAMBEN (Low Maki) (Malekula, New Hebrides)
The first half of a two-part ritual cycle of death and rebirth, native to Malekula and the Small Islands close to it, especially Vao, where it takes place one, two, or three years after *Turei Na-mbe** (setting up of new gongs). The cycle centres round the sacrifice of tusked boars, with which initiates identify themselves, seeking ritual rebirth, and life with the ancestors after death. The shortest time for *Ramben* to be completed is five or six years, the first four preparing for the final sacrifice, after which one or two years are spent by the chief sacrificers, in retreat. Dances occur at stated intervals during each year. The circular dance, *Velal*,* used during preparatory and closing stages to introduce important rites, heralds the seeking of a suitable stone for the sacrificial dolmen in the first year; in the third year it introduces the building of the dolmen; and in the fifth or sixth year it introduces the final rite which closes the cycle. Each time *Velal* is danced in strict rotation, on the home dancing-ground, by all Vao villages, at intervals of several days. During the second year, when the stone is brought from the beach to the dancing-ground, three or four important "Maki-men"

(initiates) dance *Taur Na-mbak*,* weaving a serpentine course from one side of the stone to the other. The fourth year opens with a feast and the circular *Hek-hekelean** ("Settling Down" Dance), so-called because the climax of *Ramben* is in sight, and the "Maki-men" now "settle down" seriously towards its prosecution. All villages, in rotation, dance *Hek-hekelean* at intervals of five to ten days. Two or three days after the last village has danced, people of the home-village perform *Vin-buel* ("Dance of No Consequence"), a small dance outside the sequence of ritual dances. *Hek-hekelean* is danced once more, when the date of the great sacrifice is announced, and that night the first all-night performance of *Taur Na-mbak* takes place. Thence, until the day of sacrifice, it is danced nightly, from dusk to dawn, parties from visiting villages joining in from time to time. On the eve of the great sacrifice the all-night dance is frequently interrupted by *Bot-mau*,* a women's processional dance in honour of the tusked boars to be sacrificed, performed as many times as there are boars. When the procession finally withdraws, *Taur Nam-bak* is resumed. On the day of sacrifice processions arrive dancing the heavy-footed *Na-rel*,* and there are no further dances until thirty days after the sacrifice, when the initiates emerge from retreat to perform a *Na-leng** maze dance. *Na-leng* mumming plays are also given by parties from each village in turn. The same night *Le-tean*, a song-and-dance cycle describing exploits of Maki-men, is performed. After an interval of one or two years, when the "Maki-men" are mourned, are reborn, and receive new names, the *Velal* introduces the final rite bringing the cycle to a close. It is followed after an interval of a year or two by *Maki-Ru** (High Maki), the second part of the ritual. [See *Malekula, Dances of*]

RAMBLA (Spain)
A ritual place (Arabic) where dance was performed, for divination or sibylline prophecy; from this came the term "to ramble" in wandering spech. The talking was done during the ritual dance, while "possessed" by the prophetic spirit (a variation of the Roman augur). At the end, *rematat* was chanted, meaning "There! It is finished!" The colloquial term "to rumble" means "to become aware of something kept secret" — "He's been rumbled!" (found out). So also, walking without much purpose — "to ramble"; and roses, likewise. Probably the dance term *rumba* comes from this Arabic root.

RAMMAL (Arabia), RUMAL (Urdu)
The "pattern" of the "dance in sand". *Rammali* are sand diviners; they draw astrological patterns on sand, in response to requests for "fortunes". Their art is called *Raml 'Ali* or "Ali's Sand", from their patron Imam Ali, an ancient adept. The practice itself is a "dance of the fingers". These members of the Soothsayers Guild possess a number of basic patterns by memory. In Levantine countries, they will draw appropriate patterns for the month; for the Festival, etc. In India the practice was specialised : then patterns were drafted on cotton. These large squares called *band-hanna* (ring of the year), also got the more definite name *rumal*. Finally the Thuggee cult adopted the *rumal* as the ritual implement of offering its victims (strangling with kerchief) because it was impressed with the sacred pattern of Bhowanee. From this sacrifice dancers were exempt. The Arab *rammali* are well regarded; clad like the Ulema, they follow their fraternal Gild of the Astronomers in the Alay Procession.   [Cp. *Alpona* (India)]

RAMMAL (Persian)
An itinerant conjuror, whose confederate sings and dances; also a diviner (the earlier term comes from *rumal*, or sand patterns). The *rammals* undertake "detective work" to recover stolen property.

RANELAGH (England)
Famous 18th century London Pleasure Gardens at Chelsea Village, three-quarters of a mile from Buckingham Gate and St. James's Park. Opened in 1742, they comprised the house and gardens of the late Lord Ranelagh (purchased in 1733 by Lacy — patentee of Drury Lane Theatre — and Rietti); a rectangular "canal"; grottos and "temples"; and the newly constructed Rotunda. This circular building measured 555 feet in circumference, 150 feet internal diameter, and round it were two tiers of fifty-two boxes, each holding eight people. A bandstand provided accommodation for musicians, and in 1746 an organ was added. Concerts by famous singers and musicians were held thrice weekly; displays of fireworks were given; masquerades (or *ridottos*) occurred twice a week. Tickets for masquerades cost 10/6d. and £1/1/0, but the entrance fee on ordinary nights was 2/6d., including tea, coffee, bread and butter. During intervals, or between dances, patrons promenaded round the Rotunda or in the gardens, and for some years the fame of Ranelagh eclipsed that of Vauxhall.* The approach road from Buckingham Gate was well lit; the Proprietors provided a horse patrol to guard against foot-pads. George II frequently attended masquerades, as did most of London Society. Of an open-air *ridotto* in 1749, Horace Walpole wrote : "It began at three o'clock and at five the fashionable folk began to come in. The whole garden was filled with marquees and

tents. In one corner there was a Maypole dressed with garlands and people danced round it to a tabour and pipe, and rustic music, all masked, even the bandsmen . . . On the canal was a kind of gondola, dressed with flags and streamers, filled with musicians . . . Then there were booths for tea and wine, gaming tables, and dancing, and about two thousand people . . ."[1] In 1802 Boodles Club gave a grand fête there, with lamps hung in the trees, a dance floor and a stage for ballets and short plays. But the popularity of the Gardens waned; and the last fashionable ball was held there on July 8th, 1803. A final exotic flourish occurred when Ranelagh was hired, for one day, by the Spanish Ambassador, for an elaborate *fiesta*, with Spanish dances. In 1805 the Rotunda and other buildings were sold by auction, and later demolished.   [Cp. *Redoute**]

[1] Horace Walpole's *Correspondence*. Ed. Mrs. Paget Toynbee and W. S. Lewis.
[See *The London Pleasure Gardens of the Eighteenth Century*. Warwick Wroth. 1896]

RANGASTAL (S. India)
Denotes, especially in South Kannara, the "dancing-space" used by *Yakshagana** players. The show is folk-play and dance, usually after harvest, performed by small professional travelling companies of men and boys. They occupy a hard, harvested field; erect tall posts crowned with fresh green mango leaves; and present their drama, chiefly *Karnajun*. The *Bhagavata* is their chief, as minstrel, reciter, or singer, accompanied by drums and cymbals. *Rangastal* is, in effect, a temporary stage (*ranga*) lighted by two great brass oil pots. Torches are added, for the play lasts all night from dusk to dawn. One performance is given; collection having been made, when the company packs up to travel to the next village; to eat and sleep until it is time for the next show. *Rangastal* is thus the folk version of the household ritual modes of *alpona** and *rangoli*, but it is concrete, where they are abstract in form.

RANGOLI (India)
Dance-floor pattern, used on the boards of the stage, or on the stone platform, for public performances. The *alpona** is similar, but is confined mainly to domestic usage. Compare the English *Tyler* (Masonic) or the clerical *vergire;* and the *marker*, for game of tennis. Compare also the old Egyptian *Arit**—the Roman augur's *kirke* or *templum*. There are Polynesian patterns (*tangov**) but only the Chinese *Lo-fan* has revealed an obvious manner of usage in the derivative of the mariners compass.

RANT
A 17th century English dance of uncertain origin, mentioned in Stuart publications. Music for the *Rant* occurs in the compositions of John Jenkins (1592 - 1678), and in Matthew Locke's *Melothesia* (1673). The form of the dance is unknown. The name may be an abbreviation of *Coranto*, but there is considerable difference in the rhythms of the two dances. In Old Dutch *Ranten* means to dote or rave, and one possible derivation is from the verb "to rant," suggesting a dance of wild character.

RANGLER TANZ (Austria)
A pair dance for young men, who perform a styled wrestling match. One, two or three pairs may dance simultaneously. It is an ordinary festival dance, often alternated with *schühplattler*, in which the movements suggest some likeness to expert football players.

RAPPER, RAPER (English : from Greek — *Raper* — a rod or a stick)
The wooden lath carried by Mores dancers; often misnamed as sword. The term *rapis*, though taken into Italian as *rapier*, has more affinity with *rhabdos*, the magical rod or wand; or the *lituus* (later pastoral crook or staff) used by Roman augurs. The *rapis* was brought into England by Greek missions who preceded Constantine at York. With the needle, it gives the Greek term, *raptos*, as "something sewn together", which laced forms appear in the *Mores* dances,* in the repeated intertwining. *Retoz* and *regöz* denote the pattern made; the "floor-cover" (see *Regöz**—"Three Kings' Dance") as *rhapsodos*, is "one who sews songs together". The *rapis* served to mark time and to mark spaces. The final pattern made by six rappers is the "Rose" or "Lock"—in the air. The long *rapis*, or wand, was used in some rituals to mark a circle visibly on the ground.

RAPPRESENTAZIONI (Italy)
Mediaeval term for an Italian mode of "Miracle Play" then featured as being a "representatione" or alleged historical event—in verbal contradistinction to the growing mode for presenting acted versions of Grecian or Roman legends, admitted freely to be myths. These productions appeared through Italy, in town or village as occasion served, from the 12th to the 16th centuries, roughly contemporary with the foreign propaganda versions similarly produced by Italian clerics (in their first instance) in England. The Florentine reformer Savonorola, stimulated newer performances; he compiled a *Passion* and a version of *Arte Moriendi*. as well as a *Manual of Mentale Oratione*. This work, which notably precedes the modern psycho-

analysts, reveals a curious emphasis on the mind. With its full title: *Operetta frate Giroloma de Ferrare della Oratione Mentale* (printed about 1495) it advocated "mind training", with pictures, long before the notorious Jesuit *Exercises* appeared. The traditional twelve episodes of the Pachon, following authentic traditions from Egypt and Babylonia, affirmed the "twelve actions" of the "year of the gods" seen with the Grecian Herakles. Many dances decorated some versions of these episodes. Bernado Pulci (d. 1501) found a legend of *Barlaam and Josophat*, based on the imported Buddha legend; while his wife, Antonia, wrote many more, including an arrangement of *The Prodigal Son;* and another version of *Joseph and Potiphar*, unquestionably intended for full performance. All these plays begin with the *Entry of the Angelus* (messenger) the Master of Ceremonies, who speaks or chants his *Preludis*. Many of the *Rappresentazione* were acted in dumb show, based on active mime, extended by dance and accompanied by simple music. The first printed example known is *Abbraham* (script by Maffeo Belcari), printed in 1485, after his death. *Herod and Salome* was a most popular subject; as is indicated by the numerous drawings in manuscripts, and even of carvings in churches, in wood or stone. Many of the *Todtentanz* forms were extensions of the *Arte Moriendi*. The last fading relic of the fraternity of the Batutti, who organized many representations, now remains in the Beffana celebrations of children; and the dollshouse contrivances of "Cribs" or "Stables" in toys or waxworks.

RAQA or RAQAD (Hebrew)

From *Rakadu* (Assyrian) meaning "to step with the feet", or to move in procession with stamping feet in unison. This was always a collective, or group dance, with simple instruments such as *toph* and *shofar* (drum and horn-trumpet). The *Raqa* is a reversal of the typical "marriage dance", which forms on the basis of "See and be seen"; for the funeral (at which *raqad* was most common) was "To see him out". Thus the dance moved in two forms: the circumambulation around the bier; the processional to the cemetery; and another circumambulation around the grave. The custom continued longer among the Sephardic Jews (Spain and Portugal), showing seven circles (while chanting seven supplications) in each complete ritual of the circumambulation.

RAS LILA (Manipura, India)

Is literally, "Dance Play in Circle"; and indicates a range of dances taking this basic form; yet mainly in the religious and devotional line of the Vaishnavite mythos of Krishna and Radha. They receive further names, from their due period: the three principal modes being *Maha Ras Lila*, the annual or New Year celebration (in December); the *Basant Ras Lila*, for the Spring Festival (March-April, equivalent to Easter date); and the *Kunja Ras Lila*, also called *Arbor Ras Lila* (for the Harvest Festival) at *Dasehra*. There are four additional modes of the *Ras* Dances; they include (1) *Diba Ras Lila*, which can be danced during any day (except festivals and mourning, and the *Maha Ras* periods), and with it the *Nitya Ras Lila* (the "Eternal Dance" permitted to be danced at any season. The *Natya Ras Lila* has four performers, Krishna with eight *gopis;* but the April celebration of *Osta Gopi Chyam Ras Lila* requires eight players for each, Krishna and Radha. For further details on each dance, see special paragraphs.

RACHENITZA (Bulgaria)

Popular dance, usually in 7/16 beat, following a strict rhythm, generally with a piper and one or two drummers. This general dance rhythm (with varying melodies, according to rite and season), may be heard in popular rejoicings—a wedding or a feast—and also at a funeral. In the open, extension of the dance line reveals one or other of the basic *hora** patterns—the circle, spiral, and wavy line; in this manner the group dance precedes the *Vulgari* ritual of the Netsinari sect. The *Ratchenitza*, found all over Bulgaria, usually begins as a pair dance, but often becomes general. There is much improvisation on basic steps, with displays of technique by the men, the dance sometimes becoming a contest between two or three dancers. Rhythm is marked by hand movements; in the Dobrudje region arms move in heavy emphasis, thumb and first finger of each hand held together at the tips. At weddings, the *Ratchenitza* is danced by bridesmaids and groomsmen after leaving the church, and again at various stages during the celebrations.

"RATS" (French, from German)

Name given to junior dancers of the Ballet Company at the Paris Opera and other theatres. Comes from the ancient name *rathas;* given to the junior members of Teutonic councils or gilds, from far older Iranian terms.

RAYE

A little-known dance form sometimes mentioned in 16th and 17th century literature. In Middle Dutch, *Rey* or *Reye* is given as "Round Dance", while Chaucer in his *House of Fame* (1236) refers to going to "Pypers of the Duche Tonge, To lerne . . . daunces, springes, Reyes . . ." Modern Dutch is

Peruvian Ritual Dance. Five warriors moving in marching rite. From a painted vase in the Necropolis of Ancon.
                                                                                                          PERU

Rei. Possibly allied with German *Reihen* or *Reigen;** also *reisen*, "to travel", may be a parallel word.

RAYMI (Peru)
Chief festival of ancient Peruvians, which gave this name also to the dances. They are described by Reville[1] as being violent or extremely energetic; which suggests a martial mode of action. He says that "the Incas themselves took no part in these dances, but had an Inca dance of their own, grave and measured".
[1] *Les Réligions des peuples non-civilisés.* F. Reville, Paris, 1883.

RECORDS OF DANCE
Have been devised in several distinct modes. All ritual dance is fitted both to time and place, being recorded in chant and myth, rather than by any written script. These ritual methods of design, record and memory are obscure; and still little known outside the countries and doctrines of their origin. When we arrive at the modern commercial theatre, we meet with different problems in dance : the chief needs being to (a) devise a new form of dance; (b) to record it, in its finished or produced form; and (c) to obtain accurate and complete evidence concerning its origin, so that ownership and copyright can be established. With the passing of court ballet and the progress of Theatre or stage ballet, Féuillet of Paris was one of the first to see the need for a script method. Necessarily it was done to scale; not full-scale. He sought to note and record the tracks of any single dancer, in plan, as it might appear on the stage floor. This track plan was accurate, so far as it went; but omitted all movements above the feet. Next, F. A. Zorn of Odessa, advanced on Féuillet by devising a system in which he could add the dance movements in elevation, in addition to the track plan. Then the Russian ballet teacher, V. Stepanov, produced a scheme which, limited as it was to one theatre, included the stage plan itself; and showed the positions and movements of soloists and chorus, finally including the bars of music that had been used to accompany these steps. This Stepanov system was that used by Nicolas Serguéeff to make his records of the Petipas ballets of Petersburg; from which the revivals of Ballet in London were made choreographically possible. The system devised by Rudolf Laban returned from the complete stage plan, to a decorated linear mode, with symbols to include body movements; but limited to the single dancer. The visual record made by the cinema film (if it could be quadruplicated from the same dance, in four different but simultaneous views) might be valuable in conjunction with both musical score and choreographic score. The multiple values of dance, requiring record in three dimensions of space as well as time, state a problem of great practical difficulty. The sole dance form that is fully recordable by cinema is the cut-out or painted-paper dance of the film cartoon, where the dance is created as much by the facile movement of the film as by the initially inert dancer-figures.

REDJANG (Bali)
A dance performed once a year by unmarried girls in the village of Tenganan, in the hills of East Bali,

where the conservative Bali Aga (descendants of pure Indonesian inhabitants) live and preserve tradition. The ancient, rarely-heard *gamelan selundung*, played by old men, accompanies the dance. Girls, wearing crowns decorated with flowers of beaten gold, and clad in bright silks with loose scarves attached at the waist, dance the *redjang* in a double line, arranged from the smallest children to grown girls who have not obtained a husband. The graceful flicking of scarves first to one side then the other, with a half turn of the body each time, recalls Javanese style. It is a slow dance, with long intervals between movements, when the girls stand with downcast eyes until the music indicates a change of pose. With the arrival of the boys, marriageable girls step forward one by one, modestly and with downcast eyes, to display their charms. There follows the *abuang,** when the boys choose a bride and dance before her.

REDONDILLA (Spain, Med.)
The 14th century "ballad measure" taken by Prescott[1] to be "the basis of Spanish versification" and of great antiquity. There is considerable resemblance between the early Spanish ballad and the British. The light trochaic structure of the *redondilla*, rolling on its graceful *asonante* seems to carry monotony into extreme flexibility. As with early *troubadors* and English gleemen, the ballad was usually mimed and danced, with verse, melody, and action, all in simple form. "Some graceful little songs, still chanted by the peasantry of Spain in their dances to the accompaniment of castanets, are referred by a competent critic (Condé, *de la Poesie Oriental*, M.S.) to an Arabian origin".
[1] *History of Ferdinand and Isabella.* W. H. Prescott (7th edn. p. 193. 1854).

REDOUTE (French, from Italian *ridotto*)
Public assemblies where guests danced, with or without masks. Similar assemblies appeared in Germany and England. Horace Walpole refers to "Ridotto" as an attraction at Vauxhall* and Ranelagh* (18th century). The building used in Vienna, erected in 1748 (rebuilt in stone in 1754) forms part of the Burg or Imperial Palace. There was a *Grosse* and *Kleine* Redoutensaal where, in 1795, Beethoven played at a concert of Haydn. Till about 1870 these rooms were used for concerts, and masked balls were held there during Carnival (Twelfth Night to Shrove Tuesday), some being open to the public on payment of an entrance fee; others private. Special nights were reserved for the court and nobility. Dances performed at the *Redoute* (*Redoutentanze*) were Minuets,* Allemandes,* Contredanses,* Schottisches,* Anglaises* and Landlers.* They were composed for full orchestra and published (mainly by Artaria) for pianoforte. Mozart, Haydn, Beethoven, Hummel, Woelfl, Gyrowetz and others have left dances written for these assemblies

REEL O' TULLOCH (Scotland)
This and other Scottish *Reels** in 4/4 time, come from ancient periods. The Gaelic title *Ruidhle Thulaichean* (cp. *Ruad** and *Ruelle**) affirms the circular form. This *Reel* is a variant of the Foursome Reel; they are usually danced to follow the *Strathspey,** and then break into the *Hullachan.* Some consider that this dance became known in Germany as *Der Schottische*, with which name it appeared in America; with a version called *Stealing Dance* or *Tag*, now flippantly termed the "Excuse Me!", demanding a change of partners. The nineteenth century *Schottische** was more akin to the Austrian *Landler** than to Scottish dances. The *Eightsome Reel* is relatively modern. The older name *Hullachan* is akin to the Irish *Hoolighan* or the Breton *Khorrigan*. Bagpipe music is used. Another dance *Tullochgorm* (sometimes called *Reel o' Tullochgorm*), is quoted as the earliest form of Highland Fling.

REGISSEUR (France)
Literally, "one who registers" — as for jobs, for parts, and for attendance at (a) performances, and (b) rehearsals. He is a steward or overseer; working with the producer on a variety of tasks, from watching the "stage-manager" who works on technical details of production, to collaborating with the *chef d'orchestre*, on getting musicians in (and their "band parts"). He may be entrusted with a record of a ballet (notation*), or may even make such documents. He sees that "treasury" is there in time; or reports for fines and deductions. For touring, he will co-operate in oversight of scenic and property packing and transport; and even help with that of the company. The duties and demands on a *régisseur* are numerous and onerous; they always vary and rarely remain the same, even with one company. They die young and receive no bouquets.

REILL or Short *Daunse* (Scotland. Med.)
Is a dance form midway between *revel* (or merriment) and *reel*, to perform a dance ballad (to "reel off" a list of names). In Ireland it belonged to the group name Reilly or O'Rahilly — the youth who danced round the circle or the "Great O" so often recalled in these prefixtures to so many Irish names. The crowd followed the names (of the ancestors) with claps and comments of "Really!" now adopted as an English sniff of incredulity. The dance was a *tripudium* round the circle followed by a step dance over crossed sticks at the centre

(shillelagh or else edged weapons). The un-ruly behaviour came at length to be turned to *Messe-Ruolle* and thence to Mis-Rule, with abbot as Messe Leader.

REGOS, Pron. "Raggash" (Hungary)
The band of minstrels, the *Regös* or *raggersh*, who perform their Festival Masque in the season of the New Year. A group of six to ten *Regös* will travel round a large village; or visit several small villages, presenting a carnival play, usually after nightfall, with dancing and chanting, carrying crudely fashioned lanterns. They receive small gifts and are entertained. These *Regös* are not strictly in religious legend; they are never the gypsies (*Zigeuner*), but ordinary village lads. The *Regös* perform the "Three Kings Dance" on the appropriate floor-pattern.   [See *Rapper*]

REHEARSAL (from Old French : *rehercier*, "to harrow again", to repeat)
Rehearsal of dance movement or of music; in the process of building-up a new dance, or reviving an older dance, requires the presence of (a) a ballet-master or producer, (b) a pianist or violinist; and (c) one or more dancers, in parts, but all of them in the period of completion. Rehearsal belongs only in part to *repertoire*; since it implies shaping (as well as giving instruction) on one specific dance, play, ballet, opera; and in this differs from *repetition*.* Rehearsal thus supposes that a dancer or actor or singer knows his business : it is now to be fitted to one particular production; and should not require any technical instruction. Rehearsal within the repertory is "to find again", to be refreshed.

REI DAVID, DANCA DO (Portugal)
Part of the procession held at Braga on John's Day. At intervals the procession stops while "King David" and his ten followers dance, dressed in pseudo-oriental costume. Each man plays a musical instrument as they go along the streets (violin, guitar, flute, triangle or cello), and continue to accompany themselves during the dance. With a hopping step the "King" dances down the line formed by the other ten, and returns with a back step, finishing with a pirouette. This is repeated by two of his retinue, then again by these two with the "King", while the other dancers turn and wind back to their places. The dance is first mentioned by name in 1726, although the John's Day procession at Braga is recorded in 1579, when it was much more elaborate. Included then were a *Serpe* (Serpent), and *cavallinhos fuscos* (hobby-horses); a *Mourisca** was performed and a *Dança dos pelas*, in which girls danced on the shoulders of men.

Now only the *Dança do Rei David* remains, and the *Carros dos Pastores*—a pastoral playlet performed on a decorated lorry, in which children dressed as shepherds and shepherdesses perform a simple country dance.

REIGEN (Germany)
Singentanz; also as *Reihen*; a line dance and round dance with song, a *carole*; earlier form *rihen/rihan*. Also earlier as *reige, reie, reye*, "bringing in line" (from Skt. *rekha*, "line-formed"), dances in firm line, straight and circular.

REINCARNATION
Is a primal theme for ritual and mystical dance form, all over the world, and in all periods of history. Lacking an accurate knowledge of this fundamental article of faith, we cannot understand the dynamic motives of the religious cults. This theme is presented in a thousand aspects : none of them complete, many of them now darkly obscured with superstition, especially when materialised to present a "rising from the dead" in solid physical form by the newly dead body. Genuine reincarnation affirms, but does not contradict, the subtle laws of nature. The main lesson, as the Druids of Britain taught, is obvious in the cycle of the Eternal Tree, as *Iggdrazil* in the Scandinavian scheme; as the *Tree of Life* in the Babylonian-Jewish scheme; and so on, down to the revised "Chemical Tree" of the elements, formulated by the Alchemists and half-revealed by the Russian chemist Mendeleev; and again stated in the transformative atomic-electronic mode (by disintegration) by modern physicists. As the Hindus show—partly by means of their Sacred Dance—the process is rhythmic, in expansion and contraction (local or universal), pulsating systole and diastole; producing Life and destroying Life, but forever creating Form motivated by Energy. No other mode than Dance is capable of providing the dynamic mythos that indicates (but can never state in full) the secrets of this World Dance.
[See *Sacred Dance; Magical Dance; Cosmic Ballet*]

RELAX, RELAXING
(French form *relachement*; USA form "rerlacks"; German, *mildern*; Italian, *dolce far niente*). Physiological opposite to tension, developed and used in dance. Every professional dancer must learn "how to relax", a process which begins by taking all the tense state from all muscles of the entire body. The method, more especially for "civilised persons", has to be learned; and a discipline evolved, slightly different for each individual. The cause of city nervous tension (not dancing) is found in the instinctive-emotional state, as engendered by high-

pressure living; chiefly in getting and dodging, and still remaining alive. Tension is not excess effort; we have to learn by experiment how to become tensed for many normal actions; but we forget to relax afterwards. We may watch a cat, instead of getting confused with modern pseudo-psychology and its array of futile terms.—Watch muscles and nerves.

RELIGIOUS DANCE
Has existed in every religious scheme fabricated by men. Since "religion" signifies the "binding-together" of men, it moves only in the liturgy of group ritual. Since religion seeks ever to impose discipline on the disparate souls within the group, it must operate by means of rhythmic dynamism. Without this urge, religion lapses into *dochema;* the living sap fails to rise and all leaves of orna-ment, flowers of design, fruit of understanding, cease to appear. Dance in gesture and position, in tempo and movement, is in technical control of the liturgy; so that, as Lucian's oft-quoted com-ment affirms, "They dance out their religion", because no words can compass it; every human art however joined—from architecture to drama, from music to dance—fails to arrive at any full expres-sion. Gilbert Murray pointedly remarks:[1] "The whole temple service is an elaborate allegory, a representation of the divine government of the world". Nowhere is this fact more evident than in the magnificent sacred dance of the Hindu temple. Nowhere is it more conspicuously absent than the turgid realism of the mediaeval Miracle Play; or the witless ballet form given to the Hebrew master poem of the "Initiation of Ioba". Religious dance demands integrated and meaningful movement, devoid of all personal modes of "self-expression". For this reason were the Egyptian priests masked in their solemn rituals: the individual must dis-appear within the group; and the group must be integrated into the ancient allegory.
[1] *Five Stages of Greek Religion.* Gilbert Murray (Second Edition. London 1935, p. 188). An essential work for comprehension of the meaning of ancient Greek dance.

REMOLINO (Spain)
A whirl-wind, treble *molino.* One of the basic figures of the twelve routines of the ancient *Tango.* *Moline*="a mill".

RENNINGEN (Sweden)
"Weaving Dance". A dance in 4/4 time for eight couples, showing the processes of stretching the threads, winding, weaving, movements of the shuttle, unwinding, and hanging up the finished cloth. The dance begins with the first six couples forming a circle, the remaining four dancers standing opposite to each other in the middle in the form of a cross. The ring is broken as dancers move in and out of the various patterns, singing the air on the last five bars. Costumes worn are those of the Uppland area, consisting of striped skirt and apron for the girls, with patterned shawl over red waistcoat and white blouse. On their heads they wear the typical Swedish sloping-crowned bonnet. The men wear grey jacket and hat, with red waistcoat and embroidered breeches. [Cp. *Li Tisseran,* (Provence); *Väva Vadmal* (Swe-den)]

REPETITION (France)
(Ex. Latin *repetitio,* to learn by repetition), is a stock ballet term; and signifies almost the same as the English "rehearsals". In modern French, *donner des répétitions* means "to give private les-sons". Theatre *répétition* is by no means private; yet it is not a "class", since it does not demand "exercises". The *répétiteur* is often a private tutor; but in Theatre he is in charge of the *répétition general*—the full preparation for the show; he may also be the ballet-master; but he is not thus identi-cal with *regisseur.** Indeed, *Maître répétiteur* may be no more than the junior master who acts as usher, with students, in and out of class. At times the *répétiteur* may combine jobs with ballet master or *régisseur.*
[See *Rehearsal; Regisseur; Maître de Ballet*]

"RESURRECTION" DANCE (Australian Aboriginal)
A native dance of Victoria District, Australia; the male dancers all hold green branches. With these they stroke the shoulders of the next man, in rhythmic passes, without stopping. They begin at sunset, with two long rows facing; these change to two large arcs, the ends slowly closing in, until the whole group forms a compact circular mass, facing inwards. Slowly they bow to the ground, until they are hidden by their green boughs; and so they "die"—while the traditional death chant continues. Suddenly the oldest man, as group leader, changes the tune, waves his largest branch, when the whole group leaps upwards; and they begin a long joyful "dance of resurrection", waving the green boughs high in the air.

REVELATION RITUAL DANCE (Congo)
Described as a witch doctor ritual, this Negro dance is an African Holy Inquisition; on lines less formal, but perhaps more honest, than the Spanish medi-aeval system of trial by torture. The beginning is the search for some "criminal", following an un-explained death. The witch doctor puts on his trappings, and consults the sacred amulets, human

bones, tripods or the speaking image; he lights a match, pronounces the names of suspects; if the light goes out, the culprit has been found. The maker of *daua* (magic) has been discovered. But the doctor says he needs proof. For this need, the night ritual is performed. Large quantities of *pombé* (native beer from fermented rye and bananas) are distributed; a great fire is lighted in the village clearing; and "the dance of revelation" begins. The men are drunk; they form a circle round the squatting doctor. His two female assistants stand alongside, serving the magical bowl and the pitcher of *pombé*. The dance ring slowly revolves; all men are armed with knives and spears. A pinch of some powder is added to the sacred cup; the men drink, and dance on. Weaker men begin to droop; and these fall, soon to become victims: they are despatched with the weapons. During one such ritual dance, seventeen men in a village of 150 persons were killed. Only the Holy Inquisition could rival method and result; also in the cause of ethical justice. One doctor, Kibongo, was hanged by the Belgians; the sentence could be executed only by two white policemen. This rite may be a prophylactic against some epidemic disease, met by eliminating weaker men who may be carriers of some mysterious blood derangement. It has not been unknown, in fighting of European armies, for officers to shoot "cowards" on their own side, *"pour encourager les autres"*. But: just as this witch doctor, Kibongo, was executed, it has also been known for infuriated private soldiers to eliminate some "victory at all costs" officer, before he finally destroys all his own troops. Official magic sometimes breaks down.

REVELS (London) (Mediaeval)
Held four times annually in the Inns of Court by law students and lawyers. They were named 1. *All Hallows* (September 30th); 2. *Erkenwald* (April 30th); 3. *"Purification"* (February 2nd); and 4. *Midsummer* (June 30th). These dates do not coincide now with the better known "Quarter Days". The Judges of Court danced at *Cantel-Messe* (Candlemas) February 2nd, but the Masque was the greatest feast of the year, in Winter.
[Cp. *Rouel*—Rule]

REVERENCE—1 (from Latin ceremonial)
A term used to indicate a bow, done as a salute on first entrance and sometimes on withdrawal, by females as a "curtsey" or "court-s-hey", as a mark of etiquette or social politeness. The act is rarely performed by men, except on the stage in "romantic plays", when a deep bow is accompanied by a sweeping doffing of a large hat with large feathers. The theological version is a copy of this court salute, urged as a "mark of respect", but most often an indication of servility; for it culminates in such savage rites as "kissing rings", and even "kissing the foot". In classical ballet, the ballerina uses the "reverence", sometimes to her partner, sometimes to characters of high rank in the ballet, as for example, in *The Sleeping Beauty* and *Giselle*.

REVERENCE, RIVERENZA—2 (Italy)
The ceremonial salute or greeting in beginning and ending the formal salon *danza* of the Renaissance in North Italian towns. The salute took four slightly different forms: from the most solemn, *Il Riverenza Grave* (six bars of music in *Alta Danza*); opening *riverenza* (four beats duration in *La Spagna*); short *riverenza* (one bar of six beats, in two movements only); *riverenza media* (medium, lasting eight bars instead of four) in *Canario*; when *Il Grande Riverenza* endures sixteen bars. The diminishing retains the proportion: the *riverenza grave* may be eight or sixteen beats; but the *media* will then be half, four or eight; and the *riverenza minima* runs shorter still, but never less than four beats. There was a similar *riverenza* used in formal fencing exercises; it was carried into the academies of dance (where it still is practised). In the English court it is known as the courtsey. The Italian *riverenza*, practised by the ladies, was directed also at the spectators, as well as their partners. During the two centuries of these dances, the precise periods of salute varied, as they did from one dance to another.

REVESBY PLAY (Lincolnshire, England)
Revesby has a January Plough Play that carries many ancient features, though the words now used date only from an 18th century revision. Presented as a Mumming Play, it features also a Sword Dance, close to the Morris style. The "Cosmic Dragon" is here named the Wild Worm (at other centres it was White Worm, perhaps alluding to snow or ice as "White Death"), but here the Fool has five "sons", who are named Pickel Herring; Blue Britches; Ginger Britches; Pepper Britches; and All Spice. The Fool is shewn his "image" in a mystical mirror, framed by the six linked swords (the Rose or Hexsa), and later the same "lock" of swords is used for his beheading.
[See *Sword Dance; Pickelherring*]

REZNIKA (Czechoslovakia)
A dance seen in Moravia, which includes miming said to represent the buying of an ox by a butcher, but the gestures now are so reduced as to be scarcely recognisable. Performed by young men and girls with polka and running steps, the prin-

cipal remaining piece of mime occurs when the girl places her right hand in her partner's left, palm up, he slapping it with his other hand to represent counting out coins.

RHABDOS (Greek, or in Latin *Virga*)

The ancient "magical wand" or "instrument of power" carried by chief officiants for innumerable rituals. The wand is the half-way implement between an ornamental "sign of office"—such as we have today with White Rod or Black Rod in and out of Parliament or the Palace—and the tool used in vocational action, such as the shepherd's crook—turned into the episcopal crozier, the rod or lituus used by the Roman *augur;* or still farther back, the flail carried by Egyptian kings as slave-masters. The wand entered into numerous stage ballets—as in *Giselle,* where the rhabdos of Bacchus, ivy-crowned, is carried; or in *Coppelia* in the Harvest scene. Another form is the municipal mace; and another is the rural Maypole which is carried only once.

RHAFF-DDAWNSYDD (Welsh)

Rope-dancer; or *rhaff-ddawns,* rope-dancing. From *rhaff* or *rhaffan,* a rope or cord. In two modes: (1) dancing or balancing on a tight rope—acrobatic version; (2) dancing in a circle with all dancers holding on to a ring of rope on which they pull.

RHIOL (Welsh)

"Noble". The tale of lineage, genealogy, as proclaimed by the Herald (or *Gheraldus*). This essential court activity is the technical parent of the long series of *reel* dances. Accompanied by simple pipe and tabour, the Herald "reels off" the standard account of the king's parentage, by naming his ancestors, their places, and their qualities; with the marriages. This rite was closely connected with the whole system of Chevallerie, as developed in the graphic symbolism of the Knightly Shield, Crest, and Quarterings. These were painted or drawn on wood or stone (also on some documents, and graves), but, in ritual practice, always drawn on the ground. Here the quarterings reveal the division of the space or *field* (its original title) by marriage union; so that the first emblazonry must move up, to yield space for the "other half". In the dance, the single dancers steps the requisite number of times (generations back) while the lineage is reeled off; and he moves from one quarter to another quarter. This requires most accurate counting and stepping by *rhienol* (parental line) and names of *rhieni* (ancestry) within the *rhwyll* (ring fence) as superintended by the *rhyngyll* (sergeant of dancers; the *"sir-jeant"*). In Gaelic, the same sort of tradition continued, with different terms. The general term of *reel* gained many wider references (reel of thread, to thread the steps, to do a bobbin —and the interjection "Really?" as a surprised acknowledgment). The term *rhiol* has connection with the dance from *rouelle, ruel, rouen,* and many others, implying a circular movement. *Rhiallu* implies hundred, or a thousand; or "By Goom! That's a lot!" *Rhol* is "to bluster", to make large claims, e.g. as to famous ancestry.

RHODFA-LLONG-WRTH-DDAWNS (Welsh)

Literally, the "circle" (or) gang (in) touch (in) dance. Possibly the medial terms—*Llong-wrth*— became transformed into the English "longways", but the name indicates the general circle dance, equivalent to *kolo** or *hora** in Eastern Europe, which vary in "touching hands", or "not touching hands". *Rhodfallong* is used also to mean "gangway", as in making way for the bride.

RHYTHM—1 (Greek : *Ruthmos*)

Is primarily measured movement or vibration of an object or a mode of energy; and is thus the central factor in all works of art; and one of the aims of all ritual, as well as the principal factor in Vital Balance which is the basis of all life. Rhythm is one of the three elemental *gunas* or cosmic qualities known to Hinduism: as *Rajas* (Rhythm), *Tamas* (Inertia) and *Sattvas* (Balance). All dance uses the mobility or rhythm of the body, against the inertia of the floor, to reveal innumerable passing phases of Balance against Dis-Balance. Though these ideas are prevalent in all Hindu doctrines of art and ritual, they are more readily evident in their Greek copies. Here rhythm, entangled with theories of Number, becomes apparent in two main modes: as *Ruthmos* and *A-Ruthmos*—the thing rhythmic, and the symbol of thing (number) non-rhythmic or static. Arithmetic is always a process of enumeration of things that (for this act) *do not change.* Zeno argued this assumption to absurdity; but Euclid got it in linear mode into geometry. All have been used in dance and music.

RHYTHM, RUTHMOS—2

Rhythm is an actuality in all vital existence; opposed to it we have *arithmos,* limited to integers, numbers applicable to quantities of like things; and secondarily as an aid to measuring magnitude in form, distance in Space (or Time), to approximate degrees. This *arithmos* is privative of rhythm which is continuous, and having five main versions: *arithmeo,* to count; *arithmetis,* enumeration; *arithmetikos,* one who enumerates; *arithmetos,* what is counted; and *arithmos,* as number or quantity. These terms led to wide misunderstanding of the broad alleged Pythagorean statement, that "Numbers are Things". Even if we take the less crude Aristotelian version: "Elements of Numbers compare with Elements of Things", we are ensnared in the fallacious "research" of the pseudo-mathematician (as *arithmetikos*) who enumerates endlessly those abstractions (such as "transfinite numbers") which lack contact with the *animus* of things or bodies. All this range of *a-rithmos* is, by definition, privative; it is a shadow of life and not life itself.

We turn to RUTHMOS, a vital term which has a score of affiliated versions; all of them pendant on the Herekleitan use of the verb *reo* (or *rheo*) "to flow", and used by him in his famous dictum *Panta Rhéi* — "All things flow". We look at some of the principal versions:

1. *Reo*: to flow, stream forth, to run.
2. *Ruthmizo*: to reduce, to time and measure; to form in rhythm, to modulate substance and impose on it due proportion.
3. *Erruthmezomen*: to arrange in a symmetrical or balanced order.
4. *Ruthmikos*: to be formed, to be set in due proportion, rhythmically.
5. *Ruthmos*: has seven major implications, which are
   (a) rhythm, as primary, in measured movement (natural, or art);
   (b) dancing; a modulated movement of body, in step, gait, gesture;
   (c) marching; moving the feet to regular rhythm (in groups as a rule);
   (d) music; the beat, stress, flow of rhythm in music, tempo;
   (e) poetry; rhythm as distinct from meter; or rhythm; word/meaning; sound;
   (f) prose; a harmonious flow of vocable sounds with meaning;
   (g) objects (artworks) rhythm of material, of plan, of purpose, governance by triple proportion in these aims;
6. *Eurthythmos*: formed to orderly movement;
7. *Eurthythmia*: perfect harmony (*armonia*, or the arts).

The concept of Number, Numerals, and Enumeration (Latinised terms), is the province linking vital Rhythm with *Arithmetikos*; linking Time to Events, and Forms to Space, by distance and by dimension.

We are concerned here with (a) Rhythm in bodily movement, as *Dance*; and (b) rhythm in sound, by voice and instrument, as *Music*. In each mode rhythm is obtained by opposition of two major factors. The body is opposed by the resistant floor; the musical sound is opposed or alternated by the unstruck instrument, or silence. The body has to pause after exertion, to gain poise and place for the next movement; the instrument (or voice) has to pause for the next beat, the next phrase, the next movement, in the dual structure of melody and harmony of sound. In every instance, rhythm appears as an operation, never as a concrete thing. The "thing done" may appear as a work of art; and visible rhythm marks the doing of it, as the tide leaves ripples on the sand after its rhythmic ebb and flow; but in any concrete work — a picture, a sculpture, a building — we can observe only *results* of rhythmic operation; we can even establish a new rhythm of personal observation by an active operation of search for quality, among the clues of quantity; but only in dynamic arts such as spoken or chanted poetry, dance, or music, can we observe rhythm in action, hear it in sound, and feel it at its moment of expression. Theatre is thus easier to apprehend than books, for we have immediate contact, instead of painted or carven symbols that demand imaginative reconstruction.

RHYTHM IN DANCE — 3
Like rhythm in all other genuine works of genuine art, it has not one but three definite phases. Ballet at its best may exhibit even more. Every work of art contains three different factors, which must be integrated in a single work to attain success as art: as a factor able to move or impress human imagination with wonder and delight. Every work of art is rightly biassed in favour of its own selected theme. Automatically this selection excludes all antagonistic factors; all opposition; all hindrance. But as a work of art must appear in some material form, this ideal is never reached. The dancer has always the opposition of the floor; must always exert against the pull of gravity; must always (if done for spectacle, for impression of others) appeal against the natural apathy of the watcher. Vital rhythm is the most efficient attractor. The work of art (the dance or picture or building or sculpture) contains three distinct factors: (a) *technical*, (b) *formal* or stylistic; and (c) *theme* or mood or meaning or idea. The choice of the theme begins to operate on the selection of materials and methods, the technical or visual factor. The factor of plan, design or style unites these two — the abstract idea and the concrete technology — into one single integrated work. Each factor has its own rhythms; the rhythm of working, making, shaping in *material;* the rhythm of plan or design in *style;* and the rhythm of the unfolding *theme* as its nature and meaning are gradually made clear to that "other mind" which is the attentive spectator. He receives the triple impact; he responds through his own sensitivity in

answering rhythms; now one phase (muscular-neutral), now another (imaginative-format), and then the connecting mode, the feeling-rhythm that signifies the essential "rightness" of the union, which we call sometimes the sense of beauty; which informed Greeks called *armonia*. Rhythm is not single, in work, or in worker, or in working; yet it must be integrated into an indivisible unity to attain irrefutable success. Because rhythm belongs also to time and place, to person and to period, no single work of art can possibly appeal fully to all people in any country at all times.

RICE DANCE (Borneo)

In order to ensnare the "soul", or life-energy, of the *padi* or rice, the sowing of this cereal is preceded by a masquerade among the Kayans of the Mahakam River, Central Borneo. It is danced in an open space in the village by men who themselves represent the spirits of the rice, wearing masks with goggle eyes, great teeth and ears, and beards of white goat's hair; their bodies wrapped in split banana leaves. Their leader carries a long wooden crook. At mid-day, accompanied by strict, traditional gong-rhythms, the dancers form a circle and perform various steps, waving their arms, shaking and turning their heads. Then in Indian file, headed by the leader, and each man holding the hand of the next, they move out of the village. As they walk the leader from time to time seems to hook something out of the air towards him, with the crook of his staff; which gesture is imitated by all his followers. They are catching the spirits of the rice; as these cannot make any sound, the dancers also must utter no word. The following day rice sowing begins. The Dyaks of North Borneo perform a ceremonial dance round an altar at rice-harvest time.

RIDÉE (France)

A round dance of the Vannetais district, Brittany, with variations according to locality. Accompanied by arm swings with a clearly marked rhythm of their own, the difficulty lies in synchronising arm movements with those of legs and feet. Danced in a circle moving clockwise, men and women stand alternately, hand in hand, or with little fingers linked. Only one step is used, which takes eight beats of music (in lively 2/4 or 4/4 time) to complete, and the sequence of arm movements must also end on the eighth beat. In different versions the step and tempo vary, but arm-swings remain the same. Usually danced in a circle, the *Ridée* may also go in a line, dancers following the movements of the leader. The tune is also sung by the dancers. The term *ridée* means "ripple" which motion is

seen in gently waving hands as the circle moves round, at a walking pace. There is a Ridée done at Pontivy, very similar.

RIGAUDON (France)

An old dance to lively music in 2/4 time, belonging particularly to Provence. A gay dance of the people, it found favour in chateau and palace ballrooms in the seventeenth century, being popular at the courts of Louis XIII, XIV and XV, and lasting until the Revolution in 1789. As a Court dance it lost some vitality, but took on added dignity. In England, known as the *Rigadoon*, it arrived in the last quarter of the 17th century, and became fairly popular. Some authorities state that the dance was called after Rigaud, who "invented" it; others that the name derived from *rig*, an English word meaning lively, wanton; but neither of these theories seems acceptable. In Provence, performance of the dance was forbidden in 1664 by the Provençal Parliament, but in the adjacent Dauphiné region, the *Rigaudon* still exists as a folk dance, most country fêtes ending with it. The dance contains the jumping step, or *pas de rigaudon*, peculiar to it in its earlier existence. For any number of couples, partners facing each other, it has only one figure, and is danced lightly and gracefully. The *pas de rigaudon* (a step with small jumps on the toes) is performed *sur place* by the man, the woman advancing towards him, holding her skirt on either side, with polka steps. The man salutes his partner; she makes a reverence. While the man repeats *pas de rigaudon*, the woman retreats with polka steps, then both turn anti-clockwise, each dancing their own step. The sequence is repeated, but instead of saluting his partner, the man takes her right hand and turns her anti-clockwise. In the 18th century the *Rigaudon* was given prominence by the famous dancer Camargo (1710 - 1770) who frequently performed it on the stage.

RIGOL AND RIGOLETTO (Italian, from Spanish Rico)

Dance and dance music, used for lighter intervals, between longer acts, or parts of longer works (i.e. processionals, ducal welcomes etc.), giving an opportunity for refreshments (always important in Italy). This pragmatic break originated all the *intermezzi rigoletti* numbers. Popular verses supplied apt words; sometimes not requested by the composer or players. Similar music was taken from the towns to country districts, where the quick dance *rigoletto* was fashionable; always in a *rondelet*. *Trouvères* used similar forms; but musicians established the intermezzo form, which gradually waxed important as a composition, now without the dancing, but still permitting the lessening of tension, suitable for refreshment during spectacles.

RING DANCE

One of the elemental forms of group dance, found all over the world; in all periods. Various names include *rang, rinche* or *rinke* (Irish); *ranche* (S. America), and many older names associated with *rouen, rowne* or *rowan; rouet* or *rouette; rouel, real* or *reale,* to *roussel* and *karouelle* (carol); *roon* (Scots); *rounders* (into the game). From the Orient we have *sara* or *sarah* (from *sam-sara*) and *bande,* for *sarabande; zara* or *tzaro; zero;* the Balkan group with *kolo* and *hora; kora;* thence to *chorus, chorale,* etc., and *hota* (also further west as *jota.* From Egypt comes *Min* and *Bez* or *Beth;* also *Shen* (with *Dzyan* in Asia). (From *Min* derives *min-estrel, min-ister*). The term *selah* (psalms) means "dance follows". There are many more, some central or root terms with numerous derivative forms associated with the celebrants, place, dance form or progress etc. The characteristic ring groups follow a few simple patterns (a) in the arrangement of the dancers, and (b) in the routine of the steps. Many have associated songs, chants, sacrifices, musical form. The basic circle may consist of all men; all women; or all youths; it may be simple, double or treble; it may move with all dancers in one direction; or in the opposite direction (widdershins, or *vedya-shina, vedya dak-shina*—anti-sunwise or sunwise); or two rings may move in opposition. The chosen site may have importance; on a hilltop; by a river or sea-shore; in some sacred enclosure; while the time of year for each celebration must be considered. Stonehenge in Wiltshire, was one of the great sites of religious ring dance ritual; which mode of ritual is found active in all religious systems. Associated with many ring dance forms is the central pillar or speaker, musicians, preacher, master of ceremony etc.

RINGLEADER (England)

Defined in Hollyband's *Dictionary* (1593) as the person assigned by the master of ceremonies to open a ball or lead off the dance. These dances were ring dances; the leader had to set the figures and the tempo.

RINGMOR (Scotland)

An open field dance, in spring or harvest season. A single dancer makes a large ring, marked by his heels, alternately stretched out as he circles "high and low". The dancer rises and falls on one foot— first at full height and then squatting low, until his haunches seem to touch the turf.

RINNCE FADA (Gaelic)

Literally, the "Temple of Fate", but named as *rinche* or rink (field) instead of *Teampull* (Temple). Probably derived from the *Templum Augures,* introduced into Ireland with both early systems of Christianity, but chiefly with the Latin method from Rome, which had a *templum vates,* later the Vatican Hill. Fatum became *fada* (*vada,* or way). (*Vates-cana,* "prophet-walk"). The English took up the term *rink* (field); thus we have "skating rink". The Irish continued the term, for its festival usage; and still apply this name to suites of dances. In Ireland *Rinnce Fada* was a longways dance, mentioned in 1681 in Dinely's *Voyage through the Kingdom of Ireland* as being danced by all ranks, from master to servants, one behind the other, to the accompaniment of bagpipes, Irish harp and Jews harp. An account in 1813 in Gamble's *A View of Society and Manners in the North of Ireland* describes the dancers in pairs, linked by a kerchief, following a trio of dancers similarly linked. These three then formed two arches with the kerchiefs, through which the two lines of dancers passed, cast off each side and met again at the bottom, meanwhile performing "a variety of pleasing evolutions interspersed with *entrechats* or cuts".

RISHI (Arabia)

A *harim* dance, performed by women and young girls, with the upper part of the body only. The head is constantly shaken and turned, in order to fling out the hair, and produce the maximum sound from bells attached to it. If the dancers' hair is too short, false plaits are fixed with silver hooks, over each ear, to help hold out her own hair. The dance is accompanied by drums played by other ladies of the *harim*—the hajir, with red patterns painted on each end; and small, shallow drums which are held shoulder high. But the principal sound of the dance is the jingling of bells, which are fastened to the dancer's toes and ankles, and fall in a cascade from her head-dress to her shoulders. Bells are also an important part of the costume in another *Harim* dance, *Safina.**
[Cp. *Ghedra* (Morocco)]

RITUAL DANCE

Is principally religious though many secular rituals have developed by social need. Ritual means specifically "the right act", implying also right time and place. Ritual requires suppression of individual variation "on impulse", with obedience to prescribed routine. Ritual demands accuracy in (a) position, (b) movement and (c) gesture of all those taking part in ceremonial. In origin each ritual is a concrete action, usually done by a group of people to announce and to affirm certain of its social values. Later, many parts become abstract, ornamental, and finally lose meaning. This decay is apparent in many dance forms; great elaboration of professional technique accompanies loss of genuine form and meaning. There are ritual dances (and songs which often belong to them), that express the values of the different classes of a nation —its castes and sub-castes, its professions and vocations. Many of the original acts, movements and gestures are derived from such social activities (as, e.g., "laying a foundation stone", or "marching in procession"). There are three distinct, and even different, phases. First the "movement of necessity" apparent in actual performance of some important task—for example, the "laying of the foundation stone". This masonic accomplishment was in Egypt a highly important technical requirement. The preparation of a suitable heavy stone, and the careful placing of it in the centre of the chosen site, were tasks following on extensive calculations of many kinds; while afterwards this single stone was the central pivot, from which all subsequent measurements were taken. In the second phase, when the layout of a traditional diagram plan was followed by custom rather than by calculus, there was less need felt for a centre stone; and prominence was given to corners; so that the large stones (again with technical reasons, as for utmost strength), were placed as headstones of the corner. Obviously there could not be less than four square corners; in the typical Gothic (or Latin cross) plan, there appeared twelve technical corners, then reflected as "twelve stations", by as many pillars. These supplied pivotal points in the ritual dance; winding in and out and around the pillars, as before was done with the great stones at Avebury or Stonehenge or Carnac. Finally, the "foundation stone" rite lapses into ornamental publicity; a smaller block carved with names and dates; emphasising the individuals, not the real purpose of the building or its users. The dance then vanishes.

Hindu Ritual Dance and Players. 12th century, Halebid, Mysore.   INDIA

Newer rituals have grown up in other social places; the great processional Ritual of Bureaucratic Empires is found in the Queue; its shrine is the Waiting Room; its magical parchments occur as the Form-in-Triplicate; its exactions in revenue stamps and licence fees—all pursued by rote and ritual.

RITUAL OF HEALING DANCE

Has been performed through the world in circumstances that differ immensely; but all follow one principle: the ejection of extraneous forces from an ailing human body, with a corresponding integration of personal forces to sustain the individual life in true balance. The older methods, apparently empirical in custom, achieve many remarkable results. Some combine a dance ritual with chanting and rhythmic sound, while others add or replace movement by some application of herbs. Almost invariably the ancient Medicine Man isolated his patient: he does not assemble a crowd of sufferers to exchange troubles. The tribal doctor (sometimes called without true cause "witch doctor") is often an experienced expert in the manipulation of natural energies: he may call these as *mana*,* or *orenda*, or *wakanda*, what the modernist hospital doctor calls "tone", or the theologist names "grace". The Hindu named their several modes as *prana*. Their main divergence resides in the basic mode of treatment: the hospital medicine man treats disease with drugs, vaccines, inoculations; and eventually surgery. His system is chiefly material. The tribal medicine man treats disease with a variety of energies: sensory and emotional, traditional and local. The two systems meet in the usage of herbal concoctions; many of the standard preparations of the British Pharmacopeia are inherited from the tribal medicine man or the village wizard. Broadly, the hospital doctor deals with *forms*: he speaks of microbes and bacteria, of virus and vaccines; and his ritual is one of Sterilization. He deals out death to the microbic world of amoeba. The tribal medicine man deals firstly with *energies*: he chants of the equally invisible world of demons or spirits, and summons their forces to do this or that; or he exorcises and banishes them. The two systems may eventually balance: as they do in living fact, for Soul is energy while Mind is structure, linked indissolubly together as the *Persona*, evident in several modes of consciousness. These modes perform a vital dance. The moving Soul, passionate by instinct and emotion, dances with the more durable Mind, building sensory forms into images. These twin phases dance in a mutual vitality; as the modern psychologists, Freud, Adler and Jung have shown. Finally, the mind evinces its image structure, in rhythmic patterns of sound and form and colour.

The Hôm, the Sacred Tree of the Temple of Bel. Two masked priests perform the lustration ceremonial. The Hôm is seen carved in mural panels of alabaster (painted and gilded) or as a choreographic pattern in low relief on temple pavings, where it is danced over.   BABYLONIA

RITUAL PAVEMENT (Assyria)

At Nineveh, Korsabad; was contrived in two principal modes. For many parts of the temple-palace, sunburned or kilnburned brick was laid; often in a bitumen bed. Over this were placed slabs of alabaster. For certain ritual halls (Hall of Divination) some channels were slightly sunk in a slab, possibly to contain liquids (oil or water, as in the modern Egyptian manner). In the shrine, the Sacred Tree of Life (*Asshurah*) was carved in low relief, as a ritual pattern eight or nine feet long) for ceremonial movement; with its thirty-two roads or paths.

"The pavement" (says Layard)[1] "of the chambers was formed either of alabaster slabs, covered with inscriptions recording the name and genealogy of the king; and probably the chief events of his reign; or of kiln-burnt bricks, each bearing a short inscription. Alabaster slabs were placed on a thin coating of bitumen, spread over the bottom of the chamber, even under the upright slabs forming its sides . . . Between the lions and bulls forming the entrances, was generally placed one large slab, bearing an inscription". (p. 261).

This alabaster was quarried from adjacent hills, in a darkish grey hue, soft and easy to carve. Under fire (or sun heat) it whitens; but also becomes softer. The wall reliefs were coloured, and probably part-gilded; so also the Sacred Tree, set in the floor.

[1] *Nineveh and its Remains*. A. H. Layard. (Vol. II) London, 1850.

RITUAL: PLACE AND PERSON (Hebrew from Babylonian source)

Is based on Sun-Earth orientation (as with religious architecture in its planning). The surveyor's method is to strike a circle; find the true north; or tropical east (which varies) and from the circle, to obtain the fundamental square for edifice or the rite. Thence also are obtained Numbers and Numerals; these relations are later affirmed in ritual dance. The priest thus stands, facing the East. This is called Front. On his Left hand is the North, called Hidden, or Dark; while on his Right hand is the South, called Shining. The West, behind his back, is called the reverse or Behindmost. From this basis, ritual places are situated, and persons in it officiate. The Christian church came ultimately (leaving its Greek *basilica* original form (King's Court)) to require (a) an altar at the East End (as Front), and a Great Door at the West. At the four primary points were placed the Four Arch-angellus, Apostles, Prophets etc.; with their attributions of positions and duties, in symbolism. They were the Hinges (*cardo*) or cardinals, on which the ceremonial moved. They gave Cardinal Numbers (amply indicated in static Roman Numerals, consisting of lines on squares and circles—see any clock face), and the ritual movement "round the space" was dominated by the count of Ordinal Numbers, that is: steps in *order* and relation. Cardinal gives Position and No change; while Ordinal gives Movement in due rhythm and proper order. Babylonian rituals show that due count was highly important; from them came the Greek dualism of *ruthmos* and *a-ruthmos* (arithmetic), the Moving and Non-Moving elements necessary in all ceremony and ritual. Round this circle were thus placed the Twelve Stations (divisions) of progressive ritual, balanced by their presentation in progressive myth-relation, one form as action in rite, the other form as dramatic action in dance-mime.

RITUAL POSES or MUDRA MODES

Appear frequently in the lower or physical disciplines of every religious cult. Many of them require not motion but stillness, as in the traditional poses of Gautama the Buddha; or some of the faqirs who followed similar methods. Often these poses recur at regular intervals between periods of motion (as in some Hindu-Brahmin dance). In Egypt, the student sat with updrawn knees, arms around them. Some poses are recorded, which occur during the initiation ceremonial. The Egyptian was placed in a coverless sarcophagous, with linen head-wrappings; then spread in an extended cross position. This was copied by some Gnostic sects; they placed the candidate on an oval with axial cross; there he had to be "tested" by a helper with

the cult name of Maria Magh Delilah. He had to rise after three nights of hypnotic sleep.

RIVER DANCE (Sikkim)

Lepcha folk dance performed by young men and girls, depicting a legend about the Rivers Teesta and Rangit. Girls represent the Teesta, and in serpentine pattern approach the boys, who advance with zig-zag hopping steps as the Rangit. The legend tells how the two rivers resolved to meet at a certain point and to marry. To find the way to the meeting-place the Teesta followed a snake and the Rangit a bird, which continually digressed in search of food. Arriving late the Rangit wished to turn back, but after a discussion the two rivers flowed on together. When the two lines of dancers meet they mime the legendary conversation, then continue the dance in one sinuous line. Danced in bare feet, the young men wear knee-length striped skirts, white shirts and round pillbox hats; the girls, ankle-length differently coloured skirts and short, long-sleeved jackets, their dark hair parted in the middle and arranged in plaits over the top.

ROBOT (Russian, also Czech)

Means "worker". This term came into West European use through Karel Capek's play called *R.U.R.* or *Rossum's Universal Robots*. Its theme was that of a welfare state in which all the workers would be mechanical electrical—automata, doing all the slave labour without going on strike over lodging terms or another twenty shillings an hour. Many productions of this play contained a *Robot Dance*, done to factory rhythms, not unlike some of those offered as Jazz, but with a harder syncopation.

ROBES

In prominent rituals, often have supplied the complementary floor pattern in dance movement. In particular, this fact is seen in Shield* forms and symbols. One of the basic forms is seen in the church robe, formed on an elliptical shape, bisected with two lines making a cross. This egg-shape, laid on the floor, shows the *cope* and the *drag*, at the two ends. The origin of such robes appears to occur in secret initiation rites. Laid on the floor, the *candidatus* had traced round him his "patron" and so the plain white texture received its typical overlay, in this "crossification". Simple geometry laid these lines; the rite marked the ten or twelve divisions, sometimes from the old symbols of the Zodiac; sometimes from the terrestrial circle of eight points, origin of *runes**. The Roman *toga picta* thus vied with embroidered robes of Hellenic divinities.

ROBIN ET MARIAN (French)

Named as *jeu pastorale* but once a powerful legend

—last produced (about 1420?) by Adam de la Halle. This was the last spurt of the Celtic mythos in France; its earlier mode was used by Gluck and his librettist the Italian Ranier de Calzabigi. Gluck met him in Vienna in 1761 and they contrived the new opera Orfeé—on the same theme—the story of Orpheus Lord of Music, seeking Eurydice or the return of Spring. Gluck's opera is full of choral music and ballet; like the May Games of England. Robin and Marianne came from Old Egypt; as Hru-ben-Hut and May-Iona; eventually made into historical dummies, they were put aside from our mechanical civilisation—perhaps in favour of Shop-steward and Naafi.

ROBIN HOOD (in England)
Is the residue of a very ancient Egyptian celebration of Spring, connected usually with Maut (or Maát) of the Wheat. Lost under accretions of clerical error, the original name was Hru-ben-Hud. Gradually it disintegrated into what seemed village May Day games; the only other item being the HUD FRIDAY (of interment, of sowing grain). Traditionally, Hud was the Green Man, bearer of new vegetation. Associated was the BEZ or Bessie, the Boss of the small company, the Fellahs; and then Osiris with Isis, and Mut or Maát the Earth Mother. These dance rituals became merged later with the Moeris, and Sword Dance; and especially the Egyptian Festival of Pachon (Month) which became a "Passion" and used the Great Egg symbol, for Easter. The name Hu remains widely in England: Hugh Lincoln, Plymouth Hu, Suten Hu (Kings Hu) and daily in our applause words "Hu Re" or "Hu-Ra!"—Praise Sun God!" Traditional dances are numerous and varied.

ROCK-AND-ROLL (USA)
Term emergent in 1958, to denote tribal dance of Teddy-boys, in USA cities spread rapidly to Britain, Germany (dance of Halb-Starke), even Russia (dance of stilyagi). Crude dance based on general jazz syncopation merged with local variation, according to music instruments available. Essentially a group dance of "Teenagers" or adolescents, noise and yells replace style and elegance. Not a genuine folk-dance, possessing only vitality but no meaning; no ritual or ceremony.

RODO-MONTADE; Rodomonte (French, Italian)
Rhetorical flourish of crude verse, which broke the succession of round dance (New Year Festival or Masque), when the elected king (or his Champion, supporter for the period), stood on the "mount" (a slight eminence contrived for the occasion) and declared the titles and virtues of this Monarch of the Messe Ruele. Rudo or Rodo is the circle (Ruada,

Route) and the hill is the montade or montan, used in those days by most orators. Connected with the Carole;* the "monarch" used to sing for himself.

ROKAIK (Malekula, New Hebrides)
A women's Na-leng* or figure dance, performed on the Dancing-Ground soon after dawn on the day of the great sacrifice in Maki-ru.* Danced by wives of the Maki-men (initiates) and their husbands, it is connected with the sacrifice of boars which the Maki-men are about to make. On their backs, reaching far above their heads, the women wear a large ornament called hokuri, made out of a thatch-palm leaf, the mid-rib being tied to her back and decorated with various herbs. The dancers, beating the ground with bamboos and singing, career down the Dancing-Ground and back again, waving branches called ro-mavi round and round in front of them. When the dance is over, the wives, at one end of the Dancing-Ground, drop their bamboos and run across the ground to the sea-shore. They are pursued by one, sometimes two Maki-men, waving leafy branches. This is called "beating the women", although no actual beating takes place. [See Malekula, Dances of; Maki-ru; Na-leng]

ROLANG (Tibet)
Lama ritual term for "corpse who dances", in effect related as a converse of the better-known European vampire, who walks or dances in his nightly quest for fresh blood. This ritual, it is said by travellers, was followed by shamans of the Bönpo people before the introduction of Buddhism into Tibet, though it is not necromantic. The dead man is not recalled; nor is there any seeking for prophecy. There are several modes of rolang, some similar to the Hayti preparation of the zombie; others that recall the Arabian ghul; and likewise the Jewish golem. The principal Tibetan rolang rite is a supreme test of courage, consisting of the re-animation of a corpse by the magician's own energy, until it stands up and dances. Failure ends in death of the magician. No authoritative observation of the rolang exists, though Alexandra David Neel describes it ex hypothesi; while the rite may be compared with some of the secret versions of the spiritual exercises prescribed by Ignatius of Loyola; or, more accurately, by his Jewish successors who joined his secret society. They are recalled by one of their pass-words: "Roland-for-Oliver". [See Mystics and Magicians in Tibet. A. D. Neel]

ROLLELIBUTZEN (Switzerland)
"Bell-Maskers". At Altstatten in the Rhine Valley, these masked dancers appear at Shrovetide. Wearing elaborate head-dress and many large bells (Rölleli) on a strap over the shoulder, they go

through the town led by the *Butzenkönig* (King of the Maskers), and his retinue on horseback. The *Röllelibutzen* follow in an ordered processional dance. As a relic of an ancient fertility rite, they carry squirts filled with water, with which they sprinkle spectators, especially unmarried girls. The custom of spilling water or perfume exists in various dances elsewhere, such as the Spanish *Bal del Ciri.** It occurred, too, at the *Cascarone Balls** of Old California, also a feature of pre-Lent Carnival.
[Cp. *Nüssler* (Switzerland); *Perchten* and *Schemenlaufen* (Austria); *Narren-Treffen* (Germany)]

ROMALIS (Spain)

An old Andalusian gypsy dance, similar to the *Olé*, and apparently of Arabic origin. It is a woman's solo dance. Richard Ford,[1] who travelled in Spain in the early-19th century, describes the dance as being called *Romalis* by the gypsies and *Olé* by the Spaniards. "The dance", he writes, "is closely analagous to the *Ghawasee** of the Egyptians and the *Nautch** of the Hindoos . . . The ladies . . seem to have no bones . . the whole person performs a pantomime and trembles like an aspen leaf . . . The unchanged balancing of raised hands, the tapping of feet and the serpentine quivering movements . . continue in violent action until . . all but exhausted. The spectators . . beat time with their hands in measured cadence . . . " The music of the *Romalis* is Arabic in character and has been described as "low and melancholy . . . and full of sudden pauses . . ."
[1] *Gatherings from Spain*. Richard Ford. 1846.

ROMAN RITUAL DANCES

Over the twelve centuries of the Roman kingdoms and republic, ceremonial changed; especially from its earliest modes—organised in the rituals of the Arvales Fratres—to later town systems grouped under devotion to Mars the Regulator. Each system had its annual or administrative divisions. None of them admit forms that we should immediately name today as "dance". Most of them required rhythmic ceremonial; most of them done to instrumental music with singing; so that by a close study of Roman history we can discover no less than six different systems of ritual with music. Most of these rites had strong roots, not only in the past, but in other countries, from the powerful yet obscure Etruscan influences that moved into Rome with plays and dancers (even the date is known—375 BC) to the later professional augurs, who demanded a clear space in every town and village for their prophetic ceremonial. With the augur are grouped other rites; some tend to continue down to our own time.   [See *Augurs Ritual Dance; Salii*]

ROMAN SACRED DANCE

Contemplation, or the reckoning of the *templum* was the method by which the Roman Augurs operated their sacred ritual of prognostication. Knowledge of calendars and times was, despite the revelation, still mainly hidden knowledge. The Augurs' *templum* was the predecessor of the mediaeval astrological chart or *horo-scopus* (later done by the *Episcopus* or *biskop*) set out as a compass dial in large scale. Large enough to walk in and dance around, the *templum* was oriented to the cardinal points. His assistants stood one at each of these four hinges (*cardus*) and thus got their title of cardinal. With his *lituus* he traced the symbols, after snapping the measuring cord along the transverse diameters. He then surveyed the stars, the weather and (secretly beforehand) the latest military, political and family news. Then the Augur made his speech as *profeta*. He foretold little, but sketched in general advice : "What to do". This was delivered as he moved rhythmically around his *templum*, chanting in dignified tones, on the sacred reservation atop the Capitoline Hill in Rome. Our modern terms template (a workshop guide) and temple derive from this origin.

ROMANTIC BALLET (Modern European Classification)

Can be best understood by frequent comparison with CLASSICAL BALLET, and both against MODERNIST BALLET. The original contrast began with the Renaissance consciousness of current learning, culture, and ideology, in terms of predominant scholasticism and mediaeval totalitarianism, as compared with the "re-birth of learning" that followed the (a) negative revolt against Rome and its Vaticanism, with (b) the positive turn to study of the re-discovered literary treasures of Greece and ancient Rome. Secular dance developed apace against church or clerical dance rituals; the secular drama and music emerged, clear from church or clerical uses; and with them came the idea of the modern enclosed Theatre. Displacement of theological themes in plays was marked by return to Grecian and Latin mythos. The term "Romantic Ballet" implies a genre or style of ballet, as related to its theme chiefly, which contains a romantic or fictional story, as opposed to (a) the Mythological Ballet, with Greek religious themes; or (b) the Jesuit* or School Ballet, with moral satires or danced form of "Morality Plays"; or (c) the Court Ballet, ceremonial dance or movement or etiquette considered necessary for court use. Romantic Ballet accompanied the so-called Romantic Revival or Movement that followed publication of Bishop Percy's *Reliques of Ancient Poetry*, which was avidly accepted by Sir Walter Scott, Byron,

Shelley, Heine and others who proceeded to write fiction and poems on these lines. The Romantic Ballet began with one on a Scottish legend of sylphides (*La Sylphide*, with Marie Taglioni, Paris 1832), and continued with *Giselle* and others. The technical mode of dancing remained much the same as it had been developed in the French *Academie;* with the chief change in the use of the *pointe* on the stage, also by Marie Taglioni, which step proved valuable to suggest the supernatural quality of the creatures of the elements who figure in the Romantic Ballets.

See *Le comte de Gabalis* by Abbé N. de Montfaucon de Villares, for another source of inspiration that led towards Romantic Ballet and Poetry.
[See *Themes of Ballet; Classical Ballet*]

ROMANY (Gypsy)
Since 14th Century gypsy dances and especially music have been known all over Europe. Investigation into Romany origins have been many but uncertain. It does seem that this, their own chosen name, derives from *Romeria* (Portuguese a *pilgrimage* or wandering) for that remains as their dominant characteristic. This; and their firmly held Christian faith, suggest their gradual appearance in the wake of the several Crusades. Fatherless children, with mothers speaking many sorts of language, banded in wandering groups, taking words from every country. This fact is repeated in their use of musical form and dance form, always strongly marked by the country that later Gypsies have settled in. And both music and dance receive changes. In Spain they use terms *Gita* and *Gitano* (Hindu, from *Bhagavad Gita*). They first appeared in centuries following upon Crusades; and then spread into many countries, often selling services of dance and song at festivities.

RO-MBULAT (Malekula, New Hebrides)
"Banana Leaves". A processional dance in the Small Islands off the north-east coast of Malekula, danced chiefly at night during *Turei Na-mbe** (Gong-Raising ritual) and at initiation into manhood. Formerly dancers wore "dry banana leaves" (*Ro-mbulat*), later changed to carrying leafy branches held above their heads. The refrain of the accompanying song is first sung by a man in the centre of the dancing-ground, at the same time swinging legs and arms violently forward, which movement is copied by the dancers gathered at one end of the ground, who also beat the ground violently with one foot. Then all, singing the refrain, dance to the other end of the ground with the thudding step used in *Na-rel.** The refrain ends with shouts and the dancers return to their starting-point. Meanwhile the young unmarried girls, hand-in-hand in a row at the lower edge of the dancing-ground, plunge forwards and backwards in an undulating step called "catching crabs," uttering piercing cries from time to time. When the dance and refrain have been repeated three times, the same man begins the verse of the song, which is taken up by the dancers, who remain facing him, swinging arms and marking time. Then the refrain is resumed and the dance from end to end of the dancing-ground repeated. A variant of *Ro-mbulat*, called *Kò-kòke Ro-mbulatean*, is danced during post-funeral rites for an old man. The name derives from the verb *kòke*, "to carry a bundle", referring to the green banana leaf carried by each dancer high above the head in the left hand, and the bunch of dry banana leaves held in the right hand, and beaten against the thigh in the rhythm of the dance.   [See *Malekula, Dances of*]

RONALDSHAY (Scotland)
New Year Dance. After receiving New Year gifts from their masters, the farm servants, maids and friends "see the year in" with song and dancing. There is a large stone, about ten feet high, placed upright in a plain in the Isle of North Ronaldshay. "On the first day of the year, one could see fifty or sixty villagers there assembled, dancing in the moonlight with no other music than their own singing".[1]
[1] *Account of Scotland: Orkney.* (1893)

RONCESVALLE (France)
Danse du Chevaliers, known more widely as a contest or ballet (probably the origin of *Valles* or *Valse*). Mentioned by Chaucer (in *Canterbury Tales*) to which Tyrwhitt adds his note: "An Hospital beat: Marie de Rouncyvalle in Charing, London, is mentioned in *Monast. t. ii. 443*, and there was a Runcevall Hall in Oxford. So that perhaps it was the name of some fraternity". There is a place, frontiers of Spain/France, called Roncesvalles (Cp. Rouen, centre of *Fraters*), which possibly derived its name from the spectacle there, or as headquarters of a fraternity, as did Campo-Stella (Iago Compostella) not far distant. *Rouncevaux, Roncesvalle* probably became Rounce-Cheval (of Chevaliers) in its last phase, as a permanent centre, perhaps like the "Round Table" of King Arthur, later set up at Winchester.

ROPE DANCING
Originated in technical necessity: principally in Italy during the Roman Republic. The Romans were great builders of roads and bridges: they had guilds of bridge-makers, headed by the *Pontifex Maximus*. In this work, the initial need is to cross

a river or ravine; and then to haul a rope across, preparatory to extending the arches from their banked foundations. Kite-flying (still a modern method, used in undeveloped countries), can carry over a slender string, followed by thicker and yet thicker ropes; or by descent into gully or stream, when the string is carried by a small party, the first connection is made. Following in succession, the third or fourth rope, made taut, carries the equilibrist from side to side. Certain young men, becoming highly expert, then desire to show their technical accomplishment to city folk. Thus basic necessity is converted to technical exhibition; and the rope-dancer appears. From Italy, these expert balancers spread into France and Spain, even to England; and later to Mexico (as *voladores** from Spain and Portugal), but they are little known in other lands. In Italy, and North Africa, the frequent construction of aqueducts found employment for arch-builders, with their rope-laden confederates. Wall decorations at Pompeii portray their feats, as devised for public amusement. Later these pioneer groups became the itinerant *cordeliers*. We may compare this technical basis with that of the stilt-dancers in the Landes district of France; later, taken into the towns; and, being economically useful (instead of moving ladders) in the circus-tent erection, a stilts clown was often recruited, to sling and fix the guy-ropes and stretchers of "the big top". Visitors to New York could compare the feats of steel erectors. Joseph Pennell, drawing constructors of Panama Canal, showed men being lifted by crane from the "big cut" when the dinner-whistle blew; but the rope-dancers knew how to slide down a long rope (as from the top of Saint Paul's) to the ground, in a few seconds, as a display. Technical rope-handling is now utilised by mountaineers; the earlier usage by stevedores has declined, in this languid age. The theatre version of these devices has returned in the so-called "Flying Ballet", as a modernized adaptation of the church Dance of Angels,* done on similarly concealed ropes.

ROPPO (Japan)

Kagura dance-drama, having accepted many of the conventions of the *Noh* ritual-drama (Miracle play) has allowed other rituals to be publicised. One of these, derived from Zen (Buddhist) teaching, is the "six-fold extension" in dance, named *Roppo*. This belongs to the *aragoto*, or "proud" technique. The final movements affirm the "six directions of space". Greek geometers tried to summarise these in derivations from their sculptural design methods. The Gnostics hinted at them in their phrase: "the height and the breadth, the length and the depth thereof", while the Hindu ritual dance has a routine

The Rishi Li Tieh (Kawi poet-sage). He uses the Zen ritual of Roppo (Six Directions) to send his soul-mind to the Mountains of the Immortals. From a wood engraving by Kana Tanyu, after a Noh play.
JAPAN

in *alarippu,** which expresses by *hasta** the same bases. In Japan, the *roppo* comes mostly at the conclusion of a dance: as if to say "We have given you this world (*sekai*) for your delight. Take it in your memory!" A recent English writer[1] has attempted to elucidate, an intussusception of pictorial modes, in receding dimensions.

[1] *The Serial Universe*. J. W. Dunne. London, 1934.

ROSALIA (Italian-French)

A term now confined to music, at first meaning what the performance did: namely, the musicians repeated the sequence or passage a step higher or lower, so that the singer could cease, while a dance measure was performed, usually in a ring—hence the rosary or rosalia chain. The *Carolle for crysty-messe* (15th century), which begins "The Rose es the fayrest flour of alle" has a parallel implication.

ROSCA, La (Spain—Salamanca)

Is performed solely at weddings or baptisms; or at the special *Festa de Rosca*, where the *rosca* (or *rozia*), a ring-shaped small loaf or biscuit, is set on a table top. Around this small table an expert couple perform complicated steps. (Best man and maid). The dance is begun by the man, in a prelude called *escuadra* (the square), then he is joined, beside the table, by his partner; when they dance together at the same side of the table. The bride is dressed like the images on the altar; the man uses his castanets; offers the musicians a *brindis* (a blessing and tip), and places the amphora by the base of the altar. It was formerly done solely in church.

ROSIÈRE, LA (France)
Principal figure at a Rose Festival of Picardy, held at Salency, village near Noyon, on June 8th. A village maiden is chosen on account of her spotless reputation. Formerly she was selected (it was said) by the seigneur, from a group proposed by the villagers. The girl, as *La Rosière*, was adorned with fresh rose blossoms. Her friends conducted her to church for a service (sometimes her name was mentioned by way of challenge). The evening was filled with a ball, led by the seigneur, dancing first with *La Rosière*. There is a traditional date for a Bishop (saint) Medard, on June 8th (475 - 545), but little is known. His festival has been copied in other places. A French cinema film has been made with this title; it related to a youth who gained the title, with quaint results.

ROSH HASHANA (Hebrew)
"The Head", the First of Year, celebrated First of Tishri. For the ritual, the signal was given by the *shofar* (ram's horn bugle) and the circle dance, varied by solemn processional, with the *Kedusha*.

RÖSSEL-TANZ (Roumania)
"Dance of the Horses". Used to be performed at weddings among the Saxon communities in Roumania. It may have been danced simply to entertain guests, since what significance connected it with weddings is not clear. *Rösseltanz* danced and mimed a story about two mysterious visitors (a Colonel and Lt. Colonel) to a peasant's house. Arriving at night, in a carriage drawn by two horses and a goat, they secured a night's lodging, then killed the animals, whom all ate for supper. The bones were piled on the skins, and next morning when the guests departed, they resurrected the animals merely by ordering them to get up, when skin, flesh and bones became whole again. But, owing to one of the sons having split a bone for the marrow at supper, one of the horses limped. On seeing this the Colonel flew into a rage, threatening to kill both sons, but compromised by taking them into his service as hostages. The dancing and miming of this legend (which occurs

elsewhere, with variations), made a dramatic presentation.

ROUELLE (French)
Equivalent to Saxon *Ruad*, *rad* etc.; the basic regulation or "Rule" of a ritual and hence of its dance progression. Chiefly known in the Messe-Ruelle, this formal canon governed the Winter Feast (of the Solstice) of the Crest or Crossing. Scandinavian lands had a similar guide in the Rune or Rouen; first known as the circle (or ovoid) with its elemental "Sixteen Letters" derived from their serial along the periphery, and their ordinal position (as in the Chinese *Pa-Kwa*) in opposition. For the Rune, sixteen dancers took positions each symbolising a letter; by moving into sequence, they "spelled out" words of importance. This was the basis of the *spiel* or "magic spell", obtained by dance-singing. In England, the slanders of cleric contrived to pervert the name into Misrule, so that the annually elected leader was changed from Lord of Messe Ruells to Lord of Misrule; in Scotland, the "Abbot of Unreason". The term *rouelle* then signified the "Little Wheel". It has also become *roulette*, a wheel of chance or fortune, and it was again mutilated in England into "Revel", by a mis-spell from *reuel*, and then gained a "Master of Revels" who gave the order of ceremony and dance.

ROUND DANCE
Is so universal that the dance movement or figure; the custom; the place; and the ceremony; all possess hundreds of associated names, some of them obvious, but others serving to elicit information only after close examination. Many of them begin with "r" or its converse "l", as *runa=luna*. One of the oldest is *ryan*, with its better known "Aryan" signifying "those who do not 'go round', i.e. work; hence the 'noble ones' ". In Scandinavia the dance place was the *rune* (letters and numbers spread from it; as from the *templum* of Rome), and it became Rouen. Allied are *rad, ruad, raedhe, rudra, Rahda* or *Radha* (India), all connected with *sarabanda*—the circle of life. The next group has *ruel, ruelle* (then *revel*) and *reel*—the dance, or *reel* of the spun woollen thread. Then we have *rond* and *ronde; rondelle, ronda;* next *rouet, rout, rouette* and *pi-rouette, route* (a path or way), and *riad* (Russian), all as verbs and nouns of the moving circle. *Band* or *bande;* and *kolo* or *koro*]with *choro*) are not so close to the basic *ronde* or *rand;* but they retain the definition of circles, as does the *kirke;* or the *chakram* of India. Most of these terms present facts of both form and function : they name the circle in its local mode, and suggest the time and place of ceremony.

ROUNDELAY, Rondellai (Old French—*rondelet, rondel; rondeau,* etc.)
The *rondeau* settled as a poem into a form of nine lines with a refrain following the third and ninth lines; it accompanied a slow dance form in a circle, as a secular mode of the carole; and was one of the final modes of the cultural system of *la chevallerie* or knighthood. At one time it was a ball dance; the ball was passed round the circle; and later still became competitive, to become degraded finally into a spectacular base-ball game. Associated with this dance were many ancillary terms: the *roleau* (money paid to the musicians, or the prize for singers); *roulade,* the final flourish of song; *rondeau,* another version; *ronde* or *rondelet,* similar forms.

"ROYAL DANCE" (Papua)
The climax of the *Gabé** Festival. Performed by village chiefs, its movements are slow and dignified, paying tribute to the dead. Impressiveness is enhanced by its dramatic position in the sequence of Festival dances, and by the whirling women's dance which accompanies it. (See *Amou Youmamé**). Preceded at dusk by a *Warriors' Dance** and *Women's Dance,* both violent in action but performed in silence, the *Royal Dance* begins with a dignified entry, one by one, of the chiefs. Each dancer wears a fan-shaped head-dress five or six feet high. Hundreds of feathers, graded in colour, are fixed to a bamboo frame which rests on the shoulders, bird-of-paradise plumes soaring at the top. From his shoulders hangs a cloak of parakeet and bird-of-paradise feathers, while his body bears painted designs. He carries a big hour-glass drum, one end covered with lizard skin, and beaten with the flat hand. (Drums vary from eighteen inches to four feet in length). At his elbows swing skulls of former chiefs, not yet buried and attending their last *Gabé.* Each chief is accompanied by two girls, who are an extension of the man himself, his "adornments". With one on each side, elbows touching, he walks slowly to the centre of the dancing-ground, to the rhythm of his drum-beat. Turning in each direction, he dips his plumed head-dress to the four points of the compass, then begins his dance which uses few gestures, and depends for effect upon undulations of the feather head-dress and cloak. While the chief and his two "adornments" progress with dignified grace to the other end of the dancing-ground, women continue to whirl round them in violent contrast. As one chief leaves the clearing the next enters, to perform the same grave dance, until all (about ten) have danced. Finally, each one aproaches a dais where bones of the dead are piled, and performs a brief dance before them, swaying his plumed head-dress over

them in salute. The climatic *Royal Dance* is followed till dawn by dances copying movements of birds and animals.   [See *Olové; Ourouvé*]

ROZA (Spain)
A dancing-ground, usually a newly cleared path of flat ground, marked as a circle, definitely prepared for dancing, in or near a village.   [See *Gajo*]

RUAD
Also *rued, roade, rote, rude, ruede* and *Rood.* (Cp. *Dreme of the Rood,* early English poem of mystery play). Means generally "Path", "Way", in a symbolic ritual dance where the ring indicated the circle of life. This prolific symbol existed under many names, throughout Europe; from its form *ruad* to *ruelle* and *rouen,* to *real* and *rad* or *roue, rouette,* always indicating a moving circle. Compare *Zodiack** and *Shen,* or *Rouelle.* The German *rad*=the ancient *Rath*=company on the "correct" road. In France the name survives with the "*rats*" of the Paris Opera and Ballet.

RUBANDA (Persia)
A thin gauzy cotton veil, over the face, used by dancers as, for example, in the European *ballet, Giselle;* and in *Anderin* (harim) dances. The street veil is called *chadar.*

RUEDA (Spain)
A Castilian round dance (*rueda*=wheel) most characteristically in 2/4 time, but also in 5/8 and 3/8 time. The form consists of alternate walking and dancing round the circle, dancers never touching each other.

RUGOVO WARRIORS' DANCE (Yugoslavia)
A dance from the town of Rugovo, in the Kosmet Region of Southern Serbia. Men of Rugovo were formerly professional warriors, so that several of their dances show a fighting tradition. The *Warriors' Dance,* as arranged for performance by modern folk dance groups is very impressive. Danced by two men, accompanied only by drum rhythm, it is a contest for possession of the drummer. Carrying curved swords, the two men dance in opposition to each other, with swooping almost sinuous movements, soft and catlike in mocassin boots. The drummer follows them beating the rhythm. as they move round, now crouching, now standing. The winner places his foot on the drum, while the drummer kneels, and there follows a dance by the two warriors, arms linked horizontally at shoulder height.   [Cp. *Teskoto*]

RUGGERA (Sicily)
Pantomime dance, peculiar to Messina in Sicily.

The *Ruggera* is performed by four persons—two men, and two girls, in a round. They sing, using distinctive gestures; the first round is done in silence to the instruments (bagpipes, cymbals or tamburines and castanets). For the second round, the leading girl sings a chant to the same rhythm, usually a love song (later changed by clerical guile to praise of some "saint"). There is another silent round; and next the man sings; and so they continue until eight rounds and four songs have been given. Other dancers take their places.

RUMBA (Cuba)
A dance of African Negro origin influenced by strong local rhythms and complicated syncopation. In 2/4 time, the rhythm varies, sometimes from bar to bar. In Havana, it is often danced in the poor quarters to the accompaniment of percussion instruments in the shape of pots and pans, spoons, and bottles. To the African, rhythm is more important than melody; anything handy will be used which is suitable for beating cross-rhythms and syncopations. (See *Batuque**). In the *Rumba*, emphasis is on movements of the body rather than the feet. About 1930 the *Rumba* became popular as a ballroom dance.

RUNES, Dance of the
Ritual dances of Scandinavian tribes, with Goth contacts. The ritual has affinities with the sacred augur dance of Rome, in that it is based on the dis-cussed circle. The Roman circle was marked out, first in four oriented points; then in eight; while the *Rouen* or *rune* circle was developed to sixteen. This is the number of letter-symbols in the sacred rune alphabeta (the Greek had twenty-four divisions). The ritual cussation (division) of the entire circle gave sixteen places; each with its own value; the dance led rhythmically between them. The *Beth Roune*, or House of the Rouen, had in its annual celebration, a central seat, later called 'Eth-roune, then "throne". The "letters" are short straight lines, read by their direction (or inclination) to an assumed axis, at first marked visibly. Dancers followed these to "spell out" any message, which could be read only by those initiated into the system. As in modern shorthand systems, the sound value is related to "the line" and direction of the stroke. Runic was thus a sacred shorthand, which could also be danced, by the position, duration, and direction of the steps. Some of the sword dances reveal eroded fragments of runic dance ritual.

There remain many traces of Brahmin equivalents in Sanskrit letters written in relation to geometrical symbols; also on a long thread or rosary with 108 beads.

RUNIC KNOT (Scandinavia)
The *skalds* and other wise men of Northern Europe had a dual system of notation. One called runic enscribed a circle into eight or sixteen divisions : at the end of each radius was a symbol or *litra* (made on the ground by the runic staff or crook). More complicated patterns traced the progress of the seasons and other evolutions; many such patterns still exist on stone cross forms, in Scotland or N. England, in smaller scale. Their full size mode was "danced out". A slight reminder can be seen in some Morris (*Moeries*) dances, if we trace the ground pattern followed by the feet of six men as they weave in and out. They affirm the knot (by that name) with their united short swords (rappers or *rapers*) which "make a rose" held aloft at the end of their dance.

RUNNING SET
An English square dance in quick time, preserved in villages of the Appalachian Mountains, in North America. Rediscovered there by Cecil Sharp and Maud Karpeles in 1917, it was considered by them to represent a type of country dance known in the early 17th century, but already declining in 1650 when the first edition of Playford's *The English Dancing Master** was issued, which book contained no example of the *Running Set* among its 104 dances. The Playford dances show influence of drawing-room manners, whereas the *Running Set* was danced in a freer style, without the "courtesy movements", and at greater speed. It may have been popular in the English northern counties and Scottish Lowlands, whence came the emigrants to the Southern Appalachians. The basic step is a smooth, quick running-step, and the dance may be accompanied by a fiddle playing jig-tunes; or there may be no music at all. Rhythm is marked by thrumming the bow on the fiddle, or by spectators "patting" (alternate stamping and clapping). The sequence of figures is announced by a Caller, and the area enclosed by the dancers is called the Set or the General Set. Danced by four couples (sometimes more), the *Running Set* consists of an Introduction and some fourteen figures, which follow each other without pause, the whole dance being one swift, continuous movement. Figures include "Shoot the Owl", "Chase the Squirrel", "Wild Goose-Chase", "Box the Gnat", "Bird in a Cage", "California Show Basket", and "Wind up the Ball Yarn", (or "Grapevine Twist"). In the Appalachians the *Running Set* is usually followed by a dance-game called *Tucker*. An extra man (Tucker) dances about in the centre of the Set, and tries to "capture" a lady as partners dance together. The dispossessed man then takes the centre as "Tucker", and repeats the performance. The *Running Set* is

now again danced in England, to a set of traditional tunes arranged by Ralph Vaughan Williams.

RUSALIYE (Macedonia)
The series of connected ceremonial dances that belonged to the ancient Twelve Nights Festival coincident with the Winter Solstice, and the opening of the New Year. In Macedonia, the ceremony is termed *Rusal*, and the dancers, the *Rusaliye*. They perform between Christmas and Epiphany, attired in semi-ritual costume of coat, scarf and *fustanella** (it is near the Greek border), with soft leather boots, and carrying wooden swords. The leading man, called tancar, begins in slow rhythm; body slightly bent forward with legs apart and thrust-out heels. His feet "feel the ground", as if stroking it; then vigorously his sword cuts the air. He is "breaking the path" and clearing away evil spirits; his sword is now turned downwards. The other dancers follow in the same style, in open order. The older solo dancer, who stands as master in the centre of the ring which forms, the *balta-dzija* (axe-carrier) moves slowly his silver axe, engraven with ivy leaf patterns. (Formerly this ivy was the real plant, significant of the thick woods through which he had to cut his symbolical path). The second part of the dance is extremely vigorous; with high jumps and long leaps; the swords brandished over the heads of the sick folk "helps to cure them". Many of the routines resemble those of the West European Morris Dance. The money collected is expended on various local social objectives : fountains, wells, bridge repairs, etc., for which groups of twenty or thirty dancers march from one village to the next.   [Cp. *Calusari*]

RUSH BEARING (England)
This dance became, in 19th century, attached solely to May Day. Originally rush-bearing was a vassel-age duty (required as a part of rent), whereby dry straw or green rushes were "cut and carried" to the local hall or church. This became ceremonial; then ornamented with dance. At Musgrave (West-morland) twelve village maids assembled on May Day, wearing coronals of May blossom or haw-thorn. Starting at 10 a.m. from Brough Bridge, they went with a band in procession towards the church, the rush-bearers dancing. Proceeding up the north aisle, they hung the crowns and garlands by the altar (newer dispensation), where they remained. Next came a modern service. Finally the space before the altar was cleared and, led by a fiddler, dancing began, to continue until 3 p.m. that afternoon, when adjournment was made for a minor feast or tea-fight. Royton Mores Dancers used to accompany the "Rush Procession" in Lancashire.   [See *Church Dances*]

RUSSIAN BALLET (19th century and after)
Has appeared in three distinct phases, after initial development from French, Milanese and Danish styles (1) Tsarist or court ballet, chiefly at Maryinsky Theatre in Petersburg, period of *technical* formation; (2) the Colonial Ballet Russe, centred in Paris), with S. P. Diaghilev; period of new *stylistic* formation; and (3) Soviet Russian Ballet. post 1927, period of *thematic* development. All three modes overlap to some extent. The new centre is in Moscow, Bolshoi Theatre, and Theatre School. There have been numerous imitations of the Russian Ballet; various diversions of its teaching methods, and many commercial imitations made from the principal 19th century ballets of Petersburg; many have been drastically altered, never for the better; cut or otherwise mutilated; while outside Russia the technical standard is usually second rate.

RUTUBURI (Mexico)
A ritual dance of the Tarahumara Indians, performed as an invocation to the Sun and Moon, for rain; as harvest thanksgiving; also as a curing ceremony. Formerly it was danced all night, followed at sunrise by the *Yumari,** but both dances are now combined in one called *Dutuburi*, danced out of doors in a ceremonial dance patio. Many American Indians believe that their dances were taught to their ancestors by the forest animals, *Rutuburi* being associated with the turkey. The rabbit, giant woodpecker, and the blackbird are sung to by the priest, each according to the season —the blackbird at harvest, woodpecker in winter, and rabbit during the wet season. Three crosses stand in the patio, and three priests dance three times towards and away from them. The middle priest, who is the chanter (*saweame*), shakes a rattle. Formerly both men and women took part in the dance that follows. Today in the *Dutuburi* version, the men merely walk back and forth with the centre priest while he chants. The women move in a linked arc, one behind the other, each holding with her right hand the left hand of the woman in front. With a skipping step they dance to right of the chanter and move in an anti-clockwise curve.

RUWAHINE (New Zealand)
Maori "wise woman", who instructed the girls for their initiations, and the dances that formerly belonged to this rite. She is necessarily a woman skilled in all feminine handicrafts; and is able to make the *korowai* (robe of womanhood) from the start. The ordinary term for woman is *Wahine*. One of the ancient dance floor patterns, the *taniko*, is seen now only in woven cloak patterns.

Russian Ballet. Yuri Zakharov, a leading dancer, as the evil magician in *Swan Lake* when produced by the State Academic Bolshoi Theatre for their 175th Anniversary. RUSSIA

RYMOUR (Normandy)
Term used for Minstrel* or Troubadour* in one
period; related in function to the Saxon-English
gleeman. He filled the usual offices of entertainer;
with song, recitation, and dance, varied with such
music as would accompany his chant, or give
rhythm to his dancing. The name is spelled in
many variations — as *rimer, rimmer;* and penetrated
into Scotland, even giving rise to ballads on the
profession, such as the famous *Thomas the Rhymer*
(and his visit to Fairyland). One historical rimer
was Blondell de Neslé, who accompanied Richard
I, and later went to seek his master, who was held
to ransom in jail. This was in 1193. The poetic
account is given in Provençal verse; it seems to
have been part of a *geste* or mime-dance. See
Reliques of Ancient English Poetry. Thomas Percy.

RYOKS (Java)
In Central Java, in the Sultanate of Soerakarta,
there is a mountain region where the *Ryoks*
(masked dancers) are considered indispensible to
any wedding festivity. Their elaborate masks, the
responsibility of a special group called *atoeran
ginoman*, belong to the village, and the tradition
of wearing them and skill in performing the dances,
often belongs to one family, being handed down
from father to son. In the procession of the bridegroom to the mosque, the *Ryoks* take part, one
appearing as a fantastic monster, dressed in vari-
coloured muslin and *batik* cloth, three-quarter
length frilled breeches, and wearing a lion-faced
mask with staring eyes and grinning teeth, surmounted by an immense fan-shaped head-dress of
peacock feathers, streamers and flowers. Another
Ryok supports the end of the creature's ten-foot
calico tail, as he twirls about, leaping in the air,
jumping from side to side of the road, springing
suddenly backwards. When opportunity occurs this
second dancer himself performs a solo.
[Cp. *Barong* (Bali); *Korean Lion Dance; Prüh*
(Burma)]

S

SACRED DANCE
Is interpreted to indicate (a) religious dance ritual;
(b) religious rhythmic ceremonial; and (c) performance of mythic drama, setting forth some
aspect of doctrine. These ritual dances may be
distinguished as: 1. group rituals; and 2. group
ceremonials, as compared with individual rites and
secret personal ceremonies. The difference between
group ritual and group ceremonial appears in the
intention: in the religious ritual there is a dom-

inant element of worship, directed by the group
(possibly with an experienced leader), to the deity
they hold as sacred and supreme; whereas in group
ceremonial, there may be no element of worship
but instead of this, a united feeling held among
the group, possibly for one of their own number;
as, for example, in the rites of consecration of a
bishop. Individual rites or ceremonies carry the
same distinct character: they may be guided (a)
by a mode of worship, or (b) a mode of meditation
or contemplation that does not direct devotion to
some other being. Active dances appear less frequently in these individual phases of ceremonial;
but they are not always absent. Sacred dance is
rarely new and spontaneous: on the contrary, rites
tend always to follow in the path of some ancient
custom. The group is important; the individual
appears solely as a regular officiant, or as a temporary leader, not stressing his own personality.
In this fact resides the immense difference between
ritual and drama. Sacred dance must always
exhibit the theme and purpose of dance, never the
form and movement of some private person. In
presentation of mythic drama (or dramatic myth)
these two oppositions tend to become confused,
especially in traditional legends that accumulate
about religious myth; until we see the grandeur
of true myth debased in pseudo-history.
See *The Sacred Dance.* W. O. E. Oesterley, 1923.
[See *Indian Dance; Egyptian Dance*]

SACRED TREES
Mostly with rituals and dances, appear connected
with nearly every religious system. The adoration
of the Green Shoot (as sign and symbol of returned
life) recurs annually, from the Gardens of Adonis
to the Palm branches of the christian system —
from the Sacred Palm of ancient Egypt to the
Druidic oak and Yule Log; from the Assyrian
Temple Tree with its profound symbolism (explained to privileged watchers of the dance over
the pavement carving) to the biblical Tree of Jesse,
seen in European church windows. Dance rituals
are numerous and varied; some carrying living
Branches; in some the actor dancers mime as the
Tree. Sometimes the Tree becomes a geometrical
symbol, "The Cross" and is buried in decorative
foliage The Maypole bears a "Living shoot" while
the Winter Solstice has its Fir tree.

SACRIFICIAL DANCE (Hebrew/Arabic)
W. Robertson Smith[1] observes two modes; two
extremes of ceremonial expression.
  "Another rite which admits of a twofold interpretation is the sacrificial dance. Dancing is a common expression of religious joy, as appears from
  many passages in the old testament; but the

"limping dance" of the priests of Baal (in *1. Kings xviii 26*) is associated with forms of mournful supplication. And in Syriac the same verb, in different conjugations, means 'to dance' and 'to mourn' ".

This sharp inversion is known to us, as a traditional change over a much longer period; when the funerary customs of Rome have gradually moved over to our modern expression of "fun and games", with no sort of lugubrious implication, via the French useage of *funambulist*, in the *foires*, from *funus*.

[1] *Religion of the Semites.* W. Robertson Smith. London, 1893 (p. 432).

SADLER'S WELLS THEATRE AND BALLET (London)

Following the 19th century derelict period, the Theatre building was demolished; and rebuilt in accordance with the scheme formulated by Lilian Baylis (of the Old Vic Theatre*) for a second popular centre for Drama and Opera. Her method was intended to transfer the entire company (for either production), with scenery and costumes etc., so that patrons in North London could be met (also at low prices) like those in South London. Technical omissions inhibited the smooth operation (there was no scene-dock or storage space in the new building), while the same difficulties of obtaining competent theatre people, at low fees, continued. There was no Equity then; only the Actors' Association. The Baylis scheme made no provision for ballet productions, though these were already contemplated. A small company sustained the tender project; and gradually a new idea became apparent to them; namely that opera-ballet might become real ballet. A few teachers and a few students helped; once more the ancient home of Joey Grimaldi became a centre of dance and pantomime. Eventually more ideas were acquired; then the Theatre became a working centre, a theatre with a school, or a school with a theatre; though it has been perenially lacking in adequate creative ideas. Thus we have witnessed the strange spectacle of alleged "British Ballet" basing its technical performance on Franco-Russian academic dance; and utilising 19th century Russian Ballets (of the pre-Diaghilev era) as examples of British Art; and even exporting these productions to America on this same basis. Further, in this incredible scheme, has followed the confusion of the subsidised transfer of the Sadler's Wells Ballet Company to Covent Garden, without the necessary change of name : developing more confusion by naming a second or "Junior Company" with a closely similar name. Hence there now exist (1958) two "Sadler's Wells Ballet Company" plus a newly formed junior—

junior group of expectant students. The British Council then exports rearranged copies of "Russian Classical Ballets" to the USA, as examples of British culture; and sends the second company, with the misleading title, expending large sums to provide American theatres with entertainment, subsidised by the British tax-payer.

SAFINA (Arabia)

A *harim* dance, performed by women and by small girls. With movement barely perceptible, they dance in slow progression, two by two and holding hands. Little stamps of the feet set jingling the bells on their anklets and attached to rings on the big toe, suggesting the nursery 'rhyme "rings on her fingers and bells on her toes". Many bells are worn also in the *harim* dance, *Rishi.**

SAGAR DANTZA (Basque)

"Apple Dance". A dance for five girls, accompanied only by female voices. Four girls carry an apple in each hand and dance in a square formation; the fifth girl, with a basket of apples on her head, dances between and round the other four. Moving with gentle grace, they wind through various patterns. Sometimes, facing each other in pairs, each girl moves one arm in upward, downward and lateral movements, in opposite directions to her partner, the apples held in the hand being brought gently to touch as the hands momentarily meet.

SAKALAVA (Madagascar)

Malagasy term for War Dance. A ceremonial form was performed for the New Year Festival in the courtyard of the royal palace, to include the salute to the ruler (*veloma*=salute). Music was provided by drums in several sizes, also the *valiha*, a bamboo instrument about four feet long, with sections of strong outer fibre, detached, and strained over small pieces of wood, resembling the bow of a violin. A single *valiha* gives a soft plaintive sound, somewhat like a guitar; but a number, with drums, produces a good volume of sound.

SAKARA (Nigeria)

Dance of the Ilorin tribe of Yoruba people. Usually performed by groups of eight (four men and four women in lines facing), the girls are chosen from among spectators by the Master of Ceremonies. With graceful movements, the lines meet and retire, or pass through each other. This simple dance is accompanied by calabashes; an instrument like a small violin played by plucking the strings; and a small drum nine inches across. Arranged at one side of the dancing-space, the musicians are closely surrounded by six to ten boys who sing in chorus, led by the player of the stringed instrument. The songs introduce names of many spectators, who are then expected to contribute money. Following the changing rhythms of the drum, sometimes a particularly skilful dancer, who knows the drum language, and re-acts to its "speaking", dances alone. The drummer then leaves his seat to follow him as he moves round the dancing-space, dancer and drummer watching each other closely.

SAKI ACROBATIC DANCERS (Nigera)
The only tribe of acrobatic dancers among the Yoruba people. Saki men travel in bands, performing in villages. On arrival they set up a smooth pole, about eighteen feet high. Only one or two are acrobats, the others providing the rhythm by beating gourds (called *Sekere*) ornamented with cowrie shells. At first, all dance round the pole, while an audience collects. Then the first dancer and head beater sing that they are ready to begin. Each performance has its own songs which, with the beating of gourds, tell the dancer what he should do, such as "crawl like a snail". Wearing only a piece of cloth from waist to ankles, he jumps on to the pole, clutching it with legs and body, and crawls to the top without touching it with his hands. At the top he turns upside down; and, singing loudly, crawls down the smooth pole in a snail-like spiral trail, still without the hands touching, and head first. Gourd beaters meantime dance round the foot of the pole, the leader throwing up his gourd and catching it.

SALAMBO (Hebrew/Arabic)
The "Image of Baal", also given as *Salambas*, seems related principally to the peripatetic figures that were carried in ceremonial rituals, in street processions, at the great town festivals of Baal. The name does not apply to the Oriental Aphrodite. Essentially the name appears to imply the symbol of "Him to whom submission is made", as the root *salm*, as a verb, or proper name, equals submission; this is extended in the familiar salute of Islam — the *Sala-am*, or reverence; the word, with the bow, or the raised right hand. Distantly this connects also with the mediaeval dancing figure called Salome. Her pose is frequently one of inversion; yet this is symbolic, not acrobatic. Possibly there is a relation to the Roman Saliian priests. The "great word" of Islam relates to *istalama* — "he made peace", which implies a reverence, a salutation : spoken as *Es-salamu aleikhum* with right hand on the brow, and bending forwards. The rites and procession of *Salambo* included chanting and dancing — as the "dancing Baal". See *Salammbô*. Gustave Flaubert. Paris, 1862 — a novel about Carthage.
[See *Salii; Salome, Dance of*]

SALII — 1
Dancing priests of ancient Rome, who derived their name from the leaping dances they performed. Twice a year, in March and October when the Romans sowed their corn, these priests of Mars (god of vegetation before he was god of war), danced in the Comitium at Rome, invoking also Saturn, as god of sowing. Many towns of Italy possessed a College of Salii; in Rome there were two colleges, each composed of twelve members which, says Frazer, may have referred to the twelve months of the old lunar year.[1] Wearing a bronze helmet, a sword at their side, on the left arm a shield, and in the right hand a staff with which they struck the shield, they danced through the city for several days, expelling demons of blight. Singing and clashing their shields, they danced in triple time, the rhythm being kept by a "fugelman" who pranced at the head of the procession. The *Salii* officiated each year about the 14th March, when they administered the blows with which *Mamurius Veturius** (the "Old Mars") was expelled from the city at the end of the old year, and beginning of the new year.
[1] *The Golden Bough*. Sir James Frazer. London, 1890.

Salian Dancers. An intaglio gem showing servants carrying five anchile, or shields, as used by the Salian dancers in some ceremonials (street processional period). They wore a version of *toga picta*. (Museum, Florence).   ROME

SALII — 2 (Ancient Rome)
The College of Twelve priest-dancers is said to date from Numa, devoted to rites of Mars Gradivus; selected from the patricians. They had twelve shields (each bearing *S/S* pattern) related to their duties, sometimes called *ankhiles* or *ancilia*. This term *ankhileus* seems to relate to a more ancient

name as "life-bearers" (from Egyptian *ankh*), but Ovid derives their name *Salii* (plural) from their dancing. Their principal festival of Mars was celebrated on First March, at the Mars Temple on the Palatine Hill, where they had a magnificent banquet, after passing through the city bearing the *ancilia*, singing and dancing traditional chants as they struck their shields with rods. The hymns (*Saliaria carmina*) in ancient, half-forgotten tongue, were known as *Axiamenta* (possibly "Song of the Axe", as sacred in Crete and Babylon). They had no musical instruments or musicians. Their hymns praised Mamurius Venturius (ancient god of agriculture, said to be an armourer or smith). The shape of the *ankhile* was almost an "eight" or double oval; these "shields" were born on a rod suspended between the shoulders of bearers (according to ancient gems), who were servants. This cult was distinctively masculine, as opposed to the cult of the Vestal Virgins, with the *Flamens** partaking of both sides. A second Salian College was established by Tullus Hostius, named for Quirinus, called *Salii Collini* or *Agonales*. Their effective number of Twelve compares them with the Twelve Corybantes of Crete; and other groups of the symbolical twelve. They had ranks or dignities of *praesul*, *vates*, and *magister*; which suggest derivation (through Etruscan cities) from Druidic or Cymric cults; and a possible distant parallel with the Grecian body of Muses; also nine under Apollo, and perhaps three others.

SALLE (French)

The current term *la salle*, indicates both the audience and the place where it gathers; especially the French music-hall. Ordinary dramatic work and classical ballet are equally out of place; though technical ballet exercises usurp occasional attention in English music-halls. *La Salle* is the circus of real action, as opposed to the "social dream" of drama, or fairyland ballet; with an audience predominantly adult and demanding a topical realism, at its height in pointed satire, in a tense re-action against the outer-world, with its endless impositions of rule and regulation. Dance in the music-hall offers the best opportunity for what is termed "Modern Dance", though too many dancers affect to despise the Music-hall (because they cannot meet its sharp demand for power expressed in stage art), and fail to exploit its temerarious technique.

SALOME, DANCE OF

Usually associated with a perversion of scriptural legend as a "Dance with a Gory Head", by a sparsely clad female. Any brief investigation into the meaning of the name dispels this superficial notion. Salome=*Shalom* (Hebrew) meaning "wel-

come", further exemplified in the Islamic greeting *Shalum Aleikhum!* meaning "Peace be with you", to which the reply is *Aleikum Salaam!* — "And with you Peace!" This ritual dance was a later repetition of the Babylonian "Dance of the Veils of Ishtar" (see also *Esther* or *Istar's Dance*), which symbolically possessed several layers of meaning : a seasonal one pertaining to the year (*Sol-Om-On* is here the Sun, like *Shem-Sun* is, with Delilah) and another meaning is relevant to the "birth of the soul", in which the discarded seven veils mean the gradual escape from the seven veils of the material world. The Head of Johannun on the plate means the end of the Golden Year in its circle; Herod (*Ha-Ruadas*) signifies the Keeper of the 360 "Days of the Year" (the supposed "infant victims" which he slays). The *Ruad** is the Circle of the Year; the cross in it was called Rood.

SALON (French, from Latin *salus* and *sali*)

Essentially the large room in house or palace where there was sufficient space to dance socially in groups; also the social gathering (especially in Paris) where the *grandes dames* invited the current "nice people" to assemble; commented on by Thackeray as part of the *snobisme* of the 18th century period. Taken over by the Irish, to name drinking rooms, the term was carried by them to the USA, where it appeared as *Saloon* (the genteel pronunciation of Bloomsbury) and there it remains (also on ocean liners).

SALTARELLO—1 (Italy)

A 15th and 16th century court dance, the "after-dance" to the *Passamezzo** (see *Nachtanz**). The music, in triple time, was often based on that for the first dance, which was in duple time. From *saltare*, "to jump" the name indicates the springing or hopping movements of the dance, in contrast to the *terre-à-terre* style of its companion. Antonio Cornazano's 15th-century manuscript, *Libro-dell' Arte Danzare* (in the Vatican Library) refers to the *Saltarello* as "the gayest of all dances and the Spanish call it *Alta Danza* . . ." It also formed part of the later *Balletti** as, for example, in the *Brando Alta Regina,** arranged as *Intrada*, *Contrapasso*, *Saltarello*, *Gagliarda*, all repeated and ending with a *Finale*. This *Saltarello*, in 3/2 time, was danced with hopped steps and side leaps. Partners approached each other, linked right arms and revolved twice, then changed places and circled to the left—repeated with left arms linked, and followed by a sequence with partners facing each other and dancing sideways.

SALTARELLO—2 (Italy)

An old courting dance of central Italy, belonging

to Romagna; also danced in the Marche and the Abruzzi, with many local variations. The girl holds her apron throughout the dance, which is one of retreat and pursuit; offering by the man; rejection, coy by-play, and final acceptance by the girl. The couple move in a semi-circle, tempo gradually increasing, and the dance is a mimed flirtation without set figures. In some places an accordion and small drum accompany the dance, with music in 3/8 or 6/8 time, but the drum is the principal instrument for a *Saltarello*, a vigorous drum-beat being the signal for a leap by both dancers. Said to belong specially to gardeners and vine-growers, it is performed out of doors, often with bare feet. The Neapolitan *Seccarara** alternates with or in cludes the *Saltarello*.

SALTATORE (Italian)
A dancer, or leaper; a jumper or tumbler in dancing. From *saltare* : to jump, to leap, to jump or skip. Associated terms include : *Saltazione*, jumping or leaping; *saltellare*, to leap or skip along; *salto*, a little dance, or leap; *saltato*, to have danced or jumped; *salterello*, a jumping object, a cracker, a doll; *salterio* and *saltero*, the book of psalms (which used to be chanted to dance movement); *saltetto*, a little leap in dancing; *saltabeccare* and *saltabellare*, to skip and hop along in rhythm; *saltambarco* or *saltamin-dosso*, a clown's jacket, used in dancing; *salta*, a small office or desk, where public girls went to pay priests for permission to dance; *sala*, a hall, a salon, the semi-public room where they danced.

SAMAET (Arabic)
General Egyptian term for the ritual spinning dances, as performed by sects of the Mevleveh dervishes in Africa.   [See *Dervish Dances*]

SAMBA (Brazil)
A dance in 2/4 time and lively tempo, always in the major key. Two forms exist in Brazil—the *Samba* of the countryside, which is more syncopated, faster and more vigorous; and the urban form, which has less varied rhythm. Various hybrid forms combine the *Tango*,* *Rumba** or *Foxtrot* with the Samba. The *Samba-Carioca* is a salon dance, Carioca denoting Rio de Janeiro, but the ballroom dance known in England about 1934 as the *Carioca* was "invented" by the dancing-masters. In 1938 the *Samba* became popular in American ballrooms, and in the early 1940's its popularity increased owing to the dynamic dancing of Carmen Miranda in Hollywood films. The type of *Samba* then known in European ballrooms was a modernised version of the *Maxixe*,* brought from Paris about 1921, although a *Maxixe Brésilienne*

had long been known in England. The ballroom *Samba* is mainly a non-progressive dance, with two distinctive characteristics—a gentle but rhythmic bouncing movement, and a swinging movement of the body, obtained by leaning back on forward steps and forward on backward steps.

SAMOAN DANCING
In Samoa, the word for "a dance" or "to dance" is *siva*. A *siva* is held on festive occasions, such as weddings, or when visitors from another village arrive, or for private entertainment. Boys dance after tattooing; the Manaia (Chief's son) courts his bride with dancing, and the bride dances at her wedding. At informal *sivas*, held in the family's house, children learn to dance by copying their elders, and by instructions called to them by spectators. There are no special teachers. On important occasions the largest guest house in the village is used. When a travelling party (or *malaga*) arrives from a neighbouring village, dancers divide into two sides—hosts and visitors—members of the home village completing the visitors' team if necessary. The two sides dance alternately. A group of young men in the centre of the floor play stringed instruments (formerly bamboo drums), and sing appropriate songs. Rhythm is marked by clapping or beating the ground with the knuckles. Dancers wear bark-cloth skirts or loin-cloths, flowers, shell necklaces, anklets and bracelets of leaves. A half-dozen formal claps open the dance and there are a few set endings. In between the dancer has a choice of some twenty-five or thirty figures, and two or three set transitional poses. Three definite styles—dance of the *taupo** (the village ceremonial hostess), dance of the boys, and dance of the clowns*—relate to the kind of dance and not to the status of the dancer. The individual dancer thus has three styles and many figures from which to construct his or her dance. Chiefs (who rarely dance) and older women of rank may choose between the dignified *taupo* style and the comedy dance of those accompanying them. The style of a virtuoso dancer may be copied by a youngster, but each dancer strives to develop individuality. As the night wears on, dancing becomes more provacative, so that in modern Samoa missionaries forbid converts to dance, or to watch a big night *siva*. Girls, therefore, put off joining the church until they are older "for", they say, "*laititi a'u fia siva*" —"I am but young and like to dance".
[See *Taupo's Dance; Clowns' Dance*]

SAMSARA (Hindu, Sanskrit)
The "world dance", or Nature seen as the eternal dance of human life. The Hindu doctrine visualises *Samsara* as a *Sarabande*, a veritable "prison of in-

evitable dance", which the Ego (or *Eka*, the One) is self-compelled by incessant Desire to enter and continue. The Buddhist views this as a Dance of Misery; thus he seeks to understand it, then by understanding, to gain self-release and escape from the unending World Whirl as an actor; and to gain the bliss of *Nirvana* as a spectator. The Brahman —adopting Creation as his standard rather than Dissolution—seeks, in a yet more gigantic task, to understand this World, and to subdue it. The Buddhist does not deny the gods but seeks to supersede them; the Brahman affirms the gods, and then seeks to be "with them". Either of these cosmic aims is grander than that of the ancient Egyptian or the modern Christian, or yet the Babylonian or Roman schemes. The Hindu mythos (its presentation of sublime facts under a veil of tenuous symbols, hard to understand) sees the Cosmos as a Divine Dance. This Brahman system is the only one that utilises symbols of Dance, of Dancer, and Dancing as vehicles of profound instruction by a variety of dynamic modes of ritual and worship. The Chinese *Ming* system of the "Hall of Light" admits ritual dance; but it becomes lost in Confucian conferences, where the subtleties of Tao are ossified, as surely as the crude virility of the Assyrian hordes was defeated by its own imperialism, despite the Khaldean masters who sought to teach the Dance of the Sacred Tree. Other systems we can infer only from a few separated symbols, such as the *Tangov** of Polynesia; the Twelve Trees of the British Druids; and the Cretan Mother Goddess with her ritual dance of bulls; and the Great Green Serpent of the Mexican scheme.

SANDHYA GAYATRI (India)

Literally "Evening Prayer", but, as "Dance of Shiva", signifying the God's Dance of Dissolution, as the "evening" of earthly time. *Sandhya* indicates the "twilight hour" and *Gayatri* is the famous "Sixteen-syllable-mantra" of Hindu Brahmin ritual. This mythical episode was a favourite subject with the painters of Hindostan, showing the Dance of Shiva before the assembly of all the gods; some of whom act as orchestra and chorus.   [See *Raga*]

SAND TRACINGS—1 (Malekula, New Hebrides)

Labyrinthine patterns, drawn in the sand or volcanic dust, Now drawn by men, the designs used to be made by women, and are connected with the Malekulan "Journey of the Dead". They are drawn with the finger, in one continuous line, upon a previously traced framework of straight, intersecting lines, or small circles. Once the design is begun the finger must not be lifted until the figure is complete. Although now only a pastime, these maze patterns are connected with the basic design called "The Path", said to be that drawn by the Guardian Ghost, Temes Savsap, as she guards the entrance to the Land of the Dead. When the soul of the dead man approaches, she erases half the design, which he must know how to complete, before he can enter the other land, by the path which leads through the maze. This is symbolised in the *Na-leng** dances, performed when the initiates emerge from their thirty days seclusion during the *Maki* ritual cycles.

[See *Na-leng; Ramben; Maki-ru; Malekula, dances of*. Cp. *Rangoli; Labyrinth; Alpona; Navajo; Yei-Bit-Chai*]

SAND TRACINGS—2

Primitive choreographic ritual patterns are known in traces, all over the ancient world. In Polynesia (now existing) they are known as *Ghir* (in Vao Island), *Ul* (Malekula), *Na-Leng** (the Malekulan "Maze-Dance Ritual"), *Rolu* (in Laravat, Malekula), *Na-Hal*, or "The Path" (Malekula), or *Ni-Sel* (in Atchin district). The *Nahal* is a basic traditional Labyrinthine pattern through which the dead man has to find his way to peaceful conditions. The *Tangov* is another important basic form—this is a "diamond-shape", from which, as centre, other patterns are traced. In America the Navajo* Indians make ritual paintings on a sand floor.

Arabic forms : *Rama'ali* or *rammal;**

Scandinavian basis, the *rune* and *rouen* or *Futork;*

Roman basis: (Etruscan) the *escu-ara* (square) of the Augur;

Roman (Latina) : the stone-cut alphabeta (e.g. Trajan column letters);

Hindu : (Brahmin) *yantra;*

Hindu : (popular traditional forms) *Alpona** (Bengal), *Rangoli** (Bombay);

English : Maze (planted trees, bushes, turf-cut).

[See *Navajo; Yei Bit Chai*]

SANDUNGA OR ZANDUNGA (Mexico)

A pair dance of the Isthmus of Tehuantepec performed at fiestas and other social occasions. Various legends recount the origin of the dance, but the music is said to date only from mid-19th century. The name means "beautiful and graceful woman", and seems to refer to an ideal whom every *tehuana* wishes to resemble. The women of Tehuantepec are famous for their beauty. In the form of a *Jarabe,** the dance is performed by partners facing but not touching, the girl moving haughtily with a simple waltz step, without looking at her partner, who dances round her with quick *zapateado** steps. A *marimba* (together with string and brass instruments for wedding occasions) accompanies the dance, and verses are sometimes sung, either popular or telling of frustrated love. When danced

by several couples at once, men and women form two lines facing, partners first dancing towards and away from each other, then the man following the woman round. The statuesque *tehuanas* may wear their curious but lovely fiesta costume.
[See *Llorona*; *Zandunga*]

SANGHYANG DEDARI (Bali)

A dance of exorcism, performed by two little girls during the rainy season, to exorcise evil fever spirits, by invoking spirits of the *dedari* (heavenly nymphs) *Supraba* and *Tundjung Biru* (Blue Lotus) to enter their bodies. The children are chosen for their psychic quality. Their parents are highly regarded, and exempt from certain village duties. After training, the girls go into a deep trance, during which they perform with ease dance steps which take an ordinary dancer months to learn. *Sanghyang* steps are the same as *Legong*.* In the temple, the girls, with loose hair, dressed in white skirts, with gold ear-plugs, silver anklets, bracelets and rings, kneel before the altar on either side of the priest. A brazier with three sorts of incense burns on the altar. Women singers sit in a circle round them, men in a group at the back. The jewellery is removed and put into a bowl of water, and small incense burners are placed before each girl. After a prayer, the women sing, and the girls fall into a trance, from which moment they do not open their eyes until the end of the ceremony when they are taken out of their trance. They are now regarded as goddesses. Women attendants remove the white skirts and replace them with the legong costume of gold brocade, silver belt and gold head-dress with frangipani flowers. The jewellery is put on again while the women sing. With bare hands the *sanghyang* brush the coals from the braziers. They may chase the evil spirits through the village or to another temple, but must not touch the ground outside, and are carried on men's shoulders. In the temple courtyard, they dance among the glowing fire of burning coconut shells until the fire is extinguished, or they pick up the burning embers and pour them over themselves. Then the two men, with the girls standing on their shoulders, walk round the courtyard. Their feet clinging to the men's shoulders, the girls dance from the waist up, balancing and bending back at incredible angles. The dance over, the girls are brought out of trance with more songs, and the flowers from their head-dresses distributed as amulets. Although the ceremony lasts for two hours the children show no signs of fatigue.

SANGITA (Hindu, Sanskrit; India)

The summarised term for all necessary components of worship : namely *Gita* (singing); *Vadya* (musical accompaniment), and *Natya* (dance). These are the technical terms; the liturgy itself is the *Tantra** (composed of *Mantra* (sacred verses) and *Yantra* (basic dance design), with *Raga-Rasa** (or Rhythmic Mood in Musical tone). *Tantra*, or "the doctrine" is expressed verbally by *Gitam*, and made visible by *Natyam* in symbolic mode. Full comprehension, and understanding of the place and meaning of dance in the ritual, can be gained only from full study of all six factors of the traditional ceremonial.
[See *Raga*; *Natya Veda*, *Yantra Raja*; *Tantra*]

SANJUANITO (Ecuador)

Chief dance of Ecuador, with music in the minor key, in 2/4 time. Guitars and a melancholy song in 4/4 time, accompanying the dance. *Sanjuanito* is a pair dance of subdued character, with partners facing but not touching. Each holds a kerchief in one hand, which they gently raise and lower as they dance towards and away from each other. This dance of mild flirtation resembles the gay *Zamacueca** of Chile, but in a less positive manner, and is identical with the *Huaiño** of Bolivia and Peru. Spanish coquetry is mingled with the natural passivity of the American Indian, and the melancholy character and plaintive minor-key music may be explained by the fact that, in Bolivia, the *Huaiño* was originally associated with funeral ceremonies of the Quechua Indians.
[Cp. *Tamborito* (Panama); *Jarabe* (Mexico)]

SANKETAK (Hindu)

Indicates broadly the "language of signs" which were utilised in *Kama-kala*,* as taught in the *Kama-shastras*. One modern exemplar (familiar to us) is in the Victorian usage of the "Language of Flowers", occasionally followed by florists (as, after Shakespeare : "Here's Rosemary, that's for remembrance !"). These popular symbol-systems enter into the realm of dance, especially in the more developed *Nautch** of Northern India, where a *mudra** will indicate a flower (a lotus), or an insect (a bee), in dancing some love poem. This section is known as *Bhasha Sanketak*, or Flower Language. Then *Anga Sanketak*, more closely affiliated with dancing and acting, is the "touch of parts of the body", to indicate regular notions. The "fifteen lines" made by the fingers and thumb may indicate the fifteen days of the lunar half-month; they often appear in Hindu dance, but seldom receive explanation. *Potli Sanketak* produces small bundles or packets of easily recognisable commodities (not in modern trade packs) which indicate related ideas. We have the modern fancy chocolate box, or bottle of scent, as a present to a close lady friend; culminating in necklace, or a ring as the final symbol.

Then *Vastra Sanketak* carried indications by means of selection of colour in costume. We know of the various robes in ritual colourings: white, black, violet or red. *Vastra* has importance in association with *ragmala** Hindu paintings, in relation to traditional love poems of the seasons; and consequently in their portrayal in performance of their dance expression. *Tambul Sanketak* is practically obsolete; it indicated notions carried by the folding or arrangement of *fan* or betel leaf. Finally *Pusp Sanketak* carried the usage of flowers in more specialised directions; in the form of garlands. In India, it is customary to present a welcome visitor, or some respected friend on an auspicious occasion, with a floral garland, brought and put over his head. When the dancer wears a floral garland, it may indicate other marks of rank, or season, or of function, much as the halo does in Western art.

SANTHAL DANCE (Bihar and Orissa province, India)

The Santhal tribes have remains of many traditional dances; some featured at religious festivals; others used more for pastime. Many are courtship or marriage-market dances. Full moon nights are marked by drum signals; girls rapidly assemble in best attire, ornamented with flowers in spring, or feathers in winter. Young men carrying banners, with drums, pipes and gongs, assemble in the fields. The girls take no notice; the youth approach, playing and dancing in regular lines. Girls are now swaying to and fro, linked in standing lines; they advance and retire, but do not dance or even mix with the youths; who watch them closely, selecting one or other. Later they "hold sweet converse" and get acquainted. Other dances are miniature comedies: "Indigo Reaping", or "Wives Quarrelling", or "Money-Lender Outwitted!"

SARABANDE—1

A dance of 16th and 17th centuries, known in three forms: Spanish solo dance; French Court dance; and English country dance, also performed at Court. Known in Spain at the beginning of the 16th century, it is stated in the *Historia de la Musica Española* (Madrid 1859) to have been "invented" by a dancer named Zarabanda, but this is unlikely. Others contend that the name comes from the Arabic derived word *Sarao*, meaning a dance gathering; but it may derive from the Sanskrit *Sam-sàra*, "Dance of the World", giving it an older, ritual origin. The Spanish *Sarabande* was a woman's solo, the dancer accompanying herself with song and castanets, or guitar. Its style was fiery and abandoned, some 16th century Spanish writers finding it "a disgrace, to the nation", and

calling it *el pestifero baile de Zaraband*. Towards the end of the reign of Philip II (1527-98), it was suppressed, but was later revived in more decorous style, in which form it arrived at the French Court in 1588. There, as a grave and stately court dance in triple measure, it became very popular during the 17th century. Its dignity was such that Cardinal Richelieu (1585-1642), Minister to Louis XIII, considered it suitable to dance himself, in a court ballet or masque, before Anne of Austria. He is described as wearing green velvet knee breeches with bells on his feet and using castanets, so that the dance evidently retained a Spanish flavour. When the *Sarabande* reached England, some of its gaiety returned, and it became a jolly country dance, like "Sir Roger de Coverley". The English *Sarabande* (spelt *Saraband*) was popular at the court of Charles II, who himself danced it. The first edition of Playford's *Dancing Master** (1651) gives two examples, one "longways for as many as will", one "longways for six".

SARABANDE—2 (European, from Sanskrit)

Equals *Sam-sàra*, the "whole world" (dance, or movement, of humanity); *Bhande*, the company, praising or dancing; and *bande*, the circle or ring. From the root *sara* comes also *sala* and thus *Sally* and *Sarah*, mythic dancers (*abram* who becomes *abr-ah-am* has with him *sara*, who grows to *sam-sàra* and also *samskàra*—tendencies of the world). The figure of the "world as dance" occurs in many mythic systems. Goethe has it in *Faust*:[1]

"Plunge we in Time's tumultuous dance
In rush and roll of Circumstance!"
and continues to echo (perhaps a result of his reading of Spinoza?) when Mephistopheles replies:
". . . . this whole supernal
Is made but for a god's delight.

He dwells in splendour single and eternal . . ."
which is the authentic Hindu doctrine of *Lila Maya*; again expressed by Umar-i-Khayyam in quatrains, about the "shadow-show" of the Sufi poets in Iran.
[1] *Faust*. Bayard Taylor's trans. (p. 50).

SARAO (Spain)

A 16th century Carnival dance-game, resembling the Masque in form. A lengthy dance, similar to the *Cotillon,** with a number of figures, might last a whole evening, and was given to entertain the Court after a banquet. In some of the older *Saraos*, a king or queen, selected from among the dancers, opened the ball and led the figures. *Senor Bastonero*, literally "staff-bearer", as master of ceremonies, was appointed to regulate the ball and choose the couples in later times. Every *Sarao* opened and closed with a Minuet.*

SARAGAKU (Japan)

Mediaeval development of dance rituals, miracle plays and court etiquette, which appeared from the Kamakura period (ended about 1224), during the Ashigaka period. Partly from Shinto origins, partly under the Buddhist influence of the Zen cult, it culminated about 1430, when its integrating style produced the early *Noh** Dance-Plays. *Saragaku* was formed from earlier dance rituals, including *Dengaku** (warrior memorial dances); *Kowaka; Kusemai; Ko-uta; Ennen-mai;* and *Bugaku*, the oldest of the Shinto shrine dances, which developed then into a chant-dance used also in Buddhist ceremonial. *Saragaku* developed at Shinto shrines; at Ise were three different groups of performers or schools of ritual; while at Omi, Tamba and Kawachi, similar dance liturgies ruled. In Nara, at the Kasuga shrines, four distinct groups grew up, originators of the four modern schools of Komparu, Kwanze, Hosho, and Kongo (so named from their leaders). The *Saragaku* was brought to its final form by Kiyotsugu and Seami, by revisions and additions. Military themes spread, as in *Shugen Noh* (praise of warriors) and *Yureno-Noh* or *Shoreno-Noh* forms, also propaganda for the Shoguns or military dictators, fortified with Buddhist sentiment. *Saragaku* remained chiefly at the shrines; while the *Noh* developed at the court, at first. Then the shrine priests adopted the *Saragaku* form, including all elements (see *Noh Dance-Drama**). Seami, producer of late *Saragaku* (born 1373) was patronised by Ashikaga Yoshimitsu, who was a Zen Buddhist; thence he got the meaning of Yugen; he wrote some early *Noh Plays.*

SARBA (Rumania)

Nearly as popular as the *Hora,** the *Sârba* has many variants usually in 2/4 time. Usually performed only by young men, the dance may last for an hour without stopping; tempo often increases to a dizzy speed. The form is a linked line or curve, with a "leader" at each end. Dancers are linked by placing their hands on each other's shoulders. The front leader regulates steps by special calls; when the curved chain, moving to the right, winds into a spiral, the tail leader brings the dancers back into line. Both leaders improvise new figures. Usually in a long line, the *Sârba* is also often performed by several small chains at a time. The Serbian version is called *Vlaski*. A still faster dance is the *Brâul* or *Brâuletul* ("Belt"), named after the manner in which the dancers are linked — by holding their neighbours' belts.   [Cp. *Aurresku*]

SARCOPHAGUS DANCE RITUAL (Egypt, Rome)

Reveals a striking confirmation of the real function of the most ancient Egyptian sarcophagus. Investigators into pyramid use and structure are obsessed with the supposed construction of such an immense structure as a place of burial. Hence they express dismay when they unearth one more specimen: find a sarcophagus — but empty, with no cover. They then invent wild theories, instead of investigating the plain fact, that the place is not one of burial, but of ceremonial initiation. For this solemn rite no lid is necessary; the early stone cells (for such they were) remained unadorned. Subsequent ceremonial developed the ritual dance — circumambulation of the recumbent body of the new initiate, by the hierophants and priests — which clearly suggested memorial designs of their chief positions and movements. These copies were carved and painted on the outside. Before this position, the *interior* of the royal Egyptian sarcophagus (when later imitated for a coffin), was painted with symbolical figures; nearly always the symbol of new life. Later still, these paintings were made on the walls of temples. But the two main places were: the sarcophagus and the chamber of initiation. Hence the ritual dance here received some erudite record. The later use of the pyramid (in a few instances) for final burial is similar to the gradual encroachment of extinct V.I.P.'s into Christian churches — which at first were never erected as burial places. Ritual dance in ceremonial, by this reflex in painting, and then sculpture, reveal the designs of main types of early ritual in their movement and gesture.
[See *Zodiac; Animal Dances*]

SARDANA — 1 (Catalonia, Spain)

A round dance, in which anyone may join, found all over Catalonia. Although based on the *Contrapas,** which has signs of origin in ancient Greece, the present form dates from mid-nineteenth century. N'Antoni Toron and Pep Ventura established the form of orchestra (*Cobla*), and music; while Miguel Pardas fixed the choreography. The *Sardana Cobla* consists of ten players, one with drum and *flabiol* (three-holed flute), together with wood-wind and brass instruments, a double-bass, and a tenora. The pipe-and-taborer announces commencement of the dance, and throughout sets the time, but there is no leader among the dancers. To dance the *Sardana* well one should have a facility for mental arithmetic, and it is these arithmetical intricacies lying behind an apparently simple dance which make it unique. Steps are governed by rigid rules, and the dance is divided into thirteen sections. First the introduction on the *flabiol* which calls the dancers together; then alternating sections of "shorts" (two steps left and right) and "longs" (four steps left and right), until the tenth section, the "contrapunt", when dancers stop while the flabiol plays a short melody. When the dance theme recurs, dancers move round again, repeating the "longs"; then another "contrapunt" or pause, and a final repetition of the "longs". The circle moves left and right, music alternating between grave and gay. The "longs" give an opportunity for experts to improvise, but never holding up the rhythm of the circle as a whole. In order to end each section correctly, the adept counts the number of beats in each part, since one rule decrees that no section may end with feet apart but only with a full close; another that the "longs" must not only not end with one beat over, but must end with the circle moving to the left. It is necessary to calculate how many beats will remain at the end, and how to apportion the final steps. Several variations of *Sardana* exist, differing both in number and combination of steps. It is seen at its best at Empordà, La Bisbal, Figueras, Torrella de Montgri, San Felio de Guixols and Gerona. In Barcelona it may be seen during the Feast of Nuestra Señora de la Merced (September 23 - 26) and at Tarragona on September 23rd at the Festival of Santa Tecla, but it is also danced on every possible secular occasion, as a spontaneous expression of enjoyment.

SARDANA — 2 (France)

Shows a slight variation on the Catalan dance, and is popular in the "Vallespir" (Haute Vallée du Tech), Roussillon, where it is performed on fête days. A round dance in 2/4 time, it is directed by a leader in the centre. Dancers in couples form into a circle, men and women alternating and holding hands at face height, which position is held throughout the dance. The circle swings first right then left, sometimes stopping and marking the rhythm for several bars by swinging the arms. Five different steps are used — *Le pas court*, *le pas long*, *le pas sauté* (in two ways), and *le pas combiné*, which combines a *pas sauté* with a *pas court*. The dance thus consists of a series of slight but subtle variations on a comparatively simple basic step. As in the Catalan *Sardana*, the circle makes little progress, but does slowly move through a small degree.

SARDANAPALUS (Assyrian)

Chief Priest and Ruler, equals Sar-Dana-Palas or "Tsar (Ruler of) Dance-Rituals (of) Palus", equals Palace or Temple. This ritual system, enduring down to at least 800 BC, was made known to those countries penetrated by Assyrian warriors, and by traders. They contacted the Phoenician people (People of the Palm), and they also took these rites. One great centre was the island now called Sardinia

(and other Mediterranean isles), where the worship was continued (see ancient building ruins on this Island, and at Carthage). One custom was the tribute to Dagon (Dakana), whose symbol was a Fish. From his mythos, with the fish-headdress, came the Mitra or Mitre; his tribute was fish; some being called *sardini* (for the "Tribute to Sardanas"). This was delivered after the liturgy. Many versions from this ceremonial or functional name have appeared. In some the "r" changes to "l". We know of *Sar-impi* or *Sar-amba* (dancers), *Sal-ammbo* (Sicily), *Salii* (in Rome), and *Sal's-Bori* (Place of Rite) in England. The *Sardana* dance exists, in changed form, but keeping its time (after a service) in Catalunya. It is not a recent form or a deliberate newly invented dance. Goya painted the "Burial of the Sardina", in which custom another ancient ritual is concealed. The title *Sar Danas* turned into *Sal-Dansa* and *Sultana;* and in Egypt culminated in *Sirdar*. The term "sire", is general, as the regal *tsar* is specialised. See also *Nebo-Chad-Nezzar* (an analagous title of ritual and function).

SARDINA, Burial of the (Sicily - Spain)

Is illustrated dramatically by F. Goya (the painting is now in the San Fernando Academy in Madrid) and shows a group of revellers, one with semi-mask with horns, dancing before the religious banner bearing the smiling head of the Chief Sar-dina. Like the split bishop's mitre (once a fish head, or Dakon), this traditional festival was the last distorted remnant of an ancient ceremonial; what was earlier a solemn religious ritual had become a jest for the crowd. The "Sacred Fish" was once an emblem of annual sacrifice (the Egyptian name *khepra* — kipper, the "preserved one" remains with us), as does the Teuton *blöt* (bloater) and the Hebrew *machera* (mackerel), or the Scandinavian *hring* (herring).

SATACEK, SATECKOVA (Czechoslovakia)

Circle dance in Moravia, for couples, in alternating 3/4 and 2/4 time. The two parts of the dance are repeated as often as required. Man and girl stand one behind the other, both facing the same direction. With arms flexed at the elbows, she holds two corners of a kerchief, the other two being held by the man behind her, with arms outstretched. In the first part (in triple time), the couple move round the circle anti-clockwise with a waltz step, the woman glancing back at her partner over each shoulder alternately. The second part (in quick duple time) consists of a turn by the woman under the arms, the kerchief still held taut.

SATIRE IN DANCE

An inversion of values (Saturnin) as was done in

the Festival of Saturnalia, in Satire or "Satyr plays" (Comedies). By exaggeration and caricature; burlesque or what is now called cartoon, some notable feature of an original is made to seem excessive or defective. Mediocre minds are not readily affected by comment on the ordinary "golden mean", but socially it becomes necessary frequently to comment on undue claims by rulers or officials. Then the arts of satire are properly called into use; chiefly by those who suffer from the impositions of authority. Satire is thus a denial of the propaganda of the mighty; ridicule of their magnificence and their pomp.

SATYR, SATUROI OR TITUROI (Greek mythology)
Also associated with Sileni, Fauns (Faunus) and Pans, said to be originally Pelopponnesian godlings of woods and forests. The Attic drama made them more famous in the *drama satyricon*, but they appear (as Faun) also in Italy (as at Pompeii). The early satyrs were bald-headed and long-eared; later they were more goat like, probably as companions or servants of Bacchus (in Greece) and Silenus (in Italy). Fauns were depicted with pointed ears and short tails; the Satyrs were shown with goat's feet; some had horns as well. From them were derived clerical notions of a "personal devil" though the hidden reason was their traditional lubricity as connected with the enormous energy attributed to Bacchus as a god of increase. As servants of Bacchus (Silenus or Sylvanus in Italy) they were always dancing and singing; and thus appeared in many popular triumphal processions.

SATYR'S DANCE (Greece)
From *Zattyroz*—the companions of Bacchus who danced with him. The Satyric dance was usually that of Comedy; from it developed the satirical or jocular mode of *Mimesis;* but did not so begin. These dancers appear (in mythical form) described as having long pointed ears (symbolic of their keen hearing and love of rhythm), and with a goat's tail. This tail was probably a totemic symbol; later pictures (as on vases etc.) show Satyrs with goat's legs, similar to Pan. The Satyr differed from the Greek Pan or Latin Faunus in having no horns. From this type is named the man alleged to have no moral standard (a medical term further exaggerates this original), while a type of Greek play was performed in which the Chorus danced as satyrs. In the English period of the Elizabethan Masque, Ben Jonson called for these figures to dance and join the singing chorus.   [See *Kordax*]

SATYRS (English Masque)
Characters presenting supposed ancient creatures of Grecian myths, based on the half-human and half-goat figure of the Earth god, Pan; and used by the clerics to invent their devil (Satan) figure. The makers of the Elizabethan Masques took their cue not from theology, but from Greek legend; they used Satyrs for their "antic dance", where they performed "long handsprings and large leaps of twelve feet long". Some merged with the tradition of the Wilde Man or the Wode House, the forest creatures of European legend, in "antic dance full of gesture and swift motion". They used kibby* dance, or kobold dance steps; these dances in the Masque were performed always by expert professional actor-dancers. In *a Winter's Tale* there is mention of the anti-masque of Satyrs: "Here a Dance of Twelve Satyrs, with bells on their shaggy thighs".   [See *Kordax; Satyr; Satyr's Dance*]

SAUL AND THE PROPHETS (Dance of) (Hebrew mythos)
The discipline of ritual dance that was taught and used in the Schools of the Prophets (as that of Samuel) is slightly touched on in the *Book of Samuel* (xi. 23. 24) where it says: "And he went, going thence towards Naioth in Ramah; and so he went on until he came into Naioth in Ramah; and there he stripped off his robes; and he prophesied before (the schools of) Samuel, in like manner, and he lay down (in trance) naked all that day, and that night". This meagre reference caught the attention of the modern Hebrew poet, Saul Tchernichovsky; he extended the incident into a longer poem, printed in *The Quest* (1928). There the poet sees once more *"The Dance of the Pious"* in front of the altar:

"There they leapt in their new strength and their
     might
  While the king, too, went forth with them into
     the circle"!

And as they danced in the sunlight, so this rhythm changed from the dance of prophecy into the dance of ecstacy, as

"From second to second their cleaving grew
     greater,
  Their being consumed, even higher and higher".

Until the consummation, when:
"And in one many-faced body the prophets subdued them;
  They turned right, they turned left, in dances
     most wondrous",

so that once again his soul became naked. So concludes this short and splendid poem of just over one hundred lines.

See "The Dance of Saul with the Prophets". Poem by Saul Tschernichovsky (Trans. by I. M. Lask). In *Quest Magazine.* 1928 (Pp. 192 - 196)

SAUT BASQUE

A dance of French Basque provinces, especially Basse Navarre, where it has two forms—a recreational dance in a large kitchen or on a threshing-floor; and a more ceremonial form, out of doors, following a *Cavalcade* or (in Soule province) after a *Pastorale* folk-play. On these occasions it is an honour to be the first group to dance the *Saut Basque*, the privilege sometimes being auctioned to the village which is the highest bidder. There are many different arrangements of the *Saut Basque*. Danced by men only, in a slowly moving circle, sometimes clockwise, sometimes anti-clockwise, it is a succession of steps, or "jumps", joined to form a smooth sequence. In the centre of the circle stands the leader, who "calls" the steps in their proper order, so that the dancers make an uninterrupted enchainement of the different *sauts*. In one such sequence the order is : *Pika; Sauté; Sauté eta iru; Dobla; Dobla eta iru; Erdiska; Erdiska eta iru; Luz eta ebats; Esker, Eskuin; Esker iru; Eskuin iru; Entrechats; Jo! Jo! Jo!; Erdiska fantaisie.* The men dance only with their legs and feet, arms being held stiffly at the sides. The *Saut Basque* is sometimes followed by the *Zazpi Jausiak** or "Seven Jumps", itself a once-ceremonial, or ritual dance, (see *Zevensprong;** *Siebensprung,**) but each version has its own "following dance".

SAUTER, SAUTEREUSE (France)

An acrobatic dancer; a mountebank, one who leaps. From *saut*—a leap or a bound; or *sauter*—to leap and to bound. *Saut* is a common term in French dancing schools, and a *sauterie* is a small private dance. Boys play at *saute-mouton* or leap-frog. A grasshopper in England becomes a *sauterelle* in France.

SAUTERIE (French)

A small private dance, a family dance. Connected with *saut*, to leap or bound; and *sauter*, to skip quickly. Also *sauteur* and *sauteuse* and *sautillement* (children's play) when the English "leap frog" becomes *saute mouton* (lamb's skipping). The mediaeval French term *sauter* implied a leaper in public, a mountebank; and in English became *somersault* but *somerset* becomes *faire la culbute*, or acrobatic leaps.

SAXON DANCING (England)

Was acrobatic, judging by contemporary references and drawings. Performers were *gleemen* and *glee-maidens* who entertained both populace and prince. Encouraged by the Saxon lords, they flocked to the princely halls. With the minstrels, they included dancing, tumbling and balancing in their performance, although "dancing" and "tumbling" seem to have been almost synonymous, as indicated in the Anglo-Saxon words for dancing—*hoppan* (to hop), *saltian* and *stellan* (to leap), and *tomban* (to tumble). In the chronicles of Anglo-Saxon writers, tumbling and dancing often mean the same, as in the Saxon account of "Herodias dancing before Herod", described and illustrated as vaulting and tumbling. The harp (inherited from earlier bards and scalds) was the most popular instrument used by gleemen; but violins, pipes or flutes, horns, and tabors were also played. An 8th century drawing shows two men dancing, to music of horn and trumpet; while in a 9th century Latin and Saxon MS in the Cotton Library, a young man is shown dancing solo to two flutes and a lyre. This seems to be an elegant dance, rather than contortionist. Gleemen also taught animals, such as bears, to "dance" and posture; with one of the troupe (sometimes a woman) dancing in front of the leashed animal, who pranced on its hind legs. In Norman times, the gleemen became *joculators** and *jug-glours*, who, with minstrels, continued to entertain at lordly houses. At Tutbury, in 1380, John of Gaunt had his own court of minstrels. Chaucer called the glee-maidens *tumbling-women, tomble-steres* and *tombesteres* (from *tomban*); in *Romance of the Rose* he refers to them as *saylours*, or dancers (from Latin *salio*).

SAXON DANCE IN RUMANIA

Some time in the 11th century, the Magyar ruler of Rumania invited Saxons to live in thinly-populated Transylvania, where their communities throve for several centuries, retaining their own German customs, dances, and costumes. (See *Borten Abtanz;** *Rosseltanz;** *Spiesstanz**). The young men of each village belonged successively to two groups—from confirmation to marriage to the *Bruderschaft*, after marriage to the *Nachbarschaft*. The *Bruderschaft* had at its head the *Altknecht*, chosen every year, and under him six "brothers" held posts of authority. Strict rules of the Brotherhood governed behaviour for youths, as sons, brothers, suitors—and as dancers, for strict etiquette governed the Sunday afternoon dancing. Held either at the village inn, or in the open air, permission was first sought by the Altknecht, from the pastor. To make sure that no girl was partnerless, the Altknecht sometimes arranged the couples beforehand, no youth daring to oppose his choice. At the end of each dance, the girls retired to one side of the room, boys to the other, the sexes remaining together only while the dance was in progress. Generally, only unmarried girls and youths might dance, but in some districts young married couples were permitted to continue dancing for six months after marriage, while elsewhere they might dance every fourth year! The most popular dances seem to have been similar to the *Landler** and the *Schuhplattler*,* but only at special festivals were gala costumes worn. At Pentecost there was dancing for two successive days, when the girls wore black skirts with white, embroidered aprons on the Monday, these colours being reversed on the Tuesday. On their heads they wore the *borten*—a black, flower-pot shaped hat, without crown or brim, with wide, coloured ribbons hanging to the hem of the skirt. In the massive jewelled girdle, and the *Patzel* (a large, round, silver-gilt and jewelled ornament, worn on the chest), they often displayed family heirlooms. The youths wore their best clothes, no part of which they might remove until after the second dance. Then, at a signal from the Altknecht, they could take off their jackets, while the girls removed the uncomfortable *borten*, the dances proceeding with more freedom of movement. These customs still existed in the 19th century.

SAYLER, OR SAYELERE (English)

Chaucer's reference to dance includes mention of Saylers as popular dances—"I can saute and ne sayle", among other terms used for dance, such as *tomblestere* or *hoppe*, Most of these dances were very simple in form; from one to three dancers would jig about, to the rhythm of some familiar melody, performed with pipe and tabour. The songs, especially the newly contrived parodies, which satirised local persons found at fault, were doubtless the centre of attraction; though the dance, with its phases of mime, the unspoken word and apt allusion, served to point the moral and adorn the tale in a manner that no spying priest could report in words.

SCALD, SKALD (Icelandic)

A Norse poet, comparable with Keltic *bard*. They had the duty of chanting genealogies and liturgies; with these went a solemn ritual dance procession or circle, to simple music. The word "skoll!" now used as a toast, derives thence. One of their dances had a floor pattern which we know as Runic Knot (maze*). Some ritual centres retain the name *rune* as, e.g. Rouen.

SCALE IN DANCE AND BALLET

Begins with (a) company available; (b) theme to be presented; and (c) the size of performing space. This last factor governs the basic effective scale of spectacular ballet; yet it must still be founded on the unit of human scale, the size of the single dancer. To mass the dancers: into lines, squares, circles, and other figures; may restore form and discipline to definite order, but limits the general

effects possible. Additions of banners, extended costumes, giant figures (as on stilts), or use of horses (circus; or horse-ballet; the tourney etc.), may help to achieve spectacle but does not affirm real art. Ballet which uses dance must remain within contacts of the small group: the dramatic group; or else agree to leave expression and display only acrobatic form. The effective scales of dance and ballet are few: they remain related to the group which can display theme in action, and the number of possible spectators: the distance of vision. The ancient Collosseum; or the modern American Bowl (Hollywood), or Russian "Green Stage" (Gorki Park), may accommodate each some 20,000 spectators. They extend spectacle and lose dance. Effective ballet ranges from Chamber Ballet.* (*Intime*, Television, or Concert Dance), to Arena Ballet,* with Theatre Ballet as the medial proportion. The theatre holding 2,000/3,000 spectators offers the maximum number that can see sufficiently well; or the stage action becomes too remote to maintain interest. The small theatre; for Chamber Ballet (500/800 persons) has usually a small stage (The Hermitage, Winter Palace, Leningrad, is an exception), and requires a technical change in dance, especially of classical ballet, as now received. Rarely it is possible even for a skilled producer, to be able to modify a single production to fit equally in all three scales.
[See *Arena Ballet; Chamber Ballet*]

SCALES OF DANCE, OR THE FIVE MAIN MODES

Five modes of dance movement exist in the Universe, with the human form as the central mode. The other four pass through it or "cross" in energetic transit, in rhythmic beat, and in scale of operation.

NATURE —— —— —— —— SOCIAL GROUPS

HUMAN FORM

ELECTRONIC —— —— —— —— COSMIC

The human array of dance begins and ends with the dance of a single human figure; for in that is the full range of organic control. They link with the dance of social or ritual groups, by the arrangement of many single figures in group with an endless array of patterns, rhythms, and purposes. Similar patterns appear when we search into the mysteries of the Atom; into Electron and Neutron; where we find an equally immense array of similar dance movements, disciplined by their own energies into incalculable rhythms. Of these molecules, atoms, and electrons, the human body and its motions are built. They go further, to supply the basic star dust for the whole scintillating cosmos; which moves in the fifth great mode of Dance movement; and is the one most observed by the wondering eyes of mankind. The stars dance in their courses; from them wise men of bygone centuries took their times and their tunes; and to them, they fitted solemn ritual and ceremonial, with ordered dances (and symbolized them in mythic form), in humbly submissive imitation of the stellar universe. Five modes of dance movement thus proceed in their different rhythms; all interlacing; all mutually supported, and integrally related in energy, in life, and in form. To seek and learn them, we face the mystery of the universe; it is to be resolved in the fascinating rhythms of all dance. [See *Symbol in Dance*]

SCARAMOUCHE (Italian)

A character in *Commedia delle Arte*, in Italy. From the ecclesiastical role of the Fan-bearer, in ritual; *esmoucher*, or *iscara-esmoucher*. Not being very active, the person who carried the fan tended to lounge; hence came the "moocher". This job required the wafting of the heavy incense in this or that direction; it is also hinted that he had to "keep the flies off" and in fact, a peacock feather fan became frequent in use, despite its oriental origin, in many churches.

SCENARIO (Italo-French)

A familiar theatrical term, of technical rather than literary origin, denoting the full general scheme for any theatre production, from opera to film. Thus the *scenario* includes more than the book or libretto. A Shakespeare play, as printed, is a "book"; but it is not a scenario, despite the brief stage directions. G. B. Shaw added more facts for his works; but a complete scenario should include directions for all essential sectors of the production, especially technical requirements, such as scene-plot and lighting-plot; list of essential "properties"; and carrying adequate references to (a) music, and (b) dance or "business" necessary for visual exposition. To prepare a complete scenario requires experience and intimate technical knowledge of all opportunities and limitations in the modern theatre, with special reference to the particular stage, for which some definite production is being designed. No choreographer can be completely educated for his job unless he is able to furnish such a scenario for any ballet he contemplates producing. For this reason too many ballets fail to become integrated,.

SCENERY

For Dance varies as widely as Dance; from the (1) Natural setting, cave or field, then (2) village or town street; (3) the village or church "green yard" and (4) the inn-yard, next developing; (5) the permanent "cloister". This links with (6) the church interior or the hill-side Greek theatre or (8) the court hall or manorial hall and the gild-hall. These precede the modern enclosed commercial theatre. Except the Greek stage, little was done to change appearance to provide a skena, a suggestion of another place. The singers, actors, dancers, musicians gathered and gave their work; either in (a) festival attire, (b) ritual mask or costume, or (c) caricature varied by normal attire. The city theatre, developed in parallel with the church as display centre, began to devise means of theatrical illusion by more or less material vision. Theatre became "realistic" in another sense; then the use of contrived scenery followed mechanisms and painted work. Deliberately arranged scenic settings thus provide the dancer with a Character view, suggesting Time and Place other than actuality. This is accentuated by use of selected costume (especially by masks) and then by "stage properties". The third element comes in the dance with music: all should blend. The final touch is the facial or bodily make-up. The whole setting is then illuminated: realistically or in some fanciful mode; thus a complete impact can be gained. From daylight (or night setting with torches etc.) we move by gas light to electric light, each with its different appearance on dancers and setting. We come next to the Italian Theatre, enclosed and fully arranged, with scenery drawn in perspective and done in naturalistic realism, aiming to deceive the eye Titian used a ladder, to ascend and touch painting by Peruzzi, to be sure it was not in relief. Italian painted scenery begins (15th century) with Brunelleschie and Il Cecca (for *Rappresentazioni*) in Florence; but Balthazar Peruzzi (1480 - 1536) of Siena, following Pietro del Borgo's studies in perspective, was the innovator of pictorial realism. Vasari the historian was much astonished. Some of Peruzzi's best work was for Cardinal Bibiena's piece *Calandra*, performed in the Vatican, for Leo X. (1514) for the Duchess of Mantua. Duke Alessandro of Florence had Andrea del Sarto. In 1532, the Duca got G. M. Primerani to write on *Tamar*, for which Bastiani detto Aristotile painted scenery, for a temporary theatre in the ducal courtyard. There he gave Laudi's *Commodo*. All these productions excited great interest, by report.

In 1605 and 1612 Inigo Jones went from London; with notable results in his Masques. In Venice the Opera was developed, from 1640, mythological themes.

Italian realism, switched from religious propaganda in paint to Theatre, used Opera later; so that singers and dancers brought painters on their travels when Italian Opera invaded London. French artists began round 1645; then Sir William

Davenant derived realistic scenery for the London stage; this influence continued into this century. The Bibiena brothers (Bologna 1657) developed perspective; so that Riccaboni (writing 1736) comments at length. Servandoni came to Covent Garden. This was before the romantic or pre-Raphaelite movement appeared; and Charles Kemble, Madame Vestris, Macready and Phelps led to Welby, Pugin and John Capon (1757-1827) who founded the famous "Drury Lane Style" of realism. Clarkson Stanfield and William Beverley introduced the spectacular Xmesse pantomime. Realism spread to Germany and Russia, where it remains in excellent form in the Moscow Arts Theatre.

SCHAFFLERTANZ (Germany)
A mediaeval gild dance of Münich, performed by the registered coopers of the city; an important trade, since it governed the industry in brewing. Parts of the casks were possibly used for bow or hoop dances, but this does not imply that such dances were invented by or restricted to the coopers. The *Schäfflertanz* was a garland dance performed every seven years; having seven figures called *Schlange* (serpent), *Laube* (arbour), *Kreuz* (cross), *Krone* (crown), *Kleiner Kreis* (little circle), *Chassieren* (lines), and *Reifenschwung* (hoopswing). Lasting about twenty minutes, the dance was performed with a simple polka step by twenty-five men carrying half-hoops decorated with greenery, and accompanied by two Fools. Various patterns were formed with the garlanded hoops, as suggested by the names of the figures, dancers winding in and out to make serpent, arbour, cross and crown shapes. In *Kleiner Kreis* the men formed four small circles; in *Chassieren* they advanced and retired in lines. In the final figure, two dancers standing in the middle of a circle formed by their companions, each rhythmically swung a small hoop on which stood a tumbler of wine, without spilling any or upsetting the glass. The *Schäfflertanz* is almost identical with the Hungarian *Bodnártánc*.*
[Cp. Garland dances *Jardiniero*; *Treilles* (France). Balancing Dances *Binasuan* (Phillipines); *Tari Piring* (Sumatra); *Pandanggo Sa Ilaw*; (Phillipines); *Menari Hinei* (Malaya); *Schönpart* (German); *Godalet Dantza* (Basque); *Cakewalk*; *Calinda* (USA)]

SCHEM-HA-PHORASCH—1 (Hebrew)
Given as the "Divided Name" (or extension of *Tetragrammaton**), implying the "carpet of letters"; has the number of seventy-two, which limits traditionally the number of members of the Great Sanhedrin—seventy-two men with the Chief Rabbi (73). The basis is the Hebrew letter-series (twenty-two letters) and the ten numbers. The letters are taken as Ten Male, Ten Female, and three "Mother"

Letter forms. They are "written divided", in two parallel rows; or in the secret circle (*encompassed*), which mode is similar to the Chinese *Pa-kua*, and the Hindu Sanskrit *chakram*.* Both are written on a periphery to correlate their three values: those two adjacent on each side; those reflected across the circle. This movement is the foundation of the ritual dance. They are thirty-two paths of *Yetzirah** (Formation). From such a "cosmic circle" issue all propositions concerning geometrical form and arithmetical number. From the "Black Fire and the White Fire" came their colours; the mediaeval magic that grew (in one aspect) into alchemy and also the magical ceremonial dances. Arabic/Hindu usage of these schemes resulted in the abstract computations of algebra, later developing (for example) into Infinitesimal Calculus, in its Integral and Differential modes.

Schemenlaufen at Imster. Carnival play. AUSTRIA

SCHEM-HA-PHORASCH—2 (Hebrew-Arabic)
Literally "plan of carpet"—*farrash*=carpet—linked with *Kabbalah*, as the basic letter-number scheme of the Hebrew alphabet: ten male letters with ten female letters and three genetic letters, from which numerous permutations and combinations provide leading technical terms for the script. One original form is found in the Chaldean-Babylonian "ritual of the pavement", where the "Sacred Tree" that showed the symbolical thirty-two Paths of the

Universe, was laid out in full scale as a ritual pattern. The later development of the Persian carpet provided a "Little Farrash" or carpet in small scale, sufficient for the prayers and devotions of one man alone. On this he performed that secret "Dance of the Mind" through which he was guided by means of the sacred letters formulated into key words of the scheme.
[See *Qabalah; Pattern; Sand Tracings; Tarot*]

SCHEMENLAUFEN (Austria)

"Dance of the Phantoms". A Winter - Spring masquerade held every third year, just before Lent, at Imst on the southern slopes of the Lechtaler Alps, Austrian Tyrol. Only men take part in this festival for expelling Winter and welcoming Spring. Besides a "Queen" in girlish mask, flaxen ringlets, crown and embroidered dress, the chief characters are the *Scheller* (Bell Ringers) and the *Rollers*, who always appear in pairs. Accompanying them are the *Spritzer* (Sprayer), who squirts water at the spectators from a syringe; the *Sackner* (Sack Holder) wearing a tall, pointed hat and carrying a sack of corn to throw at spectators; an old "woman" in cross-eyed mask and woolly hair, carrying a swaddled "baby" which she throws at women in the crowd, retrieving it by its string; and a crowd of "witches" in female costume, all wearing masks, some carrying besoms, some with bells tied at the waist. They dance through the streets and squares twisting their bodies continuously to jangle the bells and so dispel the evils of Winter. The *Scheller*, gorgeously dressed in knee breeches, white stockings, and a plaid shawl over a white shirt, wear a good-humoured mask with curly moustaches, and on their heads an enormous oval head-dress made of evergreens and Winter flowers. In one hand they carry a spirally striped stick surmounted by a large knob, and to their waist are attached large bells. Their companions, the *Rollers*, who "roll in" the Spring, also wear breeches and white stockings, but their mask is pale and girlish, their head-dress of Spring flowers is smaller and surmounted by three white tufts. In the right hand they carry a switch bound with ribbons, on the handle of which are threaded large, circular *pretzels* (cakes). Round their waist they wear a wide belt studded with very small bells, while from their shoulders falls a white lace veil.
[See *Perchten* (Austria); *Rölleli-butzen; Nüssler* (Switzerland); *Narrentreffen* (Germany); *Suruvakary* (Bulgaria)]

SCHNADA-HUPFELN (Austria)

Tyrolean folk-dances, often accompanied with verses; and performed usually to the rhythm of some popular *ländler** or a slow waltz. Both men and girls participate; the dance occurs at any local gathering — wedding or birthday, which gives opportunity for fun and feasting.

SCHONPART (Med. German)

General term for the 15th century Carnival Dance performed annually in Nüremberg; which is described in some detail in the works of Hans Sachs, the cobbler-poet of that city. The day's dance was led off by the *vor-tanzer*, the male elected because of his ability in dancing; he had to dance with a glass full of wine, which on the conclusion, he drank, assisted by his partner.
[Cp. *Schäfflertanz* (Germany); *Bodnártanc* (Hungary)]

SCHOOLS OF DANCE

Have been numerous and varied. Some kind of instruction in movement has invariably accompanied all tribal association, directed towards the main ends of (a) behaviour; (b) preparation for fighting, or matrimony; and (c) as a part of discipline in more advanced tribal thinking, as with religion. Rhythmic discipline evolves dance, by position and movement, chant and gesture; so that schools are inevitably the complementary structure which must precede the dance as ritual or dance as display. Thus we have (1) native schools; (2) religious schools; (3) educational schools — army etc.; (4) theatre schools; (5) ballet schools; (6) professional dance schools; (7) modern dance schools — each with variations and special features, often exhibiting high skill and marked accomplishment.

SCHOTTISCHE

A round dance for couples in 2/4 or 6/8 time. First danced in England in 1848, it musically resembled a slow Polka, and was known as the *German Polka*. Although the name means "Scottish", and the music is often composed of Scottish airs, the dance-form is related to the Austrian *Landler,** *Waltz** and *Polka.** It has no connection with the *Ecossaise.** A ballroom dance known as *Scotis español* — "Spanish Schottische" — was popular for a short time on the Continent after the 1914 - 18 war, but derived little, or nothing, from Spain.

SCHUASTAPOLKA (Austria)

In Upper Styria, this mimetic dance features the Shoe-maker's Polka, for a group of couples with a single man who is the Shoemaker. This lively dance, usually in 2/4 time is a variant of "Paul Jones", but has more mime. The odd man kneels in the centre, to imitate shoe-mending with needle and thread; he sings the current dance-song as the men move round him to clap their hands, while the girls dance round them with a walking or polka step.

The dance-song refers sometimes to the girl's dowry, naming the sum or value of her goods. As the music suddenly stops, all the men jump to find a partner; the unsuccessful one remains as the Shoemaker for the next round. Concluding the *Schuastapolka*, the band leader signals an end; when the *Lestest Shuastamann* is tossed in the air and caught (by arms or a blanket), and has to stand treat to his fellows. For the tossing, another song is chanted.   [Cp. *Owcharz* (Poland)]

Schühplattler Dance. Salzburg.   AUSTRIA

SCHÜHPLATTLER (Austria and Bavaria)
Associated particularly with the Austrian Tyrol, it is known also in Central Switzerland, as the *Gäuerler*; and in Appenzell (Eastern Switzerland), as the *Hierig*. A courting dance, to music in 3/4 time, the *Schühplattler* is said to imitate the strutting or "displaying" of the cock before the hen. While girls waltz round the room, each man dances round his partner; then men and girls waltz together, the man's hands on the girl's waist, her hands on his shoulders. Then comes the "showing-off" by the men, who perform the *Platteln* in the middle of the circle, while the girls waltz round alone. This consists of rhythmic slaps by each man of different parts of his body—thighs, buttocks, heels, knees, chest and cheeks—together with snapping fingers, clapping hands, and high jumps or hops on alternate feet. Sometimes he may turn a somersault or cartwheel. All these violent move-

ments make a syncopated rhythm personal to each dancer, yet in harmony with the rhythm of music and dance. One of the most intricate of *Schühplattler* dances is the *Haiss-plattler*; another is called *Prax-plattler*.

SCIOMACHIA (Italy)
Festivals in Rome. Cardinal du Bellay, as superintendent of the affairs of Francois I, was in Rome from 1547-48, and in the following spring devised his famous fête, called *Sciomachia*, or "dance or contest of shadows", in honour of the birth of the son of Henri II and Catherine de Medici, in March 1549. This was (says Henry Clouzot—Rabelais' biographer) "a wonderful pantomime, consisting of land-fights and water-fights, bullfights and military reviews, mythological tableaux, festivals (of ballet) and fireworks, of which master Francois (Rabelais), doubtless one of the chief organizers, had an account printed by Gryphius under the title of *Sciomachia*". This inclusive fête marks another of the developments from the style of older rejoicings, in the newer ballet form, which tended to be restricted to theatre buildings, then just appearing as edifices constructed chiefly for plays of all kinds.

SCOP AND BI-SCOP (Old English, from Greek, *sco-pas*, Latin *scope*)
An overseer of ceremonies, religious or ritual. Eventually the term became bishop, as meaning the immediate controller of miracle plays as used in the primitive church festivals in North Britain. The Greek *scopus* which was soon elevated to *episcopus*, and then *archiepiscopus*, who gradually left the immediate work to supervise orders and revenues. The term generally means always "to see' or to "make seen" (as with the Greek sculptor Scopas, who "revealed the form"). Analogous Teutonic terms developed as *spiegel* (mirror) and then *spiel* (play), whence *Gottes-Spiel*, or the "God's Play", which turned to gospel (also *spielen*, to play or sing). There was no preaching (of any modern style, talk to a crowd) in the early system; but the *parabolos* and the *spiel* were freely used at all festivals, to draw the crowd. Dances were used where language might prove a barrier; and mime conveyed what words could not suggest. Analogous in the south of England was the Minstrel, who became in time the Min-ister.

SCOTTISH DANCE (Scotland and Ireland)
Scots formerly were tribes who lived both in Northern Ireland and Southern Scotland. Earlier than this period Picts and Gaels inhabited these countries; with tribal dances peculiar to their own systems; though it seems that through all, tra-

ditions of the *Bailtinne* have endured for many centuries. We have no information on the dance form used by Picts or the Kymry visitors; while we have to go to ancient legends of Eire for any data on Scottish or Gaelic dance. In the mediaeval period, various travellers and invasions brought newer fashions; especially from France and Spain direct by sea. Some names are quoted in *The Boke called Governour* "devised by Sir Thomas Elyot, knight, London, 1546". Here he mentioned some ancient Grecian dances; and then says: "In stede of these we have now Base daunces, bergenethes, pauyons, turgions and roundes". Another contemporary short list appeared in the *Complaynt of Scotland*: "The dances consisted in one ring, licht lopene (leaping), galmonding (gambolling), stendling (striding), backuart and forduart, dans and base dansin, paureans, galzardis, turdions, braulis, buffons, with many othir licht dancis". No small part of the difficulty of tracing authentic Scottish dance forms appears in the numerous differential modes of spelling. Distorted by dialect, any French or Spanish or English familiar dance name would re-appear — by voice or from printers, in a score of guises. The diversion of the term *reel* is an outstanding example: *reel* is seen as *reuill*, but turns up as *royal*; in England the transfer of "u" to "v" gives us *revel* from *reull* (Master of Reveles), while in Gaelic it is now printed as *ruidhle*. The one thing it does *not* mean is to reel or stagger in walking. Witches were credited (*News from Scotland*, 1591) with dancing reels. See Walter Scott: *Heart of Midlothian; The Pirate* (Sword-dance); *Fair Maid of Perth* (Morrice).

SEALS (Sumerian, Babylonian, Assyrian, etc.)
Present the oldest known durable records of earliest sacred ritual dance, by notations and gesture. This primal method disappeared, lapsing into imitative temple records of receipts, regulations, trade, and deeds of gift or transfer. Most of the museum collections contain this semi-commercial and legal type of seal. Records of customs show that the personal property of every man included (a) seal and (b) walking-stick (used as a rod of known measure, and possibly a comparative weight). The seal was personal, social, and religious; it carried the functional titles of important individuals, and sometimes copied reference to ruling princes. The general shape of the seal followed that of the "place of the presence" modified by necessity of fitting the finger; and many took a cylindrical shape, used by rolling, leaving a flat embossed strip of soft wax or clay. Considerable skill was developed in making seals from fragments of hard stone; though some office seals were duplicated from burned clay or wood original matrices. Dance records show

functional positions (especially salutes and libations) with accompanying gestures; many indicate the relations of one person to another. The salute of priest to the god, of servant to the king, of the ruler to the ambassador or to the defeated foe, can all be obtained by analysis and comparison. Longer inspection reveals parts of the ritual and the processional movement most frequently used.

SEASONS (Greek)
Were presented in ritual dance by: Mercury (Spring); Apollo (Summer); Bacchus (Autumn); and Hercules (Winter). Biblical forms, less firmly traditional, are: Adam and Eve (Spring); Ruth (Summer); Joshua and Caleb (Autumn); and Deluge (Winter).

SECCARARA (Italy)
A traditional dance of Naples, which alternates with or includes, the ancient form of Saltarello;* it involved much mime and gesture, with grimace and facial distortion, accompanied by satirical songs and parodies of personal movement, familiar as normal in local celebrities.

SECT ROUGE (Haiti)
Negro Secret Society, formulated on a semi-cannibal basis; with other elements of social terrorism. West Africa was the place of origin; but the *Sect Rouge* includes influences from France; and it resembles in some details the Thuggee sect of Bhowanee, formerly prevalent in Bengal. Two other Societies are also known to exist, though closely secret in all but name: the *Cochon Gris* and the *Vinbrindingue*. All of them have ritual and processional dances, at night. Certain facts correspond with the activities of *Sociéte Siciliana*, the gangster groups so well organised by Signor Al Capone in Chicago; but the killing here was chiefly commercial; though the victims were just as dead. It was left for the Dominicans to make a theatrical spectacle out of murder for religious motives, at the *Quemadera* in Madrid. The *Sect Rouge* punishes traitors or heretics: usually by drowning, not by burning at the stake. Their dance celebrations follow a "hunting procedure" since they seek victims, like the Indian Thugs. Unlike the Nazis, they do not pretend to strict legal procedure. According to Zora Hurston, animal masks are worn in dance, and animal movements are simulated. The dancers carry lighted candles, chanting to drums; leaders, attired in red and white robes, direct the ceremonial. The refrain of one song is: *Sortie Nan Cimiterre, toute corps moni senti Manlingue*. They use the cross roads as their ground cross symbol; and again dance; more dancing follows as they approach the cemetery. Baron Croix is invoked.

Finally, they seek victims, strangling them with cords made of human intestines. The Thugs used a *ramal*; the Dominicans used torch and ropes. After a "transubstantiation" (victim is "made an animal") and the ritual *Messe*, they return home at dawn to resume their daily tasks.

SEDER (Hebrew) Pesach

The "Order" of the ritual Passover meal or Messe, with Praise over Four cups of wine (four seasons) with *Hallel* (Popular songs) and occasional solemn dance movement, sometimes by the Rabbi.

SEDNA FESTIVAL DANCE (Esquimaux of Baffin-land)

Sedna, dreaded Goddess of the Underworld, controls the weather, and unless the appropriate ceremony is held will bring sickness, bad weather, failure in hunting. At a special festival held to ensure fecundity among seals, the *Angakut* (Medicine Man), disguised as a woman and representing the power of fertility among animals, goes among the people. Held in the dancing-house, or *kagga*, the dance is formed by two lines of men and women, facing each other. Moving slowly between the lines, the *Angakut* touches first a man, then a woman with his wand, indicating that they must pair together for twenty-four hours. As the pairs move away, the *Angakut* continues dancing, and they too must dance if he touches them. After violent dancing, the *Angakut* goes into a trance, in order to visit Sedna in the Underworld; and gain her aid for the community. This is also a ceremony of the Dying Sedna, who comes to life again each year, symbolising the return of the breeding season. Another ceremonial dance is held in the *kagga* each Spring, at the time of the first deer hunt.

SEGUIDILLA (Spain)

A Spanish-Moorish dance mode, from Arabic *Seggedehiyya*, the "entry of the people" (servants, students), before the *Seggedeh*, literally the "seat", but relevant to the low dais covered with carpet, on which sits the *sheik* or the *mullah*. In Egypt, the prayer rug is always named *seggedah*, as the "place of prayer", or the "place of the master". Thus this dance was the equivalent to the Christian *pavane*,* the Gaelic *branle*,* or the Russian-Polish *polonaise*—a ceremonial dance of entry. Now considered to be primarily an Andalusian dance, it is known all over Spain, each region having its own version, with variation of steps, rhythm and music. A dance for one couple, or groups of couples, with castanets, the music is in 3/4 or 3/8 time, usually in the minor key. It is played on guitars, with sometimes a flute or violin. *Seguidilla* is also the name given to the *coplas* (verses) which accompany the

dance. Sung by the musicians, they consist of four short lines separated by an *estrebillo*, or chorus, of three lines. While the regional dances are called after their particular district, such as *Seguidillas Sevillanas* or *Malaguenas*, there are four main styles of the dance, which are : *Seguidillas Manchegas*, gay and lively (known in La Mancha at the time of Cervantes—1547-1616); *Seguidillas Boleras*, more dignified and stately, not related to the *Bolero**; *Seguidillas Gitanas*, a slow and sentimental gypsy dance; and *Seguidillas Toleadas*, in which the *Cachucha** combines to form a vigorous dance.

SEISES, LOS (Spain)

Performed now by ten boys (formerly twelve) aged twelve to thirteen, before the high altar in Seville Cathedral, at Candlemas (2nd February); Easter; the feasts of Corpus Christi (May or June); and the "Conception" (December). It was formerly also performed at Jaca in Aragon, in Majorca, Toledo, and Valencia. After service, about Vesper-time, the boys dance before the kneeling Cardinal Archbishop and clergy. A string orchestra and the cathedral organ accompany them, the music being in *Seguidilla** rhythm. In solemn measure, the dance is grave and dignified, without much movement of arms or body. There are ten figures, each having a mystical meaning, the most notable being simple and double chains in the figure 8 and double "S"—SS—. Sometimes the chain forms a circle; or the boys in double lines meet and cross, dissolve and re-form at right-angles. As they begin to dance, the boys chant; then cease singing and play castanets, which are smaller than the usual, made of ivory and worn on the middle finger instead of the thumb. For Easter and Corpus Christi the boys wear red knickerbockers and tunic; blue for the feast of the Conception, striped with gold braid, and with wings upon the shoulders. White taffeta scarves fall across the chest, fastened at the shoulder with a rosette, and stockings and shoes are white. Their tunics have lace collars and cuffs, and their damask hats of red or blue are lined with white, having a tuft of white plumes. In 1685, the story goes, a Spanish Prelate wished to suppress the dance, but the Pope decreed that it should continue until the costumes were worn out. As these have been continually repaired, they never have worn out, and so the dance remains. Origin of *Los Seises* is obscure. The first account tells of a wooden arc of the Testament carried through the cathedral in procession, accompanied by choir-boys and priests, and preceded by eight boys, dancing and singing, attired as angels and wearing garlands of flowers on their heads. In its present form, the dance dates from 1264. Since 1650 boys have been trained in the

College of San Isidore, where they enter at the age of eight or ten.

SELLINGER'S ROUND (England)

Sometimes sub-titled "Or the Beginning of the World". A 16th century round dance, one of the first to be known as a "Round" instead of the earlier "Carole".* Its name is attributed by Wm. H. Gratton Flood[1] to Sir Anthony St. Ledger, Viceroy of Ireland, who danced it there in 1540 as an Irish Hey,* and brought it to England when he retired in 1548. Flood asserts that the Irish *Hey* was the origin of the English *Round* or *Country Dance*. *Sellinger's Round* became very popular in England and the music was arranged by Dr. Wm. Byrd for the collection now called *Queen Elizabeth's Virginal Book*. That it was originally a dance round the Maypole is illustrated in a woodcut in a 17th century "Garland", which has the words "Hey for Sellinger's Round" written above the picture of dancers moving round a Maypole. The sub-title is partly explained in a comedy of 1607, called *Lingua*; the dance is frequently mentioned in 16th and 17th century literature.

[1] *History of Irish Music*. Wm. H. Gratton Flood. 1905.

SEMELE (Greece)

An older name for Koré, or Persephone. Her ritual is an ascension or new birth, or resurrection from the earth (*Zemlya* is the Russian term). Dionysus brings her, in rescue (or Perseus draws back Persephoneia) which has been deduced from pictures of a ceremonial held at Athens, on the dancing floor, dedicated "to the wild women" (the Maenads of Dionysus). There to the sound of singing, and piping, they came dancing, with scattering of spring flowers or petals from baskets. Then a priest summoned Semele from an *omphalos* (an artificial mound or mount). He "called her forth" to be attended by the young Dionysus as spirit of Spring. At Delphi, a similar rite was conducted by women called *Herois*. The circle was a merry spring dance, celebrating the Easter or Spring resurrection rituals, with Young Dionysus as the saviour, whose hand will encourage the vine. With the Romans, the dance rituals were associated with agriculture: Semele was thus invoked (now as Sylvestria) by the tasks of the year in sequence.
[See *Seasons*]

SERF BALLET (Russia)

When peasants in Russia were reduced to serfdom, and tied to their owners' land (much as conscript soldiers are tied to a regiment), the dukes and counts organised companies of servants. Cut off, during five or six months of winter, from easy travel, they lived on their country estates; and sought to provide amusement. In summer serfs did the farm labour; but the nobles also bought men and girls, likely to be skilful in playing instruments and dancing. On some estates (Ostankino for example), equipped theatres were constructed; and miniature orchestras alternated with dance performances. One or two of these serfs obtained marriage or emancipation, and joined city companies. Two Serf Theatres still exist near Moscow : one at Ostankino, north of the city, once owned by Count Sheremetiev. His classical palace (1799) has a well-equipped theatre, where his company of 170 serfs (not including the technical personnel) gave performances. Argunov was the architect. This palace was erected for Parasha Shemchugova, a talented actress, whom he later married. Now the place is a State Museum. At Arkangelskoye is the palace of Prince N. B. Yusopov, friend of Catherine II, where in a theatre built in the park, serf actors and dancers gave performances. The French architect de Gernie designed this theatre and palace.

SERIMPIS (Java)

Also given as *Srimpi*, and *Sarempi*—dancing girls, formerly belonging to the Javanese princely courts at Solo and Djokjakarta (now called Jakarta), along with the other groups called *Bedajas*.* The *Serimpis*, always operating in groups of four (as a kind of traditional quadrille basis) were the fully-trained dancing girls, who danced in costume at festivities, before the Sultan and privileged visitors. The *Serimpis* were formerly attached to Hindu temples; but with the fading of Hinduism before the advance of Islam in Java, these artists secured employment and protection in the courts on a similar basis. Their main themes are legends from *Mahabharata* and *Ramayana* with more prominence for episodes from the story of the Javanese hero-prince Pandji; also the Javanese romance cycle *Menak*. The Serimpis are (or we should, in view of revolutionary events, say *were*) "little princesses". Dancing for them was not a profession, not even a vocation, but a centre of their general education. Chosen as children, they ceased dancing at the age of fourteen. They learned by imitation only; performing stately traditional dances, with many *mudra** forms, in magnificent state costume. The accompanying song was chanted by musicians as they played. Each girl wore brown silk, bearing *batik* patterns, and the black "military skirt" over. A wide silken sash was held by gold band and diamond-studded clasp; and a *kris* (ritual dagger, with seven-curved blade), was held by the sash. Brilliant head-dress with curved helm, and rich arm ornaments, completed the costume. Feet remained bare. *Serimpis* were not permitted to perform outside the palace, though they were not prisoners. After leaving, on "retirement", they usually were married to suitors from the local nobility.   [See *Bedajas; Bayadere*]

SERPENT DANCE (Brazil, Amazon Basin)
A mating dance performed by the Indians of Amazon jungle villages. Although the men are gaily decked with brilliant feathers, the girls' chief costume consists of patterns painted on their thighs, often in the zig-zag symbol of a snake. Entering the small jungle clearing in single file, each girl's hands on the shoulders of the one in front, they slowly advance and retreat. The line, moving in sinuous curves and twists, suggests a serpentine movement. Then, with linked arms, the men dance into the arena with loud cries, and catching the hands of their partners, they begin a series of monotonous contortions of the body. The dance is accompanied by drums, beaten by older women sitting outside the circle, while everyone chants and those with "dancing-sticks" beat them on the ground.
[Cp. *Snake Dance* (Hopi); *Oenpelli Snake Dance*]

SERPENT DANCES
Exist in many countries; some follow a serpentine choric form in movement (as does the *kolo* for part of its course), while others present a masked figure of a many-legged serpent, a dragon or similar monster. Serpent dances (as *Sarpa, Naga,* etc.) follow several distinct modes or thematic meanings. One is the *zarpa,* as the unfolding of Time in rhythmic events; another (as the Chinese dragon) reveals the undulating form of the Nature power, in magnetic folds; while yet another (as the Indian *naga*) worships the snake form as a symbol of the coiled or embracing wisdom, or its power, *Kundalini.*   [See *Naga, Snake Dance*]

SET DE FLO' (USA)
A negro dance performed at wedding celebrations on plantations in the South, and the forerunner of the *Cakewalk.** This group dance in couples, opened with the woman placing her foot on her partner's knee, while he tied her shoe-string. After curtsey and bow to each other, the dance began, the men exchanging partners until all had danced. Although a pantomimic dance of work on the plantation ,it was gay in character, and allowed scope for individual display, especially for the girls. As in the *Cakewalk,* prizes of large cakes were awarded to the best performers. Movements of this dance depicted swinging a scythe, tossing hay into a wagon, hoisting a cotton-bale, rolling a barrel of tobacco, swinging an axe, and hoeing corn or cane.

The men strutted and pranced to impress; the girls sought to charm them by coquetry and graceful dancing. Improvised songs often accompanied dances. Girls were proud to "strut their stuff". One ex-slave girl is reported as saying, "Set a glass of water on my head, an' de boys would bet none spilt. Had flowers round my head, an' a big ribbon on each side, an' didn't waste a drop", which recalls the balanced strutting of the *Cakewalk* and *Calinda.**
[See *Cakewalk; Calinda; Negro Dancing in USA*]

SEVEN CHAMPIONS
Seven Saints etc., occur so frequently in Mediaeval tales, from the famous *Chanson de Roland* to the traditional tales (still used) of the Mummers of Revesby, that we must examine their underlying structure. We find that these Seven Champions (or Paladins) are newly disguised characters, now acting as Seven Champions of Christendom, but in fact operating in folk lore many centuries before. They are aligned with the "History of the Seven Sages", in Oriental lands. When we query : why there are always seven, we contact Lunar Worship extending its synthetic heroes. Thus we perceive that the famous Dance-Mime attributed to Roncevalles, is in essence a re-cast form by monastic experts in propaganda, on behalf of their Crusades (as the current aggression was then neatly labelled). The allocation of a supposed site was then necessary to give the requisite "historical basis' applied to every revamped myth; but as Roncevalles = *Rinnce-valse,* we see performance is more important than the alleged original event. The Seven Champions were thus distributed anew, in the most ancient combat of Winter (The Dark Folk, now the Moors, the current "enemy") against Summer (The Children of Light—the Monks and clerics, on the side of peace and the better way of life). The old Solstice Contest was taken over from the people's traditions, to be utilised for the papal propaganda scheme : the population was then urged to Join up and See the World, and also to Fight for Freedom (which, as usual they hadn't got), under the new generals, nominated as the Seven Champions. For the local purpose, this scheme was presented in dramatic form, in lusty songs and dance-mime, using all the technical resources furnished by Minstrel and Gleemen. From the critical opposition, developed the *Troubadours* and *Trouveres..* During this development, the older Miracle Plays (done in church and cloister) began to fail in attraction. The modern *ballet d'action* had thrown out another firm root, into the mass imagination of the people; while the religious antagonism of educated people developed the system of *La Chevallerie* with its romances of Arthur and Charlemagne. This too was

finally captured by the church and infused with theological commentary.
See *Morte d'Arthur*. Malory.

SEVEN MACCABEES (Namur, Belgium)
Version of the continental sword dance, executed to the music of pipe and tabour, each of the dancers holding the point of his neighbour's sword. This routine is familiar in England, in many traditional Morris Dances. To these games at Namur, stilt combats were added: and the general dance was extended to a contest between two Sides, called *Melans* (Blacks) and *Avreusses* (Whites or Greens). Finally this developed into a town contest with five or six hundred youths engaged on each side, but without any sort of weapons, in the great square of Namur. Music was provided by fifes, cymbals, and trumpets. This stilt struggle might last for two hours, before sufficient "wounded" compelled one side to surrender; when it was no longer a dance, but more like American football. Stilt dances are found in West Africa, India, Mexico, Austrian Tyrol.
[See *Zanco* (Mexico); *Mysore Stilt Dance* (India)]

SEVEN VIRTUES, Dance of (China)
Is mentioned by the Chinese traveller Hiuen Tsang to King Harsa in India, who wished to know details of *Dance of Seven Virtues* arranged to celebrate the suppression of a great rebellion in China (*circa*. 619 AD), and performed at the Chinese Imperial Court. With it was another famous Chinese dance-song known as *Music of Chen Wang's Victory*. This visit to India was in the 7th century AD. He came to study Hindu *yoga* (*Yoga-charya Bhumi-sastras*) and the *Tripitaka* of Buddhism; visiting Kanauj (Hindostan), where King Harsa ruled, as a famous patron of arts and philosophy; himself a poet and composer of many songs and dances. Three extant plays now attributed to him are *Ratnavali*, with *Naganda*; and *Pryadarsika*. The first named has been performed in London (1918); the dancer was Menaka.

SEVEN VIRTUES AND SEVEN VICES (Europe)
A theme of several Moralities, or church plays; produced by monks in cloisters in England or Germany, for the edification of the faithful. Some of these versions had episodic dances; usually as *interludis*.

SHADOW DANCE
Has existed in two main forms: (a) a mode of finger-dance and of puppet dance, making actual shadows; and (b) an ancestral dance, in which living dancers portray the bygone ancestral forms as dancing figures; this occurred at annual ceremonies as a mode of appeasement or of praise. The *Chayyim* mode is the Hebrew form; it continued to the last mediaeval mode of *Der Golem* (the tribal avenger). Persia retained it as a poet's duty; and then rank, or calling, as Umar-el-Khayyam, "Singer of Shadows". India knows it still at Serai-kella (small district near Eastern coast), where Chhau Dancers celebrate annually the Fight of Rama "for the ancestors". Morocco has an unrecognisable male dance of boys (as at Marrakesh) known as *Chleu*, from the same origins. Scotland has the Gaelic song or "lilt" which (translated) urges the boy "Dance to your Shadow, lad!" The last Roman form was seen in the practice of bringing waxen figures of ancestors to the funeral feasts, or in processions, following the custom of living actors who "mimicked the deceased man" in his habits. The philosophical ideas that urged these customs would take much space to formulate; but the general idea is that every man has a second form, a "lower soul" which animates him while living and dissociates but slowly when his body dies; it is reluctant to dissolve; it is thus his "shadow". If this shadow can be kept "dancing" (or animated, as in life), the soul of the man will endure longer; it will be appeased. This aim energises some of the Voodoo dances of Hayti. The custom of keeping waxen figures of royalties (as their special due) continued to the time of Elizabeth; they were kept in the Pyx (or Pax) Chapel, full-size, and fully attired in personal clothing. In time this custom was displaced by the renewed custom of making stone or metal figures as "memorials", and in modern times, the general idea continues in shadow pictures or photographs.

SHAKERS (USA)
Name given, from obscure sources, to the followers of Fox (the Lollards who knew the Arab *Zhikr*) called Quietists, said to be first led by John Wesley, but influenced by Abbé Cisneros of Montserrat (1627), whose system was developed by Madame Guyon. The term "Shaker" (in the USA) and "Quaker" (in England) is variously alleged to refer to their former habit of religious dancing, towards the end of their meetings. Their own name is Society of Friends; no dancing is to be seen now in Britain at the "Meeting House". Similar sects in Russia (as some of the Jewish sects—'*Chassidim*, in Poland) do sometimes develop their chanting into rhythmic dancing. When this mode of dance appears, it is usually a development of the earlier "processional" following a circular form round the hall, marked with short steps beaten to rhythm. Though this liturgy is immensely sincere and

devotional, there are no reports of excesses of any kind.

SHAKKYO-MONO (Japan)

Term applied to a category of dance plays, known as "Lion plays", or "Lion dances". This obscure title apparently derives from Sanskrit — *shakya* (power), here focussed in the Lion; but the Japanese word is given as the name of a "stone bridge". The full term resembles *Shakkya-Muni*, a name of the Indian Gautama Buddha ("possessor of power"). The principal legend tells of a noble who visits China, seeking the tomb of Manjusri (Manchu-Shri), the God of Justice and Reason. This disciple is himself a "lion-master". The dance was called *shishi-mai* (it featured the *Foh* animal — lion or dog). These dancing lions appear often in the Orient; in Java with Rangda;* in Tibet with the *gompa-tsam* masks; in Korea in the "Lion Dance";* in Bali as the *Barong;** in China as *Gee-ling*. They are animated often, by two men hidden in a skin, more or less realistic or symbolical, but the Japanese *Shakkyo* dance, as occurring in the *Noh* plays, is performed solo by a man. In gorgeous costume and with face heavily made up in traditional symbolic style, he wears a halo of hair and long mane reaching the ground, which he sweeps in circles round his head.
[Cp. *Barong; Korean Lion Dance; Ryoks; Prüh*]

SHAKTA-SHAKTI (India-Sanskrit)

Term implying (among other meanings) the cosmic forces in positive-negative modes, in their eternal process of circulation, given in mythos as "Dance of the Gods". As Woodroffe says:[1]

"The dance of the gods, therefore, means the action of the forms of Chit-Shakti upon the primordial and continuous cosmic stuff, by which action "dusts" appear; meaning discontinuities or centres of strain (gyrostatic or otherwise)".

He continues:

"*Rig Veda* X. 72. 6 definitely though metaphorically outlines the process by which granules or centres of strain appear in the continuous cosmic stuff. It tells how the Devatas begin to dance in the cosmic all-pervasive Water; and how grains or particles (symbolised as dust) are formed by the dance of the gods. The important Vedic parable is traceable in some of the other so-called mythologies of the world; and it represents a fundamental law of creative evolution".
[1] *World as Power*. Book V — *World as Continuity* (pp. 79 - 80). Sir John Woodroffe.

SHALAKO (N. America)

A special form of *Kachina** masked dancers; who take part in ceremonies among the Zuni* Indians. Twice the size of other *Kachinas*, these six giant *Shalako* are each animated by two men, like a Pantomime horse. Wrapped in a white blanket making a tall cylindrical shape, the men inside hold the mask on a pole at the top of this "body", so that the figure appears to be about ten feet high, towering above everyone. The mask itself is turquoise colour, with protruding eyes and snapping jaws, and is surmounted by a fan-spread of white and black feathers. A "ruff" of raven feathers is fixed below the mask, and a fox fur wraps the "shoulders" of the figure, over the blanket. Considered as sacred, the masks are consecrated with cornmeal before each ceremony. The *Shalako* perform with the *Kachinas*, on their arrival at the Winter Solstice, accompanied by *Koyemshi** (dancing clowns); and at the Summer Solstice they precede the *Kachinas*, in their departure for the spirit world. Like the *Kachinas* they are beneficent spirits.

SHAMAN (Siberia)

From the Hindu *Sramana*, men of various sects who were travelling ascetics. Like the *san-nyasins*, they had descendants, the Essenes, who lived in small communities; one sect was called *Nazar*. They had little ritual, but used united praise songs and a simple movement usually associated with daily needs — the drawing of water, preparation of food. They taught preventive rules such as times and places of eating; sleep periods varied by exercise in work. The *Sramana* became organised many centuries back as the Ice Age was receding once more and people travelled north from the central belt now made into desert. With them went the teachers.   [See *Kamlanie*]

SHANTY (England)

Is the national term for the "work-song", usually the accompaniment of action, in some task demanding application of team work. The shanty, with its linked tune and words, serve to mark the phases of labour rhythm, in movement and rest. Shanty has a simple form, like the basic carol that accompanied dance; but its technical demands require a larger number of variations on the rhythmic scheme. The chant is the religious parallel to the secular shanty; while in Java another temple mode, deeply locked in ritual, gives the name *Tjandi* to the building itself. We recall also the Hebrew *kantor* and the Latin *cante* (with the Iberian *cante hondo,** a funeral song that used to accompany the procession to the grave). There are several other associated terms of music and dance, as linked with vocational movement, either in prose rhythm, or full dance rhythm.

SHABH AL'ABID (Arabia)
"Dance of Slaves". Performed in the open, before a house where space permits. Two youths, holding hands, move quickly forward and back side by side, then in a circle, one forward and one back. This continues until a third dancer comes out, places his hand on the others, and one of the two gives up his place. The dance is accompanied on the *mizmar* by plaintive music.

SHARH DHAHERI (Arabia)
A dance for two lines of men, in the style of "Nuts in May". The poet stands between the two parallel lines, and recites a verse which the two rows repeat. Then one line advances to the other, raises hands over head as they meet, bows nearly to the ground and withdraws. This is repeated several times, till the other line takes up the dance in similar fashion. At intervals the poet sings or recites another verse. The music is rather sad.

SHARH SAIBANI (Arabia)
Men's Comedy Dance. For example, a cook's mate appears clad as an attractive female; his suitor seeks him behind the line of clapping men; and drags "her" out, or she follows bashfully. But when another dancer appears, the "lady" deserts one for the other. They carry on a Rabelaisian conversation, in extempore verse, if they can contrive such excellence. This dance is mainly slap-stick and music-hall style.

SHARH OF SUR (Oman, Arabia)
Sharh is the general name for "dance". This is a men's war dance. Two performers singing a wordless tune of mournful character, walk towards a line of ten men with sticks. The two stop and fight, leaping up, at a distance from each other; or tripping each other by sweeping the sword stick in a spiral over the ground, the other leaping clear. Then they kneel opposite and fence. When they get too close, one of the ten intervenes with his stick; and once more when the victor holds his dagger over the body of his "enemy" on the ground.

SHEAN TRIUBHAS (Scotland)
Gaelic term, translated as "Old Trews"; pronounced not as Shaun but Shann. Alleged to derive from a comic dance, done by way of contempt for an *Act of Proscription* upon Highlanders (1746) in order to suppress Jacobite tendencies. This Act forbade the wearing of Highland dress and "hodden grey trews, or knee breeches, were to be worn instead of kilt and tartan". The angry Scots would agree only on one dance thereafter (if the tale is to be credited), known as *Scottish Measure*; it has

been suggested (to be refuted by McClennan, authority on Scots Dance), that there was in the dance a kicking movement "to kick the trews off". As the whole story seems incredible, some stronger origin must be sought for the title; it is more than probable that the main steps of the dance have seen changes.

SHEBWARI (Arabia)
A wedding dance performed by men. In two facing lines ten paces apart, they bend their knees and bow their bodies forward and back, to the beating of drums. The performers sing as they dance, marking the rhythm by hand-clapping.

SHEDIM (Hebrew)
Classed as dancing nature-spirits; or "elementals" —semi-formed energies of the "five elements" from which they emanated as five distinct groups. They are comparable with the Hindu *deva-gandhara-apsara* groups. Their life is solely in action; they dance ceaselessly, conveying the main stress of their own rhythms to those entities whom they may contact. They are mentioned in the *Qabalah.** [See *Gabalis, Comte de*]

SHEIKHAT (OR CHIRATES) (Morocco)
Dancing-girls of Tiznit, South Morocco, famous for their beauty and musical skill. Rivals of the *Ghedra** dancers of Goulimine, a few miles away, they form a small guild in one "quarter" of Tiznit, in charge of older women, former dancers. Their distinctive costume, belonging only to them, is a long, stiff black robe to the feet, a white veil, earrings and bracelets. Their feet are bare. The girls, in their teens, perform in a low room of the one-storeyed houses. Before beginning the dance, it is their custom to kiss the hand of each of the spectators. Then, together, they twist their heads so as to throw off the veil, leaving the head swathed in a small silk turban or scarf. Playing the three-stringed *lutar*, or with small bells or the *neuk-sat* (small cymbals) on their fingers, and with downcast eyes, they move round the room in long, slow dances, singing as they dance.
[See *Morocco, Dances of*]

SHELAH-NA-GIG (Ireland)
Ritual dance; and dancing girl. Gerald Massey refers to this dance in his *Notes* (p. 681) where he says:[1]

"also called 'Cicily of the Branch' ".
Kohl in his *Travels in Ireland* notes that there once were women who made a profession of performing the part of the *Sheelah-na-Gig*; Their charm for bringing "good luck" was this: *"persuadent nempe ut exhibeat quod mulieres secretissimum habent".* The "holy bell" was rung at the peak moment, for

this flourish in the church mode of the Gig. This valiant symbol was carved over many church porches through Ireland. The "Branch" was relevant to the "Green Branch" typical of May First, but later transposed into the "Palm-branch" which never grew in Ireland. Italy had the quondam "Saint Cecilia" as the local form of *Sheelah-na-Gig;* with a transfer from dance to music. The *Gig* varied its dance form.

[1] *Book of Beginnings.* Gerald Massey. London, 1881.

SHEN

The primal sacred figure in ritual dance; present in every mythic scheme under scores of different names, many closely related. The Shen is the symbol of the Moon-god of ancient Harran; *S(h)in;* it is in China as *Chen;* in Mongolia as *Khen* or *Khan.* In Greece it appeared as *Omegha* and *Omicron;* while on Shakespeare's stage it was "The Great Round O". In this manner it is the circle invariably inscribed around the royal names of Egypt: for the *Phara-Oh*—the Master of the Circle. In Iranian myth it was *Dzhyan,* as in Tibet it becomes *Dzhen;* and in Japan *Zen.* Babylon had it as *Sarpanit* or *Zirpna;* which in India became *Choan* or *Chouen;* and was scattered widely in all the Iono-Iuno names of ancient Etruria and Latium; becoming John (a fictitious saint) along with *'sh-ana,* the ring of the year; and *Ianua* or Janus. All of these indicated the pure circle that was formed by the requisite number of worshippers, ritualists, priests, sacred dancers, in their willing submission to the subtle rhythms that arise in moving round and across the Primal Ring of Time. Again as symbol it figures as the Wheel of Law, the Rouelle or Rouenne; or the Wheel of Fortune, as well as the Hindu Samsara or the Bandhara of Life. The Shen is the symbolic predecessor of *khoro, karole, chorus, kolo* and *hora;* this dance again moves from ring to chain (or serpent) formation and back again. In Nature and in social form, the ring recurs again and again; when it moves as a unit, it developed into ritual and ceremony, where dance is inevitably an essential feature.   [See *Zodiac*]

SHER-SHAY (Jamaica)

Traditional festivals, solely for men, devoted to the goddess Erzulie.* Men take any female parts required in the rituals, which have an old religious basis. Possibly the term in the local *patois* is from the French *Cherchez la Femme.* This was (15th century or earlier) a slogan or password in the dying mode of La Chevallerie. The *Trouvéres* were "Finders". The ceremonial has its proper date in the Spring season; but lesser rites may recur during the year; all include singing-dancing-music.

[See *Erzulie; Xaca; Sect Rouge; Guede*]

SHIELD

As a basis of dance pattern (Ellipse or Square or Circle), is obscured by its later usage in "heraldry" as a symbol system almost forgotten in its ritual origins. Every *knecht* had his shield; often it was quartered in ritual; beyond this the genealogy of the individual obscured the richness of ritual; supporters were reduced to actionless images. Despite our inheritance in poetry (especially in Homer) of many "shields" and often full descriptions, significance of the ritual is lost. We have shields (or circles) of Denderah; of Apollo or Athéne; of Mars and Jupiter. One lingers with Britannia; some coins reflect a few elements of design; the Zodiac has retreated into astronomy. Examination of these traditions becomes essential to trace the general course of early rites in religion, with the prescribed rhythmic movement apparent in tracing the full circle (twelve "Stations"). In Gaelic, *sheiling* is the dancing place, *Sheila,* the chief girl dancer.

SHIELDS (Greek)

Of Apollo, of Achilles, or Herculeus: comprise condensed presentations of mythic drama, as combat, journey, or dance-ritual, sometimes pictured in graphic form, and given in episodic incidents on many vases used in rituals. The predominant factor is the round (or oval) form, affirming the circular journey, out and back, and serving to define the typical Twelve Labours, or Twelve Adventures, or Twelve Places, which the hero-god encounters in his progress. These shields take on three main forms, relevant to (a) terrestrial combats or trials, of the human warrior; (b) the underworld combats or dance-ritual, of the leader-hero, the Soter ("he who guides", or shows the way), and (c) the inter-cosmic combat or ritual dance which indicates the transition of the human soul, into and from Earth; into the Underworld and then expanding outwards to the Olympic heaven-world. These should be compared with the Tibetan scheme of *Khyilkhor*,* the Hindu *Mandala*,* and *chakra,*,* or the Chinese *Ming T'ang,*,* as well as the Egyptian "Journey through the Gates"; for the Greeks gained their knowledge chiefly from these more ancient sources. They were expressed in cosmic terms, by the astronomical scheme of the Twelve Mansions or Houses of the Zodiac*,*; probably first in this mode, in Babylon, but rapidly known in India, and Western China; and speedily familiar on the Plain of Salisbury.

SHIH CHING (Ancient China)

Traditional *Book of Love Poems;* classical book of ancient China, the *Book of Odes.* Selection was attributed to Confucius; he and his musicmasters of royal court admitted only three hundred pieces as worth preservation. Later candidates for Master of Ceremonial had to study them. They are fused with etiquette or forms of manners (*kuo feng* = feudal manners). These love songs are read with allegorical interpretation; their language is ancient and difficult. The necessity of expression is first by linear symmetry of words but rhythm is all important to dance expression. In the poetry of *Shih Ching*, all kinds of impressions were associated with sound of words, especially impressions of movement.[1] The voices of singers were assisted by gesture; and pantomime presented to the eye what the song was describing to the ear. This principle of ritual expression was, some centuries later, the origin of the *Noh** drama-rituals in Japan; in them we may watch today a dance form, closely parallel to that utilised in the symbolical love poems of *Shih Ching*. Those men who preserved them, who attended performances at palace ceremonies, were masters of music at princely or royal courts. *Shih Ching* poetry possessed a popular meaning, cherished by the masses; and allegorical meanings, perceived by the educated few.

> *The Young Elms (LXIII) Ch'en feng. 2.*
> "At the Eastern Gate, rise young elms
>   On the Hill of Yuan, stand oaks;
> That is the daughter of Tzu Chang
>   Who dances beneath their shade —
> On this beautiful morning they seek each other
>   Out on the southern plain —
> Let no one tarry to spin the hemp —
>   To the market, go! Dance! Dance!"

[1] *Festivals and Songs of Ancient China.* Marcel Granet. Paris.
The Hall of Light. W. E. Soothill. London, 1952.

SHIMMY (USA)

An American ballroom dance popular about 1920, accompanied by jazz, or rag-time music. Its chief characteristic was a shaking, or "shimmying" of the shoulders; the fast movement of the dance was in fox-trot style. Music considered to be an outstanding example of this type of rhythm was Zaz Confrey's piece, *Kitten on the Keys*, later used by Hindemith in a movement of his *Piano Suite "1922"*, and by Wilhelm Grosz in his *Second Dance Suite*.

SHIN KYONG (Tibet)

"Skeleton Dance". Two skeletons, male and female, in origin, and companions of Yama, perform a mystical "Dance of Death" which is reminiscent of the European *todtentanz*,* though different. Where the European "Death the Skeleton Man" comes to take typical members of social classes, these *Shin Kyong* figures are portents of a greater myth : the death of Kosmos, rather than of persons. They are pictured in the *gompa* (monastery) courts of Tibet, as in one at Deng-kar Gompa. The *Shin Kyong* are able to dance — with no muscles; they are seen as dissolving, yet they seek to continue life; and, thus creating and dying, they affirm a dialectical continuity in their *Cho-kyong* mythos (Protectors of Faith). There are many such wall pictures. The yogi dance of the *Chöd-khorlo*, though known in fact to few lamas, has many terrific traditions, supported by records of past events and imaginations of things to come. These are traditions of the *Gelüg-pa* (Yellow Robes) of the Reformed Sect, who are the most powerful group in Western Asia. They know that Death — who is *Yama*, is also Life, when seen reversed as *Maya*; so that both are equally illusions; the reality is *in* the "dance while it endures".

SHINTO (Japan)

System of religious ancestor worship, held in annual festivals, marked by performance of the ancient *Kagura** dance programme, with the mediaeval *Noh** dance drama played as mythic legends. Shinto means "The Way of the Gods" in the earth : the *Shen* (Chinese) is the symbolic hall in which the Emperor endeavoured to follow (or to point out), on behalf of the people, this commended "Way of the Gods", and prayed to the ancestors for help and guidance in finding and keeping on the Way. This has been called the *Tao*, but the mysticism associated with this erudite system has been unable to use any visual mode for exposition, other than by symbols. *Shen-Tao* developed a more pragmatic mode in Japan; and united the Buddhism imported from Korea (about 5th century AD) to provide a more philosophical system of belief. This in turn developed the rituals, culminating (14th century) in the *Noh* drama-dance.
[See *Kagura; Noh; Saragaku; Dengaku No Noh; Denmari; Gigaku; Gagaku*]

SHIP FESTIVAL AND DANCE — 1

Egypt had the annual sacred procession of the Ship, one of the most celebrated Festivals. There is a detailed record on the walls of Karnak; and more in the sanctuary of Essabona,, or the adytum of Derrie. Other depictions in relief sculpture, once magnificently coloured, appear in the Temple at Semneh; while these are repeated in numerous monuments through Egypt and Nubia. The Sacred Bark (sometimes the Solar *Baris*) appears always in the papyrus scriptures; the symbolism drawn from the realism of boats on the Nile and the idea of the Sun moving across the sky in his own sacred bark. Within the temple, this realism exchanged for ritual symbolism, in dance terms; so that the worshippers formed the barque, with their chief inside;

movement was now in chant music and gesture. This later entered Rome; the term *navis* remains to remind us of this transition of a boat to a *kirke* (coracle).

SHIP FESTIVAL AND DANCE — 2

Ruskin, writing on the old church at Torcello (predecessor of Venice) comments on the tradition of "Church = Ship". The plan follows the older Basilica (Roman court) with central nave or *navis;* and aisles on each side marked with massive shafts. There are many windows. Ruskin writes :[1]

"... the church itself was frequently symbolised under the image of a ship, of which the bishop was the pilot ... as an ark of refuge ...."

"... the raised seats and episcopal throne which occupy the curve of the apse ...."

"let him ascend the highest tier of the stern ledges that sweep round the altar of Torcello, and looking as the pilot did, along the marble ribs of the temple-ship, re-people its veined deck with the shadows of its dead mariners ...."

[1] *Stones of Venice*. J. Ruskin. (Everyman Edn. p. 23).

SHIRABYOSHI (Japan)

Female entertainers or "minstrels" of feudal Japan. They travelled the country, visiting baronial halls, where they danced, mimed, and sang or recited epic poems and heroic tales. Dressed in white, they were called "White Gliders", and wore long tunics with wide sleeves. The manipulation of these sleeves was part of the dance, and the skilled twisting of fans added its symbolic meaning (See *Ogi No Saboki**). Below the tunic were trousers, and they wore a high head-dress or hood. Sometimes a sabre was added, and a sweeping train. Although the *shirabyoshi* played drum and fife, they were often accompanied by an orchestra made up from retainers of the lord in whose house they entertained. What remains of their songs, gestures and rhythmic movement, and the symbolic handling of fans, is preserved in the traditional *Nô** drama. Three famous 12th-century *shirabyoshi* are still remembered in Japanese history. It is from these early exponents of the arts of dance and music that the *geisha** have developed.

SHIVA, DANCES OF (Southern India)

The tremendous figure of Shiva as Destroyer, pervades popular Shaivism with awe; though he is well understood as being the "Dissolver of Chains", and the "Liberator of the Soul"; just as his dark spouse Kali, in her "Dance of the Burning Ground", is seen, not as the annihilator, but as the breaker of all dark fetters. Foreign comprehension of Shiva, and of his cosmic functions, is confused by the many claims of his devotees. Formerly the great

Hindu trinity (itself a unity and inheritor of an older system — the Indivisible One, or Unknowable Brahm), was presented as Brahma the Creator, Vishnu the Preserver; with Shiva the Dissolver. Though Brahma is little featured (there are but few temples dedicated to him), the two great cults of Vishnu and Shiva each tend to claim, for their pre-eminent figure, all the functions doctrinally allotted among the three aspects of the Unity of Brahm. Their leaders know well enough these facts : and even popular devotion rarely lapses into conflict. Thus it is that at present, the great *Shiva Natyam* of the South Indian temples has taken over the technique formerly utilised (under its systematic name of *Maha-Bharata-Natyam*) by the Vaishnavites in the North. The use of the Sanskrit terms, as followed in the South, proves the technical sources. So the "Five Functions of Shiva" are gathered, from the trinity, for him and his *shakta;* and he is presented not only as the Creative Dancer and the Rhythmic Sustainer, but as the Yogic Dissolver, just as Parvati turns over to the work of Kali. In a brief chapter, A. K. Coomaraswamy[1] indicated these functions. E. J. Carpenter[2] quotes an older scholar. The system known as the Caiva-Siddhanta is the most elaborate, influential, and the most valuable of all the religions of India.

[1] *Dance of Shiva*. Dr. A. K. Coomaraswamy. New York, 1924.

[2] *Theism in Mediaeval India*. Dr. E. J. Carpenter. London, 1926.

[See *Tandava Lakshanam*. Naidu and Pantalu. Madras, 1936]

SHIVA-KALI NATYAM (India)

The *natyam* (dances) of Shiva and Kali are maintained by the Shaivist cult of Hinduism, in contrast to the dance rituals dedicated to Krishna-Radha, by the Vaishnavites (followers of Vishnu), known also as Bhagavats (devotees, praisers of Bhagavan, the highest lord). Shiva as "male", with Kali as "female", are symbolised aspects of the dissolvent rhythms of the cosmos — not as wild destroyers — but as the "inward returning wave" after the expansive power of Brahm has reached its temporal optimum. As Krishna is a symbol of emotional expansion and joy, so Shiva is a symbol of intellectual development and equilibrium. Lord Shiva is not only *Nataraja,** the Lord of Dancers, but is *Mahayogi*, the Great Thinker; and his "spouse" or *Shakta* (balancing group phases of energy, the "magnet" to his electrical pulse) who is Kali, is an aspect of Kala or Time, which engulfs all created things in its course. The profound Hindu thinkers could find no more suitable symbol than dancing images, and brief descriptions, to indicate the essentially dynamic form of the *Purana* (Hindu mythos) which factor is again asserted in the rituals known as *Tantra* (worship, liturgy, ceremonial). Not only the Dancer, but the Dance; and not only the moment of Dance but all Nature, is seen as Dancing, in this embracing nobility of universal conception, expressed at its popular end in realism, but forever linked with its abstracted end as the finest philosophy of creation, maintenance and dissolution, that the world has known. Some echo of this doctrine appears with later Greek thinkers, from Plato to Plotinus or Parmenides, and is echoed in the dark saying of Herakleitus—*Panta Rhei!* "Everything Flows!" The Gnostics were the last public teachers in Europe to retain this same doctrine; but the Bhagavats, reaching Italy and especially Provence, left their traditions, still faintly echoed in the terms of Spain as *gitana* and *gitano* (Singers of the Song of Praise or *Gita*), and the dance ring called *gavot** or *gavat* (from *Bhagavat*). In Western Europe we may recall the "Hermetic Doctrine" : — "As Above, so Below," for the infinitely great Kosmic Dance of Stars is reflected in the infinitely small Dance of Atoms. See *Dance of Shiva*. A. K. Coomaraswamy. New York, 1924.

SHLEUH BOY DANCERS (Morocco)
Shleuhs are Berbers of the Masmouda tribe. Troupes of boy dancers under a leader (the Raïs) perform in such places as the Djema el Fna, the famous square at Marrakesh. Varying in number from twelve to twenty-four, they begin their training before the age of seven, in order thoroughly to master the steps. Dressed like girls in white over coloured garments, with silver or crimson belt, they have painted faces and hennaed hands. Their heads are shaven except for one lock which, on the older boys, is wound, with many strands of coloured wool, into a turban. A large gold earring ornaments one ear. Besides high-pitched singing, the instruments accompanying the dance include the *bendir* (a single-sided tambour two feet across); the *nakus*, a metal pipe beaten with rods; the three-stringed *lutar*, and the *neuk'sat* (three small cymbals worn by the dancers—two on the thumb and first finger of the left hand, one on the second finger of the right hand). The *rebab* is played by the Raïs, who opens the performance by intoning a song, musicians joining in as the dancers form a line facing the audience. There are seven body movements, apart from the footwork—a genuflexion towards the audience and their master; double *entrechat* done while turning corners of the various figures; salutes made with the right hand; crooking of knees and salaaming movements; and the *Shtah del Khzem*, a "shiver" of the shoulders and head (called *Shtah atemshi-uji* when

done while moving forwards or backwards). One foot marks the beat, while toe and heel of the other foot do a syncopated rhythm as the dancers form a five-pointed figure. The dance is full of mime and symbolic body movements. Although apparently intent only upon each other during the dance, a passing tourist will be noticed and treated to a special solo in exchange for payment.
[See *Morocco, Dances of; Khawal* (Egypt); *Cifte Tel* (Turkey)]

SHLEUH GLIDING DANCE (Morocco)
Among the dances of the Shleuhs living in the Atlas Mountains south of Marrakesh is a circle dance performed by all men or all women. Little tapping steps bring dancers forward or backward, without the actual step being seen, giving an impression of effortless gliding. The circle moves as one unit, not as a collection of individual dancers. Spectators see continually changing patterns of flowing movement; a circle that expands and contracts, moving slowly round from right to left, like a flexible chain manipulated into different shapes. The gliding effect is aided by the long garments of both men and women which conceal the actual step. The upper part of the body is kept still, only the arms rhythmically rising and falling. Sometimes two solo dancers will perform inside the circle, advancing and retreating; and the smooth movement will be varied by a characteristic "shiver" of the hips (called *Shtah del Khzem* or *Shtah atemshi-uji* according to whether it is done while standing still, or moving backwards or forwards). The dance is accompanied by hand-clapping, high-pitched chanting, and the beat of tambours played either by musicians in the centre of the ring (themselves sitting in a small circle) or by the dancers themselves. There may be twenty tambour players, and fifty to a hundred dancers will take part in the dance, performed in a large courtyard or on the open plain.   [See *Morocco, Dances of*]

SHONE (Isle of Lewis, Scotland)
Ritual dance offerings were made to the ancient sea-god Shoné, by the islanders of Lewis at Hallowtide. They gathered in Ta Teampull Maluay (replaced later by a church). Every family furnished a peck of malt, brewed into ale. The tallest man waded into the sea, carrying a cup of ale. With waves rising to his middle, he gave a greeting to Shoné, asking for "seaware" in return; and then threw the ale in a wide circle round him. This was at dusk. He returned to shore; the company then went to Teampull, chanting en route; and inside, they made their prayer, again to Shoné. The candle was put out at a signal; they all then walked to

the appointed field (*rinnce*) to drink their ale, and feast; and then danced for the remainder of the night. At dawn they returned home, believing that due observance of the Dance and Ale of Shoné ensured them a plentiful crop. The ritual has not been known since the Reformation. [See *Sikinik*]

SHOTA RUSTAVELI (Georgia, USSR)

Is the hero of this "national epic" in the latest form, which is contemporary with the *Romance of the Rose* (also known to be completed by several authors) in Western Europe. The legend of this "Knight in the Leopard Skin" was apparently revised into its present general form in the most prosperous period, the reign of Queen Tamara in the 12th century, from much older material. The story was performed as a minstrel legend, in terms of mime-dance : the term *Shota* is equivalent to the *Chout* (of Russia) who is a minstrel (or, in the ballet *Chout*, a buffoon), and is parallel with the *Ashug* or singer-dancer of Uzbekistan; or the *Ashaq* of Persia. The name Rustaveli seems to refer to a tribe—the *velie* is the group; but the original kernel of legend may well derive from that of Bacchus in the Dionysus cult (which was deeply set in Georgia). A long and boring ballet was performed in Paris and London (Cambridge Theatre, 1947), with possible inspiration from *Panthere a'Amore* (Nicole de Margival) or even the older *Bestiare d'Amour* (Richard de Fournival).

SHOW GIRL

From German, *schau-spielerin*. American music-hall or burlesque term for girls who perform simple rhythms in scanty costume, usually for entertainment of politicians, Elks Conventions, or other brotherly gatherings away from home. American commercial managers regard this type of display as "cheesecake", meaning thereby the maximum exhibition permitted by law and local religious societies. The same commercial drive has crept into American theatre ballet; though technical ability is now, to some extent, recognised as an additional contribution to culture. The typical show-girl hopes to "make a career", but discovers that youth does not last; she is, in part, the modern development of the ancient *Torte* (now called torch) or "Dancer for Ashtarte" (Ashtoreth, the Syrian goddess of Love and Luck), or the Hebrew *kadesh* (*kaddisch*, holy, devoted etc.) and, as with the *coryphée* of the opera-ballet, does not necessarily lead an evil life any more than her less decorative sister in commercial store or office life. All this type of entertainment offers is music and movement, light and colour, without the slightest strain on the brains of the tired business men. The "show-girl" is, in general, the feminine equivalent

to the American college "sports boy" of the baseball or football field.

SHUKADE (Ecuador)

A healing dance by the *puna* (witch-doctor) of the Colorado people in the province of Esmerelda. Performed round five "magic stones" (polished lumps of black lava), this ritual dance enables the *puna* to secure a séance with "possession", making the cure by hypnosis and use of herbal concoctions. Then the *yukang* (demon of sickness) is expelled.

SIBEL, SIBYL (Wales)

An ancient Welsh dance, said to be a survival "from the Druids", but given in Bremmer's *Harpsichord and Spinnet Miscellany* (Edinburgh 1761) as *Cibel* or *Cebell*,* an English dance of the 17th century. The form of the dance is unknown, but the music suggests that it may have been a solo dance followed by a group dance, since there are no crescendos or diminuendos, the music alternating regularly with four bars *piano* and four bars *forte*. An example is given in Edward Jones' *Relicks of the Welsh Bards* (1784 and 1794). This name—used by the Greek members of the primitive (non-Latin) Christian kirke—suggests a Greek origin—as the "Speaker" in the séance; though the Sibyl continued in Italy. Michael Angelo painted one in the Sistine Chapel. The Arabic *sibel* means *fountain*.

SIBERIAN KNEELING DANCE

In the Kurile Islands, among the Kamschatka people, women perform a kneeling dance, described by S. P. Krashinikoff in *Petersburg 1764*: "They dance in this manner—two women kneel opposite each other in the middle of the room, holding a little toe in each hand. First they begin to sing (love songs) very low, moving slightly their hands and shoulders; by degrees they raise their voice and increase the motions of their bodies until they are quite out of breath. This strange entertainment, as it appeared to me, seemed greatly to delight the Kamschatdales . . ." The dance was accompanied·by a simple flute. [Cp. *Ghedra* (Morocco)]

SICILIANA; SICILIANO; SICILIENNE

A dance with music usually in the minor key, in 6/8 or 12/8 time. Frequently performed at Sicilian weddings, after the feast, to accompaniment of flute or tambourine; bagpipe or guitar; or an orchestra of two or three violins. The form is a version of the *Cushion Dance** but without the accompanying rhyme. A man, cap in hand, bows low to a lady, who dances with him, the couple being linked by a kerchief. After a vigorous dance, the man again bows and sits down, the woman continuing to pirouette by herself; then she walks round the room and chooses a partner, and so on, man and woman alternately dancing and choosing. Bride and groom dance by themselves, until towards the end of the evening, when all dance together.

SICILY, DANCING IN
In the country parts of the Island dancing retains its ceremonial character, being considered not merely as a pleasant pastime, but as part of a special ceremony, such as a wedding, and only to be indulged in in such connection. The traditional "separation of the sexes" common in Sicily does not encourage social dancing, although since the two world wars popular versions of modern ballroom dances are occasionally seen in the country, and fox-trots, tangos and rumbas have invaded the ballrooms of the towns, as they have practically the world over. Formerly the *Contradanza* (something between a quadrille and a Sir Roger de Coverley) was popular, and the *Ruggera*.* At old-fashioned weddings there was always dancing after the feast, the bride and groom leading, and each male guest dancing in turn with the bride; but traditional dances such as the *Fasola*, the *Puliciusa*, the *Chiovu*, and the *Papariana* are now almost unknown. The best known dance is the *Siciliana** popular at weddings.

SIEBENSPRUNG (Germany)
"Seven Jumps". A dance in 2/4 time, similar to the *Zevensprong** of Belgium and the Netherlands is danced by couples. At intervals the man (while jumping) makes seven movements—two with his feet, two with his knees, two with his elbows, finally touching the floor with his forehead. Meanwhile his partner pirouettes round him, and verses are sung during the dance. Similar dances are known in Denmark; and the *Saut Basque** is sometimes followed by a seven-fold leap. The ritual origin of the dance is clear from the fact that in Westphalia, in Germany, it was the custom on Easter-day for men and women to dance round a favourite oak tree. Round the tree were seven holes dug in the ground, in which the dancers did their best to land after each jump.
[See *Zazpi Jausiak* (Basque); *Spell of Seven Steps* (Ceylon); *Zevensprong* (Belgium and Netherlands)]

SIEGFRIED LIED (Faröe Islands)
The "Song of Siegfried" (Conqueror of Death), which was a solemn dance ritual and chant (probably an initiation ceremonial), similar to a short description in *Sturlunga-saga*.

SIERRA LEONE (W. Africa)
Dance follows traditional ritual and folk dances of the protectorate; and a mixture of modern variants in the colony; much like the contesting religious systems. Secret societies, as *Poro* (men's) and *Bundu** (women's) have their own dance rituals; of which fragments, incidentally repeated outside, become known. There are the traditional Initiation ceremonials, with their essential dance forms. Dancing and singing go always together; both for the ceremonial terminations, or the Muslim fête such as Id-ul-Fitr. The influence of African dance is so strong that it permeates the Europeanised sectors, as at the "Junior Diners" Club, where, according to a local writer, they sing : "Everybody, everybody! everybody ! ! likes Saturday Nights". They join hands and circle slowly round. Each member is imprisoned in turn, in the ring, where he must perform a solo dance. All are expected to join in, irrespective of rank or occupation for, they insist, "everyone likes Saturday night". The traditional dances, as those of the *Bundu*, take many forms. There is the *kabadia*, or the *buyan*, danced to the *kalangi* music with drums. The *ferenks* is a boy's dance for two; but the sword dance can be offered by any man who is able enough. The *tongoyama* is reputedly an exorcism or devil dance; while the *Fulah* dances (mostly Moslem) take acrobatic or humorous form.

SIGN LANGUAGE IN DANCE (Africa)
Prehistoric man, in the Tanga-Nyika district of Africa, seem to be the most ancient *homo sapiens*, according to excavations by Dr. L. S. B. Leakey, in the Olduvai River gorge, some sixty miles from Nairobi (where he is Curator of Croydon Museum). Skeletons have been found, estimated to date over one million years old. They belonged to the African Negro and his rivals the Pygmy tribes. They, according to Dr. Albert Churchward (in his *Origin and Evolution of Religion*, 1924) developed their use of ceremonial and ritual with dance and simple music. He writes :

"Ceremonial rites were established as the means of memorizing facts in Sign Language, when there were no written records . . in these the 'Knowledge' was acted, the Ritual was exhibited, and kept in ever living memory by continual repetition. The Mysteries, Totemic or Religious were founded on the basis of action".

Dr Churchward specifies most often the Nilotic Negro; following in succession Stellar Cult, Lunar Cult (Matriarchal) and Solar Cult (Paternal) and credits them with some, at least, of the origins of religious symbolism. These were arrayed in action; the rhythms of each ruling phase being the guide. Other recent discussions seek to find an "origin for art" but as they had no "art" (in our sense of the word), they were entirely expressive and meaningful. They possibly invented a sculpture from the basis of their Sacred Tree, painting from their Geometric designs and dance patterns. The one certainty (from the Altamira and other caves) is that they did invent a sort of art gallery, as well as their pre-historic mode of displayed ritual, which developed into both church and theatre. See *Primitive Song*. C. M. Bowra. 1962.

SIKINIK (Baffinland, N. Canada)
"Sun Dance" (Inuit, or Eskimo). This "Dance of Return of the Sun" (*Sikinik*) occurs each January. For a very few minutes the sun first appears above the horizon, to signal the "coming of light". The Inuit tribe gathers on the seashore, facing "the direction", making a huge circle. Every man carries a piece of meat. The watcher calls out the greeting: "*Auk Shuni*" ("Welcome") three times, to herald the coming of the Sun. The chief then lifts both hands high, drops them to his sides, turning from the circle. Silence follows, as the sun goes from sight; then arises the "Sun Chant", in their ritual—intoning, that begins "*Auk shu ni sikinik*" —"Be Strong, O! Sun!" when the dance continues in a slow shuffling movement. Music is made by a monotone of humming. The meat pieces are dropped on the ground where each man has held his place. The next figure of dance is the moving circle, which weaves in and out, among the meat pieces. When this dance ends, these pieces remain on the ground—marking the now-used pattern— and the men return to their daily tasks. [See *Shoné*]

SILENT "REELS" (Bosnia, Yugoslavia)
When the country was conquered by the Turks in the 16th century, they prohibited native songs and dances, which led in Bosnia to several dances being performed without any musical accompaniment. Called silent or dumb "reels", they are danced by men and women in perfect rhythm, the only sound being the jingle of many coins which adorn the costumes of the girls, and the tap of feet. At Glamoc, in the Dinaric Mountains, the dance is begun by the girls moving in a close circle. Later the men join in and tempo increases. During the dance each man vigorously shakes his partner's hand and turns her round. In Starobosansko the girls, holding their partner's hand, have to follow improvised steps performed by the men, tempo and complexity of rhythm gradually increasing. Locally these dances are said to be a test of strength and resilience in the girl, by the man who may be looking for a marriage partner.

SILVANUS (Latin Etruscan)
According to R. P. Knight, Sylvanus is identical

with Sylva—being the same word in different local spellings . . . . SLFA and SLF.

Shinto Dance of Miyajima Shrine (Inland Sea).
JAPAN

SINGKIL (Phillipines)
Belongs to the Muslim Filipinos in the Southern Islands, and was formerly learned by every girl of royal blood—possibly as an exercise in assurance and control. Pairs of bamboo poles are laid on the ground and two people, one at each end of each pair, clap them together in syncopated rhythm. The dancers step rhythmically in and out of the bamboos in a variety of patterns. *Singkil* is similar to *Tinikling,** but more elegant. Wearing embroidered skirt and tunic, gold ear-rings and a veil falling at the back to the hips from a flat headdress, the dancer carries a fan in each hand which she skilfully manipulates as she steps in and out of the clacking bamboos. Whereas *Tinikling* proceeds at vigorous speed, *Singkil* is more leisurely, the dancers moving with ease among the viciously snapping sticks. Accompanying music includes a set of gongs similar to those in a *gamelan** orchestra.
[Cp. *Tinikling; Bamboo Trap Dance* (Assam)]

SIR ROGER DE COVERLEY (England)
Used as a 19th century ballroom dance, usually the last of the evening. It is a longways figure dance for large groups, in which the jumble that often occurs, affords great cause for mirth. This is said to be an "old English country dance", and as such it is still performed in many country houses for the New Year celebrations. This folk dance first appears

recorded in Playford's *Dancing Master*, edition of 1696, along with the violin music.

SISTRUM (Sistra)

Latin name for Egyptian ritual instrument; a U-shaped bar of bent metal, furnished with a handle. From the two sides are inserted four loose bars of silver. Movement produces a light tinkle. Many Egyptian mural sculptures show singers and dancers holding a sistrum in one hand level with the shoulders. They were introduced into Rome together with the worship of Isis and Horus.

SIVA ALSO SHIVA (India)

Is the Hindu name of the cosmic god who is *Nata Raja*, King of Dancers, whose energy is displayed in universal modes, called The Seven Dances of Siva. Many fine sculptures in stone and bronze portray one or other of these dances, mostly South Indian, with symbolism within symbolism, one end in visual art—as is the dance—and the other in profound scientific relativity. The inclusive dance form is *Ananda-tandavam* (as is indicated in the frontispiece example) but the succession of dance form reveals the "Five Functions of Siva Nataraja".

1. *Kaliga-tandavam*—Symbolises Creation
2. *Gavuri-tandavam*—Rising Conservation
3. *Tiripura-tandavam*—Purification of Form/Energy
4. *Sandya-tandavam*—Maturing Conservation
5. *Urdhava-tandavam*—Period of Grace
6. *Sankara-tandavam*—Dissolution (and so into
7. *Ananda-tandavam*—Release. Salvation. Bliss.

These five functions in seven phases proceed continuously, until universal cessation returns to *Kaivalya*, Equilibrium. The Divine Dancer rests; a new impulse disturbs the perfect balance, when another process of creation begins. The *Tandava** indicates masculine formal dance; *Lasyd** does not appear in this symbolism; though Kali joins in the phase of Dissolution or Destruction, as does Siva in his final Yogi Dance *Smashana*. Ritually the Gods execute his Dance at seven great centres in temple halls—the *Sabha Sobor*—where those qualified (*adhikari*, competent) may see them, as

1. *Kanaga-sabah*, at Chidambaram
(*Ananda-tandavam*
2. *Racita-sabah*, at Madura
(*Sandya-tandavam*
3. *Sri-sabah*, at Tirupattur
(*Gavurit-tandavam*
4. *Chitra-sabah*, at Tirukuttalam
(*Tirupura-tandavam*
5. *Rattin-sabah*, at Tiruvelangdu
(*Kali-tandavam*
6. *Tambira-sabah*, at Tinneveli
(*Mouni-tandavam*

7. At all *Sabah, Universal*
(*Sankara-tandavam*

The attributes of Nataraja signify the five functions, elaborated in cosmic energy. They may be compared with other important systems. The *tiruvasi* (arch of flames) has various totals : twenty-four or thirty-two or forty-nine, according to the dance given. The arch seems originally to have been constructed of a framework supporting lighted lamps. The form is comparable with (a) the Egyptian *shen** or cartouche; (b) the Tibetan *mandala*;* (c) the Latinised mode in *vesica pisces* or halo; (d) the Chinese *trigrams*; (e) the Hebrew *schem-ha-phorasch*,* (f) the Hellenic *khoros*. The Tibetan *kyilkhor*= Tamil *koyil-khor*; and thence comes into the Mediaeval European "magic circle" (*horoscopus*) and the ovoid form of *navis* sometimes traced over the choir of a church. They appear finally in modern Tables of Atomic Energy—the dancing molecules and atoms—from Lucretius to Mendelyev and Curie, or Rutherford.

SJALASKUTTAN (Finland)

"Seal's Jump". An imitative dance of Kimito in Aboland, in the Swedish-speaking parts of Finland, with music in 3/8 time; for any number of couples standing one behind the other. The dance-style is heavy, imitating seals. In the first figure Polka-mazurka steps forward are used, and jumps with bent knees, couples alternately facing and turning away. At the end of the figure, the first couple lead down the centre, dancers ending in two lines facing. For the second figure, arms are raised at shoulder level, hands drooping from wrists, like seal's fins. In two lines, the dancers move towards each other; partners take hands (keeping elbows at shoulder height) and dance round on the spot; or they advance with a skipping step, then partners jump with feet together, men turning to left, girls to right, finishing back to back, then jumping round to face each other again. In the middle and at the end of the figure, partners dance on the spot with feet together, as long as the musician repeats the last note of the bar. In the costume for both men and women, the predominating colour is blue, instead of the more usual red.

SKAINS-MATE OR *SKEINSMATE* (English-Irish)

A *skain* was a dagger; the term meant (a) a partner in practice in fence, or (b) a partner in robbery by use of daggers. Later applied to wool-winding— another partnership, in which one pair of hands danced while the other pair remained still; and in this associated with the game of "cat's-cradle", in pattern-making by string. See Greensleaves or "Green skein"—a ravelled sleave of wool in winding—an idle dance—a sleaveless errand—a skein of sleive-silk. (*Troilus and Cressida*).

SKAKAVA (Czechoslovakia)
Was performed as a high-jump dance, by the men, while the women chanted a hymn; or sometimes an invocation.

SKANSEN (Sweden)
Peasant and Folk Dance is performed at Skansen, an extensive outdoor section of the Stockholm "Northern Museum" (founded in 1872 by Dr. Arthur Hazelius), situated on the west of Djurgardan, near Stockholm. An enclosure of forty acres contains "Sweden in miniature". Attendants are dressed in various traditional costumes. Dances are performed usually every Sunday afternoon; sometimes on week-days; sometimes for special festivals, with expert players on peasant instruments, such as the *nyckelharpa* (a hurdy-gurdy with bow); or the *kantela* (a string instrument from Finland). The dances include : *Vava vadmal** (weaving dance); *Gustafs Sköl* (with singing); *Hallingen* (acrobatic form); and *Trekarlspolskan; Dalpolskan; Frykdalspolskan; Vingakerdansen;* and *Renlanderen.* These are performed in traditional peasant costume, some by Dalecarlian peasants, and some by members of the *Svenska Folkdans sens Vanner* (a modern association organised to preserve the older traditional arts). The chief period is the Spring Festival of Skansen (late May-and-June), in which some five hundred performers take part
[See *Svenska Tans; Lekstuga*]

SKATING DANCE
Developed in Holland (especially in Friesland), where skilful skaters turned their necessary mode of winter transit (they could cover the fifteen miles from Leyden to Rotterdam in seventy-five minutes) into exhibitionist displays of every kind. From racing they turned to dancing; especially proven by "cutting figures" on the ice surface. These geometrical or floral forms remained visible for some hours, to prove their accuracy. Modern commercial "dancing on skates" has been developed not only on artificial rinks having merely three inches of solid ice, but as a theatrical display. This form becomes somewhat monotonous; movement on ice can permit little more than elemental forms of dance progression, combined with incessant turns or pirouettes. They often display a startling virtuosity; but this feat is repeated too much. On films, the "psychic distance" of the skaters makes the display even more tenuous, as a spectacle. Strutt[1] mentions that he had seen skaters in Hyde Park dance a minuet as elegantly as if they had been dancing in a ballroom.
[1] *Sports and Pastimes of the English People.* Joseph Strutt. 1898.p. 154.

SKHEMA (old Greek)
"Form or external shape", as opposed to "the Reality"; show or pretence gestures. With *Skematikos* it extends to "making steps" or "to make figures in dance". As *Skhematicon* it indicates "Figures in Dance"—that it, it was the general Greek term for what we now call "choreography" —as the basic scheme or pattern, including mime or gesticulation. Thus *Skhema* is basic dance pattern, for them, as opposed to *khoros*—it was the "thing done or shewn". *Skhematica lakonica* was the summary—Laconian figures or well-known gestures (displacing speech) traditional pattern. Farther East, this same term *lakhon* is used to denote play or playing (ritual or theatre) and is significantly, an unrolling of the *lekhon* (sometimes literally, a roll of painted linen) and the story or play may be a *Lakhos*, one of Fate or Destiny.

SKIAPODES (Ancient Greek)
Literally the "Shadowfooted" sometimes referred to a fabulous tribe in Libya; but also (a) wizarddancers (on the sand, silent) or (b) ancestral shadows, who might come when called by the sybil, or a "medium". There was a kind of *kholo, in* which the *Skiapodeoi* joined hands—by kerchieves —with the living as they moved in this magical dance—October-November.

SKIFFLE (Scuffle)
USA - English proletarian dance-song, dance-music; town equivalent to the Hobo Dance. No two groups are identical, each has its own style, but music is usually based on guitar, accordion or mandoline (Spanish, German, or Italian mode, as in Chicago, or in London). This town dance, a counter to country folk-dance, is said to have started off at "get-the-rent" parties in USA, from Negro blues, *samba*, fox-trot etc. Anthropological reports list a curious number of titles—either in dance or music; from *Barrow Boy Blues; Snow-Man* or *Cocaine Fanny* or *Coca-cola Can-can; Teddy Boys Toddle; Homosexual Hop;* or *Overtime & Strike;* also *Double Time; Buggle-off Baby!* (all in 1957 - 58). The vocal element resembles West Indian Calypso; it has a basis but peculiar parodies are frequent.

SKIRT DANCE
A theatre dance, used in comedy or ·music-hall programmes, in which long and voluminous skirts are worn, often diaphanous or slit, through which the legs are glimpsed at intervals. The 19th century re-invention (for it is as ancient as women who flirt) is often credited to the American, Loie Fuller. An American claim dates from Clara Quality, who did a Skirt Dance at Niblos Theatre, New York City, in February 1890. Loie Fuller was then danc-

ing in London, where Kate Vaughan had, a decade before, performed her Skirt Dance in the Gaiety Theatre, the Olympic and other theatres. She was one of the first dancers to recover from the "ballet recession" that occurred about 1850, when Jenny Lind brought opera "back again", and she did it by discarding the ballet uniform and using the lacy black skirt. The dance is based on the simple technique of the rising and swirling leg—a slow pirouette.

SKOBO OR SCOBO (Denmark)

A comic men's dance, satirising "inspection" (such as the kit inspection of the modern army) probably much older, from *epi-scopus*, inspector. In French an allied term *escobar* implies "to shuffle" and this all men's dance uses the chief step as a shuffled and double shuffle—to the opposite man, to push him away, to move sideways to the next man. In Prussia are families bearing the name Skibble, said to imply shuffling peasants. Children in England have a double game they call *Bobbers and Skibbie* or *Bobbes and Kibbies*; it also has bouncing with a round stone or marble.

SKOMOROKHY (Russian)

Also *Iskomorokhy*—Mediaeval "jester in song", who danced and played instruments. With "songs of the seasons" and fragments of ancient ritual songs, he added satirical cracks directed at the official church and government agents of all kinds. They appear in the opera *Sadko* (Rimsky-Korsakov). They used the *gusla* (lyre) found in all Slavonic countries (e.g. Serbia), and the *balalaika* (triangular guitar), more recently ousted by the German accordion. This jester was the chief preserver of folk-song; and in the same way, of folk-dance forms. Familiar to visitors is the *chatushka* or topical ditty, similar to the West Indian *calypso** and with no more depth or durability, it challenges the authentic folk-song, as jazz ruins the folk-dance rhythm. Formerly the *skomorokhy* was, in his rare serious hours, sometimes associated (a rebel in religion as he was in politics) with the secession from the Russian Church; and his folk-songs or melodies were used for the hymns and chanting of the Khylisty (or Khristy) and the Skoptsi sects, who seceded even farther than the Raskolniki. Their extremists, who made much use of dance ritual and song, recruited from the Mediaeval jesters, who became known as *Istriani*, or the *stranniky* (in groups) or "wanderers". Some of them covered their anarchist beliefs by touring puppet shows: also a vehicle for scarifying jests against the *tchinovniki* (officialism generally).

SKOTSE TRIJE (Netherlands)

Dutch dance, established by the Frisians, but danced all over the country, resembling the *Quadrille** in form, though the movement has a basic *Polka* step; with no hop. The *Skotse Trije* is not Scottish; it is a square dance for eight couples, danced to music in 2/4 time. The name indicates Frisian Square; but the *Trije* may long ago have meant a form with a three-step. The figures may vary with melodies (with verses, sometimes polite), as from *Schoenma-kerke* (Shoemakers' Circle), or (in West Friesland) allusions to *Bonder in het Hooi* (Lost in the Hay). Another such melody (known at Terschelling) was entitled *Japie sta stil!* (Oh! Johnnie, stand still!), highly favoured for the May Queen dances.

SKY PACER (Ancient China)

The "Song of the Sky Pacer", or the "Sky Poem of Steps in Astronomy", is one of the oldest known astronomical rhymes. Astronomy and astrology were closely linked and men who did not actually read the sky, had to know the names of the constellations. The rhyme is attributed to Tan Hsuan Tau (circa. AD 589-618), from far older sources.[1] In sum, the *Song of Sky Pacer* (or Dancer) gives an outline *aide memoire* for students: by the astronomical fixations, related to the seasons, the astrological aspects could be extracted; and thus applied to governing and agricultural needs. Thus, in effect, the Sky Pacer supplies the cosmic chart; which in reflex mode, constitutes the superior plan of the temple rites. These charts were then "danced into vision" for lesser men, by the ruler and his colleagues, in the Temple of Heaven; for "The North Pole Central Palace is the Purple *Wei* Palace", and then in due sequence come the lesser ministers of state "who follow their stars". Yet "the four sky Directors lie dark within the Bushel", though "Bright are the seven stars of the Northern Bushel; the first of its lordly Rulers is called the pure pivot". This naming (of Sirius) is recalled by the modern concept that our galaxy is revolving round that immense star Sirius, as the central pivot; though this cosmos may again be dancing round some unknown greater centre. Thus the concept hinted by Plotinus (and earlier Hindu thinkers) that the "whole Cosmos is a dancing mystery", is again contemplated in this ancient Chinese poem; and accepted as a guide to terrestrial action, in submission to the vast scheme thus glimpsed. The structure of the ceremonial; its seasons, and its purposes, as planned in Imperial China, thus all endeavoured to follow in ritual the dance of the cosmos, with each successive phase in due season. The whole Chinese religious scheme developed

from this concept; and with it, their magnificent array of ceremonial rites and dances.
[1] *The Hall of Light.* (Chapter on *The Sky Pacer*) W. E. Soothill. London, 1952.

"SLEEPY" DANCE (Mexico)

A dance of the Mayo Indians, performed in the villages of San Ignacio and Navajoa, in the early morning. It follows one of the main figures of the *Matachines,** of which it forms part. Several times during the dance, the performers pretend to sleep. The music stops, dancers drop to the ground and, during a short pause, settle down as though to sleep, with their heads on their arms. When the music begins again, softly and slowly, the *monarca* (or captain) awakens, glances round, then returns to his sleeping position. This he repeats three times, but the third time, as the music gradually becomes louder and quicker, he leaps up and begins to dance, followed by all his companions. The *"Sleepy" Dance* may have had a sun worship origin in pre-Conquest days, before being taken into a *Matachines* organization.

"SMOKING HEADS" DANCE (New Hebrides)

A solo dance, performed by an old man, at the initial ceremony of "smoking" human heads for preservation after a cannibal raid. The object of the dance was to pacify the spirit of the dead man. The old man danced very precisely, chanting in a hoarse whisper. Lifting one foot he turned slightly and very slowly put it down, then lifted the other foot and put that slowly down. While he danced, the oldest man among a group of old men squatting round a fire, held in the smoke a human head impaled on a stick, while other heads were set on stakes in the ground.

SNAKE DANCE, HOPI (North America)

The culmination of a nine-day rain ceremony organized by the Antelope and Snake Societies of the Hopi* Indians. Secret rites are held in the *kiva** for seven days. On the eighth day the first dance outside is performed; and on the ninth day the *Snake Dance* takes place, nowadays before a crowded audience of visitors. During the first four days, rattle snakes and others are collected by members of the Snake Society, who go in pairs, the first day to the north, second day to the west, third to the south, and fourth to the east. Kept in the *kiva*, the snakes are used in secret rituals, during which they are allowed to strike harmlessly, thus losing some of their poison. On the ninth day they are carried to a bower in the plaza, and members of the two societies emerge, decorated with black and white paint, wearing a kilt, many necklaces, and a bunch of red feathers on top of the head. Parading in turn four times round the plaza, the priests of each society form into two facing lines before the snake bower. The dance is performed by the Snake priests in groups of three. Grasping a snake with his teeth, one man dances down the plaza; the second man, dancing close beside him, waves a feather in front of the snake's head to distract its attention, while the third man picks up the snake as soon as it is dropped. The first dancer then returns for another snake and the dance continues. The Antelope men receive the snakes from the third member of each group. When all the reptiles are used, a circle of cornmeal is made by the Chief Snake Priest, and divided into six sections representing the four directions, zenith and nadir, (cp. *Roppo,** Japan). Into this the snakes are thrown and covered with cornmeal. The ceremony ends with each dancer seizing with his hands, as many snakes as he can hold and rushing with them out of the village, where they are released, to carry news and purpose of the ceremony to the rain gods. It is considered most authentic (as done at Walpi) to hold the snake in the mouth, near the middle of its body, without additional hold by the hands. The fangs are not removed, but expert teamwork by the three dancers, with the previous dispersion of some of the venom in the *kiva*, prevents serious accidents.

SNAKE DANCE (India)

Has several forms. The *punnagavarali* (*raga*) is the melody used by experts to bring snakes from their haunts; they are captured and taken away to some distance. This *raga* is most effectively played, it is said, during night hours from 10.30 to 1.30. The exhibition form appears when the *punna-wallah* (snake charmer) carries his own pets, and shows them for money to those interested. The reptiles respond to the melody; and they rise and seem to "dance", swaying to and fro with the rhythm of the music, played usually on a simple *bin* (gourd flute). The stage form imitates these realistic modes for spectacular effect, in performances of Hindu Dance. The same *nagaswaram* (snake tune) may be employed—but there are no snakes—while the dancer only pretends to play. Finally there are the female contortionists who wriggle in voluptuous curves, hoping that their display will be mistaken for art.

SNURREBOK (Sweden)

A village dance (translated as *Twiddle Goat*) summarised briefly as a *komisk allmogedans*, a comedy country dance, is known widely in Sweden, as well as in Denmark; and can also be seen, in much the same form, in the Netherlands. The best known variant of this *Duitsche Tanz* (German Polka) is one danced in a village called *Haaksbergen;* the dance is known as *Haakse-bergentans.* All of these village dances belong to the same group of basic forms; first there is a "showing off parade", slow and even courtly; followed by a quicker *galop* or *polka.** The company stops, at a musical signal, to exchange courtesies by bows and smiles; and then resumes. In the main, we may assign them to the "courting dances", since, in several places, the man with his partner recites to the tune, an acknowledgement that he has "been out with his girl", which seems equivalent to "publishing the banns".

SOKOL—1 (Czechoslovakia)
A social League for Gymnastic and Plastic Exercises, founded in Bohemia by Dr. Tyrs, with the underlying purpose of political work for gaining freedom from Austrian domination. Eventually, this plan succeeded, led by Dr. Masaryk, only to fall victim to the Nazi scheme. The Sokol (meaning "Eagle") gained adherents in neighbouring countries. Their displays in a great stadium in Prague were notable events, every six years. Including forms of revived Greek dance in their training, they produced versions of Greek games; but extended this to mass exercises, with as many as 18,000 men moving simultaneously. The plastic training produced in some instances very attractive results. The Sokol attracted the attention of men such as Jaques Dalcroze, Rudolf Laban; and the Russian Lesgaft,* who later developed in Petersburg a similar institution; now known as the *Lesgaft Fizkultura Technikum.* The Sokol was finally abolished in Czechoslovakia; but was partially replaced by a version of the Scout Movement, taking its names from the Russian groups, The Young Pioneers. They include plastic exercises in their training

SOKOL—2 (Czechoslovakia)
The term *sokol* comes from the Yugoslav poetry, where *sokol* means falcon, the national hero. After several attempts from 1848, following the idea of the *Sokol* (following the ideals of Jan Amos Komensky (Comenius), the educator), a change in Austrian policy (1860) gave an opening. In Prague, a Czech majority on the City Council in 1861 encouraged this cultural development. Dr. Miroslav Tyrs was the prime mover; in 1862 the body was formed, with its designation *Sokol* in 1864. Thenceforward development was continuous. While major emphasis was placed on male athleticism, for the women and then the children, considerable attention was given to "plastic gymnastics", which culminated in dance movement, of a form and style that promoted the later German Modern Dance, which copied the Czechs, after the

Fourth *Slet* in 1901 at Prague. In the Fifth *Slet* (Congress) of 1917, some "scenes" or "living pictures" were prepared. They had been in 1889 to Paris for the First *Slet.* The *Sokol* took on an international aspect; during the 1914-1918 war, they fought to gain their own national freedom, with the encouragement of Dr. Masaryk. When Hitler invaded Czechoslovakia, the *Sokols* were destroyed; but recovered after his defeat; again to be ruined by the Russians after 1940. Dr. Tyrs, as a professor of Art History, was keenly interested in the aesthetic aspect of *Sokol;* and encouraged staging of "incidents of Greek culture", as well as plastic training for women. The Nazis copied parts of their *Jugenbund* from the *Sokol* system; though adding arms (as did Mussolini), which the *Sokol* never carried or used, being a profoundly democratic organization. The *Sokol* influence on body training through Europe, and in America, has been considerable.

SOMERSAULT, ALSO SOMERSET, SOMERSAUT (Old English, from Norman French)
A show movement in acrobatic work, rarely included in ballet; never in any ballroom or salon dance; and at a few places in eccentric modes of folk dance, as at the *Mela* or Indian Festival Fair (*Holi* or *Desehra*). Somersault implies a spin or inversion of the entire body in the air. When a dozen or score of expert Chinese acrobats are performing with exact group precision, the movements gain a certain spectacular quality. The move enters into some sports such as water diving. In circus terminology, different kinds of somersaults are known as: Monkey; Lion's; Arab's; or Carp's Leap.

SON—1 (Cuba)
An old dance-song, first mentioned in 1568, and popular in the Island for centuries. About 1916-17, popular composers in Cuba turned it into a stylised, highly syncopated ballroom dance, usually with an introduction for solo singer. The folk dance, meanwhile, continues, and with negro melodies and ritualistic words added becomes the *Son Afro-Cubano;* while in Guatemala the national dance, in basic 3/4 time with cross rhythm in 6/8 time, is called *Son Guatemalteco,* or *Son Chapin.* As a ballroom dance, the *Son* remained very popular until about 1950, when the *Mamba* began to supercede every other dance in *Cuba.*

SON—2 (Mexico)
A dance-song, *son* meaning literally "sound" or a "pleasant sound". The term became attached to Mexican dance-songs about the middle of the 18th century, presumably referring to the song rather

than to the dance. *Sones* are nevertheless danced, the form being identical with the *Jarabe*,* and these two, in their simplest forms, are the basis of many Mexican folk dances. *Sones* and *Jarabes* are danced very frequently by the "ordinary folk", in their every-day or fiesta clothes. Dancers face each other without touching, the girl lifting her skirt a little at the sides, the man dancing with hands behind his back and the upper part of his body stiff. *Sones* in the State of Vera Cruz, accompanied by harp, violin and guitar with one or two male singers, are famous for their gaiety, the girl matching the vigour of the man's steps. Some of the best dancers have migrated to the City of Vera Cruz, or to Mexico City, where stylised versions of *Sones Veracruzanos* and other dances (*Huapango*,* *Sandunga*,* *Jarabe*,* etc.) may be seen.

SONAJEROS (Mexico)
"Rattlers". Name of a society of youths in Jalisco (especially the town of Tuxpan), so-called after the large rattles which they carry during their dances. The rattle (*sonaja*) is made of metal plates arranged in four groups on a thick wooden handle. Accompanied by a flute and drum, the *Sonajeros* dance in a single line, moving through lively figures and steps. The select Society of Sonajeros has about thirty carefully chosen members, of whom some fifteen dance at a time, wearing red trousers over their usual white cotton suits, which are decorated with coloured ribbons. A black apron, pointed front and back, completes the costume.

SONGS OF ASCENTS (Arabic - Jewish)
A lunar ritual, celebrating phases by means of psalms, emphasised to affirm not only the lunar rhythms in three phases, but all fifteen nights as affecting human beings; and finally their record as "symbolism revealing the inner life". The biggest performance was given by Levites in Second Temple at Jerusalem, moving up the actual fifteen steps from the Women's Court to the Inner Court of the Second Temple. They moved slowly upwards, one step at a time, bearing harps and lyres, cymbals and trumpets, as they chanted of successive phases, until on the fifteenth they reached the Full Moon Splendour; and began the reversal series as they descended—this part receiving far less acclaim and less record. The whole round has a curious resemblance to the *Gitam* or song of the *gopis* (dairymaids) who serenaded Krishna in India, also as a very old ritual belonging to lunar worship; and now extended to him as the solar lord. In *rag-mala** paintings they are seen attired, fifteen in white or silver dress, and fifteen more in darker hues or blue or green. These mark the period denoted as "Light Fortnight" and "Dark Fortnight".

There is a similar ceremony performed by the lama-priests of Tibetan monasteries; as they enter the courtyard down a flight of stone steps. The *Mishnah* states that the fifteen steps correspond exactly to the fifteen *Songs of Ascents* (contained in the book of psalms. In total, these indicated both in the book of psalms). In total, these indicated both prayers and thanks for water.
[See *Joy of the House of Water Drawing*]

SONG OF DEGREES (Hebrew)
Ritual association of chanting with the reception "into the temple" by fifteen "steps", or signs (usually referred to the lunar mansions—twenty-eight or thirty in the month, making fourteen (plus one in the centre), on each side, as in Hindu Lunar symbolism). This was developed by the Khrestiani into the "Stations of the Cross".

SONG OF SONGS (Hebrew)
Collection of ancient dance-songs (in primal dramatic form) entitled broadly as *Shir-al-Shirin* (Song of Songs), printed in English as the *Canticles*, though this "Song of Solomon" is headed in Tyndale's Bible as *Balette of Balettes*. Dr. Cheyne in the *Encyclopaedia Biblica* (art. *Canticles*), traces them to a group of Syrian dance-songs, connected with wedding festivities; which later were used by Syrian and Greek Gnostics, as a base for one of their most important religious allegories. The Hebrew *Midrash* and the *Targum* are conclusive in their proofs that *The Song of Songs* originated as an allegory. What seems clear is that the Syriac-Jewish wedding (admittedly a religious ceremony), adopted the older allegory form as a chant, to go with the dances that followed through the seven days of the wedding feast. There are parallels in India: both for the usage of *Kirtans* (as from the days of the poet-reformer Chaitanya, in praise of the Dance of Krishna and Radha), and for the *Tantrik* ritual celebration (*kaula sadhana*) of the Mystic Marriage. G. R. S. Mead gives some of the translated text; from the Greek version of *The Wedding Song of Wisdom*. Singing of *Sophia* (Wisdom) the scribe writes:

"Her mouth is opened, and softly;
  Two and thirty are they who sing her praises . . .
Her bridesmen are grouped close around her,
  Seven in number, whom she hath invited;
Her bridesmaids also are Seven,
  Who lead the Dance before her.
And Twelve are her servants before her,
  Their eyes ever seeking the Bridegroom—
That at his coming they may be filled with
    Light".

Consult works by G. R. S. Mead: *Encyclopaedia*

Biblica; Jewish Encyclopaedia (art. *Song of Songs*); *Talmud.*

SORTILEGE (of the *Khitt* at Rome)

Or "Fortune Dance" (Latin Church) was a regular practice of "drawing lots". In early stages, the *sortilege* was a "choice of officials"—a legal selection, yet done by chance, by various methods. After democracy in church was abolished by Roman bishops, offices were held by appointment from above, not election from below. Only cardinals may now vote. Thus *sortilege* became unofficial and disapproved; gradually it sunk to "bad manners" then "heresy" and then to "sin", alleged of the "witch coven" of the village. It was then murky magic. Despite denigration, the practice still continues today; having had many variegations. The original dance changed slowly. The "dividing of the cloak" by drawing lots is included in the New Testament, as being done by "Roman soldiers". Virgil is mentioned as a magician; later his book was utilised for *Sortes Virgilianus.*

SOULE, SOUL, SEALE, the Dance of

From the ancient traditions of Babylonia, every officer of note carried his own personal seal, and his seal of office. This official seal had to be attached (by contra-impression) on all official documents handled by him. This was the charter basis; done in pendant wax replica. The historical development separated the ritual from the ceremonial : the object became (in one direction) the notorious breastplate of the Jewish priests (reduction of their zodiac, with twelve stones each bearing a name and position. From these, the practice of using "birthday stones" followed). In secular usage, the seal became the Great Seal (as of the Chancellor), and continues in Britain as a basis of picturesque ceremony. In popular tradition (as in France), the ceremonial continued as a dance ritual; as at a place named from it, Soule. The reckoning of population was done in numbers of "souls". (Russia.)

SOURYAKARI (Bulgaria)

Singer-dancers of the Bulgarian New Year Festival. Leaders are (in each village), *Mont-zec* (young man) and *Mom-mei* (maiden), who follow a ritual, containing dance, chanting, and magical ceremonies; some like the English New Year period. Every male carries a branch ornamented with red ribbons, old coins, topped by the image of Sourya, the sun god of the Year. No work is done before the New Year Day; they all fast. Betrothed maids prepare *platiy* (a cake) and stick in it various roots or young plant shoots, each symbolising "house, or mill, vineyard, horse, hen, or cat, etc.", denoting the family possessions. A large old silver coin,

babka-and, is placed in the cake before cooking; it has a red silk thread tied as a cross; and is regarded as a symbol of great fortune. On the round table *paralya*, the family gather round the festal cake, with dry vegetables, corn, a lighted taper, and a censer. The ritual dance is done by the head of the family. He walks in measured tread, first in three circles, then to the "four quarters", while invocations and rhythmic chants continue. The taper is then preserved. Next they cut the cake; the objects now suggest horoscopes. After midnight, these young couples promenade the street with torches, singing and dancing along to call on friends; they are recompensed with presents and return only as dawn breaks, to their own domiciles. The sun god in India is called Surya.

SOUSEDKA (Czechoslovakia)

Village festal dance, used at weddings in Bohemia, and danced as a *ronde* in slow triple time. Traditional tunes show many variations, from which Dvorak selected three of the most popular, written in his *Slavonic Dances* (Nos. 3, 4 and 16).

SOVIET BALLET (Russia)

Continues, in all its essentials, in the technical and stylistic standard of its predecessor, the tsarist imperial ballet, as taught and performed in Moscow and Petersburg. Ballets continued during the stormy years of the Revolution from 1917, but a decade had elapsed before the first definitely Soviet ballet was produced. In 1927 the "revolutionary ballet" of *The Red Poppy* was produced in Moscow, after a preliminary version had been seen in Kharkov. Technical excellence had never faded; brilliant dancers were available, trained in the Vaganova system, chiefly in Leningrad. The Soviet ballet system includes (since 1936 officially) principles of dance advocated by Isadora Duncan, François Delsarte, Jaques Dalcroze, merged with the best that the Italian, French, or Danish schools have been able to offer. Despite the desire to produce modern themes, absence of marked creative power continued (as it had during the 19th century), though technical power was never better; and most of the older classical ballets continued to be performed. *Swan Lake* was revised only with a fuller version of original music; as was *The Sleeping Beauty* (1937). The first really new production was the masterpiece, *Bakchiserai Fontan* (1934); yet this work is based on a Pushkin poem; as was *Captive of the Caucasus* (1937). The two leading companies, with their respective academies of ballet dance and general education, thrive in Moscow and Leningrad; yet new ballets are still slow to appear. No one can accept a version of *Romeo and Juliet* (1939) as a revolutionary ballet. The most notable development has been the accession of stage artists, from the affiliated Republics of the Soviet Union, to expert tuition in ballet styles of dance; who are then used to stimulate performances of opera and ballet in the various Republican capital cities. The union of the advanced technical style with ancient local legendary themes has evoked some notable works. After Ekaterina Geltzer (who retired after her final success in *The Red Poppy*), the notable Soviet dancers have been Marina Semyonova, Olga Lepeshinskaya, and Galina Ulanova, with newer stars as Maya Plisetskaya and Raissa Struchkova. The men perform finer dancing than any western company has been able so far to show.

SPAGNOLETTO (Italy)
Cesare Negri gives *Lo Spagnoletto* as the Italian version of a Spanish rustic dance called *Espanoletas*. He taught it as a popular version, in Milan and other Italian towns, during the 16th century; and describes the dance in his book,[1] where it is danced by two couples who form a square. The form is simple and artificial; while the opening *riverenza breve in saltino* (with another at the end), seems to indicate that the rustic character of the dance has been much polished.
[1] *Nuove Inventione di Balli.* Cesare Negri. 1604.

SPANISH DANCE (Modern)
As with Ballet, many exponents of Spanish dance have permitted a flashy mode of exhibitionism to dilute the purity of style that was characteristic of the few leading dancers, especially in the style known as *Flamenco*. Vicente Escudero (one-time partner of Argentina), ventured to state his opinions in his book *Mi Baile* (*My Dance*), and, more succinctly, in a smaller publication describing *Decalogue on Pure Flamenco Dance.*[1] He deals variously with technical, emotional, and mental factors. Technically, he desires clarity of style and fusion of accent, personal with national; while rejecting foreign intrusions as incompatible with aesthetic or plastic purity. His male style demands "quiet hips"—that is, the pelvic swing must not be feminine, but reveal sobriety of response. Especially he requires the Spaniard to dance in style grave and austere; if he reveals strong passions, their expression must be achieved in reserved movements. He uses a sustained rhythm, fully appropriate to the dramatic theme of his dance, rather than seeking to display merely the personality of the dancer. The male dancer must avoid all feminine traits : the pelvic swing, thrusting arms, spreading fingers, or facile head and facial movements. He rejects the "circus style"; especially hoping for the art of dancing slowly (so much approved by Havelock Ellis in his writing on Spain), and would ignore

A Spanish "couple dance" of Aragon Province. Rondalla, usually danced by villagers at weddings.
SPAIN

artificial aids like metallic shoe heels, or special stage boards. His respect for tradition affirms that the dancer shall appear in true Spanish garb; avoiding billowing sleeves, wide-necked shirts, and fancy silk sashes. These principles could be studied with benefit by all folk-dancers.
[1] *Mi Baile* (1943) *Decalogue on Pure Flamenco.* Vincente Escudero. Madrid (1951).

SPASIRKA (Czechoslovakia)
Literally, a "walk-dance" (from German, *spaziergangen*), implying the dance of the village swain and his girl, when "going for a walk", alternately fast and slow. On the stage, it becomes a flirting dance; the music alternates in slow and quick 4/8 time. A specimen may be found in Dvorak's *Slavonic Dances* (No. 13), written as a piano duet.

SPELL OF SEVEN STEPS (Ceylon)
Is accompanied in dance by a ballad of seven quatrains—the *Hat Adiya Dola* ("Offering to Demonic"), and is given in full by Pertold[1] so that it explains the other Seven Step Dances (*Siebensprung** etc.). The *adi* (Sanskrit) is the single step. *Hat* equals "seven". This Sinhalese ritual is used

primarily as exorcism (for the invocation, or reverse, see *Pilli-Yakun-Nattima**). *Dola* or *dole* is "offering to daemonic powers" (i.e. lower nature-energies), as compared with *puda* (or *puja*) as "offering to gods—high powers"). The central part of the system is the naming or identification (by the exorcist) of the invading powers that cause the disease (it is read as a mode of "possession" rather than as any material ill), and thus creating a diagnosis or statement. The dance is then performed, to break down, one by one, each focus of evil magnetism that exists in the sick man. For this, his imagination is enlisted, by the dancer's efficient bedside manner; as he dances round to suitable rhythms. The seven quatrains are sung, making ritual steps, ending in the upspring; with offerings of seven kinds. These are prepared, laid out separately; and given in turn with a drop of lime-juice (not to the patient). It must not be assumed that by "demon" the Sinhalese doctor-magician imagines any such entity as the Roman "devil". He sees, rather, personalised "nature-forces" which have somehow found a focus in the sick man. To understand this method it is essential to know what is *Mana,** with the twin modes of *Totem** and *Tabu.** Dance is an active and essential element in this curative hypnosis combined with magnetism.
[See *Siebensprung* (Germany); *Saut Basque; Zevensprong* (Netherlands); *Zazpi Jausiak* (Basque)]
[1] Text of Ballad *Hat Adiya Dola*, by Dr. O. Pertold, in *Archiv Orientalni*. (Praha) No. 2—June 1929.

SPIELMANN (German)
Mediaeval player-minstrel. The term *spiel* has broad affiliations; basically it signifies "to play" in any form—from drama to mime-dance. One of its earlier modes is *Gottes-spiel*, meaning the Parable or Miracle Play that was shewn in Teuton lands by early Greek missions, to become even more widely known as *Goddes-spell* or gospel. The magical term "spell" is another form: this is the incantation or *out-spieling* of the magical rhythm, as the dance unfolds. Analogous is *spiegel*, meaning "mirror" in every way: applied to many early books, such as "Mirrour for Magistrates", and familiar in the name of Tyl Eulenspiegel, or "Tyl of the Owl-Mirror" (The Mirror of the Fool's Wisdom). *Das Spielman* figures in many a German poem or story; latterly he has been systematically denigrated by clerical propaganda (as with *Don Juan* and *Doktor Faust* likewise) until, quite unjustly, *Spielman* turns from the simple player to a devil dancer. *Espiel* is "to see" the play or dance. *Spiel* is to play; but *spiel-karte* is a playing card, formerly the "role" of the player, the "card of the play". *Schauspiel* is theatre-play; *schauspielhaus* is the theatre itself.

SPIESSTANZ (Rumania)
"Spit Dance". Name given by Saxon communities in Rumania to a dance performed at christenings. Two roasting-spits were crossed on the ground, and the dancer moved in and out of the "angles" or spaces. Dancers took turns to perform, the first dancer being the baby's grandfather, who would sing about how agile and nimble he was, and how well he danced. If he was too old or infirm, the godfathers started the dance, and if they were unable to do so, the midwife was paid a small sum to perform the ceremony.
[See *Saxon Dance in Rumania*]

SPORT IN DANCE
Is principally connected with modern ballroom dancing, in which there is no drama and no contest, until we enter the various competition systems. These are chiefly found in two related systems: first the national and local series of "events" divided between Professionals on one side, and Amateurs on the other, whereby a classified fame-for-the-year is attained. The other is the junior system, offering similar awards to crowds of dance students, chiefly in classes or schools. The whole emphasis is "the feat" with "correctness and style". Students may obtain a selection from a wide array of certificates, seals, medals and cups. Teachers may gain similar fame, chiefly in competing for "Championships" which rarely bring them cash but afford professional renown, which presumably in turn adds a halo of success that can be turned to advantage, to bring more pupils who will in due time, advance also in the sport. Large crowds of dancers take much interest; though attendance does not rival football or cricket or boxing events. But boxers and cricketers are not noted for paying for tuition. The *Palais de Danse* is often a local centre for this harmless and normally healthy pastime. Plums in Sport Dance are, as in other sports, relatively few. Teachers can, in London, reap a useful income from giving tuition to wealthy amateurs. They can occasionally get useful ocean vacations, by travelling, say, to South Africa, as Judges for (a) local competitions or (b) for advanced students who want to become teachers and will pay examination fees. There are also (c) lecture demonstrations, at leading hotels. London newspapers run Dance Competitions; and pay well for professional help; while the Blackpool Tower finds that dance competitions bring in crowds from their "Two Counties"—whence many of Britain's finest dancers emerge. We must regret the paltry type of "cup" obtained from trade silversmiths, and inflicted on dancers. They should at least be given a work of art—there are plenty available.

SPORTS (England)

"Dance" among legalised games. James I issued "Declaration of Sports" in 1618. This followed action by Puritans (at first in Lancashire) to enforce "strict observance" like a Jewish Sabbath. James, at the time, decided against the Puritans. Local villagers continued "Sunday Sports" having obtained "permission to use Sports after Morning Service". Hence the Declaration of Sports was published as an Order in Council, first for the Diocese of Lancashire, stating what *were* "lawful games". These games were archery, dancing, leaping and vaulting, and setting up maypoles. Regulations stated that no-one would be "allowed" to enter any sports who had not "attended service". The clerics objected to any secular supervision; the Order was withdrawn. Next came an attempt to suppress Village Wakes in Somerset. In 1633, Judge Richardson ordered cessation. Archbishops objected to the civil encroachment on "rights of clergy". People were friendly at wakes and dances, and if they had no fun "they would go into tippling houses". Charles I. republished the *Book of Sports*, but resistance was even greater, and (disapproving also of Charles), the *Declaration* was publicly burned by the Long Parliament (People's Parliament) in 1644.

SPRINGAR, SPRINGDANS (Norway)

Animated pair dance with music always in 3/4 time, but the dancers' steps form a counterpoint in different time—2/4 or 4/4. Change from one figure to the next is indicated by the leader with a stamp or hand-clap, but as there is nothing arbitrary about the number of bars for each figure, dancers obey this direction only when they are ready to do so. *Springar* has nine different steps, and is a dance in which partners show their individual qualities—the man his virility and accomplishment, the girl her skill and grace. Singing often accompanies the dance, the melody having a drone bass. *Springar* is related to the Polsdans, from which has developed the *Spring Pols.**

SPRINGER (Germany)

A jumper or dancer, a *docke;* equivalent to *sautereau* (French) or *saltarello* (Italian). A term applied mostly in mediaeval times, to the more acrobatic type of dancer, showing at the *Messe;* also a lively puppet and its dance.

SPRING FESTIVAL DANCES

Are world wide and very numerous. They should be examined in relation to the Winter Festivals: usually a Death-and-Birth story related to the Year, symbolised in mask or person. English Spring Festivals are balanced now on a May Day celebration.

Morris Dances survive in a few places. Older characters included the Robin Hood group: Robin, Marian, Frere Tuck, Little John, Will Scarlet. France had Marianne; Wales had Marion or Merion; Spain had Juan and Latin Italy had Faust (passing to Germany) while Russia had her own Little Peter (Petrushka) for Butter-week. Scandinavia had Kupalo with Höder and Baldur; France had also her Jeanne d'Arc. For all of these, suitable persons were elected to play the part for the occasion; they are not "historical characters" though at times a Jeanne of Rouen or a Robin of Sherwood would appear to attain reality, masking the individual.

SPRING POLS (Norway)

A dance of the Osterdal forest region, for couples in a circle. To lively music in 3/4 time, dancers move round a circle anti-clockwise, each couple at the same time turning clockwise. Having three figures, the dance begins with partners facing, the girl outside. Moving anti-clockwise round the circle, they proceed with running steps, followed by the *Rundpols* ("Round Pols"), in which couples turn clockwise, as in the old-fashioned *waltz.** In the second figure, *Rundpols* is preceded by a hopping step with arms swung down and across; while in the third figure the *Rundpols* follows a step in which partners let go of hands and make a turn away from each other.   [Cp. *Springer; Aattetur*]

SQUARE DANCE—1

A modern folk-dance, developed in America by a fusion of the old round and chain dances with European ballroom *Quadrilles,** *Lancers,** *Cotillons.** In square formation, the figures of the *Quadrille* were "called" by the Dancing Master, but the sequence was known to the dancers, the calling being merely a reminder. American Square Dancing gives the Caller added importance, since he controls the form of the dance. He may arrange any of the figures used in Square Dancing and the *Running Set** (a Square Dance in quicker tempo), in whatever order he chooses, since they have no set sequence. The dancers are thus dependent upon the Caller's instructions, which he shouts out in sing-song style by means of a set of jargonic rhythms. A smooth, rhythmic walk is the general movement, with a frequent pivot step. The set consists of four couples in square formation, and the figures are joined by a "connecting" figure, with which the dance usually begins and ends. Accordion; piano and fiddle; or dance band, may accompany the Square Dance, while clapping hands frequently emphasise the rhythm. In the popular "Swing" sequence, two men link to swing the girls around, lifting them off the floor. This dance form was used by Catherine Littlefield in her ballet *Barn Dance;* but the accompaniment to the *Square Dance* rarely rises to symphonic heights; or the dancing to marked virtuosity. Sometimes a pseudo-folksy "farm costume" provides a character dress for exhibition dancers.

SQUARE DANCE — 2
The typical military exercise as dance, with four sides or two opposed sides; also the "hollow square" of infantry defence. The name derives from *escu* — "the warriors" of each ancient clan in Keltic period. They had ION-escu "People of Iona", later "the Jones" or, in Rumania, the Ionescu and many other families, *escu.* Western Europe knew the *escu-ura,* who became the esquires in chivalry system; then *escu* equals shield (defence). Later *escu-ad becomes* squad; and *escu-ad-rouel* (people's circle) becomes quadrille. The military influence remains. In clerical terms, the two sides of the quire (in Greek as phon and antiphon) developed as "two voices". The typical square folk dance required two sides, set in some kind of opposition. These remain, for example, in some Morris dances; and the Abbots Bromley *Horn Dance;** and in many games. Later the barn dance took on this character of two sides; but the circular form was also joined. Modern square dances include many variants of the original square; with movements along the side; across the centre; and in parallel with male and female partners. The English children's game "Gathering Knots of May" indicates a long row which advances and retreats, using the nursery rhymes as a chant; while the ancient Greek dance called *Pyrrhic** shows the warrior type, one with lance and shield against one with dagger and shield. Much of the symbolic form is echoed in the game on the chessbord, which is a reduced scale battlefield of squares within a square.

SQUAW DANCE (Apache and Navajo Indians, New Mexico and Arizona)
Formerly, as an early item in the War Dance (precedent to raiding) came the *Squaw Dance,* which was, in effect, part of the "marriage market" or "selection ceremony", lasting three days. Young unmarried men "sang" the dance. They began drumming at dusk, on a moonlit night, chanting softly, until the round rose in volume to intense shouting. This was a signal. Tribal maidens then entered in pairs, watched by mothers; and slowly they began taking partners. Drumming changed to dancing rhythms, and the dance latterly was described as being much like "American country dance" in form and tempo. Each dance continued some ten to fifteen minutes, when the man gave some small present to the girl; maybe she returned

to the elders, or perhaps she danced again with him, swinging her fluted skirts and singing some words she recalled.

STAGE NAMES (Noms de Théâtre; Bühne-namen)
Are professionally recognised labels under which a performer chooses to dance (or sing, act, or play instruments). The practice arises from the monastic requirement of "ceasing the worldly name" and "taking on the new name" — as Brother So-and-So, or Sister What's-it, in the new environment. This custom was reinforced by internal stage professional practice (it still endures) of naming any player not by his own cognomen or praenomen, but by the character which he portrays. This was evident in the Italian *Commedia dell' Arte;* and it became most pronounced in the mediaeval gild practice in England, since when many a family has accepted and used a name that began local recognition as the name of a part in a miracle play. They are not to be confused with clan names (as in Scotland) or communal names, such as "Jones" (from Iona's) and "Smith" (from Es-mithras) or occupational names. Stage names have existed regularly in English Theatre since the Restoration period. Many players found it discreet to drop names that advertised obsolete political affiliations (Roundhead or Cavalier), or anti-clerical family tendencies (the Puritan names — Barebones, Lackluck). The invasion of Italian Opera induced some high-class English singers to visit Italy; to return with Italian cover-names, and thus to meet the induced snobbery of London, educated to accept only an Italian name as a guarantee of "Fine Art". Next the system was applied to ballet : many honest cockney girls went to Paris for a six-month tour; and returned with accent plus *nom-de-theatre;* and thus got more *reclame* and a higher salary. This practice accounts for the apparent absence of many high-class British artists of song and dance in late 18th and early 19th century lists. Finally, the advent of the Russian Ballet in 1911 led to the habit of adding "ovsky" or "ova" to English names; and a new regiment of "Russian women" spread over Europe. Thus it has been calculated that Anna Pavlova had some 2,375 "genuine Russian" pupils, now resident mostly in USA, performing, teaching or preaching. There is one technical fact that justifies a change of name. The original family name (especially Polish multi-consonantal) products, are far too long to get printed in full, or with accuracy. There is something managerial to be said for reduction of polysyllables to something that "the public can remember".

STANDARD DANCES
Are forms imposed by (a) court etiquette, as by a

chamberlain in his "conditions of admission" (see Almack*) or (b) by an academy in its system of teaching; or (c) by a professional group, usually a national body and (at least in its beginnings) usually self-appointed. These conditions may be observed in — the court presentations and court balls; the academies of ballet tuition; and in the professional associations (as, for example, in England) which endeavour to impose standard styles and forms of dance for the popular ballroom. The basic plea, like that in the horse-racing industry, is two-fold. We are told that racing exists to promote improvement of stock. So it does, but only horses for more racing, as is now parallel with the motor industry. The commercial car is not the racing car. The racehorse is not the military horse, the draught horse, or the hunting hack. The standardised ballroom dancers, urged on by competitions, with arrays of gold and silver cups, stars and commendations, produce merely more standard dancers, with more artificial style. On the other hand, an accepted "style" offers models for imitation by adolescent dancers, as a phase of their party manners, which is a necessary element in social education. In this phase, the ballroom dance is parallel to the earlier corroboree (and indeed in some USA variations, such as bepop and similar eccentricities) merges too closely with the native ceremonials. Notably in the USA, no national style of ballroom dance exists; partly because "teachers" begin with six whole months of previous training; or because the drive for "new fashions" with the necessity of going to classes to learn the slight alterations, provides a commercial twist, as in millinery. In ballroom dance, there are now four standard dances: foxtrot (faux-trotte), waltz or valse; tango and rumba. With variations, these have ruled some forty years and teachers from other nations come to copy the idea. The ballroom dance ruins folk-dance; since, beyond "correct behaviour" it has no meaning; and serves feebly in lieu of the ancient marriage market (debutantes' dance). Standards in academic or stage dance serve other necessities, notably in any new company, meeting for the first time, agreeing to dance chiefly in some known academic standard method.

STANDARDS IN DANCE
Are balanced between arbitrary imposts of persons in temporary authority; and those inherited habits, by custom, and tradition. Science is an endless search for "eternal standards" to be expressed by way of formulae, which will be entirely impersonal and non-human. No such standards can be expected or found in Dance. A standard presents an accepted norm of working operations; useful only because it is agreed. Such a standard is the English yard,

which is not accepted by the French, who perversely prefer their metre. Many commercial "standards" are blatant swindles against the consumer (as in "trade names", customs, sizes, etc.), but in Dance the standard style tends to be the familiar mode. Here we come in contact with "fashion" versus "tradition". Many dance standards have no more rational meaning than a woman's hat; but we may compare these curiosities with the natural standards of orchids or bird plumes, not forgetting that the "standard snow flake" is eternally hexagonal or star-shaped with endless variations in each example. Some standards attempt to discipline style: as in current ballroom standards of the "four dances". But this authority is itself arbitrary: a seizure of power, which some other groups deny. Yet, some technical agreement there must be, to permit of performance of any dance other than a wild solo (even academic!), and we come to the comparison with language. There is no practical "one-man language" — the poet must speak in the tongue that his hearers know; a fact too often forgotten by ballet-fakers, who try to invent "new words" instead of giving expression in new ways to familiar words and relations. Standards are thus (a) technical, (b) emotional or social, and (c) stylistic. We cannot avoid some contact with all the sides of this triangle in devising any new work of art.

STANISLAVSKI INSTITUTE (London)
Organised in London, in 1962 on the basis of the Theatre School run by George Martin, to teach and examine the Method, or "producing system" used by the great Russian Theatre Master. K. S. Stanislavski was born in Moscow in 1870, in a rich mercantile family of textile manufacturers named Alexiev. After his early education — including unbroken interest in amateur Theatre, he had the famous 1898 meeting, with his colleague Nemirovich-Danchenko, at the Slavyansky Bazaar Hotel. This building had its own small theatre attached, used by them for rehearsals and small productions. As a direct result, the Moscow Art Theatre was born. Stanislavski developed his system slowly in the wake of several Russian poets and mystics; by 1906 he had set it in its first conscious order. During this period, Nemirovich-Danchenko was working on parallel lines with opera: he desired the 'acting singer' as his colleague sought to unite dramatic realism with stage convention. In this work Alexander Gorski, of the Moscow Ballet Theatre, displayed much interest from his first arrival from Petersburg in 1898. He sought to extend the technical classicism of Petipas into the prose of gesture (or mime) allied with the poetry

of motion (or dance). There was a continual interchange of visits. The dancer Isadora Duncan and the Russian poet Alesandr Blok brought further impetus: one in performance and the other in theme. In both of these artists, the Moscow Arts Theatre displayed great interest; and Blok's play *Balagan* (*Puppet Booth*) was produced soon after Maeterlinck's *Blue Bird*. His poetic drama *Rose and Crown* had 200 rehearsals at the Art Theatre (but no public performance); closely observed by Stanislavski's students, V. Meyerhold, Alex Tairov and Nicolai Okhlopkhov. To and from Moscow and Petersburg the discussions ranged; the practice developed; and the experiments of Vera Kommissarshevskaya at her Green Theatre were seen by many dancers, not least a girl known as Agrippina Vaganova. She became in 1916 the head of the Petrograd Ballet School, where Gorski's system had been adopted. She called her development of *adagio* as *cantilena*, the 'singing dance' and it appeared in the stage work of her famous pupils Marina Semyonova, Olga Lepechinskaya, and Galina Ulanova. In this unified system, still not fully worked out, the Soviet Ballet has developed its integrated style.[1] In Moscow the work of Alex Gorski continued over a quarter of a century to his death in 1924.

[1] "... the problems of teaching young dancers the art of acting have suggested the necessity to apply Stanislavski's system to choreography ... the application of the system to choreography has long been the subject of discussion in ballet circles. The way this can be done is not yet clear". (Pages 46 - 47, *Ballet School of the Bolshoi Theatre*. Y. Bocharnikova & M. Gabovich. Moscow, 1959.)

STEP

As the basic bodily movement in all dance, may be compared with vowels and consonants in speech. The stride is the dynamic vowel movement; the contact of foot, as static step, is the formative halt; as the limitation of form by a consonant shapes the force of a vowel into intelligible speech. Step ranges from the naturalistic infant toddling, or the firm adult march of utility, to the fantasy "step" of *entrechat*, or other variations "in the air". Individual steps are disciplined by rhythm; and by their association with a group, moving in rhythm. Here it is not possible to describe, or further to define, the essential character of thousands of steps, that appear in dance through the centuries; while those of classical ballet, and of many traditional forms, are now to be found described in a series of technical books. Finally, accurate steps have to be learned from a competent teacher: that is, one who can *do* them; and who can *analyze* their form, and so explain them rationally to the student. Artificial step develops into Tap. The simplest formal step, in dance style, is that known in the Hellenic *kanon;* that of "one step = one musical note = one vocal syllable", simultaneously; which is closely equivalent to the form and construction of the military march and its music. This affirms the importance of percussion, which is so predominant in European music. Each language has its word for "step" — *pacé, pas, pada*, etc., with direct equivalent terms in music — note, beat, tala.

STEPANOV NOTATION SYSTEM (Petersburg, Russia)

Is a specialised scheme of ballet record, devised by Vladimir I. Stepanov (1866 - 1896), when he was a teacher in the Ballet Section of the Imperial Theatre School in Petersburg. With Dr. Lesgaft,* this brilliant teacher formulated his recording system; and eventually they published a book in French.[1] Among leading students of the Stepanov system were Nicolai Serguéeff and A. A. Gorsky, later of Moscow Bolshoi Theatre. All three of these men made records of the current Petipas ballets. Gorsky's volumes remain in Moscow; another set is in the archives of the Maryinsky Theatre (now Kirov Theatre, Leningrad), while Serguéeff was able to bring his set of twenty-three ballet records when he left Russia in 1920. The Stepanov system differs from other notation systems, in that it begins with the full stage and the full ballet company, with the parallel passages of music, page by page. Other systems record movements of the individual dancers; and hope to bring them together in production. Nicolai I. Serguéeff (1876 - 1952) contacted Sergei Diaghileff later in Paris (1920) and the two masters were able to reproduce *The Sleeping Beauty* ballet in London (1921) with the aid of these full records. Later the *maestro* was employed at the Sadler's Wells Ballet, where he reconstituted some Russian Petipas ballets with a much smaller company; and finally with the International Ballet (of London), where similar revivals, with more accuracy, were reproduced, until the time of his death. Though it is said that Serguéeff guarded his records with great secrecy, he permitted the present writer (and others, such as Pierre Tugal, *Danse Archives*, Paris), to examine them. An article with a reproduction of a page appeared in *Dance Magazine* (New York),[2] which shows the unique combination devised by Stepanov. From this set of records, the classical Russian ballet revival was alone made possible, in Western Europe.

[1] *Alphabet des Mouvements du Corps Humaine.* V. I. Stepanov. Paris, 1892.
[2] "Nicolai Serguéeff". W. G. Raffé. *Dance Magazine* (July 1950, pages 14, 15, 16, 35).

STEYRISCHER TANZ (Styria, Austria)
A couple dance in 3/4 time, accompanied by three-part singing and syncopated hand-clapping representing the rhythm of threshing. After waltzing, the men form a group in the centre, while the girls continue to waltz, either alone or in pairs, round the circle. In four-line verses called *Gstanzln*, one man leads the singing, the others taking the parts, while the girls continue to waltz. Each verse is followed by clapping in four rhythms — *Vorpaschen* first; *Zuahipaschen* second; *Trittern* third; *Sextern* providing syncopation. After the clapping, men and girls begin the dance again, the whole being repeated five or six times. To finish the evening the *Steyrischer Auf-Pasch* is played when, after singing and clapping, each man takes his neighbour's partner, and so continues until all have danced together. At each round small sums of money are given to the band. *Steyrischer* is the local form of the *Ländler*.*

STILT DANCE
A crude dance performed by men walking on a pair of stilts; celebrating their vocational work in showing off technical ability. Naturally such dances exist only in flat, marshy districts (e.g. Landes or La Camargue in Southern France — *bouche du Rhone*), where there is a local need for such devices to move through hunting places. Occasionally stilts have been brought into small towns for ceremonial processions; they enable the money-collectors to approach second-floor windows with their bags. For Carnival, an exaggerated clown costume, with long legs covering the wooden stilts, is thus used. In Mexico is a stilt dance called *Zanco*,* and stilt dancers are called *Monigotes*. In Dahomey, West Africa, at villages of Savalon and Paouignan bordering on Lake Moukoue, stilt-dancers perform on certain occasions. They wear multi-coloured glass beads and perform extraordinary feats. In the Austrian Tyrol at the end of Winter, boys walk on stilts from house to house. They drive out the symbol of Winter (an old witch) to make way for Spring (a young girl).
[See *Seven Maccabees* (Belgium); *Mysore Stilt Dance* (India); *Zanco* (Mexico)]

STIMULANTS for Dancers
Are used by many professionals. The great Marie Lloyd kept a dozen small "stouts" in the wings; and often would drink the lot during one evening. Some use tobacco (not commended) and others take beef-tea drinks two hours before. Mexican Indian dancers are allowed to use *mescaline* only on specially important festal occasions; South Americans chew coca leaves; others use *cacao theobroma* nut. In Europe alcohol in some mode has been a favourite for centuries; the Italian Commedia players used liqueur. Somerset knew of mead and cider for the New Year *Was-Heil* dances. Professional dancers learn not to eat or drink anything too near to any performance; they make it up afterwards. Russian dancers do not fortify their work with *vodka*; even after the show at supper, they take wine for choice. Drugs like morphia, cocaine, novocaine etc. are slow methods of suicide for any dancer. In Japan, *geisha*ered* or *maiko*redered* take tea (*chanoyu* is a tea ceremony), while the Scots have been known to imbibe *usque-baugh* ("water of life") for which the modern commercial substitute is hardly equivalent. Tatars use *yoghurt* and *koumiss* (fermented mares' milk), popular also in Yugoslavia, where numerous centenarians dance at weddings, fortified by *rakya* (plum brandy).

STORE DISPLAY DANCE (Britain, USA, etc.)
Keen publicity men have occasionally utilised performances of dance to provide a basis of advertising for some commodity or service. While it is quite common to see girls attired in special costume, acting as ushers or programme girls at notable events, the use of dance episodes for display involves more creative work. The Lentheric Perfume Co. Inc., used in USA department stores, two dancers, who performed several three- or five-minute episodes contrived to give point to one or other of the named perfumes there being sold. In Chicago a confectionary firm had similar shows. In England, the Wool Sales Board has put on shows and films, advertising wool; while Ford Motor Company ran performances during a World Fair. The development of commercial television will doubtless extend this kind of dance display; but the difficulty is always to discover — not only suitable dancers — but sufficiently striking ideas, suitable for dance form.
[See *Commercial Ballet*; *Merchandising by Dance*]

STORNELLA (Italy; mediaeval)
A melody (and its dance) usually with some verses, associated chiefly with love-songs and marital arguments. This term indicates a "mock battle" and was associated with the French *tourney* or *tournament*, an ornamental fight; performed, often with introductory music and singing, by gentlemen invested in metallic attire. The ornate coats-of-mail, now in museums, may remind us of hard facts. They weigh eighty pounds or even ninety pounds. The valiant knight had to be attired by his valet, and hoisted on to his horse (a smaller animal than our modern draught-horse); and if he was unseated, he could not easily arise. The *stornella* was the little *estorney*. The "clerks" carried on parallel terms, from which "attorney" reminds us of the costly and often

inefficient method of purchasing law to obtain justice, which still governs us. The *stornelle* were confined mostly to "matrimonial cases"—the "courts of love"—and we may associate them with procedure of the graver mode, as we link the *strombotta** (or *strombosta*) with the lower ranks of Italian citizens. Highest of all, *troubadours** and *trouveres** wrote poems, sang them and slowly danced, especially at the feasts which followed the tournament.

STRANNIKI (Russian—plural; *strannik*, singular)
The wandering Russian or Polish minstrels, who begged their way from village to village; sometimes with puppet-shows, always with some instrument (usually *balailaka*) for song and dance. The term derives from the same root as *istria* (pre-Roman, Etruscan term) for players, actors, dancers, mimes. As they appeared mostly at festivals, it became *istria-ana-ki*. They had a sort of religious bias in that they retold biblical myths; but they were most renowned for their satirical couplets, like the early Comedia players in Italy. In contrast with the Russian *skomorokhi* (jesters), the *stranniki* were unattached to any master; like the *klephta* of Greece. Thus the term, first denoting "players", gradually came to imply "wanderers". These youths and men travelled in groups of three or four; going south in the winter, returning north in the summer.

STRATHSPEY (Scotland)
A dance in 4/4 meter, thought at one time to have been the same as the *Reel*,* which later developed its own characteristics. Named *Strathspeys* are not found before the 18th century, and the title page of a book of 1780 refers to "a collection of *Strathspeys* or old *Highland Reels*". A *Reel* always follows the dancing of the *Strathspey*. Whereas the *Reel* is quick and lively and the mus'c without dotted notes, the *Strathspey* is slower, smoother, more gliding in character. Its music has many dotted notes, and a characteristic is the "Scotch Snap", when a short accented note precedes the longer note. The form of the *Strathspey* is a setting to partners and alternating "cutting the figure of eight". It begins in square formation, partners side by side. Then the men move forward and right to face their partners. There follows the figure-of-eight pattern, ending with opposite partners facing; repeated to bring own partners together again. Now popular at dance gatherings all over Scotland, the dignified ballroom *Strathspey* is a simplified version of the more elaborate Highland dance. The name is said to derive from its native place, the valley (strath) of the Spey.

STRIP PLEASE
Was long a religious custom, with many clerics, before or at least parallel with secular customs. Sometimes spectacular, sometimes as a supposed necessary ritual, adherents were asked to "Strip Please!" We may note three observances: (1) the customs of ritual baptism, for one or for a group, in early days, always adults. Thus Mrs. Becket of Canterbury was immersed in holy water by stalwart clerics; (2) When entering a convent, young girls were required to strip when "making vows" on being wedded to the church. (Philip Calderon illustrated this rite in a picture kept in The Tate Galley, London). With more dancing, especially in the *interludus*, Miracle Plays were presented to the admiring public. The play of *Adam and Eve* was a great favourite, when the ʹactors entered quite nude, retiring to obtain fig leaves after a suitable interval. Many mediaeval painters were attracted to this scene for making church paintings.

STRIP TEASE
Or to give the display its French name *cabaret naturelle* is not at all new. What is recent is the commercialisation, not only in theatre, but on seaside posters, brochures, and fashion advertising; as well as cinema film and to some extent in ballet (*Carmen*). The converse of "strip" is adornment with signs and symbols of rank and wealth. Military punishments use "stripping of rank badges" as symbols; while the church added excommunication. Here also the nuns were received in a ceremonial stripping supposed to suggest rejection of the naughty world outside (there is a painting by Calderon, in the Tate Gallery, on this topic). Art schools use the practice for the "life class" but rarely is there dance until civil relations are resumed. The church also did stripping when it arranged its "Jesus on cross" symbol (9th century, unknown before) thus inciting a horde of Spanish painters to paint naked bodies, sacred or secular. Long before this "art dance" (as the girls call it) was commercialised, priests were denounced by prophets who were not instructed in symbolism; and materialised the ritual. Our oldest myth is that of Salome or Shulamith; but the Greeks made a competition, in their legend "Judgement of Paris". Saxon England turned another myth into a pseudo-historical tale for Coventry; perhaps it was once acted at this famous centre of revelry and miracle play. Lady Godiva's legend was revived in Victorian times; but as a modern tourist attraction, has been challenged by endless "Beauty Competitions". Later still, the charming Elizabeth Chudleigh brought the "blades" to Soho Square; but in modern Paris, it became customary for artists and models to go from the Dance Halls or cafés—being somewhat heated—as dawn appeared they dived into the Seine or smaller waters. The procession after Quats

Arts Ball was considerable; no gendarmes intervened.

STROMBOTTA (Italy, 14th century)

Was, by then, principally a short poem or simple verse form, sung to musical accompaniment. This term obviously retains a diminutive mode; as "the little *strambo*" or *strombot*, and we recall the term *bottega* (even now used in London as *bodega*) meaning a local workshop, and now a public meeting place. This is a companion name to *trattoria*—the still current term in Italy for the lower-class "public house", and equivalent to the French *cabaret*. Every *trattoria* had its regular customers; and every Italian gathering tends to break into song and dance. The Northern visitors learned about the place, the custom, and the customers. They pronounced *strombotta* as *strompetta* (in English it is now "strumpet"); from which we can place these mediaeval love songs as being more or less the forerunners of the modern ballroom croon. (We also remember Stromboli is a volcano). The *strombotta* were the bawdy songs of the peasants' *trattoria*, sung by ladies of the establishment; while many of them were improvised by the local poets as they danced.

STRUNT (Scotland)

A walking or dance step, meaning a pompous and sturdy or arrogant movement. We compare *strunt* with *stunt* and *strut*; and we see it today in the circulating march of the experienced Scottish piper (especially leading some military band), as he dances to his own penetrating music.

STUART MASQUES (England)—The Dancing-Place

Held in the Hall of State in the great Palaces and country houses, masques were arranged and the hall suitably fitted up, for each occasion. At first scenes were "dispersed" at either end of the hall, but presently the action was presented on a stage at one end of the room. The audience was arranged in tiers, according to rank, the throne or "state" being placed in the centre. In 1605 for *The Masque of Blackness*, a platform on wheels about forty feet square was erected, but later the usual measurement of the stage seems to have been forty feet wide, twenty-eight feet deep, with an average depth in front of six feet. Between the "state" and the stage was the dancing-place, usually carpeted, and used either during the action, or for the dancing with which all masques ended. It was connected to the stage by steps or a sloping platform. Characters in the masque came down from the stage and danced with selected guests from the audience; sometimes they moved down to approach the throne. Thus, in Townsend's *Tempe*

Restored (1632) Harmony with the Chorus, "goes up to the State and sings", while her companions, the Influences of the Stars, "fall into their daunce, which being past they are placed on the degrees by the Lords and Ladies, where they sitt to see the Masque". The performers were themselves the lords and ladies of the Court. In the same masque the Queen herself was one of the characters, later joining the King on the "state" to watch the rest of the action. The mingling of stage characters with the audience was most common in the early masques, but remained to the end of this form of entertainment, as a reminder of the masque's beginnings in the banqueting hall, when the audience sometimes found themselves in the midst of the scene.   [See *Entrée*]

STYLE IN BALLET AND DANCE

Is so important a quality that it is essential to clarify its main relations as (a) historical, and (b) contemporary. The internal factors of Style exist in :

> *Dance form; as Stylised movement* (technical, expressional, ritual);
> *Mimetic form; as Stylised Emotional expression* (personal or related);
> *Musical form; as Stylised Sound* (instrumental, vocal, expressional);
> *Decor (Scene, costume) as Stylised accent* on Time/Place, character (colour, light).

These factors are present, or should be present, consciously considered and integrated into a completely Stylised ballet, in which these several ingredients shall agree mutually and not compete, either in expression or demand for attention. Style is essentially a non-natural convention (a series of reciprocal conventions) which for Theatre are basically non-realistic, principally by reason of subjection to the Theatre World; but mostly by the imposition of discipline by rhythmic unity. Without this embracing Rhythmic Unity of Style, a single ballet fails to synthesise its contributory parts : it remains as a set of disparate exhibitory attempts, by some four or five different artists, who thereby state their inability to understand and agree on the exposition of a single theme. In the orchestra, this lack of unison is now most frequently imposed by inadequate composers; too many "modern composers" are obviously incapable of sustaining musical theme, either in melody or harmony. To attempt to dance to such alleged music is inviting failure. *Historically :* Style marks the agreed conventions of a time-and-place. Tradition is ancient style; opposed to it is Novelty—the consciously New—which invents, diverts, or perverts Style; and in between comes Fashion, or a general mass acceptance of current convention. The primal necessity in all Styles in all arts is clarity of expression; fullness of meaning (rational or emotional), and fitness of means to end, of tools and methods to the social need. Style reveals the balancing steleyard of individual power to social comprehension. Any group of individuals who hope to arrive at social success while rejecting social meaning should be deposed.

STYLE IN DANCE

Appears in Theatre (etc.) Convention; having always a triple basis: (1) in mode of technical movement; (2) in design or plan of movement; and (3) in the unifying purpose or aim of the movement, in making clear some meaning by expression through dance. Style presupposes some agreed convention, known both to dancer and observer; or no agreed criterion can be established. Style is usually arbitrary, and rarely natural. For example, style in language requires that writer and reader shall both be acquainted with a single language, whether spoken or written, and here style resolves into a triple convention of technical expression, of formative or planned structure; with both pendant upon clarity of expression. Design of structure and method of expression must combine to permit full and clear statement of meaning. This expression becomes as essential in dance—a language of emotion visually stated—as in music, a parallel language aurally stated (again, not pre-eminently intellectual), which also must possess technique and structure. Style is thus living and valid association of three factors. We enlarge on stylistic conventions when we admit its shading into less durable forms. Novelty is the froth and ephemera of style; it may endure for a few days. Tradition, as the polar opposite of novelty, is style that has gained a solidly recognised code of group convention. Intermediate we find fashions; they are trivial departures from firm convention, from accepted and utilised style, which verge towards frivolous novelty. The currently accepted view of "choreography" leans perilously towards novelty, while its traditional basis has too long eliminated the central need for building upon some theme possessed of human meaning and value. Empty style is worse than no style at all; while a merely technical style, limited chiefly to fiddling irruptions of pseudomovement, is mainly revolting. Eclectic arts commonly muddle a variety of styles, that possess no common centre. Fine style is essentially a synthesis of technique, structure, and meaning, fitted to address its chosen audience; and thus carefully avoiding obscurity, whether by choice or default. Sources of Dance "Style" are triple:

1. *Technical*; modes or styles of movement.
    e.g. style in good golf or cricket etc.
2. *Design*; modes or styles of plan, arrangement.
    e.g. style in painting, plan of structure, of lines and masses; of light and shade; colour and tone.
3. *Theme*; mode of thematic expression.
    e.g. style of sequence, or "plot"—dramatic contrast, change of emotional stress, expectancy, suspense etc.

Before this age of rapid mass transport, local style in the arts did not spread so rapidly or disastrously. A small painting, a book, an ivory carving, could be carried, though slowly, from foreign lands; but architecture could be seen only by travel. Dance and music spread by minstrels, troubadours, bands of processional players; yet local and national styles were affected but slowly. Now, immature students go to a single school; and "take classes" in all sorts of styles; they "do" a local convention, but in a few lessons they "learn Hindu", or "do Spanish", and so contribute further to a mingling of threads and patches. Instead of firm local or national style, we suffer under formless eclecticism.

SUBSIDY

Is the beginning and end of most performances of dance and all productions of ballet: Who is to pay? From the earliest group performances, the initial problem is: to prepare and to provide; whether the feast is for a Babylonian New Year of *Zagmuk*, or a great pig-feast in the New Hebrides in Polynesia: a Stuart masque, an Italian ducal wedding, a Russian court theatre, or an Arts Council compromise. Dancers, costumes, scenic or ritual materials, and time—must all somehow be subsidised. Naturally and economically, the "money" comes from the supporting, subsidising, patronising groups. All the time, the people pay. Official elements aim to intervene: from priests to inspectors of entertainment tax. They must "have their cut". This "dance of dollars" leads to obscure and intricate manoeuvres: in Britain, the Treasury subsidises (via the Councils) the production of a very few shows. Then it proceeds to get back most of this outlay by (a) entertainment tax; (b) income tax; (c) purchase tax on many materials; (d) P.A.Y.E. tax on high wages; for (e) excessive cost of transport to and from the theatres—all to expend on the entertainment of its own stony heart—the "Best and Biggest Bangs of History". Subsidy comes out of income. When the Italian economic organisation at the Vatican was plundering England of more revenue than went to the King's Treasury (Mathew of Paris gives details), the English dancing festivials in towns and villages were self-maintained. From the "ladle" of the Morris-dance groups, to the gild-revenues; townspeople worked, rather than paid, to provide the show. Even so, they had both eyes on "pilgrim offerings" (as the tourist trade was then called), and they amiably fleeced their visitors, for cash returns, just like any modern "seaside landlady". Currency is made to move on the currents of trade; friction diminishes its value. This is the "dance of Mammon"; for this there is an anthem dedicated to *Pulex Irritans* ("tax-collectors" to you), where the words announce that "Big fleas have little fleas, that on their back do bite 'em — and these fleas have smaller fleas — and so, *ad infinitum*". Hence the whirlpool of fighters for cash, from the holders of purse-strings (or automatic printing machines), in the endeavour to "sell talent". Theatre managers call it Box Office at the other end. Where the mediaeval knight (we are told in romantic legends), "flung his purse of gold" to the itinerant minstrel who pleased him and his guests, the ducal sycophancies of Mantua or Milan were ornamented with direct plunder by active *condottierie;* the priests sharing, by selling blessings (as in Sicily), while in England the expensive masques of Ben Jonson were subsidised as directly. The continental theatre system in Paris, or Stuttgart, to Petersburg, was arranged for subsidies — municipal or regal; for the town's "opera house" as a matter of prestige. England never gave direct theatre subsidies; the only shows given free to the populace were those at Tyburn Tree; and the Lord Mayor's annual civic procession. In the USA, things were, and are, much worse. In 1925, New York City had some fifty living theatres; in 1950 these were reduced to half; none were subsidised, although various opera and ballet companies received intermittent subsidies (Kahn, Fleischmann, Samuel Insull, etc.)

Paris Opera continues to receive municipal (not state) subsidy; as do a few German, Belgian, and Danish theatres. In Russia, the regulated income and usage of the "big five theatres" now equates expenses; and subsidy for them is not needed. The 1914 rake-off ranged to a two-million ruble guarantee. Soviet theatres are often otherwise subsidised, in their formative days. Elimination of profit motive provides contracts and shows; elimination of competitive expression ensures that too many plays are dull; dance is the greatest exception. Private subsidies have in Europe sustained performances, from the Colonial Ballet Russe, to the International Ballet in England, and the Company of the Marquis de Cuevas, while Rolf de Maré carried Swedish Ballet for over a decade. Some small touring Indian companies have been subsidised; none by the Indian government.

SUITE (French)

In the Seventeenth Century, this term implied a collection of dances — and thence dance tunes — played in the same key. That is: they could be played by a small orchestra without change of instrument or alteration of key; though variation in rhythm and movement was required to sustain interest. Here the chamber music began definitely to depart towards "concert suite", and away from its essential functional connection, by the factor of dance movement, towards the modernist character of "absolute music" as an "independent art". The French suite form ran: *Prelude, Allemande,* Courante,* Sarabande,** and *Gigue.** Sometimes *Gavotte** and *Bourree** replaced *Courante* and *Sarabande.* An early *Suite,* by Auxcouste, appeared printed in Paris in 1652.

SULVASUTRAS (Sanskrit, India)

"Rules of Cord", given in commentaries and supplements of *Kalpasutras* (Time Measures), which treat of ceremonial forms for construction of sacrificial altars, according to the Vedas. The date of this script is variously assigned: R. C. Dutt gives 800 BC, while Max Muller indicates between 500 BC and 200 BC. The editions attributed to Apastambha, Budhayana, and Katayana, differ in detail; but it is certain that Hindu designers were using these technical methods of rope-measurement for buildings (including wooden theatres) at the same time as the Greeks in Athens. G. R. Kaye (*Indian Mathematics*) quotes references to "root rectangles" (from Budhayana's edition of *Sulvasutras*) which would apply to architectural form, or possibly to musical theory; but we have always to remember that written manuscripts, in India, never described the whole theory, which was reserved by every competent *guru* for his own students, on the assumption that actual demonstration was essential to convey a complete grasp of practice. Teachers of dance will agree with that notion. The *Sulvasutras* thus entered into Indian dance, first as a traditional standard for theatre form and arrangement; and then as a method of fixing a choreographic area. This factor can be seen, in the Greek versions, in the still existing Theatre of Dionysus at Athens, where the "Great Diamond" (so often mentioned as a symbol in Buddhist literature) is visible in the orchestra. These Hindu forms survive in two modes: as the *alpona** or *rangoli,** used for festival worship; and the smaller symbols of *Shri Yantra,* drawn in manuscripts, or on some parts of the temples.   [See *Alpona; Put-Ser; Pleroma*]

SUN DANCES

Have been known in all countries; they mark acceptance of solar year-time; and commemorate the four quarters of the year. Most of them have been unified with the religious schemes of their day, so that each celebration calls for a feast, called a *foire*, a *messe*, a *quatre*, or a *Yule* and a *Yohannus* (or two of each). The astronomical dates follow solstice and equinox. Here we note dance rituals that recognise the Sun as a symbol of deity, as a father-mother of all living things; as a welcome ruler in our temperate climes, but as a dangerous destroyer in tropical lands. Thus the same god evinces two sides of his single nature; and accordingly rituals vary in different places. In England Whit-Sun-Tide is celebrated as a feast. Formerly there was a common superstition that "the sun dances on this day", but that mistake was due to careless reference to the Sun Dance as if the celebration was to watch our sun moving, instead of ourselves moving in due homage. Patterns of dances formerly followed the orientation (as at Stonehenge) and many a church was oriented according to its memorial "saint" in worship. Thus the Summer solstice, allotted to Yo-Hannus (turned into "Saint John") turns the central line towards northeast; the winter solstice (to Iolo or Yule) towards south-east.

SUN DANCE (Lithuania)
Popular tradition reports in this Baltic land, that there was an important festival of the gods on the "Day of Johannus" (Midsummer Solstice). On that auspicious day, Mother Sun goes forth from her palace in a great car, drawn by three horses — golden, silver, and diamond — to meet her spouse the Moon. On her journey, she dances, emitting fiery sparks.

SUREME (Japan)
Women who act as spiritualist mediums; or, as an alternative, "perform comic dances in honour of the gods". The *Sureme-san* is, in a way, an offshoot of the *Kagura** mime-dancers; she appears in temple and towns, she is seen in the villages. They are supposed to be "possessed" both when "communicating" and when dancing.

SURSUM CORDA (Dog-Latin)
An exhortation heard during Christian church ritual, alleged to mean "Lift up your hearts", but in fact derived from a deacon's order — *Circum chorda*, in the Greek *ecclesia*. The phrase is used in eucharistic rite, being "said by the priest to the people", but was no more than a simple request to "keep moving" along the rope or cord, so that every man would have his turn. There were no seats, no servers; thus applicants had to "come to the rail". As there was no rail, they moved "by the cord". This method was a regular secular Greek practice, when officials had to clear a way in the *Agora* for some civic purpose; they used an ochre-smeared rope, and those who did not move fast enough (the evidence being the red on their garments) were admonished or fined. Thus the exhortation was for one of the ritual movements; but could not be a dance form until music was added; when it became a processional in "the preface".

SURUVAKARY (Bulgaria)
Festival dance of the New Year, performed in the districts of Radomir and Bressnik. The name indicates *Surya* (the Sun); with possibly *valkary* (*valkyrie*) as the dancing attendants (days or weeks). The date has shifted slightly; and has been tied to Vassili by clerical interest. Prominent are the big masks, five or six feet in height, invested with wings, or at least feather coverings; and topped by animal or bird heads. The male dancers carry wooden swords; and dance round the villages, not with magical intent to "compel fine crops", but as a welcome, and anticipation, of essential food. They carry a large drum; and have brass cow-bells tied to leathern belts. With them are twelve animal characters (the months), and the New Year Bride with her child, the Young Year, who is the Babe, sponsored by the Glorious Sun, born after the Old Year has died. Bride and Babe appear again with the *Kukeri* (now shifted to the Lent season), which retains the King (deputy of the Sun) and the Rites of the Spring Plough. Later the *Kukeri* merge with the *Rusalii** at the Whetsun Feast. [Cp. *Schemenlaufen* (Austria)]

SVANTEVIT, OR SUANTEVET (Old Sweden)
Dance ritual belonging to the vanished cult of the Solar God, celebrated at Arkona in the Baltic Island of Rügen, about the middle of June (for the midsummer solstice). This Slavonic cult was vanquished by the slowly spreading Latin system from Italy. About 870-880, a party of raiding monks from Corvey constructed a rival "chapel of Vitus" (copying the older name, in Latin form) much as another ancient centre in Praha (Prague, Bohemia) was adroitly changed over, when the sacred hill of the Sun-god Ghoradshany (Hradcany) was taken over in the name of "Saint Vitus", and a church erected on the demolished shrine. Dance was prominent in all these ancient rituals of worship using sun symbols. The Rhineland legends, cherished in Teutonic tradition (those of Siegfried and the Rhine-maidens; of Valhalla and the Knights of the Swan) stem from partial memories of these ceremonial rites.

SVASTIKA (Sanskrit)
From *Sva-sti-ka*, or "Good Fortune". Is an elemental

symbol of ritual notation; indicating solar direction for the *Pradakshina* or circuit ritual of the Brahmin festivals of ancient Hindu villages. Every Aryan village was planned on rectangular form (like Roman *campus*). At the centre stood the Council Tree (or Pillar) with altar of sacrifice (or tribute) at the central platform (*mandala*) or enclosure. Brahma, as "Protector of the Four Quarters", was symbolised by his pillar surmounted by the typical "four faces", one overlooking each quarter of the village; hence the pragmatic origin of the "four faces". The ritual required the march round the confines; a square dance form marked by four sharp turns, as indicated by the solar directions (*deosil*). From it in Britain was copied the *Vidya-shina*, the Way of Wisdom, later in reverse dropped to "widdershins". The "good fortune" consisted in being allowed to join the processional, all going in the same prosperous direction, chanting the *Sva-ha* and other *mantrams*. Later *stika* became "straight line" and then stick (rod) or "line of writing" (for printers, used now, as a "stick of type") *Domus-stika*; the one of the house. Every festival began with solemn ritual and ended in rejoicing with music and dancing after the feast.

SVENSKA TANS (Sweden)
Are folk dances, now preserved by frequent performance, as at *Lekstuga** meetings. The basic music revolves round the violin; and now the modern piano, for which traditional tunes have been harmonised. Nils Andersen collected a number of old dance tunes in his *Svenska Latara*; and M. P. Nilsson has *Vara Danslekar* (Dance Games). *Lekstugan* tunes are contained in a book of that name, by E. Lindelof. Besides the winter meetings (see *Lekstuga**), the famous Outdoor Folk Museum of Skansen, just outside Stockholm, organises regular folk dance performances, through the summer season. Many of the traditional melodies are associated with particular periods of folk ritual, and many have words that indicate this fact. Thus the regular march tune, *gang-latara*, belongs to mass movement (procession) at weddings or festivals. The *brudlatara* is the "bridal tune"; the *rolata*, the few minutes of rest between this actual wedding dance and the bride's departure. At her home we hear *skanlatara*, the "Good Health" or "drink-hand-out tune", and, more rarely, the *tiggarlatara*, during which the "presents are shown" (or collected together). These tunes thus belong, not to mime, but to the actual rites.   [See *Skansen*]

SWASHBUCKLER (Mediaeval English)
A frequent term in the military or sporting play of Buckler and Baton, or Sword and Buckler. The sound, similar to that alleged of the Saliian priests or Korybantes,* was a regular tattoo of the company, beating various rhythms on their own or opponent's bucklers (the round shield, or targe). They then began the military dance, keeping time with stamping feet. Fencers had a parallel term: to "swish", done by the rapid twist of the foil through the air, making a whipping sound; when next they tapped their feet to begin attack. Ruffianly attacks caused the term to degenerate; to denote boasting braggarts. They were called swinge-bucklers or rakes (roisterer). These "blades" are mentioned by Shakespeare (*Henry IV.* 2. iii. 2). In the *Milkmaids Dance,** these men sometimes kept a swash accompaniment to the Maids' tapping on their silver.

SWEDISH BALLET (Stockholm)
The Royal Opera House was instituted by Gustav III in 1773, using Italian opera and French ballet as a basis. The monarch himself acted and wrote lyrics. The *maitre de ballet* selected was Louis Gallodier from Paris; he trained a corps from available young actors; and obtained a ballet that was magnificently extravagant. Antoine Bournonville came, as a pupil of Noverre, arriving in 1781, bringing newer dramatic principles; many foreign choreographers followed, usually with French works. Swedish talent was slow to develop; but produced one master in Charles Didelot, who eventually contributed much to Russia; where he was known as Mons. Didlo. He had been first to London. Phillips Taglioni married a Swedish girl; his famous daughter Marie, was born in Stockholm (1804) and he became ballet master in 1818. Romantic Ballet was soon established, mainly by Anders Selinder, the first native master, together with Auguste Bournonville (who had also a Swedish wife), whence a link had formed between Denmark and Sweden. Now appeared Christian Johannsen — pupil of Bournonville, later to be rated high in Russian ballet circles as a master of style. Swedish Ballet passed its prime by 1860, as ballet did in France and England. Jean Borlin joined Rolf de Maré in the revival, after Fokine's visit in 1918; they started the *Ballet Suedois*, while Cieplinsky ruled at the Stockholm Opera House. In 1931 Julian Algo came in; experimenting with "Modern Ballet" in some usually violent productions. His *Visions* was shewn in London by International Ballet, but provoked no great reception. Rolfe de Maré died and *Ballet Suedois* disbanded in 1925. The essence was not Swedish, but Franco-American. There remains a good technically able group in Stockholm, lacking "something to say", while their varied reproductions sometimes appear in Gothenburg and Malmö (Municipal Theatre).

SWIMMING DANCE FORMS

Are shown in numerous "aquatic displays" which have a closer relation to elemental choreographic floor patterns than to any vertical dance. Obviously, they can provide only a flat pattern on the surface of the water. The Roman writer Martial describes, in his *Epigrams*, those he saw in his own day : —

"Young girls, disguised as nymphs, were seen in the water, sometimes sporting in a chariot like that of the fabled Nereids, grouping in most varied designs. At one time they would bring out the figure of a trident; then interlacing differently, they came together in the shape of an anchor, an oar, or a boat. This last figure, in dissolving, became transformed into the constellation of Castor and Pollux; then succeeded a sail, blown out with the wind. These swimmers could do in the water what the pantomimists did by means of their dances in combination, representing on the stage of the theatre a great variety of subjects. Such games and feats in the water could not fail to be useful in maintaining the expertness of citizens in swimming".

SWORD DANCES

These are very numerous and widespread. Every tribe or race continues some form of sword dance. In Britain the equipment of naval uniforms with swords has only recently been abolished; and Cutlass Drill is rare. Many sword dances carry specific names, e.g. the Pyrrhic Dance,* which can be consulted here. The typal forms may be analysed as :

(1) *Preparation* for war or aggression, raids, etc. Exercises with weapons; swords, lances, cutlass, spears to cultivate celerity in use; skill in handling and effective means of defence when attack is answered.

(2) *Ritual dance*, to (a) develop emotional ferocity, and (b) to cultivate tribal unity in aggression. Weakened versions of this ritual are "saluting flag", "showing colours" by marching through enemy town (or even at home) and chanting of traditional tunes, with noisy and aggressive music (as from brass bands) with firing of guns; military tattoos; now aeroplane flights.

(3) *Triumphal war dance*, the "dance of victory", waving of captured flags, of scalps (Red Indian mode) or pulling trophies and captives through streets (the Italian *trionfo*).

These three phases present the "Before", "During" and "After" phases of war; the dance rhythm changes considerably, according to the need for rejoicing or the acceptance of defeat. This contrast is shown in two modes reversed, in the military funeral : another ritual, where the procession to the grave is slow march and slow music, but the return to the barracks (after firing symbolic shots at depredating enemy spirits in the air) is done to quick march and merry music. From variations of the sword dance many later ceremonial dances have been developed. The *Morris Dance** with "swords" is probably the farthest removed from the essentially combative form of the basic military sword dance; while the modern ballet still evinces faint traces of one of its ancestral systems with weapons. [See *English Sword Dances*]

SYLVANUS (Latin - Etruscan)

Is a ritual title that covers many modes of meaning. According to R. P. Knight,[1] Sylvanus, as identical with Sylva—and (different local spellings)— equates with Pan, as the "Lord of Matter". He is called in the Orphic Hymns, as "Zeus Mover of All Things", harmonising them with the music of his

Sword Dance, Macedonia.   YUGOSLAVIA

"Winter-versus-Spring Contest" in symbolic dance terms. The creative Sylvanus versus the destructive Goat. Wall painting from the buried city of Herculaneum, reproduced in Piroli's *Antiquities*. 1804–5 (Paris).   ANCIENT ITALY

pipes. Pan is called also Pervader of the Sky. In a choral *Ode* of Sophocles, Pan is addressed as "Author and Director of the Dances of the Gods". In Roman development, Sylvanus was especially god of field and forest; his servants, the Sylphs and Sylphides; his dwelling, the sylvan depths. This tradition still remains in Teutonic countries (notably Germany and Austria), where Sylvanus becomes Silvestre, the god of the New Year, promiser of green crops. In this capacity, Sylvanus-Silvestre is leader of the Twelve Months in the Dance of the Year; and as such he is invoked on the First or New Year Day, with dance and song.
[1] *Symbolical Language of Ancient Art and Mythology*. Richard Payne Knight. New York, 1876.

SYMBOLS IN DANCE
Appear in several distinct categories. Their most obvious form is visual: in terms of choreographic design, in costume, and implements; and in scenic settings (as in the *Masque**). Less immediately notable is the use of symbolic theme; the conscious presentation of some myth or drama, with full usage of every aspect of dance to integrate dance and music, movement and colour, into one single work of theatrical art. Rarest event of all, now, is to meet any conscious mastery of symbol, formulated into dance expression for some creative work of great social art. Wagner made his attempt in terms of opera; as Shakespeare made his endeavours in dramatic poetry; but despite the urging of Noverre, no European ballet has yet been able to rise to this height. Even the "symphonic ballets" have been frustrated by absence of full creative integration. Technical ambitions, or financial limitations have inhibited a full symbolism; while mere realism defeats its own presumed objective. Secular myths are rare, while religious myths are ruined by realism (as is their doctrinal presentation), for the subtle meaning of myth and symbol is absent. Neither myth nor symbol in relation, pretends to be "the truth", so that any attempt to endow stage form with "scientific accuracy" is an admission of failure to understand Theatre and its intrinsic functions. In Hindu temple dance (when understood by a producer and when presented with economy and symbolic values) is one of the few extant modes of Dance which can and does use genuine symbolism: that is, the presentation of an unstateable truth by means of mythic forms which condense into symbols and symbolic action, affirmed by music and sharpened by mime and gesture into a fusion of delicately apprehended reality (which is *not* realism), that can be conveyed only by means of a new-created art. All symbol hides meaning, while it simultaneously reveals— to those who will accept the hidden meaning, instead of the obvious and necessarily incomplete material form.

SYMPHONIC BALLET
Is a production for which the choreographer, having a trained company of dancers available, tries to exploit the musical values of a symphony composed by a musician who is preferably dead, so that he can neither object to treatment nor claim royalties for use of his work. The method, as observed in production of one of these performances, showed that the choreographer called his group for rehearsal in a drill hall; and provisionally allotted them parts, unnamed and undescribed. Presently, the "idea began to develop", and as the gramophone records were repeated again and again, some characters began to receive labels, as Fate, or The Young Man, and the Woman in Red —and so forth. The music not being alterable except by excisions; and being more or less well-known to the public, could not be "arranged", (as M. Petipas persuaded Tschaikovsky to do, quite

legitimately, for new ballets in process of construction). The theory was that the music, if it had a known programme, might suggest a "story", and that the musical structure and phrasing would be duplicated, or reflected contrapuntally, in the structure of the ballet and the phrasing of the dance. This consummation was devoutly to be wished; but appeared in these ballets only for a few rare moments. The range of mastery of the contributory arts that compose ballet is seldom attained. The reverse of this system has so far proved impossible; that is, for a competent composer to contrive music for a ballet already marked out in terms of movement. Most choreographers who have attempted symphonic ballet have followed the composers, in ignoring the historical facts revealed in the growth of the symphony as a musical form; and instead have used the music as a basis for vague generalisations by way of theme, while avoiding the technical aridity of "abstract ballet". To add choreographic form as dance movement, whether contrapuntally or in close parallel, to musical movement, without seeking to realise more fully the original structure of the four-fold symphony, is to defeat the musicians as well as the dancers. A true symphony ballet must be fused kinetically—must be symkinetic as well as symphony. Failure to develop thematically is the most common fault in modern music; while aggressive beats and percussive noises are substituted for genuine emotional sequence; and these same errors can be seen in choreographic form, being due initially to a supposedly superior rejection of comprehensible theme. Symphony is social or group music, as opposed to soloist or individual music; so that all dance must reveal the same general character; and must be supported visually in terms of costume and decor with lighting. Full symphony expression is the final test of genuine modern ballet, as a complete art form, just as full dramatic expression is the final test of a genuine play.
See *Symphonic Ballet*. Anatole Chujoy (New York).
[See *Choreodrama; Abstract Ballet; Ballet*]

SYRTOS (Greece)
Known in classical times, and described in detail by Lucian, the *Syrtos* today has become merged with the *Kalamatianos*,* regarded as the national dance of Greece. In the *Syrtos*, a linked circle dance for men and women, the leader would break away to perform virtuoso steps, in a display of virility, while the girls danced demurely with downcast eyes. There are still many Greek dances of this type, and the name has survived as a dance style— the distinguishing measure of dances of gentle character. Greek dances are of two kinds—lively or restrained, with a third group which uses both

styles in alternation. The energetic, leaping dances of the mountains, performed mostly by men, are *pidiktos* ("leaping"); while the more solemn, lyrical dances of the lowlands and the islands, performed by both men and women, are *syrtos* ("dragging" or "creeping"). The modern *Syrtos* or *Kalamatianos*, danced in circle or chain, is seen in sophisticated Athenian ballrooms as well as in the countryside. The leader of the chain, linked by kerchiefs, draws the procession round and in and out, doing a monotonous little step. A lively version is often sung in the night clubs of the capital.

SZEKLER LEGENYES (Hungary)
"Youth Dance", formerly Recruiting Dance, which was ended in Hungary by conscription after 1848-49. Earlier it had been the custom for the best dancers of regiments to join in recruiting tours, tempting youths by bright uniforms, brilliant dance, exciting music, to "join the colours". After 1850, former recruiters did not cease dancing; though standards fell, and they could not use uniforms; while dancers could be drawn only from restricted areas, such as their own village. Then the *Körmagyar** (Hungarian circle dance), and *Csárdás** developed. *Szekler Legenyes*, with its name, was preserved in Trans-Danubian districts (near Gyor), and in Rumanian villages (between the Danube and Theiss). The dance is chiefly circular and solely male. Eastwards, similar dances became known as *Legényes* (lad=*legeny*), and later as *Csürdüngölö* (*csur* is the great barn; *dongolo*, to stamp), but this name is now applied, in jest, to any Hungarian *Szekler* dance. The Youth Dance was led off by the "best dancer" as the recruiting dance, *Verbunkos** was started by "the corporal". Each man dances opposite to a man on the far side of the ring—his distant partner. Occasionally there is a solo in centre. Dance is rapid, vigorous and athletic, while rhythmic; yet highly exhibitionistic. Play is made with clashes of heels (metal spurs also) and smacks of the high leg-boots; or of thighs or arms. Occasional sharp "dance-words" mark high points, as "hipp-hopp"—"hip-hop-hip ! !" (Dalcroze adopted this "hopp" for his affirmation of rhythmic beat, in teaching music). The traditional "praise-word" comes as "*kivagja a rezet*" —literally "He knocks out the copper!"

T

TABERNACLE (*Taberna, Taverna*, etc.)
Or Ale-house; the Jewish "Feast of Tabernacles" was the annual harvest rejoicing, with song, music and dance, coupled with the worship (*Beneth Suc-*

coth) of tribal union. The ale-house—more or less equivalent in provincial England—was the meeting not only for drink but for prayers to *Aleim*—the Jewish company of gods. Dance form was simple: circle, square or processional. The traditions are connected with those of *Ruach*, or Ark (esp. Jean d'Arc) as this was the peasant or proletarian kirke. The booths set up in any field, or near a vineyard, were called Tents of *Benoth* (Venus)—*Benoh* or *Venoh*; but in village or town the dance became the *Almonde* or *Allemande*. The Feast of Tabernacles was often denounced by the austere *Nabi* (prophet) speakers.

TABU (Polynesian term)

Literally "holy" or "must-not-be-touched". In all ritual dance of the Eastern world (not only in Polynesia) the problem of *totem* and *tabu* is present; and seems to be a principle rarely understood in Europe. This "touch" is linked with *mana*,* the power or energy most concerned. Dancers must not touch (a) each other; (b) the dancing-ground—women especially are forbidden to approach or enter; (c) certain implements used in ritual, as the *churinga* or bull-roarer. In some circumstances, as in ritual periods of *tabu*, the person may not even touch, with his fingers, his own food (Maori). The central basis of all *Totem-tabu* rites arises in the reality of *mana*, as a natural electro-magnetic force, ever-present, and ever-active, which the people understand from experience. The same energy, being a world-force, naturally exists in all countries; but mechanical energies (produced in and used by civilised communities) distract attention from these subtle powers of nature (except, perhaps, in agriculture and shipping). Rituals in the Orient have, for one of several main purposes, the business of seeking, attracting, collecting, and using this energy, they call *mana*. This energy is just as real as the cruder form we call electricity, used for driving engines and lighting lamps or disposing of fellow citizens (in USA). This crude mode is mineral or metallic Electro-Motor Force. The *mana* used by "savages" is a higher grade: namely vital E.-M. F. Medical men call, it nervous energy; it ceases to flow in plants when stems are cut; it drops in winter, in other conditions. This *mana* can be drawn, concentrated directed—it was thus the basis of the king-job, for the most powerful man was he who had, and could give, most *mana*. His job was to get it, and to conserve it, for the benefit of his tribe. Hence he must not readily touch, or be touched: the current would flow. We refrain from touching electric iron rails or copper wires of our traction systems. Iron is a metal to be avoided by the *mana*-chief; he also avoids water; he uses oil. He is *tabu*;

he is the living battery of *mana*-energy; saviour of his tribe. In dance ritual (as in Ancient Egypt), he collects more, daily; and directs its flow to his people. In some lands it is called "grace", but the common usage is lacking in principle and power. Only in surgeries is the principle of *tabu* recognised; here the "touch of danger" is called infection, or contagion; and protection is secured by "sterilization" of the microbe/demons about to attack.   [See *Mana*; *Totem*]

TAGE WEISEN (Germany: Mediaeval)

Term allotted to denote the general "watch tune" or march, played by the small band of the mediaeval town watchmen. In England the Waits or *wyghtes*, held the same office; and contributed to nightly gaiety by trumpet calls, but the regular tune (which is now replaced by the strains of the "regimental march" inheritor of the same tradition) was reserved for feasts or other special occasions.

TAGORE SCHOOL OF DANCE (Bengal, India)

Was founded (1907) by the Indian poet Rabindranath Tagore (of Calcutta), as part of his *ashram* or School for restoration of Hindu culture. Tagore found much of his material in (a) poems of Bengal, *kirtans* and his own writings; (b) ancient *raga*, music; and (c) religious or festival dances of Manipuri, which suited the predominantly lyrical quality of performances first arranged in this new school, Shantiniketan, at Bolpur in Bengal (about eighty miles north of Calcutta). The school has settled a three-year course (part of their work is in practical dance, music and learning of *mudra*, and *hasta*,* part for general education), which is attended by young sons and daughters of cultured Hindus. Some part of the dance tuition is now in *Kathak*, and *Kathakali*, styles, carried on since the death of Tagore by his family; along with training in pictorial arts. Performances have been shewn in Calcutta, Colombo, Madras, and other cities.

TAHLUL (Arabic)

Is traditional song and dance of praise on occasion of a sacrifice. Says Robertson Smith,[1] "The festal song of praise, *tahlul*, properly goes with the dance round the altar (*Psalm xxvi.* 6), for in primitive times song and dance are inseparable". Also, "in later Arabic the *tawaf*, or act of circling the sacred stone, was still a principal part of religion (though later it became a meaningless ceremony". The name *tuwaif* is still applied to the Moslem dancing-girl in Bengal or East Pakistan. [See *Tuwaif* (Pakistan)]
[1] *Religion of the Semites*. W. Robertson Smith. P. 340.

TAKACSTANC, "WEAVERS' DANCE" (Hungary)

A hopping dance, found in the Trans-Danubian district, usually performed by one man, but sometimes by two men facing each other. The symbol of their trade seems to be the handkerchief which they hold high in front of them; and, on the last beat of the music, pass it under the right and left thighs alternately, from one hand to the other. Hopping continues through the dance; the business with the handkerchief is repeated twice while hopping on the right leg, and twice on the left leg. In the region between the Danube and Tisza, it is called the Cap Dance, the same hopping dance being performed with the high sheep-skin hat of the district instead of with the handkerchief.

TALI TYING (Coimbatore, South India)
Ceremony of dedication of young dancing-girls. It was the custom among some Hindus to present to the temple, one girl from their family, as a young child. The small girl, decorated with jewels, stood upon a heap of *padi* (rice), holding the top edge of a folded cloth held before her by two dancing girls. As music was played, the dancing master moved her legs up and down in rhythm. Following this introduction the child began on the course of music and dancing. Dedication was marked by tattooing or branding, the marks being called *chank* or *chakra*. After the ceremony music was played by Kaikolan musicians.
See *Ethnographical Notes on Southern India.* E. Thurston (Madras, 1906).

TAMASHA (Indian term in Urdu from Persian)
Often used in general for "party" or "gathering for amusement", but earlier related to the entertainment of village drama and dancing; especially used now to refer to a noisy and merry popular gathering, even in the larger cities of India. The term has run into various meanings, like the English village term "bean-feast". May be related to *Tamoshanter*—as the persons engaged in providing or arranging the jollification; since the sign was the "scarlet bonnet" or woollen headcover, elsewhere favoured by itinerant entertainers.

TAMBORITO (Panama)
A pair dance in lively 2/4 time, popular during Carnival. Partners dance opposite each other, the woman sometimes circling about the man. At Parita (in the south of the Peninsula), which has a reputation for the purest form of *Tamborito*, the best dancers do not move the body above the hips, keeping time in a rhythmical restrained fashion, although the tempo of the dance increases as it proceeds. Spectators form a circle round the dancers, accompanying their movements with hand-clapping; while drummers, placed inside the circle beat the African-derived rhythm on small drums— upright and played with the hands, or horizontal

and beaten on both heads with sticks. The 17th century air accompanying the dance is usually sung by a woman soloist, followed by a choral refrain. The singing, as distinct from the dance, is called *Tonada*. In the seclusion of the home, a more subdued *Tamborito* is danced, called *Tambor de Orden* ("Ordinary Tamborito"). During Carnival (which at Parita lasts four days), the girls wear the lovely national costume—the *pollera*—derived from Spanish colonial gowns. Having a very full skirt, with wide, long-ended sash, the bodice of the dress has a frilled "off the shoulder" cape, with a large red pom-pom in front. Both skirt and cape are embroidered with traditional patterns in black or red on white. Flowers are bunched at either side of the head, but in Parita the hair ornaments, made of fish scales and artificial pearls, quiver on tiny springs as the dancer moves.

TANDAVA (Sanskrit)
Hindu ritual dance—the masculine, or positive part of the Brahmin ritual of *Samaya*. "The *Lasya** or female-dance and the *Tandava*, or male-dance, both being types of the same *Nrtya*, their identity of Avastha or condition is established". See *Saundarya-Lahari (Ocean of Beauty)*. Shankara; translated by Sastri and Ayyangar (p. 60). Madras, 1937.

TANE-TANE (Polynesian; *Mangaia*)
Royal dance of the god Tané, with symbol of sacred adze; often a stone adze, as in the Hervey Islands. Tané's "voice" comes from the big slotted drum called *kaara*. He is the drum-god and the axe-god, and presides over the erotic dance as well as war dances. Some styles of the symbolic adze are over six feet high.

TANGKA (Tibetan)
The "temple banner", which bears the mystical choreographic diagrams known as *mandala** or *khyilkhor*,* symbolising the doctrine of the "dance of the mind", in the Lama-Buddhist religious system. The scheme and its practice are ancient; possibly preceding the establishment of Buddhism in Tibet or Mongolia (Mon-Yul). They were painted in traditional ritual forms, on heavy Chinese silk. From Khotan (Eastern Turkestan), which was formerly part of Indian Empire, Aurel Stein and Le Coq found many art relics, those from Dandan-Uiliq being dated about 8th century AD. Some of these items were painted silk banners.
[Cp. *Tangov*]

TANGO (Argentina), TUNKU (Asia)
A Spanish dance, formerly a ritual (Xango or Shango, North African religious ritual). This Afro-Iberian ritual dance was once the important New

Year Feast celebration, in worship of Shango. The ritual had twelve periods which were dramatised in twelve episodes; some of the names remain, but the order is dislocated. The Arab tradition differed into *Fandango** or *Fantango*, and Moslem *Fantazzia*, while the Spanish form early went to South America; and thence came back, alleged to be an "Argentine dance"—it is so, only as a ballroom form. The figures of the earlier modes are:

1. *EL PASEO*. The promenade, arrival and around square space.
2. *EL MARCHA*. Setting to partners and slow march of the whole company.
3. *EL CORTE*. The company defines the circle of the Corte by moving round its circumference.
4. *EL MEDIO CORTE*. The leading couple demonstrate in the centre.
5. *EL CHASE* is used to follow the first couple, in figures, as they call.
6. *EL MEDIA LUNA* is half way; at half moon, the half circle now filled, defined.
7. *EL MOULINET*, the mill, *Moulin*, by movement in two opposing circles.
8. *EL FROTTADO*. Friction from the Moulinet, resolved by
9. *EL OCHO*, to centre, to "Eye" in smallest circle (=Oc; oke, oak-tree, etc.).
10. *EL ABANICO*. L'Eventail, the pigeon or "fanning out", to
11. *EL RUADE*, the Wheel, or Great Circle (the path, the Way) leading to
12. *EL CRUZADO*, the Cross, or final balance (similar to figures seen in English folk-dance, "Parson's Farewell").

Another movement, *LA VIGNE*, is really a double step or routine, used in the circular figures of La Corte or Le Moulinet. The modern form of *Tango* is quicker than the ritual form.

TANGO DAS TODTEN (Nazi Germany)
Germans are proverbially great lovers of music and the arts. This culture did not disappear in their aggressive war on Europe. Of numerous proven details, one characteristic example (1943) may suffice:

"In Yanov the tortures and the murders were carried on with musical accompaniment. An orchestra was formed of the inmates and a special tune called the 'Tango of Death' was composed. When this camp was disbanded every member of the orchestra was put to death".[1]

At the Sobitor "Reception Centre" near Lublin in Poland, the Nazi S.S. gave further evidence of their *Echt Deutsche Kulture*. The organised S.S. arranged *Abende Sänger*—evening "entertainments" in which music and dance were combined with song. Here the Jewish prisoners were compelled to sing *Give us back our Moses;* and several others played a synagogue chant.

[1] *The Scourge of the Swastika*. Lord Russell of Liverpool. London, 1954 (p. 138).

TANGO-NO-SEKKU (Japan)
Festival of Heroes, held annually about the 5th May. Dedicated to the boys of a household, sometimes called the Festival of Flags for Boys. Puppets are made, displayed in the house for the occasion, representing popular heroes in Japanese history or legend. The models of ancient armour are now merely substitute symbols, for the real armour, in which the Japanese *samurai* boys were invested on their initiation. The great symbol of this festival is an immense golden carp made of paper or cloth, sometimes ten or twenty feet long, hoisted on a flagstaff. The idea is that the sons of the family will be "as strong as the carp", who tries to swim up the waterfall.
[Cp. Girls 'Festival—*Hina Matsuri*]

TANGOV (Polynesian term)
The central diamond figure of numerous dance patterns; called also *trapezoid* (Greek) "as a *Table*"; or *trapezium* (Latin) and diamond, *carrée*. The *Tangov* is essentially formed of two equilateral triangles, placed base to base. Thus the *tangov* forms a basic frame for the curves of the European *vesica piscis* giving two centres and two cutting points. Dancers in Polynesia used the *tangov* as the initial form for making sand patterns (see *Sand Tracings**) for ritual dance; from the four angles were drawn many lines in variable convolutions. If we compare it with the regular square and rectangle (the basic figure used by the Roman augur and the Gothic architect, for their geometrical patterns), we can perceive a similar usage of integral proportions. The diamond, or *tangov*, was set down by the Greeks in the Theatre of Dionysus at Athens, in the brick paving of the orchestra. Obviously they had some definite ritual reason for displaying this simple symbol as a pattern; while we know that these regular full-scale symbols were always followed in ritual by those taking part, according to their office. As *rangov* it offers the same root as *rangoli,** in India (the stage or theatre).

TANHA (Sanskrit and Pali)
Is a basic term, equated with Desire in all its modes; but especially as *trishna* in the soul of Man. *Trishna* is *tanha* as "thirst", as urgent desire for life, experience, worldly existence in form, for which Buddhism prescribed the discipline of the Noble Eightfold Path. *Tanha* appears alike in

Brahmin doctrine and Buddhism; it is that vitalising energy which will, in the words of J. E. Carpenter "generate the Burden, the union of the Five Supports, the well-known energy of *tanha*, desire, the craving for existence, for the gratification of sense, and the pleasure of power and prosperity".[1] The profounder meanings of *Tanha* in *samsara* as the dynamism of the World Dance, imply more, for this dual energy formulates both sense-organ and sense-perception. We are in *Tanda* (Dance) again, with the triune concept of "Dancer-Dance-Dancing". This word supplies the European meaning of Dance or *Tanza*. In the Hindu system: the mythos of World Dance is projected in the immensely grand figures of the Dancing Shiva* and his alternate "spouse", the Dancing Kali, while symbols of this figurative dance are set on many a Tibetan *tangka** (temple banner). While universal *tanha*, as a cosmic energy concentrated on vitalist formation (creative evolution) appears within the soul of Man as a consciously realized thirst for experience in life; for feeling, sensation, knowledge, fame and finally wisdom with release — that same *tanha* appears, in even more massive rhythms, as the total energisation comprised in the world of nature; and apparent, to the objective view of early men, as the Soul of Nature, as a vast power to be sought, gained, mastered, and used. This power has been given many names: its rhythmic energies are perceived as periodical dances of life and form; and we know it as *mana** or *orenda*; as "grace" or as "holy spirit". Early religions sought to make contact with these energies at peak modes, not to supplicate, but to unite with and to use. For this purpose were contrived many rituals of dynamic dance form, much as canals or channels were devised for intercepting and using water for crops; for they too are athirst; and desire the water of life.

[1] *Theism in Mediaeval India*. J. Estlin Carpenter. p. 31 - 32.

TANJORI NATYAM (India)

Religious Dance of the Tanjore Temples — chiefly a ritual-dance system, following the *Bharata Natyam** style of dance; done by the *devi-dasas* (formerly), and now by affiliated dancing girls. Tanjore is one of the oldest centres of Shivaism, and thus centres its devotion on the Dancing Shiva.

TANSY DANCE (England)

Mediaeval England had a series of Easter rituals, among which *The Tansy Cake* and *Dance* came on the following Wednesday. The ceremonial was continued in Yorkshire until the late 17th century. There was a custom of "unshoeing" young men on the Monday, by the girls; which shoes were redeemed on the Wednesday by the youths, bringing small ransom presents, including a sector of Tansy Cake. The term *tansy* appears, according to one version, to derive from Greek *athanasia*, as "the death cake", and like rosemary, the "herb of remembrance", but also that of recovery. An entertainment was made, with this redemption of shoes and gift of cake, that was followed by simple folk dancing. Tansy cake had to be green. To the flour, eggs, sugar, cream and butter on which it was based, spinach leaves were added. The tansy herb was, says Selden, among the bitter herbs used by the Jews at this season.[1] Gerard's *Herball* (1633) commends tansy as a "spring medicine".

[1] *Table Talk*. John Selden.

TANTARA (Phoenicia)

Ancient dance, possibly Egyptian, related to the musical schemes that provided the music. Tara was the "sounding string" and possibly Tanis was the "Bright Goddess who Spoke" (as Titania, Tanis etc.). The instruments began with the *tara* (*tambora*, *tambourina*, *tambour*, or *tambura*), probably with one string; then came the *du-tara* (two strings) or *dutar*; the *si-tara* (Indian) with three strings; and the *chi-tara* (four-strings), which turned to *guitar*, but also *gita* (song). These traditional names throw light on development of string instruments.

TANTRA — 1 (Sanskrit)

Is the generic Hindu term for liturgy or ritual, as used in ceremonial of formal worship. The twin streams of *Tantra* and *Vedanta* run as "Practice and Theory" in the massive *Sat Darshanas* (Six Views) of Hinduism. Therefore, the *Tantrik* systems and books control the exposition of doctrine, in the various schemes of devotion, praise and worship, in almost all current Hindu worship, as the *Vedanta* controls their general doctrine as theme or content. The third exponent of religion appears in the *Puranas*, or mythic stories, which tell of the "doings of the gods", and thus supply certain thematic material, on traditions of form and figure, for the presentation of ritual dance episodes. The ritual of *Tantra* is made explicit by means of its dual ceremonial exposition in (a) *Yantra*, and (b) *Mantra*; or the visual formal arrangement of position, gesture, and relation, as combined with the chanting and musical form in sound. *Yantra* begins with statement of position and power: *Mantra* emerges as the complementary expression, in sound, of this power in action; while the Sacred Dance extends their mythic expression (by means of imagined entities, as the cosmic gods and goddesses — as *Shakta** and *Shakti*, or positive and negative universal powers) to forms more easily comprehended by the ordinary worshipper. The ad-

vanced worshipper learns to pass beyond ceremonial action and formalised devotion, into the
inner reaches of his own mind. He may still watch
Natyam; he may still engage in ceremony; he may
still voice praise, and perform music; but now he
knows what they mean and what they imply; he
has combined the *Sat Darshana* of successive
phases, into one inclusive comprehension that perforce includes himself.
[See *Natya Veda; Indian Dance; Sacred Dance;
Yantra-raja*]

TANTRA — 2 (Sanskrit)
The *Tantras* (explained in numerous works by Sir
John Woodroffe, e.g. *Principles of Tantra*) pre-
scribe ceremonial and formulae for worship, for
prayer and sacrifice, similar to the missals and
breviaries for the European Latin systems, from
the *agape* to the *messe* or supper. In these ceremonies we find rituals followed by use of position
and gesture, by chant and simple musical form. The
Tantra includes its essential factors of *Yantra* (the
elements of position and movement) with *Mantra*
(the bases of rhythm in songs of praise) for which
parallel forms can be found in European churches
and chapels, though the rhythmic element of dance
(inherited from Hebrew and Arab sources, as in
Seville) died from these rites, but developed in
India to the splendours of the *Bharata Natyam,***
or temple dance. In general we may say that
Tantra and its pragmatic ritual affords a close
parallel to the theory of Vedanta.
[See *Principles of Tantra; Introduction to Tantra.*
Sir John Woodroffe (formerly Justice of High
Court, Calcutta)]

TANTRA NUSARENA (India)
An ancient book, or code of ceremonial, noted in a
work bearing this name. From this particular cult
of ascetics, some of the rebelling Buddhist cults
(circa 350 BC) were formulated, becoming known
as Nazarene in Iran and in Syria, as they spread
from Kashmir. The *Tantra* in India presents the
practicable system of liturgy and worship, while
the Vedanta contains the theoretical or theological
side of the ancient doctrines. The *Tantrika* liturgy
was highly developed in ceremonial; and it was, in
fact, a denial of what they described as superfluous
ritual, which caused some Hindus to revolt against
the Brahmin or priestly system (and that of the
Kshattriya, of whom Gautama was one), in favour
of a far simpler system. The result was the great
Buddhist system, now itself formulated into as
many sects or cults as the Brahmins had; and with
an accumulation of complex ceremonial, spreading
into ritual and dance forms, in connection with a
vast pantheon of gods. The Nazareni did maintain a

distant and pure cult in its Syrian centres; which
they founded in Harran and on the shore of Galilee lake. Finally they merged with the Syrians, and
had the Nazar-Beth or Naxari-Beth (House). With
them were the *San-nyasa* — the "Unmarked Ones",
who denied all cults.

TANZ (Modern German)
Means *Dance;* but the origin of this word is not
exactly known. Maybe the root exists in ancient
Sanskrit or Zend, since the transition goes with the
Odin legend. Carlyle has a brief reference which
has a distinct Hindu flavour;[1] especially in relation
to one of their basic concepts of Cosmic Movement.
Grimm (he says) denies that any man Odin ever
existed. "The word Wuotan, the original form of
Odin, spread as a name of their chief divinity, over
all Teutonic nations; this word . . . means primarily
Movement, Source of Movement, Power; and is
the name of the highest god . . . Wuotan means
winding, force of movement". What the prefix
Wuo means, is "dark". It may mean Unity, or
Cosmos; "What IS" and thus the "Dancing Universe". Odin came, it was said, from the Black Sea
region, with twelve companions (according to
Eddas of Snorro). Carlyle remarks : "The World
of Nature, for every man, is the Phantasy of Himself; this world is the multiplex Image of his own
Dream" — and thence proceeds to the problem of
Odin's *Runes,* and the miracles or magic, *Runes*
comprise the Scandinavian alphabet . . . a kind of
second speech. These formative lines, when linked
with their primal circle or egg, indicate distantly
the choreographic mode of Wuotan's process of
moving, or dancing, in terms of form and position
— facts which fix sound and meaning to diagram
lines. Finally, Carlyle reminds us of our Wednesday, Wansborough, Wanstead and Wednesbury,
though he omits Edin-Burgh and the Irish Etain.
[1] *Heroes and Hero-Worship.* Thomas Carlyle.

TAO-TAO (Polynesia — Tonga or Friendly Islands)
One of the principal dances in these Islands, which
appears prominently in all their religious ceremonies. Invading missionaries have almost succeeded in destroying these traditional rites.

TAPLAS (Welsh)
A spontaneous gambol, or dance, usually referring
to a single person.

TARA (Ireland)
Historical site of the Palace of Kings in ancient
Ireland; sustained by the solid fact of a discernible
position, some twenty miles north of Dublin. Seen
from the air, it shows two great circles within containing curves of an immense S-shape, marked as

banked mounds with a central dome in one circle. This was *Teamhair na Riogh, Tara of the Kings*. There was held the *Feis* of Tara, a great assembly, with laws and judgements, feasts and dancing. Two parallel banks, seven hundred feet long, are called *Teach Miodhchuarta*, or Banquet Hall. Few firm dates are yet known. That there were ritual ceremonials, with chant and dance, seems certain from other parallel evidence; that we know next to nothing of the actual forms is equally certain; yet it was a Druid centre before the destroying Latin invasions, begun by one Padreigh; though (as with Stonehenge in Britain), the Druids were by no means the original constructors.

TARANTELLA—1 (Italy)
A courting dance of South Italy, Sicily and Sardinia, with local variations. The music, in 3/8 or 6/8 time, gradually increases speed, while partners mime a sequence of pursuit, retreat, persuasion, and final surrender, similar to that in the *Saltarello*.* Usually danced by a man and woman to accompaniment of mandolins, guitars and a drum, it is sometimes performed solo, the dancer playing castanets or tambourine. It is to this high-speed solo dance that has become attached the legend of the tarantula spider, for whose bite the dance was said to be a cure, but science now declares this insect to be no more poisonous than a wasp. The supposed victims of the spider's bite were made to dance until they dropped, exhausted, similar to the Rumanian dance of exorcism *Occhuli Draculi*.* The epidemic known as Tarantism occurred in Italy in the 15th, 16th and 17th centuries, and was similar to the mediaeval German hysterical outbursts, or dancing mania. A few songs and airs played by wandering bands of musicians to cure the afflicted (known as Tarantists) were preserved by Kircher in the 17th century, but this *Tarantella* bore little resemblance musically to the modern dance. The *Tarantella* is danced in Sicily on every possible occasion, to accompaniment of hand-

clapping, couples improvising their own figures. It is found in Capri and Sorrento, and in Apulia is known as the *Taranda*. A variation in Calabria is the shepherd's dance, the *Pecorara* or *Pasturara*. The most instinctive dance of South Italy, it is familiar to all from childhood, and babies hear the *Tarantella* rhythm sung to them while dandled on their mother's knee. A famous theatrical example was Fanny Elssler's dance in the ballet *La Tarantule*, at Paris in 1839.

TARANTELLA—2 (Italy)
Traditional Dance, named from Tarentum, but known as *Treguenda** or the *Danza alla Strega*, the magical dance of the witch-women. The place is a very ancient Greek centre; so that in AD 170, a new settlement was founded by a Christian mission from Britain, headed by one Chadval or Caedwal, at Tarentum, from which the cathedral of Tarento developed. The dance gave name and tradition to the place, from a simple magical device. The witches are said to have danced at the "three ways", weaving by their steps an invisible trap or web, to ensnare travellers at certain times. From this method came the legend of the tarantula spider; but the story grew the wrong way round. To be caught in the dancing web meant that the spider had caught the unwary victim. The modern dance, in 6/8 time, belongs chiefly to Napoli. Quack doctors so named a spider (it measures over two inches across), from an affliction (same as Vitus dance), which they alleged to be due to the "bite", and curable by performing the dance.
[See *Treguenda*]

TARANTELLA—3 (Naples, Italy)
Is said to be a notable episode of the Whitsuntide pilgrimage of Monte Virgine, near Naples, attended by perhaps 40,000 pilgrims, of whom more than half come from that city, twenty miles distant. This seems to be associated with the Madonna dell 'Arco. After "kissing the earth" by the shrine, the pilgrims don ribbons, flowers, and garlands, some held on long poles. Gay plumes and ribbons decorate the horses. At a certain point half way on return home, everybody descends and dances an old *Tarantella Danza*, which is said here to present a "love story", in action, when two dancers act as the enamoured swain and his lover; followed by carolling the popular songs of the day, mixed with an occasional traditional tune. The dance is here not merely a technically executed folk-dance.
[See *Danza dell' Arco*]

TA-RA-RA-BOOM-DE-AY (London, 19th century)
Merits inclusion within the annals of dance by reason of the extraordinary popularity of this

Tarantella.   ITALY

"dance suite" in the "Nineties" as one of the high peaks of the London Music Hall. The heroine, Lottie Collins, was featured often at the Grand Theatre, Islington, as "England's Skirt Dancer", The magical syllables of this mystic chant were devised by the poet Richard Morton, set to music by Angelo Usher, and sung by Miss Collins with indescribable gusto, assisted invariably by an audience that might include cabinet and clerical ministers. The incantation of the chorus repeats eight times the syllables "Ta-ra-ra-Boom-de-ay"; and (it was agreed by many ministers) conveyed as much common sense as most of their professional pronouncements. This was in 1891; the vigorous tribal chant endured a decade or more afterwards, to become one of the traditional chants of London costermongers (barrow boys now). The song was followed by the Skirt Dance, fast and furious. There was a polka, a waltz, and a galop in the suite (all composed by Josef Meissler), and a Polka March. *Ta-ra-ra-Boom-de-ay* was a great favourite of Thomas Hardy, the novelist.

TARASCA

From Spanish *Tarascon* (modern Spanish gives *tarascar*, to bite, like a dog). *Tarasca* was the Dragon, the enemy of the Hobby Horse; presumably the "Evil One" who fought the May Games combat (Winter *versus* Spring) supported by the black-faced hordes of Black Winter, and under command of the Black (Winter) Prince. *Tarasca* was one of the earliest victims of the two martyr risings of the old English May Games — first by the Reformation, then by the Puritans in their attack on all spectacles, religious or secular. He was not the "same character" as the Hobby Horse, but the *alter ego*. In France *Le Chevalet* (Horse) had the same opponent. In the older Portuguese idiom, *tarasco* means "wild or savage" (the furious dance), while *tarasca* indicates a "bad woman" or an old sword. There is a French village or small town, Tarascon, named from its fame as the centre of this annual ceremonial. Probably this Spanish name derived from *taurescu*, the "bull people", rather than a horse; and belonged thenceforth not to a factual rite but to a puppet performance of substitute, much as the term "marionette" is derived in France from Marian of the May Games.
[Cp. *Tewrdannckh* (Belgium)]

TARI-PIRING (Sumatra)

A dance performed by men and women, with a lighted candle in a saucer held on the palm of each hand. Beginning in a seated position, to a very smooth rhythm, dancers turn and twist arms and hands, the candle flames flickering but never going out. Presently the dancers rise, and continue weaving sinuous patterns, bodies and arms dipping and swaying, in continued, unbroken rhythm. Popular legend tells a story of a Shalendra princess who lost her ring; and explains the dance as depicting her servants searching for it at night by candle light, but the dance has a far older meaning, being an old ancestral dance. It can be called *Tari Piring* (Saucer Dance) or *Tari Lilin* (Candle Dance).
[Cp. *Menari Henei* (Malaya); *Binasuan* (Phillipines)]

TAROT — 1 (from Hebrew)

An inversion of *TORAH*, "the Law" *Tarot* is a popular (and somewhat vulgarised) idea of "The Prophets" in the sense of *Fortuna*; but this was not its origin. Four secret Qabalistic symbols became attached (through ritual usage) to the four letters *IHVH* of *Tetragrammaton*; so that from these we may deduce (a) the origin of the Tarot pack of seventy-two "playing cards" and the later amusement pack of fifty-two cards (seasons or courts of four quarters). Some of the pictorial symbols are extant:

> *The Wand* (Staff of Power) as the I or Yod;
> *The Cup* (of Libation) to H;
> *The Sword* (or Divider) to V;
> *The Shekel of Gold* (wheel) to final H.

The system of *Temurah* or Permutation gave rise to various card games. The liturgical form was ritualised on the *Deck* (or *navis* or ship), as Dance.

TAROT — 2; TARROCHI, Dance of

A popular "fortune-telling dance" active in France and Italy in the 10th to 12th centuries; associated with "playing cards" or picture-diagrams on coloured cards. These were at first painted by hand; then printed by woodblocks with colours dropped in; finally they assume the familiar form of modern "playing cards" used for sedentary games. These are not the full Tarot set of seventy-two cards or rolls formerly used for the real dance game. The name also has collapsed into "trot". The same "role by card" system is continued by the Lama monks in the Tibetan temple plays; actors who do not learn their parts are allotted painted cards; a picture of the make-up and costume on one side; the cues or leading words on the reverse (see *Three Tibetan Mysteries*). Such cards exist in India (some are round) and probably the method of the fortune telling came from India. The dance form was an early mode of the Paul-John (now Jones) with one seat less than the dancers numbered; after the ceremonial introductions, the trot was round the seats and there was then a joker, an odd-man out. This dance-drama had an earlier ritual form of which little can now be learned; possibly with the four courts belonging to the four seasons and the four "temperaments" of man.

TARTS (West Europe)

A modernised and vulgarised appellation, slanted at chorus girls in "the profession", which is the fag-end of an ancient religious Asian term, derived from Ash-Tarte, the great Assyrian Goddess of Love. The *ash-tartes* of ritual were the feminine devotees and dancers in the celebrations, including the ceremonial meal or *messe*. That gathering has left to the confectioner the generic term "tarts", for the more attractive pastries (*pasta*), while in Scotland we find another relic from the same tradition, in the tartan patterns of the kilt. The *tartan* was a high military rank in Babylon; a member of the king's retinue; he wore a checkered pattern cloak which distinguished his rank—much as now stripes, pips, and tabs indicate title. In Scotland the *tartan* is the pattern (checks of colour) while the *plaid* is the substance; usually of wool, thirty or forty inches wide and twelve yards long (at its fullest measure), drawn over the shoulders, but at night used as a wrapping. Each clan had its own tartans, used for plaids, and even for *trews*, and the women's cloak, not only in Scotland but by Irish Gaels. The Stuart shield was "checky" like tartan. The English equivalent is the *gingham* (*King-game**) checker pattern, along with the colloquial *ginks* (the older folk), and its accompaniment "high ginks or jinks" as a "fun and games" term. *High Jinks* was a charade game. At the English royal courts, Maids of Honour inherited the place and function of the religious *Ash-tartes* of ancient times; and in this manner, received their perquisites. At the ancient town of Kingston-on-Thames, where rests a Coronation Stone on which seven English monarchs were crowned, there was naturally a Court of Honour. At Richmond, village near by, a baker regularly supplied certain dainties, still known as "Maids of Honour" (even if they lack pedigree of cost and cooking). This requisition has records: The original warrant book of the Board of Green Cloth (entry by Lord Steward) says:

"June 12, 1681 : Order this day was given : that Maides of Honour should have Cherry Tarts instead of Gooseberry Tarts, it being observed that Cherrys are at three pence per pound".

TASVIR, also as TASBIR (Northern India)

The "living image" or mental image, formed in response to hearing the appropriate *raga** (melody-motif) correctly played on the right instrument at the proper time. There are two phases : the rarest is the formative response of the creative artist, who, on hearing the *raga*, is able (after making his solemn devotions to *Sri-ragini* Sarasvati (goddess of music), to project mentally a suitable pictorial form. Holding this steadily in mind, before his mental vision, he then transfers this image of the dancer to his prepared paper. The second phase is that of the observer, who hears the melody and concentrates on the painted picture. Thus he blends his aural perception with his visual perception, becoming able to receive these into his mental repertory as a single strongly organised memory-picture. He is thence initiated into the third or final phase, which he can obtain either from the melody heard, or from the picture seen. This is the ultimate reflex of creative power : he is able to cause the mental image to repeat her movement, or to continue the dance; or even to command a new dance in the same general mode. The subtle psychological process thus indicated is related to the more profound *Tantra** ritual.

TATTOO DANCE (Borneo)

Among the Kayans or Kalabits (also the Roro people of New Guinea), girls are not thought to be marriageable without tattooed designs, often on the legs, which are proudly displayed at public festivals. At the annual agricultural dance, the "gods of fertility" are invoked by troops of male dancers, each carrying a drum decorated with long streamers. From their heads hang long strings of plaited leaves; their hair is decorated with brilliant flowers. On arrival at the ground, the dance begins with peculiar crouching movements, suddenly changing in response to drum rhythms. Without warning groups of girls appear, dance through the line of men for a few minutes, then as suddenly depart. The swing of their skirts allows glimpses of beautifully tattooed thighs, certain designs meaning that they are eligible for marriage.

TAUPOS' DANCE (Samoa)

Chiefs of each village appoint a girl of their household to be the *Taupo*, or ceremonial hostess. At about fifteen or sixteen years, she holds a position of prestige, is given courtesy titles, attended by a retinue of young girls, and will later marry a chief's son from another village. It is her duty to serve older women in their social duties, to wait upon and entertain guests, and to be village hostess on ceremonial occasions. When one village visits another, the young men ceremonially wait upon the visiting *Taupo* with gifts, to sing and dance for her. Conversely, it is a mark of courtesy to a guest, for the *taupo* to dance for him .At a ceremonial *siva* (dance), the *taupo*, accompanied by her maids, leads the formal applause (chosen from a few set phrases), and may not dance until she con-

siders it time to end the party. Her highly ceremonious dance is performed with an equal number
of dancers (as clowns or jesters) on either side of
her. While mocking her dance with comic antics,
at the same time they honour the *taupo*. All their
movements are directed towards her as the central
figure, and by contrast, emphasise her grace
and beauty. She must dance with proud, remote
expression, her movements grave and dignified.
Periodically she may vary her serious expression
by an impudent grimace, but this is the only
deviation from an otherwise aloof gravity and
serenity.   [See *Samoan Dancing; Clowns' Dance*]

TAUR NA-MBAK AND TAURE (Malekula, New Hebrides)

The two most important circular dances on Malekula and the Small Islands. *Taur Na-mbak* is performed from dusk to dawn for several consecutive
nights preceding the great day of sacrifice in the
ritual cycle, *Ramben;** and *Taure* takes the same
position in the second ritual, *Maki-ru.** The two
dances are similar in form, but as *Maki-ru* is symbolically more important and visually more elaborate, *Taure* is the most important dance in the whole
long cycle of *Ramben* and *Maki-ru*, which may last
fifteen to twenty, or even thirty years. In structure
both dances follow the pattern described for
*Turei Na-mbe,** consisting of three concentric
circles of "guests", Maki-men, and women. They
alternate singing and dancing of refrain and verses
of songs. They differ from *Turei Na-mbe* only when
the guests, the innermost circle, instead of forming
a cluster, "ray out" from the centre, each "ray"
representing one village. In that formation they
dance round counter-clockwise with rapid movements, contrasting with the dignified Maki-men
(initiates), who dance more slowly, clockwise.
Taure is of ancient origin, a dance called *teur* being
known on Malekula before the growth of the
elaborate ritual cycles. Connected with veneration
of the ancestors and the sacrifice of tusked boars,
both *Taur Na-mbak* and *Taure* honour the dead
and celebrate the mystical identification of the
Maki-men with the boars to be sacrificed at the
culminating rite. "Taur" means "to mourn", but in
the sense of one life being ended and a new and
fuller life about to begin; in this connection signifying the period of seclusion after sacrifice, when
initiates are mourned by their wives, are "reborn"
and receive new names and titles. There is a subtle
distinction in the two dance names—*Taure*, coming
at the peak of the whole long, double cycle, symbolises solely the mystical death and rebirth; while
the suffix *Na-mbak* added to *Taur* in the earlier
ritual, signifies also the more earthly form of
rebirth, the outcome of the love-making which

takes place when *Taur Na-mbak* is danced throughout the night preceding the great sacrifice.
[See *Turei Na-mbe; Ramben; Maki-ru; Malekula,
dances of*]

TAWEF (Arabia)

Ritual dance in circumambulation of the Shrine of
Mekka, the Kaaba; the general approach is called
Haj or *Hajr*, and also *Yatra*. This dance or walk
ends with the traditional salute, the pilgrim's kiss
on *Hajr-ul-Aswad* (*Black Stone*) and on *Hajr-ul-
Yaman* (Brown Stone).

TAZZIA (Persian, Arabic)

The religious drama or play (done at Moharram
festival of the Shias of Islam), centred on the
"Death of Husain and Hassan", and often accompanied by processional dances. From this: *fantazzia* links with the Greek phantaze; while in Italian
tazzia came to mean a cup. An allied term *tazzie*
means a "swift runner", in general; a greyhound in
particular; or a particularly active dancer-tumbler.
A *tarr* is the accompanying guitar or banjo.

TEACHING DANCE

Requires far more than ability to dance; despite the
fallacious ideas of some critics. First the dancer
must demonstrably be able to *do* each dance; next
she must be able consciously to *explain* its form
and movement; then finally she must be able to
criticise constructively her students' endeavours.
The rare good teacher has, therefore, to be an artist
in teaching as well as an artist in dancing : indeed,
of the two powers, that in tuition is of more real
use. Textbooks are valuable as supports; an academic system is even better; but the final test is on
the stage of the theatre.

TECUANES, DANZA DE LOS (Mexico)

"Tiger Dance". Belongs to Guerrero district, famous
for its animal and mask dances. Formerly part of
a ritual for successful hunting, it is now a comedy
dance-play with definite characters, dialogue, and
the final killing of the tiger. Besides the tiger
(Tecuan) characters include hunters with dogs and
ropes, five servants, two doctors, two dogs, two
deer, four ospreys and a man dressed as a woman.
The *toucan* is played by a dancer in a striped
overall with a big tiger mask. First a set series is
danced with swift steps to lively music. Then, after
discussion about how to catch him, all set out to
hunt the tiger, which is presently captured and
brought in, his skin to be used for breeches for the
Master of the proceedings. Measurements for the
breeches are taken and the performance ends with
a dance of leave-taking, both outside and inside the

church. The English mumming play is recalled by the man-woman; and the clowning of the *tecuan* who, during the figure-dancing, skips about using his detachable tail as the "Fool" uses his bladder, to flick the dancers with. During the hunting of the tiger one man is wounded, and healed by the doctors, while humorous remarks about them are passed. This dialogue is partly in the Aztec language. [See *Macoleras*]

TELEIDDYN (Welsh)

The minstrel-harper, of the highest class, in mediaeval Wales, who travelled with his small company from court to court, from feast to feast; or was put on the staff as a regular retainer. His instrument was the *Telan* or harp; and any of his companions would, as well as dancing and reciting as a *tantawr* or "musician on strings", also play for the ladies. His object here was usually *tangnefedd*—to achieve for them a period of tranquillity. Thus his repertory tended to fill with carols as love-songs, ballads and short poems, rendered in couplets or triplets. At the other extreme came the *Ysgentyn*, the cruder buffoon of the dining-hall.

TELEVISION—Dance on

As an electro-mechanical process of mass communication, has so far proved unable—or unwilling—to produce developed modes of dance, especially fitted to its limited medium. The popular small screen used in the home first loses immensely in scale; while colour remains absent. The method is in the hands of technicians and office staff. Offerings have ranged from glimpses of stage ballet to sections of stylised folk-dance, or cabaret numbers alternating with old style music-hall turns, with an occasional glance at some festival item caught by a travelling camera. Dance is immensely outweighed by the various sports and games industries; it is rarely understood so well. Probably Television could develop a dance mode in better relation with its limited power—especially in chamber ballet with mime based on a clear story—but the chronic shortage of ideas is everywhere evident. As with music, television is hampered by loss of scale and living impact.

TERAPHIM (Assyrian-Hebrew)

Name for figures used in divination, as *Urim** and *Thummim* indicators. There were thirty-two in a set; usually they were named, in this plural, as *Teraphim* (the *Khrbu* or *Kerubhim* were the "players" or announcers). This defined number of thirty-two appears in many places, in several religious schemes. In the ancient Chinese *Pa-Kwa*, there are "thirty-two paths", or connections (from the sixty-four sides, points, positions, forces etc.). With the Chinese compass, we have the modern nautical compass; it has thirty-two points. The chessboard, now standard, has sixty-four squares with thirty-two playing figures, sixteen on each side. Possibly the *teraphim* were also made and used in two opposing sets. It is clear that a single *teraph* alone was useless for prediction or divination. As the movement is as necessary as the opposition of the forces (or qualities, meanings, indications etc.), their play resolves into a kind of ritual dance. From the existence of the "Sacred Tree" in Korsabad and Nineveh (made on a large scale), which was shown as mythic symbol on the alabaster walls; and used in ritual, as incised in the floor; we know that its "thirty-two paths" were, in fact, traversed by the priests during ceremony. These same "thirty-two paths" were revived once more in the mediaeval *Qabalah*,* and as this term indicates "permutations and combinations", once more we learn that movement is essential to read the doctrine. The Teraphim were traditional dancing-acting figures or puppets, inherited from Babylon; and used for dramatic shows; for fortune telling; and the "lares and penates" or household gods of a minor kind. They present, in a smaller scale and emphasis, copies of the more majestic figures seen in the *Five M'Gilloth*,* the chief Hebrew Festivals, where "cherubim and seraphim continually do cry" in the solemn dance rituals. The Jews naturally carried their traditions from the Diaspora, into every land; into Spain and Southern France. At Arles there was a centre, taken over by the Christians from older builders, where cloisters for miracle plays were devised. The numerous Jewish visitors (it was then, a port) referred to the place as the Santa Teraphim, which name was gradually distorted into an unknown "Saint Trophime". Similar changes occurred in the nearby town Santa Gillies. Acting-dancing puppets are famous in Java in several modes; the European mode long survived in Puppet drama, though rarely in dancing episodes. When the wooden painted figures were no longer used in actual dramatic mode (moving and nodding etc.) they were carried in street processions as holy idols, especially in Spain, with a chanted accompaniment and dances at intervals. Some of these figures are notable examples of realistic sculpture. Finally (in England) the tradition ended in such places as the famous West Front of Wells Cathedral (*circa* 1300), where some three hundred figures, fully painted and gilded, represented as many mythic persons from scriptures. Others were made at Chartres.
[See *Tarota*]

TERGUL DE FÊTE (Rumania)
A marriage market, which used to be held yearly
on 29th June at the top of the Gaina Mountain.
Treated as a general holiday, families for miles
around travelled to the market, the trousseaux of
marriageable girls carried in painted chests on
wagons drawn by the best horses or oxen. Live-
stock and beehives were also taken, and displayed
around the family tent, outside which the head of
the family sat, awaiting applications for his daughter's hand. Eligible young men, wearing a broad
leather belt holding gold and silver coins, to indicate the degree of their solvency, also attended
with their families. After bargaining, suitable terms
would be arranged, and the young couples betrothed, when general celebrations followed with
dancing and singing. The couples were married in
the following Spring.
[Cp. *Mailehen* (Germany); *Marriage Market Dance;
Tlustni Dni* (Poland)]

TERPSICHORE (Hellas)
The "Muse of Dancing", figures as one of the Nine
Muses, traditionally said to be the leaders of culture and learning in ancient Hellas. Originally
there were three — *Meleta* (Meditation); *Mneme*
(Memory); and *Aoide* (Song), as three modes of
time, for the legend is older than the Grecian
culture.

TERUK-KUTTU (South India)
Festival dance-play, performed in places through
Tamil Nad; one of the typical Indian folk-plays,
deriving generally from the religious *Bhagavata
Mela Nataka** (Festival celebrations play), and
similar to *Vithi Nataka*, as seen in Andhra; and
related to the *Yaksha Gana** performances of the
Telugu country. They are performed on a small
stage, often a temporary construction, by men
only. The stage may be a small rectangular affair
of bamboo, with back and half-wings; or a circular
earth platform, with a slight roof but no walls,
called *mandapa*, around which the audience sit on
three sides. There is no scenery except curtains.
Every actor enters, dancing; usually one by one,
according to the announcing chant of the *guru*.
Most of these modern plays are comprised within
the general group known in Ceylon as *Nadagama*.
Characters and treatment vary from place to place.

TESKOTO (Yugoslavia)
An ancient dance from the Macedonian mountains,
performed by men in a close line or curve. Their
arms are linked behind, each man grasping the
sash of his neighbours, so that the line moves as
one man, in perfect co-ordination. Accompanied
by a drummer, who takes his time from the leader

of the dance, the dancers begin slowly, gradually
building up to a climax. The leader flourishes a kerchief as he calls the changes in time and step. At
first the movements are slow and cautious, as
though the men are testing the ground before
trusting their weight to it. The drummer follows
their movements, sometimes kneeling as he beats
his rhythms, and, as the leader calls, the whole
line smoothly dips and sways. Often on one foot,
the other bent across from the knee, or at the back,
they spring up and continue their catlike, cautious
movements with perfect balance. As the tempo
increases, the leader breaks away, passes the kerchief to the next man and dances to the other end
of the line. The next man does likewise, and so on,
until the leader is in his original place, and the
dancers once more in a linked curve. The dance
ends with the drummer kneeling before the leader,
who stands on the drum and places one foot on
the drummer's head, which suggests the possible
ritual origin of the dance.
[Cp. *Rugovo Warriors Dance* (Yugoslavia)]

TETRAGRAMMATON (Greek term used in Hebrew:
   Qabbalah*)
The "four-speaker", or the "square-word"; also the
"four(th) speakings". Along with the *Sepher Yetzirah,** this generic god-name is used by Jewish
Kabbalists, as a potent symbol in their unravelling
of the occult meanings of their Bible. They assert
that if read literally these sacred books are not-
sense; that *Kabbalah* is the true key to the Bible.
The written formula of *Tetra-grammaton* requires
the ten numbers and the twenty-two letters of the
Hebrew Schem-ha-Phorasch. These are symbolised
by the *kerubim*, as the potent letter-words (of the
*Schem-ha-phorasch** — "Carpet of Letters"), in
which they are extended to seventy-two, plus a
central one (similar to the council or Great Sanhedrin). The necessary movement, to and from any
one point to any other, constitutes the primal
ritual dance. Visitors to the British Museum can
see in the Assyrian Gallery the Babylonian origin:
the Tree of Life, formulated as "three pillars"
together with the traditional "thirty-two Paths" (or
routes, influences, aspects, etc.) from one whorl
or nexus to any other. This profound symbol-
diagram (*otzharim*) was used, both on walls for
instruction and on temple floors for ritual, in the
Temples of Babylon, whence the Hebrew prophets
were graduated. In *Idra Rabba Qadisha* ("Greater
Holy Assembly"), Rabbi Simeon began:[1] "Time
for Thee, O Tetragrammaton, to lay to Thine hand
. . . Wherefore is this name employed? It is
written: Who is like unto thee among the gods
(Elohim), O Tetragrammaton". He continues: "He
who walks, going up and down . . .(*from one house*

to another) reveals the secret; but the faithful in spirit conceal the word . . . Wherefore, then, "walks?" What is this word, "Walks?" In fact, it means the ritual dance. (They are in the *Ha-Yekel* . . . the temple or palace . . .). "By nine paths, evolved from the perfect name, which is 'Tetragrammaton expressed' and 'Tetragrammaton hidden'." [2] This makes IHVH and ALHIM (*Elohim*): that is, the square place, and its seven creative spirits who "dance" therein. Their dance seeks to achieve (to reveal) "equilibrium in balance", or harmony of contraries; a fundamental qabalistical idea.

[1] *The Kabbalah Unveiled.* Trans. of *Kabbala Denudata* (*Rosenroth*) by S. L. M. Mathers.

[2] Former is written with vowel points of the latter.

TEWRDANNCKH (Belgium)
Processional display with street dancing, celebrated annually at Antwerp and other places. The name is that of a mediaeval hero—probably from a much earlier Teutonic origin, and possibly developed as the festival of the Winter Solstice. The first record of historical date is a work printed originally in Augsburg in 1519, with the title of *The Adventures of The Praiseworthy Valiant and High-renowned Knight and Hero, Lord Tewrdannckh.* This volume was reproduced by the Holbein Society (London) in 1884, in facsimile, including numerous old woodcuts.

THEATRES (European)
The covered form, appeared at the end of the Renaissance. The Greek amphitheatre could be covered; smaller structures were devised, later copied in London, at first in brick and wood. Plays, then opera or masque, permitted the inclusion of dance action. In Italy, the Teatro Olimpico was designed by Palladio for his birthplace, Vicenza. It was begun in 1579 and completed in 1584, four years after his death by Scamozzi. The first performance was *Oedipus Rex* by Sophocles. The structure, with its two-storied stage, was at first covered with a velarium, over the great auditorium of thirteen tiers. The oldest theatre in Germany is Schlosstheater et Celle, built 1674. In London, wooden theatres were replaced by stone or brick —as Her Majesty's Theatre or King's Theatre. The Great Fire and the Revolution were responsible for changes, reflected in Italian Opera and English pantomime; while the spa dance rooms (Sadler's Wells) developed into theatres.

THEATRE DANCE
The phases of development of *Theatrum* ("House of Gods"—Greek form), follows economic power, social craft ability, and agreement on usage. The earliest phase is the "reserved space"—not always that, for Homer's "dancing place" was first the threshing ground of baked brick, the only hard, clean, flat place in the locality. The area (arena) is then covered with a roof of sorts, especially in Northern lands where rain is frequent. The ritual must be sheltered; it must be unbroken, once begun. (Cricket has not yet caught up; only boxing seeks the shelter of a roof). Then comes the long period of wooden enclosures; of roped enclosures (the *corral*, the ring, the circus, the *kirke*), but stone defence walls come before public ritual. The Greek theatre was constructed of wood, often on a skilfully selected hillside (lessening necessary labour), and only in the final, most prosperous (and often most ritually careless) period, were public theatres built of stone. Precisely the same sequence appears in church structures in Europe; the (a) taking-over of buildings of the "old regime" (here the basilica); then (b) the rapid arrangement of wooden enclosures; (c) wooden buildings intended to last for more than one season; and finally (d) the stone cloister, intended as a regular and permanent church theatre; enclosed within church walls, hugging the nave—usually on south side— and entered through it—and at length deserted by public and players alike for the Inn Yard. Then the commercial roofed-in theatre (growing up alongside with princely hall and regal salon) began, completing the reversal. Greek citizens were paid to attend the public rites; London citizens fight and pay to get into them; while football or cricket competitions are regarded as world-shattering "news". Similarly, the performers in theatres are now regarded as more important than what they perform. Inversion is completed in all aspects; and London theatres are built in dirty back streets. With all these changes, the style of performance, the type of dance, changes in due keeping—the only "gods" now are in the high gallery.

THEMES FOR BALLET—1
As deliberately fabricated works of art, Ballets rarely follow in a system that is solely traditional as do folk dances; or in ceremonial form, like ritual dances; or by social fashions, in the manner of the salon. The ballet is now a commercial theatre commodity; to be designed, made, and sold. Therefore, the theme selected for presentation must be chosen with the same care as those in, for example, books or films, which depend for commercial success on multiplication of copies, followed by wide distribution. The customers come into the theatre; they must come repeatedly and in large numbers, simply to repay the initial cost of production, plus the nightly running expenses. Hence the "Manager" begins, divided by two

desires : he wants a great novelty, but he does not want it to be *too* novel, and incomprehensible. So he would like "something like the public clearly enjoyed before", only more so. He battles with the witless choreographer who "wants to express himself", but who has no experience in real creative production of social value. The "Manager" contends with the "Angel", who will furnish the finance to start a new show, if only his current lady friend can be assured of the leading part for most of the theatre evening, regardless of her real talent or previous experience. Despite all these cares, the average Manager is unable to "pick a winner" as often as the police chief can say with certainty "Who dunnit !"

THEMES FOR BALLET—2

Derive from very different sources : some from "classical ballet", which is, so to say, "in stock". Some works are based on other legends, old or new. Some ballet themes are fitted to exploit poetry; others to confiscate ready-made musical compositions, which the producer rashly guarantees "to interpret". Some shows venture on ice as a modernist novelty; not dancing but skating. Others try much thinner ice when they hire a notorious ballerina to repeat her virtuosi exhibitions, regardless of any kind of artistic or dramatic expression. Or some notorious pseudo-painter will be given another opportunity to advertise his opinion of the public from El Saqqara. Then again, public funds will be guaranteed, to send a ballet company abroad, to advertise "British art" by means of Russian revivals, for the financial benefit of American managers. Themes of any newer ballets, in such repertories, appear to be reckoned of no importance or meaning; but members of the companies may be invited out to local tea-fights, wearing costumes supplied to publicise recent feminine fashions. This device was used earlier by Serge Diaghileff, not to spend but to obtain funds for ballet from a French *couturier* (Mdme. Chanel).

THEMES OF BALLETS

(1) *French Court Ballet* adopted threadbare themes alleged to derive from Greek or Roman religious mythology. Remnants from earlier Masques were occasionally used for the Pastoral type; when nobles and ladies would promenade as shepherds and shepherdesses. The retirement of the Sun King from public practice put an end to the Greek God tradition; and Romantic Ballet began with the Bourgeois Theatre.

(2) *Romantic Ballet* found or devised stories of the supernatural creatures; and the unseen denizens of earth and water, or air and fire were presented on the ballet stage. This notion had novelty of character, if not of treatment; for none of the producers appear to have had any informed ideas of who these creatures were, or what they were supposed to do, besides dance like balletdancers. Nevertheless, the Romantic Ballets held the Theatre for a century, against the rival claims of operatic singers who retailed a different and more social vogue of romantic stories, chiefly from the novelists. Thus two kinds of fiction replaced the older myths.

(3) The Romantic *Nouvelle* culminated in Musical Comedy; recently it has had a come-back in the USA as the "Musical" where film-fun, wildwest opera, and modernist ballet combine to offer the civic glamour of the vanishing "Live Theatre" The Victorian comedies, as done by Gilbert and Sullivan, did not include dance; but conversely they carried much witty topical satire, that is conspicuously lacking from modern ballet, which is as deadly serious as Test Cricket Matches.

(4) *Modernist Dance*, claiming in group productions to be Ballet, has frequently sought to present the theme of the "social problem", and by overdoing a tenuous mode of realism, has become as incomprehensible as many other examples of alleged Modern Art (such as large stones with curious holes in them, said to symbolise the states of the mass mind, or alternatively the combat of the Libido; or repulsive masses of twisted wire, said to present some Unknown Hero or Prisoner). These ballets move in contortions of similar character : they go nowhere, they have no human meaning, social or personal; and bring us to the "Abstract".

(5) *Abstract Ballet*, apparently results from harsh economy plus complete lack of good ideas. While a French dancer states his desire for "ballet without Music", (and some critics think that his works would be as much improved without Dance), some American producers of "novelty" offer "Ballets with no Scenery", or "Ballets in practice costume"; but principally turn to Abstract Ballets, with no meaning, no purpose, or use (except to acquire a few dollars for participants in this circus), These efforts do not show genuine surrealism, as we get in (a) dreams; (b) atom-bomb propaganda; (c) certain radio efforts by Goons; (d) many political speeches; (e) Vatican dogmas; (f) some Paris fashions for women; (g) dance crooning; and many more modern symptoms of the Free World. Abstract Ballet is essentially a shoddy effort to produce effect without reality; a bargain-basement kind of art that is a caricature of the oncemagnificent realism of ballet, even when at its most sycophantic mode in the *Masque* or the *Trionfo*. Art produces many kinds of art works

for many kinds of authentic purpose; but "What is Abstract is never Art".

(6) *Horror Ballet*, following the Horror Comic, endeavours to shock by sensation, and instead of seeking beauty and pleasure by use of felicitous thematic content, substitutes an Essence of Yellow Pressure, as the news of the brave new world. Shakespeare, it is true, leaves his play *Hamlet* littered with fourteen corpses in the last Act, thereby making a "smash hit" superior to crime novels, thrillers and detection, which are modestly content with a body per chapter; a score far below that of the Road Hog Motorist. Smash and Grab alternates with Hit and Run; and the Theatre vainly tries to keep up with a pace Faster than Sound, Faster than Dancing. Faster than sense. We get the Horror Ballet. There was *Miracle in the Gorbals*: the romantic legend of a razor gang and a real modern miracle. There was *The Cage*—guaranteed front page. Several ballets deal with Witch burning (based on the unauthentic researches of Montague Summers, S. J.). There was a pornographic *Carmen*; good for a column in any Sabbath newspaper; though the exploits of Lizzie Borden in *Fall River Legend* occur off-stage.

"Lizzie Borden with an axe,
Gave her father forty whacks.
When she saw what she had done,
She gave her mother forty-one".

So goes the old Massachusets nursery rhyme; but no ballet has yet been made on the Boston theme of *Sacco and Vanzetti*; nor, from Nazi Germany, say, *"The Night of the Long Knives"*. There is a morbid occupation with blood and mud; nights on the tiles (*Le Rendezvous*). *Scheherazade* was too much for the New York police; they demanded that the "Negro Slaves" be made over to Hindus, not to offend local voters; just as the British Home Office once banned *The Mikado*; but they did not stop Maud Allan performing *Salome* with a gory head on a plate.

(7) *Mystical Ballet* refers chiefly to theme, rather than to any special manner of production and performance. From one view, *Giselle* may be termed "mystical", like *Les Sylphides*, because the general theme is magical and non-realistic. But the genuine mystical ballet (or dance) is one able to carry an impression of a spiritual quality that is beyond any superstition. Some of the Miracle Plays attempted this feat; rarely with success; but a really fine performance of *Everyman* sometimes achieves this end. The ballet of *Job*, as produced, fails largely because its real theme is obviously not understood, and William Blake has not been admitted. Pressure of technical exhibitionism (misnamed as "choreography") and "personality of the

dancer" prevent the concentrated thematic expression that is the essential need, first and last. Even in some Hindu Ballet, display has inhibited the real meaning too often. Abstract ballet is futile for this purpose; while the "fairy-tale ballet" remains at the nursery level, however well done.

THEOLOGICAL BALLETS
Have been devised to publicise favourably some doctrine of a definite sect, by way of realism, material, and factual "portrayal of events"; and in contra-distinction from Religious Ballet; which utilises a Mythic mode. We may recall recent productions: of *Job*, or *Everyman*, or interludes in *Pilgrim's Progress*; or older works such as the array of scholastic productions favoured by Jesuit propagandists during the 17th and 18th centuries in Europe. In the USA some dancers (e.g. Ruth St. Denis) have sought to arrange performances of dance in churches, but this does not make such productions theological dances or ballets. Some of them purport to show "Biblical history", by way of performing parables or legends, as if they had happened in material fact (e.g. *The Prodigal Son*, or *The Wise Virgins*). Ballet as an art of fantasy lends its character to genuine myth, but is challenged by the full realism so often sought by earnest clerics. The situation is further complicated by the apathy of the public, especially when they are asked to pay to see propaganda works intended to induce them to lead much better lives. They resent being educated or moralised; they prefer (like a famous queen) to be amused.

THERAPEUTAE (*Thera-putra; Thera-Vada; Thera-vadi*)
Earliest Judaeo-Christian sects known to have included dance in their ritual. Some writers state they are the same as the Essenes.[1] Their name is first mentioned in Maccabees (about BC 150) and by writers including Josephus, Pliny and Philo. When the "Dead Sea Scrolls" are fully translated, more may be learned of their doctrines. Buddhist missions influenced their creeds; they shunned town life; performed healing by means of herbal remedies; and maintained a strict moral discipline. And also they danced in their liturgy.

Philo of Alexandria wrote *On the Contemplative Life* (about 30 AD) including this description of the "sacred dance" of the Therapeuts (servants of God). He writes:

"The president chants a hymn; either a new one he has composed, or one from the ancient poets . . . they have meters and tunes in many trimetric epics, processional hymns, libation odes; altar chants, stationary choruses and dance-songs, all admirably measured off . . . after him, the others in bands, in order, take up the chanting, while the rest listen in silence, except when they join the refrains . . . After the banquet they keep the holy all-night festival . . . they all stand up; in the middle of the ceremony they separate, men in one band, women in the other . . . a leader is chosen for each.

. . . "they then chant hymns in many metres and melodies, sometimes in chorus, sometimes one hand beating time to the answering chant; now dancing to its music, now in processional hymns; at another time in standing songs, turning and returning in the dance . . . then when one band has feasted (as in the Bacchic rites men drink the wine unmixed) they join and one chorus is formed. . . . "So the chorus of men and women Therapeuts . . . by means of melodies in parts and harmony . . .

. . . "Thus unto morning's light, with no drowsiness, with eyes and bodies fresher than when they came, they stand at dawn, catching sight of the rising sun they raise their hands praying." This curtailed account clearly indicates the combined Feast and dance which later was called *Messe;* and compares with the strange movements sometimes today performed as "religious dance". This ritual came into Gnostic worship; one form only is slightly given by G. R. S. Mead in his *Sacred Dance of Jesus* from the *Acts of John.* The rite was known, at least in part, by Augustine and ascribed to the Priscillian sect which flourished in Spain, before the Festa Messe was reduced into a sort of Barmecide feast.
[1] Essenes—*Ya-San-Nyasa* (Buddhist ascetics with name turned to Aramaic).
[See *Dance of Jesus*]

THERSILEION (Greek—Arcadian)
The Assembly Hall and Theatre constructed in their federal capital Megalopolis, by the Thebans, about 370 BC. The Hall could hold about 6,000 persons; the Theatre contained about 20,000. The colonnade of the *Thersileion* served as a background to the stage.

THORN DANCE—1 (At Polwart-on-the-Green, Berwickshire)
In the middle of Polwart village stood two ancient thorn trees, a few yards distant. Around them, it was formerly the custom of every newly-married pair, and the company invited, to dance in a ring. Dancing, they sung; and thus originated the Scottish ballad "At Polwart on the Green".[1] The tune was used by John Gay for his opera *Polly* in 1729, but costume and dance are at least 16th century, and probably much earlier. The later words sung to the air run:

"At Polwart-on-the-Green, If you'll meet me the
    morn,
Where lasses do convene, To dance about the
    Thorn;
A kindly welcome you shall meet, Fra' her who
    likes to view,
A lover and a lad complete, the lad and lover
    you".
[1] *The Songs of Scotland* (for the tune) G. F. Graham.

THORN DANCE—2
Hawthorn, by its early pure white bloom, indicated the end of winter and firm arrival of spring. Greek girls, therefore, used the flowers as a crown at weddings; while thorn branches were used as torches after weddings, in the nuptial dances. Roman colonists in Britain held mayflower as a charm against sorcery (and used it at their altars), while Henry VII used the flower as his royal device.

"THREE BLIND MICE" (England)
A dance-song, known since 16th - 17th century; sung and danced as a round. Though printed as probably the best-known round in the world, no point of origin is certain, either for words or tune. One version was included in "Pleasant Roundelaies" in *Deuteromelia, or the Seconde Part of Musick's Melodie* (1609), as:
"Three blinde Mice, three blinde Mice,
    Dame Iulian, Dame Iulian;
The Miller and his Merrie Olde Wife
    Shee scrapt her tripe—
Licke thou the knife,
    (Three Blinde Mice) *ad lib* . . ."
The popular nursery version repeats "See how they run", and children often clap or stamp feet, as they sing or dance. These dance verses were known at Sadler's Wells Spa; and were revived more recently, with verses by a critic of ballet, as yet unpublished.

THYIADIC DANCE (Ancient Greece)
Women in the Thyiadic ritual came, in alternate years with the Delphian women, to Parnassos; to follow rites in honour of Dionysos. Pausanias gives some details: he says that they danced on their journey, on the road from Athens.[1] One place of dancing was Panopeus. This ecstatic dance is included by Aristophanes in his play *The Frogs,* as sung by the chorus of the *Mystae.* There is an invocation to Dionysus as Iacchos (or Yacchos), the Spirits of the Earth. The Thyiads (parallel to some extent with the Maenads or Menats, of Egyptian origin), were known as the "Rushing Ones" (or, in occult terms, "Those who moved direct . . . to the gods"). Pindar in the *Pythian Ode* mentioned their dancing at this annual Festi-

val of Pan. According to Herodotus, a torch procession was included. Some writers assert the Thyiades were the same as the Bacchantes. The references to "wild dances" and to "raving" doubtless hit off thus the high lights, which then (as now in the popular press) provoked most external comment.

[1] Pausanias (Book x. iv. 1, 2).

Altar top from Knossos in Crete used in ritual dance, and depicting sixteen dancers with players.

CRETE

THYRSUS (Ancient Greece)

Ritual wand carried by Dionysus and his worshippers, in the ceremonial festivals, especially by the Bacchantes. The *thyrsus* was a staff of olive wood, terminated by a fir-cone, or by a bunch of grapes, and having a double trail of vine-leaves round the upper half. Copies of the *thyrsus* are prominent in romantic ballet, in the hands of village maidens celebrating a harvest festival (as in *Giselle*) or supernatural creatures.

TIBETAN DANCE-DRAMA

A "drama week" was held annually at the Norbulingka, the Summer Palace of the Dalai Lama, outside Lhassa. For seven days religious plays were given on a stone stage in the outer garden of the Palace, the Dalai Lama watching from his window in the inner "Garden of Jewels". Before an audience of high officials and lamas, groups of male actors performed the same plays each year, with words sung in recitative, and dances performed to an orchestra of flutes and drums. The players, ordinary citizens, were actors and dancers only for this period of the year. One of the seven groups, the *Gyumalunma*, was famous for its parodies, in which the words were spoken, not sung. While holding them in high esteem, Tibetans can laugh at their own institutions, and grave abbots rocked with laughter as the *Gyumalunma* burlesqued state dignitaries and functions, such as the *Oracle Dance*.* At the end of the week, the actors were invited to perform in houses of the nobles and in monasteries, the theatrical season lasting a month.

TIBETAN RITUAL DANCE

Sacred dance appears in several modes: the "Miracle Play and Dance" in the cloister or courtyard of Gompa (Monastery) or certain suitable natural settings (sloping hillside); in Mongolia, also called *Tsam*, which equals broadly "Theatre". For the so-called devil-dance or "Dance of Death" see the *Tibetan Book of the Dead* (Evans Wentz); for some plays see *Three Tibetan Mysteries (as performed in Tibetan Monasteries)* trans. French, Jacques Bacot; English, H. I. Woolf. The ritual dance dramas are performed by monks and lamas; costumes are gorgeous; dancers are almost invariably masked; music is impressive; there is no appeal by feminine pulchritude, but solely by themes, which are familiar. Festivals attract pilgrims great distances. See *Mystics and Magicians in Tibet* (Alexander David Neel). Much of their choreographic form is founded on the great symbol *Kyilkhor** ("Wind of Energy-Collecting-Light"). One of the *Tibetan Mysteries* is *Nansal*. Nansal, the heroine, says "The spectacle I see through spiritual contemplation is excellent—the theatrical performance is a lesser spectacle". In this single phrase is given the whole aim of the sacred Theatre. The "material form" of the *kyilkhor* is the Wheel of Life (from Buddhist Wheel of Law), in which all conscient beings must dance; their problem is how to escape from the Wheel and yet live, (*Samsarabande*). The diagram is then named Mandala*: Place of Dance. It is shewn on many temple banners. Tibetan ritual dance is closely connected with the erudite symbolism of the "Great Circle" or "Great Wheel", which re-appears in all religions, with as many different names and more modes of presentation. Nearly all rituals utilise rhythmic dance and symbolic gesture. The following quotation refers to the chief Tibetan-Buddhist symbol:[1]

"Dr. L. A. Waddell, a well-known authority on Lamaism, in *Lamaism in Sikkim*, refers to the symbolism of the famous, but recently ruined, wall painting of the *Si-pa-i-korhlo (khorlo)*, or "Circle of Existence" in the Tashiding Monastery, Sikkim, as follows: 'This picture is one of the purest Buddhist emblems that the Lamas have preserved for us. By its means I have been able to restore the fragments of a circle in the ver-

andha of Ajanta Cave XVII hitherto uninterpreted and known merely as the Zodiac' ".
This *khorlo* (or *khyorkil*) is the same symbol as the *Mandala*,* the Lotus, and the *Sri Yantra*, as taken from different aspects; all of them present the world as a vast *Sangsara*, or "dance of all things together", contrasted with *Nirvana*, which is an escape from the world dance, and withdrawal from the dancing. This doctrine of the incessant world-dance (known to many ancient philosophers, including Plato — *Republic*, the *Legend of Er*.), permeats the entire symbolism of the liturgy, which aims at the awakening, development, and maturation of human consciousness, into full comprehension of incessant process of universal creation and dissolution.

[1] Quotation from *Tibetan Book of the Dead*. Ed. Dr. L. W. Evans Wentz. p. 55.

TIGHTS (Ballet)
Close-fitting long stockings, used by ballet-dancers; made in personal patterns according to specification. The most complete version is a single garment with two legs, drawn in at the waist by folding closely. The close fit gives the current name to "tight stockings". They are usually made in machine-knitted silk or nylon (or rayon and other modern artificial silks) for stage use; also hand-knitted (much thicker, usually black) for rehearsal or practice. The development of this attire is merged with the history of ballet, as public dance of spectacle, Hose were, in England to the time of Henry VIII, made of woven cloth, cut and sewn. The king's were made of wide taffeta. By chance he got a pair of silk hose from Spain. His son, Edward VI had a present from Sir Thomas Gresham —a pair of long Spanish silk stockings. For some years they continued to be rare. Then, says Stow, "in the second year of Queen Elizabeth, her silk-woman Mistress Montague, presented her majesty with a pair of black knit silk stockings for a new-years gift; the which, after a few days wearing, pleased her highness so well that she sent for Mistress Montagu; and asked her where she had them; and if she could help her to any more. Whereon she answered, saying, "I made them carefully, of purpose only for your majesty; and seeing these please you so well, I will presently set more in hand!" "Do so", quoth the queen, "for indeed I like silk stockings so well because they are pleasant, fine, and delicate, that henceforth I will wear no more cloth stockings". And from that time, to her death, the queen never wore cloth hose, but only silk stockings".[1]
Papal circles have at times become concerned with the problem of tights; Pio Nono issued a *Bull*, commanding that all stage and theatre tights should be blue only. Even puppets were not exempt. The *burattini* (puppet players) in Rome took into their repertoire melodramas and ballets. For their legs the puppets had to wear little blue tights, similar to those which the law compelled ballerinas to wear. This, despite the fact that in the earlier Vatican ballets, the usage of any tights was much debated.
Connoisseurs of ballet are generally agreed that, on aesthetic grounds (if none other) the feminine leg is far better when sheathed in glistening silk, than visible in the rawness of natural skin, however polished or stained. The painter, Leon Bakst, had for one of Fokine's ballets, the duty of adding painted pattern decoration to the legs (or tights), of one of the dancers, for each performance. Opposed to the sartorial phenomenon of Tights, is the modernist (?) fashion for "slacks". Now it is the theatre convention that directors or producers (if female) should wear slacks when at work, precisely like the females of the Chinese proletariat; but without the essential camouflage of the tutu over maternal hindquarters.

[1] Stow's *Chronical*. (1631).

TILER, ALSO TYLER, TILLER (English)
Term used by Freemasons for an official in their ritual, once a kind of initiation dance into the Order. His chief task was then to draw the floor pattern of the *G A O T U* — for this, square and compass were items practically needed. In Egyptian days, predecessors to the Masons *Putser** had to have skill to draw the geometrical forms : circle, square, triangle, and pentagon or hexagon, using the rope alone. Then to be *tiller*, meant merely "able to draw" and also to use the chain to repel unauthorised persons; and by parallel meaning, to use the rudder of the "ship" as tiller. In Paris, the Tuileries once provided a centre. Few architectural students today learn enough of "rope geometry" to be able easily "to tile the patron" (pattern). The Pentagon is favoured by modern Freemasons and appears in a large simple design in the entrance hall of the London Lodge. This figure was at the basis of all Egyptian and Greek scales for their pentatonic music.

TILLER GIRLS DANCE
Popular form of "Precision Dance", produced by training in the Dance School formerly run by John Tiller. Most of the girls came from Lancashire; after training, many of them joined continental shows in which their charm and accuracy prove a regular attraction. Their type of show blends with music-hall traditions, especially as to music and presentation in uniform costume. Apparently they were sent out "boxed in dozens". There is, with

the authentic Tiller Girl tradition, a real sense of rhythm that is not always present in more elaborate productions. The School continues, often challenged by home and foreign competition, yet still not surpassed.

TIMBILA (Chopi, Bantu, etc., Africa)
The basic percussion instrument, used in Portuguese East Africa, to accompany all dances. This developed instrument reveals a long ancestry of experiment and selection, from the timber used, to the complicated rhythmic relations obtained from an orchestra of expert players. The form and structure of the *timbila* is fully explained by Hugh Tracey, together with the basic elements of the Chopi dance.[1] The instrument is known over most of Africa, and has spread to Southern America as the *Marimba*,* while its analogue is found in Java as the *gendrang*. The empirical tuning resembles the chromatic and diatonic scales, derived possibly from simpler flutes, where the notes are got from repeated arithmetically equal divisions of the length. The male orchestra may number twenty; they do not write or read "music", but learn tone production and musical form entirely by ear; assisted by sight of dancing. They include melody and harmony. There is no non-playing conductor; they follow the orchestral leader.
[1] *Chopi Musicians*. Hugh Tracey. London, 1948.

TIME IN DANCE
Appears in three principal modes : physical, emotional, and stylistic. (1) Physical dance time is conditioned by the ability of the dancer to move in due rhythm, keeping the balance of form and speed. This is matched by the provider of music, from handclap to full orchestra. Physical tone and physical motion must meet. (2) Emotional time, seen in variation of stress, comes with expression of mood or theme; highly variable. Pain seems to endure, joy "makes time stand still"—the dancer must capture and show the range between. (3) Stylistic time pivots on visual factors; chiefly when a dance is performed as "historical" when scene and costume must blend with mime and gesture in controlled dance. Further subtleties of Time appear when action extends beyond the single dancer to the group; when from one scene in ballet, time changes must be suggested to unfold the basic theme. Time elements are less obvious in ritual than in spectacular displays.

TINI-KLING (Phillipine Islands)
Folk-dance, performed usually by girls. There are two long thin wooden bars. Two dancers on their knees hold these bars on or near the floor, right hand and left; and with the rhythm of music, open

or draw them close. This is a bird-trap. Dancers, usually singly, but sometimes in pairs, step neatly over the moving bars, dancing as "birds being caught", and avoid "losing a mark" by being hit with one or other of the two *klings*.
[Cp. *Singkil* (Phillipines); *Bamboo Trap Dance* (Assam); *Bayanihan*]

TIRANA (Spain)
A dance in 6/8 time derived from the *Fandango*,* usually accompanied by guitars, and sung in four-lined *coplas*. A famous exponent of the dance was Maria del Rosario Fernandez, who was known as "La Tirana" and was painted by Goya. The *Tirana* is found also in Portugal.

TISSERAND, LE (Provence, France)
"The Weaver". A "work" dance, describing the process of weaving. To a light framework ("the loom"), ribbons are attached representing the warp. Each taking a ribbon, the dancers move up to the frame and out again, while a single dancer, "the Weaver", makes the weft by weaving another ribbon horizontally through the vertical ones.
[See *Väva Vadmal*; *Renningen*; *Lei Courdello*]

TJAKALELE (Molucca)
War dances, done as sham fights or skirmishes, between natives of Ambon, Banda, and Ternate. The *tjakalele* has a traditional religious character, being performed only on high festival occasions. In the dance, the oldest obtainable clothing forms the costume of the warriors, who seek to impress with violent movements and high jumps, with shouting. They wear light brass helmets, copied probably from the mediaeval armour of their invading Portuguese or Dutch enemies. Preparation for the dance is long and expensive, requiring much time and attention to detail.

TJITJI INMA (Central Australia)
Boys' two-day pre-initiation ceremony, among the Pitjendadjara tribe. First is a presentation of an ancestral legend, such as the "Story of the Mountain Devil". Accounting for the colours of birds, it relates how the Mountain Devil (a spiked and banded lizard) invited birds and small reptiles to a ceremony. On arrival they paired off to decorate each other for the rituals, but owing to an accidental fire many of the splendid colours were spoilt, becoming the smokey-grey or black they are today. Only the Mountain Devil and the Banded Sleepy-Lizard escaped, and still wear their ceremonial colours. From this ceremonial corroboree, women are excluded. Newly initiated youths teach the boys (aged about 7 - 13) the dances and chants,

and symbolic body patterns representing the characters. As in the story the boys pair off to paint
each other with red ochre, charcoal and white
pipeclay. Two older boys, representing the Mountain Devil and Banded Lizard, lead the chanting,
as the lads dance towards them with high prancing
steps, showing the arrival of the creatures at the
Mountain Devil's camp. With body bent forward
at the hips, their hands move curiously over each
other in a rotatory movement. Sometimes they stop
to utter a shrill cry, then continue, ending with a
flourish before the leaders. All then go, in a close
group, to parade before the women. The second
day's ceremonies begin at dawn. Painted with
different patterns, the boys dance and mime
various incidents on the journey to the Mountain
Devil's home. Accompanied by chanting, and using
the same prancing steps, they portray a bat trying
to proceed without being noticed by a lizard; or
a reptile chasing butterflies, etc. As before, the
ceremony ends with a parade before the women.
In the evening, seated round the fire, the lads chant
while the men dance and mime humorous events
from the past, the woman sitting on the outskirts
of the circle. This is the boys' first experience of
tribal ceremony, its purpose being to start their
education in knowledge of their totemic ancestors
in the ancient "dream-time". Further instruction
in tribal law and custom continues, through several
initiations, well into manhood.
[See *Corroboree; Nakumdoit; Wilyaroo*]

TLACOLERAS (Mexico)
A mime-dance of the district of Guerrero, famous
for its animal and mask dances. (See *Tecuanes**).
The name comes from an Aztec word *tlacolol* "to
prepare the land for cultivation", and the dance
represents this process by symbolical burning of
the undergrowth. The sound of flames is represented by the cracking of whips. This may have
had some other significance, now forgotten, since
the whips are not cracked in the air, but dancers
lash each other on their padded left arms. Accompanied by violins, and led by a Captain, the men,
dressed in leather tunics and trousers, with thick
boots, masks and wide-brimmed sombreros, wind
in and out of patterns, marking the rhythm with
their whips. When, at one point, the fire is considered to have gone out, the dancers move about
whipping one another, to start it again, by the
simulated sound of flames. Dialogue sometimes
accompanies the dance. At Chilpancingo the dancers include one disguised as a dog called *la mara-
villa* ("the marvel"), who chases another representing a tiger which is supposed to be harming
the cornfields.

TLUSTNI DNI (Poland)
"The Fat Days". As in most Catholic countries,
the last days before Lent in Poland were a carnival
time, with dancing and processions. Sometimes they
were called *Ostatki*, "the remaining days", or
Zaputsy, "the empty days". Dressed in fantastic
costumes, with masks made from straw, leather or
wood, the villagers paraded through the street,
representing farm animals such as horses, goats,
and hens, and also special figures symbolic of
Winter, named Karnival, Death and Marzanna. The
last, an ancient goddess of Death, was later
drowned in effigy to mark the passing of Winter.
The Carnival of *Tlustni Dni* symbolised the returning life energy of Spring, when the most important event was the auctioning of girls. Young
men would jokingly bargain for the girl of their
choice. If, after further acquaintance, the girl was
approved, the bargain was sealed with a few coins;
and the youth was given coloured eggs at Easter,
by the girl. This was a relic of the old marriage
market.
[Cp. *Marriage Market Dance; Mailehen; Tergul de
Fête; Mardi Gras; Fasching; Fastnachsbär*]

TOBACCO CRAWL (USA)
Many old dances were founded on familiar, rhythmically repeated processes of handicraft movements. When work is done, mime in dancing uses
these same rhythms, to suggest great success, high
production, skilful work; while a similar *mimesis*
occurs in all hunting dances. When these ceremonial dances fade from the social scene, as
machines replace hard manual labour, these forms
of rhythm disappear. Other rhythmic movements
take their place. We get "machine dances" as well
as mechanical dancers. (See *Automatic Ballet
Dancer**). Occasionally a still-human reaction reveals this instinctive tendency to evoke rhythm;
even when there is no conscious intention. Here is
a modern emergence of a "Tobacco Crawl". It
appeared in the Big Brick Warehouse at Lake City,
in South Carolina. There was the mystic chant of
the auctioneer, whose sing-song recital was serious
business. In front, behind, and in the aisles, buyers
for the big tobacco companies shuffled along, in a
curious rhythmic lock-step, their pace harmonised
with the tempo of his chant, moving in a slow
procession. So a commercial ritual replaces, by a
worship of Mammon, the devotion to older gods.
A similar lock-step was shewn on the London stage,
in an American play. The lock-step was imposed
on convicts in some USA prisons; and, as publicity,
the step was displayed by gentlemen, attired in
barred blue-and-white suits, down Charing Cross
Road, to announce the play. The British Lock-Step
Shopping Crawl is the National Queue System.

TOCOTINES, LOS (Mexico)

Name given to the "flyers" in the *Juego de los Voladores** ("The Flying Game") by the Totonacs of Papantla, Vera Cruz. The ceremony takes place there annually at the five-day feast of Corpus Christi, when dancers perform both morning and afternoon. Each year a new pole is provided, and ceremonies similar to those of the Huastecas (see *Gavilan, La Danza del**) attend the felling and setting up of the tree. The *Tocotines* (four, plus the musician-Captain), are young, unmarried men, who agree to "fly" for seven years. Before performing they must fast and abstain from stimulants and women. Dressed in red suits, with a bunch of feathers and ribbons on top of a pointed hat, they wear heavy shoes, unlike the barefoot *Voladores* in other villages. Having danced before the church, they go in line to the 80-foot pole set up in the plaza, where, to the music of pipe and drum, the four men dance in a chain never turning their backs to the pole. Each movement is repeated three times, and they dance seven times around the pole. Then all climb up to the platform at the top. The Captain, sitting on the centre hub, facing east, and arching his body back, plays a melody on his flute seven times. This he repeats in each direction. Then standing up on the minute platform towards the east, he makes seven turns marking the rhythm of his melody with jumps about ten inches high. Sometimes, standing on one foot, he makes "steps" with the other in the air. When changing from one foot to another, he often makes two turns, so that each cardinal point receives fourteen turns instead of seven. After this the four *Tocotines* attach the ropes to their waists, and to a special flute melody played seven times, they fall away from the pole and begin their downward circling flight. When the Captain changes to a new tune, the four flyers alter their position. From falling head downwards, they flex their abdomens and lean backwards, until the second tune has been played seven times, when they resume their first position. When nearing the ground, they turn a somersault, and land on their feet. The Captain slides down, and all do a final dance round the pole. At Papantla and at Metepec, dancers are accompanied by a *Negrito** in place of the *Malinche** of Pahuatlan.
[See *Voladores, Juego delos; Otomi Voladores; Gavilan, Danza del*]

TODA "DANCE OF THE LORDS" (S. India)

The only dance known to the South India Toda people, a diminishing tribe living in the Nilgiri Hills. Having no musical instruments of their own, a vassal tribe (the Kothas), bring pipes, long curved trumpets, and flat tambours, to play at Toda ceremonies. The dance is performed by men at funerals and other gatherings. In the village square a small circle is formed. From other villages, Toda men come in small groups, marching with arms linked and chanting "Rhao, hao, hao". As they arrive they join the ring, until a large circle revolves slowly, with shuffling step, to the same monotonous chant. The dance continues until all visitors have arrived, then ceases. Tall and with proud bearing, the dignity of the "lords" is enhanced by the *putkûli*—a voluminous robe of white cotton, with vertical stripes of black and red, embroidered round the edge with blue.

TODTENTANZ (German)

Fourteenth century term used in Germany for the widespread West European "Dance of Death". An early printed version carries the title: *Todtentanz durch alle stendt der Menschen &c, furgebildet mit figuren. S. Gallen 1581.* Holbein became interested and engraved a series. One Latin term was *Imagines Mortis;* but there were other German names, such as *Schau-platz des Todes, oder Todtentanz* ("Theatre of Death", etc.), or *Geistliche Todts-Gedanchen* ("Spiritual Dance of Death"), and *Die Messchiliche Sterblichkeit* ("Human Mortality as Dance of Death"). The contents of these innumerable Dance-dramas was the inevitable seizure by Death of all men; popular versions appeared by way of satirical protest against the clerical emphasis they shewed in the *Horae* or Dance of Hours, and the Church Miracles and Mysteries. The approved *Dance of Death* included the popes and emperors, by way of observation that they were not spared by Death, more than the poor man.
See *The Dance of Death.* Francis Douce. 1833.
[See *Trois Vifs et Trois Morts; Danse Macabre; Misère, Danse de; Morts, Danse des*]

TOE DANCE

Is done (a) vertically on the big toe; and (b) on the "half-toe" or all five, bent at an angle with the sole; not considered as being "real toe-dancing". Stage toe-dance is confined almost exclusively to classical ballet. (American mothers of small dancing daughters firmly believe that to "rise on the toe" and to "perform an arabesque", are the two principal requirements in any "real dancing"). Stage ballet is always helped by use of specially made "blocked ballet shoes", contrived to spread the body weight over the foot. Frequently it is alleged that this dancer or that dancer "invented the toe-step", but it has been in vogue for many centuries; and is a common step in Cossack (Kashak) dances, done by men or small boys. They acquire great foot strength by "rising in the saddle", being constantly on horseback though not sitting. Visitors to Russia have witnessed Cossacks, dancing on the toe, wearing only soft leather shoes, through which the form of the feet can be seen after some wear. The stage advantage was utilised in "Romantic Ballet", being adopted to suggest a supernatural lightness (as in *La Sylphide*, etc.), but in modern times this effect is ruined by the corps-de-ballet tapping, like the sound of many clogs.

TOE-NAYA (Burma)
Is the Burmese Unicorn, and more or less equivalent to the Hobby Horse of other lines of tradition. He resembles a horse, with long fleecy hair, his single horn jutting from his brow; and below are eyes of gleaming ruby. Some of the *Toe-Naya* tribe can fly; then they are called *Naya-pyan*, or "Flying Naya". Like the Hobby Horse, the *Toe-Naya* is rarely even mentioned in oral tales or written legends; yet the villagers disguise their best dancers in suitable costumes, so that *Toe-Naya* can take the leading part in every folk-feast. With him may appear any of the other animals of Burmese folklore; five in all. These are the *Keinnara* (*Kinnara* in Hindu origins), the *Galon* (who is *Garuda* in India), and the famous Snake Spirit, the *Naga*.* The last is the miniature water-elephant, who is like a mouse only in scale, but otherwise precisely like an elephant; and real, big elephants are afraid of it. [See *Wezak; Prüh; Burmese Dance*]

TOHUNGA (New Zealand)
Maori priest or wise man, who often leads ritual; or arranges those in which he does not appear. He is guardian of the *tuaha*, the altar or "stone of power", fenced safely in its sacred place near every Maori village. Here religious ceremonial, invocations or prayers were performed, with simple circle dance movements with each *karakia* (prayer in chanted form). The *Tohunga* worked alongside the *Rangatira* or chief; rarely were both offices combined; but the *Rangatira* filled one task done elsewhere by the wise man—the recitation of chanted genealogies (*whakapapa*) as the leading *kaumata* (elder) of the tribe. The *Tohunga* is in charge of the invisible life of the tribe; which sometimes the dances were provided to stimulate.

TOM TOM (Chiefly African term)
A drum, usually described as a "kind of oriental drum", also given as *Tam-tam;* a name probably derived from the sound. Inadequate to distinguish the numerous classes of drum; or the analogous tambour and tambourine.

TOMBLESTERE (England, Saxon period)
A term denoting the exhibitionist, dancer or Tumbler, mentioned in Chaucer. He performed in or before the ale-house—whence his frequent

reward was a pot—tumbler—of the liquid there dispensed. This custom gave rise to the tip—in France still *pour-boire*—of the *garcon* who brings the drinks. Some writers think that the term was earlier prevalent, on those annual ceremonials, or *Watch for the Dead* (or "All Souls' Day"), when families would spend a memorial day in or by cemeteries (as Moslem people still do in Arab countries); and that the amusements which whiled away the long hours included the *Tomb-el-ster* or *Tomb-Dancers*.   [See *Saxon Dancing*]

TOMNAHURICH GHOST DANCE (Scotland)
By Inverness is a hill called Tomnahurich, of which there is a strange tale. Through Inverness strode two piper lads. They attracted notice, as they swore in Gaelic at cars which threatened them in narrow streets; were taken in charge; and brought before the Sheriff. Neither had seen a car before: they thought they were queer beasts. In answer to demands for information, they explained: They had come from Strathspey to pipe in Inverness. Accosted by an old man, who offered each lad a guinea and plenty of whiskey, he asked if they would pipe for his friends? They agreed; they followed the old man up Tomnahurich Hill; about half-way up they found a door, which the old man opened. There was a splendid ballroom, filled with hundreds of handsome men and beautiful women, waiting for music so that they could dance. The pipers had a dram, then began to play; and dancing went on all through the night. Then they got each man his guinea; and turned into the morning air. They showed the guineas to the sheriff—a golden spade guinea. They had not shown these to the policemen. As the sheriff touched the coins, they fell into dust. The pipers were remanded for enquiries. In the cell the minister was told, by each man, that he had not long come from the battle of Sheriffmuir; and they wanted to know about Inverness—who were these "police?" Then the guid man thought he had best make a prayer; but so soon as he uttered the holy names, the men crumbled with their pipes into dry and ancient dust. That had been a most long night in Tomnahurich Hill.

TONALPONALLI (Mexico)
Is the calendar stone of the ancient Mexicans, derived by them probably from the Toltecs. This scheme governed some of their ritual dances, by control of the seasonal reckoning whence came rhythms and positions. The Mexicans had two calendars: first for the "reckoning of the moon", regulating their religious festivals; and the other for the sun, for civil purposes. They used a time cycle of fifty-two solar years. This solar or civil

year had eighteen months of twenty days each, divided into five-day weeks, four periods. This calendar does not coincide with lunar periods; and it would seem they had difficulty in balancing the two schemes. We may compare this Mexican *Ton-alponal-li* with the Bengali *alpona*,* used as a religious ritual diagram, when we examine the scheme presented in the drawing by Vasco da Gama from this great stone, now in Mexico City. The syllable *Ton* identifies the solar deity; it occurs also in (Hindu) *tandeva* and *tan-matra*. The eighteen months were named from festivals, birds, and animal symbols, or flowers. These symbols appeared in dance rituals proper to each period.
[See *Aztec Dances*]

TONKIN (Indo-China)

Sacred songs or chants are used with dances for "raising of spirits"—that is, as an oriental mode of a spiritualist seance. Their written forms (in Chinese) comprise: (a) quatrains, usually in dialogue form; (b) sacred chants, sung by groups, usually of men; and (c) romantic tales. A chorus of boys sings, alternately with girls, for the dialogue of quatrains. These chants are accompanied by dances, which in mime form, present martial or similar episodes. Their romance forms are similar to the old French *chanson de geste*. When used in reverse procedure—namely for exorcisms—sacrifices are made at intervals; while dances remain in ring formation.
See *Etudes sur les chants et la poésie populaire des Mans du Tonkin*. M. Bonifacy. Hanoi, 1902.

TOPENG (Java)

Masked plays, in which dialogue is recited by the *Dalang* (manager), are performed by travelling companies through Java. Their form is between dance-mime and musical plays; their usual subject matter, episodes from the mythical life of the Javanese hero-prince Pandji. In recent years, much revision has been done, and though older plays continue in favour, many newer political themes have been invented, as commentary on the current situations, much as the itinerant puppet-play was used through Europe, with eloquent satires on the clerical system of plunder. Yet the religious connections are still to be seen in the outlying districts of Java. The masks are frequently made by the members of the company, even those purchased, are retouched in colour by them.

TORCH DANCES

Began with the practice of nocturnal rites, in days of pre-history. From cave illumination, to heaped fires in a forest clearing, the Torch was always a sign of human life, by its control of fire. Technical methods of securing a light, of choosing and finding some material that would give a good flame, or would last for a sufficient time; and could easily be renewed, gave these predecessors of the "electrician's mate" considerable work. Exactly how it was accomplished, we must deduce from sparse clues. In historical periods, there are references to pine torches; various tars or resins; and the wonders of the "eternal fires" that existed around Baku in Azerbaijan, fed with mineral oils, which continued until the last Fire Temple was destroyed by the Russians about 1840. In European towns, the torch was for centuries indispensable for any night dance; and even for dances held within halls. Fitted lamps, burning oil, remained scarce; but olive oil had come into use; as had *ghee* in India, along with coco-oil. The Festivals of *Moharram* (Moslem) or *Diwali* (Hindu) still affirm the splendour of the "One thousand and One Lights". In Italy, France and England, the line of servants bearing torches followed the herald's call; as the preliminary to ceremonial dance; and in time the torch entrance itself was disciplined into dance form. In Hellas, the upturned torch compared with the expiring fragment, downturned; as symbols of life and death. Races were run with "handing on the torch" literally; but in England the duty of the humble servitors (the "link-men") was to stand around the hall, or enclosure, handling a fiery and smoky torch, for the primitive purpose of giving sufficient light to watch the performance. With the wooden buildings then erected, fire insurance did not exist. Mishaps were plentiful though rarely so sudden as to kill. The Globe Theatre on Bankside caught fire; yet over a thousand spectators escaped readily. Great lamps for burning oil (in Arab countries) succeeded torches; then candles of all kinds were developed as an industry. The invention of coal-gas illumination marked for Theatre an immense change—not at first welcome. Torches are now forbidden in the theatre buildings; except the tiny electric battery; and we are now relegated to the annual occasion of a *bonne feu* (alleged to be for one, Guido Faux), and the Scottish hill torches of Baeltinne. During all these centuries, the march of the line of lighted torches has signified some coming display; but torch dances are forgotten.
[See *Fackeltanz* (Germany)]

TOROKOS TANC (Hungary)

"Turk's Dance". A burlesque dance by Hungarian soldiers at the time of the Turkish invasion of Hungary, parodying the behaviour of the Turks. Later the dance became popular on festival occasions, such as weddings, when the young men, with partners, danced round anti-clockwise. As in most

Hungarian pair dances, the girl's steps were less spectacular than the man's, but both danced with that rhythmic co-ordination of movement characteristic of Hungarian dancing, where the whole body dances, not merely the legs. As the girls turned, with their partners, in the *Törökos Tanc*, the young men performed agile steps and amusing antics. An old folk song accompanied the dance.

TOTEM DANCES (from North American Indian)
Anthropologists have constructed a vast corpus of material, related to the two phases of ritual named as *Totem* and *Tabu*,* in which it is recognised that ritual dancing has a place of high importance. Precisely what happens, they do not tell us. Freud was too much involved with modern medical magic, developing into a strange system now called psycho-analysis; but C. G. Jung, has departed from this limitation; as did Adler and Brill, in different directions. Jung's work is the most hopeful. The term *Totem* (pronounced *Tot-em*, not *toe-t'm*) was learned by John Long of London, from North American Indians, in 1791. But little of its meaning was understood, until Polynesia furnished the correlative term of *Tabu*, though the pragmatic substance of this doctrine recurs throughout Jewish doctrine (as known, for example, in the practice of *kosher* versus *tref*). Study having been confused with natural and ceremonial magic; and being conveyed in a curious theology of academic pomp, the relatively simple genuine meaning yet escapes explanation. "From time to time", says Freud, "festivals are held at which members of a totem represent or imitate, in ceremonial dances, the movement and characteristics of the totem".[1] (p.17). And again : "A member of a clan seeks to emphasise his relationship to the totem in various significant ways : he imitates an exterior similarity by dressing himself in the skin of the totem animal; by having a picture of it tattooed on himself. On the solemn occasions of birth, initiation into manhood, or funeral obsequies, this identification with the totem is carried out in deeds and words. Dances in which all the members of the tribe disguise themselves as their totem, and act like it, serve various magic and religious purposes". (p. 144). The failure of the Freudian scheme to convince ordinary intelligence, resides in its continued lack of connection with normal natural man; in his origins away from city life; and its preoccupation with the abnormal conditions. *Totem* must be integrated rationally with *Tabu*, and meaning translated into modern terms, for wider acceptance. In this endeavour, the study of dance forms, ceremonies, and doctrines will provide immensely valuable material, as yet barely surveyed.
[1] *Totem and Tabu*. Sigmund Freud. London, 1938.

TOURALOURE (colloquial French)
Now known in England (esp. musical halls) as "tooral-looral". The name began with *Compagnons de la Tour*, travelling groups of Freemasons. They used marching tunes; and kept up ballads with dance melodies, played on the Loure. From this name came *tourlourous*,* modern French for a raw recruit, a conscript soldier. The older form was linked with *tournoi*, a military tournament, always with music—often with march music and dance-songs. Cp. also *tireliera*, a money-box for collecting as at a dance show in a village; and *Tireuse de cartes*, an itinerant fortune teller.

TOURLOUROU (French, mediaeval)
A term applied to youngest military recruits; and thus used in dance-songs, when they were satirised, especially by the villagers; turning into the "nonsense refrain" of "Toor-ooral-oo!" They were termed, by their serjeant, as Jean-Jean;[1] or the Jeans of Jeans—the very young, the inexperienced, or "little wenches", while he was the Sir-Jean or Sir Jeannet. They obeyed : as *tour-rouleau*—turn-circles, in drill. The earlier *tu-ral-tu* comes from *turluru* (Italian) and *turlureau* (French), based on *loure* (French) a bagpipe; so that the phrase *toure-loure* implied a round with the bagpipe, the recruiting song and dance (as in Hungary). This was common in the 16th - 17th centuries.
[1] *Jean Bart* is a "Jack Tar" hat. French trews are named "Jeans".

TRANCE DANCES
Exist in several classes : (a) where the group dances and then moves into trance (see *Ketjak*, Java); or (b) where the group dances and moves into Ecstatic dance (see *Dervish Dance**); or (c) where one dancer first goes into trance and then gets up to dance (see *Djanger*,* Bali); or (d) where a group begins with chanting and then develops into dance movement (Jewish dance, *Kantor*; Negro dance, *Voodoo* Magical Dance; *Sibylline dance*).

TRAIPSE (West Indies, Jamaica, etc.)
Slow dance, done usually to some calypso tune, either along a street (at Fiesta time) or round a room. The dance has little form; it is a shuffle (they often have no good shoes) but moves into a kind of sexual wriggle, marking the refrain, if any. This word was also current in 19th century London; it implied going round to find a job, or selling wares door to door—this was the basic repetition step. The *traipse* compares with the *hobo*. Pope (*Dunciad. iii. 141*) defines the term "Lo, next two slip-shod muses traipse along, In lofty madness, meditating song". There may be a couple, or a

small group, but the traipse is far from the dignified processional of passacaglia of tradition.

TRAPEZIUS (Greco-Latin)
Trapa-Zeus; the "Diamond Ritual" of Zeus. The
high importance of this forgotten rite is expressed
by the prominent position given to the "diamond"
or trapesius form, in the centre of the *orchestra*
in the great Theatre of Dionysus at Athens; where
it still exists in the paving. This term was the
source of the great D (*Delta*) carved over many
temple doors in Greece. Several of these "geometric
forms" served as basic symbols of the form of
ritual; in this instance, as important as the Islamic
Arabic *Muhr-i-Suleiman*, or the Brahmin *Mahayan-
tra*, and the Christian *vesica piscis* or Allemunde.
The chorus began and ended in relation to this form
and its dynamic lines; the aim of one rite was to
indicate the "interpenetration of opposites"—at this
time, the opposition and agreement of two triangles. We may compare the *Trapezius* with the
older Babylonian "Sacred Tree" (or Thirty-two
Paths), and the *Vajra-kheddika* ("Diamond-cutting"
of the Chinese Buddhists. These dancing groups
"drew" the changing symbols before the watching
eyes of the instructed spectators; to others they
would mean little. One term (that of the "rapper"
or wooden "sword") remains with English Morris
Dancing.

TRAQUENARD (France)
Now refers to traps or trapping; in the mediaeval
sense, this *danse traquenarde* was a relic of the
display of the tourney, and its occasional "horse
ballet".* By military movement in groups, on horse
or on foot, they sought gradually to enclose or
entrap (*à la traque*) the desired prey. This particular
movement was the *traquer* (as in "beating up"
game), and in the organized method it required the
"tracking pace" of man or horse, as when held in
by snare or bridle. Hence the music has a "dotted"
rhythm, that recalls the short and snappy beats,
of horse-hoofs or men's feet. The style of *traquer*
was perhaps used in the later *masque;* when the
men surrounded the ladies, in a pretence of capture. The style of music entered the circus for a
time, but has vanished.

TRATA (Greece)
A girls' chain dance, performed at Megara (between
Athens and Corinth), on Easter Tuesday. Slow and
gentle, the movement is simple. Girls with downcast eyes, linked by their hands crossed in front,
move slowly to right and left, alternating with a
few steps backward. Singing as they dance, the
girls sometimes form several chains, which meet
and merge and separate again, as they wind in

serpentine patterns. They perform the dance out of
doors, wearing their best clothes, with caps covered
in silver coins.

TRAUERMARSCH (German)
A rhythmic funeral march which may be a slow
dance movement. For military funeral, a musical
movement in slow time is used towards the
cemetery; a sharp bugle call (Last Post) at the
interment; followed by a quick march, sometimes
even jolly, for return to barracks. *Trauer Ode*,
funeral ode by Bach (1727) is a more official example; while Schubert's *Trauer Walzer* (1821) is
less severe. Greek music had many examples. In
England we see Guards Slow March as a modern
display.

TRAUNSTEIN SWORD DANCE (Bavaria, Germany)
Takes place on Easter Monday, after the traditional
"St. George's Ride". Earliest records of the Ride
date from 1530. It is celebrated annually in several
Bavarian villages, but particularly in Traunstein,
where the tradition is maintained by a society
interested in preserving folk customs. St. George, in
armour and plumed helmet, rides in the centre of
the procession, while other riders and grooms wear
mediaeval costume. At the little Ettendorf chapel
on a nearby hill, priests consecrate horses and
riders with "holy water." The procession returns to
the Market Square where, on a specially erected
stage, the traditional Sword Dance is performed,
in hilt-and-point style by twelve or fourteen men,
as a contest between Winter and Spring. Winter,
in striped tights and hooded jerkin, carries a long
twisted stick, to fight Spring (leader of the dance)
and his followers, with their swords. These men
wear breeches and embroidered waistcoats, with
a round hat or cap. Various figures are performed.
After a long contest, Winter is defeated, and Spring
is raised on the lock of swords for all to see.

TRAVESTY
In Dance signifies a change of appearance that does
not express fundamental character. Most often, a
woman may dress as a man; a man may dress as a
woman (pantomime "dame") or in early Shakespeare plays, a boy was attired as a girl. Travesty
also enters fancy dress ball rejoicings. Basically
the French term *travestissement* means disguise;
but on stage, this is no secret. To "travesty" in other
arts may be deceitful. The use of travesty is more
subtle than at first appears; a woman may (a) dress
as a man, but (b) she may also try to suggest the
character, or (c) use the disguise but remain the
female (*Twelfth Night*). Thus Senora Macarona
(Paris Exp. 1899) appeared as a man, and as a
matador. But no bull was deceived.

TRAWEITELDANS (Belgium)
A Flemish dance from the country districts round
Antwerp, performed by men to the accompaniment
only of a drum roll. Led by a Captain (the *Traweite-
laar*), the men perform figures of a hilt-and-point
sword-dance type, holding sticks instead of swords.
The dance is complicated by the presence of a
wooden hoop. Hung on a stick, the hoop is passed
from man to man, each man passing it over his
body and dancing within its constricting band. The
end of the dance gives a feeling of triumph as the
last man frees himself from the hoop. *Traweiteldans*
is performed by a special Confraternity, and may
have had symbolical meaning.

TREE DANCES
Occur frequently in traditional rites, usually as
ceremonials of ancient religious faiths. Mannhardt
cites the celebration of May at Venlo on the Maas,
when maidens light tapers as evening comes on,
and dance round the lighted tree. At Luneberg,
wedding festivities include the dance with the
"May" adorned with lights, carried before the
bridal pair; while in the Hartz mountains, the
peasants dance round the *Johannis baum*, a
trimmed, newly cut tree, or a pyramidal wooden
structure, ornamented with wreaths of flowers or
leaves, and bearing many lights. Palgrave (in
Arabia) tells of seeing (1862 - 63) Arabian men
dancing in a mode of tree worship (in the district
of Shauwera), as they moved round a large acacia.
Burton (in *Mission to Gelele*) records devotion to
trees in the African kingdom of Whydah, where
the "second order of earth gods" is revered as living
in certain chosen trees, which are centres of a
dance ritual in annual celebrations. According to
Professor Burnet (cited in *Tree Worship*), the well-
known chorus of "Hey Derry Down" was a
Druidic chant, signifying literally, "In a circle the
oaks move round" — where we may presume that
the "oaks" were priests of that grade. Association
of trees, boughs or branches, flowers and fruits;
and straight rods or wands, with ritual dances, are
innumerable. Frazer, seeking facts anent the
Golden Bough of the Italian grove, found himself
involved in a dozen volumes; and even then he
was not finished. Some are included here; we may
begin with the *Babylonian Sacred Tree*.*

TREES (Sacred Tree)
In various religious rituals, a Tree appears as a symbol that carried various mythic doctrines. Invariably there was associated a sacred ritual dance
movement; around the isolated symbol (probably
erected like the later maypole), or over the secret
form, engraved in the pavement of the inner shrine;
and there used for priestly instruction. The "Tree

of Life" mentioned (but not described) in Genesis;
and again denoted as "Tree of Good and Evil" has
been abundantly followed in ecclesiastical symbolism, down to the Middle Ages, when it ended as
the "Tree of Jesse".* This design is closely similar
to the Hindu "Tree of Creation", illustrated in
images of Vishnu; where, in the church pattern, it
issues in the same basic fashion from the side of
Jehovah. The Miracle Play form merely illustrated
the Adam and Eve myth. The Persians had their
sacred *Haoma* from the Zoroastrian synthesis. With
the Greeks the Tree became the modest Caduceus,
carried by Hermes, the youthful dancing god or
"messenger", though Hercules had to visit the
Golden Tree of the Hesperides. The Hindu Tree
was painted or printed on cotton, or woven in
delicate textiles; and, as such, brought home by
Elizabethan voyagers, to be adopted into Jacobean
embroidery as "pretty ornament". Rome knew it
as a "Tree of the Sibyl"; and we see the Tree on
Pompeian walls, with the "Serpent" of Hygeia. In
church processional, the Tree was turned into the
Palm, as a theological symbol (from the "Great
Green Branch" celebrated by the resurrection of
Osiris and the Gardens of Adonis); and in folklore
— the secular religion cherished by the English
people — the Living Tree became the famous Maypole, symbol of re-awakening (another "Green
Man" and the "Garland of May"). In this connection, the dance has been traditionally followed
through many centuries. The Hebrew form was
lost in its dualistic form as the twin Jachin and
Boaz, partly to be seen in the original twin obelisks
of Egypt; and then secured recognition in the
Qabalah,* as a reflex of the most ancient known
form, the Assyrian *Asshurah*. Finally, the Royal
Institute of British Architects (following in Masonic
tradition), have erected the twin pillars before
their London home. There is no dance in Portland
Place !

TREGETOUR (Mediaeval French)
From old French : *tresgiat*, a juggling trick or feat
of skill with the hands, and sometimes feet as well.
The acting of such a conjuror was at one time
called his "minstrelsy", which indicates that the
minstrel dancers alternated ballad-and-dance turns
with these circus tricks. The *tregétours* were evidently one class of the great company of diversant
minstrels. This name passed into English as *trick-
ster*.

TREGUENDA (Italy)
The Sabbat with *Stregone Danza*, or "Awakening
Dance", belonging to the ancient ritual of the
Strega, the witch, for their Sabbat. The dance is
now called the *Tarantella*.* Its formation depicts (in

symbol) the construction of the "witch-web", in which magical ceremonial the *strega* hopes to lure her victim. Leland referring to this "spider dance" says:[1]

> "The *Tarantella* is a well-known dance, assigned to witches . . . It is the awakening dance at their *Treguenda* or Sabbat".

[See *Tarantella* (2)]

[1] *Etruscan Roman Remains in Popular Tradition.* Charles G. Leland. 1892.

Basque form of *Danse des Treilles*.   FRANCE

TREILLES, DANSE DES (France)

"Garland Dance". Belongs to Languedoc and still danced in the regions of Beziers and Pezenas at all important festivals. Each dancer holds a garland— a supple arc decorated with vine branches and grapes. The leader (colloquially *ortala*), carries a similarly decorated stick, which he holds in the middle. He directs the figures of the dance. The music, in lively 6/8 time, is played on a fife or oboe, and a tambourine. Dancers enter in pairs, holding the garlands over their heads, the leader in front. There follow seven figures: 1. *Le Croisement*. In single, then double column, they dance *sur place*, alternating in order of men and women, the leader in front. 2. *La Promenade*. Men and women in separate lines, the first dancer in each line takes a step forward, turns and proceeds to the end of the line—repeated until the first dancers are back in their original place. The leader remains in the middle. 3. *L'Invitation*. In separate lines, facing; the leader dancing first with the women, then with the men. 4. *Le Tunnel*. An arch is formed

by bringing the garlands together in pairs. The dancers remaining still, the leader dances through the tunnel and back again. 5. *La Tonnelle* (The Arbour). Formed by four men in square formation, holding the garlands; the girls, led by the leader, wind through the "arbour". The girls then make an arbour through which the men dance. 6. *Le Quadrille*. Two squares of four dancers each, form the "sails of a windmill", one turning clockwise the other anti-clockwise. The leader dances *sur place* between the squares. 7. *Le Salut*. In two horizontal lines, the dancers bow, inclining the garlands forward, then exit, men and women in opposite directions. In Provence this dance is called *Li Triho*.   [Cp. *Jardiniero*, *Li* (Provence)]

TRENCHMORE (England)

A longways dance of 16th and 17th centuries, included in the fifth edition of Playford's *Dancing Master* (1675). More than a hundred years earlier, in 1564, this dance is mentioned in a Morality Play by William Bulleyn, where a minstrel is described as "dancing Trenchmore and Heie de Gie". In 1584, Stanihurst remarks, "And truly they suit a Divine as well as an ape to frisk Trenchmore in a pair of buskins and a doublet". Gratton Flood considers that *Trenchmore* was the English version of the Irish *Rinnce Mor* (Great Dance) or *Rinnce Fada* (Long Dance), performed by a line of dancers in pairs.[1] That at Court and in the great houses, these two dances were performed by all the household (as was the *Cushion Dance*), is illustrated by two quotations. In Dinely's *Voyage through the Kingdom of Ireland* (1681), the dancing of *Rinnce Fada* is attributed to those who were "much addicted on holidays . . . to dance after their country fashion, that is the long dance one after another of all conditions, masters, mistresses and servants".[2] Of *Trenchmore* at the English Court in 1689, Selden's *Table Talk* says: "The Court of England is much altered. At a solemn Dancing first you had the grave Measures,* then the Corrantoes* and the Galliards,* and this is kept up with ceremony; at length the Trenchmore and the Cushion-Dance,* and . . . all the Company dance . . . So in our Court in Queen Elizabeth's time Gravity and State were kept up. In King James's time things were pretty well. But in King Charles's time there has been nothing but Trenchmore and the Cushion-dance *omnium gatherum*, tolly-polly, hoite come toite". The music for *Trenchmore* was printed in *Deuteromalia* in 1609.

[1] *History of Irish Music.* Wm. H. Gratton Flood. Dublin, 1905.

[2] See *Handbook of Irish Dance.* J. G. O'Keefe and A. O'Brian. Dublin, 1902.

[See *English Dancing Master; Playford Dances*]

TRESCONE, TRESCONA (Italy)

A dance for four couples, known since the Middle Ages, and performed in the country-side of Tuscany and Romagna at the harvest of hemp and maize. Accompanied by accordion or guitar, the dancers form a square, the women dancing *en place*, while the men, with a display of technical virtuosity, dance from one girl to the other. The rhythm increases in tempo, and in Tuscany the dance is in quick 6/8 time and known as the *Tresconeto*. In the late 19th century, the *Trescone* was a couple dance in which man or woman chose their partner by a flick of a kerchief. In the countryside, peasants enjoyed dancing it on the grass, with bare feet, during the evening.

TRIHORIS (Brittany)

Also: *Triori, Trihory, Triory*. An old round dance resembling the *Branle*,* described by Arbeau in his *Orchésographie** (1588) as being little, if at all, practised in his time. Known as the *Triory de Bretagne*, it was in light, duple time, with dancers in a linked circle moving continuously to the left, instead of the swing to right and left, usual in the *Branle*. The style of dancing was light and springy, and the steps included leaps. *Trihoris*, mentioned by Rabelais (16th century) in *Pantagruel*, belonged particularly to Lower Brittany, the *Passepied** being the popular dance of Upper Brittany.

TRIPETTOS, DANSO DEI (France)

"Dance of the Little Tripes", performed at many places in France in mediaeval centuries, usually at churches dedicated to the mythical Saint Martial or Saint Martin, a substitute figure for Bacchus, especially favoured in all vine districts. They had ended by the 19th century. Typically, Marcel* is "the wavy one". At Barjol there was a processional and circuit dance, on the "Saints Festival Day" at the time of the grape harvest. The parishioners first danced in church (formerly they first danced *to* and *around* the church, as at the first dedication of a new building) on the preceding day. On the Festival Day, the later mode of the communal dance had replaced the earliest mode; and now was performed inside the church, when the people sang:

"We shall carry them, the *petit tripettos*,
The *petit tripettos*, we shall carry them;
The *petit tripettos* for *San Marcell*".[1]

We have here a clue to the persistence of affirming group unity by (a) joining hands, (b) holding kerchieves; or (c) holding green boughs. In this endless chain dance, the knotted rope of the Cordeliers is replaced once more by *les petits tripettos*—in the proletarian form of *saucissons*. The fondness of

working people for offal dishes is known by haggis; by Lancashire black puddings; by chitterlings; and by the great variety of sausage. We recall that the London pantomimes featured Clown Joey as waving a string of sausages (whether as a bribe or a threat remains uncertain), but obviously this legendary dish has an origin. In the harvest dances, the boughs, cornstalks, or kerchieves were generally used; and the Dance for San Marcell-Martin disposes of thirty-feet strings of sausages, doubtless at first apparent in the churchyard dance round the building; and retained for the final feasting, as replacing an ancient "sacrifice of fatted meats". Formerly an ox was led in procession; then slaughtered and consumed. The procession was kept slow; at this time local betrothals were then first announced; and again, during the procession, at sundry halts, once again the refrain arose, "*Petits tripettos pour San Marcell!*"
[See *Church Dances*]

[1] *Réminiscence populaire de la Provence*. L. J. B. Feraud Beranger. Paris, 1885.

TRIPTOLEMUS (Hellenic)

Is best known as "the god in the car", and is shewn so on many Greek painted vases. He was closely connected with the ritual dances of Tholema (Tholma), and became so important that the name developed as a royal title, when it was used by the long line of Ptolemy rulers. We gain some light by a curious preservation of the title of The Earth Mother as Dolma in distant Tibet, after her ritual has faded from the Keltic days of Europe, leaving only the Dolmen or Dolmin, with a Teutonic trace in the shattered rites of the Irminsaul. The God of the Car was the God of the Agricultural Year; the economic necessities of food dominated the ritual expression in feast and festival. The Latin trace continues in Bar-Tholo-meus. The Krypto-Tholameus governed the secret rituals of the Greater Mysteries: from the Lesser Mysteries, with its potent symbol of the head of golden living corn (the last thing shown to the candidate for initiation), they turned to the more difficult wisdom of regeneration; from the field of the world to the field of the man. Dancing rituals enhanced the revelations. In most was figured the benevolent Corn Goddess, under many names according to many functions. As corn seed she went down into Hades; and rose again as the living green stem, uniting Perse-Phoneia, accompanied by the Psychopompus, the winged messenger bearing the Caduceus as the Staff of the Ritual Dance. As the secret grain of advanced man, she unites after another fashion which was never described, and forbidden to be mentioned outside the Mysteries. Only by long comparative study of living rituals with remains of those now gone, can we ascertain how sacred dance was formulated to open the mind to wisdom.

TRIPUDIUM (Ancient Rome)
Ritual dancing, especially by the augurs in their ceremonial rites in the *templum*. It is described as a tripping three-step dance, done both in slow and medium pace. The *podium* was sometimes the place of dance; and the *tri-pod* (or three-footed brazier), the central implement of the ritual circle dance. Possibly the elemental form is one of the origins of the *waltz* or *valsa* form.

TRISKELES (Hellenic name, universal symbol)
A term used by Agathokles of Syracuse (BC 359 - 20) to denote the oldest "dance symbol" in the world. The familiar form known in Britain is the sign of the Isle of Man (Manx) known as "The Three Legs". The Island of Sicily formerly used this sign, though it has nothing to do with the "near triangular shape of the island". Along with the four-armed swastika (*Sva-stika* in Sanskrit, used popularly as an emblem of "Good Luck") the *Triskele* emphasises cosmic movement; as eternal motion. The *tri-skele* has a relation to the *iso-skele* and other regular forms, used as symbols according to their inherent mathematical proportions, to denote certain cycles of time and rhythm; and is a potent symbol of every trinity. Consequently the form, with its derivations (which are numerous), was exhibited in ritual and ceremony. The doubled form, known as *Muhr-i-Suleiman*, appears in Morris* (*Moeres*) dance as "The Rose".

TROIS VIFS ET TROIS MORTS (French "Dance of Death")
A thirteenth century metrical work; version by Baudoin de Condé and Nicolas de Marginal. It seems to be the remnant of an ecclesiastical version, since *Horae ad usum Sarum* (1495) contains "three Deaths, three horsemen, with hawks and hounds" appearing to a hermit.
[See *Dance of Death; Todtentanz; Danse Macabre; Misère, Danse de; Morts, La danse des*]

TROOPING THE COLOUR (England)
An old military ceremonial, with march accompanied by music, usually a trained brass band. The pragmatic usage is to acquaint non-literate men with the Colour which they must support in combat. The modern ritual is colourful and impressive for spectators; it ends with changing the guard. The men are drawn up, with the Colour at one flank, the band at the other. Following inspection, the colour sergeant moves with full escort to slow march, along all ranks in single file. The develop-

ment of music has been accompanied by more disciplined drill for "Guards' Slow March". The term trooping derives from ancient Greek *trope* and *tropos* and refers to turning up and down each line.

TROPHIME (France)
Of Arles, Provencal centre of Mythic Players Gild in early Mediaeval period. The name derives from *Terephim* (or *Toraphim*) meaning the *Centa* (hundred, metaphorically, implying very many) of puppets and masks kept for the seasonal plays given in the Kalu-Istria (cloisters) at Arles. Reconstructed later in stone, the centre lost its real vitality and lapsed into monastic revenue-cellecting activities. The dancers of Arles are legendary (cp. Bizet's *L'Arlesienne*, etc.).

TROUBADOR — 1 (French)
Trobador (Spanish), *Trovera* (Norman) as "finders" ="Singers of Hora", *Tropes* de Hora. This term derives ultimately from the Buddhist missions of Asoka, which became known as *Thera-putae* — Fathers of Healing; or, in the later Latin-Greek, as *Theoria* or precepts of living. Through all propaganda or mission groups, the term survives in slight variations, applied to different items. The *trope* continues in musicology, as a form — but (in vulgar terms) their frequent food was tripe. The dance term *trip*, and the university term *tripos*; the *tripudium* and *tripod* of the sibyl with her prophecies and talking, are still linked. The later Greek terms *trip-tolemus* (*Trapa-Tholemus*) and the subsequent "royal name" Ptolemy, derive from the same stem; as does the Tibetan monastery name for the young men "undergrads", as *trapa*. Almost all of these terms move around the notion of presenting myths in terms of ritual and dramatic action, comparable with the parallel terms that derive from the equally powerful association of *Min* — to *minster* and *minstrel*. In England, a professional player may still be called a "good trouper", while in military parlance, the "trooping of the colour" is broadly comparable with the green baize notice board for the company.

TROUBADOUR — 2 (Old Provencal)
Name given (10th - 13th centuries) to the minstrels, or inventive poets, who wrote verses which they sang to instruments, singly or in small groups; while acting discreetly as purveyors of national news, or private information, and religious doctrines. Their dances were thus relatively of small importance, while mime or gesture, in the manner of courtly rhetoric, was more favoured. They cultivated princely manners, wrote *poesie courtoise* in lyrical form — *verso* and *canzo* — but adding, as a

contrast, the political satire characterised in *sirventes;* or the *partimen,* a debate in rhythm on an announced subject; and the *tenso* or *tenson,* an ancestor of dance form, where two singers would compare, with vivid gesture, the varied excellencies of their pursuits. Among these, as at Toulouse, the *Scientia Gai* was cultivated, including a Battel of Flowers and an award of a Golden Rose (imitated in papal circles). Their most private songs included mystical lays; the kind followed discreetly by Petrarch's *To Laura* and Dante's *To Beatrice,* when the May Festivals of Jeanne la Pucelle were suppressed. Some 2,500 poems exist; but, for them, only a tenth have melodies; and these the more public and popular specimens.

TROUBADOUR—3 (French)

From *trobador* (Provençal), as a "finder", maker, or composer (and singer) of poetry. The Provençal term is for the West European minstrel, as a wandering teller of tales, a group of whom would perform dance-mimes, especially at the courts. King René of Anjou was celebrated, not only as a patron, but himself a troubadour, during their period of fame (10th to 14th century). Cp Norman analogue *trouvère.*
[See *Rymour; Minstrel*]

TROUVERE (Northern France)

Name given (11th/13th centuries) to the inventive singer-poets. They followed the Provençal school; though based in their local religious canon; inasmuch as they carried the language as *Langue d'Oil* (Tongue of the Wheel), while the *Troubadours** used *Langue d'Oc* (Tongue of the *Oke* or Oak). These phrases belonged, as pass-words, to the systems they mainly supported; we know them as embedded "cracks", as "O.K." or "Oke!", and the Scots "Weel?" or the French affirmative *Oui!* Trouvères were used as trusted royal messengers; or sometimes they carried their "letters" in newly made verses, when they sang to a familiar melody, with appropriate gesture or dance. Eleanor of Aquitaine, about 1137, began to make use of this system; interlaced with the popular romances of *chevallerie.* Another sector of their work was the familiar "praise-song"—always recrudescent; as from the Italian *trionfo* to the sycophantic English Masque; in which some ruling person expected to receive fulsome acclamations from "his adoring subjects". Sometimes this *chanson à personnage* developed good verse and acceptable melodies; many accompany dance songs. They developed also the *Pastourelle,* dis-severed from its theological implications. Academies devoted to *trouvère* music and dance, were called *puys* (as at *Puy de Notre Dame*) meaning a "mount"—as an "Olympus".

TROY GAME—1 (Italy)

Sir James Frazer considers that the Troy Game was a Roman equivalent to an ancient dance associated with the Cretan labyrinth.[1] "Troy" or "the Troy Game" was said to have been brought to Italy by Aenaeas, and through his son, Ascanius and the Alban kings, to have descended to the Romans. It was performed by bands of youths on horse-back, and is compared by Virgil to the windings of the Cretan labyrinth. (See *Geranos,* Crane Dance**). The Game is depicted (as proved by the inscription) on an ancient Etruscan vase, which shows seven beardless warriors dancing, with two armed riders on horseback. A figure of the Cretan labyrinth is also included, which pattern Roman boys used to draw on the ground to use for playing a game, probably a miniature Troy Game. Children's games were also played in such a maze in Northern Europe and Scandinavia, where they were made of turf or stones, and traces may be found in Norway, Sweden, Denmark, Finland, Lapland and Iceland, called variously "Babylon", "Wieland's House", "Trojeborg", "Tröburg" etc. Labyrinths known as "The Road to Jerusalem" used for ritual processions were frequently inlaid in the floor of old churches, a few traces of which still remain in France and other European countries. It was Sir James Frazer's opinion that the *Troy Game* may have originated in religious ritual, connected with the sun worship of which Cnossus was a great centre. In Pompeii a variation of the *Troy Game,* called *Lusus Serpentis,* was performed by young men on horseback. A crude representation of its serpentine form was found on the front of a house in the Strada de Nola.
[See *Way to Jerusalem; Labyrinth*]
[1] *The Golden Bough.* Sir J. G. Frazer. 1919 (Part 3: "The Dying God").

TROY GAME—2 (*Ludus Troiae*)

Greek celebrations in dance-mime of the New Year Festival, equivalent to the Roman form of the Salii; the Kuretes or Corybantes in Crete and Phrygia; the Sword Dancers in Teutonic lands; the Boritza in Transylvania, East Europe; and the Morris Dancers in England; or the Maruts in Vedic mythology. The central doctrine is to be understood only by acceptance of the recognition of "reality-as-symbol" and in this feast, analysis is complicated by the varying presence of three or four strands of symbolism. While the "reality" may in some examples indicate a present "fertility wish" or "fertility-act", we cannot therefore assume that this is the most important or even a main project in the ritual drama. Hidden in the ceremonial is more or less conscious guidance by the old Gnostic precept "As above, so below", in that any creative activity involved or suggested, is there as a symbolic parallel to the kosmic operations of the same kind. This recognition is further complicated by the "realistic" projection of the Twelve Days Festival (it may now have less) to the Genius of the Year (as evident with the Salii) and thence the social values are interwoven with those of the agricultural year. Thus there are at least four strands of doctrine: the human as individual; as group; the social tribe or clan (for whom or before whom the small group performs the rite), and then the human as initiated or "saved", which attainment is again projected by the group for the social tribe. Thus the gods are mimed; they may appear masked or enrobed in disguise; there may be two sides at mimic battle; and there are often two distinct phases of ceremonial; the later part more private (as at Eleusis). The dance thus involves many features: the gods and goddesses; their forms and functions; their own group relations; their relations to humanity. The normal central feature of ritual death and ritual resurrection appears again and again, from ancient Egypt and Babylonia or India, to mediaeval and modern Europe; and within the doctrines of the greater religions, similar factors appear again, now as patent myth, now as alleged history.

TROYANATS (N. Serbia, Yugoslavia)
A circle dance in 2/4 time for men and women standing alternately, holding one another's shoulders. The circle moves to the right with very small, quick steps, the feet scarcely leaving the ground. Tiny steps in rapid tempo produce a quivering or vibration of the entire body, so that the whole group seems to shiver. This shaking movement may have come from the Turks during their long occupation of Yugoslavia. In Turkey, the Cifte Tel* employs a quivering of the shoulders and arms, and a similar "shiver" is found in the dancing of the Shleuh* boy dancers of Morocco.   [Cp. Drmes]

TSAM (Mongolian, Chinese)
Also Tscham, Sham. The open-air Theatre ground, favoured by the nomads of Western Mongolia and Tartary; also in provincial Tibet. The favoured space is the centre, for great festival occasions such as Wesak, for a tribal meeting, with games and religious plays from the Buddhist traditional repertory—a great square surrounded by black tents.   [See Tibetan Ritual Dance]

TSAMIKOS (Greece)
A chain dance for men and women, in 3/8 time, originating as a martial dance among the Klephts, or guerillas of the mountains. The men vie with each other in displays of technique, elaborating

basic steps, the leader often leaving the chain (as in the Kalamatianos*) to perform acrobatic feats. Dancers with linked hands move in an anti-clockwise direction, winding in serpentine patterns, and ending each phrase of music with a hop and twist of the free foot. When danced by women the steps are smooth and gentle. The Tsamikos is danced by crack regiments of Evzones, in their fustanella* and red-tasselled shoes and caps, particularly on Easter Sunday, but also on other occasions. The leader, while dancing alone, must throw back his head as far as possible without losing balance. Expert dancers balance a glass of water on their forehead.

TUAREG SWORD DANCE (Africa)
A male solo dance of the Tuaregs of the Air Mountains, central Sahara. Accompanied by syncopated drum beats in African style, the dancer runs up to the drum and performs a dance of quick, irregular steps, with the sword held in both hands at arms length above his head. The drum may be a millet mortar with a wet skin stretched over it; or a bowl of milk containing a half calabash, which gives a varying note according to how far the gourd is sunk.

TUKIK (Inuit, or Eskimo; Baffinland, N. Canada)
This secret Moon Dance may not be witnessed by any white man, since upon its correct ritual depends the life of the Inuit tribe which performs it. Fertility of race and animals are the central theme. When the sun has disappeared for the six-month winter, the moon is bright; and Oudluviak (the stars, the "little light") are brilliant. The Inuit men gather on the seashore (women must remain indoors), while they invoke Tukik to send down the "life that is life".

TUREI NA-MBE RITUAL (New Hebrides)
Performed in Malekula and the Small Islands of the New Hebrides, on the erection of a new set of gongs. In the Island of Vao Turei Na-mbe must be followed as soon as possible by Ramben* and Maki-Ru,* a two-part initiation ritual lasting many years. Gongs are made from hollowed tree-trunks with vertical or horizontal slits and on Vao an orchestra consists of four upright gongs led by the mother-gong, tinan; and two horizontal gongs. At various points during construction and consecration appropriate dances are performed. The same name is given both to the gong-raising ritual and to the dance performed only on those occasions. The "Maki-men" (initiates) dance this circular Turei na-mbe* during tree-felling and as the logs are ferried across from the mainland (when the dance and songs of the Na-rel* cycle are also

given); the same Gong-Raising dance is performed during trimming and shaping of the ends; and on the eve of consecration of the gongs, it is danced all night. When the gongs are finished festivities leading to their erection and consecration begin. Members of each village, in established rotation, and at intervals of several days, perform the preliminary circular dance, *Velal*.* On intervening nights, members of the home village perform the processional dance, *Ro-mbulat** (Banana Leaves). When the gongs are set up, visitors from other islands join the inhabitants of Vao for the all-night *Gong-Raising Dance (Turei Na-mbe)*, followed at dawn by the performance, in turn, by picked members of each village, of mumming plays, and a *Na-leng** figure dance by the "Maki-Men".
[See *Malekula, Dances of*]

TUREI NA-MBE (Gong-Raising Dance)
Malekula, New Hebrides. A circular dance, accompanied by singing, performed only during "Gong-Raising" (See *Turei Na-mbe Ritual**). It takes place on the dancing-ground (at one end of which a huge torch burns) throughout the night preceding consecration of new gongs. Its form consists of three concentric circles. Clustered in the centre the "guests" (from other villages) perform complicated steps facing the gongs. In their midst stand their leaders, each beating time with a bamboo stick called *Ne-mbal*. The next ring consists of "Maki-men" (initiates) who dance round, holding lighted torches. Women form the outer circle, dancing on the spot, with swift undulating movements towards the centre and back. The Maki-men are thus the only ones who move round. Before the dance begins, all dancers standing motionless, the gongs beat first the appropriate rhythm of the "leaf" or refrain, then the rhythm of the "fruit" or verse. Gongs cease and the refrain is sung by the guests, swinging arms and legs, while the silent Maki-men dance round with upraised torches. The gongs again take up the refrain; guests cease singing and perform complicated steps special to this dance, the Maki-men still progressing in a circle. After a pause the gongs sound the verse rhythm, but before the verse is sung the previous dance movements are repeated; guests again sing the refrain while marking time, the Maki-men still dancing with raised torches, the women swaying and uttering shrill cries. Suddenly all movement ceases; then, unaccompanied, the guests sing the first verse of the song, making slow dignified movements, Maki-men standing facing inwards with torches lowered to the ground and the women motionless and silent. Finally, the refrain sequence of gong rhythm, dancing and singing is performed once more. Then the whole performance of refrain and

verse is repeated until all verses of the song are sung, when another song is started and the complete cycle gone through again, continuing all night without a pause. Each song has its own tune, matching the rhythm of the dance. The four other ritual circle dances—*Velal*,* *Hek-Hekelean*,* *Taur-Na-mbak** and *Taure** have a similar form, differences lying in gong-rhythms and steps used, the last two named dances being ritually the most important.   [See *Malekula, Dances of*]

TURKISH DANCE AND MUSIC
Exists in three main systems, each slightly different from earlier Arabian or Persian schemes; though all having traces of Hindu influence, especially in the *raga** scales. Religious music is almost absent from Moslem ritual, though used in the Calls vocally; and more definitely by the dervish centres (though these have suffered from antipathy in republican times). Popular music, often of surprising excellence, is in advance of popular dance. The two principal uses are at wedding feasts, and in the town cafés; though·many village festivities call for dance and song. The so-called "Classical music" of the court is diminished (there are not so many wealthy weddings as formerly), and the *harim* entertainment dance, never very advanced in technique of movement, has lessened. In Turkish estimation, *oussul*, or rhythm, is most important; this encourages dance; but European scales have broken the smoother transitions found in *raga* music, essentially melodic. The latest leading secular music, *fasl*, has, like European chamber music, no dance associated with it; but the *Oyouns* (dances and rhythmic games) accepting traditional melodies from Thracian and Anatolian villages, use modes called *Hava*, *Kochma* and *Varsaghi*, as well as the poems chanted to *diwan*; and agricultural festivals celebrated by *Kalenderi*. There may be found, among the Secret Societies (or inner rings of the leading sects), such as the *Begtashies*; the *Ahies*; the *Kizeel* and the *Alevie*, forms of the *fasl* developed to ritual usage : in *Charki* (ring dance), a *Gazhul* (chanted poem), a *Divan* (solemn prayer, in quatrains), with *kochma* and *kerem* or *terem*. Different instruments are used. The *Sazchair*, a musical-poet, plays a *Saz* (three plucked strings), helped by percussion; *Def* or *daira* (tambour) varying his chant by playing a *Zurna* (a kind of oboe), accompanied by *Davoul* (large drum). Military music is simple : the *Mehterhane* (Prince-company) is the band, furnished with *Davoul*, *Borou* (trumpet), *Nakkara* and *Zil* (cymbals of brass). The religious dance form comes to view at the *Naurooz* (New Year) and in celebrations of "Hassan and Husain." Many elements of Turkish music penetrated into the Balkans, during a long occupa-

tion; and may be detected, even in modern Bosnian dance and music.

TURN PLATZ (German)

Literally, a turning-place, usually for dance, in the open air. The best *platz* is covered with a wooden floor; but some, where these have worn away, still bear the traditional name. Sometimes the wooden structure is elevated to a platform, so that competition dances can be watched. The name refers also to the *platz* used for any athletic event; some have been built under cover.

TUTU

The famous "ballerina skirt" seen in ever-shrinking folds about the dancers in modern ballet, as compared with Eugene Lamy's original design in tulle for the Romantic Ballet of the 1830's. The term *tutu* has no discernible origin in Europe; the word is known in Melanesia, for almost the same thing, namely a fringe of leaves devised to attach to an object, a totem, a dolmen, a tree, to denote a temporary tabu. A similar name in India referred to cotton weaving; and the name may have come to Europe with cotton.

TUWAIF (Pakistan)

Moslem term for a dancer, principally for *serai* (camps) entertainments. The term comes from Moslem-Arabic sources (and seems to be same as *waif* in England, as associated with "strays" or *istrais*, vagabond actors formerly denounced by a late Elizabethan law). They were sometimes linked with the semi-religious system of Thugee, formerly rife in Bengal and through North India, these girls being exempt ritually from attack for "sacrifice." In Taylor Meadow's book, *Confessions of a Thug*, the *tuwaif* girls are mentioned. They would compare now with the American cultural life of a gangster's Moll, though the *tuwaif* carried neither dagger nor hung "for her man", but sought only to provide him with "useful information" for which she got presents.   [See *Phansigars*]

TWELVE VIRGINS' DANCE (Greek legend)

Differs from the Hebrew version, as myth; in connection with the *Tale of Troy*. This Hellenic myth became a great favourite in the early Renaissance. The *Six Idyllia*, of the Sicilian poet Theocritus, were well known; and possibly gave impetus to the French court pastime of "playing at Shepherds". They delighted specially in the festivities of Menelaus and Helena. "They jest with the Bridegroom; they praise Hellen; they wish them joy in marriage". The twelve noble Spartan Virgins are brought in singing to the chamber door. They sing:

Hellens Epithalamion

"In Sparta long agoe, where Menelaus wore the crowne
Twelve noble Virgins, daughters to the greatest in the towne,
All dight upon their haire in Crowtoe garlands fresh and greene,
Danst at the chamber doore of Helena the Queene,
What time this Menelay, the younger Sonne of Atreus
Did marry with this louely daughter of Prince Tyndarus.
And therewithal at eve, a wedding song they jointly sung,
With such a shuffling of the feete, that all the Pallace rung".

TYBURN TREE, Dance of (London)

This former popular entertainment was grimly known, at one period, as "The Dance of Jack Ketch". The basis is uncertain; the name is said by some writers to be that of a highwayman, there executed; but others aver that Richard Jaquett was owner of the manor of Tyburn, and that hangmen received their sobriquet from "being in his service". There seems to have been one hangman called Jack Ketch, who himself executed Lord Russell and the Duke of Monmouth (1678). The hangman received one shilling plus three-half-pence for a rope; noblemen were expected to pay in advance. The Dance refers to the reaction of the guest, now obviated by modern scientific methods, at Pentonville.

TYROLIENNE (Austria)

Typical song-dance forms used—often in 19th century opera—as the folk dances of the peasants of the province of Tyrol, bordering on Italy. Dances thus show influences from both countries.

TZUYZKH (Armenia)

Mediaeval period; a special kind of mime dance, done in the Great Square (at Erivan) before the Palace for a Royal wedding. The people in general danced on these occasions, usually in great rings (kolo style) hand in hand. The *Tzuyzkh* was not one of the regular dances performed by the *Parik** or professional dancers of the country. In later times, the *sharakan* were sung; these were adaptations of church hymns revived in 13th century. Some are *narek*—merging prose and verse by poets or *Nurekatzi*. The dance song is called *Haberban*— eight verses of four-lines. Mourning dancers called *Egheramark* appear in black at funerals, singing a burial song to hand clap rhythms.

U

UATCHAT (Old Egyptian)

Literally the Watching Eye. A women's gild whose duties included watching the rate of Nile inundation; they celebrated two monthly dates: New Moon and Full Moon; they acted as midwives for the ordinary people; and some were skilled in garden or field work. The temple officers were more educated; they used the *Uatchat* or the famous Symbolic Eye. In England there was a centre, named Uatchat, now called Watchet, in Somer-Set. Their circle dances were chiefly New Moon affairs; From them came the later Town Watch — with its "setting the watch" for calendar dates; while the Death Watch beetle denotes the scarab.

UCHELLAWR (Welsh)

Mistletoe (*Mist-el-Tau*); sacred plant of the Druids (also *Uchelfal*). Traditional terms indicate the high estimation of Mistletoe and its Festival, with Druidic ritual ceremony. The bearer of the cut blossom was the *Uchelfaer*; he acted as leader also of *Uchelraith* (jury for admissions). He had *Uchelsaf* (high standing as dance leader); he had to be *Uchelwr* (householder) and recorded *Ucheliant* (elevation in rank) or *Ucheldor*. His task was *Uchelu*, to make high. The medial term accords with the Indian *chela* (pupil, follower) and is not unknown in Italy — Uccello the painter. Slight indications of his duties remain in English courts, where he is Usher; and in a few schools (Winchester) while Welsh chapels still refer to *uchelwyl*, or vespers — formerly the festival of the Solstice, *yr heulorsaf*.
[See *Mistletoe Ritual Dance*]

ULA-NO-WEO (Hawaii)

A standing *hula** in fast tempo, using a hopping step (*uwehe*). With body leaning slightly forward, knees are bent and hands hover gracefully over the knees. Gestures and movements symbolically indicate various colours, changing steps representing changing shades. Main symbol is the *ilima flower* and its brilliant "royal" yellow shades, the dance being associated with the Hawaiian Queen Kapiolani. Red, yellow and purple were royal colours.

ULI-ULI-NOHO (Hawaii)

"Gourd sitting". A *hula** in which dancers, seated on the ground, each hold in one hand a gourd rattle, decorated with brightly coloured feathers. There is no musical accompaniment beyond chanting and the beat of rattles. This *hula* depicts, by graceful movements of shoulders, arms and the upper body, the sport of surfing. The name of the accompanying chant — *Heeiha* — is that of a specially good surfing place, once popular with Hawaiian kings.

UNDUMPISHER (England)

Court clown and dancer, in the time of Elizabeth I. He was also an official, a kind of master of ceremonies for arranging the dances. He may have been called "Undumpisher" from *Dump*,* the name of a 16th century dance mentioned in Shakespeare's plays and contemporary literature.

UNGKULATEM (Siberia)

"I sing". A round dance of the Yakut people, which sometimes continues monotonously for hours, the dancers keeping up an unbroken chant. Proceeding clockwise the dancers, in one or several separate circles, move a step to the left, leaning slightly forward, then leaning backward as the right foot closes with the other. The circle of men and women with joined hands, thus moves slowly round.
[See *Yakut Wedding Dance*]

UNOTO (Kenya, E. Africa)

Initiation ceremony of Masai tribes, held every seven years. Young men of about twenty-one to twenty-eight years become adult warriors (*morans*), and, as responsible members of the tribe, able to marry and set up home. At the same ceremony older warriors retire, to become elders. Masai people, tall and proud, are of Semitic rather than African appearance. Their religious customs include much use of the mystical number forty-nine (suggesting Oriental connections). For *Unoto*, a circular village (*manyatta*) is built, of about 160 huts enclosing a circle three hundred yards diameter. On a specially selected place inside the circle is built the warrior's ceremonial hut (*esingera*). after forty-nine sacred oxen have been driven over the site. Round the *esingera* forty-nine smaller huts are occupied by forty-nine leaders of the initiates. Masai numbering some 2,000 may gather for the initiation of 500 young men. Dances are performed almost continually, by men, in mass formation. Beginning slowly, with almost static tableaux, the rhythm gradually increases until the men (each carrying upright a long stick), break rank and career across the grass in a leaping dance. Masai have no drums, their only musical instrument being the Kudu horn which accompanies the dance, together with shouts and claps to keep rhythm. Cloaks of white calico are decorated with patterns in red, yellow and black. Monkey skins and collars of vulture feathers are worn, together with bells on the legs, bead necklaces, bracelets and wooden ear-plugs. A headdress completes the costume. Usually of black ostrich plumes fixed to an oval frame which surround face and head like a halo, a few wear the *olowaru* — a tall, busby-like hat made from a lion's mane and worn as a mark of honour. In a lion hunt, the mane is awarded to the bravest warrior, who makes it into the *olowaru*, to be worn only at *Unoto*. *Morans* hunt with spears; and shields of buffalo-hide painted with red, black and white patterns which denote tribal section and age-group of the owner. Outstanding bravery is recorded by a small circular design, which may be painted on the shield only with agreement of all warriors. Young women, rubbed with red ochre, and adorned with bead necklaces and ear-rings and calico "toga", attend *Unoto* to seek a likely husband. [See *Numba*]

UP-HELLY-AA (Shetland Islands)

Modern revival of an ancient Viking Festival, performed near Scallaway in the Shetland Islands (the ancient capital town) to celebrate the Winter Solstice after the darkest day of midwinter. Now it is held on the last Tuesday in January. The Guizer Jarl (Earl of the Guizers or Actors) attired in a magnificent coat of mail with raven-winged helmet, heads the torchlight procession with the Viking galley. When the harbour is reached, a trumpet gives a signal, when the torches are hurled on this ancient symbol of "The Ship of the Solar Year" (probably Egyptian in origin), which then goes up in flames. Then follows singing and dancing which lasts until the dawn brings assurance of the returning sun. The principal item is a version of an old Sword Dance.

URIM (Hebrew)

Light, or "The Lights", or "The Light Bringers"; connotes a Hebrew term as the name of the Great Pyramid of Egypt. The Egyptian name is *Khuti* — "The Lights" — in this place four. *Urim* is used, in Hebrew scripts, chiefly to denote a "Revelation". This had several modes, from political "prophesy" to forecasts, that we should now range from "weather charts" or personal and tribal "fortune-telling". (Equivalent with the Grecian Oracles, and the Roman Augur). Thus the "divine Oracle", then named *Urim* and *Thummin*, was the means of "communication" (probably using *teraphim* or figures), with the local deity Yahveh. This ritual was associated with *Shekinah* or *Argha* of Covenant; which in one mode was drawn (*yantra**) and in another was constructed (ark or ship form). The ceremonial operation was composed of chants with ritual dances and gestures. In Hindu worship, the "Light offering", or "waving of lights" is similar. The original Khaldaean name of the Pyramid was *Urim-middin*, the "Light-Measures", so that its annexed Hebrew equivalent became "Revelation (of) Measures". This was the prag-matic purpose of accurate ritual: the dance measured the sacred surface; the "count" of steps or degrees gave the days and years; and the chant exhorted as to ethics, set in praise and prayer, for which the music and steps were measured. The popular demand for Fortune-telling continued for many centuries in the Roman church, accompanied by songs and dances. Greek usages formalised these Kaldaean/Egyptian rituals into a more rigid mode, with metre and *kanon*, for the movements of the *Xoros*; but in Jewish doctrine, the *schema* collapsed into the allegorical Levitical Breastplate (similar to the Grecian "Shield" symbol) for public use, or the *tetragrammaton* and the *schem-ha-phorasch** in *Qabalah*,* for mature mathematical "combination and permutation", similar to the modernist actuarial tables or logarithms. This takes dance beyond the possibility of ceremonial statement and spectacle; into a different field of symbolism. With the Jews (Israel and Judah) the Urim was given a mythic form, from the Allegory of Ishtara now presented as Esther, for the Feast of Purim, the Great Feast of the Spring Festival.

URIM AND THUMMIM, Dance of (Hebrew terms)

Used in symbolical divination, and, in the imitation of the Babylonian practice of the Wheel of the Sun, for "telling fortunes". The U-Rim was the circumference of the Wheel — the Rim — while the Thum was the central pole or axis on which it spun. Set into the U-Rim were numerous pegs, carved in various shapes. These were Teraph and Seraph (Teraphim* and Seraphim, plurals), similar to the Greek *angellos*, or messengers or "teller of future". The Wheel was spun round after the querent had put her question; and the position when it stopped, gave the required indications to be interpreted by the Levite in charge. Later there were dances by brilliantly costumed dancing girls, for the same general purpose. The final dance of this type is the much-changed "Musical Chairs", but during Mediaeval ages in West Europe, the Wheel of Fortune was frequently consulted in churches. Some of the early clocks (like that at Nuremburg) followed in this Wheel tradition, with figures of "disciples" coming out to "tell the hours". Popular forms with the tribes of Judea appeared in the Baal-Berith dance rituals, performed round the famous pillars of the town Ba-al, or "market-cross" centre; similar to the maypole dances of Saxon England. A faint memory of the peg and leg count continues in the parlour game of cribbage. [See *Zodiack*]

UZBEK DANCING

Although very old, dance in Uzbekistan was, until recent years, performed only by women in the seclusion of their household or, if in public, by boys taking women's parts. A very virile dance form for men has now developed, exemplified in the *Ulak*, a horsemen's dance performed by the collective farmers of the Ferghana Valley. Uzbek dancing has a great variety of rhythms, and although different characteristics develop according to districts, the style of dancing remains the same. The hands are used a great deal to convey the meaning of the dance, sometimes with great complexity of pattern. As the southern part of Uzbekistan borders Afghanistan, this may be a reflection of the Indian *mudras** which play a large part in the expression of Indian dancing. Women's dances are graceful and lyrical; the ancient *Tanovar*, which told of the hard lot of Uzbek women is now a joyful expression of their greater freedom. *Bilbak* (Kerchief) is a charming courting dance. Various group dances have developed in recent years, such as *Pakhta* (Cotton), which depicts work in the cotton fields, and *Pillia*, describing work processes in the silk-worm industry.

V

VAGANOVA BALLET TRAINING SYSTEM
Now used in all Soviet academies, Agrippina Yakolevna Vaganova (born Leningrad 1874, died 1951) was the principal creator of this brilliant system. Founded on the earlier methods of Johannsen and Petipas, she added material and method from Jaques-Dalcroze and from F. Delsarte, gained in her own training at the Maryinsky Theatre School. Further stimulated by Duncan, she was a disciple of A. A. Gorsky and his Moscow teacher K. Stanislavsky, in "dramatic method" and thus welded these elements into the re-organized school at Leningrad in her charge after 1914-1918 war. Her masterly method was justified in the first pupils to pass out including Marina Semyonova, Galina Ulanova, and Olga Lepeschinskaya. She was no less successful as a producer of ballet.

VALA (Scandinavian)
In the *Eddas*, or Northern poetry, the *Vala* is a prophetess or "speaker". The name was given to the Three Norns or "Daughters of Fate", known as *Urd* (Wurd or Weird) the Past; *Verdandai*, the Present; and *Skuld*, the Future. The *Vala* were prominent in Roman times, when Teutonic lands were invaded by the general Drusus. He met one of the Vala, named Veleda (she lived, among other places, in Praha, Bohemia, which carries her traditions), and she warned him not to cross the river Elbe. The prophetesses were known with other titles: as Idises, or Dises, and Hagedises (we recall the Greek name Dis), who appeared at forest shrines and festivals, usually with the armies. One story tells that the blood was collected into great tubs, wherein the Dises plunged their naked arms to the shoulder, previous to joining in the wild dance which ended the ceremony. In later times they were degraded to witches; and appeared on the Brocken, or Blocksberg, during *Walpurgisnacht.** The legend has the air of a "propaganda yarn", from the other side; it seems far more probable that the girls operated as camp cooks and that the well-known Teutonic taste for cooked pig was the cause of their kitchen-stained arms.

VALKYRIOR (Scandinavia)
Servants of the Twelve Goddesses who rule the Hall of Odin, Valhalla. The Valkyrior (or *Walkure*, who appear in Wagner's operas), are first "Choosers of the Brave" among those slain in battle; and servitors of these heroes at the ever-laden tables of feasting, and drinking. These legends belong to the *Edda*, or ancient Icelandic mythology; much of which is lost; and seldom studied. The Three Fates (Nurns or Norns) include Urd (Past), Verdandi (Present) and Skuld (Future), constantly invoked by the Valkyrior, in their songs to Odin and his wife Frigga. Another is Fraya, goddess of Love. Their instrument was the *gimli*, turned in old English to *gymel*, or "secret strings" (similar to Ger. *Himmel*, heaven). They are similar to the *Vili** (another Northern term). Their dance—a flight, a march, a service was termed *gangrad* (or *gang-quad*, to circle round). The word "floor"—*vingoff*, is used later by the skalds to mean Valhalla, but means literally "abode of friends"; from *vin*, friends, and *golf*, also floor or a field.

VALOIS TAPESTRIES (Uffizi Galleries, Florence)
Have valuable material in eight large hangings. They give portraits of Catherine de Medici and her family, in a setting, portraying her principal great festivals. The facts of this visual propaganda (for such it was), as suggested in 1581 by William Silent of Netherlands, who had them made at Brussels, show that the scenic settings are as accurate as are the portraits. A. Warburg first determined these main facts and Frances Yates names Lucas of Heere as designer.
See *The Valois Tapestries*. F. Yates, 1959.

VALSE (West European mode)
Is a social dance form, based on a large circle, with the minor revolutions of the twelve individuals (or pairs) in this ritual. The basic form is the Group Wall (*Waltz*) or the social group, obedient to simple

discipline of movement. To place its function, the *Valse* must be compared closely with (a) Jig; and (b) March; as being (1) personal and unrestricted, or (2) ordered and limited movement. They reflect phases of the mass mind, in relation to the mass body or human group. With the developed *valse* we come to *carole* (the song) and sonnet (the written poem), as well as the "seasons" of the year and their music (finally *sinfonia*) or the "hours" of the day and their laboured liturgy. With the opposition of social groups : of group versus group, or individual versus group; or individual versus individual; we arrive at varied modes of ritual, based principally on the basilica, with its rectangular form. Here, groups are no longer in harmony but on the border of discord or opposition : they can no longer "go round" but only advance and retreat. The typical institutional form is Law — pretending to be Justice — always against the individual : the *Boulé*, or Basilican court; the sultan's audience chamber or *diwan*; the Gothic church choir with its triple display : ritual, ceremonial, or in parable. In each of these forms, the people are set against the people. Only in the original dedication of a church does the circumambulation appear; with a faint trace in the internal processional of officiants, first into and lastly out of their ritual positions. The ballroom versions are placed under *Waltz.**

VASANTA OTSAVA (Hindu)

Spring Festival, marked by *Holika-daha* (bonfires to burn rubbish, the "spring-cleaning" of social ritual). This Festival of song and dance, says Dr. Bhagavan Das, has[1]

"in its worship of the *Chatuh-Shashti-Devi* (Goddess of the sixty-four arts) which subserve refined *Kama* — enjoyment, similarly degenerated in India. The shell of custom remains, the spirit has vanished. The refinements have gone, the coarsenesses have become accentuated. From being a carnival of delicate refinements and artistic enjoyments, it has become a carnival of indecent songs and conduct".

[1] *Krishna Avatara.* Dr. Bhagavan Das. Madras, 1924 (p. 71).

VASILCA (Rumania)

"King's Dance". In which a pig's head (boar's head) is carried as a symbol of the ending of winter; the failure of the Great Boar to bring down the revival of Spring. At New Year's Eve, a group of maskers disguised as animals make the round of the village, singing and dancing before each house. Led by Capra the Goat (in Transylvania the leader is a Stag), other animals represented are cats, and a mare. The dancers receive gifts from householders.

VATICAN BALLET (Rome)

Most Popes have encouraged theatrical display, especially in church ceremonial, painting and architecture, while strongly disapproving rival attractions. Their official or private efforts have varied considerably. Probably the most spectacular ballets were those performed within the halls of the Vatican in the reign of the Spanish Pope, Alexander Borgia VI, about the 15th century. Many details are given by the catholic historian, Dr. Pastor (*History of the Popes*), but the source quoted by McCabe in his *Popes and their Church* is the famous *Diarium* of Burchard, who was chamberlain of the papal court at that period, under Innocent, Alexander and Julius. Foreign envoys to Rome comment on these facts (*Thuasne. III. 167*, fully confirms). As an example, he mentions October 30th, 1501. "Pope Alexander", writes McCabe, "did not attend vespers . . . Alexander and his daughter Lucrezia Borgia, dined with Cesare and fifty girls, in Cesare's rooms in the Vatican. After the banquet, they danced; in one dance, they flitted round lighted candles, picking up nuts from the floor. After dancing ended, the Pope distributed prizes to servants who had won certain competitions".[1] Dances arranged for the next Pope, Julius II, were equally interesting, for his secretary, Cardinal Bibbiena had had even better experience, attaining the height of his reputation with Leo X. His own comedies (*Calendria*, e.g.) were performed, with dance interludes, in the halls of the Vatican. Entertainments continued in these forms for well over a century — from 1420 to 1520. Rome was looted in return, in 1525. Julius was a great patron of art.

[1] *The Popes and Their Church.* Joseph McCabe. London, 1918 (p. 76).
See also : *Civilisation of the Renaissance in Italy.* Jacob Burchardt. London, 1929.

VAVA VADMAL (Sweden)

A "longways dance", performed by men and women, showing the processes of weaving. In lines, facing each other, the couples move through various figures, making "weaving" patterns, at one point showing clearly the moving back and forth of the shuttle. In the modern revival of Swedish folk dance, the dancers wear the traditional costumes of their own regions.
[See *Renningen; Li Tisseran; Svenska Tans; Skansen; Lekstuga*]

VAUDEVILLE (France)

Mediaeval term for dances and dance-songs, more especially of those of the market town (*ville*), as compared with those of the *vire*, the distant mountain villages, which developed to the *vau-de-vire* or *vire-lai*. The type of the *vau-de-ville* slowly produced the characteristic market or fair theatre entertainments, which in England were taken, name as well, into the music-hall as vaudeville, or a series of brief "turns" or "numbers". (The dance term and the musical term are still followed). The *vau*, centred in the small village, grew also the *vaux* or *vogues*,* the more serious melodies and ritual-dance movements. The vaudeville dances and songs had a verse and then a few steps of jig, always done clockwise, in a small circle by the singer, to the same melody and rhythm; later varied by the patter or steps used while breaking into the topical and local jokes and satires.

VAUXHALL GARDENS (London)

First opened in 1732, following Spring Gardens on the same site, they covered the position now occupied chiefly by Waterloo Station and the Old Vic Theatre. The great period was from 1750 to 1790. Horace Walpole and his cronies frequented the Gardens, full of trees, pools of goldfish, shady walks, restaurants of the simpler type; a band-stand or rather a double stage for orchestra and singers; and wooden platforms laid out for dancing. Patrons could arrive by carriage or on foot, or by wherries to the landing stage. There the illustrious foreigner could watch the London populace enjoying the *Ridotto*. Vauxhall was "the centre of song and minstrelsy" for at the concerts plenty of good music could be heard, well played under first-rate conductors. As many as ten thousand people would gather for a *ridotto al fresco*. The Gardens changed slightly in character, due in part to change in management and control. The last period opened in 1822, as Royal Gardens, Vauxhall; and a theatre building was constructed—probably the forerunner of the Victoria Hall. More buildings inside covered growing technical entertainments— Firework Tower, Smugglers Cave; or Rotunda and Picture-room. Rope-dancing gave place to stage dancing. Vauxhall got worse and closed in 1840, but was re-opened by other optimists, finally to close, submerged by bricks and mortar, in 1859. By 1853 the Victorian *"bal masque"* had become rowdy and even a nuisance, since they continued to four or five in the morning; so that a new licence was opposed. From its Spring Gardens origin, the Gardens had attracted Londoners for some two hundred years; while most famous foreign visitors to London also saw Vauxhall.
[See *Almacks; Assemblies; Paris Gardens; Ranelagh*]

VECCHIA (Italy)

La Vecchia is literally "The Old One", or the Woman of Old Year, who was ceremonially fêted and burned at the turn of the year. She is parallel with the Gaelic *Cailleach*,* though this "Auld

Dame" was (in some earlier and more accurate ritual versions) killed and then resuscitated. This rite is similar to that of the Slaying of the Candidate in the Sword Dances; and the call on the "Ten Pound Doctor". *La Vecchia* presents a literalisation of the cleansing, or *Fevruare;* a disposal of accumulated rubbish. In other lands she is a bundle of hay; and so burned—not here as a "witch", for this, in Italy, is *strega*. La Vecchia is thus balanced with another old woman, now *La Beffana*, who is a new arrival, a bringer of presents. Theologically she presents Epiphany or the "Appearance" and humorously subserves the New Year. Both *La Vecchia* and *La Beffana* are accompanied by songs and dances; neither are specifically good or evil. Much of the dual custom has disappeared, especially in the industrial north of Italy; and remains chiefly in the *campagna*, or hill districts.

VEHICLE (British-American)

Term used by writers, chiefly on ballet, when they refer to a new production as a "vehicle for M'dlle Bronie Bronisovkaya" with the implication that the whole affair has been done solely to enhance her glory. Rarely is this sort of "appreciation" apparent concerning other arts. The portrait painter does his work to enhance not himself but his client. A costly new building is not erected "as a vehicle for architectural fantasies" but to serve some social purpose. Not many composers—even of "modern music" write to provide a "vehicle" for some instrumental player. Even writers of biographies rarely provide a vehicle for their subjects; though some books do seem to serve as propaganda for their central characters, though not as a "vehicle" for the writer. We may ask that a ballet shall aim in general to amuse, interest, or entertain the audience, whoever may be the principal dancer. Shakespeare did not write *Hamlet* as a vehicle for any film star.

VELAL (Malekula, New Hebrides)

A simple circular dance, similar in structure and position of dancers to the more important *Turei Na-mbe;** that is, three concentric circles, with the "guests" from other villages in the centre, "Makimen" (Initiates) in the middle, and an outer ring of women. Differences lie in gong-rhythms, which determine the step used, and type of song to be sung. *Velal* is a preparatory dance, performed before an important rite in the early and closing stages of three long ritual-cycles (*Turei-Na-mbe Ritual;** *Ramben;** and *Maki-ru**), on the Island of Vao and other of the Small Islands off the coast of Malekula. In each of these rituals, it announces the approach of an important event, but on the eve of the culminating rite it is replaced by a more im-

portant dance, such as *Turei Na-mbe* in the "Gong-Raising" Ritual; *Hek-hekelean** and *Taur Na-mbak** in *Ramben;** and *Taure* in *Maki-ru.** About two years after the climax of *Ramben* and *Maki-ru*, *Velal* is again performed, preceding the final rites which close the cycle. It thus leads up to and then down from the central point of the ritual.
[See *Malekula, Dances of*]

VENADO, DANZA DEL (Mexico)

"Deer Dance". Second part of the *Pascola** dances, performed at Easter by Yaqui Indians. The "deer" (*maso* in the Yaqui language) always dances with three or four *pascolas*, who impersonate coyotes or other animals who hunt the deer. The *maso* dancer has bare feet and torso, with a kilt held at the waist by a belt from which hang deer hooves. Like the *pascolas* he twists strings of *tenabari* (cocoons filled with gravel) round his legs, and carries a gourd rattle in each hand. Over his head is tied a white cloth, on which stands upright a small, stuffed deer's head (*maso koga*), decorated with flowers and red tassels, and tied under the chin with a leather strap. When the dancer bends nearly double, this head gives the impression of a deer feeding. Four musicians accompany the dance, one playing pipe and drum, one a water-drum, and two with rasps, who chant appropriate verses. With perfect imitation of the animal's movements, the *maso* gives a rthythmic impression of a deer coming into a clearing, nervously watching for enemies, becoming reassured and then feeding on the grass and drinking from the stream. While dancing he vibrates the gourd rattles in a special rhythm, emphasised by the clicking of his deer-hoof belt and cocoon anklets. The deer's tranquillity is shattered by the proximity of coyotes who, one by one, come leaping after him, finally killing him. Expert in the imitation of animal movements, the dancers bring this little drama of the forest vividly to life. The *Pascolas* are now given mainly for entertainment, and the "body" of the deer is carried to the man responsible for the fiesta, who must buy it with a bottle of liquor. Where the dance has still retained some of its ritual significance, it may continue all night. The "killing" of the *maso* occurs at dawn when the deer hides and is tracked down.

VENTRE, DANSE DU (North Africa)

Arabic female dance, parallel (in Algeria) to the wrestlers' "muscle-rippling" often exhibited in European fairs, as an example of highly localised muscle control. This it is; there is no fake. The *almeh* or *Ouled Nail** dancer may decide to add it to her accomplishments; but shows it as a rule on her classical front. Hence its vulgar appellation the "Tummy Dance" or "*Danse du Ventre*", shewn in cafés from Port Said to Casablanca; or occasionally in Marseilles. The dancer performs on a table-top, spread back on hands and feet, arched upwards. Her glossy skin shows off the rippling muscles. Her *virtuoso* feat is performed by placing a wine-glass full of liquid on one side of her "tummy," and slowly moving the muscles on each side, so that the empty glass on the opposite side is filled — without any touch of hands. Though "done to a tune", there is no more dance than is marked by the rhythm.
[See *Ouled Nail; Muscle Dance; Buffoon Dance; Cifte Tel*]

VERBUNKOS (Hungary)

A recruiting dance of the 1770's, performed by Hussars to induce young men to join the Army. This method of recruiting continued until mid-19th century, when the victorious Austrians, after the War of Independence (1848 - 49) introduced conscription. Led by the sergeant, recruiting groups went from village to village, accompanied by gypsy musicians, usually also in uniform. Forming a circle round the corporal, who indicated the sequence of movements, the young men first walked round, or clicked their spurs to establish the rhythm. After this preliminary, the first part of the dance was slow (*hallgato*), movements either being in a set order, or left to the Corporal to choose the sequence. The more complicated quick part (*friss*) included a basic step, when dancers leapt upwards and sideways; but freedom to improvise made a spectacular display of technique, especially as the young men were chosen for their prowess in the dance. Hand-clapping, heel-clicking, and striking the ankles with the hands were characteristic, the rhythm always being marked by clicking the spurs. Verses accompanying the dance were not sung but shouted to rhythm of the music. Recruiting took place when a village youth, dazzled by the splendid young men and the excitement of the dance, joined the circle. Given shako, sword, and a silver thaler, he at once became a soldier. The *Verbunkos* was thus a definite part of the military system, and since, in the recruiting gangs, advancement to the rank of corporal or sergeant depended upon skill and vigour in the dance, spirited performances were given and standards of technique remained high. After the introduction of conscription, the *Verbunkos* continued only among retired soldiers who taught it to the young men of their village, but as the dance had then lost its purpose it also lost much of its vigour. Its spirit has been best preserved in the *Legenyes* of Transylvania. By the early 19th century, the *Verbunkos* had become more regulated in the sequence of movements, and a refined version became popular as an opening dance in upper-class ballrooms.

VERGE (Latin)

Ritual-dance rod; traditional in many variant forms, from mace (*Mayze*) to wand; from stick (*stikoi*) to baton and lance. In churches, the officiant of the sacred white wand is the verger; he "draws the verge" (or border), or helps the warden to limit the area of the ceremonial. In British Parliamentary ceremonial, there remains much ornamental coming and going—as with "Black Rod" and "Mace", knocking at doors and processions to and from the bar; chiefly as moribund vestiges of factors that once were held by force. The Exchequer for centuries maintained its accounts by a counting wand or tally-stick; and thus was the stick-calendar marked off. The *Verge* was originally a signet of actual power, in the first pragmatic form, as a mode of simple direct measurement; in fact, a yard-stick, for which one well-known stick (skeptre) was held as standard. In ritual, the ceremonious act of measurement, once important, was accompanied by a chant and formulated into a semi-processional dance movement. There are many "stick-dances" with this origin. "Black Rod" belongs to the Knights of the Garland.

VERGER (Latin root)

The ritual officer who carries the rod or mace, mostly in a church. *Verga* indicates *wand;* but the later *verge* applies to the ritual function of marking the verge or path permitted. The earlier *virga* means physically, strength; or morally, virtue. It is possible that *verger* turned in French also to *berger;* the users of the path, the sheep (metaphorically) and their shepherd. In French playing cards, one named *vierge* became *virgin*.

VERISMO (Italian)

Vero: "true, real"—a term used in Western Europe as "realism", which began in Germany, partly at Stuttgart and Mannheim (ducal theatres) as a reversion from academicism and romanticism. The aim crept into every art; from painting or sculpture to dance and music, during a half century—approximately 1850 - 1900. It moded Ibsen in his plays, also Galsworthy and Shaw in England; Stanislavsky in USSR, and a whole congregation in Hollywood film industry. They have nearly all since discovered that nothing is less lifelike than imitated life— no plaster cast is a real portrait; and the social pendulum swung to the other extreme of abstraction. The *verismo* of Russia provoked the term socialist realism—from Verestchagin in painting to Meyerhold in the theatre. As art is *not* life, so artists still have to "select and reject".

VERVER (Haiti, from French)

The "pattern symbol" of the *loa* (or spirit), who is to be invoked. Comprehension of the magical usage of the *verver* in Haiti helps us to understand the similar usage of *alpona** or *rangoli** in India; the magical *rune* in Scandinavia. *Verve* is defined as "fancy"; or "life and spirit", while *etre en verve* is essentially "to be animated". Thus the doctrine is that if the correct traditional pattern is provided, then the particular *loa* (or class of *loa*) will use it as a focus of action or of materialisation. Thus the *verver* is, in reverse, equivalent to a barograph, a chart record of transit; and provides a plan, a centre, that is amenable to the desired *loa*, indicating especially its own essential norm of rhythm. This factor is one of the important components of all magical and ritual dance forms. The form is created firstly by the rhythm of the entity (as energy creates a floral form in nature), but now, with the form newly set forth, in reverse action it attracts the energy. The symbol, invigorated by the concentrated imagination of the *houngan* (priest), fills with the invoked energy, as a pipe line, properly connected and shaped, fills with water at the right time. Like the fireman's hose, it is *etre en verve*. This, in turn, communicates its force to the ritual dancers, who tend to follow the same pattern, especially if it has a circular basis. The opposite state is *veule*, to wane into weakness; this follows the temporary condition induced by the *verver;* together they are at the centre of *Vieudieu*, the "ancient worship" of the ancestors.

VESNYANKI (Ukraine)

Traditional women's holiday feast in spring-time, including many dances; some with this name. For some periods it was not customary for the men to participate fully in public festivity; so the girls danced and mimed male parts, as well as their own. While the dances follow main lines, topical improvisations add temporary flourish, especially in accompanying songs. The musical instruments are the harmonica or accordion (largely replacing the balalaika), and sometimes violin or trumpet.

VEXILLUM (Roman)

Was a regimental standard or flag; or banner carried in religious processions at festivals. In this connection, one of the *camillae** (or ritual dancers) carried the banner, as a *vexilary*. The term *vexillum* sometimes thus signified the company or troupe which had this standard heading its progress. This became Vigil (Vixil) of Knights, as they first danced and then "kept vigil" through the night. The solemn march was used at the Vigil, over the "Shield" or Arms and Crest.

VIEJITOS, LOS (Mexico)
"Little Old Men". A dance of the Tarascon Indians in the district of Michoacán. Usually performed by youths or boys masked as old men, this dance existed before the Conquest, one faint connection with Aztec* times remaining in the figure now called "Cross of the Four Stars", in which the dancers form into lines pointing to the four cardinal points. Honouring the four winds or four directions was a feature of Maya, and later Aztec, culture, as it is of the Indians of North America. Now showing Catholic influence, the dance is usually performed at religious fiestas, and on some secular occasions. With their ordinary cotton suits, sombreros and striped blanket, the dancers wear light wooden masks, representing old men with varying expressions, wispy fibre hair and an occasional beard. Each youth carries a short staff with the handle carved as an animal's head. On this staff they lean, crouched over, like infirm old men. Directed by a leader who plays a very small guitar-like instrument called a *Jarana*, they begin to dance in a semi-circle with small *zapateado** steps, their heads wagging from side to side over the sticks. There follow a series of figures in which, becoming more agile, the "old men" move in line, or circle, sometimes dancing in pairs, sometimes singly. In one figure they form into two lines facing, each line challenging the other in a display of virtuosity and clowning. This amusing dance has been seen on the London stage. In Petambo, the dancers include a *Maringuilla*—a man in woman's clothes wearing the mask of a pretty girl. She is the focus of the dance, which moves in a circle round her between each figure. Forming into two lines, each youth dances with her, and finally they bow to her in pairs, dancing a *son.** *Maringuilla* ("Little Mary") may be a Catholic innovation, or a version of the Mexican Indian *Malinche.**

VIGIL DANZA (Spain)
Before most religious festivals, the previous evening was marked by the custom of the Vigil, keeping watch. In the Spanish valleys of Jativa, Cocentaina, Albaida and Ontoniente, and many others around Valencia, there is a special dance on these occasions. Leaders move, dancing through the streets, as *el donsaina* and *el tabalet;* and where they find a door unlocked, they may enter. Any woman found within is led by her hand into the street, where she is requested to join in the dancing procession. In the movement between searches (done, it may be taken, where no offence will be expected), there is sung a frivolous song, varying from year to year, gay in tune and light in meaning (somewhat like the *calypso** of West Indies),

despite which, the church festival seems always kept in mind.

VIKIVAKA (Iceland)
A general term for Icelandic dance-songs; usually based on the round dance called *reihen* in the Saga stories; known in the Faröe Islands.
[See *Dansuringur*]

VILI (Slav; Balkans)
Comparable with the "fairy-dancers" of Western Europe, the *Vili* is known almost entirely from the famous ballet *Giselle*. This story, derived by Heine from the translated poems of Vuk Karajich sustains their supernatural character, as a band of sisters who haunt the moonlit glades, seeking to add other maidens to their number. The *Vili* appears in numerous Serbian legends, one specially as the fairy companion of Markovich. Like him, they are in fact quasi-historical; the term is from *phili* or *philoi*, the brothers, or sisters, of a fraternal band. "Vili" is current today in Ukraine and Georgia, as a family name suffix, as Dzhugashvili, descendants of a Turkomannic Dzhugash family. The *Vili* band dances in the forest clearings, from dusk to dawn, resenting masculine intervention of any kind. Colloquially the term changes to "filly"; while, very far back, it has links with servants— "ser-vila" or "sir-ventes". The *sar-vili* were ring dancers of the earlier faith of the *Ban*.
See *Tales from Servian Legends*. Vuk Stefan Karajich, Vienna 1813, and *Servia of the Servians*. Chedo Mijatovich, 1911; *Serbian Ballads*. V. S. Karajich, 1823 - 24.

VILLANELLE, VILLANELLA (French, Italian)
Dance, music and poem forms of mediaeval songs, sometimes unaccompanied, and in fairly free form; thus somewhat equivalent to the "Calypso"* known today in the West Indies. As a poem the French verse form ran to six stanzas, in nineteen lines each, using two rhymes in each verse. The dance form was simply one step to one note. Later this dance-song had a lute accompaniment; it would appear to be so named as essentially a "song of the village", or a country dance.
[See *Virelai*]

VILLANCICO (Italy)
North Italian name given by Cesare Negri to the Spanish rustic dance called *Villanos* (16th century). The figure was set for four dancers; as it was cheerful and informal, further groups of four could join.

VILLANOS (Spanish - Italian)
Was a 14th century "rustic dance" traditional in

Spain, which apparently moved from one country to the other in the celebrations of the traders who crossed by sea or land. The Italian "little name", which became *Villancico*, implies a regular dance, perhaps speeded in time while diminished in space, such as might be performed in some *trattoria*. Eventually it became, or returned to, a standard as a kind of court dance; though in France the village dance was developed as the *vau-de-ville*,* somewhat as *cake-walk** and *jazz* got accepted into "society ballroom style" in this 20th century. The *Villancico* was danced by a couple; or by two or four couples if space permitted; probably it had some association with the country fairs, appearing as a mode of courting dance. This would explain the notable introduction of numerous flourishes, always on the retreating steps.

VINGAKER DANSEU (Sweden)
A courting dance, performed by two girls and one man, each girl vying with the other, for attention of the man. Less simple than some peasant dances, this shows foreign influences in steps and style.

VINGT-QUATRE VIOLONS (France)
When the courts of Henri IV and Louis XIII were resplendent with numerous ballets and dancing, it became the custom to recruit a selected orchestra known as *Les Vingt-Quatre Violons*. This number twenty-four was copied from the *Menestriers*, whom they displaced; they became *musiciens en charge*, decked in noble uniform. Their duties included playing dance airs for the New Year Festivals, May Day, and the King's Fête; as well as any public dinners, and at the court balls. Louis XIII donated the name Band of twenty-four Violins; but when Louis XIV appointed Dumanoir as the new Roi des Violons, he was, as conductor, entitled "25-ième Violon de la Chambre". This definite number was continued, when the older bands of Menestriers were superseded (with their Roi des Menestrels) as they themselves had carried "The 24" from clerical into secular usage; from the twelve deacons and twelve canons of the ceremonial establishment, who had looked after both ritual and church plays, and played instruments before there were any violins. Louis XIV called them his *Grande Band*. In 1655, Lully organised his *Petit Band* of sixteen. In time this clerical tinge, disliked by courtiers, led to their complete change, into the *Chappelle du Roi*.
[See *Double Femmes, Les*]

VIRA (Portugal)
Generally a "longways dance for as many couples as will", with many variations. Most vigorous in Minho Province of the north, it is also danced in Beira Province, and in neighbouring hill villages of Estramadura. In Lisbon and adjacent places, the *Vira* has a circular formation. *Vira Corrido* (Beira Province) has running steps, and many rapid turns, being more elaborate in the northern part of the Province. Arms are curved slightly above the head, and fingers snapped. Drum and bagpipes, or two drums and small pipe, are the usual accompaniment. *Vira Extrapassado* (progressive turning dance) belongs to Minho district and is characterised by gradual increase and decrease of movement. Dancers carry themselves proudly with arms curved high, and fingers clicked. To music in 3/4 time, couples dance in a double line, facing each other. All sway slightly until their turn to dance, when waltz and *pas de basque* steps are used. The first couple turn each other, then turn their opposites in the next couple, gradually working down the set. When the first couple have reached the third pair, the new top couple begin, so that the gentle swaying movement slowly changes until all dancers are whirling. When the first couple has reached the bottom, they work up the set again, until all dancers have returned to their places, and the movement gradually relaxes into the original gentle swaying. Girls wear the elaborate Minho costume, with voluminous skirts, apron, head and shoulder kerchiefs, all heavily embroidered. The *Lisbon Vira* has no special costume, often being danced by the citizens in ordinary clothes. With music in 3/8 time, it is less virile than the *Extrapassado* and is for two couples in circular formation. Arms are slightly curved and fingers clicked on the first beat of the quick waltz time. Starting smoothly, the *Lisbon Vira* becomes more animated with *pas de basque* and skipping steps, and has many variations.

VIERALAI OR VIERLAY (Old French)
A dance-song, with its poem composed entirely with two rhymes; usually short lines with a refrain; or in one long line with one short line, again with a refrain. The dance movements followed the syllabic progression. The *virelai* or "Branch Song" was derived from the slow steps of the processional dance, when the green boughs or twigs (*virgatus*) were carried in the spring, in the ancient festival, taken over as "Palm Sunday". It was used in the "beating of bounds", when the *virgatus* was a trimmed rod, as used for measuring land (*virga terra*) in earlier Roman times.   [See *Villanelle*]

VIRTUOSITY
In any dance appears when performers feel that they have personally reached a high standard of technical skill which they must impose on their audience. Technical skill thus outruns the use of this same skill in a more artistic manner; in ballet,

it results in numerous "excerpts from classical ballet", (such as the "Blue Bird" number) which are deprived of what little meaning they possess when integrated; serving merely to exhibit the supposed skill (often quite inadequate and this more glaringly obvious when thus presented), of the couple. Properly, such attractions belong to music-hall or circus; they do not belong to the theatre, though they may take one slight step more, and gain a genuine use in honest commercial ballet, or as a music hall turn in competition with trained ponies and expert jugglers. In folk-dance, virtuosity appears as the desperate endeavour of the village lads to win the attention of some desired female; and their high leaps, long tourneys, or delicate stepping over the crossed swords, serves to exhibit muscular skill and control that may biologically serve the racial needs of Nature.

VISHNU-DHARMOTTARAM (India)

Part III of this ancient *Treatise on Indian Painting*, dated by Dr. Stella Kramrisch at about 500 AD, is the fullest known account of the principles followed.[1] As this small book reveals close acquaintance with the parallel art of dancing, it must be known to those who seek to perform Hindu dance. The work is cast in the form of a dialogue between Markandeya and Vajra, who asks the question in approved student mode. Remaining fragments of great mural paintings (as, for example, those at Ajanta), prove that ancient Hindu artists were masters of painting, as they were of sculpture, architecture or dancing. Vajra begins by asking about painting. He is at once told that to paint well, he must first know about dancing. Thereupon Vajra demands the rules for dancing; only to be informed that "The practice of dancing is difficult to be understood by one who is not acquainted with music. Without music dancing cannot exist at all". The persistent Vajra will not rest; he wants to know what are the rules of music. He is then told that he must learn the science of song (in fact, of *sound*, by voice and music). Now it is assumed that he departs to a *math* to learn these several arts and sciences; for he returns undaunted to his original quest; on which he now receives information. Canons of form are conserved in several extant books: first *Vishnu-Dharmottaram*; then *Brighat Samhita*; and *Sukranitisara* (favourite of sculptors), the *Citralaksahana* (for painters), and the *Ottamama-vatala*. None of these do more than offer technical facts and sets of rigid scales; they convey no dynamic principle, which has vanished from them, as it has from Indian music.
[See *Raga; Indian Dance*]
[1]*Vishnu-Dharmottaram*. Trans. by Stella Kramrisch. Calcutta, 1924.

VITHI NATAKA (South India)

Festival performances, derived from religious plays, though the ritual connection has mainly ceased. They are folk-plays with song and dancing (chiefly in *Bharata Natyam*,* especially in the symbolical *mudras**used freely),and are performed in Andhra at the Spring Festival season. The principal stock character is *Konangi* (the clown), and his associate is the Elephant God, Ganesh, who appears now as *Cellap-pillai*, still full of fun and frolic. These plays resemble generally the *Bhagavata Mela Nataka** or the Mysore *Yaksha-Gana.** The *Katha-kali** of Malabar has had some influence, chiefly in the use of *Tandava** and *Lasya** modes of the *Bharata Natyam* dance. Music is obtained from drums (often very skilful) with simple flute or pipes, and cymbals.

VITUS DANCE (Mediaeval Europe)

Alleged to be a "curse effect" or a "miracle" dance, in which the "sinner" who dances is afflicted with a disorder of nervous uncontrollable movement. Unwisely the term has been further fixed by "medical science", which accepted the calumny as a traditional term. The name is a corrupted version of *Vidya*, ritual dance, as once followed in Eastern Europe (alongside the Greek Orthodox Church but not in it) as an inheritance of Far Eastern doctrines of the Veda. (*Vidya*=knowledge, wisdom). One famous centre was in the semi-artificial hill, known now as Hradcany, in Prague, on which stands the mediaeval cathedral labelled Saint Vitus, on the highest of the seven hills of Prague. "Saint Vid" is celebrated in the mediaeval *Cycle of Kossovo*, translated (in part) by the Serbian poet Vuk Stefan Karejich.

VLÖGGELEN (Netherlands)

An Easter processional dance performed by men of Ootmarsum in north-east Holland. Using a rhythmic walking step, the *Vlöggelen* is a slow counter-part of the Whitsun *Cramignole.** A long chain of several hundred men moves slowly through the streets, singing the Easter hymn, *Christus is opgestanden* ("Christ is risen"). Each man joins one hand with the man in front, placing his other hand behind him for the man following him to grasp, and on the back of each is pinned the printed words of the hymn for the benefit of the man behind. The linked chain is led by eight men called *Poaskerls* (*Pasche-kerls*, or "Easter men").

VOCAL BALLET (English, etc.)

Or *Choral Ballet* differs from what is now ordinary stage ballet in having vocal portions, interludes, or accompaniment. Best known of modern examples is the ballet that forms part of *Prince Igor*, which Russian opera was performed in Paris in 1908. The notable dance *scena* was alternated with choral singing. Others have been (modern form) Stravinsky's *Wedding* (1923), Berner's *Wedding Bouquet*, *Facade*, and Holst's suite *Planets*. But vocal ballet is not new; it extends from *carols* or *laudi*, and was long an uneasy companion of Opera. Rutland Boughton has written several choral ballets.

VOGUE (French)

Implies "the village" and certain village ritual dances, concerned principally with spiritualist seances. The term derives from Latin *voca*, "the voice", and this ritual was so widely practised in Gaul, that it remains now in the clerical title *eveque*—"the evocator", as Bishop. Dance was invariably associated, before the beginning (processional often), and at the end, as thanks and praise. The *vogue* as *voke* was linked with the *vake* or wake; and some families gained a kind of inherited ability in trance speaking (as in the Rumanian, with the *Rusalii** at Easter), so that the name Voke or Vokes remained as a family surname. In Italy, the vague term *vecchia** has similar implication, besides its general connotation of "old" (as in the *vecchia religione*, described by Leland[1]). The dance form resembled the funeral *iota* or *jota*,* still celebrated in some country districts of Spain. Later the term entered England, to become *vaux*, and the place (always on the outskirts of a town, to avoid clerical interference) was indicated by Vauxhall. Compare similar variations on the theme of Green.
[1] *Etruscan Remains*. G. G. Leland.

VOKES (England, France)

Mediaeval dance and theatre term, widespread and inclusive in many later versions : *Vogue*—*voke*, *vaux* and *volka*. The word indicates a variety of meanings associated with dance and dance-halls. Vaux-Hall, south of the Thames in London, remains only as a name; the site is occupied by a grimy station, once a rural centre of folk merriment. A well-known theatrical family carried on the surname Vokes for over a century. The origin seems uncertain. There are versions of Folkes (Folkestone is one) also ffoulkes, as family names. German versions indicate *Volk, volkstanz;* but the French term *vogue* went into a costume term, finally indicating "fashion" or "proper dress for the day". The word may derive from in-voke; re-voke; pro-voke—as belonging to the mediaeval seance, held by "wise women", in many a village. The sport of "fortune telling" was regularly practised at village markets or fairs, while the reference to the "old folks" (sometimes "th'owd volks") clings to the idea of country village life.

VOLADORES, JUEGO DE LOS (Mexico,

"The Flying Game". (Sp. *Volar*, "to fly"; Fr. *voler*, "to fly"; Eng. *volatile*, "airy"). The Spanish name for an old dance ritual, depicted in two Aztec Codices, which survived in Tenochtitlan (later called Mexico City) for nearly a century after the Conquest. The plaza (in modern times the site of the "Thieves Market") was adapted as a bullring by the Spaniards in the 17th century, and called by them "El Volador". Today the *Flying Pole Dance* is performed by Indians from the Sierra Madre to Vera Cruz, much as it was in Aztec times. Faint memories of its ancient symbolism remain in some villages—in the ritual purification before performance, the honouring of the four cardinal points, and the ceremonies still accompanying the felling and setting up of the tree. In Tenochtitlan a tall pole was set up in the middle of the plaza, with a liana wound round it for foothold, and a small revolving platform at the top, with four ropes attached. According to old Spanish records, four "flyers" and a musician climbed to the top and, after a ceremonial dance by the musician on the tiny platform, the four men tied the ropes round their waists, launched themselves into the air, and "flew" in wide circles round the pole, down to the ground. The pole had to be high enough for the flyers to make thirteen revolutions, representing four periods of thirteen years in the Aztec fifty-two-year cycle. Dressed in brilliant feather garments, as the sacred birds associated with the gods of the four winds, who fly to the four cardinal points, the "flyers" produced the effect of the rise and fall of birds in flight by skilfully altering their centre of balance, as they do today at Papantla. In San Luis Potosi, the dancers still dress as birds, and elsewhere they wear red suits, possibly a memory of the red macaw feathers used by their ancestors. There are variations in different districts. At San Luis Potosi and at Papantla, only the musician dances, while at Pahuatlan the "flyers" dance, but not the musician. In some villages, *Malinche** or a *Negrito** accompanies the "flyers", while the ceremony has become attached to Catholic fiesta dates, but the *Juego de los Voladores* remains one of the Mexican dances with obvious pre-Conquest associations.
[See *Gavilan, La Danza del; Otomi Voladores; Tocotines, Los; Aztec Dances*]

VOLEUR (French)

The "flying rope-dancer" once so popular through France; but especially at the *Foire san Germain* in Paris. His speciality was the "flying descent" from some tall tower to the ground, usually following some spectacular dancing, posing or acrobatic work on a more or less horizontal rope. This technical ability had formerly a close connection with the clerical productions of miracle plays; the *voleur* played the part of the "heavenly angels" who suddenly appeared, bringing crowns for the deserving rich; and, in the night performance, startling the groundlings with fiery torches.

VOLTA, LA

A Court dance in 6/4 or 6/8 time, popular in England at the end of the 16th century, and a variation of the earlier *Galliard.** Italian in origin, it took its name from the figure which required several turns (*volti*), and was notorious because of the jump into the air made by the lady, with the assistance of her partner. This leap was considered very indelicate, and in France and Germany a campaign was waged against the dance, Louis XIII refusing to allow it at Court. But the dance did survive for a time in France. It is said to have been popular in Provence, and the *Nizzarda** (a "dance of Nice") was a version of the *Volta*. Most popular in England, it was a favourite of Queen Elizabeth I. She is depicted dancing the *Volta* with Lord Essex in a painting at Penshurst Place, in Kent, which shows her being assisted into the air by her partner. Thoinot Arbeau (in his *Orchésographie**—1588) instructs the student, Capriol, how to make the turns, with a high jump in each for the man; and how to help his partner to jump by raising her with his left thigh, his left arm round her, at the same time pushing against the stiff "busk" in the front part of her dress, with the other hand. The lady thus received considerable assistance for her high jump, both from her partner, and from the fashion of the day, which insisted upon a highly stiffened dress. Arbeau writes: "I leave you to judge whether it be a proper thing for a young girl to make large steps and wide movements of the legs: and whether in this volte her honour and well-being are not risked and involved . . ." He advises Capriol to "dance some other kind of dance". In England, it was known as *Lavolta, Lavaltoe* or *Levalto*, surviving into Stuart times, and was danced by Mary Stuart. It is mentioned by several Elizabethan writers, including Shakespeare.

VYEDMA (Witch) and VYEDMAK (Wizard)

In Slavonian language, is related to the Sanskrit *vidya*, knowledge, "to know", as *Veda* (or scripture, the memorised *shlokas* of the religious chant). These men, as tribal priests, sometimes referred to as *shamana* (next to *brahmans*) made astrological diagrams on the flat sand or mud or ice; but more often (within shelter) on the sheepskin drumhead (cp. the "Lapp magical drum"* to be seen in museums), which was used for their incantations.

They danced around the drum; rarely, the instrument was played by a partner; but for divination, they used highly polished "knuckle bones" from a sheep. By the vibrations made in tapping the drumhead, these white bones "danced" over the diagram inscribed on it; and, as they became arranged by the end of the selected chant, so the forecast could be made; or secret information obtained.
[See *Znahar*]

W

WAITS (or WYSHTES) (England)

A New Year Feast, now obsolete, which lasted to the 19th century as variants of "Mummers" who sang caroles,* played music and sought alms at the doors of rich people. Formerly they came into the Great Hall to perform seasonal dances. The name is given by Strabo along with Bards (*Bardoi*) and Druids (*Drui'dai*) as *Uates* (*ouateis*). In Mediaeval England (earlier in Wales) they were servants of the house; one of their functions was to bring in the dinner, moving to music and occasionally chanting. This was the secular mode of their "making the sacrifice". The name continued as Vates. In Greece the same class were known as "parasites"; their function was (after feeding freely) "to sing praises of their hosts". In the doggerel of the waits they ended always with a couplet soliciting money, with words of sycophantic praise. In Mediaeval England, the Watch was often confused with the Waits. The Celts and the Greeks were acquainted, despite the distance, and paid mutual visits. The modern term is now "waiter", and the host's gift to the parasite, called a "tip" or "tenpercent", has little relation to real service. The most recent living instance of this custom continued in Russia down to the "freeing of the serf". It was the custom to bring in the dinner with music and dance. Another variant of the custom continued while the Dutch ruled Indonesia—the dinner was brought in (all at once) by a string of "boys" to a burst of music. This ceremony had the name of *rijstafel* ("rice table").

WAKAMBA (Africa, Kenya district)

Tribal dance performed in the "reservation" into which the remaining families of the tribe have been herded. The *Wakamba* people dance for their own purpose; not for show. Women stand in two open lines; the men dance in one line facing them, making almost a closed square. Women dancers stamp their feet with precise rhythm, raising dust, bent or upright in turn, to the rhythms of eight drummers who sit with drums balanced over their knees. The men wear long cloths over short pants, in several colours; and high feathery plumes; while the women wear short, black skirts. All are bare-foot, the men laughing with glee as they spring high; the women sober and serious; all moving at arms length apart.

WALLOCH (Scotland)
The Highland *Walloch* is mentioned in Scots ballads, as in:

"O she was a cantie quean,
  Well could she dance the Highland walloch;
  How happy I, had she been mine,
  Or I been Roy of Aldivalloch".
In the ballad: "Roy's Wife of Aldivalloch".[1] The tune was earlier called *Ruffians Rants*.
[1] *The Songs of Scotland*. G. F. Graham. Edinburgh, 1855.

WALPURGIS NIGHT (Teutonic mythological system)
Is celebrated on the Eve of May First. This festival, together with the winter "Classical Masquerade" was taken by Goethe into his famous drama of *Faust*. Four Festivals of the Year were:

1. *Winter:* Sylvester-Abend — Neue Jahrs-Abend;
2. *Spring:* Walpurgis Nacht — May Eve Dance Festival;
.3 *Summer:* Johannis Nacht Feuer — Midsummer Dance Festival.
4. *Autumn: Ernte-zeit (Herbst-Messe)* — Harvest Dance Festival.

In *Faust*, the poem shows (Part I) Mephistopheles (Shadow-Lover) ruling the Feast in dark winter days; while in Part II, the Classical Masquerade gives place to Walpurgis Nacht, where *Homonculus** guides instead. In clerical hands, Walpurgis Nacht was obfuscated into the dummy of "Saint Walburga". The ancient deities of Bertha or Berchte (echoed in England by terms such as Perkins, perky, perquisite — the "presents" of Carnival), were submerged under a tide of Witches' Sabbat and other political propaganda denunciations. *Ma-phaestus-phileus* — the "Lover of Shadows", as opposed to *Ha-phaestus*, the "Lover of Unattainable Light" (Helena) were denigrated from their earlier splendour in the myths of Manichaeus, into the ineradicable legend of Doktor Faustus. These four festivals were rituals, celebrating the terrestrial seasons; also symbols of the world invisible. What Dante formulated as *Paradiso* and *Purgatorio*, Goethe partially shaped into his re-statement of Faust. Walpurgis is the purging period — formerly the Roman *Fevruare*, the great cleaning of the *Fates* (the *Parcae*), and closely resembles the

Tibetan *Bardo Thol.** The witches (or waits, *vates*) appear as time-watchers, of lunar time — markers in the hundreds of villages, unwilling to accept the imposed Kalends brought by the Roman *augurs*.
[See *Perchten; Schemenlaufen; Narren-Treffen; Witches Magical Dance; Homunculus*]

WALTZ (Fr. *Valse*)
A turning dance for couples, in triple time, which became popular in European ballrooms at the end of the 18th century. It derived from the Austrian *Ländler,** which in turn was one of the dances collectively known as *Deutsche** — rounds in triple time danced by couples in Bavaria, Tyrol, Styria, Carinthia and Upper Austria, known in the 14th century, but of earlier origin. The Italian *Danza Tedesca*, or "German Dance" refers to this type of dance. In Vienna, the popularity of the Waltz in 1776 is recorded by the Irish singer, Michael Kelly, in his *Reminiscences* (1826). At the great masked balls in the Radouten-Sale, *Ländlers* and *Deutsche* were composed by Haydn, Mozart and Beethoven, as well as lesser composers. At the end of the 18th century, the *Waltz* was the rage in France, and shortly before 1815 it reached England, where it was loudly decried as vulgar, but still achieved great popularity. In its early ballroom days it was much like the *Ländler*, but a smoother, lighter style soon replaced the more robust country dance. Tempo was quickened and a gliding step included, but the turning of couples while at the same time circling the room remained its characteristic. Early in the 19th century, an ornamental French *Waltz* developed. In contrast to the Viennese, it was danced on the point of the toe, and consisted of three figures:

1. *Slow Waltz* in 3/8 or 3/4 time, andante;
2. *Sauteuse Waltz* in 6/8, allegretto;
3. *Jeté* or *Quick Sauteuse Waltz* in 6/8, allegro.

This more theatrical dance included pirouettes and jumps, and was based on the five positions of classical ballet, as illustrated in a lithograph of 1817 by J. H. A. Randal, in which one young lady is shown poised on full pointes. The true Viennese *Waltz* had three steps to the bar, but a two-step version called *Langaus* became the craze of early 19th century Vienna. A writer of the time, Adolphe Bäuerle, complains that at the Mondschein-Saal nothing was danced but the *Langaus*, in which partners galloped at the greatest possible speed several times round the room. Josef Lanner (1801 - 43) and Johann Strauss the younger (1825 - 99) are still famous for their waltz compositions, while the elder Strauss (1804 - 1849) composed many waltzes and, with Lanner, laid the foundation for the true Viennese *Waltz*.

WANDS

Appear as instruments or implements in innumerable dances; chiefly those derived from some ritual believed to have magical power. This "rod of power" takes on many forms, ranging from the dainty "fairies wand" that is carried by a ballet dancer, to the robust "mace" which is part of the superstition of guilds, committees, city companies; and even the legislative chambers. These massive emblems are occasionally carried in or out as part of the same process. The marching regiment frequently has a band-master who twirls his mace in ornamental fashion imitated by show girls who stride on and around the stage. The regimental sceptre, the bishop's crozier, the augur's *lituus*, the Hellenic *thyrsus,** the Egyptian monarch's "flail" are all used in gesture; though the modern conductor's baton is relatively new as a light rod in the hand (since Spohr bumped his toe with the older staff). The ritual dancer as magician may carry or use some kind of wand; partly for visual effect, rarely for its pragmatic value. Stage effect, as in ballet, would be much enhanced if the dancer knew what she was supposed to be doing; and further if the wand itself was sufficiently interesting in form and appearance.

WANNEBAGO CREATION CHANT (Amerindian)

The men formerly mimed and danced the chief episodes of their Creation Legend, which combines something of the system of emanations taught in Babylon; and the copy tacked together by the Jews in the highly realistic story of the manufacture of Adam and Eve. The Wannebago legend was chanted; its acts were mimed; and the high points were danced by leading members of the tribes. Several other Indian nations have a similar Creation Legend, which they ritually re-enact.

WAPEN-REYERS (Netherlands)

Local name for Sword Dancers; though as the records are merged with *Mores* or *Moressen-dans*, the precise dance is vague. Municipal archives of Dordrecht mention a Sword Dance, dated 1392. There is one three years earlier noted at Bruges; but we do not know if it was the same, or a similar dance performed in 1389. Some of these, were linked with the May Games; and these associated with *De Covert* or the band of Robin Hood and Friar Tuck, who is known as *De Paterje* (Little Father). The Frere, with *Japie* (Little John) chose a girl to be May Queen; this custom endures in the far south in Limburg, at Valkenburg. In other places, *De Zevensprung** (Seven Jumps) is seen with the May Games, but, with Brabant *Bezom* (Broom) Dance has disappeared. A *Mores* dance has to suffer change before being permitted to associate with any church ceremony; but the northern *cintola* is retained, in the *Garland Dance* at Deventer, though not around or in, a church.

WARRIORS DANCE (Papua)

Performed by the "Night Dancers", or warriors, at dusk on the second night of the *Gabé* festival. Danced in silence, it is a representation of a raid on an enemy village. Warriors wear tapa' cloth draped round the waist to form a narrow apron in front and a "tail" behind, with black cassowary feathers on ther heads. A long black spear, held in the right hand, is violently vibrated during the dance, and some hold boar tusks between their teeth. On their bodies white paint outlines ribs and backbone, while faces bear parti-coloured designs, spots or stripes of red, black, white or yellow. In silence the men leap over the enclosing palisade into the dancing-place, and begin their assault on the "enemy", symbolised by certain small trees with resilient stems, previously planted. Each man leaps into the air, thrusts out both feet against a tree, making it bend, then lands on his feet brandishing his spear. Immediately, a second man repeats the onslaught, and so on until it snaps. When all trees are laid low the silence is broken by a song of triumph. The dance ends in sudden stillness and silence, as the men wait for the Women's Dance, *Amou Youmame** (also performed in silence), which precedes the *Royal Dance** of Chiefs, highlight of the *Gabé* festival.

WASTLERS (Mediaeval English)

Wandering musicians, dancers, and singers; a term said to derive from *wastle* (Saxon) to wander; but equally may hinge upon *wassail*, as "wassailers". This term was common in Sussex for carol-singers.

WATER PATTERNS (Persia)

Are formed on the still water of fountain basins in the open gardens, at the celebration of *Aid-i-Naurooz* (New Year's Day), by placing fresh rose petals in carefully distinct lines, straight or curved. Around this *hauz* (basin) on its low stone or marble edge, are placed continuous rows of ripe oranges. These patterns appeared on traditional printed cottons, used for dance costumes. We may compare with patterns on wedding cakes (in Britain), and bread patterns, cake patterns, etc.

WATUSSI N'TORI RITUAL DANCE (Congo)

Is celebrated in Ruanda—Urundi district, every year on July First, usually at Astrida, and is a most striking choreographic spectacle. The agile N'Tori, all dancers of exquisite virtuosity and elegance, perform at this feast. These young men, sons of chiefs and headmen, live at the court at N'yanza; receive an allowance; and their sole duty is to train for the dances, giving performances on Watussi or Belgian feast days. The chief show is a ballet called *To End All Talk*. There is a competition of two groups: between challengers and defenders, done in daylight in a huge clearing. The *Batwa* men (trained by a Watussi expert), open with entrance and salute. In a pause, the *corps-de-ballet* chant the praises of ancient Watussi heroes. The king claps his hands; the Batwa dancers resume, miming regulation tattooing rites; or dance the "Peerless men". Then, with their heads adorned with colobus monkey-fur; their bodies encased in many-coloured skirts of leopard skins; weapons bound to their wrists, come the *N'tori*. Their ballet contains many divertissements: "The Flashing One", "The Crowned Crane", or "The Invincible One". Their routines are vigorous, athletic and acrobatic, kept in perfect rhythm; yet much of the earlier symbolism has been vanquished by interfering missionaries; so that the dance becomes merely a spectacle, rather than significant ritual. The audience, led by *Bakoma* (diviners and doctors, etc.) and *Ambasciosi* (royal armourers etc.) surround the king and queen, watch this display of the *Iscyaka* (challengers) versus the *Indashyikuwa* (unconquerable; "holders of title"). They are furnished with their "props" by the armourers: including *Ikuma* (spear), *Umuheto* (bow), and *Ingabo* (shield). Most of the dance forms retain only a core of traditional ritual, for new musical instruments have combined with Belgian influences to bring many changes. There is a similarity between the system of court training of these young men (with its combination of formal etiquette, tribal regulations and military education), with the distant court system long prevalent in Java at Soerabaya.

WAVE MEKE (Fiji)
Meke is the Fijian word for "a dance". Many of them are mimetic. One such is the *Wave Meke*,* a dance for girls standing in lines and imitating the movements of the sea. Beginning quietly with the portrayal of ripples on the sand, the dance rises to a crescendo of movement as the approach of a big wave is mimed. First bending down, the girls gently smooth the ground with their hands, their fingers undulating to represent ripples. Then, swaying their bodies to and fro, they show the rhythmic flow of long rollers, their movements becoming more violent until they spring forward, clap their hands and sink to the ground with a cry, to indicate a wave breaking over the reef and coming to tranquillity in the lagoon.

Way to Jerusalem. Labyrinth, constructed near old Roman baths at Verde, showing the Christian maze version. The "Four Gates" follow the idea of the Tibetan *Mandorla*.   FRANCE

WAY TO JERUSALEM
Mediaeval European Church ritual dance, known principally as a slow chanting spiraline dance, performed in the nave of the church, over a spiral pattern laid in the floor by tiles or mosaic. The form itself is older than the name; it derives from the ancient Cretan-Graeco Labyrinthine Dance of Theseus and Ariadne; and has affinities with the Hebrew *kantor* and the practice of recounting the Psalms, which were ritual-dance-chants (cp. *Mandala** in India). The close attention of the ritualist was demanded in order to align (a) the number of steps, with (b) the pattern and its divisions, and (c) the musical form of the chant. The chant and motion must be so kept in unison that the ritualist finishes at the centre on the last syllable with the final step. There was in early Greek verse a similar attention to the measure of the step and that of the verse, with the style of music, for broadly the same general aim. Floor patterns, bearing this or similar names, still exist in French churches at Chartres, Bourges etc., while those that existed formerly, as in Paris at Nôtre Dame, have been destroyed, deliberately, or by normal wear under many feet.
[See *Mandala; Labyrinth, Alpona; Troy Game; Geranos*]

WAYANG KULIT (Java)
Also *Wajang Koelit*, Dutch rendering. Originally as

WaYang Khelute (Tamil), erroneously referred to as "leather puppets". *Wayang*=display or lesson etc. and *Kheulete*=pupil, student (later used by Europeans as *coolie* or servant). Basically, a shadow play or dance display formulated to convey Puranic (and other) ancient stories to younger students; originated in this fashion, probably in cave temples of India; and thence brought to Indonesia by Indian traders from Malabar. The system is professional. The *dalang* (story reciter) chants the incidents of each legend as he plays the puppets on sticks. They are contrived of thin leather, highly ornamental with many cut holes. These puppets are all flat, made of dried skins stretched on a slight frame; usually head and arms only will move (attached to rigid sticks), but a very few (as animal masks etc.) are larger, with snapping jaws. The round puppets (three dimensional figures) are not used for shadow plays. Glove puppets are rare. The final method is to allow older students (or lay people for modern shows) to sit on the *wayang* side, while women and youngsters or *kheulet* sit on the other side of the cotton screen on which dancing shadows are cast. From this shadow play, the full scale dance-mime plays have been developed, for bigger audiences. To see these puppet plays with native eyes, it must be understood that "shadow" implies not only the visual shadow (seen on the cotton screen, and formerly on cave walls); but the "shadow of memory", in which the revered ancestors, family or mythical persons, are once more revived and saluted. This dual purpose exists through all Asia. The categories of figures include *wayong* (human); *wayang beber* (paper); *wayang keroetjil* or *kelitik* (puppets), or the *wayang topeng* (masks). The *Wayang* appears, according to occasion and opportunity, and also balanced with expenditure, in more or less sumptuous productions; from the stately four-day series of the princely courts, to the half-hour excerpt on the roadside.

WAYZGOOSE (England)
A summer-time holiday feast, peculiar to English printers, accompanied with singing and dancing. Similar is *Tuning Goose*, in the 17th century a typical entertainment, arranged in Yorkshire, when the harvest was finished, ending in a jolly barn dance. The term *Wayzgoose* is said to derive from "ways"—a bundle of straw (perhaps the original bundle was the *kern* baby, or harvest sheaf), and the *wayz-goose* was the familiar Michael-Messe bird, fed to the last on the loose corn and stubble left after harvesting. This entertainment, now become rare, was held by the "chapel" of journeymen printers; a few friends such as writers, might be invited.

WEAVER, John (England)
John Weaver (1670 - 1760) was the "Father" of the English "Pantomime Ballet". The son of John Weaver (dancing master of Oxford University) the famous teacher, choreographer and writer was born at Shrewsbury in 1670 and named in the St. Chad church in 1673. He received his general education in the Free School. Following on the rapid spread of dancing instigated by John Playford's numerous collections (chiefly for the ballroom) John Weaver preceded Rich, who is frequently credited with the new move. Weaver produced a Mime ballet at Drury Lane Theatre in 1702, entitled *The Tavern Bilkers*, which he described as the "first entertainment that has appeared on the English stage, where the representation and story was carried on by dancing, action, and motion only". One term he used for this method was "Scenical Dancing".

His work was noticed in Paris; and Mons. Feuillet got in touch. Presently Weaver was engaged on an English translation of that master's book on *Notation*. He began to extend his work into teaching stage ballet, from the popular ballroom forms prevalent; and set up a School of Dance in Chancery Lane, near to the Lincolns Inn Field Theatre. This seems to have been the first organised school of stage dance in London. His main theme was the "Ballet d'Action" style—but the groundlings did not much appreciate the results. Feuillet's book was published in 1706. Weaver then concentrated on more productions. In 1717 he did a "new dance in fifteen couplets" named *The Union* which was performed at court for the Queen's birthday—and he found time to get married (1709).

His rivals noted his work, and—as was the custom, stole what they fancied. One John Thurmond copied his new style (Drury Lane, 1719 - 1726) while Rich jnr. reproduced *The Tavern Bilkers* in 1717, and again in 1727 with the title changed to *The Cheats*. Weaver turned from Playford, from the line which John Gay soon exploited (as in his *Beggars Opera*, 1727) to themes of mythology. He arranged *Perseus and Andromeda* (1716), *Orpheus and Euridice* (1717), *Harlequin Turned Judge* (1718) and *Cupid and Bacchus* (1719) all at Drury Lane Theatre.

Interspersed with this theatre work John Weaver turned author. His English version of *Orchesography or the Art of Dancing* (Feuillet) appeared in 1706 along with *A Small Treatise of Time and Cadence in Dancing*. He then essayed choreographic script: *The Union; a Dance Writ Down in Character* (1717) and three years later *An Essay towards an History of Dancing*. His large work was *Anatomical and Mechanical Lectures on Dancing*

(1721) compiled from his talks at his Academy of Dance. His final publication was *The History of the Mimes and Pantomimes*, in 1728. He was then about sixty — "a dapper cheerful little man". John Gay then appeared on the operatic scene, with ballads English and French and Italian. Weaver died in Shrewsbury, at about 90, and was buried February 10 at St. Chad's church. His monument was lost when the church collapsed.

WEGGIS DANCE (Switzerland)

A round dance for couples, moving anti-clockwise in a circle or double circle. A song, with yodelling refrain, accompanies the dance; and with each verse partners are changed and different steps used. Polka and hop steps with pronounced arm-swing-ing are usual. Partners hold hands, either with the girl's palms on the boy's, or arms crossed in front as in skating.

"WELCOME" DANCES (New Britain)

Action dances performed as a mark of respect to visitors. The dances belong to a particular village, which has the "copyright" of them, and may sell or hire them out. When a dance is sold, the pur-chasers are taught how to perform it, during which time they are treated with great respect and con-sideration. As a final mark of pleasure, a grant fête is organised, with distribution of presents to the performers by the village chief.
[Cp. *Hek-Hekelean* (Malekula, New Hebrides)]

WELSH DANCES

Have become almost obsolete; but some attempts have been made towards revival, notably of the *Llanover Reel*. Giraldus Cambrensis records seeing churchyard dances in 1188, in Brecon, with singing and a procession around the building. Samuel Rogers (English poet) noted that space on the north side of churches was reserved for secular sports. (The south — sunny side — was used for cloister space). Rogers saw at Swansea, in 1792, people dancing every Saturday night from Easter to Whit-sun. Some village dance-games are named: one was *Building the Bridge*; and *Twelve Curtseys to the Moon*. Full of vigorous rhythmic movement, these rituals retain their dance formation. *Mari Llwyd** is still performed in villages of Glamorgan. At Lud-low in 1875, townspeople were prosecuted for erecting a maypole. They proved that Maypole dancing had taken place on that land since Charles II. In Flintshire a Morris dance was discovered. The *Llanover Reel* is known, also, at Abercarn. The tune is in *Relicks of the Welsh Border* (Edward Jones). This dance has a longways formation. Other Welsh dances are recalled chiefly by name: *Robin Doig; Can Doli; Migildi Magaldi; Orwen y diafed*

felan; With fynd efo Deio i Dywyn; Dacw fuwch; Pant Corlan yr Wyn. At the "Dancing Gallery" of Cefn Mably, visitors are told of Sir Charles Kenyon, of whom an inscription was recorded:

> "The three best dancers in Wales,
> Sir Charles of Cefn Mably;
> Squire Lewis of the Van;
> And Sir John Carne of Ewenny. Ho! Ho!"

In the early 19th century it was the custom, after a wedding, to dance in part of the churchyard not used as a burial ground. The harper met the wedding procession at the church door and, to the tune of "Joy to the Bridegroom", led the way to the dancing place. Bride and groom then "led off" the first two dances — "The Beginning of the World" and "My Wife shall Have her Way" — which were always danced at weddings, but never on other occasions.

WEZAK (Burma)

Buddhist "Feast of Full Moon" which seems now to have settled at the "August Moon", but is, or was, celebrated in *Tazaungmon* (November) perhaps as a late Feast of Ancestors. The tradition is older than Buddhism, said to have been introduced into Burma round 700 AD, but Pagan, a chief educational centre, developed only from the 10th century (famous for Pali scholarship). In Mongolia the *Wezak* is celebrated in open spaces, in July or August. Huge frames carry legendary pictures of Buddha and Buddhism; there are ritual dances, as well as secular folk-dances by small groups. The Burmese *Wezak* abounds with mime and foolery; men dressed as animals dance through villages. Unicorns are first favourites. The puppet shows (see *Burmese Dance**) have some relation with this festival.   [See *Toe-Naya; Prüh*]

WHEEL, DANCES OF — 1

Are widely known, with numerous names. They exemplify the horizontal ring or circle, conceived as essentially moving, in relation to the vertical contrapunctum of the staff or pole. With the straight or wavy line, the transit or trajectory between two such points, or successive points on the circular line, these forms present the elemental bases of all dance direction or movement, cele-brated in many styles; but originally always in relation to the time-processes of moon, of the sun, and the pole-star, Sirius. Under some names, or familiar abbreviations used with current loss of original meaning, the dances are followed by tra-dition more than by ritual. We may take those known in Britain: the "Weel!" or "Well!" inter-jections in ordinary conversation, along with the term "Oke!" or "O.K..!" and its proletarian version

"Okey-dokey" which is possibly nearer to the medi- aeval version, that was still connected with fact. The well of the village (some villages are known as Oakham) was for centuries "dressed" along with a "queen ceremonial", and then known as a "grotto". These are references to one or other of the Great Wheels of Time; we may identify them by their numerical associations : the four-week or twenty- eight day procession is measured by the moon; or the twelve months that seemed to measure the solar year, *Week* and *weel* move in four modes; but triply with the moon phases; they affirmed the Great Mother as Diana Triformis; or as the Solar Wheel, affirmed the Father God. These terms are hidden behind our common language; as dances they linger in many traditions, whose ritual origins now seem lost. In *hora* and *kolo*, in *khoro* and *chorus*, the train of wheels moves on dancing feet. Round the pole, the oak-as-tree, the Oke of Prov- ence or the Oak of Guernica and the Weil of Gaul, we recall "weal and woe", to move or stop, until we turn to the *veel* or *vals* or *walts*, apparent in a hundred circular forms of dance.

WHEEL DANCES—2 (Europe)

Follow the same idea, originally, as those of the Orient. One Hindu doctrine saw the World as *Samsara* (Wheel of Existence)—the eternally circling round of life and death. Buddhist changes named this wheel as a "Ring of Misery", from which mortals should escape. Their later rescen- sions (since the early Buddhists, like the Puritans, discarded all ritual and all theatre), again adopted a ritual dance mode. By this rite it became possible to show in action, the ring and the manner of escape. Much later still, this rite entered Europe; and was known as *sara-bande*. The same idea had moved in Greece (whence *kolo** and *hora** forms appear in the Balkans). In that most Judaic epistle (that attributed to James) we observe the familiar Orphic phrase—the "wheel of re-birth" as *tropoxos tns yevesews*—as ch. iii. 6, proving the energizing idea of *palingenesis* to be present in doctrine; and thence used in ritual. Schopenhaur ascribed this to Indian influence. Wheel dances existed through ancient Europe, from the penetrative ideas of the Chaldaeans. Bel was celebrated in Scotland so firmly that the winter solstice rite endures today as *Bel-Tainne*, and the Summer one as *Samhain*: both marked by rings of fire, twelve in the circle, and a larger one in the centre. The dance follows : circles of males, of females, of chains in and out; and finally over the centre, the men at least per- form jumps, as a symbol and not as a "pagan sacrifice" of any kind. The Babylonian name was *gil-gul*, the world dance of the human soul; it became spoken as *heil-huil*, and thus as *quheil* and

wheel. The Scots use the password often as "Weel!", while in France the secret doctrine is echoed in *Langue-d'oel*, and the national affir- mative *Oui! Langue d'Ok* also cherished a Wheel dance, around the oaken upright pole.

WHIPPING DANCE (Sudan)

Seen in village two hundred miles south of Khar- toum. It is a test of endurance, and the scars remaining as evidence of the ordeal, are honorific marks. Accompanied by an orchestra of drums, beaten by women with hands and wrist, while others clap in rhythm, the dance begins with three men standing in line, while a fourth circles round, in time to the music, flourishing a rhinoceros hide whip in gestures of striking. It is not known exactly when he will strike, but each of the three men receives a lash that draws blood. Then the striker surrenders the whip to one of the three men; taking his place in the line. The dance con- tinues until each of the four men has wielded the whip, the suspense lying in not knowing just when the blow will fall. The striker dances round, pre- tends to strike, then with a smile wheels round and continues his dance. The watching women and girls show keen appreciation of the performance, and fortitude of the men in not flinching.
[Cp. *Maquarri* (Guiana)]

WHITE LADIES (Normandy)

These *Dames Blanches* were a kind of fairy, in the rural districts of Normandy, who lurk in ravines or by bridges. They intercepted coaches, it was said, and asked the traveller to dance with them. If they received courteous assent, all went well; but if the men were impatient and refused, *Les Dames Blanches* threw them into a ditch. The most famous Lady was La Dame d'Aprigny, who resided by Bayeux. There was in Britain a celebrated White Lady, also addicted to dancing, in the creation of the *White Lady of Avenel* by Sir Walter Scott; and one, a ghostly dancer, who appears in German castles, just before the death of the master.

WIDDERSHINS (Old English, from Sanskrit)

Compare, "right"—*dexter* v. "left"—*sinister*. The ritual dance "done sunwise" round the circle by the devotees called Vidya-sen-yas. *Vidya* (more properly *Wedya*) derives from the Hindu scriptures the *Vedas* (*Wedas*), which were taught at various times and places in Britain, thus embedding a few of the ritual terms deep into English tradition. *Widdershins* is read usually as meaning "clock- wise", and may be compared with *deosil*, or the Pahlevi term *dakshina*, meaning the "circumam- bulation". (From the *shin* part comes the quaint term "Shanks pony", meaning, one's own legs, as used in Northern England).

WIDOWS DANCING (Marquesas, Tahiti, etc.)
Herman Melville describes vaguely in his verbose account, *Typee*, his surface impressions of the customs of the inhabitants of some of the Polynesian Islands he visited, about 1840. Among these chapters he tells of the *Hoolah-hoolah* grounds (Dancing-place) and touches on the *Dancing Widows* (p. 256) of Typee Island, and the Feast of the Calabashes. The local system, according to Melville, resembles that suggested in "Scheherezade" or the Caucasian customs in Thamar's household.

WIFLER (Old English)
Also *Wiffler*: a rod or baton, used by a sergeant-major before a military band (or, earlier, the Watch) to clear the way for a march to music through the streets. The *wifel* or *wiffel* is a diminutive sword or javelin, formerly used to thrust back the "cheering crowds", and as such may be compared with (a) the drum-major's use of drum-sticks; the sergeant staff major and his ornamental gilded baton or mace (origin of "baton dance" in USA music-halls) or the ceremonial usage of "Gold Stick in Waiting" or of "Black Rod", in the goings and comings of the officers known by those names, in between the House of Commons and House of Lords. The implement thus pertains to many modes of ornamental movement in ritual; replacing such items as the rope wet with red ochre, used in Athens; or the common rope of the itinerant friars known as Cordeliers, who thus roped-off their *corral* for performance. The most modern form is the "Night stick" of the Irish policeman in New York City; but this performance has neither dance nor music.

WILDE-FRAUEN (Germany); WILD WOMEN
Are similar to the *Elle-maidens* of Scandinavia. They are a tribe of forest fairies, addicted to all the usual moonlight dancing and feasting of their companies. They are said to be very beautiful, with long flowing golden hair that turns to silver under the full moon, when they dance; and they live in remote caverns. The place known as Wunderberg, or Underberg, on the wide moorland near Salzburg in Austria, was reputed as the chief haunt of these *Wildë Frauen*. There is a local legend that the hill is hollow, with dwellings and underground gardens; where Charles V. awaits some prophesied events. There are salt mines near by.

WILL 'O THE WISP, OR WILL WITH A WISP (English. Med.)
Older name *Ignis Fatuus* and *Feu Follet* (Fr.) This "foolish fire" has been seen, floating uneasily a few feet above marshy ground—apparently as a free dancing light—especially in burial places or where much decaying matter is present. The dim glow has been attributed to carburetted hydrogen or phosphoretted hydrogen. The phenomenon may be compared with fire-flies and some fish which can emit a similar glow. It is also called bogle or bogie or boggart.

WILYAROO CEREMONY (Australia)
Initiation of a youth into manhood, among the Urabunna and other tribes of Central Australia. Connected also with blood-brotherhood, the ceremony takes place when the youth is old enough to mate. Old men of the tribe open their veins and sprinkle him with their blood, after his own flesh has been marked with ceremonial cuts along each side of the spine. Strings are tied round his arms and thumbs, and a circle of fires is lit round him on the dancing-ground. Since the ceremony is concerned with pairing, women are admitted. dancing in a circle close to the fires, while outside them the "Wilyaroo men" (i.e. initiated adults) dance in the opposite direction. After three circlings the women retire and light another fire, scattering the ashes when the ground is warm, and sit with head between knees so that they may not see the sacred bull-roarer. Leading the youth, men dance up to the bowed women, the leader swinging a bull-roarer, which is warmed in the ashes and then hidden. After removing the strings from arms and thumbs, the tribal Wilyaroo marks are drawn on the initiate's back by already initiated young men, setting the seal on his manhood. The new "brother" must then choose a woman and depart with her to the bush for a period of one to three weeks. Proud of his Wilyaroo marks, the young man thus becomes an adult and a responsible member of his tribe.   [See *Corroboree; Tjitji Inma; Nakumdoit*]

WISCHTANZ (Austria)
A recreational dance performed by men in the mountains of Styria. Danced by one or more pairs, each pair holds an alpenstock, over which they jump, and perform acrobatic movements, twisting the stick behind their backs or above their heads, but never letting go of it. *Wischtanz* is danced in slow waltz-time, to the accompaniment of zither, mouth-organ or guitar.

WITCH DANCE (Western Europe)
The term "witch" is a shift from "Watch"; it applied, during some centuries, to "Wise women" who were able to calculate "times and places" in relation chiefly to agriculture and midwifery. The multitudinous accounts of "Witch Trials" relate

principally to the political persecution of village centres, who refused to accept the Romanised political cult, miscalled "religion"—and though the trials, as such, may have been actual events, the alleged misdeeds of the "village witches" were based in theological chicanery, propaganda, and sheer malice. Instances of hysteria under such malignant persecution naturally occurred; these facts were then brought as "evidence" that the accused were "possessed of devils", for it was felt necessary (in the interests of the higher culture imported from Rome) to suppress all opposition. There had been, for centuries, in the numerous villages of England, systems of "keeping the watch", mostly by lunar observation; partly by calendar, interrupted by a much revised alien code of "saints days". The date of Easter is still so established. Roman collection of "tithe and tax" by way of imperial loot, was widespread. In the days of King John, Mathew of Paris (1245?) records that the wealth removed by papal thieving amounted to far more than the King's entire revenue. Various systems of repression were tried: propaganda by miracle plays; invention of new miracles (as at Walsingham etc.) and when scepticism extended more rapidly and more widely (as with the Lollards) then the systems of Witch Hunting and Holy Inquisition, each with its own "public spectacles" of revenge by burning. These in turn failed; the Witch Industry became obsolete (the Hungarian Diet proclaimed "There are no Witches!"), but the Society of Jesuits was next organised. Again, dance and theatre were utilised for propaganda; now in schools and colleges; while legends were propagated and reviewed, especially those of Don Juan and Doctor Faustus; and counter-propaganda was prepared—such as the *Don Quixote* by Cervantes (Sirvantes)—to sneer at the romantic chivalry system. From this Frankish cult had sprung the orders of knighthood; one especially was established in Winchester, as the Order of the Garland, by Edward III, who knew his enemies.

WITCH DANCES (Europe)

Alleged to have been performed at meetings, called Witches' Sabbaths (the Great Monthly Assembly), or at Covens (the Weekly Meeting), as a part of mediaeval superstition, which confused mental illness or occasional insanity, with economic persecution of those poor people who rejected the impudent claims of priests and others to govern their property, their work, and their lives. While much of the pseudo-legalism of "Witchcraft Trials" is undoubtedly historical, the reality of the supposed "crimes" is far from proven. Much so-called "evidence" was obtained by torture. The term is said to be derived from *wiccancraeft* (Anglo-Saxon) defined as "power, real or supposed, of producing effects beyond the natural means and operations". The induced abhorrence rests upon a firm faith in "evil spirits", which the witch is supposed to control. In fact, these "wise women" of the villages held most of their skill in the use of herbal remedies; while some in France and Italy concocted poisons. Tatarotti (*Congresso del Notturno*) cites Abbot Regino of Prume (10th century) as the first mediaeval writer to mention the "Witches Sabbath", asserting that "wicked women" attend great meetings by night, "with Diana, Goddess of the pagana, and do her bidding". Diana as Hecate (Trivia) was supposed to preside at crossroads. A Council of Treves (1310) forbade any woman to "pretend that she rode by night with Diana or Herodiana—*haec enim daemonica ilusio est*". By Herodiana was meant the daughter of Herodias, whose skill in dancing was supposed to be displayed at these assemblies. From the fifteenth century begin the persecutions by the "Holy Inquisition". These endured precisely as long as the clerics had power to dominate; witchcraft faded out, with their displacement. Dancing was always cited as an essential part of the ritual; and the Blocksberg (Harzwald) in Germany is named as a favourite centre; though many were in England and Scotland, with a few in Wales and less in Ireland. *Sabbath* is not the correct term; it is *Sabaoth* (Hosts, or Company). The perverted label Sabbath (Tsabbatha) is Hebrew and means "Rest". See *The Amber Witch* and *Sidonia the Sorceress*. William Meinhold. London, 1894.
[See *Devil Dance* (various sections); *Salome; Moon Dance*]

WITCH'S MAGICAL DANCE

(From Goethe's *Faust*) comes in *Scene VI* of the great poetic drama, in the "Witch's Kitchen". The Witch appears through flame, to meet Mephistopheles and Doctor Faust. "With fantastic gestures, she draws a magic circle . . . glasses begin to ring . . . finally she brings a great book . . . the apes are obliged to serve as reading-desk, and to hold torches. She beckons Faust to approach. Mephistopheles persuades Faust to step into the circle. The Witch begins to declaim, with much emphasis, from the book:

"See, thus it's done! Make ten of One;
And two let be; make even three
And rich thou'lt be—
Cast o'er the four! From five and six
(The witch's tricks!) Make seven and eight;
'Tis finished straight,
And nine is one; and ten is None—
This is the Witch's 'One times one!' "

Whence Goethe got this synopsis of geometrical numeration, we cannot tell; but it is a verbal spelling of the "Number process" of Pythagoras; later used in Trajan's time, to formulate the basic shapes of the great Latin alphabet. The Roman augurs used these trajectories in their *templum*. Given a clock-face (descendant of Roman time-keeping) any persistent geometer can work out this dance routine for himself, by drawing the circle and the points. But (as Mephistopheles continued), "Man usually believes, if only words he hears, that also with them goes material for thinking".[1]
[See *Walpurgis*]
[1] *Faust* : Bayard Taylor's translation. London, 1871 (p. 79).

WIWAT (Poland)

The fisherfolk of Pomerania on the Baltic coast have their own dances, in addition to the *Mazurka** and *Krakoviak** performed throughout Poland. One of these is the *Wiwat*, performed only by men, skilfully moving through the movements of the dance with a mug of beer in one hand. The men's traditional long, dark blue coat with shoulder cape, is seldom worn now in Pomerania, nor do the women wear their red or white skirts with gold embroidered black bodice.

WORK DANCES

Many genuine folk-dances have been derived from rhythmic movements first developed by necessity in performance of actual tasks. The ancient practice of easing labour by linking it with rhythm, first apparent in the emergence of simple song (possibly derived from grunts and cries of effort) turns to dance when the task is done. Then someone, perhaps inspired by mischief, mimics the clumsy attempt they have seen. This is followed by "showing off" by stress of real muscular rhythm, co-ordinated with some well-known job. When a group join together to recall technical movement in terms of mime, the art of dance appears; it is affirmed and revealed by rhythm. Thus we have weaving-dances; reaping-dances; or rope-winding dances, in almost every country. The sailors' shanty (chant) is sung while hauling on shrouds or capstan; while the oriental building workers all sing as they are hauling any material from pile to site. Conveyer belts and demands for more output have effectually killed the work dance in industrial Europe; so that the few pieces remaining are those associated with wine or olive pressing. Allied with the work dances are the Fighting Dances (which see). Elements of these may appear in traditional ritual dance (as in Abyssinian ritual), and a few hints recur in some stage dancing.

WUNTJA DANCE (Celebes Island)

A thanksgiving dance of the West Toradja tribe of central Celebes, performed at the Festival held after the crops have been harvested. Round a pole, on the branches of which are hung small bags of cooked rice, youths and girls, in a mixed circle, move with stamping steps. The girls' leader chants a song, which is taken up by the rest; then the men sing a different tune. Breaking up into couples, the dancers form two lines opposite each other, the left arm of the youth round his partner's neck. Various figures are performed, marked at intervals by whooping and stamping of the youths, to which the girls reply each time with three bows. The dance is performed at night by moon- or fire-light, the youths in silk knee-breeches, white shirts, silk scarf over one shoulder, and large coloured head-cloths. Attached to a broad band at the waist is a sheathed sword adorned with a tuft of human hair—relic of the old head-hunting days. The girls wear a flounced dress of bark cloth ornamented with squares of mica; necklaces, ear-drops, bracelets, and round the forehead a band of coloured beads reminiscent of the American Indian head-band. From the waist at the back, are suspended several egg-shaped boxes of gold, containing small bells.

X

XACA (Jamaica)

Pron. *Chaca* (Port). Also known as *Sher-Shay*.* A term signifying a ceremonial—sometimes entertainment in exoteric mode—of singing-dancing-chanting, where any female parts are performed by men. Some Jamaicans say that this term is merely patois for *Chercher*, meaning that worshippers seek to reach *Erzulie*,* who receives only masculine worship. The chants are familiar; the principal dances are *Congo* and *Mascaron*; but not *Jean Valou*, which requires partners.

XANGO OR SHANGO (W. Indies)

Ritual Dance, Afro-Brazilian, sometimes forming part of the *Candomble* Liturgy of Invocation and Healing, used by African negroes and by them imported into Spain; South America; Caribbean Islands (Hayti etc.), with a variety of slightly changed names. A blood sacrifice is made (usually a black fowl), but not "to the devil", as is said. The priest goes into a trance and is "possessed" by Xango (here called "God of Lightning") after a circle dance of prayer and praise. The other male gods are called : Oxossi, God of Green Vegetation (Osiris); Omulum, God of Healing; Okghum, God of

Fight; and the highest of all Oxala (Allah with the Arabs). Three girls are then brought in, to receive lesser deities (angels) of Yanssana. In Brazil the best known centre is in Bahia; but the Secret Societies employ a liturgy that is, by them, believed to be more forceful and effective. The Liturgy has its roots in distant Egypt and North Africa, as the worship of the Male Life Spirit of the *Ankha* (or *Mana*), which operates in a dual capacity, male and female; and in three modes: creating, maintaining and dissolving. *Xango* or *Tch-Ankho* is the Creative Male. The liturgy is essentially an invocation for increased male power, for victory in the tribe or in war with other tribes.   [See *Tango*]

Greeting of Persephone. Four Greek maidens sing and dance to announce the reunion of Persephone and Bacchus (Spring rite). From a Kylix by Hieron in the Louvre.   GREECE

XARILO (Greek)

Also as *Kharalo*, and *Charilo*; name given to the "Year Sacrifice" in successive phases: the living animal, finally the puppet Charilo, used in ritual mode for the "Birth of the Year" in Athens (BC). The latest version we have is from Plutarch, who wrote when the festival had become old; held at intervals of nine years at Delphi. With this term, we find linked a series of names: from the *Kyrilloi* as the servitors, to *Cyrillos* the soldiers and (from "one elected"), the Ruler, the Kyril. The Festival call which began the chant was *Kyrie Eleison* — "Welcome! Spring Uprising!" *Xarilia* was known by many endearing terms: "The Gracious One", or "The Spring Maiden". This worship was still lunar; as indicated in the name *Thyiades*, the maidens who bore the outcast image, and tied a rope around its neck. Here we have the Grecian origin of the Judas story: the grown Child had betrayed the Year to Winter; and had to be ejected. Here we have the ritual functions of the Graces or Charities; and from the same strong root sprang the prince-title of *Xralo*, as *Kralje*, giving us the dance-song we treasure as *Carol* or *Noel*. The allied festival was at Delphi called *Herois* (The Heroine, who was male-female, was the "Splendour of the Rising Year"), which was a *resurrectio* of Semele, coming to her climax at the first full moon after the equinox. This point is always "Easter". With *Xarilo* was associated the name Xrestos, the "Golden One", who was "born of the sea, Mare". Later the Russian name Yarilo (or Iaruelo) implied the Sun God symbol. From these roots came into Britain, with early Greek teachers, the festival of *Rouelle*, the solar wheel. As *I-O** plus *Ruello*, the Moon plus the Prince, the Feast was celebrated by dances of rejoicing. Devon has a place, Newton Saint Cyres. Rimsky Korsakov has used one form of the Russian myth in his ballad opera *Snegour-otchka*. The term exists in Cymric (now in Welsh) as *Rhywll* (also the Spring Circle of May), and gives the European foundation of the name of the Spring Prince — the *Kyril* or *Kralje* (Serbian version). Every one of these Spring Festivals was formulated in Dance and Song.   [See *Thyiadic Dance*]

XILONEN'S FESTIVAL (Aztec-Mexico)

Festival of the Ripening Corn, held in the eighth month of the Aztec year (2nd to 21st July) in honour of Xilonen, Goddess of Young Corn. On the tenth day a woman representing the goddess was sacrificed, after which everyone was free to eat the green maize. For eight consecutive evenings, from sunset to nine o'clock, men (distinguished warriors only) and women, danced and sang in the temple courts, lit with braziers and torches. Some dancers carried torches, and the women's long hair hung loose. Holding hands, or with arms round waists, they danced together, to the rhythmic beat of drums. On the ninth day Xilonen's representative was dressed in embroidered robes, red striped shoes, red feathers decorating her legs. Holding a round shield and crimson baton, she wore a paper crown ornamented with feathers, while the upper part of her face was painted red, the lower half yellow. All night she and her attendants danced and sang before the temple of Xilonen. In the morning a special dance was performed by the men with stalks of maize; while the women, wearing garlands of yellow flowers, danced with the victim, who was sacrificed at the temple of Cinteotl, Goddess of Maize.

XIPHISM (Hellenic)

The second of the four regular parts of the Hellenic *Pyrrhic** martial dance. This was the "mock fight" between youths, when the dancers performed their standard movements of combat, disciplined by the musical rhythm into display. They made a stroke with the short sword; threw a javelin or long spear; used a shield to parry; or rapid footwork to dodge and avoid a blow.   [See *Pyrrhic Dance*]

XISTERNA, BAILE DE LA (Majorca)

"Dance of the Well". A processional dance, in which the performers, moving forward with little jumps (*mateixa*), approach the well in a zig-zag path, with raised arms. Although now performed on a Catholic feast day (August 6th), it is the relic of a dance-ritual once performed in connection with the securing of abundant rain, necessary to produce good crops.

XYLOPHONE (Greek roots : *xylo* = wood; *phoneia* = sounds)

The class of percussion instruments used for dancing, known under many names : as *marimba,** or "Kaffir piano"; *gendrang*, in Java; or *timbila** in East Africa (Chopi, Bantu, etc.). The xylophone implies a graduated series of selected wooden bars, each capable of emitting a single note, arranged to form a scale. Nowhere is the origin of any xylophone scale scientifically elucidated; they appear all to be tuned empirically. This fact recurs with the metalloid series : Malayan gongs; or the ancient Chinese *lithophone,** the stone slabs (in *Museé de l'Homme*, Paris) dated some 2000 BC. The Chopi xylophone is completely explained (except for this tuning scale) by Hugh Tracey, in his treatment of Chopi music and dance.[1]
[See *Percussion Instruments; Gong; Lithophone; Gamelan*]
[1] *Chopi Musicians*. Hugh Tracey. London, 1948.

Y

YAB YUM (Tibetan)

Signified an intensional period in Dance rhythm of LIFE, as compared with *Shen-Kyong*, which indicates an abstract balancing period, during the Dance of Death in the Underworld. *Yab Yum* is the reciprocal natural tension — here exemplified in rhythmic dance, culminating in *maithuna*; thus it is simultaneously the most intense reality and the most intense delusion; while the *Shin-Kyong** indicates a different delusion in the Land of Yama (Death) as the union of the *Yab-Yum* depicts the height of *Maya* (World Illusion). Tibetan ritual designers record these in picture and sculptural form; immensely powerful symbols which hide by their apparent naturalism the eternal cosmic dance. China has an even simpler abstraction in the circular symbol known as *tai-chi*, in which the austere line of a circle continues across its own centre by a curved diameter which divides the areas in halves, returning to the periphery. The symbol is better known in Europe as *Yang-Ying*, or as "male-female" though it is no more so, in this diagram, than positive-negative of an electrical current or a vibrating magnetic field. Between the naturalistic *Yab-Yum* and the abstract *tai-chi*, we find the Chinese *Pa-Kwa*. These are used by the Chinese experts to discover local and temporary forces that affect personal and social welfare. The symbol of *Yab-Yum* was formerly used in certain religious rituals : in Greece, as the *hierogamos* or the sacred marriage. Rapidly the "games" became more important than symbolism; and this was lost, though occasionally renewed, as with the *agape* in Christian Antioch, for *Yab* = *Jahve*, as the fertile god of the paradisal world. Tibetan modes of these dances are to be seen, painted on *tang-ka** (temple ban-

Yamantaka—"Defeater of Death"—also known as Yab-Yum. Tibetan sculpture in bronze, gilded, 9½ ins. high.

TIBET

ners), where figures dance around the World of Time, the *khorlo* and its secret house, the *mandala*. [See *Shin-Kyong; Dance of Death*]

YAHE (Papua)
A dance of Western Elema people of Orokolo Bay performed during the long initiation cycle,

Hevehe.* Yahe celebrates a certain stage in the making of *hevehe* dance masks and the fixing of a new door to the *eravo* (men's lodge), and is part of the carnival pageant of *eharo** masked dancers. The form of the dance is a triple circle (cp. *Turei Na-mbe** and other dances on Malekula). In the centre cluster the drum-beaters and singers (*hivi haera*); round them move, in a slow circle, the dancers (*idihi vira*); on the outside, women and girls in swinging skirts, dance "on the spot". *Yahe* has seven groups of performers : 1. *Apa-eravarava*, special drummers; comic figures with short skirts, ankle and calf fringes of split banana leaf, their faces veiled with black cassowary plumes; 2. *Yahe-morita*, two youths in women's skirts and ornaments; 3. *Kara* ("Mangroves"), wearing head-dresses ornamented with long, tubular mangrove fruits; 4. *Kako* and *Pora* (two birds), with miniature bows, and identifying bird pictures on bark-cloth hung from their backs; 5. Several pairs of *eharo* masked dancers, representing totem animals, reptiles, etc.; 6. *Idihi vira*, the dancers proper, in elaborate costumes with magnificent head-dresses of feathers on wide-spreading frames, their faces painted in minute patterns; 7. *Hohoro* ("Fireflies"), small boys who circle round and round the whole party as it moves. Together with other dances of similar form, *Yahe* is performed in front of the *eravo*, from some time in the afternoon (with one or two interruptions) until dawn, by visiting parties from neighbouring villages. Each village presents its own dance, which differ only in their accompanying songs and costume-characters. The songs, having many verses, recount ancient myths, the characters in which are represented by the dancers. Each stanza is first sung by a leader, and then repeated by the chorus clustered round him.   [See *Poilati*]

YAKKA (S. India)
Derives from Egyptian "*a'akhu*"—meaning beatified souls or "spirit-souls", and merges with the even older concept of "earth spirits" or forms of subtle terrestrial energies "which dance" in their essential movement, as a vital expression of universal life. Thus we have a succession of "names and forms" that suffer slight changes with the current local comprehension; and with varied use or mythic expression in ritual dance. Thus we develop from *a-akhu* in Egypt to *Ya-aksha* in Arabia and thence to *Y'aksha* in ancient India and Yakka in modern India. In between, the spread to Hellas produced the cult of Iacchos or Ba-Iacchos, with the dancing Bacchantes. In India, these festival celebrations continue with *Yakshagana** dances.

YAKKAMA (Ceylon)
Is Sinhalese for "Ritual". There are many such rites, carried out by *Yakdessa* (exorcists), who endeavour by ceremonial acts to govern the nature powers thus personified; and to control tribal rituals. Chief of these is *Maha Yakkama* (Great Ritual) which is a ceremonial welcome to strangers. This one is dramatised as *Väddan Givissima* (Invitation to Veddas), in which a simple *Veddah* from India is asked : why he comes to Ceylon? He is accepted, cleansed, and feasted. Conversely in *Boru Yakkama*, a satire is performed, also in terms of mime and dance. The *Yakdessa* imitates a Brahmin, two more act as leopard and deer; the chief dancer carries a golden drum; then they copy the ritual dance that begins the *Kamkarya* Dance, considered essential in stating and marking the ceremonial rhythm of all these rites.

YAKKUN NEUTUMA (Ceylon, Southern India, Karnatik)
A ritual dance used as a means of exorcism on patients believed to be "possessed of devils", and wrongly described by ignorant missionaries as "devil dances", implying some sort of "worship of the devil". They are not. The dance ritual and rhythmic drum beating provides a therapy for reducing the afflictions of unbalanced persons; its justification appears in its frequently successful outcome. The "demons" are moved by drum rhythms (instead of microbes by drugs or x-rays) and having been required to give attention, are then finally dispossessed of their victims—in a manner almost biblical, except that rarely are the exorcised *yakshas* compelled to enter into a herd of swine and run over a cliff, as at Gadara.

YAKSHA(m) AND YAKSHI (fem) (Northern India)
In contrast with the Tamil Nad or Dekkan, knows the *Yakshis* as more or less benevolent; but rarely demonic. These attractive beings—always in human form and with no ritual mask—appear with *apsara* or *gandharva* (celestial dancers, and singers or musicians) in the celebrations of the gods. They seem to be equivalent with the nymph or naiad of European romantic mythology; they frequent streams or trees, are robust in form and show little need of drapery.

YAKSHA-GANA (Kanarese, South India)
Mime-dance (sometimes with chants), signifying "demon-combat" (the *yaksha* is the demon involved), played on festivals throughout Southern India, by small itinerant companies of men and boys. One well-known company moves in and around Bangalore in Mysore State. They use masks, or a mask-style make-up, and elaborate costume (though not always in good repair), and adopt simple but usually noisy musical accompaniment; drums, trumpet or conch, and cymbals.

YAKUT WEDDING DANCE (Siberia)

After the wedding feast, dancing and singing take place. All the young people partake, the young men singing, "Ho! boys ho! let us enjoy ourselves while we are young". The leading girl responds, "Sing aloud my throat". Then follows a musical dialogue, the boys singing "Let us dance and laugh while we are still unwed", to which the girls reply, "Let us play while we are still unwed, while we are still uncaught by the hands of men". The old women flock round, improvising verses. [See *Ungkulatem*]

YANGKO (China)

An old folk dance-drama belonging to Shensi Province, along the Hiang-Ho (Yellow River) in N.W. China, and existing up to modern times. The stories were of love and intrigue, or of heroic deeds, the theme being chanted by a leader with responses by a chorus. Love songs took the form of questions and answers by young men and girls who enacted the story, formed into two lines facing each other. A basic movement of three vigorous steps forward and one step backwards and sideways was used for entry and exit of the dancers. In between, group dances were performed, and solo dances by the principal characters in the story, to the music of drums, gongs and cymbals (later string and wind instruments). A clown was often an additional character. The leader held an open umbrella or metal rod, and the dancers moved with small, mincing steps. The style of dancing sometimes seen in Western classical ballet as representing "Chinese dancing" (e.g. in *Casse Noisette* and *Coppelia*), with dancers carrying paper umbrellas or fans and moving with tiny steps, with the first finger of each hand pointing upwards, is close to the traditional *Yangko* style of dancing. In 1937 the possibilities of this old form of dance-drama were recognised by political and military leaders, and during the war against Japan the *Yangko* dance form was developed by propaganda groups. The leader replaced his umbrella by a rifle or rake; the clown became a Japanese or a Quisling; and the lines of dancers, instead of enacting love stories about mythological or heroic characters, became farm workers, soldiers or students in stories with contemporary themes. Later, the form was still further developed, tending towards a more complex dramatic performance.

YANTRA RAJA (Hindu)

Indicates the Ruler or "King of *Yantras*". "This *yantra* (dance ritual pattern and symbol) or diagram of worship", says Sir J. Woodroffe "is similar in form . . . to the *Rudra Bhairava Yantra* . . . . *Yantra Raja* is so called in order to emphasise its importance in this particular form of *Sadhana*".[1]

The strict discipline of certain ritual Hindu worship is called *Sadhana*. For its liturgy, certain traditional diagrams are drawn (or permanently incised) on the floor of the temple. Instructions for drawing the *yantra* (since it is preferable that the worshipper should himself know how and why he draws the symbol), are given on page 130 of *The Great Liberation*, and also in *Ocean of Beauty* (very fully).[2] Compare with the Great Wheel Windows, constructed in West European cathedrals (called Great Rose Window also), with these symbols — used alike for esoteric doctrines of teaching, rendered both by ritual and by dance movement, over the prescribed patterns.

[1] *The Great Liberation* (Trans. of *Mahanirvana*) by Sir John Woodroffe.
[2] *Ocean of Beauty*. Trans. of *Saundarya-Lahari* (Shankara) by Sastri and Ayyanger.

YAO INITIATION DANCE (Central Africa)

Boys about to join the tribe as adults have a special masked dancing performance, to be done before a large audience. Boys make their own disguises, which completely hide the face and head, to prevent identification. A slip or a fall in the dance is regarded as a most unlucky prediction for the boy's future. If he falls he remains on the ground, as if dead; grass is sprinkled over him; when all spectators have departed, the lad creeps away from the spot, which is then splashed with fowls' blood.

YATRA (India)

A religious procession marked by dancing; popular still in Bengal (as for example, *Yudda Yatra*, a war-dance procession). Their words preserve the Shauraseni (Saracen) dialect; once centred in the Agra district, as a home of Krishna worship. *Yatra* has developed into a melodramatic form, in some more modern Bengali plays; but continues the older modes of realism in the use of dialect languages. The older *Yatra* remains popular in village life for religious festivals.

YAWE (Polynesia: Pacific Island of Yap)

This is the basic term for any ritual patterns; dance diagrams, or tattoo patterns of equally symbolical form; and has more recently been used to denote foreign writing. The islands of Yap, Rumung, and Gagil-Tomil, have a population of some 3,000, in several tribes or clans. Besides work-dances (done on building a house, a canoe etc.) there are festival or ancestral dances, ruined in part by successive invasions of Germans, Japanese, missionaries, and Americans. Each village has its own customary dance with chant. Men and women dance separately, always in day time. They carry elaborate head-dresses (feathers and pearly shells, bound by hisbiscus fibre) but seldom use make-up (except sometimes turmeric yellow), and no masks. Costumes exist only below the waist; mostly grass-skirts; but much use is made of *var* (rounded fragments of pearl-shell) as "favours" to give away. One women's dance has seven aside, facing, wielding bamboo or cane batons, clashed as they sing. This folk-dance presents two "sides" marked by different skirt and head-dress colours.

YEI BIT CHAI (Apache Indian — New Mexico)

"House of Soul" (similar to *Ya Beit Khai* (Arabic-Egyptian) held as annual ceremonial by several Indian tribes as a November "life ritual" covering some nine days, with singing, music, dancing, initiation of youth. Prayer for health of the People (The *Dinne*) is called *Hasjelti Dailjis* (*Hasjelti's* Medicine Dance), and begins with all the gathering; ending partly in curative activities of the sick, partly in mass initiations of boys and girls. Hasjelti and Hosthoghon — the two chief deities — ritually acted by two elders in deerskin masks (the latter dyed blue) begin at dusk, with the Medicine Priest before his *hogan* (ritual hut). Five days pass in songs of world creation; the sixth begins with the World Soul symbol, made in magnificent sand patterns, started at daylight by four young initiates, who work until long after mid-day. They use five of the thirty-five coloured sands available; black and white, red and yellow, with grey-blue, spilling the complicated designs with great skill from their fingers. This symbol has four sections: one shows the end of the earth, except one woman; the next shows her bearing a daughter, whose father was the "soul of water", and this child is in turn impregnated by solar fire, Naiyenesgenai. Third sector shows the return of the son-child to his sun-father, recording his exploits while on earth; the fourth indicates how earth was replenished by men and women, from sacred ears of corn. The song-priest sprinkles the Patterns with his benediction of sacred white meal; then the sick man is brought in, amid incense. Then follows the secret cure. The sand-painting is destroyed before dusk; but on the seventh and eighth days, more symbol pictures are made (not the same). Dances continue, in the open, through parts of each day, with drumming and chanting. After curing the sick, twelve dancers enter the chief clearing, presenting the "First Man/First Woman, six times living". Chants in falsetto, with swift dancing, fill the night. At sunrise, the Bluebird Song ends the ceremonial; all dancers unite in a circle; remove their masks; sprinkle them with pollen (generative symbol) and disperse.
[See *Sand Tracings; Rangoli; Navajo*]

YETZIRAH (Hebrew)

The *Siphra Yetzirah*, or Book of Formation, has its doctrinal analogies in the great *Ming T'ang** of early China; and the Hindu *Chakrams* of Vaishnavism. The book treats of cosmogeny, as symbolised by the ten numbers and the twenty-two letters, which here are mentioned with the "Thirty-two paths". These can be seen, visually depicted (originally in gold and colour) on the alabaster slabs of the Babylonian temples, formulated as the *Autz ha-chayiim*, or Tree of Life, the Golden Tree of Splendour.[1] The term "path" is used in several modes; but, through the *Qabalah*,* the leading broad notion is that of a hieroglyphically expressed idea, which may be attached (in a related summation or nexus of ideas) to any symbol by word or glyph, presented in plastic or graphic form. Hence the association with the stately dance ritual, in which the teaching priests moved, in symbolical costume and carrying implements, through the main acts of the cosmic drama. We see them, preserved in the British Museum slabs, attending the Sacred Tree by means of lustration and germination (from the date palm system of Arab countries). The Formations are realized, as Dances of Energies which project gradually more dense substances, matter and forms, into which the "Breath of Life" is projected as a vitalizing factor, simultaneously: so that Life is Form; and Form expresses Life. Between these two poles, moves the processive dance of incessant change. The Sacred Tree emerges from its invisible seed, presses into existence in stem and leaves and flowers, then failing but leaving newer seeds which again return. Leaves and Flowers and Fruits are the living creatures which perform their Dance of Life. See *Kabbalah Unveiled*. Trans. by S. L. M. Mathers from *Kabbala Denudata*. London (4th edn.) 1926.
[1] In British Museum (Assyrian Galleries).

YEZIDI DANCE (Syria, at Sheik Adi)

Performed by the Kaidi (Yezidi tribe) at their annual festival. They first perform a mock battle; they ascend rocks overhanging the temple of Sheik Adi; put oak twigs in the muzzles of their guns, and discharge them in the air; this preliminary continues for half an hour; they descend and again fire in the air. Next, in the courtyard, they perform a martial dance before the Bey, who stands on top of steps with his colleagues, priests and elders. At the end of the dance, a bull is led out of the temple; the Kaidi rush to convey it to the Sheik of their sect. Women make the *tahlel* (mourning cry) without ceasing. The Yezidi have an officer called *Cawell* or *Cowell*, who governs the rites; *Faqirs* (lowest class of students) and *Kotcheks*, who run the services. The Cawalls play tambourines and flutes; and carry the *Messe* (called *harisa*), a mixture of bruised wheat, milk and curds boiled to a pulp, with added butter; also at its best with sugar and cinnamon.

YIDDISH BALLET (London)

Most of the records of stage dance in East End of London lasted little longer than the dances. Jewish girls have often proved to be excellent dancers. They began locally. Many came from elementary experience beyond Aldgate to the professional schools, like Katti Lanner's or Stedman's, nearer the West End. One popular Victorian attraction was billed as a Masquerade Gala at a theatre known as Green Dragon Gardens. A poster kept in the Jewish Museum recalls the occasion in 1853. As the time was the end of Pentecost, after *Yontiff* (holiday), there were to be "No *Chootspers*" (liberties) allowed. The Gardens had been "clobbered" up; and there were *Chozonish* singers; the New Orchestra was *Gorpotzed* out (bedecked) and *shloremized* (fancy pieces) by the Bolbose (the boss or gaffer). Now comes the great draw :

"A Growser plotz which *cusht fiel Gelt* will be erected for dancing. In the course of the evening an Original Ballet, entitled *The Mershoogner Koler*, in which Phicy the Phresser and Sorah the Zouffer will sustain the principal characters introducing a *New Weasel Dance*.
Music by the Composer of *Shelomozzle cant be Pervented*.
Tight-rope Norrishcott by Mandler O'Lolly from the Stafford-shire Potteries.
The Ballroom solely for the admission of Ladies and Gentlemen in private dress. Fireworks by Brock. Admission 6d.".

As *Mershoogner Kolor* means "The Mad Bride", it seems possible that Smetana was perhaps inspired by this creation to write *The Bartered Bride?*

YOGA Training in Dance

(*Yoga*—Sanskrit=Union, Discipline, Method). Hindu *yoga* is a religious discipline which provides instruction and methods to train the *chela* (student) to govern (a) his physical body, (b) his vital body, (c) his emotions, and (d) his intellectual mind; in part by sequence; in part simultaneously. The genuine system is long and difficult; but certain extracts have been made for general development. These were used in the ancient Greek *palaestra* or halls for games; and approximate to that part of the scheme known as *hatha-yoga*, or strength-training. This portion has been superficially taken over by certain dance training schools; more especially in control of breathing by regular exercises. In India there are several schemes of *yoga*

discipline, fitted for the real needs of various types of student. The skilful master selects each scheme in correct relation to each separate student. Broadly there are two great systems (in India as elsewhere) which provide (a) for the training and acceptance of a youth *into* the adult social group; and (b) which permits for the advanced training of the far fewer adults who desire it, to move *out* of the *social* group into highly developed individual mind or soul training. This alone is regarded by many scholars as the "real yoga". Physically, the bodily training provides for control of the body for rhythmic breathing out (immobility); and control for utmost flexion; later this same contrast is required in mind control. The ritual postures are known as *asana;* and the symbolical poses are called *mudra** (or seal). The *yogi* receives training also by watching symbolic dance; and, rarely taking part in ritual dances.

YOGI DANCE (India)

Yogis do not dance. Hindu sacred dance belongs to religious ritual, which they have left behind in their search for wisdom, as a boy leaves behind school with its discipline. The competent *yogi* (*adhikari*) seeks to know and to control his body, only as a preliminary to control of mind; a task much more difficult. No longer does he watch temple dances : he has learned what they have to convey. He begins another process of discipline; at first this is another rhythmic motion, but internal and invisible :

"If the Yogi, devoted to Lotus Feet of his Guru, with heart unperturbed, mind concentrated, reads this work (supreme source of Liberation) faultless, pure, but most secret—then surely his Mind dances at the feet of the Devata".

This reference is the last verse (55) from *Shat-chakra-Nirupana*, translated by Arthur Avalon (Sir John Woodroffe) in *Kundali Shakti* (*Serpent Power*); 5th edn. 1953 (p. 488). [See *Chöd Ritual*]

YOI (N. Australia)

The Tiwi aboriginals of the Snake Bay Settlement, Melville Island, off the west coast of Arnhemland, call their *Corroboree** "Yoi", which, doubled as "Yoi-Yoi" was the old Malayan name for this Island. Describing incidents in hunting or fishing, a *Yoi* is danced and mimed by men to the accompaniment of a chant telling the story. *Tatuwali Yoi* ("Shark Yoi"), for instance, relates how a boy is chased by a shark; the shark in turn being chased by the crowd, speared and eaten. Men, decorated with red and yellow ochre, wearing topknots of dyed cockatoo feathers, and red and white goose-ball neck pendants, enact the various parts. The dance is repeated several times, each time a different man taking the role of the shark, and each repeat being preceded by the "long-call-high-call". While sometimes the rhythm is provided by a man beating two hardwood sticks together, the usual accompaniment, besides chanting, is the stamping of feet and slapping of cupped hands against buttocks. These "play-about" *Yoi* are made up by the Tiwi people. Women have their own *Yoi*, sometimes sung sitting down, without any dancing Some of the songs are of the Calypso* type, describing topical Island events. But the outstanding thing about the Melville Island *Yoi* is the "long-call-high-call", which introduces every dance. The dancers appear with arms raised, and a shiver of muscles runs along their arms and hands to their finger tips. Then the sound begins, rising up and up. One group takes up the note from the others as in the "long-call", and so it holds on very high. This shivering "high-call" passes imperceptibly from group to group without any break, in a long, sustained note. Suddenly it stops, and the dance goes on.

[See *Corroboree; Atnumokita; Tjitji-Inma; Kipara*]

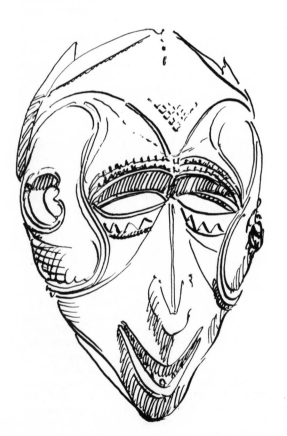

Mask used in Obi ritual dance. (B.M.)   NIGERIA

YORK MINSTER DANCES (England)
Easter was celebrated with great splendour in the Minster, by all the citizens. Down to the middle of the 17th century, companies of town apprentices, and servants of the richer gildsmen, danced solemnly in the great nave at Easter; and especially on Shrove Tuesday. The form was chiefly a round dance, some accompanied by carols or hymn tunes

YORUBA (West Africa)
Celebrates an annual Yam Festival, connected with the local Secret Society, the *Egun-Egun*. Religious in motive, being a Dance of the Dead, it is a memorial to tribal ancestors. Dancers and drummers arrive; then enter mummers, hidden in great wooden masks, carved and coloured. Some of these are contrived to mimic the former appearance of recently dead celebrities. The mummers merge with the unmasked members, dancing to welcome the "dead spirits".

YOULING (England)
In Kent there was a 16th century custom (recorded in Hasted's *History of Kent*) followed at Keston and Wickham. In Rogation Week, a number of local youths met for the ceremony, which is in essence an invocation to the rural deities of the orchard. Brand says it is supplication of Eolus, god of the soft winds, from which comes the name Youling; but it might equally be a displaced wassail rite, also addressed to the trees, as in Devon orchards. With "rough music", the youth go in procession to the orchard; and there dance round the largest tree, or several in turn, chanting:

> "Stand fast, root! Bear well, top!
> Lord send us a Youling sop!
> Every twig come apple big—
> An' every bough hold apple enow!"

After this fertility incantation, they repair to the farm, where they expect a drink and some money. The rite seems here to be part of the Rogation or Ambulation of the Parish, practised by Romans and followed by clerics, and still known at Helston in Cornwall on the 8th May, in the *Furry Dance*.*

YSGENTIN (Welsh)
A buffoon or a scaramouche; an irresponsible jester, other than an appointed or professional jester; a term sometimes indicating the goblin dance of a *bwbach* (goblin). The regular jester is *Cellwair* or *Digrifwas*.

YUEH LING (Ancient China)
The "Monthly Observances" or Ordinances, extracted from *Li Chi*, section IV, and arranged (originally) by Lu Pei-wei, who (BC 50?) edited the

already ancient Observances into *Lu Shih Ch'in;* as derived from earlier practices of three dynasties (i.e. Hsia; Shang; and Chou), and finally compiled into the state authorised version, by Ch'en Hao (AD 1261 - 1341). The Yueh-Ling were first compiled, it is believed, in the Han Dynasty period, after the destruction of the Feudal system about BC 214, when the famous "Burning of Books" was ordered. These records are regarded by W. E. Soothill as highly important, in the study of early kingship, as collateral with the whole basis of Chinese culture.[1] The *Yueh-ling* provides the record of recognised rituals, ceremonies, and rules, of which *Ming T'ang** is the living expression, in rites, month by month. By 50 BC many copies had been gathered; blended with the moral system of Confucius; influenced by Taoism and later by Buddhism. Ritual was the principal concern, affecting the ruler who operated on behalf of the people. The court and baronial rituals contained their system in terms of ceremony, music, chant, and dance form, posited in the active relations of the *Tê* and *Shen* (the pole and the circle, abstractly taken), where the king was the axle or "king-pin", as between the heavens and the realm; much as was the Pharoah (the "Great House") in ancient Egypt. This system is not so much one of "mimetic magic" as of a collection, concentration, and transfer of power, done by the conscious balance of heaven-mode and earth-king. This operation was performed in the "Hall of Light", the *Ming T'ang*. The *Li Chi* relates ceremonies and rules; the *I Li* covers principles; the *Chou Li* rounds of "The Three Rituals". The term *Li* indicates "reverence" and "sacrifice". In Chou period, the institution *Ming T'ang* reached its zenith; but rituals did not remain static, though slow changes were admitted. In all of them; position, movement, dance, and gesture are important, related to the period of year, as changed month by month. For this the pavilion was devised and so constructed. The origin was based on calendar and astronomy; the temple was thus a copy, ordered by Yueh Ling, or "what should be done" to receive and to utilise the heavenly forces.
[1] *The Hall of Light.* W. E. Soothill. London, 1952.

YUGEN (Japan)
A quality much desired in Japanese Noh-dance-drama; is praised as "flower of action" (equivalent to *rasa* in Hindu dance), revealed as unity of "picture-thought-action". For *yugen* the ordinary personality of the actor must disappear in his role. Leading Japanese critics advise: "Forget Theatre; look at *Noh.** Stand on *Noh* and receive actor; pass the actor and touch idea; on the peak of Idea you will understand the *Noh!*" Yugen abandons technique, utilises style; and arrives at essence. Linking *Yugen* and *Yukoyo* (or "mastery in rhythmic action") we have *kurai* as emotional quality of integral tension as rhythm of feeling.

YUKON ESQUIMAUX DANCES (Yukon, Alaska, N. America)
Celebrate the annual "Feast of the Dead", but with an eye on the needs of the living dancers. Rehearsals precede the ceremonies, which occupy three successive nights. First come the humorous dances; memorial, satirical, mimetic of recently dead people to assure them they are "still in memory". Men and women each have their own particular dances; but sometimes dance together, a woman in the centre of the moving ring. The second day is occupied by these group dances (most of the humorous type were done by solo experts in talk), while the last and more solemn period is filled with mask dances of the totems. One leading walrus wears a mask of that animal, and mimes its manners and habits; its pursuit and capture. The "Raven Dance" shows in a parallel fashion, the meeting and mating of the birds, by imitation in rhythm of its quick jumps and circling; by Raven Mask (leading in his costume of fur and black feathers), leaping about several women masked also as Ravens. Finally, the *shaman* performs his dance of possession, ending in a trance. From this he awakens, and assures the dancers that the ancestors have been pleased with their memorial. In return they will try to send the game towards the hunting fields.

YULE Ritual Dance (Saxon etc.)
Also as IOLO—IOno and, earlier IO-das, all signify in solar and lunar circle festival dances: four for the solar year and three for the moon. Following in Europe, traditional Bel-Taine Fire, they kept festivals of the Four Quarters; two equinoctial dates and two solstices; all marked by Fires of Celebration. The winter crossing of the ecliptic, thence known as X-Messe or the X-Feast, was turned into chrestmas; the summer date of IOno (now known to Romans, as Juno; as the other was Jove or IOve—there is no J in Latin), was disguised as the Feast of a mythical "Saint John". The Romans had Janus, made into Johannus, but marking the Two-faced Year—Departing and Coming. The Yulo Logos was the Great Festival of Winter through Northern Europe. The characteristic ritual form celebrated the famous TWELVE DAYS OF DANCING, with six days before, and six days after, the central point. This ancient symbol of TWELVE marked every aspect: the dancers, the players or minstrels (to be seen on church pillars, at Exeter, or Beverley, or at Moissac and Vezelay) were all in bands of Twelve; like Twelve Patriarch; Twelve

Prophets; Twelve Apostles; Twelve Months; Twelve Chief Greek Gods; and Twelve Symbols of the Zodiac, all of them described in a circle, indicated by a Cipher plus a vertical line—the I O symbols of the secret doctrine.   [See *Carole; Masque*]

YUMARI (Mexico)

A ritual dance of the Tarahumara Indians of the Chihuahua mountains, performed, with other dances, for the production of rain, crops and multiplication of animals. It is their belief that dances were taught to their ancestors by the animals themselves—magical prototypes who will now aid the Indians to obtain the necessities of life. Connected with the *Rutuburi,** which it followed, *Yumari* began shortly before sunrise and lasted for many hours, sometimes all day. Said to have been taught originally by the deer, it was accompanied by the chanting of the *saweame* (shaman) who, naming the animals, invokes their aid. Performed by men and women, the sexes remained apart, men moving to the left of the *saweame*, women to the right. *Yumari* does not appear to have imitated animal movements, but to have been a formal dance in which the two groups advanced and retired, crossed laterally, and moved round the dancing-place counter-clockwise, each movement being repeated three times, to chanting and shaking of rattles. Offerings of food and drink were made. Considered as a safeguard against misfortune, *Yumari* was often danced by one man near the house, while the family worked in the fields, sometimes continuing to dance all night. Before a hunt for a communal feast, each hunter danced it alone before his house for two hours, to ensure success. Today *Yumari* and *Rutuburi** are combined in one ritual dance called *Dutuburi*.

YUNNAN (China)

Lolo people in Yunnan perform a rice-sowing dance.[1] Each evening, after filling their day with planting, women assemble in groups; and proceed to dance in a meadow with youths of the village, to music of guitar and castanets. Their dances are varied and peculiar, suggesting something of Indian styles, in circle dances. After a dance period is ended, a damsel will offer a glass of rice liquor to the guest she most approves; after he takes a sip, she also drinks. Each couple follows, until all have had refreshment. Songs merge with renewed dancing in these Spring evenings.

[1] *La Province Chinoise de Yun-nan.* E. Rocher. Paris, 1879.

The Zamacueca.   PERU

Z

ZAMACUECA; Cueca (Chile)

A song-dance of Spanish origin, always in the major key, and usually in 6/8 time with the accompaniment in 3/4 time. The name is often shortened to *Cueca*. Movements of the dance are said to symbolise those of a cock and hen, to which words sung by spectators also refer, and it is generally considered that the name *Cueca* comes from *clueca*—the clucking of a hen. Partners face each other in a coquettish dance of pursuit and flight, approach and withdrawal, the girl finally allowing herself to be caught. Each dancer flourishes a kerchief. The high point of the dance, closely watched by spectators, is a kind of contest between partners. When the girl turns quickly away in retreat, the man must at the same instant turn his back on her. If he is not quick enough to turn at the same moment he earns the laughter of spectators. *Zamacueca* is accompanied by guitar, tambourine and harp, the music being in two parts, the second more lively than the first. The dance appeared in Chile in 1824, and was sometimes called *Sambacueca*, but had no relation to the Afro-Brazilian

*Samba.** A similar dance is found in Peru, Argentina and Bolivia.
[See *Marinera; Cueca; Huaiño; San Juanito; Tamborito*]

ZAMBRA

In Spain, a group name (from Arabic) for a performance of gypsy dances, such as those given by the gypsies of the Sacro Monte, Granada. The term *zambra* includes music accompanied by song, indicating a *flamenco* performance, where such dances as the *Arbola, Cachucha,** *Mosca, Panaderos* may be performed. In Andalusia, *Los Panaderos* is a version of *Bolero;** it is said to contain most of the vocational movements of the baker of bread at work. In Morocco, *Zambra* means "a revelry by night". Among cultivated Moors it is an entertainment of dancing and *cante hondo** in the Andalusian style. *Zambra* is also the name of a dance (with music for *scabelas* (flutes) and *dulzainas*) known to Moors and Spaniards from the 14th/15th century, as one performed along with the recitation or singing of the "romances". "The Moorish lady", writes Prescott,[1] "is represented there (in the courts) as an undisguised spectator of the public festivals; while her knight, bearing an embroidered mantle, or scarf, or some other token of her favour, contends openly in her presence for the prize of valour, mingles with her in the graceful dance of the *Zambra*, or sighs away his soul in moonlight serenades under her balcony."
[1] *History of Ferdinand and Isabella.* W. H. Prescott (p. 158) 7th edn. 1854.

ZAMIL DANCE (Arabia)

An almost stationary dance, in the form of a serenade, performed by men. Intended as a compliment to some exalted person, the leader of the dance sings a solo, usually a song of praise, after which the others take up the chorus. Often the singing is unaccompanied by any instruments, the performers keeping time by hand-clapping and rhythmic swinging of the body.

ZAMIN, ZAR, AND ZAN (Persian-Arabic)

Mystical dance, mentioned by the Sufi (Moslem) *kavi,* or poet, as the "Dance of Saki the Wine-Cup Bearer". This theme is a reflex of the "three great desires", of the human world; in *Zamin* (desire for land, whence comes food); *Zar* (wealth of all kinds); and *Zan* (wife and family). These, taken together, are equivalent to the Hindu *sarabande,* or the dance within *samsara* (the "Whirl of the World"); they present the embodiment of the triple fundamental desires in life. They have been theologised in Europe as, "World, Flesh and Devil"; and, again, vulgarised as "Wine, Women, and Song!"—and in all these varied modes, have been presented in dance and mime, especially in Morality Plays as the "Seven Virtues and Seven Vices".

ZANCO (Mexico)

A stilt dance performed in the Villa Alta region of Oaxaca by boys dressed as girls, who move about in perfect rhythm to the music. Stilt dancers called *Monigotes* form part of certain fiestas in some parts of Mexico. At the December festival at Patscuaro they appear in the afternoon of December 7th, eve of the festival day, in the shape of boys in white suits, wearing masks, who prance about on stilts. While at Querétaro they form part of the Christmas Eve procession, taking their place between the band and floats arranged to represent Biblical scenes. The *Monigotes* here again are boys walking on stilts, but disguised under huge cardboard figures.   [See *Stilt Dance*]

ZANDE (Southern Sudan)

Pastime dance among the Azandé; starting at sunrise in a small circular clearing, in which perhaps a dozen dancers perform. Music consists of singing, accompanied by a wooden drum, shaped like an animal. The drummer sits astride it; as if it were living. There is a lute, a kettle drum, and a simple *marimba.* The words are the general theme-song of the moment (the dance and theme change from year to year), and like the *shanty,* are sung while working. Men and women dancers hold out their hands in front, palms upward, moving their arms with the musical beat. Their feet move in a little "two-step", from side to side; with slightly moving hips, in a dance that is no more than a game. This is, the Zandé ballroom period; though they do not dance together.

ZANDUNGA (S. Mexico)

La Zandunga, sometimes given as *Sandunga,** is the traditional wedding carol of Tehuantepec. At every wedding one of the several versions is heard, with the merry yet plaintive music; and words that vary from town to village, some so robust that they could not be printed; but always with the refrain:

> La Zandunga baile, si no despietre
> Al quejoso rumor de ese harmonia
> Dejadne descansar, que estare Muerto!

which has less change from the Spanish than either music or meaning:

> Dance la Zandunga; yet if I do not awaken
> To sing its plaintive harmonies,
> Let me be silent, for I shall be dead!

La Zandunga is the symbolical bride at all weddings, and the name seems to be derived from an old Spanish version of *San-Huana* or San-Jean in the mediaeval Mystery Play, celebrated in France as Jeanne d'Arc or La Marianne; while in Tehuantepec the bride is called *La Zandunguera*. These carols are anonymous: the writers (probably many) are unknown. Another verse descants subtle mystical notes:

> Zandunga baile a tocar
> Ay madre por dios
> En la Batalla de Flores
> Mi cielo di mi corazon,

which we can translate as:

> Desiring to dance Zandunga,
> Ah, dear mother of god —
> In this battle of flowers,
> My heaven is in my heart!

for the unforgettable paradoxical refrain is, *"Mi cielo de corazon"* — "my heart is my heaven; my heaven is my heart" — over subtle variations of sequence and rhythm. The music is from marimba and flute, sometimes a soft drumming; and the dance is a simple *jarabe*.*

ZANY — 1 (Italian Med.)

A clown or fool, a jester whose dance mime sought to imitate satirically. He would mimic any well-known person, anyone "in the news" or even another member of his own company. The term is said to refer to *Zanni* = Giovanni or John; but no reason is adduced. The *sanni* came from the Orient.

ZANY — 2 (Italy, mediaeval)

Term applied to the "second clown" (now termed the *Auguste*), whose job was to "feed" or to support by answer in word and action, the principal clown or Buffoon. The word is from *sannio*; and this from *sangha*, an oriental term for "an admitted company". (The word "saint" derives from the same source; it means merely an ordinary member). *Zany* is given also as *zanny* and *sani*; plural *zannies*; and has no relation to Giovanni or Giuseppe (John or Joseph). The *Zany* played many parts, including burlesque dancing. In Britain the word has been used to denote a fool or simpleton; and thus re-spelled as *sawnie* (or "soft"). The Saxon word *selig* — "holy" — now implies someone who is "silly".

ZAPATEO (Cuba)

Derives from the *Punto* and *Guajira*, both popular Cuban dance-songs in 3/4 or 6/8 time. The name, "Zapateo" comes from a verb meaning "to strike with a shoe", and refers to the stamping steps, using heel, or toe, or the whole foot, which are included in many Latin-American dances of Spanish origin. The *Zapateo* is a cross-bred product of the *Zapateado*,* *Seguidilla** and *Guajira*.* In the Cuban style it is a sensual dance, but male and female partners strictly refrain from touching each other, the heels marking the beat, and the body being held rigid. The *Zapateo* is also danced in the Dominican Republic, where a country dance sometimes called *Sarambo* is also known as *Zapateado Montuno*; and in Chile it is mentioned in the early 18th century, when a French book of travels gave the musical notation for a Chilean *Zapateo*, in 1713.

ZAPATEADO (Spain)

Name for staccato footwork in Spanish dancing, in which the whole foot, or heel, toe or ball, strikes the ground in rhythmic stamps. The rhythm of the stamps is often syncopated, and sometimes in contrast to the music. Also the name for an Andalusian man's solo dance in triple time, in which the whole interest lies in the footwork (as also in Lancashire *Clog Dancing* and Irish *Step Dancing*). The dancer of the *Zapateado* gives a display of technical virtuosity, with lightning turns, much stamping, and sharp tapping with the heels (*taconeo*), every nuance of which is appreciated by *afficionados*. *Zapateado* steps occur also in many Latin-American dances of Spanish origin, often with variations on the fundamental rhythm.

ZAPOROSCHE (Ukraine)

Dance of the rapids — as the river there bears this name. Four men with swords perform this striking Russian dance, in a very martial manner.

ZARATHUSTRA (F. Nietzsche, Germany)

In his great poem, *Also Sprach Zarathustra*, Friedrich Nietzsche used the short name of the Iranian prophet, Zoroaster, merely as a convenient symbol of the "Overman".[1] He writes not of dancing with vision; for his attention is involved with ethics, morality, and their revolutions; just as Thomas Carlyle did not confine his attention to clothes in his *Sartor Resartus*; nor with the robes of dance. Nietzsche uses dance as a symbol of Dionysian joy; almost as it is drawn into the *Song of Solomon*.* Every student of modern dances should read this remarkable work; avoiding commentators until afterwards. Nietzsche (who was no Nazi philosopher), is the German antithesis of Karl Marx, whose interest was revolving on the same fulcrum of society and ethics; on politics as the "mass desire", and economics as "mass fulfilment"; while the poet speaks only of the fruits of a ripe civilisation. In his *Dance Song (XXXII)*, he writes:

> "Cease not your dancing, ye lovely maidens! No game spoiler hath come to you with evil eye; no enemy of maidens. . . . .
> "Upbraid me not, ye beautiful maidens, when I chasten the little god somewhat.

With tears in his eyes shall he ask you for a
dance;
    And I myself will sing a song to his dance;
A dance-song . . . . and this is the song that
Zarathustra sang when Cupid and the
maidens danced together" :

Again, in this *Second Dance Song (LIX)*:

"This is a dance over stock and stone.
I am the hunter—wilt thou be my hound—or
chamois?
. . . to the rhythm of my whip wilt thou dance
and cry?
    forget not my whip . . . . not I !"
[1] *Thus Spake Zarathustra; A Book for All and None.*
Friedrich Nietzsche (1844 - 1900). Trans. by Thomas
Common; Revised by Oscar Levy and John L.
Beevers. (Edition 1932).

ZASIALI GORALE (Lithuania)
A harvest dance, but with no mimetic action,
simply performed at harvest time. A short sequence
in waltz-time separates the figures, the dance being
performed by groups of three—a man with two
girls, or a girl with two men. The dancers form
figures of eight round each other; the girls are
turned under the man's arms; or the man, with a
girl on either side, swings first one, then the other,
with hooked elbows, as in the Czech *Kalamajka.**

ZAUBEROPER (Austria)
Literally, "Magical Opera" as a name given to stage
productions, similar to the English Fairy Pantomime. These appeared in late 18th century Viennese theatres. There was a plot, based on some
fairy-tale, with superimposed comedy passages and
ballet dances, done usually in a magnificent style
of costume and décor. The treatment sometimes
given to the fairy scenes in *Midsummer Night's
Dream* or Weber's *Oberon* was favoured; often
with dancing by children to fill some parts as fairies
or elves etc. Should a time develop, with less education for factories and offices, and more for theatre,
many children could gain practical education and
experience in similar productions, even if the effort
did not increase "production for exports".

ZAZPI JAUSIAK (Basque)
Spanish Basque dancers perform this *saut* in a ring;
men only. They pace slowly round in regular step,
waiting for a certain bar of the traditional tune.
Then they jump as high as they can. On the first
of these signals, they jump once; on the second
signal after more steps they jump up twice, coming
down on the same spot; round again and so forth;
until they arrive at the "seven jump" (*Jausiak*) bar.
Then the process reverses; and a last single jump

ends the ritual dance. Similar jump-dances are
known in other countries : Denmark, Westphalia
(Easter Day), Holland.
[See *Zevensprong; Saut Basque; Siebensprung; Spell
of Seven Steps* (Ceylon)]

ZBOJECKI (Ukraine)
A very vigorous men's dance of the Carpathian
Mountains, miming the actions of a woodcutter
during the process of felling trees. Also, a round
dance for men and women, moving anti-clockwise.

ZBOJNICKI (Poland)
Pron : *zbooinitskee*. "Robbers Dance" of the Gorale*
people, living in the Tatra Mountains, once the
stronghold of robbers and outlaws. They raided the
estates of wealthy Hungarian landowners in the
valleys, sharing the spoils with the poor, like
Robin Hood and his band. Best known is the semi-
legendary *Janosik,** a hero among Gorale in the
highlands and Slovaks in the Sub-Tatran valleys,
who was caught and executed in 1713. Many
legends are told about him. On expeditions robber
bands were accompanied by fiddlers and players of
the *kobza* (bagpipes), who played for the wild
zbojnicki. Old paintings on glass show the outlaws
wearing tall red hats, with pistols and daggers in
their belts. They danced round a fire, in pairs
facing each other; and marked the rhythm by
beating the ground with their hatchets. High point
of the dance was to leap across the fire, simultaneously draining a bottle of wine and firing a pistol.
A version of this dance, the *Goralski,** is still performed, but without the wine and pistols.

ZEMLING-CHE-SAND (Tibet)
"Birthday of the World". Annual summer festival
held in and around Lhasa. For about a week people
camp in tents among the willow groves and every
day there is dancing, singing and games. A small
group of musicians and dancers, belonging to the
city, moves from party to party giving their entertainment. Consisting of four musicians playing
Tibetan guitar, flute, fiddle and a xylophone-like
instrument and five female dancers, they perform
the national dances. Though often not young, these
women are expert in popular Tibetan dance styles,
the emphasis of which is on foot-tapping. The
dances, performed on a small wooden platform,
begin slowly but increase in speed with the music
tempo, body and arms swaying gently and gracefully. Each dancer has a nickname such as "The
Crow", "The Cat". or "The Paper Flower", just as
did the famous *Can-Can** dancers of the *Moulin
Rouge* in 19th century Paris.

ZEN—1 (Buddhist, Japanese form)

Ritual and dance, derived its inspiration from earlier Korean and Chinese Buddhism, itself from India. Primitive Buddhism sought to abolish all dance and theatre as being "sinful", but Brahmin tradition was too strong (and useful) for this attitude to endure. Every modern sect of Buddhism accepts, in varying degree, the use of rhythmic ritual in chant or song, dance or mime. Zen Buddhism was united to Japanese Shinto (Ancestor worship), with its Kagura* ritual dance of Ama-terseru, to form after a thousand years, the artistic Noh* dance-drama presentations. Yet the Noh dance adheres chiefly to the Mahayana system (Great Path), while the Zen school, using its peculiar "Sudden Method", inclines rather to the Hinayana or individualist pursuit of The Eightfold Path. Some part of the Zen ritual derives from the Chinese Shen; but the term seems to originate in the older term Dhyana (or Dhyzan) a Sanskrit-Tibetan term meaning The Path, much like the Brahmin sangsara (or "world journey"). Formerly the choreographic bases of floor pattern reflected this symbolism; but in later presentations, this guide has been eliminated by neglect.

ZEN—2 (Japan)

Is a Buddhist term for a certain sect. The idea in it is known also as Dzhen or Dzhan (Central Asia), Dhyana (Sanskrit Hindu), Jhana (in the popular Pali of ancient India), Ch'an (Chinese), Jonah or John (Gnostic doctrine), and was known also in Egypt (Shen), symbolised in abstract mode as "cartouche"—the circle or ovoid enscribed around the names of priest-kings. This symbol is the "circle of necessity", on which impossibly imaginary line we endeavour to dance out the Dance of Life. This Zen circle circumscribes the Cosmic Dance:* we may choose to dance within its unscaled range; or rest outside it, watching the crowd of dancers within; or to ignore both and move on this unmoving line. The Zen circle has no size or scale; it is what we make it; it has, therefore, no Time because it has no Space. Zen, as Johna, is a Fore-runner or Fore-Dancer, typically "dancing in the desert". Its second symbol is the "crossed circle", sometimes written or drawn as I-O-NA or I O;* and sometimes as the X that has been so much used to signify the solstice, instead of other modes of Zodiac. This Zen deals with the abstract metaphysics of the Dance; it is thus the fore-actor of Theatre: it watches and knows all acting—much as Umar-i-Khayyam had it in his brief verse. The Egyptian priest-king had this cartouche reflex inscribed in blue on the limestone paving for his temple dance-ritual: it then implied the course of his "older brother", the sun; seen now as A-ten;

and later by the Hellenes as A-théne, or Wisdom. Before Buddhism was formulated, the Brahmins had this doctrine: not as one of escape but of attainment; and Jain philosophy also broke away from rigid sacerdotal ceremonialism. The later Greeks and the nobler Romans held it as the "word of the staff", or the stoiche (like the shippe of Nippon), because they used some modes of geometry to diagramatise; instead of the tricky verbum, or the poised logos. When they retreated from Dance, they lost the vivid contact of life; and so their creed fell and failed.

See Studies in Zen. D. T. Susuki. London, 1955.

ZEVENSPRONG, DE (Netherlands and Belgium)

"Seven Jumps". Once a ritual dance performed by men round an image of "St. John". Now performed for amusement, with mock solemnity, it is a circular dance in 4/4 time, for any number of couples. Holding hands and all facing centre, dancers move round clockwise. Accompanied by singing, both dance and words are cumulative, although the "seven springs" are not jumps, but a gradual prostration of the body, the dancers finishing by lying face down on the ground. While singing the chorus, dancers, holding hands, move round with a walking step, or a polka step without a hop. On the words "Da's een", everyone stamps the right foot. Circling and chorus are repeated, then dancers cry out "Da's een, da's twee", and stamp the right foot, then the left. This continues, the chorus being repeated, and a number and movement added each time. With the seventh round, the movement is—stamp right foot, stamp left foot, kneel on right knee, kneel on both knees, right elbow on ground, both elbows on ground, lie flat on ground. The final act is to touch the ground with the forehead, followed, by the men, with a somersault. While De Zevensprong belongs to the whole of Holland, it is particularly associated with Zeeland and the Fisherfolks Fair at Volendam in the third week in October. In Belgium it often concludes village fêtes in the Entre-Sambre-et-Meuse region of the Walloon country; and is danced throughout Flanders. Counterparts exist in Spain, Denmark, Germany, and the Basque Country (see Siebensprung;* Saut Basque;* Zazpi Jausiak*); while another type requires the touching of various parts of the body during the dance (see Schuhplattler*).

[Cp. Spell of Seven Steps (Ceylon)]

ZEYBECK (Anatolia - Turkey)

A harvest dance accompanied by a song. There are two versions—one which mimes the actions of harvesting and threshing wheat; the other a round dance in 9/8 time for men and women, moving anti-clockwise. The first belongs to Western, the second to Eastern Anatolia.

ZEYBECKIKOS (Greece)
Dance-song brought to Greece about thirty years ago by refugees from Asia Minor; possibly deriving from the *Zeybeck** of Eastern Anatolia—a round dance in 9/8 time. In Athens the *Zeybeckikos*, in 9-in-a-bar time, is danced and sung in the cafés of the Port, to music of a *Bouzouki* band. Music and song begin, then one or two men will get up and dance, separately, but with intense concentration, arms raised and fingers snapping. In the *Bouzouki* band are mandolins and guitars, but the chief instrument is the Greek Lute, or *Bouzouki*, the strings being vigorously plucked. *Bouzouki* and *Zeybeckikos* music, based on old rhythms, belongs especially to the Port of Athens (as distinct from the City), being composed there, for performance in waterfront cafés. Until recently despised in the City, these dance-songs are now popular in sophisticated Athens night-clubs, while radio and gramophone records take them all over Greece.

ZEZHULICKA (Czechoslovakia)
Spring-time dance, named after the "Song of the Cuckoo" in Czechoslovakia. The form of the dance ranges from a chain pattern similar to the *mazurka*,* to the ring of the *kolo*.* A similar song-dance was known in Serbia.

ZHIKR (Arabic)
Moslem term for ritual chant, relevant also to the ritual dance practised by some sects of Dervishes (at Karouan; Cairo; formerly in Istanbul; and in other places as a weekly ceremony), and used in Java with Moslem weddings, first as a chant, and provoking a dance of celebration to round off the festivities. The Dervish Dance is done to arouse an ecstatic mood in the small circle (usually ten or twelve, men only) which moves round to a monotonous chant of *Allah-il-Allah* with a faint melody from *rebab* and flute, or flute only. The men move in a clockwise circle, slowly at first in a ring (almost but not quite, in contact) and as the pace increases they begin to turn on their own axis; and will continue for thirty or sixty minutes without stopping. The Javanese circle is less even; it forms and breaks, moves slower or quicker, according to the particular verses chosen by the company. The *Zhikr* may be compared with the *shaman* dances of Siberia, done for auto-hypnosis in exorcism or healing; and the similar practice in the so-called "devil-dances" of Ceylon, done also for exorcism. Usually, all these dances are done barefooted. Various forms of this chanting circle may be found across Northern Africa, and some have reached Hayti.

Versions that reached New Orleans with the Christian slave traffic from West Africa changed over to produce later the Negro "spirituals.", by mingling of African dance with Christian psalm tunes, with final emphasis more on part-singing than upon actual dance movement. The name got turned to "Shaker" and then "Quaker" from *Zhikr*, a term that marks a well-known sect in the USA, which followed dance in its ritual.

ZIGGURATH (Assyria)
Babylon had an important temple-shrine (as had several other Assyrian or Babylonian cities of 2000 BC to 500 BC), which was specially constructed in a stepped pyramid form. Some architects believe, without a basis of fact, that the Ziggurath was solid, with no internal chambers, because the ritual entrance was by way of a series of twenty-eight inclined planes, four to each side of the seven levels or stories. The ritual dances appear to have numbered three: first the processional approach, through the broadest streets of the city; second, the gradual ascent, in twenty-eight sections, of the privileged cortege; and lastly, the much smaller "introit" as the sibyl-priestess was escorted into the small shrine and there enthroned. The object of the height, the solitude, the ritual, was to ensure the tension required for a seance: the "enquiry to the gods" which the priestess (deep in trance) would usually afford. The basic conditions are similar for any such ceremony. The main aim was the invocation of the *Zighe* or *Zhigur*, in the *Rath*. So profound was the ritual; so long did it endure, that it has bequeathed the dance name to later generations; sharing this honour with the Hindu *Juggarnath*, a term of allied origin. The reconstruction is possible only from knowledge of fragments of ritual; of the architectural form; of the similar ceremony used by the later Greeks at Dodona; and the sacerdotal habit of combining display with secrecy. Human elements remain similar; details differ according to climate and locality; the main purpose is identical. Even the word, somewhat battered by centuries, remains in the Semite-Arab tongue, in Egypt as *ziggereet!*, the cry of the wailing women, at wedding or funeral.

ZIMBABWE (S. Africa)
Now a ruined tower, formerly an Oracle centre, built by the Bantu people—probably WaBudjga—(VaBudhlya) for whom it was the place where Charewa, the priestess, interpreted the message of the Mondoro god. Reference to earlier and allied Bushman rock and cave paintings, shows that magical or ritual dance was one of the more important occupations of these related tribes. Charles Bullock, writer of an informative item, visited rock paint-

ings in this Fort Victoria area, with Abbé Breuil, the French cave-painting expert.[1] The caves were probably then used at one end of the cult; and the other phase developed with constructed buildings like Zimbabwe (or Zambabwe) which are firmly attributed to the Bantu builders; and, as we know magical dances belong to the caves, we may reasonably assume that dances were part also of the seance rituals of Zimbabwe. The name "Zimbabwe" has a feminine quality (much as "the church" is referred to as feminine), and was ruled by *Mambo* (masculine king or chief) through *Mambah* (priestess).

[1] "Bushman Painting and Zimbabwe". Chas. Bullock,, in *NADA Rhodesia Annual*, No. 26, 1949 (p. 50).

ZINKENISTEN (Germany)

Gilds or companies (*geschaften*) of players and singers, principally at New Year; who sang carols and performed for dancers (*reigen* or *rinkeln*). They were broadly equivalent to the English waits or *wayghtes;* who were also required to act as guards.

ZION (Hebrew)

Also as Sion, whence *man-sio* and mansion, used to denote the "house" in many modes of ritual. Zion equates with the Greek Zone or Zona; all these forms indicate a regular circle, equally divided; the *davar* stands in the centre. Usually there are twelve divisions; this again is affiliated with *Zodiac,** also with Egyptian *Min-zion*, where the *davar* was the Min or standing pole, the obelisk. The circle was formed by the ritual dancers, and in circles where the *davar* was indicated by diagrams, the dance moved in regular patterns *across* the circle, especially in healing rituals. This movement produces tracks with star patterns.

ZNAHAR (fem.), ZNAHARKA (masc.) (Old Russian)

Witch, wizard; named as leaders in *shaman-brahman* tribal ritual (from the root *znat* or *zenat*, "to know", implying "those who knew how"). The term moved into Yiddish as *Schnorrors*, or the unofficial *rabbi* (see Israel Zangwill, *King of the Schnorrors*), and even into England, as "The Snark", and finally as "nark" or "one who knows and will tell". But with all terms, having the root "Giver of information". The *zenaharka* led the midnight ritual dances in certain spiritualistic seances; not necessarily evil in purport.

ZODIAK

In Ritual Dance, appears as a series of twelve symbols, as figures or signs ostensibly attributed to the starry system, against which earth and sun move; and used as the primary basis of calendrical and astronomical reckoning. Every religious system reveals this system of Twelve units of Power; sometimes in more modes than the basic symbol-pictures of the heavenly ellipse; such as the Twelve Patriarchs; Twelve Prophets; Twelve Apostles; Twelve "provinces" in some allegorical kingdom; and so on. The Babylonian system (devised presumably by the Priest caste of Khaldu), is now admitted to be the oldest of all known Zodiak systems; and is displayed always in a complete circle (or ellipse) filled by Twelve Signs or "houses" or "mansions". They are named as:

1.	*Ku (sarik-ku)*	= Aries	Ram
2.	*Te (men-nu)*	= Taurus	Bull
3.	*Masu*	= Gemini	Twins
4.	*Pul (Pul-Luku)*	= Cancer	Crab
5.	*Aru*	= Leo	Lion
6.	*Seru*	= Virgo	Virgin
7.	*Aqrabu*	= Scorpio	Scorpion
8.	*Zibanutu*	= Libra	Balance
9.	*Pa*	= Saggitarius	Archer
10.	*Enzu*	= Capricornus	Goat
11.	*Gu*	= Aquarius	Water Bearer
12.	*Zib*	= Pisces	Fishes

This series—the foundation map or plan for astronomy and its companion astrology—was laid out in large scale pattern on the temple pavement; and the "ritual-dance" which varied with each month, was performed with appropriate movement, in the correct mask-costume, with chants that affirmed instructions, praises, and prayers for the period. The circle or ellipse, which appears under many guises in all religious systems, has many names. Many of them are versions of *Shen*.

ZOHAR (Hebrew, from Assyrian)

The *Sepher Zohar* is the "Book of Splendour", or the "Book Magnificent"; it contains a number of treatises on the greater subjects of the Kabbalah. Three are available in English. These are (1) *Siphra Dzenioutha*: the Book of Concealed Mystery; (2) the *Idra Rabba Qadisha*, the Greater Holy Assembly; and (3) *Idra Zinta Qadisha*, the Lesser Holy Assembly, which is a supplement or forerunner of the second Book. There is also the *Beth Elohim* (House of the Gods, the Seven *Elohim*), which inverts later to *Beth Lehem*, the House of Bread (of the Gods), and the Book of the Revolutions of Souls; said to be, in part, on metempsychosis. These doctrinal books constitute the Dogmatic *Qabbalah**: they are all incomplete without (a) the full knowledge of the ritual; and (b) the oral accessions of the Rabbi. One of the important books is *Sepher Sephiroth*, or Book of Emanations, describing symbolically the evolution of absolute Deity into Positive-Negative existence, in the natural world, This is the doctrine of the Dance of Life, when shewn in the mode of ritual dance; and it urged the first symbolisation of that great Cosmic Ring of Dance, the Zodiac. This doctrine spread into China (*Pa-Kwa*), giving the basis of *Ming T'ang;** and westward into Syria and Greece, giving this Hebrew-Gnostic tradition, which in one form appeared ritually in the famous *Dance of Jesus** (*Acts of Johannus*).

ZOPILOTE (Mexico)

A peasant dance, recorded by Brantz Mayer as being performed while he was on an excursion, shooting the delicate birds called *zopilotes*, perched on the highest branches of cypresses in the country district near Mexico City.[1] He was secretary at the United States Legation, in 1841 - 1842. He writes: "Not the least entertainment of the evening was a song from the 'tio' (uncle), and a wild dance called the *Zopilote*, which he accomplished after several supplementary tumblers of capital pulque". It is said that twenty distinct languages were spoken within the boundaries of ancient Mexico. Names and functions of dance rituals in this country are still difficult to establish with accuracy.

[2] *Mexico*. Brantz Mayer. New York, 1844 (p. 237).

ZOPPA (Italy)

Usually *Alla Zoppa*, from Spanish *zopo*, lame or maimed, applied to syncopated style of music or dance, e.g. to rhythm of Burns' "Comin' through the rye" called Scotch snap; also as Lombardy rhythm (or *Pop goes the Weasel*).

ZOROASTRIAN (Iran)

Ritual dance, mentioned in the *Yasths* (or scripts) of this religion, as performed with *Gathas* (liturgies) in the regular ceremonial. Names of the priests caste contain origins of later dance, as *Hota* (the Sacrificing Priest).

ZULEYKA AND YUSUF (Iranian-Muslim)

Two characters whose names refer both to certain ecstatic dances of Persian Sufi devotees, and to poems which relate the legendary history of the lovers. The name Zuleyka is associated with *Suluk*, or the main doctrines of Moslem discipline (*yoga* practice). It means generally "the swift one" (there is a famous Arab hound called *suluki*); the term became vulgarised to *slick* or *sleek*), while Yusuf equals Joseph — I O seph = Wisdom of the Moon (Sephira, circle), where the symbol I O refers always to moon worship with associated ring dances. As with the parallel *ragmala* pictures in India, the poems of Zuleyka were often illustrated in beautiful symbolic paintings; and as the dance form is little known, it is from these drawings that we obtain most of our information; as the ladies of the Kangra Valley tell us about Hindu ritual and legend.

ZUNI (North America)

Pueblo* Indians in the region of the Little Colorado River, Western New Mexico. Ruled by a theocracy, the Zuni had a civil chief with minor officials chosen by a Council of six priests. Of the three sets of Zuni organizations (fifteen priesthoods; thirteen societies for curing disease; and the group organizing ceremonial), the last arranged the masked dances and "rain-making" ceremonies, some of which were held in the underground chamber, or *kiva*.* Initiation into this exclusively male group was compulsory. Many of the rites are still performed. Warriors of the once-existing scalp-taking war societies have now become civil guardians, seeing that the priests' decrees are carried out, and guarding the altar and the masked dancers, *Kachinas** and *Koyemshi*.* The Zuni year is divided by Winter and Summer Solstices, both parts having special ceremonies, which centre round rain-making and fertility of crops, living as they do in an arid plain. At the Winter Solstice there is a "cleansing of the earth", with a series of ritual dances. At the Summer Solstice, the sacred lake of the dead is visited, after which various ceremonies are held, including a rain-making ritual; and the Dance of the *Kianakwe*, or ghost people, is performed to propitiate the spirits of the dead. During the winter, *Kachinas*, or beneficient spirits, visit the earth, impersonated by masked dancers. In the *Shalako** ceremony a spectacular welcome is given them in November or December, and further ceremonies mark their departure at the Summer Solstice. During intervals between *Kachina* dances, *Koyemshi*, or dancing clowns, perform slapstick interludes. At the Summer Solstice, the *Koyemshi* dance at night with the *Kachinas;* and on September 12th they take part in a ceremonial guessing game, preceding the Red Paint Kachina Dance. Every four years there is an initiation ceremony, connected with the plumed serpent, one reminder of Toltec and Maya origins of the Zuni. Other indications lie in the honouring of the four directions by priests and *Kachina* dancers (see *Aztec Dances**) and in the sacred tribal object, the *ettonne*. Consisting of a bundle of reeds (cf. *Acatlaxque**), wrapped in cotton, the *ettonne* contains symbols of things essential to tribal life — pollen, seeds, meal and turquoise (symbol of the heavens). The *etonne*, kept by the priests, is produced only for ritual purposes. Maize was sacred to the Zuni, and the curing societies possess another sacred object, the *mili*, being a specially prepared ear of maize, sheathed in feathers.

[See *Hopi; Pueblo Indians*]

BIBLIOGRAPHY

Books on Dance, whether historical, critical, or technical can provide teacher and student with selective information. They cannot tell the student how to dance, or show the teacher how to teach dancing. Some can offer an academic outline of method; others can reveal something of the various meanings and purposes of this universal art of Dance. What a book can offer is (a) a fund of facts that may suggest ideas; (b) material with which a teacher can bring a greater sense of reality to class routine; (c) data on forms of dance used in the past for religious or social purposes, now forgotten in secular and commercial professional activities; (d) ideas for new works.

Some 3,000 works have been consulted in the collection of the data assembled in this book, the pioneer attempt at a world survey; and yet much had to be omitted. It is futile to mention 1,500 names of Greek dances, if we have no evidence of precise time and place and purpose. Many travel books are worthless, since they rarely give precise facts. Too many books by archaeologists are no more valuable; hence it is a great pleasure to find John Layard's book on *Stone Men of Malekula;* Hugh Tracey's admirable survey of African *Chopi Dance* and music; and Beryl de Zoete's enthusiastic account of *Dance in Bali.*

Ordinary academic methods have been of little value: dance is best learned by seeing performances (the Editor has seen more than 2,000, over many years) or by contacts with rituals and places, and persons.

Even modern dance description is rarely informative; films are limited; photographs give but a glimpse, until these are critically surveyed and duly associated. Cuvier's method with anatomy has suggested a comparative basis, rarely shewn by the academic boffins who rely on books which quote books that quote earlier scripts, in the naive hope that the original comment is full and factual. We have next to nothing on primitive Christian ritual dance forms and origins; we find the later emergence of theatre ballet is still confused and uncertain. These facts are reflected in an almost meaningless hence unattractive liturgy and a rarity of creative ideas in commercial theatre, together with a sad loss of integral music. We find a certain amount of military ritual with rhythmic movement; we note the popular continuity in the ballroom "Social dance" varied by appreciation of commercially devised ballet performances, concentrated chiefly upon spectacle. Critics are reduced to writing technical commentaries; the art is reduced to an enclosed sport; while "experts" when asked to lecture can offer no more than a series of anecdotes.

*

Students should consult the standard works, Encyclopaedias, and Dictionaries such as:
Encyclopædia of Religion and Ethics. Hastings.
The Jewish Encyclopaedia.
Dictionary of Religion. (several compilations)
The Golden Bough. Frazer. London, 1890
The Mystic Rose. Crawley. London, 1902
any works by Jane Ellen Harrison (e.g. *Themis)*
any works by Gilbert Murray

A limited number of the older historical printed books on various aspects of dance, beginning with Italian and French works, such as the *Orchesographie* of Arbeau.

On Hindu religions (Buddhism and Brahmanism etc.) a number of works not available in English until recent years and many of them difficult, are yet greatly rewarding.

Links between ancient dance and modern European dances from the Renaissance period onwards are few; some in architecture, sculpture, and paintings. In too many "art books" this relevance is omitted: too few modern art students are aware of the source of pictorial material in much Renaissance art—in contemporary miracle plays, masques and other spectacles, also in Japanese prints. The Byzantine church controversy—"Pictures or no pictures"—is worth examination (Finlay; Dean Stanley etc.).

On "Imaginative ideation" little is available: see Jung's work (with R. Wilhelm) *The Golden Flower;* the standard catholic work *Spiritual Exercises* (Yoga in the church); the Buddhist mode *With Mystics and Magicians in Tibet* (Alex David-Neel); also E. W. Budge's translation of the Egyptian *Per 'M-'Hru* (Book of Dead).

The entries in the Bibliography are arranged chronologically under each sub-heading.

EARLY PRINTED BOOKS ON DANCE

La Geste des Nobles Francois. Jean d'Angouleme. Paris, 1445
Trattato dell'Arte del Ballo. Guglielmo Ebreo da Pesaro. Paris, c.1460
L'Art et l'Instruction de bien dancer. Published by Michel Toulouze, Paris. c.1488
The Manner to Daunce Bace Daunces. Published by Robert Coplande. London, 1521.
Le Manuscript dit des Basses Danses de la Bibliothèque de Bourgogne. c.1523
Libro del Cortegiano. Count Baldassare Castiglione. Venice, 1528
Théâtre Francais: Vol. III *De la Conduite des Comediens.* Various hands. (3 vols) Lyons, 1574
Il Ballarino. Fabritio Caroso. Venice, 1581
Orchesographie et Traite. Thoinot Arbeau (pen name). Langres, 1588
Orchestra, or a Poem of Dancing. Sir John Davies. London, 1594
Nobilità di Dame. Fabritio Caroso. Venice, 1600
Nouve Inventioni di Balli. Cesare Negri. 1604
Terpischore. Michel Praetorius. Wolfenbüttel, 1612
De Harmonie Universelle. Marin Mersenne. Paris, 1636
The English Dancing Master. John Playford. (Numerous editions with additions, continued to 1728). London, 1650
Court Ayres. John Playford. London, 1655
Traites contre les Danses at les Comedies. St. Charles Borromée. Paris, 1664
Archaeologia Graecae (Dances of Greeks and Romans). Potter. London, 1697-99.

Choregraphie ou l'Art de d'écrire la Dance par caractères, figures et signes demonstratifs. R. A. Feuillet. Paris, 1701

Recueil de Danse. R. A. Feuillet. Paris, 1704 (Trans. John Weaver, London, 1707)

The Art of Dancing Demonstrated by Characters and Figures. P. Siris. London, 1706

Small Treatise of Time and Cadence in Dancing. John Weaver. London, 1706

Further Improvement of Dancing. John Essex. London, 1710

Further Improvement in Dancing. Edward Pemberton. London, 1711

Towards an History of Dancing. John Weaver. London, 1712

Nouveau Recueil de Danse de Bal et de celles de Ballet. L. Pécour. Paris, 1712

Neue ünd Curieuse Theatralische Tanzschul. Gregor Lambranzi. Nurnberg, 1716

Histoire de la Danse: sacrée et profane: ses progrès et ses Révolutions depuis son Origin. Bourdelot. Paris, 1724

Le Maître à Danser. P. Rameau. Paris, 1725

Abrégé de la nouvelle méthode dans l'art d'écrire ou de tracer toutes sortes de Danses de Ville. P. Rameau. Paris, 1725

De Choreis veteribus Judaeorum Diss. Zeltner, Altdorf, 1726

Tratto del Balle Nobile. George Dufort. Napoli, 1728

The Art of Dancing Explained. Kellom Tomlinson. London, 1735

The Rudiments of Genteel Behaviour. F. Nivelon. London, 1737

De Religiosis Saltationibus veteribus Judaeorum. Renz. Leipsic, 1738

Trait de Danse ancienne et moderne (3 Vols). Cahusac. Paris, 1753, Hague, 1754

Lettres sur la Danse. Jean George Noverre. Stuttgard and Lyon, 1760

Critical Observations on Dancing. Gustav A. Gallini. London, 1765.

Encyclopédie. Diderot and d'Alembert. 17 vols. "Equitation and Fencing." Paris, 1751 to 1765

Traite sur l'art de la Danse. N. Malpied. Paris, c.1770

Dictionaire de Danse. Charles Compan. Paris, 1787

Treatise on Dancing. F. J. Lambert. Norwich, 1820

Ancient Mysteries described: especially the English Miracle Plays. William Hone. London, 1823

Essai sur la Danse antique et moderne. Elise Voiart. Paris, 1825

Code of Terpsichore. Carlo Blasis. London, 1830

Dance of Death. Francis Douce. London, 1833

Petit Dictionnaire des Coulisses. Jacques Le Souffleur. Paris, 1835

Entretien sur la Danse Ancienne, Moderne, Réligieuse, Civile et Theatrale. Baron. Paris

Antique Dictionary. Trevoux. Paris

Natya Shastras. An ancient Hindu work, the oldest known book on dance. Attributed to a legendary sage, Bharata Muni, we come to more certain ground in the 11th century commentary by Abhinava Guptacarya, a Brahmin scholar in Kashmir. Scholars say he flourished about the end of the 10th century A.D. His commentary called *Bharata Natya Shastra* is the recognised source of modern Indian dance-theory.

EGYPTIAN DANCE AND RITUAL

The Book of the Master. W. Marsham Adams. London, 1898
Book of Dead: The Chapters of Coming Forth by Day. Translated by E. A. Budge. London, 1898. Revised enlarged edition, London, 1938
The Great Pyramid. D. Davidson & Aldersmith. London, 1924

GENERAL

The Science of the Emotions. Dr. Bhagavan Das. Madras, 1900; 1908; 1924
Anthropology: an Introduction to the Study of Man and Civilization. Edward B. Tylor, F.R.S. London, 1892.
History of Irish Music and Dancing. W. H. Gratton Flood. Dublin, 1905
Dance of Life. Essays on Aspects of Dance. Havelock Ellis. London, 1912
The Eurhythmics of Jaques-Dalcroze. A Series of Articles. "Introduction" by Prof. M. E. Sadler; "Rhythm as a Factor in Education"; "Moving Plastic and Dance"; "Notes from Lectures"; all by Emil Jaques-Dalcroze; "The Method; Growth and Practice" by Percy B. Ingham; "Lessons with Dalcroze" by Ethel Ingham; and "Value of Eurhythmics to Art" by M. T. H. Sadler. London, 1912; 1917.
The Splendid Wayfaring. A Survey of Art. Haldane MacFall. London, 1913
Tribal Dancing and Development. W. H. Hambly. London 1926
The Flight of the Dragon. (Rhythm in Chinese Art). Laurence Binyon. London, 1928
Ad Quadratum (On geometrical notation of Gothic architecture) Fr. Macody Lund. 2 vols. London, 1929
Eurhythmics, Art and Education. E. Jaques-Dalcroze. Translated Rothwell. London, 1930
Creative Energy. An Introduction to the Study of Yih Ching or Book of Changes. Isabel Mears. London, 1931.
Hungarian Peasant Customs. Dr. Karoly Viski. Budapest, 1932
Hungarian Dances. Dr. Karoly Viski. 1937
Nogaku. (Japanese Noh Plays) Beatrice Lane Susuki. London, 1933
Magick in Theory and Practice in four books. *The Master Therion.* Aleister Crowley. Paris, 1936
An Actor Prepares. Constantin Stanislavsky. Translated Hapgood. New York, 1936
Drama of Orokolo. F. E. Williams. 1940
Stone Men of Malekula. John Layard. London, 1942
Figures of Speech or Figures of Thought. Collected Essays on the Traditional or "Normal" view of Art. A. K. Coomaraswamy. London, 1946
The World of the Dance. (Folk Dance and Ballet in Czechoslovakia) extensively illustrated. Jan Rey. Prague, 1946
Treasury of Mexican Folkways. Frances Toor. N. York, 1947
Dances of England and France from 1450 to 1600. (with their music) Mabel Dolmetsch. London, 1949

Historical Dances for the Theatre: the Pavan and the Minuet. John Guthrie. Worthing, 1950

The Yih Ching or Book of Changes. Richard Wilhelm. Translated by Cary F. Baynes. Foreword by Dr. C. G. Jung. 2 vols. London, 1951

Gatherings from Catalonia. J. Langdon- Davies. London, 1953

Dances of Spain and Italy from 1400 to 1600. (with musical illustrations) Mabel Dolmetsch. London, 1954

Hungarian Rhapsody. (Folk Dances of Hungary) Laszlo Tarr. Budapest, 1954

Festive Papua. André Dupeyrat. (Trans. Erik de Mauny). London, 1955

HELLENIC AND ROMAN DANCE AND DANCE RITUAL

Lectures on the History of the Eastern Church. Dean A. P. Stanley. London, 1861. Everyman Library; London, 1946

An Inquiry into the Symbolical Language of Ancient Art and Mythology. Richard Payne Knight. London, 1818. New York, 1876

Decline and Fall of the Roman Empire. Edward Gibbon. Vol. II of Oxford University Press edition, 1903

Enneads of Plotinus. See *Complete Works of Plotinus.* K. S. Guthrie. New York and London, 1918

Five Stages of Greek Religion. Gilbert Murray. London, 1925. (and other works by this author).

Themis. Jane Ellen Harrison. London, 1927. (and other works by this author).

HINDU DANCE AND RITUAL

Ideals of Indian Art. E. B. Havell. London, 1911

Indian Sculpture and Painting. E. B. Havell. London, 1913

Tantra of the Great Liberation. (*Mahanirvana Tantra*). Arthur Avalon (pen-name of Sir John Woodroffe). Madras, 1913

Tantra Shastra. J. Woodroffe. Madras, 1914

Principles of Tantra. J. Woodroffe. Madras

Shakti and Shakta. J. Woodroffe. Madras

The Garland of Letters. (Studies in the Mantra Shastra). J. Woodroffe. Madras, 1922

Kamakala-vilasa. J. Woodroffe. Madras

(A knowledge of the doctrine detailed in Woodroffe's books is a basic essential to understanding Hindu Temple Dance—*Bharata Natyam*)

Ancient and Medieval Architecture in India. E. B. Havell. London, 1915

Elements of Hindu Iconography. Gopinath Rao. Madras, 1914-16

Mudras: the Ritual Hand-Poses of the Buddhist and Shiva Priests of Bali. Tyra de Kleen. London, 1924

Tibetan Book of the Dead. W. Evans Wentz. London, 1928

"Ceremonial Dances of the Sinhalese." O. Pertold. *Archiv Orientalni.* Praha, 1930

—An Enquiry into Sinhalese Folk Religion (March, 1930)
—Use of Masks—Animal Masks (June 1930)
—Ceremony: *Yakun Natta* Dance ritual (Dec. 1930)
Saundaraya Lahari. (Ocean of Beauty). Sri Samkara Bhagavat-Pada; with ritual diagrams
    by S. Sastri and T. R. S. Ayyanger. Madras, 1937
Island of Bali. Miguel Covarrubias. London, 1937
Dance and Drama in Bali. Walter Spies and Beryl de Zoete. London, 1938
Unity of Religions. Bhagavan Das. Benares, 1938
Secret of the Golden Flower. R. Wilhelm and C. G. Jung. London, 1939
Influence of Music (Sa'adyah Gaon). Trans. by H. G. Farmer. London, 1943
Ragas and Raginis: A Study of Indian Music. O. C. Gangoly. Bombay, 1949
La Danse Hindoue. Usha Chatterji. Paris 1951
Sinhalese Folk Play. E. R. Sarathchandra. Colombo, 1953
Indian Music. (2 vols) Alain Danielou. London, 1954
Trouvailles de Nedoungadou (Les Sept Danses de Siva) P. Z. Pattabiramin. Pondicherry,
    1956

PROBLEMS OF SPACE TIME AND FORM

Christian Iconography. Charles Didron. Translated. Stokes. London, 1886
Nature's Harmonious Unity. Samuel Colman. New York, 1912
The Curves of Life. Theodore A. Cook. London, 1914
Spiritual Exercises. Ignazius de Loyola. Translated by W. H. Longbridge, 1919
Proportional Form. C. A. Coan and Samuel Colman. London, 1920
Beautiful Necessity. Claude Bragdon. London, Second Edition 1923
Dynamic Symmetry (The Greek Vase). Jay Hambidge. Yale, 1924
Experiment with Time. J. W. Dunne. London, 1927
Tibetan Book of the Dead. W. Y. Evans Wentz. London, 1928
Number: The Language of Science. Tobias Danzig. London, 1930
The Serial Universe. J. W. Dunne. London, 1934
With Mystics and Magicians in Tibet. Alex. David Neel. (Penguin) London, 1936

RELIGIOUS RITUALS AND DANCE FORM

Isis Unveiled. (2 vols.) H. P. Blavatsky. New York, 1893
Religion of the Semites. W. Robertson Smith. London, 1894
Short History of Christianity. J. M. Robertson. London, 1902/1913
Pagan Christs. John M. Robertson. London, 1903
Chinese Thought. Paul Carus. Chicago, 1907
Hymn of Jesus. G. R. S. Mead. Madras, 1908
The Golden Bough. Sir J. G. Frazer. London, 1898
The Sacred Dance. W. O. E. Oesterley. Cambridge, 1923
Science and Civilization in China. (4 vols.) Joseph Needham. 1960–62

Rise, Decline and Fall of Roman Religion. James Ballantyne Hannay. London, 1925

Pagan and Christian Creeds: Their Origin and Meaning. (Chapt. XI. Ritual Dance) Edward Carpenter. London, 1929

Dress, Drink and Drums. Ernest Crawley. London, 1931

The Mystic Rose. (Study of Primitive Marriage) Ernest Crawley. London, 1931

Thus Spake Zarathustra: A Book for All and None. Friedrich Nietzsche. Translated by Common; revised Levy and Beevers. London, 1932

Christianity and Mythology. John M. Robertson. Second Edition London, 1936

ROMANTIC BALLET

Comte de Gabalis. Abbé N. de Montfaucon de Villars. Paris, 1670. English translation, London, 1913

Civilization of the Renaissance in Italy. Jacob Burckhardt. London, 1878

Letters on Dancing and Ballet. Jean George Noverre. London, 1930

A Pageant of the Dance and Ballet. Mark Edward Perugini. London, 1947 (the only single volume work of any use as a general introduction for modern Ballet)

INDEX

The Index consists of two parts. The first part is a *Geographical Index* in which the dances described in the Dictionary are listed under their country (or culture) of origin; the second part is an *Index of Subjects relating to Dance* for which entries will be found in the Dictionary. Since all entries are listed alphabetically in the body of the Dictionary, page folio numbers are not listed in the Index.

GEOGRAPHICAL INDEX

AFRICAN DANCES

BASUTO
Basuto Dances
Baloi
Mohobelo
Mokhibo
Mokorotlo
Motjeko

BANTU
Inguana
Mazya

BRITISH CAMEROONS
Mambila Moon Dance

BRITISH CENTRAL AFRICA
Anyanga
Yao

CONGO
Bakongo
Katanga
Revelation Ritual Dance
"Twelve Mask" Dance
Watussi N'tori Ritual Dance

FRENCH GUINEA
Afwi, Dance Of
Bakorogui
Korsi-Koroni Fire Dance

KENYA
Numba
Unoto
Wakamba

LIBERIA
Guere Snake Dance

NIGERIA
Ashiko
Atkinga
Bori Dancers
Elo
Hausa Dances
Ijo Ode
Kiriboto
Nigerian Social Dances
Nupe
Nupe Dances
Sakara
Saki Acrobatic Dancers
Yoruba

PORTUGUESE EAST AFRICA
Chopi Ballet
Migodo
Timbila

PORTUGUESE GUINEA
Batuque
Machol

RHODESIA
Ichimbwasa
Ichin Sengwe
Ingoma Shayama-Ombe
Kalela
Ndola
Zimbabwe

SOMALILAND
Bororoma Boromsi

SWAZILAND
Ingwala

TRANSVAAL
Domba Dance

SIERRA LEONE
Bundu
Canoe Dance
Hammock Dance

SUDAN
Abkia Funeral Dance
Bongo Dance
Dinka Virgins Dance
Doulukka
Gugu Drums
Lokuta
Mambo Dzhambo
Whipping Dance
Zande

WEST AFRICA
Danh-Sio
Habbe Dances
Obi
Awisa

ALBANIA
Arnaout

ALGERIA
Ouled Nail
Fête Des Fèves
Negro Dance
Ventre, Danse Du

AMERINDIAN
Bear Dance (Sioux)
Buffalo Dance (Dakota)
Busk (Creek)
Creek Indians
Crown Dancers (Apache)
Dakota Scalp Dance
Eagle Dance (Hopi)
Gagosa (Iroquois)
Green Corn Dance (Natchez)
Hasjelti Dailjis
Hopi Indians

Iroquois Indians
Kachinas (Pueblo)
Karok (Yuma)
Kiva (Pueblo)
Koshare (Pueblo)
Koyemshi (Pueblo)
Navajo Indians
Navajo Fire Dance
Prayer Sticks
Pueblo Indians
Shalako (Pueblo)
Snake Dance (Hopi)
Squaw Dance
Wannebago Creation Myth
Yei Bit'chi
Zuni Indians

ANDAMAN ISLANDS
Boys Initiation Dance

ARABIA
Arabian Magic Mirror
Dabke
Dervish Dance
Houri
Hagg
Kismet Al Reml
Khatmeh
Qatni Dance
Rammal
Remal
Rishi
Safina
Samet
Sharh Al'abid
Sharh Dhaheri
Sharh Saibani
Sharh of Sur
Shebwari
Tahlul
Tawef
Zamil Dance
Zhikr

ARGENTINA
Bailecito
Carnavilito
Chacerera
Cueca
Escondido
Gato
Milonga
Pericon
Tango

SUBJECTS RELATING TO DANCE

Arba-Kad-Abre
Abacus
Academy
Acrobatic Dance
Acta Pilati
Adagio
Agricultural Ritual Dances
Alchemical Ritual Dances
Allah
All Souls
Allegory
Alphabet and Dance
Altro Volta
Amour De La Hault Pleasaunce
Angel
Animal Dances
Animals in Dance
Anima-Animus
Andante
Anthropology
Arabesque Arch Dances
Arche
Archeology of Dance
Architecture of the Dance
Arena Ballet
Ark, Dance of
Ars Moriendi
Art Director
Astrological Ritual Dance
Auto-Da-Fé
Automatons, Dances of

Baladines
Ballabile
Ballatoria
Ballet
Ballet de la Cour
Ballet Geometrique
Ballon
Ballroom Dances
Barbe
Barber's Dance
Bareback Ballerina
Barrack Hack
Basic Music
Baton Dance
Bede
Beffany
Bell
Bessie
Black Mass or Messe
Blaize
Book of a Ballet
Bourgeois Ballet
Brat
Breviary

British Fire Festivals
Brownie
Bureaucratic Ballroom Dance
Byzantine Dance
Cadets Schools
Cake and Bread Dances
Calendar Dances
Calecon
Candle Dances
Cannibal Dance Rituals
Capriole
Cards, Dances of
Carmina Ecclesia
Carrousel
Castanets
Catherina
Cauldron Dances
Cecchetti System
Censor in Theatre
Cerna, Cerne
Chamber Ballet
Character Dance
Character in Dance
Charlatan
Cheironomy
Children's Dance Games and
    Songs
Chirologia
Chironomia
Choreodrama
Choreography
Choreology
Chout
Christian Dance
Christian Primitive Dance Rituals
Chylde
Circulation
Circus
Circus Ring
Cinema Film Dance
Claque
Classical Ballet
Clerici Vagantes
Cloister
Clown
Clubs, Societies, Gilds, Etc.
Cobblers Dance
Colen
Comedies-Ballets
Commercial Ballet
Communist Dance
Concert Dance
Coral Master
Corn Dances
Corps de Ballet

Cosmic Ballet
Counting Dances
Counting in Dance
Court Dance
Crambo
Dalcroze Method

Dance—Art of Movement
Dance of Death
Danse Macabre
Dance Names
Dance of Deer
Death, Dances of
Debutante
Delsarte Method
Deportment
Desguiser
Devil Dance
Diaghileff Ballet
Diagrams for Dance
Dimensionalism in Dance
Dimensions in Modern Dance
Director of Dance
Divertissement
Doll Dances
Dominics
Don Juan
Dos A Dos
Duncan Method

Ecstatic Dance
Education in Dance
Egyptian Traces in Britain
Elementals, Dance of
English Ballet
Entreé
Epidemic Dances
Ethnic Dance
Euchorics
Eurhythmics
Eurhythmics (Dolcroze)
Eurhythmy
European Ballet
Exorcism
Expositions

Fable in Dance
Fairs
Faust
Fencing and Ballet
Fiddle
Figure Dances
Figure of Eight (Lemniscate)
Film Dance
Fingers in Ballet Training
Fire Festivals
Five Positions in Ballet